MACAULAY

MACAULAY

PROSE AND POETRY

SELECTED BY G. M. YOUNG

HARVARD UNIVERSITY PRESS

Cambridge Massachusetts

1967

First published 1952

Second impression 1967

Printed in Great Britain

CONTENTS

CONTENTS

INTRODUCTION

THE volumes in this series are designed to give the reader a faithful picture of the range, and the excellences, of each writer's work. As Macaulay is pre-eminently an historian, selections from his *History of England* necessarily take the first, and fill th*e* largest, place. But even if that history had never been written, Macaulay, in virtue of the *Essays* alone, would have a secure standing among our great prose writers; and when to the *Essays* are added the speeches, and to the speeches the *Lays of Ancient Rome*, the breadth of his *œuvre*, and his mastery in each kind, are not easy to parallel in any other author, or in any age of our literature. Nor do these complete the tale, because the *Epitaph on a Jacobite* and *The Last Buccaneer* disclose yet another facet, a glimpse of poetic sensibility and refinement which, without them, we might have thought lacking from the trenchant, emphatic temper of the historian, the critic, the orator. Of that strange piece, *Tirzah and Ahirad*, every reader will judge for himself: to me it sounds as if Macaulay had set himself to write a poem which John Martin might illustrate.

One paper, by the kindness of Dr. G. M. Trevelyan, is now published for the first time—Macaulay's note of the proceedings of the Privy Council on the occasion of an attempt on the life of Queen Victoria. Apart from its historic interest it illustrates Macaulay's habit of putting everything that befell him on to paper at once, a habit which no doubt did much to sharpen his gift for historic narrative.

It is not difficult to understand why Macaulay's writing, so abundant and downright in substance, so highly coloured and so strongly cadenced, should have taken contemporaries captive. Nor is the reaction less comprehensible. When Ruskin, three years before Macaulay's death, spoke of "the beautiful, quiet, English" of Sir Arthur Helps, he anticipated the change of taste that was rapidly setting in. Macaulay is loud. He writes as if his purpose was less to convince than to silence his readers: not to win their agreement but to force their assent. Naturally, the new age rebelled, the more hotly perhaps because the large unlettered public was faithful, not caring whether their favourite was a bad historian, as Seeley said; a bully, as John Morley said; or that his verses sometimes made Matthew Arnold cry out in pain. That revolt has long died away. The last shot was fired by Lytton Strachey when he spoke of the Philistine on Parnassus. On Parnassus, truly. But it was no Philistine who wrote,

> Heard on Lavernia Scargill's whispering trees,
> And pined by Arno for my lovelier Tees;

or who could say of Dante what Dante had said of Virgil:

> Vagliami il lungo studio e il grande amore.

G.M.Y.

1800	Thomas Babington Macaulay, born at Rothley Temple, Leicestershire, 25 October, eldest son of Zachary Macaulay and Selena Mills.
1812–4	At school in Little Shelford, Cambridgeshire, and Aspenden Hall, near Buntingford, Hertfordshire.
1818	Went up to Trinity College, Cambridge.
1819	His poem, *Pompeii*, won the Chancellor's medal.
1823	First article in *Knight's Quarterly Magazine*, Spring.
1824–31	Fellow of Trinity College, Cambridge.
1825	First article in *Edinburgh Review*, August.
1826	Called to the bar.
1828	Commissioner of Bankruptcy.
1830	Liberal M.P. for Calne. Maiden speech, 5 April.
1831	First speech on Parliamentary Reform, 1 March. Pocket-borough of Calne dissolved by Reform Bill.
1832	Elected M.P. for Leeds. Commissioner, and later Secretary, of the Board of Control.
1834	Sailed for India, 15 February. Member of the Supreme Council for India until 1838.
1835	Minute on Indian Education, 2 February. President of the Commission for Composing a Criminal Code for India.
1837	Indian Criminal Code published (came into force 1862). Embarked for England, December.
1839	Began *History of England*, 9 March. M.P. for Edinburgh, June. Secretary-at-War (until 1841), September.
1840	Edward Oxford's attempt on the life of the Queen and Prince Consort, 10 June.
1841	Fall of Whig Government. General Election. Macaulay re-elected for Edinburgh, August. Resumed work on *History of England*, 5 November.
1842	*Lays of Ancient Rome*.
1843	*Critical and Historical Essays*, January.
1846	Whigs returned to office, Macaulay Paymaster-General, 30 June.
1847	General Election. Macaulay lost his seat, July.
1848	*History of England*, Volumes I and II, December.
1849	Lord Rector of Glasgow University.

1852	M.P. for Edinburgh, 13 July. Breakdown in his health, 22 July.
1854	*Speeches.*
1855	*History of England*, Volumes III and IV.
1857	Created Baron Macaulay of Rothley.
1859	Died, 28 December.
1860	Buried in Westminster Abbey, 9 January.

THE HISTORY OF ENGLAND

The first two volumes of *The History of England from the Accession of James II* were published by Longman in December 1848, though the title-pages are dated 1849. The third and fourth volumes did not appear until 1855. In 1857 Macaulay began revising these first four volumes, adding some new matter, correcting errors which had been pointed out, and taking pains to standardise spelling and typography. Volumes One and Two are especially heavily corrected. "I have no more corrections to make at present," he wrote to Longman. "I am inclined to hope that the book will be as nearly faultless, as to typographical execution, as any work of equal extent that is to be found in the world." This revised edition of Volumes One to Four was printed from the original type, much corrected, and appeared in 1858. When Macaulay died in 1859 the *History* remained unfinished. Three new chapters had been written and were ready for press; he had also left two unrevised fragments. His sister, Lady Trevelyan, edited these remains, and Longman published them as a fifth volume in 1861. The present selection follows the text of the revised edition of 1858, except in the case of the passage on Darien which comes from the fifth volume of 1861. All the original footnotes, most of them references to sources, have been omitted.

SELECTED PASSAGES

MONMOUTH'S CAMPAIGN

ON the morning of the eleventh of June [1685] the Helderenbergh, accompanied by two smaller vessels, appeared off the port of Lyme. That town is a small knot of steep and narrow alleys, lying on a coast wild, rocky, and beaten by a stormy sea. The place was then chiefly remarkable for a pier which, in the days of the Plantagenets, had been constructed of stones, unhewn and uncemented. This ancient work, known by the name of the Cob, enclosed the only haven where, in a space of many miles, the fisherman could take refuge from the tempests of the Channel.

The appearance of the three ships, foreign built and without colours, perplexed the inhabitants of Lyme; and the uneasiness increased when it was found that the Customhouse officers, who had gone on board according to usage, did not return. The town's people repaired to the cliffs, and gazed long and anxiously, but could find no solution of the mystery. At length seven boats put off from the largest of the strange vessels, and rowed to the shore. From these boats landed about eighty men, well armed and appointed. Among them were Monmouth, Grey, Fletcher, Ferguson, Wade, and Anthony Buyse, an officer who had been in the service of the Elector of Brandenburg.

Monmouth commanded silence, kneeled down on the shore, thanked God for having preserved the friends of liberty and pure religion from the perils of the sea, and implored the divine blessing on what was yet to be done by land. He then drew his sword and led his men over the cliffs into the town.

As soon as it was known under what leader and for what purpose the expedition came, the enthusiasm of the populace burst through all restraints. The little town was in an uproar with men running to and fro, and shouting "A Monmouth! a Monmouth! the Protestant religion!" Meanwhile the ensign of the adventurers, a blue

13

flag, was set up in the market place. The military stores were deposited in the town hall; and a Declaration setting forth the objects of the expedition was read from the Cross.

This Declaration, the masterpiece of Ferguson's genius, was not a grave manifesto such as ought to be put forth by a leader drawing the sword for a great public cause, but a libel of the lowest class, both in sentiment and language. It contained undoubtedly many just charges against the government. But these charges were set forth in the prolix and inflated style of a bad pamphlet; and the paper contained other charges of which the whole disgrace falls on those who made them. The Duke of York, it was positively affirmed, had burned down London, had strangled Godfrey, had cut the throat of Essex, and had poisoned the late King. On account of those villainous and unnatural crimes, but chiefly of that execrable fact, the late horrible and barbarous parricide,—such was the copiousness and such the felicity of Ferguson's diction,—James was declared a mortal and bloody enemy, a tyrant, a murderer, and an usurper. No treaty should be made with him. The sword should not be sheathed till he had been brought to condign punishment as a traitor. The government should be settled on principles favourable to liberty. All Protestant sects should be tolerated. The forfeited charters should be restored. Parliaments should be held annually, and should no longer be prorogued or dissolved by royal caprice. The only standing force should be the militia: the militia should be commanded by the Sheriffs; and the Sheriffs should be chosen by the freeholders. Finally Monmouth declared that he could prove himself to have been born in lawful wedlock, and to be, by right of blood, King of England, but that, for the present, he waived his claims, that he would leave them to the judgment of a free Parliament, and that, in the meantime, he desired to be considered only as the Captain General of the English Protestants who were in arms against tyranny and Popery.

Disgraceful as this manifesto was to those who put it forth, it was not unskilfully framed for the purpose of stimulating the passions of the vulgar. In the West the effect was great. The gentry and clergy of that part of England were indeed, with few exceptions, Tories. But the yeomen, the traders of the towns, the peasants, and the artisans, were generally animated by the old Roundhead spirit. Many of them were Dissenters, and had been goaded by petty persecution into a temper fit for desperate enterprise. The great mass of the population abhorred Popery and adored Monmouth. He was no stranger to them. His progress through Somersetshire and Devonshire in the summer of 1680 was still fresh in the

memory of all men. He was on that occasion sumptuously entertained by Thomas Thynne at Longleat Hall, then, and perhaps
still, the most magnificent country house in England. From Longleat to Exeter the hedges were lined with shouting spectators. The
roads were strewn with boughs and flowers. The multitude, in
their eagerness to see and touch their favourite, broke down the
palings of parks, and besieged the mansions where he was feasted.
When he reached Chard his escort consisted of five thousand horsemen. At Exeter all Devonshire had been gathered together to
welcome him. One striking part of the show was a company of
nine hundred young men who, clad in a white uniform, marched
before him into the city. The turn of fortune which had alienated
the gentry from his cause had produced no effect on the common
people. To them he was still the good Duke, the Protestant Duke,
the rightful heir whom a vile conspiracy kept out of his own. They
came to his standard in crowds. All the clerks whom he could
employ were too few to take down the names of the recruits. Before
he had been twenty four hours on English ground he was at the
head of fifteen hundred men. Dare arrived from Taunton with
forty horsemen of no very martial appearance, and brought encouraging intelligence as to the state of public feeling in Somersetshire.
As yet all seemed to promise well.

But a force was collecting at Bridport to oppose the insurgents.
On the thirteenth of June the red regiment of Dorsetshire militia
came pouring into that town. The Somersetshire, or yellow regiment, of which Sir William Portman, a Tory gentleman of great
note, was Colonel, was expected to arrive on the following day.
The Duke determined to strike an immediate blow. A detachment
of his troops was preparing to march to Bridport when a disastrous
event threw the whole camp into confusion.

Fletcher of Saltoun had been appointed to command the cavalry
under Grey. Fletcher was ill mounted; and indeed there were few
chargers in the camp which had not been taken from the plough.
When he was ordered to Bridport, he thought that the exigency of
the case warranted him in borrowing, without asking permission, a
fine horse belonging to Dare. Dare resented this liberty, and assailed
Fletcher with gross abuse. Fletcher kept his temper better than
any one who knew him expected. At last Dare, presuming on the
patience with which his insolence was endured, ventured to shake a
switch at the high born and high spirited Scot. Fletcher's blood
boiled. He drew a pistol and shot Dare dead. Such sudden and
violent revenge would not have been thought strange in Scotland,
where the law had always been weak, where he who did not right

himself by the strong hand was not likely to be righted at all, and where, consequently, human life was held almost as cheap as in the worst governed provinces of Italy. But the people of the southern part of the island were not accustomed to see deadly weapons used and blood spilled on account of a rude word or gesture, except in duel between gentlemen with equal arms. There was a general cry for vengeance on the foreigner who had murdered an Englishman. Monmouth could not resist the clamour. Fletcher, who, when his first burst of rage had spent itself, was overwhelmed with remorse and sorrow, took refuge on board of the Helderenbergh, escaped to the Continent, and repaired to Hungary, where he fought bravely against the common enemy of Christendom.

Situated as the insurgents were, the loss of a man of parts and energy was not easily to be repaired. Early on the morning of the following day, the fourteenth of June, Grey, accompanied by Wade, marched with about five hundred men to attack Bridport. A confused and indecisive action took place, such as was to be expected when two bands of ploughmen, officered by country gentlemen and barristers, were opposed to each other. For a time Monmouth's men drove the militia before them. Then the militia made a stand, and Monmouth's men retreated in some confusion. Grey and his cavalry never stopped till they were safe at Lyme again: but Wade rallied the infantry, and brought them off in good order.

There was a violent outcry against Grey; and some of the adventurers pressed Monmouth to take a severe course. Monmouth, however, would not listen to this advice. His lenity has been attributed by some writers to his good nature, which undoubtedly often amounted to weakness. Others have supposed that he was unwilling to deal harshly with the only peer who served in his army. It is probable, however, that the Duke, who, though not a general of the highest order, understood war very much better than the preachers and lawyers who were always obtruding their advice on him, made allowances which people altogether inexpert in military affairs never thought of making. In justice to a man who has had few defenders, it must be observed that the task, which, throughout this campaign, was assigned to Grey, was one which, if he had been the boldest and most skilful of soldiers, he could scarcely have performed in such a manner as to gain credit. He was at the head of the cavalry. It is notorious that a horse soldier requires a longer training than a foot soldier, and that the war horse requires a longer training than his rider. Something may be done with a raw infantry which has enthusiasm and animal courage: but nothing can be more helpless than a raw cavalry, consisting of yeomen and tradesmen mounted on cart horses and post horses; and such was the cavalry which Grey commanded. The wonder is, not that his men did not stand fire with resolution, not that they did not use their weapons with vigour, but that they were able to keep their seats.

Still recruits came in by hundreds. Arming and drilling went on all day. Meantime the news of the insurrection had spread fast and wide. On the evening on which the Duke landed, Gregory Alford, Mayor of Lyme, a zealous Tory, and a most bitter persecutor of Nonconformists, sent off his servants to give the alarm to the gentry of Somersetshire and Dorsetshire, and himself took horse for the West. Late at night he stopped at Honiton, and thence despatched a few hurried lines to London with the ill tidings. He then pushed on to Exeter, where he found Christopher Monk, Duke of Albemarle. This nobleman, the son and heir of George Monk, the restorer of the Stuarts, was Lord Lieutenant of Devonshire, and was then holding a muster of militia. Four thousand men of the trainbands were actually assembled under his command. He seems to have thought that, with this force, he should be able at once to crush the rebellion. He therefore marched towards Lyme.

But when, on the afternoon of Monday the fifteenth of June, he reached Axminster, he found the insurgents drawn up there to encounter him. They presented a resolute front. Four field pieces were pointed against the royal troops. The thick hedges, which on each side overhung the narrow lanes, were lined with musketeers. Albemarle, however, was less alarmed by the preparations of the enemy than by the spirit which appeared in his own ranks. Such was Monmouth's popularity among the common people of Devonshire that, if once the trainbands had caught sight of his well known face and figure, they would probably have gone over to him in a body.

Albemarle, therefore, though he had a great superiority of force, thought it advisable to retreat. The retreat soon became a rout. The whole country was strewn with the arms and uniforms which the fugitives had thrown away; and, had Monmouth urged the pursuit with vigour, he would probably have taken Exeter without a blow. But he was satisfied with the advantage which he had gained, and thought it desirable that his recruits should be better trained before they were employed in any hazardous service. He therefore marched towards Taunton, where he arrived on the eighteenth of June, exactly a week after his landing.

The Court and the Parliament had been greatly moved by the news from the West. At five in the morning of Saturday the thirteenth of June, the King had received the letter which the Mayor of Lyme had despatched from Honiton. The Privy Council was instantly called together. Orders were given that the strength of every company of infantry and of every troop of cavalry should be increased. Commissions were issued for the levying of new regiments. Alford's communication was laid before the Lords; and its substance was communicated to the Commons by a message. The Commons examined the couriers who had arrived from the West, and instantly ordered a bill to be brought in for attainting Monmouth of high treason. Addresses were voted assuring the King that both his peers and his people were determined to stand by him with life and fortune against all his enemies. At the next meeting of the Houses they ordered the declaration of the rebels to be burned by the hangman, and passed the bill of attainder through all its stages. That bill received the royal assent on the same day; and a reward of five thousand pounds was promised for the apprehension of Monmouth.

The fact that Monmouth was in arms against the government was so notorious that the bill of attainder became a law with only a faint show of opposition from one or two peers, and has seldom been severely censured even by Whig historians. Yet, when we consider how important it is that legislative and judicial functions should be kept distinct, how important it is that common fame, however strong and general, should not be received as a legal proof of guilt, how important it is to maintain the rule that no man shall be condemned to death without an opportunity of defending himself, and how easily and speedily breaches in great principles, when once made, are widened, we shall probably be disposed to think that the course taken by the Parliament was open to some objection. Neither House had before it any thing which even so corrupt a judge as Jeffreys could have directed a jury to consider as proof of Monmouth's crime. The messengers examined by the Commons were not on oath, and might therefore have related mere fictions without incurring the penalties of perjury. The Lords, who might have administered an oath, appear not to have examined any witness, and to have had no evidence before them except the letter of the Mayor of Lyme, which, in the eye of the law, was no evidence at all. Extreme danger, it is true, justifies extreme remedies. But the Act of Attainder was a remedy which could not operate till all danger was over, and which would become superfluous at the very moment at which it ceased to be null. While Monmouth was in arms it was impossible to execute him. If he should be vanquished and taken, there would be no hazard and no difficulty in trying him.

It was afterwards remembered as a curious circumstance that, among the zealous Tories who went up with the bill from the House of Commons to the bar of the Lords, was Sir John Fenwick, member for Northumberland. This gentleman, a few years later, had occasion to reconsider the whole subject, and then came to the conclusion that acts of attainder are altogether unjustifiable.

The Parliament gave other proofs of loyalty in this hour of peril. The Commons authorised the King to raise an extraordinary sum of four hundred thousand pounds for his present necessities, and, that he might have no difficulty in finding the money, proceeded to devise new imposts. The scheme of taxing houses lately built in the capital was revived and strenuously supported by the country gentlemen. It was resolved not only that such houses should be taxed, but that a bill should be brought in prohibiting the laying of any new foundations within the bills of mortality. The resolution, however, was not carried into effect. Powerful men who had land in the suburbs, and who hoped to see new streets and squares rise on their estates, exerted all their influence against the project. It was found that to adjust the details would be a work of time; and the King's wants were so pressing that he thought it necessary to quicken the movements of the House by a gentle exhortation to speed. The plan of taxing buildings was therefore relinquished; and new duties were imposed for a term of five years on foreign silks, linens, and spirits.

The Tories of the Lower House proceeded to introduce what they called a bill for the preservation of the King's person and government. They proposed that it should be high treason to say that Monmouth was legitimate, to utter any words tending to bring the person or government of the sovereign into hatred or contempt, or to make any motion in Parliament for changing the order of succession. Some of these provisions excited general disgust and alarm. The Whigs, few and weak as they were, attempted to rally, and found themselves reinforced by a considerable number of moderate and sensible Cavaliers. Words, it was said, may easily be misunderstood by a dull man. They may easily be misconstrued by a knave. What was spoken metaphorically may be apprehended literally. What was spoken ludicrously may be apprehended seriously. A particle, a tense, a mood, an emphasis, may make the whole difference between guilt and innocence. The Saviour of mankind himself, in whose blameless life malice could find no act to impeach, had been called in question for words spoken. False witnesses had suppressed a syllable which would have made it clear that those words were figurative, and had thus furnished the

Sanhedrim with a pretext under which the foulest of all judicial murders had been perpetrated. With such an example on record, who could affirm that, if mere talk were made a substantive treason, the most loyal subject would be safe? These arguments produced so great an effect that in the committee amendments were introduced which greatly mitigated the severity of the bill. But the clause which made it high treason in a member of Parliament to propose the exclusion of a prince of the blood seems to have raised no debate, and was retained. The clause was indeed altogether unimportant, except as a proof of the ignorance and inexperience of the hotheaded Royalists who thronged the House of Commons. Had they learned the first rudiments of legislation, they would have known that the enactment to which they attached so much value would be superfluous while the Parliament was disposed to maintain the order of succession, and would be repealed as soon as there was a Parliament bent on changing the order of succession.

The bill, as amended, was passed and carried up to the Lords, but did not become law. The King had obtained from the Parliament all the pecuniary assistance that he could expect; and he conceived that, while rebellion was actually raging, the loyal nobility and gentry would be of more use in their counties than at Westminster. He therefore hurried their deliberations to a close, and, on the second of July, dismissed them. On the same day the royal assent was given to a law reviving that censorship of the press which had terminated in 1679. This object was effected by a few words at the end of a miscellaneous statute which continued several expiring acts. The courtiers did not think that they had gained a triumph. The Whigs did not utter a murmur. Neither in the Lords nor in the Commons was there any division, or even, as far as can now be learned, any debate on a question which would, in our age, convulse the whole frame of society. In truth, the change was slight and almost imperceptible; for, since the detection of the Rye House plot, the liberty of unlicensed printing had existed only in name. During many months scarcely one Whig pamphlet had been published except by stealth; and by stealth such pamphlets might be published still.

The Houses then rose. They were not prorogued, but only adjourned, in order that, when they should reassemble, they might take up their business in the exact state in which they had left it.

While the Parliament was devising sharp laws against Monmouth and his partisans, he found at Taunton a reception which might well encourage him to hope that his enterprise would have a prosperous issue. Taunton, like most other towns in the south of England, was, in that age, more important than at present. Those towns have not indeed declined. On the contrary, they are, with very few exceptions, larger and richer, better built and better peopled, than in the seventeenth century. But, though they have positively advanced, they have relatively gone back. They have been far outstripped in wealth and population by the great manufacturing and commercial cities of the north, cities which, in the time of the Stuarts, were but beginning to be known as seats of industry. When Monmouth marched into Taunton it was an eminently prosperous place. Its markets were plentifully supplied. It was a celebrated seat of the woollen manufacture. The people boasted that they lived in a land flowing with milk and honey. Nor was this language held only by partial natives; for every stranger who climbed the graceful tower of Saint Mary Magdalene owned that he saw beneath him the most fertile of English valleys. It was a country rich with orchards and green pastures, among which were scattered, in gay abundance, manor houses, cottages, and village spires. The townsmen had long leaned towards Presbyterian divinity and Whig politics. In the great civil war Taunton had, through all vicissitudes, adhered to the Parliament, had been twice closely besieged by Goring, and had been twice defended with heroic valour by Robert Blake, afterwards the renowned Admiral of the Commonwealth. Whole streets had been burned down by the mortars and grenades of the Cavaliers. Food had been so scarce that the resolute governor had announced his intention of putting the garrison on rations of horse flesh. But the spirit of the town had never been subdued either by fire or by hunger.

The Restoration had produced no effect on the temper of the Taunton men. They had still continued to celebrate the anniversary of the happy day on which the siege laid to their town by the royal army had been raised; and their stubborn attachment to the old cause had excited so much fear and resentment at Whitehall that, by a royal order, their moat had been filled up, and their wall demolished to the foundation. The puritanical spirit had been kept up to the height among them by the precepts and example of one of the most celebrated of the dissenting clergy, Joseph Alleine. Alleine was the author of a tract, entitled, An Alarm to the Unconverted, which is still popular both in England and in America. From the gaol to which he was consigned by the victorious Cavaliers, he addressed to his loving friends at Taunton many epistles breathing the spirit of a truly heroic piety. His frame soon sank under the effects of study, toil, and persecution: but his memory was long cherished with exceeding love and reverence by those whom he had exhorted and catechised.

The children of the men who, forty years before, had manned the ramparts of Taunton against the Royalists, now welcomed Monmouth with transports of joy and affection. Every door and window was adorned with wreaths of flowers. No man appeared in the streets without wearing in his hat a green bough, the badge of the popular cause. Damsels of the best families in the town wove colours for the insurgents. One flag in particular was embroidered gorgeously with emblems of royal dignity, and was offered to Monmouth by a train of young girls. He received the gift with the winning courtesy which distinguished him. The lady who headed the procession presented him also with a small Bible of great price. He took it with a show of reverence. "I come," he said, "to defend the truths contained in this book, and to seal them, if it must be so, with my blood."

But, while Monmouth enjoyed the applause of the multitude, he could not but perceive, with concern and apprehension, that the higher classes were, with scarcely an exception, hostile to his undertaking, and that no rising had taken place except in the counties where he had himself appeared. He had been assured by agents, who professed to have derived their information from Wildman, that the whole Whig aristocracy was eager to take arms. Nevertheless more than a week had now elapsed since the blue standard had been set up at Lyme. Day labourers, small farmers, shopkeepers, apprentices, dissenting preachers, had flocked to the rebel camp: but not a single peer, baronet, or knight, not a single member of the House of Commons, and scarcely any esquire of sufficient note to have ever been in the commission of the peace, had joined the invaders. Ferguson, who, ever since the death of Charles, had been Monmouth's evil angel, had a suggestion ready. The Duke had put himself into a false position by declining the royal title. Had he declared himself sovereign of England, his cause would have worn a show of legality. At present it was impossible to reconcile his Declaration with the principles of the constitution. It was clear that either Monmouth or his uncle was rightful King. Monmouth did not venture to pronounce himself the rightful King, and yet denied that his uncle was so. Those who fought for James fought for the only person who ventured to claim the throne, and were therefore clearly in their duty, according to the laws of the realm. Those who fought for Monmouth fought for some unknown polity, which was to be set up by a convention not yet in existence. None could wonder that men of high rank and ample fortune stood aloof from an enterprise which threatened with destruction that system in the permanence of which they were deeply interested. If the

Duke would assert his legitimacy and assume the crown, he would at once remove this objection. The question would cease to be a question between the old constitution and a new constitution. It would be merely a question of hereditary right between two princes.

On such grounds as these Ferguson, almost immediately after the landing, had earnestly pressed the Duke to proclaim himself King; and Grey had seconded Ferguson. Monmouth had been very willing to take this advice; but Wade and other republicans had been refractory; and their chief, with his usual pliability, had yielded to their arguments. At Taunton the subject was revived. Monmouth talked in private with the dissentients, assured them that he saw no other way of obtaining the support of any portion of the aristocracy, and succeeded in extorting their reluctant consent. On the morning of the twentieth of June he was proclaimed in the market place of Taunton. His followers repeated his new title with affectionate delight. But, as some confusion might have arisen if he had been called King James the Second, they commonly used the strange appellation of King Monmouth: and by this name their unhappy favourite was often mentioned in the western counties, within the memory of persons still living.

Within twenty four hours after he had assumed the regal title, he put forth several proclamations headed with his sign manual. By one of these he set a price on the head of his rival. Another declared the Parliament then sitting at Westminster an unlawful assembly, and commanded the members to disperse. The third forbade the people to pay taxes to the usurper. The fourth pronounced Albemarle a traitor.

Albemarle transmitted these proclamations to London merely as specimens of folly and impertinence. They produced no effect, except wonder and contempt; nor had Monmouth any reason to think that the assumption of royalty had improved his position. Only a week had elapsed since he had solemnly bound himself not to take the crown till a free Parliament should have acknowledged his rights. By breaking that engagement he had incurred the imputation of levity, if not of perfidy. The class which he had hoped to conciliate still stood aloof. The reasons which prevented the great Whig lords and gentlemen from recognising him as their King were at least as strong as those which had prevented them from rallying round him as their Captain General. They disliked indeed the person, the religion, and the politics of James. But James was no longer young. His eldest daughter was justly popular. She was attached to the reformed faith. She was married to a prince who was the hereditary chief of the Protestants of the Continent, to a prince who had been bred in a republic, and whose sentiments were supposed to be such as became a constitutional King. Was it wise to incur the horrors of civil war, for the mere chance of being able to effect immediately what nature would, without bloodshed, without any violation of law, effect, in all probability, before many years should have expired? Perhaps there might be reasons for pulling down James. But what reason could be given for setting up Monmouth? To exclude a prince from the throne on account of unfitness was a course agreeable to Whig principles. But on no principle could it be proper to exclude rightful heirs, who were admitted to be, not only blameless, but eminently qualified for the highest public trust. That Monmouth was legitimate, nay, that he thought himself legitimate, intelligent men could not believe. He was therefore not merely an usurper, but an usurper of the worst sort, an impostor. If he made out any semblance of a case, he could do so only by means of forgery and perjury. All honest and sensible persons were unwilling to see a fraud which, if practised to obtain an estate, would have been punished with the scourge and the pillory, rewarded with the English crown. To the old nobility of the realm it seemed insupportable that the bastard of Lucy Walters should be set up high above the lawful descendants of the Fitzalans and De Veres. Those who were capable of looking forward must have seen that, if Monmouth should succeed in over-powering the existing government, there would still remain a war between him and the House of Orange, a war which might last longer and produce more misery than the war of the Roses, a war which might probably break up the Protestants of Europe into hostile parties, might arm England and Holland against each other, and might make both those countries an easy prey to France. The opinion, therefore, of almost all the leading Whigs seems to have been that Monmouth's enterprise could not fail to end in some great disaster to the nation, but that, on the whole, his defeat would be a less disaster than his victory.

It was not only by the inaction of the Whig aristocracy that the invaders were disappointed. The wealth and power of London had sufficed in the preceding generation, and might again suffice, to turn the scale in a civil conflict. The Londoners had formerly given many proofs of their hatred of Popery and of their affection for the Protestant Duke. He had too readily believed that, as soon as he landed, there would be a rising in the capital. But, though advices came down to him that many thousands of the citizens had been enrolled as volunteers for the good cause, nothing was done. The plain truth was that the agitators who had encouraged him to invade

England, who had promised to rise on the first signal, and who had perhaps imagined, while the danger was remote, that they should have the courage to keep their promise, lost heart when the critical time drew near. Wildman's fright was such that he seemed to have lost his understanding. The craven Danvers at first excused his inaction by saying that he would not take up arms till Monmouth was proclaimed King, and, when Monmouth had been proclaimed King, turned round and declared that good republicans were absolved from all engagements to a leader who had so shamefully broken faith. In every age the vilest specimens of human nature are to be found among demagogues.

On the day following that on which Monmouth had assumed the regal title he marched from Taunton to Bridgewater. His own spirits, it was remarked, were not high. The acclamations of the devoted thousands who surrounded him wherever he turned could not dispel the gloom which sate on his brow. Those who had seen him during his progress through Somersetshire five years before could not now observe without pity the traces of distress and anxiety on those soft and pleasing features which had won so many hearts.

Ferguson was in a very different temper. With this man's knavery was strangely mingled an eccentric vanity which resembled madness. The thought that he had raised a rebellion and bestowed a crown had turned his head. He swaggered about, brandishing his naked sword, and crying to the crowd of spectators who had assembled to see the army march out of Taunton, "Look at me! You have heard of me. I am Ferguson, the famous Ferguson, the Ferguson for whose head so many hundred pounds have been offered." And this man, at once unprincipled and brainsick, had in his keeping the understanding and the conscience of the unhappy Monmouth.

Bridgewater was one of the few towns which still had some Whig magistrates. The mayor and aldermen came in their robes to welcome the Duke, walked before him in procession to the high cross, and there proclaimed him King. His troops found excellent quarters, and were furnished with necessaries at little or no cost by the people of the town and neighbourhood. He took up his residence in the Castle, a building which had been previously honoured by royal visits. In the Castle Field his army was encamped. It now consisted of about six thousand men, and might easily have been increased to double the number, but for the want of arms. The Duke had brought with him from the Continent but a scanty supply of pikes and muskets. Many of his followers had, therefore, no other weapons than such as could be made out of the tools which they had used in husbandry or mining. Of these rude implements of war the most formidable was made by fastening the blade of a scythe erect on a strong pole. The tithing men of the country round Taunton and Bridgewater received orders to search everywhere for scythes and to bring all that could be found to the camp. It was impossible, however, even with the help of these contrivances, to supply the demand; and great numbers who were desirous to enlist were sent away.

The foot were divided into six regiments. Many of the men had been in the militia, and still wore their uniforms, red and yellow. The cavalry were about a thousand in number; but most of them had only large colts, such as were then bred in great herds on the marshes of Somersetshire for the purpose of supplying London with coach horses and cart horses. These animals were so far from being fit for any military purpose that they had not yet learned to obey the bridle, and became ungovernable as soon as they heard a gun fired or a drum beaten. A small body guard of forty young men, well armed and mounted at their own charge, attended Monmouth. The people of Bridgewater, who were enriched by a thriving coast trade, furnished him with a small sum of money.

All this time the forces of the government were fast assembling. On the west of the rebel army Albemarle still kept together a large body of Devonshire militia. On the east, the trainbands of Wiltshire had mustered under the command of Thomas Herbert, Earl of Pembroke. On the north east, Henry Somerset, Duke of Beaufort, was in arms. The power of Beaufort bore some faint resemblance to that of the great barons of the fifteenth century. He was President of Wales and Lord Lieutenant of four English counties. His official tours through the extensive region in which he represented the majesty of the throne were scarcely inferior in pomp to royal progresses. His household at Badminton was regulated after the fashion of an earlier generation. The land to a great extent round his pleasure grounds was in his own hands; and the labourers who cultivated it formed part of his family. Nine tables were every day spread under his roof for two hundred persons. A crowd of gentlemen and pages were under the orders of his steward. A whole troop of cavalry obeyed the master of the horse. The fame of the kitchen, the cellar, the kennel, and the stables was spread over all England. The gentry, many miles round, were proud of the magnificence of their great neighbour, and were at the same time charmed by his affability and good nature. He was a zealous Cavalier of the old school. At this crisis, therefore, he used his whole influence and authority in support of the crown, and occupied Bristol with the trainbands of Gloucestershire, who seem to have been better disciplined than most other troops of that description.

In the counties more remote from Somersetshire the supporters of the throne were on the alert. The militia of Sussex began to march westward, under the command of Richard, Lord Lumley, who, though he had lately been converted from the Roman Catholic religion, was still firm in his allegiance to a Roman Catholic king. James Bertie, Earl of Abingdon, called out the array of Oxfordshire. John Fell, Bishop of Oxford, who was also Dean of Christchurch, summoned the undergraduates of his University to take arms for the crown. The gownsmen crowded to give in their names. Christchurch alone furnished near a hundred pikemen and musketeers. Young noblemen and gentlemen commoners acted as officers; and the eldest son of the Lord Lieutenant was Colonel.

But it was chiefly on the regular troops that the King relied. Churchill had been sent westward with the Blues; and Feversham was following with all the forces that could be spared from the neighbourhood of London. A courier had started for Holland with a letter directing Skelton instantly to request that the three English regiments in the Dutch service might be sent to the Thames. When the request was made, the party hostile to the House of Orange, headed by the deputies of Amsterdam, again tried to cause delay. But the energy of William, who had almost as much at stake as James, and who saw Monmouth's progress with serious uneasiness, bore down opposition; and in a few days the troops sailed. The three Scotch regiments were already in England. They had arrived at Gravesend in excellent condition, and James had reviewed them on Blackheath. He repeatedly declared to the Dutch Ambassador that he had never in his life seen finer or better disciplined soldiers, and expressed the warmest gratitude to the Prince of Orange and the States for so valuable and seasonable a reinforcement. This satisfaction, however, was not unmixed. Excellently as the men went through their drill, they were not untainted with Dutch politics and Dutch divinity. One of them was shot and another flogged for drinking the Duke of Monmouth's health. It was therefore not thought advisable to place them in the post of danger. They were kept in the neighbourhood of London till the end of the campaign. But their arrival enabled the King to send to the West some infantry which would otherwise have been wanted in the capital.

While the government was thus preparing for a conflict with the rebels in the field, precautions of a different kind were not neglected.

In London alone two hundred of those persons who were thought most likely to be at the head of a Whig movement were arrested. Among the prisoners were some merchants of great note. Every man who was obnoxious to the Court went in fear. A general gloom overhung the capital. Business languished on the Exchange; and the theatres were so generally deserted that a new opera,[1] written by Dryden, and set off by decorations of unprecedented magnificence, was withdrawn, because the receipts would not cover the expenses of the performance. The magistrates and clergy were everywhere active. The Dissenters were everywhere closely observed. In Cheshire and Shropshire a fierce persecution raged: in Northamptonshire arrests were numerous; and the gaol of Oxford was crowded with prisoners. No Puritan divine, however moderate his opinions, however guarded his conduct, could feel any confidence that he should not be torn from his family and flung into a dungeon.

Meanwhile Monmouth advanced from Bridgewater, harassed through the whole march by Churchill, who appears to have done all that, with a handful of men, it was possible for a brave and skilful officer to effect. The rebel army, much annoyed both by the enemy and by a heavy fall of rain, halted in the evening of the twenty-second of June at Glastonbury. The houses of the little town did not afford shelter for so large a force. Some of the troops were therefore quartered in the churches, and others lighted their fires among the venerable ruins of the Abbey, once the wealthiest religious house in our island. From Glastonbury the Duke marched to Wells, and from Wells to Shepton Mallet.

Hitherto he seems to have wandered from place to place with no other object than that of collecting troops. It was now necessary for him to form some plan of military operations. His first scheme was to seize Bristol. Many of the chief inhabitants of that important place were Whigs. One of the ramifications of the Whig plot had extended thither. The garrison consisted only of the Gloucestershire trainbands. If Beaufort and his rustic followers could be overpowered before the regular troops arrived, the rebels would at once find themselves possessed of ample pecuniary resources: the credit of Monmouth's arms would be raised; and his friends throughout the kingdom would be encouraged to declare themselves. Bristol had fortifications which, on the north of the Avon towards Gloucesterhire, were weak, but on the south towards Somersetshire were much stronger. It was therefore determined that the attack should be made on the Gloucestershire side. But for this purpose it was necessary to take a circuitous route, and to cross the Avon at

[1] [*Albion and Albanus.*]

Keynsham. The bridge at Keynsham had been partly demolished by the militia, and was at present impassable. A detachment was therefore sent forward to make the necessary repairs. The other troops followed more slowly, and on the evening of the twenty-fourth of June halted for repose at Pensford. At Pensford they were only five miles from the Somersetshire side of Bristol; but the Gloucestershire side, which could be reached only by going round through Keynsham, was distant a long day's march.

That night was one of great tumult and expectation in Bristol. The partisans of Monmouth knew that he was almost within sight of their city, and imagined that he would be among them before daybreak. About an hour after sunset a merchantman lying at the quay took fire. Such an occurrence, in a port crowded with shipping, could not but excite great alarm. The whole river was in commotion. The streets were crowded. Seditious cries were heard amidst the darkness and confusion. It was afterwards asserted, both by Whigs and by Tories, that the fire had been kindled by the friends of Monmouth, in the hope that the trainbands would be busied in preventing the conflagration from spreading, and that in the meantime the rebel army would make a bold push, and enter the city on the Somersetshire side. If such was the design of the incendiaries, it completely failed. Beaufort, instead of sending his men to the quay, kept them all night drawn up under arms round the beautiful church of Saint Mary Redcliff, on the south of the Avon. He would see Bristol burned down, he said, nay, he would burn it down himself, rather than that it should be occupied by traitors. He was able, with the help of some regular cavalry which had joined him from Chippenham a few hours before, to prevent an insurrection. It might perhaps have been beyond his power at once to overawe the malecontents within the walls and to repel an attack from without: but no such attack was made. The fire, which caused so much commotion at Bristol, was distinctly seen at Pensford. Monmouth, however, did not think it expedient to change his plan. He remained quiet till sunrise, and then marched to Keynsham. There he found the bridge repaired. He determined to let his army rest during the afternoon, and, as soon as night came, to proceed to Bristol.

But it was too late. The King's forces were now near at hand. Colonel Oglethorpe, at the head of about a hundred men of the Life Guards, dashed into Keynsham, scattered two troops of rebel horse which ventured to oppose him, and retired after inflicting much injury and suffering little. In these circumstances it was thought necessary to relinquish the design on Bristol.

But what was to be done? Several schemes were proposed and discussed. It was suggested that Monmouth might hasten to Gloucester, might cross the Severn there, might break down the bridge behind him, and, with his right flank protected by the river, might march through Worcestershire into Shropshire and Cheshire. He had formerly made a progress through those counties, and had been received there with as much enthusiasm as in Somersetshire and Devonshire. His presence might revive the zeal of his old friends; and his army might in a few days be swollen to double its present numbers.

On full consideration, however, it appeared that this plan, though specious, was impracticable. The rebels were ill shod for such work as they had lately undergone, and were exhausted by toiling, day after day, through deep mud under heavy rain. Harassed and impeded as they would be at every stage by the enemy's cavalry, they could not hope to reach Gloucester without being overtaken by the main body of the royal troops, and forced to a general action under every disadvantage.

Then it was proposed to enter Wiltshire. Persons who professed to know that county well assured the Duke that he would be joined there by such strong reinforcements as would make it safe for him to give battle.

He took this advice, and turned towards Wiltshire. He first summoned Bath. But Bath was strongly garrisoned for the King; and Feversham was fast approaching. The rebels, therefore, made no attempt on the walls, but hastened to Philip's Norton, where they halted on the evening of the twenty-sixth of June.

Feversham followed them thither. Early on the morning of the twenty-seventh they were alarmed by tidings that he was close at hand. They got into order, and lined the hedges leading to the town.

The advanced guard of the royal army soon appeared. It consisted of about five hundred men, commanded by the Duke of Grafton, a youth of bold spirit and rough manners, who was probably eager to show that he had no share in the disloyal schemes of his half brother. Grafton soon found himself in a deep lane with fences on both sides of him, from which a galling fire of musketry was kept up. Still he pushed boldly on till he came to the entrance of Philip's Norton. There his way was crossed by a barricade, from which a third fire met him full in front. His men now lost heart, and made the best of their way back. Before they got out of the lane more than a hundred of them had been killed or wounded. Grafton's retreat was intercepted by some of the rebel cavalry: but he cut his way gallantly through them, and came off safe.

The advanced guard, thus repulsed, fell back on the main body of the royal forces. The two armies were now face to face; and a few shots were exchanged that did little or no execution. Neither side was impatient to come to action. Feversham did not wish to fight till his artillery came up, and fell back to Bradford. Monmouth, as soon as the night closed in, quitted his position, marched southward, and by daybreak arrived at Frome, where he hoped to find reinforcements.

Frome was as zealous in his cause as either Taunton or Bridgewater, but could do nothing to serve him. There had been a rising a few days before; and Monmouth's Declaration had been posted up in the market place. But the news of this movement had been carried to the Earl of Pembroke, who lay at no great distance with the Wiltshire militia. He had instantly marched to Frome, had routed a mob of rustics who, with scythes and pitchforks, attempted to oppose him, had entered the town and had disarmed the inhabitants. No weapons, therefore, were left there; nor was Monmouth able to furnish any.

The rebel army was in evil case. The march of the preceding night had been wearisome. The rain had fallen in torrents; and the roads had become mere quagmires. Nothing was heard of the promised succours from Wiltshire. One messenger brought news that Argyle's forces had been dispersed in Scotland. Another reported that Feversham, having been joined by his artillery, was about to advance. Monmouth understood war too well not to know that his followers, with all their courage and all their zeal, were no match for regular soldiers. He had till lately flattered himself with the hope that some of those regiments which he had formerly commanded would pass over to his standard: but that hope he was now compelled to relinquish. His heart failed him. He could scarcely muster firmness enough to give orders. In his misery he complained bitterly of the evil counsellors who had induced him to quit his happy retreat in Brabant. Against Wildman in particular he broke forth into violent imprecations. And now an ignominious thought rose in his weak and agitated mind. He would leave to the mercy of the government the thousands who had, at his call and for his sake, abandoned their quiet fields and dwellings. He would steal away with his chief officers, would gain some seaport before his flight was suspected, would escape to the Continent, and would forget his ambition and his shame in the arms of Lady Wentworth. He seriously discussed the scheme with his leading advisers. Some of them, trembling for their necks, listened to it with approbation:

but Grey, who, by the admission of his detractors, was intrepid everywhere except where swords were clashing and guns going off around him, opposed the dastardly proposition with great ardour, and implored the Duke to face every danger rather than requite with ingratitude and treachery the devoted attachment of the Western peasantry.

The scheme of flight was abandoned: but it was not now easy to form any plan for a campaign. To advance towards London would have been madness; for the road lay right across Salisbury Plain; and on that vast open space regular troops, and above all regular cavalry, would have acted with every advantage against undisciplined men. At this juncture a report reached the camp that the rustics of the marshes near Axbridge had risen in defence of the Protestant religion, had armed themselves with flails, bludgeons and pitchforks, and were assembling by thousands at Bridgewater. Monmouth determined to return thither, and to strengthen himself with these new allies.

The rebels accordingly proceeded to Wells, and arrived there in no amiable temper. They were, with few exceptions, hostile to Prelacy; and they showed their hostility in a way very little to their honour. They not only tore the lead from the roof of the magnificent Cathedral to make bullets, an act for which they might fairly plead the necessities of war, but wantonly defaced the ornaments of the building. Grey with difficulty preserved the altar from the insults of some ruffians who wished to carouse round it, by taking his stand before it with his sword drawn.

On Thursday, the second of July, Monmouth again entered Bridgewater, in circumstances far less cheering than those in which he had marched thence ten days before. The reinforcement which he found there was inconsiderable. The royal army was close upon him. At one moment he thought of fortifying the town; and hundreds of labourers were summoned to dig trenches and throw up mounds. Then his mind recurred to the plan of marching into Cheshire, a plan which he had rejected as impracticable when he was at Keynsham, and which assuredly was not more practicable now that he was at Bridgewater.

While he was thus wavering between projects equally hopeless, the King's forces came in sight. They consisted of about two thousand five hundred regular troops, and of about fifteen hundred of the Wiltshire militia. Early on the morning of Sunday, the fifth of July, they left Somerton, and pitched their tents that day about three miles from Bridegwater, on the plain of Sedgemoor.

Doctor Peter Mew, Bishop of Winchester, accompanied them.

This prelate had in his youth borne arms for Charles the First against the Parliament. Neither his years nor his profession had wholly extinguished his martial ardour; and he probably thought that the appearance of a father of the Protestant Church in the King's camp might confirm the loyalty of some honest men who were wavering between their horror of Popery and their horror of rebellion.

The steeple of the parish church of Bridgewater is said to be the loftiest in Somersetshire, and commands a wide view over the surrounding country. Monmouth, accompanied by some of his officers, went up to the top of the square tower from which the spire ascends, and observed through a telescope the position of the enemy. Beneath him lay a flat expanse, now rich with cornfields and apple trees, but then, as its name imports, for the most part a dreary morass. When the rains were heavy, and the Parret and its tributary streams rose above their banks, this tract was often flooded. It was indeed anciently part of that great swamp which is renowned in our early chronicles as having arrested the progress of two successive races of invaders, which long protected the Celts against the aggressions of the kings of Wessex, and which sheltered Alfred from the pursuit of the Danes. In those remote times this region could be traversed only in boats. It was a vast pool, wherein were scattered many islets of shifting and treacherous soil, overhung with rank jungle, and swarming with deer and wild swine. Even in the days of the Tudors, the traveller whose journey lay from Ilchester to Bridgewater was forced to make a circuit of several miles in order to avoid the waters. When Monmouth looked upon Sedgemoor, it had been partially reclaimed by art, and was intersected by many deep and wide trenches which, in that country, are called rhines. In the midst of the moor rose, clustering round the towers of churches, a few villages, of which the names seem to indicate that they once were surrounded by waves. In one of these villages, called Weston Zoyland, the royal cavalry lay; and Feversham had fixed his head quarters there. Many persons still living have seen the daughter of the servant girl who waited on him that day at table; and a large dish of Persian ware, which was set before him, is still carefully preserved in the neighbourhood. It is to be observed that the population of Somersetshire does not, like that of the manufacturing districts, consist of emigrants from distant places. It is by no means unusual to find farmers who cultivate the same land which their ancestors cultivated when the Plantagenets reigned in England. The Somersetshire traditions are, therefore, of no small value to a historian.

At a greater distance from Bridgewater lies the village of Middlezoy. In that village and its neighbourhood, the Wiltshire militia were quartered, under the command of Pembroke.

On the open moor, not far from Chedzoy, were encamped several battalions of regular infantry. Monmouth looked gloomily on them. He could not but remember how, a few years before, he had, at the head of a column composed of some of those very men, driven before him in confusion the fierce enthusiasts who defended Bothwell Bridge. He could distinguish among the hostile ranks that gallant band which was then called, from the name of its Colonel, Dumbarton's regiment, but which has long been known as the first of the line, and which, in all the four quarters of the world, has nobly supported its early reputation. "I know those men," said Monmouth; "they will fight. If I had but them, all would go well!"

Yet the aspect of the enemy was not altogether discouraging. The three divisions of the royal army lay far apart from one another. There was an appearance of negligence and of relaxed discipline in all their movements. It was reported that they were drinking themselves drunk with the Zoyland cider. The incapacity of Feversham, who commanded in chief, was notorious. Even at this momentous crisis he thought only of eating and sleeping. Churchill was indeed a captain equal to tasks far more arduous than that of scattering a crowd of ill armed and ill trained peasants. But the genius, which, at a later period, humbled six Marshals of France, was not now in its proper place. Feversham told Churchill little, and gave him no encouragement to offer any suggestion. The lieutenant, conscious of superior abilities and science, impatient of the control of a chief whom he despised, and trembling for the fate of the army, nevertheless preserved his characteristic self-command, and dissembled his feelings so well that Feversham praised his submissive alacrity, and promised to report it to the King.

Monmouth, having observed the disposition of the royal forces, and having been apprised of the state in which they were, conceived that a night attack might be attended with success. He resolved to run the hazard, and preparations were instantly made.

It was Sunday; and his followers, who had, for the most part, been brought up after the Puritan fashion, passed a great part of the day in religious exercises. The Castle Field, in which the army was encamped, presented a spectacle such as, since the disbanding of Cromwell's soldiers, England had never seen. The dissenting preachers who had taken arms against Popery, and some of whom had probably fought in the great civil war, prayed and preached in red coats and huge jackboots, with swords by their sides. Ferguson was one of those who harangued. He took for his text the awful imprecation by which the Israelites who dwelt beyond Jordan cleared themselves from the charge ignorantly brought against them by their brethren on the other side of the river. "The Lord God of Gods, the Lord God of Gods, he knoweth; and Israel he shall know. If it be in rebellion, or if in transgression against the Lord, save us not this day."

That an attack was to be made under cover of the night was no secret in Bridgewater. The town was full of women, who had repaired thither by hundreds from the surrounding region, to see their husbands, sons, lovers, and brothers once more. There were many sad partings that day; and many parted never to meet again. The report of the intended attack came to the ears of a young girl who was zealous for the King. Though of modest character, she had the courage to resolve that she would herself bear the intelligence to Feversham. She stole out of Bridgewater, and made her way to the royal camp. But that camp was not a place where female innocence could be safe. Even the officers, despising alike the irregular force to which they were opposed, and the negligent general who commanded them, had indulged largely in wine, and were ready for any excess of licentiousness and cruelty. One of them seized the unhappy maiden, refused to listen to her errand, and brutally outraged her. She fled in agonies of rage and shame, leaving the wicked army to its doom.

And now the time for the great hazard drew near. The night was not ill suited for such an enterprise. The moon was indeed at the full, and the northern streamers were shining brilliantly. But the marsh fog lay so thick on Sedgemoor that no object could be discerned there at the distance of fifty paces.

The clock struck eleven; and the Duke with his body guard rode out of the Castle. He was not in the frame of mind which befits one who is about to strike a decisive blow. The very children who pressed to see him pass observed, and long remembered, that his look was sad and full of evil augury. His army marched by a circuitous path, nearly six miles in length, towards the royal encampment on Sedgemoor. Part of the route is to this day called War Lane. The foot were led by Monmouth himself. The horse were confided to Grey, in spite of the remonstrances of some who remembered the mishap at Bridport. Orders were given that strict silence should be preserved, that no drum should be beaten, and no shot fired. The word by which the insurgents were to recognise one another in the darkness was Soho. It had doubtless been selected in allusion to Soho Fields in London, where their leader's palace stood.

At about one in the morning of Monday the sixth of July, the rebels were on the open moor. But between them and the enemy lay three broad rhines filled with water and soft mud. Two of these, called the Black Ditch and the Langmoor Rhine, Monmouth knew that he must pass. But, strange to say, the existence of a trench, called the Bussex Rhine, which immediately covered the royal encampment, had not been mentioned to him by any of his scouts.

The wains which carried the ammunition remained at the entrance of the moor. The horse and foot, in a long narrow column, passed the Black Ditch by a causeway. There was a similar causeway across the Langmoor Rhine; but the guide, in the fog, missed his way. There was some delay and some tumult before the error could be rectified. At length the passage was effected: but, in the confusion, a pistol went off. Some men of the Horse Guards, who were on watch, heard the report, and perceived that a great multitude was advancing through the mist. They fired their carbines, and galloped off in different directions to give the alarm. Some hastened to Weston Zoyland, where the cavalry lay. One trooper spurred to the encampment of the infantry, and cried out vehemently that the enemy was at hand. The drums of Dumbarton's regiment beat to arms; and the men got fast into their ranks. It was time; for Monmouth was already drawing up his army for action. He ordered Grey to lead the way with the cavalry, and followed himself at the head of the infantry. Grey pushed on till his progress was unexpectedly arrested by the Bussex Rhine. On the opposite side of the ditch the King's foot were hastily forming in order of battle.

"For whom are you?" called out an officer of the Foot Guards. "For the King," replied a voice from the ranks of the rebel cavalry. "For which King?" was then demanded. The answer was a shout of "King Monmouth," mingled with the war cry, which forty years before had been inscribed on the colours of the parliamentary regiments, "God with us." The royal troops instantly fired such a volley of musketry as sent the rebel horse flying in all directions. The world agreed to ascribe this ignominious rout to Grey's pusillanimity. Yet it is by no means clear that Churchill would have succeeded better at the head of men who had never before handled arms on horseback, and whose horses were unused, not only to stand fire, but to obey the rein.

A few minutes after the Duke's horse had dispersed themselves over the moor, his infantry came up running fast, and guided through the gloom by the lighted matches of Dumbarton's regiment.

Monmouth was startled by finding that a broad and profound trench lay between him and the camp which he had hoped to surprise. The insurgents halted on the edge of the rhine, and fired. Part of the royal infantry on the opposite bank returned the fire. During three quarters of an hour the roar of the musketry was incessant. The Somersetshire peasants behaved themselves as if they had been veteran soldiers, save only that they levelled their pieces too high.

But now the other divisions of the royal army were in motion. The Life Guards and Blues came pricking fast from Weston Zoyland, and scattered in an instant some of Grey's horse, who had attempted to rally. The fugitives spread a panic among their comrades in the rear, who had charge of the ammunition. The waggoners drove off at full speed, and never stopped till they were many miles from the field of battle. Monmouth had hitherto done his part like a stout and able warrior. He had been seen on foot, pike in hand, encouraging his infantry by voice and by example. But he was too well acquainted with military affairs not to know that all was over. His men had lost the advantage which surprise and darkness had given them. They were deserted by the horse and by the ammunition waggons. The King's forces were now united and in good order. Feversham had been awakened by the firing, had got out of bed, had adjusted his cravat, had looked at himself well in the glass, and had come to see what his men were doing. Meanwhile, what was of much more importance. Churchill had rapidly made an entirely new disposition of the royal infantry. The day was about to break. The event of a conflict on an open plain, by broad sunlight, could not be doubtful. Yet Monmouth should have felt that it was not for him to fly, while thousands whom affection for him had hurried to destruction were still fighting manfully in his cause. But vain hopes and the intense love of life prevailed. He saw that if he tarried the royal cavalry would soon intercept his retreat. He mounted and rode from the field.

Yet his foot, though deserted, made a gallant stand. The Life Guards attacked them on the right, the Blues on the left: but the Somersetshire clowns, with their scythes and the but ends of their muskets, faced the royal horse like old soldiers. Oglethorpe made a vigorous attempt to break them and was manfully repulsed. Sarsfield, a brave Irish officer, whose name afterwards obtained a melancholy celebrity, charged on the other flank. His men were beaten back. He was himself struck to the ground, and lay for a time as one dead. But the struggle of the hardy rustics could not last. Their powder and ball were spent. Cries were heard of "Ammunition! for God's sake ammunition!" But no ammunition was at hand. And now the King's artillery came up. It had been posted half a mile off, on the high road from Weston Zoyland to Bridgewater. So defective were then the appointments of an English army that there would have been much difficulty in dragging the great guns to the place where the battle was raging, had not the Bishop of Winchester offered his coach horses and traces for the purpose. This interference of a Christian prelate in a matter of blood has, with strange inconsistency, been condemned by some Whig writers who can see nothing criminal in the conduct of the numerous Puritan ministers then in arms against the government. Even when the guns had arrived, there was such a want of gunners that a sergeant of Dumbarton's regiment was forced to take on himself the management of several pieces. The cannon, however, though ill served, brought the engagement to a speedy close. The pikes of the rebel battalions began to shake: the ranks broke; the King's cavalry charged again, and bore down every thing before them; the King's infantry came pouring across the ditch. Even in that extremity the Mendip miners stood bravely to their arms, and sold their lives dearly. But the rout was in a few minutes complete. Three hundred of the soldiers had been killed or wounded. Of the rebels more than a thousand lay dead on the moor.

So ended the last fight, deserving the name of battle, that has been fought on English ground. The impression left on the simple inhabitants of the neighbourhood was deep and lasting. That impression, indeed, has been frequently renewed. For even in our own time the plough and the spade have not seldom turned up ghastly memorials of the slaughter, skulls, and thighbones, and strange weapons made out of implements of husbandry. Old peasants related very recently that, in their childhood, they were accustomed to play on the moor at the fight between King James's men and King Monmouth's men, and that King Monmouth's men always raised the cry of Soho.

What seems most extraordinary in the battle of Sedgemoor is that the event should have been for a moment doubtful, and that the rebels should have resisted so long. That five or six thousand colliers and ploughmen should contend during an hour with half that number of regular cavalry and infantry would now be thought a miracle. Our wonder will, perhaps, be diminished when we remember that, in the time of James the Second, the discipline of the regular army was extremely lax, and that, on the other hand, the peasantry were accustomed to serve in the militia. The difference, therefore, between a regiment of Foot Guards and a regiment of clowns just enrolled, though doubtless considerable, was by no means what it now is. Monmouth did not lead a mere mob to attack good soldiers. For his followers were not altogether without a tincture of soldiership; and Feversham's troops, when compared with English troops of our time, might almost be called a mob.

It was four o'clock: the sun was rising; and the routed army came pouring into the streets of Bridgewater. The uproar, the blood, the gashes, the ghastly figures which sank down and never rose again, spread horror and dismay through the town. The pursuers, too, were close behind. Those inhabitants who had favoured the insurrection expected sack and massacre, and implored the protection of their neighbours who professed the Roman Catholic religion, or had made themselves conspicuous by Tory politics; and it is acknowledged by the bitterest of Whig historians that this protection was kindly and generously given.

During that day the conquerors continued to chase the fugitives. The neighbouring villagers long remembered with what a clatter of horsehoofs and what a storm of curses the whirlwind of cavalry swept by. Before evening five hundred prisoners had been crowded into the parish church of Weston Zoyland. Eighty of them were wounded; and five expired within the consecrated walls. Great numbers of labourers were impressed for the purpose of burying the slain. A few, who were notoriously partial to the vanquished side, were set apart for the hideous office of quartering the captives. The tithing men of the neighbouring parishes were busied in setting up gibbets and providing chains. All this while the bells of Weston Zoyland and Chedzoy rang joyously, and the soldiers sang and rioted on the moor amidst the corpses. For the farmers of the neighbourhood had made haste, as soon as the event of the fight was known, to send hogsheads of their best cider as peace offerings to the victors.

Feversham passed for a goodnatured man: but he was a foreigner, ignorant of the laws and careless of the feelings of the English.[1] He was accustomed to the military license of France, and had learned from his great kinsman, the conqueror and devastator of the Palatinate, not indeed how to conquer, but how to devastate. A considerable number of prisoners were immediately selected for execution. Among them was a youth famous for his speed. Hopes were held out to him that his life would be spared if he could run a

[1] [Louis Duras, Earl of Feversham, was a Frenchman and a nephew of Turenne.]

race with one of the colts of the marsh. The space through which the man kept up with the horse is still marked by well known bounds on the moor, and is about three quarters of a mile. Feversham was not ashamed, after seeing the performance, to send the wretched performer to the gallows. The next day a long line of gibbets appeared on the road leading from Bridgewater to Weston Zoyland. On each gibbet a prisoner was suspended. Four of the sufferers were left to rot in irons.

Meanwhile Monmouth, accompanied by Grey, by Buyse, and by a few other friends, was flying from the field of battle. At Chedzoy he stopped a moment to mount a fresh horse and to hide his blue riband and his George. He then hastened towards the Bristol Channel. From the rising ground on the north of the field of battle he saw the flash and the smoke of the last volley fired by his deserted followers. Before six o'clock he was twenty miles from Sedgemoor. Some of his companions advised him to cross the water, and to seek refuge in Wales; and this would undoubtedly have been his wisest course. He would have been in Wales many hours before the news of his defeat was known there; and, in a country so wild, and so remote from the seat of government, might have remained long undiscovered. He determined, however, to push for Hampshire, in the hope that he might lurk in the cabins of deerstealers among the oaks of the New Forest, till means of conveyance to the Continent could be procured. He therefore, with Grey and the German, turned to the south east. But the way was beset with dangers. The three fugitives had to traverse a country in which every one already knew the event of the battle, and in which no traveller of suspicious appearance could escape a close scrutiny. They rode on all day shunning towns and villages. Nor was this so difficult as it may now appear. For men then living could remember the time when the wild deer ranged freely through a succession of·forests from the banks of the Avon in Wiltshire to the southern coast of Hampshire. At length, on Cranbourne Chase, the strength of the horses failed. They were therefore turned loose. The bridles and saddles were concealed. Monmouth and his friends procured rustic attire, disguised themselves, and proceeded on foot towards the New Forest. They passed the night in the open air: but before morning they were surrounded on every side by toils. Lord Lumley, who lay at Ringwood with a strong body of the Sussex militia, had sent forth parties in every direction. Sir William Portman, with the Somerset militia, had formed a chain of posts from the sea to the northern extremity of Dorset. At five in the morning of the seventh, Grey, who had wandered from his friends, was seized by two of the

Sussex scouts. He submitted to his fate with the calmness of one to whom suspense was more intolerable than despair. "Since we landed," he said, "I have not had one comfortable meal or one quiet night." It could hardly be doubted that the chief rebel was not far off. The pursuers redoubled their vigilance and activity. The cottages scattered over the heathy country on the boundaries of Dorsetshire and Hampshire were strictly examined by Lumley; and the clown with whom Monmouth had changed clothes was discovered. Portman came with a strong body of horse and foot to assist in the search. Attention was soon drawn to a place well fitted to shelter fugitives. It was an extensive tract of land separated by an enclosure from the open country, and divided by numerous hedges into small fields. In some of these fields the rye, the pease, and the oats were high enough to conceal a man. Others were overgrown by fern and brambles. A poor woman reported that she had seen two strangers lurking in this covert. The near prospect of reward animated the zeal of the troops. It was agreed that every man who did his duty in the search should have a share of the promised five thousand pounds. The outer fence was strictly guarded: the space within was examined with indefatigable diligence; and several dogs of quick scent were turned out among the bushes. The day closed before the work could be completed: but careful watch was kept all night. Thirty times the fugitives ventured to look through the outer hedge: but everywhere they found a sentinel on the alert: once they were seen and fired at; they then separated and concealed themselves in different hiding places.

At sunrise the next morning the search recommenced, and Buyse was found. He owned that he had parted from the Duke only a few hours before. The corn and copsewood were now beaten with more care than ever. At length a gaunt figure was discovered hidden in a ditch. The pursuers sprang on their prey. Some of them were about to fire: but Portman forbade all violence. The prisoner's dress was that of a shepherd; his beard, prematurely grey, was of several days' growth. He trembled greatly, and was unable to speak. Even those who had often seen him were at first in doubt whether this were truly the brilliant and graceful Monmouth. His pockets were searched by Portman, and in them were found, among some raw pease gathered in the rage of hunger, a watch, a purse of gold, a small treatise on fortification, an album filled with songs, receipts, prayers, and charms, and the George with which, many years before, King Charles the Second had decorated his favourite son. Messengers were instantly despatched to Whitehall with the good news, and with the George as a token that the news was true.

The prisoner was conveyed under a strong guard to Ringwood.

And all was lost; and nothing remained but that he should prepare to meet death as became one who had thought himself not unworthy to wear the crown of William the Conqueror and of Richard the Lionhearted, of the hero of Cressy and of the hero of Agincourt. The captive might easily have called to mind other domestic examples, still better suited to his condition. Within a hundred years, two sovereigns whose blood ran in his veins, one of them a delicate woman, had been placed in the same situation in which he now stood. They had shown, in the prison and on the scaffold, a virtue of which, in the season of prosperity, they had seemed incapable, and had half redeemed great crimes and errors by enduring with Christian meekness and princely dignity all that victorious enemies could inflict. Of cowardice Monmouth had never been accused; and, even had he been wanting in constitutional courage, it might have been expected that the defect would be supplied by pride and by despair. The eyes of the whole world were upon him. The latest generations would know how, in that extremity, he had borne himself. To the brave peasants of the West he owed it to show that they had not poured forth their blood for a leader unworthy of their attachment. To her who had sacrificed every thing for his sake he owed it so to bear himself that, though she might weep for him, she should not blush for him. It was not for him to lament and supplicate. His reason, too, should have told him that lamentation and supplication would be unavailing. He had done that which could never be forgiven. He was in the grasp of one who never forgave.

But the fortitude of Monmouth was not that highest sort of fortitude which is derived from reflection and from selfrespect; nor had nature given him one of those stout hearts from which neither adversity nor peril can extort any sign of weakness. His courage rose and fell with his animal spirits. It was sustained on the field of battle by the excitement of action, by the hope of victory, by the strange influence of sympathy. All such aids were now taken away. The spoiled darling of the court and of the populace, accustomed to be loved and worshipped wherever he appeared, was now surrounded by stern gaolers in whose eyes he read his doom. Yet a few hours of gloomy seclusion, and he must die a violent and shameful death. His heart sank within him. Life seemed worth purchasing by any humiliation; nor could his mind, always feeble, and now distracted by terror, perceive that humiliation must degrade, but could not save him.

As soon as he reached Ringwood he wrote to the King. The

letter was that of a man whom a craven fear had made insensible to shame. He professed in vehement terms his remorse for his treason. He affirmed that, when he promised his cousins at the Hague not to raise troubles in England, he had fully meant to keep his word. Unhappily he had afterwards been seduced from his allegiance by some horrid people who had heated his mind by calumnies and misled him by sophistry: but now he abhorred them: he abhorred himself. He begged in piteous terms that he might be admitted to the royal presence. There was a secret which he could not trust to paper, a secret which lay in a single word, and which, if he spoke that word, would secure the throne against all danger. On the following day he despatched letters, imploring the Queen Dowager and the Lord Treasurer to intercede in his behalf.

When it was known in London how he had abased himself the general surprise was great; and no man was more amazed than Barillon, who had resided in England during two bloody proscriptions, and had seen numerous victims, both of the Opposition and of the Court, submit to their fate without womanish entreaties and lamentations.

Monmouth and Grey remained at Ringwood two days. They were then carried up to London, under the guard of a large body of regular troops and militia. In the coach with the Duke was an officer whose orders were to stab the prisoner if a rescue were attempted. At every town along the road the trainbands of the neighbourhood had been mustered under the command of the principal gentry. The march lasted three days, and terminated at Vauxhall, where a regiment, commanded by George Legge, Lord Dartmouth, was in readiness to receive the prisoners. They were put on board of a state barge, and carried down the river to White-hall Stairs. Lumley and Portman had alternately watched the Duke day and night till they had brought him within the walls of the palace.

Both the demeanour of Monmouth and that of Grey, during the journey, filled all observers with surprise. Monmouth was altogether unnerved. Grey was not only calm but cheerful, talked pleasantly of horses, dogs, and field sports, and even made jocose allusions to the perilous situation in which he stood.

The King cannot be blamed for determining that Monmouth should suffer death. Every man who heads a rebellion against an established government stakes his life on the event: and rebellion was the smallest part of Monmouth's crime. He had declared against his uncle a war without quarter. In the manifesto put forth at Lyme, James had been held up to execration as an incendiary, as an assassin who had strangled one innocent man and cut the throat of another, and, lastly, as the poisoner of his own brother. To spare an enemy who had not scrupled to resort to such extremities would have been an act of rare, perhaps of blamable generosity. But to see him and not to spare him was an outrage on humanity and decency. This outrage the King resolved to commit. The arms of the prisoner were bound behind him with a silken cord; and, thus secured, he was ushered into the presence of the implacable kinsman whom he had wronged.

Then Monmouth threw himself on the ground, and crawled to the King's feet. He wept. He tried to embrace his uncle's knees with his pinioned arms. He begged for life, only life, life at any price. He owned that he had been guilty of a great crime, but tried to throw the blame on others, particularly on Argyle, who would rather have put his legs into the boots[1] than have saved his own life by such baseness. By the ties of kindred, by the memory of the late King, who had been the best and truest of brothers, the unhappy man adjured James to show some mercy. James gravely replied that this repentance was of the latest, that he was sorry for the misery which the prisoner had brought on himself, but that the case was not one for lenity. A Declaration, filled with atrocious calumnies, had been put forth. The regal title had been assumed. For treasons so aggravated there could be no pardon on this side of the grave. The poor terrified Duke vowed that he had never wished to take the crown, but had been led into that fatal error by others. As to the Declaration, he had not written it: he had not read it: he had signed it without looking at it: it was all the work of Ferguson, that bloody villain Ferguson. "Do you expect me to believe," said James, with contempt but too well merited, "that you set your hand to a paper of such moment without knowing what it contained?" One depth of infamy only remained; and even to that the prisoner descended. He was preeminently the champion of the Protestant religion. The interest of that religion had been his plea for conspiring against the government of his father, and for bringing on his country the miseries of civil war: yet he was not ashamed to hint that he was inclined to be reconciled to the Church of Rome. The King eagerly offered him spiritual assistance, but said nothing of pardon or respite. "Is there then no hope?" asked Monmouth. James turned away in silence. Then Monmouth strove to rally his courage, rose from his knees, and retired with a firmness which he had not shown since his overthrow.

Grey was introduced next. He behaved with a propriety and

[1] [An instrument of torture.]

fortitude which moved even the stern and resentful King, frankly owned himself guilty, made no excuses, and did not once stoop to ask his life. Both the prisoners were sent to the Tower by water. There was no tumult; but many thousands of people, with anxiety and sorrow in their faces, tried to catch a glimpse of the captives. The Duke's resolution failed as soon as he had left the royal presence. On his way to his prison he bemoaned himself, accused his followers, and abjectly implored the intercession of Dartmouth. "I know, my Lord, that you loved my father. For his sake, for God's sake, try if there be any room for mercy." Dartmouth replied that the King had spoken the truth, and that a subject who assumed the regal title excluded himself from all hope of pardon.

Soon after Monmouth had been lodged in the Tower, he was informed that his wife had, by the royal command, been sent to see him. She was accompanied by the Earl of Clarendon, Keeper of the Privy Seal. Her husband received her very coldly, and addressed almost all his discourse to Clarendon, whose intercession he earnestly implored. Clarendon held out no hopes; and that same evening two prelates, Turner, Bishop of Ely, and Ken, Bishop of Bath and Wells, arrived at the Tower with a solemn message from the King. It was Monday night. On Wednesday morning Monmouth was to die.

He was greatly agitated. The blood left his cheeks; and it was some time before he could speak. Most of the short time which remained to him he wasted in vain attempts to obtain, if not a pardon, at least a respite. He wrote piteous letters to the King and to several courtiers, but in vain. Some Roman Catholic divines were sent to him from Whitehall. But they soon discovered that, though he would gladly have purchased his life by renouncing the religion of which he had professed himself in an especial manner the defender, yet, if he was to die, he would as soon die without their absolution as with it.

Nor were Ken and Turner much better pleased with his frame of mind. The doctrine of nonresistance was, in their view, as in the view of most of their brethren, the distinguishing badge of the Anglican Church. The two Bishops insisted on Monmouth's owning that, in drawing the sword against the government, he had committed a great sin; and, on this point, they found him obstinately heterodox. Nor was this his only heresy. He maintained that his connection with Lady Wentworth was blameless in the sight of God. He had been married, he said, when a child. He had never cared for his Duchess. The happiness which he had not found at home he had sought in a round of loose amours, condemned by religion and morality. Henrietta had reclaimed him from a life of vice. To her he had been strictly constant. They had, by common consent, offered up fervent prayers for the divine guidance. After those prayers they had found their affection for each other strengthened; and they could then no longer doubt that, in the sight of God, they were a wedded pair. The Bishops were so much scandalised by this view of the conjugal relation that they refused to administer the sacrament to the prisoner. All that they could obtain from him was a promise that, during the single night which still remained to him, he would pray to be enlightened if he were in error.

On the Wednesday morning, at his particular request, Doctor Thomas Tenison, who then held the vicarage of Saint Martin's, and, in that important cure, had obtained the high esteem of the public, came to the Tower. From Tenison, whose opinions were known to be moderate, the Duke expected more indulgence than Ken and Turner were disposed to show. But Tenison, whatever might be his sentiments concerning nonresistance in the abstract, thought the late rebellion rash and wicked, and considered Monmouth's notion respecting marriage as a most dangerous delusion. Monmouth was obstinate. He had prayed, he said, for the divine direction. His sentiments remained unchanged; and he could not doubt that they were correct. Tenison's exhortations were in a milder tone than those of the Bishops. But he, like them, thought that he should not be justified in administering the Eucharist to one whose penitence was of so unsatisfactory a nature.

The hour drew near: all hope was over; and Monmouth had passed from pusillanimous fear to the apathy of despair. His children were brought to his room that he might take leave of them, and were followed by his wife. He spoke to her kindly, but without emotion. Though she was a woman of great strength of mind, and had little cause to love him, her misery was such that none of the bystanders could refrain from weeping. He alone was unmoved.

It was ten o'clock. The coach of the Lieutenant of the Tower was ready. Monmouth requested his spiritual advisers to accompany him to the place of execution; and they consented: but they told him that, in their judgment, he was about to die in a perilous state of mind, and that, if they attended him, it would be their duty to exhort him to the last. As he passed along the ranks of the guards he saluted them with a smile, and mounted the scaffold with a firm tread. Tower Hill was covered up to the chimney tops with an innumerable multitude of gazers, who, in awful silence, broken

only by sighs and the noise of weeping, listened for the last accents
of the darling of the people. "I shall say little," he began. "I
come here, not to speak, but to die. I die a Protestant of the Church
of England." The Bishops interrupted him, and told him that,
unless he acknowledged resistance to be sinful, he was no member
of their church. He went on to speak of his Henrietta. She was,
he said, a young lady of virtue and honour. He loved her to the
last, and he could not die without giving utterance to his feelings.
The Bishops again interfered and begged him not to use such
language. Some altercation followed. The divines have been
accused of dealing harshly with the dying man. But they appear
to have only discharged what, in their view, was a sacred duty.
Monmouth knew their principles, and, if he wished to avoid their
importunity, should have dispensed with their attendance. Their
general arguments against resistance had no effect on him. But
when they reminded him of the ruin which he had brought on his
brave and loving followers, of the blood which had been shed, of
the souls which had been sent unprepared to the great account, he
was touched, and said, in a softened voice, "I do own that. I am
sorry that it ever happened." They prayed with him long and
fervently; and he joined in their petitions till they invoked a blessing
on the King. He remained silent. "Sir," said one of the Bishops,
"do you not pray for the King with us?" Monmouth paused some
time, and, after an internal struggle, exclaimed "Amen." But it was
in vain that the prelates implored him to address to the soldiers and
to the people a few words on the duty of obedience to the government. "I will make no speeches," he exclaimed. "Only ten words,
my Lord." He turned away, called his servant, and put into the
man's hand a toothpick case, the last token of ill starred love.
"Give it," he said "to that person." He then accosted John Ketch
the executioner, a wretch who had butchered many brave and noble
victims, and whose name has, during a century and a half, been
vulgarly given to all who have succeeded him in his odious office.
"Here," said the Duke, "are six guineas for you. Do not hack me
as you did my Lord Russell. I have heard that you struck him three
or four times. My servant will give you some more gold if you do
the work well." He then undressed, felt the edge of the axe, expressed some fear that it was not sharp enough, and laid his head on
the block. The divines in the meantime continued to ejaculate with
great energy; "God accept your repentance! God accept your
imperfect repentance!"

The hangman addressed himself to his office. But he had been
disconcerted by what the Duke had said. The first blow inflicted

only a slight wound. The Duke struggled, rose from the block, and looked reproachfully at the executioner. The head sank down once more. The stroke was repeated again and again; but still the neck was not severed, and the body continued to move. Yells of rage and horror rose from the crowd. Ketch flung down the axe with a curse. "I cannot do it," he said; "my heart fails me." "Take up the axe, man," cried the sheriff. "Fling him over the rails," roared the mob. At length the axe was taken up. Two more blows extinguished the last remains of life; but a knife was used to separate the head from the shoulders. The crowd was wrought up to such an ecstasy of rage that the executioner was in danger of being torn in pieces, and was conveyed away under a strong guard.

In the meantime many handkerchiefs were dipped in the Duke's blood; for by a large part of the multitude he was regarded as a martyr who had died for the Protestant religion. The head and body were placed in a coffin covered with black velvet, and were laid privately under the communion table of Saint Peter's Chapel in the Tower. Within four years the pavement of that chancel was again disturbed, and hard by the remains of Monmouth were laid the remains of Jeffreys. In truth there is no sadder spot on the earth than that little cemetery. Death is there associated, not, as in Westminster Abbey and Saint Paul's, with genius and virtue, with public veneration and with imperishable renown; not, as in our humblest churches and churchyards, with every thing that is most endearing in social and domestic charities; but with whatever is darkest in human nature and in human destiny, with the savage triumph of implacable enemies, with the inconstancy, the ingratitude, the cowardice of friends, with all the miseries of fallen greatness and of blighted fame. Thither have been carried, through successive ages, by the rude hands of gaolers, without one mourner following, the bleeding relics of men who had been the captains of armies, the leaders of parties, the oracles of senates, and the ornaments of courts. Thither was borne, before the window where Jane Grey was praying, the mangled corpse of Guilford Dudley. Edward Seymour, Duke of Somerset, and Protector of the realm, reposes there by the brother whom he murdered. There has mouldered away the headless trunk of John Fisher, Bishop of Rochester and Cardinal of Saint Vitalis, a man worthy to have lived in a better age, and to have died in a better cause. There are laid John Dudley, Duke of Northumberland, Lord High Admiral, and Thomas Cromwell, Earl of Essex, Lord High Treasurer. There, too, is another Essex, on whom nature and fortune had lavished all their bounties in vain, and whom valour, grace, genius, royal favour, popular applause, conducted to an early and ignominious doom. Not far off sleep two chiefs of the great house of Howard, Thomas, fourth Duke of Norfolk, and Philip, eleventh Earl of Arundel. Here and there, among the thick graves of unquiet and aspiring statesmen, lie more delicate sufferers; Margaret of Salisbury, the last of the proud name of Plantagenet, and those two fair Queens who perished by the jealous rage of Henry. Such was the dust with which the dust of Monmouth mingled.

Yet a few months, and the quiet village of Toddington, in Bedfordshire, witnessed a still sadder funeral. Near that village stood an ancient and stately hall, the seat of the Wentworths. The transept of the parish church had long been their burial place. To that burial place, in the spring which followed the death of Monmouth, was borne the coffin of the young Baroness Wentworth of Nettlestede. Her family reared a sumptuous mausoleum over her remains: but a less costly memorial of her was long contemplated with far deeper interest. Her name, carved by the hand of him whom she loved too well, was, a few years ago, still discernible on a tree in the adjoining park.

It was not by Lady Wentworth alone that the memory of Monmouth was cherished with idolatrous fondness. His hold on the hearts of the people lasted till the generation which had seen him had passed away. Ribands, buckles, and other trifling articles of apparel which he had worn, were treasured up as precious relics by those who had fought under him at Sedgemoor. Old men who long survived him desired, when they were dying, that these trinkets might be buried with them. One button of gold thread which narrowly escaped this fate may still be seen at a house which overlooks the field of battle. Nay, such was the devotion of the people to their unhappy favourite that, in the face of the strongest evidence by which the fact of a death was ever verified, many continued to cherish a hope that he was still living, and that he would again appear in arms. A person, it was said, who was remarkably like Monmouth, had sacrificed himself to save the Protestant hero. The vulgar long continued, at every important crisis, to whisper that the time was at hand, and that King Monmouth would soon show himself. In 1686, a knave who had pretended to be the Duke, and had levied contributions in several villages of Wiltshire, was apprehended, and whipped from Newgate to Tyburn. In 1698, when England had long enjoyed constitutional freedom under a new dynasty, the son of an innkeeper passed himself on the yeomanry of Sussex as their beloved Monmouth, and defrauded many who were by no means of the lowest class. Five hundred pounds were collected for him. The farmers provided him with a horse. Their wives sent him baskets of chickens and ducks, and were lavish, it was said, of favours of a more tender kind; for, in gallantry at least, the counterfeit was a not unworthy representative of the original. When this impostor was thrown into prison for his fraud, his followers maintained him in luxury. Several of them appeared at the bar to countenance him when he was tried at the Horsham assizes. So long did this delusion last that, when George the Third had been some years on the English throne, Voltaire thought it necessary gravely to confute the hypothesis that the man in the iron mask was the Duke of Monmouth.

THE SEVEN BISHOPS

On the twenty-seventh of April 1688, the King put forth a second Declaration of Indulgence. In this paper he recited at length the Declaration of the preceding April. His past life, he said, ought to have convinced his people that he was not a man who could easily be induced to depart from any resolution which he had formed. But, as designing men had attempted to persuade the world that he might be prevailed on to give way in this matter, he thought it necessary to proclaim that his purpose was immutably fixed, that he was resolved to employ those only who were prepared to concur in his design, and that he had, in pursuance of that resolution, dismissed many of his disobedient servants from civil and military employments. He announced that he meant to hold a Parliament in November at the latest; and he exhorted his subjects to choose representatives who would assist him in the great work which he had undertaken.

This Declaration at first produced little sensation. It contained nothing new; and men wondered that the King should think it worth while to publish a solemn manifesto merely for the purpose of telling them that he had not changed his mind. Perhaps James was nettled by the indifference with which the announcement of his fixed resolution was received by the public, and thought that his dignity and authority would suffer unless he without delay did something novel and striking. On the fourth of May, accordingly, he made an Order in Council that his Declaration of the preceding week should be read, on two successive Sundays, at the time of divine service, by the officiating ministers of all the churches and chapels of the kingdom. In London and in the suburbs the reading was to take place on the twentieth and twenty-seventh of May, in other parts of England on the third and tenth of June. The

Bishops were directed to distribute copies of the Declaration through their respective dioceses.

When it is considered that the clergy of the Established Church, with scarcely an exception, regarded the Indulgence as a violation of the laws of the realm, as a breach of the plighted faith of the King, and as a fatal blow levelled at the interest and dignity of their own profession, it will scarcely admit of doubt that the Order in Council was intended to be felt by them as a cruel affront. It was popularly believed that Petre had avowed this intention in a coarse metaphor borrowed from the rhetoric of the East. He would, he said, make them eat dirt, the vilest and most loathsome of all dirt. But, tyrannical and malignant as the mandate was, would the Anglican priesthood refuse to obey? The King's temper was arbitrary and severe. The proceedings of the Ecclesiastical Commission were as summary as those of a court martial. Whoever ventured to resist might in a week be ejected from his parsonage, deprived of his whole income, pronounced incapable of holding any other spiritual preferment, and left to beg from door to door. If, indeed, the whole body offered an united opposition to the royal will, it was probable that even James would scarcely venture to punish ten thousand delinquents at once. But there was not time to form an extensive combination. The Order in Council was gazetted on the seventh of May. On the twentieth the Declaration was to be read in all the pulpits of London and the neighbourhood. By no exertion was it possible in that age to ascertain within a fortnight the intentions of one tenth part of the parochial ministers who were scattered over the kingdom. It was not easy to collect in so short a time the sense even of the episcopal order. It might also well be apprehended that, if the clergy refused to read the Declaration, the Protestant Dissenters would misinterpret the refusal, would despair of obtaining any toleration from the members of the Church of England, and would throw their whole weight into the scale of the Court.

The clergy therefore hesitated; and this hesitation may well be excused: for some eminent laymen, who possessed a large share of the public confidence, were disposed to recommend submission. They thought that a general opposition could hardly be expected, and that a partial opposition would be ruinous to individuals, and of little advantage to the Church and to the nation. Such was the opinion given at this time by Halifax and Nottingham. The day drew near; and still there was no concert and no formed resolution.

At this conjuncture the Protestant Dissenters of London won for themselves a title to the lasting gratitude of their country. They had hitherto been reckoned by the government as part of its strength. A few of their most active and noisy preachers, corrupted by the favours of the Court, had got up addresses in favour of the King's policy. Others, estranged by the recollection of many cruel wrongs both from the Church of England and from the House of Stuart, had seen with resentful pleasure the tyrannical prince and the tyrannical hierarchy separated by a bitter enmity, and bidding against each other for the help of sects lately persecuted and despised. But this feeling, however natural, had been indulged long enough. The time had come when it was necessary to make a choice; and the Nonconformists of the City, with a noble spirit, arrayed themselves side by side with the members of the Church in defence of the fundamental laws of the realm. Baxter, Bates, and Howe distinguished themselves by their efforts to bring about this coalition: but the generous enthusiasm which pervaded the whole Puritan body made the task easy. The zeal of the flocks outran that of the pastors. Those Presbyterian and Independent teachers who showed an inclination to take part with the King against the ecclesiastical establishment received distinct notice that, unless they changed their conduct, their congregations would neither hear them nor pay them. Alsop, who had flattered himself that he should be able to bring over a great body of his disciples to the royal side, found himself on a sudden an object of contempt and abhorrence to those who had lately revered him as their spiritual guide, sank into a deep melancholy, and hid himself from the public eye. Deputations waited on several of the London clergy imploring them not to judge of the dissenting body from the servile adulation which had lately filled the London Gazette, and exhorting them, placed as they were in the van of this great fight, to play the men for the liberties of England and for the faith delivered to the Saints. These assurances were received with joy and gratitude. Yet there was still much anxiety and much difference of opinion among those who had to decide whether, on Sunday the twentieth, they would or would not obey the King's command. The London clergy, then universally acknowledged to be the flower of their profession, held a meeting. Fifteen Doctors of Divinity were present. Tillotson, Dean of Canterbury, the most celebrated preacher of the age, came thither from a sick bed. Sherlock, Master of the Temple, Patrick, Dean of Peterborough and Rector of Saint Paul's, Covent Garden, and Stillingfleet, Archdeacon of London and Dean of Saint Paul's Cathedral, attended. The general feeling of the assembly seemed to be that it was, on the whole, advisable to obey the Order in Council. The dispute began to wax warm, and might have produced fatal consequences, if it had not been brought to a close by the firmness and wisdom of Doctor Edward Fowler, Vicar of Saint Giles's, Cripplegate, one of a small but remarkable class of divines who united that love of civil liberty which belonged to the school of Calvin with the theology of the school of Arminius. Standing up, Fowler spoke thus: "I must be plain. The question is so simple that argument can throw no new light on it, and can only beget heat. Let every man say Yes or No. But I cannot consent to be bound by the vote of the majority. I shall be sorry to cause a breach of unity. But this Declaration I cannot in conscience read." Tillotson, Patrick, Sherlock, and Stillingfleet declared that they were of the same mind. The majority yielded to the authority of a minority so respectable. A resolution by which all present pledged themselves to one another not to read the Declaration was then drawn up. Patrick was the first who set his hand to it; Fowler was the second. The paper was sent round the city, and was speedily subscribed by eighty five incumbents.

Meanwhile several of the Bishops were anxiously deliberating as to the course which they should take. On the twelfth of May a grave and learned company was assembled round the table of the Primate at Lambeth. Compton, Bishop of London, Turner, Bishop of Ely, White, Bishop of Peterborough, and Tenison, rector of Saint Martin's Parish, were among the guests. The Earl of Clarendon, a zealous and uncompromising friend of the Church, had been invited. Cartwright, Bishop of Chester, intruded himself on the meeting, probably as a spy. While he remained, no confidential communication could take place; but, after his departure, the great question of which all minds were full was propounded and discussed. The general opinion was that the Declaration ought not to be read. Letters were forthwith written to several of the most respectable prelates of the province of Canterbury, entreating them to come up without delay to London, and to strengthen the hands of their metropolitan at this conjuncture. As there was little doubt that these letters would be opened if they passed through the office in Lombard Street, they were sent by horsemen to the nearest country post towns on the different roads. The Bishop of Winchester, whose loyalty had been so signally proved at Sedgemoor, though suffering from indisposition, resolved to set out in obedience to the summons, but found himself unable to bear the motion of a coach. The letter addressed to William Lloyd, Bishop of Norwich, was, in spite of all precautions, detained by a postmaster; and that prelate, inferior to none of his brethren in courage and in zeal for the common cause of his order, did not reach London in time. His namesake, William Lloyd, Bishop of Saint Asaph, a pious, honest, and learned man, but of slender judgment, and half crazed by his persevering endeavours to extract from the Book of Daniel and from the Revelations some information about the Pope and the King of France, hastened to the capital and arrived on the sixteenth. On the following day came the excellent Ken, Bishop of Bath and Wells, Lake, Bishop of Chichester, and Sir John Trelawney, Bishop of Bristol, a baronet of an old and honourable Cornish family.

On the eighteenth a meeting of prelates and of other eminent divines was held at Lambeth. Tillotson, Tenison, Stillingfleet, Patrick, and Sherlock were present. Prayers were solemnly read before the consultation began. After long deliberation, a petition embodying the general sense was written by the Archbishop with his own hand. It was not drawn up with much felicity of style. Indeed, the cumbrous and inelegant structure of the sentences brought on Sancroft some raillery, which he bore with less patience than he showed under much heavier trials. But in substance nothing could be more skilfully framed than this memorable document. All disloyalty, all intolerance, was earnestly disclaimed. The King was assured that the Church still was, as she had ever been, faithful to the throne. He was assured also that the Bishops would, in proper place and time, as Lords of Parliament and members of the Upper House of Convocation, show that they by no means wanted tenderness for the conscientious scruples of Dissenters. But Parliament had, both in the late and in the present reign, pronounced that the sovereign was not constitutionally competent to dispense with statutes in matters ecclesiastical. The Declaration was therefore illegal; and the petitioners could not, in prudence, honour, or conscience, be parties to the solemn publishing of an illegal Declaration in the house of God, and during the time of divine service.

This paper was signed by the Archbishop and by six of his suffragans, Lloyd of Saint Asaph, Turner of Ely, Lake of Chichester, Ken of Bath and Wells, White of Peterborough, and Trelawney of Bristol. The Bishop of London, being under suspension, did not sign.

It was now late on Friday evening: and on Sunday morning the Declaration was to be read in the churches of London. It was necessary to put the paper into the King's hands without delay. The six Bishops crossed the river to Whitehall. The Archbishop, who had long been forbidden the Court, did not accompany them. Lloyd, leaving his five brethren at the house of Lord Dartmouth in the vicinity of the palace, went to Sunderland, and begged that minister to read the petition, and to ascertain when the King would be willing to receive it. Sunderland, afraid of compromising himself, refused to look at the paper, but went immediately to the royal closet. James directed that the Bishops should be admitted. He had heard from his tool Cartwright that they were disposed to obey the royal mandate, but that they wished for some little modifications in form, and that they meant to present a humble request to that effect. His Majesty was therefore in very good humour. When they knelt before him, he graciously told them to rise, took the paper from Lloyd, and said, "This is my Lord of Canterbury's hand." "Yes, sir, his own hand," was the answer. James read the petition: he folded it up; and his countenance grew dark. "This," he said, "is a great surprise to me. I did not expect this from your Church, especially from some of you. This is a standard of rebellion." The Bishops broke out into passionate professions of loyalty: but the King, as usual, repeated the same words over and over. "I tell you, this is a standard of rebellion." "Rebellion!" cried Trelawney, falling on his knees. "For God's sake, sir, do not say so hard a thing of us. No Trelawney can be a rebel. Remember that my family has fought for the crown. Remember how I served Your Majesty when Monmouth was in the West." "We put down the last rebellion," said Lake: "we shall not raise another." "We rebel!" exclaimed Turner; "we are ready to die at Your Majesty's feet." "Sir," said Ken, in a more manly tone, "I hope that you will grant to us that liberty of conscience which you grant to all mankind." Still James went on. "This is rebellion. This is a standard of rebellion. Did ever a good Churchman question the dispensing power before? Have not some of you preached for it and written for it? It is a standard of rebellion. I will have my Declaration published." "We have two duties to perform," answered Ken, "our duty to God, and our duty to Your Majesty. We honour you: but we fear God." "Have I deserved this?" said the King, more and more angry: "I who have been such a friend to your Church? I did not expect this from some of you. I will be obeyed. My Declaration shall be published. You are trumpeters of sedition. What do you do here? Go to your dioceses; and see that I am obeyed. I will keep this paper. I will not part with it. I will remember you that have signed it." "God's will be done," said Ken. "God has given me the dispensing power," said the King, "and I will maintain it. I tell you that there are still seven thousand of your Church who have not bowed the knee to Baal." The Bishops respectfully retired. That very evening the document which they had put into the hands of the King appeared word for word in print, was laid on the tables of all the coffee-houses, and was cried about the streets. Everywhere the people rose from their beds, and came out to stop the hawkers. It was said that the printer cleared a thousand pounds in a few hours by this penny broadside. This is probably an exaggeration; but it is an exaggeration which proves that the sale was enormous. How the petition got abroad is still a mystery. Sancroft declared that he had taken every precaution against publication, and that he knew of no copy except that which he had himself written, and which James had taken out of Lloyd's hand. The veracity of the Arch-bishop is beyond all suspicion. But it is by no means improbable that some of the divines who assisted in framing the petition may have remembered so short a composition accurately, and may have sent it to the press. The prevailing opinion, however, was that some person about the King had been indiscreet or treacherous. Scarcely less sensation was produced by a short letter which was written with great power of argument and language, printed secretly, and largely circulated on the same day by the post and by the common carriers. A copy was sent to every clergyman in the kingdom. The writer did not attempt to disguise the danger which those who disobeyed the royal mandate would incur: but he set forth in a lively manner the still greater danger of submission. "If we read the Declaration," said he, "we fall to rise no more. We fall unpitied and despised. We fall amidst the curses of a nation whom our compliance will have ruined." Some thought that this paper came from Holland. Others attributed it to Sherlock. But Prideaux, Dean of Norwich, who was a principal agent in dis-tributing it, believed it to be the work of Halifax.

The conduct of the prelates was rapturously extolled by the general voice: but some murmurs were heard. It was said that such grave men, if they thought themselves bound in conscience to remonstrate with the King, ought to have remonstrated earlier. Was it fair to him to leave him in the dark till within thirty six hours of the time fixed for the reading of the Declaration? Even if he wished to revoke the Order in Council, it was too late to do so. The inference seemed to be that the petition was intended, not to move the royal mind, but merely to inflame the discontents of the people. These complaints were uttterly groundless. The King had laid on the Bishops a command new, surprising, and embarrassing. It was their duty to communicate with each other, and to ascertain as far as possible the sense of the profession of which they were the heads before they took any step. They were dispersed over the whole kingdom. Some of them were distant from others a full week's journey. James allowed them only a fortnight to inform themselves, to meet, to deliberate, and to decide; and he surely had no right to think himself aggrieved because that fortnight was drawing to a close before he learned their decision. Nor is it true that they did not leave him time to revoke his order if he had been wise enough to do so. He might have called together his Council on Saturday morning, and before night it might have been known throughout London and the suburbs that he had yielded to the entreaties of the fathers of the Church. The Saturday, however, passed over without any sign of relenting on the part of the government; and the Sunday arrived, a day long remembered.

In the City and liberties of London were about a hundred parish churches. In only four of these was the Order in Council obeyed. At Saint Gregory's the Declaration was read by a divine of the name of Martin. As soon as he uttered the first words, the whole congregation rose and withdrew. At Saint Matthew's, in Friday Street, a wretch named Timothy Hall, who had disgraced his gown by acting as broker for the Duchess of Portsmouth in the sale of pardons, and who now had hopes of obtaining the vacant bishopric of Oxford, was in like manner left alone in his church. At Serjeant's Inn, in Chancery Lane, the clerk pretended that he had forgotten to bring a copy; and the Chief Justice of the King's Bench, who had attended in order to see that the royal mandate was obeyed, was forced to content himself with this excuse. Samuel Wesley, the father of John and Charles Wesley, a curate in London, took for his text that day the noble answer of the three Jews to the Chaldean tyrant; "Be it known unto thee, O King, that we will not serve thy gods, nor worship the golden image which thou hast set up." Even in the chapel of Saint James's Palace the officiating minister had the courage to disobey the order. The Westminster boys long remembered what took place that day in the Abbey. Sprat, Bishop of Rochester, officiated there as Dean. As soon as he began to read the Declaration, murmurs and the noise of people crowding out of the choir drowned his voice. He trembled so violently that men saw the paper shake in his hand. Long before he had finished, the place was deserted by all but those whose situation made it necessary for them to remain.

Never had the Church been so dear to the nation as on the afternoon of that day. The spirit of dissent seemed to be extinct. Baxter from his pulpit pronounced an eulogium on the Bishops and parochial clergy. The Dutch minister, a few hours later, wrote to inform the States General that the Anglican priesthood had risen in the estimation of the public to an incredible degree. The universal cry of the Nonconformists, he said, was that they would rather continue to be under the penal statutes than separate their cause from that of the prelates.

Another week of anxiety and agitation passed away. Sunday came again. Again the churches of the capital were thronged by hundreds of thousands. The Declaration was read nowhere except at the very few places where it had been read the week before. The minister who had officiated at the chapel in Saint James's Palace had been turned out of his situation: and a more obsequious divine appeared with the paper in his hand: but his agitation was so great that he could not articulate. In truth the feeling of the whole nation had now become such as none but the very best and noblest, or the very worst and basest, of mankind could without much discomposure encounter.

Even the King stood aghast for a moment at the violence of the tempest which he had raised. What step was he next to take? He must either advance or recede: and it was impossible to advance without peril, or to recede without humiliation. At one moment he determined to put forth a second order enjoining the clergy in high and angry terms to publish his Declaration, and menacing every one who should be refractory with instant suspension. This order was drawn up and sent to the press, then recalled, then a second time sent to the press, then recalled a second time. A different plan was suggested by some of those who were for rigorous measures. The prelates who had signed the petition might be cited before the Ecclesiastical Commission and deprived of their sees. But to this course strong objections were urged in Council. It had been announced that the Houses would be convoked before the end of the year. The Lords would assuredly treat the sentence of deprivation as a nullity, would insist that Sancroft and his fellow petitioners should be summoned to Parliament, and would refuse to acknowledge a new Archbishop of Canterbury or a new Bishop of Bath and Wells. Thus the session, which at best was likely to be sufficiently stormy, would commence with a deadly quarrel between the crown and the peers. If therefore it were thought necessary to punish the Bishops, the punishment ought to be inflicted according to the known course of English law. Sunderland had from the beginning objected, as far as he dared, to the Order in Council. He now suggested a course which, though not free from inconveniences, was the most prudent and the most dignified that a series of errors had left open to the government. The King might with grace and majesty announce to the world that he was deeply hurt by the undutiful conduct of the Church of England; but that he could not forget all the services rendered by that Church, in trying times, to his father, to his brother, and to himself; that, as a friend to the liberty of conscience, he was unwilling to deal severely by men whom conscience, ill informed indeed, and unreasonably scrupulous, might have prevented from obeying his commands; and that he would therefore leave the offenders to that punishment which their own reflections would inflict whenever they should calmly compare their recent acts with the loyal doctrines of which they had so loudly boasted. Not only Powis and Bellasyse, who had always been for moderate counsels, but Dover and Arundell, leaned towards this proposition. Jeffreys, on the other hand, maintained that the government would be disgraced if such transgressors as the seven Bishops were suffered to escape with a mere reprimand. He did not, however, wish them to be cited before the Ecclesiastical Commission, in which he sate as chief or rather as sole Judge. For the load of public hatred under which he already lay was too much even for his shameless forehead and obdurate heart; and he shrank from the responsibility which he would have incurred by pronouncing an illegal sentence on the rulers of the Church and the favourites of the nation. He therefore recommended a criminal information. It was accordingly resolved that the Archbishop and the six other petitioners should be brought before the Court of King's Bench on a charge of seditious libel. That they would be convicted it was scarcely possible to doubt. The Judges and their officers were tools of the Court. Since the old charter of the City of London had been forfeited, scarcely one prisoner whom the government was bent on bringing to punishment had been absolved by a jury. The refractory prelates would probably be condemned to ruinous fines and to long imprisonment, and would be glad to ransom themselves by serving, both in and out of Parliament, the designs of the Sovereign.

On the twenty-seventh of May it was notified to the Bishops that on the eighth of June they must appear before the King in Council. Why so long an interval was allowed we are not informed. Perhaps James hoped that some of the offenders, terrified by his displeasure, might submit before the day fixed for the reading of the Declaration in their dioceses, and might, in order to make their peace with him, persuade their clergy to obey his order. If such was his hope it was signally disappointed. Sunday the third of June came; and all parts of England followed the example of the capital. Already the Bishops of Norwich, Gloucester, Salisbury, Winchester, and Exeter had signed copies of the petition in token of their approbation. The Bishop of Worcester had refused to distribute the Declaration among his clergy. The Bishop of Hereford had distributed it: but it was generally understood that he was overwhelmed by remorse and shame for having done so. Not one parish priest in fifty complied with the Order in Council. In the great diocese of Chester, including the county of Lancaster, only three clergymen could be prevailed on by Cartwright to obey the King. In the diocese of Norwich are many hundreds of parishes. In only four of these was the Declaration read. The courtly Bishop of Rochester could not overcome the scruples of the minister of the ordinary of Chatham, who depended on the government for bread. There is still extant a pathetic letter which this honest priest sent to the Secretary of the Admiralty. "I cannot," he wrote, "reasonably expect Your Honour's protection. God's will be done. I must choose suffering rather than sin."

On the evening of the eighth of June the seven prelates, furnished by the ablest lawyers in England with full advice, repaired to the palace, and were called into the Council chamber. Their petition was lying on the table. The Chancellor took the paper up, showed it to the Archbishop, and said, "Is this the paper which Your Grace wrote, and which the six Bishops present delivered to His Majesty?" Sancroft looked at the paper, turned to the King, and spoke thus: "Sir, I stand here a culprit. I never was so before. Once I little thought that I ever should be so. Least of all could I think that I should be charged with any offence against my King: but since I am so unhappy as to be in this situation, Your Majesty will not be offended if I avail myself of my lawful right to decline saying anything which may criminate me." "This is mere chicanery," said the King. "I hope that Your Grace will not do so ill a thing as to deny your own hand." "Sir," said Lloyd, whose studies had been much among the casuists, "all divines agree that a person situated as we are may refuse to answer such a question." The King, as slow of understanding as quick of temper, could not comprehend what the prelates meant. He persisted, and was evidently becoming very angry. "Sir," said the Archbishop, "I am not bound to accuse myself. Nevertheless, if Your Majesty positively commands me to answer, I will do so in the confidence that a just and generous prince will not suffer what I say in obedience to his orders to be brought in evidence against me."

"You must not capitulate with your Sovereign," said the Chancellor. "No," said the King; "I will not give any such command. If you choose to deny your own hands, I have nothing more to say to you."

The Bishops were repeatedly sent out into the antechamber, and repeatedly called back into the Council room. At length James positively commanded them to answer the question. He did not expressly engage that their confession should not be used against them. But they, not unnaturally, supposed that, after what had passed, such an engagement was implied in his command. Sancroft acknowledged his handwriting; and his brethren followed his example. They were then interrogated about the meaning of some words in the petition, and about the letter which had been circulated with so much effect all over the kingdom: but their language was so guarded that nothing was gained by the examination. The Chancellor then told them that a criminal information would be exhibited against them in the Court of King's Bench, and called upon them to enter into recognisances. They refused. They were peers of Parliament, they said. They were advised by the best lawyers in Westminster Hall that no peer could be required to enter into a recognisance in a case of libel; and they should not think themselves justified in relinquishing the privilege of their order. The King was so absurd as to think himself personally affronted because they chose, on a legal question, to be guided by legal advice. "You believe every body," he said, "rather than me." He was indeed mortified and alarmed. For he had gone so far that, if they persisted, he had no choice left but to send them to prison; and, though he by no means foresaw all the consequences of such a step, he foresaw probably enough to disturb him. They were resolute. A warrant was therefore made out directing the Lieutenant of the Tower to keep them in safe custody, and a barge was manned to convey them down the river.

It was known all over London that the Bishops were before the Council. The public anxiety was intense. A great multitude filled the courts of Whitehall and all the neighbouring streets. Many people were in the habit of refreshing themselves at the close of a summer day with the cool air of the Thames. But on this evening the whole river was alive with wherries. When the Seven came forth under a guard, the emotions of the people broke through all restraint. Thousands fell on their knees and prayed aloud for the men who had, with the Christian courage of Ridley and Latimer, confronted a tyrant inflamed by all the bigotry of Mary. Many dashed into the stream, and, up to their waists in ooze and water, cried to the holy fathers to bless them. All down the river, from Whitehall to London Bridge, the royal barge passed between lines of boats, from which arose a shout of "God bless Your Lordships." The King, in great alarm, gave orders that the garrison of the Tower should be doubled, that the Guards should be held ready for action, and that two companies should be detached from every regiment in the kingdom, and sent up instantly to London. But the force on which he relied as the means of coercing the people shared all the feelings of the people. The very sentinels who were under arms at the Traitors' Gate reverently asked for a blessing from the martyrs whom they were to guard. Sir Edward Hales was Lieutenant of the Tower. He was little inclined to treat his prisoners with kindness. For he was an apostate from that Church for which they suffered; and he held several lucrative posts by virtue of that dispensing power against which they had protested. He learned with indignation that his soldiers were drinking the health of the Bishops. He ordered his officers to see that it was done no more. But the officers came back with a report that the thing could not be prevented, and that no other health was drunk in the garrison. Nor was it only by carousing that the troops showed their reverence for the fathers of the Church. There was such a show of devotion throughout the Tower that pious divines thanked God for bringing good out of evil, and for making the persecution of His faithful servants the means of saving many souls. All day the coaches and liveries of the first nobles of England were seen round the prison gates. Thousands of humbler spectators constantly covered Tower Hill. But among the marks of public respect and sympathy which the prelates received there was one which more than all the rest enraged and alarmed the King. He learned that a deputation of ten Nonconformist ministers had visited the Tower. He sent for four of these persons, and himself upbraided them. They courageously answered that they thought it their duty to forget past quarrels, and to stand by the men who stood by the Protestant religion.

[Here is omitted an account of the birth of the Pretender.]

The demeanour of the seven prelates meanwhile strengthened the interest which their situation excited. On the evening of the Black Friday, as it was called, on which they were committed, they reached their prison just at the hour of divine service. They instantly hastened to the chapel. It chanced that in the second lesson were these words: "In all things approving ourselves as the ministers of God, in much patience, in afflictions, in distresses, in stripes, in imprisonments." All zealous Churchmen were delighted by this coincidence, and remembered how much comfort a similar coincidence had given, near forty years before, to Charles the First at the time of his death.

On the evening of the next day, Saturday the ninth, a letter came from Sunderland enjoining the chaplain of the Tower to read the Declaration during divine service on the following morning. As the time fixed by the Order in Council for the reading in London had long expired, this proceeding of the government could be considered only as a personal insult of the meanest and most childish kind to the venerable prisoners. The chaplain refused to comply: he was dismissed from his situation; and the chapel was shut up.

The Bishops edified all who approached them by the firmness and cheerfulness with which they endured confinement, by the modesty and meekness with which they received the applauses and blessings of the whole nation, and by the loyal attachment which they professed for the persecutor who sought their destruction. They remained only a week in custody. On Friday the fifteenth of June, the first day of term, they were brought before the King's Bench. An immense throng awaited their coming. From the landing-place to the Court of Requests they passed through a lane of spectators who blessed and applauded them. "Friends," said the prisoners as they passed, "honour the King; and remember us in your prayers." These humble and pious expressions moved the hearers, even to tears. When at length the procession had made its way through the crowd into the presence of the Judges, the Attorney General exhibited the information which he had been commanded to prepare, and moved that the defendants might be ordered to plead. The counsel on the other side objected that the Bishops had been unlawfully committed, and were therefore not regularly before the Court. The question whether a peer could be required to enter into recognisances on a charge of libel was argued at great length, and decided by a majority of the Judges in favour of the crown. The prisoners then pleaded Not Guilty. That day fortnight, the twenty-ninth of June, was fixed for their trial. In the meantime they were allowed to be at large on their own recognisances. The crown lawyers acted prudently in not requiring sureties. For Halifax had arranged that twenty one temporal peers of the highest consideration should be ready to put in bail, three for each defendant; and such a manifestation of the feeling of the nobility would have been no slight blow to the government. It was also known that one of the most opulent

Dissenters of the City had begged that he might have the honour of giving security for Ken.

The Bishops were now permitted to depart to their own homes. The common people, who did not understand the nature of the legal proceedings which had taken place in the King's Bench, and who saw that their favourites had been brought to Westminster Hall in custody and were suffered to go away in freedom, imagined that the good cause was prospering. Loud acclamations were raised. The steeples of the churches sent forth joyous peals. Sprat was amazed to hear the bells of his own Abbey ringing merrily. He promptly silenced them; but his interference caused much angry muttering. The Bishops found it difficult to escape from the importunate crowd of their well-wishers. Lloyd was detained in Palace Yard by admirers who struggled to touch his hands and to kiss the skirt of his robe, till Clarendon, with some difficulty, rescued him and conveyed him home by a bypath. Cartwright, it is said, was so unwise as to mingle with the crowd. A person who saw his episcopal habit asked and received his blessing. A bystander cried out, "Do you know who blessed you?" "Surely," said he who had just been honoured by the benediction, "it was one of the Seven." "No," said the other; "it is the Popish Bishop of Chester." "Popish dog," cried the enraged Protestant; "take your blessing back again."

Such was the concourse, and such the agitation, that the Dutch Ambassador was surprised to see the day close without an insurrection. The King had been anxious and irritable. In order that he might be ready to suppress any disturbance, he had passed the morning in reviewing several battalions of infantry in Hyde Park. It is, however, by no means certain that his troops would have stood by him if he had needed their services. When Sancroft reached Lambeth, in the afternoon, he found the footguards, who were quartered in that suburb, assembled before the gate of his palace. They formed in two lines on his right and left, and asked his benediction as he went through them. He with difficulty prevented them from lighting a bonfire in honour of his return to his dwelling. There were, however, many bonfires that evening in the City. Two Roman Catholics, who were so indiscreet as to beat some boys for joining in these rejoicings, were seized by the mob, stripped naked, and ignominiously branded.

Sir Edward Hales now came to demand fees from those who had lately been his prisoners. They refused to pay anything for a detention which they regarded as illegal to an officer whose commission was, on their principles, a nullity. The Lieutenant hinted very intelligibly that, if they came into his hands again, they should be put into heavy irons and should lie on bare stones. "We are under our King's displeasure," was the answer; "and most deeply do we feel it: but a fellow subject who threatens us does but lose his breath." It is easy to imagine with what indignation the people, excited as they were, must have learned that a renegade from the Protestant faith, who held a command in defiance of the fundamental laws of England, had dared to menace divines of venerable age and dignity with all the barbarities of Lollard's Tower.

Before the day of trial the agitation had spread to the farthest corners of the island. From Scotland the Bishops received letters assuring them of the sympathy of the Presbyterians of that country, so long and so bitterly hostile to prelacy. The people of Cornwall, a fierce, bold, and athletic race, among whom there was a stronger provincial feeling than in any other part of the realm, were greatly moved by the danger of Trelawney, whom they reverenced less as a ruler of the Church than as the head of an honourable house, and the heir through twenty descents of ancestors who had been of great note before the Normans had set foot on English ground. All over the county the peasants chanted a ballad of which the burden is still remembered:

"And shall Trelawney die, and shall Trelawney die?
  Then thirty thousand Cornish boys will know the reason why."

The miners from their caverns reechoed the song with a variation:

"Then twenty thousand under ground will know the reason why."

The rustics in many parts of the country loudly expressed a strange hope which had never ceased to live in their hearts. Their Protestant Duke, their beloved Monmouth, would suddenly appear, would lead them to victory, and would tread down the King and the Jesuits under his feet.

The ministers were appalled. Even Jeffreys would gladly have retraced his steps. He charged Clarendon with friendly messages to the Bishops, and threw on others the blame of the prosecution which he had himself recommended. Sunderland again ventured to recommend concession. The late auspicious birth, he said, had furnished the King with an excellent opportunity of withdrawing from a position full of danger and inconvenience without incurring the reproach of timidity or of caprice. On such happy occasions it had been usual for sovereigns to make the hearts of subjects glad by acts of clemency; and nothing could be more advantageous to the Prince of Wales than that he should, while still in his cradle, be the peacemaker between his father and the agitated nation.

M—3

But the King's resolution was fixed. "I will go on," he said. "I have been only too indulgent. Indulgence ruined my father." The artful minister found that his advice had been formerly taken only because it had been shaped to suit the royal temper, and that, from the moment at which he began to counsel well, he began to counsel in vain. He had shown some signs of slackness in the proceeding against Magdalene College. He had recently attempted to convince the King that Tyrconnel's scheme of confiscating the property of the English colonists in Ireland was full of danger, and had, with the help of Powis and Bellasyse, so far succeeded that the execution of the design had been postponed for another year. But this timidity and scrupulosity had excited disgust and suspicion in the royal mind. The day of retribution had arrived. Sunderland was in the same situation in which his rival Rochester had been some months before. Each of the two statesmen in turn experienced the misery of clutching with an agonizing grasp, power which was perceptibly slipping away. Each in turn saw his suggestions scornfully rejected. Both endured the pain of reading displeasure and distrust in the countenance and demeanour of their master; yet both were by their country held responsible for those crimes and errors from which they had vainly endeavoured to dissuade him. While he suspected them of trying to win popularity at the expense of his authority and dignity, the public voice loudly accused them of trying to win his favour at the expense of their own honour and of the general weal. Yet, in spite of mortifications and humiliations, they both clung to office with the gripe of drowning men. Both attempted to propitiate the King by affecting a willingness to be reconciled to his Church. But there was a point at which Rochester was determined to stop. He went to the verge of apostasy: but there he recoiled: and the world, in consideration of the firmness with which he refused to take the final step, granted him a liberal amnesty for all former compliances. Sunderland, less scrupulous and less sensible of shame, resolved to atone for his late moderation, and to recover the royal confidence, by an act which, to a mind impressed with the importance of religious truth, must have appeared to be one of the most flagitious of crimes, and which even men of the world regard as the last excess of baseness. About a week before the day fixed for the great trial, it was publicly announced that he was a Papist. The King talked with delight of this triumph of divine grace. Courtiers and envoys kept their countenances as well as they could while the renegade protested that he had been long convinced of the impossibility of finding salvation out of the communion of Rome, and that his conscience would not let him rest till he had renounced the heresies in which he had been brought up. The news spread fast. At all the coffeehouses it was told how the prime minister of England, his feet bare, and a taper in his hand, had repaired to the royal chapel and knocked humbly for admittance; how a priestly voice from within had demanded who was there; how Sunderland had made answer that a poor sinner who had long wandered from the true Church implored her to receive and to absolve him; how the doors were opened; and how the neophyte partook of the holy mysteries.

This scandalous apostasy could not but heighten the interest with which the nation looked forward to the day when the fate of the seven brave confessors of the English Church was to be decided. To pack a jury was now the great object of the King. The crown lawyers were ordered to make strict inquiry as to the sentiments of the persons who were registered in the freeholders' book. Sir Samuel Astry, Clerk of the Crown, whose duty it was, in cases of this description, to select the names, was summoned to the palace, and had an interview with James in the presence of the Chancellor. Sir Samuel seems to have done his best. For, among the forty eight persons whom he nominated, were said to be several servants of the King, and several Roman Catholics. But as the counsel for the Bishops had a right to strike off twelve, these persons were removed. The crown lawyers also struck off twelve. The list was thus reduced to twenty four. The first twelve who answered to their names were to try the issue.

On the twenty-ninth of June, Westminster Hall, Old and New Palace Yard, and all the neighbouring streets to a great distance were thronged with people. Such an auditory had never before and has never since been assembled in the Court of King's Bench. Thirty five temporal peers of the realm were counted in the crowd.

All the four Judges of the Court were on the bench. Wright, who presided, had been raised to his high place over the heads of many abler and more learned men solely on account of his unscrupulous servility. Allibone was a Papist, and owed his situation to that dispensing power, the legality of which was now in question. Holloway had hitherto been a serviceable tool of the government. Even Powell, whose character for honesty stood high, had borne a part in some proceedings which it is impossible to defend. He had, in the great case of Sir Edward Hales, with some hesitation, it is true, and after some delay, concurred with the majority of the bench, and had thus brought on his character a stain which his honourable conduct on this day completely effaced.

The counsel were by no means fairly matched. The government had required from its law officers services so odious and disgraceful that all the ablest jurists and advocates of the Tory party had, one after another, refused to comply, and had been dismissed from their employments. Sir Thomas Powis, the Attorney General, was scarcely of the third rank in his profession. Sir William Williams, the Solicitor General, had great abilities and dauntless courage: but he wanted discretion; he loved wrangling; he had no command over his temper; and he was hated and despised by all political parties. The most conspicuous assistants of the Attorney and Solicitor were Serjeant Trinder, a Roman Catholic, and Sir Bartholomew Shower, Recorder of London, who had some legal learning, but whose fulsome apologies and endless repetitions were the jest of Westminster Hall. The government had wished to secure the services of Maynard: but he had plainly declared that he could not in conscience do what was asked of him.

On the other side were arrayed almost all the eminent forensic talents of the age. Sawyer and Finch, who, at the time of the accession of James, had been Attorney and Solicitor General, and who, during the persecution of the Whigs in the late reign, had served the crown with but too much vehemence and success, were of counsel for the defendants. With them were joined two persons who, since age had diminished the activity of Maynard, were reputed the two best lawyers that could be found in the Inns of Court; Pemberton, who had, in the time of Charles the Second, been Chief Justice of the King's Bench, who had been removed from his high place on account of his humanity and moderation, and who had resumed his practice at the bar; and Pollexfen, who had long been at the head of the Western circuit, and who, though he had incurred much unpopularity by holding briefs for the crown at the Bloody Assizes, and particularly by appearing against Alice Lisle, was known to be at heart a Whig, if not a republican. Sir Creswell Levinz was also there, a man of great knowledge and experience, but of singularly timid nature. He had been removed from the bench some years before, because he was afraid to serve the purposes of the government. He was now afraid to appear as the advocate of the Bishops, and had at first refused to receive their retainer: but it had been intimated to him by the whole body of attorneys who employed him that, if he declined this brief, he should never have another.

Sir George Treby, an able and zealous Whig, who had been Recorder of London under the old charter, was on the same side. Sir John Holt, a still more eminent Whig lawyer, was not retained for the defence, in consequence, it should seem, of some prejudice conceived against him by Sancroft, but was privately consulted on the case by the Bishop of London. The junior counsel for the Bishops was a young barrister named John Somers. He had no advantages of birth or fortune; nor had he yet had any opportunity of distinguishing himself before the eyes of the public: but his genius, his industry, his great and various accomplishments, were well known to a small circle of friends; and, in spite of his Whig opinions, his pertinent and lucid mode of arguing and the constant propriety of his demeanour had already secured to him the ear of the Court of King's Bench. The importance of obtaining his services had been strongly represented to the Bishops by Johnstone; and Pollexfen, it is said, had declared that no man in Westminster Hall was so well qualified to treat a historical and constitutional question as Somers.

The jury was sworn. It consisted of persons of highly respectable station. The foreman was Sir Roger Langley, a baronet of old and honourable family. With him were joined a knight and ten esquires, several of whom are known to have been men of large possessions. There were some Nonconformists in the number; for the Bishops had wisely resolved not to show any distrust of the Protestant Dissenters. One name excited considerable alarm, that of Michael Arnold. He was brewer to the palace; and it was apprehended that the government counted on his voice. The story goes that he complained bitterly of the position in which he found himself. "Whatever I do," he said, "I am sure to be half ruined. If I say Not Guilty, I shall brew no more for the King; and if I say Guilty, I shall brew no more for anybody else."

The trial then commenced, a trial which, even when coolly perused after the lapse of more than a century and a half, has all the interest of a drama. The advocates contended on both sides with far more than professional keenness and vehemence; the audience listened with as much anxiety as if the fate of every one of them was to be decided by the verdict; and the turns of fortune were so sudden and amazing that the multitude repeatedly passed in a single minute from anxiety to exultation, and back again from exultation to still deeper anxiety.

The information charged the Bishops with having written or published, in the county of Middlesex, a false, malicious, and seditious libel. The Attorney and Solicitor first tried to prove the writing. For this purpose several persons were called to speak to the hands of the Bishops. But the witnesses were so unwilling that hardly a single plain answer could be extracted from any of them. Pemberton, Pollexfen, and Levinz contended that there was no evidence to go to the jury. Two of the Judges, Holloway and Powell, declared themselves of the same opinion; and the hopes of the spectators rose high. All at once the crown lawyers announced their intention to take another line. Powis, with shame and reluctance which he could not dissemble, put into the witness box Blathwayt, a Clerk of the Privy Council, who had been present when the King interrogated the Bishops. Blathwayt swore that he had heard them own their signatures. His testimony was decisive. "Why," said Judge Holloway to the Attorney, "when you had such evidence, did you not produce it at first, without all this waste of time?" It soon appeared why the counsel for the crown had been unwilling, without absolute necessity, to resort to this mode of proof. Pemberton stopped Blathwayt, subjected him to a searching cross examination, and insisted upon having all that had passed between the King and the defendants fully related. "That is a pretty thing indeed," cried Williams. "Do you think," said Powis, "that you are at liberty to ask our witnesses any impertinent question that comes into your heads?" The advocates of the Bishops were not men to be so put down. "He is sworn," said Pollexfen, "to tell the truth and the whole truth; and an answer we must and will have." The witness shuffled, equivocated, pretended to misunderstand the questions, implored the protection of the Court. But he was in hands from which it was not easy to escape. At length the Attorney again interposed. "If," he said, "you persist in asking such a question, tell us, at least, what use you mean to make of it." Pemberton, who, through the whole trial, did his duty manfully and ably, replied without hesitation; "My Lords, I will answer Mr. Attorney. I will deal plainly with the Court. If the Bishops owned this paper under a promise from His Majesty that their confession should not be used against them, I hope that no unfair advantage will be taken of them." "You put on His Majesty what I dare hardly name," said Williams. "Since you will be so pressing, I demand, for the King, that the question may be recorded." "What do you mean, Mr. Solicitor?" said Sawyer, interposing. "I know what I mean," said the apostate: "I desire that the question may be recorded in court." "Record what you will. I am not afraid of you, Mr. Solicitor," said Pemberton. Then came a loud and fierce altercation, which Wright could with difficulty quiet. In other circumstances, he would probably have ordered the question to be recorded, and Pemberton to be committed. But on this great day the unjust Judge was overawed. He often cast a side glance towards the thick rows of Earls and Barons by whom he was watched, and before whom, in the next Parliament he might stand at the bar. He looked, a bystander said, as if all the peers present had halters in their pockets. At length Blathwayt was forced to give a full account of what had passed. It appeared that the King had entered into no express covenant with the Bishops. But it appeared also that the Bishops might not unreasonably think that there was an implied engagement. Indeed, from the unwillingness of the crown lawyers to put the Clerk of the Council into the witness box, and from the vehemence with which they objected to Pemberton's cross examination, it is plain that they were themselves of this opinion.

However, the handwriting was now proved. But a new and serious objection was raised. It was not sufficient to prove that the Bishops had written the alleged libel. It was necessary to prove also that they had written it in the county of Middlesex. And not only was it out of the power of the Attorney and Solicitor to prove this; but it was in the power of the defendants to prove the contrary. For it so happened that Sancroft had never once left the palace at Lambeth from the time when the Order in Council appeared till after the petition was in the King's hands. The whole case for the prosecution had therefore completely broken down; and the audience, with great glee, expected a speedy acquittal.

The crown lawyers then changed their ground again, abandoned altogether the charge of writing a libel, and undertook to prove that the Bishops had published a libel in the county of Middlesex. The difficulties were great. The delivery of the petition to the King was undoubtedly, in the eye of the law, a publication. But how was this delivery to be proved? No person had been present at the audience in the royal closet, except the King and the defendants. The King could not well be sworn. It was therefore only by the admissions of the defendants that the fact of publication could be established. Blathwayt was again examined, but in vain. He well remembered, he said, that the Bishops owned their hands; but he did not remember that they owned the paper which lay on the table of the Privy Council to be the same paper which they had delivered to the King, or that they were even interrogated on that point. Several other official men who had been in attendance on the Council were called, and among them Samuel Pepys, Secretary of the Admiralty; but none of them could remember that anything was said about the delivery. It was to no purpose that Williams put leading questions till the counsel on the other side declared that such twisting, such wiredrawing, was never seen in a court of justice, and till Wright himself was forced to admit that the

Solicitor's mode of examination was contrary to all rule. As witness after witness answered in the negative, roars of laughter and shouts of triumph, which the Judges did not even attempt to silence, shook the hall.

It seemed that at length this hard fight had been won. The case for the crown was closed. Had the counsel for the Bishops remained silent, an acquittal was certain; for nothing which the most corrupt and shameless Judge could venture to call legal evidence of publication had been given. The Chief Justice was beginning to charge the jury, and would undoubtedly have directed them to acquit the defendants; but Finch, too anxious to be perfectly discreet, interfered, and begged to be heard. "If you will be heard," said Wright, "you shall be heard; but you do not understand your own interests." The other counsel for the defence made Finch sit down, and begged the Chief Justice to proceed. He was about to do so, when a messenger came to the Solicitor General with news that Lord Sunderland could prove the publication, and would come down to the court immediately. Wright maliciously told the counsel for the defence that they had only themselves to thank for the turn which things had taken. The countenances of the great multitude fell. Finch was, during some hours, the most unpopular man in the country. Why could he not sit still as his betters, Sawyer, Pemberton, and Pollexfen had done? His love of meddling, his ambition to make a fine speech, had ruined everything.

Meanwhile the Lord President was brought in a sedan chair through the hall. Not a hat moved as he passed; and many voices cried out "Popish dog." He came into court pale and trembling, with eyes fixed on the ground, and gave his evidence in a faltering voice. He swore that the Bishops had informed him of their intention to present a petition to the King, and that they had been admitted into the royal closet for that purpose. This circumstance, coupled with the circumstance that, after they left the closet, there was in the King's hands a petition signed by them, was such proof as might reasonably satisfy a jury of the fact of the publication.

Publication in Middlesex was then proved. But was the paper thus published a false, malicious, and seditious libel? Hitherto the matter in dispute had been whether a fact which everybody well knew to be true could be proved according to technical rules of evidence; but now the contest became one of deeper interest. It was necessary to inquire into the limits of prerogative and liberty, into the right of the King to dispense with statutes, into the right of the subject to petition for the redress of grievances. During three hours the counsel for the petitioners argued with great force in defence of the fundamental principles of the constitution, and proved from the Journals of the House of Commons that the Bishops had affirmed no more than the truth when they represented to the King that the dispensing power which he claimed had been repeatedly declared illegal by Parliament. Somers rose last. He spoke little more than five minutes: but every word was full of weighty matter; and when he sate down his reputation as an orator and a constitutional lawyer was established. He went through the expressions which were used in the information to describe the offence imputed to the Bishops, and showed that every word, whether adjective or substantive, was altogether inappropriate. The offence imputed was a false, a malicious, a seditious libel. False the paper was not; for every fact which it set forth had been proved from the journals of Parliament to be true. Malicious the paper was not; for the defendants had not sought an occasion of strife, but had been placed by the government in such a situation that they must either oppose themselves to the royal will, or violate the most sacred obligations of conscience and honour. Seditious the paper was not; for it had not been scattered by the writers among the rabble, but delivered privately into the hands of the King alone; and a libel it was not, but a decent petition such as, by the laws of England, nay, by the laws of imperial Rome, by the laws of all civilised states, a subject who thinks himself aggrieved may with propriety present to the sovereign.

The Attorney replied shortly and feebly. The Solicitor spoke at great length and with great acrimony, and was often interrupted by the clamours and hisses of the audience. He went so far as to lay it down that no subject or body of subjects, except the Houses of Parliament, had a right to petition the King. The galleries were furious; and the Chief Justice himself stood aghast at the effrontery of this venal turncoat.

At length Wright proceeded to sum up the evidence. His language showed that the awe in which he stood of the government was tempered by the awe with which the audience, so numerous, so splendid, and so strongly excited, had impressed him. He said that he would give no opinion on the question of the dispensing power; that it was not necessary for him to do so; that he could not agree with much of the Solicitor's speech; that it was the right of the subject to petition; but that the particular petition before the Court was improperly worded, and was, in the contemplation of law, a libel. Allibone was of the same mind, but, in giving his opinion, showed such gross ignorance of law and history as brought on him the contempt of all who heard him. Holloway evaded the question of the dispensing power, but said that the petition seemed to him to be such as subjects who think themselves aggrieved are entitled to present, and therefore no libel. Powell took a bolder course. He avowed that, in his judgment, the Declaration of Indulgence was a nullity, and that the dispensing power, as lately exercised, was utterly inconsistent with all law. If these encroachments of prerogative were allowed, there was an end of Parliaments. The whole legislative authority would be in the King. "That issue, gentlemen," he said, "I leave to God and to your consciences."

It was dark before the jury retired to consider of their verdict. The night was a night of intense anxiety. Some letters are extant which were despatched during that period of suspense, and which have therefore an interest of a peculiar kind. "It is very late," wrote the Papal Nuncio; "and the decision is not yet known. The Judges and the culprits have gone to their own homes. The jury remain together. Tomorrow we shall learn the event of this great struggle."

The solicitor for the Bishops sate up all night with a body of servants on the stairs leading to the room where the jury was consulting. It was absolutely necessary to watch the officers who watched the doors; for those officers were supposed to be in the interest of the crown, and might, if not carefully observed, have furnished a courtly juryman with food, which would have enabled him to starve out the other eleven. Strict guard was therefore kept. Not even a candle to light a pipe was permitted to enter. Some basins of water for washing were suffered to pass at about four in the morning. The jurymen, raging with thirst, soon lapped up the whole. Great numbers of people walked the neighbouring streets till dawn. Every hour a messenger came from Whitehall to know what was passing. Voices, high in altercation, were repeatedly heard within the room: but nothing certain was known.

At first nine were for acquitting and three for convicting. Two of the minority soon gave way: but Arnold was obstinate. Thomas Austin, a country gentleman of great estate, who had paid close attention to the evidence and speeches, and had taken full notes, wished to argue the question. Arnold declined. He was not used, he doggedly said, to reasoning and debating. His conscience was not satisfied; and he should not acquit the Bishops. "If you come to that," said Austin, "look at me. I am the largest and strongest of the twelve; and before I find such a petition as this a libel, here I will stay till I am no bigger than a tobacco pipe." It was six in the morning before Arnold yielded. It was soon known that the jury were agreed: but what the verdict would be was still a secret.

At ten the Court again met. The crowd was greater than ever.

The jury appeared in their box; and there was a breathless stillness.

Sir Samuel Astry spoke. "Do you find the defendants, or any of them, guilty of the misdemeanour whereof they are impeached, or not guilty?" Sir Roger Langley answered, "Not Guilty." As the words were uttered, Halifax sprang up and waved his hat. At that signal, benches and galleries raised a shout. In a moment ten thousand persons, who crowded the great hall, replied with a still louder shout, which made the old oaken roof crack; and in another moment the innumerable throng without set up a third huzza, which was heard at Temple Bar. The boats which covered the Thames gave an answering cheer. A peal of gunpowder was heard on the water, and another, and another; and so, in few moments, the glad tidings went flying past the Savoy and the Friars to London Bridge, and to the forest of masts below. As the news spread, streets and squares, marketplaces and coffeehouses, broke forth into acclamations. Yet were the acclamations less strange than the weeping. For the feelings of men had been wound up to such a point that at length the stern English nature, so little used to outward signs of emotion, gave way, and thousands sobbed aloud for very joy. Meanwhile, from the outskirts of the multitude, horsemen were spurring off to bear along all the great roads intelligence of the victory of our Church and nation. Yet not even that astounding explosion could awe the bitter and intrepid spirit of the Solicitor. Striving to make himself heard above the din, he called on the Judges to commit those who had violated, by clamour, the dignity of a court of justice. One of the rejoicing populace was seized. But the tribunal felt that it would be absurd to punish a single individual for an offence common to hundreds of thousands, and dismissed him with a gentle reprimand.

It was vain to think of passing at that moment to any other business. Indeed the roar of the multitude was such that, during half an hour, scarcely a word could be heard in court. Williams got to his coach amidst a tempest of hisses and curses. Cartwright, whose curiosity was ungovernable, had been guilty of the folly and indecency of coming to Westminster in order to hear the decision. He was recognised by his sacerdotal garb and by his corpulent figure, and was hooted through the hall. "Take care," said one, "of the wolf in sheep's clothing." "Make room," cried another, "for the man with the Pope in his belly."

The acquitted prelates took refuge in the nearest chapel from the crowd which implored their blessing. Many churches were open on that morning throughout the capital; and many pious persons repaired thither. The bells of all the parishes of the City and liberties were ringing. The jury meanwhile could scarcely make their way out of the hall. They were forced to shake hands with hundreds. "God bless you!" cried the people; "God prosper your families! you have done like honest goodnatured gentlemen: you have saved us all today." As the noblemen who had appeared to support the good cause drove off, they flung from their carriage windows handfuls of money, and bade the crowd drink to the health of the King, the Bishops, and the jury.

The Attorney went with the tidings to Sunderland, who happened to be conversing with the Nuncio. "Never," said Powis, "within man's memory, have there been such shouts and such tears of joy as today." The King had that morning visited the camp on Hounslow Heath. Sunderland instantly sent a courier thither with the news. James was in Lord Feversham's tent when the express arrived. He was greatly disturbed, and exclaimed in French, "So much the worse for them." He soon set out for London. While he was present, respect prevented the soldiers from giving a loose to their feelings; but he had scarcely quitted the camp when he heard a great shouting behind him. He was surprised, and asked what that uproar meant. "Nothing," was the answer: "the soldiers are glad that the Bishops are acquitted." "Do you call that nothing?" said James. And then he repeated, "So much the worse for them."

He might well be out of temper. His defeat had been complete and most humiliating. Had the prelates escaped on account of some technical defect in the case for the crown, had they escaped because they had not written the petition in Middlesex, or because it was impossible to prove, according to the strict rules of law, that they had delivered to the King the paper for which they were called in question, the prerogative would have suffered no shock. Happily for the country, the fact of publication had been fully established. The counsel for the defence had therefore been forced to attack the dispensing power. They had attacked it with great learning, eloquence, and boldness. The advocates of the government had been by universal acknowledgment overmatched in the contest. Not a single Judge had ventured to declare that the Declaration of Indulgence was legal. One Judge had in the strongest terms pronounced it illegal. The language of the whole town was that the dispensing power had received a fatal blow. Finch, who had the day before been universally reviled, was now universally applauded. He had been unwilling, it was said, to let the case be decided in a way which would have left the great constitutional question still doubtful. He had felt that a verdict which should acquit his clients, without condemning the Declaration of Indulgence, would be but half a victory. It is certain that Finch deserved neither the reproaches which had been cast on him while the event was doubtful, nor the praises which he received when it had proved happy. It was absurd to blame him because, during the short delay which he occasioned, the crown lawyers unexpectedly discovered new evidence. It was equally absurd to suppose that he deliberately exposed his clients to risk, in order to establish a general principle; and still more absurd was it to praise him for what would have been a gross violation of professional duty.

That joyful day was followed by a not less joyful night. The Bishops, and some of their most respectable friends, in vain exerted themselves to prevent tumultuous demonstrations of public feeling. Never within the memory of the oldest, not even on that evening on which it was known through London that the army of Scotland had declared for a free Parliament, had the streets been in such a glare with bonfires. Round every bonfire crowds were drinking good health to the Bishops and confusion to the Papists. The windows were lighted with rows of candles. Each row consisted of seven; and the taper in the centre, which was taller than the rest, represented the Primate. The noise of rockets, squibs, and firearms, was incessant. One huge pile of faggots blazed right in front of the great gate of Whitehall. Others were lighted before the doors of Roman Catholic peers. Lord Arundell of Wardour wisely quieted the mob with a little money: but at Salisbury House in the Strand an attempt at resistance was made. Lord Salisbury's servants sallied out and fired: but they killed only the unfortunate beadle of the parish, who had come thither to put out the fire; and they were soon routed and driven back into the house. None of the spectacles of that night interested the common people so much as one with which they had, a few years before, been familiar, and which they now, after a long interval, enjoyed once more, the burning of the Pope. This once familiar pageant is known to our generation only by descriptions and engravings. A figure, by no means resembling those rude representations of Guy Fawkes which are still paraded on the fifth of November, but made of wax with some skill, and adorned at no small expense with robes and a tiara, was mounted on a chair resembling that in which the Bishops of Rome are still, on some great festivals, borne through Saint Peter's Church to the high altar. His Holiness was generally accompanied by a train of Cardinals and Jesuits. At his ear stood a buffoon disguised as a devil with horns and tail. No rich and zealous Protestant grudged his guinea on such an occasion, and, if rumour could be trusted, the cost of the procession was sometimes not less than a thousand pounds. After the Pope had been borne some time in state over the heads of the multitude, he was committed to the flames with loud acclamations. In the time of the popularity of Oates and Shaftesbury, this show was exhibited annually in Fleet Street before the windows of the Whig Club on the anniversary of the birth of Queen Elizabeth. Such was the celebrity of these grotesque rites, that Barillon once risked his life in order to peep at them from a hiding place. But, from the day when the Rye House Plot was discovered, till the day of the acquittal of the Bishops, the ceremony had been disused. Now, however, several Popes made their appearance in different parts of London. The Nuncio was much shocked; and the King was more hurt by this insult to his Church than by all the other affronts which he had received. The magistrates, however, could do nothing. The Sunday had dawned, and the bells of the parish churches were ringing for early prayers, before the fires began to languish and the crowds to disperse. A proclamation was speedily put forth against the rioters. Many of them, mostly young apprentices, were apprehended; but the bills were thrown out at the Middlesex sessions. The Justices, many of whom were Roman Catholics, expostulated with the grand jury and sent them three or four times back, but to no purpose.

Meanwhile the glad tidings were flying to every part of the kingdom, and were everywhere received with rapture. Gloucester, Bedford, and Lichfield, were among the places which were distinguished by peculiar zeal: but Bristol and Norwich, which stood nearest to London in population and wealth, approached nearest to London in enthusiasm on this joyful occasion.

The prosecution of the Bishops is an event which stands by itself in our history. It was the first and the last occasion on which two feelings of tremendous potency, two feelings which have generally been opposed to each other, and either of which, when strongly excited, has sufficed to convulse the state, were united in perfect harmony. Those feelings were love of the Church and love of freedom. During many generations every violent outbreak of High Church feeling, with one exception, has been unfavourable to civil liberty; every violent outbreak of zeal for liberty, with one exception, has been unfavourable to the authority and influence of the prelacy and the priesthood. In 1688 the cause of the hierarchy was for a moment that of the popular party. More than nine thousand clergymen, with the Primate and his most respectable suffragans at their head, offered themselves to endure bonds and the spoiling of their goods for the great fundamental principle of our free constitution. The effect was a coalition which included the most zealous Cavaliers, the most zealous republicans, and all the intermediate sections of the community. The spirit which had supported Hampden in the preceding generation, the spirit which, in the succeeding generation, supported Sacheverell, combined to support the Archbishop who was Hampden and Sacheverell in one. Those classes of society which are most deeply interested in the preservation of order, which in troubled times are generally most ready to strengthen the hands of government, and which have a natural antipathy to agitators, followed, without scruple, the guidance of a venerable man, the first peer of Parliament, the first minister of the Church, a Tory in politics, a saint in manners, whom tyranny had in his own despite turned into a demagogue. Many, on the other hand, who had always abhorred episcopacy, as a relic of Popery, and as an instrument of arbitrary power, now asked on bended knees the blessing of a prelate who was ready to wear fetters and to lay his aged limbs on bare stones rather than betray the interests of the Protestant religion and set the prerogative above the laws. With love of the Church and with love of freedom was mingled, at this great crisis, a third feeling which is among the most honourable peculiarities of our national character. An individual oppressed by power, even when destitute of all claim to public respect and gratitude, generally finds strong sympathy among us. Thus, in the time of our grandfathers, society was thrown into confusion by the persecution of Wilkes. We have ourselves seen the nation roused almost to madness by the wrongs of Queen Caroline. It is probable, therefore, that, even if no great political and religious interest had been staked on the event of the proceeding against the Bishops, England would not have seen, without strong emotions of pity and anger, old men of stainless virtue pursued by the vengeance of a harsh and inexorable prince who owed to their fidelity the crown which he wore.

Actuated by these sentiments our ancestors arrayed themselves against the government in one huge and compact mass. All ranks, all parties, all Protestant sects, made up that vast phalanx. In the van were the Lords Spiritual and Temporal. Then came the landed gentry and the clergy, both the Universities, all the Inns of Court, merchants, shopkeepers, farmers, the porters who plied in the streets of the great towns, the peasants who ploughed the fields. The league against the King included the very foremast[1]

---

[1] [Thus, in the first edition. The revised edition reads *foremost*, but *foremast* makes the better sense.]

men who manned his ships, the very sentinels who guarded his palace. The names of Whig and Tory were for a moment forgotten. The old Exclusionist took the old Abhorrer by the hand. Episcopalians, Presbyterians, Independents, Baptists, forgot their long feud and remembered only their common Protestantism and their common danger. Divines bred in the school of Laud talked loudly, not only of toleration, but of comprehension. The Archbishop soon after his acquittal put forth a pastoral letter which is one of the most remarkable compositions of that age. He had, from his youth up, been at war with the Nonconformists, and had repeatedly assailed them with unjust and unchristian asperity. His principal work was a hideous caricature of the Calvinistic theology. He had drawn up for the thirtieth of January and for the twenty-ninth of May forms of prayer which reflected on the Puritans in language so strong that the government had thought fit to soften it down. But now his heart was melted and opened. He solemnly enjoined the Bishops and clergy to have a very tender regard to their brethren the Protestant Dissenters, to visit them often, to entertain them hospitably, to discourse with them civilly, to persuade them, if it might be, to conform to the Church, but, if that were found impossible, to join them heartily and affectionately in exertions for the blessed cause of the Reformation.

Many pious persons in subsequent years remembered that time with bitter regret. They described it as a short glimpse of a golden age between two iron ages. Such lamentation, though natural, was not reasonable. The coalition of 1688 was produced, and could be produced, only by tyranny which approached to insanity, and by danger which threatened at once all the great institutions of the country. If there has never since been similar union, the reason is that there has never since been similar misgovernment. It must be remembered that, though concord is in itself better than discord, discord may indicate a better state of things than is indicated by concord. Calamity and peril often force men to combine. Prosperity and security often encourage them to separate.

THE ARRIVAL OF WILLIAM
AND THE FLIGHT OF JAMES

ON the sixteenth of October [1688], according to the English reckoning, was held a solemn sitting of the States of Holland. The Prince came to bid them farewell. He thanked them for the kindness with which they had watched over him when he was left an orphan child, for the confidence which they had reposed in him during his administration, and for the assistance which they had granted to him at this momentous crisis. He entreated them to believe that he had always meant and endeavoured to promote the interest of his country. He was now quitting them, perhaps never to return. If he should fall in defence of the reformed religion and of the independence of Europe, he commended his beloved wife to their care. The Grand Pensionary answered in a faltering voice; and in all that grave senate there was none who could refrain from shedding tears. But the iron stoicism of William never gave way; and he stood among his weeping friends calm and austere as if he had been about to leave them only for a short visit to his hunting grounds at Loo.

The deputies of the principal towns accompanied him to his yacht. Even the representatives of Amsterdam, so long the chief seat of opposition to his administration, joined in paying him this compliment. Public prayers were offered for him on that day in all the churches of the Hague.

In the evening he arrived at Helvoetsluys and went on board of a frigate called the Brill. His flag was immediately hoisted. It displayed the arms of Nassau quartered with those of England. The motto, embroidered in letters three feet long, was happily chosen. The House of Orange had long used the elliptical device, "I will maintain." The ellipsis was now filled up with words of high import, "The liberties of England and the Protestant religion."

The Prince had not been many hours on board when the wind became fair. On the nineteenth the armament put out to sea, and traversed, before a strong breeze, about half the distance between the Dutch and English coasts. Then the wind changed, blew hard from the west, and swelled into a violent tempest. The ships, scattered and in great distress, regained the shore of Holland as they best might. The Brill reached Helvoetsluys on the twenty-first. The Prince's fellow passengers had observed with admiration that neither peril nor mortification had for one moment disturbed his composure. He now, though suffering from sea sickness, refused to go on shore: for he conceived that, by remaining on board, he should in the most effectual manner notify to Europe that the late misfortune had only delayed for a very short time the execution of his purpose. In two or three days the fleet reassembled. One vessel only had been cast away. Not a single soldier or sailor was missing. Some horses had perished: but this loss the Prince with great expedition repaired; and, before the London Gazette had spread the news of his mishap, he was again ready to sail.

His Declaration preceded him only by a few hours. On the

first of November it began to be mentioned in mysterious whispers by the politicians of London, was passed secretly from man to man, and was slipped into the boxes of the post office. One of the agents was arrested, and the packets of which he was in charge were carried to Whitehall. The King read, and was greatly troubled. His first impulse was to hide the paper from all human eyes. He threw into the fire every copy which had been brought to him, except one; and that one he would scarcely trust out of his own hands.

The paragraph in the manifesto which disturbed him most was that in which it was said that some of the Peers, Spiritual and Temporal, had invited the Prince of Orange to invade England. Halifax, Clarendon, and Nottingham were then in London. They were immediately summoned to the palace and interrogated. Halifax, though conscious of innocence, refused at first to make any answer. "Your Majesty asks me," said he, "whether I have committed high treason. If I am suspected, let me be brought before my peers. And how can Your Majesty place any dependence on the answer of a culprit whose life is at stake? Even if I had invited His Highness over, I should without scruple plead Not Guilty." The King declared that he did not at all consider Halifax as a culprit, and that he had asked the question as one gentleman asks another who has been calumniated whether there be the least foundation for the calumny. "In that case," said Halifax, "I have no objection to aver, as a gentleman speaking to a gentleman, on my honour, which is as sacred as my oath, that I have not invited the Prince of Orange over." Clarendon and Nottingham said the same. The King was still more anxious to ascertain the temper of the Prelates. If they were hostile to him, his throne was indeed in danger. But it could not be. There was something monstrous in the supposition that any Bishop of the Church of England could rebel against his Sovereign. Compton was called into the royal closet, and asked whether he believed that there was the slightest ground for the Prince's assertion. The Bishop was in a strait; for he was himself one of the seven who had signed the invitation; and his conscience, not a very enlightened conscience, would not suffer him, it seems, to utter a direct falsehood. "Sir," he said, "I am quite confident that there is not one of my brethren who is not as guiltless as myself in this matter." The equivocation was ingenious: but whether the difference between the sin of such an equivocation and the sin of a lie be worth any expense of ingenuity may perhaps be doubted. The King was satisfied. "I fully acquit you all," he said. "But I think it necessary that you should publicly contradict the slanderous charge brought against you in the Prince's Declaration." The Bishop very naturally begged that he might be allowed to read the paper which he was required to contradict: but the King would not suffer him to look at it.

On the following day appeared a proclamation threatening with the severest punishment all who should circulate, or who should even dare to read, William's manifesto. The Primate and the few Spiritual Peers who happened to be then in London had orders to wait upon the King. Preston was in attendance with the Prince's Declaration in his hand. "My Lords," said James, "listen to this passage. It concerns you." Preston then read the sentence in which the Spiritual Peers were mentioned. The King proceeded: "I do not believe one word of this: I am satisfied of your innocence: but I think it fit to let you know of what you are accused."

The Primate, with many dutiful expressions, protested that the King did him no more than justice. "I was born in Your Majesty's allegiance. I have repeatedly confirmed that allegiance by my oath. I can have but one King at one time. I have not invited the Prince over; and I do not believe that a single one of my brethren has done so." "I am sure I have not," said Crewe of Durham. "Nor I," said Cartwright of Chester. Crewe and Cartwright might well be believed; for both had sate in the Ecclesiastical Commission. When Compton's turn came, he parried the question with an adroitness which a Jesuit might have envied. "I gave Your Majesty my answer yesterday."

James repeated again and again that he fully acquitted them all. Nevertheless it would, in his judgment, be for his service and for their own honour that they should publicly vindicate themselves. He therefore required them to draw up a paper setting forth their abhorrence of the Prince's design. They remained silent: their silence was supposed to imply consent; and they were suffered to withdraw.

Meanwhile the fleet of William was on the German Ocean. It was on the evening of Thursday the first of November that he put to sea the second time. The wind blew fresh from the east. The armament, during twelve hours, held a course towards the north-west. The light vessels sent out by the English Admiral for the purpose of obtaining intelligence brought back news which confirmed the prevailing opinion that the enemy would try to land in Yorkshire. All at once, on a signal from the Prince's ship, the whole fleet tacked, and made sail for the British Channel. The same breeze which favoured the voyage of the invaders prevented Dartmouth from coming out of the Thames. His ships were forced to strike yards and topmasts; and two of his frigates, which had gained the open sea, were shattered by the violence of the weather and driven back into the river.

Meanwhile the Dutch fleet ran fast before the gale, and reached the Straits at about ten in the morning of Saturday the third of November. William himself, in the Brill, led the way. More than six hundred vessels, with canvass spread to a favourable wind, followed in his train. The transports were in the centre. The men of war, more than fifty in number, formed an outer rampart. Herbert, with the title of Lieutenant Admiral General, commanded the whole fleet. His post was in the rear, and many English sailors, inflamed against Popery, and attracted by high pay, served under him. It was not without great difficulty that the Prince had prevailed on some Dutch officers of high reputation to submit to the authority of a stranger. But the arrangement was eminently judicious. There was, in the King's fleet, much discontent and an ardent zeal for the Protestant faith. But within the memory of old mariners the Dutch and English navies had thrice, with heroic spirit and various fortune, contended for the empire of the sea. Our sailors had not forgotten the broom with which Tromp had threatened to sweep the Channel, or the fire which De Ruyter had lighted in the dockyards of the Medway. Had the rival nations been once more brought face to face on the element of which both claimed the sovereignty, all other thoughts might have given place to mutual animosity. A bloody and obstinate battle might have been fought. Defeat would have been fatal to William's enterprise. Even victory would have deranged all his deeply meditated schemes of policy. He therefore wisely determined that the pursuers, if they overtook him, should be hailed in their own mother tongue, and adjured, by an admiral under whom they had served, and whom they esteemed, not to fight against old messmates for Popish tyranny. Such an appeal might possibly avert a conflict. If a conflict took place, one English commander would be opposed to another: nor would the pride of the islanders be wounded by learning that Dartmouth had been compelled to strike to Herbert.

Happily William's precautions were not necessary. Soon after midday he passed the Straits. His fleet spread to within a league of Dover on the north and of Calais on the south. The men of war on the extreme right and left saluted both fortresses at once. The troops appeared under arms on the decks. The flourish of trumpets, the clash of cymbals, and the rolling of drums were distinctly heard at once on the English and French shores. An innumerable company of gazers blackened the white beach of Kent. Another mighty multitude covered the coast of Picardy. Rapin de Thoyras, who, driven by persecution from his country, had taken service in the Dutch army, and now went with the Prince to England, described the spectacle, many years later, as the most magnificent and affecting that was ever seen by human eyes. At sunset the armament was off Beachy Head. Then the lights were kindled. The sea was in a blaze for many miles. But the eyes of all the steersmen were directed throughout the night to three huge lanterns which flamed on the stern of the Brill.

Meanwhile a courier had been riding post from Dover Castle to Whitehall with news that the Dutch had passed the Straits and were steering westward. It was necessary to make an immediate change in all the military arrangements. Messengers were despatched in every direction. Officers were roused from their beds at dead of night. At three on the Sunday morning there was a great muster by torchlight in Hyde Park. The King had sent several regiments northward in the expectation that William would land in Yorkshire. Expresses were despatched to recall them. All the forces except those which were necessary to keep the peace of the capital were ordered to move to the West. Salisbury was appointed as the place of rendezvous; but, as it was thought possible that Portsmouth might be the first point of attack, three battalions of guards and a strong body of cavalry set out for that fortress. In a few hours it was known that Portsmouth was safe; and these troops received orders to change their route and to hasten to Salisbury.

When Sunday the fourth of November dawned, the cliffs of the Isle of Wight were full in view of the Dutch armament. That day was the anniversary both of William's birth and of his marriage. Sail was slackened during part of the morning; and divine service was performed on board of the ships. In the afternoon and through the night the fleet held on its course. Torbay was the place where the Prince intended to land. But the morning of Monday the fifth of November was hazy. The pilot of the Brill could not discern the sea marks, and carried the fleet too far to the west. The danger was great. To return in the face of the wind was impossible. Plymouth was the next port. But at Plymouth a garrison had been posted under the command of the Earl of Bath. The landing might be opposed; and a check might produce serious consequences. There could be little doubt, moreover, that by this time the royal fleet had got out of the Thames and was hastening full sail down the Channel. Russell saw the whole extent of the peril, and exclaimed to Burnet,

"You may go to prayers, Doctor. All is over." At that moment the wind changed: a soft breeze sprang up from the south: the mist dispersed: the sun shone forth; and under the mild light of an autumnal noon, the fleet turned back, passed round the lofty cape of Berry Head, and rode safe in the harbour of Torbay.

Since William looked on that harbour its aspect has greatly changed. The amphitheatre which surrounds the spacious basin now exhibits everywhere the signs of prosperity and civilisation. At the northeastern extremity has sprung up a great watering place, to which strangers are attracted from the most remote parts of our island by the Italian softness of the air: for in that climate the myrtle flourishes unsheltered; and even the winter is milder than the Northumbrian April. The inhabitants are about ten thousand in number. The newly built churches and chapels, the baths and libraries, the hotels and public gardens, the infirmary and the museum, the white streets, rising terrace above terrace, the gay villas peeping from the midst of shrubberies and flower beds, present a spectacle widely different from any that in the seventeenth century England could show. At the opposite end of the bay lies, sheltered by Berry Head, the stirring market town of Brixham, the wealthiest seat of our fishing trade. A pier and a haven were formed there at the beginning of the present century, but have been found insufficient for the increasing traffic. The population is about six thousand souls. The shipping amounts to more than two hundred sail. The tonnage exceeds many times the tonnage of the port of Liverpool under the kings of the House of Stuart. But Torbay, when the Dutch fleet cast anchor there, was known only as a haven where ships sometimes took refuge from the tempests of the Atlantic. Its quiet shores were undisturbed by the bustle either of commerce or of pleasure; and the huts of ploughmen and fishermen were thinly scattered over what is now the site of crowded marts and of luxurious pavilions.

The peasantry of the coast of Devonshire remembered the name of Monmouth with affection, and held Popery in detestation. They therefore crowded down to the seaside with provisions and offers of service. The disembarkation instantly commenced. Sixty boats conveyed the troops to the coast. Mackay was sent on shore first with the British regiments. The Prince soon followed. He landed where the quay of Brixham now stands. The whole aspect of the place has been altered. Where we now see a port crowded with shipping, and a marketplace swarming with buyers and sellers, the waves then broke on a desolate beach; but a fragment of the rock on which the deliverer stepped from his boat has been carefully preserved, and is set up as an object of public veneration in the centre of that busy wharf.

As soon as the Prince had planted his foot on dry ground he called for horses. Two beasts, such as the small yeomen of that time were in the habit of riding, were procured from the neighbouring village. William and Schomberg mounted and proceeded to examine the country.

As soon as Burnet was on shore he hastened to the Prince. An amusing dialogue took place between them. Burnet poured forth his congratulations with genuine delight, and then eagerly asked what were his Highness's plans. Military men are seldom disposed to take counsel with gownsmen on military matters; and William regarded the interference of unprofessional advisers, in questions relating to war, with even more than the disgust ordinarily felt by soldiers on such occasions. But he was at that moment in an excellent humour, and, instead of signifying his displeasure by a short and cutting reprimand, graciously extended his hand, and answered his chaplain's question by another question: "Well, Doctor, what do you think of predestination now?" The reproof was so delicate that Burnet, whose perceptions were not very fine, did not perceive it. He answered with great fervour that he should never forget the signal manner in which Providence had favoured their undertaking.

During the first day the troops who had gone on shore had many discomforts to endure. The earth was soaked with rain. The baggage was still on board of the ships. Officers of high rank were compelled to sleep in wet clothes on the wet ground: the Prince himself had no better quarters than a hut afforded. His banner was displayed on the thatched roof; and some bedding brought from his ship was spread for him on the floor. There was some difficulty about landing the horses; and it seemed probable that this operation would occupy several days. But on the following morning the prospect cleared. The wind was gentle. The water in the bay was as even as glass. Some fishermen pointed out a place where the ships could be brought within sixty feet of the beach. This was done; and in three hours many hundreds of horses swam safely to shore.

The disembarkation had hardly been effected when the wind rose again, and swelled into a fierce gale from the west. The enemy coming in pursuit down the Channel had been stopped by the same change of weather which enabled William to land. During two days the King's fleet lay on an unruffled sea in sight of Beachy Head. At length Dartmouth was able to proceed. He passed the Isle of

Wight, and one of his ships came in sight of the Dutch topmasts in Torbay. Just at this moment he was encountered by the tempest, and compelled to take shelter in the harbour of Portsmouth. At that time James, who was not incompetent to form a judgment on a question of seamanship, declared himself perfectly satisfied that the Admiral had done all that man could do, and had yielded only to the irresistible hostility of the winds and waves. At a later period the unfortunate prince began, with little reason, to suspect Dartmouth of treachery, or at least of slackness.

The weather had indeed served the Protestant cause so well that some men of more piety than judgment fully believed the ordinary laws of nature to have been suspended for the preservation of the liberty and religion of England. Exactly a hundred years before, they said, the Armada, invincible by man, had been scattered by the wrath of God. Civil freedom and divine truth were again in jeopardy; and again the obedient elements had fought for the good cause. The wind had blown strong from the east while the Prince wished to sail down the Channel, had turned to the south when he wished to enter Torbay, had sunk to a calm during the disembarkation, and, as soon as the disembarkation was completed, had risen to a storm, and had met the pursuers in the face. Nor did men omit to remark that, by an extraordinary coincidence, the Prince had reached our shores on a day on which the Church of England commemorated, by prayer and thanksgiving, the wonderful escape of the royal House and of the three Estates from the blackest plot ever devised by Papists. Carstairs, whose suggestions were sure to meet with attention from the Prince, recommended that, as soon as the landing had been effected, public thanks should be offered to God for the protection so conspicuously accorded to the great enterprise. This advice was taken, and with excellent effect. The troops, taught to regard themselves as favourites of heaven, were inspired with new courage; and the English people formed the most favourable opinion of a general and an army so attentive to the duties of religion.

On Tuesday, the sixth of November, William's army began to march up the country. Some regiments advanced as far as Newton Abbot. A stone, set up in the midst of that little town, still marks the spot where the Prince's Declaration was solemnly read to the people. The movements of the troops were slow: for the rain fell in torrents; and the roads of England were then in a state which seemed frightful to persons accustomed to the excellent communications of Holland. William took up his quarters, during two days, at Ford, a seat of the ancient and illustrious family of Courtenay, in the neighbourhood of Newton Abbot. He was magnificently lodged and feasted there: but it is remarkable that the owner of the house, though a strong Whig, did not choose to be the first to put life and fortune in peril, and cautiously abstained from doing anything which, if the King should prevail, could be treated as a crime.

Exeter, in the meantime, was greatly agitated. Lamplugh, the Bishop, as soon as he heard that the Dutch were at Torbay, set off in terror for London. The Dean fled from the deanery. The magistrates were for the King, the body of the inhabitants for the Prince. Everything was in confusion when, on the morning of Thursday, the eighth of November, a body of troops, under the command of Mordaunt, appeared before the city. With Mordaunt came Burnet, to whom William had entrusted the duty of protecting the clergy of the Cathedral from injury and insult. The Mayor and Aldermen had ordered the gates to be closed, but yielded on the first summons. The deanery was prepared for the reception of the Prince. On the following day, Friday the ninth, he arrived. The magistrates had been pressed to receive him in state at the entrance of the city, but had steadfastly refused. The pomp of that day, however, could well spare them. Such a sight had never been seen in Devonshire. Many of the citizens went forth half a day's journey to meet the champion of their religion. All the neighbouring villages poured forth their inhabitants. A great crowd, consisting chiefly of young peasants, brandishing their cudgels, had assembled on the top of Haldon Hill, whence the army, marching from Chudleigh, first descried the rich valley of the Exe, and the two massive towers rising from the cloud of smoke which overhung the capital of the West. The road, all down the long descent and through the plain to the banks of the river, was lined, mile after mile, with spectators. From the West Gate to the Cathedral Close, the pressing and shouting on each side was such as reminded Londoners of the crowds on the Lord Mayor's day. The houses were gaily decorated. Doors, windows, balconies, and roofs were thronged with gazers. An eye accustomed to the pomp of war would have found much to criticise in the spectacle. For several toilsome marches in the rain, through roads where one who travelled on foot sank at every step up to the ankles in clay, had not improved the appearance either of the men or of their accoutrements. But the people of Devonshire, altogether unused to the splendour of well ordered camps, were overwhelmed with delight and awe. Descriptions of the martial pageant were circulated all over the kingdom. They contained much that was well fitted to gratify the vulgar appetite for the marvellous. For the Dutch army, composed of men who had been born in various climates and had served under various standards, presented an aspect at once grotesque, gorgeous, and terrible to islanders who had, in general, a very indistinct notion of foreign countries. First rode Macclesfield at the head of two hundred gentlemen, mostly of English blood, glittering in helmets and cuirasses, and mounted on Flemish war horses. Each was attended by a negro, brought from the sugar plantations on the coast of Guiana. The citizens of Exeter, who had never seen so many specimens of the African race, gazed with wonder on those black faces set off by embroidered turbans and white feathers. Then, with drawn broadswords came a squadron of Swedish horsemen in black armour and fur cloaks. They were regarded with a strange interest; for it was rumoured that they were natives of a land where the ocean was frozen and where the night lasted through half the year, and that they had themselves slain the huge bears whose skins they wore. Next, surrounded by a goodly company of gentlemen and pages, was borne aloft the Prince's banner. On its broad folds the crowd which covered the roofs and filled the windows read with delight that memorable inscription, "The Protestant religion and the liberties of England." But the acclamations redoubled when, attended by forty running footmen, the Prince himself appeared, armed on back and breast, wearing a white plume and mounted on a white charger. With how martial an air he curbed his horse, how thoughtful and commanding was the expression of his ample forehead and falcon eye, may still be seen on the canvass of Kneller. Once his grave features relaxed into a smile. It was when an ancient woman, perhaps one of those zealous Puritans who, through twenty eight years of persecution, had waited with firm faith for the consolation of Israel, perhaps the mother of some rebel who had perished in the carnage of Sedgemoor, or in the more fearful carnage of the Bloody Circuit, broke from the crowd, rushed through the drawn swords and curvetting horses, touched the hand of the deliverer, and cried out that now she was happy. Near to the Prince was one who divided with him the gaze of the multitude. That, men said, was the great Count Schomberg, the first soldier in Europe, since Turenne and Condé were gone, the man whose genius and valour had saved the Portuguese monarchy on the field of Montes Claros, the man who had earned a still higher glory by resigning the truncheon of a Marshal of France for the sake of his religion. It was not forgotten that the two heroes who, indissolubly united by their common Protestantism, were entering Exeter together, had twelve years before been opposed to each other under the walls of Maestricht, and that the energy of the young Prince had not then been found a match for the cool science of the veteran who now rode in friendship by his side. Then came a long column of the whiskered infantry of Switzerland, distinguished in all the Continental wars of two centuries by preeminent valour and discipline, but never till that week seen on English ground. And then marched a succession of bands designated, as was the fashion of that age, after their leaders, Bentinck, Solmes, and Ginkell, Talmash and Mackay. With peculiar pleasure Englishmen might look on one gallant regiment which still bore the name of the honoured and lamented Ossory. The effect of the spectacle was heightened by the recollection of more than one renowned event in which the warriors now pouring through the West Gate had borne a share. For they had seen service very different from that of the Devonshire militia or of the camp at Hounslow. Some of them had repelled the fiery onset of the French on the field of Seneff; and others had crossed swords with the infidels in the cause of Christendom on that great day when the siege of Vienna was raised. The very senses of the multitude were fooled by imagination. Newsletters conveyed to every part of the kingdom fabulous accounts of the size and strength of the invaders. It was affirmed that they were, with scarcely an exception, above six feet high, and that they wielded such huge pikes, swords, and muskets, as had never before been seen in England. Nor did the wonder of the population diminish when the artillery arrived, twenty one huge pieces of brass cannon, which were with difficulty lugged along by sixteen cart horses to each. Much curiosity was excited by a strange structure mounted on wheels. It proved to be a movable smithy, furnished with all tools and materials necessary for repairing arms and carriages. But nothing caused so much admiration as the bridge of boats, which was laid with great speed on the Exe for the conveyance of waggons and afterwards as speedily taken to pieces and carried away. It was made, if report said true, after a pattern contrived by the Christians who were warring against the Great Turk on the Danube. The foreigners inspired as much good will as admiration. Their politic leader took care to distribute the quarters in such a manner as to cause the smallest possible inconvenience to the inhabitants of Exeter and of the neighbouring villages. The most rigid discipline was maintained. Not only were pillage and outrage effectually prevented, but the troops were required to demean themselves with civility towards all classes. Those who had formed their notions of an army from the conduct of Kirke and his Lambs were amazed to see soldiers who never swore at a landlady or took an egg without paying for it. In return for this moderation the people furnished the troops with provisions in great abundance and at reasonable prices.

Much depended on the course which, at this great crisis, the clergy of the Church of England might take; and the members of the Chapter of Exeter were the first who were called upon to declare their sentiments. Burnet informed the Canons, now left without a head by the flight of the Dean, that they could not be permitted to use the prayer for the Prince of Wales, and that a solemn service must be performed in honour of the safe arrival of the Prince. The Canons did not choose to appear in their stalls; but some of the choristers and prebendaries attended. William repaired in military state to the Cathedral. As he passed under the gorgeous screen, that renowned organ, scarcely surpassed by any of those which are the boast of his native Holland, gave out a peal of triumph. He mounted the Bishop's seat, a stately throne rich with the carving of the fifteenth century. Burnet stood below; and a crowd of warriors and nobles appeared on the right hand and on the left. The singers, robed in white, sang the Te Deum. When the chaunt was over, Burnet read the Prince's Declaration: but as soon as the first words were uttered, prebendaries and singers crowded in all haste out of the choir. At the close Burnet cried in a loud voice, "God save the Prince of Orange!" and many fervent voices answered, "Amen."

On Sunday, the eleventh of November, Burnet preached before the Prince in the Cathedral, and dilated on the signal mercy vouchsafed by God to the English Church and nation. At the same time a singular event happened in a humbler place of worship. Ferguson resolved to preach at the Presbyterian meeting house. The minister and elders would not consent: but the turbulent and halfwitted knave, fancying that the times of Fleetwood and Harrison were come again, forced the door, went through the congregation sword in hand, mounted the pulpit, and there poured forth a fiery invective against the King. The time for such follies had gone by; and this exhibition excited nothing but derision and disgust.

While these things were passing in Devonshire the ferment was great in London. The Prince's Declaration, in spite of all precautions, was now in every man's hands. On the sixth of November James, still uncertain on what part of the coast the invaders had landed, summoned the Primate and three other Bishops, Compton of London, White of Peterborough, and Sprat of Rochester, to a conference in the closet. The King listened graciously while the prelates made warm professions of loyalty, and assured them that he did not suspect them. "But where," said he, "is the paper that you were to bring me?" "Sir," answered Sancroft, "we have brought no paper. We are not solicitous to clear our fame to the world. It is no new thing to us to be reviled and falsely accused. Our consciences acquit us: Your Majesty acquits us; and we are satisfied." "Yes," said the King; "but a declaration from you is necessary to my service." He then produced a copy of the Prince's manifesto. "See," he said, "how you are mentioned here." "Sir," answered one of the Bishops, "not one person in five hundred believes this manifesto to be genuine." "No!" cried the King fiercely: "then those five hundred would bring the Prince of Orange to cut my throat." "God forbid," exclaimed the prelates in concert. But the King's understanding, never very clear, was now quite bewildered. One of his peculiarities was that, whenever his opinion was not adopted, he fancied that his veracity was questioned. "This paper not genuine!" he exclaimed, turning over the leaves with his hands. "Am I not worthy to be believed? Is my word not to be taken?" "At all events, sir," said one of the Bishops, "this is not an ecclesiastical matter. It lies within the sphere of the civil power. God has entrusted Your Majesty with the sword: and it is not for us to invade your functions." Then the Archbishop, with that gentle and temperate malice which inflicts the deepest wounds, declared that he must be excused from setting his hand to any political document. "I and my brethren, sir," he said, "have already smarted severely for meddling with affairs of state; and we shall be very cautious how we do so again. We once subscribed a petition of the most harmless kind: we presented it in the most respectful manner; and we found that we had committed a high offence. We were saved from ruin only by the merciful protection of God. And, sir, the ground then taken by Your Majesty's Attorney and Solicitor was that, out of Parliament, we were private men, and that it was criminal presumption in private men to meddle with politics. They attacked us so fiercely that for my part I gave myself over for lost." "I thank you for that, my Lord of Canterbury," said the King: "I should have hoped that you would not have thought yourself lost by falling into my hands." Such a speech might have become the mouth of a merciful sovereign, but it came with bad grace from a prince who had burned a woman alive for harbouring one of his flying enemies, from a prince round whose knees his own nephew had clung in vain agonies of supplication. The Archbishop was not to be so silenced. He resumed his story, and recounted the insults which the creatures of the Court had offered to the Church of England, among which some ridicule thrown on his own style occupied a conspicuous place. The King had nothing to say but that there was no use in repeating old grievances, and that he had hoped that these things had been quite forgotten. He, who never forgot the smallest injury that he had suffered, could not understand how others should remember for a few weeks the most deadly injuries that he had inflicted.

At length the conversation came back to the point from which it had wandered. The King insisted on having from the Bishops a paper declaring their abhorrence of the Prince's enterprise. They, with many professions of the most submissive loyalty, pertinaciously refused. The Prince, they said, asserted that he had been invited by temporal as well as by spiritual peers. The imputation was common. Why should not the purgation be common also? "I see how it is," said the King. "Some of the temporal peers have been with you, and have persuaded you to cross me in this matter." The Bishops solemnly averred that it was not so. But it would, they said, seem strange that, on a question involving grave political and military considerations, the temporal peers should be entirely passed over, and the prelates alone should be required to take a prominent part. "But this," said James, "is my method. I am your King. It is for me to judge what is best. I will go my own way; and I call on you to assist me." The Bishops assured him that they would assist him in their proper department, as Christian ministers with their prayers, and as peers of the realm with their advice in his Parliament. James, who wanted neither the prayers of heretics nor the advice of Parliaments, was bitterly disappointed. After a long altercation, "I have done," he said; "I will urge you no further. Since you will not help me, I must trust to myself and to my own arms."

The Bishops had hardly left the royal presence, when a courier arrived with the news that on the preceding day the Prince of Orange had landed in Devonshire. During the following week London was violently agitated. On Sunday, the eleventh of November, a rumour was circulated that knives, gridirons, and caldrons, intended for the torturing of heretics, were concealed in the monastery which had been established under the King's protection at Clerkenwell. Great multitudes assembled round the building, and were about to demolish it, when a military force arrived. The crowd was dispersed and several of the rioters were slain. An inquest sate on the bodies, and came to a decision which strongly indicated the temper of the public mind. The jury found that certain loyal and well disposed persons, who had gone to put down the meetings of traitors and public enemies at a mass house, had been wilfully murdered by the soldiers; and this strange verdict was signed by all the jurors. The ecclesiastics at Clerkenwell, naturally alarmed by these symptoms of popular feeling, were desirous to place their property in safety. They succeeded in removing most of their furniture before any report of their intentions got abroad. But at length the suspicions of the rabble were excited. The two last carts were stopped in Holborn, and all that they contained was publicly burned in the middle of the street. So great was the alarm among the Catholics that all their places of worship were closed, except those which belonged to the royal family and to foreign Ambassadors.

On the whole, however, things as yet looked not unfavourably for James. The invaders had been more than a week on English ground. Yet no man of note had joined them. No rebellion had broken out in the north or the east. No servant of the crown appeared to have betrayed his trust. The royal army was assembling fast at Salisbury, and, though inferior in discipline to that of William, was superior in numbers.

The Prince was undoubtedly surprised and mortified by the slackness of those who had invited him to England. By the common people of Devonshire, indeed, he had been received with every sign of good will: but no nobleman, no gentleman of high consideration, had yet repaired to his quarters. The explanation of this singular fact is probably to be found in the circumstance that he had landed in a part of the island where he had not been expected. His friends in the north had made their arrangements for a rising, on the supposition that he would be among them with an army. His friends in the west had made no arrangements at all, and were naturally disconcerted at finding themselves suddenly called upon to take the lead in a movement so important and perilous. They had also fresh in their recollection, and indeed full in their sight, the disastrous consequences of rebellion, gibbets, heads, mangled quarters, families still in deep mourning for brave sufferers who had loved their country well but not wisely. After a warning so terrible and so recent, some hesitation was natural. It was equally natural, however, that William, who, trusting to promises from England, had put to hazard, not only his own fame and fortunes, but also the prosperity and independence of his native land, should feel deeply mortified. He was, indeed, so indignant, that he talked of falling back to Torbay, reembarking his troops, returning to Holland, and leaving those who had betrayed him to the fate which they deserved. At length, on Monday, the twelfth of November, a gentleman named Burrington, who resided in the neighbourhood of Crediton, joined the Prince's standard, and his example was followed by several of his neighbours.

Men of higher consequence had already set out from different parts of the country for Exeter. The first of these was John Lord Lovelace, distinguished by his taste, by his magnificence, and by the audacious and intemperate vehemence of his Whiggism. He had been five or six times arrested for political offences. The last crime laid to his charge was, that he had contemptuously denied the validity of a warrant, signed by a Roman Catholic Justice of the Peace. He had been brought before the Privy Council and strictly examined, but to little purpose. He resolutely refused to criminate himself; and the evidence against him was insufficient. He was dismissed; but, before he retired, James exclaimed in great heat, "My Lord, this is not the first trick that you have played me." "Sir," answered Lovelace, with undaunted spirit, "I never played any trick to Your Majesty, or to any other person. Whoever has accused me to Your Majesty of playing tricks is a liar." Lovelace had subsequently been admitted into the confidence of those who planned the Revolution. His mansion, built by his ancestors out of the spoils of Spanish galleons from the Indies, rose on the ruins of a house of Our Lady in that beautiful valley through which the Thames, not yet defiled by the precincts of a great capital, nor rising and falling with the flow and ebb of the sea, rolls under woods of beech round the gentle hills of Berkshire. Beneath the stately saloon, adorned by Italian pencils, was a subterraneous vault, in which the bones of ancient monks had sometimes been found. In this dark chamber some zealous and daring opponents of the government had held many midnight conferences during that anxious time when England was impatiently expecting the Protestant wind. The season for action had now arrived. Lovelace, with seventy followers, well armed and mounted, quitted his dwelling, and directed his course westward. He reached Gloucestershire without difficulty. But Beaufort, who governed that county, was exerting all his great authority and influence in support of the crown. The militia had been called out. A strong party had been posted at Cirencester. When Lovelace arrived there he was informed that he could not be suffered to pass. It was necessary for him either to relinquish his undertaking or to fight his way through. He resolved to force a passage; and his friends and tenants stood gallantly by him. A sharp conflict took place. The militia lost an officer and six or seven men; but at length the followers of Lovelace were overpowered: he was made a prisoner, and sent to Gloucester Castle.

Others were more fortunate. On the day on which the skirmish took place at Cirencester, Richard Savage, Lord Colchester, son and heir of the Earl Rivers, and father, by a lawless amour, of that unhappy poet whose misdeeds and misfortunes form one of the darkest portions of literary history, came with between sixty and seventy horse to Exeter. With him arrived the bold and turbulent Thomas Wharton. A few hours later came Edward Russell, son of the Earl of Bedford, and brother of the virtuous nobleman whose blood had been shed on the scaffold. Another arrival still more important was speedily announced. Colchester, Wharton, and Russell belonged to that party which had been constantly opposed to the Court. James Bertie, Earl of Abingdon, had, on the contrary, been regarded as a supporter of arbitrary government. He had been true to James in the days of the Exclusion Bill. He had, as Lord Lieutenant of Oxfordshire, acted with vigour and severity against the adherents of Monmouth, and had lighted bonfires to celebrate the defeat of Argyle. But dread of Popery had driven him into opposition and rebellion. He was the first peer of the realm who made his appearance at the quarters of the Prince of Orange.

But the King had less to fear from those who openly arrayed themselves against his authority, than from the dark conspiracy which had spread its ramifications through his army and his family. Of that conspiracy Churchill, unrivalled in sagacity and address, endowed by nature with a certain cool intrepidity which never failed him either in fighting or lying, high in military rank, and high in the favour of the Princess Anne, must be regarded as the soul. It was not yet time for him to strike the decisive blow. But even thus early he inflicted, by the instrumentality of a subordinate agent, a wound, serious if not deadly, on the royal cause.

Edward, Viscount Cornbury, eldest son of the Earl of Clarendon, was a young man of slender abilities, loose principles, and violent temper. He had been early taught to consider his relationship to the Princess Anne as the groundwork of his fortunes, and had been exhorted to pay her assiduous court. It had never occurred to his father that the hereditary loyalty of the Hydes could run any risk of contamination in the household of the King's favourite daughter: but in that household the Churchills held absolute sway; and Cornbury became their tool. He commanded one of the regiments of dragoons which had been sent westward. Such dispositions had been made that, on the fourteenth of November, he was, during a few hours, the senior officer at Salisbury, and all the troops assembled there were subject to his authority. It seems extraordinary that, at such a crisis, the army on which everything depended should have been left, even for a moment, under the command of a young Colonel, who had neither abilities nor experience. There can be little doubt that so strange an arrangement was the result of deep design, and as little doubt to what head and to what heart the design is to be imputed.

Suddenly three of the regiments of cavalry which had assembled at Salisbury were ordered to march westward. Cornbury put himself at their head, and conducted them first to Blandford and thence to Dorchester. From Dorchester, after a halt of an hour or two, they set out for Axminster. Some of the officers began to be uneasy, and demanded an explanation of these strange movements. Cornbury replied that he had instructions to make a night attack on some troops whom the Prince of Orange had posted at Honiton. But suspicion was awake. Searching questions were put, and were evasively answered. At last Cornbury was pressed to produce his orders. He perceived, not only that it would be impossible for him to carry over all the three regiments, as he had hoped, but that he was himself in a situation of considerable peril. He accordingly stole away with a few followers to the Dutch quarters. Most of his troops returned to Salisbury: but some who had been detached from the main body, and who had no suspicion of the designs of their commander, proceeded to Honiton. There they found themselves in the midst of a large force which was fully prepared to receive them. Resistance was impossible. Their leader pressed them to take service under William. A gratuity of a month's pay was offered to them, and was by most of them accepted.

The news of these events reached London on the fifteenth. James had been on the morning of that day in high good humour. Bishop Lamplugh had just presented himself at court on his arrival from Exeter, and had been most graciously received. "My Lord," said the King, "you are a genuine old Cavalier." The archbishopric of York, which had now been vacant more than two years and a half, was immediately bestowed on Lamplugh as the reward of loyalty. That afternoon, just as the King was sitting down to dinner, arrived an express with the tidings of Cornbury's defection. James turned away from his untasted meal, swallowed a crust of bread and a glass of wine, and retired to his closet. He afterwards learned that, as he was rising from table, several of the Lords in whom he reposed the greatest confidence were shaking hands and congratulating each other in the adjoining gallery. When the news was carried to the Queen's apartments she and her ladies broke out into tears and loud cries of sorrow.

The blow was indeed a heavy one. It was true that the direct loss to the crown and the direct gain to the invaders hardly amounted to two hundred men and as many horses. But where could the King henceforth expect to find those sentiments in which consists the strength of states and of armies? Cornbury was the heir of a house conspicuous for its attachment to monarchy. His father Clarendon, his uncle Rochester, were men whose loyalty was supposed to be proof to all temptation. What must be the strength of that feeling against which the most deeply rooted hereditary prejudices were of no avail, of that feeling which could reconcile a young officer of high birth to desertion, aggravated by breach of trust and by gross falsehood? That Cornbury was not a man of brilliant parts or enterprising temper made the event more alarming. It was impossible to doubt that he had in some quarter a powerful and artful prompter. Who that prompter was soon became evident. In the meantime no man in the royal camp could feel assured that he was not surrounded by traitors. Political rank, military rank, the honour of a nobleman, the honour of a soldier, the strongest professions, the purest Cavalier blood, could no longer afford security. Every man might reasonably doubt whether every order which he received from his superior was not meant to serve the purposes of the enemy. That prompt obedience without which an army is merely a rabble was necessarily at an end. What discipline could there be among soldiers who had just been saved from a snare by refusing to follow their commanding officer on a secret expedition, and by insisting on a sight of his orders?

Cornbury was soon kept in countenance by a crowd of deserters superior to him in rank and capacity: but during a few days he stood alone in his shame, and was bitterly reviled by many who afterwards imitated his example and envied his dishonourable precedence. Among these was his own father. The first outbreak of Clarendon's rage and sorrow was highly pathetic. "Oh God!" he ejaculated, "that a son of mine should be a rebel!" A fortnight later he made up his mind to be a rebel himself. Yet it would be unjust to pronounce him a mere hypocrite. In revolutions men live fast: the experience of years is crowded into hours: old habits of thought and action are violently broken; and novelties, which at first sight inspire dread and disgust become in a few days familiar, endurable, attractive. Many men of far purer virtue and higher spirit than Clarendon were prepared, before that memorable year ended, to do what they would have pronounced wicked and infamous when it began.

The unhappy father composed himself as well as he could, and sent to ask a private audience of the King. It was granted. James said, with more than his usual graciousness, that he from his heart pitied Cornbury's relations, and should not hold them at all accountable for the crime of their unworthy kinsman. Clarendon went home, scarcely daring to look his friends in the face. Soon, however, he learned with surprise that the act which had, as he at first thought, for ever dishonoured his family was applauded by some persons of high station. His niece, the Princess of Denmark, asked him why he shut himself up. He answered that he had been overwhelmed with confusion by his son's villany. Anne seemed not at all to understand this feeling. "People," she said, "are very uneasy about Popery. I believe that many of the army will do the same."

And now the King, greatly disturbed, called together the principal officers who were still in London. Churchill, who was about this time promoted to the rank of Lieutenant General, made his appearance with that bland serenity which neither peril nor infamy could ever disturb. The meeting was attended by Henry Fitzroy, Duke of Grafton, whose audacity and activity made him conspicuous among the natural children of Charles the Second. Grafton was colonel of the first regiment of Foot Guards. He seems to have been at this time completely under Churchill's influence, and was prepared to desert the royal standard as soon as the favourable moment should arrive. Two other traitors were in the circle, Kirke and Trelawney, who commanded those two fierce and lawless bands then known as the Tangier regiments. Both of them had, like the other Protestant officers of the army, long seen with extreme displeasure the partiality which the King had shown to members of his own Church; and Trelawney remembered with bitter resentment the persecution of his brother the Bishop of Bristol. James addressed the assembly in language worthy of a better man and of a better cause. It might be, he said, that some of the officers had conscientious scruples about fighting for him. If so, he was willing to receive back their commissions. But he adjured them as gentlemen and soldiers not to imitate the shameful example of Cornbury. All seemed moved; and none more than Churchill. He was the first to vow with well feigned enthusiasm that he would shed the last drop of his blood in the service of his gracious master: Grafton was loud and forward in similar protestations; and the example was followed by Kirke and Trelawney.

Deceived by these professions, the King prepared to set out for Salisbury. Before his departure he was informed that a considerable number of peers, temporal and spiritual, desired to be admitted to an audience. They came, with Sancroft at their head, to present a petition, praying that a free and legal Parliament might be called, and that a negotiation might be opened with the Prince of Orange.

The history of this petition is curious. The thought seems to have occurred at once to two great chiefs of parties who had long been rivals and enemies, Rochester and Halifax. They both, independently of one another, consulted the Bishops. The Bishops warmly approved of the suggestion. It was then proposed that a general meeting of peers should be called to deliberate on the form of an address to the King. It was term time; and in term time men of rank and fashion then lounged every day in Westminster Hall as they now lounge in the clubs of Pall Mall and Saint James's Street. Nothing could be easier than for the Lords who assembled there to step aside into some adjoining room and to hold a consultation. But unexpected difficulties arose. Halifax became first cold and then adverse. It was his nature to discover objections to everything; and on this occasion his sagacity was quickened by rivalry. The scheme, which he had approved while he regarded it as his own, began to displease him as soon as he found that it was also the scheme of Rochester, by whom he had been long thwarted and at length supplanted, and whom he disliked as much as it was in his easy nature to dislike anybody. Nottingham was at that time much under the influence of Halifax. They both declared that they would not join in the address if Rochester signed it. Clarendon expostulated in vain. "I mean no disrespect," said Halifax, "to my Lord Rochester: but he has been a member of the Ecclesiastical Commission: the proceedings of that Court must soon be the subject of a very serious inquiry; and it is not fit that one who has sate there should take any part in our proceedings." Nottingham, with strong expressions of personal esteem for Rochester, avowed the same opinion. The authority of the two dissentient Lords prevented several other noblemen from sub- scribing the address; but the Hydes and the Bishops persisted. Nineteen signatures were procured; and the petitioners waited in a body on the King.

He received their address ungraciously. He assured them, indeed, that he passionately desired the meeting of a free Parlia- ment; and he promised them, on the faith of a King, that he would call one as soon as the Prince of Orange should have left the island. "But how," said he, "can a Parliament be free when an enemy is in the kingdom, and can return near a hundred votes?" To the prelates he spoke with peculiar acrimony. "I could not," he said, "prevail on you the other day to declare against this invasion: but you are ready enough to declare against me. Then you would not meddle with politics. You have no scruple about meddling now. You have excited this rebellious temper among your flocks; and now you foment it. You would be better employed in teaching them how to obey than in teaching me how to govern." He was much incensed against his nephew Grafton, whose signature stood next to that of Sancroft, and said to the young man, with great asperity, "You know nothing about religion: you care nothing about it; and yet, forsooth, you must pretend to have a conscience." "It is true, sir," answered Grafton, with impudent frankness, "that I have very little conscience: but I belong to a party which has a great deal."

Bitter as was the King's language to the petitioners, it was far less bitter than that which he held after they had withdrawn. He had done, he said, far too much already in the hope of satisfying an undutiful and ungrateful people. He had always hated the thought of concession: but he had suffered himself to be talked over; and now he, like his father before him, had found that concession only made subjects more encroaching. He would yield nothing more, not an atom; and, after his fashion, he vehemently repeated many times, "Not an atom." Not only would he make no overtures to the invaders, but he would receive none. If the Dutch sent flags of truce, the first messenger should be dismissed without an answer; the second should be hanged. In such a mood James set out for Salisbury. His last act before his departure was to appoint a Council of five Lords to represent him in London during his absence. Of the five, two were Papists, and by law incapable of office. Joined with them was Jeffreys, a Protestant indeed, but more detested by the nation than any Papist. To the other two members of this board, Preston and Godolphin, no serious objection could be made. On the day on which the King left London the Prince of Wales was sent to Portsmouth. That fortress was strongly garrisoned, and was under the government of Berwick. The fleet commanded by Dartmouth lay close at hand: and it was supposed that, if things went ill, the royal infant would, without difficulty, be conveyed from Portsmouth to France.

On the nineteenth James reached Salisbury, and took up his quarters in the episcopal palace. Evil news was now fast pouring in upon him from all sides. The western counties had at length risen. As soon as the news of Cornbury's desertion was known, many wealthy landowners took heart and hastened to Exeter. Among them was Sir William Portman of Bryanstone, one of the greatest men in Dorsetshire, and Sir Francis Warre of Hestercombe, whose interest was great in Somersetshire. But the most important of the new comers was Seymour, who had recently inherited a baronetcy which added nothing to his dignity, and who, in birth, in politica influence, and in parliamentary abilities, was beyond comparison the foremost among the Tory gentlemen of England. At his first audience he is said to have exhibited his characteristic pride in a way which surprised and amused the Prince. "I think, Sir Edward," said William, meaning to be very civil, "that you are of the family of the Duke of Somerset." "Pardon me, sir," said Sir Edward, who never forgot that he was the head of the elder branch of the Seymours: "the Duke of Somerset is of my family."

The quarters of William now began to present the appearance of a court. More than sixty men of rank and fortune were lodged at Exeter; and the daily display of rich liveries, and of coaches drawn by six horses in the Cathedral Close, gave to that quiet precinct something of the splendour and gaiety of Whitehall. The common people were eager to take arms; and it would have been easy to form many battalions of infantry. But Schomberg, who thought little of soldiers fresh from the plough, maintained that, if the expedition could not succeed without such help, it would not succeed at all; and William, who had as much professional feeling as Schomberg, concurred in this opinion. Commissions therefore for raising new regiments were very sparingly given; and none but picked recruits were enlisted.

It was now thought desirable that the Prince should give a public reception to the whole body of noblemen and gentlemen who had assembled at Exeter. He addressed them in a short but dignified and well considered speech. He was not, he said, acquainted with the faces of all whom he saw. But he had a list of their names, and knew how high they stood in the estimation of their country. He gently chid their tardiness, but expressed a confident hope that it was not yet too late to save the kingdom. "Therefore," he said, "gentlemen, friends, and fellow Protestants, we bid you and all your followers most heartily welcome to our court and camp."

Seymour, a keen politician, long accustomed to the tactics of faction, saw in a moment that the party which had begun to rally round the Prince stood in need of organisation. It was as yet, he said, a mere rope of sand: no common object had been publicly and formally avowed: nobody was pledged to anything. As soon as the assembly at the deanery broke up, he sent for Burnet, and suggested that an association should be formed, and that all the English adherents of the Prince should put their hands to an instrument binding them to be true to their leader and to each other. Burnet carried the suggestion to the Prince and to Shrewsbury, by both of whom it was approved. A meeting was held in the Cathedral. A short paper drawn up by Burnet was produced, approved, and eagerly signed. The subscribers engaged to pursue in concert the objects set forth in the Prince's Declaration; to stand by him and by each other; to take signal vengeance on all who should make any attempt on his person; and, even if such an attempt should unhappily succeed, to persist in their undertaking till the liberties and the religion of the nation should be effectually secured.

About the same time a messenger arrived at Exeter from the Earl of Bath, who commanded at Plymouth. Bath declared that he placed himself, his troops, and the fortress which he governed at the Prince's disposal. The invaders therefore had now not a single enemy in their rear.

While the West was thus rising to confront the King, the North was all in a flame behind him. On the sixteenth Delamere took arms in Cheshire. He convoked his tenants, called upon them to stand by him, promised that, if they fell in the cause, their leases should be renewed to their children, and exhorted every one who had a good horse either to take the field, or to provide a substitute. He appeared at Manchester with fifty men armed and mounted, and his force had trebled before he reached Boaden Downs.

The neighbouring counties were violently agitated. It had been arranged that Danby should seize York, and that Devonshire should appear at Nottingham. At Nottingham no resistance was anticipated. But at York there was a small garrison under the command of Sir John Reresby. Danby acted with rare dexterity. A meeting of the gentry and freeholders of Yorkshire had been summoned for the twenty-second of November to address the King on the state of affairs. All the Deputy Lieutenants of the three Ridings, several noblemen, and a multitude of opulent esquires and substantial yeomen had been attracted to the provincial capital. Four troops of militia had been drawn out under arms to preserve the public peace. The Common Hall was crowded with freeholders, and the discussion had begun, when a cry was suddenly raised that the Papists were up, and were slaying the Protestants. The Papists of York were much more likely to be employed in seeking for hiding places than in attacking enemies who outnumbered them in the proportion of a hundred to one. But at that time no story of Popish atrocity could be so wild and marvellous as not to find ready belief. The meeting separated in dismay. The whole city was in confusion. At this moment Danby at the head of about a hundred horsemen rode up to the militia, and raised the cry "No Popery! A free Parliament! The Protestant religion!" The militia echoed the shout. The garrison was instantly surprised and disarmed. The governor was placed under arrest. The gates were closed. Sentinels were placed everywhere. The populace was suffered to pull down a Roman Catholic chapel; but no other harm appears to have been done. On the following morning the Guildhall was crowded with the first gentlemen of the shire, and with the principal magistrates of the city. The Lord Mayor was placed in the chair. Danby proposed a Declaration setting forth the reasons which had induced the friends of the constitution and of the Protestant religion to rise in arms. This Declaration was eagerly adopted, and received in a few hours the signatures of six peers, of five baronets, of six knights, and of many gentlemen of high consideration.

Devonshire meantime, at the head of a great body of friends and dependents, quitted the palace which he was rearing at Chatsworth, and appeared in arms at Derby. There he formally delivered to the municipal authorities a paper stating the reasons which had moved him to this enterprise. He then proceeded to Nottingham, which soon became the head quarters of the Northern insurrection. Here a proclamation was put forth couched in bold and severe terms. The name of rebellion, it was said, was a bugbear which could frighten no reasonable man. Was it rebellion to defend those laws and that religion which every king of England bound himself by oath to maintain? How that oath had lately been observed was a question on which, it was to be hoped, a free Parliament would soon pronounce. In the meantime, the insurgents declared that they held it to be not rebellion, but legitimate self defence, to resist a tyrant who knew no law but his own will. The Northern rising became every day more formidable. Four powerful and wealthy Earls, Manchester, Stamford, Rutland, and Chesterfield, repaired to Nottingham, and were joined there by Lord Cholmondeley and by Lord Grey de Ruthyn.

All this time the hostile armies in the south were approaching each other. The Prince of Orange, when he learned that the King had arrived at Salisbury, thought it time to leave Exeter. He placed that city and the surrounding country under the government of Sir Edward Seymour, and set out on Wednesday the twenty-first of November, escorted by many of the most considerable gentlemen of the western counties, for Axminster, where he remained several days.

The King was eager to fight; and it was obviously his interest to do so. Every hour took away something from his own strength, and added something to the strength of his enemies. It was most important, too, that his troops should be blooded. A great battle, however it might terminate, could not but injure the Prince's popularity. All this William perfectly understood, and determined to avoid an action as long as possible. It is said that, when Schomberg was told that the enemy were advancing and were determined to fight, he answered, with the composure of a tactician confident in his skill, "That will be just as we may choose." It was, however, impossible to prevent all skirmishing between the advanced guards of the armies. William was desirous that in such skirmishing nothing might happen which could wound the pride or rouse the vindictive feelings of the nation which he meant to deliver. He therefore, with admirable prudence, placed his British regiments in the situations where there was most risk of collision. The outposts of the royal army were Irish. The consequence was that, in the little combats of this short campaign, the invaders had on their side the hearty sympathy of all Englishmen.

The first of these encounters took place at Wincanton. Mackay's regiment, composed of British soldiers, lay near a body of the King's Irish troops, commanded by their countryman, the gallant Sarsfield. Mackay sent out a small party under a lieutenant named Campbell, to procure horses for the baggage. Campbell found what he wanted at Wincanton, and was just leaving that town on his return, when a strong detachment of Sarsfield's troops approached. The Irish were four to one: but Campbell resolved to fight it out to the last. With a handful of resolute men he took his stand in the road. The rest of his soldiers lined the hedges which overhung the highway on the right and on the left. The enemy came up. "Stand," cried Campbell; "for whom are you?" "I am for King James," answered the leader of the other party. "And I for the Prince of Orange," cried Campbell. "We will prince you," answered the Irishman with a curse. "Fire!" exclaimed Campbell; and a sharp fire was instantly poured in from both the hedges. The King's troops received three well aimed volleys before they could make any return. At length they succeeded in carrying one of the hedges; and would have overpowered the little band which was opposed to them, had not the country people, who mortally hated the Irish, given a false alarm that more of the Prince's troops were coming up. Sarsfield recalled his men and fell back; and Campbell proceeded on his march unmolested with the baggage horses. This affair, creditable undoubtedly to the valour and discipline of the Prince's army, was magnified by report into a victory won against great odds by British Protestants over Popish barbarians who had been brought from Connaught to oppress our island.

A few hours after this skirmish an event took place which put an end to all risk of a more serious struggle between the armies. Churchill and some of his principal accomplices were assembled at Salisbury. Two of the conspirators, Kirke and Trelawney, had proceeded to Warminster, where their regiments were posted. All was ripe for the execution of the long meditated treason.

Churchill advised the King to visit Warminster, and to inspect the troops stationed there. James assented; and his coach was at the door of the episcopal palace when his nose began to bleed violently. He was forced to postpone his expedition and to put himself under medical treatment. Three days elapsed before the hemorrhage was entirely subdued; and during those three days alarming rumours reached his ears.

It was impossible that a conspiracy so widely spread as that of which Churchill was the head could be kept altogether secret. There was no evidence which could be laid before a jury or a court martial; but strange whispers wandered about the camp. Feversham, who held the chief command, reported that there was a bad spirit in the army. It was hinted to the King that some who were near his person were not his friends, and that it would be a wise precaution to send Churchill and Grafton under a guard to Portsmouth. James rejected this counsel. A propensity to suspicion was not among his vices. Indeed the confidence which he reposed in professions of fidelity and attachment was such as might rather have been expected from a goodhearted and inexperienced stripling than from a politician who was far advanced in life, who had seen much of the world, who had suffered much from villanous arts, and whose own character was by no means a favourable specimen of human nature. It would be difficult to mention any other man who, having himself so little scruple about breaking faith with his neighbours, was so slow to believe that his neighbours could break faith with him. Nevertheless the reports which he had received of the state of his army disturbed him greatly. He was now no longer impatient for a battle. He even began to think of retreating. On the evening of Saturday, the twenty-fourth of November, he called a council of war. The meeting was attended by those officers against whom he had been most earnestly cautioned. Feversham expressed an opinion that it was desirable to fall back. Churchill argued on the other side. The consultation lasted till midnight. At length the King declared that he had decided for a retreat. Churchill saw or imagined that he was distrusted, and, though gifted with a rare self command, could not conceal his uneasiness. Before the day broke he fled to the Prince's quarters, accompanied by Grafton.

Churchill left behind him a letter of explanation. It was written with that decorum which he never failed to preserve in the midst of guilt and dishonour. He acknowledged that he owed everything to the royal favour. Interest, he said, and gratitude impelled him in the same direction. Under no other government could he hope to be so great and prosperous as he had been: but all such considerations must yield to a paramount duty. He was a Protestant; and he could not conscientiously draw his sword against the Protestant cause. As to the rest he would ever be ready to hazard life and fortune in defence of the sacred person and of the lawful rights of his gracious master.

Next morning all was confusion in the royal camp. The King's friends were in dismay. His enemies could not conceal their exultation. The consternation of James was increased by news which arrived on the same day from Warminster. Kirke, who commanded at that post, had refused to obey orders which he had received from Salisbury. There could no longer be any doubt that he too was in league with the Prince of Orange. It was rumoured that he had actually gone over with all his troops to the enemy: and the rumour, though false, was, during some hours, fully believed. A new light flashed on the mind of the unhappy King. He thought that he understood why he had been pressed, a few days before, to visit Warminster. There he would have found himself helpless, at the mercy of the conspirators, and in the vicinity of the hostile outposts. Those who might have attempted to defend him would have been easily overpowered. He would have been carried a prisoner to the head quarters of the invading army. Perhaps some still blacker treason might have been committed; for men who have once engaged in a wicked and perilous enterprise are no longer their own masters, and are often impelled, by a fatality which is part of their just punishment, to crimes such as they would at first have shuddered to contemplate. Surely it was not without the special intervention of some guardian Saint that a King devoted to the Catholic Church had, at the very moment when he was blindly hastening to captivity, perhaps to death, been suddenly arrested by what he had then thought a disastrous malady.

All these things confirmed James in the resolution which he had taken on the preceding evening. Orders were given for an immediate retreat. Salisbury was in an uproar. The camp broke up with the confusion of a flight. No man knew whom to trust or whom to obey. The material strength of the army was little diminished: but its moral strength had been destroyed. Many whom shame would have restrained from leading the way to the Prince's quarters were eager to imitate an example which they never would have set; and many, who would have stood by their King while he appeared to be resolutely advancing against the invaders, felt no inclination to follow a receding standard.

James went that day as far as Andover. He was attended by his son in law Prince George, and by the Duke of Ormond. Both were among the conspirators, and would probably have accompanied Churchill, had he not, in consequence of what had passed at the council of war, thought it expedient to take his departure suddenly. The impenetrable stupidity of Prince George served his turn on this occasion better than cunning would have done. It was his habit, when any news was told him, to exclaim in French, "Est-il-possible?" "Is it possible?" This catchword was now of great use to him. "Est-il-possible?" he cried, when he had been made to understand that Churchill and Grafton were missing. And when the ill tidings came from Warminster he again ejaculated, "Est-il-possible?"

Prince George and Ormond were invited to sup with the King at Andover. The meal must have been a sad one. The King was overwhelmed by his misfortunes. His son in law was the dullest of companions. "I have tried Prince George sober," said Charles the Second; "and I have tried him drunk; and, drunk or sober, there is nothing in him." Ormond, who was through life taciturn and bashful, was not likely to be in high spirits at such a moment. At length the repast terminated. The King retired to rest. Horses were in waiting for the Prince and Ormond, who, as soon as they left the table, mounted and rode off. They were accompanied by the Earl of Drumlanrig, eldest son of the Duke of Queensberry. The defection of this young nobleman was no insignificant event. For Queensberry was the head of the Protestant Episcopalians of Scotland, a class compared with whom the bitterest English Tories might be called Whiggish; and Drumlanrig himself was Lieutenant Colonel of Dundee's regiment of horse, a band more detested by the Whigs than even Kirke's Lambs. This fresh calamity was announced to the King on the following morning. He was less disturbed by the news than might have been expected. The shock which he had undergone twenty four hours before had prepared him for almost any disaster; and it was impossible to be seriously angry with Prince George, who was hardly an accountable being, for having yielded to the arts of such a tempter as Churchill. "What!" said James, "Is Est-il-possible gone too? After all, a good trooper would have been a greater loss." In truth the King's whole anger seems, at this time, to have been concentrated, and not without cause, on one object. He set off for London, breathing vengeance against Churchill, and learned, on arriving, a new crime of the archdeceiver. The Princess Anne had been some hours missing.

Anne, who had no will but that of the Churchills, had been induced by them to notify under her own hand to William, a week before, her approbation of his enterprise. She assured him that she was entirely in the hands of her friends, and that she would remain in the palace, or take refuge in the City, as they might determine. On Sunday the twenty-fifth of November, she, and those who thought for her, were under the necessity of coming to a sudden resolution. That afternoon a courier from Salisbury brought tidings that Churchill had disappeared, that he had been accompanied by Grafton, that Kirke had proved false, and that the royal forces were in full retreat. There was, as usually happened when great news, good or bad, arrived in town, a great crowd that evening in the galleries of Whitehall. Curiosity and anxiety sate on every face. The Queen broke forth into natural expressions of indignation against the chief traitor, and did not altogether spare his too partial mistress. The sentinels were doubled round that part of the palace which Anne occupied. The Princess was in dismay. In a few hours her father would be at Westminster. It was not likely that he would treat her personally with severity; but that he would permit her any longer to enjoy the society of her friend was not to be hoped. It could hardly be doubted that Sarah would be placed under arrest, and would be subjected to a strict examination by shrewd and rigorous inquisitors. Her papers would be seized. Perhaps evidence affecting her life might be discovered. If so, the worst might well be dreaded. The vengeance of the implacable King knew no distinction of sex. For offences much smaller than those which might probably be brought home to Lady Churchill he had sent women to the scaffold and the stake. Strong affection braced the feeble mind of the Princess. There was no tie which she would not break, no risk which she would not run, for the object of her idolatrous affection. "I will jump out of the window," she cried, "rather than be found here by my father." The favourite undertook to manage an escape. She communicated in all haste with some of the chiefs of the conspiracy. In a few hours everything was arranged. That evening Anne retired to her chamber as usual. At dead of night she rose, and, accompanied by her friend Sarah and two other female attendants, stole down the back stairs in a dressing gown and slippers. The fugitives gained the open street unchallenged. A hackney coach was in waiting for them there. Two men guarded the humble vehicle. One of them was Compton, Bishop of London, the Princess's old tutor: the other was the magnificent and accomplished Dorset, whom the extremity of the public danger had roused from his luxurious repose. The coach drove instantly to Aldersgate Street, where the town residence of the Bishops of London then stood, within the shadow of their Cathedral. There the Princess passed the night. On the following morning she set out for Epping Forest. In that wild tract Dorset possessed a venerable mansion, which has long since been destroyed. In his hospitable dwelling, the favourite resort, during many years, of wits and poets, the fugitives made a short stay. They could not safely attempt to reach William's quarters; for the road thither lay through a country occupied by the royal forces. It was therefore determined that Anne should take refuge with the northern insurgents. Compton wholly laid aside, for the time, his sacerdotal character. Danger and conflict had rekindled in him all the military ardour which he had felt twenty eight years before, when he rode in the Life Guards. He preceded the Princess's carriage in a buff coat and jackboots, with a sword at his side and pistols in his holsters. Long before she reached Nottingham, she was surrounded by a body guard of gentlemen who volunteered to escort her. They invited the Bishop to act as their colonel; and he consented with an alacrity which gave great scandal to rigid Churchmen, and did not much raise his character even in the opinion of Whigs.

When, on the morning of the twenty-sixth, Anne's apartment was found empty, the consternation was great in Whitehall. While the Ladies of her Bedchamber ran up and down the courts of the palace, screaming and wringing their hands, while Lord Craven, who commanded the Foot Guards, was questioning the sentinels in the gallery, while the Chancellor was sealing up the papers of the Churchills, the Princess's nurse broke into the royal apartments crying out that the dear lady had been murdered by the Papists. The news flew to Westminster Hall. There the story was that Her Highness had been hurried away by force to a place of confinement. When it could no longer be denied that her flight had been voluntary, numerous fictions were invented to account for it. She had been grossly insulted: she had been threatened: nay, though she was in that situation in which woman is entitled to peculiar tenderness, she had been beaten by her cruel stepmother. The populace, which years of misrule had made suspicious and irritable, was so much excited by these calumnies that the Queen was scarcely safe. Many Roman Catholics, and some Protestant Tories whose loyalty was proof to all trials, repaired to the palace that they might be in readiness to defend her in the event of an outbreak. In the midst of this distress and terror arrived the news of Prince George's flight. The courier who brought these evil tidings was fast followed by the King himself. The evening was closing in when James arrived, and was informed that his daughter had disappeared. After all that he had suffered this affliction forced a cry of misery from his lips. "God help me!" he said; "my own children have forsaken me."

That evening he sate in Council with his principal ministers till a late hour. It was determined that he should summon all the Lords Spiritual and Temporal who were then in London to attend him on the following day, and that he should solemnly ask their advice. Accordingly, on the afternoon of Tuesday the twenty-seventh, the Lords met in the diningroom of the palace. The assembly consisted of nine prelates and between thirty and forty noblemen, all Protestants. The two Secretaries of State, Middleton and Preston, though not peers of England, were in attendance. The King himself presided. The traces of severe bodily and mental suffering were discernible in his countenance and deportment. He opened the proceedings by referring to the petition which had been put into his hands just before he set out for Salisbury. The prayer of that petition was that he would convoke a free Parliament. Situated as he then was, he had not, he said, thought it right to comply. But, during his absence from London, great changes had taken place. He had also observed that his people everywhere seemed anxious that the Houses should meet. He had therefore commanded the attendance of his faithful Peers, in order to ask their counsel.

For a time there was silence. Then Oxford, whose pedigree, unrivalled in antiquity and splendour, gave him a kind of primacy in the meeting, said that, in his opinion those Lords who had signed the petition to which His Majesty had referred ought now to explain their views.

These words called up Rochester. He defended the petition, and declared that he still saw no hope for the throne or the country, but in a Parliament. He would not, he said, venture to affirm that, in so disastrous an extremity, even that remedy would be efficacious: but he had no other remedy to propose. He added that it might be advisable to open a negotiation with the Prince of Orange. Jeffreys and Godolphin followed; and both declared that they agreed with Rochester.

Then Clarendon rose, and, to the astonishment of all who remembered his loud professions of loyalty, and the agony of shame and sorrow into which he had been thrown, only a few days before, by the news of his son's defection, broke forth into a vehement invective against tyranny and Popery. "Even now," he said, "His Majesty is raising in London a regiment into which no Protestant is admitted." "That is not true," cried James in great agitation from the head of the board. Clarendon persisted, and left this offensive topic only to pass to a topic still more offensive. He accused the unfortunate King of pusillanimity. Why retreat from Salisbury? Why not try the event of a battle? Could people be blamed for submitting to the invader when they saw their sovereign run away at the head of his army? James felt these insults keenly, and remembered them long. Indeed even Whigs thought the language of Clarendon indecent and ungenerous. Halifax spoke in a very different tone. During several years of peril he had defended with admirable ability the civil and ecclesiastical constitution of his country against the prerogative. But his serene intellect, singularly unsusceptible of enthusiasm, and singularly averse to extremes, began to lean towards the cause of royalty at the very moment at which those noisy Royalists who had lately execrated the Trimmers as little better than rebels were everywhere rising in rebellion. It was his ambition to be, at this conjuncture, the peacemaker between the throne and the nation. His talents and character fitted him for that office; and, if he failed, the failure is to be ascribed to causes against which no human skill could contend, and chiefly to the folly, faithlessness, and obstinacy of the Prince whom he tried to save.

Halifax now gave utterance to much unpalatable truth, but with a delicacy which brought on him the reproach of flattery from spirits too abject to understand that what would justly be called flattery when offered to the powerful is a debt of humanity to the fallen. With many expressions of sympathy and deference, he declared it to be his opinion that the King must make up his mind to great sacrifices. It was not enough to convoke a Parliament or to open a negotiation with the Prince of Orange. Some at least of the grievances of which the nation complained should be instantly redressed without waiting till redress was demanded by the Houses or by the captain of the hostile army. Nottingham, in language equally respectful, declared that he agreed with Halifax. The chief concessions which these Lords pressed the King to make were three. He ought, they said, forthwith to dismiss all Roman Catholics from office, to separate himself wholly from France, and to grant an unlimited amnesty to those who were in arms against him. The last of these propositions, it should seem, admitted of no dispute. For, though some of those who were banded together against the King had acted towards him in a manner which might not unreasonably excite his bitter resentment, it was more likely that he would soon be at their mercy than that they would ever be at his. It would have been childish to open a negotiation with William, and yet to denounce vengeance against men whom William could not without infamy abandon. But the clouded understanding and implacable temper of James held out long against the arguments of those who laboured to convince him that it would be wise to pardon offences which he could not punish. "I cannot do it," he exclaimed: "I must make examples, Churchill above all; Churchill whom I raised so high. He and he alone has done all this. He has corrupted my army. He has corrupted my child. He would have put me into the hands of the Prince of Orange, but for God's special providence. My Lords, you are strangely anxious for the safety of traitors. None of you troubles himself about my safety." In answer to this burst of impotent anger, those who had recommended the amnesty represented with profound respect, but with firmness, that a prince attacked by powerful enemies can be safe only by conquering or by conciliating. "If Your Majesty, after all that has happened, has still any hope of safety in arms, we have done: but if not, you can be safe only by regaining the affections of your people." After long and animated debate the King broke up the meeting. "My Lords," he said, "you have used great freedom: but I do not take it ill of you. I have made up my mind on one point. I shall call a Parliament. The other suggestions which have been offered are of grave importance; and you will not be surprised that I take a night to reflect on them before I decide."

At first James seemed disposed to make excellent use of the time which he had taken for consideration. The Chancellor was directed to issue writs convoking a Parliament for the thirteenth of January. Halifax was sent for to the closet, had a long audience, and spoke with much more freedom than he had thought it decorous to use in the presence of a large assembly. He was informed that he had been appointed a Commissioner to treat with the Prince of Orange. With him were joined Nottingham and Godolphin. The King declared that he was prepared to make great sacrifices for the sake of peace. Halifax answered that great sacrifices would doubtless be required. "Your Majesty," he said, "must not expect that those who have the power in their hands will consent to any terms which would leave the laws at the mercy of the prerogative." With this distinct explanation of his views, he accepted the Commission which the King wished him to undertake. The concessions which a few hours before had been so obstinately refused were now made in the most liberal manner. A proclamation was put forth by which the King not only granted a free pardon to all who were in rebellion against him, but declared them eligible to be members of the approaching Parliament. It was not even required as a condition of eligibility that they should lay down their arms. The same Gazette which announced that the Houses were about to meet contained a notification that Sir Edward Hales, who, as a Papist, as a renegade, as the foremost champion of the dispensing power, and as the harsh gaoler of the Bishops, was one of the most unpopular men in the realm, had ceased to be Lieutenant of the Tower, and had been succeeded by his late prisoner, Bevil Skelton, who, though he held no high place in the esteem of his countrymen, was at least not disqualified by law for public trust.

But these concessions were meant only to blind the Lords and the nation to the King's real designs. He had secretly determined that, even in this extremity, he would yield nothing. On the very day on which he issued the proclamation of amnesty, he fully explained his intentions to Barillon. "This negotiation," said James, "is a mere feint. I must send Commissioners to my nephew, that I may gain time to ship off my wife and the Prince of Wales. You know the temper of my troops. None but the Irish will stand by me; and the Irish are not in sufficient force to resist the enemy. A Parliament would impose on me conditions which I could not endure. I should be forced to undo all that I have done for the Catholics, and to break with the King of France. As soon, therefore, as the Queen and my child are safe, I will leave England and take refuge in Ireland, in Scotland, or with your master."

Already James had made preparations for carrying this scheme into effect. Dover had been sent to Portsmouth with instructions to take charge of the Prince of Wales; and Dartmouth, who commanded the fleet there, had been ordered to obey Dover's directions in all things concerning the royal infant, and to have a yacht manned by trusty sailors in readiness to sail for France at a moment's notice. The King now sent positive orders that the child should instantly be conveyed to the nearest Continental port. Next to the Prince of Wales the chief object of anxiety was the Great Seal. To that symbol of kingly authority our jurists have always ascribed a peculiar and almost mysterious importance. It is held that, if the Keeper of the Seal should affix it, without taking the royal pleasure, to a patent of peerage or to a pardon, though he may be guilty of a high offence, the instrument cannot be questioned by any court of law, and can be annulled only by an Act of Parliament. James seems to have been afraid that his enemies might get this organ of his will into their hands, and might thus give a legal validity to acts which might affect him injuriously. Nor will his apprehensions be thought unreasonable when it is remembered that, exactly a hundred years later, the Great Seal of a King was used, with the assent of Lords and Commons, and with the approbation of many great statesmen and lawyers, for the purpose of transferring his prerogatives to his son. Lest the talisman which possessed such formidable powers should be abused, James determined that it should be kept within a few yards of his own closet. Jeffreys was therefore ordered to quit the costly mansion which he had lately built in Duke Street, and to take up his residence in a small apartment at Whitehall.

The King had made all his preparations for flight, when an unexpected impediment compelled him to postpone the execution of his design. His agents at Portsmouth began to entertain scruples. Even Dover, though a member of the Jesuitical cabal, showed signs of hesitation. Dartmouth was still less disposed to comply with the royal wishes. He was zealous for the crown, and had done all that he could do, with a disaffected fleet, and in the face of an adverse wind, to prevent the Dutch from landing in England: but he was also zealous for the Established Church, and was by no means friendly to the policy of that government of which he was the defender. The mutinous temper of the officers and men under his command had caused him much anxiety; and he had been greatly relieved by the news that a free Parliament had been convoked, and that Commissioners had been named to treat with the Prince of Orange. The joy was clamorous throughout the fleet. An address, warmly thanking the King for these gracious concessions to public feeling, was drawn up on board of the flag ship. The Admiral signed first. Thirty eight Captains wrote their names under his. This paper on its way to Whitehall crossed the messenger who brought to Portsmouth the order that the Prince of Wales should instantly be conveyed to France. Dartmouth learned, with bitter grief and resentment, that the free Parliament, the general amnesty, the negotiation, were all parts of a great fraud on the nation, and that in this fraud he was expected to be an accomplice. His conduct on this occasion was the most honourable part of a not very honourable life. In a sensible and spirited letter he declared that he had already carried his obedience to the furthest point to which a Protestant and an Englishman could go. To put the heir apparent of the British crown into the hands of Lewis would be nothing less than treason against the monarchy. The nation, already too much alienated from the Sovereign, would be roused to madness. The Prince of Wales would either not return at all, or would return attended by a French army. If His Royal Highness remained in the island, the worst that could be apprehended was that he would be brought up a member of the national Church; and that he might be so brought up ought to be the prayer of every loyal subject. Dartmouth concluded by declaring that he would risk his life in defence of the throne, but that he would be no party to the transporting of the Prince into France.

This letter deranged all the projects of James. He learned too that he could not on this occasion expect from his admiral even passive obedience. For Dartmouth had gone so far as to station several sloops at the mouth of the harbour of Portsmouth with orders to suffer no vessel to pass out unexamined. A change of plan was necessary. The child must be brought back to London, and sent thence to France. An interval of some days must elapse before this could be done. During that interval the public mind must be amused by the hope of a Parliament and the semblance of a negotiation. Writs were sent out for the elections. Trumpeters went backward and forward between the capital and the Dutch head quarters. At length passes for the King's Commissioners arrived; and the three Lords set out on their embassy.

They left the capital in a state of fearful distraction. The passions which, during three troubled years, had been gradually gathering force, now, emancipated from the restraint of fear, and stimulated by victory and sympathy, showed themselves without disguise, even in the precincts of the royal dwelling. The Grand Jury of Middlesex found a bill against the Earl of Salisbury for turning Papist. The Lord Mayor ordered the houses of the Roman Catholics of the city to be searched for arms. The mob broke into the house of one respectable merchant who held the unpopular faith, in order to ascertain whether he had not run a mine from his cellars under the neighbouring parish church, for the purpose of blowing up parson and congregation. The hawkers bawled about the streets a hue and cry after Father Petre, who had withdrawn himself, and not before it was time, from his apartments in Whitehall. Wharton's celebrated song, with many additional verses, was chaunted more loudly than ever in all the streets of the capital. The very sentinels who guarded the palace hummed, as they paced their rounds,

> " The English confusion to Popery drink,
>   Lillibullero bullen a la."

The secret presses of London worked without ceasing. Many papers daily came into circulation by means which the magistracy could not discover, or would not check. One of these has been preserved from oblivion by the skilful audacity with which it was written, and by the immense effect which it produced. It purported to be a supplemental declaration under the hand and seal of the Prince of Orange: but it was written in a style very different from that of his genuine manifesto. Vengeance alien from the usages of Christian and civilised nations was denounced against all Papists who should dare to espouse the royal cause. They should be treated, not as soldiers or gentlemen, but as freebooters. The ferocity and licentiousness of the invading army, which had hitherto been restrained with a strong hand, should be let loose on them. Good Protestants, and especially those who inhabited the capital, were adjured, as they valued all that was dear to them, and commanded, on peril of the Prince's highest displeasure, to seize, disarm, and imprison their Roman Catholic neighbours. This document, it is said, was found by a Whig bookseller one morning under his shop door. He made haste to print it. Many copies were dispersed by the post, and passed rapidly from hand to hand. Discerning readers had no difficulty in pronouncing it a forgery devised by some unquiet and unprincipled adventurer, such as, in troubled times, are always busy in the foulest and darkest offices of faction. But the multitude was completely duped. Indeed to such a height had national and religious feeling been excited against the Irish Papists that most of those who believed the spurious proclamation to be genuine were inclined to applaud it as a seasonable exhibition of vigour. When it was known that no such document had really proceeded from William, men asked anxiously what impostor had so daringly and so successfully personated His Highness. Some suspected Ferguson, others Johnson. At length, after the lapse of twenty seven years, Hugh Speke avowed the forgery, and demanded from the House of Brunswick a reward for so eminent a service rendered to the Protestant religion. He asserted, in the tone of a man who conceives himself to have done something eminently virtuous and honourable, that, when the Dutch invasion had thrown Whitehall into consternation, he had offered his services to the Court, had pretended to be estranged from the Whigs, and had promised to act as a spy upon them; that he had thus obtained admittance to the royal closet, had vowed fidelity, had been promised large pecuniary rewards, and had procured blank passes which enabled him to travel backwards and forwards across the hostile outposts. All these things he protested that he had done solely in order that he might, unsuspected, aim a deadly blow at the government, and produce a violent outbreak of popular feeling against the Roman Catholics. The forged proclamation he claimed as one of his contrivances: but whether his claim were well founded may be doubted. He delayed to make it so long that we may reasonably suspect him of having waited for the death of those who could confute him; and he produced no evidence but his own.

While these things happened in London, every post from every part of the country brought tidings of some new insurrection. Lumley had seized Newcastle. The inhabitants had welcomed him with transport. The statue of the King, which stood on a lofty pedestal of marble, had been pulled down and hurled into the Tyne. The third of December was long remembered at Hull as the Town-taking day. That place had a garrison commanded by Lord Langdale, a Roman Catholic. The Protestant officers concerted with the magistracy a plan of revolt: Langdale and his adherents were arrested; and soldiers and citizens united in declaring for the Protestant religion and a free Parliament.

The Eastern counties were up. The Duke of Norfolk, attended by three hundred gentlemen armed and mounted, appeared in the stately marketplace of Norwich. The Mayor and Aldermen met him there, and engaged to stand by him against Popery and arbitrary power. Lord Herbert of Cherbury and Sir Edward Harley took up arms in Worcestershire. Bristol, the second city of the realm, opened its gates to Shrewsbury. Trelawney, the Bishop, who had entirely unlearned in the Tower the doctrine of nonresistance, was the first to welcome the Prince's troops. Such was the temper of the inhabitants that it was thought unnecessary to leave any garrison among them. The people of Gloucester rose and delivered Lovelace from confinement. An irregular army soon gathered round him. Some of his horsemen had only halters for bridles. Many of his infantry had only clubs for weapons. But this force, such as it was, marched unopposed through counties once devoted to the House of Stuart, and at length entered Oxford in triumph. The magistrates came in state to welcome the insurgents. The University itself, exasperated by recent injuries, was little disposed to pass censures on rebellion. Already some of the Heads of Houses had despatched one of their number to assure the Prince of Orange that they were cordially with him, and that they would gladly coin their plate for his service. The Whig chief, therefore, rode through the capital of Toryism amidst general acclamation. Before him the drums beat Lillibullero. Behind him came a long stream of horse and foot. The whole High Street was gay with orange ribands. For already the orange riband had the double signification which, after the lapse of one hundred and sixty years, it still retains. Already it was the emblem to the Protestant Englishman of civil and religious freedom, to the Roman Catholic Celt of subjugation and persecution.

While foes were thus rising up all round the King, friends were fast shrinking from his side. The idea of resistance had become familiar to every mind. Many, who had been struck with horror when they heard of the first defections now blamed themselves for having been so slow to discern the signs of the times. There was no longer any difficulty or danger in repairing to William. The King, in calling on the nation to elect representatives, had, by implication, authorised all men to repair to the places where they had votes or interest; and many of those places were already occupied by invaders or insurgents. Clarendon eagerly caught at this opportunity of deserting the falling cause. He knew that his speech in the Council of Peers had given deadly offence; and he was mortified by finding that he was not to be one of the royal Commissioners. He had estates in Wiltshire; and he determined that his son, the son of whom he had lately spoken with grief and horror, should be a candidate for that county. Under pretence of looking after the election, Clarendon set out for the West. He was speedily followed by the Earl of Oxford, and by others who had hitherto disclaimed all connection with the Prince's enterprise.

By this time the invaders, steadily though slowly advancing, were within seventy miles of London. Though midwinter was approaching the weather was fine: the way was pleasant; and the turf of Salisbury Plain seemed luxuriously smooth to men who had been toiling through the miry ruts of the Devonshire and Somersetshire highways. The route of the army lay close by Stonehenge; and regiment after regiment halted to examine that mysterious ruin, celebrated all over the Continent as the greatest wonder of our island. William entered Salisbury with the same military pomp which he had displayed at Exeter, and was lodged there in the palace which the King had occupied a few days before.

The Prince's train was now swelled by the Earls of Clarendon and Oxford, and by other men of high rank, who had, till within a few days, been considered as zealous Royalists. Van Citters also made his appearance at the Dutch head quarters. He had been during some weeks almost a prisoner in his house near Whitehall, under the constant observation of relays of spies. Yet, in spite of those spies, or perhaps by their help, he had succeeded in obtaining full and accurate intelligence of all that passed in the palace; and now, full fraught with valuable information about men and things, he came to assist the deliberations of William.

Thus far the Prince's enterprise had prospered beyond the anticipations of the most sanguine. And now, according to the general law which governs human affairs, prosperity began to produce disunion. The Englishmen assembled at Salisbury were divided into two parties. One party consisted of Whigs who had always regarded the doctrines of passive obedience and of indefeasible hereditary right as slavish superstitions. Many of them had passed years in exile. All had been long shut out from participation in the favours of the crown. They now exulted in the near prospect of greatness and of vengeance. Burning with resentment, flushed with victory and hope, they would hear of no compromise. Nothing less than the deposition of the tyrant would content them; nor can it be disputed that herein they were perfectly consistent. They had exerted themselves, nine years earlier, to exclude him from the throne, because they thought it likely that he would be a bad King. It could therefore scarcely be expected that they would willingly leave him on the throne, now that he had turned out a far worse King than any reasonable man could have anticipated.

On the other hand, not a few of William's followers were zealous Tories, who had, till very recently, held the doctrine of non-resistance in the most absolute form, but whose faith in that doctrine had, for a moment, given way to the strong passions excited by the ingratitude of the King and by the peril of the Church. No situation could be more painful or perplexing than that of the old Cavalier who found himself in arms against the throne. The scruples which had not prevented him from repairing to the Dutch camp began to torment him cruelly as soon as he was there. His mind misgave him that he had committed a crime. At all events he had exposed himself to reproach, by acting in diametrical opposition to the professions of his whole life. He felt insurmountable disgust for his new allies. They were people whom, ever since he could remember, he had been reviling and persecuting, Presbyterians, Independents, Anabaptists, old soldiers of Cromwell, brisk boys of Shaftesbury, accomplices in the Rye House plot, captains of the Western insurrection. He naturally wished to find out some salvo which might sooth his conscience, which might vindicate his consistency, and which might put a distinction between him and the crew of schismatical rebels whom he had always despised and abhorred, but with whom he was now in danger of being confounded. He therefore disclaimed, with vehemence, all thought of taking the crown from that anointed head which the ordinance of heaven and the fundamental laws of the realm had made sacred. His dearest wish was to see a reconciliation effected on terms which would not lower the royal dignity. He was no traitor. He was not, in truth, resisting the kingly authority. He was in arms only because he was convinced that the best service which could be rendered to the throne was to rescue His Majesty, by a little gentle coercion, from the hands of wicked counsellors.

The evils which the mutual animosity of these factions tended to produce were, to a great extent, averted by the ascendency and by the wisdom of the Prince. Surrounded by eager disputants, officious advisers, abject flatterers, vigilant spies, malicious talebearers, he remained serene and inscrutable. He preserved silence while silence was possible. When he was forced to speak, the earnest and peremptory tone in which he uttered his well weighed opinions soon silenced everybody else. Whatever some of his too zealous adherents might say, he uttered not a word indicating any design on the English crown. He was doubtless well aware that between him and that crown were still interposed obstacles which no prudence might be able to surmount, and which a single false step would make insurmountable. His only chance of obtaining the splendid prize was not to seize it rudely, but to wait till, without any appearance of exertion or stratagem on his part, his secret wish should be accomplished by the force of circumstances, by the blunders of his opponents, and by the free choice of the Estates of the Realm. Those who ventured to interrogate him learned nothing, and yet could not accuse him of shuffling. He quietly referred them to his Declaration, and assured them that his views had undergone no change since that instrument had been drawn up. So skilfully did he manage his followers that their discord seems rather to have strengthened than to have weakened his hands: but it broke forth with violence when his control was withdrawn, interrupted the harmony of convivial meetings, and did not respect even the sanctity of the house of God. Clarendon, who tried to hide from others and from himself, by an ostentatious display of loyal sentiments, the plain fact that he was a rebel, was shocked to hear some of his new associates laughing over their wine at the royal amnesty which had just been graciously offered to them. They wanted no pardon, they said. They would make the King ask pardon before they had done with him. Still more alarming and disgusting to every good Tory was an incident which happened at Salisbury Cathedral. As soon as the officiating minister began to read the collect for the King, Burnet, among whose many good qualities selfcommand and a fine sense of the becoming cannot be reckoned, rose from his knees, sate down in his stall, and uttered some contemptuous noises which disturbed the devotions of the whole congregation.

In a short time the factions which divided the Prince's camp had an opportunity of measuring their strength. The royal Commissioners were on their way to him. Several days had elapsed since they had been appointed; and it was thought strange that, in a case of such urgency, there should be such delay. But in truth neither James nor William was desirous that negotiations should speedily commence; for James wished only to gain time sufficient for sending his wife and son into France; and the position of William became every day more commanding. At length the Prince caused it to be notified to the Commissioners that he would meet them at Hungerford. He probably selected this place because, lying at an equal distance from Salisbury and from Oxford, it was well situated for a rendezvous of his most important adherents. At Salisbury were those noblemen and gentlemen who had accompanied him from Holland or had joined him in the West; and at Oxford were many chiefs of the Northern insurrection.

Late on Thursday, the sixth of December, he reached Hungerford. The little town was soon crowded with men of rank and note who came thither from opposite quarters. The Prince was escorted by a strong body of troops. The northern Lords brought with them hundreds of irregular cavalry, whose accoutrements and horsemanship moved the mirth of men accustomed to the splendid aspect and exact movements of regular armies.

While the Prince lay at Hungerford a sharp encounter took place between two hundred and fifty of his troops and six hundred Irish who were posted at Reading. The superior discipline of the invaders was signally proved on this occasion. Though greatly outnumbered, they, at one onset, drove the King's forces in confusion through the streets of the town into the marketplace. There the Irish attempted to rally; but being vigorously attacked in front and fired upon at the same time by the inhabitants from the windows of the neighbouring houses, they soon lost heart, and fled with the loss of their colours and of fifty men. Of the conquerors only five fell. The satisfaction which this news gave to the Lords and gentlemen who had joined William was unmixed. There was nothing in what had happened to gall their national feelings. The Dutch had not beaten the English, but had assisted an English town to free itself from the insupportable dominion of the Irish.

On the morning of Saturday, the eighth of December, the King's Commissioners reached Hungerford. The Prince's body guard was drawn up to receive them with military respect. Bentinck welcomed them, and proposed to conduct them immediately to his master. They expressed a hope that the Prince would favour them with a private audience; but they were informed that he had resolved to hear them and answer them in public. They were ushered into his bedchamber, where they found him surrounded by a crowd of noblemen and gentlemen. Halifax, whose rank, age, and abilities entitled him to precedence, was spokesman. The proposition which the Commissioners had been instructed to make was that the points in dispute should be referred to the Parliament for which the writs were already sealing, and that in the mean time the Prince's army would not come within thirty or forty miles of London. Halifax, having explained that this was the basis on which he and his colleagues were prepared to treat, put into William's hands a letter from the King, and retired. William opened the letter and seemed unusually moved. It was the first letter which he had received from his father in law since they had become avowed enemies. Once they had been on good terms and had written to each other familiarly; nor had they, even when they had begun to regard each other with suspicion and aversion, banished from their correspondence those forms of kindness which persons nearly related by blood and marriage commonly use. The letter which the Commissioners had brought was drawn up by a secretary in diplomatic form and in the French language. "I have had many letters from the King," said William, "but they were all in English, and in his own hand." He spoke with a sensibility which he was little in the habit of displaying. Perhaps he thought at that moment how much reproach his enterprise, just, beneficent, and necessary as it was, must bring on him and on the wife who was devoted to him. Perhaps he repined at the hard fate which had placed him in such a situation that he could fulfil his public duties only by breaking through domestic ties, and envied the happier condition of those who are not responsible for the welfare of nations and Churches. But such thoughts, if they rose in his mind, were firmly suppressed. He requested the Lords and gentlemen whom he had convoked on this occasion to consult together, unrestrained by his presence, as to the answer which ought to be returned. To himself, however, he reserved the power of deciding in the last resort, after hearing their opinion. He then left them and retired to Littlecote Hall, a manor house situated about two miles off, and renowned down to our own times, not more on account of its venerable architecture

ARRIVAL OF WILLIAM AND FLIGHT OF JAMES 125

and furniture than on account of a horrible and mysterious crime which was perpetrated there in the days of the Tudors.

Before he left Hungerford he was told that Halifax had expressed a great desire to see Burnet. In this desire there was nothing strange; for Halifax and Burnet had long been on terms of friendship. No two men, indeed, could resemble each other less. Burnet was utterly destitute of delicacy and tact. Halifax's taste was fastidious, and his sense of the ludicrous morbidly quick. Burnet viewed every act and every character through a medium distorted and coloured by party spirit. The tendency of Halifax's mind was always to see the faults of his allies more strongly than the faults of his opponents. Burnet was, with all his infirmities, and through all the vicissitudes of a life passed in circumstances not very favourable to piety, a sincerely pious man. The sceptical and sarcastic Halifax lay under the imputation of infidelity. Halifax therefore often incurred Burnet's indignant censure; and Burnet was often the butt of Halifax's keen and polished pleasantry. Yet they were drawn to each other by a mutual attraction, liked each other's conversation, appreciated each other's abilities, interchanged opinions freely, and interchanged also good offices in perilous times. It was not, however, merely from personal regard that Halifax now wished to see his old acquaintance. The Commissioners must have been anxious to know what was the Prince's real aim. He had refused to see them in private; and little could be learned from what he might say in a formal and public interview. Almost all those who were admitted to his confidence were men taciturn and impenetrable as himself. Burnet was the only exception. He was notoriously garrulous and indiscreet. Yet circumstances had made it necessary to trust him; and he would doubtless, under the dexterous management of Halifax, have poured out secrets as fast as words. William knew this well, and, when he was informed that Halifax was asking for the Doctor, could not refrain from exclaiming, "If they get together there will be fine tattling." Burnet was forbidden to see the Commissioners in private; but he was assured in very courteous terms that his fidelity was regarded by the Prince as above all suspicion; and, that there might be no ground for complaint, the prohibition was made general.

That afternoon the noblemen and gentlemen whose advice William had asked met in the great room of the principal inn at Hungerford. Oxford was placed in the chair; and the King's overtures were taken into consideration. It soon appeared that the assembly was divided into two parties, a party anxious to come to terms with the King, and a party bent on his destruction. The latter party had the numerical superiority: but it was observed that Shrewsbury, who of all the English nobles was supposed to enjoy the largest share of William's confidence, though a Whig, sided on this occasion with the Tories. After much altercation the question was put. The majority was for rejecting the proposition which the royal Commissioners had been instructed to make. The resolution of the assembly was reported to the Prince at Littlecote. On no occasion during the whole course of his eventful life did he show more prudence and selfcommand. He could not wish the negotiation to succeed. But he was far too wise a man not to know that, if unreasonable demands made by him should cause it to fail, public feeling would no longer be on his side. He therefore overruled the opinion of his too eager followers, and declared his determination to treat on the basis proposed by the King. Many of the Lords and gentlemen assembled at Hungerford remonstrated: a whole day was spent in bickering: but William's purpose was immovable. He declared himself willing to refer all the questions in dispute to the Parliament which had just been summoned, and not to advance within forty miles of London. On his side he made some demands which even those who were least disposed to commend him allowed to be moderate. He insisted that the existing statutes should be obeyed till they should be altered by competent authority, and that all persons who held offices without a legal qualification should be forthwith dismissed. The deliberations of the Parliament, he justly conceived, could not be free if it was to sit surrounded by Irish regiments while he and his army lay at a distance of several marches. He therefore thought it reasonable that, since his troops were not to advance within forty miles of London on the west, the King's troops should fall back as far to the east. There would thus be, round the spot where the Houses were to meet, a wide circle of neutral ground. Within that circle, indeed, there were two fastnesses of great importance to the people of the capital, the Tower, which commanded their dwellings, and Tilbury Fort, which commanded their maritime trade. It was impossible to leave these places ungarrisoned. William therefore proposed that they should be temporarily entrusted to the care of the City of London. It might possibly be convenient that, when the Parliament assembled, the King should repair to Westminster with a body guard. The Prince announced that, in that case, he should claim the right of repairing thither also with an equal number of soldiers. It seemed to him just that, while military operations were suspended, both the armies should be considered as alike engaged in the service of the English nation, and should be alike maintained out of the

English revenue. Lastly, he required some guarantee that the King would not take advantage of the armistice for the purpose of introducing a French force into England. The point where there was most danger was Portsmouth. The Prince did not insist that this important fortress should be delivered up to him, but proposed that it should, during the truce, be under the government of an officer in whom both himself and James could confide.

The propositions of William were framed with a punctilious fairness, such as might have been expected rather from a disinterested umpire pronouncing an award than from a victorious prince dictating to a helpless enemy. No fault could be found with them by the partisans of the King. But among the Whigs there was much murmuring. They wanted no reconciliation with their old master. They thought themselves absolved from all allegiance to him. They were not disposed to recognise the authority of a Parliament convoked by his writ. They were averse to an armistice; and they could not conceive why, if there was to be an armistice, it should be an armistice on equal terms. By all the laws of war the stronger party had a right to take advantage of his strength; and what was there in the character of James to justify any extraordinary indulgence? Those who reasoned thus little knew from how elevated a point of view, and with how discerning an eye, the leader whom they censured contemplated the whole situation of England and Europe. They were eager to ruin James, and would therefore either have refused to treat with him on any conditions, or have imposed on him conditions insupportably hard. To the success of William's vast and profound scheme of policy it was necessary that James should ruin himself by rejecting conditions ostentatiously liberal. The event proved the wisdom of the course which the majority of the Englishmen at Hungerford were inclined to condemn.

On Sunday, the ninth of December, the Prince's demands were put in writing, and delivered to Halifax. The Commissioners dined at Littlecote. A splendid assemblage had been invited to meet them. The old hall, hung with coats of mail which had seen the wars of the Roses, and with portraits of gallants who had adorned the court of Philip and Mary, was now crowded with Peers and Generals. In such a throng a short question and answer might be exchanged without attracting notice. Halifax seized this opportunity, the first which had presented itself, of extracting all that Burnet knew or thought. "What is it that you want?" said the dexterous diplomatist: "do you wish to get the King into your power?" "Not at all," said Burnet: "we would not do the least harm to his person." "And if he were to go away?" said Halifax. "There is nothing," said Burnet, "so much to be wished." There can be no doubt that Burnet expressed the general sentiment of the Whigs in the Prince's camp. They were all desirous that James should fly from the country: but only a few of the wisest among them understood how important it was that his flight should be ascribed by the nation to his own folly and perverseness, and not to harsh usage and well grounded apprehension. It seems probable that, even in the extremity to which he was now reduced, all his enemies united would have been unable to effect his complete overthrow had he not been his own worst enemy: but, while his Commissioners were labouring to save him, he was labouring as earnestly to make all their efforts useless.

His plans were at length ripe for execution. The pretended negotiation had answered its purpose. On the same day on which the three Lords reached Hungerford the Prince of Wales arrived at Westminster. It had been intended that he should come over London Bridge; and some Irish troops were sent to Southwark to meet him. But they were received by a great multitude with such hooting and execration that they thought it advisable to retire with all speed. The poor child crossed the Thames at Kingston, and was brought into Whitehall so privately that many believed him to be still at Portsmouth.

To send him and the Queen out of the country without delay was now the first object of James. But who could be trusted to manage the escape? Dartmouth was the most loyal of Protestant Tories; and Dartmouth had refused. Dover was a creature of the Jesuits; and even Dover had hesitated. It was not very easy to find an Englishman of rank and honour who would undertake to place the heir apparent of the English crown in the hands of the King of France. In these circumstances, James bethought him of a French nobleman who then resided in London, Antonine Count of Lauzun. Of this man it has been said that his life was stranger than the dreams of other people. At an early age he had been the intimate associate of Lewis, and had been encouraged to expect the highest employments under the French crown. Then his fortunes had undergone an eclipse. Lewis had driven from him the friend of his youth with bitter reproaches, and had, it was said, scarcely refrained from adding blows. The fallen favourite had been sent prisoner to a fortress: but he had emerged from his confinement, had again enjoyed the smiles of his master, and had gained the heart of one of the greatest ladies in Europe, Anna Maria, daughter of Gaston Duke of Orleans, granddaughter of King Henry the

Fourth, and heiress of the immense domains of the house of Mont-pensier. The lovers were bent on marriage. The royal consent was obtained. During a few hours Lauzun was regarded by the court as an adopted member of the house of Bourbon. The portion which the princess brought with her might well have been an object of competition to sovereigns; three great dukedoms, an independent principality with its own mint and with its own tribunals, and an income greatly exceeding the whole revenue of the kingdom of Scotland. But this splendid prospect had been overcast. The match had been broken off. The aspiring suitor had been, during many years, shut up in a remote castle. At length Lewis relented. Lauzun was forbidden to appear in the royal presence, but was allowed to enjoy liberty at a distance from the court. He visited England, and was well received at the palace of James and in the fashionable circles of London; for in that age the gentlemen of France were regarded throughout Europe as models of grace; and many Chevaliers and Viscounts, who had never been admitted to the interior circle at Versailles, found themselves objects of general curiosity and admiration at Whitehall. Lauzun was in every respect the man for the present emergency. He had courage and a sense of honour, had been accustomed to eccentric adventures, and, with the keen observation and ironical pleasantry of a finished man of the world, had a strong propensity to knight errantry. All his national feelings and all his personal interests impelled him to undertake the adventure from which the most devoted subjects of the English crown seemed to shrink. As the guardian, at a perilous crisis, of the Queen of Great Britain and of the Prince of Wales, he might return with honour to his native land: he might once more be admitted to see Lewis dress and dine, and might, after so many vicissitudes, recommence, in the decline of life, the strangely fascinating chase of royal favour.

Animated by such feelings, Lauzun eagerly accepted the high trust which was offered to him. The arrangements for the flight were promptly made: a vessel was ordered to be in readiness at Gravesend: but to reach Gravesend was not easy. The City was in a state of extreme agitation. The slightest cause sufficed to bring a crowd together. No foreigner could appear in the streets without risk of being stopped, questioned, and carried before a magistrate as a Jesuit in disguise. It was, therefore, necessary to take the road on the south of the Thames. No precaution which could quiet suspicion was omitted. The King and Queen retired to rest as usual. When the palace had been some time profoundly quiet, James rose and called a servant who was in attendance. "You will find," said the King, "a man at the door of the antechamber: bring him hither." The servant obeyed, and Lauzun was ushered into the royal bedchamber. "I confide to you," said James, "my Queen and my son; everything must be risked to carry them into France." Lauzun, with a truly chivalrous spirit, returned thanks for the dangerous honour which had been conferred on him, and begged permission to avail himself of the assistance of his friend Saint Victor, a gentleman of Provence, whose courage and faith had been often tried. The services of so valuable an assistant were readily accepted. Lauzun gave his hand to Mary. Saint Victor wrapped up in his warm cloak the ill fated heir of so many Kings. The party stole down the back stairs, and embarked in an open skiff. It was a miserable voyage. The night was bleak: the rain fell: the wind roared: the water was rough: at length the boat reached Lambeth; and the fugitives landed near an inn, where a coach and horses were in waiting. Some time elapsed before the horses could be harnessed. Mary, afraid that her face might be known, would not enter the house. She remained with her child, cowering for shelter from the storm under the tower of Lambeth Church, and distracted by terror whenever the ostler approached her with his lantern. Two of her women attended her, one who gave suck to the Prince, and one whose office was to rock his cradle; but they could be of little use to their mistress; for both were foreigners who could hardly speak the English language, and who shuddered at the rigour of the English climate. The only consolatory circumstance was that the little boy was well, and uttered not a single cry. At length the coach was ready. Saint Victor followed it on horseback. The fugitives reached Gravesend safely, and embarked in the yacht which waited for them. They found there Lord Powis and his wife. Three Irish officers were also on board. These men had been sent thither in order that they might assist Lauzun in any desperate emergency; for it was thought not impossible that the captain of the ship might prove false; and it was fully determined that, on the first suspicion of treachery, he should be stabbed to the heart. There was, however, no necessity for violence. The yacht proceeded down the river with a fair wind; and Saint Victor, having seen her under sail, spurred back with the good news to Whitehall.

On the morning of Monday the tenth of December, the King learned that his wife and son had begun their voyage with a fair prospect of reaching their destination. About the same time a courier arrived at the palace with despatches from Hungerford. Had James been a little more discerning, or a little less obstinate, those despatches would have induced him to reconsider all his plans. The Commissioners wrote hopefully. The conditions proposed by the conqueror were strangely liberal. The King himself could not refrain from exclaiming that they were more favourable than he could have expected. He might indeed not unreasonably suspect that they had been framed with no friendly design: but this mattered nothing; for, whether they were offered in the hope that, by closing with them, he would lay the ground for a happy reconciliation, or, as is more likely, in the hope that, by rejecting them, he would exhibit himself to the whole nation as utterly unreasonable and incorrigible, his course was equally clear. In either case his policy was to accept them promptly and to observe them faithfully.

But it soon appeared that William had perfectly understood the character with which he had to deal, and, in offering those terms which the Whigs at Hungerford had censured as too indulgent, had risked nothing. The solemn farce by which the public had been amused since the retreat of the royal army from Salisbury was prolonged during a few hours. All the Lords who were still in the capital were invited to the palace that they might be informed of the progress of the negotiation which had been opened by their advice. Another meeting of Peers was appointed for the following day. The Lord Mayor and the Sheriffs of London were also summoned to attend the King. He exhorted them to perform their duties vigorously, and owned that he had thought it expedient to send his wife and child out of the country, but assured them that he would himself remain at his post. While he uttered this unkingly and unmanly falsehood, his fixed purpose was to depart before daybreak. Already he had entrusted his most valuable movables to the care of several foreign Ambassadors. His most important papers had been deposited with the Tuscan minister. But before the flight there was still something to be done. The tyrant pleased himself with the thought that he might avenge himself on a people who had been impatient of his despotism by inflicting on them at parting all the evils of anarchy. He ordered the Great Seal and the writs for the new Parliament to be brought to his apartment. The writs he threw into the fire. Some which had been already sent out he annulled by an instrument drawn up in legal form. To Feversham he wrote a letter which could be understood only as a command to disband the army. Still, however, he concealed, even from his chief ministers, his intention of absconding. Just before he retired he directed Jeffreys to be in the closet early on the morrow, and, while stepping into bed, whispered to Mulgrave that the news from Hungerford was highly satisfactory. Everybody withdrew except the Duke of Northumberland. This young man, a natural son of Charles the Second by the Duchess of Cleveland, commanded a troop of Life Guards, and was a Lord of the Bedchamber. It seems to have been then the custom of the court that, in the Queen's absence, a Lord of the Bedchamber should sleep on a pallet in the King's room; and it was Northumberland's turn to perform this duty.

At three in the morning of Tuesday the eleventh of December, James rose, took the Great Seal in his hand, laid his commands on Northumberland not to open the door of the bedchamber till the usual hour, and disappeared through a secret passage, the same passage probably through which Huddleston had been brought to the bedside of the late King. Sir Edward Hales was in attendance with a hackney coach. James was conveyed to Millbank where he crossed the Thames in a small wherry. As he passed Lambeth he flung the Great Seal into the midst of the stream, where, after many months, it was accidentally caught by a fishing net and dragged up.

At Vauxhall he landed. A carriage and horses had been stationed there for him; and he immediately took the road towards Sheerness, where a hoy belonging to the Custom House had been ordered to await his arrival.

LONDONDERRY

THE other great fastness of Protestantism was a place of more importance. Eighty years before, during the troubles caused by the last struggle of the houses of O'Neil and O'Donnel against the authority of James the First, the ancient city of Derry had been surprised by one of the native chiefs: the inhabitants had been slaughtered, and the houses reduced to ashes. The insurgents were speedily put down and punished: the government resolved to restore the ruined town: the Lord Mayor, Aldermen, and Common Council of London were invited to assist in the work; and King James the First made over to them in their corporate capacity the ground covered by the ruins of the old Derry, and about six thousand acres in the neighbourhood.

This country, then uncultivated and uninhabited, is now enriched by industry, embellished by taste, and pleasing even to eyes accustomed to the well tilled fields and stately manor houses of England. A new city soon arose which, on account of its connection with the capital of the empire, was called Londonderry. The buildings covered the summit and slope of a hill which overlooked the broad stream of the Foyle, then whitened by vast flocks of wild swans. On the highest ground stood the Cathedral, a church which, though erected when the secret of Gothic architecture was lost, and though ill qualified to sustain a comparison with the awful temples of the middle ages, is not without grace and dignity. Near the Cathedral rose the Palace of the Bishop, whose see was one of the most valuable in Ireland. The city was in form nearly an ellipse; and the principal streets formed a cross, the arms of which met in a square called the Diamond. The original houses have been either rebuilt or so much repaired that their ancient character can no longer be traced; but many of them were standing within living memory. They were in general two stories in height; and some of them had stone staircases on the outside. The dwellings were encompassed by a wall of which the whole circumference was little less than a mile. On the bastions were planted culverins and sakers presented by the wealthy guilds of London to the colony. On some of these ancient guns, which have done memorable service to a great cause, the devices of the Fishmongers' Company, of the Vintners' Company, and of the Merchant Tailors' Company are still discernible.

The inhabitants were Protestants of Anglosaxon blood. They were indeed not all of one country or of one church: but Englishmen and Scotchmen, Episcopalians and Presbyterians, seem to have generally lived together in friendship, a friendship which is sufficiently explained by their common antipathy to the Irish race and to the Popish religion. During the rebellion of 1641, Londonderry had resolutely held out against the native chieftains, and had been repeatedly besieged in vain. Since the Restoration the city had prospered. The Foyle, when the tide was high, brought up ships of large burden to the quay. The fisheries throve greatly. The nets, it was said, were sometimes so full that it was necessary to fling back multitudes of fish into the waves. The quantity of salmon caught annually was estimated at eleven hundred thousand pounds' weight.

The people of Londonderry shared in the alarm which, towards the close of the year 1688, was general among the Protestants settled in Ireland. It was known that the aboriginal peasantry of the neighbourhood were laying in pikes and knives. Priests had been haranguing in a style of which, it must be owned, the Puritan part of the Anglosaxon colony had little right to complain, about the slaughter of the Amalekites, and the judgments which Saul had brought on himself by sparing one of the proscribed race. Rumours from various quarters and anonymous letters in various hands agreed in naming the ninth of December as the day fixed for the extirpation of the strangers. While the minds of the citizens were agitated by these reports, news came that a regiment of twelve hundred Papists, commanded by a Papist, Alexander Macdonnell, Earl of Antrim, had received orders from the Lord Deputy to occupy Londonderry, and was already on the march from Coleraine. The consternation was extreme. Some were for closing the gates and resisting; some for submitting; some for temporising. The corporation had, like the other corporations of Ireland, been remodelled. The magistrates were men of low station and character. Among them was only one person of Anglosaxon extraction; and he had turned Papist. In such rulers the inhabitants could place no confidence. The Bishop, Ezekiel Hopkins, resolutely adhered to the political doctrines which he had preached during many years, and exhorted his flock to go patiently to the slaughter rather than incur the guilt of disobeying the Lord's Anointed. Antrim was meanwhile drawing nearer and nearer. At length the citizens saw from the walls his troops arrayed on the opposite shore of the Foyle. There was then no bridge: but there was a ferry which kept up a constant communication between the two banks of the river; and by this ferry a detachment from Antrim's regiment crossed. The officers presented themselves at the gate, produced a warrant directed to the Mayor and Sheriffs, and demanded admittance and quarters for his Majesty's soldiers.

Just at this moment thirteen young apprentices, most of whom appear, from their names, to have been of Scottish birth or descent, flew to the guard room, armed themselves, seized the keys of the city, rushed to the Ferry Gate, closed it in the face of the King's officers, and let down the portcullis. James Morison, a citizen more advanced in years, addressed the intruders from the top of the wall and advised them to be gone. They stood in consultation before the gate till they heard him cry, "Bring a great gun this way." They then thought it time to get beyond the range of shot. They retreated, reembarked, and rejoined their comrades on the other side of the river. The flame had already spread. The whole city was up. The other gates were secured. Sentinels paced the ramparts everywhere. The magazines were opened. Muskets and gunpowder were distributed. Messengers were sent, under cover of the following night, to the Protestant gentlemen of the neighbouring counties. The bishop expostulated in vain. It is indeed probable that the vehement and daring young Scotchmen who had taken the lead on this occasion had little respect for his office. One of them broke in on a discourse with which he interrupted the military preparations by exclaiming, "A good sermon, my lord; a very good sermon; but we have not time to hear it just now."

The Protestants of the neighbourhood promptly obeyed the summons of Londonderry. Within forty eight hours hundreds of horse and foot came by various roads to the city. Antrim, not thinking himself strong enough to risk an attack, or not disposed to take on himself the responsibility of commencing a civil war without further orders, retired with his troops to Coleraine.

[A passage is here omitted: Tyrconnel called the Irish peasantry to arms to defend the Catholic Church from King William, and there was a violent insurrection against the Protestants in Ireland.]

In Leinster, Munster and Connaught, it was utterly impossible for the English settlers, few as they were and dispersed, to offer any effectual resistance to this terrible outbreak of the aboriginal population. Charleville, Mallow, Sligo, fell into the hands of the natives. Bandon, where the Protestants had mustered in considerable force, was reduced by Lieutenant General Macarthy, an Irish officer who was descended from one of the most illustrious Celtic houses, and who had long served, under a feigned name, in the French army. The people of Kenmare held out in their little fastness till they were attacked by three thousand regular soldiers, and till it was known that several pieces of ordnance were coming to batter down the turf wall which surrounded the agent's house. Then at length a capitulation was concluded. The colonists were suffered to embark in a small vessel scantily supplied with food and water. They had no experienced navigator on board: but after a voyage of a fortnight, during which they were crowded together like slaves in a Guinea ship, and suffered the extremity of thirst and hunger, they reached Bristol in safety. When such was the fate of the towns, it was evident that the country seats which the Protestant landowners had recently fortified in the three southern provinces could no longer be defended. Many families submitted, delivered up their arms, and thought themselves happy in escaping with life. But many resolute and highspirited gentlemen and yeomen were determined to perish rather than yield. They packed up such valuable property as could easily be carried away, burned whatever they could not remove, and, well armed and mounted, set out for those spots in Ulster which were the strongholds of their race and of their faith. The flower of the Protestant population of Munster and Connaught found shelter at Enniskillen. Whatever was bravest and most truehearted in Leinster took the road to Londonderry.

In the camp[1] it was generally expected that Londonderry would fall without a blow. Rosen confidently predicted that the mere sight of the Irish army would terrify the garrison into submission. But Richard Hamilton, who knew the temper of the colonists better, had misgivings. The assailants were sure of one important ally within the walls. Lundy, the Governor, professed the Protestant religion, and had joined in proclaiming William and Mary; but he was in secret communication with the enemies of his Church and of the Sovereigns to whom he had sworn fealty. Some have suspected that he was a concealed Jacobite, and that he had affected to acquiesce in the Revolution only in order that he might be better able to assist in bringing about a Restoration: but it is probable that his conduct is rather to be attributed to faintheartedness and poverty of spirit than to zeal for any public cause. He seems to have thought resistance hopeless; and in truth, to a military eye, the defences of Londonderry appeared contemptible. The fortifications consisted of a simple wall overgrown with grass and weeds: there was no ditch even before the gates: the drawbridges had long been neglected: the chains were rusty and could scarcely be used: the parapets and towers were built after a fashion which might well move disciples of Vauban to laughter; and these feeble defences were on almost every side commanded by heights. Indeed those who laid out the city had never meant that it should be able to stand a regular siege, and had contented themselves with throwing up works sufficient to protect the inhabitants against a tumultuary attack of the Celtic peasantry. Avaux assured Louvois that a single French battalion would easily storm such a fastness. Even if the place should, notwithstanding all disadvantages, be able to repel a large army directed by the science and experience of generals who had served under Condé and Turenne, hunger must soon bring the contest to an end. The stock of provisions was small; and the population had been swollen to seven or eight times the ordinary number by a multitude of colonists flying from the rage of the natives.

Lundy, therefore, from the time when the Irish army entered Ulster, seems to have given up all thought of serious resistance. He talked so despondingly that the citizens and his own soldiers murmured against him. He seemed, they said, to be bent on discouraging them. Meanwhile the enemy drew daily nearer and nearer; and it was known that James himself was coming to take the command of his forces.

[1] [The Jacobite camp besieging Londonderry. It had been commanded by Richard Hamilton, but James had just arrived and had placed two French generals, Rosen and Maumont, over him.]

Just at this moment a glimpse of hope appeared. On the fourteenth of April ships from England anchored in the bay. They had
on board two regiments which had been sent, under the command
of a Colonel named Cunningham, to reinforce the garrison.
Cunningham and several of his officers went on shore and conferred
with Lundy. Lundy dissuaded them from landing their men. The
place, he said, could not hold out. To throw more troops into it
would therefore be worse than useless: for the more numerous the
garrison, the more prisoners would fall into the hands of the enemy.
The best thing that the two regiments could do would be to sail
back to England. He meant, he said, to withdraw himself privately;
and the inhabitants must then try to make good terms for themselves.

He went through the form of holding a council of war: but from
this council he excluded all those officers of the garrison whose
sentiments he knew to be different from his own. Some who had
ordinarily been summoned on such occasions, and who now came
uninvited, were thrust out of the room. Whatever the Governor
said was echoed by his creatures. Cunningham and Cunningham's
companions could scarcely venture to oppose their opinion to that
of a person whose local knowledge was necessarily far superior to
theirs, and whom they were by their instructions directed to obey.
One brave soldier murmured. "Understand this," he said: "to
give up Londonderry is to give up Ireland." But his objections
were contemptuously overruled. The meeting broke up. Cunningham and his officers returned to the ships, and made preparations
for departing. Meanwhile Lundy privately sent a messenger to the
head quarters of the enemy, with assurances that the city should be
peaceably surrendered on the first summons.

But as soon as what had passed in the council of war was whispered about the streets, the spirit of the soldiers and citizens
swelled up high and fierce against the dastardly and perfidious chief
who had betrayed them. Many of his own officers declared that
they no longer thought themselves bound to obey him. Voices
were heard threatening, some that his brains should be blown out,
some that he should be hanged on the walls. A deputation was sent
to Cunningham imploring him to assume the command. He
excused himself on the plausible ground that his orders were to
take directions in all things from the Governor. Meanwhile it was
rumoured that the persons most in Lundy's confidence were
stealing out of the town one by one. Long after dusk on the evening
of the seventeenth it was found that the gates were open and that
the keys had disappeared. The officers who made the discovery

took on themselves to change the passwords and to double the guards. The night, however, passed over without any assault.

After some anxious hours the day broke. The Irish, with James at their head, were now within four miles of the city. A tumultuous council of the chief inhabitants was called. Some of them vehemently reproached the Governor to his face with his treachery. He had sold them, they cried, to their deadliest enemy: he had refused admission to the force which good King William had sent to defend them. While the altercation was at the height, the sentinels who paced the ramparts announced that the vanguard of the hostile army was in sight. Lundy had given orders that there should be no firing: but his authority was at an end. Two gallant soldiers, Major Henry Baker and Captain Adam Murray, called the people to arms. They were assisted by the eloquence of an aged clergyman, George Walker, rector of the parish of Donaghmore, who had, with many of his neighbours, taken refuge in Londonderry. The whole crowded city was moved by one impulse. Soldiers, gentlemen, yeomen, artisans, rushed to the walls and manned the guns. James, who, confident of success, had approached within a hundred yards of the southern gate, was received with a shout of "No surrender," and with a fire from the nearest bastion. An officer of his staff fell dead by his side. The King and his attendants made all haste to get out of reach of the cannon balls. Lundy, who was now in imminent danger of being torn limb from limb by those whom he had betrayed, hid himself in an inner chamber. There he lay during the day, and at night, with the generous and politic connivance of Murray and Walker, made his escape in the disguise of a porter. The part of the wall from which he let himself down is still pointed out; and people still living talk of having tasted the fruit of a pear tree which assisted him in his descent. His name is, to this day, held in execration by the Protestants of the North of Ireland; and his effigy is still annually hung and burned by them with marks of abhorrence similar to those which in England are appropriated to Guy Fawkes.

And now Londonderry was left destitute of all military and of all civil government. No man in the town had a right to command any other: the defences were weak: the provisions were scanty: an incensed tyrant and a great army were at the gates. But within was that which has often, in desperate extremities, retrieved the fallen fortunes of nations. Betrayed, deserted, disorganised, unprovided with resources, begirt with enemies, the noble city was still no easy conquest. Whatever an engineer might think of the strength of the ramparts, all that was most intelligent, most courageous, most high-spirited among the Englishry of Leinster and of Northern Ulster was crowded behind them. The number of men capable of bearing arms within the walls was seven thousand; and the whole world could not have furnished seven thousand men better qualified to meet a terrible emergency with clear judgment, dauntless valour, and stubborn patience. They were all zealous Protestants; and the Protestantism of the majority was tinged with Puritanism. They had much in common with that sober, resolute, and Godfearing class out of which Cromwell had formed his unconquerable army. But the peculiar situation in which they had been placed had developed in them some qualities which, in the mother country, might possibly have remained latent. The English inhabitants of Ireland were an aristocratic caste, which had been enabled, by superior civilisation, by close union, by sleepless vigilance, by cool intrepidity, to keep in subjection a numerous and hostile population. Almost every one of them had been in some measure trained both to military and to political functions. Almost every one was familiar with the use of arms, and was accustomed to bear a part in the administration of justice. It was remarked by contemporary writers that the colonists had something of the Castilian haughtiness of manner, though none of the Castilian indolence, that they spoke English with remarkable purity and correctness, and that they were, both as militiamen and as jurymen, superior to their kindred in the mother country. In all ages, men situated as the Anglosaxons in Ireland were situated have had peculiar vices and peculiar virtues, the vices and virtues of masters, as opposed to the vices and virtues of slaves. The member of a dominant race is, in his dealings with the subject race, seldom indeed fraudulent,—for fraud is the resource of the weak,—but imperious, insolent, and cruel. Towards his brethren, on the other hand, his conduct is generally just, kind, and even noble. His selfrespect leads him to respect all who belong to his own order. His interest impels him to cultivate a good understanding with those whose prompt, strenuous, and courageous assistance may at any moment be necessary to preserve his property and life. It is a truth ever present to his mind that his own wellbeing depends on the ascendency of the class to which he belongs. His very selfishness therefore is sublimed into public spirit: and this public spirit is stimulated to fierce enthusiasm by sympathy, by the desire of applause, and by the dread of infamy. For the only opinion which he values is the opinion of his fellows; and in their opinion devotion to the common cause is the most sacred of duties. The character, thus formed, has two aspects. Seen on one side, it must be regarded by every well constituted mind with disapprobation. Seen on the other, it irresistibly extorts applause. The Spartan, smiting and spurning the wretched Helot, moves our disgust. But the same Spartan, calmly dressing his hair, and uttering his concise jests, on what he well knows to be his last day, in the pass of Thermopylæ, is not to be contemplated without admiration. To a superficial observer it may seem strange that so much evil and so much good should be found together. But in truth the good and the evil, which at first sight appear almost incompatible, are closely connected, and have a common origin. It was because the Spartan had been taught to revere himself as one of a race of sovereigns, and to look down on all that was not Spartan as of an inferior species, that he had no fellow feeling for the miserable serfs who crouched before him, and that the thought of submitting to a foreign master, or of turning his back before an enemy, never, even in the last extremity, crossed his mind. Something of the same character, compounded of tyrant and hero, has been found in all nations which have domineered over more numerous nations. But it has nowhere in modern Europe shown itself so conspicuously as in Ireland. With what contempt, with what antipathy, the ruling minority in that country long regarded the subject majority may be best learned from the hateful laws which, within the memory of men still living, disgraced the Irish statute book. Those laws were at length annulled: but the spirit which had dictated them survived them, and even at this day sometimes breaks out in excesses pernicious to the commonwealth and dishonourable to the Protestant religion. Nevertheless it is impossible to deny that the English colonists have had, with too many of the faults, all the noblest virtues of a sovereign caste. The faults have, as was natural, been most offensively exhibited in times of prosperity and security: the virtues have been most resplendent in times of distress and peril; and never were those virtues more signally displayed than by the defenders of Londonderry, when their Governor had abandoned them, and when the camp of their mortal enemy was pitched before their walls.

No sooner had the first burst of the rage excited by the perfidy of Lundy spent itself than those whom he had betrayed proceeded, with a gravity and prudence worthy of the most renowned senates, to provide for the order and defence of the city. Two governors were elected, Baker and Walker. Baker took the chief military command. Walker's especial business was to preserve internal tranquillity, and to dole out supplies from the magazines. The inhabitants capable of bearing arms were distributed into eight regiments. Colonels, captains, and subordinate officers were appointed. In a few hours every man knew his post, and was ready to repair to it as soon as the beat of the drum was heard. That machinery, by which Oliver had, in the preceding generation, kept up among his soldiers so stern and so pertinacious an enthusiasm, was again employed with not less success. Preaching and praying occupied a large part of every day. Eighteen clergymen of the Established Church and seven or eight nonconformist ministers were within the walls. They all exerted themselves indefatigably to rouse and sustain the spirit of the people. Among themselves there was for the time entire harmony. All disputes about church government, postures, ceremonies, were forgotten. The Bishop, having found that his lectures on passive obedience were derided even by the Episcopalians, had withdrawn himself, first to Raphoe, and then to England, and was preaching in a chapel in London. On the other hand, a Scotch fanatic named Hewson, who had exhorted the Presbyterians not to ally themselves with such as refused to subscribe the Covenant, had sunk under the well merited disgust and scorn of the whole Protestant community. The aspect of the Cathedral was remarkable. Cannon were planted on the summit of the broad tower which has since given place to a tower of different proportions. Ammunition was stored in the vaults. In the choir the liturgy of the Anglican Church was read every morning. Every afternoon the Dissenters crowded to a simpler worship.

James had waited twenty four hours, expecting, as it should seem, the performance of Lundy's promises; and in twenty four hours the arrangements for the defence of Londonderry were complete. On the evening of the nineteenth of April, a trumpeter came to the southern gate, and asked whether the engagements into which the Governor had entered would be fulfilled. The answer was that the men who guarded these walls had nothing to do with the Governor's engagements, and were determined to resist to the last.

On the following day a messenger of higher rank was sent, Claude Hamilton, Lord Strabane, one of the few Roman Catholic peers of Ireland. Murray, who had been appointed to the command of one of the eight regiments into which the garrison was distributed, advanced from the gate to meet the flag of truce; and a short conference was held. Strabane had been authorised to make large promises. The citizens should have a free pardon for all that was past if they would submit to their lawful Sovereign. Murray himself should have a colonel's commission, and a thousand pounds in money. "The men of Londonderry," answered Murray, "have done nothing that requires a pardon, and own no Sovereign but King William and Queen Mary. It will not be safe for your Lordship to stay longer, or to return on the same errand. Let me have the honour of seeing you through the lines."

James had been assured, and had fully expected, that the city would yield as soon as it was known that he was before the walls. Finding himself mistaken, he broke loose from the control of Melfort, and determined to return instantly to Dublin. Rosen accompanied the King. The direction of the siege was entrusted to Maumont. Richard Hamilton was second, and Pusignan third, in command.

The operations now commenced in earnest. The besiegers began by battering the town. It was soon on fire in several places. Roofs and upper stories of houses fell in, and crushed the inmates. During a short time the garrison, many of whom had never before seen the effect of a cannonade, seemed to be discomposed by the crash of chimneys, and by the heaps of ruin mingled with disfigured corpses. But familiarity with danger and horror produced in a few hours the natural effect. The spirit of the people rose so high that their chiefs thought it safe to act on the offensive. On the twenty-first of April a sally was made under the command of Murray. The Irish stood their ground resolutely; and a furious and bloody contest took place. Maumont, at the head of a body of cavalry, flew to the place where the fight was raging. He was struck in the head by a musket ball, and fell a corpse. The besiegers lost several other officers, and about two hundred men, before the colonists could be driven in. Murray escaped with difficulty. His horse was killed under him; and he was beset by enemies: but he was able to defend himself till some of his friends made a rush from the gate to his rescue, with old Walker at their head.

In consequence of the death of Maumont, Richard Hamilton was once more commander of the Irish army. His exploits in that post did not raise his reputation. He was a fine gentleman and a brave soldier; but he had no pretensions to the character of a great general, and had never, in his life, seen a siege. Pusignan had more science and energy. But Pusignan survived Maumont little more than a fortnight. At four in the morning of the sixth of May, the garrison made another sally, took several flags, and killed many of the besiegers. Pusignan, fighting gallantly, was shot through the body. The wound was one which a skilful surgeon might have cured: but there was no such surgeon in the Irish camp; and the communication with Dublin was slow and irregular. The poor Frenchman died, complaining bitterly of the barbarous ignorance and negligence which had shortened his days. A medical man, who had been sent down express from the capital, arrived after the funeral. James, in consequence, as it should seem, of this disaster, established a daily post between Dublin Castle and Hamilton's head quarters. Even by this conveyance letters did not travel very expeditiously: for the couriers went on foot; and, from fear probably of the Enniskilleners, took a circuitous route from military post to military post.

May passed away: June arrived; and still Londonderry held out. There had been many sallies and skirmishes with various success: but, on the whole, the advantage had been with the garrison. Several officers of note had been carried prisoners into the city; and two French banners, torn after hard fighting from the besiegers, had been hung as trophies in the chancel of the Cathedral. It seemed that the siege must be turned into a blockade. But before the hope of reducing the town by main force was relinquished, it was determined to make a great effort. The point selected for assault was an outwork called Windmill Hill, which was not far from the southern gate. Religious stimulants were employed to animate the courage of the forlorn hope. Many volunteers bound themselves by oath to make their way into the works or to perish in the attempt. Captain Butler, son of the Lord Mountgarret, undertook to lead the sworn men to the attack. On the walls the colonists were drawn up in three ranks. The office of those who were behind was to load the muskets of those who were in front. The Irish came on boldly and with a fearful uproar, but after long and hard fighting were driven back. The women of Londonderry were seen amidst the thickest fire serving out water and ammunition to their husbands and brothers. In one place, where the wall was only seven feet high, Butler and some of his sworn men succeeded in reaching the top; but they were all killed or made prisoners. At length, after four hundred of the Irish had fallen, their chiefs ordered a retreat to be sounded.

Nothing was left but to try the effect of hunger. It was known that the stock of food in the city was but slender. Indeed it was thought strange that the supplies should have held out so long. Every precaution was now taken against the introduction of provisions. All the avenues leading to the city by land were closely guarded. On the south were encamped, along the left bank of the Foyle, the horsemen who had followed Lord Galmoy from the valley of the Barrow. Their chief was of all the Irish captains the most dreaded and the most abhorred by the Protestants. For he had disciplined his men with rare skill and care; and many frightful stories were told of his barbarity and perfidy. Long lines of tents, occupied by the infantry of Butler and O'Neil, of Lord Slane and Lord Gormanstown, by Nugent's Westmeath men, by Eustace's Kildare men, and by Cavanagh's Kerry men, extended northward till they again approached the water side. The river was fringed with forts and batteries, which no vessel could pass without great peril. After some time it was determined to make the security still more complete by throwing a barricade across the stream, about a mile and a half below the city. Several boats full of stones were sunk. A row of stakes was driven into the bottom of the river. Large pieces of fir wood, strongly bound together, formed a boom which was more than a quarter of a mile in length, and which was firmly fastened to both shores, by cables a foot thick. A huge stone, to which the cable on the left bank was attached, was removed many years later, for the purpose of being polished and shaped into a column. But the intention was abandoned, and the rugged mass still lies, not many yards from its original site, amidst the shades which surround a pleasant country house named Boom Hall. Hard by is the well from which the besiegers drank. A little further off is the burial ground where they laid their slain, and where even in our own time the spade of the gardener has struck upon many skulls and thighbones at a short distance beneath the turf and flowers.

[A passage is here omitted. It concludes with an account of the successful partisan war waged by the Enniskillen Protestants against the native population.]

Yet, in the midst of success and plenty, the Enniskilleners were tortured by a cruel anxiety for Londonderry. They were bound to the defenders of that city, not only by religious and national sympathy, but by common interest. For there could be no doubt that, if Londonderry fell, the whole Irish army would instantly march in irresistible force upon Lough Erne. Yet what could be done? Some brave men were for making a desperate attempt to relieve the besieged city; but the odds were too great. Detachments however were sent which infested the rear of the blockading army, cut off supplies, and, on one occasion, carried away the horses of three entire troops of cavalry. Still the line of posts which surrounded Londonderry by land remained unbroken. The river was still strictly closed and guarded. Within the walls the distress had become extreme. So early as the eighth of June horseflesh was almost the only meat which could be purchased; and of horseflesh the supply was scanty. It was necessary to make up the deficiency with tallow; and even tallow was doled out with a parsimonious hand.

On the fifteenth of June a gleam of hope appeared. The sentinels on the top of the Cathedral saw sails nine miles off in the bay of Lough Foyle. Thirty vessels of different sizes were counted. Signals were made from the steeples and returned from the mast heads, but were imperfectly understood on both sides. At last a messenger from the fleet eluded the Irish sentinels, dived under the boom, and informed the garrison that Kirke had arrived from England with troops, arms, ammunition, and provisions, to relieve the city.

In Londonderry expectation was at the height: but a few hours of feverish joy were followed by weeks of misery. Kirke thought it unsafe to make any attempt, either by land or by water, on the lines of the besiegers, and retired to the entrance of Lough Foyle, where, during several weeks, he lay inactive.

And now the pressure of famine became every day more severe. A strict search was made in all the recesses of all the houses of the city; and some provisions, which had been concealed in cellars by people who had since died or made their escape, were discovered and carried to the magazines. The stock of cannon balls was almost exhausted; and their place was supplied by brickbats coated with lead. Pestilence began, as usual, to make its appearance in the train of hunger. Fifteen officers died of fever in one day. The Governor Baker was among those who sank under the disease. His place was supplied by Colonel John Mitchelburne.

Meanwhile it was known at Dublin that Kirke and his squadron were on the coast of Ulster. The alarm was great at the Castle. Even before this news arrived, Avaux had given it as his opinion that Richard Hamilton was unequal to the difficulties of the situation. It had therefore been resolved that Rosen should take the chief command. He was now sent down with all speed.

On the nineteenth of June he arrived at the head quarters of the besieging army. At first he attempted to undermine the walls; but his plan was discovered; and he was compelled to abandon it after a sharp fight, in which more than a hundred of his men were slain. Then his fury rose to a strange pitch. He, an old soldier, a Marshal of France in expectancy, trained in the school of the greatest generals, accustomed, during many years, to scientific war, to be baffled by a mob of country gentlemen, farmers, shopkeepers, who were protected only by a wall which any good engineer would at once have pronounced untenable! He raved, he blasphemed, in a language of his own, made up of all the dialects spoken from the Baltic to the Atlantic. He would raze the city to the ground: he would spare no living thing; no, not the young girls; not the babies at the breast. As to the leaders, death was too light a punishment for them: he would rack them: he would roast them alive. In his rage he ordered a shell to be flung into the town with a letter containing a horrible menace. He would, he said, gather into one body all the Protestants who had remained at their homes between Charlemont and the sea, old men, women, children, many of them near in blood and affection to the defenders of Londonderry. No protection, whatever might be the authority by which it had been given, should be respected. The multitude thus brought together should be driven under the walls of Londonderry, and should there be starved to death in the sight of their countrymen, their friends, their kinsmen. This was no idle threat. Parties were instantly sent out in all directions to collect victims. At dawn, on the morning of the second of July, hundreds of Protestants, who were charged with no crime, who were incapable of bearing arms, and many of whom had protections granted by James, were dragged to the gates of the city. It was imagined that the piteous sight would quell the spirit of the colonists. But the only effect was to rouse that spirit to still greater energy. An order was immediately put forth that no man should utter the word Surrender on pain of death; and no man uttered that word. Several prisoners of high rank were in the town. Hitherto they had been well treated, and had received as good rations as were measured out to the garrison. They were now closely confined. A gallows was erected on one of the bastions; and a message was conveyed to Rosen, requesting him to send a confessor instantly to prepare his friends for death. The prisoners in great dismay wrote to the savage Livonian, but received no answer. They then addressed themselves to their countryman, Richard Hamilton. They were willing, they said, to shed their blood for their King; but they thought it hard to die the ignominious death of thieves in consequence of the barbarity of their own companions in arms. Hamilton, though a man of lax principles, was not cruel. He had been disgusted by the inhumanity of Rosen, but, being only second in command, could not venture to express publicly all that he thought. He however remonstrated strongly. Some Irish officers felt on this occasion as it was natural that brave men should feel, and declared, weeping with pity and indignation, that they should never cease to have in their ears the cries of the poor women and children who had been driven at the point of the pike to die of famine between the camp and the city. Rosen persisted during forty eight hours. In that time many unhappy creatures perished: but Londonderry held out as resolutely as ever; and he saw that his crime was likely to produce nothing but hatred and obloquy. He at length gave way, and suffered the survivors to withdraw. The garrison then took down the gallows which had been erected on the bastion.

When the tidings of these events reached Dublin, James, though by no means prone to compassion, was startled by an atrocity of which the civil wars of England had furnished no example, and was displeased by learning that protections, given by his authority, and guaranteed by his honour, had been publicly declared to be nullities. He complained to the French ambassador, and said, with a warmth which the occasion fully justified, that Rosen was a barbarous Muscovite. Melfort could not refrain from adding that, if Rosen had been an Englishman, he would have been hanged. Avaux was utterly unable to understand this effeminate sensibility. In his opinion, nothing had been done that was at all reprehensible; and he had some difficulty in commanding himself when he heard the King and the secretary blame, in strong language, an act of whole-some severity. In truth the French ambassador and the French general were well paired. There was a great difference doubtless, in appearance and manner, between the handsome, graceful, and refined diplomatist, whose dexterity and suavity had been re-nowned at the most polite courts of Europe, and the military adventurer, whose look and voice reminded all who came near him that he had been born in a half savage country, that he had risen from the ranks, and that he had once been sentenced to death for marauding. But the heart of the diplomatist was really even more callous than that of the soldier.

Rosen was recalled to Dublin; and Richard Hamilton was again left in the chief command. He tried gentler means than those which had brought so much reproach on his predecessor. No trick, no lie, which was thought likely to discourage the starving garrison was spared. One day a great shout was raised by the whole Irish camp. The defenders of Londonderry were soon informed that the army of James was rejoicing on account of the fall of Enniskillen. They were told that they had now no chance of being relieved, and were exhorted to save their lives by capitulating. They consented to negotiate. But what they asked was, that they should be permitted to depart armed and in military array, by land or by water at their choice. They demanded hostages for the exact fulfilment of these conditions, and insisted that the hostages should be sent on board of the fleet which lay in Lough Foyle. Such terms Hamilton durst not grant: the Governors would abate nothing: the treaty was broken off; and the conflict recommenced.

By this time July was far advanced; and the state of the city was, hour by hour, becoming more frightful. The number of the inhabitants had been thinned more by famine and disease than by the fire of the enemy. Yet that fire was sharper and more constant than ever. One of the gates was beaten in: one of the bastions was laid in ruins; but the breaches made by day were repaired by night with indefatigable activity. Every attack was still repelled. But the fighting men of the garrison were so much exhausted that they could scarcely keep their legs. Several of them, in the act of striking at the enemy, fell down from mere weakness. A very small quantity of grain remained, and was doled out by mouthfuls. The stock of salted hides was considerable, and by gnawing them the garrison appeased the rage of hunger. Dogs, fattened on the blood of the slain who lay unburied round the town, were luxuries which few could afford to purchase. The price of a whelp's paw was five shillings and sixpence. Nine horses were still alive, and but barely alive. They were so lean that little meat was likely to be found upon them. It was, however, determined to slaughter them for food. The people perished so fast that it was impossible for the survivors to perform the rites of sepulture. There was scarcely a cellar in which some corpse was not decaying. Such was the extremity of distress, that the rats who came to feast in those hideous dens were eagerly hunted and greedily devoured. A small fish, caught in the river, was not to be purchased with money. The only price for which such a treasure could be obtained was some handfuls of oatmeal. Leprosies, such as strange and unwholesome diet engenders, made existence a constant torment. The whole city was poisoned by the stench exhaled from the bodies of the dead and of the half dead. That there should be fits of discontent and insubordination among men enduring such misery was inevitable. At one moment it was suspected that Walker had laid up somewhere a secret store of food, and was revelling in private, while he exhorted others to suffer resolutely for the good cause. His house was strictly examined: his innocence was fully proved: he regained his popularity; and the garrison, with death in near prospect, thronged to the cathedral to hear him preach, drank in his earnest eloquence with delight, and went forth from the house of God with haggard faces and tottering steps, but with spirit still unsubdued. There were, indeed, some secret plottings. A very few obscure traitors opened communications with the enemy. But it was necessary that all such dealings should be carefully concealed. None dared to utter publicly any words save words of defiance and stubborn resolution. Even in that extremity the general cry was "No surrender." And there were not wanting voices which, in low tones, added, "First the horses and hides; and then the prisoners; and then each other." It was afterwards related, half in jest, yet not without a horrible mixture of earnest, that a corpulent citizen, whose bulk presented a strange contrast to the skeletons which surrounded him, thought it expedient to conceal himself from the numerous eyes which followed him with cannibal looks whenever he appeared in the streets.

It was no slight aggravation of the sufferings of the garrison that all this time the English ships were seen far off in Lough Foyle. Communication between the fleet and the city was almost impossible. One diver who had attempted to pass the boom was drowned. Another was hanged. The language of signals was hardly intelligible. On the thirteenth of July, however, a piece of paper sewed up in a cloth button came to Walker's hands. It was a letter from Kirke, and contained assurances of speedy relief. But more than a fortnight of intense misery had since elapsed; and the hearts of the most sanguine were sick with deferred hope. By no art could the provisions which were left be made to hold out two days more.

Just at this time Kirke received from England a despatch, which contained positive orders that Londonderry should be relieved. He accordingly determined to make an attempt which, as far as appears, he might have made, with at least an equally fair prospect of success, six weeks earlier.

Among the merchant ships which had come to Lough Foyle under his convoy was one called the Mountjoy. The master, Micaiah Browning, a native of Londonderry, had brought from England a large cargo of provisions. He had, it is said, repeatedly remonstrated against the inaction of the armament. He now eagerly volunteered to take the first risk of succouring his fellow citizens; and his offer was accepted. Andrew Douglas, master of the Phœnix, who had on board a great quantity of meal from Scotland, was willing to share the danger and the honour. The two merchantmen were to be escorted by the Dartmouth, a frigate of thirty six guns, commanded by Captain John Leake, afterwards an admiral of great fame.

It was the twenty-eighth of July. The sun had just set: the evening sermon in the cathedral was over; and the heartbroken congregation had separated; when the sentinels on the tower saw the sails of three vessels coming up the Foyle. Soon there was a stir in the Irish camp. The besiegers were on the alert for miles along both shores. The ships were in extreme peril: for the river was low; and the only navigable channel ran very near to the left bank, where the head quarters of the enemy had been fixed, and where the batteries were most numerous. Leake performed his duty with a skill and spirit worthy of his noble profession, exposed his frigate to cover the merchantmen, and used his guns with great effect. At length the little squadron came to the place of peril. Then the Mountjoy took the lead, and went right at the boom. The huge barricade cracked and gave way: but the shock was such that the Mountjoy rebounded, and stuck in the mud. A yell of triumph rose from the banks: the Irish rushed to their boats, and were preparing to board; but the Dartmouth poured on them a well directed broadside, which threw them into disorder. Just then the Phœnix dashed at the breach which the Mountjoy had made, and was in a moment within the fence. Meantime the tide was rising fast. The Mountjoy began to move, and soon passed safe through the broken stakes and floating spars. But her brave master was no more. A shot from one of the batteries had struck him; and he died by the most enviable of all deaths, in sight of the city which was his birthplace, which was his home, and which had just been saved by his courage and selfdevotion from the most frightful form of destruction. The night had closed in before the conflict at the boom began: but the flash of the guns was seen, and the noise heard, by the lean and ghastly multitude which covered the walls of the city. When the Mountjoy grounded, and when the shout of triumph rose from the Irish on both sides of the river, the hearts of the besieged died within them. One who endured the unutterable anguish of that moment has told us that they looked fearfully livid in each other's eyes. Even after the barricade had been passed, there was a terrible half hour of suspense. It was ten o'clock before the ships arrived at the quay. The whole population was there to welcome them. A screen made of casks filled with earth was hastily thrown up to protect the landing place from the batteries on the other side of the river; and then the work of unloading began. First were rolled on shore barrels containing six thousand bushels of meal. Then came great cheeses, casks of beef, flitches of bacon, kegs of butter, sacks of pease and biscuit, ankers of brandy. Not many hours before, half a pound of tallow and three quarters of a pound of salted hide had been weighed out with niggardly care to every fighting man. The ration which each now received was three pounds of flour, two pounds of beef, and a pint of pease. It is easy to imagine with what tears grace was said over the suppers of that evening. There was little sleep on either side of the wall. The bonfires shone bright along the whole circuit of the ramparts. The Irish guns continued to roar all night; and all night the bells of the rescued city made answer to the Irish guns with a peal of joyous defiance. Through the three following days the batteries of the enemy continued to play. But, on the third night, flames were seen arising from the camp; and, when the first of August dawned, a line of smoking ruins marked the site lately occupied by the huts of the besiegers; and the citizens saw far off the long column of pikes and standards retreating up the left bank of the Foyle towards Strabane.

So ended this great siege, the most memorable in the annals of the British Isles. It had lasted a hundred and five days. The garrison had been reduced from about seven thousand effective men to about three thousand. The loss of the besiegers cannot be precisely ascertained. Walker estimated it at eight thousand men. It is certain from the despatches of Avaux that the regiments which returned from the blockade had been so much thinned that many of them were not more than two hundred strong. Of thirty six French gunners who had superintended the cannonading, thirty one had been killed or disabled. The means both of attack and of defence had undoubtedly been such as would have moved the great warriors of the Continent to laughter; and this is the very circumstance which gives so peculiar an interest to the history of the contest. It was a contest, not between engineers, but between nations; and the victory remained with the nation which, though inferior in number, was superior in civilisation, in capacity for self-government, and in stubbornness of resolution.

As soon as it was known that the Irish army had retired, a deputation from the city hastened to Lough Foyle, and invited Kirke to take the command. He came accompanied by a long train of officers, and was received in state by the two Governors, who delivered up to him the authority which, under the pressure of necessity, they had assumed. He remained only a few days; but he had time to show enough of the incurable vices of his character to disgust a population distinguished by austere morals and ardent public spirit. There was, however, no outbreak. The city was in the highest good humour. Such quantities of provisions had been landed from the fleet, that there was in every house a plenty never before known. A few days earlier a man had been glad to obtain for twenty pence a mouthful of carrion scraped from the bones of a starved horse. A pound of good beef was now sold for three half-pence. Meanwhile all hands were busied in removing corpses which had been thinly covered with earth, in filling up the holes which the shells had ploughed in the ground, and in repairing the battered roofs of the houses. The recollection of past dangers and privations, and the consciousness of having deserved well of the English nation and of all Protestant Churches, swelled the hearts of the townspeople with honest pride. That pride grew stronger when they received from William a letter acknowledging, in the most affectionate language, the debt which he owed to the brave and trusty citizens of his good city. The whole population crowded to the Diamond to hear the royal epistle read. At the close all the guns on the ramparts sent forth a voice of joy: all the ships in the river made answer: barrels of ale were broken up; and the health of Their Majesties was drunk with shouts and volleys of musketry.

Five generations have since passed away; and still the wall of Londonderry is to the Protestants of Ulster what the trophy of Marathon was to the Athenians. A lofty pillar, rising from a bastion which bore during many weeks the heaviest fire of the enemy, is seen far up and far down the Foyle. On the summit is the statue of Walker, such as when, in the last and most terrible emergency, his eloquence roused the fainting courage of his brethren. In one hand he grasps a Bible. The other, pointing down the river, seems to direct the eyes of his famished audience to the English topmasts in the distant bay. Such a monument was well deserved: yet it was scarcely needed: for in truth the whole city is to this day a monument of the great deliverance. The wall is carefully preserved; nor would any plea of health or convenience be held by the inhabitants sufficient to justify the demolition of that sacred enclosure which, in the evil time, gave shelter to their race and their religion. The summit of the ramparts forms a pleasant walk. The bastions have been turned into little gardens. Here and there, among the shrubs and flowers, may be seen the old culverins which scattered bricks, cased with lead, among the Irish ranks. One antique gun, the gift of the Fishmongers of London, was distinguished, during the hundred and five memorable days, by the loudness of its report, and still bears the name of Roaring Meg. The cathedral is filled with relics and trophies. In the vestibule is a huge shell, one of many hundreds of shells which were thrown into the city. Over the altar are still seen the French flagstaves, taken by the garrison in a desperate sally. The white ensigns of the House of Bourbon have long been dust: but their place has been supplied by new banners, the work of the fairest hands of Ulster. The anniversary of the day on which the gates were closed, and the anniversary of the day on which the siege was raised, have been down to our own time celebrated by salutes, processions, banquets, and sermons: Lundy has been executed in effigy; and the sword, said by tradition to be that of Maumont, has, on great occasions, been carried in triumph. There is still a Walker Club and a Murray Club. The humble tombs of the Protestant captains have been carefully sought out, repaired, and embellished. It is impossible not to respect the sentiment which indicates itself by these tokens. It is a sentiment which belongs to the higher and purer part of human nature, and which adds not a little to the strength of states. A people which takes no pride in the noble achievements of remote ancestors will never achieve any thing worthy to be remembered with pride by remote descendants. Yet it is impossible for the moralist or the statesman to look with unmixed complacency on the solemnities with which Londonderry commemorates her deliverance, and on the honours which she pays to those who saved her. Unhappily the animosities of her brave champions have descended with their glory. The faults which are ordinarily found in dominant castes and dominant sects have not seldom shown themselves without disguise at her festivities; and even with the expressions of pious gratitude which have resounded from her pulpits have too often been mingled words of wrath and defiance.

BOYNE

WHEN William caught sight of the valley of the Boyne, he could not suppress an exclamation and a gesture of delight. He had been apprehensive that the enemy would avoid a decisive action, and would protract the war till the autumnal rains should return with pestilence in their train. He was now at ease. It was plain that the contest would be sharp and short. The pavilion of James was pitched on the eminence of Donore. The flags of the House of Stuart and of the House of Bourbon waved together in defiance on the walls of Drogheda. All the southern bank of the river was lined by the camp and batteries of the hostile army. Thousands of armed men were moving about among the tents; and every one, horse soldier or foot soldier, French or Irish, had a white badge in his hat. That colour had been chosen in compliment to the House of Bourbon. "I am glad to see you, gentlemen," said the King, as his keen eye surveyed the Irish lines. "If you escape me now, the fault will be mine."

Each of the contending princes had some advantages over his rival. James, standing on the defensive, behind entrenchments, with a river before him, had the stronger position: but his troops were inferior both in number and in quality to those which were opposed to him. He probably had thirty thousand men. About a third part of this force consisted of excellent French infantry and excellent Irish cavalry. But the rest of his army was the scoff of all Europe. The Irish dragoons were bad; the Irish foot worse. It was said that their ordinary way of fighting was to discharge their pieces once, and then to run away bawling "Quarter," and "Murder." Their inefficiency was, in that age, commonly imputed, both by their enemies and by their allies, to natural poltroonery. How little ground there was for such an imputation has since been signally proved by many brave achievements in every part of the globe. It ought indeed, even in the seventeenth century, to have occurred to reasonable men, that a race which furnished some of the best horse soldiers in the world, would certainly, with judicious training, furnish good foot soldiers. But the Irish foot soldiers had not merely not been well trained: they had been elaborately ill trained. The greatest of our generals repeatedly and emphatically declared that even the admirable army which fought its way, under his command, from Torres Vedras to Toulouse, would, if he had suffered it to contract habits of pillage, have become, in a few weeks, unfit for all military purposes. What then was likely to be the character of troops who, from the day on which they enlisted, were not merely permitted, but invited, to supply the deficiencies of pay by marauding? They were, as might have been expected, a mere mob, furious indeed and clamorous in their zeal for the cause which they had espoused, but incapable of opposing a stedfast resistance to a well ordered force. In truth, all that the discipline, if it is to be so called, of James's army had done for the Celtic kerne had been to debase and enervate him. After eighteen months of nominal soldiership, he was positively farther from being a soldier than on the day on which he quitted his hovel for the camp.

William had under his command near thirty six thousand men, born in many lands, and speaking many tongues. Scarcely one Protestant Church, scarcely one Protestant nation, was unrepresented in the army which a strange series of events had brought to fight for the Protestant religion in the remotest island of the west. About half the troops were natives of England. Ormond was there with the Life Guards, and Oxford with the Blues. Sir John Lanier, an officer who had acquired military experience on the Continent, and whose prudence was held in high esteem, was at the head of the Queen's regiment of horse, now the First Dragoon Guards. There were Beaumont's foot, who had, in defiance of the mandate of James, refused to admit Irish papists among them, and Hastings's foot, who had, on the disastrous day of Killiecrankie, maintained the military reputation of the Saxon race. There were the two Tangier battalions, hitherto known only by deeds of violence and rapine, but destined to begin on the following morning a long career of glory. Two fine English regiments, which had been in the service of the States General, and had often looked death in the face under William's leading, followed him in this campaign, not only as their general, but as their native King. They now rank as the fifth and sixth of the line. The former was led by an officer who had no skill in the higher parts of military science, but whom the whole army allowed to be the bravest of all the brave, John Cutts. The Scotch footguards marched under the command of their countryman James Douglas. Conspicuous among the Dutch troops were Portland's and Ginkell's Horse, and Solmes's Blue regiment, consisting of two thousand of the finest infantry in Europe. Germany had sent to the field some warriors, sprung from her noblest houses. Prince George of Hesse Darmstadt, a gallant youth, who was serving his apprenticeship in the military art, rode near the King. A strong brigade of Danish mercenaries was commanded by Duke Charles Frederic of Wurtemberg. It was reported that of all the soldiers of William these were most dreaded by the Irish. For centuries of Saxon domination had not effaced the recollection of the violence and cruelty of the Scandinavian sea kings; and an ancient prophecy that the Danes would one day destroy the children of the soil was still repeated with superstitious horror. Among the foreign auxiliaries were a Brandenburg regiment and a Finland regiment. But in that great array, so variously composed, were two bodies of men animated by a spirit peculiarly fierce and implacable, the Huguenots of France thirsting for the blood of the French, and the Englishry of Ireland impatient to trample down the Irish. The ranks of the refugees had been effectually purged of spies and traitors, and were made up of men such as had contended in the preceding century against the power of the House of Valois and the genius of the House of Lorraine. All the boldest spirits of the unconquerable colony had repaired to William's camp. Mitchelburne was there with the stubborn defenders of Londonderry, and Wolseley with the warriors who had raised the unanimous shout of "Advance" on the day of Newton Butler. Sir Albert Conyngham, the ancester of the noble family whose seat now overlooks the field of battle, had brought from the neighbourhood of Lough Erne a gallant regiment of dragoons which still glories in the name of Enniskillen, and which has proved on the shores of the Euxine that it has not degenerated since the day of the Boyne.

Walker, notwithstanding his advanced age and his peaceful profession, accompanied the men of Londonderry, and tried to animate their zeal by exhortation and by example. He was now a great prelate. Ezekiel Hopkins had taken refuge from Popish persecutors and Presbyterian rebels in the city of London, had brought himself to swear allegiance to the government, had obtained a cure, and had died in the performance of the humble duties of a parish priest. William, on his march through Louth, learned that the rich see of Derry was at his disposal. He instantly made choice of Walker to be the new Bishop. The brave old man, during the few hours of life which remained to him, was overwhelmed with salutations and congratulations. Unhappily he had, during the siege in which he had so highly distinguished himself, contracted a passion for war; and he easily persuaded himself that, in indulging this passion, he was discharging a duty to his country and his religion. He ought to have remembered that the peculiar circumstances which had justified him in becoming a combatant had ceased to exist, and that, in a disciplined army led by generals of long experience and great fame, a fighting divine was likely to give less help than scandal. The Bishop elect was determined to be wherever danger was; and the way in which he exposed himself excited the extreme disgust of his royal patron, who hated a meddler almost as much as a coward. A soldier who ran away from a battle and a gownsman who pushed himself into a battle were the two objects which most strongly excited William's spleen.

It was still early in the day. The King rode slowly along the northern bank of the river, and closely examined the position of the Irish, from whom he was sometimes separated by an interval of little more than two hundred feet. He was accompanied by Schomberg, Ormond, Sidney, Solmes, Prince George of Hesse, Coningsby, and others. "Their army is but small," said one of the Dutch officers. Indeed it did not appear to consist of more than sixteen thousand men. But it was well known, from the reports brought by deserters, that many regiments were concealed from view by the undulations of the ground. "They may be stronger than they look," said William; "but, weak or strong, I will soon know all about them."

At length he alighted at a spot nearly opposite to Oldbridge, sate down on the turf to rest himself, and called for breakfast. The sumpter horses were unloaded: the canteens were opened; and a tablecloth was spread on the grass. The place is marked by an obelisk, built while many veterans who could well remember the events of that day were still living.

While William was at his repast, a group of horsemen appeared close to the water on the opposite shore. Among them his attendants could discern some who had once been conspicuous at reviews in Hyde Park and at balls in the gallery of Whitehall, the youthful Berwick, the small, fairhaired Lauzun, Tyrconnel, once admired by maids of honour as the model of manly vigour and beauty, but now bent down by years and crippled by gout, and, overtopping all, the stately head of Sarsfield.

The chiefs of the Irish army soon discovered that the person who, surrounded by a splendid circle, was breakfasting on the opposite bank, was the Prince of Orange. They sent for artillery. Two field pieces, screened from view by a troop of cavalry, were brought down almost to the brink of the river, and placed behind a hedge. William, who had just risen from his meal, and was again in the saddle, was the mark of both guns. The first shot struck one of the holsters of Prince George of Hesse, and brought his horse to the ground. "Ah!" cried the King; "the poor Prince is killed." As the words passed his lips, he was himself hit by a second ball, a sixpounder. It merely tore his coat, grazed his shoulder, and drew two or three ounces of blood. Both armies saw that the shot had taken effect; for the King sank down for a moment on his horse's neck. A yell of exultation rose from the Irish camp. The English and their allies were in dismay. Solmes flung himself prostrate on the earth, and burst into tears. But William's deportment soon reassured his friends. "There is no harm done," he said: "but the bullet came quite near enough." Coningsby put his handkerchief to the wound: a surgeon was sent for: a plaster was applied; and the King, as soon as the dressing was finished, rode round all the posts of his army amidst loud acclamations. Such was the energy of his spirit that, in spite of his feeble health, in spite of his recent hurt, he was that day nineteen hours on horseback.

A cannonade was kept up on both sides till the evening. William observed with especial attention the effect produced by the Irish shots on the English regiments which had never been in action, and declared himself satisfied with the result. "All is right," he said: "they stand fire well." Long after sunset he made a final inspection of his forces by torchlight, and gave orders that every thing should be ready for forcing a passage across the river on the morrow. Every soldier was to put a green bough in his hat. The baggage and great coats were to be left under a guard. The word was Westminster.

The King's resolution to attack the Irish was not approved by all his lieutenants. Schomberg, in particular, pronounced the experiment too hazardous, and, when his opinion was overruled, retired to his tent in no very good humour. When the order of battle was delivered to him, he muttered that he had been more used to give such orders than to receive them. For this little fit of sullenness, very pardonable in a general who had won great victories when his master was still a child, the brave veteran made, on the following morning, a noble atonement.

The first of July [1690] dawned, a day which has never since returned without exciting strong emotions of very different kinds in the two populations which divide Ireland. The sun rose bright and cloudless. Soon after four both armies were in motion. William ordered his right wing, under the command of Meinhart Schomberg, one of the Duke's sons, to march to the bridge of Slane, some miles up the river, to cross there, and to turn the left flank of the Irish army. Meinhart Schomberg was assisted by Portland and Douglas. James, anticipating some such design, had already sent to the bridge a regiment of dragoons, commanded by Sir Neil O'Neil. O'Neil behaved himself like a brave gentleman: but he soon received a mortal wound: his men fled; and the English right wing passed the river.

This move made Lauzun uneasy. What if the English right wing should get into the rear of the army of James? About four miles south of the Boyne was a place called Duleek, where the road to Dublin was so narrow, that two cars could not pass each other, and where on both sides of the road lay a morass which afforded no firm footing. If Meinhart Schomberg should occupy this spot, it would be impossible for the Irish to retreat. They must either conquer, or be cut off to a man. Disturbed by this apprehension, the French general marched with his countrymen and with Sarsfield's horse in the direction of Slane Bridge. Thus the fords near Oldbridge were left to be defended by the Irish alone.

It was now near ten o'clock. William put himself at the head of his left wing, which was composed exclusively of cavalry, and prepared to pass the river not far above Drogheda. The centre of his army, which consisted almost exclusively of foot, was entrusted to the command of Schomberg, and was marshalled opposite to Oldbridge. At Oldbridge had been collected the whole Irish army, foot, dragoons, and horse, Sarsfield's regiment alone excepted. The Meath bank bristled with pikes and bayonets. A fortification had been made by French engineers out of the hedges and buildings; and a breast work had been thrown up close to the water side. Tyrconnel was there; and under him were Richard Hamilton and Antrim.

Schomberg gave the word. Solmes's Blues were the first to move. They marched gallantly, with drums beating, to the brink of the Boyne. Then the drums stopped; and the men, ten abreast, descended into the water. Next plunged Londonderry and Enniskillen. A little to the left of Londonderry and Enniskillen, Caillemot crossed, at the head of a long column of French refugees. A little to the left of Caillemot and his refugees, the main body of the English infantry struggled through the river, up to their armpits in water. Still further down the stream the Danes found another ford. In a few minutes the Boyne, for a quarter of a mile, was alive with muskets and green boughs.

It was not till the assailants had reached the middle of the channel that they became aware of the whole difficulty and danger of the service in which they were engaged. They had as yet seen little more than half the hostile army. Now whole regiments of foot and horse seemed to start out of the earth. A wild shout of defiance rose from the whole shore: during one moment the event seemed doubtful: but the Protestants pressed resolutely forward; and in another moment the whole Irish line gave way. Tyrconnel looked on in helpless despair. He did not want personal courage: but his military skill was so small that he hardly ever reviewed his regiment in the Phœnix Park without committing some blunder; and to rally the ranks which were breaking all round him was no task for a general who had survived the energy of his body and of his mind, and yet had still the rudiments of his profession to learn. Several of his best officers fell while vainly endeavouring to prevail on their soldiers to look the Dutch Blues in the face. Richard Hamilton ordered a body of foot to fall on the French refugees, who were still deep in water. He led the way, and, accompanied by some courageous gentlemen, advanced, sword in hand, into the river. But neither his commands nor his example could infuse valour into that mob of cowstealers. He was left almost alone, and retired from the bank in despair. Further down the river, Antrim's division ran like sheep at the approach of the English column. Whole regiments flung away arms, colours and cloaks, and scampered off to the hills without striking a blow or firing a shot.

It required many years and many heroic exploits to take away the reproach which that ignominious rout left on the Irish name. Yet, even before the day closed, it was abundantly proved that the reproach was unjust. Richard Hamilton put himself at the head of the cavalry, and, under his command, they made a gallant, though an unsuccessful attempt to retrieve the day. They maintained a desperate fight in the bed of the river with Solmes's Blues. They drove the Danish brigade back into the stream. They fell impetuously on the Huguenot regiments, which, not being provided with pikes, then ordinarily used by foot to repel horse, began to give ground. Caillemot, while encouraging his fellow exiles, received a mortal wound in the thigh. Four of his men carried him back across the ford to his tent. As he passed, he continued to urge forward the rear ranks which were still up to the breast in the water. "On; on; my lads! to glory! to glory!" Schomberg, who had remained on the northern bank, and who had thence watched the progress of his troops with the eye of a general, now thought that the emergency required from him the personal exertion of a soldier. Those who stood about him besought him in vain to put on his cuirass. Without defensive armour he rode through the river, and rallied the refugees whom the fall of Caillemot had dismayed. "Come on," he cried in French, pointing to the Popish squadrons; "come on, gentlemen: there are your persecutors." Those were his last words. As he spoke, a band of Irish horsemen rushed upon him and encircled him for a moment. When they retired, he was on the ground. His friends raised him; but he was already a corpse. Two sabre wounds were on his head; and a bullet from a carbine was lodged in his neck. Almost at the same moment Walker, while exhorting the colonists of Ulster to play the men, was shot dead. During near half an hour the battle continued to rage along the southern shore of the river. All was smoke, dust and din. Old soldiers were heard to say that they had seldom seen sharper work in the Low Countries. But, just at this conjuncture, William came up with the left wing. He had found much difficulty in crossing. The tide was running fast. His charger had been forced to swim, and had been almost lost in the mud. As soon as the King was on firm ground he took his sword in his left hand,—for his right arm was stiff with his wound and his bandage,—and led his men to the place where the fight was the hottest. His arrival decided the fate of the day. Yet the Irish horse retired fighting obstinately. It was long remembered among the Protestants of Ulster that, in the midst of the tumult, William rode to the head of the Enniskilleners. "What will you do for me?" he cried. He was not immediately recognised; and one trooper, taking him for an enemy, was about to fire. William gently put aside the carbine. "What," said he, "do you not know your friends?" "It is His Majesty," said the Colonel. The ranks of sturdy Protestant yeomen set up a shout of joy. "Gentlemen," said William, "you shall be my guards to day. I have heard much of you. Let me see something of you." One of the most remarkable peculiarities of this man, ordinarily so saturnine and reserved, was that danger acted on him like wine, opened his heart, loosened his tongue, and took away all appearance of constraint from his manner. On this memorable day he was seen wherever the peril was greatest. One ball struck the cap of his pistol: another carried off the heel of his jackboot: but his lieutenants in vain implored him to retire to some station from which he could give his orders without exposing a life so valuable to Europe. His troops, animated by his example, gained ground fast. The Irish cavalry made their last stand at a house called Plottin Castle, about a mile and a half south of Old-bridge. There the Enniskilleners were repelled with the loss of fifty men, and were hotly pursued, till William rallied them and turned the chase back. In this encounter Richard Hamilton, who had done all that could be done by valour to retrieve a reputation forfeited by perfidy,[1] was severely wounded, taken prisoner, and instantly brought, through the smoke and over the carnage, before the prince whom he had foully wronged. On no occasion did the character of William show itself in a more striking manner. "Is this business over?" he said; "or will your horse make more fight?" "On my honour, Sir," answered Hamilton, "I believe that they will." "Your honour!" muttered William; "your honour!" That half suppressed exclamation was the only revenge which he condescended to take for an injury for which many sovereigns, far more affable and gracious in their ordinary deportment, would have exacted a terrible retribution. Then, restraining himself, he ordered his own surgeon to look to the hurts of the captive.

And now the battle was over. Hamilton was mistaken in thinking that his horse would continue to fight. Whole troops had been cut to pieces. One fine regiment had only thirty unwounded men left. It was enough that these gallant soldiers had disputed the field till they were left without support, or hope, or guidance, till their bravest leader was a captive, and till their King had fled.

GLENCOE

MAC IAN dwelt in the mouth of a ravine situated not far from the southern shore of Lochleven, an arm of the sea which deeply indents the western coast of Scotland, and separates Argyleshire from Invernesshire. Near his house were two or three small hamlets inhabited by his tribe. The whole population which he governed

---

[1] [Richard Hamilton had been sent over to Ireland on parole by William. But he had broken his word and become one of James's generals.]

was not supposed to exceed two hundred souls. In the neighbour-hood of the little cluster of villages was some copsewood and some pasture land: but a little further up the defile no sign of population or of fruitfulness was to be seen. In the Gaelic tongue Glencoe signifies the Glen of Weeping: and in truth that pass is the most dreary and melancholy of all the Scottish passes, the very Valley of the Shadow of Death. Mists and storms brood over it through the greater part of the finest summer; and even on those rare days when the sun is bright, and when there is no cloud in the sky, the impres-sion made by the landscape is sad and awful. The path lies along a stream which issues from the most sullen and gloomy of mountain pools. Huge precipices of naked stone frown on both sides. Even in July the streaks of snow may often be discerned in the rifts near the summits. All down the sides of the crags heaps of ruin mark the headlong paths of the torrents. Mile after mile the traveller looks in vain for the smoke of one hut, for one human form wrapped in a plaid, and listens in vain for the bark of a shepherd's dog, or the bleat of a lamb. Mile after mile the only sound that indicates life is the faint cry of a bird of prey from some stormbeaten pinnacle of rock. The progress of civilisation, which has turned so many wastes into fields yellow with harvests or gay with apple blossoms, has only made Glencoe more desolate. All the science and industry of a peaceful age can extract nothing valuable from that wilderness: but, in an age of violence and rapine, the wilderness itself was valued on account of the shelter which it afforded to the plunderer and his plunder. Nothing could be more natural than that the clan to which this rugged desert belonged should have been noted for predatory habits. For, among the Highlanders generally, to rob was thought at least as honourable an employment as to cultivate the soil; and, of all the Highlanders, the Macdonalds of Glencoe had the least productive soil, and the most convenient and secure den of robbers. Successive governments had tried to punish this wild race: but no large force had ever been employed for that purpose; and a small force was easily resisted or eluded by men familiar with every recess and every outlet of the natural fortress in which they had been born and bred. The people of Glencoe would probably have been less troublesome neighbours if they had lived among their own kindred. But they were an outpost of the Clan Donald, separated from every other branch of their own family, and almost surrounded by the domains of the hostile race of Diarmid. They were impelled by hereditary enmity, as well as by want, to live at the expense of the tribe of Campbell. Breadalbane's property had suffered greatly from their depredations; and he was not of a temper to forgive such injuries. When, therefore, the Chief of Glencoe made his appearance at the congress in Glenorchy, he was ungraciously received. The Earl, who ordinarily bore himself with the solemn dignity of a Castilian grandee, forgot, in his resentment, his wonted gravity, forgot his public character, forgot the laws of hospitality, and, with angry reproaches and menaces, demanded reparation for the herds which had been driven from his lands by Mac Ian's followers. Mac Ian was seriously apprehensive of some personal outrage, and was glad to get safe back to his own glen. His pride had been wounded; and the promptings of interest concurred with those of pride. As the head of a people who lived by pillage, he had strong reasons for wishing that the country might continue to be in a perturbed state. He had little chance of receiving one guinea of the money which was to be distributed among the malecontents. For his share of that money would scarcely meet Breadalbane's demands for compensation; and there could be little doubt that, whoever might be unpaid, Breadalbane would take care to pay himself. Mac Ian therefore did his best to dissuade his allies from accepting terms from which he could himself expect no benefit; and his influence was not small. His own vassals, indeed, were few in number: but he came of the best blood of the Highlands: he had kept up a close connection with his more powerful kinsmen; nor did they like him the less because he was a robber; for he never robbed them; and that robbery, merely as robbery, was a wicked and disgraceful act, had never entered into the mind of any Celtic chief. Mac Ian was therefore held in high esteem by the confederates. His age was venerable: his aspect was majestic; and he possessed in large measure those intellectual qualities which, in rude societies, give men an ascendency over their fellows. Breadalbane found himself, at every step of the negotiation, thwarted by the arts of his old enemy, and abhorred the name of Glencoe more and more every day.

But the government did not trust solely to Breadalbane's diplomatic skill. The authorities at Edinburgh put forth a proclamation exhorting the clans to submit to King William and Queen Mary, and offering pardon to every rebel who, on or before the thirty-first of December 1691, should swear to live peaceably under the government of their Majesties. It was announced that those who should hold out after that day would be treated as enemies and traitors. Warlike preparations were made, which showed that the threat was meant in earnest. The Highlanders were alarmed, and, though the pecuniary terms had not been satisfactorily settled, thought it prudent to give the pledge which was demanded of them.

No chief, indeed, was willing to set the example of submission. Glengarry blustered, and pretended to fortify his house. "I will not," said Lochiel, "break the ice. That is a point of honour with me. But my tacksmen and people may use their freedom." His tacksmen and people understood him, and repaired by hundreds to the Sheriff to take the oaths. The Macdonalds of Sleat, Clanronald, Keppoch, and even Glengarry, imitated the Camerons; and the chiefs, after trying to outstay each other as long as they durst, imitated their vassals.

The thirty-first of December arrived; and still the Macdonalds of Glencoe had not come in. The punctilious pride of Mac Ian was doubtless gratified by the thought that he had continued to defy the government after the boastful Glengarry, the ferocious Keppoch, the magnanimous Lochiel had yielded: but he bought his gratification dear.

At length, on the thirty-first of December, he repaired to Fort William, accompanied by his principal vassals, and offered to take the oaths. To his dismay he found that there was in the fort no person competent to administer them. Colonel Hill, the Governor, was not a magistrate; nor was there any magistrate nearer than Inverary. Mac Ian, now fully sensible of the folly of which he had been guilty in postponing to the very last moment an act on which his life and his estate depended, set off for Inverary in great distress. He carried with him a letter from Hill to the Sheriff of Argyleshire, Sir Colin Campbell of Ardkinglass, a respectable gentleman, who, in the late reign, had suffered severely for his Whig principles. In this letter the Colonel expressed a goodnatured hope that, even out of season, a lost sheep, and so fine a lost sheep, would be gladly received. Mac Ian made all the haste in his power, and did not stop even at his own house, though it lay nigh to the road. But at that time a journey through Argyleshire in the depth of winter was necessarily slow. The old man's progress up steep mountains and along boggy valleys was obstructed by snow storms; and it was not till the sixth of January that he presented himself before the Sheriff at Inverary. The Sheriff hesitated. His power, he said, was limited by the terms of the proclamation; and he did not see how he could swear a rebel who had not submitted within the prescribed time. Mac Ian begged earnestly and with tears that he might be sworn. His people, he said, would follow his example. If any of them proved refractory, he would himself send the recusant to prison, or ship him off for Flanders. His entreaties and Hill's letter overcame Sir Colin's scruples. The oath was administered; and a certificate was transmitted to the Council at Edinburgh, setting forth the special circumstances which had induced the Sheriff to do what he knew not to be strictly regular.

The news that Mac Ian had not submitted within the prescribed time was received with cruel joy by three powerful Scotchmen who were then at the English Court. Breadalbane had gone up to London at Christmas in order to give an account of his stewardship. There he met his kinsman Argyle. Argyle was, in personal qualities, one of the most insignificant of the long line of nobles who have borne that great name. He was the descendant of eminent men, and the parent of eminent men. He was the grandson of one of the ablest of Scottish politicians; the son of one of the bravest and most truehearted of Scottish patriots; the father of one Mac Callum More renowned as a warrior and as an orator, as the model of every courtly grace, and as the judicious patron of arts and letters, and of another Mac Callum More distinguished by talents for business and command, and by skill in the exact sciences. Both of such an ancestry and of such a progeny Argyle was unworthy. He had even been guilty of the crime, common enough among Scottish politicians, but in him singularly disgraceful, of tampering with the agents of James while professing loyalty to William. Still Argyle had the importance inseparable from high rank, vast domains, extensive feudal rights, and almost boundless patriarchal authority. To him, as to his cousin Breadalbane, the intelligence that the tribe of Glencoe was out of the protection of the law was most gratifying; and the Master of Stair more than sympathised with them both.

The feeling of Argyle and Breadalbane is perfectly intelligible. They were the heads of a great clan; and they had an opportunity of destroying a neighbouring clan with which they were at deadly feud. Breadalbane had received peculiar provocation. His estate had been repeatedly devastated; and he had just been thwarted in a negotiation of high moment. Unhappily there was scarcely any excess of ferocity for which a precedent could not be found in Celtic tradition. Among all warlike barbarians revenge is esteemed the most sacred of duties and the most exquisite of pleasures; and so it had long been esteemed among the Highlanders. The history of the clans abounds with frightful tales, some perhaps fabulous or exaggerated, some certainly true, of vindictive massacres and assassinations. The Macdonalds of Glengarry, for example, having been affronted by the people of a parish near Inverness, surrounded the parish church on a Sunday, shut the doors, and burned the whole congregation alive. While the flames were raging, the hereditary musician of the murderers mocked the shrieks of the perishing crowd with the notes of his bagpipe. A band of Macgregors, having cut off the head of an enemy, laid it, the mouth filled with bread and cheese, on his sister's table, and had the satisfaction of seeing her go mad with horror at the sight. They then carried the ghastly trophy in triumph to their chief. The whole clan met under the roof of an ancient church. Every one in turn laid his hand on the dead man's scalp, and vowed to defend the slayers. The inhabitants of Eigg seized some Macleods, bound them hand and foot, and turned them adrift in a boat to be swallowed up by the waves, or to perish of hunger. The Macleods retaliated by driving the population of Eigg into a cavern, lighting a fire at the entrance, and suffocating the whole race, men, women and children. It is much less strange that the two great Earls of the house of Campbell, animated by the passions of Highland chieftains, should have planned a Highland revenge, than that they should have found an accomplice, and something more than an accomplice, in the Master of Stair.

The Master of Stair was one of the first men of his time, a jurist, a statesman, a fine scholar, an eloquent orator. His polished manners and lively conversation were the delight of aristocratical societies; and none who met him in such societies would have thought it possible that he could bear the chief part in any atrocious crime. His political principles were lax, yet not more lax than those of most Scotch politicians of that age. Cruelty had never been imputed to him. Those who most disliked him did him the justice to own that, where his schemes of policy were not concerned, he was a very goodnatured man. There is not the slightest reason to believe that he gained a single pound Scots by the act which has covered his name with infamy. He had no personal reason to wish the Glencoe men any ill. There had been no feud between them and his family. His property lay in a district where their tartan was never seen. Yet he hated them with a hatred as fierce and implacable as if they had laid waste his fields, burned his mansion, murdered his child in the cradle.

To what cause are we to ascribe so strange an antipathy? This question perplexed the Master's contemporaries; and any answer which may now be offered ought to be offered with diffidence. The most probable conjecture is that he was actuated by an inordinate, an unscrupulous, a remorseless zeal for what seemed to him to be the interest of the state. This explanation may startle those who have not considered how large a proportion of the blackest crimes recorded in history is to be ascribed to ill regulated public spirit. We daily see men do for their party, for their sect, for their country, for their favourite schemes of political and social reform, what they would not do to enrich or to avenge themselves. At a temptation directly addressed to our private cupidity or to our private animosity, whatever virtue we have takes the alarm. But virtue itself may contribute to the fall of him who imagines that it is in his power, by violating some general rule of morality, to confer an important benefit on a church, on a commonwealth, on mankind. He silences the remonstrances of conscience, and hardens his heart against the most touching spectacles of misery, by repeating to himself that his intentions are pure, that his objects are noble, that he is doing a little evil for the sake of a great good. By degrees he comes altogether to forget the turpitude of the means in the excellence of the end, and at length perpetrates without one internal twinge acts which would shock a buccaneer. There is no reason to believe that Dominic would, for the best archbishopric in Christendom, have incited ferocious marauders to plunder and slaughter a peaceful and industrious population, that Everard Digby would, for a dukedom, have blown a large assembly of people into the air, or that Robespierre would have murdered for hire one of the thousands whom he murdered from philanthropy.

The Master of Stair seems to have proposed to himself a truly great and good end, the pacification and civilisation of the Highlands. He was, by the acknowledgment of those who most hated him, a man of large views. He justly thought it monstrous that a third part of Scotland should be in a state scarcely less savage than New Guinea, that letters of fire and sword should, through a third part of Scotland, be, century after century, a species of legal process, and that no attempt should be made to apply a radical remedy to such evils. The independence affected by a crowd of petty sovereigns, the contumacious resistance which they were in the habit of offering to the authority of the Crown and of the Court of Session, their wars, their robberies, their fireraisings, their practice of exacting black mail from people more peaceable and more useful than themselves, naturally excited the disgust and indignation of an enlightened and politic gownsman, who was, both by the constitution of his mind and by the habits of his profession, a lover of law and order. His object was no less than a complete dissolution and reconstruction of society in the Highlands, such a dissolution and reconstruction as, two generations later, followed the battle of Culloden. In his view the clans, as they existed, were the plagues of the kingdom; and of all the clans the worst was that which inhabited Glencoe. He had, it is said, been particularly struck by a frightful instance of the lawlessness and ferocity of those marauders. One of them, who had been concerned in some act of violence or rapine, had given information against his companions. He had been bound to a tree and murdered. The old chief had given the first stab; and scores of dirks had then been plunged into the wretch's body. By the mountaineers such an act was probably regarded as a legitimate exercise of patriarchal jurisdiction. To the Master of Stair it seemed that people among whom such things were done and were approved ought to be treated like a pack of wolves, snared by any device, and slaughtered without mercy. He was well read in history, and doubtless knew how great rulers had, in his own and other countries, dealt with such banditti. He doubtless knew with what energy and what severity James the Fifth had put down the mosstroopers of the border, how the chief of Henderland had been hung over the gate of the castle in which he had prepared a banquet for the King; how John Armstrong and his thirty six horsemen, when they came forth to welcome their sovereign, had scarcely been allowed time to say a single prayer before they were all tied up and turned off. Nor probably was the Secretary ignorant of the means by which Sixtus the Fifth had cleared the ecclesiastical state of outlaws. The eulogists of that great pontiff tell us that there was one formidable gang which could not be dislodged from a stronghold among the Apennines. Beasts of burden were therefore loaded with poisoned food and wine, and sent by a road which ran close to the fastness. The robbers sallied forth, seized the prey, feasted and died; and the pious old Pope exulted greatly when he heard that the corpses of thirty ruffians, who had been the terror of many peaceful villages, had been found lying among the mules and packages. The plans of the Master of Stair were conceived in the spirit of James and of Sixtus; and the rebellion of the mountaineers furnished what seemed to be an excellent opportunity for carrying those plans into effect. Mere rebellion, indeed, he could have easily pardoned. On Jacobites, as Jacobites, he never showed any inclination to bear hard. He hated the Highlanders, not as enemies of this or that dynasty, but as enemies of law, of industry, and of trade. In his private correspondence he applied to them the short and terrible form of words in which the implacable Roman pronounced the doom of Carthage. His project was no less than this, that the whole hill country from sea to sea, and the neighbouring islands, should be wasted with fire and sword, that the Camerons, the Macleans, and all the branches of the race of Macdonald, should be rooted out. He therefore looked with no friendly eye on schemes of reconciliation, and, while others were hoping that a little money would set everything right, hinted very intelligibly his opinion that whatever money was to be laid out on the clans would be best laid out in the form of bullets and bayonets. To the last moment he continued to flatter himself that the rebels would be obstinate, and would thus furnish him with a plea for accomplishing that great social revolution on which his heart was set. The letter is still extant in which he directed the commander of the forces in Scotland how to act if the Jacobite chiefs should not come in before the end of December. There is something strangely terrible in the calmness and conciseness with which the instructions are given. "Your troops will destroy entirely the country of Lochaber, Lochiel's lands, Keppoch's, Glengarry's and Glencoe's. Your power shall be large enough. I hope the soldiers will not trouble the government with prisoners."

This despatch had scarcely been sent off when news arrived in London that the rebel chiefs, after holding out long, had at last appeared before the Sheriffs and taken the oaths. Lochiel, the most eminent man among them, had not only declared that he would live and die a true subject to King William, but had announced his intention of visiting England, in the hope of being permitted to kiss His Majesty's hand. In London it was announced exultingly that all the clans had submitted; and the announcement was generally thought most satisfactory. But the Master of Stair was bitterly disappointed. The Highlands were then to continue to be what they had been, the shame and curse of Scotland. A golden opportunity of subjecting them to the law had been suffered to escape, and might never return. If only the Macdonalds would have stood out, nay, if an example could but have been made of the two worst Macdonalds, Keppoch and Glencoe, it would have been something. But it seemed that even Keppoch and Glencoe, marauders who in any well governed country would have been hanged thirty years before, were safe. While the Master was brooding over thoughts like these, Argyle brought him some comfort. The report that Mac Ian had taken the oaths within the prescribed time was erroneous. The Secretary was consoled. One clan, then, was at the mercy of the government, and that clan the most lawless of all. One great act of justice, nay of charity, might be performed. One terrible and memorable example might be made.

Yet there was a difficulty. Mac Ian had taken the oaths. He had taken them, indeed, too late to be entitled to plead the letter of the royal promise: but the fact that he had taken them was one which evidently ought to have been brought under consideration before his fate was decided. By a dark intrigue, of which the history is but imperfectly known, but which was, in all probability, directed by the Master of Stair, the evidence of Mac Ian's tardy submission was suppressed. The certificate which the Sheriff of Argyleshire had transmitted to the Council at Edinburgh, was never laid before the Board, but was privately submitted to some persons high in office, and particularly to Lord President Stair, the father of the Secretary. These persons pronounced the certificate irregular, and, indeed, absolutely null; and it was cancelled.

Meanwhile the Master of Stair was forming, in concert with Breadalbane and Argyle, a plan for the destruction of the people of Glencoe. It was necessary to take the King's pleasure, not, indeed, as to the details of what was to be done, but as to the question whether Mac Ian and his people should or should not be treated as rebels out of the pale of the ordinary law. The Master of Stair found no difficulty in the royal closet. William had, in all probability, never heard the Glencoe men mentioned except as banditti. He knew that they had not come in by the prescribed day. That they had come in after that day he did not know. If he paid any attention to the matter, he must have thought that so fair an opportunity of putting an end to the devastations and depredations from which a quiet and industrious population had suffered so much ought not to be lost.

An order was laid before him for signature. He signed it, but, if Burnet may be trusted, did not read it. Whoever has seen anything of public business knows that princes and ministers daily sign, and indeed must sign, documents which they have not read; and of all documents a document relating to a small tribe of mountaineers, living in a wilderness not set down in any map, was least likely to interest a Sovereign whose mind was full of schemes on which the fate of Europe might depend. But, even on the supposition that he read the order to which he affixed his name, there seems to be no reason for blaming him. That order, directed to the Commander of the Forces in Scotland, runs thus: "As for Mac Ian of Glencoe and that tribe, if they can be well distinguished from the other Highlanders, it will be proper, for the vindication of public justice, to extirpate that set of thieves." These words naturally bear a sense perfectly innocent, and would, but for the horrible event which followed, have been universally understood in that sense. It is undoubtedly one of the first duties of every government to extirpate gangs of thieves. This does not mean that every thief ought to be treacherously assassinated in his sleep, or even that every thief ought to be put to death after a fair trial, but that every gang, as a gang, ought to be completely broken up, and that whatever severity is indispensably necessary for that end ought to be used. It is in this sense that we praise the Marquess of Hastings for extirpating the Pindarees, and Lord William Bentinck for extirpating the Thugs. If William had read and weighed the words which were submitted to him by his Secretary, he would probably have understood them to mean that Glencoe was to be occupied by troops, that resistance, if resistance were attempted, was to be put down with a strong hand, that severe punishment was to be inflicted on those leading members of the clan who could be proved to have been guilty of great crimes, that some active young freebooters, who were more used to handle the broad sword than the plough, and who did not seem likely to settle down into quiet labourers, were to be sent to the army in the Low Countries, that others were to be transported to the American plantations, and that those Macdonalds who were suffered to remain in their native valley were to be disarmed and required to give hostages for good behaviour. A plan very nearly resembling this had, we know, actually been the subject of much discussion in the political circles of Edinburgh. There can be little doubt that William would have deserved well of his people if he had, in this manner, extirpated not only the tribe of Mac Ian, but every Highland tribe whose calling was to steal cattle and burn houses.

The extirpation planned by the Master of Stair was of a different kind. His design was to butcher the whole race of thieves, the whole damnable race. Such was the language in which his hatred vented itself. He studied the geography of the wild country which surrounded Glencoe, and made his arrangements with infernal skill. If possible, the blow must be quick, and crushing, and altogether unexpected. But if Mac Ian should apprehend danger and should attempt to take refuge in the territories of his neighbours, he must find every road barred. The pass of Rannoch must be secured. The Laird of Weems, who was powerful in Strath Tay, must be told that, if he harbours the outlaws, he does so at his peril. Breadalbane promised to cut off the retreat of the fugitives on one side, Mac Callum More on another. It was fortunate, the Secretary wrote, that it was winter. This was the time to maul the wretches. The nights were so long, the mountain tops so cold and stormy, that even the hardiest men could not long bear exposure to the open air without a roof or a spark of fire. That the women and the children could find shelter in the desert was quite impossible. While he wrote thus, no thought that he was committing a great wickedness crossed his mind. He was happy in the approbation of his own conscience. Duty, justice, nay charity and mercy, were the names under which he disguised his cruelty; nor is it by any means improbable that the disguise imposed upon himself.

Hill, who commanded the forces assembled at Fort William, was not entrusted with the execution of the design. He seems to have been a humane man; he was much distressed when he learned that the government was determined on severity; and it was probably thought that his heart might fail him in the most critical moment. He was directed to put a strong detachment under the orders of his second in command, Lieutenant Colonel Hamilton. To Hamilton a significant hint was conveyed that he had now an excellent opportunity of establishing his character in the estimation of those who were at the head of affairs. Of the troops entrusted to him a large proportion were Campbells, and belonged to a regiment lately raised by Argyle, and called by Argyle's name. It was probably thought that, on such an occasion, humanity might prove too strong for the mere habit of military obedience, and that little reliance could be placed on hearts which had not been ulcerated by a feud such as had long raged between the people of Mac Ian and the people of Mac Callum More.

Had Hamilton marched openly against the Glencoe men and put them to the edge of the sword, the act would probably not have wanted apologists, and most certainly would not have wanted precedents. But the Master of Stair had strongly recommended a different mode of proceeding. If the least alarm were given, the nest of robbers would be found empty; and to hunt them down in so wild a region would, even with all the help that Breadalbane and Argyle could give, be a long and difficult business. "Better," he wrote, "not meddle with them than meddle to no purpose. When the thing is resolved, let it be secret and sudden." He was obeyed; and it was determined that the Glencoe men should perish, not by military execution, but by the most dastardly and perfidious form of assassination.

On the first of February a hundred and twenty soldiers of Argyle's regiment, commanded by a captain named Campbell and a lieutenant named Lindsay, marched to Glencoe. Captain Campbell was commonly called in Scotland Glenlyon, from the pass in which his property lay. He had every qualification for the service on which he was employed, an unblushing forehead, a smooth lying tongue, and a heart of adamant. He was also one of the few Campbells who were likely to be trusted and welcomed by the Macdonalds: for his niece was married to Alexander, the second son of Mac Ian.

The sight of the red coats approaching caused some anxiety among the population of the valley. John, the eldest son of the Chief, came, accompanied by twenty clansmen, to meet the strangers, and asked what this visit meant. Lieutenant Lindsay answered that the soldiers came as friends, and wanted nothing but quarters. They were kindly received, and were lodged under the thatched roofs of the little community. Glenlyon and several of his men were taken into the house of a tacksman who was named, from the cluster of cabins over which he exercised authority, Inverriggen. Lindsay was accommodated nearer to the abode of the old chief. Auchintriater, one of the principal men of the clan, who governed the small hamlet of Auchnaion, found room there for a party commanded by a serjeant named Barbour. Provisions were liberally supplied. There was no want of beef, which had probably fattened in distant pastures; nor was any payment demanded: for in hospitality, as in thievery, the Gaelic marauders rivalled the Bedouins. During twelve days the soldiers lived familiarly with the people of the glen. Old Mac Ian, who had before felt many misgivings as to the relation in which he stood to the government, seems to have been pleased with the visit. The officers passed much of their time with him and his family. The long evenings were cheerfully spent by the peat fire with the help of some packs of cards which had found their way to that remote corner of the world, and of some French brandy which was probably part of James's farewell gift to his Highland supporters. Glenlyon appeared to be warmly attached to his niece and her husband Alexander. Every day he came to their house to take his morning draught. Meanwhile he observed with minute attention all the avenues by which, when the signal for the slaughter should be given, the Macdonalds might attempt to escape to the hills; and he reported the result of his observations to Hamilton.

Hamilton fixed five o'clock in the morning of the thirteenth of February for the deed. He hoped that, before that time, he should reach Glencoe with four hundred men, and should have stopped all the earths in which the old fox and his two cubs,—so Mac Ian and his sons were nicknamed by the murderers,—could take refuge. But, at five precisely, whether Hamilton had arrived or not, Glenlyon was to fall on, and to slay every Macdonald under seventy.

The night was rough. Hamilton and his troops made slow progress, and were long after their time. While they were contending with the wind and snow, Glenlyon was supping and playing at cards with those whom he meant to butcher before daybreak. He and Lieutenant Lindsay had engaged themselves to dine with the old Chief on the morrow.

Late in the evening a vague suspicion that some evil was intended crossed the mind of the Chief's eldest son. The soldiers were evidently in a restless state; and some of them uttered strange exclamations. Two men, it is said, were overheard whispering. "I do not like this job," one of them muttered: "I should be glad to fight the Macdonalds. But to kill men in their beds—" "We must do as we are bid," answered another voice. "If there is any thing wrong, our officers must answer for it." John Macdonald was so uneasy that, soon after midnight, he went to Glenlyon's quarters. Glenlyon and his men were all up, and seemed to be getting their arms ready for action. John, much alarmed, asked what these preparations meant. Glenlyon was profuse of friendly assurances. "Some of Glengarry's people have been harrying the country. We are getting ready to march against them. You are quite safe. Do you think that, if you were in any danger, I should not have given a hint to your brother Sandy and his wife?" John's suspicions were quieted. He returned to his house, and lay down to rest.

It was five in the morning. Hamilton and his men were still some miles off; and the avenues which they were to have secured were open. But the orders which Glenlyon had received were precise; and he began to execute them at the little village where he was himself quartered. His host Inverrigen and nine other Macdonalds were dragged out of their beds, bound hand and foot, and murdered. A boy twelve years old clung round the Captain's legs, and begged hard for life. He would do any thing: he would go any where: he would follow Glenlyon round the world. Even Glenlyon, it is said, showed signs of relenting: but a ruffian named Drummond shot the child dead.

At Auchnaion the tacksman Auchintriater was up early that morning, and was sitting with eight of his family round the fire, when a volley of musketry laid him and seven of his companions dead or dying on the floor. His brother, who alone had escaped unhurt, called to Serjeant Barbour, who commanded the slayers, and asked as a favour to be allowed to die in the open air. "Well," said the Serjeant, "I will do you that favour for the sake of your meat which I have eaten." The mountaineer, bold, athletic, and favoured by the darkness, came forth, rushed on the soldiers who were about to level their pieces at him, flung his plaid over their faces, and was gone in a moment.

Meanwhile Lindsay had knocked at the door of the old Chief and had asked for admission in friendly language. The door was opened. Mac Ian, while putting on his clothes and calling to his servants to bring some refreshment for his visitors, was shot through the head. Two of his attendants were slain with him. His wife was already up and dressed in such finery as the princesses of the rude Highland glens were accustomed to wear. The assassins pulled off her clothes and trinkets. The rings were not easily taken from her fingers: but a soldier tore them away with his teeth. She died on the following day.

The statesman, to whom chiefly this great crime is to be ascribed, had planned it with consummate ability: but the execution was complete in nothing but in guilt and infamy. A succession of blunders saved three fourths of the Glencoe men from the fate of their chief. All the moral qualities which fit men to bear a part in a massacre Hamilton and Glenlyon possessed in perfection. But neither seems to have had much professional skill. Hamilton had arranged his plan without making allowance for bad weather, and this at a season when, in the Highlands, the weather was very likely to be bad. The consequence was that the fox earths, as he called them, were not stopped in time. Glenlyon and his men committed the error of despatching their hosts with firearms instead of using the cold steel. The peal and flash of gun after gun gave notice, from three different parts of the valley at once, that murder was doing. From fifty cottages the half naked peasantry fled under cover of the night to the recesses of their pathless glen. Even the sons of Mac Ian, who had been especially marked out for destruction, contrived to escape. They were roused from sleep by faithful servants. John, who, by the death of his father, had become the patriarch of the tribe, quitted his dwelling just as twenty soldiers with fixed bayonets marched up to it. It was broad day long before Hamilton arrived. He found the work not even half performed. About thirty corpses lay wallowing in blood on the dunghills before the doors. One or two women were seen among the number, and a yet more fearful and piteous sight, a little hand, which had been lopped in the tumult of the butchery from some infant. One aged Macdonald was found alive. He was probably too infirm to fly, and, as he was above seventy, was not included in the orders under which Glenlyon had acted. Hamilton murdered the old man in cold blood. The deserted hamlets were then set on fire; and the troops departed, driving away with them many sheep and goats, nine hundred kine, and two hundred of the small shaggy ponies of the Highlands.

It is said, and may but too easily be believed, that the sufferings of the fugitives were terrible. How many old men, how many women with babes in their arms, sank down and slept their last sleep in the snow; how many, having crawled, spent with toil and hunger, into nooks among the precipices, died in those dark holes, and were picked to the bone by the mountain ravens, can never be known. But it is probable that those who perished by cold, weariness and want were not less numerous than those who were slain by the assassins. When the troops had retired, the Macdonalds crept out of the caverns of Glencoe, ventured back to the spot where the huts had formerly stood, collected the scorched corpses from among the smoking ruins, and performed some rude rites of sepulture. The tradition runs that the hereditary bard of the tribe took his seat on a rock which overhung the place of slaughter, and poured forth a long lament over his murdered brethren and his desolate home. Eighty years later that sad dirge was still repeated by the population of the valley.

The survivors might well apprehend that they had escaped the shot and the sword only to perish by famine. The whole domain was a waste. Houses, barns, furniture, implements of husbandry, herds, flocks, horses, were gone. Many months must elapse before the clan would be able to raise on its own ground the means of supporting even the most miserable existence.

It may be thought strange that these events should not have been instantly followed by a burst of execration from every part of the civilised world. The fact, however, is that years elapsed before the public indignation was thoroughly awakened, and that months elapsed before the blackest part of the story found credit even among the enemies of the government. That the massacre should not have been mentioned in the London Gazettes, in the Monthly Mercuries, which were scarcely less courtly than the Gazettes, or in pamphlets licensed by official censors, is perfectly intelligible. But that no allusion to it should be found in private journals and letters, writen by persons free from all restraint, may seem extraordinary. There is not a word on the subject in Evelyn's Diary. In Narcissus Luttrell's Diary is a remarkable entry made five weeks after the butchery. The letters from Scotland, he says, described that kingdom as perfectly tranquil, except that there was still some grumbling about ecclesiastical questions. The Dutch ministers regularly reported all the Scotch news to their government. They thought it worth while, about this time, to mention that a collier had been taken by a privateer near Berwick, that the Edinburgh mail had been robbed, that a whale, with a tongue seventeen feet long and seven feet broad, had been stranded near Aberdeen. But it is not hinted in any of their despatches that there was any rumour of any extraordinary occurrence in the Highlands. Reports that some of the Macdonalds had been slain did indeed, in about three weeks, travel through Edinburgh up to London. But these reports were vague and contradictory; and the very worst of them was far from coming up to the horrible truth. The Whig version of the story was that the old robber Mac Ian had laid an ambuscade for the soldiers, that he had been caught in his own snare, and that he and some of his clan had fallen sword in hand. The Jacobite version, written at Edinburgh on the twenty-third of March, appeared in the Paris Gazette of the seventh of April. Glenlyon, it was said, had been sent with a detachment from Argyle's regiment, under cover of darkness, to surprise the inhabitants of Glencoe, and had killed thirty six men and boys and four women. In this there was nothing very strange or shocking. A night attack on a gang of freebooters occupying a strong natural fortress may be a perfectly legitimate military operation; and, in the obscurity and confusion of such an attack, the most humane man may be so unfortunate as to shoot a woman or a child. The circumstances which give a peculiar character to the slaughter of Glencoe, the breach of faith, the breach of hospitality, the twelve days of feigned friendship and conviviality, of morning calls, of social meals, of healthdrinking, of cardplaying, were not mentioned by the Edinburgh correspondent of the Paris Gazette; and we may therefore confidently infer that those circumstances were as yet unknown even to inquisitive and busy malecontents residing in the Scottish capital within a hundred miles of the spot where the deed had been done. In the south of the island the matter produced, as far as can now be judged, scarcely any sensation. To the Londoner of those days Appin was what Caffraria or Borneo is to us. He was not more moved by hearing that some Highland thieves had been surprised and killed than we are by hearing that a band of Amakosah cattle stealers has been cut off, or that a bark full of Malay pirates has been sunk. He took it for granted that nothing had been done in Glencoe beyond what was doing in many other glens. There might have been violence; but it had been in a land of violence. There had been a night brawl, one of a hundred night brawls, between the Macdonalds and the Campbells; and the Campbells had knocked the Macdonalds on the head.

By slow degrees the whole came out. From a letter written at Edinburgh before the end of April, it appears that the horrible story was already current among the Jacobites of that city. In the summer Argyle's regiment was quartered in the south of England, and some of the men made strange confessions, over their ale, about what they had been forced to do in the preceding winter. The nonjurors soon got hold of the clue, and followed it resolutely: their secret presses went to work; and at length, near a year after the crime had been committed, it was published to the world. But the world was long incredulous. The habitual mendacity of the Jacobite libellers had brought on them an appropriate punishment. Now, when, for the first time, they told the truth, they were supposed to be romancing. They complained bitterly that the story, though perfectly authentic, was regarded by the public as a factious lie. So late as the year 1695, Hickes, in a tract in which he endeavoured to defend his darling tale of the Theban legion against the unanswerable argument drawn from the silence of historians, remarked that it might well be doubted whether any historian would make mention of the massacre of Glencoe. There were in England, he said, many thousands of well educated men who had never heard of that massacre, or who regarded it as a mere fable.

Nevertheless the punishment of some of the guilty began very early. Hill, who indeed can hardly be called guilty, was much disturbed. Breadalbane, hardened as he was, felt the stings of conscience or the dread of retribution. A few days after the Macdonalds had returned to their old dwellingplace, his steward visited the ruins of the house of Glencoe, and endeavoured to persuade the sons of the murdered chief to sign a paper declaring that they held the Earl guiltless of the blood which had been shed. They were assured that, if they would do this, all His Lordship's great influence should be employed to obtain for them from the Crown a free pardon and a remission of all forfeitures. Glenlyon did his best to assume an air of unconcern. He made his appearance in the most fashionable coffeehouse at Edinburgh, and talked loudly and self-complacently about the important service in which he had been engaged among the mountains. Some of his soldiers, however, who observed him closely, whispered that all this bravery was put on. He was not the man that he had been before that night. The form of his countenance was changed. In all places, at all hours, whether he waked or slept, Glencoe was for ever before him.

But, whatever apprehensions might disturb Breadalbane, whatever spectres might haunt Glenlyon, the Master of Stair had neither fear nor remorse. He was indeed mortified: but he was mortified only by the blunders of Hamilton and by the escape of so many of the damnable breed. "Do right, and fear nobody;" such is the language of his letters. "Can there be a more sacred duty than to rid the country of thieving? The only thing that I regret is that any got away."

LA HOGUE

TOURVILLE had with him only his own squadron, consisting of forty four ships of the line. But he had received positive orders to protect the descent on England, and not to decline a battle. Though these orders had been given before it was known at Versailles that the Dutch and English fleets had joined, he was not disposed to take on himself the responsibility of disobedience. He still remembered with bitterness the reprimand which his extreme caution had drawn upon him after the fight of Beachy Head. He would not again be told that he was a timid and unenterprising commander, that he had no courage but the vulgar courage of a common sailor. He was also persuaded that the odds against him were rather apparent than real. He believed, on the authority of James and Melfort, that the English seamen, from the flag officers down to the cabin boys, were Jacobites. Those who fought would fight with half a heart; and there would probably be numerous desertions at the most critical moment. Animated by such hopes he sailed from Brest, steered first towards the north east, came in sight of the coast of Dorsetshire, and then struck across the Channel towards La Hogue, where the army which he was to convoy to England had already begun to embark on board of the transports. He was within a few leagues of Barfleur when, before sunrise, on the morning of the nineteenth of May [1692], he saw the great armament of the allies stretching along the eastern horizon. He determined to bear down on them. By eight the two lines of battle were formed; but it was eleven before the firing began. It soon became plain that the English, from the Admiral downwards, were resolved to do their duty. Russell had visited all his ships, and exhorted all his crews. "If your commanders play false," he said, "overboard with them, and with myself the first." There was no defection. There was no slackness. Carter was the first who broke the French line. He was struck by a splinter of one of his own yard arms, and fell dying on the deck. He would not be carried below. He would not let go his sword. "Fight the ship," were his last words: "fight the ship as long as she can swim." The battle lasted till four in the afternoon. The roar of the guns was distinctly heard more than twenty miles off by the army which was encamped on the coast of Normandy. During the earlier part of the day the wind was favourable to the French: they were opposed to only half of the allied fleet; and against that half they maintained the conflict with their usual courage and with more than their usual seamanship. After a hard and doubtful fight of five hours, Tourville thought that enough had been done to maintain the honour of the white flag, and began to draw off. But by this time the wind had veered, and was with the allies. They were now able to avail themselves of their great superiority of force. They came on fast. The retreat of the French became a flight. Tourville fought his own ship desperately. She was named, in allusion to Lewis's favourite emblem, the Royal Sun, and was widely renowned as the finest vessel in the world. It was reported among the English sailors that she was adorned with an image of the Great King, and that he appeared there, as he appeared in the Place of Victories, with vanquished nations in chains beneath his feet. The gallant ship, surrounded by enemies, lay like a great fortress on the sea, scattering death on every side from her hundred and four portholes. She was so formidably manned that all attempts to board her failed. Long after sunset, she got clear of her assailants, and, with all her scuppers spouting blood, made for the coast of Normandy. She had suffered so much that Tourville hastily removed his flag to a ship of ninety guns which was named the Ambitious. By this time his fleet was scattered far over the sea. About twenty of his smallest ships made their escape by a road which was too perilous for any courage but the courage of despair. In the double darkness of night and of a thick sea fog, they ran, with all their sails spread, through the boiling waves and treacherous rocks of the Race of Alderney, and, by a strange good fortune, arrived without a single disaster at Saint Maloes. The pursuers did not venture to follow the fugitives into that terrible strait, the place of innumerable shipwrecks.

Those French vessels which were too bulky to venture into the Race of Alderney fled to the havens of the Cotentin. The Royal Sun and two other three-deckers reached Cherburg in safety. The Ambitious, with twelve other ships, all first rates or second rates, took refuge in the Bay of La Hogue, close to the headquarters of the army of James.

The three ships which had fled to Cherburg were closely chased by an English squadron under the command of Delaval. He found them hauled up into shoal water where no large man of war could get at them. He therefore determined to attack them with his fire-ships and boats. The service was gallantly and successfully performed. In a short time the Royal Sun and her two consorts were burned to ashes. Part of the crews escaped to the shore; and part fell into the hands of the English.

Meanwhile Russell with the greater part of his victorious fleet had blockaded the Bay of La Hogue. Here, as at Cherburg, the French men of war had been drawn up into shallow water. They lay close to the camp of the army which was destined for the invasion of England. Six of them were moored under a fort named Lisset. The rest lay under the guns of another fort named Saint Vaast, where James had fixed his headquarters, and where the British flag, variegated by the crosses of Saint George and Saint Andrew, hung by the side of the white flag of France. Marshal Bellefonds had planted several batteries which, it was thought, would deter the boldest enemy from approaching either Fort Lisset or Fort Saint Vaast. James, however, who knew something of English seamen, was not perfectly at ease, and proposed to send strong bodies of soldiers on board of the ships. But Tourville would not consent to put such a slur on his profession.

Russell meanwhile was preparing for an attack. On the afternoon of the twenty-third of May all was ready. A flotilla consisting of sloops, of fireships, and of two hundred boats, was entrusted to the command of Rooke. The whole armament was in the highest spirits. The rowers, flushed by success, and animated by the thought that they were going to fight under the eyes of the French and Irish troops who had been assembled for the purpose of subjugating England, pulled manfully and with loud huzzas towards the six huge wooden castles which lay close to Fort Lisset. The French, though an eminently brave people, have always been more liable to sudden panics than their phlegmatic neighbours the English and Germans. On this day there was a panic both in the fleet and in the army. Tourville ordered his sailors to man their boats, and would have led them to encounter the enemy in the bay. But his example and his exhortations were vain. His boats turned round and fled in confusion. The ships were abandoned. The cannonade from Fort Lisset was so feeble and ill directed that it did no execution. The regiments on the beach, after wasting a few musket shots, drew off. The English boarded the men of war, set them on fire, and having performed this great service without the loss of a single life, retreated at a late hour with the retreating tide. The bay was in a blaze during the night; and now and then a loud explosion announced that the flames had reached a powder room or a tier of loaded guns. At eight the next morning the tide came back strong; and with the tide came back Rooke and his two hundred boats. The enemy made a faint attempt to defend the vessels which were near Fort Saint Vaast. During a few minutes the batteries did some execution among the crews of our skiffs: but the struggle was soon over. The French poured fast out of their ships on one side: the English poured in as fast on the other, and, with loud shouts, turned the captured guns against the shore. The batteries

were speedily silenced. James and Melfort, Bellefonds and Tourville, looked on in helpless despondency while the second conflagration proceeded. The conquerors, leaving the ships of war in
flames, made their way into an inner basin where many transports
lay. Eight of these vessels were set on fire. Several were taken in
tow. The rest would have been either destroyed or carried off, had
not the sea again begun to ebb. It was impossible to do more; and
the victorious flotilla slowly retired, insulting the hostile camp with
a thundering chant of "God save the King."

Thus ended, at noon on the twenty-fourth of May, the great
conflict which had raged during five days over a wide extent of sea
and shore. One English fireship had perished in its calling. Sixteen
French men of war, all noble vessels, and eight of them three-
deckers, had been sunk or burned down to the water-edge. The
battle is called, from the place where it terminated, the battle of La
Hogue.

STEINKIRK

IN the month of July [1692] William's headquarters were at Lambeque. About six miles off, at Steinkirk, Luxemburg had encamped
with the main body of his army; and about six miles further off
lay a considerable force commanded by the Marquess of Boufflers,
one of the best officers in the service of Lewis.

The country between Lambeque and Steinkirk was intersected
by innumerable hedges and ditches; and neither army could
approach the other without passing through several long and
narrow defiles. Luxemburg had therefore little reason to apprehend that he should be attacked in his entrenchments; and he felt
assured that he should have ample notice before any attack was
made: for he had succeeded in corrupting an adventurer named
Millevoix, who was chief musician and private secretary of the
Elector of Bavaria. This man regularly sent to the French headquarters authentic information touching the designs of the allies.

The Marshal, confident in the strength of his position and in the
accuracy of his intelligence, lived in his tent as he was accustomed
to live in his hotel at Paris. He was at once a valetudinarian and a
voluptuary; and, in both characters, he loved his ease. He scarcely
ever mounted his horse. Light conversation and cards occupied
most of his hours. His table was luxurious; and, when he had sate
down to supper, it was a service of danger to disturb him. Some
scoffers remarked that in his military dispositions he was not guided
exclusively by military reasons, that he generally contrived to en-

trench himself in some place where the veal and the poultry were remarkably good, and that he was always solicitous to keep open such communications with the sea as might ensure him, from September to April, a regular supply of Sandwich oysters. If there were any agreeable women in the neighbourhood of his camp, they were generally to be found at his banquets. It may easily be supposed that, under such a commander, the young princes and nobles of France vied with one another in splendour and gallantry.

While he was amusing himself after his wonted fashion, the confederate princes discovered that their counsels were betrayed. A peasant picked up a letter which had been dropped, and carried it to the Elector of Bavaria. It contained full proofs of the guilt of Millevoix. William conceived a hope that he might be able to take his enemies in the snare which they had laid for him. The perfidious secretary was summoned to the royal presence and taxed with his crime. A pen was put into his hand: a pistol was held to his breast; and he was commanded to write on pain of instant death. His letter, dictated by William, was conveyed to the French camp. It apprised Luxemburg that the allies meant to send out a strong foraging party on the next day. In order to protect this party from molestation, some battalions of infantry, accompanied by artillery, would march by night to occupy the defiles which lay between the armies. The Marshal read, believed, and went to rest, while William urged forward the preparations for a general assault on the French lines.

The whole allied army was under arms while it was still dark. In the grey of the morning, Luxemburg was awakened by scouts, who brought tidings that the enemy was advancing in great force. He at first treated the news very lightly. His correspondent, it seemed, had been, as usual, diligent and exact. The Prince of Orange had sent out a detachment to protect his foragers, and this detachment had been magnified by fear into a great host. But one alarming report followed another fast. All the passes, it was said, were choked with multitudes of foot, horse, and artillery, under the banners of England and of Spain, of the United Provinces and of the Empire; and every column was moving towards Steinkirk. At length the Marshal rose, got on horseback, and rode out to see what was doing.

By this time the vanguard of the allies was close to his outposts. About half a mile in advance of his army was encamped a brigade named from the province of Bourbonnais. These troops had to bear the first brunt of the onset. Amazed and panickstricken, they were swept away in a moment, and ran for their lives, leaving their tents and seven pieces of cannon to the assailants.

Thus far William's plans had been completely successful: but now fortune began to turn against him. He had been misinformed as to the nature of the ground which lay between the station of the brigade of Bourbonnais and the main encampment of the enemy. He had expected that he should be able to push forward without a moment's pause, that he should find the French army in a state of wild disorder, and that his victory would be easy and complete. But his progress was obstructed by several fences and ditches: there was a short delay; and a short delay sufficed to frustrate his design. Luxemburg was the very man for such a conjuncture. He had committed great faults: he had kept careless guard: he had trusted implicitly to information which had proved false: he had neglected information which had proved true: one of his divisions was flying in confusion: the other divisions were unprepared for action. That crisis would have paralysed the faculties of an ordinary captain: it only braced and stimulated those of Luxemburg. His mind, nay his sickly and distorted body, seemed to derive health and vigour from disaster and dismay. In a short time he had disposed every thing. The French army was in battle order. Conspicuous in that great array were the household troops of Lewis, the most renowned body of fighting men in Europe; and at their head appeared, glittering in lace and embroidery hastily thrown on and half fastened, a crowd of young princes and lords who had just been roused by the trumpet from their couches or their revels, and who had hastened to look death in the face with the gay and festive intrepidity characteristic of French gentlemen. Highest in rank among these highborn warriors was a lad of sixteen, Philip Duke of Chartres, son of the Duke of Orleans, and nephew of the King of France. It was with difficulty and by importunate solicitation that the gallant boy had extorted Luxemburg's permission to be where the fire was hottest. Two other youths of royal blood, Lewis Duke of Bourbon, and Armand Prince of Conti, showed a spirit worthy of their descent. With them was a descendant of one of the bastards of Henry the Fourth, Lewis Duke of Vendome, a man sunk in indolence and in the foulest vice, yet capable of exhibiting on a great occasion the qualities of a great soldier. Berwick, who was beginning to earn for himself an honourable name in arms, was there; and at his side rode Sarsfield, whose courage and ability earned, on that day, the esteem of the whole French army. Meanwhile Luxemburg had sent off a pressing message to summon Boufflers. But the message was needless. Boufflers had heard the firing, and, like a brave and intelligent captain, was already hastening towards the point from which the sound came.

Though the assailants had lost all the advantage which belongs to a surprise, they came on manfully. In the front of the battle were the British commanded by Count Solmes. The division which was to lead the way was Mackay's. He was to have been supported, according to William's plan, by a strong body of foot and horse. Though most of Mackay's men had never before been under fire, their behaviour gave promise of Blenheim and Ramilies. They first encountered the Swiss, who held a distinguished place in the French army. The fight was so close and desperate that the muzzles of the muskets crossed. The Swiss were driven back with fearful slaughter. More than eighteen hundred of them appear from the French returns to have been killed or wounded. Luxemburg afterwards said that he had never in his life seen so furious a struggle. He collected in haste the opinion of the generals who surrounded him. All thought that the emergency was one which could be met by no common means. The King's household must charge the English. The Marshal gave the word; and the household, headed by the princes of the blood, came on, flinging their muskets back on their shoulders. "Sword in hand," was the cry through all the ranks of that terrible brigade: "sword in hand. No firing. Do it with the cold steel." After a long and bloody contest, the English were borne down. They never ceased to repeat that, if Solmes had done his duty by them, they would have beaten even the household. But Solmes gave them no effective support. He pushed forward some cavalry which, from the nature of the ground, could do little or nothing. His infantry he would not suffer to stir. They could do no good, he said; and he would not send them to be slaughtered. Ormond was eager to hasten to the assistance of his countrymen, but was not permitted. Mackay sent a pressing message to represent that he and his men were left to certain destruction: but all was vain. "God's will be done," said the brave veteran. He died as he had lived, like a good Christian and a good soldier. With him fell Douglas and Lanier, two generals distinguished among the conquerors of Ireland. Mountjoy too was among the slain. After languishing three years in the Bastille, he had just been exchanged for Richard Hamilton, and, having been converted to Whiggism by wrongs more powerful than all the arguments of Locke and Sidney, had instantly hastened to join William's camp as a volunteer. Five fine regiments were entirely cut to pieces. No part of this devoted band would have escaped but for the courage and conduct of Auverquerque, who came to the rescue in the moment of extremity with two fresh battalions. The gallant manner in which he brought off the remains of Mackay's division was long remembered and talked of with grateful admiration by the British camp fires. The ground where the conflict had raged was piled with corpses; and those who buried the slain remarked that almost all the wounds had been given in close fighting by the sword or the bayonet.

It was said that William so far forgot his wonted stoicism as to utter a passionate exclamation at the way in which the English regiments had been sacrificed. Soon, however, he recovered his equanimity, and determined to fall back. It was high time: for the French army was every moment becoming stronger, as the regiments commanded by Boufflers came up in rapid succession. The allied army returned to Lambeque unpursued and in unbroken order.

The French owned that they had about seven thousand men killed and wounded. The loss of the allies had been little, if at all, greater. The relative strength of the armies was what it had been on the preceding day; and they continued to occupy their old positions. But the moral effect of the battle was great. The splendour of William's fame grew pale. Even his admirers were forced to own that, in the field, he was not a match for Luxemburg. In France the news was received with transports of joy and pride. The Court, the Capital, even the peasantry of the remotest provinces, gloried in the impetuous valour which had been displayed by so many youths, the heirs of illustrious names. It was exultingly and fondly repeated all over the kingdom that the young Duke of Chartres could not by any remonstrances be kept out of danger, that a ball had passed through his coat, that he had been wounded in the shoulder. The people lined the roads to see the princes and nobles who returned from Steinkirk. The jewellers devised Steinkirk buckles: the perfumers sold Steinkirk powder. But the name of the field of battle was peculiarly given to a new species of collar. Lace neckcloths were then worn by men of fashion; and it had been usual to arrange them with great care. But at the terrible moment when the brigade of Bourbonnais was flying before the onset of the allies, there was no time for foppery; and the finest gentlemen of the Court came spurring to the front of the line of battle with their rich cravats in disorder. It therefore became a fashion among the beauties of Paris to wear round their necks kerchiefs of the finest lace studiously disarranged; and these kerchiefs were called Steinkirks.

LANDEN

THOUGH the French army in the Netherlands had been weakened by the departure of the forces commanded by the Dauphin and Boufflers, and though the allied army was daily strengthened by the arrival of fresh troops, Luxemburg still had a superiority of force; and that superiority he increased by an adroit stratagem. He marched towards Liege, and made as if he were about to form the siege of that city. William was uneasy, and the more uneasy because he knew that there was a French party among the inhabitants. He quitted his position near Louvain, advanced to Nether Hespen, and encamped there with the river Gette in his rear. On his march he learned that Huy had opened its gates to the French. The news increased his anxiety about Liege, and determined him to send thither a force sufficient to overawe malecontents within the city, and to repel any attack from without. This was exactly what Luxemburg had expected and desired. His feint had served its purpose. He turned his back on the fortress which had hitherto seemed to be his object, and hastened towards the Gette. William, who had detached more than twenty thousand men, and who had but fifty thousand left in his camp, was alarmed by learning from his scouts, on the eighteenth of July [1693], that the French General, with near eighty thousand, was close at hand.

It was still in the King's power, by a hasty retreat, to put between his army and the enemy the narrow, but deep, waters of the Gette, which had lately been swollen by rains. But the site which he occupied was strong; and it could easily be made still stronger. He set all his troops to work. Ditches were dug, mounds thrown up, palisades fixed in the earth. In a few hours the ground wore a new aspect; and the King trusted that he should be able to repel the attack even of a force greatly outnumbering his own. Nor was it without much appearance of reason that he felt this confidence. When the morning of the nineteenth of July broke, the bravest men of Lewis's army looked gravely and anxiously on the fortress which had suddenly sprung up to arrest their progress. The allies were protected by a breastwork. Here and there along the entrenchments were formed little redoubts and half moons. A hundred pieces of cannon were disposed along the ramparts. On the left flank, the village of Romsdorff rose close to the little stream of Landen, from which the English have named the disastrous day. On the right was the village of Neerwinden. Both villages were, after the fashion of the Low Countries, surrounded by moats and fences; and, within these enclosures, the little plots of ground occupied by different families were separated by mud walls five feet in height and a foot in thickness. All these barricades William had repaired and strengthened. Saint Simon, who, after the battle, surveyed the ground, could hardly, he tells us, believe that defences so extensive and so formidable could have been created with such rapidity.

Luxemburg, however, was determined to try whether even this position could be maintained against the superior numbers and the impetuous valour of his soldiers. Soon after sunrise the roar of the cannon began to be heard. William's batteries did much execution before the French artillery could be so placed as to return the fire. It was eight o'clock before the close fighting began. The village of Neerwinden was regarded by both commanders as the point on which every thing depended. There an attack was made by the French left wing commanded by Montchevreuil, a veteran officer of high reputation, and by Berwick, who, though young, was fast rising to an eminent place among the captains of his time. Berwick led the onset, and forced his way into the village, but was soon driven out again with a terrible carnage. His followers fled or perished: he, while trying to rally them, and cursing them for not doing their duty better, was surrounded by foes. He concealed his white cockade, and hoped to be able, by the help of his native tongue, to pass himself off as an officer of the English army. But his face was recognised by one of his mother's brothers, George Churchill, who held on that day the command of a brigade. A hurried embrace was exchanged between the kinsmen; and the uncle conducted the nephew to William, who, as long as every thing seemed to be going well, remained in the rear. The meeting of the King and the captive, united by such close domestic ties, and divided by such inexpiable injuries, was a strange sight. Both behaved as became them. William uncovered, and addressed to his prisoner a few words of courteous greeting. Berwick's only reply was a solemn bow. The King put on his hat: the Duke put on his hat; and the cousins parted for ever.

By this time the French, who had been driven in confusion out of Neerwinden, had been reinforced by a division under the command of the Duke of Bourbon, and came gallantly back to the attack. William, well aware of the importance of this post, gave orders that troops should move thither from other parts of his line. The second conflict was long and bloody. The assailants again forced an entrance into the village. They were again driven out with immense slaughter, and showed little inclination to return to the charge.

Meanwhile the battle had been raging all along the entrenchments of the allied army. Again and again Luxemburg brought up
his troops within pistolshot of the breastwork: but he could bring
them no nearer. Again and again they recoiled from the heavy fire
which was poured on their front and on their flanks. It seemed that
all was over. Luxemburg retired to a spot which was out of gun-
shot, and summoned a few of his chief officers to a consultation.
They talked together during some time; and their animated gestures
were observed with deep interest by all who were within sight.

At length Luxemburg formed his decision. A last attempt must
be made to carry Neerwinden; and the invincible household troops,
the conquerors of Steinkirk, must lead the way.

The household troops came on in a manner worthy of their long
and terrible renown. A third time Neerwinden was taken. A third
time William tried to retake it. At the head of some English regiments he charged the guards of Lewis with such fury that, for the
first time in the memory of the oldest warrior, that far famed band
was driven back. It was only by the strenuous exertions of
Luxemburg, of the Duke of Chartres, and of the Duke of Bourbon,
that the broken ranks were rallied. But by this time the centre and
left of the allied army had been so much thinned for the purpose
of supporting the conflict at Neerwinden that the entrenchments
could no longer be defended on other points. A little after four in
the afternoon the whole line gave way. All was havoc and confusion. Solmes had received a mortal wound, and fell, still alive,
into the hands of the enemy. The English soldiers, to whom his
name was hateful, accused him of having in his sufferings shown
pusillanimity unworthy of a soldier. The Duke of Ormond was
struck down in the press; and in another moment he would have
been a corpse, had not a rich diamond on his finger caught the eye
of one of the French guards, who justly thought that the owner of
such a jewel would be a valuable prisoner. The Duke's life was
saved; and he was speedily exchanged for Berwick. Ruvigny,
animated by the true refugee hatred of the country which had cast
him out, was taken fighting in the thickest of the battle. Those into
whose hands he had fallen knew him well, and knew that, if they
carried him to their camp, his head would pay for that treason to
which persecution had driven him. With admirable generosity
they pretended not to recognise him, and suffered him to make his
escape in the tumult.

It was only on such occasions as this that the whole greatness of
William's character appeared. Amidst the rout and uproar, while
arms and standards were flung away, while multitudes of fugitives

were choking up the bridges and fords of the Gette or perishing in
its waters, the King, having directed Talmash to superintend the
retreat, put himself at the head of a few brave regiments, and by
desperate efforts arrested the progress of the enemy. His risk was
greater than that which others ran. For he could not be persuaded
either to encumber his feeble frame with a cuirass, or to hide the
ensigns of the garter. He thought his star a good rallying point for
his own troops, and only smiled when he was told that it was a good
mark for the enemy. Many fell on his right hand and on his left.
Two led horses, which in the field always closely followed his
person, were struck dead by cannon shots. One musket ball passed
through the curls of his wig, another through his coat: a third
bruised his side and tore his blue riband to tatters. Many years
later greyheaded old pensioners who crept about the arcades and
alleys of Chelsea Hospital used to relate how he charged at the head
of Galway's horse, how he dismounted four times to put heart into
the infantry, how he rallied one corps which seemed to be shrinking:
"That is not the way to fight, gentlemen. You must stand close up
to them. Thus, gentlemen, thus." "You might have seen him,"—
thus an eye witness wrote, only four days after the battle,—"with his
sword in his hand, throwing himself upon the enemy. It is certain
that one time among the rest, he was seen at the head of two
English regiments, and that he fought seven with these two in sight
of the whole army, driving them before him above a quarter of an
hour. Thanks be to God that preserved him." The enemy pressed
on him so close that it was with difficulty that he at length made his
way over the Gette. A small body of brave men, who shared his
peril to the last, could hardly keep off the pursuers as he crossed
the bridge.

Never, perhaps, was the change which the progress of civilisation
has produced in the art of war more strikingly illustrated than on
that day. Ajax beating down the Trojan leader with a rock which
two ordinary men could scarcely lift, Horatius defending the bridge
against an army, Richard the Lionhearted spurring along the whole
Saracen line without finding an enemy to stand his assault, Robert
Bruce crushing with one blow the helmet and head of Sir Henry
Bohun in sight of the whole array of England and Scotland, such
are the heroes of a dark age. In such an age bodily vigour is the
most indispensable qualification of a warrior. At Landen two poor
sickly beings, who, in a rude state of society, would have been
regarded as too puny to bear any part in combats, were the souls of
two great armies. In some heathen countries they would have been
exposed while infants. In Christendom they would, six hundred

years earlier, have been sent to some quiet cloister. But their lot had fallen on a time when men had discovered that the strength of the muscles is far inferior in value to the strength of the mind. It is probable that, among the hundred and twenty thousand soldiers who were marshalled round Neerwinden under all the standards of Western Europe, the two feeblest in body were the hunchbacked dwarf who urged forward the fiery onset of France, and the asthmatic skeleton who covered the slow retreat of England.

The French were victorious: but they had bought their victory dear. More than ten thousand of the best troops of Lewis had fallen. Neerwinden was a spectacle at which the oldest soldiers stood aghast. The streets were piled breast high with corpses. Among the slain were some great lords and some renowned warriors. Montchevreuil was there, and the mutilated trunk of the Duke of Uzes, first in order of precedence among the whole aristocracy of France. Thence too Sarsfield was borne desperately wounded to a pallet from which he never rose again. The Court of Saint Germains had conferred on him the empty title of Earl of Lucan; but history knows him by the name which is still dear to the most unfortunate of nations. The region, renowned as the battle-field, through many ages, of the greatest powers of Europe, has seen only two more terrible days, the day of Malplaquet and the day of Waterloo. During many months the ground was strewn with skulls and bones of men and horses, and with fragments of hats and shoes, saddles and holsters. The next summer the soil, fertilised by twenty thousand corpses, broke forth into millions of poppies. The traveller who, on the road from Saint Tron to Tirlemont, saw that vast sheet of rich scarlet spreading from Landen to Neerwinden, could hardly help fancying that the figurative prediction of the Hebrew prophet was literally accomplished, that the earth was disclosing her blood, and refusing to cover the slain.

There was no pursuit, though the sun was still high in the heaven when William crossed the Gette. The conquerors were so much exhausted by marching and fighting that they could scarcely move; and the horses were in even worse condition than the men. The Marshal thought it necessary to allow some time for rest and refreshment. The French nobles unloaded their sumpter horses, supped gaily, and pledged one another in Champagne amidst the heaps of dead; and, when night fell, whole brigades gladly lay down to sleep in their ranks on the field of battle. The inactivity of Luxemburg did not escape censure. None could deny that he had in the action shown great skill and energy. But some complained that he wanted patience and perseverance. Others whispered that he had no wish to bring to an end a war which made him necessary to a Court where he had never, in time of peace, found favour or even justice. Lewis, who on this occasion was perhaps not altogether free from some emotions of jealousy, contrived, it was reported, to mingle with the praise which he bestowed on his lieutenant blame which, though delicately expressed, was perfectly intelligible. "In the battle," he said, "the Duke of Luxemburg behaved like Condé; and since the battle the Prince of Orange has behaved like Turenne."

In truth the ability and vigour with which William repaired his terrible defeat might well excite admiration. "In one respect," said the Admiral Coligni, "I may claim superiority over Alexander, over Scipio, over Cæsar. They won great battles, it is true. I have lost four great battles; and yet I show to the enemy a more formidable front than ever." The blood of Coligni ran in the veins of William; and with the blood had descended the unconquerable spirit which could derive from failure as much glory as happier commanders owed to success. The defeat of Landen was indeed a heavy blow. The King had a few days of cruel anxiety. If Luxemburg pushed on, all was lost. Louvain must fall, and Mechlin, and Nieuport, and Ostend. The Batavian frontier would be in danger. The cry for peace throughout Holland might be such as neither States General nor Stadtholder would be able to resist. But there was delay; and a very short delay was enough for William. From the field of battle he made his way through the multitude of fugitives to the neighbourhood of Louvain, and there began to collect his scattered forces. His character is not lowered by the anxiety which, at that moment, the most disastrous of his life, he felt for the two persons who were dearest to him. As soon as he was safe, he wrote to assure his wife of his safety. In the confusion of the flight he had lost sight of Portland, who was then in very feeble health, and had therefore run more than the ordinary risks of war. A short note which the King sent to his friend a few hours later is still extant. "Though I hope to see you this evening, I cannot help writing to tell you how rejoiced I am that you got off so well. God grant that your health may soon be quite restored. These are great trials, which he has been pleased to send me in quick succession. I must try to submit to his pleasure without murmuring, and to deserve his anger less."

William's forces rallied fast. Large bodies of troops which he had, perhaps imprudently, detached from his army while he supposed that Liege was the object of the enemy, rejoined him by forced marches. Three weeks after his defeat he held a review a few miles from Brussels. The number of men under arms was greater than on the morning of the bloody day of Landen: their appearance was soldierlike; and their spirit seemed unbroken. William now wrote to Heinsius that the worst was over. "The crisis," he said, "has been a terrible one. Thank God that it has ended thus." He did not, however, think it prudent to try at that time the event of another pitched field. He therefore suffered the French to besiege and take Charleroy; and this was the only advantage which they derived from the most sanguinary battle fought in Europe during the seventeenth century.

RECOINAGE

TILL the reign of Charles the Second our coin had been struck by a process as old as the thirteenth century. Edward the First had invited hither skilful artists from Florence, which, in his time, was to London what London, in the time of William the Third, was to Moscow. During many generations, the instruments which were then introduced into our mint continued to be employed with little alteration. The metal was divided with shears, and afterwards shaped and stamped by the hammer. In these operations much was left to the hand and eye of the workman. It necessarily happened that some pieces contained a little more and some a little less than the just quantity of silver: few pieces were exactly round; and the rims were not marked. It was therefore in the course of years discovered that to clip the coin was one of the easiest and most profitable kinds of fraud. In the reign of Elizabeth it had been thought necessary to enact that the clipper should be, as the coiner had long been, liable to the penalties of high treason. The practice of paring down money, however, was far too lucrative to be so checked; and, about the time of the Restoration, people began to observe that a large proportion of the crowns, halfcrowns and shillings which were passing from hand to hand had undergone some slight mutilation.

That was a time fruitful of experiments and inventions in all the departments of science. A great improvement in the mode of shaping and striking the coin was suggested. A mill, which to a great extent superseded the human hand, was set up in the Tower of London. This mill was worked by horses, and would doubtless be considered by modern engineers as a rude and feeble machine. The pieces which it produced, however, were among the best in Europe. It was not easy to counterfeit them; and, as their shape was exactly circular, and their edges were inscribed with a legend, clipping was not to be apprehended. The hammered coins and the milled coins were current together. They were received without distinction in public, and consequently in private, payments. The financiers of that age seem to have expected that the new money, which was excellent, would soon displace the old money which was much impaired. Yet any man of plain understanding might have known that, when the State treats perfect coin and light coin as of equal value, the perfect coin will not drive the light coin out of circulation, but will itself be driven out. A clipped crown, on English ground, went as far in the payment of a tax or a debt as a milled crown. But the milled crown, as soon as it had been flung into the crucible or carried across the Channel, became much more valuable than the clipped crown. It might therefore have been predicted, as confidently as any thing can be predicted which depends on the human will, that the inferior pieces would remain in the only market in which they could fetch the same price as the superior pieces, and that the superior pieces would take some form or fly to some place in which some advantage could be derived from their superiority.

The politicians of that age, however, generally overlooked these very obvious considerations. They marvelled exceedingly that every body should be so perverse as to use light money in preference to good money. In other words, they marvelled that nobody chose to pay twelve ounces of silver when ten would serve the turn. The horse in the Tower still paced his rounds. Fresh waggon loads of choice money still came forth from the mill; and still they vanished as fast as they appeared. Great masses were melted down; great masses exported; great masses hoarded: but scarcely one new piece was to be found in the till of a shop, or in the leathern bag which the farmer carried home from the cattle fair. In the receipts and payments of the Exchequer the milled money did not exceed ten shillings in a hundred pounds. A writer of that age mentions the case of a merchant who, in a sum of thirty five pounds, received only a single halfcrown in milled silver. Meanwhile the shears of the clippers were constantly at work. The coiners too multiplied and prospered: for the worse the current money became the more easily it was imitated. During many years this evil went on increasing. At first it was disregarded: but it at length became an insupportable curse to the country. It was to no purpose that the rigorous laws against coining and clipping were rigorously executed. At every session that was held at the Old Bailey terrible examples were made. Hurdles, with four, five, six wretches convicted of counterfeiting or mutilating the money of the realm, were dragged month after month up Holborn Hill. One morning seven men were hanged and a woman burned for clipping. But all was vain. The gains were such as to lawless spirits seemed more than proportioned to the risks. Some clippers were said to have made great fortunes. One in particular offered six thousand pounds for a pardon. His bribe was indeed rejected; but the fame of his riches did much to counteract the effect which the spectacle of his death was designed to produce. Nay the severity of the punishment gave encouragement to the crime. For the practice of clipping, pernicious as it was, did not excite in the common mind a detestation resembling that with which men regard murder, arson, robbery, even theft. The injury done by the whole body of clippers to the whole society was indeed immense: but each particular act of clipping was a trifle. To pass a halfcrown, after paring a pennyworth of silver from it, seemed a minute, an almost imperceptible, fault. Even while the nation was crying out most loudly under the distress which the state of the currency had produced, every individual who was capitally punished for contributing to bring the currency into that state had the general sympathy on his side. Constables were unwilling to arrest the offenders. Justices were unwilling to commit. Witnesses were unwilling to tell the whole truth. Juries were unwilling to pronounce the word Guilty. The convictions, therefore, numerous as they might seem, were few indeed when compared with the offences; and the offenders who were convicted looked on themselves as murdered men, and were firm in the belief that their sin, if sin it were, was as venial as that of a schoolboy who goes nutting in the wood of a neighbour. All the eloquence of the ordinary could seldom induce them to conform to the wholesome usage of acknowledging in their dying speeches the enormity of their wickedness.

The evil proceeded with constantly accelerating velocity. At length in the autumn of 1695 it could hardly be said that the country possessed, for practical purposes, any measure of the value of commodities. It was a mere chance whether what was called a shilling was really tenpence, sixpence or a groat. The results of some experiments which were tried at that time deserve to be mentioned. The officers of the Exchequer weighed fifty seven thousand two hundred pounds of hammered money which had recently been paid in. The weight ought to have been above two hundred and twenty thousand ounces. It proved to be under one hundred and fourteen thousand ounces. Three eminent London goldsmiths were invited to send a hundred pounds each in current silver to be tried by the balance. Three hundred pounds ought to have weighed about twelve hundred ounces. The actual weight proved to be six hundred and twenty four ounces. The same test was applied in various parts of the kingdom. It was found that a hundred pounds, which should have weighed about four hundred ounces, did actually weigh at Bristol two hundred and forty ounces, at Cambridge two hundred and three, at Exeter one hundred and eighty, and at Oxford only one hundred and sixteen. There were, indeed, some northern districts into which the clipped money had only begun to find its way. An honest Quaker, who lived in one of these districts, recorded, in some notes which are still extant, the amazement with which, when he travelled southward, shopkeepers and innkeepers stared at the broad and heavy halfcrowns with which he paid his way. They asked whence he came, and where such money was to be found. The guinea which he purchased for twenty two shillings at Lancaster bore a different value at every stage of his journey. When he reached London it was worth thirty shillings, and would indeed have been worth more had not the government fixed that rate as the highest at which gold should be received in the payment of taxes.

The evils produced by this state of the currency were not such as have generally been thought worthy to occupy a prominent place in history. Yet it may well be doubted whether all the misery which had been inflicted on the English nation in a quarter of a century by bad Kings, bad Ministers, bad Parliaments and bad Judges, was equal to the misery caused in a single year by bad crowns and bad shillings. Those events which furnish the best themes for pathetic or indignant eloquence are not always those which most affect the happiness of the great body of the people. The misgovernment of Charles and James, gross as it had been, had not prevented the common business of life from going steadily and prosperously on. While the honour and independence of the State were sold to a foreign power, while chartered rights were invaded, while funda- mental laws were violated, hundreds of thousands of quiet, honest and industrious families laboured and traded, ate their meals and lay down to rest, in comfort and security. Whether Whigs or Tories, Protestants or Jesuits were uppermost, the grazier drove his beasts to market: the grocer weighed out his currants: the draper measured out his broadcloth: the hum of buyers and sellers was as loud as ever in the towns: the harvest home was celebrated as joyously as ever in the hamlets: the cream overflowed the pails of Cheshire: the apple juice foamed in the presses of Herefordshire: the piles of crockery glowed in the furnaces of the Trent; and the barrows of coal rolled fast along the timber railways of the Tyne. But when the great instrument of exchange became thoroughly deranged, all trade, all industry, were smitten as with a palsy. The evil was felt daily and hourly in almost every place and by almost every class, in the dairy and on the threshing floor, by the anvil and by the loom, on the billows of the ocean and in the depths of the mine. Nothing could be purchased without a dispute. Over every counter there was wrangling from morning to night. The workman and his employer had a quarrel as regularly as the Saturday came round. On a fair day or a market day the clamours, the reproaches, the taunts, the curses, were incessant; and it was well if no booth was overturned and no head broken. No merchant would contract to deliver goods without making some stipulation about the quality of the coin in which he was to be paid. Even men of business were often bewildered by the confusion into which all pecuniary transactions were thrown. The simple and the careless were pillaged without mercy by extortioners whose demands grew even more rapidly than the money shrank. The price of the necessaries of life, of shoes, of ale, of oatmeal, rose fast. The labourer found that the bit of metal, which, when he received it, was called a shilling, would hardly, when he wanted to purchase a pot of beer or a loaf of rye bread, go as far as sixpence. Where artisans of more than usual intelligence were collected together in great numbers, as in the dockyard at Chatham, they were able to make their complaints heard and to obtain some redress. But the ignorant and helpless peasant was cruelly ground between one class which would give money only by tale and another which would take it only by weight. Yet his sufferings hardly exceeded those of the unfortunate race of authors. Of the way in which obscure writers were treated we may easily form a judgment from the letters, still extant, of Dryden to his bookseller Tonson. One day Tonson sends forty brass shillings, to say nothing of clipped money. Another day he pays a debt with pieces so bad that none of them will go. The great poet sends them all back, and demands in their place guineas at twenty nine shillings each. "I expect," he says in one letter, "good silver, not such as I have had formerly." "If you have any silver that will go," he says in another letter, "my wife will be glad of it. I lost thirty shillings or more by the last payment of fifty pounds." These complaints and demands, which have been preserved from destruction only by the eminence of the writer, are doubtless merely a fair sample of the correspondence which filled all the mail bags of England during several months.

In the midst of the public distress one class prospered greatly, the bankers; and among the bankers none could in skill or in luck bear a comparison with Charles Duncombe. He had been, not many years before, a goldsmith of very moderate wealth. He had probably, after the fashion of his craft, plied for customers under the arcades of the Royal Exchange, had saluted merchants with profound bows, and had begged to be allowed the honour of keeping their cash. But so dexterously did he now avail himself of the opportunities of profit which the general confusion of prices gave to a moneychanger, that, at the moment when the trade of the kingdom was depressed to the lowest point, he laid down near ninety thousand pounds for the estate of Helmsley in the North Riding of Yorkshire. That great property had, in a troubled time, been bestowed by the Commons of England on their victorious general Fairfax, and had been part of the dower which Fairfax's daughter had brought to the brilliant and dissolute Buckingham. Thither Buckingham, having wasted in mad intemperance, sensual and intellectual, all the choicest bounties of nature and of fortune, had carried the feeble ruins of his fine person and of his fine mind; and there he had closed his chequered life under that humble roof and on that coarse pallet which the great satirist of the succeeding generation described in immortal verse. The spacious domain passed to a new race; and in a few years a palace more splendid and costly than had ever been inhabited by the magnificent Villiers rose amidst the beautiful woods and waters which had been his, and was called by the once humble name of Duncombe.

Since the Revolution the state of the currency had been repeatedly discussed in Parliament. In 1689 a committee of the Commons had been appointed to investigate the subject, but had made no report. In 1690 another committee had reported that immense quantities of silver were carried out of the country by Jews, who, it was said, would do anything for profit. Schemes were formed for encouraging the importation and discouraging the exportation of the precious metals. One foolish bill after another was brought in and dropped. At length, in the beginning of the year 1695, the question assumed so serious an aspect that the Houses applied themselves to it in earnest. The only practical result of their deliberations, however, was a new penal law which, it was hoped, would prevent the clipping of the hammered coin and the melting and exporting of the milled coin. It was enacted that every person who informed against a clipper should be entitled to a reward of forty pounds, that every clipper who informed against two clippers should be entitled to a pardon, and that whoever should be found in possession of silver filings or parings should be burned in the cheek with a redhot iron. Certain officers were empowered to search for bullion. If bullion were found in a house or on board of a ship, the burden of proving that it had never been part of the money of the realm was thrown on the owner. If he failed in making out a satisfactory history of every ingot he was liable to severe penalties. This Act was, as might have been expected, altogether ineffective. During the following summer and autumn, the coins went on dwindling, and the cry of distress from every county in the realm became louder and more piercing.

But happily for England there were among her rulers some who clearly perceived that it was not by halters and branding irons that her decaying industry and commerce could be restored to health. The state of the currency had during some time occupied the serious attention of four eminent men closely connected by public and private ties. Two of them were politicians who had never, in the midst of official and parliamentary business, ceased to love and honour philosophy; and two were philosophers, in whom habits of abstruse meditation had not impaired the homely good sense without which even genius is mischievous in politics. Never had there been an occasion which more urgently required both practical and speculative abilities; and never had the world seen the highest practical and the highest speculative abilities united in an alliance so close, so harmonious, and so honourable as that which bound Somers and Montague to Locke and Newton.

It is much to be lamented that we have not a minute history of the conferences of the men to whom England owed the restoration of her currency and the long series of prosperous years which dates from that restoration. It would be interesting to see how the pure gold of scientific truth found by the two philosophers was mingled by the two statesmen with just that quantity of alloy which was necessary for the working. It would be curious to study the many plans which were propounded, discussed and rejected, some as inefficacious, some as unjust, some as too costly, some as too hazardous, till at length a plan was devised of which the wisdom was proved by the best evidence, complete success.

Newton has left to posterity no exposition of his opinions touching the currency. But the tracts of Locke on this subject are happily still extant; and it may be doubted whether in any of his writings, even in those ingenious and deeply meditated chapters on language which form perhaps the most valuable part of the Essay on the Human Understanding, the force of his mind appears more conspicuously. Whether he had ever been acquainted with Dudley North is not known. In moral character the two men bore little resemblance to each other. They belonged to different parties. Indeed, had not Locke taken shelter from tyranny in Holland, it is by no means impossible that he might have been sent to Tyburn by a jury which Dudley North had packed. Intellectually, however, there was much in common between the Tory and the Whig. They had laboriously thought out, each for himself, a theory of political economy, substantially the same with that which Adam Smith afterwards expounded. Nay, in some respects the theory of Locke and North was more complete and symmetrical than that of their illustrious successor. Adam Smith has often been justly blamed for maintaining, in direct opposition to all his own principles, that the rate of interest ought to be regulated by the State; and he is the more blamable because, long before he was born, both Locke and North had taught that it was as absurd to make laws fixing the price of money as to make laws fixing the price of cutlery or of broad-cloth.

Dudley North died in 1693. A short time before his death he published, without his name, a small tract which contains a concise sketch of a plan for the restoration of the currency. This plan appears to have been substantially the same with that which was afterwards fully developed and ably defended by Locke.

One question, which was doubtless the subject of many anxious deliberations, was whether any thing should be done while the war lasted. In whatever way the restoration of the coin might be effected, great sacrifices must be made, either by the whole community or by a part of the community. And to call for such sacrifices at a time when the nation was already paying taxes such as, ten years before, no financier would have thought it possible to raise, was undoubtedly a course full of danger. Timorous politicians were for delay: but the deliberate conviction of the great Whig leaders was that something must be hazarded, or that every thing was lost. Montague, in particular, is said to have expressed in strong language his determination to kill or cure. If indeed there had been any hope that the evil would merely continue to be what it was, it might have been wise to defer till the return of peace an experiment which must severely try the strength of the body politic. But the evil was one which daily made progress almost visible to the eye. There might have been a recoinage in 1694 with half the risk which must be run in 1696; and, great as would be the risk in 1696, that risk would be doubled if the recoinage were postponed till 1698.

Those politicians whose voice was for delay gave less trouble than another set of politicians, who were for a general and immediate recoinage, but who insisted that the new shilling should be worth only ninepence or ninepence halfpenny. At the head of this party

was William Lowndes, Secretary of the Treasury, and member of
Parliament for the borough of Seaford, a most respectable and
industrious public servant, but much more versed in the details of
his office than in the higher parts of political philosophy. He was
not in the least aware that a piece of metal with the King's head on
it was a commodity of which the price was governed by the same
laws which govern the price of a piece of metal fashioned into a
spoon or a buckle, and that it was no more in the power of Parliament to make the kingdom richer by calling a crown a pound than
to make the kingdom larger by calling a furlong a mile. He seriously
believed, incredible as it may seem, that, if the ounce of silver were
divided into seven shillings instead of five, foreign nations would
sell us their wines and their silks for a smaller number of ounces.
He had a considerable following, composed partly of dull men who
really believed what he told them, and partly of shrewd men who
were perfectly willing to be authorised by law to pay a hundred
pounds with eighty. Had his arguments prevailed, the evils of a
vast confiscation would have been added to all the other evils which
afflicted the nation: public credit, still in its tender and sickly
infancy, would have been destroyed; and there would have been
much risk of a general mutiny of the fleet and army. Happily
Lowndes was completely refuted by Locke in a paper drawn up
for the use of Somers. Somers was delighted with this little treatise,
and desired that it might be printed. It speedily became the text
book of all the most enlightened politicians in the kingdom, and
may still be read with pleasure and profit. The effect of Locke's
forcible and perspicuous reasoning is greatly heightened by his
evident anxiety to get at the truth, and by the singularly generous
and grateful courtesy with which he treats an antagonist of powers
far inferior to his own. Flamsteed, the Astronomer Royal, described the controversy well by saying that the point in dispute was
whether five was six or only five.

Thus far Somers and Montague entirely agreed with Locke: but
as to the manner in which the restoration of the currency ought to
be effected there was some difference of opinion. Locke recommended, as Dudley North had recommended, that the King should
by proclamation fix a near day after which the hammered money
should in all payments pass only by weight. The advantages of this
plan were doubtless great and obvious. It was most simple, and, at
the same time, most efficient. What searching, fining, branding,
hanging, burning, had failed to do would be done in an instant.
The clipping of the hammered pieces, the melting of the milled
pieces would cease. Great quantities of good coin would come

forth from secret drawers and from behind the panels of wainscots. The mutilated silver would gradually flow into the mint, and would come forth again in a form which would make mutilation impossible. In a short time the whole currency of the realm would be in a sound state; and, during the progress of this great change, there would never at any moment be any scarcity of money.

These were weighty considerations; and to the joint authority of North and Locke on such a question great respect is due. Yet it must be owned that their plan was open to one serious objection, which did not indeed altogether escape their notice, but of which they seem to have thought too lightly. The restoration of the currency was a benefit to the whole community. On what principle then was the expense of restoring the currency to be borne by a part of the community? It was most desirable doubtless that the words pound and shilling should again have a fixed signification, that every man should know what his contracts meant and what his property was worth. But was it just to attain this excellent end by means of which the effect would be that every farmer who had put by a hundred pounds to pay his rent, every trader who had scraped together a hundred pounds to meet his acceptances, would find his hundred pounds reduced in a moment to fifty or sixty? It was not the fault of such a farmer or of such a trader that his crowns and halfcrowns were not of full weight. The government itself was to blame. The evil which the State had caused the State was bound to repair; and it would evidently have been wrong to throw the charge of the reparation on a particular class, merely because that class was so situated that it could conveniently be pillaged. It would have been as reasonable to require the timber merchants to bear the whole cost of fitting out the Channel fleet, or the gunsmiths to bear the whole cost of supplying arms to the regiments in Flanders, as to restore the currency of the kingdom at the expense of those individuals in whose hands the clipped silver happened at a particular moment to be.

Locke declared that he regretted the loss which, if his advice were taken, would fall on the holders of the short money. But it appeared to him that the nation must make a choice between evils. And in truth it was much easier to lay down the general proposition that the expenses of restoring the currency ought to be borne by the public than to devise any mode in which they could without extreme inconvenience and danger be so borne. Was it to be announced that every person who should within a term of a year or half a year carry to the mint a clipped crown should receive in exchange for it a milled crown, and that the difference between the value of the two pieces should be made good out of the public purse? That would be to offer a premium for clipping. The shears would be more busy than ever. The short money would every day become shorter. The difference which the taxpayers would have to make good would probably be greater by a million at the end of the term than at the beginning: and the whole of this million would go to reward malefactors. If only a very short time were allowed for the bringing in of the hammered coin, the danger of further clipping would be reduced to little or nothing; but another danger would be incurred. The silver would flow into the mint so much faster than it could possibly flow out, that there must during some months be a grievous scarcity of money.

A singularly bold and ingenious expedient occurred to Somers and was approved by William. It was that a proclamation should be prepared with great secresy, and published at once in all parts of the kingdom. This proclamation was to announce that hammered coins would thenceforth pass only by weight. But every possessor of such coins was to be invited to deliver them up within three days, in a sealed packet, to the public authorities. The coins were to be examined, numbered, weighed, and returned to the owner with a promissory note entitling him to receive from the Treasury at a future time the difference between the actual quantity of silver in his pieces and the quantity of silver which, according to the standard, those pieces ought to have contained. Had this plan been adopted an immediate stop would have been put to the clipping, the melting and the exporting; and the expense of the restoration of the currency would have been borne, as was right, by the public. The inconvenience arising from a scarcity of money would have been of very short duration: for the mutilated pieces would have been detained only till they could be told and weighed: they would then have been sent back into circulation; and the recoinage would have taken place gradually and without any perceptible suspension or disturbance of trade. But against these great advantages were to be set off hazards, which Somers was prepared to brave, but from which it is not strange that politicians of less elevated character should have shrunk. The course which he recommended to his colleagues was indeed the safest for the country, but was by no means the safest for themselves. His plan could not be successful unless the execution was sudden: the execution could not be sudden if the previous sanction of Parliament were asked and obtained; and to take a step of such fearful importance without the previous sanction of Parliament was to run the risk of censure, impeachment, imprisonment, ruin. The King and the Lord Keeper were alone in the Council. Even Montague quailed; and it was determined to do nothing without the authority of the legislature. Montague undertook to submit to the Commons a scheme, which was not indeed without dangers and inconveniences, but which was probably the best which he could hope to carry.

On the twenty-second of November the Houses met. Foley was on that day again chosen Speaker. On the following day he was presented and approved. The King opened the session with a speech very skilfully framed. He congratulated his hearers on the success of the campaign on the Continent. That success he attributed, in language which must have gratified their feelings, to the bravery of the English army. He spoke of the evils which had arisen from the deplorable state of the coin, and of the necessity of applying a speedy remedy. He intimated very plainly his opinion that the expense of restoring the currency ought to be borne by the State: but he declared that he referred the whole matter to the wisdom of his Great Council. Before he concluded he addressed himself particularly to the newly elected House of Commons, and warmly expressed his approbation of the excellent choice which his people had made. The speech was received with a low but very significant hum of assent both from above and from below the bar, and was as favourably received by the public as by the Parliament. In the Commons an address of thanks was moved by Wharton, faintly opposed by Musgrave, adopted without a division, and carried up by the whole House to Kensington. At the palace the loyalty of the crowd of gentlemen showed itself in a way which would now be thought hardly consistent with senatorial gravity. When refreshments were handed round in the antechamber, the Speaker filled his glass, and proposed two toasts, the health of King William, and confusion to King Lewis; and both were drunk with loud acclamations. Yet near observers could perceive that, though the representatives of the nation were as a body zealous for civil liberty and for the Protestant religion, and though they were prepared to endure every thing rather than see their country again reduced to vassalage, they were anxious and dispirited. All were thinking of the state of the coin: all were saying that something must be done; and all acknowledged that they did not know what could be done. "I am afraid," said a member who expressed what many felt, "that the nation can bear neither the disease nor the cure."

There was indeed a minority by which the difficulties and dangers of that crisis were seen with malignant delight; and of that minority the keenest, boldest and most factious leader was Howe, whom poverty had made more acrimonious than ever. He moved that the

House should resolve itself into a Committee on the State of the Nation; and the Ministry,—for that word may now with propriety be used,—readily consented. Indeed the great question touching the currency could not be brought forward more conveniently than in such a Committee. When the Speaker had left the chair, Howe harangued against the war as vehemently as he had in former years harangued for it. He called for peace, peace on any terms. The nation, he said, resembled a wounded man, fighting desperately on, with blood flowing in torrents. During a short time the spirit might bear up the frame: but faintness must soon come on. No moral energy could long hold out against physical exhaustion. He found very little support. The great majority of his hearers were fully determined to put every thing to hazard rather than submit to France. It was sneeringly remarked that the state of his own finances had suggested to him the image of a man bleeding to death, and that, if a cordial were administered to him in the form of a salary, he would trouble himself little about the drained veins of the commonwealth. "We did not," said the Whig orators, "degrade ourselves by suing for peace when our flag was chased out of our own Channel, when Tourville's fleet lay at anchor in Torbay, when the Irish nation was in arms against us, when every post from the Netherlands brought news of some disaster, when we had to contend against the genius of Louvois in the Cabinet and of Luxemburg in the field. And are we to turn suppliants now, when no hostile squadron dares to show itself even in the Mediterranean, when our arms are victorious on the Continent, when God has removed the great statesman and the great soldier whose abilities long frustrated our efforts, and when the weakness of the French administration indicates, in a manner not to be mistaken, the ascendency of a female favourite?" Howe's suggestion was contemptuously rejected; and the Committee proceeded to take into consideration the state of the currency.

Meanwhile the newly liberated presses of the capital never rested a moment. Innumerable pamphlets and broadsides about the coin lay on the counters of the booksellers, and were thrust into the hands of members of Parliament in the lobby. In one of the most curious and amusing of these pieces Lewis and his ministers are introduced, expressing the greatest alarm lest England should make herself the richest country in the world by the simple expedient of calling ninepence a shilling, and confidently predicting that, if the old standard were maintained, there would be another revolution. Some writers vehemently objected to the proposition that the public should bear the expense of restoring the currency: some urged the government to take this opportunity of assimilating the money of England to the money of neighbouring nations: one projector was for coining guilders; another for coining dollars.

Within the walls of Parliament the debates continued during several anxious days. At length Montague, after defeating, first those who were for letting things remain unaltered till the peace, and then those who were for the little shilling, carried eleven resolutions in which the outlines of his own plan were set forth. It was resolved that the money of the kingdom should be recoined according to the old standard both of weight and of fineness; that all the new pieces should be milled; that the loss on the clipped pieces should be borne by the public; that a time should be fixed after which no clipped money should pass, except in payments to the government; and that a later time should be fixed, after which no clipped money should pass at all. What divisions took place in the Committee cannot be ascertained. When the resolutions were reported there was one division. It was on the question whether the old standard of weight should be maintained. The Noes were a hundred and fourteen; the Ayes two hundred and twenty five.

It was ordered that a bill founded on the resolutions should be brought in. A few days later the Chancellor of the Exchequer explained to the Commons, in a Committee of Ways and Means, the plan by which he proposed to meet the expense of the recoinage. It was impossible to estimate with precision the charge of making good the deficiencies of the clipped money. But it was certain that at least twelve hundred thousand pounds would be required. Twelve hundred thousand pounds the Bank of England undertook to advance on good security. It was a maxim received among financiers that no security which the government could offer was so good as the old hearth money had been. That tax, odious as it was to the great majority of those who paid it, was remembered with regret at the Treasury and in the City. It occurred to the Chancellor of the Exchequer that it might be possible to devise an impost on houses, which might be not less productive nor less certain than the hearth money, but which might press less heavily on the poor, and might be collected by a less vexatious process. The number of hearths in a house could not be ascertained without domiciliary visits. The windows a collector might count without passing the threshold. Montague proposed that the inhabitants of cottages, who had been cruelly harassed by the chimney men, should be altogether exempted from the new duty. His plan was approved by the Committee of Ways and Means, and was sanctioned by the House without a division. Such was the origin of the window tax, a tax which, though doubtless a great evil, must be considered as a blessing when compared with the curse from which it was the means of rescuing the nation.

Thus far things had gone smoothly. But now came a crisis which required the most skilful steering. The news that the Parliament and the government were determined on a reform of the currency produced an ignorant panic among the common people. Every man wished to get rid of his clipped crowns and halfcrowns. No man liked to take them. There were brawls approaching to riots in half the streets of London. The Jacobites, always full of joy and hope in a day of adversity and public danger, ran about with eager looks and noisy tongues. The health of King James was publicly drunk in taverns and on ale benches. Many members of Parliament, who had hitherto supported the government, began to waver; and, that nothing might be wanting to the difficulties of the conjuncture, a dispute on a point of privilege arose between the Houses. The Recoinage Bill, framed in conformity with Montague's resolutions, had gone up to the Peers and had come back with amendments, some of which, in the opinion of the Commons, their Lordships had no right to make. The emergency was too serious to admit of delay. Montague brought in a new bill, which was in fact his former bill modified in some points to meet the wishes of the Lords: the Lords, though not perfectly contented with the new bill, passed it without any alteration; and the royal assent was immediately given. The fourth of May, a date long remembered over the whole kingdom and especially in the capital, was fixed as the day on which the government would cease to receive the clipped money in payment of taxes.

The principles of the Recoinage Act are excellent. But some of the details, both of that Act and of a supplementary Act which was passed at a later period of the session, seem to prove that Montague had not fully considered what legislation can, and what it cannot, effect. For example, he persuaded the Parliament to enact that it should be penal to give or take more than twenty two shillings for a guinea. It may be confidently affirmed that this enactment was not suggested or approved by Locke. He well knew that the high price of gold was not the evil which afflicted the State, but merely a symptom of that evil, and that a fall in the price of gold would inevitably follow, and could by no human power or ingenuity be made to precede, the recoinage of the silver. In fact, the penalty seems to have produced no effect whatever. Till the milled silver was in circulation, the guinea continued, in spite of the law, to pass for thirty shillings. When the milled silver became plentiful, the guinea fell; and did not stop at twenty two shillings, but continued till it reached twenty one shillings and sixpence.

Early in February the panic which had been caused by the first debates on the currency subsided; and, from that time till the fourth of May, the want of money was not very severely felt. The recoinage began. Ten furnaces were erected in the garden behind the Treasury, which was then a part of Whitehall, and which lay between the Banquetting House and the river. Every day huge heaps of pared and defaced crowns and shillings were turned into massy ingots which were instantly sent off to the mint in the Tower.

DARIEN

IT is necessary to go back some years for the purpose of tracing the origin and progress of this quarrel. Few portions of our history are more interesting or instructive: but few have been more obscured and distorted by passion and prejudice. The story is an exciting one; and it has generally been told by writers whose judgment had been perverted by strong national partiality. Their invectives and lamentations have still to be temperately examined; and it may well be doubted whether, even now, after the lapse of more than a century and a half, feelings hardly compatible with temperate examination will not be stirred up in many minds by the name of Darien. In truth that name is associated with calamities so cruel that the recollection of them may not unnaturally disturb the equipoise even of a fair and sedate mind.

The man who brought these calamities on his country was not a mere visionary or a mere swindler. He was that William Paterson whose name is honourably associated with the auspicious commencement of a new era in English commerce and in English finance. His plan of a national bank, having been examined and approved by the most eminent statesmen who sate in the Parliament house at Westminster and by the most eminent merchants who walked the Exchange of London, had been carried into execution with signal success. He thought, and perhaps thought with reason, that his services had been ill requited. He was, indeed, one of the original Directors of the great corporation which owed its existence to him; but he was not reelected. It may easily be believed that his colleagues, citizens of ample fortune and of long experience in the practical part of trade, aldermen, wardens of companies, heads of firms well known in every Burse throughout the civilised world, were not well pleased to see among them in Grocers' Hall a foreign adventurer whose whole capital consisted in an inventive brain and a persuasive tongue. Some of them were probably weak enough to dislike him for being a Scot: some were probably mean enough to be jealous of his parts and knowledge: and even persons who were not unfavourably disposed to him might have discovered, before they had known him long, that, with all his cleverness, he was deficient in common sense; that his mind was full of schemes which, at the first glance, had a specious aspect, but which, on closer examination, appeared to be impracticable or pernicious; and that the benefit which the public had derived from one happy project formed by him would be very dearly purchased if it were taken for granted that all his other projects must be equally happy. Disgusted by what he considered as the ingratitude of the English, he repaired to the Continent, in the hope that he might be able to interest the traders of the Hanse Towns and the princes of the German Empire in his plans. From the Continent he returned unsuccessful to London; and then at length the thought that he might be more justly appreciated by his countrymen than by strangers seems to have risen in his mind. Just at this time he fell in with Fletcher of Saltoun, who happened to be in England. These eccentric men soon became intimate. Each of them had his monomania; and the two monomanias suited each other perfectly. Fletcher's whole soul was possessed by a sore, jealous, punctilious patriotism. His heart was ulcerated by the thought of the poverty, the feebleness, the political insignificance of Scotland, and of the indignities which she had suffered at the hand of her powerful and opulent neighbour. When he talked of her wrongs his dark meagre face took its sternest expression: his habitual frown grew blacker; and his eyes flashed more than their wonted fire. Paterson, on the other hand, firmly believed himself to have discovered the means of making any state which would follow his counsel great and prosperous in a time which, when compared with the life of an individual, could hardly be called long, and which, in the life of a nation, was but as a moment. There is not the least reason to believe that he was dishonest. Indeed he would have found more difficulty in deceiving others had he not begun by deceiving himself. His faith in his own schemes was strong even to martyrdom; and the eloquence with which he illustrated and defended them had all the charm of sincerity and of enthusiasm. Very seldom has any blunder committed by fools, or any villany devised by impostors, brought on any society miseries so great as the dreams of these two friends, both of them men of integrity and both of them men of parts, were destined to bring on Scotland.

In 1695 the pair went down together to their native country.

The Parliament of that country was then about to meet under the presidency of Tweeddale, an old acquaintance and country neighbour of Fletcher. On Tweeddale the first attack was made. He was a shrewd, cautious, old politician. Yet it should seem that he was not able to hold out against the skill and energy of the assailants. Perhaps, however, he was not altogether a dupe. The public mind was at that moment violently agitated. Men of all parties were clamouring for an inquiry into the slaughter of Glencoe. There was reason to fear that the session which was about to commence would be stormy. In such circumstances the Lord High Commissioner might think that it would be prudent to appease the anger of the Estates by offering an almost irresistible bait to their cupidity. If such was the policy of Tweeddale, it was, for the moment, eminently successful. The Parliament, which met burning with indignation, was soothed into good humour. The blood of the murdered Macdonalds continued to cry for vengeance in vain. The schemes of Paterson, brought forward under the patronage of the ministers of the Crown, were sanctioned by the unanimous voice of the Legislature.

The great projector was the idol of the whole nation. Men spoke to him with more profound respect than to the Lord High Commissioner. His antechamber was crowded with solicitors desirous to catch some drops of that golden shower of which he was supposed to be the dispenser. To be seen walking with him in the High Street, to be honoured by him with a private interview of a quarter of an hour, were enviable distinctions. He, after the fashion of all the false prophets who have deluded themselves and others, drew new faith in his own lie from the credulity of his disciples. His countenance, his voice, his gestures, indicated boundless self-importance. When he appeared in public he looked,—such is the language of one who probably had often seen him,—like Atlas conscious that a world was on his shoulders. But the airs which he gave himself only heightened the respect and admiration which he inspired. His demeanour was regarded as a model. Scotchmen who wished to be thought wise looked as like Paterson as they could.

His plan, though as yet disclosed to the public only by glimpses, was applauded by all classes, factions and sects, lords, merchants, advocates, divines, Whigs and Jacobites, Cameronians and Episcopalians. In truth, of all the ten thousand bubbles of which history has preserved the memory, none was ever more skilfully puffed into existence; none ever soared higher, or glittered more brilliantly; and none ever burst with a more lamentable explosion.

There was, however, a certain mixture of truth in the magnificent day dream which produced such fatal effects.

Scotland was, indeed, not blessed with a mild climate or a fertile soil. But the richest spots that had ever existed on the face of the earth had been spots quite as little favoured by nature. It was on a bare rock, surrounded by deep sea, that the streets of Tyre were piled up to a dizzy height. On that sterile crag were woven the robes of Persian satraps and Sicilian tyrants: there were fashioned silver bowls and chargers for the banquets of kings: and there Pomeranian amber was set in Lydian gold to adorn the necks of queens. In the warehouses were collected the fine linen of Egypt and the odorous gums of Arabia; the ivory of India, and the tin of Britain. In the port lay fleets of great ships which had weathered the storms of the Euxine and the Atlantic. Powerful and wealthy colonies in distant parts of the world looked up with filial reverence to the little island; and despots, who trampled on the laws and outraged the feelings of all the nations between the Hydaspes and the Ægean, condescended to court the population of that busy hive. At a later period, on a dreary bank formed by the soil which the Alpine streams swept down to the Adriatic, rose the palaces of Venice. Within a space which would not have been thought large enough for one of the parks of a rude northern baron were collected riches far exceeding those of a northern kingdom. In almost every one of the private dwellings which fringed the Great Canal were to be seen plate, mirrors, jewellery, tapestry, paintings, carving, such as might move the envy of the master of Holyrood. In the arsenal were munitions of war sufficient to maintain a contest against the whole power of the Ottoman Empire. And, before the grandeur of Venice had declined, another commonwealth, still less favoured, if possible, by nature, had rapidly risen to a power and opulence which the whole civilised world contemplated with envy and admiration. On a desolate marsh overhung by fogs and exhaling diseases, a marsh where there was neither wood nor stone, neither firm earth nor drinkable water, a marsh from which the ocean on one side and the Rhine on the other were with difficulty kept out by art, was to be found the most prosperous community in Europe. The wealth which was collected within five miles of the Stadthouse of Amsterdam would purchase the fee simple of Scotland. And why should this be? Was there any reason to believe that nature had bestowed on the Phœnician, on the Venetian, or on the Hollander, a larger measure of activity, of ingenuity, of forethought, of self command, than on the citizen of Edinburgh or Glasgow? The truth was that, in all those qualities which conduce to success in life, and especially in commercial life, the Scot had never been surpassed; perhaps he had never been equalled. All that was necessary was that his energy should take a proper direction; and a proper direction Paterson undertook to give.

His esoteric project was the original project of Christopher Columbus, extended and modified. Columbus had hoped to establish a communication between our quarter of the world and India across the great western ocean. But he was stopped by an unexpected obstacle. The American continent, stretching far north and far south into cold and inhospitable regions, presented what seemed an insurmountable barrier to his progress; and, in the same year in which he first set foot on that continent, Gama reached Malabar by doubling the Cape of Good Hope. The consequence was that during two hundred years the trade of Europe with the remoter parts of Asia had been carried on by rounding the immense peninsula of Africa. Paterson now revived the project of Columbus, and persuaded himself and others that it was possible to carry that project into effect in such a manner as to make his country the greatest emporium that had ever existed on our globe.

For this purpose it was necessary to occupy in America some spot which might be a resting place between Scotland and India. It was true that almost every habitable part of America had already been seized by some European power. Paterson, however, imagined that one province, the most important of all, had been overlooked by the short-sighted cupidity of vulgar politicians and vulgar traders. The isthmus which joined the two great continents of the New World remained, according to him, unappropriated. Great Spanish vice-royalties, he said, lay on the east and on the west; but the mountains and forests of Darien were abandoned to rude tribes which followed their own usages and obeyed their own princes. He had been in that part of the world, in what character was not quite clear. Some said that he had gone thither to convert the Indians, and some that he had gone thither to rob the Spaniards. But, missionary or pirate, he had visited Darien, and had brought away none but delightful recollections. The havens, he averred, were capacious and secure: the sea swarmed with turtle: the country was so mountainous that, within nine degrees of the equator, the climate was temperate; and yet the inequalities of the ground offered no impediment to the conveyance of goods. Nothing would be easier than to construct roads along which a string of mules or a wheeled carriage might in the course of a single day pass from sea to sea. The soil was, to the depth of several feet, a rich black mould, on which a profusion of valuable herbs and fruits grew spontaneously, and on which all the choicest productions of tropical regions might easily be raised by human industry and art; and yet the exuberant fertility of the earth had not tainted the purity of the air. Considered merely as a place of residence, the isthmus was a paradise. A colony placed there could not fail to prosper, even if it had no wealth except what was derived from agriculture. But agriculture was a secondary object in the colonization of Darien. Let but that precious neck of land be occupied by an intelligent, an enterprising, a thrifty race; and, in a few years, the whole trade between India and Europe must be drawn to that point. The tedious and perilous passage round Africa would soon be abandoned. The merchant would no longer expose his cargoes to the mountainous billows and capricious gales of the Antarctic seas. The greater part of the voyage from Europe to Darien, and the whole voyage from Darien to the richest kingdoms of Asia, would be a rapid yet easy gliding before the trade winds over blue and sparkling waters. The voyage back across the Pacific would, in the latitude of Japan, be almost equally speedy and pleasant. Time, labour, money, would be saved. The returns would come in more quickly. Fewer hands would be required to navigate the ships. The loss of a vessel would be a rare event. The trade would increase fast. In a short time it would double; and it would all pass through Darien. Whoever possessed that door of the sea, that key of the universe,—such were the bold figures which Paterson loved to employ,—would give law to both hemispheres; and would, by peaceful arts, without shedding one drop of blood, establish an empire as splendid as that of Cyrus or Alexander. Of the kingdoms of Europe, Scotland was, as yet, the poorest and the least considered. If she would but occupy Darien, if she would but become one great free port, one great warehouse for the wealth which the soil of Darien might produce, and for the still greater wealth which would be poured into Darien from Canton and Siam, from Ceylon and the Moluccas, from the mouths of the Ganges and the Gulf of Cambay, she would at once take her place in the first rank among nations. No rival would be able to contend with her either in the West Indian or in the East Indian trade. The beggarly country, as it had been insolently called by the inhabitants of warmer and more fruitful regions, would be the great mart for the choicest luxuries, sugar, rum, coffee, chocolate, tobacco, the tea and porcelain of China, the muslin of Dacca, the shawls of Cashmere, the diamonds of Golconda, the pearls of Karrack, the delicious birds' nests of Nicobar, cinnamon and pepper, ivory and sandal wood. From Scotland would come all the finest jewels and brocade worn by duchesses at the balls of St. James's and Versailles. From Scotland would come all the saltpetre which would furnish the means of war to the fleets and armies of contending potentates. And on all the vast riches which would be constantly passing through the little kingdom a toll would be paid which would remain behind. There would be a prosperity such as might seem fabulous, a prosperity of which every Scotchman, from the peer to the cadie, would partake. Soon, all along the now desolate shores of the Forth and Clyde, villas and pleasure grounds would be as thick as along the edges of the Dutch canals. Edinburgh would vie with London and Paris; and the baillie of Glasgow or Dundee would have as stately and well furnished a mansion, and as fine a gallery of pictures, as any burgomaster of Amsterdam.

This magnificent plan was at first but partially disclosed to the public. A colony was to be planted: a vast trade was to be opened between both the Indies and Scotland: but the name of Darien was as yet pronounced only in whispers by Paterson and by his most confidential friends. He had however shown enough to excite boundless hopes and desires. How well he succeeded in inspiring others with his own feelings is sufficiently proved by the memorable Act to which the Lord High Commissioner gave the Royal sanction on the 26th of June 1695. By this Act some persons who were named, and such other persons as should join with them, were formed into a corporation, which was to be named the Company of Scotland trading to Africa and the Indies. The amount of the capital to be employed was not fixed by law; but it was provided that one half of the stock at least must be held by Scotchmen resident in Scotland, and that no stock which had been originally held by a Scotchman resident in Scotland should ever be transferred to any but a Scotchman resident in Scotland. An entire monopoly of the trade with Asia, Africa and America, for a term of thirty one years, was granted to the Company. All goods imported by the Company were during twenty one years to be duty free, with the exception of foreign sugar and tobacco. Sugar and tobacco grown on the Company's own plantations were exempted from all taxation. Every member and every servant of the Company was to be privileged against impressment and arrest. If any of these privileged persons was impressed or arrested, the Company was authorised to release him, and to demand the assistance both of the civil and of the military power. The Company was authorised to take possession of unoccupied territories in any part of Asia, Africa or America, and there to plant colonies, to build towns and forts, to impose taxes, and to provide magazines, arms and ammunition, to raise troops, to wage war, to conclude treaties; and the King was made to promise that, if any foreign state should injure the Company, he would interpose, and would, at the public charge, obtain reparation. Lastly it was provided that, in order to give greater security and solemnity to this most exorbitant grant, the whole substance of the Act should be set forth in Letters Patent to which the Chancellor was directed to put the Great Seal without delay.

The letters were drawn: the Great Seal was affixed: the subscription books were opened; the shares were fixed at a hundred pounds sterling each; and from the Pentland Firth to the Solway Firth every man who had a hundred pounds was impatient to put down his name. About two hundred and twenty thousand pounds were actually paid up. This may not, at first sight, appear a large sum to those who remember the bubbles of 1825 and of 1845, and would assuredly not have sufficed to defray the charge of three months of war with Spain. Yet the effort was marvellous when it may be affirmed with confidence that the Scotch people voluntarily contributed for the colonisation of Darien a larger proportion of their substance than any other people ever, in the same space of time, voluntarily contributed to any commercial undertaking. A great part of Scotland was then as poor and rude as Iceland now is. There were five or six shires which did not altogether contain so many guineas and crowns as were tossed about every day by the shovels of a single goldsmith in Lombard Street. Even the nobles had very little ready money. They generally took a large part of their rents in kind, and were thus able, on their own domains, to live plentifully and hospitably. But there were many esquires in Kent and Somersetshire who received from their tenants a greater quantity of gold and silver than a Duke of Gordon or a Marquess of Atholl drew from extensive provinces. The pecuniary remuneration of the clergy was such as would have moved the pity of the most needy curate who thought it a privilege to drink his ale and smoke his pipe in the kitchen of an English manor house. Even in the fertile Merse there were parishes of which the minister received only from four to eight pounds sterling in cash. The official income of the Lord President of the Court of Session was only five hundred a year; that of the Lord Justice Clerk only four hundred a year. The land tax of the whole kingdom was fixed some years later by the Treaty of Union at little more than half the land tax of the single county of Norfolk. Four hundred thousand pounds probably bore as great a ratio to the wealth of Scotland then as forty millions would bear now.

The list of the members of the Darien Company deserves to be examined. The number of shareholders was about fourteen hundred. The largest quantity of stock registered in one name was three thousand pounds. The heads of three noble houses took three thousand pounds each, the Duke of Hamilton, the Duke of Queensbury and Lord Belhaven, a man of ability, spirit and patriotism, who had entered into the design with enthusiasm not inferior to that of Fletcher. Argyle held fifteen hundred pounds. John Dalrymple, but too well known as the Master of Stair, had just succeeded to his father's title and estate, and was now Viscount Stair. He put down his name for a thousand pounds. The number of Scotch peers who subscribed was between thirty and forty. The City of Edinburgh, in its corporate capacity, took three thousand pounds, the City of Glasgow three thousand, the City of Perth two thousand. But the great majority of the subscribers contributed only one hundred or two hundred pounds each. A very few divines who were settled in the capital or in other large towns were able to purchase shares. It is melancholy to see in the roll the name of more than one professional man whose paternal anxiety led him to lay out probably all his hardly earned savings in purchasing a hundred pound share for each of his children. If, indeed, Paterson's predictions had been verified, such a share would, according to the notions of that age and country, have been a handsome portion for the daughter of a writer or a surgeon.

That the Scotch are a people eminently intelligent, wary, resolute and self possessed is obvious to the most superficial observation. That they are a people peculiarly liable to dangerous fits of passion and delusions of the imagination is less generally acknowledged, but is not less true. The whole kingdom seemed to have gone mad. Paterson had acquired an influence resembling rather that of the founder of a new religion, that of a Mahomet, that of a Joseph Smith, than that of a commercial projector. Blind faith in a religion, fanatical zeal for a religion, are too common to astonish us. But such faith and zeal seem strangely out of place in the transactions of the money market. It is true that we are judging after the event. But before the event materials sufficient for the forming of a sound judgment were within the reach of all who cared to use them. It seems incredible that men of sense, who had only a vague and general notion of Paterson's scheme, should have staked everything on the success of that scheme. It seems more incredible still that men to whom the details of that scheme had been confided should not have looked into any of the common books of history or geography in which an account of Darien might have been found, and should not have asked themselves the simple question, whether

Spain was likely to endure a Scotch colony in the heart of her Transatlantic dominions. It was notorious that she claimed the sovereignty of the isthmus on specious, nay on solid, grounds. A Spaniard had been the first discoverer of the coast of Darien. A Spaniard had built a town and established a government on that coast. A Spaniard had, with great labour and peril, crossed the mountainous neck of land, had seen rolling beneath him the vast Pacific, never before revealed to European eyes, had descended, sword in hand, into the waves up to his girdle, and had there solemnly taken possession of sea and shore in the name of the Crown of Castile. It was true that the region which Paterson described as a paradise had been found by the first Castilian settlers to be a land of misery and death. The poisonous air, exhaled from rank jungle and stagnant water, had compelled them to remove to the neighbouring haven of Panama; and the Red Indians had been contemptuously permitted to live after their own fashion on the pestilential soil. But that soil was still considered, and might well be considered, by Spain as her own. In many countries there were tracts of morass, of mountain, of forest, in which governments did not think it worth while to be at the expense of maintaining order, and in which rude tribes enjoyed by connivance a kind of independence. It was not necessary for the members of the Company of Scotland trading to Africa and the Indies to look very far for an example. In some highland districts, not more than a hundred miles from Edinburgh, dwelt clans which had always regarded the authority of King, Parliament, Privy Council and Court of Session, quite as little as the aboriginal population of Darien regarded the authority of the Spanish Viceroys and Audiences. Yet it would surely have been thought an outrageous violation of public law in the King of Spain to take possession of Appin and Lochaber. And would it be a less outrageous violation of public law in the Scots to seize on a province in the very centre of his possessions, on the plea that this province was in the same state in which Appin and Lochaber had been during centuries?

So grossly unjust was Paterson's scheme; and yet it was less unjust than impolitic. Torpid as Spain had become, there was still one point on which she was exquisitely sensitive. The slightest encroachment of any other European power even on the outskirts of her American dominions sufficed to disturb her repose and to brace her paralysed nerves. To imagine that she would tamely suffer adventurers from one of the most insignificant kingdoms of the Old World to form a settlement in the midst of her empire, within a day's sail of Portobello on one side and of Carthagena on the other, was ludicrously absurd. She would have been just as likely to let them take possession of the Escurial. It was, therefore, evident that, before the new Company could even begin its commercial operations, there must be a war with Spain and a complete triumph over Spain. What means had the Company of waging such a war, and what chance of achieving such a triumph? The ordinary revenue of Scotland in time of peace was between sixty and seventy thousand a year. The extraordinary supplies granted to the Crown during the war with France had amounted perhaps to as much more. Spain, it is true, was no longer the Spain of Pavia and Lepanto. But, even in her decay, she possessed in Europe resources which exceeded thirty fold those of Scotland; and in America, where the struggle must take place, the disproportion was still greater. The Spanish fleets and arsenals were doubtless in wretched condition. But there were Spanish fleets; there were Spanish arsenals. The galleons, which sailed every year from Seville to the neighbourhood of Darien and from the neighbourhood of Darien back to Seville, were in tolerable condition, and formed, by themselves, a considerable armament. Scotland had not a single ship of the line, nor a single dockyard where such a ship could be built. A marine sufficient to overpower that of Spain must be, not merely equipped and manned, but created. An armed force sufficient to defend the isthmus against the whole power of the viceroyalties of Mexico and Peru must be sent over five thousand miles of ocean. What was the charge of such an expedition likely to be? Oliver had, in the preceding generation, wrested a West Indian island from Spain: but, in order to do this, Oliver, a man who thoroughly understood the administration of war, who wasted nothing, and who was excellently served, had been forced to spend, in a single year, on his navy alone, twenty times the ordinary revenue of Scotland; and, since his days, war had been constantly becoming more and more costly.

It was plain that Scotland could not alone support the charge of a contest with the enemy whom Paterson was bent on provoking. And what assistance was she likely to have from abroad? Undoubtedly the vast colonial empire and the narrow colonial policy of Spain were regarded with an evil eye by more than one great maritime power. But there was no great maritime power which would not far rather have seen the isthmus between the Atlantic and the Pacific in the hands of Spain than in the hands of the Darien Company. Lewis could not but dread whatever tended to aggrandise a state governed by William. To Holland the East India trade was as the apple of her eye. She had been the chief gainer by the discoveries of Gama; and it might be expected that she would do all that could be done by craft, and, if need were, by violence, rather than suffer any rival to be to her what she had been to Venice. England remained; and Paterson was sanguine enough to flatter himself that England might be induced to lend her powerful aid to the Company. He and Lord Belhaven repaired to London, opened an office in Clement's Lane, formed a Board of Directors auxiliary to the Central Board at Edinburgh, and invited the capitalists of the Royal Exchange to subscribe for the stock which had not been reserved for Scotchmen resident in Scotland. A few moneyed men were allured by the bait: but the clamour of the City was loud and menacing; and from the City a feeling of indignation spread fast through the country. In this feeling there was undoubtedly a large mixture of evil. National antipathy operated on some minds, religious antipathy on others. But it is impossible to deny that the anger which Paterson's schemes excited throughout the south of the island was, in the main, just and reasonable. Though it was not yet generally known in what precise spot his colony was to be planted, there could be little doubt that he intended to occupy some part of America; and there could be as little doubt that such occupation would be resisted. There would be a maritime war; and such a war Scotland had no means of carrying on. The state of her finances was such that she must be quite unable to fit out even a single squadron of moderate size. Before the conflict had lasted three months, she would have neither money nor credit left. These things were obvious to every coffeehouse politician; and it was impossible to believe that they had escaped the notice of men so able and well informed as some who sate in the Privy Council and Parliament at Edinburgh. In one way only could the conduct of these schemers be explained. They meant to make a dupe and a tool of the Southron. The two British kingdoms were so closely connected, physically and politically, that it was scarcely possible for one of them to be at peace with a power with which the other was at war. If the Scotch drew King William into a quarrel, England must, from regard to her own dignity which was bound up with his, support him in it. She was to be tricked into a bloody and expensive contest in the event of which she had no interest; nay, into a contest in which victory would be a greater calamity to her than defeat. She was to lavish her wealth and the lives of her seamen, in order that a set of cunning foreigners might enjoy a monopoly by which she would be the chief sufferer. She was to conquer and defend provinces for this Scotch Corporation; and her reward was to be that her merchants were to be undersold, her customers decoyed away, her exchequer beggared. There would by an end to the disputes between the old East India Company and the new East India Company; for both Companies would be ruined alike. The two great springs of revenue would be dried up together. What would be the receipt of the Customs, what of the Excise, when vast magazines of sugar, rum, tobacco, coffee, chocolate, tea, spices, silks, muslins, all duty free, should be formed along the estuaries of the Forth and of the Clyde, and along the border from the mouth of the Esk to the mouth of the Tweed? What army, what fleet, would be sufficient to protect the interests of the government and of the fair trader when the whole kingdom of Scotland should be turned into one great smuggling establishment? Paterson's plan was simply this, that England should first spend millions in defence of the trade of his Company, and should then be plundered of twice as many millions by means of that very trade.

The cry of the city and of the nation was soon echoed by the legislature. When the Parliament met for the first time after the general election of 1695, Rochester called the attention of the Lords to the constitution and designs of the Company. Several witnesses were summoned to the bar, and gave evidence which produced a powerful effect on the House. "If these Scots are to have their way," said one peer, "I shall go and settle in Scotland, and not stay here to be made a beggar." The Lords resolved to represent strongly to the King the injustice of requiring England to exert her power in support of an enterprise which, if successful, must be fatal to her commerce and to her finances. A representation was drawn up and communicated to the Commons. The Commons eagerly concurred, and complimented the Peers on the promptitude with which their Lordships had, on this occasion, stood forth to protect the public interests. The two Houses went up together to Kensington with the address. William had been under the walls of Namur when the Act for incorporating the Company had been touched with his sceptre at Edinburgh, and had known nothing about that Act till his attention had been called to it by the clamour of his English subjects. He now said, in plain terms, that he had been ill served in Scotland, but that he would try to find a remedy for the evil which had been brought to his notice. The Lord High Commissioner Tweeddale and Secretary Johnstone were immediately dismissed. But the Act which had been passed by their management still continued to be law in Scotland; nor was it in their master's power to undo what they had done.

The Commons were not content with addressing the throne. They instituted an inquiry into the proceedings of the Scotch

Company in London. Belhaven made his escape to his own country, and was there beyond the reach of the Serjeant-at-Arms. But Paterson and some of his confederates were severely examined. It soon appeared that the Board which was sitting in Clement's Lane had done things which were certainly imprudent and perhaps illegal. The Act of Incorporation empowered the directors to take and to administer to their servants an oath of fidelity. But that Act was on the south of the Tweed a nullity. Nevertheless the directors had, in the heart of the City of London, taken and administered this oath, and had thus, by implication, asserted that the powers conferred on them by the legislature of Scotland accompanied them to England. It was resolved that they had been guilty of a high crime and misdemeanour, and that they should be impeached. A committee was appointed to frame articles of impeachment; but the task proved a difficult one; and the prosecution was suffered to drop, not however till the few English capitalists who had at first been friendly to Paterson's project had been terrified into renouncing all connection with him.

Now, surely, if not before, Paterson ought to have seen that his project could end in nothing but shame to himself and ruin to his worshippers. From the first it had been clear that England alone could protect his company against the enmity of Spain; and it was now clear that Spain would be a less formidable enemy than England. It was impossible that his plan could excite greater indignation in the Council of the Indies at Madrid, or in the House of Trade at Seville, than it had excited in London. Unhappily he was given over to a strong delusion; and the blind multitude eagerly followed their blind leader. Indeed his dupes were maddened by that which should have sobered them. The proceedings of the Parliament which sate at Westminster, proceedings just and reasonable in substance, but in manner doubtless harsh and insolent, had roused the angry passions of a nation, feeble indeed in numbers and in material resources, but eminently high spirited. The proverbial pride of the Scotch was too much for their proverbial shrewdness. The votes of the English Lords and Commons were treated with marked contempt. The populace of Edinburgh burned Rochester in effigy. Money was poured faster than ever into the treasury of the Company. A stately house, in Milne Square, then the most modern and fashionable part of Edinburgh, was purchased and fitted up at once as an office and a warehouse. Ships adapted both for war and for trade were required: but the means of building such ships did not exist in Scotland; and no firm in the south of the island was disposed to enter into a contract which might not improbably be considered by the House of Commons as an impeachable offence. It was necessary to have recourse to the dockyards of Amsterdam and Hamburg. At an expense of fifty thousand pounds a few vessels were procured, the largest of which would hardly have ranked as sixtieth in the English navy; and with this force, a force not sufficient to keep the pirates of Sallee in check, the Company threw down the gauntlet to all the maritime powers in the world.

It was not till the summer of 1698 that all was ready for the expedition which was to change the face of the globe. The number of seamen and colonists who embarked at Leith was twelve hundred. Of the colonists many were younger sons of honourable families, or officers who had been disbanded since the peace. It was impossible to find room for all who were desirous of emigrating. It is said that some persons who had vainly applied for a passage hid themselves in dark corners about the ships, and, when discovered, refused to depart, clung to the rigging, and were at last taken on shore by main force. This infatuation is the more extraordinary because few of the adventurers knew to what place they were going. All that was quite certain was that a colony was to be planted somewhere, and to be named Caledonia. The general opinion was that the fleet would steer for some part of the coast of America. But this opinion was not universal. At the Dutch Embassy in Saint James's Square there was an uneasy suspicion that the new Caledonia would be founded among those Eastern spice islands with which Amsterdam had long carried on a lucrative commerce.

The supreme direction of the expedition was entrusted to a Council of Seven. Two Presbyterian chaplains and a precentor were on board. A cargo had been laid in which was afterwards the subject of much mirth to the enemies of the Company, slippers innumerable, four thousand periwigs of all kinds from plain bobs to those magnificent structures which, in that age, towered high above the foreheads and descended to the elbows of men of fashion, bales of Scotch woollen stuffs which nobody within the tropics could wear, and many hundreds of English bibles which neither Spaniard nor Indian could read. Paterson, flushed with pride and hope, not only accompanied the expedition, but took with him his wife, a comely dame, whose heart he had won in London, where she had presided over one of the great coffeehouses in the neighbourhood of the Royal Exchange. At length on the twenty-fifth of July the ships, followed by many tearful eyes, and commended to heaven in many vain prayers, sailed out of the estuary of the Forth.

The voyage was much longer than a voyage to the Antipodes

now is; and the adventurers suffered much. The rations were scanty: there were bitter complaints both of the bread and of the meat; and, when the little fleet, after passing round the Orkneys and Ireland, touched at Madeira, those gentlemen who had fine clothes among their baggage were glad to exchange embroidered coats and laced waistcoats for provisions and wine. From Madeira the adventurers ran across the Atlantic, landed on an uninhabited islet lying between Porto Rico and St. Thomas, took possession of this desolate spot in the name of the Company, set up a tent, and hoisted the white cross of St. Andrew. Soon, however, they were warned off by an officer who was sent from St. Thomas to inform them that they were trespassing on the territory of the King of Denmark. They proceeded on their voyage, having obtained the services of an old buccaneer who knew the coast of Central America well. Under his pilotage they anchored on the first of November close to the Isthmus of Darien. One of the greatest princes of the country soon came on board. The courtiers who attended him, ten or twelve in number, were stark naked: but he was distinguished by a red coat, a pair of cotton drawers, and an old hat. He had a Spanish name, spoke Spanish, and affected the grave deportment of a Spanish don. The Scotch propitiated Andreas, as he was called, by a present of a new hat blazing with gold lace, and assured him that, if he would trade with them, they would treat him better than the Castilians had done.

A few hours later the chiefs of the expedition went on shore, took formal possession of the country, and named it Caledonia. They were pleased with the aspect of a small peninsula about three miles in length and a quarter of a mile in breadth, and determined to fix here the city of New Edinburgh, destined, as they hoped, to be the great emporium of both Indies. The peninsula terminated in a low promontory of about thirty acres, which might easily be turned into an island by digging a trench. The trench was dug; and on the ground thus separated from the main land a fort was constructed: fifty guns were placed on the ramparts; and within the enclosure houses were speedily built and thatched with palm leaves.

Negotiations were opened with the chieftains, as they were called, who governed the neighbouring tribes. Among these savage rulers were found as insatiable a cupidity, as watchful a jealousy, and as punctilious a pride, as among the potentates whose disputes had seemed likely to make the Congress of Ryswick eternal. One prince hated the Spaniards because a fine rifle had been taken away from him by the Governor of Portobello on the plea that such a weapon was too good for a red man. Another loved the Spaniards because they had given him a stick tipped with silver. On the whole, the new comers succeeded in making friends of the aboriginal race. One mighty monarch, the Lewis the Great of the isthmus, who wore with pride a cap of white reeds lined with red silk and adorned with an ostrich feather, seemed well inclined to the strangers, received them hospitably in a palace built of canes and covered with palmetto royal, and regaled them with calabashes of a sort of ale brewed from Indian corn and potatoes. Another chief set his mark to a treaty of peace and alliance with the colony. A third consented to become a vassal of the Company, received with great delight a commission embellished with gold thread and flowered riband, and swallowed to the health of his new masters not a few bumpers of their own brandy.

Meanwhile the internal government of the colony was organised according to a plan devised by the directors at Edinburgh. The settlers were divided into bands of fifty or sixty: each band chose a representative; and thus was formed an assembly which took the magnificent name of Parliament. This Parliament speedily framed a curious code. The first article provided that the precepts, instructions, examples, commands and prohibitions expressed and contained in the Holy Scriptures should have the full force and effect of laws in New Caledonia, an enactment which proves that those who drew it up either did not know what the Holy Scriptures contained or did not know what a law meant. There is another provision which shows not less clearly how far these legislators were from understanding the first principles of legislation. "Benefits received and good services done shall always be generously and thankfully compensated, whether a prior bargain hath been made or not; and, if it shall happen to be otherwise, and the Benefactor obliged justly to complain of the ingratitude, the Ungrateful shall in such case be obliged to give threefold satisfaction at the least." An article much more creditable to the little Parliament, and much needed in a community which was likely to be constantly at war, prohibits, on pain of death, the violation of female captives.

By this time all the Antilles and all the shores of the Gulf of Mexico were in a ferment. The new colony was the object of universal hatred. The Spaniards began to fit out armaments. The chiefs of the French dependencies in the West Indies eagerly offered assistance to the Spaniards. The governors of the English settlements put forth proclamations interdicting all communication with this nest of buccaneers. Just at this time, the Dolphin, a vessel of fourteen guns, which was the property of the Scotch

Company, was driven on shore by stress of weather under the walls of Carthagena. The ship and cargo were confiscated, the crew imprisoned and put in irons. Some of the sailors were treated as slaves, and compelled to sweep the streets and to work on the fortifications. Others, and among them the captain, were sent to Seville to be tried for piracy. Soon an envoy with a flag of truce arrived at Carthagena, and, in the name of the Council of Caledonia, demanded the release of the prisoners. He delivered to the authorities a letter threatening them with the vengeance of the King of Great Britain, and a copy of the Act of Parliament by which the Company had been created. The Castilian governor, who probably knew that William, as Sovereign of England, would not, and, as Sovereign of Scotland, could not, protect the squatters who had occupied Darien, flung away both letter and Act of Parliament with a gesture of contempt, called for a guard, and was with difficulty dissuaded from throwing the messenger into a dungeon. The Council of Caledonia, in great indignation, issued letters of mark and reprisal against Spanish vessels. What every man of common sense must have foreseen had taken place. The Scottish flag had been but a few months planted on the walls of New Edinburgh; and already a war, which Scotland, without the help of England, was utterly unable to sustain, had begun.

By this time it was known in Europe that the mysterious voyage of the adventurers from the Forth had ended at Darien. The ambassador of the Catholic King repaired to Kensington, and complained bitterly to William of this outrageous violation of the law of nations. Preparations were made in the Spanish ports for an expedition against the intruders; and in no Spanish port were there more fervent wishes for the success of that expedition than in the cities of London and Bristol. In Scotland, on the other hand, the exultation was boundless. In the parish churches all over the kingdom the ministers gave public thanks to God for having vouchsafed thus far to protect and bless the infant colony. At some places a day was set apart for religious exercises on this account. In every borough bells were rung; bonfires were lighted; and candles were placed in the windows at night. During some months all the reports which arrived from the other side of the Atlantic were such as to excite hope and joy in the north of the island, and alarm and envy in the south. The colonists, it was asserted, had found rich gold mines, mines in which the precious metal was far more abundant and in a far purer state than on the coast of Guinea. Provisions were plentiful. The rainy season had not proved unhealthy. The settlement was well fortified. Sixty guns were mounted on the ramparts. An immense crop of Indian corn was expected. The aboriginal tribes were friendly. Emigrants from various quarters were coming in. The population of Caledonia had already increased from twelve hundred to ten thousand. The riches of the country,—these are the words of a newspaper of that time,—were great beyond imagination. The mania in Scotland rose to the highest point. Munitions of war and implements of agriculture were provided in large quantities. Multitudes were impatient to emigrate to the land of promise.

In August 1699 four ships, with thirteen hundred men on board, were despatched by the Company to Caledonia. The spiritual care of these emigrants was entrusted to divines of the Church of Scotland. One of these was that Alexander Shields whose Hind Let Loose proves that in his zeal for the Covenant he had forgotten the Gospel. To another, John Borland, we owe the best account of the voyage which is now extant. The General Assembly had charged the chaplains to divide the colonists into congregations, to appoint ruling elders, to constitute a presbytery, and to labour for the propagation of divine truth among the Pagan inhabitants of Darien. The second expedition sailed as the first had sailed, amidst the acclamations and blessings of all Scotland. During the earlier part of September the whole nation was dreaming a delightful dream of prosperity and glory; and triumphing, somewhat maliciously, in the vexation of the English. But, before the close of that month, it began to be rumoured about Lombard Street and Cheapside that letters had arrived from Jamaica with strange news. The colony from which so much had been hoped and dreaded was no more. It had disappeared from the face of the earth. The report spread to Edinburgh, but was received there with scornful incredulity. It was an impudent lie devised by some Englishmen who could not bear to see that, in spite of the votes of the English Parliament, in spite of the proclamations of the governors of the English colonies, Caledonia was waxing great and opulent. Nay, the inventor of the fable was named. It was declared to be quite certain that Secretary Vernon was the man. On the fourth of October was put forth a vehement contradiction of the story. On the fifth the whole truth was known. Letters were received from New York announcing that a few miserable men, the remains of the colony which was to have been the garden, the warehouse, the mart, of the whole world, their bones peeping through their skin, and hunger and fever written in their faces, had arrived in the Hudson.

The grief, the dismay and the rage of those who had a few hours before fancied themselves masters of all the wealth of both Indies may easily be imagined. The Directors, in their fury, lost all self command, and, in their official letters, railed at the betrayers of Scotland, the white-livered deserters. The truth is that those who used these hard words were far more deserving of blame than the wretches whom they had sent to destruction, and whom they now reviled for not staying to be utterly destroyed. Nothing had happened but what might easily have been foreseen. The Company had, in childish reliance on the word of an enthusiastic projector, and in defiance of facts known to every educated man in Europe, taken it for granted that emigrants born and bred within ten degrees of the Arctic Circle would enjoy excellent health within ten degrees of the Equator. Nay, statesmen and scholars had been deluded into the belief that a country which, as they might have read in books so common as those of Hakluyt and Purchas, was noted even among tropical countries for its insalubrity, and had been abandoned by the Spaniards solely on account of its insalubrity, was a Montpelier. Nor had any of Paterson's dupes considered how colonists from Fife or Lothian, who had never in their lives known what it was to feel the heat of a distressing midsummer day, could endure the labour of breaking clods and carrying burdens under the fierce blaze of a vertical sun. It ought to have been remembered that such colonists would have to do for themselves what English, French, Dutch, and Spanish colonists employed Negroes or Indians to do for them. It was seldom indeed that a white freeman in Barbadoes or Martinique, in Guiana or at Panama, was employed in severe bodily labour. But the Scotch who settled at Darien must at first be without slaves, and must therefore dig the trench round their town, build their houses, cultivate their fields, hew wood, and draw water, with their own hands. Such toil in such an atmosphere was too much for them. The provisions which they had brought out had been of no good quality, and had not been improved by lapse of time or by change of climate. The yams and plantains did not suit stomachs accustomed to good oatmeal. The flesh of wild animals and the green fat of the turtle, a luxury then unknown in Europe, went but a small way; and supplies were not to be expected from any foreign settlement. During the cool months, however, which immediately followed the occupation of the isthmus there were few deaths. But, before the equinox, disease began to make fearful havoc in the little community. The mortality gradually rose to ten or twelve a day. Both the clergymen who had accompanied the expedition died. Paterson buried his wife in that soil which, as he had assured his too credulous countrymen, exhaled health and vigour. He was himself stretched on his pallet by an intermittent fever. Still he would not admit that the climate of his promised land was bad. There could not be a purer air. This was merely the seasoning which people who passed from one country to another must expect. In November all would be well again. But the rate at which the emigrants died was such that none of them seemed likely to live till November. Those who were not laid on their beds were yellow, lean, feeble, hardly able to move the sick and to bury the dead, and quite unable to repel the expected attack of the Spaniards. The cry of the whole community was that death was all around them, and that they must, while they still had strength to weigh an anchor or spread a sail, fly to some less fatal region. The men and provisions were equally distributed among three ships, the Caledonia, the Unicorn, and the Saint Andrew. Paterson, though still too ill to sit in the Council, begged hard that he might be left behind with twenty or thirty companions to keep up a show of possession, and to await the next arrivals from Scotland. So small a number of people, he said, might easily subsist by catching fish and turtles. But his offer was disregarded: he was carried, utterly helpless, on board of the Saint Andrew; and the vessels stood out to sea.

The voyage was horrible. Scarcely any Guinea slave ship has ever had such a middle passage. Of two hundred and fifty persons who were on board of the Saint Andrew, one hundred and fifty fed the sharks of the Atlantic before Sandy Hook was in sight. The Unicorn lost almost all its officers, and about a hundred and forty men. The Caledonia, the healthiest ship of the three, threw overboard a hundred corpses. The squalid survivors, as if they were not sufficiently miserable, raged fiercely against one another. Charges of incapacity, cruelty, brutal insolence, were hurled backward and forward. The rigid Presbyterians attributed the calamities of the colony to the wickedness of Jacobites, Prelatists, Sabbath-breakers, Atheists, who hated in others that image of God which was wanting in themselves. The accused malignants, on the other hand, complained bitterly of the impertinence of meddling fanatics and hypocrites. Paterson was cruelly reviled, and was unable to defend himself. He had been completely prostrated by bodily and mental suffering. He looked like a skeleton. His heart was broken. His inventive faculties and his plausible eloquence were no more; and he seemed to have sunk into second childhood.

Meanwhile the second expedition had been on the seas. It reached Darien about four months after the first settlers had fled.

The new comers had fully expected to find a flourishing young town, secure fortifications, cultivated fields, and a cordial welcome. They found a wilderness. The castle of New Edinburgh was in ruins. The huts had been burned. The site marked out for the proud capital which was to have been the Tyre, the Venice, the Amsterdam of the eighteenth century was overgrown with jungle, and inhabited only by the sloth and the baboon. The hearts of the adventurers sank within them. For their fleet had been fitted out, not to plant a colony, but to recruit a colony already planted and supposed to be prospering. They were therefore worse provided with every necessary of life than their predecessors had been. Some feeble attempts, however, were made to restore what had perished. A new fort was constructed on the old ground; and within the ramparts was built a hamlet, consisting of eighty or ninety cabins, generally of twelve feet by ten. But the work went on languidly. The alacrity which is the effect of hope, the strength which is the effect of union, were alike wanting to the little community. From the councillors down to the humblest settlers all was despondency and discontent. The stock of provisions was scanty. The stewards embezzled great part of it. The rations were small; and soon there was a cry that they were unfairly distributed. Factions were formed. Plots were laid. One ringleader of the malecontents was hanged. The Scotch were generally, as they still are, a religious people; and it might therefore have been expected that the influence of the divines to whom the spiritual charge of the colony had been confided would have been employed with advantage for the preserving of order and the calming of evil passions. Unfortunately those divines seem to have been at war with almost all the rest of the society. They described their companions as the most profligate of mankind, and declared that it was impossible to constitute a presbytery according to the directions of the General Assembly; for that persons fit to be ruling elders of a Christian Church were not to be found among the twelve or thirteen hundred emigrants. Where the blame lay it is now impossible to decide. All that can with confidence be said is that either the clergymen must have been most unreasonably and most uncharitably austere, or the laymen must have been most unfavourable specimens of the nation and class to which they belonged.

It may be added that the provision by the General Assembly for the spiritual wants of the colony was as defective as the provision made for temporal wants by the directors of the Company. Nearly one third of the emigrants who sailed with the second expedition were Highlanders, who did not understand a word of English; and not one of the four chaplains could speak a word of Gaelic. It was only through interpreters that a pastor could communicate with a large portion of the Christian flock of which he had charge. Even by the help of interpreters he could not impart religious instruction to those heathen tribes which the Church of Scotland had solemnly recommended to his care. In fact, the colonists left behind them no mark that baptized men had set foot on Darien, except a few Anglo-Saxon curses, which, having been uttered more frequently and with greater energy than any other words in our language, had caught the ear and been retained in the memory of the native population of the isthmus.

The months which immediately followed the arrival of the new comers were the coolest and most salubrious of the year. But, even in those months, the pestilential influence of a tropical sun, shining on swamps rank with impenetrable thickets of black mangroves, began to be felt. The mortality was great; and it was but too clear that, before the summer was far advanced, the second colony would, like the first, have to choose between death and flight. But the agony of the inevitable dissolution was shortened by violence. A fleet of eleven vessels under the flag of Castile anchored off New Edinburgh. At the same time an irregular army of Spaniards, creoles, negroes, mulattoes and Indians marched across the isthmus from Panama; and the fort was blockaded at once by sea and land.

A drummer soon came with a message from the besiegers, but a message which was utterly unintelligible to the besieged. Even after all that we have seen of the perverse imbecility of the directors of the Company, it must be thought strange that they should have sent a colony to a remote part of the world, where it was certain that there must be constant intercourse, peaceable or hostile, with Spaniards, and yet should not have taken care that there should be in the whole colony a single person who knew a little Spanish.

With some difficulty a negotiation was carried on in such French and such Latin as the two parties could furnish. Before the end of March a treaty was signed by which the Scotch bound themselves to evacuate Darien in fourteen days; and on the eleventh of April they departed, a much less numerous body than when they arrived. In little more than four months, although the healthiest months of the year, three hundred men out of thirteen hundred had been swept away by disease. Of the survivors very few lived to see their native country again. Two of the ships perished at sea. Many of the adventurers, who had left their homes flushed with hopes of speedy opulence, were glad to hire themselves out to the planters of Jamaica, and laid their bones in that land of exile. Shields died there, worn out and heart broken. Borland was the only minister who came back. In his curious and interesting narrative, he expresses his feelings, after the fashion of the school in which he had been bred, by grotesque allusions to the Old Testament, and by a profusion of Hebrew words. On his first arrival, he tells us, he found New Edinburgh a Ziklag. He had subsequently been compelled to dwell in the tents of Kedar. Once, indeed, during his sojourn, he had fallen in with a Beer-lahai-roi, and had set up his Ebenezer: but in general Darien was to him a Magor Missabib, a Kibroth-hattaavah. The sad story is introduced with the words in which a great man of old, delivered over to the malice of the Evil Power, was informed of the death of his children and of the ruin of his fortunes: "I alone am escaped to tell thee."

ESSAYS
HISTORICAL, LITERARY AND CONTROVERSIAL

SEVEN of the essays which follow were first printed in the *Edinburgh Review*. The dates of the issues in which they appeared are as follow:

Machiavelli: March 1827.
Mill on Government: March 1829.
Moore's Life of Byron: June 1830.
William Pitt, Earl of Chatham: January 1834.
Gladstone on Church and State: April 1839.
Lord Clive: January 1840.
Warren Hastings: October 1841.

Unauthorised American volumes of Macaulay's essays from the *Edinburgh Review* began appearing in 1841, and he felt obliged to bring out an authoritative edition, *Critical and Historical Essays, Contributed to the Edinburgh Review*, which Longman published in three volumes in 1843. Macaulay made no serious changes in the text, his object being

> that every Essay should now appear as it probably would have appeared when it was first published, if [the author] had then been allowed an additional day or two to revise the proof-sheets, with the assistance of a good library.

This text has been followed in all the essays mentioned above except the review of Mill's *Essay on Government*, which Macaulay omitted with one or two others from the *Critical and Historical Essays*

> not because he is disposed to retract a single doctrine which they contain; but because he is unwilling to offer what might be regarded as an affront to the memory of one from whose opinions he still widely dissents, but to whose talents and virtues he admits that he formerly did not do justice. Serious as are the faults of the Essay on Government, a critic, while noticing those faults, should have abstained from using contemptuous language respecting the historian of British India.

The text here used is therefore that of the *Edinburgh Review*.

The two remaining essays, on Samuel Johnson and William Pitt, were written in December 1856 and January 1859 for the eighth edition of the *Encyclopædia Britannica* (Adam and Charles Black, 1853–61). They are reprinted here from the text of the copy at Britannica House, which the present publishers of the *Encyclopædia* have kindly made available.

ESSAYS

I. *Historical Essays*

MACHIAVELLI

(MARCH 1827)

Œuvres complètes de MACHIAVEL, *traduites par* J. V. PÉRIER, Paris, 1825.

THOSE who have attended to the practice of our literary tribunal are well aware that, by means of certain legal fictions similar to those of Westminster Hall, we are frequently enabled to take cognisance of cases lying beyond the sphere of our original jurisdiction. We need hardly say, therefore, that in the present instance M. Périer is merely a Richard Roe, who will not be mentioned in any subsequent stage of the proceedings, and whose name is used for the sole purpose of bringing Machiavelli into court.

We doubt whether any name in literary history be so generally odious as that of the man whose character and writings we now propose to consider. The terms in which he is commonly described would seem to import that he was the Tempter, the Evil Principle, the discoverer of ambition and revenge, the original inventor of perjury, and that, before the publication of his fatal Prince, there had never been a hypocrite, a tyrant, or a traitor, a simulated virtue, or a convenient crime. One writer gravely assures us that Maurice of Saxony learned all his fraudulent policy from that execrable volume. Another remarks that, since it was translated into Turkish, the Sultans have been more addicted than formerly to the custom of strangling their brothers. Lord Lyttelton charges the poor Florentine with the manifold treasons of the House of Guise, and with the massacre of St. Bartholomew. Several authors have hinted that the Gunpowder Plot is to be primarily attributed to his doctrines, and seem to think that his effigy ought to be substituted for that of Guy Faux, in those processions by which the ingenuous youth of England annually commemorate the preservation of the Three Estates. The Church of Rome has pronounced his works accursed things. Nor have our

235

own countrymen been backward in testifying their opinion of his merits. Out of his surname they have coined an epithet for a knave, and out of his Christian name a synonyme for the Devil.[1]

It is indeed scarcely possible for any person not well acquainted with the history and literature of Italy to read without horror and amazement the celebrated treatise which has brought so much obloquy on the name of Machiavelli. Such a display of wickedness, naked yet not ashamed, such cool, judicious, scientific atrocity, seem rather to belong to a fiend than to the most depraved of men. Principles which the most hardened ruffian would scarcely hint to his most trusted accomplice, or avow, without the disguise of some palliating sophism, even to his own mind, are professed without the slightest circumlocution, and assumed as the fundamental axioms of all political science.

It is not strange that ordinary readers should regard the author of such a book as the most depraved and shameless of human beings. Wise men, however, have always been inclined to look with great suspicion on the angels and dæmons of the multitude: and in the present instance, several circumstances have led even superficial observers to question the justice of the vulgar decision. It is notorious that Machiavelli was, through life, a zealous republican. In the same year in which he composed his manual of King-craft, he suffered imprisonment and torture in the cause of public liberty. It seems inconceivable that the martyr of freedom should have designedly acted as the apostle of tyranny. Several eminent writers have, therefore, endeavoured to detect in this unfortunate performance some concealed meaning, more consistent with the character and conduct of the author than that which appears at the first glance.

One hypothesis is that Machiavelli intended to practise on the young Lorenzo de Medici a fraud similar to that which Sunderland is said to have employed against our James the Second, and that he urged his pupil to violent and perfidious measures, as the surest means of accelerating the moment of deliverance and revenge. Another supposition, which Lord Bacon seems to countenance, is that the treatise was merely a piece of grave irony, intended to warn nations against the arts of ambitious men. It would be easy to show that neither of these solutions is consistent with many

---

[1] Nick Machiavel had ne'er a trick,
  Tho' he gave his name to our old Nick.
                    Hudibras, Part III. Canto I.
But, we believe, there is a schism on this subject among the antiquarians.

passages in The Prince itself.   But the most decisive refutation is that which is furnished by the other works of Machiavelli. In all the writings which he gave to the public, and in all those which the research of editors has, in the course of three centuries, discovered, in his Comedies, designed for the entertainment of the multitude, in his Comments on Livy, intended for the perusal of the most enthusiastic patriots of Florence, in his History, inscribed to one of the most amiable and estimable of the Popes, in his public despatches, in his private memoranda, the same obliquity of moral principle for which The Prince is so severely censured is more or less discernible. We doubt whether it would be possible to find, in all the many volumes of his compositions, a single expression indicating that dissimulation and treachery had ever struck him as discreditable.

After this, it may seem ridiculous to say that we are acquainted with few writings which exhibit so much elevation of sentiment, so pure and warm a zeal for the public good, or so just a view of the duties and rights of citizens, as those of Machiavelli. Yet so it is. And even from The Prince itself we could select many passages in support of this remark. To a reader of our age and country this inconsistency is, at first, perfectly bewildering. The whole man seems to be an enigma, a grotesque assemblage of incongruous qualities, selfishness and generosity, cruelty and benevolence, craft and simplicity, abject villany and romantic heroism. One sentence is such as a veteran diplomatist would scarcely write in cipher for the direction of his most confidential spy; the next seems to be extracted from a theme composed by an ardent schoolboy on the death of Leonidas. An act of dexterous perfidy, and an act of patriotic self-devotion, call forth the same kind and the same degree of respectful admiration. The moral sensibility of the writer seems at once to be morbidly obtuse and morbidly acute. Two characters altogether dissimilar are united in him. They are not merely joined, but interwoven. They are the warp and the woof of his mind; and their combination, like that of the variegated threads in shot silk, gives to the whole texture a glancing and ever changing appearance. The explanation might have been easy, if he had been a very weak or a very affected man. But he was evidently neither the one nor the other. His works prove, beyond all contradiction, that his understanding was strong, his taste pure, and his sense of the ridiculous exquisitely keen.

This is strange: and yet the strangest is behind. There is no reason whatever to think, that those amongst whom he lived saw any thing shocking or incongruous in his writings. Abundant proofs remain of the high estimation in which both his works and his person were held by the most respectable among his contemporaries. Clement the Seventh patronised the publication of those very books which the Council of Trent, in the following generation, pronounced unfit for the perusal of Christians. Some members of the democratical party censured the Secretary for dedicating The Prince to a patron who bore the unpopular name of Medici. But to those immoral doctrines which have since called forth such severe reprehensions no exception appears to have been taken. The cry against them was first raised beyond the Alps, and seems to have been heard with amazement in Italy. The earliest assailant, as far as we are aware, was a countryman of our own, Cardinal Pole. The author of the Anti-Machiavelli was a French Protestant.

It is, therefore, in the state of moral feeling among the Italians of those times that we must seek for the real explanation of what seems most mysterious in the life and writings of this remarkable man. As this is a subject which suggests many interesting considerations, both political and metaphysical, we shall make no apology for discussing it at some length.

During the gloomy and disastrous centuries which followed the downfall of the Roman Empire, Italy had preserved, in a far greater degree than any other part of Western Europe, the traces of ancient civilisation. The night which descended upon her was the night of an Arctic summer. The dawn began to reappear before the last reflection of the preceding sunset had faded from the horizon. It was in the time of the French Merovingians and of the Saxon Heptarchy that ignorance and ferocity seemed to have done their worst. Yet even then the Neapolitan provinces, recognising the authority of the Eastern Empire, preserved something of Eastern knowledge and refinement. Rome, protected by the sacred character of her Pontiffs, enjoyed at least comparative security and repose. Even in those regions where the sanguinary Lombards had fixed their monarchy, there was incomparably more of wealth, of information, of physical comfort, and of social order, than could be found in Gaul, Britain, or Germany.

That which most distinguished Italy from the neighbouring countries was the importance which the population of the towns, at a very early period, began to acquire. Some cities had been founded in wild and remote situations, by fugitives who had escaped from the rage of the barbarians. Such were Venice and Genoa, which preserved their freedom by their obscurity, till they became able to preserve it by their power. Other cities seem to have retained, under all the changing dynasties of invaders, under Odoacer and Theodoric, Narses and Alboin, the municipal institutions which had been conferred on them by the liberal policy of the Great Republic. In provinces which the central government was too feeble either to protect or to oppress, these institutions gradually acquired stability and vigour. The citizens, defended by their walls, and governed by their own magistrates and their own by-laws, enjoyed a considerable share of republican independence. Thus a strong democratic spirit was called into action. The Carlovingian sovereigns were too imbecile to subdue it. The generous policy of Otho encouraged it. It might perhaps have been suppressed by a close coalition between the Church and the Empire. It was fostered and invigorated by their disputes. In the twelfth century it attained its full vigour, and, after a long and doubtful conflict, triumphed over the abilities and courage of the Swabian Princes.

The assistance of the Ecclesiastical Power had greatly contributed to the success of the Guelfs. That success would, however, have been a doubtful good, if its only effect had been to substitute a moral for a political servitude, and to exalt the Popes at the expense of the Cæsars. Happily the public mind of Italy had long contained the seeds of free opinions, which were now rapidly developed by the genial influence of free institutions. The people of that country had observed the whole machinery of the church, its saints and its miracles, its lofty pretensions and its splendid ceremonial, its worthless blessings and its harmless curses, too long and too closely to be duped. They stood behind the scenes on which others were gazing with childish awe and interest. They witnessed the arrangement of the pullies, and the manufacture of the thunders. They saw the natural faces and heard the natural voices of the actors. Distant nations looked on the Pope as the vicegerent of the Almighty, the oracle of the All-wise, the umpire from whose decisions, in the disputes either of theologians or of kings, no Christian ought to appeal. The Italians were acquainted with all the follies of his youth, and with all the dishonest arts by which he had attained power. They knew how often he had employed the keys of the church to release himself from the most sacred engagements, and its wealth to pamper his mistresses and nephews. The doctrines and rites of the established religion they treated with decent reverence. But though they still called themselves Catholics, they had ceased to be Papists. Those spiritual arms which carried terror into the palaces and camps of the proudest sovereigns excited only contempt in the immediate neighbourhood of the Vatican.

Alexander, when he commanded our Henry the Second to submit
to the lash before the tomb of a rebellious subject, was himself an
exile. The Romans, apprehending that he entertained designs
against their liberties, had driven him from their city; and, though
he solemnly promised to confine himself for the future to his
spiritual functions, they still refused to readmit him.

In every other part of Europe, a large and powerful privileged
class trampled on the people and defied the government. But, in
the most flourishing parts of Italy, the feudal nobles were reduced
to comparative insignificance. In some districts they took shelter
under the protection of the powerful commonwealths which they
were unable to oppose, and gradually sank into the mass of burghers.
In other places they possessed great influence; but it was an influence widely different from that which was exercised by the
aristocracy of any Transalpine kingdom. They were not petty
princes, but eminent citizens. Instead of strengthening their fastnesses among the mountains, they embellished their palaces in the
market-place. The state of society in the Neapolitan dominions, and
in some parts of the Ecclesiastical State, more nearly resembled that
which existed in the great monarchies of Europe. But the governments of Lombardy and Tuscany, through all their revolutions,
preserved a different character. A people, when assembled in a
town, is far more formidable to its rulers than when dispersed over
a wide extent of country. The most arbitrary of the Cæsars found
it necessary to feed and divert the inhabitants of their unwieldy
capital at the expense of the provinces. The citizens of Madrid
have more than once besieged their sovereign in his own palace,
and extorted from him the most humiliating concessions. The
Sultans have often been compelled to propitiate the furious rabble
of Constantinople with the head of an unpopular Vizier. From the
same cause there was a certain tinge of democracy in the monarchies and aristocracies of Northern Italy.

Thus liberty, partially indeed and transiently, revisited Italy;
and with liberty came commerce and empire, science and taste, all
the comforts and all the ornaments of life. The Crusades, from
which the inhabitants of other countries gained nothing but relics
and wounds, brought to the rising commonwealths of the Adriatic
and Tyrrhene seas a large increase of wealth, dominion, and knowledge. The moral and the geographical position of those commonwealths enabled them to profit alike by the barbarism of the West
and by the civilisation of the East. Italian ships covered every sea.
Italian factories rose on every shore. The tables of Italian money-
changers were set in every city. Manufactures flourished. Banks

were established. The operations of the commercial machine were facilitated by many useful and beautiful inventions. We doubt whether any country of Europe, our own excepted, have at the present time reached so high a point of wealth and civilisation as some parts of Italy had attained four hundred years ago. Historians rarely descend to those details from which alone the real state of a community can be collected. Hence posterity is too often deceived by the vague hyperboles of poets and rhetoricians, who mistake the splendour of a court for the happiness of a people. Fortunately, John Villani has given us an ample and precise account of the state of Florence in the early part of the fourteenth century. The revenue of the Republic amounted to three hundred thousand florins, a sum which, allowing for the depreciation of the precious metals, was at least equivalent to six hundred thousand pounds sterling; a larger sum than England and Ireland, two centuries ago, yielded annually to Elizabeth. The manufacture of wool alone employed two hundred factories and thirty thousand workmen. The cloth annually produced sold, at an average, for twelve hundred thousand florins; a sum fully equal, in exchangeable value, to two millions and a half of our money. Four hundred thousand florins were annually coined. Eighty banks conducted the commercial operations, not of Florence only, but of all Europe. The transactions of these establishments were sometimes of a magnitude which may surprise even the contemporaries of the Barings and the Rothschilds. Two houses advanced to Edward the Third of England upwards of three hundred thousand marks, at a time when the mark contained more silver than fifty shillings of the present day, and when the value of silver was more than quadruple of what it now is. The city and its environs contained a hundred and seventy thousand inhabitants. In the various schools about ten thousand children were taught to read; twelve hundred studied arithmetic; six hundred received a learned education.

The progress of elegant literature and of the fine arts was proportioned to that of the public prosperity. Under the despotic successors of Augustus, all the fields of the intellect had been turned into arid wastes, still marked out by formal boundaries, still retaining the traces of old cultivation, but yielding neither flowers nor fruit. The deluge of barbarism came. It swept away all the landmarks. It obliterated all the signs of former tillage. But it fertilised while it devastated. When it receded, the wilderness was as the garden of God, rejoicing on every side, laughing, clapping its hands, pouring forth, in spontaneous abundance, every thing brilliant, or fragrant, or nourishing. A new language, characterized by simple sweetness and simple energy, had attained perfection. No tongue ever furnished more gorgeous and vivid tints to poetry; nor was it long before a poet appeared, who knew how to employ them. Early in the fourteenth century came forth the Divine Comedy, beyond comparison the greatest work of imagination which had appeared since the poems of Homer. The following generation produced indeed no second Dante: but it was eminently distinguished by general intellectual activity. The study of the Latin writers had never been wholly neglected in Italy. But Petrarch introduced a more profound, liberal, and elegant scholarship, and communicated to his countrymen that enthusiasm for the literature, the history, and the antiquities of Rome, which divided his own heart with a frigid mistress and a more frigid Muse. Boccaccio turned their attention to the more sublime and graceful models of Greece.

From this time, the admiration of learning and genius became almost an idolatry among the people of Italy. Kings and republics, cardinals and doges, vied with each other in honouring and flattering Petrarch. Embassies from rival states solicited the honour of his instructions. His coronation agitated the Court of Naples and the people of Rome as much as the most important political transaction could have done. To collect books and antiques, to found professorships, to patronise men of learning, became almost universal fashions among the great. The spirit of literary research allied itself to that of commercial enterprise. Every place to which the merchant princes of Florence extended their gigantic traffic, from the bazars of the Tigris to the monasteries of the Clyde, was ransacked for medals and manuscripts. Architecture, painting, and sculpture, were munificently encouraged. Indeed it would be difficult to name an Italian of eminence, during the period of which we speak, who, whatever may have been his general character, did not at least affect a love of letters and of the arts.

Knowledge and public prosperity continued to advance together. Both attained their meridian in the age of Lorenzo the Magnificent. We cannot refrain from quoting the splendid passage, in which the Tuscan Thucydides describes the state of Italy at that period. "Ridotta tutta in somma pace e tranquillità, coltivata non meno ne' luoghi più montuosi e più sterili che nelle pianure e regioni più fertili, nè sottoposta ad altro imperio che de' suoi medesimi, non solo era abbondantissima d'abitatori e di ricchezze; ma illustrata sommamente dalla magnificenza di molti principi, dallo splendore di molte nobilissime e bellissime città, dalla sedia e maestà della religione, fioriva d' uomini prestantissimi nell' amministrazione delle cose pubbliche, e d'ingegni molto nobili in tutte le scienze, ed in qualunque arte preclara ed industriosa." When we peruse this just and splendid description, we can scarcely persuade ourselves that we are reading of times in which the annals of England and France present us only with a frightful spectacle of poverty, barbarity, and ignorance. From the oppressions of illiterate masters, and the sufferings of a degraded peasantry, it is delightful to turn to the opulent and enlightened States of Italy, to the vast and magnificent cities, the ports, the arsenals, the villas, the museums, the libraries, the marts filled with every article of comfort or luxury, the factories swarming with artisans, the Apennines covered with rich cultivation up to their very summits, the Po wafting the harvests of Lombardy to the granaries of Venice, and carrying back the silks of Bengal and the furs of Siberia to the palaces of Milan. With peculiar pleasure, every cultivated mind must repose on the fair, the happy, the glorious Florence, the halls which rang with the mirth of Pulci, the cell where twinkled the midnight lamp of Politian, the statues on which the young eye of Michael Angelo glared with the frenzy of a kindred inspiration, the gardens in which Lorenzo meditated some sparkling song for the May-day dance of the Etrurian virgins. Alas, for the beautiful city! Alas, for the wit and the learning, the genius and the love!

> "Le donne, e i cavalier, gli affanni, e gli agi,
>   Che ne 'nvogliava amore e cortesia
>   Là dove i cuor son fatti sì malvagi."

A time was at hand, when all the seven vials of the Apocalypse were to be poured forth and shaken out over those pleasant countries, a time of slaughter, famine, beggary, infamy, slavery, despair.

In the Italian States, as in many natural bodies, untimely decrepitude was the penalty of precocious maturity. Their early greatness, and their early decline, are principally to be attributed to the same cause, the preponderance which the towns acquired in the political system.

In a community of hunters or of shepherds, every man easily and necessarily becomes a soldier. His ordinary avocations are perfectly compatible with all the duties of military service. However remote may be the expedition on which he is bound, he finds it easy to transport with him the stock from which he derives his subsistence. The whole people is an army; the whole year a march. Such was the state of society which facilitated the gigantic conquests of Attila and Tamerlane.

But a people which subsists by the cultivation of the earth is in a very different situation. The husbandman is bound to the soil on which he labours. A long campaign would be ruinous to him. Still his pursuits are such as give to his frame both the active and the passive strength necessary to a soldier. Nor do they, at least in the infancy of agricultural science, demand his uninterrupted attention. At particular times of the year he is almost wholly unemployed, and can, without injury to himself, afford the time necessary for a short expedition. Thus the legions of Rome were supplied during its earlier wars. The season during which the fields did not require the presence of the cultivators sufficed for a short inroad and a battle. These operations, too frequently interrupted to produce decisive results, yet served to keep up among the people a degree of discipline and courage which rendered them, not only secure, but formidable. The archers and billmen of the middle ages, who, with provisions for forty days at their backs, left the fields for the camp, were troops of the same description.

But when commerce and manufactures begin to flourish a great change takes place. The sedentary habits of the desk and the loom render the exertions and hardships of war insupportable. The business of traders and artisans requires their constant presence and attention. In such a community there is little superfluous time; but there is generally much superfluous money. Some members of the society are, therefore, hired to relieve the rest from a task inconsistent with their habits and engagements.

The history of Greece is, in this, as in many other respects, the best commentary on the history of Italy. Five hundred years before the Christian era, the citizens of the republics round the Ægean Sea formed perhaps the finest militia that ever existed. As wealth and refinement advanced, the system underwent a gradual alteration. The Ionian States were the first in which commerce and the arts were cultivated, and the first in which the ancient discipline decayed. Within eighty years after the battle of Platæa, mercenary troops were every where plying for battles and sieges. In the time of Demosthenes, it was scarcely possible to persuade or compel the Athenians to enlist for foreign service. The laws of Lycurgus prohibited trade and manufactures. The Spartans, therefore, continued to form a national force long after their neighbours had begun to hire soldiers. But their military spirit declined with their singular institutions. In the second century before Christ, Greece contained only one nation of warriors, the savage highlanders of Ætolia, who were some generations behind their countrymen in civilisation and intelligence.

All the causes which produced these effects among the Greeks acted still more strongly on the modern Italians. Instead of a power like Sparta, in its nature warlike, they had amongst them an ecclesiastical state, in its nature pacific. Where there are numerous slaves, every freeman is induced by the strongest motives to familiarise himself with the use of arms. The commonwealths of Italy did not, like those of Greece, swarm with thousands of these household enemies. Lastly, the mode in which military operations were conducted during the prosperous times of Italy was peculiarly unfavourable to the formation of an efficient militia. Men covered with iron from head to foot, armed with ponderous lances, and mounted on horses of the largest breed, were considered as composing the strength of an army. The infantry was regarded as comparatively worthless, and was neglected till it became really so. These tactics maintained their ground for centuries in most parts of Europe. That foot soldiers could withstand the charge of heavy cavalry was thought utterly impossible, till, towards the close of the fifteenth century, the rude mountaineers of Switzerland dissolved the spell, and astounded the most experienced generals by receiving the dreaded shock on an impenetrable forest of pikes.

The use of the Grecian spear, the Roman sword, or the modern bayonet, might be acquired with comparative ease. But nothing short of the daily exercise of years could train the man at arms to support his ponderous panoply, and manage his unwieldy weapon. Throughout Europe this most important branch of war became a separate profession. Beyond the Alps, indeed, though a profession, it was not generally a trade. It was the duty and the amusement of a large class of country gentlemen. It was the service by which they held their lands, and the diversion by which, in the absence of mental resources, they beguiled their leisure. But in the Northern States of Italy, as we have already remarked, the growing power of the cities, where it had not exterminated this order of men, had completely changed their habits. Here, therefore, the practice of employing mercenaries became universal, at a time when it was almost unknown in other countries.

When war becomes the trade of a separate class, the least dangerous course left to a government is to form that class into a standing army. It is scarcely possible, that men can pass their lives in the service of one state, without feeling some interest in its greatness. Its victories are their victories. Its defeats are their defeats. The contract loses something of its mercantile character. The services of the soldier are considered as the effects of patriotic zeal, his pay as the tribute of national gratitude. To betray the power which employs him, to be even remiss in its service, are in his eyes the most atrocious and degrading of crimes.

When the princes and commonwealths of Italy began to use hired troops, their wisest course would have been to form separate military establishments. Unhappily this was not done. The mercenary warriors of the Peninsula, instead of being attached to the service of different powers, were regarded as the common property of all. The connection between the state and its defenders was reduced to the most simple and naked traffic. The adventurer brought his horse, his weapons, his strength, and his experience, into the market. Whether the King of Naples or the Duke of Milan, the Pope or the Signory of Florence, struck the bargain, was to him a matter of perfect indifference. He was for the highest wages and the longest term. When the campaign for which he had contracted was finished, there was neither law nor punctilio to prevent him from instantly turning his arms against his late masters. The soldier was altogether disjoined from the citizen and from the subject.

The natural consequences followed. Left to the conduct of men who neither loved those whom they defended nor hated those whom they opposed, who were often bound by stronger ties to the army against which they fought than to the state which they served, who lost by the termination of the conflict, and gained by its prolongation, war completely changed its character. Every man came into the field of battle impressed with the knowledge that, in a few days, he might be taking the pay of the power against which he was then employed, and fighting by the side of his enemies against his associates. The strongest interests and the strongest feelings concurred to mitigate the hostility of those who had lately been brethren in arms, and who might soon be brethren in arms once more. Their common profession was a bond of union not to be forgotten even when they were engaged in the service of contending parties. Hence it was that operations, languid and indecisive beyond any recorded in history, marches and counter-marches, pillaging expeditions and blockades, bloodless capitulations and equally bloodless combats, make up the military history of Italy during the course of nearly two centuries. Mighty armies fight from sunrise to sunset. A great victory is won. Thousands of prisoners are taken; and hardly a life is lost. A pitched battle seems to have been really less dangerous than an ordinary civil tumult.

Courage was now no longer necessary even to the military character. Men grew old in camps, and acquired the highest renown by their warlike achievements, without being once required to face serious danger. The political consequences are too well known.

The richest and most enlightened part of the world was left un-defended to the assaults of every barbarous invader, to the brutality of Switzerland, the insolence of France, and the fierce rapacity of Arragon. The moral effects which followed from this state of things, were still more remarkable.

Among the rude nations which lay beyond the Alps, valour was absolutely indispensable. Without it, none could be eminent; few could be secure. Cowardice was, therefore, naturally considered as the foulest reproach. Among the polished Italians, enriched by commerce, governed by law, and passionately attached to literature, every thing was done by superiority of intelligence. Their very wars, more pacific than the peace of their neighbours, required rather civil than military qualifications. Hence, while courage was the point of honour in other countries, ingenuity became the point of honour in Italy.

From these principles were deduced, by processes strictly analogous, two opposite systems of fashionable morality. Through the greater part of Europe, the vices which peculiarly belong to timid dispositions, and which are the natural defence of weakness, fraud and hypocrisy, have always been most disreputable. On the other hand, the excesses of haughty and daring spirits have been treated with indulgence, and even with respect. The Italians regarded with corresponding lenity those crimes which require self-command, address, quick observation, fertile invention, and profound knowledge of human nature.

Such a prince as our Henry the Fifth would have been the idol of the North. The follies of his youth, the selfish ambition of his manhood, the Lollards roasted at slow fires, the prisoners massacred on the field of battle, the expiring lease of priestcraft renewed for another century, the dreadful legacy of a causeless and hopeless war bequeathed to a people who had no interest in its event, every thing is forgotten but the victory of Agincourt. Francis Sforza, on the other hand, was the model of Italian heroes. He made his employers and his rivals alike his tools. He first overpowered his open enemies by the help of faithless allies; he then armed himself against his allies with the spoils taken from his enemies. By his incomparable dexterity, he raised himself from the precarious and dependent situation of a military adventurer to the first throne of Italy. To such a man much was forgiven, hollow friendship, un-generous enmity, violated faith. Such are the opposite errors which men commit, when their morality is not a science but a taste, when they abandon eternal principles for accidental associations.

We have illustrated our meaning by an instance taken from

history. We will select another from fiction. Othello murders his wife; he gives orders for the murder of his lieutenant; he ends by murdering himself. Yet he never loses the esteem and affection of Northern readers. His intrepid and ardent spirit redeems every thing. The unsuspecting confidence with which he listens to his adviser, the agony with which he shrinks from the thought of shame, the tempest of passion with which he commits his crimes, and the haughty fearlessness with which he avows them, give an extraordinary interest to his character. Iago, on the contrary, is the object of universal loathing. Many are inclined to suspect that Shakspeare has been seduced into an exaggeration unusual with him, and has drawn a monster who has no archetype in human nature. Now we suspect, that an Italian audience, in the fifteenth century, would have felt very differently. Othello would have inspired nothing but detestation and contempt. The folly with which he trusts the friendly professions of a man whose promotion he had obstructed, the credulity with which he takes unsupported assertions, and trivial circumstances, for unanswerable proofs, the violence with which he silences the exculpation till the exculpation can only aggravate his misery, would have excited the abhorrence and disgust of the spectators. The conduct of Iago they would assuredly have condemned; but they would have condemned it as we condemn that of his victim. Something of interest and respect would have mingled with their disapprobation. The readiness of the traitor's wit, the clearness of his judgment, the skill with which he penetrates the dispositions of others and conceals his own, would have insured to him a certain portion of their esteem.

So wide was the difference between the Italians and their neighbours. A similar difference existed between the Greeks of the second century before Christ, and their masters the Romans. The conquerors, brave and resolute, faithful to their engagements, and strongly influenced by religious feelings, were, at the same time, ignorant, arbitrary, and cruel. With the vanquished people were deposited all the art, the science, and the literature of the Western world. In poetry, in philosophy, in painting, in architecture, in sculpture, they had no rivals. Their manners were polished, their perceptions acute, their invention ready; they were tolerant, affable, humane; but of courage and sincerity they were almost utterly destitute. Every rude centurion consoled himself for his intellectual inferiority, by remarking that knowledge and taste seemed only to make men atheists, cowards, and slaves. The distinction long continued to be strongly marked, and furnished an admirable subject for the fierce sarcasms of Juvenal.

The citizen of an Italian commonwealth was the Greek of the time of Juvenal, and the Greek of the time of Pericles, joined in one. Like the former, he was timid and pliable, artful and mean. But, like the latter, he had a country. Its independence and prosperity were dear to him. If his character were degraded by some base crimes, it was, on the other hand, ennobled by public spirit and by an honourable ambition.

A vice sanctioned by the general opinion is merely a vice. The evil terminates in itself. A vice condemned by the general opinion produces a pernicious effect on the whole character. The former is a local malady, the latter a constitutional taint. When the reputation of the offender is lost, he too often flings the remains of his virtue after it in despair. The Highland gentleman who, a century ago, lived by taking black mail from his neighbours, committed the same crime for which Wild was accompanied to Tyburn by the huzzas of two hundred thousand people. But there can be no doubt that he was a much less depraved man than Wild. The deed for which Mrs. Brownrigg was hanged sinks into nothing, when compared with the conduct of the Roman who treated the public to a hundred pair of gladiators. Yet we should greatly wrong such a Roman if we supposed that his disposition was as cruel as that of Mrs. Brownrigg. In our own country, a woman forfeits her place in society by what, in a man, is too commonly considered as an honourable distinction, and, at worst, as a venial error. The consequence is notorious. The moral principle of a woman is frequently more impaired by a single lapse from virtue than that of a man by twenty years of intrigues. Classical antiquity would furnish us with instances stronger, if possible, than those to which we have referred.

We must apply this principle to the case before us. Habits of dissimulation and falsehood, no doubt, mark a man of our age and country as utterly worthless and abandoned. But it by no means follows that a similar judgment would be just in the case of an Italian of the middle ages. On the contrary, we frequently find those faults which we are accustomed to consider as certain indications of a mind altogether depraved, in company with great and good qualities, with generosity, with benevolence, with disinterestedness. From such a state of society, Palamedes, in the admirable dialogue of Hume, might have drawn illustrations of his theory as striking as any of those with which Fourli furnished him. These are not, we well know, the lessons which historians are generally most careful to teach, or readers most willing to learn. But they are not therefore useless. How Philip disposed his troops at

Chæronea, where Hannibal crossed the Alps, whether Mary blew up Darnley, or Siquier shot Charles the Twelfth, and ten thousand other questions of the same description, are in themselves unimportant. The inquiry may amuse us, but the decision leaves us no wiser. He alone reads history aright who, observing how powerfully circumstances influence the feelings and opinions of men, how often vices pass into virtues and paradoxes into axioms, learns to distinguish what is accidental and transitory in human nature from what is essential and immutable.

In this respect no history suggests more important reflections than that of the Tuscan and Lombard commonwealths. The character of the Italian statesman seems, at first sight, a collection of contradictions, a phantom as monstrous as the portress of hell in Milton, half divinity, half snake, majestic and beautiful above, grovelling and poisonous below. We see a man whose thoughts and words have no connexion with each other, who never hesitates at an oath when he wishes to seduce, who never wants a pretext when he is inclined to betray. His cruelties spring, not from the heat of blood, or the insanity of uncontrolled power, but from deep and cool meditation. His passions, like well trained troops, are impetuous by rule, and in their most headstrong fury never forget the discipline to which they have been accustomed. His whole soul is occupied with vast and complicated schemes of ambition: yet his aspect and language exhibit nothing but philosophical moderation. Hatred and revenge eat into his heart: yet every look is a cordial smile, every gesture a familiar caress. He never excites the suspicion of his adversaries by petty provocations. His purpose is disclosed only when it is accomplished. His face is unruffled, his speech is courteous, till vigilance is laid asleep, till a vital point is exposed, till a sure aim is taken; and then he strikes, for the first and last time. Military courage, the boast of the sottish German, of the frivolous and prating Frenchman, of the romantic and arrogant Spaniard, he neither possesses nor values. He shuns danger, not because he is insensible to shame, but because, in the society in which he lives, timidity has ceased to be shameful. To do an injury openly is, in his estimation, as wicked as to do it secretly, and far less profitable. With him the most honourable means are those which are the surest, the speediest, and the darkest. He cannot comprehend how a man should scruple to deceive those whom he does not scruple to destroy. He would think it madness to declare open hostilities against rivals whom he might stab in a friendly embrace, or poison in a consecrated wafer.

Yet this man, black with the vices which we consider as most

loathsome, traitor, hypocrite, coward, assassin, was by no means
destitute even of those virtues which we generally consider as indicating superior elevation of character. In civil courage, in perseverance, in presence of mind, those barbarous warriors, who were
foremost in the battle or the breach, were far his inferiors. Even
the dangers which he avoided with a caution almost pusillanimous
never confused his perceptions, never paralysed his inventive
faculties, never wrung out one secret from his smooth tongue and
his inscrutable brow. Though a dangerous enemy, and a still more
dangerous accomplice, he could be a just and beneficent ruler.
With so much unfairness in his policy, there was an extraordinary
degree of fairness in his intellect. Indifferent to truth in the transactions of life, he was honestly devoted to truth in the researches
of speculation. Wanton cruelty was not in his nature. On the
contrary, where no political object was at stake, his disposition was
soft and humane. The susceptibility of his nerves and the activity
of his imagination inclined him to sympathise with the feelings of
others, and to delight in the charities and courtesies of social life.
Perpetually descending to actions which might seem to mark a
mind diseased through all its faculties, he had nevertheless an
exquisite sensibility, both for the natural and the moral sublime,
for every graceful and every lofty conception. Habits of petty
intrigue and dissimulation might have rendered him incapable of
great general views, but that the expanding effect of his philosophical studies counteracted the narrowing tendency. He had
the keenest enjoyment of wit, eloquence, and poetry. The fine arts
profited alike by the severity of his judgment, and by the liberality
of his patronage. The portraits of some of the remarkable Italians
of those times are perfectly in harmony with this description.
Ample and majestic foreheads, brows strong and dark, but not
frowning, eyes of which the calm full gaze, while it expresses
nothing, seems to discern every thing, cheeks pale with thought
and sedentary habits, lips formed with feminine delicacy, but com-
pressed with more than masculine decision, mark out men at once
enterprising and timid, men equally skilled in detecting the purposes of others, and in concealing their own, men who must have
been formidable enemies and unsafe allies, but men, at the same
time, whose tempers were mild and equable, and who possessed an
amplitude and subtlety of intellect which would have rendered
them eminent either in active or in contemplative life, and fitted
them either to govern or to instruct mankind.

Every age and every nation has certain characteristic vices, which
prevail almost universally, which scarcely any person scruples to

avow, and which even rigid moralists but faintly censure. Succeeding generations change the fashion of their morals, with the fashion of their hats and their coaches; take some other kind of wickedness under their patronage, and wonder at the depravity of their ancestors. Nor is this all. Posterity, that high court of appeal which is never tired of eulogising its own justice and discernment, acts on such occasions like a Roman dictator after a general mutiny. Finding the delinquents too numerous to be all punished, it selects some of them at hazard, to bear the whole penalty of an offence in which they are not more deeply implicated than those who escape. Whether decimation be a convenient mode of military execution, we know not; but we solemnly protest against the introduction of such a principle into the philosophy of history.

In the present instance, the lot has fallen on Machiavelli, a man whose public conduct was upright and honourable, whose views of morality, where they differed from those of the persons around him, seemed to have differed for the better, and whose only fault was, that, having adopted some of the maxims then generally received, he arranged them more luminously, and expressed them more forcibly, than any other writer.

Having now, we hope, in some degree cleared the personal character of Machiavelli, we come to the consideration of his works. As a poet, he is not entitled to a high place; but his comedies deserve attention.

The Mandragola, in particular, is superior to the best of Goldoni, and inferior only to the best of Molière. It is the work of a man who, if he had devoted himself to the drama, would probably have attained the highest eminence, and produced a permanent and salutary effect on the national taste. This we infer, not so much from the degree, as from the kind of its excellence. There are compositions which indicate still greater talent, and which are perused with still greater delight, from which we should have drawn very different conclusions. Books quite worthless are quite harmless. The sure sign of the general decline of an art is the frequent occurrence, not of deformity, but of misplaced beauty. In general, tragedy is corrupted by eloquence, and comedy by wit.

The real object of the drama is the exhibition of human character. This, we conceive, is no arbitrary canon, originating in local and temporary associations, like those canons which regulate the number of acts in a play, or of syllables in a line. To this fundamental law every other regulation is subordinate. The situations which most signally develop character form the best plot. The mother tongue of the passions is the best style.

This principle, rightly understood, does not debar the poet from any grace of composition. There is no style in which some man may not, under some circumstances, express himself. There is therefore no style which the drama rejects, none which it does not occasionally require. It is in the discernment of place, of time, and of person, that the inferior artists fail. The fantastic rhapsody of Mercutio, the elaborate declamation of Antony, are, where Shakspeare has placed them, natural and pleasing. But Dryden would have made Mercutio challenge Tybalt, in hyperboles as fanciful as those in which he describes the chariot of Mab. Corneille would have represented Antony as scolding and coaxing Cleopatra with all the measured rhetoric of a funeral oration.

No writers have injured the Comedy of England so deeply as Congreve and Sheridan. Both were men of splendid wit and polished taste. Unhappily, they made all their characters in their own likeness. Their works bear the same relation to the legitimate drama which a transparency bears to a painting. There are no delicate touches, no hues imperceptibly fading into each other: the whole is lighted up with an universal glare. Outlines and tints are forgotten in the common blaze which illuminates all. The flowers and fruits of the intellect abound; but it is the abundance of a jungle, not of a garden, unwholesome, bewildering, unprofitable from its very plenty, rank from its very fragrance. Every fop, every boor, every valet, is a man of wit. The very butts and dupes, Tattle, Witwould, Puff, Acres, outshine the whole Hotel of Rambouillet. To prove the whole system of this school erroneous, it is only necessary to apply the test which dissolved the enchanted Florimel, to place the true by the false Thalia, to contrast the most celebrated characters which have been drawn by the writers of whom we speak with the Bastard in King John, or the Nurse in Romeo and Juliet. It was not surely from want of wit that Shakspeare adopted so different a manner. Benedick and Beatrice throw Mirabel and Millamant into the shade. All the good sayings of the facetious houses of Absolute and Surface might have been clipped from the single character of Falstaff without being missed. It would have been easy for that fertile mind to have given Bardolph and Shallow as much wit as Prince Hal, and to have made Dogberry and Verges retort on each other in sparkling epigrams. But he knew that such indiscriminate prodigality was, to use his òwn admirable language, "from the purpose of playing, whose end, both at the first and now, was, and is, to hold, as it were, the mirror up to Nature."

This digression will enable our readers to understand what we mean when we say that, in the Mandragola, Machiavelli has proved that he completely understood the nature of the dramatic art, and possessed talents which would have enabled him to excel in it. By the correct and vigorous delineation of human nature, it produces interest without a pleasing or skilful plot, and laughter without the least ambition of wit. The lover, not a very delicate or generous lover, and his adviser the parasite, are drawn with spirit. The hypocritical confessor is an admirable portrait. He is, if we mistake not, the original of Father Dominic, the best comic character of Dryden. But old Nicias is the glory of the piece. We cannot call to mind any thing that resembles him. The follies which Molière ridicules are those of affectation, not those of fatuity. Coxcombs and pedants, not absolute simpletons, are his game. Shakspeare has indeed a vast assortment of fools; but the precise species of which we speak is not, if we remember right, to be found there. Shallow is a fool. But his animal spirits supply, to a certain degree, the place of cleverness. His talk is to that of Sir John what soda water is to champagne. It has the effervescence, though not the body or the flavour. Slender and Sir Andrew Aguecheek are fools, troubled with an uneasy consciousness of their folly, which, in the latter, produces meekness and docility, and in the former, awkwardness, obstinacy, and confusion. Cloten is an arrogant fool, Osric a foppish fool, Ajax a savage fool; but Nicias is, as Thersites says of Patroclus, a fool positive. His mind is occupied by no strong feeling; it takes every character, and retains none; its aspect is diversified, not by passions, but by faint and transitory semblances of passion, a mock joy, a mock fear, a mock love, a mock pride, which chase each other like shadows over its surface, and vanish as soon as they appear. He is just idiot enough to be an object, not of pity or horror, but of ridicule. He bears some resemblance to poor Calandrino, whose mishaps, as recounted by Boccaccio, have made all Europe merry for more than four centuries. He perhaps resembles still more closely Simon da Villa, to whom Bruno and Buffalmacco promised the love of the Countess Civillari. Nicias is, like Simon, of a learned profession; and the dignity with which he wears the doctoral fur, renders his absurdities infinitely more grotesque. The old Tuscan is the very language for such a being. Its peculiar simplicity gives even to the most forcible reasoning and the most brilliant wit an infantine air, generally delightful, but to a foreign reader sometimes a little ludicrous. Heroes and statesmen seem to lisp when they use it. It becomes Nicias incomparably, and renders all his silliness infinitely more silly.

We may add, that the verses with which the Mandragola is

interspersed, appear to us to be the most spirited and correct of all
that Machiavelli has written in metre. He seems to have entertained the same opinion; for he has introduced some of them in
other places. The contemporaries of the author were not blind to
the merits of this striking piece. It was acted at Florence with the
greatest success. Leo the Tenth was among its admirers, and by
his order it was represented at Rome.[1]

The Clizia is an imitation of the Casina of Plautus, which is itself
an imitation of the lost κληρουμένοι of Diphilus. Plautus was, unquestionably, one of the best Latin writers; but the Casina is by no
means one of his best plays; nor is it one which offers great facilities
to an imitator. The story is as alien from modern habits of life, as
the manner in which it is developed from the modern fashion of
composition. The lover remains in the country and the heroine
in her chamber during the whole action, leaving their fate to be
decided by a foolish father, a cunning mother, and two knavish
servants. Machiavelli has executed his task with judgment and
taste. He has accommodated the plot to a different state of society,
and has very dexterously connected it with the history of his own
times. The relation of the trick put on the doting old lover is exquisitely humorous. It is far superior to the corresponding passage
in the Latin comedy, and scarcely yields to the account which
Falstaff gives of his ducking.

Two other comedies without titles, the one in prose, the other
in verse, appear among the works of Machiavelli. The former is
very short, lively enough, but of no great value. The latter we can
scarcely believe to be genuine. Neither its merits nor its defects
remind us of the reputed author. It was first printed in 1796, from
a manuscript discovered in the celebrated library of the Strozzi.
Its genuineness, if we have been rightly informed, is established
solely by the comparison of hands. Our suspicions are strengthened
by the circumstance, that the same manuscript contained a description of the plague of 1527, which has also, in consequence, been
added to the works of Machiavelli. Of this last composition, the
strongest external evidence would scarcely induce us to believe him
guilty. Nothing was ever written more detestable in matter and
manner. The narrations, the reflections, the jokes, the lamentations, are all the very worst of their respective kinds, at once trite
and affected, threadbare tinsel from the Rag-fairs and Monmouth-

---

[1] Nothing can be more evident than that Paulus Jovius designates the
Mandragola under the name of the Nicias. We should not have noticed
what is so perfectly obvious, were it not that this natural and palpable
misnomer has led the sagacious and industrious Bayle into a gross error.

streets of literature. A foolish schoolboy might write such a piece, and, after he had written it, think it much finer than the incomparable introduction of the Decameron. But that a shrewd statesman, whose earliest works are characterised by manliness of thought and language, should, at near sixty years of age, descend to such puerility, is utterly inconceivable.

The little novel of Belphegor is pleasantly conceived, and pleasantly told. But the extravagance of the satire in some measure injures its effect. Machiavelli was unhappily married; and his wish to avenge his own cause and that of his brethren in misfortune, carried him beyond even the license of fiction. Jonson seems to have combined some hints taken from this tale, with others from Boccaccio, in the plot of The Devil is an Ass, a play which, though not the most highly finished of his compositions, is perhaps that which exhibits the strongest proofs of genius.

The political correspondence of Machiavelli, first published in 1767, is unquestionably genuine, and highly valuable. The unhappy circumstances in which his country was placed during the greater part of his public life gave extraordinary encouragement to diplomatic talents. From the moment that Charles the Eighth descended from the Alps, the whole character of Italian politics was changed. The governments of the Peninsula ceased to form an independent system. Drawn from their old orbit by the attraction of the larger bodies which now approached them, they became mere satellites of France and Spain. All their disputes, internal and external, were decided by foreign influence. The contests of opposite factions were carried on, not as formerly in the senate-house or in the market-place, but in the antechambers of Louis and Ferdinand. Under these circumstances, the prosperity of the Italian States depended far more on the ability of their foreign agents, than on the conduct of those who were entrusted with the domestic administration. The ambassador had to discharge functions far more delicate than transmitting orders of knighthood, introducing tourists, or presenting his brethren with the homage of his high consideration. He was an advocate to whose management the dearest interests of his clients were intrusted, a spy clothed with an inviolable character. Instead of consulting, by a reserved manner and ambiguous style, the dignity of those whom he represented, he was to plunge into all the intrigues of the court at which he resided, to discover and flatter every weakness of the prince, and of the favourite who governed the prince, and of the lacquey who governed the favourite. He was to compliment the mistress and bribe the confessor, to panegyrize or supplicate, to laugh or weep, to accommodate himself to every caprice, to lull every suspicion, to treasure every hint, to be every thing, to observe every thing, to endure every thing. High as the art of political intrigue had been carried in Italy, these were times which required it all.

On these arduous errands Machiavelli was frequently employed. He was sent to treat with the King of the Romans and with the Duke of Valentinois. He was twice ambassador at the Court of Rome, and thrice at that of France. In these missions, and in several others of inferior importance, he acquitted himself with great dexterity. His despatches form one of the most amusing and instructive collections extant. The narratives are clear and agreeably written; the remarks on men and things clever and judicious. The conversations are reported in a spirited and characteristic manner. We find ourselves introduced into the presence of the men who, during twenty eventful years, swayed the destinies of Europe. Their wit and their folly, their fretfulness and their merriment are exposed to us. We are admitted to overhear their chat, and to watch their familiar gestures. It is interesting and curious to recognise, in circumstances which elude the notice of historians, the feeble violence and shallow cunning of Louis the Twelfth; the bustling insignificance of Maximilian, cursed with an impotent pruriency for renown, rash yet timid, obstinate yet fickle, always in a hurry, yet always too late; the fierce and haughty energy which gave dignity to the eccentricities of Julius; the soft and graceful manners which masked the insatiable ambition and the implacable hatred of Cæsar Borgia.

We have mentioned Cæsar Borgia. It is impossible not to pause for a moment on the name of a man in whom the political morality of Italy was so strongly personified, partially blended with the sterner lineaments of the Spanish character. On two important occasions Machiavelli was admitted to his society; once, at the moment when Cæsar's splendid villany achieved its most signal triumph, when he caught in one snare and crushed at one blow all his most formidable rivals; and again when, exhausted by disease and overwhelmed by misfortunes, which no human prudence could have averted, he was the prisoner of the deadliest enemy of his house. These interviews between the greatest speculative and the greatest practical statesman of the age are fully described in the correspondence, and form perhaps the most interesting part of it. From some passages in The Prince, and perhaps also from some indistinct traditions, several writers have supposed a connexion between those remarkable men much closer than ever existed. The Envoy has even been accused of prompting the crimes of the artful and merciless tyrant. But from the official documents it is clear that their intercourse, though ostensibly amicable, was in reality hostile. It cannot be doubted, however, that the imagination of Machiavelli was strongly impressed, and his speculations on government coloured, by the observations which he made on the singular character and equally singular fortunes of a man who under such disadvantages had achieved such exploits; who, when sensuality, varied through innumerable forms, could no longer stimulate his sated mind, found a more powerful and durable excitement in the intense thirst of empire and revenge; who emerged from the sloth and luxury of the Roman purple the first prince and general of the age; who, trained in an unwarlike profession, formed a gallant army out of the dregs of an unwarlike people; who, after acquiring sovereignty by destroying his enemies, acquired popularity by destroying his tools; who had begun to employ for the most salutary ends the power which he had attained by the most atrocious means; who tolerated within the sphere of his iron despotism no plunderer or oppressor but himself; and who fell at last amidst the mingled curses and regrets of a people of whom his genius had been the wonder, and might have been the salvation. Some of those crimes of Borgia which to us appear the most odious would not, from causes which we have already considered, have struck an Italian of the fifteenth century with equal horror. Patriotic feeling also might induce Machiavelli to look with some indulgence and regret on the memory of the only leader who could have defended the independence of Italy against the confederate spoilers of Cambray.

On this subject Machiavelli felt most strongly. Indeed the expulsion of the foreign tyrants, and the restoration of that golden age which had preceded the irruption of Charles the Eighth, were projects which, at that time, fascinated all the master-spirits of Italy. The magnificent vision delighted the great but ill-regulated mind of Julius. It divided with manuscripts and sauces, painters and falcons, the attention of the frivolous Leo. It prompted the generous treason of Morone. It imparted a transient energy to the feeble mind and body of the last Sforza. It excited for one moment an honest ambition in the false heart of Pescara. Ferocity and insolence were not among the vices of the national character. To the discriminating cruelties of politicians, committed for great ends on select victims, the moral code of the Italians was too indulgent. But though they might have recourse to barbarity as an expedient, they did not require it as a stimulant. They turned with loathing from the atrocity of the strangers who seemed to love blood for its own sake, who, not content with subjugating, were impatient to destroy, who found a fiendish pleasure in razing magnificent cities, cutting the throats of enemies who cried for quarter, or suffocating an unarmed population by thousands in the caverns to which it had fled for safety. Such were the cruelties which daily excited the terror and disgust of a people among whom, till lately, the worst that a soldier had to fear in a pitched battle was the loss of his horse and the expense of his ransom. The swinish intemperance of Switzerland, the wolfish avarice of Spain, the gross licentiousness of the French, indulged in violation of hospitality, of decency, of love itself; the wanton inhumanity which was common to all the invaders, had made them objects of deadly hatred to the inhabitants of the Peninsula. The wealth which had been accumulated during centuries of prosperity and repose was rapidly melting away. The intellectual superiority of the oppressed people only rendered them more keenly sensible of their political degradation. Literature and taste, indeed, still disguised with a flush of hectic loveliness and brilliancy the ravages of an incurable decay. The iron had not yet entered into the soul. The time was not yet come when eloquence was to be gagged, and reason to be hoodwinked, when the harp of the poet was to be hung on the willows of Arno, and the right hand of the painter to forget its cunning. Yet a discerning eye might even then have seen that genius and learning would not long survive the state of things from which they had sprung, and that the great men whose talents gave lustre to that melancholy period had been formed under the influence of happier days, and would leave no successors behind them. The times which shine with the greatest splendour in literary history are not always those to which the human mind is most indebted. Of this we may be convinced, by comparing the generation which follows them with that which had preceded them. The first fruits which are reaped under a bad system often spring from seed sown under a good one. Thus it was, in some measure, with the Augustan age. Thus it was with the age of Raphael and Ariosto, of Aldus and Vida.

Machiavelli deeply regretted the misfortunes of his country, and clearly discerned the cause and the remedy. It was the military system of the Italian people which had extinguished their valour and discipline, and left their wealth an easy prey to every foreign plunderer. The Secretary projected a scheme, alike honourable to his heart and to his intellect, for abolishing the use of mercenary troops, and for organizing a national militia.

The exertions which he made to effect this great object ought alone to rescue his name from obloquy. Though his situation and his habits were pacific, he studied with intense assiduity the theory of war. He made himself master of all its details. The Florentine government entered into his views. A council of war was appointed. Levies were decreed. The indefatigable minister flew from place to place in order to superintend the execution of his design. The times were, in some respects, favourable to the experiment. The system of military tactics had undergone a great revolution. The cavalry was no longer considered as forming the strength of an army. The hours which a citizen could spare from his ordinary employments, though by no means sufficient to familiarise him with the exercise of a man-at-arms, might render him an useful foot-soldier. The dread of a foreign yoke, of plunder, massacre, and conflagration, might have conquered that repugnance to military pursuits which both the industry and the idleness of great towns commonly generate. For a time the scheme promised well. The new troops acquitted themselves respectably in the field. Machiavelli looked with parental rapture on the success of his plan, and began to hope that the arms of Italy might once more be formidable to the barbarians of the Tagus and the Rhine. But the tide of misfortune came on before the barriers which should have withstood it were prepared. For a time, indeed, Florence might be considered as peculiarly fortunate. Famine and sword and pestilence had devasted the fertile plains and stately cities of the Po. All the curses denounced of old against Tyre seemed to have fallen on Venice. Her merchants already stood afar off, lamenting for their great city. The time seemed near when the sea-weed should overgrow her silent Rialto, and the fisherman wash his nets in her deserted arsenal. Naples had been four times conquered and reconquered by tyrants equally indifferent to its welfare, and equally greedy for its spoils. Florence, as yet, had only to endure degradation and extortion, to submit to the mandates of foreign powers, to buy over and over again, at an enormous price, what was already justly her own, to return thanks for being wronged, and to ask pardon for being in the right. She was at length deprived of the blessings even of this infamous and servile repose. Her military and political institutions were swept away together. The Medici returned, in the train of foreign invaders, from their long exile. The policy of Machiaveili was abandoned; and his public services were requited with poverty, imprisonment, and torture.

The fallen statesman still clung to his project with unabated ardour. With the view of vindicating it from some popular objections and of refuting some prevailing errors on the subject of military science, he wrote his seven books on the Art of War. This excellent work is in the form of a dialogue. The opinions of the writer are put into the mouth of Fabrizio Colonna, a powerful nobleman of the Ecclesiastical State, and an officer of distinguished merit in the service of the king of Spain. Colonna visits Florence on his way from Lombardy to his own domains. He is invited to meet some friends at the house of Cosimo Rucellai, an amiable and accomplished young man, whose early death Machiavelli feelingly deplores. After partaking of an elegant entertainment, they retire from the heat into the most shady recesses of the garden. Fabrizio is struck by the sight of some uncommon plants. Cosimo says that, though rare in modern days, they are frequently mentioned by the classical authors, and that his grandfather, like many other Italians, amused himself with practising the ancient methods of gardening. Fabrizio expresses his regret that those who, in later times, affected the manners of the old Romans should select for imitation the most trifling pursuits. This leads to a conversation on the decline of military discipline and on the best means of restoring it. The institution of the Florentine militia is ably defended; and several improvements are suggested in the details.

The Swiss and the Spaniards were, at that time, regarded as the best soldiers in Europe. The Swiss battalion consisted of pikemen, and bore a close resemblance to the Greek phalanx. The Spaniards, like the soldiers of Rome, were armed with the sword and the shield. The victories of Flamininus and Æmilius over the Macedonian kings seem to prove the superiority of the weapons used by the legions. The same experiment had been recently tried with the same result at the battle of Ravenna, one of those tremendous days into which human folly and wickedness compress the whole devastation of a famine or a plague. In that memorable conflict, the infantry of Arragon, the old companions of Gonsalvo, deserted by all their allies, hewed a passage through the thickest of the imperial pikes, and effected an unbroken retreat, in the face of the gendarmerie of De Foix, and the renowned artillery of Este. Fabrizio, or rather Machiavelli, proposes to combine the two systems, to arm the foremost lines with the pike for the purpose of repulsing cavalry, and those in the rear with the sword, as being a weapon better adapted for every other purpose. Throughout the work, the author expresses the highest admiration of the military science of the ancient Romans, and the greatest contempt for the maxims which had been in vogue amongst the Italian commanders of the preceding generation. He prefers infantry to cavalry, and fortified camps to fortified towns. He is inclined to substitute rapid movements and decisive engagements for the languid and dilatory operations of his countrymen. He attaches very little importance to the invention of gunpowder. Indeed he seems to think that it ought scarcely to produce any change in the mode of arming or of disposing troops. The general testimony of historians, it must be allowed, seems to prove that the ill-constructed and ill-served artillery of those times, though useful in a siege, was of little value on the field of battle.

Of the tactics of Machiavelli we will not venture to give an opinion: but we are certain that his book is most able and interesting. As a commentary on the history of his times, it is invaluable. The ingenuity, the grace, and the perspicuity of the style, and the eloquence and animation of particular passages must give pleasure even to readers who take no interest in the subject.

The Prince and the Discourses on Livy were written after the fall of the Republican Government. The former was dedicated to the Young Lorenzo de Medici. This circumstance seems to have disgusted the contemporaries of the writer far more than the doctrines which have rendered the name of the work odious in later times. It was considered as an indication of political apostasy. The fact however seems to have been that Machiavelli, despairing of the liberty of Florence, was inclined to support any government which might preserve her independence. The interval which separated a democracy and a despotism, Soderini and Lorenzo, seemed to vanish when compared with the difference between the former and the present state of Italy, between the security, the opulence, and the repose which she had enjoyed under its native rulers, and the misery in which she had been plunged since the fatal year in which the first foreign tyrant had descended from the Alps. The noble and pathetic exhortation with which The Prince concludes shows how strongly the writer felt upon this subject.

The Prince traces the progress of an ambitious man, the Discourses the progress of an ambitious people. The same principles on which, in the former work, the elevation of an individual is explained, are applied, in the latter, to the longer duration and more complex interests of a society. To a modern statesman the form of the Discourses may appear to be puerile. In truth Livy is not an historian on whom implicit reliance can be placed, even in cases where he must have possessed considerable means of information. And the first Decade, to which Machiavelli has confined himself, is scarcely entitled to more credit than our Chronicle of British Kings who reigned before the Roman invasion. But the commentator is indebted to Livy for little more than a few texts which he might as easily have extracted from the Vulgate or the Decameron. The whole train of thought is original.

On the peculiar immorality which has rendered The Prince unpopular, and which is almost equally discernible in the Discourses, we have already given our opinion at length. We have attempted to show that it belonged rather to the age than to the man, that it was a partial taint, and by no means implied general depravity. We cannot however deny that it is a great blemish, and that it considerably diminishes the pleasure which, in other respects, those works must afford to every intelligent mind.

It is, indeed, impossible to conceive a more healthful and vigorous constitution of the understanding than that which these works indicate. The qualities of the active and the contemplative statesman appear to have been blended in the mind of the writer into a rare and exquisite harmony. His skill in the details of business had not been acquired at the expense of his general powers. It had not rendered his mind less comprehensive; but it had served to correct his speculations, and to impart to them that vivid and practical character which so widely distinguishes them from the vague theories of most political philosophers.

Every man who has seen the world knows that nothing is so useless as a general maxim. If it be very moral and very true, it may serve for a copy to a charity-boy. If, like those of Rochefoucault, it be sparkling and whimsical, it may make an excellent motto for an essay. But few indeed of the many wise apophthegms which have been uttered, from the time of the Seven Sages of Greece to that of Poor Richard, have prevented a single foolish action. We give the highest and the most peculiar praise to the precepts of Machiavelli when we say that they may frequently be of real use in regulating conduct, not so much because they are more just or more profound than those which might be culled from other authors, as because they can be more readily applied to the problems of real life.

There are errors in these works. But they are errors which a writer, situated like Machiavelli, could scarcely avoid. They arise, for the most part, from a single defect which appears to us to pervade his whole system. In his political scheme, the means had been more deeply considered than the ends. The great principle, that societies and laws exist only for the purpose of increasing the sum of private happiness, is not recognised with sufficient clearness. The good of the body, distinct from the good of the members, and sometimes hardly compatible with the good of the members, seems to be the object which he proposes to himself. Of all political fallacies, this has perhaps had the widest and the most mischievous operation. The state of society in the little commonwealths of Greece, the close connexion and mutual dependence of the citizens, and the severity of the laws of war, tended to encourage an opinion which, under such circumstances, could hardly be called erroneous. The interests of every individual were inseparably bound up with those of the state. An invasion destroyed his corn-fields and vine-yards, drove him from his home, and compelled him to encounter all the hardships of a military life. A treaty of peace restored him to security and comfort. A victory doubled the number of his slaves. A defeat perhaps made him a slave himself. When Pericles, in the Peloponnesian war, told the Athenians that, if their country triumphed, their private losses would speedily be repaired, but that, if their arms failed of success, every individual amongst them would probably be ruined, he spoke no more than the truth. He spoke to men whom the tribute of vanquished cities supplied with food and clothing, with the luxury of the bath and the amusements of the theatre, on whom the greatness of their country conferred rank, and before whom the members of less prosperous communities trembled; to men who, in case of a change in the public fortunes, would, at least, be deprived of every comfort and every distinction which they enjoyed. To be butchered on the smoking ruins of their city, to be dragged in chains to a slave-market, too see one child torn from them to dig in the quarries of Sicily, and another to guard the harams of Persepolis, these were the frequent and probable consequences of national calamities. Hence, among the Greeks, patriotism became a governing principle, or rather an ungovernable passion. Their legislators and their philosophers took it for granted that, in providing for the strength and greatness of the state, they sufficiently provided for the happi-ness of the people. The writers of the Roman empire lived under despots, into whose dominion a hundred nations were melted down, and whose gardens would have covered the little commonwealths of Phlius and Platæa. Yet they continued to employ the same language, and to cant about the duty of sacrificing every thing to a country to which they owed nothing.

Causes similar to those which had influenced the disposition of the Greeks operated powerfully on the less vigorous and daring char-acter of the Italians. The Italians, like the Greeks, were members of small communities. Every man was deeply interested in the welfare of the society to which he belonged, a partaker in its wealth and its poverty, in its glory and its shame. In the age of Machiavelli this was peculiarly the case. Public events had produced an im-mense sum of misery to private citizens. The Northern invaders had brought want to their boards, infamy to their beds, fire to their roofs, and the knife to their throats. It was natural that a man who lived in times like these should overrate the importance of those measures by which a nation is rendered formidable to its neighbours, and undervalue those which make it prosperous within itself.

Nothing is more remarkable in the political treatises of Machiavelli than the fairness of mind which they indicate. It appears where the author is in the wrong, almost as strongly as where he is in the right. He never advances a false opinion because it is new or splendid, because he can clothe it in a happy phrase, or defend it by an ingenious sophism. His errors are at once explained by a reference to the circumstances in which he was placed. They evidently were not sought out; they lay in his way, and could scarcely be avoided. Such mistakes must necessarily be committed by early speculators in every science.

In this respect it is amusing to compare The Prince and the Discourses with the Spirit of Laws. Montesquieu enjoys, perhaps, a wider celebrity than any political writer of modern Europe. Something he doubtless owes to his merit, but much more to his fortune. He had the good luck of a Valentine. He caught the eye of the French nation, at the moment when it was waking from the long sleep of political and religious bigotry; and, in consequence, he became a favourite. The English, at that time, considered a Frenchman who talked about constitutional checks and fundamental laws as a prodigy not less astonishing than the learned pig or the musical infant. Specious but shallow, studious of effect, indifferent to truth, eager to build a system, but careless of collecting those materials out of which alone a sound and durable system can be built, the lively President constructed theories as rapidly and as slightly as card-houses, no sooner projected than completed, no sooner completed than blown away, no sooner blown away than forgotten. Machiavelli errs only because his experience, acquired in a very peculiar state of society, could not always enable him to calculate the effect of institutions differing from those of which he had observed the operation. Montesquieu errs, because he has a fine thing to say, and is resolved to say it. If the phænomena which lie before him will not suit his purpose, all history must be ransacked. If nothing established by authentic testimony can be racked or chipped to suit his Procrustean hypothesis, he puts up with some monstrous fable about Siam, or Bantam, or Japan, told by writers compared with whom Lucian and Gulliver were veracious, liars by a double right, as travellers and as Jesuits.

Propriety of thought, and propriety of diction, are commonly found together. Obscurity and affectation are the two greatest faults of style. Obscurity of expression generally springs from confusion of ideas; and the same wish to dazzle at any cost which produces affectation in the manner of a writer is likely to produce sophistry in his reasonings. The judicious and candid mind of Machiavelli shows itself in his luminous, manly, and polished language. The style of Montesquieu, on the other hand, indicates in every page a lively and ingenious, but an unsound mind. Every trick of expression, from the mysterious conciseness of an oracle to the flippancy of a Parisian coxcomb, is employed to disguise the fallacy of some positions, and the triteness of others. Absurdities are brightened into epigrams; truisms are darkened into enigmas. It is with difficulty that the strongest eye can sustain the glare with which some parts are illuminated, or penetrate the shade in which others are concealed.

The political works of Machiavelli derive a peculiar interest from the mournful earnestness which he manifests whenever he touches on topics connected with the calamities of his native land. It is difficult to conceive any situation more painful than that of a great man, condemned to watch the lingering agony of an exhausted country, to tend it during the alternate fits of stupefaction and raving which precede its dissolution, and to see the symptoms of vitality disappear one by one, till nothing is left but coldness, darkness, and corruption. To this joyless and thankless duty was Machiavelli called. In the energetic language of the prophet, he was "mad for the sight of his eyes which he saw," disunion in the council, effeminacy in the camp, liberty extinguished, commerce decaying, national honour sullied, an enlightened and flourishing people given over to the ferocity of ignorant savages. Though his opinions had not escaped the contagion of that political immorality which was common among his countrymen, his natural disposition seems to have been rather stern and impetuous than pliant and artful. When the misery and degradation of Florence and the foul outrage which he had himself sustained recur to his mind, the smooth craft of his profession and his nation is exchanged for the honest bitterness of scorn and anger. He speaks like one sick of the calamitous times and abject people among whom his lot is cast. He pines for the strength and glory of ancient Rome, for the fasces of Brutus and the sword of Scipio, the gravity of the curule chair, and the bloody pomp of the triumphal sacrifice. He seems to be transported back to the days when eight hundred thousand Italian warriors sprung to arms at the rumour of a Gallic invasion. He breathes all the spirit of those intrepid and haughty senators who forgot the dearest ties of nature in the claims of public duty, who looked with disdain on the elephants and on the gold of Pyrrhus, and listened with unaltered composure to the tremendous tidings of Cannæ. Like an ancient temple deformed by the barbarous architecture of a later age, his character acquires an interest from the very circumstances which debase it. The original proportions are rendered more striking by the contrast which they present to the mean and incongruous additions.

The influence of the sentiments which we have described was not apparent in his writings alone. His enthusiasm, barred from the career which it would have selected for itself, seems to have found a vent in desperate levity. He enjoyed a vindictive pleasure in outraging the opinions of a society which he despised. He became careless of the decencies which were expected from a man so highly distinguished in the literary and political world. The sarcastic bitterness of his conversation disgusted those who were more inclined to accuse his licentiousness than their own degeneracy, and who were unable to conceive the strength of those emotions which are concealed by the jests of the wretched, and by the follies of the wise.

The historical works of Machiavelli still remain to be considered. The life of Castruccio Castracani will occupy us for a very short time, and would scarcely have demanded our notice, had it not attracted a much greater share of public attention than it deserves. Few books, indeed, could be more interesting than a careful and judicious account, from such a pen, of the illustrious Prince of Lucca, the most eminent of those Italian chiefs, who, like Pisistratus and Gelon, acquired a power felt rather than seen, and resting, not on law or on prescription, but on the public favour and on their great personal qualities. Such a work would exhibit to us the real nature of that species of sovereignty, so singular and so often misunderstood, which the Greeks denominated tyranny, and which, modified in some degree by the feudal system, reappeared in the commonwealths of Lombardy and Tuscany. But this little composition of Machiavelli is in no sense a history. It has no pretensions to fidelity. It is a trifle, and not a very successful trifle. It is scarcely more authentic than the novel of Belphegor, and is very much duller.

The last great work of this illustrious man was the history of his native city. It was written by command of the Pope, who, as chief of the house of Medici, was at that time sovereign of Florence. The characters of Cosmo, of Piero, and of Lorenzo, are, however, treated with a freedom and impartiality equally honourable to the writer and to the patron. The miseries and humiliations of dependence, the bread which is more bitter than every other food, the stairs which are more painful than every other ascent, had not broken the spirit of Machiavelli. The most corrupting post in a corrupting profession had not depraved the generous heart of Clement.

The History does not appear to be the fruit of much industry or research. It is unquestionably inaccurate. But it is elegant, lively, and picturesque, beyond any other in the Italian language. The reader, we believe, carries away from it a more vivid and a more faithful impression of the national character and manners than from more correct accounts. The truth is, that the book belongs rather to ancient than to modern literature. It is in the style, not of Davila and Clarendon, but of Herodotus and Tacitus. The classical histories may almost be called romances founded in fact. The relation is, no doubt, in all its principal points, strictly true. But the numerous little incidents which heighten the interest, the words, the gestures, the looks, are evidently furnished by the imagination of the author. The fashion of later times is different. A more exact narrative is given by the writer. It may be doubted whether more exact notions are conveyed to the reader. The best portraits are perhaps those in which there is a slight mixture of caricature, and we are not certain, that the best histories are not those in which a little of the exaggeration of fictitious narrative is judiciously employed. Something is lost in accuracy; but much is gained in effect. The fainter lines are neglected; but the great characteristic features are imprinted on the mind for ever.

The History terminates with the death of Lorenzo de' Medici. Machiavelli had, it seems, intended to continue his narrative to a later period. But his death prevented the execution of his design; and the melancholy task of recording the desolation and shame of Italy devolved on Guicciardini.

Machiavelli lived long enough to see the commencement of the last struggle for Florentine liberty. Soon after his death monarchy was finally established, not such a monarchy as that of which Cosmo had laid the foundations deep in the institutions and feelings of his countrymen, and which Lorenzo had embellished with the trophies of every science and every art; but a loathsome tyranny, proud and mean, cruel and feeble, bigotted and lascivious. The character of Machiavelli was hateful to the new masters of Italy; and those parts of his theory which were in strict accordance with their own daily practice afforded a pretext for blackening his memory. His works were misrepresented by the learned, misconstrued by the ignorant, censured by the church, abused, with all the rancour of simulated virtue, by the tools of a base government, and the priests of a baser superstition. The name of the man whose genius had illuminated all the dark places of policy, and to whose patriotic wisdom an oppressed people had owed their last chance of emancipation and revenge, passed into a proverb of infamy. For more than two hundred years his bones lay undistinguished. At length, an English nobleman paid the last honours to the greatest statesman of Florence. In the church of Santa Croce a monument was erected to his memory, which is contemplated with reverence by all who can distinguish the virtues of a great mind through the corruptions of a degenerate age, and which will be approached with still deeper homage when the object to which his public life was devoted shall be attained, when the foreign yoke shall be broken, when a second Procida shall avenge the wrongs of Naples, when a happier Rienzi shall restore the good estate of Rome, when the streets of Florence and Bologna shall again resound with their ancient war cry, *Popolo; popolo; muoiano i tiranni!*

WILLIAM PITT, EARL OF CHATHAM

(JANUARY 1834)

A History of the Right Honourable William Pitt, Earl of Chatham, containing his Speeches in Parliament, a considerable portion of his Correspondence when Secretary of State, upon French, Spanish, and American Affairs, never before published; and an Account of the principal Events and Persons of his time, connected with his Life, Sentiments, and Administration. By the REV. FRANCIS THACKERAY, A.M. 2 vols. 4to. London: 1827.

THOUGH several years have elapsed since the publication of this work, it is still, we believe, a new publication to most of our readers. Nor are we surprised at this. The book is large, and the style heavy. The information which Mr. Thackeray has obtained from the State Paper Office is new; but much of it is very uninteresting. The rest of his narrative is very little better than Gifford's or Tomline's Life of the second Pitt, and tells us little or nothing that may not be found quite as well told in the Parliamentary History, the Annual Register, and other works equally common.

Almost every mechanical employment, it is said, has a tendency to injure some one or other of the bodily organs of the artisan. Grinders of cutlery die of consumption; weavers are stunted in their growth; smiths become blear-eyed. In the same manner almost every intellectual employment has a tendency to produce some intellectual malady. Biographers, translators, editors, all, in short, who employ themselves in illustrating the lives or the writings of others, are peculiarly exposed to the *Lues Boswelliana*, or disease of admiration. But we scarcely remember ever to have seen a patient so far gone in this distemper as Mr. Thackeray. He is not satisfied with forcing us to confess that Pitt was a great orator, a vigorous minister, an honourable and high-spirited gentleman. He will have it, that all virtues and all accomplishments met in his hero. In spite of Gods, men, and columns, Pitt must be a poet, a poet capable of producing a heroic poem of the first order; and we are assured that we ought to find many charms in such lines as these:—

> "Midst all the tumults of the warring sphere,
>   My light-charged bark may haply *glide*;
> Some gale may waft, some conscious thought shall cheer,
>   And the small freight unanxious *glide*."[1]

Pitt was in the army for a few months in time of peace. Mr. Thackeray accordingly insists on our confessing that, if the young cornet had remained in the service, he would have been one of the ablest commanders that ever lived. But this is not all. Pitt, it seems, was not merely a great poet *in esse*, and a great general *in posse*, but a finished example of moral excellence, the just man made perfect. He was in the right when he attempted to establish an inquisition, and to give bounties for perjury, in order to get Walpole's head. He was in the right when he declared Walpole to have been an excellent minister. He was in the right when, being in Opposition, he maintained that no peace ought to be made with Spain, till she should formally renounce the right of search. He was in the right when, being in office, he silently acquiesced in a treaty by which Spain did not renounce the right of search. When he left the Duke of Newcastle, when he coalesced with the Duke of Newcastle, when he thundered against subsidies, when he lavished subsidies with unexampled profusion, when he execrated the Hanoverian connexion, when he declared that Hanover ought to be as dear to us as Hampshire, he was still invariably speaking the language of a virtuous and enlightened statesman.

The truth is that there scarcely ever lived a person who had so little claim to this sort of praise as Pitt. He was undoubtedly a great man. But his was not a complete and well-proportioned greatness. The public life of Hampden or of Somers resembles a regular drama, which can be criticized as a whole, and every scene

---

[1] The quotation is faithfully made from Mr. Thackeray. Perhaps Pitt wrote *guide* in the fourth line.

of which is to be viewed in connexion with the main action. The public life of Pitt, on the other hand, is a rude though striking piece, a piece abounding in incongruities, a piece without any unity of plan, but redeemed by some noble passages, the effect of which is increased by the tameness or extravagance of what precedes and of what follows. His opinions were unfixed. His conduct at some of the most important conjunctures of his life was evidently determined by pride and resentment. He had one fault, which of all human faults is most rarely found in company with true greatness. He was extremely affected. He was an almost solitary instance of a man of real genius, and of a brave, lofty, and commanding spirit, without simplicity of character. He was an actor in the Closet, an actor at Council, an actor in Parliament; and even in private society he could not lay aside his theatrical tones and attitudes. We know that one of the most distinguished of his partisans often complained that he could never obtain admittance to Lord Chatham's room till every thing was ready for the representation, till the dresses and properties were all correctly disposed, till the light was thrown with Rembrandt-like effect on the head of the illustrious performer, till the flannels had been arranged with the air of a Grecian drapery, and the crutch placed as gracefully as that of Belisarius or Lear.

Yet, with all his faults and affectations, Pitt had, in a very extraordinary degree, many of the elements of greatness. He had splendid talents, strong passions, quick sensibility, and vehement enthusiasm for the grand and the beautiful. There was something about him which ennobled tergiversation itself. He often went wrong, very wrong. But, to quote the language of Wordsworth,

> "He still retained,
> 'Mid such abasement, what he had received
> From nature, an intense and glowing mind."

In an age of low and dirty prostitution, in the age of Doddington and Sandys, it was something to have a man who might perhaps, under some strong excitement, have been tempted to ruin his country, but who never would have stooped to pilfer from her, a man whose errors arose, not from a sordid desire of gain, but from a fierce thirst for power, for glory, and for vengeance. History owes to him this attestation, that, at a time when any thing short of direct embezzlement of the public money was considered as quite fair in public men, he showed the most scrupulous disinterestedness; that, at a time when it seemed to be generally taken for granted that Government could be upheld only by the basest and most immoral arts, he appealed to the better and nobler parts of human nature, that he made a brave and splendid attempt to do, by means of public opinion, what no other statesman of his day thought it possible to do, except by means of corruption, that he looked for support, not, like the Pelhams, to a strong aristocratical connexion, not, like Bute, to the personal favour of the Sovereign, but to the middle class of Englishmen, that he inspired that class with a firm confidence in his integrity and ability, that, backed by them, he forced an unwilling court and an unwilling oligarchy to admit him to an ample share of power, and that he used his power in such a manner as clearly proved him to have sought it, not for the sake of profit or patronage, but from a wish to establish for himself a great and durable reputation by means of eminent services rendered to the state.

The family of Pitt was wealthy and respectable. His grandfather was Governor of Madras, and brought back from India that celebrated diamond which the Regent Orleans, by the advice of Saint-Simon, purchased for upwards of two millions of livres, and which is still considered as the most precious of the crown jewels of France. Governor Pitt bought estates and rotten boroughs, and sat in the House of Commons for Old Sarum. His son Robert was at one time member for Old Sarum, and at another for Oakhampton. Robert had two sons. Thomas, the elder, inherited the estates and the parliamentary interest of his father. The second was the celebrated William Pitt.

He was born in November 1708. About the early part of his life little more is known than that he was educated at Eton, and that at seventeen he was entered at Trinity College Oxford. During the second year of his residence at the University, George the First died; and the event was, after the fashion of that generation, celebrated by the Oxonians in many very middling copies of verses. On this occasion Pitt published some Latin lines, which Mr. Thackeray has preserved. They prove that the young student had but a very limited knowledge even of the mechanical part of his art. All true Etonians will hear with concern that their illustrious schoolfellow is guilty of making the first syllable in *labenti* short.[1] The matter of the poem is as worthless as that of any college exercise that was ever written before or since. There is, of course, much about Mars, Themis, Neptune, and Cocytus. The Muses are earnestly entreated to weep over the urn of Cæsar; for Cæsar, says

[1] So Mr. Thackeray has printed the poem. But it may be charitably hoped that Pitt wrote *labanti*.

the Poet, loved the Muses; Cæsar, who could not read a line of Pope, and who loved nothing but punch and fat women.

Pitt had been, from his school-days, cruelly tormented by the gout, and was at last advised to travel for his health. He accordingly left Oxford without taking a degree, and visited France and Italy. He returned, however, without having received much benefit from his excursion, and continued, till the close of his life, to suffer most severely from his constitutional malady.

His father was now dead, and had left very little to the younger children. It was necessary that William should choose a profession. He decided for the army, and a cornet's commission was procured for him in the Blues.

But, small as his fortune was, his family had both the power and the inclination to serve him. At the general election of 1734, his elder brother Thomas was chosen both for Old Sarum and for Oakhampton. When Parliament met in 1735, Thomas made his election to serve for Oakhampton, and William was returned for Old Sarum.

Walpole had now been, during fourteen years, at the head of affairs. He had risen to power under the most favourable circumstances. The whole of the Whig party, of that party which professed peculiar attachment to the principles of the Revolution, and which exclusively enjoyed the confidence of the reigning house, had been united in support of his administration. Happily for him, he had been out of office when the South-Sea Act was passed; and, though he does not appear to have foreseen all the consequences of that measure, he had strenuously opposed it, as he opposed all the measures, good and bad, of Sunderland's administration. When the South-Sea Company were voting dividends of fifty per cent, when a hundred pounds of their stock were selling for eleven hundred pounds, when Threadneedle Street was daily crowded with the coaches of dukes and prelates, when divines and philosophers turned gamblers, when a thousand kindred bubbles were daily blown into existence, the periwig company, and the Spanish-jackass company, and the quicksilver-fixation company, Walpole's calm good sense preserved him from the general infatuation. He condemned the prevailing madness in public, and turned a considerable sum by taking advantage of it in private. When the crash came, when ten thousand families were reduced to beggary in a day, when the people, in the frenzy of their rage and despair, clamoured, not only against the lower agents in the juggle, but against the Hanoverian favourites, against the English ministers, against the King himself, when Parliament met, eager for confiscation and blood, when members of the House of Commons proposed that the directors should be treated like parricides in ancient Rome, tied up in sacks, and thrown into the Thames, Walpole was the man on whom all parties turned their eyes. Four years before he had been driven from power by the intrigues of Sunderland and Stanhope, and the lead in the House of Commons had been intrusted to Craggs and Aislabie. Stanhope was no more. Aislabie was expelled from Parliament on account of his disgraceful conduct regarding the South-Sea scheme. Craggs was saved by a timely death from a similar mark of infamy. A large minority in the House of Commons voted for a severe censure on Sunderland who, finding it impossible to withstand the force of the prevailing sentiment, retired from office, and outlived his retirement but a very short time. The schism which had divided the Whig party was now completely healed. Walpole had no opposition to encounter except that of the Tories; and the Tories were naturally regarded by the King with the strongest suspicion and dislike.

For a time business went on with a smoothness and a despatch such as had not been known since the days of the Tudors. During the session of 1724, for example, there was hardly a single division except on private bills. It is not impossible that, by taking the course which Pelham afterwards took, by admitting into the Government all the rising talents and ambition of the Whig party, and by making room here and there for a Tory not unfriendly to the House of Brunswick, Walpole might have averted the tremendous conflict in which he passed the later years of his administration, and in which he was at length vanquished. The Opposition which overthrew him was an Opposition created by his own policy, by his own insatiable love of power.

In the very act of forming his Ministry he turned one of the ablest and most attached of his supporters into a deadly enemy. Pulteney had strong public and private claims to a high situation in the new arrangement. His fortune was immense. His private character was respectable. He was already a distinguished speaker. He had acquired official experience in an important post. He had been, through all changes of fortune, a consistent Whig. When the Whig party was split into two sections, Pulteney had resigned a valuable place, and had followed the fortunes of Walpole. Yet, when Walpole returned to power, Pulteney was not invited to take office. An angry discussion took place between the friends. The minister offered a peerage. It was impossible for Pulteney not to discern the motive of such an offer. He indignantly refused to accept it. For some time he continued to brood over his wrongs, and to watch for an opportunity of revenge. As soon as a favourable conjuncture arrived he joined the minority, and became the greatest leader of Opposition that the House of Commons had ever seen.

Of all the Members of the Cabinet Carteret was the most eloquent and accomplished. His talents for debate were of the first order; his knowledge of foreign affairs was superior to that of any living statesman; his attachment to the Protestant succession was undoubted. But there was not room in one Government for him and Walpole. Carteret retired, and was, from that time forward, one of the most persevering and formidable enemies of his old colleague.

If there was any man with whom Walpole could have consented to make a partition of power, that man was Lord Townshend. They were distant kinsmen by birth, near kinsmen by marriage. They had been friends from childhood. They had been schoolfellows at Eton. They were country-neighbours in Norfolk. They had been in office together under Godolphin. They had gone into Opposition together when Harley rose to power. They had been persecuted by the same House of Commons. They had, after the death of Anne, been recalled together to office. They had again been driven out together by Sunderland, and had again come back together when the influence of Sunderland had declined. Their opinions on public affairs almost always coincided. They were both men of frank, generous, and compassionate natures. Their intercourse had been for many years affectionate and cordial. But the ties of blood, of marriage, and of friendship, the memory of mutual services, the memory of common triumphs and common disasters, were insufficient to restrain that ambition which domineered over all the virtues and vices of Walpole. He was resolved, to use his own metaphor, that the firm of the house should be, not Townshend and Walpole, but Walpole and Townshend. At length the rivals proceeded to personal abuse before a large company, seized each other by the collar, and grasped their swords. The women squalled. The men parted the combatants. By friendly intervention the scandal of a duel between cousins, brothersin-law, old friends, and old colleagues, was prevented. But the disputants could not long continue to act together. Townshend retired, and, with rare moderation and public spirit, refused to take any part in politics. He could not, he said, trust his temper. He feared that the recollection of his private wrongs might impel him to follow the example of Pulteney, and to oppose measures which he thought generally beneficial to the country. He therefore never visited London after his resignation, but passed the closing years of his life in dignity and repose among his trees and pictures at Rainham.

Next went Chesterfield. He too was a Whig and a friend of the Protestant succession. He was an orator, a courtier, a wit, and a man of letters. He was at the head of *ton* in days when, in order to be at the head of *ton*, it was not sufficient to be dull and supercilious. It was evident that he submitted impatiently to the ascendency of Walpole. He murmured against the Excise Bill. His brothers voted against it in the House of Commons. The minister acted with characteristic caution and characteristic energy; caution in the conduct of public affairs; energy where his own supremacy was concerned. He withdrew his Bill, and turned out all his hostile or wavering colleagues. Chesterfield was stopped on the great staircase of St. James's, and summoned to deliver up the staff which he bore as Lord Steward of the Household. A crowd of noble and powerful functionaries, the Dukes of Montrose and Bolton, Lord Burlington, Lord Stair, Lord Cobham, Lord Marchmont, Lord Clinton, were at the same time dismissed from the service of the Crown.

Not long after these events the Opposition was reinforced by the Duke of Argyle, a man vainglorious indeed and fickle, but brave, eloquent, and popular. It was in a great measure owing to his exertions that the Act of Settlement had been peaceably carried into effect in England immediately after the death of Anne, and that the Jacobite rebellion which, during the following year, broke out in Scotland, had been suppressed. He too carried over to the minority the aid of his great name, his talents, and his paramount influence in his native country.

In each of these cases taken separately, a skilful defender of Walpole might perhaps make out a case for him. But when we see that during a long course of years all the footsteps are turned the same way, that all the most eminent of those public men who agreed with the minister in their general views of policy left him, one after another, with sore and irritated minds, we find it impossible not to believe that the real explanation of the phænomenon is to be found in the words of his son, "Sir Robert Walpole loved power so much that he would not endure a rival." Hume has described this famous minister with great felicity in one short sentence,—"moderate in exercising power, not equitable in engrossing it." Kind-hearted, jovial, and placable as Walpole was, he was yet a man with whom no person of high pretensions and high spirit could long continue to act. He had, therefore, to stand

against an Opposition containing all the most accomplished statesmen of the age, with no better support than that which he received
from persons like his brother Horace or Henry Pelham, whose
industrious mediocrity gave no cause for jealousy, or from clever
adventurers, whose situation and character diminished the dread
which their talents might have inspired. To this last class belonged
Fox, who was too poor to live without office; Sir William Yonge, of
whom Walpole himself said, that nothing but such parts could
buoy up such a character, and that nothing but such a character
could drag down such parts; and Winnington, whose private morals
lay, justly or unjustly, under imputations of the worst kind.

The discontented Whigs were, not perhaps in number, but
certainly in ability, experience, and weight, by far the most important part of the Opposition. The Tories furnished little more
than rows of ponderous foxhunters, fat with Staffordshire or
Devonshire ale, men who drank to the king over the water and
believed that all the fundholders were Jews, men whose religion
consisted in hating the Dissenters, and whose political researches
had led them to fear, like Squire Western, that their land might be
sent over to Hanover to be put in the sinking-fund. The eloquence
of these zealous squires, the remnant of the once formidable
October Club, seldom went beyond a hearty Aye or No. Very few
members of this party had distinguished themselves much in
Parliament, or could, under any circumstances, have been called
to fill any high office; and those few had generally, like Sir William
Wyndham, learned in the company of their new associates the
doctrines of toleration and political liberty, and might indeed with
strict propriety be called Whigs.

It was to the Whigs in Opposition, the patriots, as they were
called, that the most distinguished of the English youth who at this
season entered into public life attached themselves. These inexperienced politicians felt all the enthusiasm which the name of
liberty naturally excites in young and ardent minds. They conceived that the theory of the Tory Opposition and the practice of
Walpole's Government were alike inconsistent with the principles
of liberty. They accordingly repaired to the standard which
Pulteney had set up. While opposing the Whig minister, they professed a firm adherence to the purest doctrines of Whiggism. He
was the schismatic; they were the true Catholics, the peculiar
people, the depositaries of the orthodox faith of Hampden and
Russell, the one sect which, amidst the corruptions generated by
time and by the long possession of power, had preserved inviolate
the principles of the Revolution. Of the young men who attached

themselves to this portion of the Opposition the most distinguished were Lyttelton and Pitt.

When Pitt entered Parliament, the whole political world was attentively watching the progress of an event which soon added great strength to the Opposition, and particularly to that section of the Opposition in which the young statesman enrolled himself. The Prince of Wales was gradually becoming more and more estranged from his father and his father's ministers, and more and more friendly to the patriots.

Nothing is more natural than that, in a monarchy where a constitutional Opposition exists, the heir-apparent of the throne should put himself at the head of that Opposition. He is impelled to such a course by every feeling of ambition and of vanity. He cannot be more than second in the estimation of the party which is in. He is sure to be the first member of the party which is out. The highest favour which the existing administration can expect from him is that he will not discard them. But, if he joins the Opposition, all his associates expect that he will promote them; and the feelings which men entertain towards one from whom they hope to obtain great advantages which they have not are far warmer than the feelings with which they regard one who, at the very utmost, can only leave them in possession of what they already have. An heir-apparent, therefore, who wishes to enjoy, in the highest perfection, all the pleasure that can be derived from eloquent flattery and profound respect will always join those who are struggling to force themselves into power. This is, we believe, the true explanation of a fact which Lord Granville attributed to some natural peculiarity in the illustrious house of Brunswick. "This family," said he at Council, we suppose after his daily half-gallon of Burgundy, "always has quarrelled, and always will quarrel, from generation to generation." He should have known something of the matter; for he had been a favourite with three successive generations of the royal house. We cannot quite admit his explanation; but the fact is indisputable. Since the accession of George the First, there have been four Princes of Wales, and they have all been almost constantly in Opposition.

Whatever might have been the motives which induced Prince Frederick to join the party opposed to Sir Robert Walpole, his support infused into many members of that party a courage and an energy of which they stood greatly in need. Hitherto it had been impossible for the discontented Whigs not to feel some misgivings when they found themselves dividing, night after night, with uncompromising Jacobites who were known to be in constant com-

munication with the exiled family, or with Tories who had impeached Somers, who had murmured against Harley and St. John
as too remiss in the cause of the Church and the landed interest,
and who, if they were not inclined to attack the reigning family,
yet considered the introduction of that family as, at best, only the
less of two great evils, as a necessary but painful and humiliating
preservative against Popery. The minister might plausibly say that
Pulteney and Carteret, in the hope of gratifying their own appetite
for office and for revenge, did not scruple to serve the purposes of
a faction hostile to the Protestant succession. The appearance of
Frederick at the head of the patriots silenced this reproach. The
leaders of the Opposition might now boast that their course was
sanctioned by a person as deeply interested as the King himself in
maintaining the Act of Settlement, and that, instead of serving the
purposes of the Tory party, they had brought that party over to
the side of Whiggism. It must indeed be admitted that, though both
the King and the Prince behaved in a manner little to their honour,
though the father acted harshly, the son disrespectfully, and both
childishly, the royal family was rather strengthened than weakened
by the disagreement of its two most distinguished members. A
large class of politicians, who had considered themselves as placed
under sentence of perpetual exclusion from office, and who, in their
despair, had been almost ready to join in a counter-revolution, as
the only mode of removing the proscription under which they lay,
now saw with pleasure an easier and safer road to power opening
before them, and thought it far better to wait till, in the natural
course of things, the Crown should descend to the heir of the
House of Brunswick, than to risk their lands and their necks in a
rising for the House of Stuart. The situation of the royal family
resembled the situation of those Scotch families in which father and
son took opposite sides during the rebellion, in order that, come
what might, the estate might not be forfeited.

In April 1736 Frederick was married to the Princess of Saxe
Gotha, with whom he afterwards lived on terms very similar to
those on which his father had lived with Queen Caroline. The
Prince adored his wife, and thought her in mind and person the
most attractive of her sex. But he thought that conjugal fidelity was
an unprincely virtue; and, in order to be like Henry the Fourth and
the Regent Orleans, he affected a libertinism for which he had no
taste, and frequently quitted the only woman whom he loved for
ugly and disagreeable mistresses.

The address which the House of Commons presented to the
King on occasion of the Prince's marriage was moved, not by the

minister, but by Pulteney, the leader of the Whigs in Opposition. It was on this motion that Pitt, who had not broken silence during the session in which he took his seat, addressed the House for the first time. "A contemporary historian," says Mr. Thackeray, "describes Mr. Pitt's first speech as superior even to the models of ancient eloquence. According to Tindal, it was more ornamented than the speeches of Demosthenes, and less diffuse than those of Cicero." This unmeaning phrase has been a hundred times quoted. That it should ever have been quoted, except to be laughed at, is strange. The vogue which it has obtained may serve to show in how slovenly a way most people are content to think. Did Tindal, who first used it, or Archdeacon Coxe and Mr. Thackeray, who have borrowed it, ever in their lives hear any speaking which did not deserve the same compliment? Did they ever hear speaking less ornamented than that of Demosthenes, or more diffuse than that of Cicero? We know no living orator, from Lord Brougham down to Mr. Hunt, who is not entitled to the same eulogy. It would be no very flattering compliment to a man's figure to say, that he was taller than the Polish Count, and shorter than Giant O'Brien, fatter than the *Anatomie Vivante*, and more slender than Daniel Lambert.

Pitt's speech, as it is reported in the Gentleman's Magazine, certainly deserves Tindal's compliment, and deserves no other. It is just as empty and wordy as a maiden speech on such an occasion might be expected to be. But the fluency and the personal advantages of the young orator instantly caught the ear and eye of his audience. He was, from the day of his first appearance, always heard with attention; and exercise soon developed the great powers which he possessed.

In our time, the audience of a member of Parliament is the nation. The three or four hundred persons who may be present while a speech is delivered may be pleased or disgusted by the voice and action of the orator; but, in the reports which are read the next day by hundreds of thousands, the difference between the noblest and the meanest figure, between the richest and the shrillest tones, between the most graceful and the most uncouth gesture, altogether vanishes. A hundred years ago, scarcely any report of what passed within the walls of the House of Commons was suffered to get abroad. In those times, therefore, the impression which a speaker might make on the persons who actually heard him was every thing. His fame out of doors depended entirely on the report of those who were within the doors. In the Parliaments of that time, therefore, as in the ancient commonwealths, those qualifications which en-

hance the immediate effect of a speech, were far more important
ingredients in the composition of an orator than at present. All
those qualifications Pitt possessed in the highest degree. On the
stage, he would have been the finest Brutus or Coriolanus ever seen.
Those who saw him in his decay, when his health was broken, when
his mind was untuned, when he had been removed from that
stormy assembly of which he thoroughly knew the temper and over
which he possessed unbounded influence to a small, a torpid, and
an unfriendly audience, say that his speaking was then, for the most
part, a low, monotonous muttering, audible only to those who sate
close to him, that, when violently excited, he sometimes raised his
voice for a few minutes, but that it soon sank again into an unintelligible murmur. Such was the Earl of Chatham; but such was
not William Pitt. His figure, when he first appeared in Parliament,
was strikingly graceful and commanding, his features high and
noble, his eye full of fire. His voice, even when it sank to a whisper,
was heard to the remotest benches; and when he strained it to its
full extent, the sound rose like the swell of the organ of a great
cathedral, shook the house with its peal, and was heard through
lobbies and down staircases, to the Court of Requests and the
precincts of Westminster Hall. He cultivated all these eminent
advantages with the most assiduous care. His action is described
by a very malignant observer as equal to that of Garrick. His play
of countenance was wonderful: he frequently disconcerted a hostile
orator by a single glance of indignation or scorn. Every tone, from
the impassioned cry to the thrilling aside, was perfectly at his command. It is by no means improbable that the pains which he took to
improve his great personal advantages had, in some respects, a
prejudicial operation, and tended to nourish in him that passion
for theatrical effect which, as we have already remarked, was one of
the most conspicuous blemishes in his character.

But it was not solely or principally to outward accomplishments
that Pitt owed the vast influence which, during nearly thirty years,
he exercised over the House of Commons. He was undoubtedly a
great orator; and, from the descriptions of his contemporaries, and
the fragments of his speeches which still remain, it is not difficult
to discover the nature and extent of his oratorical powers.

He was no speaker of set speeches. His few prepared discourses
were complete failures. The elaborate panegyric which he pronounced on General Wolfe was considered as the very worst of all
his performances. "No man," says a critic who had often heard
him, "ever knew so little what he was going to say." Indeed his
facility amounted to a vice. He was not the master, but the slave

of his own speech. So little self-command had he when once he felt the impulse, that he did not like to take part in a debate when his mind was full of an important secret of state. "I must sit still," he once said to Lord Shelburne on such an occasion; "for, when once I am up, every thing that is in my mind comes out."

Yet he was not a great debater. That he should not have been so when first he entered the House of Commons is not strange. Scarcely any person has ever become so without long practice, and many failures. It was by slow degrees, as Burke said, that the late Mr. Fox became the most brilliant and powerful debater that ever lived. Mr. Fox himself attributed his own success to the resolution which he formed when very young, of speaking, well or ill, at least once every night. "During five whole sessions," he used to say, "I spoke every night but one; and I regret only that I did not speak on that night too." Indeed, with the exception of Mr. Stanley, whose knowledge of the science of parliamentary defence resembles an instinct, it would be difficult to name any eminent debater who has not made himself a master of his art at the expense of his audience.

But as this art is one which even the ablest men have seldom acquired without long practice, so it is one which men of respectable abilities, with assiduous and intrepid practice, seldom fail to acquire. It is singular that in such an art, Pitt, a man of splendid talents, of great fluency, of great boldness, a man whose whole life was passed in parliamentary conflict, a man who, during several years, was the leading minister of the Crown in the House of Commons, should never have attained to high excellence. He spoke without premeditation; but his speech followed the course of his own thoughts and not the course of the previous discussion. He could, indeed, treasure up in his memory some detached expression of a hostile orator, and make it the text for lively ridicule or solemn reprehension. Some of the most celebrated bursts of his eloquence were called forth by an unguarded word, a laugh, or a cheer. But this was the only sort of reply in which he appears to have excelled. He was perhaps the only great English orator who did not think it any advantage to have the last word, and who generally spoke by choice before his most formidable opponents. His merit was almost entirely rhetorical. He did not succeed either in exposition or in refutation; but his speeches abounded with lively illustrations, striking apophthegms, well told anecdotes, happy allusions, passionate appeals. His invective and sarcasm were terrific. Perhaps no English orator was ever so much feared.

But that which gave most effect to his declamation was the air of sincerity, of vehement feeling, of moral elevation, which belonged to all that he said. His style was not always in the purest taste. Several contemporary judges pronounced it too florid. Walpole, in the midst of the rapturous eulogy which he pronounces on one of Pitt's greatest orations, owns that some of the metaphors were too forced. Some of Pitt's quotations and classical stories are too trite for a clever schoolboy. But these were niceties for which the audience cared little. The enthusiasm of the orator infected all who heard him; his ardour and his noble bearing put fire into the most frigid conceit, and gave dignity to the most puerile allusion.

His powers soon began to give annoyance to the Government; and Walpole determined to make an example of the patriotic cornet. Pitt was accordingly dismissed from the service. Mr. Thackeray says that the minister took this step, because he plainly saw that it would have been vain to think of buying over so honourable and disinterested an opponent. We do not dispute Pitt's integrity; but we do not know what proof he had given of it when he was turned out of the army; and we are sure that Walpole was not likely to give credit for inflexible honesty to a young adventurer who had never had an opportunity of refusing any thing. The truth is, that it was not Walpole's practice to buy off enemies. Mr. Burke truly says, in the Appeal to the Old Whigs, that Walpole gained very few over from the Opposition. Indeed that great minister knew his business far too well. He knew that for one mouth which is stopped with a place, fifty other mouths will be instantly opened. He knew that it would have been very bad policy in him to give the world to understand that more was to be got by thwarting his measures than by supporting them. These maxims are as old as the origin of parliamentary corruption in England. Pepys learned them, as he tells us, from the counsellors of Charles the Second.

Pitt was no loser. He was made Groom of the Bedchamber to the Prince of Wales, and continued to declaim against the ministers with unabated violence and with increasing ability. The question of maritime right, then agitated between Spain and England, called forth all his powers. He clamoured for war with a vehemence which it is not easy to reconcile with reason or humanity, but which appears to Mr. Thackeray worthy of the highest admiration. We will not stop to argue a point on which we had long thought that all well-informed people were agreed. We could easily show, we think, that, if any respect be due to international law, if right, where societies of men are concerned, be any thing but another name for might, if we do not adopt the doctrine of the Buccaneers, which seems to be also the doctrine of Mr. Thackeray, that treaties mean nothing within thirty degrees of the line, the war with Spain was

altogether unjustifiable. But the truth is, that the promoters of
that war have saved the historian the trouble of trying them. They
have pleaded guilty. "I have seen," says Burke, "and with some
care examined, the original documents concerning certain important
transactions of those times. They perfectly satisfied me of the
extreme injustice of that war, and of the falsehood of the colours
which Walpole, to his ruin, and guided by a mistaken policy,
suffered to be daubed over that measure. Some years after, it was
my fortune to converse with many of the principal actors against
that minister, and with those who principally excited that clamour.
None of them, no not one, did in the least defend the measure, or
attempt to justify their conduct. They condemned it as freely as
they would have done in commenting upon any proceeding in
history in which they were totally unconcerned." Pitt, on subsequent occasions, gave ample proof that he was one of those tardy
penitents. But his conduct, even where it appeared most criminal
to himself, appears admirable to his biographer.

The elections of 1741 were unfavourable to Walpole; and after
a long and obstinate struggle he found it necessary to resign. The
Duke of Newcastle and Lord Hardwicke opened a negotiation with
the leading patriots, in the hope of forming an administration on a
Whig basis. At this conjuncture, Pitt and those persons who were
most nearly connected with him, acted in a manner very little to
their honour. They attempted to come to an understanding with
Walpole, and offered, if he would use his influence with the King
in their favour, to screen him from prosecution. They even went
so far as to engage for the concurrence of the Prince of Wales. But
Walpole knew that the assistance of the Boys, as he called the young
patriots, would avail him nothing if Pulteney and Carteret should
prove intractable, and would be superfluous if the great leaders of
the Opposition could be gained. He, therefore, declined the pro-
posal. It is remarkable that Mr. Thackeray, who has thought it
worth while to preserve Pitt's bad college verses, has not even
alluded to this story, a story which is supported by strong testimony,
and which may be found in so common a book as Coxe's Life of
Walpole.

The new arrangements disappointed almost every member of the
Opposition, and none more than Pitt. He was not invited to become
a placeman; and he therefore stuck firmly to his old trade of patriot.
Fortunate it was for him that he did so. Had he taken office at this
time, he would in all probability have shared largely in the unpopularity of Pulteney, Sandys, and Carteret. He was now the
fiercest and most implacable of those who called for vengeance on

Walpole. He spoke with great energy and ability in favour of the most unjust and violent propositions which the enemies of the fallen minister could invent. He urged the House of Commons to appoint a secret tribunal for the purpose of investigating the conduct of the late first Lord of the Treasury. This was done. The great majority of the inquisitors were notoriously hostile to the accused statesman. Yet they were compelled to own that they could find no fault in him. They therefore called for new powers, for a bill of indemnity to witnesses, or, in plain words, for a bill to reward all who might give evidence, true or false, against the Earl of Orford. This bill Pitt supported, Pitt, who had himself offered to be a screen between Lord Orford and public justice. These are melancholy facts. Mr. Thackeray omits them, or hurries over them as fast as he can; and, as eulogy is his business, he is in the right to do so. But, though there are many parts of the life of Pitt which it is more agreeable to contemplate, we know none more instructive. What must have been the general state of political morality, when a young man, considered, and justly considered, as the most public-spirited and spotless statesman of his time, could attempt to force his way into office by means so disgraceful!

The Bill of Indemnity was rejected by the Lords. Walpole withdrew himself quietly from the public eye; and the ample space which he had left vacant was soon occupied by Carteret. Against Carteret Pitt began to thunder with as much zeal as he had ever manifested against Sir Robert. To Carteret he transferred most of the hard names which were familiar to his eloquence, sole minister, wicked minister, odious minister, execrable minister. The chief topic of Pitt's invective was the favour shown to the German dominions of the House of Brunswick. He attacked with great violence, and with an ability which raised him to the very first rank among the Parliamentary speakers, the practice of paying Hanoverian troops with English money. The House of Commons had lately lost some of its most distinguished ornaments. Walpole and Pulteney had accepted peerages; Sir William Wyndham was dead; and among the rising men none could be considered as, on the whole, a match for Pitt.

During the recess of 1744, the old Duchess of Marlborough died. She carried to her grave the reputation of being decidedly the best hater of her time. Yet her love had been infinitely more destructive than her hatred. More than thirty years before, her temper had ruined the party to which she belonged and the husband whom she adored. Time had made her neither wiser nor kinder. Whoever was at any moment great and prosperous was the object of her fiercest detestation. She had hated Walpole: she now hated Carteret. Pope, long before her death, predicted the fate of her vast property.

> "To heirs unknown descends the unguarded store,
> Or wanders, heaven-directed, to the poor."

Pitt was then one of the poor; and to him Heaven directed a portion of the wealth of the haughty Dowager. She left him a legacy of ten thousand pounds, in consideration of "the noble defence he had made for the support of the laws of England, and to prevent the ruin of his country."

The will was made in August. The Duchess died in October. In November Pitt was a courtier. The Pelhams had forced the King, much against his will, to part with Lord Carteret, who had now become Earl Granville. They proceeded, after this victory, to form the Government on that basis, called by the cant name of "the broad bottom." Lyttelton had a seat at the Treasury, and several other friends of Pitt were provided for. But Pitt himself was, for the present, forced to be content with promises. The King resented most highly some expressions which the ardent orator had used in the debate on the Hanoverian troops. But Newcastle and Pelham expressed the strongest confidence that time and their exertions would soften the royal displeasure.

Pitt, on his part, omitted nothing that might facilitate his admission to office. He resigned his place in the household of Prince Frederick, and, when Parliament met, exerted his eloquence in support of the Government. The Pelhams were really sincere in their endeavours to remove the strong prejudices which had taken root in the King's mind. They knew that Pitt was not a man to be deceived with ease or offended with impunity. They were afraid that they should not be long able to put him off with promises. Nor was it their interest so to put him off. There was a strong tie between him and them. He was the enemy of their enemy. The brothers hated and dreaded the eloquent, aspiring, and imperious Granville. They had traced his intrigues in many quarters. They knew his influence over the royal mind. They knew that, as soon as a favourable opportunity should arrive, he would be recalled to the head of affairs. They resolved to bring things to a crisis; and the question on which they took issue with their master was, whether Pitt should or should not be admitted to office? They chose their time with more skill than generosity. It was when rebellion was actually raging in Britain, when the Pretender was master of the northern extremity of the island, that they tendered their resignations. The King found himself deserted, in one day, by the whole strength of that party which had placed his family on the throne. Lord Granville tried to form a government; but it soon appeared that the Parliamentary interest of the Pelhams was irresistible; and that the King's favourite statesman could count only on about thirty Lords and eighty members of the House of Commons. The scheme was given up. Granville went away laughing. The ministers came back stronger than ever; and the King was now no longer able to refuse any thing that they might be pleased to demand. He could only mutter that it was very hard that Newcastle, who was not fit to be chamberlain to the most insignificant prince in Germany, should dictate to the King of England.

One concession the ministers graciously made. They agreed that Pitt should not be placed in a situation in which it would be necessary for him to have frequent interviews with the King. Instead, therefore, of making their new ally Secretary-at-War, as they had intended, they appointed him Vice-Treasurer of Ireland, and in a few months promoted him to the office of Paymaster of the Forces.

This was, at that time, one of the most lucrative offices in the Government. The salary was but a small part of the emolument which the Paymaster derived from his place. He was allowed to keep a large sum, which, even in time of peace, was seldom less than one hundred thousand pounds, constantly in his hands; and the interest on this sum he might appropriate to his own use. This practice was not secret, nor was it considered as disreputable. It was the practice of men of undoubted honour, both before and after the time of Pitt. He, however, refused to accept one farthing beyond the salary which the law had annexed to his office. It had been usual for foreign princes who received the pay of England to give to the Paymaster of the Forces a small per centage on the subsidies. These ignominious vails Pitt resolutely declined.

Disinterestedness of this kind was, in his days, very rare. His conduct surprised and amused politicians. It excited the warmest admiration throughout the body of the people. In spite of the inconsistencies of which Pitt had been guilty, in spite of the strange contrast between his violence in Opposition and his tameness in office, he still possessed a large share of the public confidence. The motives which may lead a politician to change his connexions or his general line of conduct are often obscure; but disinterestedness in pecuniary matters every body can understand. Pitt was thenceforth considered as a man who was proof to all sordid temptations. If he acted ill, it might be from an error in judgment; it might be from resentment; it might be from ambition. But, poor as he was, he had vindicated himself from all suspicion of covetousness.

Eight quiet years followed, eight years during which the minority, which had been feeble ever since Lord Granville had been over-thrown, continued to dwindle till it became almost invisible. Peace was made with France and Spain in 1748. Prince Frederick died in 1751; and with him died the very semblance of Opposition. All the most distinguished survivors of the party which had supported Walpole and of the party which had opposed him were united under his successor. The fiery and vehement spirit of Pitt had for a time been laid to rest. He silently acquiesced in that very system of Continental measures which he had lately condemned. He ceased to talk disrespectfully about Hanover. He did not object to the treaty with Spain, though that treaty left us exactly where we had been when he uttered his spirit-stirring harangues against the pacific policy of Walpole. Now and then glimpses of his former self appeared; but they were few and transient. Pelham knew with whom he had to deal, and felt that an ally, so little used to control, and so capable of inflicting injury, might well be indulged in an occasional fit of waywardness.

Two men, little, if at all, inferior to Pitt in powers of mind, held, like him, subordinate offices in the government. One of these, Murray, was successively Solicitor-General and Attorney-General. This distinguished person far surpassed Pitt in correctness of taste, in power of reasoning, in depth and variety of knowledge. His parliamentary eloquence never blazed into sudden flashes of dazzling brilliancy; but its clear, placid, and mellow splendour was never for an instant overclouded. Intellectually he was, we believe, fully equal to Pitt; but he was deficient in the moral qualities to which Pitt owed most of his success. Murray wanted the energy, the courage, the all-grasping and all-risking ambition, which make men great in stirring times. His heart was a little cold, his temper cautious even to timidity, his manners decorous even to formality. He never exposed his fortunes or his fame to any risk which he could avoid. At one time he might, in all probability, have been Prime Minister. But the object of his wishes was the judicial bench. The situation of Chief Justice might not be so splendid as that of First Lord of the Treasury; but it was dignified; it was quiet; it was secure; and therefore it was the favourite situation of Murray.

Fox, the father of the great man whose mighty efforts in the cause of peace, of truth, and of liberty, have made that name immortal, was Secretary-at-War. He was a favourite with the King, with the Duke of Cumberland, and with some of the most powerful members of the great Whig connexion. His parliamentary talents were of the highest order. As a speaker, he was in almost all respects the very opposite of Pitt. His figure was ungraceful; his face, as Reynolds and Nollekens have preserved it to us, indicated a strong understanding; but the features were coarse, and the general aspect dark and lowering. His manner was awkward; his delivery was hesitating; he was often at a stand for want of a word; but as a debater, as a master of that keen, weighty, manly logic, which is suited to the discussion of political questions, he has perhaps never been surpassed except by his son. In reply he was as decidedly superior to Pitt as in declamation he was Pitt's inferior. Intellectually, the balance was nearly even between the rivals. But here, again, the moral qualities of Pitt turned the scale. Fox had undoubtedly many virtues. In natural disposition, as well as in talents, he bore a great resemblance to his more celebrated son. He had the same sweetness of temper, the same strong passions, the same openness, boldness, and impetuosity, the same cordiality towards friends, the same placability towards enemies. No man was more warmly or justly beloved by his family or by his associates. But unhappily he had been trained in a bad political school, in a school, the doctrines of which were, that political virtue is the mere coquetry of political prostitution, that every patriot has his price, that government can be carried on only by means of corruption, and that the state is given as a prey to statesmen. These maxims were too much in vogue throughout the lower ranks of Walpole's party, and were too much encouraged by Walpole himself, who, from contempt of what is in our day vulgarly called *humbug*, often ran extravagantly and offensively into the opposite extreme. The loose political morality of Fox presented a remarkable contrast to the ostentatious purity of Pitt. The nation distrusted the former, and placed implicit confidence in the latter. But almost all the statesmen of the age had still to learn that the confidence of the nation was worth having. While things went on quietly, while there was no Opposition, while every thing was given by the favour of a small ruling junto, Fox had a decided advantage over Pitt; but when dangerous times came, when Europe was convulsed with war, when Parliament was broken up into factions, when the public mind was violently excited, the favourite of the people rose to supreme power, while his rival sank into insignificance.

Early in the year 1754 Henry Pelham died unexpectedly. "Now I shall have no more peace," exclaimed the old King, when he heard the news. He was in the right. Pelham had succeeded in bringing together and keeping together all the talents of the kingdom. By his death, the highest post to which an English subject can aspire was left vacant; and, at the same moment, the influence which had yoked together and reined in so many turbulent and ambitious spirits was withdrawn.

Within a week after Pelham's death, it was determined that the Duke of Newcastle should be placed at the head of the Treasury; but the arrangement was still far from complete. Who was to be the leading Minister of the Crown in the House of Commons? Was the office to be intrusted to a man of eminent talents? And would not such a man in such a place demand and obtain a larger share of power and patronage than Newcastle would be disposed to concede? Was a mere drudge to be employed? And what probability was there that a mere drudge would be able to manage a large and stormy assembly, abounding with able and experienced men?

Pope has said of that wretched miser Sir John Cutler,

> "Cutler saw tenants break and houses fall
> For very want: he could not build a wall."

Newcastle's love of power resembled Cutler's love of money. It was an avarice which thwarted itself, a penny-wise and pound-foolish cupidity. An immediate outlay was so painful to him that he would not venture to make the most desirable improvement. If he could have found it in his heart to cede at once a portion of his authority, he might probably have ensured the continuance of what remained. But he thought it better to construct a weak and rotten government, which tottered at the smallest breath, and fell in the first storm, than to pay the necessary price for sound and durable materials. He wished to find some person who would be willing to accept the lead of the House of Commons on terms similar to those on which Secretary Craggs had acted under Sunderland, five-and-thirty years before. Craggs could hardly be called a minister. He was a mere agent for the minister. He was not trusted with the higher secrets of state, but obeyed implicitly the directions of his superior, and was, to use Doddington's expression, merely Lord Sunderland's man. But times were changed. Since the days of Sunderland, the importance of the House of Commons had been constantly on the increase. During many years, the person who conducted the business of the Government in that House had almost always been Prime Minister. Under these circumstances, it was not to be supposed that any person who possessed the talents necessary for the situation, would stoop to accept it on such terms as Newcastle was disposed to offer.

Pitt was ill at Bath; and, had he been well and in London, neither the King nor Newcastle would have been disposed to make any overtures to him. The cool and wary Murray had set his heart on professional objects. Negotiations were opened with Fox. Newcastle behaved like himself, that is to say, childishly and basely. The proposition which he made was, that Fox should be Secretary of State, with the lead of the House of Commons; that the disposal of the secret-service-money, or, in plain words, the business of buying members of Parliament, should be left to the First Lord of the Treasury; but that Fox should be exactly informed of the way in which this fund was employed.

To these conditions Fox assented. But the next day every thing was in confusion. Newcastle had changed his mind. The conversation which took place between Fox and the Duke is one of the most curious in English history. "My brother," said Newcastle, "when he was at the Treasury, never told any body what he did with the secret-service-money. No more will I." The answer was obvious. Pelham had been, not only First Lord of the Treasury, but also manager of the House of Commons; and it was therefore unnecessary for him to confide to any other person his dealings with the members of that house. "But how," said Fox, "can I lead in the Commons without information on this head? How can I talk to gentlemen when I do not know which of them have received gratifications and which have not? And who," he continued, "is to have the disposal of places?"—"I myself," said the Duke.—"How then am I to manage the House of Commons?"—"Oh, let the members of the House of Commons come to me." Fox then mentioned the general election which was approaching, and asked how the ministerial boroughs were to be filled up. "Do not trouble yourself," said Newcastle; "that is all settled." This was too much for human nature to bear. Fox refused to accept the Secretaryship of State on such terms; and the Duke confided the management of the House of Commons to a dull, harmless man, whose name is almost forgotten in our time, Sir Thomas Robinson.

When Pitt returned from Bath he affected great moderation, though his haughty soul was boiling with resentment. He did not complain of the manner in which he had been passed by, but said openly that, in his opinion, Fox was the fittest man to lead the House of Commons. The rivals, reconciled by their common interest and their common enmities, concerted a plan of operations for the next session. "Sir Thomas Robinson lead us!" said Pitt to Fox. "The Duke might as well send his jack-boot to lead us."

The elections of 1754 were favourable to the administration. But the aspect of foreign affairs was threatening. In India the English and the French had been employed, ever since the peace of Aix-la-Chapelle, in cutting each other's throats. They had lately taken to the same practice in America. It might have been foreseen that stirring times were at hand, times which would call for abilities very different from those of Newcastle and Robinson.

In November the Parliament met; and before the end of that month the new Secretary of State had been so unmercifully baited by the Paymaster of the Forces and the Secretary-at-War that he was thoroughly sick of his situation. Fox attacked him with great force and acrimony. Pitt affected a kind of contemptuous tenderness for Sir Thomas, and directed his attacks principally against Newcastle. On one occasion, he asked in tones of thunder whether Parliament sat only to register the edicts of one too-powerful subject? The Duke was scared out of his wits. He was afraid to dismiss the mutineers; he was afraid to promote them; but it was absolutely necessary to do something. Fox, as the less proud and intractable of the refractory pair, was preferred. A seat in the Cabinet was offered to him, on condition that he would give efficient support to the ministry in Parliament. In an evil hour for his fame and his fortunes he accepted the offer, and abandoned his connexion with Pitt, who never forgave this desertion.

Sir Thomas, assisted by Fox, contrived to get through the business of the year without much trouble. Pitt was waiting his time. The negotiations pending between France and England took every day a more unfavourable aspect. Towards the close of the session the King sent a message to inform the House of Commons that he had found it necessary to make preparations for war. The House returned an address of thanks, and passed a vote of credit. During the recess, the old animosity of both nations was inflamed by a series of disastrous events. An English force was cut off in America; and several French merchantmen were taken in the West Indian seas. It was plain that an appeal to arms was at hand.

The first object of the King was to secure Hanover; and Newcastle was disposed to gratify his master. Treaties were concluded, after the fashion of those times, with several petty German princes, who bound themselves to find soldiers if England would find money; and, as it was suspected that Frederic the Second had set his heart on the electoral dominions of his uncle, Russia was hired to keep Prussia in awe.

When the stipulations of these treaties were made known, there arose throughout the kingdom a murmur from which a judicious observer might easily prognosticate the approach of a tempest. Newcastle encountered strong opposition, even from those whom he had always considered as his tools. Legge, the Chancellor of the Exchequer, refused to sign the Treasury warrants which were necessary to give effect to the treaties. Those persons who were supposed to possess the confidence of the young Prince of Wales and of his mother held very menacing language. In this perplexity Newcastle sent for Pitt, hugged him, patted him, smirked at him, wept over him, and lisped out the highest compliments and the most splendid promises. The King, who had hitherto been as sulky as possible, would be civil to him at the levee; he should be brought into the Cabinet; he should be consulted about every thing; if he would only be so good as to support the Hessian subsidy in the House of Commons. Pitt coldly declined the proffered seat in the Cabinet, expressed the highest love and reverence for the King, and said that, if his Majesty felt a strong personal interest in the Hessian treaty, he would so far deviate from the line which he had traced out for himself as to give that treaty his support. "Well, and the Russian subsidy," said Newcastle. "No," said Pitt, "not a system of subsidies." The Duke summoned Lord Hardwicke to his aid; but Pitt was inflexible. Murray would do nothing. Robinson could do nothing. It was necessary to have recourse to Fox. He became Secretary of State, with the full authority of a leader in the House of Commons; and Sir Thomas was pensioned off on the Irish establishment.

In November 1755 the Houses met. Public expectation was wound up to the height. After ten quiet years there was to be an Opposition, countenanced by the heir-apparent of the throne, and headed by the most brilliant orator of the age. The debate on the address was long remembered as one of the greatest parliamentary conflicts of that generation. It began at three in the afternoon, and lasted till five the next morning. It was on this night that Gerard Hamilton delivered that single speech from which his nickname was derived. His eloquence threw into the shade every orator except Pitt, who declaimed against the subsidies for an hour and a half with extraordinary energy and effect. Those powers which had formerly spread terror through the majorities of Walpole and Carteret were now displayed in their highest perfection before an audience long unaccustomed to such exhibitions. One fragment of this celebrated oration remains in a state of tolerable preservation. It is the comparison between the coalition of Fox and Newcastle, and the junction of the Rhone and the Saone. "At Lyons," said Pitt, "I was taken to see the place where the two rivers meet, the one gentle, feeble, languid, and, though languid, yet of no depth, the other a boisterous and impetuous torrent; but different as they are, they meet at last." The amendment moved by the Opposition was rejected by a great majority; and Pitt and Legge were immediately dismissed from their offices.

During several months the contest in the House of Commons was extremely sharp. Warm debates took place on the estimates, debates still warmer on the subsidiary treaties. The Government succeeded in every division; but the fame of Pitt's eloquence, and the influence of his lofty and determined character, continued to increase through the Session; and the events which followed the prorogation made it utterly impossible for any other person to manage the Parliament or the country.

The war began in every part of the world with events disastrous to England, and even more shameful than disastrous. But the most humiliating of these events was the loss of Minorca. The Duke of Richelieu, an old fop who had passed his life from sixteen to sixty in seducing women for whom he cared not one straw, landed on that island, and succeeded in reducing it. Admiral Byng was sent from Gibraltar to throw succours into Port-Mahon; but he did not think fit to engage the French squadron, and sailed back without having effected his purpose. The people were inflamed to madness. A storm broke forth, which appalled even those who remembered the days of Excise and of South-Sea. The shops were filled with libels and caricatures. The walls were covered with placards. The city of London called for vengeance, and the cry was echoed from every corner of the kingdom. Dorsetshire, Huntingdonshire, Bedfordshire, Buckinghamshire, Somersetshire, Lancashire, Suffolk, Shropshire, Surrey, sent up strong addresses to the throne, and instructed their representatives to vote for a strict inquiry into the causes of the late disasters. In the great towns the feeling was as strong as in the counties. In some of the instructions it was even recommended that the supplies should be stopped.

The nation was in a state of angry and sullen despondency, almost unparalleled in history. People have, in all ages, been in the habit of talking about the good old times of their ancestors, and the degeneracy of their contemporaries. This is in general merely a cant. But in 1756 it was something more. At this time appeared Brown's Estimate, a book now remembered only by the allusions in Cowper's Table Talk and in Burke's Letters on a Regicide Peace. It was universally read, admired, and believed. The author fully convinced his readers that they were a race of cowards and scoundrels; that nothing could save them; that they were on the point of being enslaved by their enemies, and that they richly deserved their fate. Such were the speculations to which ready credence was given at the outset of the most glorious war in which England had ever been engaged.

Newcastle now began to tremble for his place, and for the only thing which was dearer to him than his place, his neck. The people were not in a mood to be trifled with. Their cry was for blood. For this once they might be contented with the sacrifice of Byng. But what if fresh disasters should take place? What if an unfriendly sovereign should ascend the throne? What if a hostile House of Commons should be chosen?

At length, in October, the decisive crisis came. The new Secretary of State had been long sick of the perfidy and levity of the First Lord of the Treasury, and began to fear that he might be made a scapegoat to save the old intriguer who, imbecile as he seemed, never wanted dexterity where danger was to be avoided. Fox threw up his office. Newcastle had recourse to Murray; but Murray had now within his reach the favourite object of his ambition. The situation of Chief-Justice of the King's Bench was vacant; and the Attorney-General was fully resolved to obtain it, or to go into Opposition. Newcastle offered him any terms, the Duchy of Lancaster for life, a tellership of the Exchequer, any amount of pension, two thousand a year, six thousand a year. When the ministers found that Murray's mind was made up, they pressed for delay, the delay of a session, a month, a week, a day. Would he only make his appearance once more in the House of Commons? Would he only speak in favour of the address? He was inexorable, and peremptorily said that they might give or withhold the Chief-Justiceship, but that he would be Attorney-General no longer.

Newcastle now contrived to overcome the prejudices of the King, and overtures were made to Pitt, through Lord Hardwicke. Pitt knew his power, and showed that he knew it. He demanded as an indispensable condition that Newcastle should be altogether excluded from the new arrangement.

The Duke was now in a state of ludicrous distress. He ran about chattering and crying, asking advice and listening to none. In the meantime, the Session drew near. The public excitement was unabated. Nobody could be found to face Pitt and Fox in the House of Commons. Newcastle's heart failed him, and he tendered his resignation.

The King sent for Fox, and directed him to form the plan of an administration in concert with Pitt. But Pitt had not forgotten old injuries, and positively refused to act with Fox.

The King now applied to the Duke of Devonshire, and this mediator succeeded in making an arrangement. He consented to take the Treasury. Pitt became Secretary of State, with the lead of the House of Commons. The Great Seal was put into commission. Legge returned to the Exchequer; and Lord Temple, whose sister Pitt had lately married, was placed at the head of the Admiralty.

It was clear from the first that this administration would last but a very short time. It lasted not quite five months; and, during those five months, Pitt and Lord Temple were treated with rudeness by the King, and found but feeble support in the House of Commons. It is a remarkable fact, that the Opposition prevented the reelection of some of the new ministers. Pitt, who sat for one of the boroughs which were in the Pelham interest, found some difficulty in obtaining a seat after his acceptance of the seals. So destitute was the new Government of that sort of influence without which no government could then be durable. One of the arguments most frequently urged against the Reform Bill was that, under a system of popular representation, men whose presence in the House of Commons was necessary to the conducting of public business might often find it impossible to find seats. Should this inconvenience ever be felt, there cannot be the slightest difficulty in devising and applying a remedy. But those who threatened us with this evil ought to have remembered that, under the old system, a great man called to power at a great crisis by the voice of the whole nation was in danger of being excluded, by an aristocratical cabal, from that House of which he was the most distinguished ornament.

The most important event of this short administration was the trial of Byng. On that subject public opinion is still divided. We think the punishment of the Admiral altogether unjust and absurd. Treachery, cowardice, ignorance amounting to what lawyers have called *crassa ignorantia*, are fit objects of severe penal inflictions. But Byng was not found guilty of treachery, of cowardice, or of gross ignorance of his profession. He died for doing what the most loyal subject, the most intrepid warrior, the most experienced seaman, might have done. He died for an error in judgment, an error, such as the greatest commanders, Frederic, Napoleon, Wellington, have often committed, and have often acknowledged. Such errors are not proper objects of punishment, for this reason, that the punishing of such errors tends not to prevent them, but to produce

them. The dread of an ignominious death may stimulate sluggishness to exertion, may keep a traitor to his standard, may prevent a
coward from running away, but it has no tendency to bring out
those qualities which enable men to form prompt and judicious
decisions in great emergencies. The best marksman may be
expected to fail when the apple which is to be his mark is set on
his child's head. We cannot conceive anything more likely to
deprive an officer of his self-possession at the time when he most
needs it than the knowledge that, if the judgment of his superiors
should not agree with his, he will be executed with every circumstance of shame. Queens, it has often been said, run far greater
risk in childbed than private women, merely because their medical
attendants are more anxious. The surgeon who attended Marie
Louise was altogether unnerved by his emotions. "Compose yourself," said Bonaparte; "imagine that you are assisting a poor girl in
the Faubourg St. Antoine." This was surely a far wiser course than
that of the Eastern king in the Arabian Nights' Entertainments,
who proclaimed that the physicians who failed to cure his daughter
should have their heads chopped off. Bonaparte knew mankind
well; and, as he acted towards this surgeon, he acted towards his
officers. No sovereign was ever so indulgent to mere errors of
judgment; and it is certain that no sovereign ever had in his service
so many military men fit for the highest commands.

Pitt acted a brave and honest part on this occasion. He ventured
to put both his power and his popularity to hazard, and spoke
manfully for Byng, both in Parliament and in the royal presence.
But the King was inexorable. "The House of Commons, Sir," said
Pitt, "seems inclined to mercy." "Sir," answered the King, "you
have taught me to look for the sense of my people in other places
than the House of Commons." The saying has more point than
most of those which are recorded of George the Second, and,
though sarcastically meant, contains a high and just compliment
to Pitt.

The King disliked Pitt, but absolutely hated Temple. The new
Secretary of State, his Majesty said, had never read Vatel, and was
tedious and pompous, but respectful. The First Lord of the
Admiralty was grossly impertinent. Walpole tells one story, which,
we fear, is much too good to be true. He assures us that Temple
entertained his royal master with an elaborate parallel between
Byng's behaviour at Minorca, and his Majesty's behaviour at
Oudenarde, in which the advantage was all on the side of the
Admiral.

This state of things could not last. Early in April, Pitt and all his friends were turned out, and Newcastle was summoned to St. James's. But the public discontent was not extinguished. It had subsided when Pitt was called to power. But it still glowed under the embers; and it now burst at once into a flame. The stocks fell. The Common Council met. The freedom of the city was voted to Pitt. All the greatest corporate towns followed the example. "For some weeks," says Walpole, "it rained gold boxes."

This was the turning point of Pitt's life. It might have been expected that a man of so haughty and vehement a nature, treated so ungraciously by the Court, and supported so enthusiastically by the people, would have eagerly taken the first opportunity of showing his power and gratifying his resentment; and an opportunity was not wanting. The members for many counties and large towns had been instructed to vote for an inquiry into the circumstances which had produced the miscarriage of the preceding year. A motion for inquiry had been carried in the House of Commons, without opposition; and, a few days after Pitt's dismissal, the investigation commenced. Newcastle and his colleagues obtained a vote of acquittal; but the minority was so strong that they could not venture to ask for a vote of approbation, as they had at first intended; and it was thought by some shrewd observers that, if Pitt had exerted himself to the utmost of his power, the inquiry might have ended in a censure, if not in an impeachment.

Pitt showed on this occasion a moderation and self-government which were not habitual to him. He had found by experience, that he could not stand alone. His eloquence and his popularity had done much, very much for him. Without rank, without fortune, without borough interest, hated by the King, hated by the aristocracy, he was a person of the first importance in the state. He had been suffered to form a ministry, and to pronounce sentence of exclusion on all his rivals, on the most powerful nobleman of the Whig party, on the ablest debater in the House of Commons. And he now found that he had gone too far. The English Constitution was not, indeed, without a popular element. But other elements generally predominated. The confidence and admiration of the nation might make a statesman formidable at the head of an Opposition, might load him with framed and glazed parchments and gold boxes, might possibly, under very peculiar circumstances, such as those of the preceding year, raise him for a time to power. But, constituted as Parliament then was, the favourite of the people could not depend on a majority in the people's own House. The Duke of Newcastle, however contemptible in morals, manners, and understanding, was a dangerous enemy. His rank, his wealth, his unrivalled parliamentary interest, would alone have made him important. But this was not all. The Whig aristocracy regarded him as their leader. His long possession of power had given him a kind of prescriptive right to possess it still. The House of Commons had been elected when he was at the head of affairs. The members for the ministerial boroughs had all been nominated by him. The public offices swarmed with his creatures.

Pitt desired power, and he desired it, we really believe, from high and generous motives. He was, in the strict sense of the word, a patriot. He had none of that philanthropy which the great French writers of his time preached to all the nations of Europe. He loved England as an Athenian loved the City of the Violet Crown, as a Roman loved the City of the Seven Hills. He saw his country insulted and defeated. He saw the national spirit sinking. Yet he knew what the resources of the empire, vigorously employed, could effect; and he felt that he was the man to employ them vigorously. "My Lord," he said to the Duke of Devonshire, "I am sure that I can save this country, and that nobody else can."

Desiring, then, to be in power, and feeling that his abilities and the public confidence were not alone sufficient to keep him in power against the wishes of the Court and of the aristocracy, he began to think of a coalition with Newcastle.

Newcastle was equally disposed to a reconciliation. He, too, had profited by his recent experience. He had found that the Court and the aristocracy, though powerful, were not every thing in the state. A strong oligarchical connexion, a great borough interest, ample patronage, and secret-service-money, might, in quiet times, be all that a minister needed; but it was unsafe to trust wholly to such support in time of war, of discontent, and of agitation. The composition of the House of Commons was not wholly aristocratical; and, whatever be the composition of large deliberative assemblies, their spirit is always in some degree popular. Where there are free debates, eloquence must have admirers, and reason must make converts. Where there is a free press, the governors must live in constant awe of the opinions of the governed.

Thus these two men, so unlike in character, so lately mortal enemies, were necessary to each other. Newcastle had fallen in November, for want of that public confidence which Pitt possessed and of that parliamentary support which Pitt was better qualified than any man of his time to give. Pitt had fallen in April, for want of that species of influence which Newcastle had passed his whole life in acquiring and hoarding. Neither of them had power enough to support himself. Each of them had power enough to overturn the other. Their union would be irresistible. Neither the King nor any party in the state would be able to stand against them.

Under these circumstances, Pitt was not disposed to proceed to extremities against his predecessors in office. Something, however, was due to consistency; and something was necessary for the preservation of his popularity. He did little; but that little he did in such a manner as to produce great effect. He came down to the House in all the pomp of gout, his legs swathed in flannels, his arm dangling in a sling. He kept his seat, through several fatiguing days, in spite of pain and languor. He uttered a few sharp and vehement sentences; but, during the greater part of the discussion, his language was unusually gentle.

When the inquiry had terminated without a vote either of approbation or of censure, the great obstacle to a coalition was removed. Many obstacles, however, remained. The King was still rejoicing in his deliverance from the proud and aspiring minister who had been forced on him by the cry of the nation. His Majesty's indignation was excited to the highest point when it appeared that Newcastle who had, during thirty years, been loaded with marks of royal favour, and who had bound himself, by a solemn promise, never to coalesce with Pitt, was meditating a new perfidy. Of all the statesmen of that age, Fox had the largest share of royal favour. A coalition between Fox and Newcastle was the arrangement which the King wished to bring about. But the Duke was too cunning to fall into such a snare. As a speaker in Parliament, Fox might perhaps be, on the whole, as useful to an administration as his great rival; but he was one of the most unpopular men in England. Then, again, Newcastle felt all that jealousy of Fox which, according to the proverb, generally exists between two of a trade. Fox would certainly intermeddle with that department which the Duke was most desirous to reserve entire to himself, the jobbing department. Pitt, on the other hand, was quite willing to leave the drudgery of corruption to any who might be inclined to undertake it.

During eleven weeks England remained without a ministry; and in the meantime Parliament was sitting, and a war was raging. The prejudices of the King, the haughtiness of Pitt, the jealousy, levity, and treachery of Newcastle, delayed the settlement. Pitt knew the Duke too well to trust him without security. The Duke loved power too much to be inclined to give security. While they were haggling, the King was in vain attempting to produce a final rupture between them, or to form a Government without them. At one time he applied to Lord Waldégrave, an honest and sensible man, but unpractised in affairs. Lord Waldégrave had the courage to accept the Treasury, but soon found that no administration formed by him had the smallest chance of standing a single week.

At length the King's pertinacity yielded to the necessity of the case. After exclaiming with great bitterness, and with some justice, against the Whigs, who ought, he said, to be ashamed to talk about liberty while they submitted to be the footmen of the Duke of Newcastle, his Majesty submitted. The influence of Leicester House prevailed on Pitt to abate a little, and but a little, of his high demands; and all at once, out of the chaos in which parties had for some time been rising, falling, meeting, separating, arose a government as strong at home as that of Pelham, as successful abroad as that of Godolphin.

Newcastle took the Treasury. Pitt was Secretary of State, with the lead in the House of Commons, and with the supreme direction of the war and of foreign affairs. Fox, the only man who could have given much annoyance to the new Government, was silenced with the office of Paymaster, which, during the continuance of that war, was probably the most lucrative place in the whole Government. He was poor, and the situation was tempting; yet it cannot but seem extraordinary that a man who had played a first part in politics, and whose abilities had been found not unequal to that part, who had sat in the Cabinet, who had led the House of Commons, who had been twice intrusted by the King with the office of forming a ministry, who was regarded as the rival of Pitt, and who at one time seemed likely to be a successful rival, should have consented, for the sake of emolument, to take a subordinate place, and to give silent votes for all the measures of a government to the deliberations of which he was not summoned.

The first measures of the new administration were characterized rather by vigour than by judgment. Expeditions were sent against different parts of the French coast with little success. The small island of Aix was taken, Rochefort threatened, a few ships burned in the harbour of St. Maloes, and a few guns and mortars brought home as trophies from the fortifications of Cherbourg. But soon conquests of a very different kind filled the kingdom with pride and rejoicing. A succession of victories, undoubtedly brilliant, and, as it was thought, not barren, raised to the highest point the fame of the minister to whom the conduct of the war had been intrusted. In July 1758 Louisburg fell. The whole island of Cape Breton was reduced. The fleet to which the court of Versailles had confided the defence of French America was destroyed. The captured standards were borne in triumph from Kensington Palace to the city, and were suspended in St. Paul's Church, amidst the roar of guns and kettle-drums, and the shouts of an immense multitude. Addresses of congratulation came in from all the great towns of England. Parliament met only to decree thanks and monuments, and to bestow, without one murmur, supplies more than double of those which had been given during the war of the Grand Alliance.

The year 1759 opened with the conquest of Goree. Next fell Guadaloupe; then Ticonderoga; then Niagara. The Toulon squadron was completely defeated by Boscawen off Cape Lagos. But the greatest exploit of the year was the achievement of Wolfe on the heights of Abraham. The news of his glorious death and of the fall of Quebec reached London in the very week in which the Houses met. All was joy and triumph. Envy and faction were forced to join in the general applause. Whigs and Tories vied with each other in extolling the genius and energy of Pitt. His colleagues were never talked of or thought of. The House of Commons, the nation, the colonies, our allies, our enemies, had their eyes fixed on him alone.

Scarcely had Parliament voted a monument to Wolfe when another great event called for fresh rejoicings. The Brest fleet, under the command of Conflans, had put out to sea. It was overtaken by an English squadron under Hawke. Conflans attempted to take shelter close under the French coast. The shore was rocky: the night was black: the wind was furious: the waves of the Bay of Biscay ran high. But Pitt had infused into every branch of the service a spirit which had long been unknown. No British seaman was disposed to err on the same side with Byng. The pilot told Hawke that the attack could not be made without the greatest danger. "You have done your duty in remonstrating," answered Hawke; "I will answer for every thing. I command you to lay me alongside the French admiral." Two French ships of the line struck. Four were destroyed. The rest hid themselves in the rivers of Britanny.

The year 1760 came; and still triumph followed triumph. Montreal was taken; the whole province of Canada was subjugated; the French fleets underwent a succession of disasters in the seas of Europe and America.

In the mean time conquests equalling in rapidity, and far surpassing in magnitude, those of Cortes and Pizarro, had been achieved in the East. In the space of three years the English had founded a mighty empire. The French had been defeated in every part of India. Chandernagore had surrendered to Clive, Pondicherry to Coote. Throughout Bengal, Bahar, Orissa, and the Carnatic, the authority of the East India Company was more absolute than that of Acbar or Aurungzebe had ever been.

On the continent of Europe the odds were against England. We had but one important ally, the King of Prussia; and he was attacked, not only by France, but also by Russia and Austria. Yet even on the Continent the energy of Pitt triumphed over all difficulties. Vehemently as he had condemned the practice of subsidising foreign princes, he now carried that practice farther than Carteret himself would have ventured to do. The active and able Sovereign of Prussia received such pecuniary assistance as enabled him to maintain the conflict on equal terms against his powerful enemies. On no subject had Pitt ever spoken with so much eloquence and ardour as on the mischiefs of the Hanoverian connexion. He now declared, not without much show of reason, that it would be unworthy of the English people to suffer their King to be deprived of his electoral dominions in an English quarrel. He assured his countrymen that they should be no losers, and that he would conquer America for them in Germany. By taking this line he conciliated the King, and lost no part of his influence with the nation. In Parliament, such was the ascendency which his eloquence, his success, his high situation, his pride, and his intrepidity had obtained for him, that he took liberties with the House of which there had been no example, and which have never since been imitated. No orator could there venture to reproach him with inconsistency. One unfortunate man made the attempt, and was so much disconcerted by the scornful demeanour of the minister that he stammered, stopped, and sat down. Even the old Tory country gentlemen, to whom the very name of Hanover had been odious, gave their hearty Ayes to subsidy after subsidy. In a lively contemporary satire, much more lively indeed than delicate, this remarkable conversion is not unhappily described.

> "No more they make a fiddle-faddle
> About a Hessian horse or saddle.
> No more of continental measures;
> No more of wasting British treasures.
> Ten millions, and a vote of credit,
> 'Tis right. He can't be wrong who did it."

The success of Pitt's continental measures was such as might have been expected from their vigour. When he came into power, Hanover was in imminent danger; and, before he had been in office three months, the whole electorate was in the hands of France.

But the face of affairs was speedily changed. The invaders were driven out. An army, partly English, partly Hanoverian, partly composed of soldiers furnished by the petty princes of Germany, was placed under the command of Prince Ferdinand of Brunswick. The French were beaten in 1758 at Crevelt. In 1759, they received a still more complete and humiliating defeat at Minden.

In the mean time, the nation exhibited all the signs of wealth and prosperity. The merchants of London had never been more thriving. The importance of several great commercial and manufacturing towns, of Glasgow in particular, dates from this period. The fine inscription on the monument of Lord Chatham in Guildhall records the general opinion of the citizens of London, that under his administration commerce had been "united with and made to flourish by war."

It must be owned that these signs of prosperity were in some degree delusive. It must be owned that some of our conquests were rather splendid than useful. It must be owned that the expense of the war never entered into Pitt's consideration. Perhaps it would be more correct to say that the cost of his victories increased the pleasure with which he contemplated them. Unlike other men in his situation, he loved to exaggerate the sums which the nation was laying out under his direction. He was proud of the sacrifices and efforts which his eloquence and his success had induced his countrymen to make. The price at which he purchased faithful service and complete victory, though far smaller than that which his son, the most profuse and incapable of war ministers, paid for treachery, defeat, and shame, was long and severely felt by the nation.

Even as a war minister, Pitt is scarcely entitled to all the praise which his contemporaries lavished on him. We, perhaps from ignorance, cannot discern in his arrangements any appearance of profound or dexterous combination. Several of his expeditions, particularly those which were sent to the coast of France, were at once costly and absurd. Our Indian conquests, though they add to the splendour of the period during which he was at the head of affairs, were not planned by him. He had undoubtedly great energy, great determination, great means at his command. His temper was enterprising; and, situated as he was, he had only to follow his temper. The wealth of a rich nation, the valour of a brave nation were ready to support him in every attempt.

In one respect, however, he deserved all the praise that he has ever received. The success of our arms was perhaps owing less to the skill of his dispositions than to the national resources and the national spirit. But that the national spirit rose to the emergency, that the national resources were contributed with unexampled cheerfulness, this was undoubtedly his work. The ardour of his soul had set the whole kingdom on fire. It inflamed every soldier who dragged the cannon up the heights of Quebec, and every sailor who boarded the French ships among the rocks of Britanny. The minister, before he had been long in office, had imparted to the commanders whom he employed his own impetuous, adventurous, and defying character. They, like him, were disposed to risk every thing, to play double or quits to the last, to think nothing done while any thing remained undone, fail rather than not to attempt. For the errors of rashness there might be indulgence. For over-caution, for faults like those of Lord George Sackville, there was no mercy. In other times, and against other enemies, this mode of warfare might have failed. But the state of the French government and of the French nation gave every advantage to Pitt. The fops and intriguers of Versailles were appalled and bewildered by his vigour. A panic spread through all ranks of society. Our enemies soon considered it as a settled thing that they were always to be beaten. Thus victory begot victory; till, at last, wherever the forces of the two nations met, they met with disdainful confidence on the one side, and with a craven fear on the other.

The situation which Pitt occupied at the close of the reign of George the Second was the most enviable ever occupied by any public man in English history. He had conciliated the King; he domineered over the House of Commons; he was adored by the people; he was admired by all Europe. He was the first Englishman of his time; and he had made England the first country in the world. The Great Commoner, the name by which he was often designated, might look down with scorn on coronets and garters. The nation was drunk with joy and pride. The Parliament was as quiet as it had been under Pelham. The old party distinctions were almost effaced; nor was their place yet supplied by distinctions of a still more important kind. A new generation of country squires and rectors had arisen who knew not the Stuarts. The Dissenters were tolerated; the Catholics not cruelly persecuted. The Church was drowsy and indulgent. The great civil and religious conflict which began at the Reformation seemed to have terminated in universal repose. Whigs and Tories, Churchmen and Puritans, spoke with equal reverence of the constitution, and with equal enthusiasm of the talents, virtues, and services of the minister.

A few years sufficed to change the whole aspect of affairs. A nation convulsed by faction, a throne assailed by the fiercest invective, a House of Commons hated and despised by the nation, England set against Scotland, Britain set against America, a rival legislature sitting beyond the Atlantic, English blood shed by English bayonets, our armies capitulating, our conquests wrested from us, our enemies hastening to take vengeance for past humiliation, our flag scarcely able to maintain itself in our own seas, such was the spectacle which Pitt lived to see. But the history of this great revolution requires far more space than we can at present bestow. We leave the Great Commoner in the zenith of his glory. It is not impossible that we may take some other opportunity of tracing his life to its melancholy, yet not inglorious close.

LORD CLIVE

(JANUARY 1840)

The Life of Robert Lord Clive; collected from the Family Papers, communicated by the Earl of Powis. By MAJOR-GENERAL SIR JOHN MALCOLM, K.C.B. 3 vols. 8vo. London: 1836.

WE have always thought it strange that, while the history of the Spanish empire in America is familiarly known to all the nations of Europe, the great actions of our countrymen in the East should, even among ourselves, excite little interest. Every schoolboy knows who imprisoned Montezuma, and who strangled Atahualpa. But we doubt whether one in ten, even among English gentlemen of highly cultivated minds, can tell who won the battle of Buxar, who perpetrated the massacre of Patna, whether Sujah Dowlah ruled in Oude or in Travancore, or whether Holkar was a Hindoo or a Mussulman. Yet the victories of Cortes were gained over savages who had no letters, who were ignorant of the use of metals, who had not broken in a single animal to labour, who wielded no better weapons than those which could be made out of sticks, flints, and fish-bones, who regarded a horse-soldier as a monster, half man and half beast, who took a harquebusier for a sorcerer, able to scatter the thunder and lightning of the skies. The people of India, when we subdued them, were ten times as numerous as the Americans whom the Spaniards vanquished, and were at the same time quite as highly civilised as the victorious Spaniards. They had reared cities larger and fairer than Saragossa or Toledo, and buildings more beautiful and costly than the cathedral of Seville. They could show bankers richer than the richest firms of Barcelona or Cadiz, viceroys whose splendour far surpassed that of Ferdinand the Catholic, myriads of cavalry and long trains of artillery which would have astonished the Great Captain. It might have been expected, that every Englishman who takes any interest in any part of history would be curious to know how a handful of his country-men, separated from their home by an immense ocean, subjugated, in the course of a few years, one of the greatest empires in the world. Yet, unless we greatly err, this subject is, to most readers, not only insipid, but positively distasteful.

Perhaps the fault lies partly with the historians. Mr. Mill's book, though it has undoubtedly great and rare merit, is not sufficiently animated and picturesque to attract those who read for amusement. Orme, inferior to no English historian in style and power of painting, is minute even to tediousness. In one volume he allots, on an average, a closely printed quarto page to the events of every forty-eight hours. The consequence is, that his narrative, though one of the most authentic and one of the most finely written in our language, has never been very popular, and is now scarcely ever read.

We fear that the volumes before us will not much attract those readers whom Orme and Mill have repelled. The materials placed at the disposal of Sir John Malcolm by the late Lord Powis were indeed of great value. But we cannot say that they have been very skilfully worked up. It would, however, be unjust to criticize with severity a work which, if the author had lived to complete and revise it, would probably have been improved by condensation and by a better arrangement. We are more disposed to perform the pleasing duty of expressing our gratitude to the noble family to which the public owes so much useful and curious information.

The effect of the book, even when we make the largest allowance for the partiality of those who have furnished and of those who have digested the materials, is, on the whole, greatly to raise the character of Lord Clive. We are far indeed from sympathizing with Sir John Malcolm, whose love passes the love of biographers, and who can see nothing but wisdom and justice in the actions of his idol. But we are at least equally far from concurring in the severe judgment of Mr. Mill, who seems to us to show less discrimination in his account of Clive than in any other part of his valuable work. Clive, like most men who are born with strong passions and tried by strong temptations, committed great faults. But every person who takes a fair and enlightened view of his whole career must admit that our island, so fertile in heroes and statesmen, has scarcely ever produced a man more truly great either in arms or in council.

The Clives had been settled, ever since the twelfth century, on an estate of no great value, near Market-Drayton, in Shropshire.

In the reign of George the First, this moderate but ancient inheritance was possessed by Mr. Richard Clive, who seems to have been a plain man of no great tact or capacity. He had been bred to the law, and divided his time between professional business and the avocations of a small proprietor. He married a lady from Manchester, of the name of Gaskill, and became the father of a very numerous family. His eldest son, Robert, the founder of the British empire in India, was born at the old seat of his ancestors on the twenty-ninth of September 1725.

Some lineaments of the character of the man were early discerned in the child. There remain letters written by his relations when he was in his seventh year; and from these letters it appears that, even at that early age, his strong will and his fiery passions, sustained by a constitutional intrepidity which sometimes seemed hardly compatible with soundness of mind, had begun to cause great uneasiness to his family. "Fighting," says one of his uncles, "to which he is out of measure addicted, gives his temper such a fierceness and imperiousness, that he flies out on every trifling occasion." The old people of the neighbourhood still remember to have heard from their parents how Bob Clive climbed to the top of the lofty steeple of Market-Drayton, and with what terror the inhabitants saw him seated on a stone spout near the summit. They also relate how he formed all the idle lads of the town into a kind of predatory army, and compelled the shopkeepers to submit to a tribute of apples and halfpence, in consideration of which he guaranteed the security of their windows. He was sent from school to school, making very little progress in his learning, and gaining for himself every where the character of an exceedingly naughty boy. One of his masters, it is said, was sagacious enough to prophesy that the idle lad would make a great figure in the world. But the general opinion seems to have been that poor Robert was a dunce, if not a reprobate. His family expected nothing good from such slender parts and such a headstrong temper. It is not strange, therefore, that they gladly accepted for him, when he was in his eighteenth year, a writership in the service of the East India Company, and shipped him off to make a fortune or to die of a fever at Madras.

Far different were the prospects of Clive from those of the youths whom the East India College now annually sends to the Presidencies of our Asiatic empire. The Company was then purely a trading corporation. Its territory consisted of a few square miles, for which rent was paid to the native governments. Its troops were scarcely numerous enough to man the batteries of three or four ill-constructed forts, which had been erected for the protection of the warehouses. The natives, who composed a considerable part of these little garrisons, had not yet been trained in the discipline of Europe, and were armed, some with swords and shields, some with bows and arrows. The business of the servant of the Company was not, as now, to conduct the judicial, financial, and diplomatic business of a great country, but to take stock, to make advances to weavers, to ship cargoes, and above all to keep an eye on private traders who dared to infringe the monopoly. The younger clerks were so miserably paid that they could scarcely subsist without incurring debt; the elder enriched themselves by trading on their own account; and those who lived to rise to the top of the service often accumulated considerable fortunes.

Madras, to which Clive had been appointed, was, at this time, perhaps the first in importance of the Company's settlements. In the preceding century, Fort St. George had arisen on a barren spot beaten by a raging surf; and in the neighbourhood a town, inhabited by many thousands of natives, had sprung up, as towns spring up in the East, with the rapidity of the prophet's gourd. There were already in the suburbs many white villas, each surrounded by its garden, whither the wealthy agents of the Company retired, after the labours of the desk and the warehouse, to enjoy the cool breeze which springs up at sunset from the Bay of Bengal. The habits of these mercantile grandees appear to have been more profuse, luxurious, and ostentatious, than those of the high judicial and political functionaries who have succeeded them. But comfort was far less understood. Many devices which now mitigate the heat of the climate, preserve health, and prolong life, were unknown. There was far less intercourse with Europe than at present. The voyage by the Cape, which in our time has often been performed within three months, was then very seldom accomplished in six, and was sometimes protracted to more than a year. Consequently, the Anglo-Indian was then much more estranged from his country, much more addicted to Oriental usages, and much less fitted to mix in society after his return to Europe, than the Anglo-Indian of the present day.

Within the fort and its precincts, the English governors exercised, by permission of the native rulers, an extensive authority, such as every great Indian landowner exercised within his own domain. But they had never dreamed of claiming independent power. The surrounding country was governed by the Nabob of the Carnatic, a deputy of the Viceroy of the Deccan, commonly called the Nizam, who was himself only a deputy of the mighty prince designated by our ancestors as the Great Mogul. Those names, once so august and formidable, still remain. There is still a Nabob of the Carnatic, who lives on a pension allowed to him by the English out of the revenues of the province which his ancestors ruled. There is still a Nizam, whose capital is overawed by a British cantonment, and to whom a British resident gives, under the name of advice, commands which are not to be disputed. There is still a Mogul, who is permitted to play at holding courts and receiving petitions, but who has less power to help or hurt than the youngest civil servant of the Company.

Clive's voyage was unusually tedious even for that age. The ship remained some months at the Brazils, where the young adventurer picked up some knowledge of Portuguese, and spent all his pocket-money. He did not arrive in India till more than a year after he had left England. His situation at Madras was most painful. His funds were exhausted. His pay was small. He had contracted debts. He was wretchedly lodged, no small calamity in a climate which can be made tolerable to an European only by spacious and well placed apartments. He had been furnished with letters of recommendation to a gentleman who might have assisted him; but when he landed at Fort St. George he found that this gentleman had sailed for England. The lad's shy and haughty disposition withheld him from introducing himself to strangers. He was several months in India before he became acquainted with a single family. The climate affected his health and spirits. His duties were of a kind ill suited to his ardent and daring character. He pined for his home, and in his letters to his relations expressed his feelings in language softer and more pensive than we should have expected, either from the waywardness of his boyhood, or from the inflexible sternness of his later years. "I have not enjoyed," says he, "one happy day since I left my native country:" and again, "I must confess, at intervals, when I think of my dear native England, it affects me in a very particular manner. . . . If I should be so far blest as to revisit again my own country, but more especially Manchester, the centre of all my wishes, all that I could hope or desire for would be presented before me in one view."

One solace he found of the most respectable kind. The Governor possessed a good library, and permitted Clive to have access to it. The young man devoted much of his leisure to reading, and acquired at this time almost all the knowledge of books that he ever possessed. As a boy he had been too idle, as a man he soon became too busy, for literary pursuits.

But neither climate nor poverty, neither study nor the sorrows of a home-sick exile, could tame the desperate audacity of his spirit. He behaved to his official superiors as he had behaved to his schoolmasters, and was several times in danger of losing his situation. Twice, while residing in the Writers' Buildings, he attempted to destroy himself; and twice the pistol which he snapped at his own head failed to go off. This circumstance, it is said, affected him as a similar escape affected Wallenstein. After satisfying himself that the pistol was really well loaded, he burst forth into an exclamation that surely he was reserved for something great.

About this time an event which at first seemed likely to destroy all his hopes in life suddenly opened before him a new path to eminence. Europe had been, during some years, distracted by the war of the Austrian succession. George the Second was the steady ally of Maria Theresa. The house of Bourbon took the opposite side. Though England was even then the first of maritime powers, she was not, as she has since become, more than a match on the sea for all the nations of the world together; and she found it difficult to maintain a contest against the united navies of France and Spain. In the eastern seas France obtained the ascendency. Labourdonnais, governor of Mauritius, a man of eminent talents and virtues, conducted an expedition to the continent of India in spite of the opposition of the British fleet, landed, assembled an army, appeared before Madras, and compelled the town and fort to capitulate. The keys were delivered up; the French colours were displayed on Fort St. George; and the contents of the Company's warehouses were seized as prize of war by the conquerors. It was stipulated by the capitulation that the English inhabitants should be prisoners of war on parole, and that the town should remain in the hands of the French till it should be ransomed. Labourdonnais pledged his honour that only a moderate ransom should be required.

But the success of Labourdonnais had awakened the jealousy of his countryman, Dupleix, governor of Pondicherry. Dupleix, moreover, had already begun to revolve gigantic schemes, with which the restoration of Madras to the English was by no means compatible. He declared that Labourdonnais had gone beyond his powers; that conquests made by the French arms on the continent of India were at the disposal of the governor of Pondicherry alone; and that Madras should be rased to the ground. Labourdonnais was compelled to yield. The anger which the breach of the capitulation excited among the English was increased by the ungenerous manner in which Dupleix treated the principal servants of the Company. The governor and several of the first gentlemen of Fort St. George were carried under a guard to Pondicherry, and conducted through the town in a triumphal procession under the eyes of fifty thousand spectators. It was with reason thought that this gross violation of public faith absolved the inhabitants of Madras from the engagements into which they had entered with Labour-donnais. Clive fled from the town by night in the disguise of a Mussulman, and took refuge at Fort St. David, one of the small English settlements subordinate to Madras.

The circumstances in which he was now placed naturally led him to adopt a profession better suited to his restless and intrepid spirit than the business of examining packages and casting accounts. He solicited and obtained an ensign's commission in the service of the Company, and at twenty-one entered on his military career. His personal courage, of which he had, while still a writer, given signal proof by a desperate duel with a military bully who was the terror of Fort St. David, speedily made him conspicuous even among hundreds of brave men. He soon began to show in his new calling other qualities which had not before been discerned in him, judgment, sagacity, deference to legitimate authority. He distinguished himself highly in several operations against the French, and was particularly noticed by Major Lawrence, who was then considered as the ablest British officer in India.

Clive had been only a few months in the army when intelligence arrived that peace had been concluded between Great Britain and France. Dupleix was in consequence compelled to restore Madras to the English Company; and the young ensign was at liberty to resume his former business. He did indeed return for a short time to his desk. He again quitted it in order to assist Major Lawrence in some petty hostilities with the natives, and then again returned to it. While he was thus wavering between a military and a commercial life, events took place which decided his choice. The politics of India assumed a new aspect. There was peace between the English and French Crowns; but there arose between the English and French Companies trading to the East a war most eventful and important, a war in which the prize was nothing less than the magnificent inheritance of the house of Tamerlane.

The empire which Baber and his Moguls reared in the sixteenth century was long one of the most extensive and splendid in the world. In no European kingdom was so large a population subject to a single prince, or so large a revenue poured into the treasury. The beauty and magnificence of the buildings erected by the sovereigns of Hindostan, amazed even travellers who had seen St. Peter's. The innumerable retinues and gorgeous decorations which surrounded the throne of Delhi dazzled even eyes which were accustomed to the pomp of Versailles. Some of the great viceroys who held their posts by virtue of commissions from the Mogul ruled as many subjects as the King of France or the Emperor of Germany. Even the deputies of these deputies might well rank, as to extent of territory and amount of revenue, with the Grand Duke of Tuscany, or the Elector of Saxony.

There can be little doubt that this great empire, powerful and prosperous as it appears on a superficial view, was yet, even in its best days, far worse governed than the worst governed parts of Europe now are. The administration was tainted with all the vices of Oriental despotism and with all the vices inseparable from the domination of race over race. The conflicting pretensions of the princes of the royal house produced a long series of crimes and public disasters. Ambitious lieutenants of the sovereign sometimes aspired to independence. Fierce tribes of Hindoos, impatient of a foreign yoke, frequently withheld tribute, repelled the armies of the government from the mountain fastnesses, and poured down in arms on the cultivated plains. In spite, however, of much constant maladministration, in spite of occasional convulsions which shook the whole frame of society, this great monarchy, on the whole, retained, during some generations, an outward appearance of unity, majesty, and energy. But, throughout the long reign of Aurungzebe, the state, notwithstanding all that the vigour and policy of the prince could effect, was hastening to dissolution. After his death, which took place in the year 1707, the ruin was fearfully rapid. Violent shocks from without cooperated with an incurable decay which was fast proceeding within; and in a few years the empire had undergone utter decomposition.

The history of the successors of Theodosius bears no small analogy to that of the successors of Aurungzebe. But perhaps the fall of the Carlovingians furnishes the nearest parallel to the fall of the Moguls. Charlemagne was scarcely interred when the imbecility and the disputes of his descendants began to bring contempt on themselves and destruction on their subjects. The wide dominion of the Franks was severed into a thousand pieces. Nothing more than a nominal dignity was left to the abject heirs of an illustrious name, Charles the Bald, and Charles the Fat, and Charles the Simple. Fierce invaders, differing from each other in race, language, and religion, flocked, as if by concert, from the farthest corners of the earth, to plunder provinces which the government could no longer defend. The pirates of the Northern Sea extended their ravages from the Elbe to the Pyrenees, and at length fixed their seat in the rich valley of the Seine. The Hungarian, in whom the trembling monks fancied that they recognised the Gog or Magog of prophecy, carried back the plunder of the cities of Lombardy to the depth of the Pannonian forests. The Saracen ruled in Sicily, desolated the fertile plains of Campania, and spread terror even to the walls of Rome. In the midst of these sufferings, a great internal change passed upon the empire. The corruption of death began to ferment into new forms of life. While the great body, as a whole, was torpid and passive, every separate member began to feel with a sense, and to move with an energy all its own. Just here, in the most barren and dreary tract of European history, all feudal privileges, all modern nobility, take their source. It is to this point that we trace the power of those princes who, nominally vassals, but really independent, long governed, with the titles of dukes, marquesses, and counts, almost every part of the dominions which had obeyed Charlemagne.

Such or nearly such was the change which passed on the Mogul empire during the forty years which followed the death of Aurung-zebe. A succession of nominal sovereigns, sunk in indolence and debauchery, sauntered away life in secluded palaces, chewing bang, fondling concubines, and listening to buffoons. A succession of ferocious invaders descended through the western passes, to prey on the defenceless wealth of Hindostan. A Persian conqueror crossed the Indus, marched through the gates of Delhi, and bore away in triumph those treasures of which the magnificence had astounded Roe and Bernier, the Peacock Throne, on which the richest jewels of Golconda had been disposed by the most skilful hands of Europe, and the inestimable Mountain of Light, which, after many strange vicissitudes, lately shone in the bracelet of Runjeet Sing, and is now destined to adorn the hideous idol of Orissa. The Afghan soon followed to complete the work of devastation which the Persian had begun. The warlike tribes of Rajpootana threw off the Mussulman yoke. A band of mercenary soldiers occupied Rohilcund. The Seiks ruled on the Indus. The Jauts spread dismay along the Jumna. The highlands which border on the western sea-coast of India poured forth a yet more formidable race, a race which was long the terror of every native power, and which, after many desperate and doubtful struggles, yielded only to the fortune and genius of England. It was under the reign of Aurungzebe that this wild clan of plunderers first descended from their mountains; and soon after his death, every corner of his wide empire learned to tremble at the mighty name of the Mahrattas. Many fertile viceroyalties were entirely subdued by them. Their dominions stretched across the peninsula from sea to sea. Mahratta captains reigned at Poonah, at Gualior, in Guzerat, in Berar, and in Tanjore. Nor did they, though they had become great sovereigns, therefore cease to be freebooters. They still retained the predatory habits of their forefathers. Every region which was not subject to their rule was wasted by their incursions. Wherever their kettle-drums were heard, the peasant threw his bag of rice on his shoulder, hid his small savings in his girdle, and fled with his wife and children to the mountains or the jungles, to the milder neighbour-hood of the hyæna and the tiger. Many provinces redeemed their harvests by the payment of an annual ransom. Even the wretched phantom who still bore the imperial title stooped to pay this ignominious black-mail. The camp-fires of one rapacious leader were seen from the walls of the palace of Delhi. Another, at the head of his innumerable cavalry, descended year after year on the rice-fields of Bengal. Even the European factors trembled for their magazines. Less than a hundred years ago, it was thought necessary to fortify Calcutta against the horsemen of Berar; and the name of the Mahratta ditch still preserves the memory of the danger.

Wherever the viceroys of the Mogul retained authority they became sovereigns. They might still acknowledge in words the superiority of the house of Tamerlane; as a Count of Flanders or a Duke of Burgundy might have acknowledged the superiority of the most helpless driveller among the later Carlovingians. They might occasionally send to their titular sovereign a complimentary present, or solicit from him a title of honour. In truth, however, they were no longer lieutenants removable at pleasure, but indepen-dent hereditary princes. In this way originated those great Mussul-man houses which formerly ruled Bengal and the Carnatic, and those which still, though in a state of vassalage, exercise some of the powers of royalty at Lucknow and Hyderabad.

In what was this confusion to end? Was the strife to continue during centuries? Was it to terminate in the rise of another great monarchy? Was the Mussulman or the Mahratta to be the Lord of India? Was another Baber to descend from the mountains, and to lead the hardy tribes of Cabul and Chorasan against a wealthier and less warlike race? None of these events seemed improbable. But scarcely any man, however sagacious, would have thought it possible that a trading company, separated from India by fifteen thousand miles of sea, and possessing in India only a few acres for purposes of commerce, would, in less than a hundred years, spread its empire from Cape Comorin to the eternal snow of the Hima-layas; would compel Mahratta and Mahommedan to forget their mutual feuds in common subjection; would tame down even those wild races which had resisted the most powerful of the Moguls; and, having united under its laws a hundred millions of subjects, would carry its victorious arms far to the east of the Burrampooter, and far to the west of the Hydaspes, dictate terms of peace at the gates of Ava, and seat its vassal on the throne of Candahar.

The man who first saw that it was possible to found an European empire on the ruins of the Mogul monarchy was Dupleix. His restless, capacious, and inventive mind had formed this scheme, at a time when the ablest servants of the English Company were busied only about invoices and bills of lading. Nor had he only proposed to himself the end. He had also a just and distinct view of the means by which it was to be attained. He clearly saw that the greatest force which the princes of India could bring into the field would be no match for a small body of men trained in the discipline, and guided by the tactics, of the West. He saw also that the natives of India might, under European commanders, be formed into armies, such as Saxe or Frederic would be proud to command. He was perfectly aware that the most easy and convenient way in which an European adventurer could exercise sovereignty in India, was to govern the motions, and to speak through the mouth of some glittering puppet dignified by the title of Nabob or Nizam. The arts both of war and policy, which a few years later were employed with such signal success by the English, were first understood and practised by this ingenious and aspiring Frenchman.

The situation of India was such that scarcely any aggression could be without a pretext, either in old laws or in recent practice. All rights were in a state of utter uncertainty; and the Europeans who took part in the disputes of the natives confounded the confusion, by applying to Asiatic politics the public law of the West and analogies drawn from the feudal system. If it was convenient to treat a Nabob as an independent prince, there was an excellent plea for doing so. He was independent in fact. If it was convenient to treat him as a mere deputy of the Court of Delhi, there was no difficulty; for he was so in theory. If it was convenient to consider his office as an hereditary dignity, or as a dignity held during life only, or as a dignity held only during the good pleasure of the Mogul, arguments and precedents might be found for every one of those views. The party who had the heir of Baber in their hands represented him as the undoubted, the legitimate, the absolute sovereign, whom all subordinate authorities were bound to obey. The party against whom his name was used did not want plausible pretexts for maintaining that the empire was *de facto* dissolved, and that, though it might be decent to treat the Mogul with respect, as a venerable relic of an order of things which had passed away, it was absurd to regard him as the real master of Hindostan.

In the year 1748, died one of the most powerful of the new masters of India, the great Nizam al Mulk, Viceroy of the Deccan. His authority descended to his son, Nazir Jung. Of the provinces subject to this high functionary, the Carnatic was the wealthiest and the most extensive. It was governed by an ancient Nabob, whose name the English corrupted into Anaverdy Khan.

But there were pretenders to the government both of the viceroyalty and of the subordinate province. Mirzapha Jung, a grandson of Nizam al Mulk, appeared as the competitor of Nazir Jung. Chunda Sahib, son-in-law of a former Nabob of the Carnatic, disputed the title of Anaverdy Khan. In the unsettled state of Indian law, it was easy for both Mirzapha Jung and Chunda Sahib to make out something like a claim of right. In a society altogether disorganized, they had no difficulty in finding greedy adventurers to follow their standards. They united their interests, invaded the Carnatic, and applied for assistance to the French, whose fame had been raised by their success against the English in the recent war on the coast of Coromandel.

Nothing could have happened more pleasing to the subtle and ambitious Dupleix. To make a Nabob of the Carnatic, to make a Viceroy of the Deccan, to rule under their names the whole of southern India; this was indeed an attractive prospect. He allied himself with the pretenders, and sent four hundred French soldiers, and two thousand sepoys, disciplined after the European fashion, to the assistance of his confederates. A battle was fought. The French distinguished themselves greatly. Anaverdy Khan was defeated and slain. His son, Mahommed Ali, who was afterwards well known in England as the Nabob of Arcot, and who owes to the eloquence of Burke a most unenviable immortality, fled with a scanty remnant of his army to Trichinopoly; and the conquerors became at once masters of almost every part of the Carnatic.

This was but the beginning of the greatness of Dupleix. After some months of fighting, negotiation, and intrigue, his ability and good fortune seemed to have prevailed every where. Nazir Jung perished by the hands of his own followers; Mirzapha Jung was master of the Deccan; and the triumph of French arms and French policy was complete. At Pondicherry all was exultation and festivity. Salutes were fired from the batteries, and *Te Deum* sung in the churches. The new Nizam came thither to visit his allies; and the ceremony of his installation was performed there with great pomp. Dupleix, dressed in the garb worn by Mahommedans of the highest rank, entered the town in the same palanquin with the Nizam, and, in the pageant which followed, took precedence of all the court. He was declared Governor of India from the river Kristna to Cape Comorin, a country about as large as France, with authority superior even to that of Chunda Sahib. He was entrusted with the command of seven thousand cavalry. It was announced that no mint would be suffered to exist in the Carnatic except that at Pondicherry. A large portion of the treasures which former Viceroys of the Deccan had accumulated found its way into the coffers of the French governor. It was rumoured that he had received two hundred thousand pounds sterling in money, besides many valuable jewels. In fact, there could scarcely be any limit to his gains. He now ruled thirty millions of people with almost absolute power. No honour or emolument could be obtained from the government but by his intervention. No petition, unless signed by him, was perused by the Nizam.

Mirzapha Jung survived his elevation only a few months. But another prince of the same house was raised to the throne by French influence, and ratified all the promises of his predecessor. Dupleix was now the greatest potentate in India. His countrymen boasted that his name was mentioned with awe even in the chambers of the palace of Delhi. The native population looked with amazement on the progress which, in the short space of four years, an European adventurer had made towards dominion in Asia. Nor was the vainglorious Frenchman content with the reality of power. He loved to display his greatness with arrogant ostentation before the eyes of his subjects and of his rivals. Near the spot where his policy had obtained its chief triumph, by the fall of Nazir Jung and the elevation of Mirzapha, he determined to erect a column, on the four sides of which four pompous inscriptions, in four languages, should proclaim his glory to all the nations of the East. Medals stamped with emblems of his successes were buried beneath the foundations of this stately pillar, and round it arose a town bearing the haughty name of Dupleix Fatihabad, which is, being interpreted, the City of the Victory of Dupleix.

The English had made some feeble and irresolute attempts to stop the rapid and brilliant career of the rival Company, and continued to recognise Mahommed Ali as Nabob of the Carnatic. But the dominions of Mahommed Ali consisted of Trichinopoly alone; and Trichinopoly was now invested by Chunda Sahib and his French auxiliaries. To raise the siege seemed impossible. The small force which was then at Madras had no commander. Major Lawrence had returned to England; and not a single officer of established character remained in the settlement. The natives had learned to look with contempt on the mighty nation which was soon to conquer and to rule them. They had seen the French colours flying on Fort St. George; they had seen the chiefs of the English factory led in triumph through the streets of Pondicherry; they had seen the arms and counsels of Dupleix everywhere successful, while the opposition which the authorities of Madras had made to his progress, had served only to expose their own weakness, and to heighten his glory. At this moment, the valour and genius of an obscure English youth suddenly turned the tide of fortune.

Clive was now twenty-five years old. After hesitating for some time between a military and a commercial life, he had at length been placed in a post which partook of both characters, that of commissary to the troops, with the rank of captain. The present emergency called forth all his powers. He represented to his superiors that, unless some vigorous effort were made, Trichinopoly would fall, the house of Anaverdy Khan would perish, and the French would become the real masters of the whole peninsula of India. It was absolutely necessary to strike some daring blow. If an attack were made on Arcot, the capital of the Carnatic, and the favourite residence of the Nabobs, it was not impossible that the siege of Trichinopoly would be raised. The heads of the English settlement, now thoroughly alarmed by the success of Dupleix, and apprehensive that, in the event of a new war between France and Great Britain, Madras would be instantly taken and destroyed, approved of Clive's plan, and intrusted the execution of it to himself. The young captain was put at the head of two hundred English soldiers, and three hundred sepoys, armed and disciplined after the European fashion. Of the eight officers who commanded this little force under him, only two had ever been in action, and four of the eight were factors of the Company, whom Clive's example had induced to offer their services. The weather was stormy; but Clive pushed on, through thunder, lightning, and rain, to the gates of Arcot. The garrison, in a panic, evacuated the fort, and the English entered it without a blow.

But Clive well knew that he should not be suffered to retain undisturbed possession of his conquest. He instantly began to collect provisions, to throw up works, and to make preparations for sustaining a siege. The garrison, which had fled at his approach, had now recovered from its dismay, and, having been swollen by large reinforcements from the neighbourhood to a force of three thousand men, encamped close to the town. At dead of night, Clive marched out of the fort, attacked the camp by surprise, slew great numbers, dispersed the rest, and returned to his quarters without having lost a single man.

The intelligence of these events was soon carried to Chunda Sahib who, with his French allies, was besieging Trichinopoly. He immediately detached four thousand men from his camp, and sent them to Arcot. They were speedily joined by the remains of the force which Clive had lately scattered. They were further strengthened by two thousand men from Vellore, and by a still more important reinforcement of a hundred and fifty French soldiers whom Dupleix despatched from Pondicherry. The whole of this army, amounting to about ten thousand men, was under the command of Rajah Sahib, son of Chunda Sahib.

Rajah Sahib proceeded to invest the fort of Arcot, which seemed quite incapable of sustaining a siege. The walls were ruinous, the ditches dry, the ramparts too narrow to admit the guns, the battlements too low to protect the soldiers. The little garrison had been greatly reduced by casualties. It now consisted of a hundred and twenty Europeans and two hundred sepoys. Only four officers were left; the stock of provisions was scanty; and the commander, who had to conduct the defence under circumstances so discouraging, was a young man of five and twenty, who had been bred a book-keeper.

During fifty days the siege went on. During fifty days the young captain maintained the defence, with a firmness, vigilance, and ability which would have done honour to the oldest marshal in Europe. The breach, however, increased day by day. The garrison began to feel the pressure of hunger. Under such circumstances, any troops so scantily provided with officers might have been expected to show signs of insubordination; and the danger was peculiarly great in a force composed of men differing widely from each other in extraction, colour, language, manners, and religion. But the devotion of the little band to its chief surpassed any thing that is related of the Tenth Legion of Cæsar, or of the Old Guard of Napoleon. The sepoys came to Clive, not to complain of their scanty fare, but to propose that all the grain should be given to the Europeans, who required more nourishment than the natives of Asia. The thin gruel, they said, which was strained away from the rice, would suffice for themselves. History contains no more touching instance of military fidelity, or of the influence of a commanding mind.

An attempt made by the government of Madras to relieve the place had failed. But there was hope from another quarter. A body of six thousand Mahrattas, half soldiers, half robbers, under the command of a chief named Morari Row, had been hired to assist Mahommed Ali; but thinking the French power irresistible, and the triumph of Chunda Sahib certain, they had hitherto remained inactive on the frontiers of the Carnatic. The fame of the defence of Arcot roused them from their torpor. Morari Row declared that he had never before believed that Englishmen could fight, but that he would willingly help them since he saw that they had spirit to help themselves. Rajah Sahib learned that the Mahrattas were in motion. It was necessary for him to be expeditious. He first tried negotiation. He offered large bribes to Clive, which were rejected with scorn. He vowed that, if his proposals were not accepted, he would instantly storm the fort, and put every man in it to the sword. Clive told him in reply, with characteristic haughtiness, that his father was an usurper, that his army was a rabble, and that he would do well to think twice before he sent such poltroons into a breach defended by English soldiers.

Rajah Sahib determined to storm the fort. The day was well suited to a bold military enterprise. It was the great Mahommedan festival which is sacred to the memory of Hosein the son of Ali. The history of Islam contains nothing more touching than the event which gave rise to that solemnity. The mournful legend relates how the chief of the Fatimites, when all his brave followers had perished round him, drank his latest draught of water, and uttered his latest prayer, how the assassins carried his head in triumph, how the tyrant smote the lifeless lips with his staff, and how a few old men recollected with tears that they had seen those lips pressed to the lips of the Prophet of God. After the lapse of near twelve centuries, the recurrence of this solemn season excites the fiercest and saddest emotions in the bosoms of the devout Moslem of India. They work themselves up to such agonies of rage and lamentation that some, it is said, have given up the ghost from the mere effect of mental excitement. They believe that whoever, during this festival, falls in arms against the infidels, atones by his death for all the sins of his life, and passes at once to the garden of the Houris. It was at this time that Rajah Sahib determined to assault Arcot. Stimulating drugs were employed to aid the effect of religious zeal, and the besiegers, drunk with enthusiasm, drunk with bang, rushed furiously to the attack.

Clive had received secret intelligence of the design, had made his arrangements, and, exhausted by fatigue, had thrown himself on his bed. He was awakened by the alarm, and was instantly at his post. The enemy advanced driving before them elephants whose foreheads were armed with iron plates. It was expected that the gates would yield to the shock of these living battering-rams. But the huge beasts no sooner felt the English musket-balls than they turned round, and rushed furiously away, tramping on the multitude which had urged them forward. A raft was launched on the water which filled one part of the ditch. Clive, perceiving that his gunners at that post did not understand their business, took the management of a piece of artillery himself, and cleared the raft in a few minutes. Where the moat was dry, the assailants mounted with great boldness; but they were received with a fire so heavy and so well-directed, that it soon quelled the courage even of fanaticism and of intoxication. The rear ranks of the English kept the front ranks supplied with a constant succession of loaded muskets, and every shot told on the living mass below. After three desperate onsets, the besiegers retired behind the ditch.

The struggle lasted about an hour. Four hundred of the assailants fell. The garrison lost only five or six men. The besieged passed an anxious night, looking for a renewal of the attack. But when day broke, the enemy were no more to be seen. They had retired, leaving to the English several guns and a large quantity of ammunition.

The news was received at Fort St. George with transports of joy and pride. Clive was justly regarded as a man equal to any command. Two hundred English soldiers, and seven hundred sepoys were sent to him, and with this force he instantly commenced offensive operations. He took the fort of Timery, effected a junction with a division of Morari Row's army, and hastened, by forced marches, to attack Rajah Sahib, who was at the head of about five thousand men, of whom three hundred were French. The action was sharp; but Clive gained a complete victory. The military chest of Rajah Sahib fell into the hands of the conquerors. Six hundred sepoys, who had served in the enemy's army, came over to Clive's quarters, and were taken into the British service. Conjeveram surrendered without a blow. The governor of Arnee deserted Chunda Sahib, and recognised the title of Mahommed Ali.

Had the entire direction of the war been entrusted to Clive, it would probably have been brought to a speedy close. But the timidity and incapacity which appeared in all the movements of the English, except where he was personally present, protracted the struggle. The Mahrattas muttered that his soldiers were of a different race from the British whom they found elsewhere. The effect of this languor was that in no long time Rajah Sahib, at the head of a considerable army, in which were four hundred French troops, appeared almost under the guns of Fort St. George, and laid waste the villas and gardens of the gentlemen of the English settlement. But he was again encountered and defeated by Clive. More than a hundred of the French were killed or taken, a loss more serious than that of thousands of natives. The victorious army marched from the field of battle to Fort St. David. On the road lay the City of the Victory of Dupleix, and the stately monument which was designed to commemorate the triumphs of France in the East. Clive ordered both the city and the monument to be rased to the ground. He was induced, we believe, to take this step, not by personal or national malevolence, but by a just and profound policy. The town and its pompous name, the pillar and its vaunting inscriptions, were among the devices by which Dupleix had laid the public mind of India under a spell. This spell it was Clive's business to break. The natives had been taught that France was confessedly the first power in Europe, and that the English did not presume to dispute her supremacy. No measure could be more effectual for the removing of this delusion than the public and solemn demolition of the French trophies.

The government of Madras, encouraged by these events, determined to send a strong detachment, under Clive, to reinforce the garrison of Trichinopoly. But just at this conjuncture, Major Lawrence arrived from England, and assumed the chief command. From the waywardness and impatience of control which had characterized Clive, both at school and in the counting-house, it might have been expected that he would not, after such achievements, act with zeal and good humour in a subordinate capacity. But Lawrence had early treated him with kindness; and it is bare justice to Clive to say that, proud and overbearing as he was, kindness was never thrown away upon him. He cheerfully placed himself under the orders of his old friend, and exerted himself as strenuously in the second post as he could have done in the first. Lawrence well knew the value of such assistance. Though himself gifted with no intellectual faculty higher than plain good sense, he fully appreciated the powers of his brilliant coadjutor. Though he had made a methodical study of military tactics, and, like all men regularly bred to a profession, was disposed to look with disdain on interlopers, he had yet liberality enough to acknowledge that Clive was an exception to common rules. "Some people," he wrote, "are pleased to term Captain Clive fortunate and lucky; but, in my opinion, from the knowledge I have of the gentleman, he deserved and might expect from his conduct every thing as it fell out;—a man of an undaunted resolution, of a cool temper, and of a presence of mind which never left him in the greatest danger—

born a soldier; for, without a military education of any sort, or much conversing with any of the profession, from his judgment and good sense, he led on an army like an experienced officer and a brave soldier, with a prudence that certainly warranted success."

The French had no commander to oppose to the two friends. Dupleix, not inferior in talents for negotiation and intrigue to any European who has borne a part in the revolutions of India, was not qualified to direct in person military operations. He had not been bred a soldier, and had no inclination to become one. His enemies accused him of personal cowardice; and he defended himself in a strain worthy of Captain Bobadil. He kept away from shot, he said, because silence and tranquillity were propitious to his genius, and he found it difficult to pursue his meditations amidst the noise of fire-arms. He was thus under the necessity of entrusting to others the execution of his great warlike designs; and he bitterly complained that he was ill served. He had indeed been assisted by one officer of eminent merit, the celebrated Bussy. But Bussy had marched northward with the Nizam, and was fully employed in looking after his own interests, and those of France, at the court of that prince. Among the officers who remained with Dupleix, there was not a single man of capacity; and many of them were boys, at whose ignorance and folly the common soldiers laughed.

The English triumphed every where. The besiegers of Trichinopoly were themselves besieged and compelled to capitulate. Chunda Sahib fell into the hands of the Mahrattas, and was put to death, at the instigation probably of his competitor, Mahommed Ali. The spirit of Dupleix, however, was unconquerable, and his resources inexhaustible. From his employers in Europe, he no longer received help or countenance. They condemned his policy. They gave him no pecuniary assistance. They sent him for troops only the sweepings of the galleys. Yet still he persisted, intrigued, bribed, promised, lavished his private fortune, strained his credit, procured new diplomas from Delhi, raised up new enemies to the government of Madras on every side, and found tools even among the allies of the English Company. But all was in vain. Slowly, but steadily, the power of Britain continued to increase, and that of France to decline.

The health of Clive had never been good during his residence in India; and his constitution was now so much impaired that he determined to return to England. Before his departure he undertook a service of considerable difficulty, and performed it with his usual vigour and dexterity. The forts of Covelong and Chingleput were occupied by French garrisons. It was determined to send a force against them. But the only force available for this purpose was of such a description that no officer but Clive would risk his reputation by commanding it. It consisted of five hundred newly-levied sepoys, and two hundred recruits who had just landed from England, and who were the worst and lowest wretches that the Company's crimps could pick up in the flash-houses of London. Clive, ill and exhausted as he was, undertook to make an army of this undisciplined rabble, and marched with them to Covelong. A shot from the fort killed one of these extraordinary soldiers; on which all the rest faced about and ran away, and it was with the greatest difficulty that Clive rallied them. On another occasion, the noise of a gun terrified the sentinels so much that one of them was found, some hours later, at the bottom of a well. Clive gradu-ally accustomed them to danger, and, by exposing himself con-stantly in the most perilous situations, shamed them into courage. He at length succeeded in forming a respectable force out of his unpromising materials. Covelong fell. Clive learned that a strong detachment was marching to relieve it from Chingleput. He took measures to prevent the enemy from learning that they were too late, laid an ambuscade for them on the road, killed a hundred of them with one fire, took three hundred prisoners, pursued the fugitives to the gates of Chingleput, laid siege instantly to that fastness, reputed one of the strongest in India, made a breach, and was on the point of storming when the French commandant capitulated and retired with his men.

Clive returned to Madras victorious, but in a state of health which rendered it impossible for him to remain there long. He married at this time a young lady of the name of Maskelyne, sister of the eminent mathematician, who long held the post of Astrono-mer Royal. She is described as handsome and accomplished; and her husband's letters, it is said, contain proofs that he was devotedly attached to her.

Almost immediately after the marriage, Clive embarked with his bride for England. He returned a very different person from the poor slighted boy who had been sent out ten years before to seek his fortune. He was only twenty-seven; yet his country already respected him as one of her first soldiers. There was then general peace in Europe. The Carnatic was the only part of the world where the Eng-lish and French were in arms against each other. The vast schemes of Dupleix had excited no small uneasiness in the city of London; and the rapid turn of fortune, which was chiefly owing to the courage and talents of Clive, had been hailed with great delight. The young captain was known at the India House by the honourable nickname of General Clive, and was toasted by that appellation at the feasts of the Directors. On his arrival in England, he found himself an object of general interest and admiration. The East India Company thanked him for his services in the warmest terms, and bestowed on him a sword set with diamonds. With rare delicacy, he refused to receive this token of gratitude, unless a similar compliment were paid to his friend and commander, Lawrence.

It may easily be supposed that Clive was most cordially welcomed home by his family, who were delighted by his success, though they seem to have been hardly able to comprehend how their naughty idle Bobby had become so great a man. His father had been singularly hard of belief. Not until the news of the defence of Arcot arrived in England was the old gentleman heard to growl out that, after all, the booby had something in him. His expressions of approbation became stronger and stronger as news arrived of one brilliant exploit after another; and he was at length immoderately fond and proud of his son.

Clive's relations had very substantial reasons for rejoicing at his return. Considerable sums of prize-money had fallen to his share; and he had brought home a moderate fortune, part of which he expended in extricating his father from pecuniary difficulties, and in redeeming the family estate. The remainder he appears to have dissipated in the course of about two years. He lived splendidly, dressed gaily even for those times, kept a carriage and saddle horses, and, not content with these ways of getting rid of his money, resorted to the most speedy and effectual of all modes of evacuation, a contested election followed by a petition.

At the time of the general election of 1754, the government was in a very singular state. There was scarcely any formal opposition. The Jacobites had been cowed by the issue of the last rebellion. The Tory party had fallen into utter contempt. It had been deserted by all the men of talents who had belonged to it, and had scarcely given a symptom of life during some years. The small faction which had been held together by the influence and promises of Prince Frederic, had been dispersed by his death. Almost every public man of distinguished talents in the kingdom, whatever his early connections might have been, was in office, and called himself a Whig. But this extraordinary appearance of concord was quite delusive. The administration itself was distracted by bitter enmities and conflicting pretensions. The chief object of its members was to depress and supplant each other. The prime minister, Newcastle, weak, timid, jealous, and perfidious, was at once detested and despised by some of the most important members of his government, and by none more than by Henry Fox, the Secretary at War. This able, daring, and ambitious man seized every opportunity of crossing the First Lord of the Treasury, from whom he well knew that he had little to dread and little to hope; for Newcastle was through life equally afraid of breaking with men of parts and of promoting them.

Newcastle had set his heart on returning two members for St. Michael, one of those wretched Cornish boroughs which were swept away by the Reform Act in 1832. He was opposed by Lord Sandwich, whose influence had long been paramount there; and Fox exerted himself strenuously in Sandwich's behalf. Clive, who had been introduced to Fox, and very kindly received by him, was brought forward on the Sandwich interest, and was returned. But a petition was presented against the return, and was backed by the whole influence of the Duke of Newcastle.

The case was heard, according to the usage of that time, before a committee of the whole House. Questions respecting elections were then considered merely as party questions. Judicial impartiality was not even affected. Sir Robert Walpole was in the habit of saying openly that, in election battles, there ought to be no quarter. On the present occasion the excitement was great. The matter really at issue was, not whether Clive had been properly or improperly returned, but whether Newcastle or Fox was to be master of the New House of Commons, and consequently first minister. The contest was long and obstinate, and success seemed to lean sometimes to one side and sometimes to the other. Fox put forth all his rare powers of debate, beat half the lawyers in the House at their own weapons, and carried division after division against the whole influence of the Treasury. The committee decided in Clive's favour. But when the resolution was reported to the House, things took a different course. The remnant of the Tory Opposition, contemptible as it was, had yet sufficient weight to turn the scale between the nicely balanced parties of Newcastle and Fox. Newcastle the Tories could only despise. Fox they hated, as the boldest and most subtle politician and the ablest debater among the Whigs, as the steady friend of Walpole, as the devoted adherent of the Duke of Cumberland. After wavering till the last moment, they determined to vote in a body with the Prime Minister's friends. The consequence was that the House, by a small majority, rescinded the decision of the committee, and Clive was unseated.

Ejected from Parliament, and straitened in his means, he natur-ally began to look again towards India. The Company and the

Government were eager to avail themselves of his services. A treaty favourable to England had indeed been concluded in the Carnatic. Dupleix had been superseded, and had returned with the wreck of his immense fortune to Europe, where calumny and chicanery soon hunted him to his grave. But many signs indicated that a war between France and Great Britain was at hand; and it was therefore thought desirable to send an able commander to the Company's settlements in India. The Directors appointed Clive governor of Fort St. David. The King gave him the commission of a lieutenant-colonel in the British army, and in 1755 he again sailed for Asia.

The first service on which he was employed after his return to the East was the reduction of the stronghold of Gheriah. This fortress, built on a craggy promontory, and almost surrounded by the ocean, was the den of a pirate named Angria, whose barks had long been the terror of the Arabian Gulf. Admiral Watson, who commanded the English squadron in the Eastern seas, burned Angria's fleet, while Clive attacked the fastness by land. The place soon fell, and a booty of a hundred and fifty thousand pounds sterling was divided among the conquerors.

After this exploit, Clive proceeded to his government of Fort St. David. Before he had been there two months, he received intelligence which called forth all the energy of his bold and active mind.

Of the provinces which had been subject to the house of Tamerlane, the wealthiest was Bengal. No part of India possessed such natural advantages both for agriculture and for commerce. The Ganges, rushing through a hundred channels to the sea, has formed a vast plain of rich mould which, even under the tropical sky, rivals the verdure of an English April. The rice fields yield an increase such as is elsewhere unknown. Spices, sugar, vegetable oils, are produced with marvellous exuberance. The rivers afford an inexhaustible supply of fish. The desolate islands along the sea-coast, overgrown by noxious vegetation, and swarming with deer and tigers, supply the cultivated districts with abundance of salt. The great stream which fertilises the soil is, at the same time, the chief highway of Eastern commerce. On its banks, and on those of its tributary waters, are the wealthiest marts, the most splendid capitals, and the most sacred shrines of India. The tyranny of man had for ages struggled in vain against the overflowing bounty of nature. In spite of the Mussulman despot and of the Mahratta freebooter, Bengal was known through the East as the garden of Eden, as the rich kingdom. Its population multiplied exceedingly.

Distant provinces were nourished from the overflowing of its granaries; and the noble ladies of London and Paris were clothed in the delicate produce of its looms. The race by whom this rich tract was peopled, enervated by a soft climate and accustomed to peaceful avocations, bore the same relation to other Asiatics which the Asiatics generally bear to the bold and energetic children of Europe. The Castilians have a proverb, that in Valencia the earth is water and the men women; and the description is at least equally applicable to the vast plain of the Lower Ganges. Whatever the Bengalee does he does languidly. His favourite pursuits are sedentary. He shrinks from bodily exertion; and, though voluble in dispute, and singularly pertinacious in the war of chicane, he seldom engages in a personal conflict, and scarcely ever enlists as a soldier. We doubt whether there be a hundred genuine Bengalees in the whole army of the East India Company. There never, perhaps, existed a people so thoroughly fitted by nature and by habit for a foreign yoke.

The great commercial companies of Europe had long possessed factories in Bengal. The French were settled, as they still are, at Chandernagore on the Hoogley. Higher up the stream the Dutch traders held Chinsurah. Nearer to the sea, the English had built Fort William. A church and ample warehouses rose in the vicinity. A row of spacious houses, belonging to the chief factors of the East India Company, lined the banks of the river; and in the neighbourhood had sprung up a large and busy native town, where some Hindoo merchants of great opulence had fixed their abode. But the tract now covered by the palaces of Chowringhee contained only a few miserable huts thatched with straw. A jungle, abandoned to water-fowl and alligators, covered the site of the present Citadel, and the Course, which is now daily crowded at sunset with the gayest equipages of Calcutta. For the ground on which the settlement stood, the English, like other great landholders, paid rent to the government; and they were, like other great landholders, permitted to exercise a certain jurisdiction within their domain.

The great province of Bengal, together with Orissa and Bahar, had long been governed by a viceroy, whom the English called Aliverdy Khan, and who, like the other viceroys of the Mogul, had become virtually independent. He died in 1756, and the sovereignty descended to his grandson, a youth under twenty years of age, who bore the name of Surajah Dowlah. Oriental despots are perhaps the worst class of human beings; and this unhappy boy was one of the worst specimens of his class. His understanding was naturally feeble, and his temper naturally unamiable. His education had been such as would have enervated even a vigorous intellect and perverted even a generous disposition. He was unreasonable, because nobody ever dared to reason with him, and selfish, because he had never been made to feel himself dependent on the good-will of others. Early debauchery had unnerved his body and his mind. He indulged immoderately in the use of ardent spirits, which inflamed his weak brain almost to madness. His chosen companions were flatterers, sprung from the dregs of the people, and recommended by nothing but buffoonery and servility. It is said that he had arrived at that last stage of human depravity, when cruelty becomes pleasing for its own sake, when the sight of pain as pain, where no advantage is to be gained, no offence punished, no danger averted, is an agreeable excitement. It had early been his amusement to torture beasts and birds; and, when he grew up, he enjoyed with still keener relish the misery of his fellow-creatures.

From a child Surajah Dowlah had hated the English. It was his whim to do so; and his whims were never opposed. He had also formed a very exaggerated notion of the wealth which might be obtained by plundering them; and his feeble and uncultivated mind was incapable of perceiving that the riches of Calcutta, had they been even greater than he imagined, would not compensate him for what he must lose, if the European trade, of which Bengal was a chief seat, should be driven by his violence to some other quarter. Pretexts for a quarrel were readily found. The English, in expectation of a war with France, had begun to fortify their settlement without special permission from the Nabob. A rich native whom he longed to plunder, had taken refuge at Calcutta, and had not been delivered up. On such grounds as these Surajah Dowlah marched with a great army against Fort William.

The servants of the Company at Madras had been forced by Dupleix to become statesmen and soldiers. Those in Bengal were still mere traders, and were terrified and bewildered by the approaching danger. The governor, who had heard much of Surajah Dowlah's cruelty, was frightened out of his wits, jumped into a boat, and took refuge in the nearest ship. The military commandant thought that he could not do better than follow so good an example. The fort was taken after a feeble resistance; and great numbers of the English fell into the hands of the conquerors. The Nabob seated himself with regal pomp in the principal hall of the factory, and ordered Mr. Holwell, the first in rank among the prisoners, to be brought before him. His Highness abused the insolence of the English, and grumbled at the smallness of the treasure which he had found; but promised to spare their lives, and retired to rest.

Then was committed that great crime, memorable for its singular atrocity, memorable for the tremendous retribution by which it was followed. The English captives were left at the mercy of the guards; and the guards determined to secure them for the night in the prison of the garrison, a chamber known by the fearful name of the Black Hole. Even for a single European malefactor, that dungeon would, in such a climate, have been too close and narrow. The space was only twenty feet square. The air-holes were small and obstructed. It was the summer solstice, the season when the fierce heat of Bengal can scarcely be rendered tolerable to natives of England by lofty halls and by the constant waving of fans. The number of the prisoners was one hundred and forty-six. When they were ordered to enter the cell, they imagined that the soldiers were joking; and, being in high spirits on account of the promise of the Nabob to spare their lives, they laughed and jested at the absurdity of the notion. They soon discovered their mistake. They expostulated; they entreated; but in vain. The guards threatened to cut down all who hesitated. The captives were driven into the cell at the point of the sword, and the door was instantly shut and locked upon them.

Nothing in history or fiction, not even the story which Ugolino told in the sea of everlasting ice, after he had wiped his bloody lips on the scalp of his murderer, approaches the horrors which were recounted by the few survivors of that night. They cried for mercy. They strove to burst the door. Holwell who, even in that extremity, retained some presence of mind, offered large bribes to the gaolers. But the answer was that nothing could be done without the Nabob's orders, that the Nabob was asleep, and that he would be angry if anybody woke him. Then the prisoners went mad with despair. They trampled each other down, fought for the places at the windows, fought for the pittance of water with which the cruel mercy of the murderers mocked their agonies, raved, prayed, blasphemed, implored the guards to fire among them. The gaolers in the mean time held lights to the bars, and shouted with laughter at the frantic struggles of their victims. At length the tumult died away in low gaspings and moanings. The day broke. The Nabob had slept off his debauch, and permitted the door to be opened. But it was some time before the soldiers could make a lane for the survivors, by piling up on each side the heaps of corpses on which the burning climate had already begun to do its loathsome work. When at length a passage was made, twenty-three ghastly figures, such as their own mothers would not have known, staggered one by one out of the charnel-house. A pit was instantly dug. The dead bodies, a hundred and twenty-three in number, were flung into it promiscuously, and covered up.

But these things which, after the lapse of more than eighty years, cannot be told or read without horror, awakened neither remorse nor pity in the bosom of the savage Nabob. He inflicted no punishment on the murderers. He shewed no tenderness to the survivors. Some of them, indeed, from whom nothing was to be got, were suffered to depart; but those from whom it was thought that any thing could be extorted were treated with execrable cruelty. Holwell, unable to walk, was carried before the tyrant, who reproached him, threatened him, and sent him up the country in irons, together with some other gentlemen who were suspected of knowing more than they chose to tell about the treasures of the Company. These persons, still bowed down by the sufferings of that great agony, were lodged in miserable sheds, and fed only with grain and water, till at length the intercessions of the female relations of the Nabob procured their release. One Englishwoman had survived that night. She was placed in the haram of the Prince at Moorshedabad.

Surajah Dowlah, in the mean time, sent letters to his nominal sovereign at Delhi, describing the late conquest in the most pompous language. He placed a garrison in Fort William, forbade any Englishman to dwell in the neighbourhood, and directed that, in memory of his great actions, Calcutta should thenceforward be called Alinagore, that is to say, the Port of God.

In August the news of the fall of Calcutta reached Madras, and excited the fiercest and bitterest resentment. The cry of the whole settlement was for vengeance. Within forty-eight hours after the arrival of the intelligence it was determined that an expedition should be sent to the Hoogley, and that Clive should be at the head of the land forces. The naval armament was under the command of Admiral Watson. Nine hundred English infantry, fine troops and full of spirit, and fifteen hundred sepoys, composed the army which sailed to punish a Prince who had more subjects than Louis the Fifteenth or the Empress Maria Theresa. In October the expedition sailed; but it had to make its way against adverse winds, and did not reach Bengal till December.

The Nabob was revelling in fancied security at Moorshedabad. He was so profoundly ignorant of the state of foreign countries that he often used to say that there were not ten thousand men in all Europe; and it had never occurred to him as possible, that the English would dare to invade his dominions. But, though undisturbed by any fear of their military power, he began to miss them greatly. His revenues fell off; and his ministers succeeded in making him understand that a ruler may sometimes find it more profitable to protect traders in the open enjoyment of their gains than to put them to the torture for the purpose of discovering hidden chests of gold and jewels. He was already disposed to permit the Company to resume its mercantile operations in his country, when he received the news that an English armament was in the Hoogley. He instantly ordered all his troops to assemble at Moorshedabad, and marched towards Calcutta.

Clive had commenced operations with his usual vigour. He took Budgebudge, routed the garrison of Fort William, recovered Calcutta, stormed and sacked Hoogley. The Nabob, already disposed to make some concessions to the English, was confirmed in his pacific disposition by these proofs of their power and spirit. He accordingly made overtures to the chiefs of the invading armament, and offered to restore the factory, and to give compensation to those whom he had despoiled.

Clive's profession was war; and he felt that there was something discreditable in an accommodation with Surajah Dowlah. But his power was limited. A committee, chiefly composed of servants of the Company who had fled from Calcutta, had the principal direction of affairs; and these persons were eager to be restored to their posts and compensated for their losses. The government of Madras, apprised that war had commenced in Europe, and apprehensive of an attack from the French, became impatient for the return of the armament. The promises of the Nabob were large, the chances of a contest doubtful; and Clive consented to treat, though he expressed his regret that things should not be concluded in so glorious a manner as he could have wished.

With this negotiation commences a new chapter in the life of Clive. Hitherto he had been merely a soldier, carrying into effect, with eminent ability and valour, the plans of others. Henceforth he is to be chiefly regarded as a statesman; and his military movements are to be considered as subordinate to his political designs. That in his new capacity he displayed great talents, and obtained great success, is unquestionable. But it is also unquestionable, that the transactions in which he now began to take a part have left a stain on his moral character.

We can by no means agree with Sir John Malcolm, who is obstinately resolved to see nothing but honour and integrity in the conduct of his hero. But we can as little agree with Mr. Mill, who has gone so far as to say that Clive was a man "to whom deception, when it suited his purpose, never cost a pang." Clive seems to us to have been constitutionally the very opposite of a knave, bold even to temerity, sincere even to indiscretion, hearty in friendship, open in enmity. Neither in his private life, nor in those parts of his public life in which he had to do with his countrymen, do we find any signs of a propensity to cunning. On the contrary, in all the disputes in which he was engaged as an Englishman against Englishmen, from his boxing-matches at school to those stormy altercations at the India House and in Parliament amidst which his later years were passed, his very faults were those of a high and magnanimous spirit. The truth seems to have been that he considered Oriental politics as a game in which nothing was unfair. He knew that the standard of morality among the natives of India differed widely from that established in England. He knew that he had to deal with men destitute of what in Europe is called honour, with men who would give any promise without hesitation and break any promise without shame, with men who would unscrupulously employ corruption, perjury, forgery, to compass their ends. His letters show that the great difference between Asiatic and European morality was constantly in his thoughts. He seems to have imagined, most erroneously in our opinion, that he could effect nothing against such adversaries, if he was content to be bound by ties from which they were free, if he went on telling truth, and hearing none, if he fulfilled, to his own hurt, all his engagements with confederates who never kept an engagement that was not to their advantage. Accordingly this man, in the other parts of his life an honourable English gentleman and soldier, was no sooner matched against an Indian intriguer, than he became himself an Indian intriguer, and descended, without scruple, to falsehood, to hypocritical caresses, to the substitution of documents, and to the counterfeiting of hands.

The negotiations between the English and the Nabob were carried on chiefly by two agents, Mr. Watts, a servant of the Company, and a Bengalee of the name of Omichund. This Omichund had been one of the wealthiest native merchants resident at Calcutta, and had sustained great losses in consequence of the Nabob's expedition against that place. In the course of his commercial transactions, he had seen much of the English, and was peculiarly qualified to serve as a medium of communication between them and a native court. He possessed great influence with his own race, and had in large measure the Hindoo talents, quick observation, tact, dexterity, perseverance, and the Hindoo vices, servility, greediness, and treachery.

The Nabob behaved with all the faithlessness of an Indian statesman, and with all the levity of a boy whose mind had been enfeebled by power and self-indulgence. He promised, retracted, hesitated, evaded. At one time he advanced with his army in a threatening manner towards Calcutta; but when he saw the resolute front which the English presented, he fell back in alarm, and consented to make peace with them on their own terms. The treaty was no sooner concluded than he formed new designs against them. He intrigued with the French authorities at Chandernagore. He invited Bussy to march from the Deccan to the Hoogley, and to drive the English out of Bengal. All this was well known to Clive and Watson. They determined accordingly to strike a decisive blow, and to attack Chandernagore, before the force there could be strengthened by new arrivals, either from the south of India or from Europe. Watson directed the expedition by water, Clive by land. The success of the combined movements was rapid and complete. The fort, the garrison, the artillery, the military stores, all fell into the hands of the English. Near five hundred European troops were among the prisoners.

The Nabob had feared and hated the English, even while he was still able to oppose to them their French rivals. The French were now vanquished; and he began to regard the English with still greater fear and still greater hatred. His weak and unprincipled mind oscillated between servility and insolence. One day he sent a large sum to Calcutta, as part of the compensation due for the wrongs which he had committed. The next day he sent a present of jewels to Bussy, exhorting that distinguished officer to hasten to protect Bengal "against Clive, the daring in war, on whom," says his highness, "may all bad fortune attend." He ordered his army to march against the English. He countermanded his orders. He tore Clive's letters. He then sent answers in the most florid language of compliment. He ordered Watts out of his presence, and threatened to impale him. He again sent for Watts, and begged pardon for the insult. In the mean time, his wretched maladministration, his folly, his dissolute manners, and his love of the lowest company, had disgusted all classes of his subjects, soldiers, traders, civil functionaries, the proud and ostentatious Mahommedans, the timid, supple, and parsimonious Hindoos. A formidable confederacy was formed against him, in which were included Roydullub, the minister of finance, Meer Jaffier, the principal commander of the troops, and Jugget Seit, the richest banker in India. The plot was confided to the English agents, and a communication was opened between the malcontents at Moorshedabad and the committee at Calcutta.

In the committee there was much hesitation; but Clive's voice was given in favour of the conspirators, and his vigour and firmness bore down all opposition. It was determined that the English should lend their powerful assistance to depose Surajah Dowlah, and to place Meer Jaffier on the throne of Bengal. In return, Meer Jaffier promised ample compensation to the Company and its servants, and a liberal donative to the army, the navy, and the committee. The odious vices of Surajah Dowlah, the wrongs which the English had suffered at his hands, the dangers to which our trade must have been exposed had he continued to reign, appear to us fully to justify the resolution of deposing him. But nothing can justify the dissimulation which Clive stooped to practise. He wrote to Surajah Dowlah in terms so affectionate that they for a time lulled that weak prince into perfect security. The same courier who carried this "soothing letter," as Clive calls it, to the Nabob, carried to Mr. Watts a letter in the following terms: "Tell Meer Jaffier to fear nothing. I will join him with five thousand men who never turned their backs. Assure him I will march night and day to his assistance, and stand by him as long as I have a man left."

It was impossible that a plot which had so many ramifications should long remain entirely concealed. Enough reached the ears of the Nabob to arouse his suspicions. But he was soon quieted by the fictions and artifices which the inventive genius of Omichund produced with miraculous readiness. All was going well; the plot was nearly ripe; when Clive learned that Omichund was likely to play false. The artful Bengalee had been promised a liberal compensation for all that he had lost at Calcutta. But this would not satisfy him. His services had been great. He held the thread of the whole intrigue. By one word breathed in the ear of Surajah Dowlah, he could undo all that he had done. The lives of Watts, of Meer Jaffier, of all the conspirators, were at his mercy; and he determined to take advantage of his situation and to make his own terms. He demanded three hundred thousand pounds sterling as the price of his secrecy and of his assistance. The committee, incensed by the treachery and appalled by the danger, knew not what course to take. But Clive was more than Omichund's match in Omichund's own arts. The man, he said, was a villain. Any artifice which would defeat such knavery was justifiable. The best course would be to promise what was asked. Omichund would soon be at their mercy; and then they might punish him by withholding from him, not only the bribe which he now demanded, but also the compensation which all the other sufferers of Calcutta were to receive.

His advice was taken. But how was the wary and sagacious

Hindoo to be deceived? He had demanded that an article touching his claims should be inserted in the treaty between Meer Jaffier and the English, and he would not be satisfied unless he saw it with his own eyes. Clive had an expedient ready. Two treaties were drawn up, one on white paper, the other on red, the former real, the latter fictitious. In the former Omichund's name was not mentioned; the latter, which was to be shown to him, contained a stipulation in his favour.

But another difficulty arose. Admiral Watson had scruples about signing the red treaty. Omichund's vigilance and acuteness were such that the absence of so important a name would probably awaken his suspicions. But Clive was not a man to do anything by halves. We almost blush to write it. He forged Admiral Watson's name.

All was now ready for action. Mr. Watts fled secretly from Moorshedabad. Clive put his troops in motion, and wrote to the Nabob in a tone very different from that of his previous letters. He set forth all the wrongs which the British had suffered, offered to submit the points in dispute to the arbitration of Meer Jaffier, and concluded by announcing that, as the rains were about to set in, he and his men would do themselves the honour of waiting on his highness for an answer.

Surajah Dowlah instantly assembled his whole force, and marched to encounter the English. It had been agreed that Meer Jaffier should separate himself from the Nabob, and carry over his division to Clive. But, as the decisive moment approached, the fears of the conspirator overpowered his ambition. Clive had advanced to Cossimbuzar; the Nabob lay with a mighty power a few miles off at Plassey; and still Meer Jaffier delayed to fulfil his engagements, and returned evasive answers to the earnest remonstrances of the English general.

Clive was in a painfully anxious situation. He could place no confidence in the sincerity or in the courage of his confederate: and, whatever confidence he might place in his own military talents, and in the valour and discipline of his troops, it was no light thing to engage an army twenty times as numerous as his own. Before him lay a river over which it was easy to advance, but over which, if things went ill, not one of his little band would ever return. On this occasion, for the first and for the last time, his dauntless spirit, during a few hours, shrank from the fearful responsibility of making a decision. He called a council of war. The majority pronounced against fighting; and Clive declared his concurrence with the majority. Long afterwards, he said that he had never called but one council of war, and that, if he had taken the advice of that council, the British would never have been masters of Bengal. But scarcely had the meeting broken up when he was himself again. He retired alone under the shade of some trees, and passed near an hour there in thought. He came back determined to put every thing to the hazard, and gave orders that all should be in readiness for passing the river on the morrow.

The river was passed; and, at the close of a toilsome day's march, the army, long after sunset, took up its quarters in a grove of mango-trees near Plassey, within a mile of the enemy. Clive was unable to sleep: he heard, through the whole night, the sound of drums and cymbals from the vast camp of the Nabob. It is not strange that even his stout heart should now and then have sunk, when he reflected against what odds, and for what a prize, he was in a few hours to contend.

Nor was the rest of Surajah Dowlah more peaceful. His mind, at once weak and stormy, was distracted by wild and horrible apprehensions. Appalled by the greatness and nearness of the crisis, distrusting his captains, dreading every one who approached him, dreading to be left alone, he sat gloomily in his tent, haunted, a Greek poet would have said, by the furies of those who had cursed him with their last breath in the Black Hole.

The day broke, the day which was to decide the fate of India. At sunrise the army of the Nabob, pouring through many openings from the camp, began to move towards the grove where the English lay. Forty thousand infantry, armed with firelocks, pikes, swords, bows and arrows, covered the plain. They were accompanied by fifty pieces of ordnance of the largest size, each tugged by a long team of white oxen, and each pushed on from behind by an elephant. Some smaller guns, under the direction of a few French auxiliaries, were perhaps more formidable. The cavalry were fifteen thousand, drawn, not from the effeminate population of Bengal, but from the bolder race which inhabits the northern provinces; and the practised eye of Clive could perceive that both the men and the horses were more powerful than those of the Carnatic. The force which he had to oppose to this great multitude consisted of only three thousand men. But of these nearly a thousand were English; and all were led by English officers, and trained in the English discipline. Conspicuous in the ranks of the little army were the men of the Thirty-Ninth Regiment, which still bears on its colours, amidst many honourable additions won under Wellington in Spain and Gascony, the name of Plassey, and the proud motto, *Primus in Indis*.

The battle commenced with a cannonade in which the artillery of the Nabob did scarcely any execution, while the few field-pieces of the English produced great effect. Several of the most distinguished officers in Surajah Dowlah's service fell. Disorder began to spread through his ranks. His own terror increased every moment. One of the conspirators urged on him the expediency of retreating. The insidious advice, agreeing as it did with what his own terrors suggested, was readily received. He ordered his army to fall back, and this order decided his fate. Clive snatched the moment, and ordered his troops to advance. The confused and dispirited multitude gave way before the onset of disciplined valour. No mob attacked by regular soldiers was ever more completely routed. The little band of Frenchmen, who alone ventured to confront the English, were swept down the stream of fugitives. In an hour the forces of Surajah Dowlah were dispersed, never to reassemble. Only five hundred of the vanquished were slain. But their camp, their guns, their baggage, innumerable waggons, innumerable cattle, remained in the power of the conquerors. With the loss of twenty-two soldiers killed and fifty wounded, Clive had scattered an army of near sixty thousand men, and subdued an empire larger and more populous than Great Britain.

Meer Jaffier had given no assistance to the English during the action. But, as soon as he saw that the fate of the day was decided, he drew off his division of the army, and, when the battle was over, sent his congratulations to his ally. The next morning he repaired to the English quarters, not a little uneasy as to the reception which awaited him there. He gave evident signs of alarm when a guard was drawn out to receive him with the honours due to his rank. But his apprehensions were speedily removed. Clive came forward to meet him, embraced him, saluted him as Nabob of the three great provinces of Bengal, Bahar, and Orissa, listened graciously to his apologies, and advised him to march without delay to Moorshedabad.

Surajah Dowlah had fled from the field of battle with all the speed with which a fleet camel could carry him, and arrived at Moorshedabad in little more than twenty-four hours. There he called his councillors round him. The wisest advised him to put himself into the hands of the English, from whom he had nothing worse to fear than deposition and confinement. But he attributed this suggestion to treachery. Others urged him to try the chance of war again. He approved the advice, and issued orders accordingly. But he wanted spirit to adhere even during one day to a manly resolution. He learned that Meer Jaffier had arrived; and his terrors became insupportable. Disguised in a mean dress, with a casket of jewels in his hand, he let himself down at night from a window of his palace, and, accompanied by only two attendants, embarked on the river for Patna.

In a few days Clive arrived at Moorshedabad, escorted by two hundred English soldiers and three hundred sepoys. For his residence had been assigned a palace, which was surrounded by a garden so spacious that all the troops who accompanied him could conveniently encamp within it. The ceremony of the installation of Meer Jaffier was instantly performed. Clive led the new Nabob to the seat of honour, placed him on it, presented to him, after the immemorial fashion of the East, an offering of gold, and then, turning to the natives who filled the hall, congratulated them on the good fortune which had freed them from a tyrant. He was compelled on this occasion to use the services of an interpreter; for it is remarkable that, long as he resided in India, intimately acquainted as he was with Indian politics and with the Indian character, and adored as he was by his Indian soldiery, he never learned to express himself with facility in any Indian language. He is said indeed to have been sometimes under the necessity of employing, in his intercourse with natives of India, the smattering of Portuguese which he had acquired, when a lad, in Brazil.

The new sovereign was now called upon to fulfil the engagements into which he had entered with his allies. A conference was held at the house of Jugget Seit, the great banker, for the purpose of making the necessary arrangements. Omichund came thither, fully believing himself to stand high in the favour of Clive who, with dissimulation surpassing even the dissimulation of Bengal, had up to that day treated him with undiminished kindness. The white treaty was produced and read. Clive then turned to Mr. Scrafton, one of the servants of the Company, and said in English, "It is now time to undeceive Omichund." "Omichund," said Mr. Scrafton in Hindostanee, "the red treaty is a trick. You are to have nothing." Omichund fell back insensible into the arms of his attendants. He revived; but his mind was irreparably ruined. Clive, who, though little troubled by scruples of conscience in his dealings with Indian politicians, was not inhuman, seems to have been touched. He saw Omichund a few days later, spoke to him kindly, advised him to make a pilgrimage to one of the great temples of India, in the hope that change of scene might restore his health, and was even disposed, notwithstanding all that had passed, again to employ his talents in the public service. But, from the moment of that sudden shock, the unhappy man sank gradually into idiocy. He, who had formerly been distinguished by the strength of his understanding and the simplicity of his habits, now squandered the remains of his fortune on childish trinkets, and loved to exhibit himself dressed in rich garments, and hung with precious stones. In this abject state he languished a few months, and then died.

We should not think it necessary to offer any remarks for the purpose of directing the judgment of our readers with respect to this transaction, had not Sir John Malcolm undertaken to defend it in all its parts. He regrets, indeed, that it was necessary to employ means so liable to abuse as forgery; but he will not admit than any blame attaches to those who deceived the deceiver. He thinks that the English were not bound to keep faith with one who kept no faith with them, and that, if they had fulfilled their engagements with the wily Bengalee, so signal an example of successful treason would have produced a crowd of imitators. Now, we will not discuss this point on any rigid principles of morality. Indeed, it is quite unnecessary to do so; for, looking at the question as a question of expediency in the lowest sense of the word, and using no arguments but such as Machiavelli might have employed in his conferences with Borgia, we are convinced that Clive was altogether in the wrong, and that he committed, not merely a crime, but a blunder. That honesty is the best policy is a maxim which we firmly believe to be generally correct, even with respect to the temporal interest of individuals; but, with respect to societies, the rule is subject to still fewer exceptions, and that for this reason, that the life of societies is longer than the life of individuals. It is possible to mention men who have owed great worldly prosperity to breaches of private faith. But we doubt whether it be possible to mention a state which has on the whole been a gainer by a breach of public faith. The entire history of British India is an illustration of the great truth, that it is not prudent to oppose perfidy to perfidy, and that the most efficient weapon with which men can encounter falsehood is truth. During a long course of years, the English rulers of India, surrounded by allies and enemies whom no engagement could bind, have generally acted with sincerity and uprightness; and the event has proved that sincerity and uprightness are wisdom. English valour and English intelligence have done less to extend and to preserve our Oriental empire than English veracity. All that we could have gained by imitating the doublings, the evasions, the fictions, the perjuries which have been employed against us, is as nothing, when compared with what we have gained by being the one power in India on whose word reliance can be placed. No oath which superstition can devise, no hostage however precious, inspires a hundredth part of the confidence which is produced by the "yea, yea," and "nay, nay," of a British envoy. No fastness, however strong by art or nature, gives to its inmates a security like that enjoyed by the chief who, passing through the territories of powerful and deadly enemies, is armed with the British guarantee. The mightiest princes of the East can scarcely, by the offer of enormous usury, draw forth any portion of the wealth which is concealed under the hearths of their subjects. The British Government offers little more than four per cent.; and avarice hastens to bring forth tens of millions of rupees from its most secret repositories. A hostile monarch may promise mountains of gold to our sepoys, on condition that they will desert the standard of the Company. The Company promises only a moderate pension after a long service. But every sepoy knows that the promise of the Company will be kept: he knows that if he lives a hundred years his rice and salt are as secure as the salary of the Governor-General: and he knows that there is not another state in India which would not, in spite of the most solemn vows, leave him to die of hunger in a ditch as soon as he had ceased to be useful. The greatest advantage which a government can possess is to be the one trustworthy government in the midst of governments which nobody can trust. This advantage we enjoy in Asia. Had we acted during the last two generations on the principles which Sir John Malcolm appears to have considered as sound, had we, as often as we had to deal with people like Omichund, retaliated by lying, and forging, and breaking faith, after their fashion, it is our firm belief that no courage or capacity could have upheld our empire.

Sir John Malcolm admits that Clive's breach of faith could be justified only by the strongest necessity. As we think that breach of faith not only unnecessary, but most inexpedient, we need hardly say that we altogether condemn it.

Omichund was not the only victim of the revolution. Surajah Dowlah was taken a few days after his flight, and was brought before Meer Jaffier. There he flung himself on the ground in convulsions of fear, and with tears and loud cries implored the mercy which he had never shown. Meer Jaffier hesitated; but his son Meeran, a youth of seventeen, who in feebleness of brain and savageness of nature greatly resembled the wretched captive, was implacable. Surajah Dowlah was led into a secret chamber, to which in a short time the ministers of death were sent. In this act the English bore no part; and Meer Jaffier understood so much of their feelings, that he thought it necessary to apologise to them for having avenged them on their most malignant enemy.

The shower of wealth now fell copiously on the Company and its servants. A sum of eight hundred thousand pounds sterling, in coined silver, was sent down the river from Moorshedabad to Fort William. The fleet which conveyed this treasure consisted of more than a hundred boats, and performed its triumphal voyage with flags flying and music playing. Calcutta, which a few months before had been desolate, was now more prosperous than ever. Trade revived; and the signs of affluence appeared in every English house. As to Clive, there was no limit to his acquisitions but his own moderation. The treasury of Bengal was thrown open to him. There were piled up, after the usage of Indian princes, immense masses of coin, among which might not seldom be detected the florins and byzants with which, before any European ship had turned the Cape of Good Hope, the Venetians purchased the stuffs and spices of the East. Clive walked between heaps of gold and silver, crowned with rubies and diamonds, and was at liberty to help himself. He accepted between two and three hundred thousand pounds.

The pecuniary transactions between Meer Jaffier and Clive were sixteen years later condemned by the public voice, and severely criticised in Parliament. They are vehemently defended by Sir John Malcolm. The accusers of the victorious general represented his gains as the wages of corruption, or as plunder extorted at the point of the sword from a helpless ally. The biographer, on the other hand, considers these great acquisitions as free gifts, honourable alike to the donor and to the receiver, and compares them to the rewards bestowed by foreign powers on Marlborough, on Nelson, and on Wellington. It had always, he says, been customary in the East to give and receive presents; and there was, as yet, no Act of Parliament positively prohibiting English functionaries in India from profiting by this Asiatic usage. This reasoning, we own, does not quite satisfy us. We do not suspect Clive of selling the interests of his employers or his country; but we cannot acquit him of having done what, if not in itself evil, was yet of evil example. Nothing is more clear than that a general ought to be the servant of his own government, and of no other. It follows that whatever rewards he receives for his services ought to be given either by his own government, or with the full knowledge and approbation of his own government. This rule ought to be strictly maintained even with respect to the merest bauble, with respect to a cross, a medal, or a yard of coloured riband. But how can any government be well served, if those who command its forces are at liberty, without its permission, without its privity, to accept princely fortunes from its allies? It is idle to say that there was then no Act of Parliament prohibiting the practice of taking presents from Asiatic sovereigns. It is not on the Act which was passed at a later period for the purpose of preventing any such taking of presents, but on grounds which were valid before that Act was passed, on grounds of common law and common sense, that we arraign the conduct of Clive. There is no Act that we know of, prohibiting the Secretary of State for Foreign Affairs from being in the pay of continental powers. But it is not the less true that a Secretary who should receive a secret pension from France would grossly violate his duty, and would deserve severe punishment. Sir John Malcolm compares the conduct of Clive with that of the Duke of Wellington. Suppose,—and we beg pardon for putting such a supposition even for the sake of argument,—that the Duke of Wellington had, after the campaign of 1815, and while he commanded the army of occupation in France, privately accepted two hundred thousand pounds from Louis the Eighteenth, as a mark of gratitude for the great services which his Grace had rendered to the House of Bourbon; what would be thought of such a transaction? Yet the statute-book no more forbids the taking of presents in Europe now than it forbade the taking of presents in Asia then.

At the same time, it must be admitted that, in Clive's case, there were many extenuating circumstances. He considered himself as the general, not of the Crown, but of the Company. The Company had, by implication at least, authorised its agents to enrich themselves by means of the liberality of the native princes, and by other means still more objectionable. It was hardly to be expected that the servant should entertain stricter notions of his duty than were entertained by his masters. Though Clive did not distinctly acquaint his employers with what had taken place, and request their sanction, he did not, on the other hand, by studied conceal-ment, show that he was conscious of having done wrong. On the contrary, he avowed with the greatest openness that the Nabob's bounty had raised him to affluence. Lastly, though we think that he ought not in such a way to have taken any thing, we must admit that he deserves praise for having taken so little. He accepted twenty lacs of rupees. It would have cost him only a word to make the twenty forty. It was a very easy exercise of virtue to declaim in England against Clive's rapacity; but not one in a hundred of his accusers would have shown so much self-command in the treasury of Moorshedabad.

Meer Jaffier could be upheld on the throne only by the hand which had placed him on it. He was not, indeed, a mere boy; nor had he been so unfortunate as to be born in the purple. He was not therefore quite so imbecile or quite so depraved as his predecessor had been. But he had none of the talents or virtues which his post required; and his son and heir, Meeran, was another Surajah Dowlah. The recent revolution had unsettled the minds of men. Many chiefs were in open insurrection against the new Nabob. The viceroy of the rich and powerful province of Oude who, like the other viceroys of the Mogul, was now in truth an independent sovereign, menaced Bengal with invasion. Nothing but the talents and authority of Clive could support the tottering government. While things were in this state a ship arrived with despatches which had been written at the India House before the news of the battle of Plassey had reached London. The Directors had determined to place the English settlements in Bengal under a government constituted in the most cumbrous and absurd manner; and, to make the matter worse, no place in the arrangement was assigned to Clive. The persons who were selected to form this new government, greatly to their honour, took on themselves the responsibility of disobeying these preposterous orders, and invited Clive to exercise the supreme authority. He consented; and it soon appeared that the servants of the Company had only anticipated the wishes of their employers. The Directors, on receiving news of Clive's brilliant success, instantly appointed him governor of their possessions in Bengal, with the highest marks of gratitude and esteem. His power was now boundless, and far surpassed even that which Dupleix had attained in the south of India. Meer Jaffier regarded him with slavish awe. On one occasion, the Nabob spoke with severity to a native chief of high rank, whose followers had been engaged in a brawl with some of the Company's sepoys. "Are you yet to learn," he said, "who that Colonel Clive is, and in what station God has placed him?" The chief, who, as a famous jester and an old friend of Meer Jaffier, could venture to take liberties, answered, "I affront the Colonel! I, who never get up in the morning without making three low bows to his jackass!" This was hardly an exaggeration. Europeans and natives were alike at Clive's feet. The English regarded him as the only man who could force Meer Jaffier to keep his engagements with them. Meer Jaffier regarded him as the only man who could protect the new dynasty against turbulent subjects and encroaching neighbours.

It is but justice to say that Clive used his power ably and vigorously for the advantage of his country. He sent forth an expedition against the tract lying to the north of the Carnatic. In this tract the French still had the ascendency; and it was important to dislodge them. The conduct of the enterprise was entrusted to an officer of the name of Forde, who was then little known, but in whom the keen eye of the governor had detected military talents of a high order. The success of the expedition was rapid and splendid.

While a considerable part of the army of Bengal was thus engaged at a distance, a new and formidable danger menaced the western frontier. The Great Mogul was a prisoner at Delhi in the hands of a subject. His eldest son, named Shah Alum, destined to be, during many years, the sport of adverse fortune, and to be a tool in the hands, first of the Mahrattas, and then of the English, had fled from the palace of his father. His birth was still revered in India. Some powerful princes, the Nabob of Oude in particular, were inclined to favour him. Shah Alum found it easy to draw to his standard great numbers of the military adventurers with whom every part of the country swarmed. An army of forty thousand men, of various races and religions, Mahrattas, Rohillas, Jauts, and Afghans, was speedily assembled round him; and he formed the design of overthrowing the upstart whom the English had elevated to a throne, and of establishing his own authority throughout Bengal, Orissa, and Bahar.

Meer Jaffier's terror was extreme; and the only expedient which occurred to him was to purchase, by the payment of a large sum of money, an accommodation with Shah Alum. This expedient had been repeatedly employed by those who, before him, had ruled the rich and unwarlike provinces near the mouth of the Ganges. But Clive treated the suggestion with a scorn worthy of his strong sense and dauntless courage. "If you do this," he wrote, "you will have the Nabob of Oude, the Mahrattas, and many more, come from all parts of the confines of your country, who will bully you out of money till you have none left in your treasury. I beg your excellency will rely on the fidelity of the English, and of those troops which are attached to you." He wrote in a similar strain to the governor of Patna, a brave native soldier, whom he highly esteemed. "Come to no terms; defend your city to the last. Rest assured that the English are stanch and firm friends, and that they never desert a cause in which they have once taken a part."

He kept his word. Shah Alum had invested Patna, and was on the point of proceeding to storm, when he learned that the Colonel was advancing by forced marches. The whole army which was approaching consisted of only four hundred and fifty Europeans, and two thousand five hundred sepoys. But Clive and his Englishmen were now objects of dread over all the East. As soon as his advanced guard appeared, the besiegers fled before him. A few

French adventurers who were about the person of the prince advised him to try the chance of battle; but in vain. In a few days this great army, which had been regarded with so much uneasiness by the court of Moorshedabad, melted away before the mere terror of the British name.

The conqueror returned in triumph to Fort William. The joy of Meer Jaffier was as unbounded as his fears had been, and led him to bestow on his preserver a princely token of gratitude. The quit-rent which the East India Company was bound to pay to the Nabob for the extensive lands held by them to the south of Calcutta amounted to near thirty thousand pounds sterling a year. The whole of this splendid estate, sufficient to support with dignity the highest rank of the British peerage, was now conferred on Clive for life.

This present we think Clive justified in accepting. It was a present which, from its very nature, could be no secret. In fact, the Company itself was his tenant, and, by its acquiescence, signified its approbation of Meer Jaffier's grant.

But the gratitude of Meer Jaffier did not last long. He had for some time felt that the powerful ally who had set him up might pull him down, and had been looking round for support against the formidable strength by which he had himself been hitherto sup-ported. He knew that it would be impossible to find among the natives of India any force which would look the Colonel's little army in the face. The French power in Bengal was extinct. But the fame of the Dutch had anciently been great in the Eastern seas; and it was not yet distinctly known in Asia how much the power of Holland had declined in Europe. Secret communications passed between the court of Moorshedabad, and the Dutch factory at Chinsurah; and urgent letters were sent from Chinsurah, exhorting the government of Batavia to fit out an expedition which might balance the power of the English in Bengal. The authorities of Batavia, eager to extend the influence of their country, and still more eager to obtain for themselves a share of the wealth which had recently raised so many English adventurers to opulence, equipped a powerful armament. Seven large ships from Java arrived un-expectedly in the Hoogley. The military force on board amounted to fifteen hundred men, of whom about one half were Europeans. The enterprise was well timed. Clive had sent such large detach-ments to oppose the French in the Carnatic that his army was now inferior in number to that of the Dutch. He knew that Meer Jaffier secretly favoured the invaders. He knew that he took on himself a serious responsibility if he attacked the forces of a friendly power;

that the English ministers could not wish to see a war with Holland added to that in which they were already engaged with France; that they might disavow his acts; that they might punish him. He had recently remitted a great part of his fortune to Europe, through the Dutch East India Company; and he had therefore a strong interest in avoiding any quarrel. But he was satisfied, that if he suffered the Batavian armament to pass up the river and to join the garrison of Chinsurah, Meer Jaffier would throw himself into the arms of these new allies, and that the English ascendency in Bengal would be exposed to most serious danger. He took his resolution with characteristic boldness, and was most ably seconded by his officers, particularly by Colonel Forde, to whom the most important part of the operations was entrusted. The Dutch attempted to force a passage. The English encountered them both by land and water. On both elements the enemy had a great superiority of force. On both they were signally defeated. Their ships were taken. Their troops were put to a total rout. Almost all the European soldiers, who constituted the main strength of the invading army, were killed or taken. The conquerors sat down before Chinsurah; and the chiefs of that settlement, now thoroughly humbled, consented to the terms which Clive dictated. They engaged to build no fortifications, and to raise no troops beyond a small force necessary for the police of their factories; and it was distinctly provided that any violation of these covenants should be punished with instant expulsion from Bengal.

Three months after this great victory, Clive sailed for England. At home, honours and rewards awaited him, not indeed equal to his claims or to his ambition, but still such as, when his age, his rank in the army, and his original place in society are considered, must be pronounced rare and splendid. He was raised to the Irish peerage, and encouraged to expect an English title. George the Third, who had just ascended the throne, received him with great distinction. The ministers paid him marked attention; and Pitt, whose influence in the House of Commons and in the country was unbounded, was eager to mark his regard for one whose exploits had contributed so much to the lustre of that memorable period. The great orator had already in Parliament described Clive as a heaven-born general, as a man who, bred to the labour of the desk, had displayed a military genius which might excite the admiration of the King of Prussia. There were then no reporters in the gallery; but these words, emphatically spoken by the first statesman of the age, had passed from mouth to mouth, had been transmitted to Clive in Bengal, and had greatly delighted and flattered him.

Indeed, since the death of Wolfe, Clive was the only English general of whom his countrymen had much reason to be proud. The Duke of Cumberland had been generally unfortunate; and his single victory, having been gained over his countrymen, and used with merciless severity, had been more fatal to his popularity than his many defeats. Conway, versed in the learning of his profession, and personally courageous, wanted vigour and capacity. Granby, honest, generous, and as brave as a lion, had neither science nor genius. Sackville, inferior in knowledge and abilities to none of his contemporaries, had incurred, unjustly as we believe, the imputation most fatal to the character of a soldier. It was under the command of a foreign general that the British had triumphed at Minden and Warburg. The people therefore, as was natural, greeted with pride and delight a captain of their own, whose native courage and self-taught skill had placed him on a level with the great tacticians of Germany.

The wealth of Clive was such as enabled him to vie with the first grandees of England. There remains proof that he had remitted more than a hundred and eighty thousand pounds through the Dutch East India Company, and more than forty thousand pounds through the English Company. The amount which he had sent home through private houses was also considerable. He had invested great sums in jewels, then a very common mode of remittance from India. His purchases of diamonds, at Madras alone, amounted to twenty-five thousand pounds. Besides a great mass of ready money, he had his Indian estate, valued by himself at twenty-seven thousand a-year. His whole annual income, in the opinion of Sir John Malcolm, who is desirous to state it as low as possible, exceeded forty thousand pounds; and incomes of forty thousand pounds at the time of the accession of George the Third were at least as rare as incomes of a hundred thousand pounds now. We may safely affirm that no Englishman who started with nothing has ever, in any line of life, created such a fortune at the early age of thirty-four.

It would be unjust not to add that Clive made a creditable use of his riches. As soon as the battle of Plassey had laid the foundation of his fortune, he sent ten thousand pounds to his sisters, bestowed as much more on other poor friends and relations, ordered his agent to pay eight hundred a-year to his parents, and to insist that they should keep a carriage, and settled five hundred a-year on his old commander Lawrence, whose means were very slender. The whole sum which Clive expended in this manner may be calculated at fifty thousand pounds.

He now set himself to cultivate Parliamentary interest. His purchases of land seem to have been made in a great measure with that view, and, after the general election of 1761, he found himself in the House of Commons, at the head of a body of dependents whose support must have been important to any administration. In English politics, however, he did not take a prominent part. His first attachments, as we have seen, were to Mr. Fox; at a later period he was attracted by the genius and success of Mr. Pitt; but finally he connected himself in the closest manner with George Grenville. Early in the session of 1764, when the illegal and impolitic persecution of that worthless demagogue Wilkes had strongly excited the public mind, the town was amused by an anecdote, which we have seen in some unpublished memoirs of Horace Walpole. Old Mr. Richard Clive, who, since his son's elevation, had been introduced into society for which his former habits had not well fitted him, presented himself at the levee. The King asked him where Lord Clive was. "He will be in town very soon," said the old gentleman, loud enough to be heard by the whole circle, "and then your Majesty will have another vote."

But in truth all Clive's views were directed towards the country in which he had so eminently distinguished himself as a soldier and a statesman; and it was by considerations relating to India that his conduct as a public man in England was regulated. The power of the Company, though an anomaly, is in our time, we are firmly persuaded, a beneficial anomaly. In the time of Clive, it was not merely an anomaly, but a nuisance. There was no Board of Control. The Directors were for the most part mere traders, ignorant of general politics, ignorant of the peculiarities of the empire which had strangely become subject to them. The Court of Proprietors, wherever it chose to interfere, was able to have its way. That court was more numerous, as well as more powerful than at present; for then every share of five hundred pounds conferred a vote. The meetings were large, stormy, even riotous, the debates indecently virulent. All the turbulence of a Westminster election, all the trickery and corruption of a Grampound election, disgraced the proceedings of this assembly on questions of the most solemn importance. Fictitious votes were manufactured on a gigantic scale. Clive himself laid out a hundred thousand pounds in the purchase of stock, which he then divided among nominal proprietors on whom he could depend, and whom he brought down in his train to every discussion and every ballot. Others did the same, though not to quite so enormous an extent.

The interest taken by the public of England in Indian questions was then far greater than at present, and the reason is obvious. At present a writer enters the service young; he climbs slowly; he is fortunate if, at forty-five, he can return to his country with an annuity of a thousand a-year, and with savings amounting to thirty thousand pounds. A great quantity of wealth is made by English functionaries in India; but no single functionary makes a very large fortune, and what is made is slowly, hardly, and honestly earned. Only four or five high political offices are reserved for public men from England. The residencies, the secretaryships, the seats in the boards of revenue and in the Sudder courts, are all filled by men who have given the best years of life to the service of the Company; nor can any talents however splendid or any connexions however powerful obtain those lucrative posts for any person who has not entered by the regular door, and mounted by the regular gradations. Seventy years ago, less money was brought home from the East than in our time. But it was divided among a very much smaller number of persons, and immense sums were often accumulated in a few months. Any Englishman, whatever his age might be, might hope to be one of the lucky emigrants. If he made a good speech in Leadenhall Street, or published a clever pamphlet in defence of the chairman, he might be sent out in the Company's service, and might return in three or four years as rich as Pigot or as Clive. Thus the India House was a lottery-office, which invited every body to take a chance, and held out ducal fortunes as the prizes destined for the lucky few. As soon as it was known that there was a part of the world where a lieutenant-colonel had one morning received as a present an estate as large as that of the Earl of Bath or the Marquis of Rockingham, and where it seemed that such a trifle as ten or twenty thousand pounds was to be had by any British functionary for the asking, society began to exhibit all the symptoms of the South Sea year, a feverish excitement, an ungovernable impatience to be rich, a contempt for slow, sure, and moderate gains.

At the head of the preponderating party in the India House, had long stood a powerful, able, and ambitious Director of the name of Sulivan. He had conceived a strong jealousy of Clive, and remembered with bitterness the audacity with which the late governor of Bengal had repeatedly set at nought the authority of the distant Directors of the Company. An apparent reconciliation took place after Clive's arrival; but enmity remained deeply rooted in the hearts of both. The whole body of Directors was then chosen annually. At the election of 1763, Clive attempted to break down the power of the dominant faction. The contest was carried on with a violence which he describes as tremendous. Sulivan was victorious, and hastened to take his revenge. The grant of rent which Clive had received from Meer Jaffier was, in the opinion of the best English lawyers, valid. It had been made by exactly the same authority from which the Company had received their chief possessions in Bengal, and the Company had long acquiesced in it. The Directors, however, most unjustly determined to confiscate it, and Clive was forced to file a bill in Chancery against them.

But a great and sudden turn in affairs was at hand. Every ship from Bengal had for some time brought alarming tidings. The internal misgovernment of the province had reached such a point that it could go no further. What, indeed, was to be expected from a body of public servants exposed to temptation such that, as Clive once said, flesh and blood could not bear it, armed with irresistible power, and responsible only to the corrupt, turbulent, distracted, ill-informed Company, situated at such a distance that the average interval between the sending of a despatch and the receipt of an answer was above a year and a half? Accordingly, during the five years which followed the departure of Clive from Bengal, the misgovernment of the English was carried to a point such as seems hardly compatible with the very existence of society. The Roman proconsul, who, in a year or two, squeezed out of a province the means of rearing marble palaces and baths on the shores of Campania, of drinking from amber, of feasting on singing birds, of exhibiting armies of gladiators and flocks of camelopards, the Spanish viceroy, who, leaving behind him the curses of Mexico or Lima, entered Madrid with a long train of gilded coaches, and of sumpter-horses trapped and shod with silver, were now outdone. Cruelty, indeed, properly so called, was not among the vices of the servants of the Company. But cruelty itself could hardly have produced greater evils than sprang from their unprincipled eagerness to be rich. They pulled down their creature, Meer Jaffier. They set up in his place another Nabob, named Meer Cossim. But Meer Cossim had talents and a will; and, though sufficiently inclined to oppress his subjects himself, he could not bear to see them ground to the dust by oppressions which yielded him no profit, nay, which destroyed his revenue in its very source. The English accordingly pulled down Meer Cossim, and set up Meer Jaffier again; and Meer Cossim, after revenging himself by a massacre surpassing in atrocity that of the Black Hole, fled to the dominions of the Nabob of Oude. At every one of these revolutions, the new prince divided among his foreign masters whatever could be scraped together from the treasury of his fallen predecessor. The immense population of his dominions was given up as a prey to those who had made him a sovereign, and who could unmake him. The servants of the Company obtained, not for their employers, but for themselves, a monopoly of almost the whole internal trade. They forced the natives to buy dear and to sell cheap. They insulted with impunity the tribunals, the police, and the fiscal authorities of the country. They covered with their protection a set of native dependents who ranged through the provinces, spreading desolation and terror wherever they appeared. Every servant of a British factor was armed with all the power of his master; and his master was armed with all the power of the Company. Enormous fortunes were thus rapidly accumulated at Calcutta, while thirty millions of human beings were reduced to the extremity of wretchedness. They had been accustomed to live under tyranny, but never under tyranny like this. They found the little finger of the Company thicker than the loins of Surajah Dowlah. Under their old masters they had at least one resource: when the evil became insupportable, the people rose and pulled down the government. But the English government was not to be so shaken off. That government, oppressive as the most oppressive form of barbarian despotism, was strong with all the strength of civilisation. It resembled the government of evil Genii, rather than the government of human tyrants. Even despair could not inspire the soft Bengalee with courage to confront men of English breed, the hereditary nobility of mankind, whose skill and valour had so often triumphed in spite of tenfold odds. The unhappy race never attempted resistance. Sometimes they submitted in patient misery. Sometimes they fled from the white man, as their fathers had been used to fly from the Mahratta; and the palanquin of the English traveller was often carried through silent villages and towns, which the report of his approach had made desolate.

The foreign lords of Bengal were naturally objects of hatred to all the neighbouring powers; and to all the haughty race presented a dauntless front. Their armies, every where outnumbered, were every where victorious. A succession of commanders, formed in the school of Clive, still maintained the fame of their country. "It must be acknowledged," says the Mussulman historian of those times, "that this nation's presence of mind, firmness of temper, and undaunted bravery, are past all question. They join the most resolute courage to the most cautious prudence; nor have they their equals in the art of ranging themselves in battle array and fighting in order. If to so many military qualifications they knew how to join the arts of government, if they exerted as much ingenuity and solicitude in relieving the people of God, as they do in whatever concerns their military affairs, no nation in the world would be preferable to them, or worthier of command. But the people under their dominion groan every where, and are reduced to poverty and distress. Oh God! come to the assistance of thine afflicted servants, and deliver them from the oppressions which they suffer."

It was impossible, however, that even the military establishment should long continue exempt from the vices which pervaded every other part of the government. Rapacity, luxury, and the spirit of insubordination, spread from the civil service to the officers of the army, and from the officers to the soldiers. The evil continued to grow till every mess-room became the seat of conspiracy and cabal, and till the sepoys could be kept in order only by wholesale executions.

At length the state of things in Bengal began to excite uneasiness at home. A succession of revolutions; a disorganized administration; the natives pillaged, yet the Company not enriched; every fleet bringing back fortunate adventurers who were able to purchase manors and to build stately dwellings, yet bringing back also alarming accounts of the financial prospects of the government; war on the frontiers; disaffection in the army; the national character disgraced by excesses resembling those of Verres and Pizarro; such was the spectacle which dismayed those who were conversant with Indian affairs. The general cry was that Clive, and Clive alone, could save the empire which he had founded.

This feeling manifested itself in the strongest manner at a very full General Court of Proprietors. Men of all parties, forgetting their feuds and trembling for their dividends, exclaimed that Clive was the man whom the crisis required, that the oppressive proceedings which had been adopted respecting his estate ought to be dropped, and that he ought to be entreated to return to India.

Clive rose. As to his estate, he said, he would make such propositions to the Directors as would, he trusted, lead to an amicable settlement. But there was a still greater difficulty. It was proper to tell them that he never would undertake the government of Bengal while his enemy Sulivan was chairman of the Company. The tumult was violent. Sulivan could scarcely obtain a hearing. An overwhelming majority of the assembly was on Clive's side. Sulivan wished to try the result of a ballot. But, according to the by-laws of the Company, there can be no ballot except on a requisition signed by nine proprietors; and, though hundreds were present, nine persons could not be found to set their hands to such a requisition.

Clive was in consequence nominated Governor and Commander-in-Chief of the British possessions in Bengal. But he adhered to his declaration, and refused to enter on his office till the event of the next election of Directors should be known. The contest was obstinate; but Clive triumphed. Sulivan, lately absolute master of the India House, was within a vote of losing his own seat; and both the chairman and the deputy-chairman were friends of the new governor.

Such were the circumstances under which Lord Clive sailed for the third and last time to India. In May 1765 he reached Calcutta; and he found the whole machine of government even more fearfully disorganized than he had anticipated. Meer Jaffier, who had some time before lost his eldest son Meeran, had died while Clive was on his voyage out. The English functionaries at Calcutta had already received from home strict orders not to accept presents from the native princes. But, eager for gain, and unaccustomed to respect the commands of their distant, ignorant, and negligent masters, they again set up the throne of Bengal to sale. About one hundred and forty thousand pounds sterling were distributed among nine of the most powerful servants of the Company; and, in consideration of this bribe, an infant son of the deceased Nabob was placed on the seat of his father. The news of the ignominious bargain met Clive on his arrival. In a private letter, written immediately after his landing to an intimate friend, he poured out his feelings in language which, proceeding from a man so daring, so resolute, and so little given to theatrical display of sentiment, seems to us singularly touching. "Alas!" he says, "how is the English name sunk! I could not avoid paying the tribute of a few tears to the departed and lost fame of the British nation—irrecoverably so, I fear. However, I do declare, by that great Being who is the searcher of all hearts, and to whom we must be accountable if there be a hereafter, that I am come out with a mind superior to all corruption, and that I am determined to destroy these great and growing evils, or perish in the attempt."

The Council met, and Clive stated to them his full determination to make a thorough reform, and to use for that purpose the whole of the ample authority, civil and military, which had been confided to him. Johnstone, one of the boldest and worst men in the assembly, made some show of opposition. Clive interrupted him, and haughtily demanded whether he meant to question the power of the new government. Johnstone was cowed, and disclaimed any such intention. All the faces round the board grew long and pale; and not another syllable of dissent was uttered.

Clive redeemed his pledge. He remained in India about a year and a half; and in that short time effected one of the most extensive, difficult, and salutary reforms that ever was accomplished by any statesman. This was the part of his life on which he afterwards looked back with most pride. He had it in his power to triple his already splendid fortune: to connive at abuses while pretending to remove them; to conciliate the good-will of all the English in Bengal, by giving up to their rapacity a helpless and timid race, who knew not where lay the island which sent forth their oppressors, and whose complaints had little chance of being heard across fifteen thousand miles of ocean. He knew that, if he applied himself in earnest to the work of reformation, he should raise every bad passion in arms against him. He knew how unscrupulous, how implacable, would be the hatred of those ravenous adventurers who, having counted on accumulating in a few months fortunes sufficient to support peerages, should find all their hopes frustrated. But he had chosen the good part; and he called up all the force of his mind for a battle far harder than that of Plassey. At first success seemed hopeless; but soon all obstacles began to bend before that iron courage and that vehement will. The receiving of presents from the natives was rigidly prohibited. The private trade of the servants of the Company was put down. The whole settlement seemed to be set, as one man, against these measures. But the inexorable governor declared that, if he could not find support at Fort William, he would procure it elsewhere, and sent for some civil servants from Madras to assist him in carrying on the administration. The most factious of his opponents he turned out of their offices. The rest submitted to what was inevitable; and in a very short time all resistance was quelled.

But Clive was far too wise a man not to see that the recent abuses were partly to be ascribed to a cause which could not fail to produce similar abuses as soon as the pressure of his strong hand was withdrawn. The Company had followed a mistaken policy with respect to the remuneration of its servants. The salaries were too low to afford even those indulgences which are necessary to the health and comfort of Europeans in a tropical climate. To lay by a rupee from such scanty pay was impossible. It could not be supposed that men of even average abilities would consent to pass the best years of life in exile, under a burning sun, for no other consideration than these stinted wages. It had accordingly been understood, from a very early period, that the Company's agents were at liberty to enrich themselves by their private trade. This practice had been seriously injurious to the commercial interests of the corporation. That very intelligent observer, Sir Thomas Roe, in the reign of James the First, strongly urged the Directors to apply a remedy to the abuse. "Absolutely prohibit the private trade," said he; "for your business will be better done. I know this is harsh. Men profess they come not for bare wages. But you will take away this plea if you give great wages to their content; and then you know what you part from."

In spite of this excellent advice, the Company adhered to the old system, paid low salaries, and connived at the indirect gains of the agents. The pay of a member of Council was only three hundred pounds a-year. Yet it was notorious that such a functionary could not live in India for less than ten times that sum; and it could not be expected that he would be content to live even handsomely in India without laying up something against the time of his return to England. This system, before the conquest of Bengal, might affect the amount of the dividends payable to the proprietors, but could do little harm in any other way. But the Company was now a ruling body. Its servants might still be called factors, junior merchants, senior merchants. But they were in truth proconsuls, proprætors, procurators of extensive regions. They had immense power. Their regular pay was universally admitted to be insufficient. They were, by the ancient usage of the service, and by the implied permission of their employers, warranted in enriching themselves by indirect means; and this had been the origin of the frightful oppression and corruption which had desolated Bengal. Clive saw clearly that it was absurd to give men power, and to require them to live in penury. He justly concluded that no reform could be effectual which should not be coupled with a plan for liberally remunerating the civil servants of the Company. The Directors, he knew, were not disposed to sanction any increase of the salaries out of their own treasury. The only course which remained open to the governor was one which exposed him to much misrepresentation, but which we think him fully justified in adopting. He appropriated to the support of the service the monopoly of salt, which has formed, down to our own time, a principal head of Indian revenue; and he divided the proceeds according to a scale which seems to have been not unreasonably fixed. He was in consequence accused by his enemies, and has been accused by historians, of disobeying his instructions, of violating his promises, of authorizing that very abuse which it was his special mission to destroy, namely, the trade of the Company's servants. But every discerning and impartial judge will admit, that there was really nothing in common between the system which he set up and that which he was sent to destroy. The monopoly of salt had been a source of revenue to the governments of India before Clive was born. It continued to be so long after his death. The civil servants were clearly entitled to a maintenance out of the revenue; and all that Clive did was to charge a particular portion of the revenue with their maintenance. He thus, while he put an end to the practices by which gigantic fortunes had been rapidly accumulated, gave to every British functionary employed in the East the means of slowly, but surely, acquiring a competence. Yet, such is the injustice of mankind that none of those acts which are the real stains of his life has drawn on him so much obloquy as this measure, which was in truth a reform necessary to the success of all his other reforms.

He had quelled the opposition of the civil service: that of the army was more formidable. Some of the retrenchments which had been ordered by the Directors affected the interests of the military service; and a storm arose, such as even Cæsar would not willingly have faced. It was no light thing to encounter the resistance of those who held the power of the sword, in a country governed only by the sword. Two hundred English officers engaged in a conspiracy against the government, and determined to resign their commissions on the same day, not doubting that Clive would grant any terms rather than see the army, on which alone the British empire in the East rested, left without commanders. They little knew the unconquerable spirit with which they had to deal. Clive had still a few officers round his person on whom he could rely. He sent to Fort St. George for a fresh supply. He gave commissions even to mercantile agents who were disposed to support him at this crisis; and he sent orders that every officer who resigned should be instantly brought up to Calcutta. The conspirators found that they had miscalculated. The governor was inexorable. The troops were steady. The sepoys, over whom Clive had always possessed extraordinary influence, stood by him with unshaken fidelity. The leaders in the plot were arrested, tried, and cashiered. The rest, humbled and dispirited, begged to be permitted to withdraw their resignations. Many of them declared their repentance even with tears. The younger offenders Clive treated with lenity. To the ringleaders he was inflexibly severe; but his severity was pure from all taint of private malevolence. While he sternly upheld the just authority of his office, he passed by personal insults and injuries with magnanimous disdain. One of the conspirators was accused of having planned the assassination of the governor; but Clive would not listen to the charge. "The officers," he said, "are Englishmen, not assassins."

While he reformed the civil service and established his authority over the army, he was equally successful in his foreign policy. His landing on Indian ground was the signal for immediate peace. The Nabob of Oude, with a large army, lay at that time on the frontier of Bahar. He had been joined by many Afghans and Mahrattas, and there was no small reason to expect a general coalition of all the native powers against the English. But the name of Clive quelled in an instant all opposition. The enemy implored peace in the humblest language, and submitted to such terms as the new governor chose to dictate.

At the same time, the government of Bengal was placed on a new footing. The power of the English in that province had hitherto been altogether undefined. It was unknown to the ancient constitution of the empire, and it had been ascertained by no compact. It resembled the power which, in the last decrepitude of the Western Empire, was exercised over Italy by the great chiefs of foreign mercenaries, the Ricimers and the Odoacers, who put up and pulled down at their pleasure a succession of insignificant princes, dignified with the names of Cæsar and Augustus. But as in Italy, so in India, the warlike strangers at length found it expedient to give to a domination which had been established by arms the sanction of law and ancient prescription. Theodoric thought it politic to obtain from the distant court of Byzantium a commission appointing him ruler of Italy; and Clive, in the same manner, applied to the Court of Delhi for a formal grant of the powers of which he already possessed the reality. The Mogul was absolutely helpless; and, though he murmured, had reason to be well pleased that the English were disposed to give solid rupees which he never could have extorted from them, in exchange for a few Persian characters which cost him nothing. A bargain was speedily struck; and the titular sovereign of Hindostan issued a warrant, empowering the Company to collect and administer the revenues of Bengal, Orissa, and Bahar.

There was still a Nabob, who stood to the British authorities in the same relation in which the last drivelling Chilperics and Childerics of the Merovingian line stood to their able and vigorous Mayors of the Palace, to Charles Martel and to Pepin. At one time Clive had almost made up his mind to discard this phantom altogether; but he afterwards thought that it might be convenient still to use the name of the Nabob, particularly in dealings with other European nations. The French, the Dutch, and the Danes, would, he conceived, submit far more readily to the authority of the native Prince, whom they had always been accustomed to respect, than to that of a rival trading corporation. This policy may, at that time, have been judicious. But the pretence was soon found to be too flimsy to impose on anybody; and it was altogether laid aside. The heir of Meer Jaffier still resides at Moorshedabad, the ancient capital of his house, still bears the title of Nabob, is still accosted by the English as "Your Highness," and is still suffered to retain a portion of the regal state which surrounded his ancestors. A pension of a hundred and sixty thousand pounds a-year is annually paid to him by the government. His carriage is surrounded by guards, and preceded by attendants with silver maces. His person and his dwelling are exempted from the ordinary authority of the ministers of justice. But he has not the smallest share of political power, and is, in fact, only a noble and wealthy subject of the Company.

It would have been easy for Clive, during his second administration in Bengal, to accumulate riches such as no subject in Europe possessed. He might indeed, without subjecting the rich inhabitants of the province to any pressure beyond that to which their mildest rulers had accustomed them, have received presents to the amount of three hundred thousand pounds a-year. The neighbouring princes would gladly have paid any price for his favour. But he appears to have strictly adhered to the rules which he had laid down for the guidance of others. The Rajah of Benares offered him diamonds of great value. The Nabob of Oude pressed him to accept a large sum of money and a casket of costly jewels. Clive courteously, but peremptorily refused: and it should be observed that he made no merit of his refusal, and that the facts did not come to light till after his death. He kept an exact account of his salary, of his share of the profits accruing from the trade in salt, and of those presents which, according to the fashion of the East, it would be churlish to refuse. Out of the sum arising from these resources, he defrayed the expenses of his situation. The surplus he divided among a few attached friends who had accompanied him to India. He always boasted, and, as far as we can judge, he boasted with truth, that his last administration diminished instead of increasing his fortune.

One large sum indeed he accepted. Meer Jaffier had left him by will above sixty thousand pounds sterling in specie and jewels: and the rules which had been recently laid down extended only to presents from the living, and did not affect legacies from the dead. Clive took the money, but not for himself. He made the whole over to the Company, in trust for officers and soldiers invalided in their service. The fund which still bears his name owes its origin to this princely donation.

After a stay of eighteen months, the state of his health made it necessary for him to return to Europe. At the close of January 1767 he quitted for the last time the country on whose destinies he had exercised so mighty an influence.

His second return from Bengal was not, like his first, greeted by the acclamations of his countrymen. Numerous causes were already at work which embittered the remaining years of his life and hurried him to an untimely grave. His old enemies at the India House were still powerful and active; and they had been reinforced by a large band of allies whose violence far exceeded their own. The whole crew of pilferers and oppressors from whom he had rescued Bengal persecuted him with the implacable rancour which belongs to such abject natures. Many of them even invested their property in India stock, merely that they might be better able to annoy the man whose firmness had set bounds to their rapacity. Lying newspapers were set up for no purpose but to abuse him; and the temper of the public mind was then such, that these arts, which under ordinary circumstances would have been ineffectual against truth and merit, produced an extraordinary impression.

The great events which had taken place in India had called into existence a new class of Englishmen, to whom their countrymen gave the name of Nabobs. These persons had generally sprung from families neither ancient nor opulent; they had generally been sent at an early age to the East; and they had there acquired large fortunes, which they had brought back to their native land. It was natural that, not having had much opportunity of mixing with the best society, they should exhibit some of the awkwardness and some of the pomposity of upstarts. It was natural that, during their sojourn in Asia, they should have acquired some tastes and habits surprising, if not disgusting, to persons who never had quitted Europe. It was natural that, having enjoyed great consideration in the East, they should not be disposed to sink into obscurity at home; and as they had money, and had not birth or high connexion, it was natural that they should display a little obtrusively the single advantage which they possessed. Wherever they settled there was a kind of feud between them and the old nobility and gentry, similar to that which raged in France between the farmer-general and the marquis. This enmity to the aristocracy long continued to distinguish the servants of the Company. More than twenty years after the time of which we are now speaking, Burke pronounced that among the Jacobins might be reckoned "the East Indians almost to a man, who cannot bear to find that their present importance does not bear a proportion to their wealth."

The Nabobs soon became a most unpopular class of men. Some of them had in the East displayed eminent talents, and rendered great services to the state; but at home their talents were not shown to advantage, and their services were little known. That they had sprung from obscurity, that they had acquired great wealth, that they exhibited it insolently, that they spent it extravagantly, that they raised the price of every thing in their neighbourhood, from fresh eggs to rotten boroughs, that their liveries outshone those of dukes, that their coaches were finer than that of the Lord Mayor, that the examples of their large and ill governed households corrupted half the servants in the country, that some of them, with all their magnificence, could not catch the tone of good society, but, in spite of the stud and the crowd of menials, of the plate and the Dresden china, of the venison and the Burgundy, were still low men; these were things which excited, both in the class from which they had sprung and in the class into which they attempted to force themselves, the bitter aversion which is the effect of mingled envy and contempt. But when it was also rumoured that the fortune which had enabled its possessor to eclipse the Lord-Lieutenant on the race-ground, or to carry the county against the head of a house as old as Domesday Book, had been accumulated by violating public faith, by deposing legitimate princes, by reducing whole provinces to beggary, all the higher and better as well as all the low and evil parts of human nature were stirred against the wretch who had obtained by guilt and dishonour the riches which he now lavished with arrogant and inelegant profusion. The unfortunate Nabob seemed to be made up of those foibles against which comedy has pointed the most merciless ridicule, and of those crimes which have thrown the deepest gloom over tragedy, of Turcaret and Nero, of Monsieur Jourdain and Richard the Third. A tempest of execration and derision, such as can be compared only to that outbreak of public feeling against the Puritans which took place at the time of the Restoration, burst on the servants of the Company. The humane man was horror-struck at the way in which they had got their money, the thrifty man at the way in which they spent it. The dilettante sneered at their want of taste. The maccaroni blackballed them as vulgar fellows. Writers the most unlike in sentiment and style, Methodists and libertines, philosophers and buffoons, were for once on the same side. It is hardly too much to say that, during a space of about thirty years, the whole lighter literature of England was coloured by the feelings which we have described. Foote brought on the stage an Anglo-Indian chief, dissolute, ungenerous, and tyrannical, ashamed of the humble friends of his youth, hating the aristocracy, yet childishly eager to be numbered among them, squandering his wealth on pandars and flatterers, tricking out his chairmen with the most costly hothouse flowers, and astounding the ignorant with jargon about rupees, lacs, and jaghires. Mackenzie, with more delicate humour, depicted a plain country family raised by the Indian acquisitions of one of its members to sudden opulence, and exciting derision by an awkward mimicry of the manners of the great. Cowper, in that lofty expostulation which glows with the very spirit of the Hebrew poets, placed the oppression of India foremost in the list of those national crimes for which God had punished England with years of disastrous war, with discomfiture in her own seas, and with the loss of her transatlantic empire. If any of our readers will take the trouble to search in the dusty recesses of circulating libraries for some novel published sixty years ago, the chance is that the villain or sub-villain of the story will prove to be a savage old Nabob, with an immense fortune, a tawny complexion, a bad liver, and a worse heart.

Such, as far as we can now judge, was the feeling of the country respecting Nabobs in general. And Clive was eminently the Nabob, the ablest, the most celebrated, the highest in rank, the highest in fortune, of all the fraternity. His wealth was exhibited in a manner which could not fail to excite odium. He lived with great magnificence in Berkeley Square. He reared one palace in Shropshire and another at Claremont. His parliamentary influence might vie with that of the greatest families. But in all this splendour and power envy found something to sneer at. On some of his relations wealth and dignity seem to have sat as awkwardly as on Mackenzie's Margery Mushroom. Nor was he himself, with all his great qualities, free from those weaknesses which the satirists of that age represented as characteristic of his whole class. In the field, indeed, his habits were remarkably simple. He was constantly on horseback, was never seen but in his uniform, never wore silk, never entered a palanquin, and was content with the plainest fare. But when he was no longer at the head of an army, he laid aside this Spartan temperance for the ostentatious luxury of a Sybarite. Though his person was ungraceful, and though his harsh features were redeemed from vulgar ugliness only by their stern, dauntless, and commanding expression, he was fond of rich and gay clothing, and replenished his wardrobe with absurd profusion. Sir John Malcolm gives us a letter worthy of Sir Matthew Mite, in which Clive orders "two hundred shirts, the best and finest that can be got for love or money." A few follies of this description, grossly exaggerated by report, produced an unfavourable impression on the public mind. But this was not the worst. Black stories, of which the greater part were pure inventions, were circulated respecting his conduct in the East. He had to bear the whole odium, not only of those bad acts to which he had once or twice stooped, but of all the bad acts of all the English in India, of bad acts committed when he was absent, nay, of bad acts which he had manfully opposed and severely punished. The very abuses against which he had waged an honest, resolute, and successful war, were laid to his account. He was, in fact, regarded as the personification of all the vices and weaknesses which the public, with or without reason, ascribed to the English adventurers in Asia. We have ourselves heard old men, who knew nothing of his history, but who still retained the prejudices conceived in their youth, talk of him as an incarnate fiend. Johnson always held this language. Brown, whom Clive employed to lay out his pleasure grounds, was amazed to see in the house of his noble employer a chest which had once been filled with gold from the treasury of Moorshedabad, and could not understand how the conscience of the criminal could suffer him to sleep with such an object so near to his bedchamber. The peasantry of Surrey looked with mysterious horror on the stately house which was rising at Claremont, and whispered that the great wicked lord had ordered the walls to be made so thick in order to keep out the devil, who would one day carry him bodily away. Among the gaping clowns who drank in this frightful story was a worthless ugly lad of the name of Hunter, since widely known as William Huntington, S.S.; and the superstition which was strangely mingled with the knavery of that remarkable impostor seems to have derived no small nutriment from the tales which he heard of the life and character of Clive.

In the mean time, the impulse which Clive had given to the administration of Bengal was constantly becoming fainter and fainter. His policy was to a great extent abandoned; the abuses which he had suppressed began to revive; and at length the evils which a bad government had engendered were aggravated by one of those fearful visitations which the best government cannot avert. In the summer of 1770, the rains failed; the earth was parched up; the tanks were empty; the rivers shrank within their beds; and a famine, such as is known only in countries where every household depends for support on its own little patch of cultivation, filled the whole valley of the Ganges with misery and death. Tender and delicate women, whose veils had never been lifted before the public gaze, came forth from the inner chambers in which Eastern jealousy had kept watch over their beauty, threw themselves on the earth before the passers-by, and, with loud wailings, implored a handful of rice for their children. The Hoogley every day rolled down thousands of corpses close to the porticoes and gardens of the English conquerors. The very streets of Calcutta were blocked up by the dying and the dead. The lean and feeble survivors had not energy enough to bear the bodies of their kindred to the funeral pile or to the holy river, or even to scare away the jackals and vultures, who fed on human remains in the face of day. The extent of the mortality was never ascertained; but it was popularly reckoned by millions. This melancholy intelligence added to the excitement which already prevailed in England on Indian subjects. The proprietors of East India stock were uneasy about their dividends. All men of common humanity were touched by the calamities of our unhappy subjects; and indignation soon began to mingle itself with pity. It was rumoured that the Company's servants had created the famine by engrossing all the rice of the country; that they had sold grain for eight, ten, twelve times the price at which they had bought it; that one English functionary who, the year before, was not worth a hundred guineas, had, during that season of misery, remitted sixty thousand pounds to London. These charges we believe to have been unfounded. That servants of the Company had ventured, since Clive's departure, to deal in rice, is probable. That, if they dealt in rice, they must have gained by the scarcity, is certain. But there is no reason for thinking that they either produced or aggravated an evil which physical causes sufficiently explain. The outcry which was raised against them on this occasion was, we suspect, as absurd as the imputations which, in times of dearth at home, were once thrown by statesmen and judges, and are still thrown by two or three old women, on the corn factors. It was, however, so loud and so general that it appears to have imposed even on an intellect raised so high above vulgar prejudices as that of Adam Smith. What was still more extraordinary, these unhappy events greatly increased the unpopularity of Lord Clive. He had been some years in England when the famine took place. None of his measures had the smallest tendency to produce such a calamity. If the servants of the Company had traded in rice, they had done so in direct contravention of the rule which he had laid down, and, while in power, had resolutely enforced. But, in the eyes of his countrymen, he was, as we have said, the Nabob, the Anglo-Indian character personified; and, while he was building and planting in Surrey, he was held responsible for all the effects of a dry season in Bengal.

Parliament had hitherto bestowed very little attention on our

Eastern possessions. Since the death of George the Second, a rapid succession of weak administrations, each of which was in turn flattered and betrayed by the Court, had held the semblance of power. Intrigues in the palace, riots in the capital, and insurrectionary movements in the American colonies, had left the advisers of the crown little leisure to study Indian politics. Where they did interfere, their interference was feeble and irresolute. Lord Chatham, indeed, during the short period of his ascendency in the councils of George the Third, had meditated a bold and sweeping measure respecting the acquisitions of the Company. But his plans were rendered abortive by the strange malady which about that time began to overcloud his splendid genius.

At length, in 1772, it was generally felt that Parliament could no longer neglect the affairs of India. The Government was stronger than any which had held power since the breach between Mr. Pitt and the great Whig connexion in 1761. No pressing question of domestic or European policy required the attention of public men. There was a short and delusive lull between two tempests. The excitement produced by the Middlesex election was over; the discontents of America did not yet threaten civil war; the financial difficulties of the Company brought on a crisis; the ministers were forced to take up the subject; and the whole storm, which had long been gathering, now broke at once on the head of Clive.

His situation was indeed singularly unfortunate. He was hated throughout the country, hated at the India House, hated, above all, by those wealthy and powerful servants of the Company, whose rapacity and tyranny he had withstood. He had to bear the double odium of his bad and of his good actions, of every Indian abuse and of every Indian reform. The state of the political world was such that he could count on the support of no powerful connexion. The party to which he had belonged, that of George Grenville, had been hostile to the Government, and yet had never cordially united with the other sections of the Opposition, with the little band which still followed the fortunes of Lord Chatham, or with the large and respectable body of which Lord Rockingham was the acknowledged leader. George Grenville was now dead: his followers were scattered; and Clive, unconnected with any of the powerful factions which divided the Parliament, could reckon only on the votes of those members who were returned by himself. His enemies, particularly those who were the enemies of his virtues, were unscrupulous, ferocious, implacable. Their malevolence aimed at nothing less than the utter ruin of his fame and fortune. They wished to see him expelled from Parliament, to see his spurs chopped off, to see his estate confiscated; and it may be doubted whether even such a result as this would have quenched their thirst for revenge.

Clive's parliamentary tactics resembled his military tactics. Deserted, surrounded, outnumbered, and with every thing at stake, he did not even deign to stand on the defensive, but pushed boldly forward to the attack. At an early stage of the discussions on Indian affairs he rose, and in a long and elaborate speech vindicated himself from a large part of the accusations which had been brought against him. He is said to have produced a great impression on his audience. Lord Chatham who, now the ghost of his former self, loved to haunt the scene of his glory, was that night under the gallery of the House of Commons, and declared that he had never heard a finer speech. It was subsequently printed under Clive's direction, and, when the fullest allowance has been made for the assistance which he may have obtained from literary friends, proves him to have possessed, not merely strong sense and a manly spirit, but talents both for disquisition and declamation which assiduous culture might have improved into the highest excellence. He confined his defence on this occasion to the measures of his last administration, and succeeded so far that his enemies thenceforth thought it expedient to direct their attacks chiefly against the earlier part of his life.

The earlier part of his life unfortunately presented some assailable points to their hostility. A committee was chosen by ballot to inquire into the affairs of India; and by this committee the whole history of that great revolution which threw down Surajah Dowlah and raised Meer Jaffier was sifted with malignant care. Clive was subjected to the most unsparing examination and cross-examination, and afterwards bitterly complained that he, the Baron of Plassey, had been treated like a sheep-stealer. The boldness and ingenuousness of his replies would alone suffice to show how alien from his nature were the frauds to which, in the course of his Eastern negotiations, he had sometimes descended. He avowed the arts which he had employed to deceive Omichund, and resolutely said that he was not ashamed of them, and that, in the same circumstances, he would again act in the same manner. He admitted that he had received immense sums from Meer Jaffier; but he denied that, in doing so, he had violated any obligation of morality or honour. He laid claim, on the contrary, and not without some reason, to the praise of eminent disinterestedness. He described in vivid language the situation in which his victory had placed him; a great prince dependent on his pleasure; an opulent city afraid of being given up to plunder; wealthy bankers bidding against each other for his smiles; vaults piled with gold and jewels thrown open to him alone. "By God, Mr. Chairman," he exclaimed, "at this moment I stand astonished at my own moderation."

The inquiry was so extensive that the Houses rose before it had been completed. It was continued in the following session. When at length the committee had concluded its labours, enlightened and impartial men had little difficulty in making up their minds as to the result. It was clear that Clive had been guilty of some acts which it is impossible to vindicate without attacking the authority of all the most sacred laws which regulate the intercourse of individuals and of states. But it was equally clear that he had displayed great talents, and even great virtues; that he had rendered eminent services both to his country and to the people of India; and that it was in truth not for his dealings with Meer Jaffier nor for the fraud which he had practised on Omichund, but for his determined resistance to avarice and tyranny, that he was now called in question.

Ordinary criminal justice knows nothing of set-off. The greatest desert cannot be pleaded in answer to a charge of the slightest transgression. If a man has sold beer on Sunday morning, it is no defence that he has saved the life of a fellow-creature at the risk of his own. If he has harnessed a Newfoundland dog to his little child's carriage, it is no defence that he was wounded at Waterloo. But it is not in this way that we ought to deal with men who, raised far above ordinary restraints, and tried by far more than ordinary temptations, are entitled to a more than ordinary measure of indulgence. Such men should be judged by their contemporaries as they will be judged by posterity. Their bad actions ought not, indeed, to be called good; but their good and bad actions ought to be fairly weighed; and, if on the whole the good preponderate, the sentence ought to be one, not merely of acquittal, but of approbation. Not a single great ruler in history can be absolved by a judge who fixes his eye inexorably on one or two unjustifiable acts. Bruce the deliverer of Scotland, Maurice the deliverer of Germany, William the deliverer of Holland, his great descendant the deliverer of England, Murray the good regent, Cosmo the father of his country, Henry the Fourth of France, Peter the Great of Russia, how would the best of them pass such a scrutiny? History takes wider views; and the best tribunal for great political cases is the tribunal which anticipates the verdict of history.

Reasonable and moderate men of all parties felt this in Clive's case. They could not pronounce him blameless; but they were not disposed to abandon him to that low-minded and rancorous pack who had run him down and were eager to worry him to death. Lord North, though not very friendly to him, was not disposed to go to extremities against him. While the inquiry was still in progress, Clive, who had some years before been created a Knight of the Bath, was installed with great pomp in Henry the Seventh's Chapel. He was soon after appointed Lord-Lieutenant of Shropshire. When he kissed hands, George the Third, who had always been partial to him, admitted him to a private audience, talked to him half an hour on Indian politics, and was visibly affected when the persecuted general spoke of his services and of the way in which they had been requited.

At length the charges came in a definite form before the House of Commons. Burgoyne, chairman of the committee, a man of wit, fashion, and honour, an agreeable dramatic writer, an officer whose courage was never questioned and whose skill was at that time highly esteemed, appeared as the accuser. The members of the administration took different sides; for in that age all questions were open questions except such as were brought forward by the Government, or such as implied some censure on the Government. Thurlow, the Attorney-General, was among the assailants. Wedderburne, the Solicitor-General, strongly attached to Clive, defended his friend with extraordinary force of argument and language. It is a curious circumstance that, some years later, Thurlow was the most conspicuous champion of Warren Hastings, while Wedderburne was among the most unrelenting persecutors of that great though not faultless statesman. Clive spoke in his own defence at less length and with less art than in the preceding year, but with much energy and pathos. He recounted his great actions and his wrongs; and, after bidding his hearers remember that they were about to decide not only on his honour but on their own, he retired from the House.

The Commons resolved that acquisitions made by the arms of the State belong to the State alone, and that it is illegal in the servants of the State to appropriate such acquisitions to themselves. They resolved that this wholesome rule appeared to have been systematically violated by the English functionaries in Bengal. On a subsequent day they went a step farther, and resolved that Clive had, by means of the power which he possessed as commander of the British forces in India, obtained large sums from Meer Jaffier. Here the House stopped. They had voted the major and minor of Burgoyne's syllogism; but they shrank from drawing the logical conclusion. When it was moved that Lord Clive had abused his powers, and set an evil example to the servants of the public, the previous question was put and carried. At length, long after the sun had risen on an animated debate, Wedderburne moved that Lord Clive had at the same time rendered great and meritorious services to his country; and this motion passed without a division.

The result of this memorable inquiry appears to us, on the whole, honourable to the justice, moderation, and discernment of the Commons. They had indeed no great temptation to do wrong. They would have been very bad judges of an accusation brought against Jenkinson or against Wilkes. But the question respecting Clive was not a party question; and the House accordingly acted with the good sense and good feeling which may always be expected from an assembly of English gentlemen, not blinded by faction.

The equitable and temperate proceedings of the British Parliament were set off to the greatest advantage by a foil. The wretched government of Louis the Fifteenth had murdered, directly or indirectly, almost every Frenchman who had served his country with distinction in the East. Labourdonnais was flung into the Bastile, and, after years of suffering, left it only to die. Dupleix, stripped of his immense fortune, and broken-hearted by humiliating attendance in antechambers, sank into an obscure grave. Lally was dragged to the common place of execution with a gag between his lips. The Commons of England, on the other hand, treated their living captain with that discriminating justice which is seldom shown except to the dead. They laid down sound general principles; they delicately pointed out where he had deviated from those principles; and they tempered the gentle censure with liberal eulogy. The contrast struck Voltaire, always partial to England, and always eager to expose the abuses of the Parliaments of France. Indeed he seems, at this time, to have meditated a history of the conquest of Bengal. He mentioned his design to Dr. Moore when that amusing writer visited him at Ferney. Wedderburne took great interest in the matter, and pressed Clive to furnish materials. Had the plan been carried into execution, we have no doubt that Voltaire would have produced a book containing much lively and picturesque narrative, many just and humane sentiments poignantly expressed, many grotesque blunders, many sneers at the Mosaic chronology, much scandal about the Catholic missionaries, and much sublime theophilanthropy, stolen from the New Testament, and put into the mouths of virtuous and philosophical Brahmins.

Clive was now secure in the enjoyment of his fortune and his honours. He was surrounded by attached friends and relations; and he had not yet passed the season of vigorous bodily and mental exertion. But clouds had long been gathering over his mind, and now settled on it in thick darkness. From early youth he had been subject to fits of that strange melancholy "which rejoiceth exceedingly and is glad when it can find the grave." While still a writer at Madras, he had twice attempted to destroy himself. Business and prosperity had produced a salutary effect on his spirits. In India, while he was occupied by great affairs, in England, while wealth and rank had still the charm of novelty, he had borne up against his constitutional misery. But he had now nothing to do, and nothing to wish for. His active spirit in an inactive situation drooped and withered like a plant in an uncongenial air. The malignity with which his enemies had pursued him, the indignity with which he had been treated by the committee, the censure, lenient as it was, which the House of Commons had pronounced, the knowledge that he was regarded by a large portion of his countrymen as a cruel and perfidious tyrant, all concurred to irritate and depress him. In the mean time, his temper was tried by acute physical suffering. During his long residence in tropical climates, he had contracted several painful distempers. In order to obtain ease he called in the help of opium; and he was gradually enslaved by this treacherous ally. To the last, however, his genius occasionally flashed through the gloom. It was said that he would sometimes, after sitting silent and torpid for hours, rouse himself to the discussion of some great question, would display in full vigour all the talents of the soldier and the statesman, and would then sink back into his melancholy repose.

The disputes with America had now become so serious that an appeal to the sword seemed inevitable; and the ministers were desirous to avail themselves of the services of Clive. Had he still been what he was when he raised the siege of Patna, and annihilated the Dutch army and navy at the mouth of the Ganges, it is not improbable that the resistance of the Colonists would have been put down, and that the inevitable separation would have been deferred for a few years. But it was too late. His strong mind was fast sinking under many kinds of suffering. On the twenty-second of November 1774, he died by his own hand. He had just completed his forty-ninth year.

In the awful close of so much prosperity and glory, the vulgar saw only a confirmation of all their prejudices; and some men of real piety and genius so far forgot the maxims both of religion and of philosophy as confidently to ascribe the mournful event to the just vengeance of God, and to the horrors of an evil conscience. It is with very different feelings that we contemplate the spectacle of a great mind ruined by the weariness of satiety, by the pangs of wounded honour, by fatal diseases, and more fatal remedies.

Clive committed great faults; and we have not attempted to disguise them. But his faults, when weighed against his merits, and viewed in connexion with his temptations, do not appear to us to deprive him of his right to an honourable place in the estimation of posterity.

From his first visit to India dates the renown of the English arms in the East. Till he appeared, his countrymen were despised as mere pedlars, while the French were revered as a people formed for victory and command. His courage and capacity dissolved the charm. With the defence of Arcot commences that long series of Oriental triumphs which closes with the fall of Ghizni. Nor must we forget that he was only twenty-five years old when he approved himself ripe for military command. This is a rare if not a singular distinction. It is true that Alexander, Condé, and Charles the Twelfth, won great battles at a still earlier age; but those princes were surrounded by veteran generals of distinguished skill, to whose suggestions must be attributed the victories of the Granicus, of Rocroi, and of Narva. Clive, an inexperienced youth, had yet more experience than any of those who served under him. He had to form himself, to form his officers, and to form his army. The only man, as far as we recollect, who at an equally early age ever gave equal proof of talents for war, was Napoleon Bonaparte.

From Clive's second visit to India dates the political ascendency of the English in that country. His dexterity and resolution realised, in the course of a few months, more than all the gorgeous visions which had floated before the imagination of Dupleix. Such an extent of cultivated territory, such an amount of revenue, such a multitude of subjects, was never added to the dominion of Rome by the most successful proconsul. Nor were such wealthy spoils ever borne under arches of triumph, down the Sacred Way, and through the crowded Forum, to the threshold of Tarpeian Jove. The fame of those who subdued Antiochus and Tigranes grows dim when compared with the splendour of the exploits which the young English adventurer achieved at the head of an army not equal in numbers to one half of a Roman legion.

From Clive's third visit to India dates the purity of the administration of our Eastern empire. When he landed in Calcutta in 1765, Bengal was regarded as a place to which Englishmen were sent only to get rich, by any means, in the shortest possible time. He first made dauntless and unsparing war on that gigantic system of oppression, extortion, and corruption. In that war he manfully put to hazard his ease, his fame, and his splendid fortune. The same sense of justice which forbids us to conceal or extenuate the faults of his earlier days compels us to admit that those faults were nobly repaired. If the reproach of the Company and of its servants has been taken away, if in India the yoke of foreign masters, else-where the heaviest of all yokes, has been found lighter than that of any native dynasty, if to that gang of public robbers which formerly spread terror through the whole plain of Bengal has succeeded a body of functionaries not more highly distinguished by ability and diligence than by integrity, disinterestedness, and public spirit, if we now see such men as Munro, Elphinstone, and Metcalfe, after leading victorious armies, after making and deposing kings, return, proud of their honourable poverty, from a land which once held out to every greedy factor the hope of boundless wealth, the praise is in no small measure due to Clive. His name stands high on the roll of conquerors. But it is found in a better list, in the list of those who have done and suffered much for the happiness of mankind. To the warrior, history will assign a place in the same rank with Lucullus and Trajan. Nor will she deny to the reformer a share of that veneration with which France cherishes the memory of Turgot, and with which the latest generations of Hindoos will contemplate the statue of Lord William Bentinck.

WARREN HASTINGS

(OCTOBER 1841)

Memoirs of the Life of Warren Hastings, first Governor-General of Bengal. Compiled from Original Papers, by the Rev. G. R. GLEIG, M.A. 3 vols. 8vo. London: 1841.

THIS book seems to have been manufactured in pursuance of a contract, by which the representatives of Warren Hastings, on the one part, bound themselves to furnish papers, and Mr. Gleig, on the other part, bound himself to furnish praise. It is but just to say that the covenants on both sides have been most faithfully kept; and the result is before us in the form of three big bad volumes, full of undigested correspondence and undiscerning panegyric.

If it were worth while to examine this performance in detail, we could easily make a long article by merely pointing out inaccurate statements, inelegant expressions, and immoral doctrines. But it would be idle to waste criticism on a bookmaker; and, whatever credit Mr. Gleig may have justly earned by former works, it is as a bookmaker, and nothing more, that he now comes before us.

More eminent men than Mr. Gleig have written nearly as ill as he, when they have stooped to similar drudgery. It would be unjust to estimate Goldsmith by the History of Greece, or Scott by the Life of Napoleon. Mr. Gleig is neither a Goldsmith nor a Scott; but it would be unjust to deny that he is capable of something better than these Memoirs. It would also, we hope and believe, be unjust to charge any Christian minister with the guilt of deliberately maintaining some propositions which we find in this book. It is not too much to say that Mr. Gleig has written several passages, which bear the same relation to the Prince of Machiavelli that the Prince of Machiavelli bears to the Whole Duty of Man, and which would excite amazement in a den of robbers, or on board of a schooner of pirates. But we are willing to attribute these offences to haste, to thoughtlessness, and to that disease of the understanding which may be called the *Furor Biographicus*, and which is to writers of lives what the *goître* is to an Alpine shepherd, or dirt-eating to a Negro slave.

We are inclined to think that we shall best meet the wishes of our readers, if, instead of dwelling on the faults of this book, we attempt to give, in a way necessarily hasty and imperfect, our own view of the life and character of Mr. Hastings. Our feeling towards him is not exactly that of the House of Commons which impeached him in 1787; neither is it that of the House of Commons which uncovered and stood up to receive him in 1813. He had great qualities, and he rendered great services to the state. But to represent him as a man of stainless virtue is to make him ridiculous; and from regard for his memory, if from no other feeling, his friends would have done well to lend no countenance to such puerile adulation. We believe that, if he were now living, he would have sufficient judgment and sufficient greatness of mind to wish to be shown as he was. He must have known that there were dark spots on his fame. He might also have felt with pride that the splendour of his fame would bear many spots. He would have preferred, we are confident, even the severity of Mr. Mill to the puffing of Mr. Gleig. He would have wished posterity to have a likeness of him, though an unfavourable likeness, rather than a daub at once insipid and unnatural, resembling neither him nor any body else. "Paint me as I am," said Oliver Cromwell, while sitting to young Lely. "If you leave out the scars and wrinkles, I will not pay you a shilling." Even in such a trifle, the great Protector showed both his good sense and his magnanimity. He did not wish all that was characteristic in his countenance to be lost, in the vain attempt to give him the regular features and smooth blooming cheeks of the curl-pated minions of James the First. He was content that his face should go forth marked with all the blemishes which had been put on it by time, by war, by sleepless nights, by anxiety, perhaps by remorse; but with valour, policy, authority, and public care written in all its princely lines. If men truly great knew their own interest, it is thus that they would wish their minds to be portrayed.

Warren Hastings sprang from an ancient and illustrious race. It has been affirmed that his pedigree can be traced back to the great Danish sea-king, whose sails were long the terror of both coasts of the British channel, and who, after many fierce and doubtful struggles, yielded at last to the valour and genius of Alfred. But the undoubted splendour of the line of Hastings needs no illustration from fable. One branch of that line wore, in the fourteenth century, the coronet of Pembroke. From another branch sprang the renowned Chamberlain, the faithful adherent of the White Rose, whose fate has furnished so striking a theme both to poets and to historians. His family received from the Tudors the earldom of Huntingdon, which, after long dispossession, was regained in our time by a series of events scarcely paralleled in romance.

The lords of the manor of Daylesford, in Worcestershire, claimed to be considered as the heads of this distinguished family. The main stock, indeed, prospered less than some of the younger shoots. But the Daylesford family, though not ennobled, was wealthy and highly considered, till, about two hundred years ago, it was overwhelmed by the great ruin of the civil war. The Hastings of that time was a zealous cavalier. He raised money on his lands, sent his plate to the mint at Oxford, joined the royal army, and, after spending half his property in the cause of King Charles, was glad to ransom himself by making over most of the remaining half to Speaker Lenthal. The old seat at Daylesford still remained in the family; but it could no longer be kept up; and in the following generation it was sold to a merchant of London.

Before this transfer took place, the last Hastings of Daylesford had presented his second son to the rectory of the parish in which the ancient residence of the family stood. The living was of little value; and the situation of the poor clergyman, after the sale of the estate, was deplorable. He was constantly engaged in lawsuits about his tithes with the new lord of the manor, and was at length utterly ruined. His eldest son, Howard, a well-conducted young man, obtained a place in the Customs. The second son, Pynaston, an idle worthless boy, married before he was sixteen, lost his wife in two years, and died in the West Indies, leaving to the care of his unfortunate father a little orphan, destined to strange and memorable vicissitudes of fortune.

Warren, the son of Pynaston, was born on the sixth of December 1732. His mother died a few days later, and he was left dependent on his distressed grandfather. The child was early sent to the village school, where he learned his letters on the same bench with the sons of the peasantry. Nor did any thing in his garb or fare indicate that his life was to take a widely different course from that of the young rustics with whom he studied and played. But no cloud could overcast the dawn of so much genius and so much ambition. The very ploughmen observed, and long remembered, how kindly little Warren took to his book. The daily sight of the lands which his ancestors had possessed, and which had passed into the hands of strangers, filled his young brain with wild fancies and projects. He loved to hear stories of the wealth and greatness of his progenitors, of their splendid housekeeping, their loyalty, and their valour. On one bright summer day, the boy, then just seven years old, lay on the bank of the rivulet which flows through the old domain of his house to join the Isis. There, as three-score and ten years later he told the tale, rose in his mind a scheme which, through all the turns of his eventful career, was never abandoned. He would recover the estate which had belonged to his fathers. He would be Hastings of Daylesford. This purpose, formed in infancy and poverty, grew stronger as his intellect expanded and as his fortune rose. He pursued his plan with that calm but indomitable force of will which was the most striking peculiarity of his character. When, under a tropical sun, he ruled fifty millions of Asiatics, his hopes, amidst all the cares of war, finance, and legislation, still pointed to Daylesford. And when his long public life, so singularly chequered with good and evil, with glory and obloquy, had at length closed for ever, it was to Daylesford that he retired to die.

When he was eight years old, his uncle Howard determined to take charge of him, and to give him a liberal education. The boy went up to London, and was sent to a school at Newington, where he was well taught but ill fed. He always attributed the smallness of his stature to the hard and scanty fare of this seminary. At ten he was removed to Westminster school, then flourishing under the care of Dr. Nichols. Vinny Bourne, as his pupils affectionately called him, was one of the masters. Churchill, Colman, Lloyd, Cumberland, Cowper, were among the students. With Cowper, Hastings formed a friendship which neither the lapse of time, nor a wide dissimilarity of opinions and pursuits, could wholly dissolve. It does not appear that they ever met after they had grown to manhood. But forty years later, when the voices of many great orators were crying for vengeance on the oppressor of India, the shy and secluded poet could image to himself Hastings the Governor-General only as the Hastings with whom he had rowed on the Thames and played in the cloister, and refused to believe that so good-tempered a fellow could have done any thing very wrong. His own life had been spent in praying, musing, and rhyming among the water-liles of the Ouse. He had preserved in no common measure the innocence of childhood. His spirit had indeed been severely tried, but not by temptations which impelled him to any gross violation of the rules of social morality. He had never been attacked by combinations of powerful and deadly enemies. He had never been compelled to make a choice between innocence and greatness, between crime and ruin. Firmly as he held in theory the doctrine of human depravity, his habits were such that he was unable to conceive how far from the path of right even kind and noble natures may be hurried by the rage of conflict and the lust of dominion.

Hastings had another associate at Westminster of whom we shall have occasion to make frequent mention, Elijah Impey. We know little about their school days. But, we think, we may safely venture to guess that, whenever Hastings wished to play any trick more than usually naughty, he hired Impey with a tart or a ball to act as fag in the worst part of the prank.

Warren was distinguished among his comrades as an excellent swimmer, boatman, and scholar. At fourteen he was first in the examination for the foundation. His name in gilded letters on the walls of the dormitory still attests his victory over many older competitors. He stayed two years longer at the school, and was looking forward to a studentship at Christ Church, when an event happened which changed the whole course of his life. Howard Hastings died, bequeathing his nephew to the care of a friend and distant relation, named Chiswick. This gentleman, though he did not absolutely refuse the charge, was desirous to rid himself of it as soon as possible. Dr. Nichols made strong remonstrances against the cruelty of interrupting the studies of a youth who seemed likely to be one of the first scholars of the age. He even offered to bear the expense of sending his favourite pupil to Oxford. But Mr. Chiswick was inflexible. He thought the years which had already been wasted on hexameters and pentameters quite sufficient. He had it in his power to obtain for the lad a writership in the service of the East India Company. Whether the young adventurer, when once shipped off, made a fortune, or died of a liver complaint, he equally ceased to be a burden to any body. Warren was accordingly removed from Westminster school, and placed for a few months at a commercial academy, to study arithmetic and book-keeping. In January 1750, a few days after he had completed his seventeenth year, he sailed for Bengal, and arrived at his destination in the October following.

He was immediately placed at a desk in the Secretary's office at Calcutta, and laboured there during two years. Fort William was then a purely commercial settlement. In the south of India the encroaching policy of Dupleix had transformed the servants of the English company, against their will, into diplomatists and generals. The war of the succession was raging in the Carnatic; and the tide had been suddenly turned against the French by the genius of young Robert Clive. But in Bengal the European settlers, at peace with the natives and with each other, were wholly occupied with ledgers and bills of lading.

After two years passed in keeping accounts at Calcutta, Hastings was sent up the country to Cossimbazar, a town which lies on the Hoogly, about a mile from Moorshedabad, and which then bore to Moorshedabad a relation, if we may compare small things with great, such as the city of London bears to Westminster. Moorshedabad was the abode of the prince who, by an authority ostensibly derived from the Mogul, but really independent, ruled the three great provinces of Bengal, Orissa, and Bahar. At Moorshedabad were the court, the haram, and the public offices. Cossimbazar was a port and a place of trade, renowned for the quantity and excellence of the silks which were sold in its marts, and constantly receiving and sending forth fleets of richly laden barges. At this important point, the Company had established a small factory subordinate to that of Fort William. Here, during several years, Hastings was employed in making bargains for stuffs with native brokers. While he was thus engaged, Surajah Dowlah succeeded to the government, and declared war against the English. The defenceless settlement of Cossimbazar, lying close to the tyrant's capital, was instantly seized. Hastings was sent a prisoner to Moorshedabad, but, in consequence of the humane intervention of the servants of the Dutch Company, was treated with indulgence. Meanwhile the Nabob marched on Calcutta; the governor and the commandant fled; the town and citadel were taken, and most of the English prisoners perished in the Black Hole.

In these events originated the greatness of Warren Hastings. The fugitive governor and his companions had taken refuge on the dreary islet of Fulda, near the mouth of the Hoogly. They were naturally desirous to obtain full information respecting the proceedings of the Nabob; and no person seemed so likely to furnish it as Hastings, who was a prisoner at large in the immediate neighbourhood of the court. He thus became a diplomatic agent, and soon established a high character for ability and resolution. The treason which at a later period was fatal to Surajah Dowlah was already in progress; and Hastings was admitted to the deliberations of the conspirators. But the time for striking had not arrived. It was necessary to postpone the execution of the design; and Hastings, who was now in extreme peril, fled to Fulda.

Soon after his arrival at Fulda, the expedition from Madras, commanded by Clive, appeared in the Hoogly. Warren, young, intrepid, and excited probably by the example of the Commander of the Forces who, having like himself been a mercantile agent of the Company, had been turned by public calamities into a soldier, determined to serve in the ranks. During the early operations of the war he carried a musket. But the quick eye of Clive soon perceived that the head of the young volunteer would be more useful than his arm. When, after the battle of Plassey, Meer Jaffier was proclaimed Nabob of Bengal, Hastings was appointed to reside at the court of the new prince as agent for the Company.

He remained at Moorshedabad till the year 1761, when he became a member of Council, and was consequently forced to reside at Calcutta. This was during the interval between Clive's first and second administration, an interval which has left on the fame of the East India Company a stain, not wholly effaced by many years of just and humane government. Mr. Vansittart, the Governor, was at the head of a new and anomalous empire. On the one side was a band of English functionaries, daring, intelligent, eager to be rich. On the other side was a great native population, helpless, timid, accustomed to crouch under oppression. To keep the stronger race from preying on the weaker, was an undertaking which tasked to the utmost the talents and energy of Clive. Vansittart, with fair intentions, was a feeble and inefficient ruler. The master caste, as was natural, broke loose from all restraint; and then was seen what we believe to be the most frightful of all spectacles, the strength of civilisation without its mercy. To all other despotism there is a check, imperfect indeed, and liable to gross abuse, but still sufficient to preserve society from the last extreme of misery. A time comes when the evils of submission are obviously greater than those of resistance, when fear itself begets a sort of courage, when a convulsive burst of popular rage and despair warns tyrants not to presume too far on the patience of mankind. But against misgovernment such as then afflicted Bengal it was impossible to struggle. The superior intelligence and energy of the dominant class made their power irresistible. A war of Bengalees against Englishmen was like a war of sheep against wolves, of men against dæmons. The only protection which the conquered could find was in the moderation, the clemency, the enlarged policy of the conquerors. That protection, at a later period, they found. But at first English power came among them unaccompanied by English morality. There was an interval between the time at which they became our subjects, and the time at which we began to reflect that we were bound to discharge towards them the duties of rulers. During that interval, the business of a servant of the Company was simply to wring out of the natives a hundred or two hundred thousand pounds as speedily as possible, that he might return home before his constitution had suffered from the heat, to marry a peer's daughter, to buy rotten boroughs in Cornwall, and to give balls in St. James's Square. Of the conduct of Hastings at this time, little is known; but the little that is known, and the circumstance that little is known, must be considered as honourable to him. He could not protect the natives: all that he could do was to abstain from plundering and oppressing them; and this he appears to have done. It is certain that at this time he continued poor; and it is equally certain, that by cruelty and dishonesty he might easily have become rich. It is certain that he was never charged with having borne a share in the worst abuses which then prevailed; and it is almost equally certain that, if he had borne a share in those abuses, the able and bitter enemies who afterwards persecuted him would not have failed to discover and to proclaim his guilt. The keen, severe, and even malevolent scrutiny to which his whole public life was subjected, a scrutiny unparalleled, as we believe, in the history of mankind, is in one respect advantageous to his reputation. It brought many lamentable blemishes to light; but it entitles him to be considered pure from every blemish which has not been brought to light.

The truth is that the temptations to which so many English functionaries yielded in the time of Mr. Vansittart were not temptations addressed to the ruling passions of Warren Hastings. He was not squeamish in pecuniary transactions; but he was neither sordid nor rapacious. He was far too enlightened a man to look on a great empire merely as a buccaneer would look on a galleon. Had his heart been much worse than it was, his understanding would have preserved him from that extremity of baseness. He was an unscrupulous, perhaps an unprincipled statesman; but still he was a statesman, and not a freebooter.

In 1764 Hastings returned to England. He had realized only a very moderate fortune; and that moderate fortune was soon reduced to nothing, partly by his praiseworthy liberality, and partly by his mismanagement. Towards his relations he appears to have acted very generously. The greater part of his savings he left in Bengal, hoping probably to obtain the high usury of India. But high usury and bad security generally go together; and Hastings lost both interest and principal.

He remained four years in England. Of his life at this time very little is known. But it has been asserted, and is highly probable, that liberal studies and the society of men of letters occupied a great part of his time. It is to be remembered to his honour, that in days when the languages of the East were regarded by other servants of the Company merely as the means of communicating with weavers and money-changers, his enlarged and accomplished mind sought in Asiatic learning for new forms of intellectual enjoyment, and for new views of government and society. Perhaps, like most persons who have paid much attention to departments of knowledge which lie out of the common track, he was inclined to overrate the value of his favourite studies. He conceived that the cultivation of Persian literature might with advantage be made a part of the liberal education of an English gentleman; and he drew up a plan with that view. It is said that the University of Oxford, in which Oriental learning had never, since the revival of letters, been wholly neglected, was to be the seat of the institution which he contemplated. An endowment was expected from the munificence of the Company; and professors thoroughly competent to interpret Hafiz and Ferdusi were to be engaged in the East. Hastings called on Johnson, with the hope, as it should seem, of interesting in this project a man who enjoyed the highest literary reputation, and who was particularly connected with Oxford. The interview appears to have left on Johnson's mind a most favourable impression of the talents and attainments of his visiter. Long after, when Hastings was ruling the immense population of British India, the old philosopher wrote to him, and referred in the most courtly terms, though with great dignity, to their short but agreeable intercourse.

Hastings soon began to look again towards India. He had little to attach him to England; and his pecuniary embarrassments were great. He solicited his old masters the Directors for employment. They acceded to his request, with high compliments both to his abilities and to his integrity, and appointed him a Member of Council at Madras. It would be unjust not to mention that, though forced to borrow money for his outfit, he did not withdraw any portion of the sum which he had appropriated to the relief of his distressed relations. In the spring of 1769 he embarked on board of the Duke of Grafton, and commenced a voyage distinguished by incidents which might furnish matter for a novel.

Among the passengers in the Duke of Grafton was a German of the name of Imhoff. He called himself a baron; but he was in distressed circumstances, and was going out to Madras as a portrait-painter, in the hope of picking up some of the pagodas which were then lightly got and as lightly spent by the English in India. The baron was accompanied by his wife, a native, we have somewhere read, of Archangel. This young woman who, born under the Arctic circle, was destined to play the part of a Queen under the tropic of Cancer, had an agreeable person, a cultivated mind, and manners in the highest degree engaging. She despised her husband heartily, and, as the story which we have to tell sufficiently proves, not without reason. She was interested by the conversation and flattered by the attentions of Hastings. The situation was indeed perilous. No place is so propitious to the formation either of close friendships, or of deadly enmities as an Indiaman. There are very few people who do not find a voyage which lasts several months insupportably dull. Any thing is welcome which may break that long monotony, a sail, a shark, an albatross, a man overboard. Most passengers find some resource in eating twice as many meals as on land. But the great devices for killing the time are quarrelling and flirting. The facilities for both these exciting pursuits are great. The inmates of the ship are thrown together far more than in any country-seat or boarding-house. None can escape from the rest except by imprisoning himself in a cell in which he can hardly turn. All food, all exercise, is taken in company. Ceremony is to a great extent banished. It is every day in the power of a mischievous person to inflict innumerable annoyances; it is every day in the power of an amiable person to confer little services. It not seldom happens that serious distress and danger call forth in genuine beauty and deformity heroic virtues and abject vices which, in the ordinary intercourse of good society, might remain during many years unknown even to intimate associates. Under such circumstances met Warren Hastings and the Baroness Imhoff, two persons whose accomplishments would have attracted notice in any court of Europe. The gentleman had no domestic ties. The lady was tied to a husband for whom she had no regard, and who had no regard for his own honour. An attachment sprang up, which was soon strengthened by events such as could hardly have occurred on land. Hastings fell ill. The baroness nursed him with womanly tenderness, gave him his medicines with her own hand, and even sat up in his cabin while he slept. Long before the Duke of Grafton reached Madras, Hastings was in love. But his love was of a most characteristic description. Like his hatred, like his ambition, like all his passions, it was strong, but not impetuous. It was calm, deep, earnest, patient of delay, unconquerable by time. Imhoff was called into council by his wife and his wife's lover. It was arranged that the baroness should institute a suit for a divorce in the courts of Franconia, that the baron should afford every facility to the proceeding, and that, during the years which might elapse before the sentence should be pronounced, they should continue to live together. It was also agreed that Hastings should bestow some very substantial marks of gratitude on the complaisant husband, and should, when the marriage was dissolved, make the lady his wife, and adopt the children whom she had already born to Imhoff.

We are not inclined to judge either Hastings or the baroness severely. There was undoubtedly much to extenuate their fault. But we can by no means concur with the Reverend Mr. Gleig, who carries his partiality to so injudicious an extreme, as to describe the conduct of Imhoff, conduct the baseness of which is the best excuse for the lovers, as "wise and judicious."

At Madras, Hastings found the trade of the Company in a very disorganized state. His own tastes would have led him rather to political than to commercial pursuits: but he knew that the favour of his employers depended chiefly on their dividends, and that their dividends depended chiefly on the investment. He therefore, with great judgment, determined to apply his vigorous mind for a time to this department of business, which had been much neglected, since the servants of the Company had ceased to be clerks, and had become warriors and negotiators.

In a very few months he effected an important reform. The Directors notified to him their high approbation, and were so much pleased with his conduct that they determined to place him at the head of the government of Bengal. Early in 1772 he quitted Fort St. George for his new post. The Imhoffs, who were still man and wife, accompanied him, and lived at Calcutta "on the same wise and judicious plan,"—we quote the words of Mr. Gleig,—which they had already followed during more than two years.

When Hastings took his seat at the head of the council-board, Bengal was still governed according to the system which Clive had devised, a system which was, perhaps, skilfully contrived for the purpose of facilitating and concealing a great revolution, but which, when that revolution was complete and irrevocable, could produce nothing but inconvenience. There were two governments, the real and the ostensible. The supreme power belonged to the Company, and was in truth the most despotic power that can be conceived. The only restraint on the English masters of the country was that which their own justice and humanity imposed on them. There was no constitutional check on their will, and resistance to them was utterly hopeless.

But, though thus absolute in reality, the English had not yet assumed the style of sovereignty. They held their territories as vassals of the throne of Delhi; they raised their revenues as collectors appointed by the imperial commission; their public seal was inscribed with the imperial titles; and their mint struck only the imperial coin.

There was still a nabob of Bengal, who stood to the English rulers of his country in the same relation in which Augustulus stood to Odoacer, or the last Merovingians to Charles Martel and Pepin. He lived at Moorshedabad, surrounded by princely magnificence. He was approached with outward marks of reverence, and his name was used in public instruments. But in the government of the country he had less real share than the youngest writer or cadet in the Company's service.

The English council which represented the Company at Calcutta was constituted on a very different plan from that which has since been adopted. At present the Governor is, as to all executive measures, absolute. He can declare war, conclude peace, appoint public functionaries or remove them, in opposition to the unanimous sense of those who sit with him in council. They are, indeed, entitled to know all that is done, to discuss all that is done, to advise, to remonstrate, to send protests to England. But it is with the governor that the supreme power resides, and on him that the whole responsibility rests. This system, which was introduced by Mr. Pitt and Mr. Dundas in spite of the strenuous opposition of Mr. Burke, we conceive to be on the whole the best that was ever devised for the government of a country where no materials can be found for a representative constitution. In the time of Hastings the governor had only one vote in council, and, in case of an equal division, a casting vote. It therefore happened not unfrequently that he was overruled on the gravest questions; and it was possible that he might be wholly excluded, for years together, from the real direction of public affairs.

The English functionaries at Fort William had as yet paid little or no attention to the internal government of Bengal. The only branch of politics about which they much busied themselves was negotiation with the native princes. The police, the administration of justice, the details of the collection of revenue, they almost entirely neglected. We may remark that the phraseology of the Company's servants still bears the traces of this state of things. To this day they always use the word "political" as synonymous with "diplomatic." We could name a gentleman still living, who was described by the highest authority as an invaluable public servant, eminently fit to be at the head of the internal administration of a whole presidency, but unfortunately quite ignorant of all political business.

The internal government of Bengal the English rulers delegated to a great native minister, who was stationed at Moorshedabad. All military affairs, and, with the exception of what pertains to mere ceremonial, all foreign affairs, were withdrawn from his control; but the other departments of the administration were entirely confided to him. His own stipend amounted to near a hundred thousand pounds sterling a-year. The personal allowance of the nabobs, amounting to more than three hundred thousand pounds a-year, passed through the minister's hands, and was, to a great extent, at his disposal. The collection of the revenue, the administration of justice, the maintenance of order, were left to this high functionary; and for the exercise of his immense power he was responsible to none but the British masters of the country.

A situation so important, lucrative, and splendid, was naturally an object of ambition to the ablest and most powerful natives. Clive had found it difficult to decide between conflicting pretensions. Two candidates stood out prominently from the crowd, each of them the representative of a race and of a religion.

The one was Mahommed Reza Khan, a Mussulman of Persian extraction, able, active, religious after the fashion of his people, and highly esteemed by them. In England he might perhaps have been regarded as a corrupt and greedy politician. But, tried by the lower standard of Indian morality, he might be considered as a man of integrity and honour.

His competitor was a Hindoo Brahmin whose name has, by a terrible and melancholy event, been inseparably associated with that of Warren Hastings, the Maharajah Nuncomar. This man had played an important part in all the revolutions which, since the time of Surajah Dowlah, had taken place in Bengal. To the consideration which in that country belongs to high and pure caste, he added the weight which is derived from wealth, talents, and experience. Of his moral character it is difficult to give a notion to those who are acquainted with human nature only as it appears in our island. What the Italian is to the Englishman, what the Hindoo is to the Italian, what the Bengalee is to other Hindoos, that was Nuncomar to other Bengalees. The physical organization of the Bengalee is feeble even to effeminacy. He lives in a constant vapour bath. His pursuits are sedentary, his limbs delicate, his movements languid. During many ages he has been trampled upon by men of bolder and more hardy breeds. Courage, independence, veracity, are qualities to which his constitution and his situation are equally unfavourable. His mind bears a singular analogy to his body. It is weak even to helplessness, for purposes of manly resistance; but its suppleness and its tact move the children of sterner climates to admiration not unmingled with contempt. All those arts which are the natural defence of the weak are more familiar to this subtle race than to the Ionian of the time of Juvenal, or to the Jew of the dark ages. What the horns are to the buffalo, what the paw is to the tiger, what the sting is to the bee, what beauty, according to the old Greek song, is to woman, deceit is to the Bengalee. Large promises, smooth excuses, elaborate tissues of circumstantial falsehood, chicanery, perjury, forgery, are the weapons, offensive and defensive, of the people of the Lower Ganges. All those millions do not furnish one sepoy to the armies of the Company. But as usurers, as money-changers, as sharp legal practitioners, no class of human beings can bear a comparison with them. With all his softness, the Bengalee is by no means placable in his enmities or prone to pity. The pertinacity with which he adheres to his purposes yields only to the immediate pressure of fear. Nor does he lack a certain kind of courage which is often wanting in his masters. To inevitable evils he is sometimes found to oppose a passive fortitude, such as the Stoics attributed to their ideal sage. An European warrior who rushes on a battery of cannon with a loud hurrah will sometimes shriek under the surgeon's knife, and fall into an agony of despair at the sentence of death. But the Bengalee who would see his country overrun, his house laid in ashes, his children murdered or dishonoured, without having the spirit to strike one blow, has yet been known to endure torture with the firmness of Mucius, and to mount the scaffold with the steady step and even pulse of Algernon Sydney.

In Nuncomar, the national character was strongly and with exaggeration personified. The Company's servants had repeatedly detected him in the most criminal intrigues. On one occasion he brought a false charge against another Hindoo, and tried to substantiate it by producing forged documents. On another occasion it was discovered that, while professing the strongest attachment to the English, he was engaged in several conspiracies against them, and in particular that he was the medium of a correspondence between the court of Delhi and the French authorities in the Carnatic. For these and similar practices he had been long detained in confinement. But his talents and influence had not only procured his liberation, but had obtained for him a certain degree of consideration even among the British rulers of his country.

Clive was extremely unwilling to place a Mussulman at the head of the administration of Bengal. On the other hand, he could not bring himself to confer immense power on a man to whom every sort of villany had repeatedly been brought home. Therefore, though the nabob, over whom Nuncomar had by intrigue acquired great influence, begged that the artful Hindoo might be intrusted with the government, Clive, after some hesitation, decided honestly and wisely in favour of Mahommed Reza Khan, who had held his high office seven years when Hastings became Governor. An infant son of Meer Jaffier was now nabob; and the guardianship of the young prince's person had been confided to the minister.

Nuncomar, stimulated at once by cupidity and malice, had been constantly attempting to undermine his successful rival. This was not difficult. The revenues of Bengal, under the administration established by Clive, did not yield such a surplus as had been anticipated by the Company; for, at that time, the most absurd notions were entertained in England respecting the wealth of India. Palaces of porphyry, hung with the richest brocade, heaps of pearls and diamonds, vaults from which pagodas and gold mohurs were measured out by the bushel, filled the imagination even of men of business. Nobody seemed to be aware of what nevertheless was most undoubtedly the truth, that India was a poorer country than countries which in Europe are reckoned poor, than Ireland, for example, or than Portugal. It was confidently believed by lords of the treasury and members for the city that Bengal would not only defray its own charges, but would afford an increased dividend to the proprietors of India stock, and large relief to the English finances. These absurd expectations were disappointed; and the directors, naturally enough, chose to attribute the disappointment rather to the mismanagement of Mahommed Reza Khan than to their own ignorance of the country intrusted to their care. They were confirmed in their error by the agents of Nuncomar; for Nuncomar had agents even in Leadenhall Street. Soon after Hastings reached Calcutta, he received a letter addressed by the Court of Directors, not to the council generally, but to himself in particular. He was directed to remove Mahommed Reza Khan, to arrest him, together with all his family and all his partisans, and to institute a strict inquiry into the whole administration of the province. It was added that the Governor would do well to avail himself of the assistance of Nuncomar in the investigation. The vices of Nuncomar were acknowledged. But even from his vices, it was said, much advantage might at such a conjuncture be derived; and, though he could not safely be trusted, it might still be proper to encourage him by hopes of reward.

The Governor bore no good will to Nuncomar. Many years before, they had known each other at Moorshedabad; and then a quarrel had risen between them which all the authority of their superiors could hardly compose. Widely as they differed in most points, they resembled each other in this, that both were men of unforgiving natures. To Mahommed Reza Khan, on the other hand, Hastings had no feelings of hostility. Nevertheless he proceeded to execute the instructions of the Company with an alacrity which he never showed, except when instructions were in perfect conformity with his own views. He had, wisely as we think, determined to get rid of the system of double government in Bengal. The orders of the directors furnished him with the means of effecting his purpose, and dispensed him from the necessity of discussing the matter with his council. He took his measures with his usual vigour and dexterity. At midnight, the palace of Mahommed Reza Khan at Moorshedabad was surrounded by a battalion of sepoys. The minister was roused from his slumbers, and informed that he was a prisoner. With the Mussulman gravity, he bent his head and submitted himself to the will of God. He fell not alone. A chief named Schitab Roy had been intrusted with the government of Bahar. His valour and his attachment to the English had more than once been signally proved. On that memorable day on which the people of Patna saw from their walls the whole army of the Mogul scattered by the little band of Captain Knox, the voice of the British conquerors assigned the palm of gallantry to the brave Asiatic. "I never," said Knox, when he introduced Schitab Roy, covered with blood and dust, to the English functionaries assembled in the factory, "I never saw a native fight so before." Schitab Roy was involved in the ruin of Mahommed Reza Khan, was removed from office, and was placed under arrest. The members of the council received no intimation of these measures till the prisoners were on their road to Calcutta.

The inquiry into the conduct of the minister was postponed on different pretences. He was detained in an easy confinement during many months. In the mean time, the great revolution which Hastings had planned was carried into effect. The office of minister was abolished. The internal administration was transferred to the servants of the Company. A system, a very imperfect system, it is true, of civil and criminal justice, under English superintendence, was established. The nabob was no longer to have even an ostensible share in the government; but he was still to receive a considerable annual allowance, and to be surrounded with the state of sovereignty. As he was an infant, it was necessary to provide guardians for his person and property. His person was entrusted to a lady of his father's haram, known by the name of the Munny Begum. The office of treasurer of the household was bestowed on a son of Nuncomar, named Goordas. Nuncomar's services were wanted, yet he could not safely be trusted with power; and Hastings thought it a masterstroke of policy to reward the able and unprincipled parent by promoting the inoffensive child.

The revolution completed, the double government dissolved, the Company installed in the full sovereignty of Bengal, Hastings had no motive to treat the late ministers with rigour. Their trial had been put off on various pleas till the new organization was complete. They were then brought before a committee, over which the Governor presided. Schitab Roy was speedily acquitted with honour. A formal apology was made to him for the restraint to which he had been subjected. All the Eastern marks of respect were bestowed on him. He was clothed in a robe of state, presented with jewels and with a richly harnessed elephant, and sent back to his government at Patna. But his health had suffered from confinement; his high spirit had been cruelly wounded; and soon after his liberation he died of a broken heart.

The innocence of Mahommed Reza Khan was not so clearly established. But the Governor was not disposed to deal harshly. After a long hearing, in which Nuncomar appeared as the accuser, and displayed both the art and the inveterate rancour which distinguished him, Hastings pronounced that the charges had not been made out, and ordered the fallen minister to be set at liberty.

Nuncomar had purposed to destroy the Mussulman administration, and to rise on its ruin. Both his malevolence and his cupidity had been disappointed. Hastings had made him a tool, had used him for the purpose of accomplishing the transfer of the government from Moorshedabad to Calcutta, from native to European hands. The rival, the enemy, so long envied, so implacably persecuted, had been dismissed unhurt. The situation so long and ardently desired had been abolished. It was natural that the Governor should be from that time an object of the most intense hatred to the vindictive Brahmin. As yet, however, it was necessary to suppress such feelings. The time was coming when that long animosity was to end in a desperate and deadly struggle.

In the mean time, Hastings was compelled to turn his attention to foreign affairs. The object of his diplomacy was at this time simply to get money. The finances of his government were in an embarrassed state; and this embarrassment he was determined to relieve by some means, fair or foul. The principle which directed all his dealings with his neighbours is fully expressed by the old motto of one of the great predatory families of Teviotdale, "Thou shalt want ere I want." He seems to have laid it down, as a fundamental proposition which could not be disputed, that, when he had not as many lacs of rupees as the public service required, he was to take them from any body who had. One thing, indeed, is to be said in excuse for him. The pressure applied to him by his employers at home, was such as only the highest virtue could have withstood, such as left him no choice except to commit great wrongs, or to resign his high post and with that post all his hopes of fortune and distinction. The directors, it is true, never enjoined or applauded any crime. Far from it. Whoever examines their letters written at that time will find there many just and humane sentiments, many excellent precepts, in short, an admirable code of political ethics. But every exhortation is modified or nullified by a demand for money. "Govern leniently, and send more money; practise strict justice and moderation towards neighbouring powers, and send more money;" this is in truth the sum of almost all the instructions that Hastings ever received from home. Now these instructions, being interpreted, mean simply, "Be the father and the oppressor of the people; be just and unjust, moderate and rapacious." The directors dealt with India, as the church, in the good old times, dealt with a heretic. They delivered the victim over to the executioners, with an earnest request that all possible tenderness might be shown. We by no means accuse or suspect those who framed these despatches of hypocrisy. It is probable that, writing fifteen thousand miles from the place where their orders were to be carried into effect, they never perceived the gross inconsistency of which they were guilty. But the inconsistency was at once manifest to their lieutenant at Calcutta who, with an empty treasury, with an unpaid army, with his own salary often in arrear, with deficient crops, with government tenants daily running away, was called upon to remit home another half million without fail. Hastings saw that it was absolutely necessary for him to disregard either the moral discourses or the pecuniary requisitions of his employers. Being forced to disobey them in something, he had to consider what kind of disobedience they would most readily pardon; and he correctly judged that the safest course would be to neglect the sermons and to find the rupees.

A mind so fertile as his, and so little restrained by conscientious scruples, speedily discovered several modes of relieving the financial embarrassments of the government. The allowance of the Nabob of Bengal was reduced at a stroke from three hundred and twenty thousand pounds a-year to half that sum. The Company had bound itself to pay near three hundred thousand pounds a-year to the Great Mogul, as a mark of homage for the provinces which he had intrusted to their care; and they had ceded to him the districts of Corah and Allahabad. On the plea that the Mogul was not really independent, but merely a tool in the hands of others, Hastings determined to retract these concessions. He accordingly declared that the English would pay no more tribute, and sent troops to occupy Allahabad and Corah. The situation of these places was such, that there would be little advantage and great expense in retaining them. Hastings, who wanted money and not territory, determined to sell them. A purchaser was not wanting. The rich province of Oude had, in the general dissolution of the Mogul Empire, fallen to the share of the great Mussulman house by which it is still governed. About twenty years ago, this house, by the permission of the British government, assumed the royal title; but, in the time of Warren Hastings, such an assumption would have been considered by the Mahommedans of India as a monstrous impiety. The Prince of Oude, though he held the power, did not venture to use the style of sovereignty. To the appellation of Nabob or Viceroy, he added that of Vizier of the monarchy of Hindostan, just as in the last century the Electors of Saxony and Brandenburg, though independent of the Emperor, and often in arms against him, were proud to style themselves his grand Chamberlain and Grand Marshal. Sujah Dowlah, then Nabob Vizier, was on excellent terms with the English. He had a large treasure. Allahabad and Corah were so situated that they might be of use to him and could be of none to the Company. The buyer and seller soon came to an understanding; and the provinces which had been torn from the Mogul were made over to the government of Oude for about half a million sterling.

But there was another matter still more important to be settled by the Vizier and the Governor. The fate of a brave people was to be decided. It was decided in a manner which has left a lasting stain on the fame of Hastings and of England.

The people of Central Asia had always been to the inhabitants of

India what the warriors of the German forests were to the subjects of the decaying monarchy of Rome. The dark, slender, and timid Hindoo shrank from a conflict with the strong muscle and resolute spirit of the fair race, which dwelt beyond the passes. There is reason to believe that, at a period anterior to the dawn of regular history, the people who spoke the rich and flexible Sanscrit came from regions lying far beyond the Hyphasis and the Hystaspes, and imposed their yoke on the children of the soil. It is certain that, during the last ten centuries, a succession of invaders descended from the west on Hindostan; nor was the course of conquest ever turned back towards the setting sun, till that memorable campaign in which the cross of Saint George was planted on the walls of Ghizni.

The Emperors of Hindostan themselves came from the other side of the great mountain ridge; and it had always been their practice to recruit their army from the hardy and valiant race from which their own illustrious house sprang. Among the military adventurers who were allured to the Mogul standards from the neighbourhood of Cabul and Candahar, were conspicuous several gallant bands, known by the name of the Rohillas. Their services had been rewarded with large tracts of land, fiefs of the spear, if we may use an expression drawn from an analogous state of things, in that fertile plain through which the Ramgunga flows from the snowy heights of Kumaon to join the Ganges. In the general confusion which followed the death of Aurungzebe, the warlike colony became virtually independent. The Rohillas were distinguished from the other inhabitants of India by a peculiarly fair complexion. They were more honourably distinguished by courage in war, and by skill in the arts of peace. While anarchy raged from Lahore to Cape Comorin, their little territory enjoyed the blessings of repose under the guardianship of valour. Agriculture and commerce flourished among them; nor were they negligent of rhetoric and poetry. Many persons now living have heard aged men talk with regret of the golden days when the Afghan princes ruled in the vale of Rohilcund.

Sujah Dowlah had set his heart on adding this rich district to his own principality. Right, or show of right, he had absolutely none. His claim was in no respect better founded than that of Catherine to Poland, or that of the Bonaparte family to Spain. The Rohillas held their country by exactly the same title by which he held his, and had governed their country far better than his had ever been governed. Nor were they a people whom it was perfectly safe to attack. Their land was indeed an open plain, destitute of natural defences; but their veins were full of the high blood of Affghanistan. As soldiers, they had not the steadiness which is seldom found except in company with strict discipline; but their impetuous valour had been proved on many fields of battle. It was said that their chiefs, when united by common peril, could bring eighty thousand men into the field. Sujah Dowlah had himself seen them fight, and wisely shrank from a conflict with them. There was in India one army, and only one, against which even those proud Caucasian tribes could not stand. It had been abundantly proved that neither tenfold odds, nor the martial ardour of the boldest Asiatic nations, could avail aught against English science and resolution. Was it possible to induce the Governor of Bengal to let out to hire the irresistible energies of the imperial people, the skill against which the ablest chiefs of Hindostan were helpless as infants, the discipline which had so often triumphed over the frantic struggles of fanaticism and despair, the unconquerable British courage which is never so sedate and stubborn as towards the close of a doubtful and murderous day?

This was what the Nabob Vizier asked, and what Hastings granted. A bargain was soon struck. Each of the negotiators had what the other wanted. Hastings was in need of funds to carry on the government of Bengal, and to send remittances to London; and Sujah Dowlah had an ample revenue. Sujah Dowlah was bent on subjugating the Rohillas; and Hastings had at his disposal the only force by which the Rohillas could be subjugated. It was agreed that an English army should be lent to the Nabob Vizier, and that, for the loan, he should pay four hundred thousand pounds sterling, besides defraying all the charge of the troops while employed in his service.

"I really cannot see," says the Reverend Mr. Gleig, "upon what grounds, either of political or moral justice, this proposition deserves to be stigmatized as infamous." If we understand the meaning of words, it is infamous to commit a wicked action for hire, and it is wicked to engage in war without provocation. In this particular war, scarcely one aggravating circumstance was wanting. The object of the Rohilla war was this, to deprive a large population, who had never done us the least harm, of a good government, and to place them, against their will, under an execrably bad one. Nay, even this is not all. England now descended far below the level even of those petty German princes who, about the same time, sold us troops to fight the Americans. The hussar-mongers of Hesse and Anspach had at least the assurance that the expeditions on which their soldiers were to be employed would be conducted in conformity with the humane rules of civilised warfare. Was the Rohilla war likely to be so conducted? Did the Governor stipulate that it should be so conducted? He well knew what Indian warfare was. He well knew that the power which he covenanted to put into Sujah Dowlah's hands, would, in all probability, be atrociously abused; and he required no guarantee, no promise that it should not be so abused. He did not even reserve to himself the right of withdrawing his aid in case of abuse, however gross. Mr. Gleig repeats Major Scott's absurd plea, that Hastings was justified in letting out English troops to slaughter the Rohillas, because the Rohillas were not of Indian race, but a colony from a distant country. What were the English themselves? Was it for them to proclaim a crusade for the expulsion of all intruders from the countries watered by the Ganges? Did it lie in their mouths to contend that a foreign settler who establishes an empire in India is a *caput lupinum?* What would they have said if any other power had, on such a ground, attacked Madras or Calcutta, without the slightest provocation? Such a defence was wanting to make the infamy of the transaction complete. The atrocity of the crime, and the hypocrisy of the apology, are worthy of each other.

One of the three brigades of which the Bengal army consisted was sent under Colonel Champion to join Sujah Dowlah's forces. The Rohillas expostulated, entreated, offered a large ransom, but in vain. They then resolved to defend themselves to the last. A bloody battle was fought. "The enemy," says Colonel Champion, "gave proof of a good share of military knowledge; and it is impossible to describe a more obstinate firmness of resolution than they displayed." The dastardly sovereign of Oude fled from the field. The English were left unsupported; but their fire and their charge were irresistible. It was not, however, till the most distinguished chiefs had fallen, fighting bravely at the head of their troops, that the Rohilla ranks gave way. Then the Nabob Vizier and his rabble made their appearance, and hastened to plunder the camp of the valiant enemies, whom they had never dared to look in the face. The soldiers of the Company, trained in an exact discipline, kept unbroken order, while the tents were pillaged by these worthless allies. But many voices were heard to exclaim, "We have had all the fighting, and those rogues are to have all the profit."

Then the horrors of Indian war were let loose on the fair valleys and cities of Rohilcund. The whole country was in a blaze. More than a hundred thousand people fled from their homes to pestilential jungles, preferring famine, and fever, and the haunts of tigers, to the tyranny of him, to whom an English and a Christian government had, for shameful lucre, sold their substance, and their blood, and the honour of their wives and daughters. Colonel Champion remonstrated with the Nabob Vizier, and sent strong representations to Fort William; but the Governor had made no conditions as to the mode in which the war was to be carried on. He had troubled himself about nothing but his forty lacs; and, though he might disapprove of Sujah Dowlah's wanton barbarity, he did not think himself entitled to interfere, except by offering advice. This delicacy excites the admiration of the reverend biographer. "Mr. Hastings," he says, "could not himself dictate to the Nabob, nor permit the commander of the Company's troops to dictate how the war was to be carried on." No, to be sure. Mr. Hastings had only to put down by main force the brave struggles of innocent men fighting for their liberty. Their military resistance crushed, his duties ended; and he had then only to fold his arms and look on, while their villages were burned, their children butchered, and their women violated. Will Mr. Gleig seriously maintain this opinion? Is any rule more plain than this, that whoever voluntarily gives to another irresistible power over human beings is bound to take order that such power shall not be barbarously abused? But we beg pardon of our readers for arguing a point so clear.

We hasten to the end of this sad and disgraceful story. The war ceased. The finest population in India was subjected to a greedy, cowardly, cruel tyrant. Commerce and agriculture languished. The rich province which had tempted the cupidity of Sujah Dowlah became the most miserable part even of his miserable dominions. Yet is the injured nation not extinct. At long intervals gleams of its ancient spirit have flashed forth; and even at this day, valour, and self-respect, and a chivalrous feeling rare among Asiatics, and a bitter remembrance of the great crime of England, distinguish that noble Afghan race. To this day they are regarded as the best of all sepoys at the cold steel; and it was very recently remarked, by one who had enjoyed great opportunities of observation, that the only natives of India to whom the word "gentleman" can with perfect propriety be applied are to be found among the Rohillas.

Whatever we may think of the morality of Hastings, it cannot be denied that the financial results of his policy did honour to his talents. In less than two years after he assumed the government, he had, without imposing any additional burdens on the people subject to his authority, added about four hundred and fifty thousand pounds to the annual income of the Company, besides procuring about a million in ready money. He had also relieved the finances of Bengal from military expenditure, amounting to near a quarter of a million a year, and had thrown that charge on the Nabob of Oude. There can be no doubt that this was a result which, if it had been obtained by honest means, would have entitled him to the warmest gratitude of his country, and which, by whatever means obtained, proved that he possessed great talents for administration.

In the mean time, Parliament had been engaged in long and grave discussions on Asiatic affairs. The ministry of Lord North, in the session of 1773, introduced a measure which made a considerable change in the constitution of the Indian government. This law, known by the name of the Regulating Act, provided that the presidency of Bengal should exercise a control over the other possessions of the Company; that the chief of that presidency should be styled Governor-General; that he should be assisted by four Councillors; and that a supreme court of judicature, consisting of a chief justice and three inferior judges, should be established at Calcutta. This court was made independent of the Governor-General and Council, and was entrusted with a civil and criminal jurisdiction of immense and, at the same time, of undefined extent.

The Governor-General and Councillors were named in the act, and were to hold their situations for five years. Hastings was to be the first Governor-General. One of the four new Councillors, Mr. Barwell, an experienced servant of the Company, was then in India. The other three, General Clavering, Mr. Monson, and Mr. Francis, were sent out from England.

The ablest of the new Councillors was, beyond all doubt, Philip Francis. His acknowledged compositions prove that he possessed considerable eloquence and information. Several years passed in the public offices had formed him to habits of business. His enemies have never denied that he had a fearless and manly spirit; and his friends, we are afraid, must acknowledge that his estimate of himself was extravagantly high, that his temper was irritable, that his deportment was often rude and petulant, and that his hatred was of intense bitterness and long duration.

It is scarcely possible to mention this eminent man without adverting for a moment to the question which his name at once suggests to every mind. Was he the author of the Letters of Junius? Our own firm belief is that he was. The evidence is, we think, such as would support a verdict in a civil, nay, in a criminal proceeding. The handwriting of Junius is the very peculiar handwriting of Francis, slightly disguised. As to the position, pursuits, and connexions of Junius, the following are the most important facts which can be considered as clearly proved: first, that he was acquainted with the technical forms of the secretary of state's office; secondly, that he was intimately acquainted with the business of the war-office; thirdly, that he, during the year 1770, attended debates in the House of Lords, and took notes of speeches, particularly of the speeches of Lord Chatham; fourthly, that he bitterly resented the appointment of Mr. Chamier to the place of deputy secretary-at-war; fifthly, that he was bound by some strong tie to the first Lord Holland. Now, Francis passed some years in the secretary of state's office. He was subsequently chief clerk of the war-office. He repeatedly mentioned that he had himself, in 1770, heard speeches of Lord Chatham; and some of these speeches were actually printed from his notes. He resigned his clerkship at the war-office from resentment at the appointment of Mr. Chamier. It was by Lord Holland that he was first introduced into the public service. Now, here are five marks, all of which ought to be found in Junius. They are all five found in Francis. We do not believe that more than two of them can be found in any other person whatever. If this argument does not settle the question, there is an end of all reasoning on circumstantial evidence.

The internal evidence seems to us to point the same way. The style of Francis bears a strong resemblance to that of Junius; nor are we disposed to admit, what is generally taken for granted, that the acknowledged compositions of Francis are very decidedly inferior to the anonymous letters. The argument from inferiority, at all events, is one which may be urged with at least equal force against every claimant that has ever been mentioned, with the single exception of Burke: and it would be a waste of time to prove that Burke was not Junius. And what conclusion, after all, can be drawn from mere inferiority? Every writer must produce his best work; and the interval between his best work and his second best work may be very wide indeed. Nobody will say that the best letters of Junius are more decidedly superior to the acknowledged works of Francis than three or four of Corneille's tragedies to the rest, than three or four of Ben Jonson's comedies to the rest, than the Pilgrim's Progress to the other works of Bunyan, than Don Quixote to the other works of Cervantes. Nay, it is certain that the Man in the Mask, whoever he may have been, was a most unequal writer. To go no further than the letters which bear the signature of Junius; the letter to the king, and the letters to Horne Tooke, have little in common, except the asperity; and asperity was an ingredient seldom wanting either in the writings or in the speeches of Francis.

Indeed, one of the strongest reasons for believing that Francis was Junius is the moral resemblance between the two men. It is not difficult, from the letters which, under various signatures, are known to have been written by Junius, and from his dealings with Woodfall and others, to form a tolerably correct notion of his character. He was clearly a man not destitute of real patriotism and magnanimity, a man whose vices were not of a sordid kind. But he must also have been a man in the highest degree arrogant and insolent, a man prone to malevolence, and prone to the error of mistaking his malevolence for public virtue. "Doest thou well to be angry?" was the question asked in old time of the Hebrew prophet. And he answered, "I do well." This was evidently the temper of Junius; and to this cause we attribute the savage cruelty which disgraces several of his letters. No man is so merciless as he who, under a strong self-delusion, confounds his antipathies with his duties. It may be added that Junius, though allied with the democratic party by common enmities, was the very opposite of a democratic politician. While attacking individuals with a ferocity which perpetually violated all the laws of literary warfare, he regarded the most defective parts of old institutions with a respect amounting to pedantry, pleaded the cause of Old Sarum with fervour, and contemptuously told the capitalists of Manchester and Leeds that, if they wanted votes, they might buy land and become freeholders of Lancashire and Yorkshire. All this, we believe, might stand, with scarcely any change, for a character of Philip Francis.

It is not strange that the great anonymous writer should have been willing at that time to leave the country which had been so powerfully stirred by his eloquence. Every thing had gone against him. That party which he clearly preferred to every other, the party of George Grenville, had been scattered by the death of its chief; and Lord Suffolk had led the greater part of it over to the ministerial benches. The ferment produced by the Middlesex election had gone down. Every faction must have been alike an object of aversion to Junius. His opinions on domestic affairs separated him from the ministry; his opinions on colonial affairs from the opposition. Under such circumstances, he had thrown down his pen in misanthropical despair. His farewell letter to Woodfall bears date the nineteenth of January 1773. In that letter, he declared that he must be an idiot to write again; that he had meant well by the cause and the public; that both were given up; that there were not ten men who would act steadily together on any question. "But it is all alike," he added, "vile and contemptible. You have never flinched that I know of; and I shall always rejoice to hear of your prosperity." These were the last words of Junius. In a year from that time, Philip Francis was on his voyage to Bengal.

With the three new Councillors came out the judges of the Supreme Court. The chief justice was Sir Elijah Impey. He was an old acquaintance of Hastings; and it is probable that the Governor-General, if he had searched through all the inns of court, could not have found an equally serviceable tool. But the members of Council were by no means in an obsequious mood. Hastings greatly disliked the new form of government, and had no very high opinion of his coadjutors. They had heard of this, and were disposed to be suspicious and punctilious. When men are in such a frame of mind, any trifle is sufficient to give occasion for dispute. The members of Council expected a salute of twenty-one guns from the batteries of Fort William. Hastings allowed them only seventeen. They landed in ill-humour. The first civilities were exchanged with cold reserve. On the morrow commenced that long quarrel which, after distracting British India, was renewed in England, and in which all the most eminent statesmen and orators of the age took active part on one or the other side.

Hastings was supported by Barwell. They had not always been friends. But the arrival of the new members of Council from England naturally had the effect of uniting the old servants of the Company. Clavering, Monson, and Francis formed the majority. They instantly wrested the government out of the hands of Hastings; condemned, certainly not without justice, his late dealings with the Nabob Vizier; recalled the English agent from Oude, and sent thither a creature of their own; ordered the brigade which had conquered the unhappy Rohillas to return to the Company's territories; and instituted a severe inquiry into the conduct of the war. Next, in spite of the Governor-General's remonstrances, they proceeded to exercise, in the most indiscreet manner, their new authority over the subordinate presidencies; threw all the affairs of Bombay into confusion; and interfered, with an incredible union of rashness and feebleness, in the intestine disputes of the Mahratta government. At the same time, they fell on the internal administration of Bengal and attacked the whole fiscal and judicial system, a system which was undoubtedly defective, but which it was very improbable that gentlemen fresh from England would be competent to amend. The effect of their reforms was that all protection to life and property was withdrawn, and that gangs of robbers plundered and slaughtered with impunity in the very suburbs of Calcutta. Hastings continued to live in the Government-house, and to draw the salary of Governor-General. He continued even to take the lead at the council-board in the transaction of ordinary business; for his opponents could not but feel that he knew much of which they were ignorant, and that he decided, both surely and speedily, many questions which to them would have been hopelessly puzzling. But the higher powers of government and the most valuable patronage had been taken from him.

The natives soon found this out. They considered him as a fallen man; and they acted after their kind. Some of our readers may have seen, in India, a cloud of crows pecking a sick vulture to death, no bad type of what happens in that country, as often as fortune deserts one who has been great and dreaded. In an instant, all the sycophants who had lately been ready to lie for him, to forge for him, to pandar for him, to poison for him, hasten to purchase the favour of his victorious enemies by accusing him. An Indian government has only to let it be understood that it wishes a particular man to be ruined; and, in twenty-four hours, it will be furnished with grave charges, supported by depositions so full and circumstantial that any person unaccustomed to Asiatic mendacity would regard them as decisive. It is well if the signature of the destined victim is not counterfeited at the foot of some illegal compact, and if some treasonable paper is not slipped into a hiding-place in his house. Hastings was now regarded as helpless. The power to make or mar the fortune of every man in Bengal had passed, as it seemed, into the hands of the new councillors. Immediately charges against the Governor-General began to pour in. They were eagerly welcomed by the majority who, to do them justice, were men of too much honour knowingly to countenance false accusations, but who were not sufficiently acquainted with the East to be aware that, in that part of the world, a very little encouragement from power will call forth, in a week, more Oateses, and Bedloes, and Dangerfields, than Westminster Hall sees in a century.

It would have been strange indeed if, at such a juncture, Nuncomar had remained quiet. That bad man was stimulated at once by malignity, by avarice, and by ambition. Now was the time to be avenged on his old enemy, to wreak a grudge of seventeen years, to establish himself in the favour of the majority of the Council, to become the greatest native in Bengal. From the time of the arrival of the new Councillors, he had paid the most marked court to them, and had in consequence been excluded, with all indignity, from the Government-house. He now put into the hands of Francis, with great ceremony, a paper containing several charges of the most serious description. By this document Hastings was accused of putting offices up to sale, and of receiving bribes for suffering offenders to escape. In particular, it was alleged that Mohammed Reza Khan had been dismissed with impunity, in consideration of a great sum paid to the Governor-General.

Francis read the paper in Council. A violent altercation followed. Hastings complained in bitter terms of the way in which he was treated, spoke with contempt of Nuncomar and of Nuncomar's accusation, and denied the right of the council to sit in judgment on the governor. At the next meeting of the Board, another communication from Nuncomar was produced. He requested that he might be permitted to attend the council, and that he might be heard in support of his assertions. Another tempestuous debate took place. The Governor-General maintained that the council-room was not a proper place for such an investigation; that from persons who were heated by daily conflict with him he could not expect the fairness of judges; and that he could not, without betraying the dignity of his post, submit to be confronted with such a man as Nuncomar. The majority, however, resolved to go into the charges. Hastings rose, declared the sitting at an end, and left the room, followed by Barwell. The other members kept their seats, voted themselves a council, put Clavering in the chair, and ordered Nuncomar to be called in. Nuncomar not only adhered to the original charges, but, after the fashion of the East, produced a large supplement. He stated that Hastings had received a great sum for appointing Rajah Goordas treasurer of the Nabob's household, and for committing the care of his Highness's person to the Munny Begum. He put in a letter purporting to bear the seal of the Munny Begum, for the purpose of establishing the truth of his story. The seal, whether forged, as Hastings affirmed, or genuine, as we are rather inclined to believe, proved nothing. Nuncomar, as every body knows who knows India, had only to tell the Munny Begum that such a letter would give pleasure to the majority of the council, in order to procure her attestation. The majority, however, voted that the charge was made out; that Hastings had corruptly received between thirty and forty thousand poinds; and that he ought to be compelled to refund.

The general feeling among the English in Bengal was strongly in favour of the Governor-General. In talents for business, in knowledge of the country, in general courtesy of demeanour, he was decidedly superior to his persecutors. The servants of the Company were naturally disposed to side with the most distinguished member of their own body against a clerk from the war-office, who, profoundly ignorant of the native languages and the native character, took on himself to regulate every department of the administration. Hastings, however, in spite of the general sympathy of his countrymen, was in a most painful situation. There was still an appeal to higher authority in England. If that authority took part with his enemies, nothing was left to him but to throw up his office. He accordingly placed his resignation in the hands of his agent in London, Colonel Macleane. But Macleane was instructed not to produce the resignation, unless it should be fully ascertained that the feeling at the India House was adverse to the Governor-General.

The triumph of Nuncomar seemed to be complete. He held a daily levee, to which his countrymen resorted in crowds, and to which, on one occasion, the majority of the Council condescended to repair. His house was an office for the purpose of receiving charges against the Governor-General. It was said that, partly by threats, and partly by wheedling, the villanous Brahmin had induced many of the wealthiest men of the province to send in complaints. But he was playing a perilous game. It was not safe to drive to despair a man of such resource and of such determination as Hastings. Nuncomar, with all his acuteness, did not understand the nature of the institutions under which he lived. He saw that he had with him the majority of the body which made treaties, gave places, raised taxes. The separation between political and judicial functions was a thing of which he had no conception. It had probably never occurred to him that there was in Bengal an authority perfectly independent of the council, an authority which could protect one whom the council wished to destroy, and send to the gibbet one whom the council wished to protect. Yet such was the fact. The Supreme Court was, within the sphere of its own duties, altogether independent of the Government. Hastings, with his usual sagacity, had seen how much advantage he might derive from possessing himself of this stronghold; and he had acted accordingly. The Judges, especially the Chief Justice, were hostile to the majority of the council. The time had now come for putting this formidable machinery into action.

On a sudden, Calcutta was astounded by the news that Nuncomar had been taken up on a charge of felony, committed, and thrown into the common jail. The crime imputed to him was that six years before he had forged a bond. The ostensible prosecutor was a native. But it was then, and still is, the opinion of every body, idiots and biographers excepted, that Hastings was the real mover in the business.

The rage of the majority rose to the highest point. They protested against the proceedings of the Supreme Court, and sent several urgent messages to the Judges, demanding that Nuncomar should be admitted to bail. The Judges returned haughty and resolute answers. All that the Council could do was to heap honours and emoluments on the family of Nuncomar; and this they did. In the mean time the assizes commenced; a true bill was found; and Nuncomar was brought before Sir Elijah Impey and a jury composed of Englishmen. A great quantity of contradictory swearing, and the necessity of having every word of the evidence interpreted, protracted the trial to a most unusual length. At last a verdict of guilty was returned, and the Chief Justice pronounced sentence of death on the prisoner.

Mr. Gleig is so strangely ignorant as to imagine that the Judges had no further discretion in the case, and that the power of extending mercy to Nuncomar resided with the Council. He therefore throws on Francis and Francis's party the whole blame of what followed. We should have thought that a gentleman who has published five or six bulky volumes on Indian affairs might have taken the trouble to inform himself as to the fundamental principles of the Indian Government. The Supreme Court had, under the Regulating Act, the power to respite criminals till the pleasure of the Crown should be known. The Council had, at that time, no power to interfere.

That Impey ought to have respited Nuncomar we hold to be perfectly clear. Whether the whole proceeding was not illegal, is a question. But it is certain that, whatever may have been, according to technical rules of construction, the effect of the statute under which the trial took place, it was most unjust to hang a Hindoo for forgery. The law which made forgery capital in England was passed without the smallest reference to the state of society in India. It was unknown to the natives of India. It had never been put in execution among them, certainly not for want of delinquents. It was in the highest degree shocking to all their notions. They were not accustomed to the distinction which many circumstances, peculiar to our own state of society, have led us to make between forgery and other kinds of cheating. The counterfeiting of a seal was, in their estimation, a common act of swindling; nor had it ever crossed their minds that it was to be punished as severely as gang-robbery or assassination. A just judge would, beyond all doubt, have reserved the case for the consideration of the sovereign. But Impey would not hear of mercy or delay.

The excitement among all classes was great. Francis and Francis's few English adherents described the Governor-General and the Chief Justice as the worst of murderers. Clavering, it was said, swore that, even at the foot of the gallows, Nuncomar should be rescued. The bulk of the European society, though strongly attached to the Governor-General, could not but feel compassion for a man who, with all his crimes, had so long filled so large a space in their sight, who had been great and powerful before the British empire in India began to exist, and to whom, in the old times, governors and members of council, then mere commercial factors, had paid court for protection. The feeling of the Hindoos was infinitely stronger. They were, indeed, not a people to strike one blow for their countryman. But his sentence filled them with sorrow and dismay. Tried even by their low standard of morality, he was a bad man. But, bad as he was, he was the head of their race and religion, a Brahmin of the Brahmins. He had inherited the purest and highest caste. He had practised with the greatest punctuality all those ceremonies to which the superstitious Bengalees ascribe far more importance than to the correct discharge of the social duties. They felt, therefore, as a devout Catholic in the dark ages would have felt, at seeing a prelate of the highest dignity sent to the gallows by a secular tribunal. According to their old national laws, a Brahmin could not be put to death for any crime whatever. And the crime for which Nuncomar was about to die was regarded by them in much the same light in which the selling of an unsound horse, for a sound price, is regarded by a Yorkshire jockey.

The Mussulmans alone appear to have seen with exultation the fate of the powerful Hindoo, who had attempted to rise by means of the ruin of Mahommed Reza Khan. The Mahommedan historian of those times takes delight in aggravating the charge. He assures us that in Nuncomar's house a casket was found containing counterfeits of the seals of all the richest men of the province. We have never fallen in with any other authority for this story, which in itself is by no means improbable.

The day drew near; and Nuncomar prepared himself to die with that quiet fortitude with which the Bengalee, so effeminately timid in personal conflict, often encounters calamities for which there is no remedy. The sheriff, with the humanity which is seldom wanting in an English gentleman, visited the prisoner on the eve of the execution, and assured him that no indulgence, consistent with the law, should be refused to him. Nuncomar expressed his gratitude with great politeness and unaltered composure. Not a muscle of his face moved. Not a sigh broke from him. He put his finger to his forehead, and calmly said that fate would have its way, and that there was no resisting the pleasure of God. He sent his compliments to Francis, Clavering, and Monson, and charged them to protect Rajah Goordas who was about to become the head of the Brahmins of Bengal. The sheriff withdrew, greatly agitated by what had passed, and Nuncomar sat composedly down to write notes and examine accounts.

The next morning, before the sun was in his power, an immense concourse assembled round the place where the gallows had been set up. Grief and horror were on every face; yet to the last the multitude could hardly believe that the English really purposed to take the life of the great Brahmin. At length the mournful procession came through the crowd. Nuncomar sat up in his palanquin, and looked round him with unaltered serenity. He had just parted from those who were most nearly connected with him. Their cries and contortions had appalled the European ministers of justice, but had not produced the smallest effect on the iron stoicism of the prisoner. The only anxiety which he expressed was that men of his own priestly caste might be in attendance to take charge of his corpse. He again desired to be remembered to his friends in the Council, mounted the scaffold with firmness, and gave the signal to the executioner. The moment that the drop fell, a howl of sorrow and despair rose from the innumerable spectators. Hundreds turned away their faces from the polluting sight, fled with loud wailings towards the Hoogley, and plunged into its holy waters, as if to purify themselves from the guilt of having looked on such a crime. These feelings were not confined to Calcutta. The whole province was greatly excited; and the population of Dacca, in particular, gave strong signs of grief and dismay.

Of Impey's conduct it is impossible to speak too severely. We have already said that, in our opinion, he acted unjustly in refusing to respite Nuncomar. No rational man can doubt that he took this course in order to gratify the Governor-General. If we had ever had any doubts on that point, they would have been dispelled by a letter which Mr. Gleig has published. Hastings, three or four years later, described Impey as the man "to whose support he was at one time indebted for the safety of his fortune, honour, and reputation." These strong words can refer only to the case of Nuncomar; and they must mean that Impey hanged Nuncomar in order to support Hastings. It is, therefore, our deliberate opinion that Impey, sitting as a judge, put a man unjustly to death in order to serve a political purpose.

But we look on the conduct of Hastings in a somewhat different light. He was struggling for fortune, honour, liberty, all that makes life valuable. He was beset by rancorous and unprincipled enemies.

From his colleagues he could expect no justice. He cannot be blamed for wishing to crush his accusers. He was indeed bound to use only legitimate means for that end. But it was not strange that he should have thought any means legitimate which were pronounced legitimate by the sages of the law, by men whose peculiar duty it was to deal justly between adversaries, and whose education might be supposed to have peculiarly qualified them for the discharge of that duty. Nobody demands from a party the unbending equity of a judge. The reason that judges are appointed is, that even a good man cannot be trusted to decide a cause in which he is himself concerned. Not a day passes on which an honest prosecutor does not ask for what none but a dishonest tribunal would grant. It is too much to expect that any man, when his dearest interests are at stake, and his strongest passions excited, will, as against himself, be more just than the sworn dispensers of justice. To take an analogous case from the history of our own island: suppose that Lord Stafford, when in the Tower on suspicion of being concerned in the Popish plot, had been apprised that Titus Oates had done something which might, by a questionable construction, be brought under the head of felony. Should we severely blame Lord Stafford, in the supposed case, for causing a prosecution to be instituted, for furnishing funds, for using all his influence to intercept the mercy of the Crown? We think not. If a judge, indeed, from favour to the Catholic lords, were to strain the law in order to hang Oates, such a judge would richly deserve impeachment. But it does not appear to us that the Catholic lord, by bringing the case before the judge for decision, would materially overstep the limits of a just self-defence.

While, therefore, we have not the least doubt that this memorable execution is to be attributed to Hastings, we doubt whether it can with justice be reckoned among his crimes. That his conduct was dictated by a profound policy is evident. He was in a minority in Council. It was possible that he might long be in a minority. He knew the native character well. He knew in what abundance accusations are certain to flow in against the most innocent inhabitant of India who is under the frown of power. There was not in the whole black population of Bengal a place-holder, a place-hunter, a government tenant, who did not think that he might better himself by sending up a deposition against the Governor-General. Under these circumstances, the persecuted statesman resolved to teach the whole crew of accusers and witnesses that, though in a minority at the council board, he was still to be feared. The lesson which he gave them was indeed a lesson not to be forgotten. The head of the combination which had been formed against him, the richest, the most powerful, the most artful, of the Hindoos, distinguished by the favour of those who then held the government, fenced round by the superstitious reverence of millions, was hanged in broad day before many thousands of people. Every thing that could make the warning impressive, dignity in the sufferer, solemnity in the proceeding, was found in this case. The helpless rage and vain struggles of the Council made the triumph more signal. From that moment the conviction of every native was that it was safer to take the part of Hastings in a minority than that of Francis in a majority, and that he who was so venturous as to join in running down the Governor-General might chance, in the phrase of the Eastern poet, to find a tiger, while beating the jungle for a deer. The voices of a thousand informers were silenced in an instant. From that time, whatever difficulties Hastings might have to encounter, he was never molested by accusations from natives of India.

It is a remarkable circumstance that one of the letters of Hastings to Dr. Johnson bears date a very few hours after the death of Nuncomar. While the whole settlement was in commotion, while a mighty and ancient priesthood were weeping over the remains of their chief, the conqueror in that deadly grapple sat down, with characteristic self-possession, to write about the Tour to the Hebrides, Jones's Persian Grammar, and the history, traditions, arts, and natural productions of India.

In the mean time, intelligence of the Rohilla war, and of the first disputes between Hastings and his colleagues, had reached London. The directors took part with the majority, and sent out a letter filled with severe reflections on the conduct of Hastings. They condemned, in strong but just terms, the iniquity of undertaking offensive wars merely for the sake of pecuniary advantages. But they utterly forgot that, if Hastings had by illicit means obtained pecuniary advantages, he had done so, not for his own benefit, but in order to meet their demands. To enjoin honesty, and to insist on having what could not be honestly got, was then the constant practice of the Company. As Lady Macbeth says of her husband, they "would not play false, and yet would wrongly win."

The Regulating Act, by which Hastings had been appointed Governor-General for five years, empowered the Crown to remove him on an address from the Company. Lord North was desirous to procure such an address. The three members of Council who had been sent out from England were men of his own choice. General Clavering, in particular, was supported by a large parliamentary connexion, such as no cabinet could be inclined to disoblige. The wish of the minister was to displace Hastings, and to put Clavering at the head of the government. In the Court of Directors parties were very nearly balanced. Eleven voted against Hastings; ten for him. The Court of Proprietors was then convened. The great sale-room presented a singular appearance. Letters had been sent by the Secretary of the Treasury, exhorting all the supporters of government who held India stock to be in attendance. Lord Sandwich marshalled the friends of the administration with his usual dexterity and alertness. Fifty peers and privy-councillors, seldom seen so far eastward, were counted in the crowd. The debate lasted till midnight. The opponents of Hastings had a small superiority on the division; but a ballot was demanded; and the result was that the Governor-General triumphed by a majority of above a hundred votes over the combined efforts of the directors and the cabinet. The ministers were greatly exasperated by this defeat. Even Lord North lost his temper, no ordinary occurrence with him, and threatened to convoke parliament before Christmas, and to bring in a bill for depriving the Company of all political power, and for restricting it to its old business of trading in silks and teas.

Colonel Macleane, who through all this conflict had zealously supported the cause of Hastings, now thought that his employer was in imminent danger of being turned out, branded with parliamentary censure, perhaps prosecuted. The opinion of the crown lawyers had already been taken respecting some parts of the Governor-General's conduct. It seemed to be high time to think of securing an honourable retreat. Under these circumstances, Macleane thought himself justified in producing the resignation with which he had been intrusted. The instrument was not in very accurate form; but the directors were too eager to be scrupulous. They accepted the resignation, fixed on Mr. Wheler, one of their own body, to succeed Hastings, and sent out orders that General Clavering, as senior member of Council, should exercise the functions of Governor-General till Mr. Wheler should arrive.

But, while these things were passing in England, a great change had taken place in Bengal. Monson was no more. Only four members of the government were left. Clavering and Francis were on one side, Barwell and the Governor-General on the other; and the Governor-General had the casting vote. Hastings, who had been during two years destitute of all power and patronage, became at once absolute. He instantly proceeded to retaliate on his adversaries. Their measures were reversed: their creatures were displaced. A new valuation of the lands of Bengal, for the purposes of taxation, was ordered; and it was provided that the whole inquiry should be conducted by the Governor-General, and that all the letters relating to it should run in his name. He began, at the same time, to revolve vast plans of conquest and dominion, plans which he lived to see realised, though not by himself. His project was to form subsidiary alliances with the native princes, particularly with those of Oude and Berar, and thus to make Britain the paramount power in India. While he was meditating these great designs, arrived the intelligence that he had ceased to be Governor-General, that his resignation had been accepted, that Wheler was coming out immediately, and that, till Wheler arrived, the chair was to be filled by Clavering.

Had Hastings still been in a minority, he would probably have retired without a struggle; but he was now the real, master of British India, and he was not disposed to quit his high place. He asserted that he had never given any instructions which could warrant the steps taken at home. What his instructions had been, he owned he had forgotten. If he had kept a copy of them he had mislaid it. But he was certain that he had repeatedly declared to the Directors that he would not resign. He could not see how the court, possessed of that declaration from himself, could receive his resignation from the doubtful hands of an agent. If the resignation were invalid, all the proceedings which were founded on that resignation were null, and Hastings was still Governor-General.

He afterwards affirmed that, though his agents had not acted in conformity with his instructions, he would nevertheless have held himself bound by their acts, if Clavering had not attempted to seize the supreme power by violence. Whether this assertion were or were not true, it cannot be doubted that the imprudence of Clavering gave Hastings an advantage. The General sent for the keys of the fort and of the treasury, took possession of the records, and held a council at which Francis attended. Hastings took the chair in another apartment, and Barwell sat with him. Each of the two parties had a plausible show of right. There was no authority entitled to their obedience within fifteen thousand miles. It seemed that there remained no way of settling the dispute except an appeal to arms; and from such an appeal Hastings, confident of his influence over his countrymen in India, was not inclined to shrink. He directed the officers of the garrison of Fort William and of all the neighbouring stations to obey no orders but his. At the same time, with admirable judgment, he offered to submit the case to the Supreme Court, and to abide by its decision. By making this proposition he risked nothing; yet it was a proposition which his opponents could hardly reject. Nobody could be treated as a criminal for obeying what the judges should solemnly pronounce to be the lawful government. The boldest man would shrink from taking arms in defence of what the judges should pronounce to be usurpation. Clavering and Francis, after some delay, unwillingly consented to abide by the award of the court. The court pronounced that the resignation was invalid, and that therefore Hastings was still Governor-General under the Regulating Act; and the defeated members of the Council, finding that the sense of the whole settlement was against them, acquiesced in the decision.

About this time arrived the news that, after a suit which had lasted several years, the Franconian courts had decreed a divorce between Imhoff and his wife. The Baron left Calcutta, carrying with him the means of buying an estate in Saxony. The lady became Mrs. Hastings. The event was celebrated by great festivities; and all the most conspicuous persons at Calcutta, without distinction of parties, were invited to the Government-house. Clavering, as the Mahommedan chronicler tells the story, was sick in mind and body, and excused himself from joining the splendid assembly. But Hastings whom, as it should seem, success in ambition and in love had put into high good-humour, would take no denial. He went himself to the General's house, and at length brought his vanquished rival in triumph to the gay circle which surrounded the bride. The exertion was too much for a frame broken by mortification as well as by disease. Clavering died a few days later.

Wheler, who came out expecting to be Governor-General, and was forced to content himself with a seat at the Council Board, generally voted with Francis. But the Governor-General, with Barwell's help and his own casting vote, was still the master. Some change took place at this time in the feeling both of the Court of Directors and of the Ministers of the Crown. All designs against Hastings were dropped; and, when his original term of five years expired, he was quietly reappointed. The truth is that the fearful dangers to which the public interests in every quarter were now exposed made both Lord North and the Company unwilling to part with a Governor whose talents, experience, and resolution, enmity itself was compelled to acknowledge.

The crisis was indeed formidable. That great and victorious empire, on the throne of which George the Third had taken his seat eighteen years before, with brighter hopes than had attended the accession of any of the long line of English sovereigns, had, by the most senseless misgovernment, been brought to the verge of ruin. In America millions of Englishmen were at war with the country from which their blood, their language, their religion, and their institutions were derived, and to which, but a short time before, they had been as strongly attached as the inhabitants of Norfolk and Leicestershire. The great powers of Europe, humbled to the dust by the vigour and genius which had guided the councils of George the Second, now rejoiced in the prospect of a signal revenge. The time was approaching when our island, while struggling to keep down the United States of America, and pressed with a still nearer danger by the too just discontents of Ireland, was to be assailed by France, Spain, and Holland, and to be threatened by the armed neutrality of the Baltic; when even our maritime supremacy was to be in jeopardy; when hostile fleets were to command the Straits of Calpe and the Mexican Sea; when the British flag was to be scarcely able to protect the British Channel. Great as were the faults of Hastings, it was happy for our country that at that conjuncture, the most terrible through which she has ever passed, he was the ruler of her Indian dominions.

An attack by sea on Bengal was little to be apprehended. The danger was that the European enemies of England might form an alliance with some native power, might furnish that power with troops, arms, and ammunition, and might thus assail our possessions on the side of the land. It was chiefly from the Mahrattas that Hastings anticipated danger. The original seat of that singular people was the wild range of hills which runs along the western coast of India. In the reign of Aurungzebe the inhabitants of those regions, led by the great Sevajee, began to descend on the possessions of their wealthier and less warlike neighbours. The energy, ferocity, and cunning of the Mahrattas, soon made them the most conspicuous among the new powers which were generated by the corruption of the decaying monarchy. At first they were only robbers. They soon rose to the dignity of conquerors. Half the provinces of the empire were turned into Mahratta principalities. Freebooters, sprung from low castes, and accustomed to menial employments, became mighty Rajahs. The Bonslas, at the head of a band of plunderers, occupied the vast region of Berar. The Guicowar, which is, being interpreted, the Herdsman, founded that dynasty which still reigns in Guzerat. The houses of Scindia and Holkar waxed great in Malwa. One adventurous captain made his nest on the impregnable rock of Gooti. Another became the lord of the thousand villages which are scattered among the green rice-fields of Tanjore.

That was the time, throughout India, of double government. The form and the power were every where separated. The Mussulman nabobs who had become sovereign princes, the Vizier in Oude, and the Nizam at Hyderabad, still called themselves the viceroys of the house of Tamerlane. In the same manner the Mahratta states, though really independent of each other, pretended to be members of one empire. They all acknowledged, by words and ceremonies, the supremacy of the heir of Sevajee, a *roi fainéant* who chewed bang and toyed with dancing girls in a state prison at Sattara, and of his Peshwa or mayor of the palace, a great hereditary magistrate, who kept a court with kingly state at Poonah, and whose authority was obeyed in the spacious provinces of Aurungabad and Bejapoor.

Some months before war was declared in Europe, the government of Bengal was alarmed by the news that a French adventurer, who passed for a man of quality, had arrived at Poonah. It was said that he had been received there with great distinction, that he had delivered to the Peshwa letters and presents from Louis the Sixteenth, and that a treaty, hostile to England, had been concluded between France and the Mahrattas.

Hastings immediately resolved to strike the first blow. The title of the Peshwa was not undisputed. A portion of the Mahratta nation was favourable to a pretender. The Governor-General determined to espouse this pretender's interest, to move an army across the peninsula of India, and to form a close alliance with the chief of the house of Bonsla, who ruled Berar, and who, in power and dignity, was inferior to none of the Mahratta princes.

The army had marched, and the negotiations with Berar were in progress, when a letter from the English consul at Cairo brought the news that war had been proclaimed both in London and Paris. All the measures which the crisis required were adopted by Hastings without a moment's delay. The French factories in Bengal were seized. Orders were sent to Madras that Pondicherry should instantly be occupied. Near Calcutta, works were thrown up which were thought to render the approach of a hostile force impossible. A maritime establishment was formed for the defence of the river. Nine new battalions of sepoys were raised, and a corps of native artillery was formed out of the hardy Lascars of the Bay of Bengal. Having made these arrangements, the Governor-General with calm confidence pronounced his presidency secure from all attack, unless the Mahrattas should march against it in conjunction with the French.

The expedition which Hastings had sent westward was not so speedily or completely successful as most of his undertakings. The commanding officer procrastinated. The authorities at Bombay blundered. But the Governor-General persevered. A new commander repaired the errors of his predecessor. Several brilliant actions spread the military renown of the English through regions where no European flag had ever been seen. It is probable that, if a new and more formidable danger had not compelled Hastings to change his whole policy, his plans respecting the Mahratta empire would have been carried into complete effect.

The authorities in England had wisely sent out to Bengal, as commander of the forces and member of the council, one of the most distinguished soldiers of that time. Sir Eyre Coote had, many years before, been conspicuous among the founders of the British empire in the East. At the council of war which preceded the battle of Plassey, he earnestly recommended, in opposition to the majority, that daring course which, after some hesitation, was adopted, and which was crowned with such splendid success. He subsequently commanded in the south of India against the brave and unfortunate Lally, gained the decisive battle of Wandewash over the French and their native allies, took Pondicherry, and made the English power supreme in the Carnatic. Since those great exploits near twenty years had elapsed. Coote had no longer the bodily activity which he had shown in earlier days; nor was the vigour of his mind altogether unimpaired. He was capricious and fretful, and required much coaxing to keep him in good-humour. It must, we fear, be added that the love of money had grown upon him, and that he thought more about his allowances, and less about his duties, than might have been expected from so eminent a member of so noble a profession. Still he was perhaps the ablest officer that was then to be found in the British army. Among the native soldiers his name was great and his influence unrivalled. Nor is he yet forgotten by them. Now and then a white-bearded old sepoy may still be found, who loves to talk of Porto Novo and Pollilore. It is but a short time since one of those aged men came to present a memorial to an English officer, who holds one of the highest employments in India. A print of Coote hung in the room. The veteran recognised at once that face and figure which he had not seen for more than half a century, and, forgetting his salam to the living, halted, drew himself up, lifted his hand, and with solemn reverence paid his military obeisance to the dead.

Coote, though he did not, like Barwell, vote constantly with the Governor-General, was by no means inclined to join in systematic opposition, and on most questions concurred with Hastings, who did his best, by assiduous courtship, and by readily granting the most exorbitant allowances, to gratify the strongest passions of the old soldier.

It seemed likely at this time that a general reconciliation would put an end to the quarrels which had, during some years, weakened and disgraced the government of Bengal. The dangers of the empire might well induce men of patriotic feeling,—and of patriotic feeling neither Hastings nor Francis was destitute,—to forget private enmities, and to cooperate heartily for the general good. Coote had never been concerned in faction. Wheler was thoroughly tired of it. Barwell had made an ample fortune, and, though he had promised that he would not leave Calcutta while his help was needed in Council, was most desirous to return to England, and exerted himself to promote an arrangement which would set him at liberty. A compact was made, by which Francis agreed to desist from opposition, and Hastings engaged that the friends of Francis should be admitted to a fair share of the honours and emoluments of the service. During a few months after this treaty there was apparent harmony at the council-board.

Harmony, indeed, was never more necessary; for at this moment internal calamities, more formidable than war itself, menaced Bengal. The authors of the Regulating Act of 1773 had established two independent powers, the one judicial, the other political; and, with a carelessness scandalously common in English legislation, had omitted to define the limits of either. The judges took advantage of the indistinctness, and attempted to draw to themselves supreme authority, not only within Calcutta, but through the whole of the great territory subject to the presidency of Fort William. There are few Englishmen who will not admit that the English law, in spite of modern improvements, is neither so cheap nor so speedy as might be wished. Still, it is a system which has grown up among us. In some points, it has been fashioned to suit our feelings; in others, it has gradually fashioned our feelings to suit itself. Even to its worst evils we are accustomed; and therefore, though we may complain of them, they do not strike us with the horror and dismay which would be produced by a new grievance of smaller severity. In India the case is widely different. English law, transplanted to that country, has all the vices from which we suffer here; it has them all in a far higher degree; and it has other vices, compared with which the worst vices from which we suffer are trifles. Dilatory here, it is far more dilatory in a land where the help of an interpreter is needed by every judge and by every advocate. Costly here, it is far more costly in a land into which the legal practitioners must be imported from an immense distance. All English labour in India, from the labour of the Governor-General and the Commander-in-Chief, down to that of a groom or a watchmaker, must be paid for at a higher rate than at home. No man will be banished, and banished to the torrid zone, for nothing. The rule holds good with respect to the legal profession. No English barrister will work, fifteen thousand miles from all his friends, with the thermometer at ninety-six in the shade, for the emoluments which will content him in Chambers that overlook the Thames. Accordingly, the fees at Calcutta are about three times as great as the fees of Westminster Hall; and this, though the people of India are, beyond all comparison, poorer than the people of England. Yet the delay and the expense, grievous as they are, form the smallest part of the evil which English law, imported without modifications into India, could not fail to produce. The strongest feelings of our nature, honour, religion, female modesty, rose up against the innovation. Arrest on mesne process was the first step in most civil proceedings; and to a native of rank arrest was not merely a restraint, but a foul personal indignity. Oaths were required in every stage of every suit; and the feeling of a quaker about an oath is hardly stronger than that of a respectable native. That the apartments of a woman of quality should be entered by strange men, or that her face should be seen by them, are, in the East, intolerable outrages, outrages which are more dreaded than death, and which can be expiated only by the shedding of blood. To these outrages the most distinguished families of Bengal, Bahar, and Orissa, were now exposed. Imagine what the state of our own country would be, if a jurisprudence were on a sudden introduced among us, which should be to us what our jurisprudence was to our Asiatic subjects. Imagine what the state of our country would be, if it were enacted that any man, by merely swearing that a debt was due to him, should acquire a right to insult the persons of men of the most honourable and sacred callings and of women of the most shrinking delicacy, to horsewhip a general officer, to put a bishop in the stocks, to treat ladies in the way which called forth the blow of Wat Tyler. Something like this was the effect of the attempt which the Supreme Court made to extend its jurisdiction over the whole of the Company's territory.

A reign of terror began, of terror heightened by mystery; for even that which was endured was less horrible than that which was anticipated. No man knew what was next to be expected from this strange tribunal. It came from beyond the black water, as the people of India, with mysterious horror, call the sea. It consisted of judges not one of whom was familiar with the usages of the millions over whom they claimed boundless authority. Its records were kept in unknown characters; its sentences were pronounced in unknown sounds. It had already collected round itself an army of the worst part of the native population, informers, and false witnesses, and common barrators, and agents of chicane, and, above all, a banditti of bailiffs' followers, compared with whom the retainers of the worst English spunging-houses, in the worst times, might be considered as upright and tender-hearted. Many natives, highly considered among their countrymen, were seized, hurried up to Calcutta, flung into the common jail, not for any crime even imputed, not for any debt that had been proved, but merely as a precaution till their cause should come to trial. There were instances in which men of the most venerable dignity, persecuted without a cause by extortioners, died of rage and shame in the gripe of the vile alguazils of Impey. The harams of noble Mahommedans, sanctuaries respected in the East by governments which respected nothing else, were burst open by gangs of bailiffs. The Mussulmans, braver and less accustomed to submission than the Hindoos, sometimes stood on their defence; and there were instances in which they shed their blood in the doorway, while defending, sword in hand, the sacred apartments of their women. Nay, it seemed as if even the faint-hearted Bengalee, who had crouched at the feet of Surajah Dowlah, who had been mute during the administration of Vansittart, would at length find courage in despair. No Mahratta invasion had ever spread through the province such dismay as this inroad of English lawyers. All the injustice of former oppressors, Asiatic and European, appeared as a blessing when compared with the justice of the Supreme Court.

Every class of the population, English and native, with the exception of the ravenous pettifoggers who fattened on the misery and terror of an immense community, cried out loudly against this fearful oppression. But the judges were immoveable. If a bailiff was resisted, they ordered the soldiers to be called out. If a servant of the Company, in conformity with the orders of the government, withstood the miserable catchpoles who, with Impey's writs in their hands, exceeded the insolence and rapacity of gang-robbers, he was flung into prison for a contempt. The lapse of sixty years, the virtue and wisdom of many eminent magistrates who have during that time administered justice in the Supreme Court, have not effaced from the minds of the people of Bengal the recollection of those evil days.

The members of the government were, on this subject, united as one man. Hastings had courted the judges; he had found them useful instruments. But he was not disposed to make them his own masters, or the masters of India. His mind was large; his knowledge of the native character most accurate. He saw that the system pursued by the Supreme Court was degrading to the government and ruinous to the people; and he resolved to oppose it manfully. The consequence was, that the friendship, if that be the proper word for such a connexion, which had existed between him and Impey, was for a time completely dissolved. The government placed itself firmly between the tyrannical tribunal and the people. The Chief Justice proceeded to the wildest excesses. The Governor-General and all the members of Council were served with writs, calling on them to appear before the King's justices, and to answer for their public acts. This was too much. Hastings, with just scorn, refused to obey the call, set at liberty the persons wrongfully detained by the Court, and took measures for resisting the outrageous proceedings of the sheriffs' officers, if necessary, by the sword. But he had in view another device which might prevent the necessity of an appeal to arms. He was seldom at a loss for an expedient; and he knew Impey well. The expedient, in this case, was a very simple one, neither more nor less than a bribe. Impey was, by act of Parliament, a judge, independent of the government of Bengal, and entitled to a salary of eight thousand a-year. Hastings proposed to make him also a judge in the Company's service, removable at the pleasure of the government of Bengal; and to give him, in that capacity, about eight thousand a-year more. It was understood that, in consideration of this new salary, Impey would desist from urging the high pretensions of his court. If he did urge these pretensions, the government could, at a moment's notice, eject him from the new place which had been created for him. The bargain was struck; Bengal was saved; an appeal to force was averted; and the Chief Justice was rich, quiet, and infamous.

Of Impey's conduct it is unnecessary to speak. It was of a piece with almost every part of his conduct that comes under the notice of history. No other such judge has dishonoured the English ermine, since Jefferies drank himself to death in the Tower. But we cannot agree with those who have blamed Hastings for this transaction. The case stood thus. The negligent manner in which the Regulating Act had been framed put it in the power of the Chief Justice to throw a great country into the most dreadful confusion. He was determined to use his power to the utmost, unless he was paid to be still; and Hastings consented to pay him. The necessity was to be deplored. It is also to be deplored that pirates should be able to exact ransom, by threatening to make their captives walk the plank. But to ransom a captive from pirates has always been held a humane and Christian act; and it would be absurd to charge the payer of the ransom with corrupting the virtue of the corsair. This, we seriously think, is a not unfair illustration of the relative position of Impey, Hastings, and the people of India. Whether it was right in Impey to demand or to accept a price for powers which, if they really belonged to him, he could not abdicate, which, if they did not belong to him, he ought never to have usurped, and which in neither case he could honestly sell, is one question. It is quite another question, whether Hastings was not right to give any sum, however large, to any man, however worthless, rather than either surrender millions of human beings to pillage, or rescue them by civil war.

Francis strongly opposed this arrangement. It may, indeed, be suspected that personal aversion to Impey was as strong a motive with Francis as regard for the welfare of the province. To a mind burning with resentment it might seem better to leave Bengal to the oppressors than to redeem it by enriching them. It is not improbable, on the other hand, that Hastings may have been the more willing to resort to an expedient agreeable to the Chief Justice, because that high functionary had already been so serviceable, and might, when existing dissensions were composed, be serviceable again.

But it was not on this point alone that Francis was now opposed to Hastings. The peace between them proved to be only a short and hollow truce, during which their mutual aversion was constantly becoming stronger. At length an explosion took place. Hastings publicly charged Francis with having deceived him, and with having induced Barwell to quit the service by insincere promises. Then came a dispute, such as frequently arises even between honourable men, when they may make important agreements by mere verbal communication. An impartial historian will probably be of opinion that they had misunderstood each other; but their minds were so much embittered that they imputed to each other nothing less than deliberate villany. "I do not," said Hastings, in a minute recorded on the Consultations of the Government, "I do not trust to Mr. Francis's promises of candour, convinced that he is incapable of it. I judge of his public conduct by his private, which I have found to be void of truth and honour." After the Council had risen, Francis put a challenge into the Governor-General's hand. It was instantly accepted. They met, and fired. Francis was shot through the body. He was carried to a neighbouring house, where it appeared that the wound, though severe, was not mortal. Hastings inquired repeatedly after his enemy's health, and proposed to call on him; but Francis coldly declined the visit. He had a proper sense, he said, of the Governor-General's politeness, but could not consent to any private interview. They could meet only at the Council-board.

In a very short time it was made signally manifest to how great a danger the Governor-General had, on this occasion, exposed his country. A crisis arrived with which he, and he alone, was competent to deal. It is not too much to say that, if he had been taken from the head of affairs, the years 1780 and 1781 would have been as fatal to our power in Asia as to our power in America.

The Mahrattas had been the chief objects of apprehension to Hastings. The measures which he had adopted for the purpose of breaking their power, had at first been frustrated by the errors of those whom he was compelled to employ; but his perseverance and ability seemed likely to be crowned with success, when a far more formidable danger showed itself in a distant quarter.

About thirty years before this time, a Mahommedan soldier had begun to distinguish himself in the wars of Southern India. His education had been neglected; his extraction was humble. His father had been a petty officer of revenue; his grandfather a wandering dervise. But though thus meanly descended, though ignorant even of the alphabet, the adventurer had no sooner been placed at the head of a body of troops than he approved himself a man born for conquest and command. Among the crowd of chiefs who were struggling for a share of India, none could compare with him in the qualities of the captain and the statesman. He became a general; he became a sovereign. Out of the fragments of old principalities, which had gone to pieces in the general wreck, he formed for himself a great, compact, and vigorous empire. That empire he ruled with the ability, severity, and vigilance of Louis the Eleventh. Licentious in his pleasures, implacable in his revenge, he had yet enlargement of mind enough to perceive how much the prosperity of subjects adds to the strength of governments. He was an oppressor; but he had at least the merit of protecting his people against all oppression except his own. He was now in extreme old age; but his intellect was as clear, and his spirit as high, as in the prime of manhood. Such was the great Hyder Ali, the founder of the Mahommedan kingdom of Mysore, and the most formidable enemy with whom the English conquerors of India have ever had to contend.

Had Hastings been governor of Madras, Hyder would have been either made a friend, or vigorously encountered as an enemy.

Unhappily the English authorities in the south provoked their powerful neighbour's hostility, without being prepared to repel it. On a sudden, an army of ninety thousand men, far superior in discipline and efficiency to any other native force that could be found in India, came pouring through those wild passes which, worn by mountain torrents, and dark with jungle, lead down from the table-land of Mysore to the plains of the Carnatic. This great army was accompanied by a hundred pieces of cannon; and its movements were guided by many French officers, trained in the best military schools of Europe.

Hyder was every where triumphant. The sepoys in many British garrisons flung down their arms. Some forts were surrendered by treachery, and some by despair. In a few days the whole open country north of the Coleroon had submitted. The English inhabitants of Madras could already see by night, from the top of Mount St. Thomas, the eastern sky reddened by a vast semicircle of blazing villages. The white villas, to which our countrymen retire after the daily labours of government and of trade, when the cool evening breeze springs up from the bay, were now left without inhabitants; for bands of the fierce horsemen of Mysore had already been seen prowling among the tulip-trees, and near the gay verandas. Even the town was not thought secure, and the British merchants and public functionaries made haste to crowd themselves behind the cannon of Fort St. George.

There were the means indeed of assembling an army which might have defended the presidency, and even driven the invader back to his mountains. Sir Hector Munro was at the head of one considerable force; Baillie was advancing with another. United, they might have presented a formidable front even to such an enemy as Hyder. But the English commanders, neglecting those fundamental rules of the military art of which the propriety is obvious even to men who have never received a military education, deferred their junction, and were separately attacked. Baillie's detachment was destroyed. Munro was forced to abandon his baggage, to fling his guns into the tanks, and to save himself by a retreat which might be called a flight. In three weeks from the commencement of the war, the British empire in southern India had been brought to the verge of ruin. Only a few fortified places remained to us. The glory of our arms had departed. It was known that a great French expedition might soon be expected on the coast of Coromandel England, beset by enemies on every side, was in no condition to protect such remote dependencies.

Then it was that the fertile genius and serene courage of Hastings achieved their most signal triumph. A swift ship, flying before the south-west monsoon, brought the evil tidings in few days to Calcutta. In twenty-four hours the Governor-General had framed a complete plan of policy adapted to the altered state of affairs. The struggle with Hyder was a struggle for life and death. All minor objects must be sacrificed to the preservation of the Carnatic. The disputes with the Mahrattas must be accommodated. A large military force and a supply of money must be instantly sent to Madras. But even these measures would be insufficient, unless the war, hitherto so grossly mismanaged, were placed under the direction of a vigorous mind. It was no time for trifling. Hastings determined to resort to an extreme exercise of power, to suspend the incapable governor of Fort St. George, to send Sir Eyre Coote to oppose Hyder, and to entrust that distinguished general with the whole administration of the war.

In spite of the sullen opposition of Francis, who had now recovered from his wound, and had returned to the Council, the Governor-General's wise and firm policy was approved by the majority of the board. The reinforcements were sent off with great expedition, and reached Madras before the French armament arrived in the Indian seas. Coote, broken by age and disease, was no longer the Coote of Wandewash; but he was still a resolute and skilful commander. The progress of Hyder was arrested; and in a few months the great victory of Porto Novo retrieved the honour of the English arms.

In the meantime Francis had returned to England, and Hastings was now left perfectly unfettered. Wheler had gradually been relaxing in his opposition, and, after the departure of his vehement and implacable colleague, cooperated heartily with the Governor-General, whose influence over the British in India, always great, had, by the vigour and success of his recent measures, been considerably increased.

But, though the difficulties arising from factions within the Council were at an end, another class of difficulties had become more pressing than ever. The financial embarrassment was extreme. Hastings had to find the means, not only of carrying on the government of Bengal, but of maintaining a most costly war against both Indian and European enemies in the Carnatic, and of making remittances to England. A few years before this time he had obtained relief by plundering the Mogul and enslaving the Rohillas; nor were the resources of his fruitful mind by any means exhausted.

His first design was on Benares, a city which in wealth, population, dignity, and sanctity, was among the foremost of Asia. It was commonly believed that half a million of human beings was crowded into that labyrinth of lofty alleys, rich with shrines, and minarets, and balconies, and carved oriels, to which the sacred apes clung by hundreds. The traveller could scarcely make his way through the press of holy mendicants and not less holy bulls. The broad and stately flights of steps which descended from these swarming haunts to the bathing-places along the Ganges were worn every day by the footsteps of an innumerable multitude of worshippers. The schools and temples drew crowds of pious Hindoos from every province where the Brahminical faith was known. Hundreds of devotees came thither every month to die: for it was believed that a peculiarly happy fate awaited the man who should pass from the sacred city into the sacred river. Nor was superstition the only motive which allured strangers to that great metropolis. Commerce had as many pilgrims as religion. All along the shores of the venerable stream lay great fleets of vessels laden with rich merchandize. From the looms of Benares went forth the most delicate silks that adorned the balls of St. James's and of the *Petit Trianon*; and, in the bazars, the muslins of Bengal and the sabres of Oude were mingled with the jewels of Golconda and the shawls of Cashmere. This rich capital, and the surrounding tract, had long been under the immediate rule of a Hindoo prince, who rendered homage to the Mogul emperors. During the great anarchy of India, the lords of Benares became independent of the court of Delhi, but were compelled to submit to the authority of the Nabob of Oude. Oppressed by this formidable neighbour, they invoked the protection of the English. The English protection was given; and at length the Nabob Vizier, by a solemn treaty, ceded all his rights over Benares to the Company. From that time the Rajah was the vassal of the government of Bengal, acknowledged its supremacy, and engaged to send an annual tribute to Fort William. This tribute Cheyte Sing, the reigning prince, had paid with strict punctuality.

Respecting the precise nature of the legal relation between the Company and the Rajah of Benares, there has been much warm and acute controversy. On the one side, it has been maintained that Cheyte Sing was merely a great subject on whom the superior power had a right to call for aid in the necessities of the empire. On the other side, it has been contended that he was an independent prince, that the only claim which the Company had upon him was for a fixed tribute, and that, while the fixed tribute was regularly paid, as it assuredly was, the English had no more right to exact any further contribution from him than to demand subsidies from

Holland or Denmark. Nothing is easier than to find precedents and analogies in favour of either view.

Our own impression is that neither view is correct. It was too much the habit of English politicians to take it for granted that there was in India a known and definite constitution by which questions of this kind were to be decided. The truth is that, during the interval which elapsed between the fall of the house of Tamerlane and the establishment of the British ascendency, there was no such constitution. The old order of things had passed away; the new order of things was not yet formed. All was transition, confusion, obscurity. Every body kept his head as he best might, and scrambled for whatever he could get. There have been similar seasons in Europe. The time of the dissolution of the Carlovingian empire is an instance. Who would think of seriously discussing the question, what extent of pecuniary aid and of obedience Hugh Capet had a constitutional right to demand from the Duke of Britanny or the Duke of Normandy? The words "constitutional right" had, in that state of society, no meaning. If Hugh Capet laid hands on all the possessions of the Duke of Normandy, this might be unjust and immoral; but it would not be illegal, in the sense in which the ordinances of Charles the Tenth were illegal. If, on the other hand, the Duke of Normandy made war on Hugh Capet, this might be unjust and immoral; but it would not be illegal in the sense in which the expedition of Prince Louis Buonaparte was illegal.

Very similar to this was the state of India sixty years ago. Of the existing governments not a single one could lay claim to legitimacy, or could plead any other title than recent occupation. There was scarcely a province in which the real sovereignty and the nominal sovereignty were not disjoined. Titles and forms were still retained which implied that the heir of Tamerlane was an absolute ruler, and that the Nabobs of the provinces were his lieutenants. In reality, he was a captive. The Nabobs were in some places independent princes. In other places, as in Bengal and the Carnatic, they had, like their master, become mere phantoms, and the Company was supreme. Among the Mahrattas again the heir of Sevajee still kept the title of Rajah; but he was a prisoner, and his prime minister, the Peshwa, had become the hereditary chief of the state. The Peshwa, in his turn, was fast sinking into the same degraded situation to which he had reduced the Rajah. It was, we believe, impossible to find, from the Himalayas to Mysore, a single government which was at once a government *de facto* and a government *de jure*, which possessed the physical means of making itself feared by its neighbours and subjects, and which had at the same time the authority derived from law and long prescription.

Hastings clearly discerned, what was hidden from most of his contemporaries, that such a state of things gave immense advantages to a ruler of great talents and few scruples. In every international question that could arise, he had his option between the *de facto* ground and the *de jure* ground; and the probability was that one of those grounds would sustain any claim that it might be convenient for him to make, and enable him to resist any claim made by others. In every controversy, accordingly, he resorted to the plea which suited his immediate purpose, without troubling himself in the least about consistency; and thus he scarcely ever failed to find what, to persons of short memories and scanty information, seemed to be a justification for what he wanted to do. Sometimes the nabob of Bengal is a shadow, sometimes a monarch. Sometimes the Vizier is a mere deputy, sometimes an independent potentate. If it is expedient for the Company to show some legal title to the revenues of Bengal, the grant under the seal of the Mogul is brought forward as an instrument of the highest authority. When the Mogul asks for the rents which were reserved to him by that very grant, he is told that he is a mere pageant, that the English power rests on a very different foundation from a charter given by him, that he is welcome to play at royalty as long as he likes, but that he must expect no tribute from the real masters of India.

It is true that it was in the power of others, as well as of Hastings, to practise this legerdemain; but in the controversies of governments, sophistry is of little use unless it be backed by power. There is a principle which Hastings was fond of asserting in the strongest terms, and on which he acted with undeviating steadiness. It is a principle which, we must own, though it may be grossly abused, can hardly be disputed in the present state of public law. It is this, that where an ambiguous question arises between two governments, there is, if they cannot agree, no appeal except to force, and that the opinion of the stronger must prevail. Almost every question was ambiguous in India. The English government was the strongest in India. The consequences are obvious. The English government might do exactly what it chose.

The English government now chose to wring money out of Cheyte Sing. It had formerly been convenient to treat him as a sovereign prince; it was now convenient to treat him as a subject. Dexterity inferior to that of Hastings could easily find, in the general chaos of laws and customs, arguments for either course. Hastings wanted a great supply. It was known that Cheyte Sing had a large revenue, and it was suspected that he had accumulated a treasure. Nor was he a favourite at Calcutta. He had, when the Governor-General was in great difficulties, courted the favour of Francis and Clavering. Hastings who, less we believe from evil passions than from policy, seldom left an injury unpunished, was not sorry that the fate of Cheyte Sing should teach neighbouring princes the same lesson which the fate of Nuncomar had already impressed on the inhabitants of Bengal.

In 1778, on the first breaking out of the war with France, Cheyte Sing was called upon to pay, in addition to his fixed tribute, an extraordinary contribution of fifty thousand pounds. In 1779, an equal sum was exacted. In 1780, the demand was renewed. Cheyte Sing, in the hope of obtaining some indulgence, secretly offered the Governor-General a bribe of twenty thousand pounds. Hastings took the money; and his enemies have maintained that he took it intending to keep it. He certainly concealed the transaction, for a time, both from the Council in Bengal and from the Directors at home; nor did he ever give any satisfactory reason for the concealment. Public spirit, or the fear of detection, however, determined him to withstand the temptation. He paid over the bribe to the Company's treasury, and insisted that the Rajah should instantly comply with the demands of the English government. The Rajah, after the fashion of his countrymen, shuffled, solicited, and pleaded poverty. The grasp of Hastings was not to be so eluded. He added to the requisition another ten thousand pounds as a fine for delay, and sent troops to exact the money.

The money was paid. But this was not enough. The late events in the south of India had increased the financial embarrassments of the Company. Hastings was determined to plunder Cheyte Sing, and, for that end, to fasten a quarrel on him. Accordingly, the Rajah was now required to keep a body of cavalry for the service of the British government. He objected and evaded. This was exactly what the Governor-General wanted. He had now a pretext for treating the wealthiest of his vassals as a criminal. "I resolved," —these are the words of Hastings himself,—"to draw from his guilt the means of relief to the Company's distresses, to make him pay largely for his pardon, or to exact a severe vengeance for past delinquency." The plan was simply this, to demand larger and larger contributions till the Rajah should be driven to remonstrate, then to call his remonstrance a crime, and to punish him by confiscating all his possessions.

Cheyte Sing was in the greatest dismay. He offered two hundred thousand pounds to propitiate the British government. But

Hastings replied that nothing less than half a million would be accepted. Nay, he began to think of selling Benares to Oude, as he had formerly sold Allahabad and Rohilcund. The matter was one which could not be well managed at a distance; and Hastings resolved to visit Benares.

Cheyte Sing received his liege lord with every mark of reverence, came near sixty miles, with his guards, to meet and escort the illustrious visiter, and expressed his deep concern at the displeasure of the English. He even took off his turban, and laid it in the lap of Hastings, a gesture which in India marks the most profound submission and devotion. Hastings behaved with cold and repulsive severity. Having arrived at Benares, he sent to the Rajah a paper containing the demands of the government of Bengal. The Rajah, in reply, attempted to clear himself from the accusations brought against him. Hastings, who wanted money and not excuses, was not to be put off by the ordinary artifices of Eastern negotiation. He instantly ordered the Rajah to be arrested and placed under the custody of two companies of sepoys.

In taking these strong measures, Hastings scarcely showed his usual judgment. It is probable that, having had little opportunity of personally observing any part of the population of India, except the Bengalees, he was not fully aware of the difference between their character and that of the tribes which inhabit the upper provinces. He was now in a land far more favourable to the vigour of the human frame than the Delta of the Ganges; in a land fruitful of soldiers, who have been found worthy to follow English battalions to the charge and into the breach. The Rajah was popular among his subjects. His administration had been mild; and the prosperity of the district which he governed presented a striking contrast to the depressed state of Bahar under our rule, and a still more striking contrast to the misery of the provinces which were cursed by the tyranny of the Nabob Vizier. The national and religious prejudices with which the English were regarded throughout India were peculiarly intense in the metropolis of the Brahminical superstition. It can therefore scarcely be doubted that the Governor-General, before he outraged the dignity of Cheyte Sing by an arrest, ought to have assembled a force capable of bearing down all opposition. This had not been done. The handful of sepoys who attended Hastings would probably have been sufficient to overawe Moorshedabad, or the Black Town of Calcutta. But they were unequal to a conflict with the hardy rabble of Benares. The streets surrounding the palace were filled by an immense multitude, of whom a large proportion, as is usual in Upper India, wore arms. The tumult became a fight, and the fight a massacre. The English officers defended themselves with desperate courage against overwhelming numbers, and fell, as became them, sword in hand. The sepoys were butchered. The gates were forced. The captive prince, neglected by his gaolers during the confusion, discovered an outlet which opened on the precipitous bank of the Ganges, let himself down to the water by a string made of the turbans of his attendants, found a boat, and escaped to the opposite shore.

If Hastings had, by indiscreet violence, brought himself into a difficult and perilous situation, it is only just to acknowledge that he extricated himself with even more than his usual ability and presence of mind. He had only fifty men with him. The building in which he had taken up his residence was on every side blockaded by the insurgents. But his fortitude remained unshaken. The Rajah from the other side of the river sent apologies and liberal offers. They were not even answered. Some subtle and enterprizing men were found who undertook to pass through the throng of enemies, and to convey the intelligence of the late events to the English cantonments. It is the fashion of the natives of India to wear large earrings of gold. When they travel, the rings are laid aside, lest the precious metal should tempt some gang of robbers; and, in place of the ring, a quill or a roll of paper is inserted in the orifice to prevent it from closing. Hastings placed in the ears of his messengers letters rolled up in the smallest compass. Some of these letters were addressed to the commanders of the English troops. One was written to assure his wife of his safety. One was to the envoy whom he had sent to negotiate with the Mahrattas. Instructions for the negotiation were needed; and the Governor-General framed them in that situation of extreme danger, with as much composure as if he had been writing in his palace at Calcutta.

Things, however, were not yet at the worst. An English officer of more spirit than judgment, eager to distinguish himself, made a premature attack on the insurgents beyond the river. His troops were entangled in narrow streets, and assailed by a furious population. He fell, with many of his men; and the survivors were forced to retire.

This event produced the effect which has never failed to follow every check, however slight, sustained in India by the English arms. For hundreds of miles round, the whole country was in commotion. The entire population of the district of Benares took arms. The fields were abandoned by the husbandmen, who thronged to defend their prince. The infection spread to Oude. The oppressed people of that province rose up against the Nabob Vizier, refused to pay their imposts, and put the revenue officers to flight. Even Bahar was ripe for revolt. The hopes of Cheyte Sing began to rise. Instead of imploring mercy in the humble style of a vassal, he began to talk the language of a conqueror, and threatened, it was said, to sweep the white usurpers out of the land. But the English troops were now assembling fast. The officers, and even the private men, regarded the Governor-General with enthusiastic attachment, and flew to his aid with an alacrity which, as he boasted, had never been shown on any other occasion. Major Popham, a brave and skilful soldier who had highly distinguished himself in the Mahratta war, and in whom the Governor-General reposed the greatest confidence, took the command. The tumultuary army of the Rajah was put to rout. His fastnesses were stormed. In a few hours, above thirty thousand men left his standard, and returned to their ordinary avocations. The unhappy prince fled from his country for ever. His fair domain was added to the British dominions. One of his relations indeed was appointed rajah; but the Rajah of Benares was henceforth to be, like the Nabob of Bengal, a mere pensioner.

By this revolution, an addition of two hundred thousand pounds a-year was made to the revenues of the Company. But the immediate relief was not as great as had been expected. The treasure laid up by Cheyte Sing had been popularly estimated at a million sterling. It turned out to be about a fourth part of that sum; and, such as it was, it was seized by the army and divided as prize-money.

Disappointed in his expectations from Benares, Hastings was more violent than he would otherwise have been, in his dealings with Oude. Sujah Dowlah had long been dead. His son and successor, Asaph-ul-Dowlah, was one of the weakest and most vicious even of Eastern princes. His life was divided between torpid repose and the most odious forms of sensuality. In his court there was boundless waste, throughout his dominions wretchedness and disorder. He had been, under the skilful management of the English government, gradually sinking from the rank of an independent prince to that of a vassal of the Company. It was only by the help of a British brigade that he could be secure from the aggressions of neighbours who despised his weakness, and from the vengeance of subjects who detested his tyranny. A brigade was furnished; and he engaged to defray the charge of paying and maintaining it. From that time his independence was at an end. Hastings was not a man to lose the advantage which he had thus gained. The Nabob soon began to complain of the burden which he had undertaken to bear. His revenues, he said, were falling off;

his servants were unpaid; he could no longer support the expense of the arrangement which he had sanctioned. Hastings would not listen to these representations. The Vizier, he said, had invited the Government of Bengal to send him troops, and had promised to pay for them. The troops had been sent. How long the troops were to remain in Oude was a matter not settled by the treaty. It remained, therefore, to be settled between the contracting parties. But the contracting parties differed. Who then must decide? The stronger.

Hastings also argued that, if the English force was withdrawn, Oude would certainly become a prey to anarchy, and would probably be overrun by a Mahratta army. That the finances of Oude were embarrassed he admitted. But he contended, not without reason, that the embarrassment was to be attributed to the incapacity and vices of Asaph-ul-Dowlah himself, and that, if less were spent on the troops, the only effect would be that more would be squandered on worthless favourites.

Hastings had intended, after settling the affairs of Benares, to visit Lucknow, and there to confer with Asaph-ul-Dowlah. But the obsequious courtesy of the Nabob Vizier prevented this visit. With a small train he hastened to meet the Governor-General. An interview took place in the fortress which, from the crest of the precipitous rock of Chunar, looks down on the waters of the Ganges.

At first sight it might appear impossible that the negotiation should come to an amicable close. Hastings wanted an extraordinary supply of money. Asaph-ul-Dowlah wanted to obtain a remission of what he already owed. Such a difference seemed to admit of no compromise. There was, however, one course satisfactory to both sides, one course by which it was possible to relieve the finances both of Oude and of Bengal; and that course was adopted. It was simply this, that the Governor-General and the Nabob Vizier should join to rob a third party; and the third party whom they determined to rob was the parent of one of the robbers.

The mother of the late Nabob, and his wife, who was the mother of the present Nabob, were known as the Begums or Princesses of Oude. They had possessed great influence over Sujah Dowlah, and had, at his death, been left in possession of a splendid dotation. The domains of which they received the rents and administered the government were of wide extent. The treasure hoarded by the late Nabob, a treasure which was popularly estimated at near three millions sterling, was in their hands. They continued to occupy his favourite palace at Fyzabad, the Beautiful Dwelling; while Asaph-ul-Dowlah held his court in the stately Lucknow, which he had built for himself on the shores of the Goomti, and had adorned with noble mosques and colleges.

Asaph-ul-Dowlah had already extorted considerable sums from his mother. She had at length appealed to the English; and the English had interfered. A solemn compact had been made, by which she consented to give her son some pecuniary assistance, and he in his turn promised never to commit any further invasion of her rights. This compact was formerly guaranteed by the government of Bengal. But times had changed; money was wanted; and the power which had given the guarantee was not ashamed to instigate the spoiler to excesses such that even he shrank from them.

It was necessary to find some pretext for a confiscation inconsistent, not merely with plighted faith, not merely with the ordinary rules of humanity and justice, but also with that great law of filial piety which, even in the wildest tribes of savages, even in those more degraded communities which wither under the influence of a corrupt half-civilization, retains a certain authority over the human mind. A pretext was the last thing that Hastings was likely to want. The insurrection at Benares had produced disturbances in Oude. These disturbances it was convenient to impute to the Princesses. Evidence for the imputation there was scarcely any; unless reports wandering from one mouth to another, and gaining something by every transmission, may be called evidence. The accused were furnished with no charge; they were permitted to make no defence; for the Governor-General wisely considered that, if he tried them, he might not be able to find a ground for plundering them. It was agreed between him and the Nabob Vizier that the noble ladies should, by a sweeping measure of confiscation, be stripped of their domains and treasures for the benefit of the Company, and that the sums thus obtained should be accepted by the government of Bengal in satisfaction of its claims on the government of Oude.

While Asaph-ul-Dowlah was at Chunar, he was completely subjugated by the clear and commanding intellect of the English statesman. But, when they had separated, the Vizier began to reflect with uneasiness on the engagement into which he had entered. His mother and grandmother protested and implored. His heart, deeply corrupted by absolute power and licentious pleasures, yet not naturally unfeeling, failed him in this crisis. Even the English resident at Lucknow, though hitherto devoted to Hastings, shrank from extreme measures. But the Governor-General was inexorable. He wrote to the resident in terms of the greatest severity, and declared that, if the spoliation which had been agreed upon were not instantly carried into effect, he would himself go to Lucknow, and do that from which feebler minds recoil with dismay. The resident, thus menaced, waited on his Highness, and insisted that the treaty of Chunar should be carried into full and immediate effect. Asaph-ul-Dowlah yielded, making at the same time a solemn protestation that he yielded to compulsion. The lands were resumed; but the treasure was not so easily obtained. It was necessary to use violence. A body of the Company's troops marched to Fyzabad, and forced the gates of the palace. The Princesses were confined to their own apartments. But still they refused to submit. Some more stringent mode of coercion was to be found. A mode was found of which, even at this distance of time, we cannot speak without shame and sorrow.

There were at Fyzabad two ancient men, belonging to that unhappy class which a practice, of immemorial antiquity in the East, has excluded from the pleasures of love and from the hope of posterity. It has always been held in Asiatic courts that beings thus estranged from sympathy with their kind are those whom princes may most safely trust. Sujah Dowlah had been of this opinion. He had given his entire confidence to the two eunuchs; and after his death they remained at the head of the household of his widow.

These men were, by the orders of the British government, seized, imprisoned, ironed, starved almost to death, in order to extort money from the Princesses. After they had been two months in confinement, their health gave way. They implored permission to take a little exercise in the garden of their prison. The officer who was in charge of them stated that, if they were allowed this indulgence, there was not the smallest chance of their escaping, and that their irons really added nothing to the security of the custody in which they were kept. He did not understand the plan of his superiors. Their object in these inflictions was not security but torture; and all mitigation was refused. Yet this was not the worst. It was resolved by an English government that these two infirm old men should be delivered to the tormentors. For that purpose they were removed to Lucknow. What horrors their dungeon there witnessed can only be guessed. But there remains on the records of Parliament this letter, written by a British resident to a British soldier.

"Sir, the Nabob having determined to inflict corporal punishment upon the prisoners under your guard, this is to desire that his officers, when they shall come, may have free access to the prisoners, and be permitted to do with them as they shall see proper."

While these barbarities were perpetrated at Lucknow, the Princesses were still under duresse at Fyzabad. Food was allowed to enter their apartments only in such scanty quantities that their female attendants were in danger of perishing with hunger. Month after month this cruelty continued, till at length, after twelve hundred thousand pounds had been wrung out of the Princesses, Hastings began to think that he had really got to the bottom of their revenue, and that no rigour could extort more. Then at length the wretched men who were detained at Lucknow regained their liberty. When their irons were knocked off, and the doors of their prison opened, their quivering lips, the tears which ran down their cheeks, and the thanksgivings which they poured forth to the common Father of Mussulmans and Christians, melted even the stout hearts of the English warriors who stood by.

There is a man to whom the conduct of Hastings, through the whole of these proceedings, appears not only excusable but laudable. There is a man who tells us that he "must really be pardoned if he ventures to characterize as something preeminently ridiculous and wicked, the sensibility which would balance against the preservation of British India a little personal suffering, which was applied only so long as the sufferers refused to deliver up a portion of that wealth, the whole of which their own and their mistresses' treason had forfeited." We cannot, we must own, envy the reverend biographer, either his singular notion of what constitutes preeminent wickedness, or his equally singular perception of the preeminently ridiculous. Is this the generosity of an English soldier? Is this the charity of a Christian priest? Could neither Mr. Gleig's professions teach him the first rudiments of morality? Or is morality a thing which may be well enough in sermons, but which has nothing to do with biography?

But we must not forget to do justice to Sir Elijah Impey's conduct on this occasion. It was not indeed easy for him to intrude himself into a business so entirely alien from all his official duties. But there was something inexpressibly alluring, we must suppose, in the peculiar rankness of the infamy which was then to be got at Lucknow. He hurried thither as fast as relays of palankin-bearers could carry him. A crowd of people came before him with affidavits against the Begums, ready drawn in their hands. Those affidavits he did not read. Some of them, indeed, he could not read; for they were in the dialects of Northern India, and no interpreter was employed.[1] He administered the oath to the deponents, with all

[1] This passage has been slightly altered. As it originally stood, Sir Elijah Impey was described as ignorant of all the native languages in which the depositions were drawn. A writer who apparently has had access to some private source of information has contradicted this state-

possible expedition, and asked not a single question, not even whether they had perused the statements to which they swore. This work performed, he got again into his palankin, and posted back to Calcutta, to be in time for the opening of term. The cause was one which, by his own confession, lay altogether out of his jurisdiction. Under the charter of justice, he had no more right to inquire into crimes committed by natives in Oude than the Lord President of the Court of Session of Scotland to hold an assize at Exeter. He had no right to try the Begums, nor did he pretend to try them. With what object, then, did he undertake so long a journey? Evidently in order that he might give, in an irregular manner, that sanction which in a regular manner he could not give, to the crimes of those who had recently hired him; and in order that a confused mass of testimony which he did not sift, which he did not even read, might acquire an authority not properly belonging to it, from the signature of the highest judicial functionary in India.

The time was approaching, however, when he was to be stripped of that robe which has never, since the Revolution, been disgraced so foully as by him. The state of India had for some time occupied much of the attention of the British Parliament. Towards the close of the American war, two committees of the Commons sat on Eastern affairs. In one Edmund Burke took the lead. The other was under the presidency of the able and versatile Henry Dundas, then Lord Advocate of Scotland. Great as are the changes which, during the last sixty years, have taken place in our Asiatic dominions, the reports which those committees laid on the table of the House will still be found most interesting and instructive.

There was as yet no connexion between the Company and either of the great parties in the state. The ministers had no motive to defend Indian abuses. On the contrary, it was for their interest to show, if possible, that the government and patronage of our Oriental empire might, with advantage, be transferred to themselves. The votes therefore, which, in consequence of the reports made by the two committees, were passed by the Commons, breathed the spirit of stern and indignant justice. The severest epithets were applied

---

ment, and has asserted that Sir Elijah knew Persian and Bengalee. Some of the depositions were certainly in Persian. Those therefore Sir Elijah might have read if he had chosen to do so. But others were in the vernacular dialects of Upper India, with which it is not alleged that he had any acquaintance. Why the Bengalee is mentioned it is not easy to guess. Bengalee at Lucknow would have been as useless as Portuguese in Switzerland.

to several of the measures of Hastings, especially to the Rohilla war; and it was resolved, on the motion of Mr. Dundas, that the Company ought to recall a Governor-General who had brought such calamities on the Indian people, and such dishonour on the British name. An act was passed for limiting the jurisdiction of the Supreme Court. The bargain which Hastings had made with the Chief Justice was condemned in the strongest terms; and an address was presented to the king, praying that Impey might be ordered home to answer for his misdeeds.

Impey was recalled by a letter from the Secretary of State. But the proprietors of India Stock resolutely refused to dismiss Hastings from their service, and passed a resolution affirming, what was undeniably true, that they were entrusted by law with the right of naming and removing their Governor-General, and that they were not bound to obey the directions of a single branch of the legislature with respect to such nomination or removal.

Thus supported by his employers, Hastings remained at the head of the government of Bengal till the spring of 1785. His administration, so eventful and stormy, closed in almost perfect quiet. In the Council there was no regular opposition to his measures. Peace was restored to India. The Mahratta war had ceased. Hyder was no more. A treaty had been concluded with his son, Tippoo; and the Carnatic had been evacuated by the armies of Mysore. Since the termination of the American war, England had no European enemy or rival in the Eastern seas.

On a general review of the long administration of Hastings, it is impossible to deny that, against the great crimes by which it is blemished, we have to set off great public services. England had passed through a perilous crisis. She still, indeed, maintained her place in the foremost rank of European powers; and the manner in which she had defended herself against fearful odds had inspired surrounding nations with a high opinion both of her spirit and of her strength. Nevertheless, in every part of the world, except one, she had been a loser. Not only had she been compelled to acknowledge the independence of thirteen colonies peopled by her children, and to conciliate the Irish by giving up the right of legislating for them; but, in the Mediterranean, in the Gulf of Mexico, on the coast of Africa, on the continent of America, she had been compelled to cede the fruits of her victories in former wars. Spain regained Minorca and Florida; France regained Senegal, Goree, and several West Indian Islands. The only quarter of the world in which Britain had lost nothing was the quarter in which her interests had been committed to the care of Hastings. In spite of the utmost exertions both of European and Asiatic enemies, the power of our country in the East had been greatly augmented. Benares was subjected; the Nabob Vizier reduced to vassalage. That our influence had been thus extended, nay, that Fort William and Fort St. George had not been occupied by hostile armies, was owing, if we may trust the general voice of the English in India, to the skill and resolution of Hastings.

His internal administration, with all its blemishes, gives him a title to be considered as one of the most remarkable men in our history. He dissolved the double government. He transferred the direction of affairs to English hands. Out of a frightful anarchy, he educed at least a rude and imperfect order. The whole organization by which justice was dispensed, revenue collected, peace maintained, throughout a territory not inferior in population to the dominions of Louis the Sixteenth or of the Emperor Joseph, was formed and superintended by him. He boasted that every public office, without exception, which existed when he left Bengal was his creation. It is quite true that this system, after all the improvements suggested by the experience of sixty years, still needs improvement, and that it was at first far more defective than it now is. But whoever seriously considers what it is to construct from the beginning the whole of a machine so vast and complex as a government will allow that what Hastings effected deserves high admiration. To compare the most celebrated European ministers to him seems to us as unjust as it would be to compare the best baker in London with Robinson Crusoe, who, before he could bake a single loaf, had to make his plough and his harrow, his fences and his scarecrows, his sickle and his flail, his mill and his oven.

The just fame of Hastings rises still higher, when we reflect that he was not bred a statesman; that he was sent from school to a counting-house; and that he was employed during the prime of his manhood as a commercial agent, far from all intellectual society.

Nor must we forget that all, or almost all, to whom, when placed at the head of affairs, he could apply for assistance, were persons who owed as little as himself, or less than himself, to education. A minister in Europe finds himself, on the first day on which he commences his functions, surrounded by experienced public servants, the depositaries of official traditions. Hastings had no such help. His own reflection, his own energy, were to supply the place of all Downing Street and Somerset House. Having had no facilities for learning, he was forced to teach. He had first to form himself, and then to form his instruments; and this not in a single department, but in all the departments of the administration.

It must be added that, while engaged in this most arduous task, he was constantly trammelled by orders from home, and frequently borne down by a majority in council. The preservation of an Empire from a formidable combination of foreign enemies, the construction of a government in all its parts, were accomplished by him, while every ship brought out bales of censure from his employers, and while the records of every consultation were filled with acrimonious minutes by his colleagues. We believe that there never was a public man whose temper was so severely tried; not Marlborough, when thwarted by the Dutch Deputies; not Wellington, when he had to deal at once with the Portuguese Regency, the Spanish Juntas, and Mr. Percival. But the temper of Hastings was equal to almost any trial. It was not sweet; but it was calm. Quick and vigorous as his intellect was, the patience with which he endured the most cruel vexations, till a remedy could be found, resembled the patience of stupidity. He seems to have been capable of resentment, bitter and long-enduring; yet his resentment so seldom hurried him into any blunder that it may be doubted whether what appeared to be revenge was any thing but policy.

The effect of his singular equanimity was that he always had the full command of all the resources of one of the most fertile minds that ever existed. Accordingly, no complication of perils and embarrassments could perplex him. For every difficulty he had a contrivance ready; and, whatever may be thought of the justice and humanity of some of his contrivances, it is certain that they seldom failed to serve the purpose for which they were designed.

Together with this extraordinary talent for devising expedients, Hastings possessed, in a very high degree, another talent scarcely less necessary to a man in his situation; we mean the talent for conducting political controversy. It is as necessary to an English statesman in the East that he should be able to write, as it is to a minister in this country that he should be able to speak. It is chiefly by the oratory of a public man here that the nation judges of his powers. It is from the letters and reports of a public man in India that the dispensers of patronage form their estimate of him. In each case, the talent which receives peculiar encouragement is developed, perhaps at the expense of the other powers. In this country, we sometimes hear men speak above their abilities. It is not very unusual to find gentlemen in the Indian service who write above their abilities. The English politician is a little too much of a debater; the Indian politician a little too much of an essayist.

Of the numerous servants of the Company who have distinguished themselves as framers of minutes and despatches, Hastings stands at the head. He was indeed the person who gave to the official writing of the Indian governments the character which it still retains. He was matched against no common antagonist. But even Francis was forced to acknowledge, with sullen and resentful candour, that there was no contending against the pen of Hastings. And, in truth, the Governor-General's power of making out a case, of perplexing what it was inconvenient that people should understand, and of setting in the clearest point of view whatever would bear the light, was incomparable. His style must be praised with some reservation. It was in general forcible, pure, and polished; but it was sometimes, though not often, turgid, and, on one or two occasions, even bombastic. Perhaps the fondness of Hastings for Persian literature may have tended to corrupt his taste.

And, since we have referred to his literary tastes, it would be most unjust not to praise the judicious encouragement which, as a ruler, he gave to liberal studies and curious researches. His patronage was extended, with prudent generosity, to voyages, travels, experiments, publications. He did little, it is true, towards introducing into India the learning of the West. To make the young natives of Bengal familiar with Milton and Adam Smith, to substitute the geography, astronomy, and surgery of Europe for the dotages of the Brahminical superstition, or for the imperfect science of ancient Greece transfused through Arabian expositions, this was a scheme reserved to crown the beneficent administration of a far more virtuous ruler. Still, it is impossible to refuse high commendation to a man who, taken from a ledger to govern an empire, overwhelmed by public business, surrounded by people as busy as himself, and separated by thousands of leagues from almost all literary society, gave, both by his example and by his munificence, a great impulse to learning. In Persian and Arabic literature he was deeply skilled. With the Sanscrit he was not himself acquainted; but those who first brought that language to the knowledge of European students owed much to his encouragement. It was under his protection that the Asiatic Society commenced its honourable career. That distinguished body selected him to be its first president; but, with excellent taste and feeling, he declined the honour in favour of Sir William Jones. But the chief advantage which the students of Oriental letters derived from his patronage remains to be mentioned. The Pundits of Bengal had always looked with great jealousy on the attempts of foreigners to pry into those mysteries which were locked up in the sacred dialect. Their religion had been persecuted by the Mahommedans. What they knew of the spirit of the Portuguese government might warrant them in apprehending persecution from Christians. That apprehension, the wisdom and moderation of Hastings removed. He was the first foreign ruler who succeeded in gaining the confidence of the hereditary priests of India, and who induced them to lay open to English scholars the secrets of the old Brahminical theology and jurisprudence.

It is indeed impossible to deny that, in the great art of inspiring large masses of human beings with confidence and attachment, no ruler ever surpassed Hastings. If he had made himself popular with the English by giving up the Bengalees to extortion and oppression, or if, on the other hand, he had conciliated the Bengalees and alienated the English, there would have been no cause for wonder. What is peculiar to him is that, being the chief of a small band of strangers who exercised boundless power over a great indigenous population, he made himself beloved both by the subject many and by the dominant few. The affection felt for him by the civil service was singularly ardent and constant. Through all his disasters and perils, his brethren stood by him with steadfast loyalty. The army, at the same time, loved him as armies have seldom loved any but the greatest chiefs who have led them to victory. Even in his disputes with distinguished military men, he could always count on the support of the military profession. While such was his empire over the hearts of his countrymen, he enjoyed among the natives a popularity, such as other governors have perhaps better merited, but such as no other governor has been able to attain. He spoke their vernacular dialects with facility and precision. He was intimately acquainted with their feelings and usages. On one or two occasions, for great ends, he deliberately acted in defiance of their opinion; but on such occasions he gained more in their respect than he lost in their love. In general, he carefully avoided all that could shock their national or religious prejudices. His administration was indeed in many respects faulty; but the Bengalee standard of good government was not high. Under the Nabobs, the hurricane of Mahratta cavalry had passed annually over the rich alluvial plain. But even the Mahratta shrank from a conflict with the mighty children of the sea; and the immense rice-harvests of the Lower Ganges were safely gathered in, under the protection of the English sword. The first English conquerors had been more rapacious and merciless even than the Mahrattas; but that generation had passed away. Defective as was the police, heavy as were the public burdens, it is probable that the oldest man in Bengal could not recollect a season of equal security and prosperity. For the first time within living memory, the province was placed under a government strong enough to prevent others from robbing, and not inclined to play the robber itself. These things inspired good-will. At the same time, the constant success of Hastings and the manner in which he extricated himself from every difficulty made him an object of superstitious admiration; and the more than regal splendour which he sometimes displayed dazzled a people who have much in common with children. Even now, after the lapse of more than fifty years, the natives of India still talk of him as the greatest of the English; and nurses sing children to sleep with a jingling ballad about the fleet horses and richly caparisoned elephants of Sahib Warren Hostein.

The gravest offences of which Hastings was guilty did not affect his popularity with the people of Bengal; for those offences were committed against neighbouring states. Those offences, as our readers must have perceived, we are not disposed to vindicate; yet, in order that the censure may be justly apportioned to the transgression, it is fit that the motive of the criminal should be taken into consideration. The motive which prompted the worst acts of Hastings was misdirected and ill-regulated public spirit. The rules of justice, the sentiments of humanity, the plighted faith of treaties, were in his view as nothing, when opposed to the immediate interests of the state. This is no justification, according to the principles either of morality, or of what we believe to be identical with morality, namely, far-sighted policy. Nevertheless the common sense of mankind, which in questions of this sort seldom goes far wrong, will always recognise a distinction between crimes which originate in an inordinate zeal for the commonwealth, and crimes which originate in selfish cupidity. To the benefit of this distinction Hastings is fairly entitled. There is, we conceive, no reason to suspect that the Rohilla war, the revolution of Benares, or the spoliation of the Princesses of Oude, added a rupee to his fortune. We will not affirm that, in all pecuniary dealings, he showed that punctilious integrity, that dread of the faintest appearance of evil, which is now the glory of the Indian civil service. But when the school in which he had been trained and the temptations to which he was exposed are considered, we are more inclined to praise him for his general uprightness with respect to money, than rigidly to blame him for a few transactions which would now be called indelicate and irregular, but which even now would hardly be designated as corrupt. A rapacious man he certainly was not. Had he been so, he would infallibly have returned to his country the richest subject in Europe. We speak within compass, when we say that, without applying any extraordinary pressure, he might easily have obtained from the zemindars of the Company's provinces and from neighbouring princes, in the course of thirteen years, more than three millions sterling, and might have outshone the splendour of Carlton House and of the *Palais Royal*. He brought home a fortune such as a Governor-General, fond of state, and careless of thrift, might easily, during so long a tenure of office, save out of his legal salary. Mrs. Hastings, we are afraid, was less scrupulous. It was generally believed that she accepted presents with great alacrity, and that she thus formed, without the connivance of her husband, a private hoard amounting to several lacs of rupees. We are the more inclined to give credit to this story, because Mr. Gleig, who cannot but have heard it, does not, as far as we have observed, notice or contradict it.

The influence of Mrs. Hastings over her husband was indeed such that she might easily have obtained much larger sums than she was ever accused of receiving. At length her health began to give way; and the Governor-General, much against his will, was compelled to send her to England. He seems to have loved her with that love which is peculiar to men of strong minds, to men whose affection is not easily won or widely diffused. The talk of Calcutta ran for some time on the luxurious manner in which he fitted up the round-house of an Indiaman for her accommodation, on the profusion of sandal-wood and carved ivory which adorned her cabin, and on the thousands of rupees which had been expended in order to procure for her the society of an agreeable female companion during the voyage. We may remark here that the letters of Hastings to his wife are exceedingly characteristic. They are tender, and full of indications of esteem and confidence; but, at the same time, a little more ceremonious than is usual in so intimate a relation. The solemn courtesy with which he compliments "his elegant Marian" reminds us now and then of the dignified air with which Sir Charles Grandison bowed over Miss Byron's hand in the cedar parlour.

After some months Hastings prepared to follow his wife to England. When it was announced that he was about to quit his office, the feeling of the society which he had so long governed manifested itself by many signs. Addresses poured in from Europeans and Asiatics, from civil functionaries, soldiers, and traders. On the day on which he delivered up the keys of office, a crowd of friends and admirers formed a lane to the quay where he embarked. Several barges escorted him far down the river; and some attached friends refused to quit him till the low coast of Bengal was fading from the view, and till the pilot was leaving the ship.

Of his voyage little is known, except that he amused himself with books and with his pen; and that, among the compositions by which he beguiled the tediousness of that long leisure, was a pleasing imitation of Horace's *Otium Divos rogat*. This little poem was inscribed to Mr. Shore, afterwards Lord Teignmouth, a man of whose integrity, humanity, and honour, it is impossible to speak too highly; but who, like some other excellent members of the civil service, extended to the conduct of his friend Hastings an indulgence of which his own conduct never stood in need.

The voyage was, for those times, very speedy. Hastings was little more than four months on the sea. In June 1785, he landed at Plymouth, posted to London, appeared at Court, paid his respects in Leadenhall Street, and then retired with his wife to Cheltenham.

He was greatly pleased with his reception. The King treated him with marked distinction. The Queen, who had already incurred much censure on account of the favour which, in spite of the ordinary severity of her virtue, she had shown to the "elegant Marian," was not less gracious to Hastings. The Directors received him in a solemn sitting; and their chairman read to him a vote of thanks which they had passed without one dissentient voice. "I find myself," said Hastings, in a letter written about a quarter of a year after his arrival in England, "I find myself every where, and universally, treated with evidences, apparent even to my own observation, that I possess the good opinion of my country."

The confident and exulting tone of his correspondence about this time is the more remarkable, because he had already received ample notice of the attack which was in preparation. Within a week after he landed at Plymouth, Burke gave notice in the House of Commons of a motion seriously affecting a gentleman lately returned from India. The session, however, was then so far advanced, that it was impossible to enter on so extensive and important a subject.

Hastings, it is clear, was not sensible of the danger of his position. Indeed that sagacity, that judgment, that readiness in devising expedients, which had distinguished him in the East, seemed now to have forsaken him; not that his abilities were at all impaired; not that he was not still the same man who had triumphed over Francis and Nuncomar, who had made the Chief Justice and the Nabob Vizier his tools, who had deposed Cheyte Sing, and repelled Hyder Ali. But an oak, as Mr. Grattan finely said, should not be transplanted at fifty. A man who, having left England when a boy, returns to it after thirty or forty years passed in India, will find, be his talents what they may, that he has much both to learn and to unlearn before he can take a place among English statesmen. The working of a representative system, the war of parties, the arts of debate, the influence of the press, are startling novelties to him. Surrounded on every side by new machines and new tactics, he is as much bewildered as Hannibal would have been at Waterloo, or Themistocles at Trafalgar. His very acuteness deludes him. His very vigour causes him to stumble. The more correct his maxims, when applied to the state of society to which he is accustomed, the more certain they are to lead him astray. This was strikingly the case with Hastings. In India he had a bad hand; but he was master of the game, and he won every stake. In England he held excellent cards, if he had known how to play them; and it was chiefly by his own errors that he was brought to the verge of ruin.

Of all his errors the most serious was perhaps the choice of a champion. Clive, in similar circumstances, had made a singularly happy selection. He put himself into the hands of Wedderburn, afterwards Lord Loughborough, one of the few great advocates who have also been great in the House of Commons. To the defence of Clive, therefore, nothing was wanting, neither learning nor knowledge of the world, neither forensic acuteness nor that eloquence which charms political assemblies. Hastings entrusted his interests to a very different person, a major in the Bengal army, named Scott. This gentleman had been sent over from India some time before as the agent of the Governor-General. It was rumoured that his services were rewarded with Oriental munificence; and we believe that he received much more than Hastings could conveniently spare. The Major obtained a seat in Parliament, and was there regarded as the organ of his employer. It was evidently impossible that a gentleman so situated could speak with the authority which belongs to an independent position. Nor had the agent of Hastings the talents necessary for obtaining the ear of an assembly which, accustomed to listen to great orators, had naturally become fastidious. He was always on his legs; he was very tedious; and he had only one topic, the merits and wrongs of Hastings. Every body who knows the House of Commons will easily guess what followed. The Major was soon considered as the greatest bore of his time. His exertions were not confined to Parliament. There was hardly a day on which the newspapers did not contain some puff upon Hastings, signed *Asiaticus* or *Bengalensis*, but known to be written by the indefatigable Scott; and hardly a month in which some bulky pamphlet on the same subject, and from the same pen, did not pass to the trunk-makers and the pastry-cooks. As to this gentleman's capacity for conducting a delicate question through Parliament, our readers will want no evidence beyond that which they will find in letters preserved in these volumes. We will give a single specimen of his temper and judgment. He designated the greatest man then living as "that reptile Mr. Burke."

In spite, however, of this unfortunate choice, the general aspect of affairs was favourable to Hastings. The King was on his side. The Company and its servants were zealous in his cause. Among public men he had many ardent friends. Such were Lord Mansfield, who had outlived the vigour of his body, but not that of his mind; and Lord Lansdowne, who, though unconnected with any party, retained the importance which belongs to great talents and knowledge. The ministers were generally believed to be favourable to the late Governor-General. They owed their power to the clamour which had been raised against Mr. Fox's East India Bill. The authors of that bill, when accused of invading vested rights, and of setting up powers unknown to the constitution, had defended themselves by pointing to the crimes of Hastings, and by arguing that abuses so extraordinary justified extraordinary measures. Those who, by opposing that bill, had raised themselves to the head of affairs, would naturally be inclined to extenuate the evils which had been made the plea for administering so violent a remedy; and such, in fact, was their general disposition. The Lord Chancellor Thurlow, in particular, whose great place and force of intellect gave him a weight in the government inferior only to that of Mr. Pitt, espoused the cause of Hastings with indecorous violence. Mr. Pitt, though he had censured many parts of the Indian system, had studiously abstained from saying a word against the late chief of the Indian government. To Major Scott, indeed, the young minister had in private extolled Hastings as a great, a wonderful man, who had the highest claims on the government. There was only one objection to granting all that so eminent a servant of the public could ask. The resolution of censure still remained on the journals of the House of Commons. That resolution was, indeed, unjust; but, till it was rescinded, could the minister advise the King to bestow any mark of approbation on the person censured? If Major Scott is to be trusted, Mr. Pitt declared that this was the only reason which prevented the government from conferring a peerage on the late Governor-General. Mr. Dundas was the only important member of the administration who was deeply committed to a different view of the subject. He had moved the resolutions which created the difficulty; but even from him little was to be apprehended. Since he presided over the committee on Eastern affairs, great changes had taken place. He was surrounded by new allies; he had fixed his hopes on new objects; and whatever may have been his good qualities,—and he had many,—flattery itself never reckoned rigid consistency in the number.

From the ministry, therefore, Hastings had every reason to expect support; and the ministry was very powerful. The opposition was loud and vehement against him. But the opposition, though formidable from the wealth and influence of some of its members, and from the admirable talents and eloquence of others, was outnumbered in parliament, and odious throughout the country. Nor, as far as we can judge, was the opposition generally desirous to engage in so serious an undertaking as the impeachment of an Indian Governor. Such an impeachment must last for years. It must impose on the chiefs of the party an immense load of labour. Yet it could scarcely, in any manner, affect the event of the great political game. The followers of the coalition were therefore more inclined to revile Hastings than to prosecute him. They lost no opportunity of coupling his name with the names of the most hateful tyrants of whom history makes mention. The wits of Brookes's aimed their keenest sarcasms both at his public and at his domestic life. Some fine diamonds which he had presented, as it was rumoured, to the royal family, and a certain richly carved ivory bed which the Queen had done him the honour to accept from him, were favourite subjects of ridicule. One lively poet proposed, that the great acts of the fair Marian's present husband should be immortalized by the pencil of his predecessor; and that Imhoff should be employed to embellish the House of Commons with paintings of the bleeding Rohillas, of Nuncomar swinging, of Cheyte Sing letting himself down to the Ganges. Another, in an exquisitely humorous parody of Virgil's third eclogue, propounded the question, what that mineral could be of which the rays had power to make the most austere of princesses the friend of a wanton. A third described, with gay malevolence, the gorgeous appearance of Mrs. Hastings at St. James's, the galaxy of jewels, torn from Indian Begums, which adorned her head-dress, her necklace gleaming with future votes, and the depending questions that shone upon her ears. Satirical attacks of this description, and perhaps a motion for a vote of censure, would have satisfied the great body of the opposition. But there were two men whose indignation was not to be so appeased, Philip Francis and Edmund Burke.

Francis had recently entered the House of Commons, and had already established a character there for industry and talent. He laboured indeed under one most unfortunate defect, want of fluency. But he occasionally expressed himself with a dignity and energy worthy of the greatest orators. Before he had been many days in parliament, he incurred the bitter dislike of Pitt, who constantly treated him with as much asperity as the laws of debate would allow. Neither lapse of years nor change of scene had mitigated the enmities which Francis had brought back from the East. After his usual fashion, he mistook his malevolence for virtue, nursed it, as preachers tell us that we ought to nurse our good dispositions, and paraded it, on all occasions, with Pharisaical ostentation.

The zeal of Burke was still fiercer; but it was far purer. Men unable to understand the elevation of his mind have tried to find out some discreditable motive for the vehemence and pertinacity which he showed on this occasion. But they have altogether failed. The idle story that he had some private slight to revenge has long been given up, even by the advocates of Hastings. Mr. Gleig supposes that Burke was actuated by party spirit, that he retained a bitter remembrance of the fall of the coalition, that he attributed that fall to the exertions of the East India interest, and that he considered Hastings as the head and the representative of that interest. This explanation seems to be sufficiently refuted by a reference to dates. The hostility of Burke to Hastings commenced long before the coalition; and lasted long after Burke had become a strenuous supporter of those by whom the coalition had been defeated. It began when Burke and Fox, closely allied together, were attacking the influence of the crown, and calling for peace with the American republic. It continued till Burke, alienated from Fox, and loaded with the favours of the crown, died, preaching a crusade against the French republic. It seems absurd to attribute to the events of 1784 an enmity which began in 1781, and which retained undiminished force long after persons far more deeply implicated than Hastings in the events of 1784 had been cordially forgiven. And why should we look for any other explanation of Burke's conduct than that which we find on the surface? The plain truth is that Hastings had committed some great crimes, and that the thought of those crimes made the blood of Burke boil in his veins. For Burke was a man in whom compassion for suffering, and hatred of injustice and tyranny, were as strong as in Las Casas or Clarkson. And although in him, as in Las Casas and in Clarkson, these noble feelings were alloyed with the infirmity which belongs to human nature, he is, like them, entitled to this great praise, that he devoted years of intense labour to the service of a people with whom he had neither blood nor language, neither religion nor manners in common, and from whom no requital, no thanks, no applause could be expected.

His knowledge of India was such as few, even of those Europeans

who have passed many years in that country, have attained, and
such as certainly was never attained by any public man who had
not quitted Europe. He had studied the history, the laws, and the
usages of the East with an industry, such as is seldom found united
to so much genius and so much sensibility. Others have perhaps
been equally laborious, and have collected an equal mass of
materials. But the manner in which Burke brought his higher
powers of intellect to work on statements of facts, and on tables of
figures, was peculiar to himself. In every part of those huge bales
of Indian information which repelled almost all other readers, his
mind, at once philosophical and poetical, found something to
instruct or to delight. His reason analysed and digested those vast
and shapeless masses; his imagination animated and coloured them.
Out of darkness, and dulness, and confusion, he formed a multitude
of ingenious theories and vivid pictures. He had, in the highest
degree, that noble faculty whereby man is able to live in the past
and in the future, in the distant and in the unreal. India and its
inhabitants were not to him, as to most Englishmen, mere names
and abstractions, but a real country and a real people. The burning
sun, the strange vegetation of the palm and the cocoa-tree, the rice-
field, the tank, the huge trees, older than the Mogul empire, under
which the village crowds assemble, the thatched roof of the
peasant's hut, the rich tracery of the mosque where the imaum prays
with his face to Mecca, the drums, and banners, and gaudy idols,
the devotee swinging in the air, the graceful maiden, with the
pitcher on her head, descending the steps to the river-side, the
black faces, the long beards, the yellow streaks of sect, the turbans
and the flowing robes, the spears and the silver maces, the elephants
with their canopies of state, the gorgeous palankin of the prince,
and the close litter of the noble lady, all those things were to him as
the objects amidst which his own life had been passed, as the objects
which lay on the road between Beaconsfield and St. James's Street.
All India was present to the eye of his mind, from the halls where
suitors laid gold and perfumes at the feet of sovereigns to the wild
moor where the gipsy camp was pitched, from the bazars, humming
like bee-hives with the crowd of buyers and sellers, to the jungle
where the lonely courier shakes his bunch of iron rings to scare
away the hyænas. He had just as lively an idea of the insurrection
at Benares as of Lord George Gordon's riots, and of the execution
of Nuncomar as of the execution of Dr. Dodd. Oppression in
Bengal was to him the same thing as oppression in the streets of
London.

He saw that Hastings had been guilty of some most unjustifiable acts. All that followed was natural and necessary in a mind like Burke's. His imagination and his passions, once excited, hurried him beyond the bounds of justice and good sense. His reason, powerful as it was, became the slave of feelings which it should have controlled. His indignation, virtuous in its origin, acquired too much of the character of personal aversion. He could see no mitigating circumstance, no redeeming merit. His temper which, though generous and affectionate, had always been irritable, had now been made almost savage by bodily infirmities and mental vexations. Conscious of great powers and great virtues, he found himself, in age and poverty, a mark for the hatred of a perfidious court and a deluded people. In Parliament his eloquence was out of date. A young generation, which knew him not, had filled the House. Whenever he rose to speak, his voice was drowned by the unseemly interruptions of lads who were in their cradles when his orations on the Stamp Act called forth the applause of the great Earl of Chatham. These things had produced on his proud and sensitive spirit an effect at which we cannot wonder. He could no longer discuss any question with calmness, or make allowance for honest differences of opinion. Those who think that he was more violent and acrimonious in debates about India than on other occasions are ill informed respecting the last years of his life. In the discussions on the Commercial Treaty with the Court of Versailles, on the Regency, on the French Revolution, he showed even more virulence than in conducting the impeachment. Indeed it may be remarked that the very persons who called him a mischievous maniac, for condemning in burning words the Rohilla war and the spoliation of the Begums, exalted him into a prophet as soon as he began to declaim, with greater vehemence, and not with greater reason, against the taking of the Bastile and the insults offered to Marie Antoinette. To us he appears to have been neither a maniac in the former case, nor a prophet in the latter, but in both cases a great and good man, led into extravagance by a tempestuous sensibility which domineered over all his faculties.

It may be doubted whether the personal antipathy of Francis, or the nobler indignation of Burke, would have led their party to adopt extreme measures against Hastings, if his own conduct had been judicious. He should have felt that, great as his public services had been, he was not faultless; and should have been content to make his escape, without aspiring to the honours of a triumph. He and his agent took a different view. They were impatient for the rewards which, as they conceived, were deferred only till Burke's attack should be over. They accordingly resolved to force a decisive action with an enemy for whom, if they had been wise, they would have made a bridge of gold. On the first day of the session of 1786, Major Scott reminded Burke of the notice given in the preceding year, and asked whether it was seriously intended to bring any charge against the late Governor-General. This challenge left no course open to the Opposition, except to come forward as accusers, or to acknowledge themselves calumniators. The administration of Hastings had not been so blameless, nor was the great party of Fox and North so feeble, that it could be prudent to venture on so bold a defiance. The leaders of the Opposition instantly returned the only answer which they could with honour return; and the whole party was irrevocably pledged to a prosecution.

Burke began his operations by applying for Papers. Some of the documents for which he asked were refused by the ministers, who, in the debate, held language such as strongly confirmed the prevailing opinion, that they intended to support Hastings. In April, the charges were laid on the table. They had been drawn by Burke with great ability, though in a form too much resembling that of a pamphlet. Hastings was furnished with a copy of the accusation; and it was intimated to him that he might, if he thought fit, be heard in his own defence at the bar of the Commons.

Here again Hastings was pursued by the same fatality which had attended him ever since the day when he set foot on English ground. It seemed to be decreed that this man, so politic and so successful in the East, should commit nothing but blunders in Europe. Any judicious adviser would have told him that the best thing which he could do would be to make an eloquent, forcible, and affecting oration at the bar of the House; but that, if he could not trust himself to speak, and found it necessary to read, he ought to be as concise as possible. Audiences accustomed to extemporaneous debating of the highest excellence are always impatient of long written compositions. Hastings, however, sat down as he would have done at the Government-house in Bengal, and prepared a paper of immense length. That paper, if recorded on the consultations of an Indian administration, would have been justly praised as a very able minute. But it was now out of place. It fell flat, as the best written defence must have fallen flat, on an assembly accustomed to the animated and strenuous conflicts of Pitt and Fox. The members, as soon as their curiosity about the face and demeanour of so eminent a stranger was satisfied, walked away to dinner, and left Hastings to tell his story till midnight to the clerks and the sergeant-at-arms.

All preliminary steps having been duly taken, Burke, in the

beginning of June, brought forward the charge relating to the Rohilla war. He acted discreetly in placing this accusation in the van; for Dundas had formerly moved, and the House had adopted, a resolution condemning, in the most severe terms, the policy followed by Hastings with regard to Rohilcund. Dundas had little, or rather nothing, to say in defence of his own consistency; but he put a bold face on the matter, and opposed the motion. Among other things, he declared that, though he still thought the Rohilla war unjustifiable, he considered the services which Hastings had subsequently rendered to the state as sufficient to atone even for so great an offence. Pitt did not speak, but voted with Dundas; and Hastings was absolved by a hundred and nineteen votes against sixty-seven.

Hastings was now confident of victory. It seemed, indeed, that he had reason to be so. The Rohilla war was, of all his measures, that which his accusers might with greatest advantage assail. It had been condemned by the Court of Directors. It had been condemned by the House of Commons. It had been condemned by Mr. Dundas, who had since become the chief minister of the Crown for Indian affairs. Yet Burke, having chosen this strong ground, had been completely defeated on it. That, having failed here, he should succeed on any point, was generally thought impossible. It was rumoured at the clubs and coffee-houses that one or perhaps two more charges would be brought forward, that if, on those charges, the sense of the House of Commons should be against impeachment, the Opposition would let the matter drop, that Hastings would be immediately raised to the peerage, decorated with the star of the Bath, sworn of the privy council, and invited to lend the assistance of his talents and experience to the India board. Lord Thurlow indeed, some months before, had spoken with contempt of the scruples which prevented Pitt from calling Hastings to the House of Lords; and had even said, that if the Chancellor of the Exchequer was afraid of the Commons, there was nothing to prevent the Keeper of the Great Seal from taking the royal pleasure about a patent of peerage. The very title was chosen. Hastings was to be Lord Daylesford. For, through all changes of scene and changes of fortune, remained unchanged his attachment to the spot which had witnessed the greatness and the fall of his family, and which had borne so great a part in the first dreams of his young ambition.

But in a very few days these fair prospects were overcast. On the thirteenth of June, Mr. Fox brought forward, with great ability and eloquence, the charge respecting the treatment of Cheyte Sing.

M—15

Francis followed on the same side. The friends of Hastings were in high spirits when Pitt rose. With his usual abundance and felicity of language, the minister gave his opinion on the case. He maintained that the Governor-General was justified in calling on the Rajah of Benares for pecuniary assistance, and in imposing a fine when that assistance was contumaciously withheld. He also thought that the conduct of the Governor-General during the insurrection had been distinguished by ability and presence of mind. He censured, with great bitterness, the conduct of Francis, both in India and in Parliament, as most dishonest and malignant. The necessary inference from Pitt's arguments seemed to be that Hastings ought to be honourably acquitted; and both the friends and the opponents of the minister expected from him a declaration to that effect. To the astonishment of all parties, he concluded by saying that, though he thought it right in Hastings to fine Cheyte Sing for contumacy, yet the amount of the fine was too great for the occasion. On this ground, and on this ground alone, did Mr. Pitt, applauding every other part of the conduct of Hastings with regard to Benares, declare that he should vote in favour of Mr. Fox's motion.

The House was thunderstruck; and it well might be so. For the wrong done to Cheyte Sing, even had it been as flagitious as Fox and Francis contended, was a trifle when compared with the horrors which had been inflicted on Rohilcund. But if Mr. Pitt's view of the case of Cheyte Sing were correct, there was no ground for an impeachment, or even for a vote of censure. If the offence of Hastings was really no more than this, that, having a right to impose a mulct, the amount of which mulct was not defined, but was left to be settled by his discretion, he had, not for his own advantage, but for that of the state, demanded too much, was this an offence which required a criminal proceeding of the highest solemnity, a criminal proceeding, to which, during sixty years, no public functionary had been subjected? We can see, we think, in what way a man of sense and integrity might have been induced to take any course respecting Hastings, except the course which Mr. Pitt took. Such a man might have thought a great example necessary, for the preventing of injustice, and for the vindicating of the national honour, and might, on that ground, have voted for impeachment both on the Rohilla charge, and on the Benares charge. Such a man might have thought that the offences of Hastings had been atoned for by great services, and might, on that ground, have voted against the impeachment on both charges. With great diffidence, we give it as our opinion that the most correct course would, on the whole, have been to impeach on the Rohilla charge, and to acquit on the Benares charge. Had the Benares charge appeared to us in the same light in which it appeared to Mr. Pitt, we should, without hesitation, have voted for acquittal on that charge. The one course which it is inconceivable that any man of a tenth part of Mr. Pitt's abilities can have honestly taken was the course which he took. He acquitted Hastings on the Rohilla charge. He softened down the Benares charge till it became no charge at all; and then he pronounced that it contained matter for impeachment.

Nor must it be forgotten that the principal reason assigned by the ministry for not impeaching Hastings on account of the Rohilla war was this, that the delinquencies of the early part of his administration had been atoned for by the excellence of the later part. Was it not most extraordinary that men who had held this language could afterwards vote that the later part of his administration furnished matter for no less than twenty articles of impeachment? They first represented the conduct of Hastings in 1780 and 1781 as so highly meritorious that, like works of supererogation in the Catholic theology, it ought to be efficacious for the cancelling of former offences; and they then prosecuted him for his conduct in 1780 and 1781.

The general astonishment was the greater, because, only twenty-four hours before, the members on whom the minister could depend had received the usual notes from the treasury, begging them to be in their places and to vote against Mr. Fox's motion. It was asserted by Mr. Hastings that, early on the morning of the very day on which the debate took place, Dundas called on Pitt, woke him, and was closeted with him many hours. The result of this conference was a determination to give up the late Governor-General to the vengeance of the Opposition. It was impossible even for the most powerful minister to carry all his followers with him in so strange a course. Several persons high in office, the Attorney-General, Mr. Grenville, and Lord Mulgrave, divided against Mr. Pitt. But the devoted adherents who stood by the head of the government without asking questions, were sufficiently numerous to turn the scale. A hundred and nineteen members voted for Mr. Fox's motion; seventy-nine against it. Dundas silently followed Pitt.

That good and great man, the late William Wilberforce, often related the events of this remarkable night. He described the amazement of the House, and the bitter reflections which were muttered against the Prime Minister by some of the habitual supporters of government. Pitt himself appeared to feel that his conduct required some explanation. He left the treasury bench, sat for some time next to Mr. Wilberforce, and very earnestly declared that he had found it impossible, as a man of conscience, to stand any longer by Hastings. The business, he said, was too bad. Mr. Wilberforce, we are bound to add, fully believed that his friend was sincere, and that the suspicions to which this mysterious affair gave rise were altogether unfounded.

Those suspicions, indeed, were such as it is painful to mention. The friends of Hastings, most of whom, it is to be observed, generally supported the administration, affirmed that the motive of Pitt and Dundas was jealousy. Hastings was personally a favourite with the King. He was the idol of the East India Company and of its servants. If he were absolved by the Commons, seated among the Lords, admitted to the Board of Control, closely allied with the strong-minded and imperious Thurlow, was it not almost certain that he would soon draw to himself the entire management of Eastern affairs? Was it not possible that he might become a formidable rival in the cabinet? It had probably got abroad that very singular communications had taken place between Thurlow and Major Scott, and that, if the First Lord of the Treasury was afraid to recommend Hastings for a peerage, the Chancellor was ready to take the responsibility of that step on himself. Of all ministers, Pitt was the least likely to submit with patience to such an encroachment on his functions. If the Commons impeached Hastings, all danger was at an end. The proceeding, however it might terminate, would probably last some years. In the meantime, the accused person would be excluded from honours and public employments, and could scarcely venture even to pay his duty at court. Such were the motives attributed by a great part of the public to the young minister, whose ruling passion was generally believed to be avarice of power.

The prorogation soon interrupted the discussions respecting Hastings. In the following year, those discussions were resumed. The charge touching the spoliation of the Begums was brought forward by Sheridan, in a speech which was so imperfectly reported that it may be said to be wholly lost, but which was, without doubt, the most elaborately brilliant of all the productions of his ingenious mind. The impression which it produced was such as has never been equalled. He sat down, not merely amidst cheering, but amidst the loud clapping of hands, in which the Lords below the bar and the strangers in the gallery joined. The excitement of the House was such that no other speaker could obtain a hearing; and the debate was adjourned. The ferment spread fast through the town. Within four and twenty hours, Sheridan was offered a thousand pounds for the copyright of the speech, if he would himself correct it for the press. The impression made by this remarkable display of eloquence on severe and experienced critics, whose discernment may be supposed to have been quickened by emulation, was deep and permanent. Mr. Windham, twenty years later, said that the speech deserved all its fame, and was, in spite of some faults of taste, such as were seldom wanting either in the literary or in the parliamentary performances of Sheridan, the finest that had been delivered within the memory of man. Mr. Fox, about the same time, being asked by the late Lord Holland what was the best speech ever made in the House of Commons, assigned the first place, without hesitation, to the great oration of Sheridan on the Oude charge.

When the debate was resumed, the tide ran so strongly against the accused that his friends were coughed and scraped down. Pitt declared himself for Sheridan's motion; and the question was carried by a hundred and seventy-five votes against sixty-eight.

The Opposition, flushed with victory and strongly supported by the public sympathy, proceeded to bring forward a succession of charges relating chiefly to pecuniary transactions. The friends of Hastings were discouraged, and, having now no hope of being able to avert an impeachment, were not very strenuous in their exertions. At length the House, having agreed to twenty articles of charge, directed Burke to go before the Lords, and to impeach the late Governor-General of High Crimes and Misdemeanours. Hastings was at the same time arrested by the Sergeant-at-arms, and carried to the bar of the Peers.

The session was now within ten days of its close. It was, therefore, impossible that any progress could be made in the trial till the next year. Hastings was admitted to bail; and further proceedings were postponed till the Houses should re-assemble.

When Parliament met in the following winter, the Commons proceeded to elect a committee for managing the impeachment. Burke stood at the head; and with him were associated most of the leading members of the Opposition. But when the name of Francis was read a fierce contention arose. It was said that Francis and Hastings were notoriously on bad terms, that they had been at feud during many years, that on one occasion their mutual aversion had impelled them to seek each other's lives, and that it would be improper and indelicate to select a private enemy to be a public accuser. It was urged on the other side with great force, particularly by Mr. Windham, that impartiality, though the first duty of a judge, had never been reckoned among the qualities of an advocate; that in the ordinary administration of criminal justice among the English, the aggrieved party, the very last person who ought to be admitted into the jury-box, is the prosecutor; that what was wanted in a manager was, not that he should be free from bias, but that he should be able, well informed, energetic, and active. The ability and information of Francis were admitted; and the very animosity with which he was reproached, whether a virtue or a vice, was at least a pledge for his energy and activity. It seems difficult to refute these arguments. But the inveterate hatred borne by Francis to Hastings had excited general disgust. The House decided that Francis should not be a manager. Pitt voted with the majority, Dundas with the minority.

In the meantime, the preparations for the trial had proceeded rapidly; and on the thirteenth of February, 1788, the sittings of the Court commenced. There have been spectacles more dazzling to the eye, more gorgeous with jewellery and cloth of gold, more attractive to grown-up children, than that which was then exhibited at Westminster; but, perhaps, there never was a spectacle so well calculated to strike a highly cultivated, a reflecting, an imaginative mind. All the various kinds of interest which belong to the near and to the distant, to the present and to the past, were collected on one spot, and in one hour. All the talents and all the accomplishments which are developed by liberty and civilisation were now displayed, with every advantage that could be derived both from cooperation and from contrast. Every step in the proceedings carried the mind either backward, through many troubled centuries, to the days when the foundations of our constitution were laid; or far away, over boundless seas and deserts, to dusky nations living under strange stars, worshipping strange gods, and writing strange characters from right to left. The High Court of Parliament was to sit according to forms handed down from the days of the Plantagenets, on an Englishman accused of exercising tyranny over the lord of the holy city of Benares, and over the ladies of the princely house of Oude.

The place was worthy of such a trial. It was the great hall of William Rufus, the hall which had resounded with acclamations at the inauguration of thirty kings, the hall which had witnessed the just sentence of Bacon and the just absolution of Somers, the hall where the eloquence of Strafford had for a moment awed and melted a victorious party inflamed with just resentment, the hall where Charles had confronted the High Court of Justice with the placid courage which has half redeemed his fame. Neither military nor civil pomp was wanting. The avenues were lined with grenadiers. The streets were kept clear by cavalry. The peers, robed in gold and ermine, were marshalled by the heralds under Garter King-at-arms. The judges in their vestments of state attended to give advice on points of law. Near a hundred and seventy lords, three fourths of the Upper House as the Upper House then was, walked in solemn order from their usual place of assembling to the tribunal. The junior baron present led the way, George Eliott, Lord Heath-field, recently ennobled for his memorable defence of Gibraltar against the fleets and armies of France and Spain. The long procession was closed by the Duke of Norfolk, Earl Marshal of the realm, by the great dignitaries, and by the brothers and sons of the King. Last of all came the Prince of Wales, conspicuous by his fine person and noble bearing. The grey old walls were hung with scarlet. The long galleries were crowded by an audience such as has rarely excited the fears or the emulation of an orator. There were gathered together, from all parts of a great, free, enlightened, and prosperous empire, grace and female loveliness, wit and learning, the representatives of every science and of every art. There were seated round the Queen the fair-haired young daughters of the house of Brunswick. There the Ambassadors of great Kings and Commonwealths gazed with admiration on a spectacle which no other country in the world could present. There Siddons, in the prime of her majestic beauty, looked with emotion on a scene surpassing all the imitations of the stage. There the historian of the Roman Empire thought of the days when Cicero pleaded the cause of Sicily against Verres, and when, before a senate which still retained some show of freedom, Tacitus thundered against the oppressor of Africa. There were seen, side by side, the greatest painter and the greatest scholar of the age. The spectacle had allured Reynolds from that easel which has preserved to us the thoughtful foreheads of so many writers and statesmen, and the sweet smiles of so many noble matrons. It had induced Parr to suspend his labours in that dark and profound mine from which he had extracted a vast treasure of erudition, a treasure too often buried in the earth, too often paraded with injudicious and inelegant ostentation, but still precious, massive, and splendid. There appeared the voluptuous charms of her to whom the heir of the throne had in secret plighted his faith. There too was she, the beautiful mother of a beautiful race, the Saint Cecilia whose delicate features, lighted up by love and music, art has rescued from the common decay. There were the members of that brilliant society which quoted, criticized, and exchanged repartees, under the rich peacock-hangings of Mrs. Montague. And there the ladies whose lips, more persuasive than those of Fox himself, had carried the Westminster election against palace and treasury, shone round Georgiana Duchess of Devonshire.

The Sergeants made proclamation. Hastings advanced to the bar, and bent his knee. The culprit was indeed not unworthy of that great presence. He had ruled an extensive and populous country, had made laws and treaties, had sent forth armies, had set up and pulled down princes. And in his high place he had so borne himself, that all had feared him, that most had loved him, and that hatred itself could deny him no title to glory, except virtue. He looked like a great man, and not like a bad man. A person small and emaciated, yet deriving dignity from a carriage which, while it indicated deference to the court, indicated also habitual self-possession and self-respect, a high and intellectual forehead, a brow pensive, but not gloomy, a mouth of inflexible decision, a face pale and worn, but serene, on which was written, as legibly as under the picture in the council-chamber at Calcutta, *Mens æqua in arduis*; such was the aspect with which the great proconsul presented himself to his judges.

His counsel accompanied him, men all of whom were afterwards raised by their talents and learning to the highest posts in their profession, the bold and strong-minded Law, afterwards Chief Justice of the King's Bench; the more humane and eloquent Dallas, afterwards Chief Justice of the Common Pleas; and Plomer who, near twenty years later, successfully conducted in the same high court the defence of Lord Melville, and subsequently became Vice-chancellor and Master of the Rolls.

But neither the culprit nor his advocates attracted so much notice as the accusers. In the midst of the blaze of red drapery, a space had been fitted up with green benches and tables for the Commons. The managers, with Burke at their head, appeared in full dress. The collectors of gossip did not fail to remark that even Fox, generally so regardless of his appearance, had paid to the illustrious tribunal the compliment of wearing a bag and sword. Pitt had refused to be one of the conductors of the impeachment; and his commanding, copious, and sonorous eloquence was wanting to that great muster of various talents. Age and blindness had unfitted Lord North for the duties of a public prosecutor; and his friends were left without the help of his excellent sense, his tact, and his urbanity. But, in spite of the absence of these two distinguished members of the Lower House, the box in which the managers stood contained an array of speakers such as perhaps had not appeared together since the great age of Athenian eloquence. There were Fox and Sheridan, the English Demosthenes and the English Hyperides. There was Burke, ignorant, indeed, or negligent of the art of adapting his reasonings and his style to the capacity and taste of his hearers, but in amplitude of comprehension and richness of imagination superior to every orator, ancient or modern. There, with eyes reverentially fixed on Burke, appeared the finest gentleman of the age, his form developed by every manly exercise, his face beaming with intelligence and spirit, the ingenious, the chivalrous, the high-souled Windham. Nor, though surrounded by such men, did the youngest manager pass unnoticed. At an age when most of those who distinguish themselves in life are still contending for prizes and fellowships at college, he had won for himself a conspicuous place in parliament. No advantage of fortune or connexion was wanting that could set off to the height his splendid talents and his unblemished honour. At twenty-three he had been thought worthy to be ranked with the veteran statesmen who appeared as the delegates of the British Commons, at the bar of the British nobility. All who stood at that bar, save him alone, are gone, culprit, advocates, accusers. To the generation which is now in the vigour of life, he is the sole representative of a great age which has passed away. But those who, within the last ten years, have listened with delight, till the morning sun shone on the tapestries of the House of Lords, to the lofty and animated eloquence of Charles Earl Grey, are able to form some estimate of the powers of a race of men among whom he was not the foremost.

The charges and the answers of Hastings were first read. This ceremony occupied two whole days, and was rendered less tedious than it would otherwise have been by the silver voice and just emphasis of Cowper, the clerk of the court, a near relation of the amiable poet. On the third day Burke rose. Four sittings were occupied by his opening speech, which was intended to be a general introduction to all the charges. With an exuberance of thought and a splendour of diction which more than satisfied the highly raised expectation of the audience, he described the character and institutions of the natives of India, recounted the circumstances in which the Asiatic empire of Britain had originated, and set forth the constitution of the Company and of the English Presidencies. Having thus attempted to communicate to his hearers an idea of Eastern society, as vivid as that which existed in his own mind, he proceeded to arraign the administration of Hastings as systematically conducted in defiance of morality and public law. The energy and pathos of the great orator extorted expressions of unwonted admiration from the stern and hostile Chancellor, and, for a moment, seemed to pierce even the resolute heart of the defendant. The ladies in the galleries, unaccustomed to such displays of eloquence, excited by the solemnity of the occasion, and perhaps not unwilling to display their taste and sensibility, were in a state of uncontrollable emotion. Handkerchiefs were pulled out; smelling-bottles were handed round; hysterical sobs and screams were heard; and Mrs. Sheridan was carried out in a fit. At length the orator concluded. Raising his voice till the old arches of Irish oak resounded, "Therefore," said he, "hath it with all confidence been ordered by the Commons of Great Britain, that I impeach Warren Hastings of high crimes and misdemeanours. I impeach him in the name of the Commons' House of Parliament whose trust he has betrayed. I impeach him in the name of the English nation, whose ancient honour he has sullied. I impeach him in the name of the people of India, whose rights he has trodden under foot, and whose country he has turned into a desert. Lastly, in the name of human nature itself, in the name of both sexes, in the name of every age, in the name of every rank, I impeach the common enemy and oppressor of all!"

When the deep murmur of various emotions had subsided, Mr. Fox rose to address the Lords respecting the course of proceeding to be followed. The wish of the accusers was that the Court would bring to a close the investigation of the first charge before the second was opened. The wish of Hastings and of his counsel was that the managers should open all the charges, and produce all the evidence for the prosecution, before the defence began. The Lords retired to their own House to consider the question. The Chancellor took the side of Hastings. Lord Loughborough, who was now in opposition, supported the demand of the managers. The division showed which way the inclination of the tribunal leaned. A majority of near three to one decided in favour of the course for which Hastings contended.

When the Court sat again, Mr. Fox, assisted by Mr. Grey, opened the charge respecting Cheyte Sing, and several days were spent in reading papers and hearing witnesses. The next article was that relating to the Princesses of Oude. The conduct of this part of the case was intrusted to Sheridan. The curiosity of the public to hear him was unbounded. His sparkling and highly finished declamation lasted two days; but the Hall was crowded to suffocation during the whole time. It was said that fifty guineas had been paid for a single ticket. Sheridan, when he concluded, contrived, with a knowledge of stage-effect which his father might have envied, to sink back, as if exhausted, into the arms of Burke, who hugged him with the energy of generous admiration.

June was now far advanced. The session could not last much longer; and the progress which had been made in the impeachment was not very satisfactory. There were twenty charges. On two only of these had even the case for the prosecution been heard: and it was now a year since Hastings had been admitted to bail.

The interest taken by the public in the trial was great when the Court began to sit, and rose to the height when Sheridan spoke on the charge relating to the Begums. From that time the excitement went down fast. The spectacle had lost the attraction of novelty. The great displays of rhetoric were over. What was behind was not of a nature to entice men of letters from their books in the morning, or to tempt ladies who had left the masquerade at two to be out of bed before eight. There remained examinations and cross-examinations. There remained statements of accounts. There remained the reading of papers, filled with words unintelligible to English ears, with lacs and crores, zemindars and aumils, sunnuds and perwannahs, jaghires and nuzzurs. There remained bickerings, not always carried on with the best taste or with the best temper, between the managers of the impeachment and the counsel for the defence, particularly between Mr. Burke and Mr. Law. There remained the endless marches and countermarches of the Peers between their house and the Hall: for as often as a point of law was to be discussed, their lordships retired to discuss it apart; and the consequence was, as a peer wittily said, that the judges walked and the trial stood still.

It is to be added that, in the spring of 1788 when the trial commenced, no important question, either of domestic or foreign policy, excited the public mind. The proceeding in Westminster Hall, therefore, naturally attracted most of the attention of Parliament and of the public. It was the one great event of that season. But in the following year the King's illness, the debates on the Regency, the expectation of a change of Ministry, completely diverted public attention from Indian affairs; and within a fortnight after George the Third had returned thanks in St. Paul's for his recovery, the States-General of France met at Versailles. In the midst of the agitation produced by these events, the impeachment was for a time almost forgotten.

The trial in the Hall went on languidly. In the session of 1788, when the proceedings had the interest of novelty, and when the Peers had little other business before them, only thirty-five days were given to the impeachment. In 1789, the Regency Bill occupied the Upper House till the session was far advanced. When the King recovered the circuits were beginning. The judges left town; the Lords waited for the return of the oracles of jurisprudence; and the consequence was that during the whole year only seventeen days were given to the case of Hastings. It was clear that the matter would be protracted to a length unprecedented in the annals of criminal law.

In truth, it is impossible to deny that impeachment, though it is a fine ceremony, and though it may have been useful in the seventeenth century, is not a proceeding from which much good can now be expected. Whatever confidence may be placed in the decisions of the Peers on an appeal arising out of ordinary litigation, it is certain that no man has the least confidence in their impartiality, when a great public functionary, charged with a great state crime, is brought to their bar. They are all politicians. There is hardly one among them whose vote on an impeachment may not be confidently predicted before a witness has been examined; and, even if it were possible to rely on their justice, they would still be quite unfit to try such a cause as that of Hastings. They sit only during half the year. They have to transact much legislative and much judicial business. The law-lords, whose advice is required to guide the unlearned majority, are employed daily in administering justice elsewhere. It is impossible, therefore, that during a busy session, the Upper House should give more than a few days to an impeachment. To expect that their Lordships would give up partridge-shooting, in order to bring the greatest delinquent to speedy justice, or to relieve accused innocence by speedy acquittal, would be unreasonable indeed. A well constituted tribunal, sitting regularly six days in the week, and nine hours in the day, would have brought the trial of Hastings to a close in less than three months. The Lords had not finished their work in seven years.

The result ceased to be matter of doubt, from the time when the Lords resolved that they would be guided by the rules of evidence which are received in the inferior courts of the realm. Those rules, it is well known, exclude much information which would be quite sufficient to determine the conduct of any reasonable man, in the most important transactions of private life. Those rules, at every assizes, save scores of culprits whom judges, jury, and spectators, firmly believe to be guilty. But when those rules were rigidly applied to offences committed many years before, at the distance of many thousand miles, conviction was, of course, out of the question. We do not blame the accused and his counsel for availing themselves of every legal advantage in order to obtain an acquittal. But it is clear that an acquittal so obtained cannot be pleaded in bar of the judgment of history.

Several attempts were made by the friends of Hastings to put a stop to the trial. In 1789 they proposed a vote of censure upon Burke, for some violent language which he had used respecting the death of Nuncomar and the connexion between Hastings and Impey. Burke was then unpopular in the last degree both with the House and with the country. The asperity and indecency of some expressions which he had used during the debates on the Regency had annoyed even his warmest friends. The vote of censure was carried; and those who had moved it hoped that the managers would resign in disgust. Burke was deeply hurt. But his zeal for what he considered as the cause of justice and mercy triumphed over his personal feelings. He received the censure of the house with dignity and meekness, and declared that no personal mortification or humiliation should induce him to flinch from the sacred duty which he had undertaken.

In the following year the Parliament was dissolved; and the friends of Hastings entertained a hope that the new House of Commons might not be disposed to go on with the impeachment. They began by maintaining that the whole proceeding was terminated by the dissolution. Defeated on this point, they made a direct motion that the impeachment should be dropped; but they were defeated by the combined forces of the Government and the Opposition. It was, however, resolved that, for the sake of expedition, many of the articles should be withdrawn. In truth, had not some such measure been adopted, the trial would have lasted till the defendant was in his grave.

At length, in the spring of 1795, the decision was pronounced, near eight years after Hastings had been brought by the Sergeant-at-arms of the Commons to the bar of the Lords. On the last day of this great procedure the public curiosity, long suspended, seemed to be revived. Anxiety about the judgment there could be none; for it had been fully ascertained that there was a great majority for the defendant. Nevertheless many wished to see the pageant, and the hall was as much crowded as on the first day. But those who, having been present on the first day, now bore a part in the proceedings of the last, were few; and most of those few were altered men.

As Hastings himself said, the arraignment had taken place before one generation, and the judgment was pronounced by another. The spectator could not look at the woolsack, or at the red benches of the Peers, or at the green benches of the Commons, without seeing something that reminded him of the instability of all human things, of the instability of power and fame and life, of the more lamentable instability of friendship. The great seal was borne before Lord Loughborough who, when the trial commenced, was a fierce opponent of Mr. Pitt's government, and who was now a member of that government, while Thurlow, who presided in the court when it first sat, estranged from all his old allies, sat scowling among the junior barons. Of about a hundred and sixty nobles who walked in the procession on the first day, sixty had been laid in their family vaults. Still more affecting must have been the sight of the managers' box. What had become of that fair fellowship, so closely bound together by public and private ties, so resplendent with every talent and accomplishment? It had been scattered by calamities more bitter than the bitterness of death. The great chiefs were still living, and still in the full vigour of their genius. But their friendship was at an end. It had been violently and publicly dissolved, with tears and stormy reproaches. If those men, once so dear to each other, were now compelled to meet for the purpose of managing the impeachment, they met as strangers whom public business had brought together, and behaved to each other with cold and distant civility. Burke had in his vortex whirled away Windham. Fox had been followed by Sheridan and Grey.

Only twenty-nine Peers voted. Of these only six found Hastings guilty on the charges relating to Cheyte Sing and to the Begums. On other charges, the majority in his favour was still greater. On some, he was unanimously absolved. He was then called to the bar, was informed from the woolsack that the Lords had acquitted him, and was solemnly discharged. He bowed respectfully, and retired.

We have said that the decision had been fully expected. It was also generally approved. At the commencement of the trial there had been a strong and indeed unreasonable feeling against Hastings. At the close of the trial, there was a feeling equally strong and equally unreasonable in his favour. One cause of the change was, no doubt, what is commonly called the fickleness of the multitude, but what seems to us to be merely the general law of human nature. Both in individuals and in masses violent excitement is always followed by remission, and often by reaction. We are all inclined to depreciate whatever we have overpraised, and, on the other hand, to show undue indulgence where we have shown undue rigour. It was thus in the case of Hastings. The length of his trial, moreover, made him an object of compassion. It was thought, and not without reason, that, even if he was guilty, he was still an ill-used man, and that an impeachment of eight years was more than a sufficient punishment. It was also felt that, though, in the ordinary course of criminal law, a defendant is not allowed to set off his good actions against his crimes, a great political cause should be tried on different principles, and that a man who had governed an empire during thirteen years might have done some very reprehensible things, and yet might be on the whole deserving of rewards and honours rather than of fine and imprisonment. The press, an instrument neglected by the prosecutors, was used by Hastings and his friends with great effect. Every ship, too, that arrived from Madras or Bengal brought a cuddy full of his admirers. Every gentleman from India spoke of the late Governor-General as having deserved better, and having been treated worse, than any man living. The effect of this testimony, unanimously given by all persons who knew the East, was naturally very great. Retired members of the Indian services, civil and military, were settled in all corners of the kingdom. Each of them was, of course, in his own little circle, regarded as an oracle on an Indian question; and they were, with scarcely one exception, the zealous advocates of Hastings. It is to be added, that the numerous addresses to the late Governor-General, which his friends in Bengal obtained from the natives and transmitted to England, made a considerable impression. To these addresses we attach little or no importance. That Hastings was beloved by the people whom he governed is true; but the eulogies of pundits, zemindars, Mahommedan doctors, do not prove it to be true. For an English collector or judge would have found it easy to induce any native who could write to sign a panegyric on the most odious ruler that ever was in India. It was said that at Benares, the very place at which the acts set forth in the first article of impeachment had been committed, the natives had erected a temple to Hastings; and this story excited a strong sensation in England. Burke's observations on the apotheosis were admirable. He saw no reason for astonishment, he said, in the incident which had been represented as so striking. He knew something of the mythology of the Brahmins. He knew that, as they worshipped some gods from love, so they worshipped others from fear. He knew that they erected shrines, not only to the benignant deities of light and plenty, but also to the fiends who preside over small-pox and murder. Nor did he at all dispute the claim of Mr. Hastings to be admitted into such a Pantheon. This reply has always struck us as one of the finest that ever was made in Parliament. It is a grave and forcible argument, decorated by the most brilliant wit and fancy.

Hastings was, however, safe. But in every thing except character he would have been far better off if, when first impeached, he had at once pleaded guilty, and paid a fine of fifty thousand pounds. He was a ruined man. The legal expenses of his defence had been enormous. The expenses which did not appear in his attorney's bill were perhaps larger still. Great sums had been paid to Major Scott. Great sums had been laid out in bribing newspapers, rewarding pamphleteers, and circulating tracts. Burke, so early as 1790, declared in the House of Commons that twenty thousand pounds had been employed in corrupting the press. It is certain that no controversial weapon, from the gravest reasoning to the coarsest ribaldry, was left unemployed. Logan defended the accused governor with great ability in prose. For the lovers of verse, the speeches of the managers were burlesqued in Simpkin's letters. It is, we are afraid, indisputable that Hastings stooped so low as to court the aid of that malignant and filthy baboon John Williams, who called himself Anthony Pasquin. It was necessary to subsidise such allies largely. The private hoards of Mrs. Hastings had disappeared. It is said that the banker to whom they had been intrusted had failed. Still, if Hastings had practised strict economy, he would, after all his losses, have had a moderate competence; but in the management of his private affairs he was imprudent. The dearest wish of his heart had always been to regain Daylesford. At length, in the very year in which his trial commenced, the wish was accomplished; and the domain, alienated more than seventy years before, returned to the descendant of its old lords. But the manor-house was a ruin; and the grounds round it had, during many years, been utterly neglected. Hastings proceeded to build, to plant, to form a sheet of water, to excavate a grotto; and, before he was dismissed from the bar of the House of Lords, he had expended more than forty thousand pounds in adorning his seat.

The general feeling both of the directors and of the proprietors of the East India Company was that he had great claims on them, that his services to them had been eminent, and that his misfortunes had been the effect of his zeal for their interest. His friends in Leadenhall Street proposed to reimburse him for the costs of his trial, and to settle on him an annuity of five thousand pounds a-year. But the consent of the Board of Control was necessary; and at the head of the Board of Control was Mr. Dundas, who had himself been a party to the impeachment, who had, on that account, been reviled with great bitterness by the adherents of Hastings, and who, therefore, was not in a very complying mood. He refused to consent to what the Directors suggested. The Directors remonstrated. A long controversy followed. Hastings, in the mean time, was reduced to such distress, that he could hardly pay his weekly bills.

At length a compromise was made. An annuity of four thousand a-year was settled on Hastings; and, in order to enable him to meet pressing demands, he was to receive ten years' annuity in advance. The Company was also permitted to lend him fifty thousand pounds, to be repaid by instalments, without interest. This relief, though given in the most absurd manner, was sufficient to enable the retired governor to live in comfort, and even in luxury, if he had been a skilful manager. But he was careless and profuse, and was more than once under the necessity of applying to the Company for assistance, which was liberally given.

He had security and affluence, but not the power and dignity which, when he landed from India, he had reason to expect. He had then looked forward to a coronet, a red riband, a seat at the Council Board, an office at Whitehall. He was then only fifty-two, and might hope for many years of bodily and mental vigour. The case was widely different when he left the bar of the Lords. He was now too old a man to turn his mind to a new class of studies and duties. He had no chance of receiving any mark of royal favour while Mr. Pitt remained in power; and, when Mr. Pitt retired, Hastings was approaching his seventieth year.

Once, and only once, after his acquittal, he interfered in politics; and that interference was not much to his honour. In 1804 he exerted himself strenuously to prevent Mr. Addington, against whom Fox and Pitt had combined, from resigning the Treasury. It is difficult to believe that a man so able and energetic as Hastings can have thought that, when Bonaparte was at Boulogne with a great army, the defence of our island could safely be entrusted to a ministry which did not contain a single person whom flattery could describe as a great statesman. It is also certain that, on the important question which had raised Mr. Addington to power, and on which he differed from both Fox and Pitt, Hastings, as might have been expected, agreed with Fox and Pitt, and was decidedly opposed to Addington. Religious intolerance has never been the vice of the Indian service, and certainly was not the vice of Hastings. But Mr. Addington had treated him with marked favour. Fox had been a principal manager of the impeachment. To Pitt it was owing that there had been an impeachment; and Hastings, we fear, was on this occasion guided by personal considerations, rather than by a regard to the public interest.

The last twenty-four years of his life were chiefly passed at Daylesford. He amused himself with embellishing his grounds, riding fine Arab horses, fattening prize-cattle, and trying to rear Indian animals and vegetables in England. He sent for seeds of a very fine custard-apple, from the garden of what had once been his own villa, among the green hedgerows of Allipore. He tried also to naturalise in Worcestershire the delicious leechee, almost the only fruit of Bengal which deserves to be regretted even amidst the plenty of Covent Garden. The Mogul emperors, in the time of their greatness, had in vain attempted to introduce into Hindostan the goat of the table-land of Thibet, whose down supplies the looms of Cashmere with the materials of the finest shawls. Hastings tried, with no better fortune, to rear a breed at Daylesford; nor does he seem to have succeeded better with the cattle of Bootan, whose tails are in high esteem as the best fans for brushing away the mosquitoes.

Literature divided his attention with his conservatories and his menagerie. He had always loved books, and they were now necessary to him. Though not a poet, in any high sense of the word, he wrote neat and polished lines with great facility, and was fond of exercising this talent. Indeed, if we must speak out, he seems to have been more of a Trissotin than was to be expected from the powers of his mind, and from the great part which he had played in life. We are assured in these Memoirs that the first thing which he did in the morning was to compose a copy of verses. When the family and guests assembled, the poem made its appearance as regularly as the eggs and rolls; and Mr. Gleig requires us to believe that, if from any accident Hastings came to the breakfast-table without one of his charming performances in his hand, the omission was felt by all as a grievous disappointment. Tastes differ widely. For ourselves, we must say that, however good the breakfasts at Daylesford may have been,—and we are assured that the tea was of the most aromatic flavour, and that neither tongue nor venison-pasty was wanting,—we should have thought the reckoning high if we had been forced to earn our repast by listening every day to a new madrigal or sonnet composed by our host. We are glad, however, that Mr. Gleig has preserved this little feature of character, though we think it by no means a beauty. It is good to be often reminded of the inconsistency of human nature, and to learn to look without wonder or disgust on the weaknesses which are found in the strongest minds. Dionysius in old times, Frederic in the last century, with capacity and vigour equal to the conduct of the greatest affairs, united all the little vanities and affectations of provincial blue-stockings. These great examples may console the admirers of Hastings for the affliction of seeing him reduced to the level of the Hayleys and Sewards.

When Hastings had passed many years in retirement, and had

long outlived the common age of men, he again became for a short time an object of general attention. In 1813 the charter of the East India Company was renewed; and much discussion about Indian affairs took place in Parliament. It was determined to examine witnesses at the bar of the Commons; and Hastings was ordered to attend. He had appeared at that bar once before. It was when he read his answer to the charges which Burke had laid on the table. Since that time twenty-seven years had elapsed; public feeling had undergone a complete change; the nation had now forgotten his faults, and remembered only his services. The reappearance, too, of a man who had been among the most distinguished of a generation that had passed away, who now belonged to history, and who seemed to have risen from the dead, could not but produce a solemn and pathetic effect. The Commons received him with acclamations, ordered a chair to be set for him, and, when he retired, rose and uncovered. There were, indeed, a few who did not sympathize with the general feeling. One or two of the managers of the impeachment were present. They sate in the same seats which they had occupied when they had been thanked for the services which they had rendered in Westminster Hall: for, by the courtesy of the House, a member who has been thanked in his place is considered as having a right always to occupy that place. These gentlemen were not disposed to admit that they had employed several of the best years of their lives in persecuting an innocent man. They accordingly kept their seats, and pulled their hats over their brows; but the exceptions only made the prevailing enthusiasm more remarkable. The Lords received the old man with similar tokens of respect. The University of Oxford conferred on him the degree of Doctor of Laws; and, in the Sheldonian theatre, the undergraduates welcomed him with tumultuous cheering.

These marks of public esteem were soon followed by marks of royal favour. Hastings was sworn of the Privy Council, and was admitted to a long private audience of the Prince Regent, who treated him very graciously. When the Emperor of Russia and the King of Prussia visited England, Hastings appeared in their train both at Oxford and in the Guildhall of London, and, though surrounded by a crowd of princes and great warriors, was every where received by the public with marks of respect and admiration. He was presented by the Prince Regent both to Alexander and to Frederick William; and his Royal Highness went so far as to declare in public that honours far higher than a seat in the Privy Council were due, and would soon be paid, to the man who had saved the British dominions in Asia. Hastings now confidently expected a peerage; but, from some unexplained cause, he was again disappointed.

He lived about four years longer, in the enjoyment of good spirits, of faculties not impaired to any painful or degrading extent, and of health such as is rarely enjoyed by those who attain such an age. At length, on the twenty-second of August 1818, in the eighty-sixth year of his age, he met death with the same tranquil and decorous fortitude which he had opposed to all the trials of his various and eventful life.

With all his faults,—and they were neither few nor small,—only one cemetery was worthy to contain his remains. In that temple of silence and reconciliation where the enmities of twenty genera-tions lie buried, in the Great Abbey which has during many ages afforded a quiet resting-place to those whose minds and bodies have been shattered by the contentions of the Great Hall, the dust of the illustrious accused should have mingled with the dust of the illustrious accusers. This was not to be. Yet the place of interment was not ill chosen. Behind the chancel of the parish-church of Daylesford, in earth which already held the bones of many chiefs of the house of Hastings, was laid the coffin of the greatest man who has ever borne that ancient and widely extended name. On that very spot probably, fourscore years before, the little Warren, meanly clad and scantily fed, had played with the children of ploughmen. Even then his young mind had revolved plans which might be called romantic. Yet, however romantic, it is not likely that they had been so strange as the truth. Not only had the poor orphan retrieved the fallen fortunes of his line. Not only had he repurchased the old lands, and rebuilt the old dwelling. He had preserved and extended an empire. He had founded a polity. He had administered government and war with more than the capacity of Richelieu. He had patronised learning with the judicious liberality of Cosmo. He had been attacked by the most formidable combination of enemies that ever sought the destruction of a single victim; and over that combination, after a struggle of ten years, he had triumphed. He had at length gone down to his grave in the fulness of age, in peace, after so many troubles, in honour, after so much obloquy.

Those who look on his character without favour or malevolence will pronounce that, in the two great elements of all social virtue, in respect for the rights of others, and in sympathy for the sufferings of others, he was deficient. His principles were somewhat lax. His heart was somewhat hard. But while we cannot with truth describe him either as a righteous or as a merciful ruler, we cannot regard without admiration the amplitude and fertility of his intellect, his rare talents for command, for administration, and for controversy, his dauntless courage, his honourable poverty, his fervent zeal for the interests of the state, his noble equanimity, tried by both extremes of fortune, and never disturbed by either.

WILLIAM PITT

(JANUARY 1859)

WILLIAM PITT, the second son of William Pitt, Earl of Chatham, and of Lady Hester Grenville, daughter of Hester, Countess Temple, was born on the 28th of May 1759. The child inherited a name which, at the time of his birth, was the most illustrious in the civilised world, and was pronounced by every Englishman with pride, and by every enemy of England with mingled admiration and terror. During the first year of his life, every month had its illuminations and bonfires, and every wind brought some messenger charged with joyful tidings and hostile standards. In Westphalia the English infantry won a great battle which arrested the armies of Louis the Fifteenth in the midst of a career of conquest: Boscawen defeated one French fleet on the coast of Portugal: Hawke put to flight another in the Bay of Biscay: Johnson took Niagara: Amherst took Ticonderoga: Wolfe died by the most enviable of deaths under the walls of Quebec: Clive destroyed a Dutch armament in the Hooghley, and established the English supremacy in Bengal: Coote routed Lally at Wandewash, and established the English supremacy in the Carnatic. The nation, while loudly applauding the successful warriors, considered them all, on sea and on land, in Europe, in America, and in Asia, merely as instruments which received their direction from one superior mind. It was the great William Pitt, the great commoner, who had vanquished French marshals in Germany, and French admirals on the Atlantic; who had conquered for his country one great empire on the frozen shores of Ontario, and another under the tropical sun near the mouths of the Ganges. It was not in the nature of things that popularity such as he at this time enjoyed should be permanent. That popularity had lost its gloss before his children were old enough to understand that their father was a great man. He was at length placed in situations in which neither his talents for administration nor his talents for debate appeared to the best advantage. The energy and decision which had eminently fitted him for the direction of war were not needed in time of peace. The lofty and spirit-stirring eloquence which had made him supreme in the House of Commons, often fell dead on the House of Lords. A cruel malady racked his joints, and left his joints only to fall on his nerves and on his brain. During the closing years of his life, he was odious to the court, and yet was not on cordial terms with the great body of the opposition. Chatham was only the ruin of Pitt, but an awful and majestic ruin, not to be contemplated by any man of sense and feeling without emotions resembling those which are excited by the remains of the Parthenon and of the Coliseum. In one respect the old statesman was eminently happy. Whatever might be the vicissitudes of his public life, he never failed to find peace and love by his own hearth. He loved all his children, and was loved by them; and, of all his children, the one of whom he was fondest and proudest was his second son.

The child's genius and ambition displayed themselves with a rare and almost unnatural precocity. At seven, the interest which he took in grave subjects, the ardour with which he pursued his studies, and the sense and vivacity of his remarks on books and on events, amazed his parents and instructors. One of his sayings of this date was reported to his mother by his tutor. In August 1766, when the world was agitated by the news that Mr. Pitt had become Earl of Chatham, little William exclaimed, "I am glad that I am not the eldest son. I want to speak in the House of Commons like papa." A letter is extant in which Lady Chatham, a woman of considerable abilities, remarked to her lord, that their younger son at twelve had left far behind him his elder brother, who was fifteen. "The fineness," she wrote, "of William's mind makes him enjoy with the greatest pleasure what would be above the reach of any other creature of his small age." At fourteen the lad was in intellect a man. Hayley, who met him at Lyme in the summer of 1773, was astonished, delighted, and somewhat overawed, by hearing wit and wisdom from so young a mouth. The poet, indeed, was afterwards sorry that his shyness had prevented him from submitting the plan of an extensive literary work, which he was then meditating, to the judgment of this extraordinary boy. The boy, indeed, had already written a tragedy, bad of course, but not worse than the tragedies of his friend. This piece is still preserved at Chevening, and is in some respects highly curious. There is no love. The whole plot is political; and it is remarkable that the interest, such as it is, turns on a contest about a regency. On one side is a faithful servant of the Crown, on the other an ambitious and unprincipled conspirator. At length the king, who had been missing, reappears, resumes his power, and rewards the faithful defender of his rights. A reader who should judge only by internal evidence would have no hesitation in pronouncing that the play was written by some Pittite poetaster at the time of the rejoicings for the recovery of George the Third in 1789.

The pleasure with which William's parents observed the rapid development of his intellectual powers was alloyed by apprehensions about his health. He shot up alarmingly fast; he was often ill, and always weak; and it was feared that it would be impossible to rear a stripling so tall, so slender, and so feeble. Port wine was prescribed by his medical advisers; and it is said that he was, at fourteen, accustomed to take this agreeable physic in quantities which would, in our abstemious age, be thought much more than sufficient for any full-grown man. This regimen, though it would probably have killed ninety-nine boys out of a hundred, seems to have been well suited to the peculiarities of William's constitution; for at fifteen he ceased to be molested by disease, and, though never a strong man, continued, during many years of labour and anxiety, of nights passed in debate and of summers passed in London, to be a tolerably healthy one. It was probably on account of the delicacy of his frame that he was not educated like other boys of the same rank. Almost all the eminent English statesmen and orators to whom he was afterwards opposed or allied, North, Fox, Shelburne, Windham, Grey, Wellesley, Grenville, Sheridan, Canning, went through the training of great public schools. Lord Chatham had himself been a distinguished Etonian; and it is seldom that a distinguished Etonian forgets his obligations to Eton. But William's infirmities required a vigilance and tenderness such as could be found only at home. He was therefore bred under the paternal roof. His studies were superintended by a clergyman named Wilson; and those studies, though often interrupted by illness, were prosecuted with extraordinary success. Before the lad had completed his fifteenth year, his knowledge both of the ancient languages and of mathematics was such as very few men of eighteen then carried up to college. He was therefore sent, towards the close of the year 1773, to Pembroke Hall, in the university of Cambridge. So young a student required much more than the ordinary care which a college tutor bestows on undergraduates. The governor, to whom the direction of William's academical life was confided, was a bachelor of arts named Pretyman, who had been senior wrangler in the preceding year, and who, though not a man of prepossessing appearance or brilliant parts, was eminently acute and laborious, a sound scholar, and an excellent geometrician. At Cambridge, Pretyman was, during more than two years, the inseparable companion, and indeed almost the only companion, of his pupil. A close and lasting friendship sprang up between the pair. The disciple was able, before he completed his twenty-eighth year, to make his preceptor bishop of Lincoln and dean of St. Paul's; and the preceptor showed his gratitude by writing a Life of the disciple, which enjoys the distinction of being the worst biographical work of its size in the world.

Pitt, till he graduated, had scarcely one acquaintance, attended chapel regularly morning and evening, dined every day in hall, and never went to a single evening party. At seventeen, he was admitted, after the bad fashion of those times, by right of birth, without any examination, to the degree of Master of Arts. But he continued during some years to reside at college, and to apply himself vigorously, under Pretyman's direction, to the studies of the place, while mixing freely in the best academic society.

The stock of learning which Pitt laid in during this part of his life was certainly very extraordinary. In fact, it was all that he ever possessed; for he very early became too busy to have any spare time for books. The work in which he took the greatest delight was Newton's Principia. His liking for mathematics, indeed, amounted to a passion, which, in the opinion of his instructors, themselves distinguished mathematicians, required to be checked rather than encouraged. The acuteness and readiness with which he solved problems was pronounced by one of the ablest of the moderators, who in those days presided over the disputations in the schools, and conducted the examinations of the Senate-House, to be unrivalled in the university. Nor was the youth's proficiency in classical learning less remarkable. In one respect, indeed, he appeared to disadvantage when compared with even second-rate and third-rate men from public schools. He had never, while under Wilson's care, been in the habit of composing in the ancient languages; and he therefore never acquired that knack of versification which is sometimes possessed by clever boys whose knowledge of the language and literature of Greece and Rome is very superficial. It would have been utterly out of his power to produce such charming elegiac lines as those in which Wellesley bade farewell to Eton, or such Virgilian hexameters as those in which Canning described the pilgrimage to Mecca. But it may be doubted whether any scholar has ever, at twenty, had a more solid and profound knowledge of the two great tongues of the old civilised world. The facility with which he penetrated the meaning of the most intricate sentences in the Attic writers astonished veteran critics. He had set his heart on being intimately acquainted with all the extant poetry of Greece, and was not satisfied till he had mastered Lycophron's Cassandra, the most obscure work in the whole range of ancient literature. This strange rhapsody, the difficulties of which have perplexed and repelled many excellent scholars, "he read," says his preceptor, "with an ease at first sight, which, if I had not witnessed it, I should have thought beyond the compass of human intellect."

To modern literature Pitt paid comparatively little attention. He knew no living language except French; and French he knew very imperfectly. With a few of the best English writers he was intimate, particularly with Shakespeare and Milton. The debate in Pandemonium was, as it well deserved to be, one of his favourite passages; and his early friends used to talk, long after his death, of the just emphasis and the melodious cadence with which they had heard him recite the incomparable speech of Belial. He had indeed been carefully trained from infancy in the art of managing his voice, a voice naturally clear and deep-toned. His father, whose oratory owed no small part of its effect to that art, had been a most skilful and judicious instructor. At a later period, the wits of Brookes's, irritated by observing, night after night, how powerfully Pitt's sonorous elocution fascinated the rows of country gentlemen, reproached him with having been "taught by his dad on a stool."

His education, indeed, was well adapted to form a great parliamentary speaker. One argument often urged against those classical studies which occupy so large a part of the early life of every gentleman bred in the south of our island is, that they prevent him from acquiring a command of his mother tongue, and that it is not unusual to meet with a youth of excellent parts, who writes Ciceronian Latin prose and Horatian Latin Alcaics, but who would find it impossible to express his thoughts in pure, perspicuous, and forcible English. There may perhaps be some truth in this observation. But the classical studies of Pitt were carried on in a peculiar manner, and had the effect of enriching his English vocabulary, and of making him wonderfully expert in the art of constructing correct English sentences. His practice was to look over a page or two of a Greek or Latin author, to make himself master of the meaning, and then to read the passage straight forward into his own language. This practice, begun under his first teacher Wilson, was continued under Pretyman. It is not strange that a young man of great abilities, who had been exercised daily in this way during ten years, should have acquired an almost unrivalled power of putting his thoughts, without premeditation, into words well selected and well arranged.

Of all the remains of antiquity, the orations were those on which he bestowed the most minute examination. His favourite employment was to compare harangues on opposite sides of the same question, to analyse them, and to observe which of the arguments of the first speaker were refuted by the second, which were evaded, and which were left untouched. Nor was it only in books that he at this time studied the art of parliamentary fencing. When he was at home, he had frequent opportunities of hearing important debates at Westminster; and he heard them, not only with interest and enjoyment, but with a close scientific attention resembling that with which a diligent pupil at Guy's Hospital watches every turn of the hand of a great surgeon through a difficult operation. On one of these occasions, Pitt, a youth whose abilities were as yet known only to his own family and to a small knot of college friends, was introduced on the steps of the throne in the House of Lords to Fox, who was his senior by eleven years, and who was already the greatest debater, and one of the greatest orators, that had appeared in England. Fox used afterwards to relate that, as the discussion proceeded, Pitt repeatedly turned to him, and said, "But surely, Mr. Fox, that might be met thus;" or, "Yes; but he lays himself open to this retort." What the particular criticisms were Fox had forgotten; but he said that he was much struck at the time by the precocity of a lad who, through the whole sitting, seemed to be thinking only how all the speeches on both sides could be answered.

One of the young man's visits to the House of Lords was a sad and memorable era in his life. He had not quite completed his nineteenth year, when, on the 7th of April, 1778, he attended his father to Westminster. A great debate was expected. It was known that France had recognised the independence of the United States. The Duke of Richmond was about to declare his opinion that all thought of subjugating those states ought to be relinquished. Chatham had always maintained that the resistance of the colonies to the mother country was justifiable. But he conceived, very erroneously, that on the day on which their independence should be acknowledged the greatness of England would be at an end. Though sinking under the weight of years and infirmities, he determined, in spite of the entreaties of his family, to be in his place. His son supported him to a seat. The excitement and exertion were too much for the old man. In the very act of addressing the peers, he fell back in convulsions. A few weeks later his corpse was borne, with gloomy pomp, from the Painted Chamber to the Abbey. The favourite child and namesake of the deceased statesman followed the coffin as chief mourner, and saw it deposited in the transept where his own was destined to lie.

His elder brother, now Earl of Chatham, had means sufficient, and barely sufficient, to support the dignity of the peerage. The other members of the family were poorly provided for. William had little more than three hundred a year. It was necessary for him to follow a profession. He had already begun to eat his terms. In the spring of 1780 he came of age. He then quitted Cambridge, was called to the bar, took chambers in Lincoln's Inn, and joined the western circuit. In the autumn of that year a general election took place; and he offered himself as a candidate for the university; but he was at the bottom of the poll. It is said that the grave doctors, who then sate, robed in scarlet, on the benches of Golgotha, thought it great presumption in so young a man to solicit so high a distinction. He was, however, at the request of a hereditary friend, the Duke of Rutland, brought into Parliament by Sir James Lowther for the borough of Appleby.

The dangers of the country were at that time such as might well have disturbed even a constant mind. Army after army had been sent in vain against the rebellious colonists of North America. On pitched fields of battle the advantage had been with the disciplined troops of the mother country. But it was not on pitched fields of battle that the event of such a contest could be decided. An armed nation, with hunger and the Atlantic for auxiliaries, was not to be subjugated. Meanwhile the House of Bourbon, humbled to the dust a few years before by the genius and vigour of Chatham, had seized the opportunity of revenge. France and Spain were united against us, and had recently been joined by Holland. The command of the Mediterranean had been for a time lost. The British flag had been scarcely able to maintain itself in the British Channel. The northern powers professed neutrality; but their neutrality had a menacing aspect. In the East, Hyder had descended on the Carnatic, had destroyed the little army of Baillie, and had spread terror even to the ramparts of Fort Saint George. The discontents of Ireland threatened nothing less than civil war. In England the authority of the government had sunk to the lowest point. The King and the House of Commons were alike unpopular. The cry for parliamentary reform was scarcely less loud and vehement than in the autumn of 1830. Formidable associations, headed, not by ordinary demagogues, but by men of high rank, stainless character, and distinguished ability, demanded a revision of the representative system. The populace, emboldened by the impotence and irresolution of the government, had recently broken loose from all restraint, besieged the chambers of the legislature, hustled peers, hunted bishops, attacked the residences of ambassadors, opened prisons, burned and pulled down houses. London had presented during some days the aspect of a city taken by storm; and it had been necessary to form a camp among the trees of Saint James's Park.

In spite of dangers and difficulties abroad and at home, George the Third, with a firmness which had little affinity with virtue or with wisdom, persisted in his determination to put down the American rebels by force of arms; and his ministers submitted their judgment to his. Some of them were probably actuated merely by selfish cupidity; but their chief, Lord North, a man of high honour, amiable temper, winning manners, lively wit, and excellent talents both for business and for debate, must be acquitted of all sordid motives. He remained at a post from which he had long wished and had repeatedly tried to escape, only because he had not sufficient fortitude to resist the entreaties and reproaches of the King, who silenced all arguments by passionately asking whether any gentleman, any man of spirit, could have the heart to desert a kind master in the hour of extremity.

The opposition consisted of two parties which had once been hostile to each other, and which had been very slowly, and, as it soon appeared, very imperfectly reconciled, but which at this conjuncture seemed to act together with cordiality. The larger of these parties consisted of the great body of the Whig aristocracy. Its head was Charles, Marquess of Rockingham, a man of sense and virtue, and in wealth and parliamentary interest equalled by very few of the English nobles, but afflicted with a nervous timidity which prevented him from taking a prominent part in debate. In the House of Commons, the adherents of Rockingham were led by Fox, whose dissipated habits and ruined fortunes were the talk of the whole town, but whose commanding genius, and whose sweet, generous, and affectionate disposition, extorted the admiration and love of those who most lamented the errors of his private life. Burke, superior to Fox in largeness of comprehension, in extent of knowledge, and in splendour of imagination, but less skilled in that kind of logic and in that kind of rhetoric which convince and persuade great assemblies, was willing to be the lieutenant of a young chief who might have been his son.

A smaller section of the opposition was composed of the old followers of Chatham. At their head was William, Earl of Shelburne, distinguished both as a statesman and as a lover of science and letters. With him were leagued Lord Camden, who had formerly held the Great Seal, and whose integrity, ability, and constitutional knowledge commanded the public respect; Barré, an eloquent and acrimonious declaimer; and Dunning, who had long held the first place at the English bar. It was to this party that Pitt was naturally attracted.

On the 26th of February 1781 he made his first speech in favour of Burke's plan of economical reform. Fox stood up at the same moment, but instantly gave way. The lofty yet animated deportment of the young member, his perfect self-possession, the readiness with which he replied to the orators who had preceded him, the silver tones of his voice, the perfect structure of his unpremeditated sentences, astonished and delighted his hearers. Burke, moved even to tears, exclaimed, "It is not a chip of the old block; it is the old block itself." "Pitt will be one of the first men in Parliament," said a member of the opposition to Fox. "He is so already," answered Fox, in whose nature envy had no place. It is a curious fact, well remembered by some who were very recently living, that soon after this debate Pitt's name was put up by Fox at Brookes's.

On two subsequent occasions during that session Pitt addressed the House, and on both fully sustained the reputation which he had acquired on his first appearance. In the summer, after the prorogation, he again went the western circuit, held several briefs, and acquitted himself in such a manner that he was highly complimented by Buller from the bench, and by Dunning at the bar.

On the 27th of November the Parliament reassembled. Only forty-eight hours before had arrived tidings of the surrender of Cornwallis and his army; and it had consequently been necessary to rewrite the royal speech. Every man in the kingdom, except the King, was now convinced that it was mere madness to think of conquering the United States. In the debate on the report of the address, Pitt spoke with even more energy and brilliancy than on any former occasion. He was warmly applauded by his allies; but it was remarked that no person on his own side of the house was so loud in eulogy as Henry Dundas, the Lord Advocate of Scotland, who spoke from the ministerial ranks. That able and versatile politician distinctly foresaw the approaching downfall of the government with which he was connected, and was preparing to make his own escape from the ruin. From that night dates his connection with Pitt, a connection which soon became a close intimacy, and which lasted till it was dissolved by death.

About a fortnight later, Pitt spoke in the committee of supply on the army estimates. Symptoms of dissension had begun to appear on the Treasury bench. Lord George Germaine, the Secretary of State who was especially charged with the direction of the war in America, had held language not easily to be reconciled with declarations made by the First Lord of the Treasury. Pitt noticed the discrepancy with much force and keenness. Lord George and Lord North began to whisper together; and Welbore Ellis, an ancient placeman who had been drawing salary almost every quarter since the days of Henry Pelham, bent down between them to put in a word. Such interruptions sometimes discompose veteran speakers. Pitt stopped, and, looking at the group, said, with admirable readiness, "I shall wait till Nestor has composed the dispute between Agamemnon and Achilles."

After several defeats, or victories hardly to be distinguished from defeats, the ministry resigned. The King, reluctantly and un-graciously, consented to accept Rockingham as first minister. Fox and Shelburne became Secretaries of State. Lord John Cavendish, one of the most upright and honourable of men, was made Chancellor of the Exchequer. Thurlow, whose abilities and force of character had made him the dictator of the House of Lords, continued to hold the great seal.

To Pitt was offered, through Shelburne, the Vice-Treasurership of Ireland, one of the easiest and most highly paid places in the gift of the Crown; but the offer was, without hesitation, declined. The young statesman had resolved to accept no post which did not entitle him to a seat in the cabinet: and a few days later, he announced that resolution in the House of Commons. It must be remembered that the cabinet was then a much smaller and more select body than at present. We have seen cabinets of sixteen. In the time of our grandfathers a cabinet of ten or eleven was thought inconveniently large. Seven was an usual number. Even Burke, who had taken the lucrative office of Paymaster, was not in the cabinet. Many therefore thought Pitt's declaration indecent. He himself was sorry that he had made it. The words, he said in private, had escaped him in the heat of speaking; and he had no sooner uttered them than he would have given the world to recall them. They, however, did him no harm with the public. The second William Pitt, it was said, had shown that he had inherited the spirit, as well as the genius, of the first. In the son, as in the father, there might perhaps be too much pride; but there was nothing low or sordid. It might be called arrogance in a young barrister, living in chambers on three hundred a year, to refuse a salary of five thousand a year, merely because he did not choose to bind himself to speak or vote for plans which he had no share in framing; but surely such arrogance was not very far removed from virtue.

Pitt gave a general support to the administration of Rockingham, but omitted, in the meantime, no opportunity of courting that

Ultra-Whig party which the persecution of Wilkes and the Middlesex election had called into existence, and which the disastrous events of the war, and the triumph of republican principles in America, had made formidable both in numbers and in temper. He supported a motion for shortening the duration of Parliaments. He made a motion for a committee to examine into the state of the representation, and, in the speech by which that motion was introduced, avowed himself the enemy of the close boroughs, the strongholds of that corruption to which he attributed all the calamities of the nation, and which, as he phrased it in one of those exact and sonorous sentences of which he had a boundless command, had grown with the growth of England and strengthened with her strength, but had not diminished with her diminution or decayed with her decay. On this occasion he was supported by Fox. The motion was lost by only twenty votes in a house of more than three hundred members. The reformers never again had so good a division till the year 1831.

The new administration was strong in abilities, and was more popular than any administration which had held office since the first year of George the Third, but was hated by the King, hesitatingly supported by the Parliament, and torn by internal dissensions. The Chancellor was disliked and distrusted by almost all his colleagues. The two Secretaries of State regarded each other with no friendly feeling. The line between their departments had not been traced with precision; and there were consequently jealousies, encroachments, and complaints. It was all that Rockingham could do to keep the peace in his cabinet; and, before the cabinet had existed three months, Rockingham died.

In an instant all was confusion. The adherents of the deceased statesman looked on the Duke of Portland as their chief. The King placed Shelburne at the head of the Treasury. Fox, Lord John Cavendish, and Burke, immediately resigned their offices; and the new prime minister was left to constitute a government out of very defective materials. His own parliamentary talents were great; but he could not be in the place where parliamentary talents were most needed. It was necessary to find some member of the House of Commons who could confront the great orators of the opposition; and Pitt alone had the eloquence and the courage which were required. He was offered the great place of Chancellor of the Exchequer, and he accepted it. He had scarcely completed his twenty-third year.

The Parliament was speedily prorogued. During the recess, a negotiation for peace which had been commenced under Rockingham was brought to a successful termination. England acknowledged the independence of her revolted colonies; and she ceded to her European enemies some places in the Mediterranean and in the Gulf of Mexico. But the terms which she obtained were quite as advantageous and honourable as the events of the war entitled her to expect, or as she was likely to obtain by persevering in a contest against immense odds. All her vital parts, all the real sources of her power, remained uninjured. She preserved even her dignity; for she ceded to the House of Bourbon only part of what she had won from that House in previous wars. She retained her Indian empire undiminished; and, in spite of the mightiest efforts of two great monarchies, her flag still waved on the rock of Gibraltar. There is not the slightest reason to believe that Fox, if he had remained in office, would have hesitated one moment about concluding a treaty on such conditions. Unhappily that great and most amiable man was, at this crisis, hurried by his passions into an error which made his genius and his virtues, during a long course of years, almost useless to his country.

He saw that the great body of the House of Commons was divided into three parties, his own, that of North, and that of Shelburne; that none of those three parties was large enough to stand alone; that, therefore, unless two of them united, there must be a miserably feeble administration, or, more probably, a rapid succession of miserably feeble administrations, and this at a time when a strong government was essential to the prosperity and respectability of the nation. It was then necessary and right that there should be a coalition. To every possible coalition there were objections. But, of all possible coalitions, that to which there were the fewest objections was undoubtedly a coalition between Shelburne and Fox. It would have been generally applauded by the followers of both. It might have been made without any sacrifice of public principle on the part of either. Unhappily, recent bickerings had left in the mind of Fox a profound dislike and distrust of Shelburne. Pitt attempted to mediate, and was authorised to invite Fox to return to the service of the Crown. "Is Lord Shelburne," said Fox, "to remain prime minister?" Pitt answered in the affirmative. "It is impossible that I can act under him," said Fox. "Then negotiation is at an end," said Pitt; "for I cannot betray him." Thus the two statesmen parted. They were never again in a private room together.

As Fox and his friends would not treat with Shelburne, nothing remained to them but to treat with North. That fatal coalition which is emphatically called "The Coalition" was formed. Not three quarters of a year had elapsed since Fox and Burke had threatened North with impeachment, and had described him, night after night, as the most arbitrary, the most corrupt, the most incapable of ministers. They now allied themselves with him for the purpose of driving from office a statesman with whom they cannot be said to have differed as to any important question. Nor had they even the prudence and the patience to wait for some occasion on which they might, without inconsistency, have combined with their old enemies in opposition to the government. That nothing might be wanting to the scandal, the great orators, who had, during seven years, thundered against the war, determined to join with the authors of that war in passing a vote of censure on the peace.

The Parliament met before Christmas 1782. But it was not till January 1783 that the preliminary treaties were signed. On the 17th of February they were taken into consideration by the House of Commons. There had been, during some days, floating rumours that Fox and North had coalesced; and the debate indicated but too clearly that those rumours were not unfounded. Pitt was suffering from indisposition: he did not rise till his own strength and that of his hearers were exhausted; and he was consequently less successful than on any former occasion. His admirers owned that his speech was feeble and petulant. He so far forgot himself as to advise Sheridan to confine himself to amusing theatrical audiences. This ignoble sarcasm gave Sheridan an opportunity of retorting with great felicity. "After what I have seen and heard to-night," he said, "I really feel strongly tempted to venture on a competition with so great an artist as Ben Jonson, and to bring on the stage a second Angry Boy." On a division, the address proposed by the supporters of the government was rejected by a majority of sixteen.

But Pitt was not a man to be disheartened by a single failure, or to be put down by the most lively repartee. When, a few days later, the opposition proposed a resolution directly censuring the treaties, he spoke with an eloquence, energy, and dignity, which raised his fame and popularity higher than ever. To the coalition of Fox and North he alluded in language which drew forth tumultuous applause from his followers. "If," he said, "this ill-omened and unnatural marriage be not yet consummated, I know of a just and lawful impediment; and, in the name of the public weal, I forbid the banns."

The ministers were again left in a minority; and Shelburne consequently tendered his resignation. It was accepted; but the King struggled long and hard before he submitted to the terms

M—16

dictated by Fox, whose faults he detested, and whose high spirit and powerful intellect he detested still more. The first place at the board of Treasury was repeatedly offered to Pitt: but the offer, though tempting, was steadfastly declined. The young man, whose judgment was as precocious as his eloquence, saw that his time was coming, but was not come, and was deaf to royal importunities and reproaches. His Majesty, bitterly complaining of Pitt's faint-heartedness, tried to break the coalition. Every art of seduction was practised on North, but in vain. During several weeks the country remained without a government. It was not till all devices had failed, and till the aspect of the House of Commons became threatening, that the King gave way. The Duke of Portland was declared First Lord of the Treasury. Thurlow was dismissed. Fox and North became Secretaries of State, with power ostensibly equal. But Fox was the real prime minister.

The year was far advanced before the new arrangements were completed; and nothing very important was done during the remainder of the session. Pitt, now seated on the opposition bench, brought the question of parliamentary reform a second time under the consideration of the Commons. He proposed to add to the House at once a hundred county members and several members for metropolitan districts, and to enact that every borough of which an election committee should report that the majority of voters appeared to be corrupt should lose the franchise. The motion was rejected by 293 votes to 149.

After the prorogation, Pitt visited the Continent for the first and last time. His travelling companion was one of his most intimate friends, a young man of his own age, who had already distinguished himself in Parliament by an engaging natural eloquence, set off by the sweetest and most exquisitely modulated of human voices, and whose affectionate heart, caressing manners, and brilliant wit, made him the most delightful of companions, William Wilberforce. That was the time of Anglomania in France; and at Paris the son of the great Chatham was absolutely hunted by men of letters and women of fashion, and forced, much against his will, into political disputation. One remarkable saying which dropped from him during this tour has been preserved. A French gentleman expressed some surprise at the immense influence which Fox, a man of pleasure, ruined by the dice-box and the turf, exercised over the English nation. "You have not," said Pitt, "been under the wand of the magician."

In November 1783 the Parliament met again. The government had irresistible strength in the House of Commons, and seemed to be scarcely less strong in the House of Lords, but was, in truth, surrounded on every side by dangers. The King was impatiently waiting for the moment at which he could emancipate himself from a yoke which galled him so severely that he had more than once seriously thought of retiring to Hanover; and the King was scarcely more eager for a change than the nation. Fox and North had committed a fatal error. They ought to have known that coalitions between parties which have long been hostile can succeed only when the wish for coalition pervades the lower ranks of both. If the leaders unite before there is any disposition to union among the followers, the probability is that there will be a mutiny in both camps, and that the two revolted armies will make a truce with each other, in order to be revenged on those by whom they think that they have been betrayed. Thus it was in 1783. At the beginning of that eventful year, North had been the recognised head of the old Tory party, which, though for a moment prostrated by the disastrous issue of the American war, was still a great power in the state. To him the clergy, the universities, and that large body of country gentlemen whose rallying cry was "Church and King," had long looked up with respect and confidence. Fox had, on the other hand, been the idol of the Whigs, and of the whole body of Protestant dissenters. The coalition at once alienated the most zealous Tories from North, and the most zealous Whigs from Fox. The University of Oxford, which had marked its approbation of North's orthodoxy by electing him chancellor, the city of London, which had been during two and twenty years at war with the Court, were equally disgusted. Squires and rectors, who had inherited the principles of the cavaliers of the preceding century, could not forgive their old leader for combining with disloyal subjects in order to put a force on the sovereign. The members of the Bill of Rights Society and of the Reform Associations were enraged by learning that their favourite orator now called the great champion of tyranny and corruption his noble friend. Two great multitudes were at once left without any head, and both at once turned their eyes on Pitt. One party saw in him the only man who could rescue the King; the other saw in him the only man who could purify the Parliament. He was supported on one side by Archbishop Markham, the preacher of divine right, and by Jenkinson, the captain of the Prætorian band of the King's friends; on the other side by Jebb and Priestley, Sawbridge and Cartwright, Jack Wilkes and Horne Tooke. On the benches of the House of Commons, however, the ranks of the ministerial majority were unbroken; and that any statesman would venture to brave such a majority was thought impossible. No prince of the Hanoverian line had ever, under any provocation, ventured to appeal from the representative body to the constituent body. The ministers, therefore, notwithstanding the sullen looks and muttered words of displeasure with which their suggestions were received in the closet, notwithstanding the roar of obloquy which was rising louder and louder every day from every corner of the island, thought themselves secure.

Such was their confidence in their strength that, as soon as the Parliament had met, they brought forward a singularly bold and original plan for the government of the British territories in India. What was proposed was that the whole authority, which till that time had been exercised over those territories by the East India Company, should be transferred to seven commissioners who were to be named by Parliament, and were not to be removable at the pleasure of the Crown. Earl Fitzwilliam, the most intimate personal friend of Fox, was to be chairman of this board; and the eldest son of North was to be one of the members.

As soon as the outlines of the scheme were known, all the hatred which the coalition had excited burst forth with an astounding explosion. The question which ought undoubtedly to have been considered as paramount to every other was, whether the proposed change was likely to be beneficial or injurious to the thirty millions of people who were subject to the Company. But that question cannot be said to have been even seriously discussed. Burke, who, whether right or wrong in the conclusions to which he came, had at least the merit of looking at the subject in the right point of view, vainly reminded his hearers of that mighty population whose daily rice might depend on a vote of the British Parliament. He spoke, with even more than his wonted power of thought and language, about the desolation of Rohilcund, about the spoliation of Benares, about the evil policy which had suffered the tanks of the Carnatic to go to ruin; but he could scarcely obtain a hearing. The contending parties, to their shame it must be said, would listen to none but English topics. Out of doors the cry against the ministry was almost universal. Town and country were united. Corporations exclaimed against the violation of the charter of the greatest corporation in the realm. Tories and democrats joined in pronouncing the proposed board an unconstitutional body. It was to consist of Fox's nominees. The effect of his bill was to give, not to the Crown, but to him personally, whether in office or in opposition, an enormous power, a patronage sufficient to counterbalance the patronage of the Treasury and of the Admiralty, and to decide the elections for fifty boroughs. He knew, it was said, that he was hateful alike to King and people; and he had devised a plan which would make him independent of both. Some nicknamed him Cromwell, and some Carlo Khan. Wilberforce, with his usual felicity of expression, and with very unusual bitterness of feeling, described the scheme as the genuine offspring of the coalition, as marked with the features of both its parents, the corruption of one and the violence of the other. In spite of all opposition, however, the bill was supported in every stage by great majorities, was rapidly passed, and was sent up to the Lords. To the general astonishment, when the second reading was moved in the Upper House, the opposition proposed an adjournment, and carried it by eighty-seven votes to seventy-nine. The cause of this strange turn of fortune was soon known. Pitt's cousin, Earl Temple, had been in the royal closet, and had there been authorised to let it be known that His Majesty would consider all who voted for the bill as his enemies. The ignominious commission was performed, and instantly a troop of Lords of the Bedchamber, of Bishops who wished to be translated, and of Scotch peers who wished to be re-elected, made haste to change sides. On a later day, the Lords rejected the bill. Fox and North were immediately directed to send their seals to the palace by their Under Secretaries; and Pitt was appointed First Lord of the Treasury and Chancellor of the Exchequer.

The general opinion was, that there would be an immediate dissolution. But Pitt wisely determined to give the public feeling time to gather strength. On this point he differed from his kinsman Temple. The consequence was, that Temple, who had been appointed one of the Secretaries of State, resigned his office forty-eight hours after he had accepted it, and thus relieved the new government from a great load of unpopularity: for all men of sense and honour, however strong might be their dislike of the India Bill, disapproved of the manner in which that bill had been thrown out. Temple carried away with him the scandal which the best friends of the new government could not but lament. The fame of the young prime minister preserved its whiteness. He could declare with perfect truth that, if unconstitutional machinations had been employed, he had been no party to them.

He was, however, surrounded by difficulties and dangers. In the House of Lords, indeed, he had a majority; nor could any orator of the opposition in that assembly be considered as a match for Thurlow, who was now again Chancellor, or for Camden, who cordially supported the son of his old friend Chatham. But in the other House there was not a single eminent speaker among the

official men who sate round Pitt. His most useful assistant was
Dundas, who, though he had not eloquence, had sense, knowledge,
readiness, and boldness. On the opposite benches was a powerful
majority, led by Fox, who was supported by Burke, North, and
Sheridan. The heart of the young minister, stout as it was, almost
died within him. He could not once close his eyes on the night
which followed Temple's resignation. But, whatever his internal
emotions might be, his language and deportment indicated nothing
but unconquerable firmness and haughty confidence in his own
powers. His contest against the House of Commons lasted from
the 17th of December 1783 to the 8th of March 1784. In sixteen
divisions the opposition triumphed. Again and again the King was
requested to dismiss his ministers. But he was determined to go to
Germany rather than yield. Pitt's resolution never wavered. The
cry of the nation in his favour became vehement and almost furious.
Addresses assuring him of public support came up daily from every
part of the kingdom. The freedom of the city of London was
presented to him in a gold box. He went in state to receive this
mark of distinction. He was sumptuously feasted in Grocers' Hall;
and the shopkeepers of the Strand and Fleet Street illuminated
their houses in his honour. These things could not but produce an
effect within the walls of Parliament. The ranks of the majority
began to waver; a few passed over to the enemy; some skulked
away; many were for capitulating while it was still possible to
capitulate with the honours of war. Negotiations were opened with
the view of forming an administration on a wide basis; but they
had scarcely been opened when they were closed. The opposition
demanded, as a preliminary article of the treaty, that Pitt should
resign the Treasury; and with this demand Pitt steadfastly refused
to comply. While the contest was raging, the Clerkship of the Pells,
a sinecure place for life, worth three thousand a year, and tenable
with a seat in the House of Commons, became vacant. The
appointment was with the Chancellor of the Exchequer: nobody
doubted that he would appoint himself; and nobody could have
blamed him if he had done so: for such sinecure offices had always
been defended on the ground that they enabled a few men of
eminent abilities and small incomes to live without any profession,
and to devote themselves to the service of the state. Pitt, in spite of
the remonstrances of his friends, gave the Pells to his father's old
adherent, Colonel Barré, a man distinguished by talent and
eloquence, but poor and afflicted with blindness. By this arrangement a pension which the Rockingham administration had granted
to Barré was saved to the public. Never was there a happier stroke

of policy. About treaties, wars, expeditions, tariffs, budgets, there will always be room for dispute. The policy which is applauded by half the nation may be condemned by the other half. But pecuniary disinterestedness everybody comprehends. It is a great thing for a man who has only three hundred a year to be able to show that he considers three thousand a year as mere dirt beneath his feet, when compared with the public interest and the public esteem. Pitt had his reward. No minister was ever more rancorously libelled; but, even when he was known to be overwhelmed with debt, when millions were passing through his hands, when the wealthiest magnates of the realm were soliciting him for marquisates and garters, his bitterest enemies did not dare to accuse him of touching unlawful gain.

At length the hard fought fight ended. A final remonstrance, drawn up by Burke with admirable skill, was carried on the 8th of March by a single vote in a full House. Had the experiment been repeated, the supporters of the coalition would probably have been in a minority. But the supplies had been voted; the Mutiny Bill had been passed; and the Parliament was dissolved.

The popular constituent bodies all over the country were in general enthusiastic on the side of the new government. A hundred and sixty of the supporters of the coalition lost their seats. The First Lord of the Treasury himself came in at the head of the poll for the University of Cambridge. His young friend, Wilberforce, was elected Knight of the great shire of York, in opposition to the whole influence of the Fitzwilliams, Cavendishes, Dundases, and Saviles. In the midst of such triumphs Pitt completed his twenty-fifth year. He was now the greatest subject that England had seen during many generations. He domineered absolutely over the cabinet, and was the favourite at once of the Sovereign, of the Parliament, and of the nation. His father had never been so powerful, nor Walpole, nor Marlborough.

This narrative has now reached a point, beyond which a full history of the life of Pitt would be a history of England, or rather of the whole civilised world; and for such a history this is not the proper place. Here a very slight sketch must suffice; and in that sketch prominence will be given to such points as may enable a reader who is already acquainted with the general course of events to form a just notion of the character of the man on whom so much depended.

It we wish to arrive at a correct judgment of Pitt's merits and defects, we must never forget that he belonged to a peculiar class of statesmen, and that he must be tried by a peculiar standard. It is not easy to compare him fairly with such men as Ximenes and Sully, Richelieu and Oxenstiern, John de Witt and Warren Hastings. The means by which those politicians governed great communities were of quite a different kind from those which Pitt was under the necessity of employing. Some talents, which they never had any opportunity of showing that they possessed, were developed in him to an extraordinary degree. In some qualities, on the other hand, to which they owe a large part of their fame, he was decidedly their inferior. They transacted business in their closets, or at boards where a few confidential councillors sate. It was his lot to be born in an age and in a country in which parliamentary government was completely established; his whole training from infancy was such as fitted him to bear a part in parliamentary government; and, from the prime of his manhood to his death, all the powers of his vigorous mind were almost constantly exerted in the work of parliamentary government. He accordingly became the greatest master of the whole art of parliamentary government that has ever existed, a greater than Montague or Walpole, a greater than his father Chatham or his rival Fox, a greater than either of his illustrious successors Canning and Peel.

Parliamentary government, like every other contrivance of man, has its advantages and its disadvantages. On the advantages there is no need to dilate. The history of England during the hundred and seventy years which have elapsed since the House of Commons became the most powerful body in the state, her immense and still growing prosperity, her freedom, her tranquillity, her greatness in arts, in sciences, and in arms, her maritime ascendency, the marvels of her public credit, her American, her African, her Australian, her Asiatic empires, sufficiently prove the excellence of her institutions. But those institutions, though excellent, are assuredly not perfect. Parliamentary government is government by speaking. In such a government, the power of speaking is the most highly prized of all the qualities which a politician can possess; and that power may exist, in the highest degree, without judgment, without fortitude, without skill in reading the characters of men or the signs of the times, without any knowledge of the principles of legislation or of political economy, and without any skill in diplomacy or in the administration of war. Nay, it may well happen that those very intellectual qualities which give a peculiar charm to the speeches of a public man may be incompatible with the qualities which would fit him to meet a pressing emergency with promptitude and firmness. It was thus with Charles Townshend. It was thus with Windham. It was a privilege to listen to those accomplished and ingenious orators. But in a perilous crisis they would have been found far inferior in all the qualities of rulers to such a man as Oliver Cromwell, who talked nonsense, or as William the Silent, who did not talk at all. When parliamentary government is established, a Charles Townshend or a Windham will almost always exercise much greater influence than such men as the great Protector of England, or as the founder of the Batavian commonwealth. In such a government, parliamentary talent, though quite distinct from the talents of a good executive or judicial officer, will be a chief qualification for executive and judicial office. From the Book of Dignities a curious list might be made out of Chancellors ignorant of the principles of equity, and First Lords of the Admiralty ignorant of the principles of navigation, of Colonial ministers who could not repeat the names of the Colonies, of Lords of the Treasury who did not know the difference between funded and unfunded debt, and of Secretaries of the India Board who did not know whether the Mahrattas were Mahometans or Hindoos. On these grounds, some persons, incapable of seeing more than one side of a question, have pronounced parliamentary government a positive evil, and have maintained that the administration would be greatly improved if the power, now exercised by a large assembly, were transferred to a single person. Men of sense will probably think the remedy very much worse than the disease, and will be of opinion that there would be small gain in exchanging Charles Townshend and Windham for the Prince of the Peace, or the poor slave and the dog Steenie.

Pitt was emphatically the man of parliamentary government, the type of his class, the minion, the child, the spoiled child, of the House of Commons. For the House of Commons he had a hereditary, an infantine love. Through his whole boyhood, the House of Commons was never out of his thoughts, or out of the thoughts of his instructors. Reciting at his father's knee, reading Thucydides and Cicero into English, analysing the great Attic speeches on the Embassy and on the Crown, he was constantly in training for the conflicts of the House of Commons. He was a distinguished member of the House of Commons at twenty-one. The ability which he had displayed in the House of Commons made him the most powerful subject in Europe before he was twenty-five. It would have been happy for himself and for his country if his elevation had been deferred. Eight or ten years, during which he would have had leisure and opportunity for reading and reflection, for foreign travel, for social intercourse and free exchange of thought on equal terms with a great variety of companions, would have supplied what, without any fault on his part, was wanting to his powerful intellect. He had all the knowledge that he could be expected to have; that is to say, all the knowledge that a man can acquire while he is a student at Cambridge, and all the knowledge that a man can acquire when he is First Lord of the Treasury and Chancellor of the Exchequer. But the stock of general information which he brought from college, extraordinary for a boy, was far inferior to what Fox possessed, and beggarly when compared with the massy, the splendid, the various treasures laid up in the large mind of Burke. After Pitt became minister, he had no leisure to learn more than was necessary for the purposes of the day which was passing over him. What was necessary for those purposes such a man could learn with little difficulty. He was surrounded by experienced and able public servants. He could at any moment command their best assistance. From the stores which they produced his vigorous mind rapidly collected the materials for a good parliamentary case: and that was enough. Legislation and administration were with him secondary matters. To the work of framing statutes, of negotiating treaties, of organising fleets and armies, of sending forth expeditions, he gave only the leavings of his time and the dregs of his fine intellect. The strength and sap of his mind were all drawn in a different direction. It was when the House of Commons was to be convinced and persuaded that he put forth all his powers.

Of those powers we must form our estimate chiefly from tradition; for of all the eminent speakers of the last age Pitt has suffered most from the reporters. Even while he was still living, critics remarked that his eloquence could not be preserved, that he must be heard to be appreciated. They more than once applied to him the sentence in which Tacitus describes the fate of a senator whose rhetoric was admired in the Augustan age: "Haterii canorum illud et profluens cum ipso simul exstinctum est." There is, however, abundant evidence that nature had bestowed on Pitt the talents of a great orator; and those talents had been developed in a very peculiar manner, first by his education, and secondly by the high official position to which he rose early, and in which he passed the greater part of his public life.

At his first appearance in Parliament he showed himself superior to all his contemporaries in command of language. He could pour forth a long succession of round and stately periods, without premeditation, without ever pausing for a word, without ever repeating a word, in a voice of silver clearness, and with a pronunciation so articulate that not a letter was slurred over. He had less amplitude of mind and less richness of imagination than Burke, less ingenuity than Windham, less wit than Sheridan, less perfect mastery of dialectical fence, and less of that highest sort of eloquence which consists of reason and passion fused together, than Fox. Yet the almost unanimous judgment of those who were in the habit of listening to that remarkable race of men placed Pitt, as a speaker, above Burke, above Windham, above Sheridan, and not below Fox. His declamation was copious, polished, and splendid. In power of sarcasm he was probably not surpassed by any speaker, ancient or modern; and of this formidable weapon he made merciless use. In two parts of the oratorical art which are of the highest value to a minister of state he was singularly expert. No man knew better how to be luminous or how to be obscure. When he wished to be understood, he never failed to make himself understood. He could with ease present to his audience, not perhaps an exact or profound, but a clear, popular, and plausible view of the most extensive and complicated subject. Nothing was out of place; nothing was forgotten; minute details, dates, sums of money, were all faithfully preserved in his memory. Even intricate questions of finance, when explained by him, seemed clear to the plainest man among his hearers. On the other hand, when he did not wish to be explicit,—and no man who is at the head of affairs always wishes to be explicit,—he had a marvellous power of saying nothing in language which left on his audience the impression that he had said a great deal. He was at once the only man who could open a budget without notes, and the only man who, as Windham said, could speak that most elaborately evasive and unmeaning of human compositions, a King's speech, without premeditation.

The effect of oratory will always to a great extent depend on the character of the orator. There perhaps never were two speakers whose eloquence had more of what may be called the race, more of the flavour imparted by moral qualities, than Fox and Pitt. The speeches of Fox owe a great part of their charm to that warmth and softness of heart, that sympathy with human suffering, that admiration for everything great and beautiful, and that hatred of cruelty and injustice, which interest and delight us even in the most defective reports. No person, on the other hand, could hear Pitt without perceiving him to be a man of high, intrepid, and commanding spirit, proudly conscious of his own rectitude and of his own intellectual superiority, incapable of the low vices of fear and envy, but too prone to feel and to show disdain. Pride, indeed, pervaded the whole man, was written in the harsh, rigid lines of his face, was marked by the way in which he walked, in which he sate, in which he stood, and, above all, in which he bowed. Such pride, of course, inflicted many wounds. It may confidently be affirmed that there cannot be found, in all the ten thousand invectives written against Fox, a word indicating that his demeanour had ever made a single personal enemy. On the other hand, several men of note who had been partial to Pitt, and who to the last continued to approve his public conduct and to support his administration, Cumberland, for example, Boswell, and Matthias, were so much irritated by the contempt with which he treated them, that they complained in print of their wrongs. But his pride, though it made him bitterly disliked by individuals, inspired the great body of his followers in Parliament and throughout the country with respect and confidence. They took him at his own valuation. They saw that his self-esteem was not that of an upstart, who was drunk with good luck and with applause, and who, if fortune turned, would sink from arrogance into abject humility. It was that of the magnanimous man so finely described by Aristotle in the Ethics, of the man who thinks himself worthy of great things, being in truth worthy. It sprang from a consciousness of great powers and great virtues, and was never so conspicuously displayed as in the midst of difficulties and dangers which would have unnerved and bowed down any ordinary mind. It was closely connected, too, with an ambition which had no mixture of low cupidity. There was something noble in the cynical disdain with which the mighty minister scattered riches and titles to right and left among those who valued them, while he spurned them out of his own way. Poor himself, he was surrounded by friends on whom he had bestowed three thousand, six thousand, ten thousand a year. Plain Mister himself, he had made more lords than any three ministers that had preceded him. The garter, for which the first dukes in the kingdom were contending, was repeatedly offered to him, and offered in vain.

The correctness of his private life added much to the dignity of his public character. In the relations of son, brother, uncle, master, friend, his conduct was exemplary. In the small circle of his intimate associates, he was amiable, affectionate, even playful. They loved him sincerely; they regretted him long; and they would hardly admit that he who was so kind and gentle with them could be stern and haughty with others. He indulged, indeed, somewhat too freely in wine, which he had early been directed to take as a medicine, and which use had made a necessary of life to him. But it was very seldom that any indication of undue excess could be detected in his tones or gestures; and, in truth, two bottles of port were little more to him than two dishes of tea. He had, when he was first introduced into the clubs of Saint James's Street, shown a strong taste for play; but he had the prudence and the resolution to stop before this taste had acquired the strength of habit. From the passion which generally exercises the most tyrannical dominion over the young he possessed an immunity, which is probably to be ascribed partly to his temperament and partly to his situation. His constitution was feeble: he was very shy; and he was very busy. The strictness of his morals furnished such buffoons as Peter Pindar and Captain Morris with an inexhaustible theme for merriment of no very delicate kind. But the great body of the middle class of Englishmen could not see the joke. They warmly praised the young statesman for commanding his passions, and for covering his frailties, if he had frailties, with decorous obscurity, and would have been very far indeed from thinking better of him if he had vindicated himself from the taunts of his enemies by taking under his protection a Nancy Parsons or a Marianne Clark.

No part of the immense popularity which Pitt long enjoyed is to be attributed to the eulogies of wits and poets. It might have been naturally expected that a man of genius, of learning, of taste, an orator whose diction was often compared to that of Tully, the representative, too, of a great university, would have taken a peculiar pleasure in befriending eminent writers, to whatever political party they might have belonged. The love of literature had induced Augustus to heap benefits on Pompeians, Somers to be the protector of nonjurors, Harley to make the fortunes of Whigs. But it could not move Pitt to show any favour even to Pittites. He was doubtless right in thinking that, in general, poetry, history and philosophy ought to be suffered, like calico and cutlery, to find their proper price in the market, and that to teach men of letters to look habitually to the state for their recompense is bad for the state and bad for letters. Assuredly nothing can be more absurd or mischievous than to waste the public money in bounties for the purpose of inducing people who ought to be weighing out grocery or measuring out drapery to write bad or middling books. But, though the sound rule is that authors should be left to be remunerated by their readers, there will, in every generation, be a few exceptions to this rule. To distinguish these special cases from the mass is an employment well worthy of the faculties of a great and accomplished ruler; and Pitt would assuredly have had little difficulty in finding such cases. While he was in power, the greatest philologist of the age, his own contemporary at Cambridge, was reduced to earn a livelihood by the lowest literary drudgery, and to spend in writing squibs for the Morning Chronicle years to which we might have owed an all but perfect text of the whole tragic and comic drama of Athens. The greatest historian of the age, forced by poverty to leave his country, completed his immortal work on the shores of Lake Leman. The political heterodoxy of Porson, and the religious heterodoxy of Gibbon, may perhaps be pleaded in defence of the minister by whom those eminent men were neglected. But there were other cases in which no such excuse could be set up. Scarcely had Pitt obtained possession of unbounded power when an aged writer of the highest eminence, who had made very little by his writings, and who was sinking into the grave under a load of infirmities and sorrows, wanted five or six hundred pounds to enable him, during the winter or two which might still remain to him, to draw his breath more easily in the soft climate of Italy. Not a farthing was to be obtained; and before Christmas the author of the English Dictionary and of the Lives of the Poets had gasped his last in the river fog and coal smoke of Fleet Street. A few months after the death of Johnson appeared the Task, incomparably the best poem that any Englishman then living had produced—a poem, too, which could hardly fail to excite in a well constituted mind a feeling of esteem and compassion for the poet, a man of genius and virtue, whose means were scanty, and whom the most cruel of all the calamities incident to humanity had made incapable of supporting himself by vigorous and sustained exertion. Nowhere had Chatham been praised with more enthusiasm, or in verse more worthy of the subject, than in the Task. The son of Chatham, however, contented himself with reading and admiring the book, and left the author to starve. The pension which, long after, enabled poor Cowper to close his melancholy life, unmolested by duns and bailiffs, was obtained for him by the strenuous kindness of Lord Spencer. What a contrast between the way in which Pitt acted towards Johnson and the way in which Lord Grey acted towards his political enemy Scott, when Scott, worn out by misfortune and disease, was advised to try the effect of the Italian air! What a contrast between the way in which Pitt acted towards Cowper and the way in which Burke, a poor man and out of place, acted towards Crabbe! Even Dundas, who made no pretensions to literary taste, and was content to be considered as a hard-headed and somewhat coarse man of business, was, when compared with his eloquent and classically educated friend, a Mæcenas or a Leo. Dundas made Burns an exciseman, with seventy pounds a year; and this was more than Pitt, during his long tenure of power, did for the encouragement of letters. Even those who may think that

is, in general, no part of the duty of a government to reward literary merit will hardly deny that a government, which has much lucrative church preferment in its gift, is bound, in distributing that preferment, not to overlook divines whose writings have rendered great service to the cause of religion. But it seems never to have occurred to Pitt that he lay under any such obligation. All the theological works of all the numerous bishops whom he made and translated are not, when put together, worth fifty pages of the Horæ Paulinæ, of the Natural Theology, or of the View of the Evidences of Christianity. But on Paley the all-powerful minister never bestowed the smallest benefice. Artists Pitt treated as contemptuously as writers. For painting he did simply nothing. Sculptors, who had been selected to execute monuments voted by Parliament, had to haunt the ante-chambers of the Treasury during many years before they could obtain a farthing from him. One of them, after vainly soliciting the minister for payment during fourteen years, had the courage to present a memorial to the King, and thus obtained tardy and ungracious justice. Architects it was absolutely necessary to employ; and the worst that could be found seem to have been employed. Not a single fine public building of any kind or in any style was erected during his long administration. It may be confidently affirmed that no ruler whose abilities and attainments would bear any comparison with his has ever shown such cold disdain for what is excellent in arts and letters.

His first administration lasted seventeen years. That long period is divided by a strongly marked line into two almost exactly equal parts. The first part ended and the second began in the autumn of 1792. Throughout both parts Pitt displayed in the highest degree the talents of a parliamentary leader. During the first part he was a fortunate and, in many respects, a skilful administrator. With the difficulties which he had to encounter during the second part he was altogether incapable of contending: but his eloquence and his perfect mastery of the tactics of the House of Commons concealed his incapacity from the multitude.

The eight years which followed the general election of 1784 were as tranquil and prosperous as any eight years in the whole history of England. Neighbouring nations which had lately been in arms against her, and which had flattered themselves that, in losing her American colonies, she had lost a chief source of her wealth and of her power, saw, with wonder and vexation, that she was more wealthy and more powerful than ever. Her trade increased. Her manufactures flourished. Her exchequer was full to overflowing. Very idle apprehensions were generally entertained, that the public debt, though much less than a third of the debt which we now bear with ease, would be found too heavy for the strength of the nation. Those apprehensions might not perhaps have been easily quieted by reason. But Pitt quieted them by a juggle. He succeeded in persuading first himself, and then the whole nation, his opponents included, that a new sinking fund, which, so far as it differed from former sinking funds, differed for the worse, would, by virtue of some mysterious power of propagation belonging to money, put into the pocket of the public creditor great sums not taken out of the pocket of the tax-payer. The country, terrified by a danger which was no danger, hailed with delight and boundless confidence a remedy which was no remedy. The minister was almost universally extolled as the greatest of financiers. Meanwhile both the branches of the House of Bourbon found that England was as formidable an antagonist as she had ever been. France had formed a plan for reducing Holland to vassalage. But England interposed; and France receded. Spain interrupted by violence the trade of our merchants with the regions near the Oregon. But England armed, and Spain receded. Within the island there was profound tranquillity. The King was, for the first time, popular. During the twenty-three years which had followed his accession he had not been loved by his subjects. His domestic virtues were acknowledged. But it was generally thought that the good qualities by which he was distinguished in private life were wanting to his political character. As a Sovereign, he was resentful, unforgiving, stubborn, cunning. Under his rule the country had sustained cruel disgraces and disasters; and every one of those disgraces and disasters was imputed to his strong antipathies, and to his perverse obstinacy in the wrong. One statesman after another complained that he had been induced by royal caresses, entreaties, and promises, to undertake the direction of affairs at a difficult conjuncture, and that, as soon as he had, not without sullying his fame and alienating his best friends, served the turn for which he was wanted, his ungrateful master began to intrigue against him, and to canvass against him. Grenville, Rockingham, Chatham, men of widely different characters, but all three upright and high-spirited, agreed in thinking that the Prince under whom they had successively held the highest place in the government was one of the most insincere of mankind. His confidence was reposed, they said, not in those known and responsible counsellors to whom he had delivered the seals of office, but in secret advisers who stole up the back stairs into his closet. In Parliament, his ministers, while defending themselves against the attacks of the opposition in front, were perpetually, at his instigation, assailed on the flank or in the rear by a vile band of mercenaries who called themselves his friends. These men constantly, while in possession of lucrative places in his service, spoke and voted against bills which he had authorised the First Lord of the Treasury or the Secretary of State to bring in. But from the day on which Pitt was placed at the head of affairs there was an end of secret influence. His haughty and aspiring spirit was not to be satisfied with the mere show of power. Any attempt to undermine him at Court, any mutinous movement among his followers in the House of Commons, was certain to be at once put down. He had only to tender his resignation; and he could dictate his own terms. For he, and he alone, stood between the King and the Coalition. He was therefore little less than Mayor of the Palace. The nation loudly applauded the King for having the wisdom to repose entire confidence in so excellent a minister. His Majesty's private virtues now began to produce their full effect. He was generally regarded as the model of a respectable country gentleman, honest, goodnatured, sober, religious. He rose early: he dined temperately: he was strictly faithful to his wife: he never missed church; and at church he never missed a response. His people heartily prayed that he might long reign over them; and they prayed the more heartily because his virtues were set off to the best advantage by the vices and follies of the Prince of Wales, who lived in close intimacy with the chiefs of the opposition.

How strong this feeling was in the public mind appeared signally on one great occasion. In the autumn of 1788 the King became insane. The opposition, eager for office, committed the great indiscretion of asserting that the heir apparent had, by the fundamental laws of England, a right to be Regent with the full powers of royalty. Pitt, on the other hand, maintained it to be the constitutional doctrine that, when a Sovereign is, by reason of infancy, disease, or absence, incapable of exercising the regal functions, it belongs to the estates of the realm to determine who shall be the vicegerent, and with what portion of the executive authority such vicegerent shall be entrusted. A long and violent contest followed, in which Pitt was supported by the great body of the people with as much enthusiasm as during the first months of his administration. Tories with one voice applauded him for defending the sick-bed of a virtuous and unhappy Sovereign against a disloyal faction and an undutiful son. Not a few Whigs applauded him for asserting the authority of Parliaments and the principles of the Revolution, in opposition to a doctrine which seemed to have too much affinity with the servile theory of indefeasible hereditary right. The middle class, always zealous on the side of decency and the domestic virtues, looked forward with dismay to a reign resembling that of Charles II. The palace, which had now been, during thirty years, the pattern of an English home, would be a public nuisance, a school of profligacy. To the good King's repast of mutton and lemonade, despatched at three o'clock, would succeed midnight banquets, from which the guests would be carried home speechless. To the backgammon board at which the good King played for a little silver with his equerries, would succeed faro tables from which young patricians who had sate down rich would rise up beggars. The drawing-room, from which the frown of the Queen had repelled a whole generation of frail beauties, would now be again what it had been in the days of Barbara Palmer and Louisa de Querouaille. Nay, severely as the public reprobated the Prince's many illicit attachments, his one virtuous attachment was reprobated more severely still. Even in grave and pious circles his Protestant mistresses gave less scandal than his Popish wife. That he must be Regent nobody ventured to deny. But he and his friends were so unpopular that Pitt could, with general approbation, propose to limit the powers of the Regent by restrictions to which it would have been impossible to subject a Prince beloved and trusted by the country. Some interested men, fully expecting a change of administration, went over to the opposition. But the majority, purified by these desertions, closed its ranks, and presented a more firm array than ever to the enemy. In every division Pitt was victorious. When at length, after a stormy interregnum of three months, it was announced, on the very eve of the inauguration of the Regent, that the King was himself again, the nation was wild with delight. On the evening of the day on which His Majesty resumed his functions, a spontaneous illumination, the most general that had ever been seen in England, brightened the whole vast space from Highgate to Tooting, and from Hammersmith to Greenwich. On the day on which he returned thanks in the cathedral of his capital, all the horses and carriages within a hundred miles of London were too few for the multitudes which flocked to see him pass through the streets. A second illumination followed, which was even superior to the first in magnificence. Pitt with difficulty escaped from the tumultuous kindness of an innumerable multitude which insisted on drawing his coach from Saint Paul's Churchyard to Downing Street. This was the moment at which his fame and fortune may be said to have reached the zenith. His influence in the closet was as great as that of Carr or Villiers had been. His dominion over the Parliament was more absolute than that of Walpole or Pelham had been. He was at the same time as high in the favour of the populace as ever Wilkes or Sacheverell had been. Nothing did more to raise his character than his noble poverty. It was well known that, if he had been dismissed from office after more than five years of boundless power, he would hardly have carried out with him a sum sufficient to furnish the set of chambers in which, as he cheerfully declared, he meant to resume the practice of the law. His admirers, however, were by no means disposed to suffer him to depend on daily toil for his daily bread. The voluntary contributions which were awaiting his acceptance in the city of London alone would have sufficed to make him a rich man. But it may be doubted whether his haughty spirit would have stooped to accept a provision so honourably earned and so honourably bestowed.

To such a height of power and glory had this extraordinary man risen at twenty-nine years of age. And now the tide was on the turn. Only ten days after the triumphant procession to Saint Paul's, the States-General of France, after an interval of a hundred and seventy-four years, met at Versailles.

The nature of the great Revolution which followed was long very imperfectly understood in this country. Burke saw much further than any of his contemporaries: but whatever his sagacity descried was refracted and discoloured by his passions and his imagination. More than three years elapsed before the principles of the English administration underwent any material change. Nothing could as yet be milder or more strictly constitutional than the minister's domestic policy. Not a single act indicating an arbitrary temper or a jealousy of the people could be imputed to him. He had never applied to Parliament for any extraordinary powers. He had never used with harshness the ordinary powers entrusted by the constitution to the executive government. Not a single state prosecution which would even now be called oppressive had been instituted by him. Indeed, the only oppressive state prosecution instituted during the first eight years of his administration was that of Stockdale, which is to be attributed, not to the government, but to the chiefs of the opposition. In office, Pitt had redeemed the pledges which he had, at his entrance into public life, given to the supporters of parliamentary reform. He had, in 1785, brought forward a judicious plan for the improvement of the representative system, and had prevailed on the King, not only to refrain from talking against that plan, but to recommend it to the Houses in a speech from the throne.[1] This attempt failed; but there can be little doubt

[1] The speech with which the King opened the session of 1785, concluded with an assurance that His Majesty would heartily concur in every measure which could tend to secure the true principles of the constitution. These words were at the time understood to refer to Pitt's Reform Bill.

that, if the French Revolution had not produced a violent reaction of public feeling, Pitt would have performed, with little difficulty and no danger, that great work which, at a later period, Lord Grey could accomplish only by means which for a time loosened the very foundations of the commonwealth. When the atrocities of the slave trade were first brought under the consideration of Parliament, no abolitionist was more zealous than Pitt. When sickness prevented Wilberforce from appearing in public, his place was most efficiently supplied by his friend the minister. A humane bill, which mitigated the horrors of the middle passage, was, in 1788, carried by the eloquence and determined spirit of Pitt, in spite of the opposition of some of his own colleagues; and it ought always to be remembered to his honour that, in order to carry that bill, he kept the Houses sitting, in spite of many murmurs, long after the business of the government had been done, and the Appropriation Act passed. In 1791 he cordially concurred with Fox in maintaining the sound constitutional doctrine, that an impeachment is not terminated by a dissolution. In the course of the same year the two great rivals contended side by side in a far more important cause. They are fairly entitled to divide the high honour of having added to our statute-book the inestimable law which places the liberty of the press under the protection of juries. On one occasion, and one alone, Pitt, during the first half of his long administration, acted in a manner unworthy of an enlightened Whig. In the debate on the Test Act, he stooped to gratify the master whom he served, the university which he represented, and the great body of clergymen and country gentlemen on whose support he rested, by talking, with little heartiness, indeed, and with no asperity, the language of a Tory. With this single exception, his conduct from the end of 1783 to the middle of 1792 was that of an honest friend of civil and religious liberty.

Nor did anything, during that period, indicate that he loved war, or harboured any malevolent feelings against any neighbouring nation. Those French writers who have represented him as a Hannibal sworn in childhood by his father to bear eternal hatred to France, as having, by mysterious intrigues and lavish bribes, instigated the leading Jacobins to commit those excesses which dishonoured the Revolution, as having been the real author of the first coalition, know nothing of his character or of his history. So far was he from being a deadly enemy to France, that his laudable attempts to bring about a closer connection with that country by means of a wise and liberal treaty of commerce brought on him the severe censure of the opposition. He was told in the House of Commons that he was a degenerate son, and that his partiality for the hereditary foes of our island was enough to make his great father's bones stir under the pavement of the Abbey.

And this man, whose name, if he had been so fortunate as to die in 1792, would now have been associated with peace, with freedom, with philanthropy, with temperate reform, with mild and constitutional administration, lived to associate his name with arbitrary government, with harsh laws harshly executed, with alien bills, with gagging bills, with suspensions of the Habeas Corpus Act, with cruel punishments inflicted on some political agitators, with unjustifiable prosecutions instituted against others, and with the most costly and most sanguinary wars of modern times. He lived to be held up to obloquy as the stern oppressor of England, and the indefatigable disturber of Europe. Poets, contrasting his earlier with his later years, likened him sometimes to the apostle who kissed in order to betray, and sometimes to the evil angels who kept not their first estate. A satirist of great genius introduced the fiends of Famine, Slaughter, and Fire, proclaiming that they had received their commission from One whose name was formed of four letters, and promising to give their employer ample proofs of gratitude. Famine would gnaw the multitude till they should rise up against him in madness. The demon of Slaughter would impel them to tear him from limb to limb. But Fire boasted that she alone could reward him as he deserved, and that she would cling round him to all eternity. By the French press and the French tribune every crime that disgraced and every calamity that afflicted France was ascribed to the monster Pitt and his guineas. While the Jacobins were dominant, it was he who had corrupted the Gironde, who had raised Lyons and Bordeaux against the Convention, who had suborned Paris to assassinate Lepelletier, and Cecilia Regnault to assassinate Robespierre. When the Thermidorian reaction came, all the atrocities of the Reign of Terror were imputed to him. Collot D'Herbois and Fouquier Tinville had been his pensioners. It was he who had hired the murderers of September, who had dictated the pamphlets of Marat and the Carmagnoles of Barrere, who had paid Lebon to deluge Arras with blood, and Carrier to choke the Loire with corpses.

The truth is, that he liked neither war nor arbitrary government. He was a lover of peace and freedom, driven, by a stress against which it was hardly possible for any will or any intellect to struggle, out of the course to which his inclinations pointed, and for which his abilities and acquirements fitted him, and forced into a policy repugnant to his feelings and unsuited to his talents.

The charge of apostasy is grossly unjust. A man ought no more to be called an apostate because his opinions alter with the opinions of the great body of his contemporaries than he ought to be called an oriental traveller because he is always going round from west to east with the globe and everything that is upon it. Between the spring of 1789 and the close of 1792, the public mind of England underwent a great change. If the change of Pitt's sentiments attracted peculiar notice, it was not because he changed more than his neighbours; for in fact he changed less than most of them; but because his position was far more conspicuous than theirs, because he was, till Bonaparte appeared, the individual who filled the greatest space in the eyes of the inhabitants of the civilised world. During a short time the nation, and Pitt, as one of the nation, looked with interest and approbation on the French Revolution. But soon vast confiscations, the violent sweeping away of ancient institutions, the domination of clubs, the barbarities of mobs maddened by famine and hatred, produced a reaction here. The court, the nobility, the gentry, the clergy, the manufacturers, the merchants, in short, nineteen twentieths of those who had good roofs over their heads and good coats on their backs, became eager and intolerant Antijacobins. This feeling was at least as strong among the minister's adversaries as among his supporters. Fox in vain attempted to restrain his followers. All his genius, all his vast personal influence, could not prevent them from rising up against him in general mutiny. Burke set the example of revolt; and Burke was in no long time joined by Portland, Spencer, Fitzwilliam, Loughborough, Carlisle, Malmesbury, Windham, Elliot. In the House of Commons, the followers of the great Whig statesman and orator diminished from about a hundred and sixty to fifty. In the House of Lords he had but ten or twelve adherents left. There can be no doubt that there would have been a similar mutiny on the ministerial benches if Pitt had obstinately resisted the general wish. Pressed at once by his master and by his colleagues, by old friends and by old opponents, he abandoned, slowly and reluctantly, the policy which was dear to his heart. He laboured hard to avert the European war. When the European war broke out, he still flattered himself that it would not be necessary for this country to take either side. In the spring of 1792 he congratulated the Parliament on the prospect of long and profound peace, and proved his sincerity by proposing large remissions of taxation. Down to the end of that year he continued to cherish the hope that England might be able to preserve neutrality. But the passions which raged on both sides of the Channel were not to be restrained. The republicans who ruled France were inflamed by a fanaticism resembling that of the

Mussulmans who, with the Koran in one hand and the sword in the other, went forth, conquering and converting, eastward to the Bay of Bengal, and westward to the Pillars of Hercules. The higher and middle classes of England were animated by zeal not less fiery than that of the Crusaders who raised the cry of *Deus vult* at Clermont. The impulse which drove the two nations to a collision was not to be arrested by the abilities or by the authority of any single man. As Pitt was in front of his fellows, and towered high above them, he seemed to lead them. But in fact he was violently pushed on by them, and, had he held back but a little more than he did, would have been thrust out of their way or trampled under their feet.

He yielded to the current: and from that day his misfortunes began. The truth is that there were only two consistent courses before him. Since he did not choose to oppose himself, side by side with Fox, to the public feeling, he should have taken the advice of Burke, and should have availed himself of that feeling to the full extent. If it was impossible to preserve peace, he should have adopted the only policy which could lead to victory. He should have proclaimed a Holy War for religion, morality, property, order, public law, and should have thus opposed to the Jacobins an energy equal to their own. Unhappily he tried to find a middle path; and he found one which united all that was worst in both extremes. He went to war: but he would not understand the peculiar character of that war. He was obstinately blind to the plain fact, that he was contending against a state which was also a sect, and that the new quarrel between England and France was of quite a different kind from the old quarrel about colonies in America and fortresses in the Netherlands. He had to combat frantic enthusiasm, boundless ambition, restless activity, the wildest and most audacious spirit of innovation; and he acted as if he had to deal with the harlots and fops of the old Court of Versailles, with Madame de Pompadour and the Abbé de Bernis. It was pitiable to hear him, year after year, proving to an admiring audience that the wicked Republic was exhausted, that she could not hold out, that her credit was gone, and her assignats were not worth more than the paper of which they were made; as if credit was necessary to a government of which the principle was rapine, as if Alboin could not turn Italy into a desert till he had negotiated a loan at five per cent., as if the exchequer bills of Attila had been at par. It was impossible that a man who so completely mistook the nature of a contest could carry on that contest successfully. Great as Pitt's abilities were, his military administration was that of a driveller. He was at the head of a nation engaged in a struggle for life and death, of a nation eminently distinguished by all the physica and all the moral qualities which make excellent soldiers. The resources at his command were unlimited. The Parliament was even more ready to grant him men and money than he was to ask for them. In such an emergency, and with such means, such a statesman as Richelieu, as Louvois, as Chatham, as Wellesley, would have created in a few months one of the finest armies in the world, and would soon have discovered and brought forward generals worthy to command such an army. Germany might have been saved by another Blenheim; Flanders recovered by another Ramilies; another Poitiers might have delivered the Royalist and Catholic provinces of France from a yoke which they abhorred, and might have spread terror even to the barriers of Paris. But the fact is, that, after eight years of war, after a vast destruction of life, after an expenditure of wealth far exceeding the expenditure of the American war, of the Seven Years' War, of the war of the Austrian Succession, and of the war of the Spanish Succession united, the English army, under Pitt, was the laughing-stock of all Europe. It could not boast of one single brilliant exploit. It had never shown itself on the Continent but to be beaten, chased, forced to reembark, or forced to capitulate. To take some sugar island in the West Indies, to scatter some mob of half naked Irish peasants, such were the most splendid victories won by the British troops under Pitt's auspices.

The English navy no mismanagement could ruin. But during a long period whatever mismanagement could do was done. The Earl of Chatham, without a single qualification for high public trust, was made, by fraternal partiality, First Lord of the Admiralty, and was kept in that great post during two years of a war in which the very existence of the state depended on the efficiency of the fleet. He continued to doze away and trifle away the time which ought to have been devoted to the public service, till the whole mercantile body, though generally disposed to support the government, complained bitterly that our flag gave no protection to our trade. Fortunately he was succeeded by George Earl Spencer, one of those chiefs of the Whig party who, in the great schism caused by the French Revolution, had followed Burke. Lord Spencer, though inferior to many of his colleagues as an orator, was decidedly the best administrator among them. To him it was owing that a long and gloomy succession of days of fasting, and, most emphatically, of humiliation, was interrupted, twice in the short space of eleven months, by days of thanksgiving for great victories.

It may seem paradoxical to say that the incapacity which Pitt showed in all that related to the conduct of the war is, in some

sense, the most decisive proof that he was a man oᴸ very extraordinary abilities. Yet this is the simple truth. For assuredly one-
tenth part of his errors and disasters would have been fatal to the
power and influence of any minister who had not possessed, in
the highest degree, the talents of a parliamentary leader. While his
schemes were confounded, while his predictions were falsified,
while the coalitions which he had laboured to form were falling to
pieces, while the expeditions which he had sent forth at enormous
cost were ending in rout and disgrace, while the enemy against
whom he was feebly contending was subjugating Flanders and
Brabant, the Electorate of Mentz, the Electorate of Treves, Holland,
Piedmont, Liguria, Lombardy, his authority over the House of Commons was constantly becoming more and more absolute. There was
his empire. There were his victories, his Lodi and his Arcola, his
Rivoli and his Marengo. If some great misfortune, a pitched battle
lost by the allies, the annexation of a new department to the French
Republic, a sanguinary insurrection in Ireland, a mutiny in the fleet,
a panic in the city, a run on the bank, had spread dismay through the
ranks of his majority, that dismay lasted only till he rose from the
Treasury bench, drew up his haughty head, stretched his arm with
commanding gesture, and poured forth, in deep and sonorous tones,
the lofty language of inextinguishable hope and inflexible resolution. Thus, through a long and calamitous period, every disaster
that happened without the walls of Parliament was regularly
followed by a triumph within them. At length he had no longer an
opposition to encounter. Of the great party which had contended
against him during the first eight years of his administration more
than one half now marched under his standard, with his old competitor the Duke of Portland at their head; and the rest had, after
many vain struggles, quitted the field in despair. Fox had retired
to the shades of St. Anne's Hill, and had there found, in the society
of friends whom no vicissitude could estrange from him, of a woman
whom he tenderly loved, and of the illustrious dead of Athens, of
Rome, and of Florence, ample compensation for all the misfortunes
of his public life. Session followed session with scarcely a single
division. In the eventful year 1799, the largest minority that could
be mustered against the government was twenty-five.

In Pitt's domestic policy there was at this time assuredly no want
of vigour. While he offered to French Jacobinism a resistance so
feeble that it only encouraged the evil which he wished to suppress,
he put down English Jacobinism with a strong hand. The Habeas
Corpus Act was repeatedly suspended. Public meetings were
placed under severe restraints. The government obtained from

Parliament power to send out of the country aliens who were suspected of evil designs; and that power was not suffered to be idle.
Writers who propounded doctrines adverse to monarchy and
aristocracy were proscribed and punished without mercy. It was
hardly safe for a republican to avow his political creed over his
beefsteak and his bottle of port at a chop-house. The old laws of
Scotland against sedition, laws which were considered by Englishmen as barbarous, and which a succession of governments had
suffered to rust, were now furbished up and sharpened anew. Men
of cultivated minds and polished manners were, for offences which
at Westminster would have been treated as mere misdemeanours,
sent to herd with felons at Botany Bay. Some reformers, whose
opinions were extravagant, and whose language was intemperate,
but who had never dreamed of subverting the government by
physical force, were indicted for high treason, and were saved from
the gallows only by the righteous verdicts of juries. This severity
was at the time loudly applauded by alarmists whom fear had made
cruel, but will be seen in a very different light by posterity. The
truth is, that the Englishmen who wished for a revolution were,
even in number, not formidable, and, in everything but number,
a faction utterly contemptible, without arms, or funds, or plans, or
organisation, or leader. There can be no doubt that Pitt, strong as
he was in the support of the great body of the nation, might easily
have repressed the turbulence of the discontented minority by
firmly yet temperately enforcing the ordinary law. Whatever
vigour he showed during this unfortunate part of his life was vigour
out of place and season. He was all feebleness and languor in his
conflict with the foreign enemy who was really to be dreaded, and
reserved all his energy and resolution for the domestic enemy who
might safely have been despised.

One part only of Pitt's conduct during the last eight years of the
eighteenth century deserves high praise. He was the first English
minister who formed great designs for the benefit of Ireland. The
manner in which the Roman Catholic population of that unfortunate
country had been kept down during many generations seemed to
him unjust and cruel; and it was scarcely possible for a man of his
abilities not to perceive that, in a contest against the Jacobins, the
Roman Catholics were his natural allies. Had he been able to do
all that he wished, it is probable that a wise and liberal policy would
have averted the rebellion of 1798. But the difficulties which he
encountered were great, perhaps insurmountable; and the Roman
Catholics were, rather by his misfortune than by his fault, thrown
into the hands of the Jacobins. There was a third great rising of

the Irishry against the Englishry, a rising not less formidable than the risings of 1641 and 1689. The Englishry remained victorious; and it was necessary for Pitt, as it had been necessary for Oliver Cromwell and William of Orange before him, to consider how the victory should be used. It is only just to his memory to say that he formed a scheme of policy, so grand and so simple, so righteous and so humane, that it would alone entitle him to a high place among statesmen. He determined to make Ireland one kingdom with England, and, at the same time, to relieve the Roman Catholic laity from civil disabilities, and to grant a public maintenance to the Roman Catholic clergy. Had he been able to carry these noble designs into effect, the Union would have been an Union indeed. It would have been inseparably associated in the minds of the great majority of Irishmen with civil and religious freedom; and the old Parliament in College Green would have been regretted only by a small knot of discarded jobbers and oppressors, and would have been remembered by the body of the nation with the loathing and contempt due to the most tyrannical and the most corrupt assembly that had ever sate in Europe. But Pitt could execute only one half of what he had projected. He succeeded in obtaining the consent of the Parliaments of both kingdoms to the Union; but that reconciliation of races and sects, without which the Union could exist only in name, was not accomplished. He was well aware that he was likely to find difficulties in the closet. But he flattered himself that, by cautious and dexterous management, those difficulties might be overcome. Unhappily, there were traitors and sycophants in high place who did not suffer him to take his own time and his own way, but prematurely disclosed his scheme to the King, and disclosed it in the manner most likely to irritate and alarm a weak and diseased mind. His Majesty absurdly imagined that his Coronation oath bound him to refuse his assent to any bill for relieving Roman Catholics from civil disabilities. To argue with him was impossible. Dundas tried to explain the matter, but was told to keep his Scotch metaphysics to himself. Pitt, and Pitt's ablest colleagues, resigned their offices. It was necessary that the King should make a new arrangement. But by this time his anger and distress had brought back the malady which had, many years before, incapacitated him for the discharge of his functions. He actually assembled his family, read the Coronation oath to them, and told them that, if he broke it, the Crown would immediately pass to the House of Savoy. It was not until after an interregnum of several weeks that he regained the full use of his small faculties, and that a ministry after his own heart was at length formed.

The materials out of which he had to construct a government were neither solid nor splendid. To that party, weak in numbers, but strong in every kind of talent, which was hostile to the domestic and foreign policy of his late advisers, he could not have recourse. For that party, while it differed from his late advisers on every point on which they had been honoured with his approbation, cordially agreed with them as to the single matter which had brought on them his displeasure. All that was left to him was to call up the rear ranks of the old ministry to form the front rank of a new ministry. In an age pre-eminently fruitful of parliamentary talents, a cabinet was formed containing hardly a single man who, in parliamentary talents, could be considered as even of the second rate. The most important offices in the state were bestowed on decorous and laborious mediocrity. Henry Addington was at the head of the Treasury. He had been an early, indeed a hereditary, friend of Pitt, and had by Pitt's influence been placed, while still a young man, in the chair of the House of Commons. He was universally admitted to have been the best speaker that had sate in that chair since the retirement of Onslow. But nature had not bestowed on him very vigorous faculties; and the highly respectable situation which he had long occupied with honour had rather un-fitted than fitted him for the discharge of his new duties. His business had been to bear himself evenly between contending factions. He had taken no part in the war of words; and he had always been addressed with marked deference by the great orators who thundered against each other from his right and from his left. It was not strange that, when, for the first time, he had to encounter keen and vigorous antagonists, who dealt hard blows without the smallest ceremony, he should have been awkward and unready, or that the air of dignity and authority which he had acquired in his former post, and of which he had not divested himself, should have made his helplessness laughable and pitiable. Nevertheless, during many months, his power seemed to stand firm. He was a favourite with the King, whom he resembled in narrowness of mind, and to whom he was more obsequious than Pitt had ever been. The nation was put into high good humour by a peace with France. The enthusiasm with which the upper and middle classes had rushed into the war had spent itself. Jacobinism was no longer formidable. Everywhere there was a strong reaction against what was called the atheistical and anarchical philosophy of the eighteenth century. Bonaparte, now First Consul, was busied in constructing out of the ruins of old institutions a new ecclesiastical establishment and a new order of knighthood. That nothing less than the dominion of the whole civilised world would satisfy his selfish ambition was not yet suspected; nor did even wise men see any reason to doubt that he might be as safe a neighbour as any prince of the House of Bourbon had been. The treaty of Amiens was therefore hailed by the great body of the English people with extravagant joy. The popularity of the minister was for the moment immense. His want of parliamentary ability was, as yet, of little consequence: for he had scarcely any adversary to encounter. The old opposition, delighted by the peace, regarded him with favour. A new opposition had indeed been formed by some of the late ministers, and was led by Grenville in the House of Lords, and by Windham in the House of Commons. But the new opposition could scarcely muster ten votes, and was regarded with no favour by the country. On Pitt the ministers relied as on their firmest support. He had not, like some of his colleagues, retired in anger. He had expressed the greatest respect for the conscientious scruple which had taken possession of the royal mind; and he had promised his successors all the help in his power. In private his advice was at their service. In Parliament he took his seat on the bench behind them; and, in more than one debate, defended them with powers far superior to their own. The King perfectly understood the value of such assistance. On one occasion, at the palace, he took the old minister and the new minister aside. "If we three," he said, "keep together, all will go well."

But it was hardly possible, human nature being what it is, and, more especially, Pitt and Addington being what they were, that this union should be durable. Pitt, conscious of superior powers, imagined that the place which he had quitted was now occupied by a mere puppet which he had set up, which he was to govern while he suffered it to remain, and which he was to fling aside as soon as he wished to resume his old position. Nor was it long before he began to pine for the power which he had relinquished. He had been so early raised to supreme authority in the state, and had enjoyed that authority so long, that it had become necessary to him. In retirement his days passed heavily. He could not, like Fox, forget the pleasures and cares of ambition in the company of Euripides or Herodotus. Pride restrained him from intimating, even to his dearest friends, that he wished to be again minister. But he thought it strange, almost ungrateful, that his wish had not been divined, that it had not been anticipated, by one whom he regarded as his deputy.

Addington, on the other hand, was by no means inclined to descend from his high position. He was, indeed, under a delusion much resembling that of Abon Hassan in the Arabian tale. His brain was turned by his short and unreal Caliphate. He took his elevation quite seriously, attributed it to his own merit, and considered himself as one of the great triumvirate of English statesmen, as worthy to make a third with Pitt and Fox.

Such being the feelings of the late minister and of the present minister, a rupture was inevitable; and there was no want of persons bent on making that rupture speedy and violent. Some of these persons wounded Addington's pride by representing him as a lacquey, sent to keep a place on the Treasury bench till his master should find it convenient to come. Others took every opportunity of praising him at Pitt's expense. Pitt had waged a long, a bloody, a costly, an unsuccessful war. Addington had made peace. Pitt had suspended the constitutional liberties of Englishmen. Under Addington those liberties were again enjoyed. Pitt had wasted the public resources. Addington was carefully nursing them. It was sometimes but too evident that these compliments were not unpleasing to Addington. Pitt became cold and reserved. During many months he remained at a distance from London. Meanwhile his most intimate friends, in spite of his declarations that he made no complaint, and that he had no wish for office, exerted themselves to effect a change of ministry. His favourite disciple, George Canning, young, ardent, ambitious, with great powers and great virtues, but with a temper too restless and a wit too satirical for his own happiness, was indefatigable. He spoke; he wrote; he intrigued; he tried to induce a large number of the supporters of the government to sign a round robin desiring a change; he made game of Addington and of Addington's relations in a succession of lively pasquinades. The minister's partisans retorted with equal acrimony, if not with equal vivacity. Pitt could keep out of the affray only by keeping out of politics altogether; and this it soon became impossible for him to do. Had Napoleon, content with the first place among the sovereigns of the Continent, and with a military reputation surpassing that of Marlborough or of Turenne, devoted himself to the noble task of making France happy by mild administration and wise legislation, our country might have long continued to tolerate a government of fair intentions and feeble abilities. Unhappily, the treaty of Amiens had scarcely been signed, when the restless ambition and the insupportable insolence of the First Consul convinced the great body of the English people that the peace, so eagerly welcomed, was only a precarious armistice. As it became clearer and clearer that a war for the dignity, the independence, the very existence of the nation was at hand, men looked with increasing uneasiness on the weak and languid cabinet which would have to contend against an enemy who united more than the power of Lewis the Great to more than the genius of Frederick the Great. It is true that Addington might easily have been a better war minister than Pitt, and could not possibly have been a worse. But Pitt had cast a spell on the public mind. The eloquence, the judgment, the calm and disdainful firmness, which he had, during many years, displayed in Parliament, deluded the world into the belief that he must be eminently qualified to super-intend every department of politics; and they imagined, even after the miserable failures of Dunkirk, of Quiberon, and of the Helder, that he was the only statesman who could cope with Bonaparte. This feeling was nowhere stronger than among Addington's own colleagues. The pressure put on him was so strong that he could not help yielding to it: yet, even in yielding, he showed how far he was from knowing his own place. His first proposition was, that some insignificant nobleman should be First Lord of the Treasury and nominal head of the administration, and that the real power should be divided between Pitt and himself, who were to be secretaries of state. Pitt, as might have been expected, refused even to discuss such a scheme, and talked of it with bitter mirth. "Which secretaryship was offered to you?" his friend Wilberforce asked. "Really," said Pitt, "I had not the curiosity to inquire." Addington was frightened into bidding higher. He offered to resign the Treasury to Pitt, on condition that there should be no extensive change in the Government. But Pitt would listen to no such terms. Then came a dispute such as often arises after negotiations orally conducted, even when the negotiators are men of strict honour. Pitt gave one account of what had passed; Addington gave another: and, though the discrepancies were not such as necessarily implied any intentional violation of truth on either side, both were greatly exasperated.

Meanwhile the quarrel with the First Consul had come to a crisis. On the 16th of May 1803, the King sent a message calling on the House of Commons to support him in withstanding the ambitious and encroaching policy of France; and, on the 22nd, the House took the message into consideration.

Pitt had now been living many months in retirement. There had been a general election since he had spoken in Parliament, and there were two hundred members who had never heard him. It was known that on this occasion he would be in his place, and curiosity was wound up to the highest point. Unfortunately, the short-hand writers were, in consequence of some mistake, shut out on that day from the gallery, so that the newspapers contained only a very meagre report of the proceedings. But several accounts of what passed are extant; and of those accounts the most interesting is contained in an unpublished letter, written by a very young member, John William Ward, afterwards Earl of Dudley. When Pitt rose, he was received with loud cheering. At every pause in his speech there was a burst of applause. The peroration is said to have been one of the most animated and magnificent ever heard in Parliament. "Pitt's speech," Fox wrote a few days later, "was admired very much, and very justly. I think it was the best he ever made in that style." The debate was adjourned; and on the second night Fox replied in an oration which, as the most zealous Pittites were forced to acknowledge, left the palm of eloquence doubtful. Addington made a pitiable appearance between the two great rivals; and it was observed that Pitt, while exhorting the Commons to stand resolutely by the executive government against France, said not a word indicating esteem or friendship for the prime minister.

War was speedily declared. The First Consul threatened to invade England at the head of the conquerors of Belgium and Italy, and formed a great camp near the Straits of Dover. On the other side of those Straits the whole population of our island was ready to rise up as one man in defence of the soil. At this conjuncture, as at some other great conjunctures in our history, the conjuncture of 1660, for example, and the conjuncture of 1688, there was a general disposition among honest and patriotic men to forget old quarrels, and to regard as a friend every person who was ready, in the existing emergency, to do his part towards the saving of the state. A coalition of all the first men in the country would, at that moment, have been as popular as the coalition of 1783 had been unpopular. Alone in the kingdom the King looked with perfect complacency on a cabinet in which no man superior to himself in genius was to be found, and was so far from being willing to admit all his ablest subjects to office that he was bent on excluding them all.

A few months passed before the different parties which agreed in regarding the government with dislike and contempt came to an understanding with each other. But in the spring of 1804 it became evident that the weakest of ministries would have to defend itself against the strongest of oppositions, an opposition made up of three oppositions, each of which would, separately, have been formidable from ability, and which, when united, were also formidable from number. The party which had opposed the peace, headed by Grenville and Windham, and the party which had opposed the renewal of the war, headed by Fox, concurred in thinking that the men now in power were incapable of either making a good peace or waging a vigorous war. Pitt had, in 1802, spoken for peace against the party of Grenville, and had, in 1803, spoken for war against the party of Fox. But of the capacity of the cabinet, and especially of its chief, for the conduct of great affairs, he thought as meanly as either Fox or Grenville. Questions were easily found on which all the enemies of the government could act cordially together. The unfortunate First Lord of the Treasury, who had, during the earlier months of his administration, been supported by Pitt on one side, and by Fox on the other, now had to answer Pitt, and to be answered by Fox. Two sharp debates, followed by close divisions, made him weary of his post. It was known, too, that the Upper House was even more hostile to him than the Lower, that the Scotch representative peers wavered, that there were signs of mutiny among the Bishops. In the cabinet itself there was discord, and, worse than discord, treachery. It was necessary to give way: the ministry was dissolved; and the task of forming a government was entrusted to Pitt.

Pitt was of opinion that there was now an opportunity, such as had never before offered itself, and such as might never offer itself again, of uniting in the public service, on honourable terms, all the eminent talents of the kingdom. The passions to which the French Revolution had given birth were extinct. The madness of the innovator and the madness of the alarmist had alike had their day. Jacobinism and Antijacobinism had gone out of fashion together. The most liberal statesman did not think that season propitious for schemes of parliamentary reform; and the most conservative statesman could not pretend that there was any occasion for gagging bills and suspensions of the Habeas Corpus Act. The great struggle for independence and national honour occupied all minds; and those who were agreed as to the duty of maintaining that struggle with vigour might well postpone to a more convenient time all disputes about matters comparatively unimportant. Strongly impressed by these considerations, Pitt wished to form a ministry including all the first men in the country. The Treasury he reserved for himself; and to Fox he proposed to assign a share of power little inferior to his own.

The plan was excellent: but the King would not hear of it. Dull, obstinate, unforgiving, and, at that time, half mad, he positively refused to admit Fox into his service. Anybody else, even men who had gone as far as Fox, or further than Fox, in what His Majesty considered as Jacobinism, Sheridan, Grey, Erskine, should be graciously received; but Fox never. During several hours Pitt laboured in vain to reason down this senseless antipathy. That he was perfectly sincere there can be no doubt; but it was not enough to be sincere; he should have been resolute. Had he declared himself determined not to take office without Fox, the royal obstinacy would have given way, as it gave way, a few months later, when opposed to the immutable resolution of Lord Grenville. In an evil hour Pitt yielded. He flattered himself with the hope that, though he consented to forego the aid of his illustrious rival, there would still remain ample materials for the formation of an efficient ministry. That hope was cruelly disappointed. Fox entreated his friends to leave personal considerations out of the question, and declared that he would support, with the utmost cordiality, an efficient and patriotic ministry from which he should be himself excluded. Not only his friends, however, but Grenville and Grenville's adherents, answered, with one voice, that the question was not personal, that a great constitutional principle was at stake, and that they would not take office while a man eminently qualified to render service to the commonwealth was placed under a ban merely because he was disliked at Court. All that was left to Pitt was to construct a government out of the wreck of Addington's feeble administration. The small circle of his personal retainers furnished him with a very few useful assistants, particularly Dundas, who had been created Viscount Melville, Lord Harrowby, and Canning.

Such was the inauspicious manner in which Pitt entered on his second administration. The whole history of that administration was of a piece with the commencement. Almost every month brought some new disaster or disgrace. To the war with France was soon added a war with Spain. The opponents of the minister were numerous, able, and active. His most useful coadjutors he soon lost. Sickness deprived him of the help of Lord Harrowby. It was discovered that Lord Melville had been guilty of highly culpable laxity in transactions relating to public money. He was censured by the House of Commons, driven from office, ejected from the Privy Council, and impeached of high crimes and misdemeanours. The blow fell heavy on Pitt. It gave him, he said in Parliament, a deep pang; and, as he uttered the word pang, his lip quivered, his voice shook; he paused, and his hearers thought that he was about to burst into tears. Such tears shed by Eldon would have moved nothing but laughter. Shed by the warm-hearted and open-hearted Fox, they would have moved sympathy, but would have caused no surprise. But a tear from Pitt would have been something portentous. He suppressed his emotion, however, and proceeded with his usual majestic self-possession.

His difficulties compelled him to resort to various expedients. At one time Addington was persuaded to accept office with a peerage; but he brought no additional strength to the government. Though he went through the form of reconciliation, it was impossible for him to forget the past. While he remained in place he was jealous and punctilious; and he soon retired again. At another time Pitt renewed his efforts to overcome his master's aversion to Fox; and it was rumoured that the King's obstinacy was gradually giving way. But, meanwhile, it was impossible for the minister to conceal from the public eye the decay of his health, and the constant anxiety which gnawed at his heart. His sleep was broken. His food ceased to nourish him. All who passed him in the Park, all who had interviews with him in Downing Street, saw misery written in his face. The peculiar look which he wore during the last months of his life was often pathetically described by Wilberforce, who used to call it the Austerlitz look.

Still the vigour of Pitt's intellectual faculties, and the intrepid haughtiness of his spirit, remained unaltered. He had staked everything on a great venture. He had succeeded in forming another mighty coalition against the French ascendency. The united forces of Austria, Russia and England might, he hoped, oppose an insurmountable barrier to the ambition of the common enemy. But the genius and energy of Napoleon prevailed. While the English troops were preparing to embark for Germany, while the Russian troops were slowly coming up from Poland, he, with rapidity unprecedented in modern war, moved a hundred thousand men from the shores of the Ocean to the Black Forest, and compelled a great Austrian army to surrender at Ulm. To the first faint rumours of this calamity Pitt would give no credit. He was irritated by the alarms of those around him. "Do not believe a word of it," he said: "it is all a fiction." The next day he received a Dutch newspaper containing the capitulation. He knew no Dutch. It was Sunday; and the public offices were shut. He carried the paper to Lord Malmesbury, who had been Minister in Holland; and Lord Malmesbury translated it. Pitt tried to bear up; but the shock was too great; and he went away with death in his face.

The news of the battle of Trafalgar arrived four days later, and seemed for a moment to revive him. Forty-eight hours after that most glorious and most mournful of victories had been announced to the country came the Lord Mayor's day; and Pitt dined at Guildhall. His popularity had declined. But on this occasion the multitude, greatly excited by the recent tidings, welcomed him enthusiastically, took off his horses in Cheapside, and drew his carriage up King Street. When his health was drunk, he returned thanks in two or three of those stately sentences of which he had a boundless command. Several of those who heard him laid up his words in their hearts; for they were the last words that he ever uttered in public: "Let us hope that England, having saved herself by her energy, may save Europe by her example."

This was but a momentary rally. Austerlitz soon completed what Ulm had begun. Early in December Pitt had retired to Bath, in the hope that he might there gather strength for the approaching session. While he was languishing there on his sofa arrived the news that a decisive battle had been fought and lost in Moravia, that the coalition was dissolved, that the Continent was at the feet of France. He sank down under the blow. Ten days later, he was so emaciated that his most intimate friends hardly knew him. He came up from Bath by slow journeys, and, on the 11th of January 1806, reached his villa at Putney. Parliament was to meet on the 21st. On the 20th was to be the parliamentary dinner at the house of the First Lord of the Treasury in Downing Street; and the cards were already issued. But the days of the great minister were numbered. The only chance for his life, and that a very slight chance, was, that he should resign his office, and pass some months in profound repose. His colleagues paid him very short visits, and carefully avoided political conversation. But his spirit, long accustomed to dominion, could not, even in that extremity, relinquish hopes which everybody but himself perceived to be vain. On the day on which he was carried into his bedroom at Putney, the Marquess Wellesley, whom he had long loved, whom he had sent to govern India, and whose administration had been eminently able, energetic, and successful, arrived in London after an absence of eight years. The friends saw each other once more. There was an affectionate meeting, and a last parting. That it was a last parting Pitt did not seem to be aware. He fancied himself to be recovering, talked on various subjects cheerfully, and with an unclouded mind, and pronounced a warm and discerning eulogium on the Marquess's brother Arthur. "I never," he said, "met with any military man with whom it was so satisfactory to converse." The excitement and exertion of this interview were too much for the sick man. He fainted away; and Lord Wellesley left the house, convinced that the close was fast approaching.

And now members of Parliament were fast coming up to London. The chiefs of the opposition met for the purpose of considering the course to be taken on the first day of the session. It was easy to guess what would be the language of the King's speech, and of the address which would be moved in answer to that speech. An amendment condemning the policy of the government had been prepared, and was to have been proposed in the House of Commons by Lord Henry Petty, a young nobleman who had already won for himself that place in the esteem of his country which, after the lapse of more than half a century, he still retains. He was unwilling, however, to come forward as the accuser of one who was incapable of defending himself. Lord Grenville, who had been informed of Pitt's state by Lord Wellesley, and had been deeply affected by it, earnestly recommended forbearance; and Fox, with characteristic generosity and good nature, gave his voice against attacking his now helpless rival. "Sunt lacrymæ rerum," he said, "et mentem mortalia tangunt." On the first day, therefore, there was no debate. It was rumoured that evening that Pitt was better. But on the following morning his physicians pronounced that there were no hopes. The commanding faculties of which he had been too proud were beginning to fail. His old tutor and friend, the Bishop of Lincoln, informed him of his danger, and gave such religious advice and consolation as a confused and obscured mind could receive. Stories were told of devout sentiments fervently uttered by the dying man. But these stories found no credit with anybody who knew him. Wilberforce pronounced it impossible that they could be true. "Pitt," he added, "was a man who always said less than he thought on such topics." It was asserted in many after-dinner speeches, Grub Street elegies, and academic prize poems and prize declamations, that the great minister died exclaiming, "Oh my country!" This is a fable; but it is true that the last words which he uttered, while he knew what he said, were broken exclamations about the alarming state of public affairs. He ceased to breathe on the morning of the 23rd of January 1806, the twenty-fifth anniversary of the day on which he first took his seat in Parliament. He was in his forty-seventh year, and had been, during near nineteen years, First Lord of the Treasury, and undisputed chief of the administration. Since parliamentary government was established in England, no English statesman has held supreme power so long. Walpole, it is true, was First Lord of the Treasury during more than twenty years, but it was not till Walpole had been some time First Lord of the Treasury that he could be properly called Prime Minister.

It was moved in the House of Commons that Pitt should be honoured with a public funeral and a monument. The motion was opposed by Fox in a speech which deserves to be studied as a model of good taste and good feeling. The task was the most invidious that ever an orator undertook: but it was performed with a humanity and delicacy which were warmly acknowledged by the mourning friends of him who was gone. The motion was carried by 288 votes to 89.

The 22nd of February was fixed for the funeral. The corpse, having lain in state during two days in the Painted Chamber, was borne with great pomp to the northern transept of the Abbey. A splendid train of princes, nobles, bishops, and privy councillors followed. The grave of Pitt had been made near to the spot where his great father lay, near also the spot where his great rival was soon to lie. The sadness of the assistants was beyond that of ordinary mourners. For he whom they were committing to the dust had died of sorrows and anxieties of which none of the survivors could be altogether without a share. Wilberforce, who carried the banner before the hearse, described the awful ceremony with deep feeling. As the coffin descended into the earth, he said, the eagle face of Chatham from above seemed to look down with consternation into the dark house which was receiving all that remained of so much power and glory.

All parties in the House of Commons readily concurred in voting forty thousand pounds to satisfy the demands of Pitt's creditors. Some of his admirers seemed to consider the magnitude of his embarrassments as a circumstance highly honourable to him; but men of sense will probably be of a different opinion. It is far better, no doubt, that a great minister should carry his contempt of money to excess than that he should contaminate his hands with unlawful gain. But it is neither right nor becoming in a man to whom the public has given an income more than sufficient for his comfort and dignity to bequeath to that public a great debt, the effect of mere negligence and profusion. As First Lord of the Treasury and Chancellor of the Exchequer, Pitt never had less than six thousand a year, besides an excellent house. In 1792 he was forced by his royal master's friendly importunity to accept for life the office of Warden of the Cinque Ports, with near four thousand a year more. He had neither wife nor child: he had no needy relations: he had no expensive tastes: he had no long election bills. Had he given but a quarter of an hour a week to the regulation of his household, he would have kept his expenditure within bounds. Or, if he could not spare even a quarter of an hour a week for that purpose, he had numerous friends, excellent men of business, who would have been proud to act as his stewards. One of those friends, the chief of a great commercial house in the city, made an attempt to put the establishment in Downing Street to rights; but in vain. He found that the waste of the servants' hall was almost fabulous. The quantity of butcher's meat charged in the bills was nine hundred-weight a week. The consumption of poultry, of fish, and of tea was in proportion. The character of Pitt would have stood higher if, with the disinterestedness of Pericles and of De Witt, he had united their dignified frugality.

The memory of Pitt has been assailed, times innumerable, often justly, often unjustly; but it has suffered much less from his assailants than from his eulogists. For, during many years, his name was the rallying cry of a class of men with whom, at one of those terrible conjunctures which confound all ordinary distinctions, he was accidentally and temporarily connected, but to whom, on almost all great questions of principle, he was diametrically opposed. The haters of parliamentary reform called themselves Pittites, not choosing to remember that Pitt made three motions for parliamentary reform, and that, though he thought that such a reform could not safely be made while the passions excited by the French revolution were raging, he never uttered a word indicating that he should not be prepared at a more convenient season to bring the question forward a fourth time. The toast of Protestant ascendency was drunk on Pitt's birthday by a set of Pittites who could not but be aware that Pitt had resigned his office because he could not carry Catholic emancipation. The defenders of the Test Act called themselves Pittites, though they could not be ignorant that Pitt had laid before George the Third unanswerable reasons for abolishing the Test Act. The enemies of free trade called themselves Pittites, though Pitt was far more deeply imbued with the doctrines of Adam Smith than either Fox or Grey. The very negro-drivers invoked the name of Pitt, whose eloquence was never more conspicuously displayed than when he spoke of the wrongs of the negro. This mythical Pitt, who resembles the genuine Pitt as little as the Charlemagne of Ariosto resembles the Charlemagne of Eginhard, has had his day. History will vindicate the real man from calumny disguised under the semblance of adulation, and will exhibit him as what he was, a minister of great talents, honest intentions, and liberal opinions, pre-eminently qualified, intellectually and morally, for the part of a parliamentary leader, and capable of administering, with prudence and moderation, the government of a prosperous and tranquil country, but unequal to surprising and terrible emergencies, and liable, in such emergencies, to err grievously, both on the side of weakness and on the side of violence.

II. *Literary Essays*

MOORE'S LIFE OF LORD BYRON

(JUNE 1830)

Letters and Journals of Lord Byron; with Notices of his Life. By THOMAS
MOORE, Esq. 2 vols. 4to. London: 1830.

WE have read this book with the greatest pleasure. Considered
merely as a composition, it deserves to be classed among the best
specimens of English prose which our age has produced. It contains, indeed, no single passage equal to two or three which we
could select from the Life of Sheridan. But, as a whole, it is immeasurably superior to that work. The style is agreeable, clear, and
manly, and, when it rises into eloquence, rises without effort or
ostentation. Nor is the matter inferior to the manner. It would be
difficult to name a book which exhibits more kindness, fairness, and
modesty. It has evidently been written, not for the purpose of
showing, what, however, it often shows, how well its author can
write, but for the purpose of vindicating, as far as truth will permit,
the memory of a celebrated man who can no longer vindicate himself. Mr. Moore never thrusts himself between Lord Byron and the
public. With the strongest temptations to egotism, he has said no
more about himself than the subject absolutely required.

A great part, indeed the greater part, of these volumes, consists
of extracts from the Letters and Journals of Lord Byron; and it is
difficult to speak too highly of the skill which has been shown in the
selection and arrangement. We will not say that we have not occasionally remarked in these two large quartos an anecdote which
should have been omitted, a letter which should have been suppressed, a name which should have been concealed by asterisks, or
asterisks which do not answer the purpose of concealing the name.
But it is impossible, on a general survey, to deny that the task has
been executed with great judgment and great humanity. When we
consider the life which Lord Byron had led, his petulance, his
irritability, and his communicativeness, we cannot but admire the
dexterity with which Mr. Moore has contrived to exhibit so much
of the character and opinions of his friend, with so little pain to the
feelings of the living.

The extracts from the journals and correspondence of Lord
Byron are in the highest degree valuable, not merely on account of
the information which they contain respecting the distinguished

man by whom they were written, but on account also of their rare merit as compositions. The Letters, at least those which were sent from Italy, are among the best in our language. They are less affected than those of Pope and Walpole; they have more matter in them than those of Cowper. Knowing that many of them were not written merely for the person to whom they were directed, but were general epistles, meant to be read by a large circle, we expected to find them clever and spirited, but deficient in ease. We looked with vigilance for instances of stiffness in the language and awkwardness in the transitions. We have been agreeably disappointed; and we must confess that, if the epistolary style of Lord Byron was artificial, it was a rare and admirable instance of that highest art which cannot be distinguished from nature.

Of the deep and painful interest which this book excites no abstract can give a just notion. So sad and dark a story is scarcely to be found in any work of fiction; and we are little disposed to envy the moralist who can read it without being softened.

The pretty fable by which the Duchess of Orleans illustrated the character of her son the Regent might, with little change, be applied to Byron. All the fairies, save one, had been bidden to his cradle. All the gossips had been profuse of their gifts. One had bestowed nobility, another genius, a third beauty. The malignant elf who had been uninvited came last, and, unable to reverse what her sisters had done for their favourite, had mixed up a curse with every blessing. In the rank of Lord Byron, in his understanding, in his character, in his very person, there was a strange union of opposite extremes. He was born to all that men covet and admire. But in every one of those eminent advantages which he possessed over others was mingled something of misery and debasement. He was sprung from a house, ancient indeed and noble, but degraded and impoverished by a series of crimes and follies which had attained a scandalous publicity. The kinsman whom he succeeded had died poor, and, but for merciful judges, would have died upon the gallows. The young peer had great intellectual powers; yet there was an unsound part in his mind. He had naturally a generous and feeling heart; but his temper was wayward and irritable. He had a head which statuaries loved to copy, and a foot the deformity of which the beggars in the streets mimicked. Distinguished at once by the strength and by the weakness of his intellect, affectionate yet perverse, a poor lord, and a handsome cripple, he required, if ever man required, the firmest and the most judicious training. But, capriciously as nature had dealt with him, the parent to whom the office of forming his character was intrusted was more capricious still. She passed from paroxysms of rage to paroxysms of tenderness. At one time she stifled him with her caresses: at another time she insulted his deformity. He came into the world; and the world treated him as his mother had treated him, sometimes with fondness, sometimes with cruelty, never with justice. It indulged him without discrimination, and punished him without discrimination. He was truly a spoiled child, not merely the spoiled child of his parent, but the spoiled child of nature, the spoiled child of fortune, the spoiled child of fame, the spoiled child of society. His first poems were received with a contempt which, feeble as they were, they did not absolutely deserve. The poem which he published on his return from his travels was, on the other hand, extolled far above its merit. At twenty-four he found himself on the highest pinnacle of literary fame, with Scott, Wordsworth, Southey, and a crowd of other distinguished writers beneath his feet. There is scarcely an instance in history of so sudden a rise to so dizzy an eminence.

Every thing that could stimulate, and every thing that could gratify the strongest propensities of our nature, the gaze of a hundred drawing-rooms, the acclamations of the whole nation, the applause of applauded men, the love of lovely women, all this world and all the glory of it were at once offered to a youth to whom nature had given violent passions, and whom education had never taught to control them. He lived as many men live who have no similar excuse to plead for their faults. But his countrymen and his countrywomen would love him and admire him. They were resolved to see in his excesses only the flash and outbreak of that same fiery mind which glowed in his poetry. He attacked religion; yet in religious circles his name was mentioned with fondness, and in many religious publications his works were censured with singular tenderness. He lampooned the Prince Regent; yet he could not alienate the Tories. Every thing, it seemed, was to be forgiven to youth, rank, and genius.

Then came the reaction. Society, capricious in its indignation as it had been capricious in its fondness, flew into a rage with its froward and petted darling. He had been worshipped with an irrational idolatry. He was persecuted with an irrational fury. Much has been written about those unhappy domestic occurrences which decided the fate of his life. Yet nothing is, nothing ever was, positively known to the public, but this, that he quarrelled with his lady, and that she refused to live with him. There have been hints in abundance, and shrugs and shakings of the head, and "Well, well, we know," and "We could an if we would," and "If we list to speak," and "There be that might an they list." But we are not aware that there is before the world, substantiated by credible, or even by tangible evidence, a single fact indicating that Lord Byron was more to blame than any other man who is on bad terms with his wife. The professional men whom Lady Byron consulted were undoubtedly of opinion that she ought not to live with her husband. But it is to be remembered that they formed that opinion without hearing both sides. We do not say, we do not mean to insinuate, that Lady Byron was in any respect to blame. We think that those who condemn her on the evidence which is now before the public are as rash as those who condemn her husband. We will not pronounce any judgment, we cannot, even in our own minds, form any judgment, on a transaction which is so imperfectly known to us. It would have been well if, at the time of the separation, all those who knew as little about the matter then as we know about it now had shown that forbearance which, under such circumstances, is but common justice.

We know no spectacle so ridiculous as the British public in one of its periodical fits of morality. In general, elopements, divorces, and family quarrels, pass with little notice. We read the scandal, talk about it for a day, and forget it. But once in six or seven years our virtue becomes outrageous. We cannot suffer the laws of religion and decency to be violated. We must make a stand against vice. We must teach libertines that the English people appreciate the importance of domestic ties. Accordingly some unfortunate man, in no respect more depraved than hundreds whose offences have been treated with lenity, is singled out as an expiatory sacrifice. If he has children, they are to be taken from him. If he has a profession, he is to be driven from it. He is cut by the higher orders, and hissed by the lower. He is, in truth, a sort of whipping-boy, by whose vicarious agonies all the other transgressors of the same class are, it is supposed, sufficiently chastised. We reflect very complacently on our own severity, and compare with great pride the high standard of morals established in England with the Parisian laxity. At length our anger is satiated. Our victim is ruined and heart-broken. And our virtue goes quietly to sleep for seven years more.

It is clear that those vices which destroy domestic happiness ought to be as much as possible repressed. It is equally clear that they cannot be repressed by penal legislation. It is therefore right and desirable that public opinion should be directed against them. But it should be directed against them uniformly, steadily, and temperately, not by sudden fits and starts. There should be one weight and one measure. Decimation is always an objectionable mode of punishment. It is the resource of judges too indolent and hasty to investigate facts and to discriminate nicely between shades of guilt. It is an irrational practice, even when adopted by military tribunals. When adopted by the tribunal of public opinion, it is infinitely more irrational. It is good that a certain portion of disgrace should constantly attend on certain bad actions. But it is not good that the offenders should merely have to stand the risks of a lottery of infamy, that ninety-nine out of every hundred should escape, and that the hundredth, perhaps the most innocent of the hundred, should pay for all. We remember to have seen a mob assembled in Lincoln's Inn to hoot a gentleman against whom the most oppressive proceeding known to the English law was then in progress. He was hooted because he had been an indifferent and unfaithful husband, as if some of the most popular men of the age, Lord Nelson for example, had not been indifferent and unfaithful husbands. We remember a still stronger case. Will posterity believe that, in an age in which men whose gallantries were universally known, and had been legally proved, filled some of the highest offices in the state and in the army, presided at the meetings of religious and benevolent institutions, were the delight of every society, and the favourites of the multitude, a crowd of moralists went to the theatre, in order to pelt a poor actor for disturbing the conjugal felicity of an alderman? What there was in the circumstances either of the offender or of the sufferer to vindicate the zeal of the audience, we could never conceive. It has never been supposed that the situation of an actor is peculiarly favourable to the rigid virtues, or that an alderman enjoys any special immunity from injuries such as that which on this occasion roused the anger of the public. But such is the justice of mankind.

In these cases the punishment was excessive; but the offence was known and proved. The case of Lord Byron was harder. True Jedwood justice was dealt out to him. First came the execution, then the investigation, and last of all, or rather not at all, the accusation. The public, without knowing any thing whatever about the transactions in his family, flew into a violent passion with him, and proceeded to invent stories which might justify its anger. Ten or twenty different accounts of the separation, inconsistent with each other, with themselves, and with common sense, circulated at the same time. What evidence there might be for any one of these, the virtuous people who repeated them neither knew nor cared. For in fact these stories were not the causes, but the effects of the public indignation. They resembled those loathsome slanders which Lewis Goldsmith, and other abject libellers of the same class, were in the habit of publishing about Bonaparte; such as that he poisoned a girl with arsenic when he was at the military school, that he hired a grenadier to shoot Dessaix at Marengo, that he filled St. Cloud with all the pollutions of Capreæ. There was a time when anecdotes like these obtained some credence from persons who, hating the French emperor without knowing why, were eager to believe any thing which might justify their hatred. Lord Byron fared in the same way. His countrymen were in a bad humour with him. His writings and his character had lost the charm of novelty. He had been guilty of the offence which, of all offences, is punished most severely; he had been over-praised; he had excited too warm an interest; and the public, with its usual justice, chastised him for its own folly. The attachments of the multitude bear no small resemblance to those of the wanton enchantress in the Arabian Tales, who, when the forty days of her fondness were over, was not content with dismissing her lovers, but condemned them to expiate, in loathsome shapes, and under cruel penances, the crime of having once pleased her too well.

The obloquy which Byron had to endure was such as might well have shaken a more constant mind. The newspapers were filled with lampoons. The theatres shook with execrations. He was excluded from circles where he had lately been the observed of all observers. All those creeping things that riot in the decay of nobler natures hastened to their repast; and they were right; they did after their kind. It is not every day that the savage envy of aspiring dunces is gratified by the agonies of such a spirit, and the degradation of such a name.

The unhappy man left his country for ever. The howl of contumely followed him across the sea, up the Rhine, over the Alps; it gradually waxed fainter; it died away; those who had raised it began to ask each other, what, after all, was the matter about which they had been so clamorous, and wished to invite back the criminal whom they had just chased from them. His poetry became more popular than it had ever been; and his complaints were read with tears by thousands and tens of thousands who had never seen his face.

He had fixed his home on the shores of the Adriatic, in the most picturesque and interesting of cities, beneath the brightest of skies, and by the brightest of seas. Censoriousness was not the vice of the neighbours whom he had chosen. They were a race corrupted by a bad government and a bad religion, long renowned for skill in the arts of voluptuousness, and tolerant of all the caprices of sensuality. From the public opinion of the country of his adoption, he had nothing to dread. With the public opinion of the country of his birth, he was at open war. He plunged into wild and desperate excesses, ennobled by no generous or tender sentiment. From his Venetian haram he sent forth volume after volume, full of eloquence, of wit, of pathos, of ribaldry, and of bitter disdain. His health sank under the effects of his intemperance. His hair turned grey. His food ceased to nourish him. A hectic fever withered him up. It seemed that his body and mind were about to perish together.

From this wretched degradation he was in some measure rescued by a connexion, culpable indeed, yet such as, if it were judged by the standard of morality established in the country where he lived, might be called virtuous. But an imagination polluted by vice, a temper embittered by misfortune, and a frame habituated to the fatal excitement of intoxication, prevented him from fully enjoying the happiness which he might have derived from the purest and most tranquil of his many attachments. Midnight draughts of ardent spirits and Rhenish wines had begun to work the ruin of his fine intellect. His verse lost much of the energy and condensation which had distinguished it. But he would not resign, without a struggle, the empire which he had exercised over the men of his generation. A new dream of ambition arose before him; to be the chief of a literary party; to be the great mover of an intellectual revolution; to guide the public mind of England from his Italian retreat, as Voltaire had guided the public mind of France from the villa of Ferney. With this hope, as it should seem, he established The Liberal. But, powerfully as he had affected the imaginations of his contemporaries, he mistook his own powers if he hoped to direct their opinions; and he still more grossly mistook his own disposition, if he thought that he could long act in concert with other men of letters. The plan failed, and failed ignominiously. Angry with himself, angry with his coadjutors, he relinquished it, and turned to another project, the last and noblest of his life.

A nation, once the first among the nations, preeminent in knowledge, preeminent in military glory, the cradle of philosophy, of eloquence, and of the fine arts, had been for ages bowed down under a cruel yoke. All the vices which oppression generates, the abject vices which it generates in those who submit to it, the ferocious vices which it generates in those who struggle against it, had deformed the character of that miserable race. The valour which had won the great battle of human civilisation, which had saved Europe, which had subjugated Asia, lingered only among pirates and robbers. The ingenuity, once so conspicuously displayed in every department of physical and moral science, had been depraved into a timid and servile cunning. On a sudden this degraded people had risen on their oppressors. Discountenanced or betrayed by the surrounding potentates, they had found in themselves something of that which might well supply the place of all foreign assistance, something of the energy of their fathers.

As a man of letters, Lord Byron could not but be interested in the event of this contest. His political opinions, though, like all his opinions, unsettled, leaned strongly towards the side of liberty. He had assisted the Italian insurgents with his purse, and, if their struggle against the Austrian government had been prolonged, would probably have assisted them with his sword. But to Greece he was attached by peculiar ties. He had when young resided in that country. Much of his most splendid and popular poetry had been inspired by its scenery and by its history. Sick of inaction, degraded in his own eyes by his private vices and by his literary failures, pining for untried excitement and honourable distinction, he carried his exhausted body and his wounded spirit to the Grecian camp.

His conduct in his new situation showed so much vigour and good sense as to justify us in believing that, if his life had been prolonged, he might have distinguished himself as a soldier and a politician. But pleasure and sorrow had done the work of seventy years upon his delicate frame. The hand of death was upon him: he knew it; and the only wish which he uttered was that he might die sword in hand.

This was denied to him. Anxiety, exertion, exposure, and those fatal stimulants which had become indispensable to him, soon stretched him on a sick bed, in a strange land, amidst strange faces, without one human being that he loved near him. There, at thirty-six, the most celebrated Englishman of the nineteenth century closed his brilliant and miserable career.

We cannot even now retrace those events without feeling something of what was felt by the nation, when it was first known that the grave had closed over so much sorrow and so much glory; something of what was felt by those who saw the hearse, with its long train of coaches, turn slowly northward, leaving behind it that cemetery which had been consecrated by the dust of so many great poets, but of which the doors were closed against all that remained of Byron. We well remember that, on that day, rigid moralists could not refrain from weeping for one so young, so illustrious, so unhappy, gifted with such rare gifts, and tried by such strong temptations. It is unnecessary to make any reflections. The history carries its moral with it. Our age has indeed been fruitful of warnings to the eminent, and of consolations to the obscure. Two men have died within our recollection, who, at a time of life at which many people have hardly completed their education, had raised themselves, each in his own department, to the height of glory. One of them died at Longwood; the other at Missolonghi.

It is always difficult to separate the literary character of a man who lives in our own time from his personal character. It is peculiarly difficult to make this separation in the case of Lord Byron. For it is scarcely too much to say, that Lord Byron never wrote without some reference, direct or indirect, to himself. The interest excited by the events of his life mingles itself in our minds, and probably in the minds of almost all our readers, with the interest which properly belongs to his works. A generation must pass away before it will be possible to form a fair judgment of his books, considered merely as books. At present they are not only books, but relics. We will however venture, though with unfeigned diffidence, to offer some desultory remarks on his poetry.

His lot was cast in the time of a great literary revolution. That poetical dynasty which had dethroned the successors of Shakspeare and Spenser was, in its turn, dethroned by a race who represented themselves as heirs of the ancient line, so long dispossessed by usurpers. The real nature of this revolution has not, we think, been comprehended by the great majority of those who concurred it it.

Wherein especially does the poetry of our times differ from that of the last century? Ninety-nine persons out of a hundred would answer that the poetry of the last century was correct, but cold and mechanical, and that the poetry of our time, though wild and irregular, presented far more vivid images, and excited the passions far more strongly than that of Parnell, of Addison, or of Pope. In the same manner we constantly hear it said, that the poets of the age of Elizabeth had far more genius, but far less correctness, than those of the age of Anne. It seems to be taken for granted, that there is some incompatibility, some antithesis between correctness and creative power. We rather suspect that this notion arises merely from an abuse of words, and that it has been the parent of many of the fallacies which perplex the science of criticism.

What is meant by correctness in poetry? If by correctness be meant the conforming to rules which have their foundation in truth and in the principles of human nature, then correctness is only another name for excellence. If by correctness be meant the conforming to rules purely arbitrary, correctness may be another name for dulness and absurdity.

A writer who describes visible objects falsely and violates the propriety of character, a writer who makes the mountains "nod their drowsy heads" at night, or a dying man take leave of the world with a rant like that of Maximin, may be said, in the high and just sense of the phrase, to write incorrectly. He violates the first great law of his art. His imitation is altogether unlike the thing imitated. The four poets who are most eminently free from incorrectness of this description are Homer, Dante, Shakspeare, and Milton. They are, therefore, in one sense, and that the best sense, the most correct of poets.

When it is said that Virgil, though he had less genius than Homer, was a more correct writer, what sense is attached to the word correctness? Is it meant that the story of the Æneid is developed more skilfully than that of the Odyssey? that the Roman describes the face of the external world, or the emotions of the mind, more accurately than the Greek? that the characters of Achates and Mnestheus are more nicely discriminated, and more consistently supported, than those of Achilles, of Nestor, and of Ulysses? The fact incontestably is that, for every violation of the fundamental laws of poetry which can be found in Homer, it would be easy to find twenty in Virgil.

Troilus and Cressida is perhaps of all the plays of Shakspeare that which is commonly considered as the most incorrect. Yet it seems to us infinitely more correct, in the sound sense of the term, than what are called the most correct plays of the most correct dramatists. Compare it, for example, with the Iphigénie of Racine. We are sure that the Greeks of Shakspeare bear a far greater resemblance than the Greeks of Racine to the real Greeks who besieged Troy; and for this reason, that the Greeks of Shakspeare are human beings, and the Greeks of Racine mere names, mere words printed in capitals at the head of paragraphs of declamation. Racine, it is true, would have shuddered at the thought of making a warrior at the siege of Troy quote Aristotle. But of what use is it to avoid a single anachronism, when the whole play is one anachronism, the sentiments and phrases of Versailles in the camp of Aulis?

In the sense in which we are now using the word correctness, we think that Sir Walter Scott, Mr. Wordsworth, Mr. Coleridge, are far more correct poets than those who are commonly extolled as the models of correctness, Pope, for example, and Addison. The single description of a moonlight night in Pope's Iliad contains more inaccuracies than can be found in all the Excursion. There is not a single scene in Cato, in which all that conduces to poetical illusion, all the propriety of character, of language, of situation, is not more grossly violated than in any part of the Lay of the Last Minstrel. No man can possibly think that the Romans of Addison resemble the real Romans so closely as the moss-troopers of Scott resemble the real moss-troopers. Watt Tinlinn and William of Deloraine are not, it is true, persons of so much dignity as Cato. But the dignity of the persons represented has as little to do with the correctness of poetry as with the correctness of painting. We prefer a gipsy by Reynolds to his Majesty's head on a signpost, and a Borderer by Scott to a Senator by Addison.

In what sense, then, is the word correctness used by those who say, with the author of the Pursuits of Literature, that Pope was the most correct of English Poets, and that next to Pope came the late Mr. Gifford? What is the nature and value of that correctness, the praise of which is denied to Macbeth, to Lear, and to Othello, and given to Hoole's translations and to all the Seatonian prize-poems? We can discover no eternal rule, no rule founded in reason and in the nature of things, which Shakspeare does not observe much more strictly than Pope. But if by correctness be meant the conforming to a narrow legislation which, while lenient to the *mala in se*, multiplies, without the shadow of a reason, the *mala prohibita*, if by correctness be meant a strict attention to certain ceremonious observances, which are no more essential to poetry than etiquette to good government, or than the washings of a Pharisee to devotion, then, assuredly, Pope may be a more correct poet than Shakspeare; and, if the code were a little altered, Colley Cibber might be a more correct poet than Pope. But it may well be doubted whether this kind of correctness be a merit, nay, whether it be not an absolute fault.

It would be amusing to make a digest of the irrational laws which bad critics have framed for the government of poets. First in celebrity and in absurdity stand the dramatic unities of place and time. No human being has ever been able to find any thing that could, even by courtesy, be called an argument for these unities, except that they have been deduced from the general practice of the Greeks. It requires no very profound examination to discover that the Greek dramas, often admirable as compositions, are, as exhibitions of human character and human life, far inferior to the English plays of the age of Elizabeth. Every scholar knows that the dramatic part of the Athenian tragedies was at first subordinate to the lyrical part. It would, therefore, have been little less than a miracle if the laws of the Athenian stage had been found to suit plays in which there was no chorus. All the greatest masterpieces of the dramatic art have been composed in direct violation of the unities, and could never have been composed if the unities had not been violated. It is clear, for example, that such a character as that of Hamlet could never have been developed within the limits to which Alfieri confined himself. Yet such was the reverence of literary men during the last century for these unities that Johnson who, much to his honour, took the opposite side, was, as he says, "frightened at his own temerity," and "afraid to stand against the authorities which might be produced against him."

There are other rules of the same kind without end. "Shakspeare," says Rymer, "ought not to have made Othello black; for the hero of a tragedy ought always to be white." "Milton," says another critic, "ought not to have taken Adam for his hero; for the hero of an epic poem ought always to be victorious." "Milton," says another, "ought not to have put so many similes into his first book; for the first book of an epic poem ought always to be the most unadorned. There are no similes in the first book of the Iliad." "Milton," says another, "ought not to have placed in an epic poem such lines as these:—

" 'While thus I called, and strayed I knew not whither.' "

And why not? The critic is ready with a reason, a lady's reason. "Such lines," says he, "are not, it must be allowed, unpleasing to the ear; but the redundant syllable ought to be confined to the drama, and not admitted into epic poetry." As to the redundant syllable in heroic rhyme on serious subjects, it has been, from the time of Pope downward, proscribed by the general consent of all the correct school. No magazine would have admitted so incorrect a couplet as that of Drayton;

"As when we lived untouch'd with these disgraces,
    When as our kingdom was our dear embraces."

Another law of heroic rhyme, which, fifty years ago, was considered as fundamental, was, that there should be a pause, a comma at least, at the end of every couplet. It was also provided that there should never be a full stop except at the end of a line. Well do we remember to have heard a most correct judge of poetry revile Mr. Rogers for the incorrectness of that most sweet and graceful passage,

"Such grief was ours,—it seems but yesterday,—
When in thy prime, wishing so much to stay,
'Twas thine, Maria, thine without a sigh
At midnight in a sister's arms to die.
Oh thou wert lovely; lovely was thy frame,
And pure thy spirit as from heaven it came:
And when recalled to join the blest above
Thou diedst a victim to exceeding love,
Nursing the young to health. In happier hours,
When idle Fancy wove luxuriant flowers,
Once in thy mirth thou bad'st me write on thee;
And now I write what thou shalt never see."

Sir Roger Newdigate is fairly entitled, we think, to be ranked among the great critics of this school. He made a law that none of the poems written for the prize which he established at Oxford should exceed fifty lines. This law seems to us to have at least as much foundation in reason as any of those which we have mentioned; nay, much more, for the world, we believe, is pretty well agreed in thinking that the shorter a prize-poem is, the better.

We do not see why we should not make a few more rules of the same kind; why we should not enact that the number of scenes in every act shall be three or some multiple of three, that the number of lines in every scene shall be an exact square, that the *dramatis personæ* shall never be more or fewer than sixteen, and that, in heroic rhymes, every thirty-sixth line shall have twelve syllables. If we were to lay down these canons, and to call Pope, Goldsmith, and Addison incorrect writers for not having complied with our whims, we should act precisely as those critics act who find incorrectness in the magnificent imagery and the varied music of Coleridge and Shelley.

The correctness which the last century prized so much resembles the correctness of those pictures of the garden of Eden which we see in old Bibles. We have an exact square, enclosed by the rivers Pison, Gihon, Hiddekel, and Euphrates, each with a convenient bridge in the centre, rectangular beds of flowers, a long canal, neatly bricked and railed in, the tree of knowledge, clipped like one of the limes behind the Tuilleries, standing in the centre of the grand alley, the snake twined round it, the man on the right hand, the woman on the left, and the beasts drawn up in an exact circle round them. In one sense the picture is correct enough. That is to say, the squares are correct; the circles are correct: the man and the woman are in a most correct line with the tree; and the snake forms a most correct spiral.

But if there were a painter so gifted that he could place on the canvass that glorious paradise, seen by the interior eye of him whose outward sight had failed with long watching and labouring for liberty and truth, if there were a painter who could set before us the mazes of the sapphire brook, the lake with its fringe of myrtles, the flowery meadows, the grottoes overhung by vines, the forests shining with Hesperian fruit and with the plumage of gorgeous birds, the massy shade of that nuptial bower which showered down roses on the sleeping lovers, what should we think of a connoisseur who should tell us that this painting, though finer than the absurd picture in the old Bible, was not so correct? Surely we should answer, It is both finer and more correct; and it is finer because it is more correct. It is not made up of correctly drawn diagrams; but it is a correct painting, a worthy representation of that which it is intended to represent.

It is not in the fine arts alone that this false correctness is prized by narrow-minded men, by men who cannot distinguish means from ends, or what is accidental from what is essential. M. Jourdain admired correctness in fencing. "You had no business to hit me then. You must never thrust in quart till you have thrust in tierce." M. Tomès liked correctness in medical practice. "I stand up for Artemius. That he killed his patient is plain enough. But still he acted quite according to rule. A man dead is a man dead; and there is an end of the matter. But if rules are to be broken, there is no saying what consequences may follow." We have heard of an old German officer, who was a great admirer of correctness in military operations. He used to revile Bonaparte for spoiling the science of war, which had been carried to such exquisite perfection by Marshal Daun. "In my youth we used to march and countermarch all the summer without gaining or losing a square league, and then we went into winter quarters. And now comes an ignorant, hotheaded young man, who flies about from Boulogne to Ulm, and from Ulm to the middle of Moravia, and fights battles in December. The whole system of his tactics is monstrously incorrect." The world is of opinion, in spite of critics like these, that the end of fencing is to hit, that the end of medicine is to cure, that the end of war is to conquer, and that those means are the most correct which best accomplish the ends.

And has poetry no end, no eternal and immutable principles? Is poetry, like heraldry, mere matter of arbitrary regulation? The heralds tell us that certain scutcheons and bearings denote certain conditions, and that to put colours on colours, or metals on metals, is false blazonry. If all this were reversed, if every coat of arms in

Europe were new fashioned, if it were decreed that or should never be placed but on argent, or argent but on or, that illegitimacy should be denoted by a lozenge, and widowhood by a bend, the new science would be just as good as the old science, because both the new and the old would be good for nothing. The mummery of Portcullis and Rouge Dragon, as it has no other value than that which caprice has assigned to it, may well submit to any laws which caprice may impose on it. But it is not so with that great imitative art, to the power of which all ages, the rudest and the most enlightened, bear witness. Since its first great masterpieces were produced, every thing that is changeable in this world has been changed. Civilisation has been gained, lost, gained again. Religions, and languages, and forms of government, and usages of private life, and modes of thinking, all have undergone a succession of revolutions. Every thing has passed away but the great features of nature, and the heart of man, and the miracles of that art of which it is the office to reflect back the heart of man and the features of nature. Those two strange old poems, the wonder of ninety generations, still retain all their freshness. They still command the veneration of minds enriched by the literature of many nations and ages. They are still, even in wretched translations, the delight of schoolboys. Having survived ten thousand capricious fashions, having seen successive codes of criticism become obsolete, they still remain to us, immortal with the immortality of truth, the same when perused in the study of an English scholar as when they were first chanted at the banquets of the Ionian princes.

Poetry is, as was said more than two thousand years ago, imitation. It is an art analogous in many respects to the art of painting, sculpture, and acting. The imitations of the painter, the sculptor, and the actor, are, indeed, within certain limits, more perfect than those of the poet. The machinery which the poet employs consists merely of words; and words cannot, even when employed by such an artist as Homer or Dante, present to the mind images of visible objects quite so lively and exact as those which we carry away from looking on the works of the brush and the chisel. But, on the other hand, the range of poetry is infinitely wider than that of any other imitative art, or than that of all the other imitative arts together. The sculptor can imitate only form; the painter only form and colour; the actor, until the poet supplies him with words, only form, colour, and motion. Poetry holds the outer world in common with the other arts. The heart of man is the province of poetry, and of poetry alone. The painter, the sculptor, and the actor can exhibit no more of human passion and character than that small portion which overflows into the gesture and the face, always an imperfect, often a deceitful, sign of that which is within. The deeper and more complex parts of human nature can be exhibited by means of words alone. Thus the objects of the imitation of poetry are the whole external and the whole internal universe, the face of nature, the vicissitudes of fortune, man as he is in himself, man as he appears in society, all things which really exist, all things of which we can form an image in our minds by combining together parts of things which really exist. The domain of this imperial art is commensurate with the imaginative faculty.

An art essentially imitative ought not surely to be subjected to rules which tend to make its imitations less perfect than they otherwise would be; and those who obey such rules ought to be called, not correct, but incorrect artists. The true way to judge of the rules by which English poetry was governed during the last century is to look at the effects which they produced.

It was in 1780 that Johnson completed his Lives of the Poets. He tells us in that work that, since the time of Dryden, English poetry had shown no tendency to relapse into its original savageness, that its language had been refined, its numbers tuned, and its sentiments improved. It may perhaps be doubted whether the nation had any great reason to exult in the refinements and improvements which gave it Douglas for Othello, and the Triumphs of Temper for the Fairy Queen.

It was during the thirty years which preceded the appearance of Johnson's Lives that the diction and versification of English poetry were, in the sense in which the word is commonly used, most correct. Those thirty years are, as respects poetry, the most deplorable part of our literary history. They have indeed bequeathed to us scarcely any poetry which deserves to be remembered. Two or three hundred lines of Gray, twice as many of Goldsmith, a few stanzas of Beattie and Collins, a few strophes of Mason, and a few clever prologues and satires, were the masterpieces of this age of consummate excellence. They may all be printed in one volume, and that volume would be by no means a volume of extraordinary merit. It would contain no poetry of the very highest class, and little which could be placed very high in the second class. The Paradise Regained or Comus would outweigh it all.

At last, when poetry had fallen into such utter decay that Mr. Hayley was thought a great poet, it began to appear that the excess of the evil was about to work the cure. Men became tired of an insipid conformity to a standard which derived no authority from nature or reason. A shallow criticism had taught them to ascribe a superstitious value to the spurious correctness of poetasters. A deeper criticism brought them back to the true correctness of the first great masters. The eternal laws of poetry regained their power, and the temporary passions which had superseded those laws went after the wig of Lovelace and the hoop of Clarissa.

It was in a cold and barren season that the seeds of that rich harvest which we have reaped were first sown. While poetry was every year becoming more feeble and more mechanical, while the monotonous versification which Pope had introduced, no longer redeemed by his brilliant wit and his compactness of expression, palled on the ear of the public, the great works of the old masters were every day attracting more and more of the admiration which they deserved. The plays of Shakspeare were better acted, better edited, and better known than they had ever been. Our fine ancient ballads were again read with pleasure, and it became a fashion to imitate them. Many of the imitations were altogether contemptible. But they showed that men had at least begun to admire the excellence which they could not rival. A literary revolution was evidently at hand. There was a ferment in the minds of men, a vague craving for something new, a disposition to hail with delight any thing which might at first sight wear the appearance of originality. A reforming age is always fertile of impostors. The same excited state of public feeling which produced the great separation from the see of Rome produced also the excesses of the Anabaptists. The same stir in the public mind of Europe which overthrew the abuses of the old French government, produced the Jacobins and Theophilanthropists. Macpherson and Della Crusca were to the true reformers of English poetry what Knipperdoling was to Luther, or Clootz to Turgot. The success of Chatterton's forgeries and of the far more contemptible forgeries of Ireland showed that people had begun to love the old poetry well, though not wisely. The public was never more disposed to believe stories without evidence, and to admire books without merit. Any thing which could break the dull monotony of the correct school was acceptable.

The forerunner of the great restoration of our literature was Cowper. His literary career began and ended at nearly the same time with that of Alfieri. A comparison between Alfieri and Cowper may, at first sight, appear as strange as that which a loyal Presbyterian minister is said to have made in 1745 between George the Second and Enoch. It may seem that the gentle, shy, melancholy Calvinist, whose spirit had been broken by fagging at school,

who had not courage to earn a livelihood by reading the titles of
bills in the House of Lords, and whose favourite associates were a
blind old lady and an evangelical divine, could have nothing in
common with the haughty, ardent, and voluptuous nobleman, the
horse-jockey, the libertine, who fought Lord Ligonier in Hyde
Park, and robbed the Pretender of his queen. But though the
private lives of these remarkable men present scarcely any points
of resemblance, their literary lives bear a close analogy to each
other. They both found poetry in its lowest state of degradation,
feeble, artificial, and altogether nerveless. They both possessed
precisely the talents which fitted them for the task of raising it from
that deep abasement. They cannot, in strictness, be called great
poets. They had not in any very high degree the creative power,

"The vision and the faculty divine;"

but they had great vigour of thought, great warmth of feeling, and
what, in their circumstances, was above all things important, a
manliness of taste which approached to roughness. They did not
deal in mechanical versification and conventional phrases. They
wrote concerning things the thought of which set their hearts on
fire; and thus what they wrote, even when it wanted every other
grace, had that inimitable grace which sincerity and strong passion
impart to the rudest and most homely compositions. Each of them
sought for inspiration in a noble and affecting subject, fertile of
images which had not yet been hackneyed. Liberty was the muse
of Alfieri, Religion was the muse of Cowper. The same truth is
found in their lighter pieces. They were not among those who
deprecated the severity, or deplored the absence, of an unreal
mistress in melodious commonplaces. Instead of raving about
imaginary Chloes and Sylvias, Cowper wrote of Mrs. Unwin's
knitting-needles. The only love verses of Alfieri were addressed to
one whom he truly and passionately loved. "Tutte le rime amorose
che seguono," says he, "tutte sono per essa, e ben sue, e di lei
solamente; poichè mai d' altra donna per certo non canterò."

These great men were not free from affectation. But their affectation was directly opposed to the affectation which generally prevailed. Each of them expressed, in strong and bitter language, the
contempt which he felt for the effeminate poetasters who were in
fashion both in England and in Italy. Cowper complains that

"Manner is all in all, whate'er is writ,
    The substitute for genius, taste, and wit."

He praised Pope; yet he regretted that Pope had

> "Made poetry a mere mechanic art,
> And every warbler had his tune by heart."

Alfieri speaks with similar scorn of the tragedies of his predecessors. "Mi cadevano dalle mani per la languidezza, trivialità e prolissità dei modi e del verso, senza parlare poi della snervatezza dei pensieri· Or perchè mai questa nostra divina lingua, sì maschia anco, ed energica, e feroce, in bocca di Dante, dovrà ella farsi così sbiadata ed eunuca nel dialogo tragico?"

To men thus sick of the languid manner of their contemporaries ruggedness seemed a venial fault, or rather a positive merit. In their hatred of meretricious ornament, and of what Cowper calls "creamy smoothness," they erred on the opposite side. Their style was too austere, their versification too harsh. It is not easy, however, to overrate the service which they rendered to literature. The intrinsic value of their poems is considerable. But the example which they set of mutiny against an absurd system was invaluable. The part which they performed was rather that of Moses than that of Joshua. They opened the house of bondage; but they did not enter the promised land.

During the twenty years which followed the death of Cowper, the revolution in English poetry was fully consummated. None of the writers of this period, not even Sir Walter Scott, contributed so much to the consummation as Lord Byron. Yet Lord Byron contributed to it unwillingly, and with constant self-reproach and shame. All his tastes and inclinations led him to take part with the school of poetry which was going out against the school which was coming in. Of Pope himself he spoke with extravagant admiration. He did not venture directly to say that the little man of Twickenham was a greater poet than Shakspeare or Milton: but he hinted pretty clearly that he thought so. Of his contemporaries, scarcely any had so much of his admiration as Mr. Gifford who, considered as a poet, was merely Pope, without Pope's wit and fancy, and whose satires are decidedly inferior in vigour and poignancy to the very imperfect juvenile performance of Lord Byron himself. He now and then praised Mr. Wordsworth and Mr. Coleridge, but ungraciously and without cordiality. When he attacked them, he brought his whole soul to the work. Of the most elaborate of Mr. Wordsworth's poems he could find nothing to say, but that it was "clumsy, and frowsy, and his aversion." Peter Bell excited his spleen to such a degree that he evoked the shades of Pope and Dryden, and demanded of them whether it were possible that such trash could evade contempt? In his heart he thought his own Pilgrimage of Harold inferior to his Imitation of Horace's Art of Poetry, a feeble echo of Pope and Johnson. This insipid performance he repeatedly designed to publish, and was withheld only by the solicitations of his friends. He has distinctly declared his approbation of the unities, the most absurd laws by which genius was ever held in servitude. In one of his works, we think in his Letter to Mr. Bowles, he compares the poetry of the eighteenth century to the Parthenon, and that of the nineteenth to a Turkish mosque, and boasts that, though he had assisted his contemporaries in building their grotesque and barbarous edifice, he had never joined them in defacing the remains of a chaster and more graceful architecture. In another letter, he compares the change which had recently passed on English poetry to the decay of Latin poetry after the Augustan age. In the time of Pope, he tells his friends, it was all Horace with us. It is all Claudian now.

For the great old masters of the art he had no very enthusiastic veneration. In his letter to Mr. Bowles he uses expressions which clearly indicate that he preferred Pope's Iliad to the original. Mr. Moore confesses that his friend was no very fervent admirer of Shakspeare. Of all the poets of the first class, Lord Byron seems to have admired Dante and Milton most. Yet in the fourth canto of Childe Harold he places Tasso, a writer not merely inferior to them, but of quite a different order of mind, on at least a footing of equality with them. Mr. Hunt is, we suspect, quite correct in saying that Lord Byron could see little or no merit in Spenser.

But Byron the critic and Byron the poet were two very different men. The effects of the noble writer's theory may indeed often be traced in his practice. But his disposition led him to accommodate himself to the literary taste of the age in which he lived; and his talents would have enabled him to accommodate himself to the taste of any age. Though he said much of his contempt for mankind, and though he boasted that amidst the inconstancy of fortune and of fame he was all-sufficient to himself, his literary career indicated nothing of that lonely and unsocial pride which he affected. We cannot conceive him, like Milton or Wordsworth, defying the criticism of his contemporaries, retorting their scorn, and labouring on a poem in the full assurance that it would be unpopular, and in the full assurance that it would be immortal. He has said, by the mouth of one of his heroes, in speaking of political greatness, that "he must serve who fain would sway;" and this he assigns as a reason for not entering into political life. He did not consider that the sway which he had exercised in literature had been purchased by servitude, by the sacrifice of his own taste to the taste of the public.

He was the creature of his age; and whenever he had lived he would have been the creature of his age. Under Charles the First Byron would have been more quaint than Donne. Under Charles the Second the rants of Byron's rhyming plays would have pitted it, boxed it, and galleried it, with those of any Bayes or Bilboa. Under George the First the monotonous smoothness of Byron's versification and the terseness of his expression would have made Pope himself envious.

As it was, he was the man of the last thirteen years of the eighteenth century, and of the first twenty-three years of the nineteenth century. He belonged half to the old, and half to the new school of poetry. His personal taste led him to the former; his thirst of praise to the latter; his talents were equally suited to both. His fame was a common ground on which the zealots of both sides, Gifford, for example, and Shelley, might meet. He was the representative, not of either literary party, but of both at once, and of their conflict, and of the victory by which that conflict was terminated. His poetry fills and measures the whole of the vast interval through which our literature has moved since the time of Johnson. It touches the Essay on Man at the one extremity, and the Excursion at the other.

There are several parallel instances in literary history. Voltaire, for example, was the connecting link between the France of Louis the Fourteenth and the France of Louis the Sixteenth, between Racine and Boileau on the one side, and Condorcet and Beaumarchais on the other. He, like Lord Byron, put himself at the head of an intellectual revolution, dreading it all the time, murmuring at it, sneering at it, yet choosing rather to move before his age in any direction than to be left behind and forgotten. Dryden was the connecting link between the literature of the age of James the First, and the literature of the age of Anne. Oromasdes and Arimanes fought for him. Arimanes carried him off. But his heart was to the last with Oromasdes. Lord Byron was, in the same manner, the mediator between two generations, between two hostile poetical sects. Though always sneering at Mr. Wordsworth, he was yet, though perhaps unconsciously, the interpreter between Mr. Wordsworth and the multitude. In the Lyrical Ballads and the Excursion Mr. Wordsworth appeared as the high priest of a worship of which Nature was the idol. No poems have ever indicated a more exquisite perception of the beauty of the outer world, or a more passionate love and reverence for that beauty. Yet they were not popular; and it is not likely that they ever will be popular as the poetry of Sir Walter Scott is popular. The feeling which pervaded them was too deep for general sympathy. Their style was often too mysterious for general comprehension. They made a few esoteric disciples, and many scoffers. Lord Byron founded what may be called an exoteric Lake school; and all the readers of verse in England, we might say in Europe, hastened to sit at his feet. What Mr. Wordsworth had said like a recluse, Lord Byron said like a man of the world, with less profound feeling, but with more perspicuity, energy, and conciseness. We would refer our readers to the last two cantos of Childe Harold and to Manfred, in proof of these observations.

Lord Byron, like Mr. Wordsworth, had nothing dramatic in his genius. He was indeed the reverse of a great dramatist, the very antithesis to a great dramatist. All his characters, Harold looking on the sky, from which his country and the sun are disappearing together, the Giaour, standing apart in the gloom of the side-aisle, and casting a haggard scowl from under his long hood at the crucifix and the censer, Conrad leaning on his sword by the watch-tower, Lara smiling on the dancers, Alp gazing steadily on the fatal cloud as it passes before the moon, Manfred wandering among the precipices of Berne, Azzo on the judgment seat, Ugo at the bar, Lambro frowning on the siesta of his daughter and Juan, Cain presenting his unacceptable offering, are essentially the same. The varieties are varieties merely of age, situation, and outward show. If ever Lord Byron attempted to exhibit men of a different kind, he always made them either insipid or unnatural. Selim is nothing. Bonnivart is nothing. Don Juan, in the first and best cantos, is a feeble copy of the Page in the Marriage of Figaro. Johnson, the man whom Juan meets in the slave-market, is a most striking failure. How differently would Sir Walter Scott have drawn a bluff, fearless Englishman, in such a situation! The portrait would have seemed to walk out of the canvass.

Sardanapalus is more coarsely drawn than any dramatic personage that we can remember. His heroism and his effeminacy, his contempt of death, and his dread of a weighty helmet, his kingly resolution to be seen in the foremost ranks, and the anxiety with which he calls for a looking-glass, that he may be seen to advantage, are contrasted, it is true, with all the point of Juvenal. Indeed the hint of the character seems to have been taken from what Juvenal says of Otho:

"Speculum civilis sarcina belli.
Nimirum summi ducis est occidere Galbam,
Et curare cutem summi constantia civis,
Bedriaci in campo spolium affectare Palati,
Et pressum in faciem digitis extendere panem."

These are excellent lines in a satire. But it is not the business of the dramatist to exhibit characters in this sharp antithetical way. It is not thus that Shakspeare makes Prince Hal rise from the rake of Eastcheap into the hero of Shrewsbury, and sink again into the rake of Eastcheap. It is not thus that Shakspeare has exhibited the union of effeminacy and valour in Antony. A dramatist cannot commit a greater error than that of following those pointed descriptions of character, in which satirists and historians indulge so much. It is by rejecting what is natural that satirists and historians produce these striking characters. Their great object generally is to ascribe to every man as many contradictory qualities as possible: and this is an object easily attained. By judicious selection and judicious exaggeration, the intellect and the disposition of any human being might be described as being made up of nothing but startling contrasts. If the dramatist attempts to create a being answering to one of these descriptions, he fails, because he reverses an imperfect analytical process. He produces, not a man, but a personified epigram. Very eminent writers have fallen into this snare. Ben Jonson has given us a Hermogenes, taken from the lively lines of Horace; but the inconsistency which is so amusing in the satire appears unnatural and disgusts us in the play. Sir Walter Scott has committed a far more glaring error of the same kind in the novel of Peveril. Admiring, as every judicious reader must admire, the keen and vigorous lines in which Dryden satirised the Duke of Buckingham, Sir Walter attempted to make a Duke of Buckingham to suit them, a real living Zimri; and he made, not a man, but the most grotesque of all monsters. A writer who should attempt to introduce into a play or a novel such a Wharton as the Wharton of Pope, or a Lord Hervey answering to Sporus, would fail in the same manner.

But to return to Lord Byron; his women, like his men, are all of one breed. Haidee is a half-savage and girlish Julia; Julia is a civilised and matronly Haidee. Leila is a wedded Zuleika, Zuleika a virgin Leila. Gulnare and Medora appear to have been intentionally opposed to each other. Yet the difference is a difference of situation only. A slight change of circumstances would, it should seem, have sent Gulnare to the lute of Medora, and armed Medora with the dagger of Gulnare.

It is hardly too much to say, that Lord Byron could exhibit only one man and only one woman, a man proud, moody, cynical, with defiance on his brow, and misery in his heart, a scorner of his kind, implacable in revenge, yet capable of deep and strong affection; a woman all softness and gentleness, loving to caress and to be caressed, but capable of being transformed by passion into a tigress.

Even these two characters, his only two characters, he could not exhibit dramatically. He exhibited them in the manner, not of Shakspeare, but of Clarendon. He analysed them; he made them analyse themselves; but he did not make them show themselves. We are told, for example, in many lines of great force and spirit, that the speech of Lara was bitterly sarcastic, that he talked little of his travels, that, if he was much questioned about them, his answers became short, and his brow gloomy. But we have none of Lara's sarcastic speeches or short answers. It is not thus that the great masters of human nature have portrayed human beings. Homer never tells us that Nestor loved to relate long stories about his youth. Shakspeare never tells us that in the mind of Iago every thing that is beautiful and endearing was associated with some filthy and debasing idea.

It is curious to observe the tendency which the dialogue of Lord Byron always has to lose its character of dialogue, and to become soliloquy. The scenes between Manfred and the Chamois-hunter, between Manfred and the Witch of the Alps, between Manfred and the Abbot, are instances of this tendency. Manfred, after a few unimportant speeches, has all the talk to himself. The other interlocutors are nothing more than good listeners. They drop an occasional question or ejaculation which sets Manfred off again on the inexhaustible topic of his personal feelings. If we examine the fine passages in Lord Byron's dramas, the description of Rome, for example, in Manfred, the description of a Venetian revel in Marino Faliero, the concluding invective which the old doge pronounces against Venice, we shall find that there is nothing dramatic in these speeches, that they derive none of their effect from the character or situation of the speaker, and that they would have been as fine, or finer, if they had been published as fragments of blank verse by Lord Byron. There is scarcely a speech in Shakspeare of which the same could be said. No skilful reader of the plays of Shakspeare can endure to see what are called the fine things taken out, under the name of "Beauties" or of "Elegant Extracts," or to hear any single passage, "To be or not to be," for example, quoted as a sample of the great poet. "To be or not to be" has merit undoubtedly as a composition. It would have merit if put into the mouth of a chorus. But its merit as a composition vanishes when compared with its merit as belonging to Hamlet. It is not too much to say that the great plays of Shakspeare would lose less by being deprived of all the passages which are commonly called the fine passages, than those passages lose by being read separately from the play. This is perhaps the highest praise which can be given to a dramatist.

On the other hand, it may be doubted whether there is, in all Lord Byron's plays, a single remarkable passage which owes any portion of its interest or effect to its connexion with the characters or the action. He has written only one scene, as far as we can recollect, which is dramatic even in manner, the scene between Lucifer and Cain. The conference is animated, and each of the interlocutors has a fair share of it. But this scene, when examined, will be found to be a confirmation of our remarks. It is a dialogue only in form. It is a soliloquy in essence. It is in reality a debate carried on within one single unquiet and sceptical mind. The questions and the answers, the objections and the solutions, all belong to the same character.

A writer who showed so little dramatic skill in works professedly dramatic was not likely to write narrative with dramatic effect. Nothing could indeed be more rude and careless than the structure of his narrative poems. He seems to have thought, with the hero of the Rehearsal, that the plot was good for nothing but to bring in fine things. His two longest works, Childe Harold and Don Juan, have no plan whatever. Either of them might have been extended to any length, or cut short at any point. The state in which the Giaour appears illustrates the manner in which all Byron's poems were constructed. They are all, like the Giaour, collections of fragments; and, though there may be no empty spaces marked by asterisks, it is still easy to perceive, by the clumsiness of the joining, where the parts for the sake of which the whole was composed end and begin.

It was in description and meditation that Byron excelled. "Description," as he said in Don Juan, "was his forte." His manner is indeed peculiar, and is almost unequalled; rapid, sketchy, full of vigour; the selection happy; the strokes few and bold. In spite of the reverence which we feel for the genius of Mr. Wordsworth, we cannot but think that the minuteness of his descriptions often diminishes their effect. He has accustomed himself to gaze on nature with the eye of a lover, to dwell on every feature, and to mark every change of aspect. Those beauties which strike the most negligent observer, and those which only a close attention discovers, are equally familiar to him and are equally prominent in his poetry. The proverb of old Hesiod, that half is often more than the whole, is eminently applicable to description. The policy of the Dutch, who cut down most of the precious trees in the Spice Islands, in order to raise the value of what remained, was a policy which poets would do well to imitate. It was a policy which no poet understood better than Lord Byron. Whatever his faults might be, he was never, while his mind retained its vigour, accused of prolixity.

His descriptions, great as was their intrinsic merit, derived their principal interest from the feeling which always mingled with them. He was himself the beginning, the middle, and the end, of all his own poetry, the hero of every tale, the chief object in every landscape. Harold, Lara, Manfred, and a crowd of other characters, were universally considered merely as loose incognitos of Byron; and there is every reason to believe that he meant them to be so considered. The wonders of the outer world, the Tagus, with the mighty fleets of England riding on its bosom, the towers of Cintra overhanging the shaggy forest of cork-trees and willows, the glaring marble of Pentelicus, the banks of the Rhine, the glaciers of Clarens, the sweet Lake of Leman, the dell of Egeria with its summer-birds and rustling lizards, the shapeless ruins of Rome overgrown with ivy and wall-flowers, the stars, the sea, the mountains, all were mere accessaries, the background to one dark and melancholy figure.

Never had any writer so vast a command of the whole eloquence of scorn, misanthropy, and despair. That Marah was never dry. No art could sweeten, no draughts could exhaust, its perennial waters of bitterness. Never was there such variety in monotony as that of Byron. From maniac laughter to piercing lamentation, there was not a single note of human anguish of which he was not master. Year after year, and month after month, he continued to repeat that to be wretched is the destiny of all; that to be eminently wretched is the destiny of the eminent; that all the desires by which we are cursed lead alike to misery, if they are not gratified, to the misery of disappointment, if they are gratified, to the misery of satiety. His heroes are men who have arrived by different roads at the same goal of despair, who are sick of life, who are at war with society, who are supported in their anguish only by an unconquerable pride resembling that of Prometheus on the rock or of Satan in the burning marl, who can master their agonies by the force of their will, and who, to the last, defy the whole power of earth and heaven. He always described himself as a man of the same kind with his favourite creations, as a man whose heart had been withered, whose capacity for happiness was gone and could not be restored, but whose invincible spirit dared the worst that could befall him here or hereafter.

How much of this morbid feeling sprang from an original disease of the mind, how much from real misfortune, how much from the nervousness of dissipation, how much was fanciful, how much was merely affected, it is impossible for us, and would probably have been impossible for the most intimate friends of Lord Byron, to decide. Whether there ever existed, or can ever exist, a person answering to the description which he gave of himself, may be doubted: but that he was not such a person is beyond all doubt. It is ridiculous to imagine that a man whose mind was really imbued with scorn of his fellow-creatures would have published three or four books every year in order to tell them so; or that a man who could say with truth that he neither sought sympathy nor needed it would have admitted all Europe to hear his farewell to his wife, and his blessings on his child. In the second canto of Childe Harold, he tells us that he is insensible to fame and obloquy.

> "Ill may such contest now the spirit move,
>   Which heeds nor keen reproof nor partial praise."

Yet we know on the best evidence that, a day or two before he published these lines, he was greatly, indeed childishly, elated by the compliments paid to his maiden speech in the House of Lords.

We are far, however, from thinking that his sadness was altogether feigned. He was naturally a man of great sensibility; he had been ill educated; his feelings had been early exposed to sharp trials; he had been crossed in his boyish love; he had been mortified by the failure of his first literary efforts; he was straitened in pecuniary circumstances; he was unfortunate in his domestic relations; the public treated him with cruel injustice; his health and spirits suffered from his dissipated habits of life; he was, on the whole, an unhappy man. He early discovered that, by parading his unhappiness before the multitude, he produced an immense sensation. The world gave him every encouragement to talk about his mental sufferings. The interest which his first confessions excited induced him to affect much that he did not feel; and the affectation probably reacted on his feelings. How far the character in which he exhibited himself was genuine, and how far theatrical, it would probably have puzzled himself to say.

There can be no doubt that this remarkable man owed the vast influence which he exercised over his contemporaries at least as much to his gloomy egotism as to the real power of his poetry. We never could very clearly understand how it is that egotism, so unpopular in conversation, should be so popular in writing; or how it is that men who affect in their compositions qualities and feelings which they have not impose so much more easily on their contemporaries than on posterity. The interest which the loves of Petrarch excited in his own time, and the pitying fondness with which half Europe looked upon Rousseau, are well known. To readers of our age, the love of Petrarch seems to have been love of that kind which breaks no hearts, and the sufferings of Rousseau to have deserved laughter rather than pity, to have been partly counterfeited, and partly the consequences of his own perverseness and vanity.

What our grandchildren may think of the character of Lord Byron, as exhibited in his poetry, we will not pretend to guess. It is certain, that the interest which he excited during his life is without a parallel in literary history. The feeling with which young readers of poetry regarded him can be conceived only by those who have experienced it. To people who are unacquainted with real calamity, "nothing is so dainty sweet as lovely melancholy." This faint image of sorrow has in all ages been considered by young gentlemen as an agreeable excitement. Old gentlemen and middle-aged gentlemen have so many real causes of sadness that they are rarely inclined "to be as sad as night only for wantonness." Indeed they want the power almost as much as the inclination. We know very few persons engaged in active life who, even if they were to procure stools to be melancholy upon, and were to sit down with all the premeditation of Master Stephen, would be able to enjoy much of what somebody calls the "ecstasy of woe."

Among that large class of young persons whose reading is almost entirely confined to works of imagination, the popularity of Lord Byron was unbounded. They bought pictures of him; they treasured up the smallest relics of him; they learned his poems by heart, and did their best to write like him, and to look like him. Many of them practised at the glass, in the hope of catching the curl of the upper lip, and the scowl of the brow, which appear in some of his portraits. A few discarded their neckcloths in imitation of their great leader. For some years the Minerva press sent forth no novel without a mysterious, unhappy, Lara-like peer. The number of hopeful under-graduates and medical students who became things of dark imaginings, on whom the freshness of the heart ceased to fall like dew, whose passions had consumed themselves to dust, and to whom the relief of tears was denied, passes all calculation. This was not the worst. There was created in the minds of many of these enthusiasts, a pernicious and absurd association between intellectual power and moral depravity. From the poetry of Lord Byron they drew a system of ethics, compounded of misanthropy and voluptuousness, a system in which the two great commandments were, to hate your neighbour, and to love your neighbour's wife.

This affectation has passed away; and a few more years will destroy whatever yet remains of that magical potency which once belonged to the name of Byron. To us he is still a man, young, noble, and unhappy. To our children he will be merely a writer; and their impartial judgment will appoint his place among writers, without regard to his rank or to his private history. That his poetry will undergo a severe sifting, that much of what has been admired by his contemporaries will be rejected as worthless, we have little doubt. But we have as little doubt that, after the closest scrutiny, there will still remain much that can only perish with the English language.

SAMUEL JOHNSON

(DECEMBER 1856)

SAMUEL JOHNSON, one of the most eminent English writers of the eighteenth century, was the son of Michael Johnson, who was, at the beginning of that century, a magistrate of Lichfield, and a bookseller of great note in the midland counties. Michael's abilities and attainments seem to have been considerable. He was so well acquainted with the contents of the volumes which he exposed to sale, that the country rectors of Staffordshire and Worcestershire thought him an oracle on points of learning. Between him and the clergy, indeed, there was a strong religious and political sympathy. He was a zealous churchman, and, though he had qualified himself for municipal office by taking the oaths to the sovereigns in possession, was to the last a Jacobite in heart. At his house, a house which is still pointed out to every traveller who visits Lichfield, Samuel was born on the 18th of September 1709. In the child, the physical, intellectual, and moral peculiarities which afterwards distinguished the man were plainly discernible; great muscular strength accompanied by much awkwardness and many infirmities; great quickness of parts, with a morbid propensity to sloth and procrastination; a kind and generous heart, with a gloomy and irritable temper. He had inherited from his ancestors a scrofulous taint, which it was beyond the power of medicine to remove. His parents were weak enough to believe that the royal touch was a specific for this malady. In his third year he was taken up to London, inspected by the court surgeon, prayed over by the court chaplains, and stroked and presented with a piece of gold by Queen Anne. One of his earliest recollections was that of a stately lady in a diamond stomacher and a long black hood. Her hand was applied in vain. The boy's features, which were originally noble and not irregular, were distorted by his malady. His cheeks were deeply scarred. He lost for a time the sight of one eye; and he saw but very imperfectly with the other. But the force of his mind overcame every impediment. Indolent as he was, he acquired knowledge with such ease and rapidity, that at every school to which he was sent he was soon the best scholar. From sixteen to eighteen he resided at home, and was left to his own devices. He learned much at this time, though his studies were without guidance and without plan. He ransacked his father's shelves, dipped into a multitude of books, read what was interesting, and passed over what was dull. An ordinary lad would have acquired little or no useful knowledge in such a way: but much that was dull to ordinary lads was interesting to Samuel. He read little Greek; for his proficiency in that language was not such that he could take much pleasure in the masters of Attic poetry and eloquence. But he had left school a good Latinist, and he soon acquired, in the large and miscellaneous library of which he now had the command, an extensive knowledge of Latin literature. That Augustan delicacy of taste, which is the boast of the great public schools of England, he never possessed. But he was early familiar with some classical writers, who were quite unknown to the best scholars in the sixth form at Eton. He was peculiarly attracted by the works of the great restorers of learning. Once, while searching for some apples, he found a huge folio volume of Petrarch's works. The name excited his curiosity, and he eagerly devoured hundreds of pages. Indeed, the diction and versification of his own Latin compositions show that he had paid at least as much attention to modern copies from the antique as to the original models.

While he was thus irregularly educating himself, his family was sinking into hopeless poverty. Old Michael Johnson was much better qualified to pore upon books, and to talk about them, than to trade in them. His business declined: his debts increased: it was with difficulty that the daily expenses of his household were defrayed. It was out of his power to support his son at either university; but a wealthy neighbour offered assistance; and, in reliance on promises which proved to be of very little value, Samuel was entered at Pembroke College, Oxford. When the young scholar presented himself to the rulers of that society, they were amazed not more by his ungainly figure and eccentric manners than by the quantity of extensive and curious information which he had picked up during many months of desultory, but not unprofitable study. On the first day of his residence he surprised his teachers by quoting Macrobius; and one of the most learned among them declared, that he had never known a freshman of equal attainments.

At Oxford, Johnson resided during about three years. He was poor, even to raggedness; and his appearance excited a mirth and a pity, which were equally intolerable to his haughty spirit. He was driven from the quadrangle of Christ Church by the sneering looks which the members of that aristocratical society cast at the holes in his shoes. Some charitable person placed a new pair at his door; but he spurned them away in a fury. Distress made him, not servile, but reckless and ungovernable. No opulent gentleman commoner, panting for one-and-twenty, could have treated the academical authorities with more gross disrespect. The needy scholar was generally to be seen under the gate of Pembroke, a gate now adorned with his effigy, haranguing a circle of lads, over whom, in spite of his tattered gown and dirty linen, his wit and audacity gave him an undisputed ascendency. In every mutiny against the discipline of the college he was the ringleader. Much was pardoned, however, to a youth so highly distinguished by abilities and acquirements. He had early made himself known by turning Pope's Messiah into Latin verse. The style and rhythm, indeed, were not exactly Virgilian; but the translation found many admirers, and was read with pleasure by Pope himself.

The time drew near at which Johnson would, in the ordinary course of things, have become a Bachelor of Arts: but he was at the end of his resources. Those promises of support on which he had relied had not been kept. His family could do nothing for him. His debts to Oxford tradesmen were small indeed, yet larger than he could pay. In the autumn of 1731, he was under the necessity of quitting the university without a degree. In the following winter his father died. The old man left but a pittance; and of that pittance almost the whole was appropriated to the support of his widow. The property to which Samuel succeeded amounted to no more than twenty pounds.

His life, during the thirty years which followed, was one hard struggle with poverty. The misery of that struggle needed no aggravation, but was aggravated by the sufferings of an unsound body and an unsound mind. Before the young man left the university, his hereditary malady had broken forth in a singularly cruel form. He had become an incurable hypochondriac. He said long after that he had been mad all his life, or at least not perfectly sane; and, in truth, eccentricities less strange than his have often been thought grounds sufficient for absolving felons, and for setting aside wills. His grimaces, his gestures, his mutterings, sometimes diverted and sometimes terrified people who did not know him. At a dinner table he would, in a fit of absence, stoop down and twitch off a lady's shoe. He would amaze a drawing room by suddenly ejaculating a clause of the Lord's Prayer. He would conceive an unintelligible aversion to a particular alley, and perform a great circuit rather than see the hateful place. He would set his heart on touching every post in the streets through which he walked. If by any chance he missed a post, he would go back a hundred yards and repair the omission. Under the influence of his disease, his senses became morbidly torpid, and his imagination morbidly active. At one time he would stand poring on the town clock without being able to tell the hour. At another, he would distinctly hear his mother, who was many miles off, calling him by his name. But this was not the worst. A deep melancholy took possession of him, and gave a dark tinge to all his views of human nature and of human destiny. Such wretchedness as he endured has driven many men to shoot themselves or drown themselves. But he was under no temptation to commit suicide. He was sick of life; but he was afraid of death; and he shuddered at every sight or sound which reminded him of the inevitable hour. In religion he found but little comfort during his long and frequent fits of dejection; for his religion partook of his own character. The light from heaven shone on him indeed, but not in a direct line, or with its own pure splendour. The rays had to struggle through a disturbing medium; they reached him refracted, dulled and discoloured by the thick gloom which had settled on his soul; and, though they might be sufficiently clear to guide him, were too dim to cheer him.

With such infirmities of body and of mind, this celebrated man was left, at two-and-twenty, to fight his way through the world. He remained during about five years in the midland counties. At Lichfield, his birth-place and his early home, he had inherited some friends and acquired others. He was kindly noticed by Henry Hervey, a gay officer of noble family, who happened to be quartered there. Gilbert Walmesley, registrar of the ecclesiastical court of the diocese, a man of distinguished parts, learning, and knowledge of the world, did himself honour by patronising the young adventurer, whose repulsive person, unpolished manners, and squalid garb moved many of the petty aristocracy of the neighbourhood to laughter or to disgust. At Lichfield, however, Johnson could find no way of earning a livelihood. He became usher of a grammar school in Leicestershire; he resided as a humble companion in the house of a country gentleman; but a life of dependence was insupportable to his haughty spirit. He repaired to Birmingham, and there earned a few guineas by literary drudgery. In that town he printed a translation, little noticed at the time, and long forgotten, of a Latin book about Abyssinia. He then put forth proposals for publishing by subscription the poems of Politian, with notes containing a history of modern Latin verse; but subscriptions did not come in; and the volume never appeared.

While leading this vagrant and miserable life, Johnson fell in love. The object of his passion was Mrs. Elizabeth Porter, a widow who had children as old as himself. To ordinary spectators, the lady appeared to be a short, fat, coarse woman, painted half an inch thick, dressed in gaudy colours, and fond of exhibiting provincial airs and graces which were not exactly those of the Queensberrys and Lepels. To Johnson, however, whose passions were strong, whose eyesight was too weak to distinguish ceruse from natural bloom, and who had seldom or never been in the same room with a woman of real fashion, his Titty, as he called her, was the most beautiful, graceful and accomplished of her sex. That his admiration was unfeigned cannot be doubted; for she was as poor as himself. She accepted, with a readiness which did her little honour, the addresses of a suitor who might have been her son. The marriage, however, in spite of occasional wranglings, proved happier than might have been expected. The lover continued to be under the illusions of the wedding-day till the lady died in her sixty-fourth year. On her monument he placed an inscription extolling the charms of her person and of her manners; and, when long after her decease, he had occasion to mention her, he exclaimed, with a tenderness half ludicrous, half pathetic, "Pretty creature!"

His marriage made it necessary for him to exert himself more strenuously than he had hitherto done. He took a house in the neighbourhood of his native town, and advertised for pupils. But eighteen months passed away; and only three pupils came to his academy. Indeed, his appearance was so strange, and his temper so violent, that his schoolroom must have resembled an ogre's den. Nor was the tawdry painted grandmother whom he called his Titty well qualified to make provision for the comfort of young gentlemen. David Garrick, who was one of the pupils, used, many years later, to throw the best company of London into convulsions of laughter by mimicking the endearments of this extraordinary pair.

At length Johnson, in the twenty-eighth year of his age, determined to seek his fortune in the capital as a literary adventurer. He set out with a few guineas, three acts of the tragedy of Irene in manuscript, and two or three letters of introduction from his friend Walmesley.

Never since literature became a calling in England had it been a less gainful calling than at the time when Johnson took up his residence in London. In the preceding generation a writer of eminent merit was sure to be munificently rewarded by the government. The least that he could expect was a pension or a sinecure place; and, if he showed any aptitude for politics, he might hope to be a member of parliament, a lord of the treasury, an ambassador, a secretary of state. It would be easy, on the other hand, to name several writers of the nineteenth century of whom the least successful has received forty thousand pounds from the booksellers. But Johnson entered on his vocation in the most dreary part of the dreary interval which separated two ages of prosperity. Literature had ceased to flourish under the patronage of the great, and had not begun to flourish under the patronage of the public. One man of letters, indeed, Pope, had acquired by his pen what was then considered as a handsome fortune, and lived on a footing of equality with nobles and ministers of state. But this was a solitary exception. Even an author whose reputation was established, and whose works were popular, such an author as Thomson, whose Seasons were in every library, such an author as Fielding, whose Pasquin had had a greater run than any drama since The Beggar's Opera, was sometimes glad to obtain, by pawning his best coat, the means of dining on tripe at a cookshop underground, where he could wipe his hands, after his greasy meal, on the back of a Newfoundland dog. It is easy, therefore, to imagine what humiliations and privations must have awaited the novice who had still to earn a name. One of the publishers to whom Johnson applied for employment measured with a scornful eye that athletic though uncouth frame, and exclaimed, "You had better get a porter's knot, and carry trunks." Nor was the advice bad; for a porter was likely to be as plentifully fed, and as comfortably lodged, as a poet.

Some time appears to have elapsed before Johnson was able to form any literary connection from which he could expect more than bread for the day which was passing over him. He never forgot the generosity with which Hervey, who was now residing in London, relieved his wants during this time of trial. "Harry Hervey," said the old philosopher many years later, "was a vicious man; but he was very kind to me. If you call a dog Hervey, I shall love him." At Hervey's table Johnson sometimes enjoyed feasts which were made more agreeable by contrast. But in general he dined, and thought that he dined well, on sixpenny worth of meat, and a pennyworth of bread, at an alehouse near Drury Lane.

The effect of the privations and sufferings which he endured at this time was discernible to the last in his temper and his deportment. His manners had never been courtly. They now became almost savage. Being frequently under the necessity of wearing shabby coats and dirty shirts, he became a confirmed sloven. Being often very hungry when he sat down to his meals, he contracted a habit of eating with ravenous greediness. Even to the end of his life, and even at the tables of the great, the sight of food affected him as it affects wild beasts and birds of prey. His taste in cookery, formed in subterranean ordinaries and *Alamode* beefshops, was far from delicate. Whenever he was so fortunate as to have near him a hare that had been kept too long, or a meat pie made with rancid butter, he gorged himself with such violence that his veins swelled, and the moisture broke out on his forehead. The affronts which his poverty emboldened stupid and low-minded men to offer to him would have broken a mean spirit into sycophancy, but made him rude even to ferocity. Unhappily the insolence which, while it was defensive, was pardonable, and in some sense respectable, accompanied him into societies where he was treated with courtesy and kindness. He was repeatedly provoked into striking those who had taken liberties with him. All the sufferers, however, were wise enough to abstain from talking about their beatings, except Osborne, the most rapacious and brutal of booksellers, who proclaimed everywhere that he had been knocked down by the huge fellow whom he had hired to puff the Harleian Library.

About a year after Johnson had begun to reside in London, he was fortunate enough to obtain regular employment from Cave, an enterprising and intelligent bookseller, who was proprietor and editor of the Gentleman's Magazine. That journal, just entering on the ninth year of its long existence, was the only periodical work in the kingdom which then had what would now be called a large circulation. It was indeed, the chief source of parliamentary intelligence. It was not then safe, even during a recess, to publish an account of the proceedings of either House without some disguise. Cave, however, ventured to entertain his readers with what he called Reports of the Debates of the Senate of Lilliput.

France was Blefuscu; London was Mildendo: pounds were sprugs: the Duke of Newcastle was the Nardac secretary of state: Lord Hardwicke was the Hurgo Hickrad; and William Pulteney was Wingul Pulnub. To write the speeches was, during several years, the business of Johnson. He was generally furnished with notes, meagre indeed, and inaccurate, of what had been said; but sometimes he had to find arguments and eloquence both for the ministry and for the opposition. He was himself a Tory, not from rational conviction—for his serious opinion was that one form of government was just as good or as bad as another—but from mere passion, such as inflamed the Capulets against the Montagues, or the Blues of the Roman circus against the Greens. In his infancy he had heard so much talk about the villanies of the Whigs, and the dangers of the Church, that he had become a furious partisan when he could scarcely speak. Before he was three he had insisted on being taken to hear Sacheverell preach at Lichfield Cathedral, and had listened to the sermon with as much respect, and probably with as much intelligence, as any Staffordshire squire in the congregation. The work which had been begun in the nursery had been completed by the university. Oxford, when Johnson resided there, was the most Jacobitical place in England; and Pembroke was one of the most Jacobitical colleges in Oxford. The prejudices which he brought up to London were scarcely less absurd than those of his own Tom Tempest. Charles II. and James II. were two of the best kings that ever reigned. Laud, a poor creature who never did, said, or wrote any thing indicating more than the ordinary capacity of an old woman, was a prodigy of parts and learning over whose tomb Art and Genius still continued to weep. Hampden deserved no more honourable name than that of "the zealot of rebellion." Even the ship money, condemned not less decidedly by Falkland and Clarendon than by the bitterest Roundheads, Johnson would not pronounce to have been an unconstitutional impost. Under a government the mildest that had ever been known in the world under a government which allowed to the people an unprecedented liberty of speech and action, he fancied that he was a slave; he assailed the ministry with obloquy which refuted itself, and regretted the lost freedom and happiness of those golden days in which a writer who had taken but one-tenth part of the license allowed to him would have been pilloried, mangled with the shears, whipped at the cart's tail, and flung into a noisome dungeon to die. He hated dissenters and stock-jobbers, the excise and the army, septennial parliaments, and continental connections. He long had an aversion to the Scotch, an aversion of which he could not remember the commencement, but which, he owned, had probably originated in his abhorrence of the conduct of the nation during the Great Rebellion. It is easy to guess in what manner debates on great party questions were likely to be reported by a man whose judgment was so much disordered by party spirit. A show of fairness was indeed necessary to the prosperity of the Magazine. But Johnson long afterwards owned that, though he had saved appearances, he had taken care that the Whig dogs should not have the best of it; and, in fact, every passage which has lived, every passage which bears the marks of his higher faculties, is put into the mouth of some member of the opposition.

A few weeks after Johnson had entered on these obscure labours, he published a work which at once placed him high among the writers of his age. It is probable that what he had suffered during his first year in London had often reminded him of some parts of that noble poem in which Juvenal had described the misery and degradation of a needy man of letters, lodged among the pigeons' nests in the tottering garrets which overhung the streets of Rome. Pope's admirable imitations of Horace's Satires and Epistles had recently appeared, were in every hand, and were by many readers thought superior to the originals. What Pope had done for Horace, Johnson aspired to do for Juvenal. The enterprise was bold, and yet judicious. For between Johnson and Juvenal there was much in common, much more certainly than between Pope and Horace.

Johnson's London appeared without his name in May 1738. He received only ten guineas for this stately and vigorous poem: but the sale was rapid, and the success complete. A second edition was required within a week. Those small critics who are always desirous to lower established reputations ran about proclaiming that the anonymous satirist was superior to Pope in Pope's own peculiar department of literature. It ought to be remembered, to the honour of Pope, that he joined heartily in the applause with which the appearance of a rival genius was welcomed. He made inquiries about the author of London. Such a man, he said, could not long be concealed. The name was soon discovered; and Pope, with great kindness, exerted himself to obtain an academical degree and the mastership of a grammar school for the poor young poet. The attempt failed, and Johnson remained a bookseller's hack.

It does not appear that these two men, the most eminent writer of the generation which was going out, and the most eminent writer of the generation which was coming in, ever saw each other. They lived in very different circles, one surrounded by dukes and earls, the other by starving pamphleteers and indexmakers. Among

Johnson's associates at this time may be mentioned Boyse, who, when his shirts were pledged, scrawled Latin verses sitting up in bed with his arms through two holes in his blanket, who composed very respectable sacred poetry when he was sober, and who was at last run over by a hackney coach when he was drunk; Hoole, surnamed the metaphysical tailor, who, instead of attending to his measures, used to trace geometrical diagrams on the board where he sate cross-legged; and the penitent impostor, George Psalmanazar, who, after poring all day, in a humble lodging, on the folios of Jewish rabbis and Christian fathers, indulged himself at night with literary and theological conversation at an alehouse in the city. But the most remarkable of the persons with whom at this time Johnson consorted, was Richard Savage, an earl's son, a shoemaker's apprentice, who had seen life in all its forms, who had feasted among blue ribands in Saint James's Square, and had lain with fifty pounds weight of irons on his legs in the condemned ward of Newgate. This man had, after many vicissitudes of fortune, sunk at last into abject and hopeless poverty. His pen had failed him. His patrons had been taken away by death, or estranged by the riotous profusion with which he squandered their bounty, and the ungrateful insolence with which he rejected their advice. He now lived by begging. He dined on venison and Champagne whenever he had been so fortunate as to borrow a guinea. If his questing had been unsuccessful, he appeased the rage of hunger with some scraps of broken meat, and lay down to rest under the Piazza of Covent Garden in warm weather, and, in cold weather, as near as he could get to the furnace of a glass house. Yet, in his misery, he was still an agreeable companion. He had an inexhaustible store of anecdotes about that gay and brilliant world from which he was now an outcast. He had observed the great men of both parties in hours of careless relaxation, had seen the leaders of opposition without the mask of patriotism, and had heard the prime minister roar with laughter and tell stories not over decent. During some months Savage lived in the closest familiarity with Johnson; and then the friends parted, not without tears. Johnson remained in London to drudge for Cave. Savage went to the West of England, lived there as he had lived everywhere, and, in 1743, died, penniless and heartbroken, in Bristol gaol.

Soon after his death, while the public curiosity was strongly excited about his extraordinary character, and his not less extraordinary adventures, a life of him appeared widely different from the catchpenny lives of eminent men which were then a staple article of manufacture in Grub Street. The style was indeed deficient in ease and variety; and the writer was evidently too partial to the Latin element of our language. But the little work, with all its faults, was a masterpiece. No finer specimen of literary biography existed in any language, living or dead; and a discerning critic might have confidently predicted that the author was destined to be the founder of a new school of English eloquence.

The Life of Savage was anonymous; but it was well known in literary circles that Johnson was the writer. During the three years which followed, he produced no important work; but he was not, and indeed could not be, idle. The fame of his abilities and learning continued to grow. Warburton pronounced him a man of parts and genius; and the praise of Warburton was then no light thing. Such was Johnson's reputation that, in 1747, several eminent booksellers combined to employ him in the arduous work of preparing a Dictionary of the English Language, in two folio volumes. The sum which they agreed to pay him was only fifteen hundred guineas; and out of this sum he had to pay several poor men of letters who assisted him in the humbler parts of his task.

The Prospectus of the Dictionary he addressed to the Earl of Chesterfield. Chesterfield had long been celebrated for the politeness of his manners, the brilliancy of his wit, and the delicacy of his taste. He was acknowledged to be the finest speaker in the House of Lords. He had recently governed Ireland, at a momentous conjuncture, with eminent firmness, wisdom, and humanity; and he had since become Secretary of State. He received Johnson's homage with the most winning affability, and requited it with a few guineas, bestowed doubtless in a very graceful manner, but was by no means desirous to see all his carpets blackened with the London mud, and his soups and wines thrown to right and left over the gowns of fine ladies and the waistcoats of fine gentlemen, by an absent, awkward scholar, who gave strange starts and uttered strange growls, who dressed like a scarecrow, and ate like a cormorant. During some time Johnson continued to call on his patron, but, after being repeatedly told by the porter that his lordship was not at home, took the hint, and ceased to present himself at the inhospitable door.

Johnson had flattered himself that he should have completed his Dictionary by the end of 1750; but it was not till 1755 that he at length gave his huge volumes to the world. During the seven years which he passed in the drudgery of penning definitions and marking quotations for transcriptions, he sought for relaxation in literary labour of a more agreeable kind. In 1749 he published the Vanity of Human Wishes, an excellent imitation of the Tenth Satire of

Juvenal. It is in truth not easy to say whether the palm belongs to the ancient or to the modern poet. The couplets in which the fall of Wolsey is described, though lofty and sonorous, are feeble when compared with the wonderful lines which bring before us all Rome in tumult on the day of the fall of Sejanus, the laurels on the doorposts, the white bull stalking towards the Capitol, the statues rolling down from their pedestals, the flatterers of the disgraced minister running to see him dragged with a hook through the streets, and to have a kick at his carcase before it is hurled into the Tiber. It must be owned too that in the concluding passage the Christian moralist has not made the most of his advantages, and has fallen decidedly short of the sublimity of his Pagan model. On the other hand, Juvenal's Hannibal must yield to Johnson's Charles; and Johnson's vigorous and pathetic enumeration of the miseries of a literary life must be allowed to be superior to Juvenal's lamentation over the fate of Demosthenes and Cicero.

For the copyright of the Vanity of Human Wishes Johnson received only fifteen guineas.

A few days after the publication of this poem, his tragedy, begun many years before, was brought on the stage. His pupil, David Garrick, had, in 1741, made his appearance on a humble stage in Goodman's Fields, had at once risen to the first place among actors, and was now, after several years of almost uninterrupted success, manager of the Drury Lane Theatre. The relation between him and his old preceptor was of a very singular kind. They repelled each other strongly, and yet attracted each other strongly. Nature had made them of very different clay; and circumstances had fully brought out the natural peculiarities of both. Sudden prosperity had turned Garrick's head. Continued adversity had soured Johnson's temper. Johnson saw with more envy than became so great a man the villa, the plate, the china, the Brussels carpet, which the little mimic had got by repeating, with grimaces and gesticulations, what wiser men had written; and the exquisitely sensitive vanity of Garrick was galled by the thought that, while all the rest of the world was applauding him, he could obtain from one morose cynic, whose opinion it was impossible to despise, scarcely any compliment not acidulated with scorn. Yet the two Lichfield men had so many early recollections in common, and sympathized with each other on so many points on which they sympathized with nobody else in the vast population of the capital, that, though the master was often provoked by the monkey-like impertinence of the pupil, and the pupil by the bearish rudeness of the master, they remained friends till they were parted by death. Garrick now brought Irene out, with alterations sufficient to displease the author, yet not sufficient to make the piece pleasing to the audience. The public, however, listened with little emotion, but with much civility, to five acts of monotonous declamation. After nine representations the play was withdrawn. It is, indeed, altogether unsuited to the stage, and, even when perused in the closet, will be found hardly worthy of the author. He had not the slightest notion of what blank verse should be. A change in the last syllable of every other line would make the versification of the Vanity of Human Wishes closely resemble the versification of Irene. The poet, however, cleared, by his benefit nights, and by the sale of the copyright of his tragedy, about three hundred pounds, then a great sum in his estimation.

About a year after the representation of Irene, he began to publish a series of short essays on morals, manners, and literature. This species of composition had been brought into fashion by the success of the Tatler, and by the still more brilliant success of the Spectator. A crowd of small writers had vainly attempted to rival Addison. The Lay Monastery, the Censor, the Freethinker, the Plain Dealer, the Champion, and other works of the same kind, had had their short day. None of them had obtained a permanent place in our literature; and they are now to be found only in the libraries of the curious. At length Johnson undertook the adventure in which so many aspirants had failed. In the thirty-sixth year after the appearance of the last number of the Spectator appeared the first number of the Rambler. From March 1750 to March 1752, this paper continued to come out every Tuesday and Saturday.

From the first the Rambler was enthusiastically admired by a few eminent men. Richardson, when only five numbers had appeared, pronounced it equal, if not superior, to the Spectator. Young and Hartley expressed their approbation not less warmly. Bubb Dodington, among whose many faults indifference to the claims of genius and learning cannot be reckoned, solicited the acquaintance of the writer. In consequence probably of the good offices of Dodington, who was then the confidential adviser of Prince Frederic, two of his Royal Highness's gentlemen carried a gracious message to the printing office, and ordered seven copies for Leicester House. But these overtures seem to have been very coldly received. Johnson had had enough of the patronage of the great to last him all his life, and was not disposed to haunt any other door as he had haunted the door of Chesterfield.

By the public the Rambler was at first very coldly received. Though the price of a number was only twopence, the sale did not amount to five hundred. The profits were therefore very small.

But as soon as the flying leaves were collected and reprinted they became popular. The author lived to see thirteen thousand copies spread over England alone. Separate editions were published for the Scotch and Irish markets. A large party pronounced the style perfect, so absolutely perfect that in some essays it would be impossible for the writer himself to alter a single word for the better. Another party, not less numerous, vehemently accused him of having corrupted the purity of the English tongue. The best critics admitted that his diction was too monotonous, too obviously artificial, and now and then turgid even to absurdity. But they did justice to the acuteness of his observations on morals and manners, to the constant precision and frequent brilliancy of his language, to the weighty and magnificent eloquence of many serious passages, and to the solemn yet pleasing humour of some of the lighter papers. On the question of precedence between Addison and Johnson, a question which, seventy years ago, was much disputed, posterity has pronounced a decision from which there is no appeal. Sir Roger, his chaplain and his butler, Will Wimble and Will Honeycomb, the Vision of Mirza, the Journal of the Retired Citizen, the Everlasting Club, the Dunmow Flitch, the Loves of Hilpah and Shalum, the Visit to the Exchange, and the Visit to the Abbey, are known to everybody. But many men and women, even of highly cultivated minds, are unacquainted with Squire Bluster and Mrs. Busy, Quisquilius and Venustulus, the Allegory of Wit and Learning, the Chronicle of the Revolutions of a Garret, and the sad fate of Aningait and Ajut.

The last Rambler was written in a sad and gloomy hour. Mrs. Johnson had been given over by the physicians. Three days later she died. She left her husband almost broken-hearted. Many people had been surprised to see a man of his genius and learning stooping to every drudgery, and denying himself almost every comfort, for the purpose of supplying a silly, affected old woman with superfluities, which she accepted with but little gratitude. But all his affection had been concentrated on her. He had neither brother nor sister, neither son nor daughter. To him she was beautiful as the Gunnings, and witty as Lady Mary. Her opinion of his writings was more important to him than the voice of the pit of Drury Lane Theatre or the judgment of the Monthly Review. The chief support which had sustained him through the most arduous labour of his life was the hope that she would enjoy the fame and the profit which he anticipated from his Dictionary. She was gone; and in that vast labyrinth of streets, peopled by eight hundred thousand human beings, he was alone. Yet it was necessary for him to set himself, as he expressed it, doggedly to work. After three more laborious years, the Dictionary was at length complete.

It had been generally supposed that this great work would be dedicated to the eloquent and accomplished nobleman to whom the Prospectus had been addressed. He well knew the value of such a compliment; and therefore, when the day of publication drew near, he exerted himself to sooth, by a show of zealous and at the same time of delicate and judicious kindness, the pride which he had so cruelly wounded. Since the Ramblers had ceased to appear, the town had been entertained by a journal called The World, to which many men of high rank and fashion contributed. In two successive numbers of The World, the Dictionary was, to use the modern phrase, puffed with wonderful skill. The writings of Johnson were warmly praised. It was proposed that he should be invested with the authority of a Dictator, nay, of a Pope, over our language, and that his decisions about the meaning and the spelling of words should be received as final. His two folios, it was said, would of course be bought by everybody who could afford to buy them. It was soon known that these papers were written by Chesterfield. But the just resentment of Johnson was not to be so appeased. In a letter written with singular energy and dignity of thought and language, he repelled the tardy advances of his patron. The Dictionary came forth without a dedication. In the preface the author truly declared that he owed nothing to the great, and described the difficulties with which he had been left to struggle so forcibly and pathetically that the ablest and most malevolent of all the enemies of his fame, Horne Tooke, never could read that passage without tears.

The public, on this occasion, did Johnson full justice, and something more than justice. The best lexicographer may well be content if his productions are received by the world with cold esteem. But Johnson's Dictionary was hailed with an enthusiasm such as no similar work has ever excited. It was indeed the first dictionary which could be read with pleasure. The definitions show so much acuteness of thought and command of language, and the passages quoted from poets, divines, and philosophers, are so skilfully selected, that a leisure hour may always be very agreeably spent in turning over the pages. The faults of the book resolve themselves, for the most part, into one great fault. Johnson was a wretched etymologist. He knew little or nothing of any Teutonic language except English, which indeed, as he wrote it, was scarcely a Teutonic language; and thus he was absolutely at the mercy of Junius and Skinner.

The Dictionary, though it raised Johnson's fame, added nothing to his pecuniary means. The fifteen hundred guineas which the booksellers had agreed to pay him had been advanced and spent before the last sheets issued from the press. It is painful to relate that, twice in the course of the year which followed the publication of this great work, he was arrested and carried to spunging-houses, and that he was twice indebted for his liberty to his excellent friend Richardson. It was still necessary for the man who had been formally saluted by the highest authority as Dictator of the English language to supply his wants by constant toil. He abridged his Dictionary. He proposed to bring out an edition of Shakspeare by subscription; and many subscribers sent in their names, and laid down their money; but he soon found the task so little to his taste that he turned to more attractive employments. He contributed many papers to a new monthly journal, which was called the Literary Magazine. Few of these papers have much interest; but among them was the very best thing that he ever wrote, a master-piece both of reasoning and of satirical pleasantry, the review of Jenyns's Inquiry into the Nature and Origin of Evil.

In the spring of 1758 Johnson put forth the first of a series of essays, entitled The Idler. During two years these essays continued to appear weekly. They were eagerly read, widely circulated, and, indeed, impudently pirated while they were still in the original form, and had a large sale when collected into volumes. The Idler may be described as a second part of the Rambler, somewhat livelier and somewhat weaker than the first part.

While Johnson was busied with his Idlers, his mother, who had accomplished her ninetieth year, died at Lichfield. It was long since he had seen her; but he had not failed to contribute largely, out of his small means, to her comfort. In order to defray the charges of her funeral, and to pay some debts which she had left, he wrote a little book in a single week, and sent off the sheets to the press without reading them over. A hundred pounds were paid to him for the copyright; and the purchasers had great cause to be pleased with their bargain; for the book was Rasselas.

The success of Rasselas was great, though such ladies as Miss Lydia Languish must have been grievously disappointed when they found that the new volume from the circulating library was little more than a dissertation on the author's favourite theme, the Vanity of Human Wishes; that the Prince of Abyssinia was without a mistress, and the Princess without a lover; and that the story set the hero and the heroine down exactly where it had taken them up. The style was the subject of much eager controversy. The Monthly

Review and the Critical Review took different sides. Many readers pronounced the writer a pompous pedant, who would never use a word of two syllables where it was possible to use a word of six, and who could not make a waiting woman relate her adventures without balancing every noun with another noun, and every epithet with another epithet. Another party, not less zealous, cited with delight numerous passages in which weighty meaning was expressed with accuracy and illustrated with splendour. And both the censure and the praise were merited.

About the plan of Rasselas little was said by the critics; and yet the faults of the plan might seem to invite severe criticism. Johnson has frequently blamed Shakspeare for neglecting the proprieties of time and place, and for ascribing to one age or nation the manners and opinions of another. Yet Shakspeare has not sinned in this way more grievously than Johnson. Rasselas and Imlac, Nekayah and Pekuah, are evidently meant to be Abyssinians of the eighteenth century: for the Europe which Imlac describes is the Europe of the eighteenth century; and the inmates of the Happy Valley talk familiarly of that law of gravitation which Newton discovered, and which was not fully received even at Cambridge till the eighteenth century. What a real company of Abyssinians would have been may be learned from Bruce's Travels. But Johnson, not content with turning filthy savages, ignorant of their letters, and gorged with raw steaks cut from living cows, into philosophers as eloquent and enlightened as himself or his friend Burke, and into ladies as highly accomplished as Mrs. Lennox or Mrs. Sheridan, transferred the whole domestic system of England to Egypt. Into a land of harems, a land of polygamy, a land where women are married without ever being seen, he introduced the flirtations and jealousies of our ball-rooms. In a land where there is boundless liberty of divorce, wedlock is described as the indissoluble compact. "A youth and maiden meeting by chance, or brought together by artifice, exchange glances, reciprocate civilities, go home, and dream of each other. Such," says Rasselas, "is the common process of marriage." Such it may have been, and may still be, in London, but assuredly not at Cairo. A writer who was guilty of such improprieties had little right to blame the poet who made Hector quote Aristotle, and represented Julio Romano as flourishing in the days of the oracle of Delphi.

By such exertions as have been described, Johnson supported himself till the year 1762. In that year a great change in his circumstances took place. He had from a child been an enemy of the reigning dynasty. His Jacobite prejudices had been exhibited with little disguise both in his works and in his conversation. Even in his massy and elaborate Dictionary, he had, with a strange want of taste and judgment, inserted bitter and contumelious reflections on the Whig party. The excise, which was a favourite resource of Whig financiers, he had designated as a hateful tax. He had railed against the commissioners of excise in language so coarse that they had seriously thought of prosecuting him. He had with difficulty been prevented from holding up the Lord Privy Seal by name as an example of the meaning of the word "renegade." A pension he had defined as pay given to a state hireling to betray his country; a pensioner as a slave of state hired by a stipend to obey a master. It seemed unlikely that the author of these definitions would himself be pensioned. But that was a time of wonders. George the Third had ascended the throne; and had, in the course of a few months, disgusted many of the old friends and conciliated many of the old enemies of his house. The city was becoming mutinous. Oxford was becoming loyal. Cavendishes and Bentincks were murmuring. Somersets and Wyndhams were hastening to kiss hands. The head of the treasury was now Lord Bute, who was a Tory, and could have no objection to Johnson's Toryism. Bute wished to be thought a patron of men of letters; and Johnson was one of the most eminent and one of the most needy men of letters in Europe. A pension of three hundred a year was graciously offered, and with very little hesitation accepted.

This event produced a change in Johnson's whole way of life. For the first time since his boyhood he no longer felt the daily goad urging him to the daily toil. He was at liberty, after thirty years of anxiety and drudgery, to indulge his constitutional indolence, to lie in bed till two in the afternoon, and to sit up talking till four in the morning, without fearing either the printer's devil or the sheriff's officer.

One laborious task indeed he had bound himself to perform. He had received large subscriptions for his promised edition of Shakspeare; he had lived on those subscriptions during some years; and he could not without disgrace omit to perform his part of the contract. His friends repeatedly exhorted him to make an effort; and he repeatedly resolved to do so. But, notwithstanding their exhortations and his resolutions, month followed month, year followed year, and nothing was done. He prayed fervently against his idleness; he determined, as often as he received the sacrament, that he would no longer doze away and trifle away his time; but the spell under which he lay resisted prayer and sacrament. His private notes at this time are made up of self-reproaches. "My indolence," he wrote on Easter eve in 1764, "has sunk into grosser sluggishness. A kind of strange oblivion has overspread me, so that I know not what has become of the last year." Easter 1765 came, and found him still in the same state. "My time," he wrote, "has been unprofitably spent, and seems as a dream that has left nothing behind. My memory grows confused, and I know not how the days pass over me." Happily for his honour, the charm which held him captive was at length broken by no gentle or friendly hand. He had been weak enough to pay serious attention to a story about a ghost which haunted a house in Cock Lane, and had actually gone himself, with some of his friends, at one in the morning, to St. John's Church, Clerkenwell, in the hope of receiving a communication from the perturbed spirit. But the spirit, though adjured with all solemnity, remained obstinately silent; and it soon appeared that a naughty girl of eleven had been amusing herself by making fools of so many philosophers. Churchill, who, confident in his powers, drunk with popularity, and burning with party spirit, was looking for some man of established fame and Tory politics to insult, celebrated the Cock Lane Ghost in three cantos, nicknamed Johnson Pomposo, asked where the book was which had been so long promised and so liberally paid for, and directly accused the great moralist of cheating. This terrible word proved effectual; and in October 1765 appeared, after a delay of nine years, the new edition of Shakspeare.

This publication saved Johnson's character for honesty, but added nothing to the fame of his abilities and learning. The preface, though it contains some good passages, is not in his best manner. The most valuable notes are those in which he had an opportunity of showing how attentively he had during many years observed human life and human nature. The best specimen is the note on the character of Polonius. Nothing so good is to be found even in Wilhelm Meister's admirable examination of Hamlet. But here praise must end. It would be difficult to name a more slovenly, a more worthless, edition of any great classic. The reader may turn over play after play without finding one happy conjectural emendation, or one ingenious and satisfactory explanation of a passage which had baffled preceding commentators. Johnson had, in his Prospectus, told the world that he was peculiarly fitted for the task which he had undertaken, because he had, as a lexicographer, been under the necessity of taking a wider view of the English language than any of his predecessors. That his knowledge of our literature was extensive is indisputable. But, unfortunately, he had altogether neglected that very part of our literature with which it is especially desirable that an editor of Shakspeare should be conversant. It is dangerous to assert a negative. Yet little will be risked by the assertion, that in the two folio volumes of the English Dictionary there is not a single passage quoted from any dramatist of the Elizabethan age, except Shakspeare and Ben. Even from Ben the quotations are few. Johnson might easily, in a few months, have made himself well acquainted with every old play that was extant. But it never seems to have occurred to him that this was a necessary preparation for the work which he had undertaken. He would doubtless have admitted that it would be the height of absurdity in a man who was not familiar with the works of Æschylus and Euripides to publish an edition of Sophocles. Yet he ventured to publish an edition of Shakspeare, without having ever in his life, as far as can be discovered, read a single scene of Massinger, Ford, Decker, Webster, Marlow, Beaumont, or Fletcher. His detractors were noisy and scurrilous. Those who most loved and honoured him had little to say in praise of the manner in which he had discharged the duty of a commentator. He had, however, acquitted himself of a debt which had long lain heavy on his conscience, and he sank back into the repose from which the sting of satire had roused him. He long continued to live upon the fame which he had already won. He was honoured by the University of Oxford with a Doctor's degree, by the Royal Academy with a professorship, and by the King with an interview, in which his Majesty most graciously expressed a hope that so excellent a writer would not cease to write. In the interval, however, between 1765 and 1775 Johnson published only two or three political tracts, the longest of which he could have produced in forty-eight hours, if he had worked as he worked on the Life of Savage and on Rasselas.

But, though his pen was now idle, his tongue was active. The influence exercised by his conversation, directly upon those with whom he lived, and indirectly on the whole literary world, was altogether without a parallel. His colloquial talents were indeed of the highest order. He had a strong sense, quick discernment, wit, humour, immense knowledge of literature and of life, and an infinite store of curious anecdotes. As respected style, he spoke far better than he wrote. Every sentence which dropped from his lips was as correct in structure as the most nicely balanced period of the Rambler. But in his talk there were no pompous triads, and little more than a fair proportion of words in *osity* and *ation*. All was simplicity, ease, and vigour. He uttered his short, weighty, and pointed sentences with a power of voice, and a justness and energy of emphasis, of which the effect was rather increased than diminished by the rollings of his huge form, and by the asthmatic gaspings and puffings in which the peals of his eloquence generally ended. Nor did the laziness which made him unwilling to sit down to his desk prevent him from giving instruction or entertainment orally. To discuss questions of taste, of learning, of casuistry, in language so exact and so forcible that it might have been printed without the alteration of a word, was to him no exertion, but a pleasure. He loved, as he said, to fold his legs and have his talk out. He was ready to bestow the overflowings of his full mind on anybody who would start a subject, on a fellow-passenger in a stage coach, or on the person who sate at the same table with him in an eating house. But his conversation was nowhere so brilliant and striking as when he was surrounded by a few friends, whose abilities and knowledge enabled them, as he once expressed it, to send him back every ball that he threw. Some of these, in 1764, formed themselves into a club, which gradually became a formidable power in the commonwealth of letters. The verdicts pronounced by this conclave on new books were speedily known over all London, and were sufficient to sell off a whole edition in a day, or to condemn the sheets to the service of the trunk-maker and the pastrycook. Nor shall we think this strange when we consider what great and various talents and acquirements met in the little fraternity. Goldsmith was the representative of poetry and light literature, Reynolds of the arts, Burke of political eloquence and political philosophy. There, too, were Gibbon, the greatest historian, and Jones, the greatest linguist, of the age. Garrick brought to the meetings his inexhaustible pleasantry, his incomparable mimicry, and his consummate knowledge of stage effect. Among the most constant attendants were two high-born and high-bred gentlemen, closely bound together by friendship, but of widely different characters and habits; Bennet Langton, distinguished by his skill in Greek literature, by the orthodoxy of his opinions, and by the sanctity of his life; and Topham Beauclerk, renowned for his amours, his knowledge of the gay world, his fastidious taste, and his sarcastic wit. To predominate over such a society was not easy. Yet even over such a society Johnson predominated. Burke might indeed have disputed the supremacy to which others were under the necessity of submitting. But Burke, though not generally a very patient listener, was content to take the second part when Johnson was present; and the club itself, consisting of so many eminent men, is to this day popularly designated as Johnson's Club.

Among the members of this celebrated body was one to whom it has owed the greater part of its celebrity, yet who was regarded with little respect by his brethren, and had not without difficulty obtained a seat among them. This was James Boswell, a young Scotch lawyer, heir to an honourable name and a fair estate. That he was a coxcomb and a bore, weak, vain, pushing, curious, garrulous, was obvious to all who were acquainted with him. That he could not reason, that he had no wit, no humour, no eloquence, is apparent from his writings. And yet his writings are read beyond the Mississippi, and under the Southern Cross, and are likely to be read as long as the English exists, either as a living or as a dead language. Nature had made him a slave and an idolater. His mind resembled those creepers which the botanists call parasites, and which can subsist only by clinging round the stems and imbibing the juices of stronger plants. He must have fastened himself on somebody. He might have fastened himself on Wilkes, and have become the fiercest patriot in the Bill of Rights Society. He might have fastened himself on Whitfield, and have become the loudest field preacher among the Calvinistic Methodists. In a happy hour he fastened himself on Johnson. The pair might seem ill matched. For Johnson had early been prejudiced against Boswell's country. To a man of Johnson's strong understanding and irritable temper, the silly egotism and adulation of Boswell must have been as teasing as the constant buzz of a fly. Johnson hated to be questioned; and Boswell was eternally catechizing him on all kinds of subjects, and sometimes propounded such questions as, "What would you do, sir, if you were locked up in a tower with a baby?" Johnson was a water drinker; and Boswell was a winebibber, and indeed little better than a habitual sot. It was impossible that there should be perfect harmony between two such companions. Indeed, the great man was sometimes provoked into fits of passion in which he said things which the small man, during a few hours, seriously resented. Every quarrel, however, was soon made up. During twenty years the disciple continued to worship the master: the master continued to scold the disciple, to sneer at him, and to love him. The two friends ordinarily resided at a great distance from each other. Boswell practised in the Parliament House of Edinburgh, and could pay only occasional visits to London. During those visits his chief business was to watch Johnson, to discover all Johnson's habits, to turn the conversation to subjects about which Johnson was likely to say something remarkable, and to fill quarto note books with minutes of what Johnson had said. In this way were gathered the materials, out of which was afterwards constructed the most interesting biographical work in the world.

Soon after the club began to exist, Johnson formed a connection less important indeed to his fame, but much more important to his happiness, than his connection with Boswell. Henry Thrale, one of the most opulent brewers in the kingdom, a man of sound and cultivated understanding, rigid principles, and liberal spirit, was married to one of those clever, kind-hearted, engaging, vain, pert young women, who are perpetually doing or saying what is not exactly right, but who, do or say what they may, are always agreeable. In 1765 the Thrales became acquainted with Johnson, and the acquaintance ripened fast into friendship. They were astonished and delighted by the brilliancy of his conversation. They were flattered by finding that a man so widely celebrated preferred their house to any other in London. Even the peculiarities which seemed to unfit him for civilised society, his gesticulations, his rollings, his puffings, his mutterings, the strange way in which he put on his clothes, the ravenous eagerness with which he devoured his dinner, his fits of melancholy, his fits of anger, his frequent rudeness, his occasional ferocity, increased the interest which his new associates took in him. For these things were the cruel marks left behind by a life which had been one long conflict with disease and with adversity. In a vulgar hack writer such oddities would have excited only disgust. But in a man of genius, learning, and virtue, their effect was to add pity to admiration and esteem. Johnson soon had an apartment at the brewery in Southwark, and a still more pleasant apartment at the villa of his friends on Streatham Common. A large part of every year he passed in those abodes, abodes which must have seemed magnificent and luxurious indeed, when compared with the dens in which he had generally been lodged. But his chief pleasures were derived from what the astronomer of his Abyssinian tale called "the endearing elegance of female friendship." Mrs. Thrale rallied him, soothed him, coaxed him, and, if she sometimes provoked him by her flippancy, made ample amends by listening to his reproofs with angelic sweetness of temper. When he was diseased in body and in mind, she was the most tender of nurses. No comfort that wealth could purchase, no contrivance that womanly ingenuity, set to work by womanly compassion, could devise, was wanting to his sick room. He requited her kindness by an affection pure as the affection of a father, yet delicately tinged with a gallantry, which, though awkward, must have been more flattering than the attentions of a crowd of the fools who gloried in the names, now obsolete, of Buck and Maccaroni. It should seem that a full half of Johnson's life, during about sixteen years, was passed under the roof of the Thrales. He accompanied the family sometimes to Bath, and sometimes to Brighton, once to Wales, and once to Paris. But he had at the same time a house in one of the narrow and gloomy courts on the north of Fleet Street. In the garrets was his library, a large and miscellaneous collection of books, falling to pieces and begrimed with dust. On a lower floor he sometimes, but very rarely, regaled a friend with a plain dinner, a veal pie, or a leg of lamb and spinage, and a rice pudding. Nor was the dwelling uninhabited during his long absences. It was the home of the most extraordinary assemblage of inmates that ever was brought together. At the head of the establishment Johnson had placed an old lady named Williams, whose chief recommendations were her blindness and her poverty. But, in spite of her murmurs and reproaches, he gave an asylum to another lady who was as poor as herself, Mrs. Desmoulins, whose family he had known many years before in Staffordshire. Room was found for the daughter of Mrs. Desmoulins, and for another destitute damsel, who was generally addressed as Miss Carmichael, but whom her generous host called Polly. An old quack doctor named Levett, who bled and dosed coal-heavers and hackney coachmen, and received for fees crusts of bread, bits of bacon, glasses of gin, and sometimes a little copper, completed this strange menagerie. All these poor creatures were at constant war with each other, and with Johnson's negro servant Frank. Sometimes, indeed, they transferred their hostilities from the servant to the master, complained that a better table was not kept for them, and railed or maundered till their benefactor was glad to make his escape to Streatham, or to the Mitre Tavern. And yet he, who was generally the haughtiest and most irritable of mankind, who was but too prompt to resent anything which looked like a slight on the part of a purse-proud bookseller, or of a noble and powerful patron, bore patiently from mendicants, who, but for his bounty, must have gone to the workhouse, insults more provoking than those for which he had knocked down Osborne and bidden defiance to Chesterfield. Year after year Mrs. Williams and Mrs. Desmoulins, Polly and Levett, continued to torment him and to live upon him.

The course of life which has been described was interrupted in Johnson's sixty-fourth year by an important event. He had early read an account of the Hebrides, and had been much interested by learning that there was so near him a land peopled by a race which was still as rude and simple as in the middle ages. A wish to become intimately acquainted with a state of society so utterly unlike all that he had ever seen frequently crossed his mind. But it is not probable that his curiosity would have overcome his habitual sluggishness, and his love of the smoke, the mud, and the cries of

London, had not Boswell importuned him to attempt the adventure, and offered to be his squire. At length, in August 1773, Johnson crossed the Highland line, and plunged courageously into what was then considered, by most Englishmen, as a dreary and perilous wilderness. After wandering about two months through the Celtic region, sometimes in rude boats which did not protect him from the rain, and sometimes on small shaggy poneys which could hardly bear his weight, he returned to his old haunts with a mind full of new images and new theories. During the following year he employed himself in recording his adventures. About the beginning of 1775, his Journey to the Hebrides was published, and was, during some weeks, the chief subject of conversation in all circles in which any attention was paid to literature. The book is still read with pleasure. The narrative is entertaining; the speculations, whether sound or unsound, are always ingenious; and the style, though too stiff and pompous, is somewhat easier and more graceful than that of his early writings. His prejudice against the Scotch had at length become little more than matter of jest; and whatever remained of the old feeling had been effectually removed by the kind and respectful hospitality with which he had been received in every part of Scotland. It was, of course, not to be expected that an Oxonian Tory should praise the Presbyterian polity and ritual, or that an eye accustomed to the hedgerows and parks of England should not be struck by the bareness of Berwickshire and East Lothian. But even in censure Johnson's tone is not unfriendly. The most enlightened Scotchmen, with Lord Mansfield at their head, were well pleased. But some foolish and ignorant Scotchmen were moved to anger by a little unpalatable truth which was mingled with much eulogy, and assailed him whom they chose to consider as the enemy of their country with libels much more dishonourable to their country than anything that he had ever said or written. They published paragraphs in the newspapers, articles in the magazines, sixpenny pamphlets, five shilling books. One scribbler abused Johnson for being blear-eyed; another for being a pensioner: a third informed the world that one of the Doctor's uncles had been convicted of felony in Scotland, and had found that there was in that country one tree capable of supporting the weight of an Englishman. Macpherson, whose Fingal had been proved in the Journey to be an impudent forgery, threatened to take vengeance with a cane. The only effect of this threat was that Johnson reiterated the charge of forgery in the most contemptuous terms, and walked about, during some time, with a cudgel, which, if the impostor had not been too wise to encounter it, would assuredly have descended upon him, to borrow the sublime language of his own epic poem, "like a hammer on the red son of the furnace."

Of other assailants Johnson took no notice whatever. He had early resolved never to be drawn into controversy; and he adhered to his resolution with a steadfastness which is the more extraordinary, because he was, both intellectually and morally, of the stuff of which controversialists are made. In conversation, he was a singularly eager, acute, and pertinacious disputant. When at a loss for good reasons, he had recourse to sophistry; and when heated by altercation, he made unsparing use of sarcasm and invective. But when he took his pen in his hand, his whole character seemed to be changed. A hundred bad writers misrepresented him and reviled him; but not one of the hundred could boast of having been thought by him worthy of a refutation, or even of a retort. The Kenricks, Campbells, MacNicols, and Hendersons, did their best to annoy him, in the hope that he would give them importance by answering them. But the reader will in vain search his works for any allusion to Kenrick or Campbell, to MacNicol or Henderson. One Scotchman, bent on vindicating the fame of Scotch learning, defied him to the combat in a detestable Latin hexameter.

"Maxime, si tu vis, cupio contendere tecum."

But Johnson took no notice of the challenge. He had learned, both from his own observation and from literary history, in which he was deeply read, that the place of books in the public estimation is fixed, not by what is written about them, but by what is written in them; and that an author whose works are likely to live is very unwise if he stoops to wrangle with detractors whose works are certain to die. He always maintained that fame was a shuttlecock which could be kept up only by being beaten back, as well as beaten forward, and which would soon fall if there were only one battledore. No saying was oftener in his mouth than that fine apophthegm of Bentley, that no man was ever written down but by himself.

Unhappily, a few months after the appearance of the Journey to the Hebrides, Johnson did what none of his envious assailants could have done, and to a certain extent succeeded in writing himself down. The disputes between England and her American colonies had reached a point at which no amicable adjustment was possible. Civil war was evidently impending; and the ministers seem to have thought that the eloquence of Johnson might with advantage be employed to inflame the nation against the opposition here, and against the rebels beyond the Atlantic. He had already written two or three tracts in defence of the foreign and domestic policy of the government; and those tracts, though hardly worthy of him, were much superior to the crowd of pamphlets which lay on the counters of Almon and Stockdale. But his Taxation No Tyranny was a pitiable failure. The very title was a silly phrase, which can have been recommended to his choice by nothing but a jingling alliteration which he ought to have despised. The arguments were such as boys use in debating societies. The pleasantry was as awkward as the gambols of a hippopotamus. Even Boswell was forced to own that, in this unfortunate piece, he could detect no trace of his master's powers. The general opinion was that the strong faculties which had produced the Dictionary and the Rambler were beginning to feel the effect of time and of disease, and that the old man would best consult his credit by writing no more.

But this was a great mistake. Johnson had failed, not because his mind was less vigorous than when he wrote Rasselas in the evenings of a week, but because he had foolishly chosen, or suffered others to choose for him, a subject such as he would at no time have been competent to treat. He was in no sense a statesman. He never willingly read or thought or talked about affairs of state. He loved biography, literary history, the history of manners; but political history was positively distasteful to him. The question at issue between the colonies and the mother country was a question about which he had really nothing to say. He failed, therefore, as the greatest men must fail when they attempt to do that for which they are unfit; as Burke would have failed if Burke had tried to write comedies like those of Sheridan; as Reynolds would have failed if Reynolds had tried to paint landscapes like those of Wilson. Happily, Johnson soon had an opportunity of proving most signally that his failure was not to be ascribed to intellectual decay.

On Easter eve 1777, some persons, deputed by a meeting which consisted of forty of the first booksellers in London, called upon him. Though he had some scruples about doing business at that season, he received his visitors with much civility. They came to inform him that a new edition of the English poets, from Cowley downwards, was in contemplation, and to ask him to furnish short biographical prefaces. He readily undertook the task, a task for which he was pre-eminently qualified. His knowledge of the literary history of England since the Restoration was unrivalled. That knowledge he had derived partly from books, and partly from sources which had long been closed; from old Grub Street traditions; from the talk of forgotten poetasters and pamphleteers who had long been lying in parish vaults; from the recollections of such men as Gilbert Walmesley, who had conversed with the wits of Button; Cibber, who had mutilated the plays of two generations of dramatists; Orrery, who had been admitted to the society of Swift; and Savage, who had rendered services of no very honourable kind to Pope. The biographer therefore sate down to his task with a mind full of matter. He had at first intended to give only a paragraph to every minor poet, and only four or five pages to the greatest name. But the flood of anecdote and criticism overflowed the narrow channel. The work, which was originally meant to consist only of a few sheets, swelled into ten volumes, small volumes, it is true, and not closely printed. The first four appeared in 1779, the remaining six in 1781.

The Lives of the Poets are, on the whole, the best of Johnson's works. The narratives are as entertaining as any novel. The remarks on life and on human nature are eminently shrewd and profound. The criticisms are often excellent, and, even when grossly and provokingly unjust, well deserve to be studied. For, however erroneous they may be, they are never silly. They are the judgments of a mind trammelled by prejudice and deficient in sensibility, but vigorous and acute. They therefore generally contain a portion of valuable truth which deserves to be separated from the alloy; and, at the very worst, they mean something, a praise to which much of what is called criticism in our time has no pretensions.

Savage's Life Johnson reprinted nearly as it had appeared in 1744. Whoever, after reading that life, will turn to the other lives will be struck by the difference of style. Since Johnson had been at ease in his circumstances he had written little and had talked much. When, therefore, he, after the lapse of years, resumed his pen, the mannerism which he had contracted while he was in the constant habit of elaborate composition was less perceptible than formerly; and his diction frequently had a colloquial ease which it had formerly wanted. The improvement may be discerned by a skilful critic in the Journey to the Hebrides, and in the Lives of the Poets is so obvious that it cannot escape the notice of the most careless reader.

Among the lives the best are perhaps those of Cowley, Dryden, and Pope. The very worst is, beyond all doubt, that of Gray.

This great work at once became popular. There was, indeed, much just and much unjust censure: but even those who were loudest in blame were attracted by the book in spite of themselves. Malone computed the gains of the publishers at five or six thousand pounds. But the writer was very poorly remunerated. Intending at first to write very short prefaces, he had stipulated for only two hundred guineas. The booksellers, when they saw how far his performance had surpassed his promise, added only another hundred. Indeed, Johnson, though he did not despise, or affect to despise money, and though his strong sense and long experience ought to have qualified him to protect his own interests, seems to have been singularly unskilful and unlucky in his literary bargains. He was generally reputed the first English writer of his time. Yet several writers of his time sold their copyrights for sums such as he never ventured to ask. To give a single instance, Robertson received four thousand five hundred pounds for the History of Charles V.; and it is no disrespect to the memory of Robertson to say that the History of Charles V. is both a less valuable and a less amusing book than the Lives of the Poets.

Johnson was now in his seventy-second year. The infirmities of age were coming fast upon him. That inevitable event of which he never thought without horror was brought near to him; and his whole life was darkened by the shadow of death. He had often to pay the cruel price of longevity. Every year he lost what could never be replaced. The strange dependents to whom he had given shelter, and to whom, in spite of their faults, he was strongly attached by habit, dropped off one by one; and, in the silence of his home, he regretted even the noise of their scolding matches. The kind and generous Thrale was no more; and it would have been well if his wife had been laid beside him. But she survived to be the laughing-stock of those who had envied her, and to draw from the eyes of the old man who had loved her beyond anything in the world tears far more bitter than he would have shed over her grave. With some estimable and many agreeable qualities, she was not made to be independent. The control of a mind more steadfast than her own was necessary to her respectability. While she was restrained by her husband, a man of sense and firmness, indulgent to her taste in trifles, but always the undisputed master of his house, her worst offences had been impertinent jokes, white lies, and short fits of pettishness ending in sunny good humour. But he was gone; and she was left an opulent widow of forty, with strong sensibility, volatile fancy, and slender judgment. She soon fell in love with a music-master from Brescia, in whom nobody but herself could discover anything to admire. Her pride, and perhaps some better feelings, struggled hard against this degrading passion. But the struggle irritated her nerves, soured her temper, and at length endangered her health. Conscious that her choice was one which Johnson could not approve, she became desirous to escape from his inspection. Her manner towards him changed. She was sometimes cold and sometimes petulant. She did not conceal her joy when he left Streatham; she never pressed him to return; and, if he came unbidden, she received him in a manner which convinced him that he was no longer a welcome guest. He took the very intelligible hints which she gave. He read, for the last time, a chapter of the Greek Testament in the library which had been formed by himself. In a solemn and tender prayer he commended the house and its inmates to the Divine protection, and, with emotions which choked his voice and convulsed his powerful frame, left for ever that beloved home for the gloomy and desolate house behind Fleet Street, where the few and evil days which still remained to him were to run out. Here, in June 1783, he had a paralytic stroke, from which, however, he recovered, and which does not appear to have at all impaired his intellectual faculties. But other maladies came thick upon him. His asthma tormented him day and night. Dropsical symptoms made their appearance. While sinking under a complication of diseases, he heard that the woman whose friendship had been the chief happiness of sixteen years of his life had married an Italian fiddler; that all London was crying shame upon her; and that the newspapers and magazines were filled with allusions to the Ephesian matron, and the two pictures in Hamlet. He vehemently said that he would try to forget her existence. He never uttered her name. Every memorial of her which met his eye he flung into the fire. She meanwhile fled from the laughter and hisses of her countrymen and countrywomen to a land where she was unknown, hastened across Mount Cenis, and learned, while passing a merry Christmas of concerts and lemonade parties at Milan, that the great man with whose name hers is inseparably associated had ceased to exist.

He had, in spite of much mental and much bodily affliction, clung vehemently to life. The feeling described in that fine but gloomy paper which closes the series of his Idlers seemed to grow stronger in him as his last hour drew near. He fancied that he should be able to draw his breath more easily in a southern climate, and would probably have set out for Rome and Naples, but for his fear of the expense of the journey. That expense, indeed, he had the means of defraying; for he had laid up about two thousand pounds, the fruit of labours which had made the fortune of several publishers. But he was unwilling to break in upon this hoard, and he seems to have wished even to keep its existence a secret. Some of his friends hoped that the government might be induced to increase his pension to six hundred pounds a-year: but this hope was disappointed; and he resolved to stand one English winter more. That winter was his last. His legs grew weaker; his breath grew shorter; the fatal water gathered fast, in spite of incisions which he, courageous against pain, but timid against death, urged his surgeons to make deeper and deeper. Though the tender care which had mitigated his sufferings during months of sickness at Streatham was withdrawn, he was not left desolate. The ablest physicians and surgeons attended him, and refused to accept fees from him. Burke parted from him with deep emotion. Windham sate much in the sick room, arranged the pillows, and sent his own servant to watch a night by the bed. Frances Burney, whom the old man had cherished with fatherly kindness, stood weeping at the door; while Langton, whose piety eminently qualified him to be an adviser and comforter at such a time, received the last pressure of his friend's hand within. When at length the moment, dreaded through so many years, came close, the dark cloud passed away from Johnson's mind. His temper became unusually patient and gentle; he ceased to think with terror of death, and of that which lies beyond death; and he spoke much of the mercy of God, and of the propitiation of Christ. In this serene frame of mind he died on the 13th of December, 1784. He was laid, a week later, in Westminster Abbey, among the eminent men of whom he had been the historian,—Cowley and Denham, Dryden and Congreve, Gay, Prior, and Addison.

Since his death the popularity of his works—the Lives of the Poets, and perhaps, the Vanity of Human Wishes, excepted—has greatly diminished. His Dictionary has been altered by editors till it can scarcely be called his. An allusion to his Rambler or his Idler is not readily apprehended in literary circles. The fame even of Rasselas has grown somewhat dim. But though the celebrity of the writings may have declined, the celebrity of the writer, strange to say, is as great as ever. Boswell's book has done for him more than the best of his own books could do. The memory of other authors is kept alive by their works. But the memory of Johnson keeps many of his works alive. The old philosopher is still among us in the brown coat with the metal buttons and the shirt which ought to be at wash, blinking, puffing, rolling his head, drumming with his fingers, tearing his meat like a tiger, and swallowing his tea in oceans. No human being who has been more than seventy years in the grave is so well known to us. And it is but just to say that our intimate acquaintance with what he himself would have called the anfractuosities of his intellect and of his temper serves only to strengthen our conviction that he was both a great and a good man.

III. *Controversial Essays*

MILL ON GOVERNMENT
(MARCH 1829)

Essays on Government, Jurisprudence, the Liberty of the Press, Prisons and Prison Discipline, Colonies, the Law of Nations, and Education. By JAMES MILL, Esq. author of the History of British India. Reprinted by permission from the Supplement to the Encyclopædia Britannica. (Not for sale.) London, 1828.

OF those philosophers who call themselves Utilitarians, and whom others generally call Benthamites, Mr. Mill is, with the exception of the illustrious founder of the sect, by far the most distinguished. The little work now before us contains a summary of the opinions held by this gentleman and his brethren on several subjects most important to society. All the seven Essays, of which it consists, abound in curious matter. But at present we intend to confine our remarks to the Treatise on Government, which stands first in the volume. On some future occasion, we may perhaps attempt to do justice to the rest.

It must be owned, that, to do justice to any composition of Mr. Mill is not, in the opinion of his admirers, a very easy task. They do not, indeed, place him in the same rank with Mr. Bentham; but the terms in which they extol the disciple, though feeble when compared with the hyperboles of adoration employed by them in speaking of the master, are as strong as any sober man would allow himself to use concerning Locke or Bacon. The Essay before us is perhaps the most remarkable of the works to which Mr. Mill owes his fame. By the members of his sect, it is considered as perfect and unanswerable. Every part of it is an article of their faith; and the damnatory clauses, in which their creed abounds far beyond any theological symbol with which we are acquainted, are strong and full against all who reject any portion of what is so irrefragably established. No man, they maintain, who has understanding sufficient to carry him through the first proposition of Euclid, can read this master-piece of demonstration, and honestly declare that he remains unconvinced.

We have formed a very different opinion of this work. We think that the theory of Mr. Mill rests altogether on false principles, and that even on those false principles he does not reason logically. Nevertheless, we do not think it strange that his speculations

579

should have filled the Utilitarians with admiration. We have been for some time past inclined to suspect that these people, whom some regard as the lights of the world, and others as incarnate demons, are in general ordinary men, with narrow understandings, and little information. The contempt which they express for elegant literature, is evidently the contempt of ignorance. We apprehend that many of them are persons who, having read little or nothing, are delighted to be rescued from the sense of their own inferiority by some teacher, who assures them that the studies which they have neglected are of no value, puts five or six phrases into their mouths, lends them an odd number of the Westminster Review, and in a month transforms them into philosophers. Mingled with these smatterers, whose attainments just suffice to elevate them from the insignificance of dunces to the dignity of bores, and to spread dismay among their pious aunts and grandmothers, there are, we well know, many well-meaning men, who have really read and thought much; but whose reading and meditation have been almost exclusively confined to one class of subjects; and who, consequently, though they possess much valuable knowledge respecting those subjects, are by no means so well qualified to judge of a great system as if they had taken a more enlarged view of literature and society.

Nothing is more amusing or instructive than to observe the manner in which people, who think themselves wiser than all the rest of the world, fall into snares which the simple good sense of their neighbours detects and avoids. It is one of the principal tenets of the Utilitarians, that sentiment and eloquence serve only to impede the pursuit of truth. They therefore affect a quakerly plainness, or rather a cynical negligence and impurity of style. The strongest arguments, when clothed in brilliant language, seem to them so much wordy nonsense. In the mean time they surrender their understandings, with a facility found in no other party, to the meanest and most abject sophisms, provided those sophisms come before them disguised with the externals of demonstration. They do not seem to know that logic has its illusions as well as rhetoric,— that a fallacy may lurk in a syllogism as well as in a metaphor.

Mr. Mill is exactly the writer to please people of this description. His arguments are stated with the utmost affectation of precision; his divisions are awfully formal; and his style is generally as dry as that of Euclid's Elements. Whether this be a merit, we must be permitted to doubt. Thus much is certain, that the ages in which the true principles of philosophy were least understood, were those in which the ceremonial of logic was most strictly observed, and that the time from which we date the rapid progress of the experimental sciences was also the time at which a less exact and formal way of writing came into use.

The style which the Utilitarians admire, suits only those subjects on which it is possible to reason *a priori*. It grew up with the verbal sophistry which flourished during the dark ages. With that sophistry it fell before the Baconian philosophy, in the day of the great deliverance of the human mind. The inductive method not only endured, but required greater freedom of diction. It was impossible to reason from phenomena up to principles, to mark slight shades of difference in quality, or to estimate the comparative effect of two opposite considerations between which there was no common measure, by means of the naked and meagre jargon of the schoolmen. Of those schoolmen Mr. Mill has inherited both the spirit and the style. He is an Aristotelian of the fifteenth century, born out of due season. We have here an elaborate treatise on Government, from which, but for two or three passing allusions, it would not appear that the author was aware that any governments actually existed among men. Certain propensities of Human Nature are assumed; and from these premises the whole science of Politics is synthetically deduced! We can scarcely persuade ourselves that we are not reading a book written before the time of Bacon and Galileo,—a book written in those days in which physicians reasoned from the nature of heat to the treatment of fever, and astronomers proved syllogistically that the planets could have no independent motion,—because the heavens were incorruptible, and nature abhorred a vacuum!

The reason, too, which Mr. Mill has assigned for taking this course strikes us as most extraordinary.

"Experience," says he, "if we look only at the outside of the facts, appears to be *divided* on this subject. Absolute monarchy, under Neros and Caligulas, under such men as the Emperors of Morocco and Sultans of Turkey, is the scourge of human nature. On the other side, the people of Denmark, tired out with the oppression of an aristocracy, resolved that their king should be absolute; and, under their absolute monarch, are as well governed as any people in Europe."

This Mr. Mill actually gives as a reason for pursuing the *a priori* method. But, in our judgment, the very circumstances which he mentions, irresistibly prove that the *a priori* method is altogether unfit for investigations of this kind, and that the only way to arrive at the truth is by induction. *Experience* can never be divided, or even appear to be divided, except with reference to some hypothesis.

When we say that one fact is inconsistent with another fact, we mean only that it is inconsistent with *the theory* which we have founded on that other fact. But, if the fact be certain, the unavoidable conclusion is that our theory is false; and, in order to correct it, we must reason back from an enlarged collection of facts to principles.

Now here we have two governments which, by Mr. Mill's own account, come under the same head in his *theoretical* classification. It is evident, therefore, that, by reasoning on that theoretical classification, we shall be brought to the conclusion that these two forms of government must produce the same effects. But Mr. Mill himself tells us that they do not produce the same effects. Hence he infers that the only way to get at truth is to place implicit confidence in that chain of proof *a priori*, from which it appears that they must produce the same effects! To believe at once in a theory, and in a fact which contradicts it, is an exercise of faith sufficiently hard: But, to believe in a theory *because* a fact contradicts it, is what neither philosopher nor pope ever before required. This, however, is what Mr. Mill demands of us. He seems to think that if all despots, without exception, governed ill, it would be unnecessary to prove, by a synthetical argument, what would then be sufficiently clear from experience. But as some despots will be so perverse as to govern well, he finds himself compelled to prove the impossibility of their governing well, by that synthetical argument, which would have been superfluous had not the facts contradicted it. He reasons *a priori*, because the phenomena are not what, by reasoning *a priori*, he will prove them to be. In other words, he reasons *a priori*, because, by so reasoning, he is certain to arrive at a false conclusion!

In the course of the examination to which we propose to subject the speculations of Mr. Mill, we shall have to notice many other curious instances of that turn of mind which the passage above quoted indicates.

The first chapter of his Essay relates to the ends of government. The conception on this subject, he tell us, which exists in the minds of most men is vague and undistinguishing. He first assumes, justly enough, that the end of government is "to increase to the utmost the pleasures, and diminish to the utmost the pains, which men derive from each other." He then proceeds to show, with great form, that "the greatest possible happiness of society is attained by insuring to every man the greatest possible quantity of the produce of his labour." To effect this is, in his opinion, the end of government. It is remarkable that Mr. Mill, with all his affected display of precision, has here given a description of the ends of government far less precise than that which is in the mouths of the vulgar. The first man with whom Mr. Mill may travel in a stage-coach, will tell him that government exists for the protection of the *persons* and property of men. But Mr. Mill seems to think that the preservation of property is the first and only object. It is true, doubtless, that many of the injuries which are offered to the persons of men, proceed from a desire to possess their property. But the practice of vindictive assassination as it has existed in some parts of Europe—the practice of fighting wanton and sanguinary duels, like those of the sixteenth and seventeenth centuries, in which bands of seconds risked their lives as well as the principals;—these practices, and many others which might be named, are evidently injurious to society; and we do not see how a government which tolerated them could be said "to diminish to the utmost the pains which men derive from each other." Therefore, according to Mr. Mill's very correct assumption, such a government would not perfectly accomplish the end of its institution. Yet such a government might, as far as we can perceive, "insure to every man the greatest possible quantity of the produce of his labour." Therefore such a government might, according to Mr. Mill's subsequent doctrine, perfectly accomplish the end of its institution. The matter is not of much consequence, except as an instance of that slovenliness of thinking which is often concealed beneath a peculiar ostentation of logical neatness.

Having determined the ends, Mr. Mill proceeds to consider the means. For the preservation of property, some portion of the community must be intrusted with power. This is Government; and the question is, how are those to whom the necessary power is intrusted to be prevented from abusing it?

Mr. Mill first passes in review the simple forms of government. He allows that it would be inconvenient, if not physically impossible, that the whole community should meet in a mass; it follows, therefore, that the powers of government cannot be directly exercised by the people. But he sees no objection to pure and direct Democracy, except the difficulty which we have mentioned.

"The community," says he, "cannot have an interest opposite to its interests. To affirm this would be a contradiction in terms. The community within itself, and with respect to itself, can have no sinister interest. One community may intend the evil of another; never its own. This is an indubitable proposition, and one of great importance."

Mr. Mill then proceeds to demonstrate, that a purely Aristocratical form of government is necessarily bad.

"The reason for which government exists, is, that one man, if stronger than another, will take from him whatever that other possesses and he desires. But if one man will do this, so will several. And if powers are put into the hands of a comparatively small number, called an aristocracy,—powers which make them stronger than the rest of the community, they will take from the rest of the community as much as they please of the objects of desire. They will thus defeat the very end for which government was instituted. The unfitness, therefore, of an aristocracy to be intrusted with the powers of government, rests on demonstration."

In exactly the same manner Mr. Mill proves absolute monarchy to be a bad form of government.

"If government is founded upon this as a law of human nature, that a man, if able, will take from others any thing which they have and he desires, it is sufficiently evident, that when a man is called a king he does not change his nature; so that when he has got power to enable him to take from every man what he pleases, he will take whatever he pleases. To suppose that he will not, is to affirm that government is unnecessary, and that human beings will abstain from injuring one another of their own accord.

"It is very evident that this reasoning extends to every modification of the smaller number. Whenever the powers of government are placed in any hands other than those of the community, whether those of one man, of a few, or of several, those principles of human nature which imply that government is at all necessary, imply that those persons will make use of them to defeat the very end for which government exists."

But is it not possible that a king or an aristocracy may soon be saturated with the objects of their desires, and may then protect the community in the enjoyment of the rest? Mr. Mill answers in the negative. He proves, with great pomp, that every man desires to have the actions of every other correspondent to his will. Others can be induced to conform to our will only by motives derived from pleasure or from pain. The infliction of pain is of course direct injury; and even if it take the milder course, in order to produce obedience by motives derived from pleasure, the government must confer favours. But, as there is no limit to its desire of obedience, there will be no limit to its disposition to confer favours; and, as it can confer favours only by plundering the people, there will be no limit to its disposition to plunder the people. "It is therefore not true, that there is in the mind of a king, or in the minds of an aristocracy, any point of saturation with the objects of desire."

Mr. Mill then proceeds to show, that as monarchical and oligarchical governments can influence men by motives drawn from pain, as well as by motives drawn from pleasure, they will carry their cruelty, as well as their rapacity, to a frightful extent. As he seems greatly to admire his own reasonings on this subject, we think it but fair to let him speak for himself.

"The chain of inference in this case is close and strong to a most unusual degree. A man desires that the actions of other men shall be instantly and accurately correspondent to his will. He desires that the actions of the greatest possible number shall be so. Terror is the grand instrument. Terror can work only through assurance that evil will follow any failure of conformity between the will and the actions willed. Every failure must therefore be punished. As there are no bounds to the mind's desire of its pleasure, there are, of course, no bounds to its desire of perfection in the instruments of that pleasure. There are, therefore, no bounds to its desire of exactness in the conformity between its will and the actions willed; and by consequence to the strength of that terror which is its procuring cause. Every the most minute failure must be visited with the heaviest infliction; and as failure in extreme exactness must frequently happen, the occasions of cruelty must be incessant.

"We have thus arrived at several conclusions of the highest possible importance. We have seen that the principle of human nature, upon which the necessity of government is founded, the propensity of one man to possess himself of the objects of desire at the cost of another, leads on, by infallible sequence, where power over a community is attained, and nothing checks, not only to that degree of plunder which leaves the members (excepting always the recipients and instruments of the plunder) the bare means of subsistence, but to that degree of cruelty which is necessary to keep in existence the most intense terrors."

Now, no man who has the least knowledge of the real state of the world, either in former ages or at the present moment, can possibly be convinced, though he may perhaps be bewildered, by arguments like these. During the last two centuries, some hundreds of absolute princes have reigned in Europe. Is it true, that their cruelty has kept in existence the most intense degree of terror, that their rapacity has left no more than the bare means of subsistence to any of their subjects, their ministers and soldiers excepted? Is this true of all of them? Of one half of them? Of one tenth part of them? Of a single one? Is it true, in the full extent, even of Philip the Second, of Lewis the Fifteenth, or of the Emperor Paul? But it is scarcely necessary to quote history. No man of common sense, however ignorant he may be of books, can be imposed on by Mr. Mill's argument; because no man of common sense can live among his fellow-creatures for a day without seeing innumerable facts which contradict it. It is our business, however, to point out its fallacy; and happily the fallacy is not very recondite.

We grant that rulers will take as much as they can of the objects of their desires; and that, when the agency of other men is necessary to that end, they will attempt by all means in their power to enforce the prompt obedience of such men. But what are the objects of human desire? Physical pleasure, no doubt, in part. But the mere appetites which we have in common with the animals, would be gratified almost as cheaply and easily as those of the animals are gratified, if nothing were given to taste, to ostentation, or to the affections. How small a portion of the income of a gentleman in easy circumstances is laid out merely in giving pleasurable sensations to the body of the possessor! The greater part even of what is spent on his kitchen and his cellar, goes not to titillate his palate, but to keep up his character for hospitality, to save him from the reproach of meanness in housekeeping, and to cement the ties of good neighbourhood. It is clear, that a king or an aristocracy may be supplied to satiety with mere corporal pleasures, at an expense which the rudest and poorest community would scarcely feel.

Those tastes and propensities which belong to us as reasoning and imaginative beings are not indeed so easily gratified. There is, we admit, no point of saturation with objects of desire which come under this head. And therefore the argument of Mr. Mill will be just, unless there be something in the nature of the objects of desire themselves which is inconsistent with it. Now, of these objects there is none which men in general seem to desire more than the good opinion of others. The hatred and contempt of the public are generally felt to be intolerable. It is probable, that our regard for the sentiments of our fellow-creatures springs by association from a sense of their ability to hurt or to serve us. But be this as it may, it is notorious, that when the habit of mind of which we speak has once been formed, men feel extremely solicitous about the opinions of those by whom it is most improbable, nay, absolutely impossible, that they should ever be in the slightest degree injured or benefited. The desire of posthumous fame, and the dread of posthumous reproach and execration, are feelings from the influence of which scarcely any man is perfectly free, and which in many men are powerful and constant motives of action. As we are afraid that, if we handle this part of the argument after our own manner, we shall incur the reproach of sentimentality, a word which, in the sacred language of the Benthamites, is synonymous with idiocy, we will quote what Mr. Mill himself says on the subject, in his Treatise on Jurisprudence.

"Pains from the moral source are the pains derived from the unfavourable sentiments of mankind. . . . . These pains are capable of rising to a height with which hardly any other pains incident to our nature can be compared. There is a certain degree of unfavourableness in the sentiments of his fellow-creatures, under which hardly any man, not below the standard of humanity, can endure to live.

"The importance of this powerful agency, for the prevention of injurious acts, is too obvious to need to be illustrated. If sufficiently at command, it would almost supersede the use of other means. . . . .

"To know how to direct the unfavourable sentiments of mankind, it is necessary to know in as complete, that is, in as comprehensive, a way as possible, what it is which gives them birth. Without entering into the metaphysics of the question, it is a sufficient practical answer, for the present purpose, to say that the unfavourable sentiments of man are excited by every thing which hurts them."

It is strange that a writer who considers the pain derived from the unfavourable sentiments of others as so acute, that, if sufficiently at command, it would supersede the use of the gallows and the tread-mill, should take no notice of this most important restraint, when discussing the question of Government. We will attempt to deduce a theory of politics in the mathematical form, in which Mr. Mill delights, from the premises with which he has himself furnished us.

PROPOSITION I. THEOREM.

No rulers will do any thing which may hurt the people.

This is the thesis to be maintained; and the following we humbly offer to Mr. Mill, as its syllogistic demonstration.

No rulers will do that which produces pain to themselves.

But the unfavourable sentiments of the people will give pain to them.

Therefore no rulers will do any thing which may excite the unfavourable sentiments of the people.

But the unfavourable sentiments of the people are excited by every thing which hurts them.

Therefore no rulers will do any thing which may hurt the people, which was the thing to be proved.

Having thus, as we think, not unsuccessfully imitated Mr. Mill's logic, we do not see why we should not imitate, what is at least equally perfect in its kind, his self-complacency, and proclaim our Ἕυρηκα in his own words: "The chain of inference, in this case, is close and strong to a most unusual degree."

The fact is, that, when men, in treating of things which cannot be circumscribed by precise definitions, adopt this mode of reasoning, when once they begin to talk of power, happiness, misery, pain, pleasure, motives, objects of desire, as they talk of lines and numbers, there is no end to the contradictions and absurdities into which they fall. There is no proposition so monstrously untrue in morals or politics that we will not undertake to prove it, by something which shall sound like a logical demonstration, from admitted principles.

Mr. Mill argues, that if men are not inclined to plunder each other, government is unnecessary; and that, if they are so inclined, the powers of government, when intrusted to a small number of them, will necessarily be abused. Surely it is not by propounding dilemmas of this sort, that we are likely to arrive at sound conclusions in any moral science. The whole question is a question of degree. If all men preferred the moderate approbation of their neighbours, to any degree of wealth or grandeur, or sensual pleasure, government would be unnecessary. If all men desired wealth so intensely as to be willing to brave the hatred of their fellow-creatures for sixpence, Mr. Mill's argument against monarchies and aristocracies would be true to the full extent. But the fact is, that all men have some desires which impel them to injure their neighbours, and some desires which impel them to benefit their neighbours. Now, if there were a community consisting of two classes of men, one of which should be principally influenced by the one set of motives and the other by the other, government would clearly be necessary to restrain the class which was eager for plunder, and careless of reputation: and yet the powers of government might be safely intrusted to the class which was chiefly actuated by the love of approbation. Now, it might, with no small plausibility be maintained, that, in many countries, *there are* two classes which, in some degree, answer to this description; that the poor compose the class which government is established to restrain; and the people of some property the class to which the powers of government may without danger be confided. It might be said that a man who can barely earn a livelihood by severe labour, is under stronger temptations to pillage others than a man who enjoys many luxuries. It might be said that a man who is lost in the crowd is less likely to have the fear of public opinion before his eyes, than a man whose station and mode of living render him conspicuous. We do not assert all this. We only say, that it was Mr. Mill's business to prove the contrary; and that, not having proved the contrary, he is not entitled to say, "that those principles which imply that government is at all necessary, imply that an aristocracy will make use of its power to defeat the end for which governments exist." This is not true, unless it be true that a rich man is as likely to covet the goods of his neighbours as a poor man; and that a poor man is as likely to be solicitous about the opinions of his neighbours as a rich man.

But we do not see that, by reasoning *a priori* on such subjects as these, it is possible to advance one single step. We know that every man has some desires which he can gratify only by hurting his neighbours, and some which he can gratify only by pleasing them. Mr. Mill has chosen to look only at one-half of human nature, and to reason on the motives which impel men to oppress and despoil others, as if they were the only motives by which men could possibly be influenced. We have already shown that, by taking the other half of the human character, and reasoning on it as if it were the whole, we can bring out a result diametrically opposite to that at which Mr. Mill has arrived. We can, by such a process, easily prove that any form of government is good, or that all government is superfluous.

We must now accompany Mr. Mill on the next stage of his argument. Does any combination of the three simple forms of government afford the requisite securities against the abuse of power? Mr. Mill complains that those who maintain the affirmative generally beg the question, and proceeds to settle the point by proving, after his fashion, that no combination of the three simple forms, or of any two of them, can possibly exist.

"From the principles which we have already laid down it follows that, of the objects of human desire, and, speaking more definitely, of the means to the ends of human desire, namely, wealth and power, each party will endeavour to obtain as much as possible.
"If any expedient presents itself to any of the supposed parties effectual to this end, and not opposed to any preferred object of pursuit, we may infer, with certainty, that it will be adopted.   One effectual expedient is not more effectual than obvious. Any two of the parties, by combining may swallow up the third. That such combination will take place appears to be as certain as any thing which depends upon human will; because there are strong motives in favour of it, and none that can be conceived in opposition to it. . . . . The mixture of three of the kinds of government, it is thus evident, cannot possibly exist. . . . . It may be proper to enquire, whether an union may not be possible of two of them. . . .
"Let us first suppose, that monarchy is united with aristocracy. Their power is equal or not equal. If it is not equal, it follows, as a necessary consequence, from the principles which we have already established, that the stronger will take from the weaker till it en-

grosses the whole. The only question therefore is, What will happen when the power is equal?

"In the first place, it seems impossible that such equality should ever exist. How is it to be established? or, By what criterion is it to be ascertained? If there is no such criterion, it must, in all cases, be the result of chance. If so, the chances against it are as infinity to one. The idea, therefore, is wholly chimerical and absurd. . . .

"In this doctrine of the mixture of the simple forms of government is included the celebrated theory of the balance among the component parts of a government. By this it is supposed that, when a government is composed of monarchy, aristocracy, and democracy, they balance one another, and by mutual checks produce good government. A few words will suffice to show that, if any theory deserves the epithets of 'wild, visionary, and chimerical,' it is that of the balance. If there are three powers, How is it possible to prevent two of them from combining to swallow up the third?

"The analysis which we have already performed will enable us to trace rapidly the concatenation of causes and effects in this imagined case.

"We have already seen that the interest of the community, considered in the aggregate, or in the democratical point of view, is, that each individual should receive protection; and that the powers which are constituted for that purpose should be employed exclusively for that purpose. . . . . We have also seen that the interest of the king and of the governing aristocracy is directly the reverse. It is to have unlimited power over the rest of the community, and to use it for their own advantage. In the supposed case of the balance of the monarchical, aristocratical, and democratical powers, it cannot be for the interest of either the monarchy or the aristocracy to combine with the democracy; because it is the interest of the democracy, or community at large, that neither the king nor the aristocracy should have one particle of power, or one particle of the wealth of the community, for their own advantage.

"The democracy or community have all possible motives to endeavour to prevent the monarchy and aristocracy from exercising power, or obtaining the wealth of the community for their own advantage. The monarchy and aristocracy have all possible motives for endeavouring to obtain unlimited power over the persons and property of the community. The consequence is inevitable: they have all possible motives for combining to obtain that power."

If any part of this passage be more eminently absurd than another, it is, we think, the argument by which Mr. Mill proves that there cannot be an union of monarchy and aristocracy. Their power, he says, must be equal or not equal. But of equality there is no criterion. Therefore the chances against its existence are as infinity to one. If the power be not equal, then it follows, from the principles of human nature, that the stronger will take from the weaker, till it has engrossed the whole.

Now, if there be no criterion of equality between two portions of power, there can be no common measure of portions of power. Therefore it is utterly impossible to compare them together. But where two portions of power are of the same kind, there is no difficulty in ascertaining, sufficiently for all practical purposes, whether they are equal or unequal. It is easy to judge whether two men run equally fast, or can lift equal weights. Two arbitrators, whose joint decision is to be final, and neither of whom can do any thing without the assent of the other, possess equal power. Two electors, each of whom has a vote for a borough, possess, in that respect, equal power. If not, all Mr. Mill's political theories fall to the ground at once. For, if it be impossible to ascertain whether two portions of power are equal, he never can show that, even under a system of universal suffrage, a minority might not carry every thing their own way, against the wishes and interests of the majority.

Where there are two portions of power differing in kind, there is, we admit, no criterion of equality. But then, in such a case, it is absurd to talk, as Mr. Mill does, about the stronger and the weaker. Popularly, indeed, and with reference to some particular objects, these words may very fairly be used. But to use them mathematically is altogether improper. If we are speaking of a boxing-match, we may say that some famous bruiser has greater bodily power than any man in England. If we are speaking of a panto-mime, we may say the same of some very agile Harlequin. But it would be talking nonsense to say, in general, that the power of Harlequin either exceeded that of the pugilist, or fell short of it.

If Mr. Mill's argument be good as between different branches of a legislature, it is equally good as between sovereign powers. Every government, it may be said, will, if it can, take the objects of its desires from every other. If the French government can subdue England, it will do so. If the English government can subdue France, it will do so. But the power of England and France is either equal or not equal. The chance that it is not exactly equal is as infinity to one, and may safely be left out of the account; and then the stronger will infallibly take from the weaker till the weaker is altogether enslaved.

Surely the answer to all this hubbub of unmeaning words is the plainest possible. For some purposes, France is stronger than England. For some purposes, England is stronger than France. For some, neither has any power at all. France has the greater population, England the greater capital; France has the greater army, England the greater fleet. For an expedition to Rio Janeiro or the

Philippines, England has the greater power. For a war on the Po or the Danube, France has the greater power. But neither has power sufficient to keep the other in quiet subjection for a month. Invasion would be very perilous; the idea of complete conquest on either side utterly ridiculous. This is the manly and sensible way of discussing such questions. The *ergo*, or rather the *argal*, of Mr. Mill cannot impose on a child. Yet we ought scarcely to say this; for we remember to have heard *a child* ask whether Bonaparte was stronger than an elephant!

Mr. Mill reminds us of those philosophers of the sixteenth century, who, having satisfied themselves *a priori* that the rapidity with which bodies descended to the earth varied exactly as their weights, refused to believe the contrary on the evidence of their own eyes and ears. The British constitution, according to Mr. Mill's classification, is a mixture of monarchy and aristocracy; one House of Parliament being composed of hereditary nobles, and the other almost entirely chosen by a privileged class, who possess the elective franchise on account of their property, or their connexion with certain corporations. Mr. Mill's argument proves that, from the time that these two powers were mingled in our government, that is, from the very first dawn of our history, one or the other must have been constantly encroaching. According to him, moreover, all the encroachments must have been on one side. For the first encroachment could only have been made by the stronger; and that first encroachment would have made the stronger stronger still. It is, therefore, matter of absolute demonstration, that either the Parliament was stronger than the Crown in the reign of Henry VIII., or that the Crown was stronger than the Parliament in 1641. "Hippocrate dira ce que lui plaira," says the girl in Moliere; "mais le cocher est mort." Mr. Mill may say what he pleases; but the English constitution is still alive. That, since the Revolution the Parliament has possessed great power in the state, is what nobody will dispute. The King, on the other hand, can create new peers, and can dissolve Parliaments. William sustained severe mortifications from the House of Commons, and was, indeed, unjustifiably oppressed. Anne was desirous to change a ministry which had a majority in both Houses. She watched her moment for a dissolution, created twelve Tory peers, and succeeded. Thirty years later, the House of Commons drove Walpole from his seat. In 1784, George III. was able to keep Mr. Pitt in office in the face of a majority of the House of Commons. In 1804, the apprehension of a defeat in Parliament compelled the same King to part from his most favoured minister. But, in 1807, he was able to do exactly what Anne had done nearly a hundred years before. Now, had the power of the King increased during the intervening century, or had it remained stationary? Is it possible that the one lot among the infinite number should have fallen to us? If not, Mr. Mill has proved that one of the two parties must have been constantly taking from the other. Many of the ablest men in England think that the influence of the Crown has, on the whole, increased since the reign of Anne. Others think that the Parliament has been growing in strength. But of this there is no doubt, that both sides possessed great power then, and possess great power now. Surely, if there were the least truth in the argument of Mr. Mill, it could not possibly be a matter of doubt, at the end of a hundred and twenty years, whether the one side or the other had been the gainer.

But we ask pardon. We forgot that a fact, irreconcilable with Mr. Mill's theory, furnishes, in his opinion, the strongest reason for adhering to the theory. To take up the question in another manner, is it not plain that there may be two bodies, each possessing a perfect and entire power, which cannot be taken from it without its own concurrence? What is the meaning of the words stronger and weaker, when applied to such bodies as these? The one may, indeed, by physical force, altogether destroy the other. But this is not the question. A third party, a general of their own, for example, may, by physical force, subjugate them both: Nor is there any form of government, Mr. Mill's Utopian democracy not excepted, secure from such an occurrence. We are speaking of the powers with which the constitution invests the two branches of the legislature; and we ask Mr. Mill how, on his own principles, he can maintain that one of them will be able to encroach on the other, if the consent of the other be necessary to such encroachment?

Mr. Mill tells us that, if a government be composed of the three simple forms, which he will not admit the British constitution to be, two of the component parts will inevitably join against the third. Now, if two of them combine and act as one, this case evidently resolves itself into the last; and all the observations which we have just made will fully apply to it. Mr. Mill says, that "any two of the parties, by combining, may swallow up the third;" and afterwards asks, "How it is possible to prevent two of them from combining to swallow up the third?" Surely Mr. Mill must be aware that in politics two is not always the double of one. If the concurrence of all the three branches of the legislature be necessary to every law, each branch will possess constitutional power sufficient to protect it against any thing but that physical force, from which no form of government is secure. Mr. Mill reminds us of the Irishman, who could not be brought to understand how one juryman could possibly starve out eleven others.

But is it certain that two of the branches of the legislature will combine against the third? "It appears to be as certain," says Mr. Mill, "as any thing which depends upon human will; because there are strong motives in favour of it, and none that can be conceived in opposition to it." He subsequently sets forth what these motives are. The interest of the democracy is, that each individual should receive protection. The interest of the King and the aristocracy is, to have all the power that they can obtain, and to use it for their own ends. Therefore the King and the aristocracy have all possible motives for combining against the people. If our readers will look back to the passage quoted above, they will see that we represent Mr. Mill's argument quite fairly.

Now we should have thought that, without the help of either history or experience, Mr. Mill would have discovered, by the light of his own logic, the fallacy which lurks, and indeed scarcely lurks, under this pretended demonstration. The interest of the King may be opposed to that of the people. But is it identical with that of the aristocracy? In the very page which contains this argument, intended to prove that the King and the aristocracy will coalesce against the people, Mr. Mill attempts to show that there is so strong an opposition of interest between the King and the aristocracy, that if the powers of government are divided between them, the one will inevitably usurp the power of the other. If so, he is not entitled to conclude that they will combine to destroy the power of the people, merely because their interests may be at variance with those of the people. He is bound to show, not merely that in all communities the interest of a king must be opposed to that of the people, but also that, in all communities, it must be more directly opposed to the interest of the people than to the interest of the aristocracy. But he has not shown this. Therefore he has not proved his proposition on his own principles. To quote history would be a mere waste of time. Every schoolboy, whose studies have gone so far as the Abridgements of Goldsmith, can mention instances in which sovereigns have allied themselves with the people against the aristocracy, and in which the nobles have allied themselves with the people against the sovereign. In general, when there are three parties, every one of which has much to fear from the others, it is not found that two of them combine to plunder the third. If such a combination be formed, it scarcely ever effects its purpose. It soon becomes evident which member of the coalition is likely to be the greater gainer by the transaction. He becomes an object of jealousy to his ally, who, in all probability, changes sides, and compels him to restore what he has taken. Everybody knows how Henry VIII. trimmed between Francis and the Emperor Charles. But it is idle to cite examples of the operation of a principle which is illustrated in almost every page of history, ancient or modern, and to which almost every state in Europe has, at one time or another, been indebted for its independence.

Mr. Mill has now, as he conceives, demonstrated that the simple forms of government are bad, and that the mixed forms cannot possibly exist. There is still, however, it seems, a hope for mankind.

"In the grand discovery of modern times, the system of representation, the solution of all the difficulties, both speculative and practical, will perhaps be found. If it cannot, we seem to be forced upon the extraordinary conclusion, that good government is impossible. For, as there is no individual or combination of individuals, except the community itself, who would not have an interest in bad government, if intrusted with its powers, and as the community itself is incapable of exercising those powers, and must intrust them to certain individuals, the conclusion is obvious: the community itself must check those individuals; else they will follow their interest, and produce bad government. But how is it the community can check? The community can act only when assembled; and when assembled, it is incapable of acting. The community, however, can choose representatives."

The next question is—How must the representative body be constituted? Mr. Mill lays down two principles, about which, he says, "it is unlikely that there will be any dispute."

"First, The checking body must have a degree of power sufficient for the business of checking.

"Secondly, It must have an identity of interest with the community. Otherwise, it will make a mischievous use of its power."

The first of these propositions certainly admits of no dispute. As to the second, we shall hereafter take occasion to make some remarks on the sense in which Mr. Mill understands the words, "interest of the community."

It does not appear very easy, on Mr. Mill's principles, to find out any mode of making the interest of the representative body identical with that of the constituent body. The plan proposed by Mr. Mill is simply that of very frequent election. "As it appears," says he, "that limiting the duration of their power is a security against the sinister interest of the people's representatives, so it appears that it is the only security of which the nature of the case admits." But all the arguments by which Mr. Mill has proved monarchy and aristocracy to be pernicious, will, as it appears to us, equally prove this security to be no security at all. Is it not clear that the representatives, as soon as they are elected, are an aristocracy, with an interest opposed to the interest of the community? Why should they not pass a law for extending the term of their power from one year to ten years, or declare themselves senators for life? If the whole legislative power is given to them, they will be constitutionally competent to do this. If part of the legislative power is withheld from them, to whom is that part given? Is the people to retain it, and to express its assent or dissent in primary assemblies? Mr. Mill himself tells us that the community can only act when assembled, and that, when assembled, it is incapable of acting. Or is it to be provided, as in some of the American republics, that no change in the fundamental laws shall be made without the consent of a convention, specially elected for the purpose? Still the difficulty recurs: Why may not the members of the convention betray their trust, as well as the members of the ordinary legislature? When private men, they may have been zealous for the interests of the community. When candidates, they may have pledged themselves to the cause of the constitution. But as soon as they are a convention, as soon as they are separated from the people, as soon as the supreme power is put into their hands, commences that interest opposite to the interest of the community, which must, according to Mr. Mill, produce measures opposite to the interests of the community. We must find some other means, therefore, of checking this check upon a check; some other prop to carry the tortoise, that carries the elephant, that carries the world.

We know well that there is no real danger in such a case. But there is no danger, only because there is no truth in Mr. Mill's principles. If men were what he represents them to be, the letter of the very constitution which he recommends would afford no safeguard against bad government. The real security is this, that legislators will be deterred by the fear of resistance and of infamy, from acting in the manner which we have described. But restraints, exactly the same in kind, and differing only in degree, exist in all forms of government. That broad line of distinction which Mr. Mill tries to point out between monarchies and aristocracies on the one side, and democracies on the other, has in fact no existence. In no form of government is there an absolute identity of interest between the people and their rulers. In every form of government, the rulers stand in some awe of the people. The fear of resistance and the sense of shame operate, in a certain degree, on the most absolute kings and the most illiberal oligarchies. And nothing but the fear of resistance and the sense of shame preserves the freedom of the most democratic communities from the encroachments of their annual and biennial delegates.

We have seen how Mr. Mill proposes to render the interest of the representative body identical with that of the constituent body. The next question is, in what manner the interest of the constituent body is to be rendered identical with that of the community. Mr. Mill shows that a minority of the community, consisting even of many thousands, would be a bad constituent body, and, indeed, merely a numerous aristocracy.

"The benefits of the representative system," says he, "are lost, in all cases in which the interests of the choosing body are not the same with those of the community. It is very evident, that if the community itself were the choosing body, the interest of the community and that of the choosing body would be the same."

On these grounds Mr. Mill recommends that all males of mature age, rich and poor, educated and ignorant, shall have votes. But why not the women too? This question has often been asked in parliamentary debate, and has never, to our knowledge, received a plausible answer. Mr. Mill escapes from it as fast as he can. But we shall take the liberty to dwell a little on the words of the oracle. "One thing," says he, "is pretty clear, that all those individuals whose interests are involved in those of other individuals, may be struck off without inconvenience. . . . . In this light Women may be regarded, the interest of almost all of whom is involved either in that of their fathers, or in that of their husbands."

If we were to content ourselves with saying, in answer to all the arguments in Mr. Mill's Essay, that the interest of a king is involved in that of the community, we should be accused, and justly, of talking nonsense. Yet such an assertion would not, as far as we can perceive, be more unreasonable than that which Mr. Mill has here ventured to make. Without adducing one fact, without taking the trouble to perplex the question by one sophism, he placidly dogmatizes away the interest of one half of the human race. If there be a word of truth in history, women have always been, and still are, over the greater part of the globe, humble companions, playthings, captives, menials, beasts of burden. Except in a few happy and highly civilized communities, they are strictly in a state of personal slavery. Even in those countries where they are best treated, the laws are generally unfavourable to them, with respect to almost all the points in which they are most deeply interested.

Mr. Mill is not legislating for England or the United States; but for mankind. Is then the interest of a Turk the same with that of the girls who compose his haram? Is the interest of a Chinese the same with that of the woman whom he harnesses to his plough? Is the interest of an Italian the same with that of the daughter whom he devotes to God? The interest of a respectable Englishman may be said, without any impropriety, to be identical with that of his wife. But why is it so? Because human nature is *not* what Mr. Mill conceives it to be; because civilized men, pursuing their own happiness in a social state, are not Yahoos fighting for carrion; because there is a pleasure in being loved and esteemed, as well as in being feared and servilely obeyed. Why does not a gentleman restrict his wife to the bare maintenance which the law would compel him to allow her, that he may have more to spend on his personal pleasures? Because, if he loves her, he has pleasure in seeing her pleased; and because, even if he dislikes her, he is unwilling that the whole neighbourhood should cry shame on his meanness and ill-nature. Why does not the legislature, altogether composed of males, pass a law to deprive women of all civil privileges whatever, and reduce them to the state of slaves? By passing such a law, they would gratify what Mr. Mill tells us is an inseparable part of human nature, the desire to possess unlimited power of inflicting pain upon others. That they do not pass such a law, though they have the power to pass it, and that no man in England wishes to see such a law passed, proves that the desire to possess unlimited power of inflicting pain is not inseparable from human nature.

If there be in this country an identity of interest between the two sexes, it cannot possibly arise from any thing but the pleasure of being loved, and of communicating happiness. For, that it does not spring from the mere instinct of sex, the treatment which women experience over the greater part of the world abundantly proves. And if it be said that our laws of marriage have produced it, this only removes the argument a step further; for those laws have been made by males. Now, if the kind feelings of one half of the species be a sufficient security for the happiness of the other, why may not the kind feelings of a monarch or an aristocracy be sufficient at least to prevent them from grinding the people to the very utmost of their power?

If Mr. Mill will examine why it is that women are better treated in England than in Persia, he may perhaps find out, in the course of his enquiries, why it is that the Danes are better governed than the subjects of Caligula.

We now come to the most important practical question in the whole Essay. Is it desirable that all males arrived at years of discretion should vote for representatives, or should a pecuniary qualification be required? Mr. Mill's opinion is, that the lower the qualification the better; and that the best system is that in which there is none at all.

"The qualification," says he, "must either be such as to embrace the majority of the population, or something less than the majority. Suppose, in the first place, that it embraces the majority, the question is, whether the majority would have an interest in oppressing those who, upon this supposition, would be deprived of political power? If we reduce the calculation to its elements, we shall see that the interest which they would have of this deplorable kind, though it would be something, would not be very great. Each man of the majority, if the majority were constituted the governing body, would have something less than the benefit of oppressing a single man. If the majority were twice as great as the minority, each man of the majority would only have one half the benefit of oppressing a single man. . . . . Suppose, in the second place, that the qualification did not admit a body of electors so large as the majority, in that case, taking again the calculation in its elements, we shall see that each man would have a benefit equal to that derived from the oppression of more than one man; and that, in proportion as the elective body constituted a smaller and smaller minority, the benefit of misrule to the elective body would be increased, and bad government would be insured."

The first remark which we have to make on this argument is, that, by Mr. Mill's own account, even a government in which every human being should vote would still be defective. For, under a system of universal suffrage, the majority of the electors return the representative, and the majority of the representatives make the law. The whole people may vote, therefore, but only the majority govern. So that, by Mr. Mill's own confession, the most perfect system of government conceivable is one in which the interest of the ruling body to oppress, though not great, is something.

But is Mr. Mill in the right, when he says that such an interest could not be very great? We think not. If, indeed, every man in the community possessed an equal share of what Mr. Mill calls the objects of desire, the majority would probably abstain from plundering the minority. A large minority would offer a vigorous resistance; and the property of a small minority would not repay the other members of the community for the trouble of dividing it. But it happens that in all civilized communities there is a small minority of rich men, and a great majority of poor men. If there were a thousand men with ten pounds a-piece, it would not be worth while for nine hundred and ninety of them to rob ten, and it would be a bold attempt for six hundred of them to rob four hundred.

But if ten of them had a hundred thousand pounds a-piece, the case would be very different. There would then be much to be got, and nothing to be feared.

"That one human being will desire to render the person and property of another subservient to his pleasures, notwithstanding the pain or loss of pleasure which it may occasion to that other individual, is," according to Mr. Mill, "the foundation of government." That the property of the rich minority can be made subservient to the pleasures of the poor majority, will scarcely be denied. But Mr. Mill proposes to give the poor majority power over the rich minority. Is it possible to doubt to what, on his own principles, such an arrangement must lead?

It may perhaps be said that, in the long run, it is for the interest of the people that property should be secure, and that therefore they will respect it. We answer thus:—It cannot be pretended that it is not for the immediate interest of the people to plunder the rich. Therefore, even if it were quite certain that, in the long run, the people would, as a body, lose by doing so, it would not necessarily follow that the fear of remote ill consequences would overcome the desire of immediate acquisitions. Every individual might flatter himself that the punishment would not fall on him. Mr. Mill himself tell us, in his Essay on Jurisprudence, that no quantity of evil which is remote and uncertain will suffice to prevent crime.

But we are rather inclined to think that it would, on the whole, be for the interest of the majority to plunder the rich. If so, the Utilitarians will say, that the rich *ought* to be plundered. We deny the inference. For, in the first place, if the object of government be the greatest happiness of the greatest number, the intensity of the suffering which a measure inflicts must be taken into consideration, as well as the number of the sufferers. In the next place, we have to notice one most important distinction which Mr. Mill has altogether overlooked. Throughout his Essay, he confounds the community with the species. He talks of the greatest happiness of the greatest number: but when we examine his reasonings, we find that he thinks only of the greatest number of a single generation.

Therefore, even if we were to concede, that all those arguments of which we have exposed the fallacy, are unanswerable, we might still deny the conclusion at which the essayist arrives. Even if we were to grant that he had found out the form of government which is best for the majority of the people now living on the face of the earth, we might still without inconsistency maintain that form of government to be pernicious to mankind. It would still be incumbent on Mr. Mill to prove that the interest of every generation is identical with the interest of all succeeding generations. And how on his own principles he could do this we are at a loss to conceive.

The case, indeed, is strictly analogous to that of an aristocratic government. In an aristocracy, says Mr. Mill, the few, being invested with the powers of government, can take the objects of their desires from the people. In the same manner, every generation in turn can gratify itself at the expense of posterity,—priority of time, in the latter case, giving an advantage exactly corresponding to that which superiority of station gives in the former. That an aristocracy will abuse its advantage, is, according to Mr. Mill, matter of demonstration. Is it not equally certain, that the whole people will do the same; that, if they have the power, they will commit waste of every sort on the estate of mankind, and transmit it to posterity impoverished and desolated?

How is it possible for any person who holds the doctrines of Mr. Mill to doubt that the rich, in a democracy such as that which he recommends, would be pillaged as unmercifully as under a Turkish Pacha? It is no doubt for the interest of the next generation, and it may be for the remote interest of the present generation, that property should be held sacred. And so no doubt it will be for the interest of the next Pacha, and even for that of the present Pacha, if he should hold office long, that the inhabitants of his Pachalik should be encouraged to accumulate wealth. Scarcely any despotic sovereign has plundered his subjects to a large extent, without having reason before the end of his reign to regret it. Every body knows how bitterly Louis the Fourteenth, towards the close of his life, lamented his former extravagance. If that magnificent prince had not expended millions on Marli and Versailles, and tens of millions on the aggrandizement of his grandson, he would not have been compelled at last to pay servile court to low-born money-lenders, to humble himself before men on whom, in the days of his pride, he would not have vouchsafed to look, for the means of supporting even his own household. Examples to the same effect might easily be multiplied. But despots, we see, do plunder their subjects, though history and experience tell them, that by prematurely exacting the means of profusion, they are in fact devouring the seed-corn, from which the future harvest of revenue is to spring. Why then should we suppose that the people will be deterred from procuring immediate relief and enjoyment by the fear of distant calamities, of calamities which perhaps may not be fully felt till the times of their grand-children?

These conclusions are strictly drawn from Mr. Mill's own principles: and, unlike most of the conclusions which he has himself drawn from those principles, they are not, as far as we know, contradicted by facts. The case of the United States is not in point. In a country where the necessaries of life are cheap and the wages of labour high, where a man who has no capital but his legs and arms may expect to become rich by industry and frugality, it is not very decidedly even for the immediate advantage of the poor to plunder the rich; and the punishment of doing so would very speedily follow the offence. But in countries in which the great majority live from hand to mouth, and in which vast masses of wealth have been accumulated by a comparatively small number, the case is widely different. The immediate want is, at particular seasons, craving, imperious, irresistible. In our own time it has steeled men to the fear of the gallows, and urged them on the point of the bayonet. And, if these men had at their command that gallows, and those bayonets, which now scarcely restrain them, what is to be expected? Nor is this state of things one which can exist only under a bad government. If there be the least truth in the doctrines of the school to which Mr. Mill belongs, the increase of population will necessarily produce it every where. The increase of population is accelerated by good and cheap government. Therefore, the better the government, the greater is the inequality of conditions: and the greater the inequality of conditions, the stronger are the motives which impel the populace to spoliation. As for America, we appeal to the twentieth century.

It is scarcely necessary to discuss the effects which a general spoliation of the rich would produce. It may indeed happen, that where a legal and political system full of abuses is inseparably bound up with the institution of property, a nation may gain by a single convulsion, in which both perish together. The price is fearful: But if, when the shock is over, a new order of things should arise under which property may enjoy security, the industry of individuals will soon repair the devastation. Thus we entertain no doubt that the revolution was, on the whole, a most salutary event for France. But would France have gained if, ever since the year 1793, she had been governed by a democratic convention? If Mr. Mill's principles be sound, we say that almost her whole capital would by this time have been annihilated. As soon as the first explosion was beginning to be forgotten, as soon as wealth again began to germinate, as soon as the poor again began to compare their cottages and sallads with the hotels and banquets of the rich, there would have been another scramble for property, another maximum, another general confiscation, another reign of terror.

Four or five such convulsions following each other, at intervals of ten or twelve years, would reduce the most flourishing countries of Europe to the state of Barbary or the Morea.

The civilized part of the world has now nothing to fear from the hostility of savage nations. Once the deluge of barbarism has passed over it, to destroy and to fertilize; and in the present state of mankind we enjoy a full security against that calamity. That flood will no more return to cover the earth. But is it possible that, in the bosom of civilization itself, may be engendered the malady which shall destroy it? Is it possible that institutions may be established which, without the help of earthquake, of famine, of pestilence, or of the foreign sword, may undo the work of so many ages of wisdom and glory, and gradually sweep away taste, literature, science, commerce, manufactures, everything but the rude arts necessary to the support of animal life? Is it possible that, in two or three hundred years, a few lean and half-naked fishermen may divide with owls and foxes the ruins of the greatest European cities—may wash their nets amidst the relics of her gigantic docks, and build their huts out of the capitals of her stately cathedrals? If the principles of Mr. Mill be sound, we say, without hesitation, that the form of government which he recommends will assuredly produce all this. But if these principles be unsound, if the reasonings by which we have opposed them be just, the higher and middling orders are the natural representatives of the human race. Their interest may be opposed, in some things, to that of their poorer contemporaries, but it is identical with that of the innumerable generations which are to follow.

Mr. Mill concludes his Essay, by answering an objection often made to the project of universal suffrage—that the people do not understand their own interests. We shall not go through his arguments on this subject, because, till he has proved, that it is for the interest of the people to respect property, he only makes matters worse, by proving that they understand their interests. But we cannot refrain from treating our readers with a delicious *bonne bouche* of wisdom, which he has kept for the last moment.

"The opinions of that class of the people who are below the middle rank are formed, and their minds are directed, by that intelligent, that virtuous rank, who come the most immediately in contact with them, who are in the constant habit of intimate communication with them, to whom they fly for advice and assistance in all their numerous difficulties, upon whom they feel an immediate and daily dependence in health and in sickness, in infancy and in old age, to whom their children look up as models for their imitation, whose opinions they hear daily repeated, and account it their honour to adopt. There can be no doubt that the middle rank, which gives to science, to art, and to legislation itself, their most distinguished ornaments, and is the chief source of all that has exalted and refined human nature, is that portion of the community, of which, if the basis of representation were ever so far extended, the opinion would ultimately decide. Of the people beneath them, a vast majority would be sure to be guided by their advice and example."

This single paragraph is sufficient to upset Mr. Mill's theory. Will the people act against their own interest? Or will the middle rank act against its own interest? Or is the interest of the middle rank identical with the interest of the people? If the people act according to the directions of the middle rank, as Mr. Mill says that they assuredly will, one of these three questions must be answered in the affirmative. But if any one of the three be answered in the affirmative, his whole system falls to the ground. If the interest of the middle rank be identical with that of the people, why should not the powers of government be intrusted to that rank? If the powers of government were intrusted to that rank, there would evidently be an aristocracy of wealth; and "to constitute an aristocracy of wealth, though it were a very numerous one, would," according to Mr. Mill, "leave the community without protection, and exposed to all the evils of unbridled power." Will not the same motives which induce the middle classes to abuse one kind of power, induce them to abuse another? If their interest be the same with that of the people, they will govern the people well. If it be opposite to that of the people, they will advise the people ill. The system of universal suffrage, therefore, according to Mr. Mill's own account, is only a device for doing circuitously, what a representative system, with a pretty high qualification, would do directly.

So ends this celebrated Essay. And such is this philosophy, for which the experience of three thousand years is to be discarded; this philosophy, the professors of which speak as if it had guided the world to the knowledge of navigation and alphabetical writing; as if, before its dawn, the inhabitants of Europe had lived in caverns and eaten each other! We are sick, it seems, like the children of Israel, of the objects of our old and legitimate worship. We pine for a new idolatry. All that is costly and all that is ornamental in our intellectual treasures must be delivered up, and cast into the furnace—and there comes out this Calf!

Our readers can scarcely mistake our object in writing this

article. They will not suspect us of any disposition to advocate the cause of absolute monarchy, or of any narrow form of oligarchy, or to exaggerate the evils of popular government. Our object at present is, not so much to attack or defend any particular system of polity, as to expose the vices of a kind of reasoning utterly unfit for moral and political discussions; of a kind of reasoning which may so readily be turned to purposes of falsehood that it ought to receive no quarter, even when by accident it may be employed on the side of truth.

Our objection to the Essay of Mr. Mill is fundamental. We believe that it is utterly impossible to deduce the science of government from the principles of human nature.

What proposition is there respecting human nature which is absolutely and universally true? We know of only one: and that is not only true, but identical; that men always act from self-interest. This truism the Utilitarians proclaim with as much pride as if it were new, and as much zeal as if it were important. But in fact, when explained, it means only that men, if they can, will do as they choose. When we see the actions of a man, we know with certainty what he thinks his interest to be. But it is impossible to reason with certainty from what *we* take to be his interest to his actions. One man goes without a dinner, that he may add a shilling to a hundred thousand pounds: another runs in debt to give balls and masquerades. One man cuts his father's throat to get possession of his old clothes: another hazards his own life to save that of an enemy. One man volunteers on a forlorn hope: another is drummed out of a regiment for cowardice. Each of these men has, no doubt, acted from self-interest. But we gain nothing by knowing this, except the pleasure, if it be one, of multiplying useless words. In fact, this principle is just as recondite, and just as important, as the great truth that whatever is, is. If a philosopher were always to state facts in the following form—"There is a shower: but whatever is, is; therefore, there is a shower," his reasoning would be perfectly sound; but we do not apprehend that it would materially enlarge the circle of human knowledge. And it is equally idle to attribute any importance to a proposition which, when interpreted, means only that a man had rather do what he had rather do.

If the doctrine, that men always act from self-interest, be laid down in any other sense than this—if the meaning of the word self-interest be narrowed so as to exclude any one of the motives which may by possibility act on any human being,—the proposition ceases to be identical; but at the same time it ceases to be true.

What we have said of the word self-interest applies to all the synonymes and circumlocutions which are employed to convey the same meaning; pain and pleasure, happiness and misery, objects of desire, and so forth.

The whole art of Mr. Mill's Essay consists in one simple trick of legerdemain. It consists in using words of the sort which we have been describing, first in one sense and then in another. Men will take the objects of their desire if they can. Unquestionably:— but this is an identical proposition: For an object of desire means merely a thing which a man will procure if he can. Nothing can possibly be inferred from a maxim of this kind. When we see a man take something, we shall know that it was an object of his desire. But till then, we have no means of judging with certainty what he desires, or what he will take. The general proposition, however, having been admitted, Mr. Mill proceeds to reason as if men had no desires but those which can be gratified only by spoliation and oppression. It then becomes easy to deduce doctrines of vast importance from the original axiom. The only misfortune is, that by thus narrowing the meaning of the word desire, the axiom becomes false, and all the doctrines consequent upon it are false likewise.

When we pass beyond those maxims which it is impossible to deny without a contradiction in terms, and which, therefore, do not enable us to advance a single step in practical knowledge, we do not believe that it is possible to lay down a single general rule respecting the motives which influence human actions. There is nothing which may not, by association or by comparison, become an object either of desire or of aversion. The fear of death is generally considered as one of the strongest of our feelings. It is the most formidable sanction which legislators have been able to devise. Yet it is notorious that, as Lord Bacon has observed, there is no passion by which that fear has not been often overcome. Physical pain is indisputably an evil: yet it has been often endured, and even welcomed. Innumerable martyrs have exulted in torments which made the spectators shudder; and, to use a more homely illustration, there are few wives who do not long to be mothers.

Is the love of approbation a stronger motive than the love of wealth? It is impossible to answer this question generally, even in the case of an individual with whom we are very intimate. We often say, indeed, that a man loves fame more than money, or money more than fame. But this is said in a loose and popular sense; for there is scarcely a man who would not endure a few sneers for a great sum of money, if he were in pecuniary distress; and scarcely a man, on the other hand, who, if he were in flourishing circumstances, would expose himself to the hatred and contempt of the public for a trifle. In order, therefore, to return a precise answer even about a single human being, we must know what is the amount of the sacrifice of reputation demanded, and of the pecuniary advantage offered, and in what situation the person to whom the temptation is proposed stands at the time. But when the question is propounded generally about the whole species, the impossibility of answering is still more evident. Man differs from man; generation from generation; nation from nation. Education, station, sex, age, accidental associations, produce infinite shades of variety.

Now, the only mode in which we can conceive it possible to deduce a theory of government from the principles of human nature, is this. We must find out what are the motives which, in a particular form of government, impel rulers to bad measures, and what are those which impel them to good measures. We must then compare the effect of the two classes of motives; and according as we find the one or the other to prevail, we must pronounce the form of government in question good or bad.

Now let it be supposed that, in aristocratical and monarchical states, the desire of wealth and other desires of the same class always tend to produce misgovernment, and that the love of approbation and other kindred feelings always tend to produce good government. Then, if it be impossible, as we have shown that it is, to pronounce generally which of the two classes of motives is the more influential, it is impossible to find out, *a priori*, whether a monarchical or aristocratical form of government be good or bad.

Mr. Mill has avoided the difficulty of making the comparison, by very coolly putting all the weights into one of the scales,—by reasoning as if no human being had ever sympathized with the feelings, been gratified by the thanks, or been galled by the execrations, of another.

The case, as we have put it, is decisive against Mr. Mill; and yet we have put it in a manner far too favourable to him. For, in fact, it is impossible to lay it down as a general rule that the love of wealth in a sovereign always produces misgovernment, or the love of approbation good government. A patient and far-sighted ruler, for example, who is less desirous of raising a great sum immediately than of securing an unencumbered and progressive revenue, will, by taking off restraints from trade and giving perfect security to property, encourage accumulation and entice capital from foreign countries. The commercial policy of Prussia, which is perhaps superior to that of any country in the world, and which puts to shame the absurdities of our republican brethren on the other side of the Atlantic, has probably sprung from the desire of an absolute ruler to enrich himself. On the other hand, when the popular estimate of virtues and vices is erroneous, which is too often the case, the love of approbation leads sovereigns to spend the wealth of the nation on useless shows, or to engage in wanton and destructive wars. If then we can neither compare the strength of two motives, nor determine with certainty to what description of actions either motive will lead, how can we possibly deduce a theory of government from the nature of man?

How, then, are we to arrive at just conclusions on a subject so important to the happiness of mankind? Surely by that method, which, in every experimental science to which it has been applied, has signally increased the power and knowledge of our species,— by that method for which our new philosophers would substitute quibbles scarcely worthy of the barbarous respondents and opponents of the middle ages,—by the method of Induction;—by observing the present state of the world,—by assiduously studying the history of past ages,—by sifting the evidence of facts,—by carefully combining and contrasting those which are authentic,— by generalizing with judgment and diffidence,—by perpetually bringing the theory which we have constructed to the test of new facts,—by correcting, or altogether abandoning it, according as those new facts prove it to be partially or fundamentally unsound. Proceeding thus,—patiently,—diligently,—candidly,—we may hope to form a system as far inferior in pretension to that which we have been examining and as far superior to it in real utility, as the prescriptions of a great physician, varying with every stage of every malady, and with the constitution of every patient, to the pill of the advertising quack which is to cure all human beings, in all climates, of all diseases.

This is that noble Science of Politics, which is equally removed from the barren theories of the Utilitarian sophists, and from the petty craft, so often mistaken for statesmanship by minds grown narrow in habits of intrigue, jobbing, and official etiquette;—which, of all sciences, is the most important to the welfare of nations, —which of all sciences most tends to expand and invigorate the mind,—which draws nutriment and ornament from every part of philosophy and literature, and dispenses, in return, nutriment and ornament to all. We are sorry and surprised when we see men of good intentions and good natural abilities abandon this healthful and generous study to pore over speculations like those which we have been examining. And we should heartily rejoice to find that our remarks had induced any person of this description to employ, in researches of real utility, the talents and industry which are now wasted on verbal sophisms, wretched of their wretched kind.

As to the greater part of the sect, it is, we apprehend, of little consequence, what they study, or under whom. It would be more amusing, to be sure, and more reputable, if they would take up the old republican cant, and declaim about Brutus and Timoleon, the duty of killing tyrants, and the blessedness of dying for liberty. But, on the whole, they might have chosen worse. They may as well be Utilitarians as jockeys or dandies. And though quibbling about self-interest and motives, and objects of desire, and the greatest happiness of the greatest number, is but a poor employment for a grown man, it certainly hurts the health less than hard drinking, and the fortune less than high play: it is not much more laughable than phrenology, and is immeasurably more humane than cock-fighting.

GLADSTONE ON CHURCH AND STATE

(APRIL 1839)

The State in its Relations with the Church. By W. E. GLADSTONE, Esq., Student of Christ Church, and M.P. for Newark. 8vo. Second Edition. London: 1839.

THE author of this volume is a young man of unblemished character, and of distinguished parliamentary talents, the rising hope of those stern and unbending Tories, who follow, reluctantly and mutinously, a leader, whose experience and eloquence are indispensable to them, but whose cautious temper and moderate opinions they abhor. It would not be at all strange if Mr. Gladstone were one of the most unpopular men in England. But we believe that we do him no more than justice when we say that his abilities and his demeanour have obtained for him the respect and good will of all parties. His first appearance in the character of an author is therefore an interesting event; and it is natural that the gentle wishes of the public should go with him to his trial.

We are much pleased, without any reference to the soundness or unsoundness of Mr. Gladstone's theories, to see a grave and elaborate treatise on an important part of the Philosophy of Government proceed from the pen of a young man who is rising to eminence in the House of Commons. There is little danger that people engaged in the conflicts of active life will be too much addicted to general speculation. The opposite vice is that which most easily besets them. The times and tides of business and debate tarry for no man. A politician must often talk and act before he has thought and read. He may be very ill-informed respecting a question; all his notions about it may be vague and inaccurate; but speak he must; and if he is a man of talents, of tact, and of intrepidity, he soon finds that, even under such circumstances, it is possible to speak successfully. He finds that there is a great difference between the effect of written words, which are perused and reperused in the stillness of the closet, and the effect of spoken words which, set off by the graces of utterance and gesture, vibrate for a single moment on the ear. He finds that he may blunder without much chance of being detected, that he may reason sophistically, and escape unrefuted. He finds that, even on knotty questions of trade and legislation, he can, without reading ten pages, or thinking ten minutes, draw forth loud plaudits, and sit down with the credit of having made an excellent speech. Lysias, says Plutarch, wrote a defence for a man who was to be tried before one of the Athenian tribunals. Long before the defendant had learned the speech by heart, he became so much dissatisfied with it that he went in great distress to the author. "I was delighted with your speech the first time I read it; but I liked it less the second time, and still less the third time; and now it seems to me to be no defence at all." "My good friend," said Lysias, "you quite forget that the judges are to hear it only once." The case is the same in the English parliament. It would be as idle in an orator to waste deep meditation and long research on his speeches, as it would be in the manager of a theatre to adorn all the crowd of courtiers and ladies who cross over the stage in a procession with real pearls and diamonds. It is not by accuracy or profundity that men become the masters of great assemblies. And why be at the charge of providing logic of the best quality, when a very inferior article will be equally acceptable? Why go as deep into a question as Burke, only in order to be, like Burke, coughed down, or left speaking to green benches and red boxes? This has long appeared to us to be the most serious of the evils which are to be set off against the many blessings of popular government. It is a fine and true saying of Bacon, that reading makes a full man, talking a ready man, and writing an exact man. The tendency of institutions like those of England is to encourage readiness in public men, at the expense both of fulness and of exactness. The keenest and most vigorous minds of every generation, minds often admirably fitted for the investigation of truth, are habitually employed in producing arguments, such as no man of sense would ever put into a treatise intended for publication, arguments which are just good enough to be used once, when aided by fluent delivery and pointed language. The habit of discussing questions in this way necessarily reacts on the intellects of our ablest men; particularly of those who are introduced into parliament at a very early age, before their minds have expanded to full maturity. The talent for debate is developed in such men to a degree which, to the multitude, seems as marvellous as the performances of an Italian *improvisatore*. But they are fortunate indeed if they retain unimpaired the faculties which are required for close reasoning or for enlarged speculation. Indeed we should sooner expect a great original work on political science, such a work, for example, as the Wealth of Nations, from an apothecary in a country town, or from a minister in the Hebrides, than from a statesman who, ever since he was one-and-twenty, had been a distinguished debater in the House of Commons.

We therefore hail with pleasure, though assuredly not with unmixed pleasure, the appearance of this work. That a young politician should, in the intervals afforded by his parliamentary avocations, have constructed and propounded, with much study and mental toil, an original theory on a great problem in politics, is a circumstance which, abstracted from all consideration of the soundness or unsoundness of his opinions, must be considered as highly creditable to him. We certainly cannot wish that Mr. Gladstone's doctrines may become fashionable among public men. But we heartily wish that his laudable desire to penetrate beneath the surface of questions, and to arrive, by long and intent meditation, at the knowledge of great general laws, were much more fashionable than we at all expect it to become.

Mr. Gladstone seems to us to be, in many respects, exceedingly well qualified for philosophical investigation. His mind is of large grasp; nor is he deficient in dialectical skill. But he does not give his intellect fair play. There is no want of light, but a great want of what Bacon would have called dry light. Whatever Mr. Gladstone sees is refracted and distorted by a false medium of passions and prejudices. His style bears a remarkable analogy to his mode of thinking, and indeed exercises great influence on his mode of thinking. His rhetoric, though often good of its kind, darkens and perplexes the logic which it should illustrate. Half his acuteness and diligence, with a barren imagination and a scanty vocabulary, would have saved him from almost all his mistakes. He has one gift most dangerous to a speculator, a vast command of a kind of language, grave and majestic, but of vague and uncertain import; of a kind of language which affects us much in the same way in which the lofty diction of the chorus of Clouds affected the simple-hearted Athenian.

ᾧ γῆ τοῦ φθέγματος, ὡς ἱερὸν, καὶ σεμνὸν, καὶ τερατῶδες.

When propositions have been established, and nothing remains but to amplify and decorate them, this dim magnificence may be in place. But if it is admitted into a demonstration, it is very much worse than absolute nonsense; just as that transparent haze, through which the sailor sees capes and mountains of false sizes and in false bearings, is more dangerous than utter darkness. Now, Mr. Gladstone is fond of employing the phraseology of which we speak in those parts of his work which require the utmost perspicuity and precision of which human language is capable; and in this way, he deludes first himself, and then his readers. The foundations of his theory, which ought to be buttresses of adamant, are made out of the flimsy materials which are fit only for perorations. This fault is one which no subsequent care or industry can correct. The more strictly Mr. Gladstone reasons on his premises, the more absurd are the conclusions which he brings out; and, when at last his good sense and good nature recoil from the horrible practical inferences to which his theory leads, he is reduced sometimes to take refuge in arguments inconsistent with his fundamental doctrines, and sometimes to escape from the legitimate consequences of his false principles, under cover of equally false history.

It would be unjust not to say that this book, though not a good book, shows more talent than many good books. It abounds with eloquent and ingenious passages. It bears the signs of much patient thought. It is written throughout with excellent taste and excellent temper; nor does it, so far as we have observed, contain one expression unworthy of a gentleman, a scholar, or a Christian. But the doctrines which are put forth in it appear to us, after full and calm consideration, to be false, to be in the highest degree pernicious, and to be such as, if followed out in practice to their legitimate consequences, would inevitably produce the dissolution of society: and for this opinion we shall proceed to give our reasons with that freedom which the importance of the subject requires, and which Mr. Gladstone, both by precept and by example, invites us to use, but, we hope, without rudeness, and, we are sure, without malevolence.

Before we enter on an examination of this theory, we wish to guard ourselves against one misconception. It is possible that some persons who have read Mr. Gladstone's book carelessly, and others who have merely heard in conversation, or seen in a newspaper, that the member for Newark has written in defence of the Church of England against the supporters of the voluntary system, may imagine that we are writing in defence of the voluntary system, and that we desire the abolition of the Established Church. This is not the case. It would be as unjust to accuse us of attacking the Church, because we attack Mr. Gladstone's doctrines, as it would be to accuse Locke of wishing for anarchy, because he refuted Filmer's patriarchal theory of government, or to accuse Blackstone of recommending the confiscation of ecclesiastical property, because he denied that the right of the rector to tithe was derived from the Levitical law. It is to be observed, that Mr. Gladstone rests his case on entirely new grounds, and does not differ more widely from us than from some of those who have hitherto been considered as the most illustrious champions of the Church. He is not content with the Ecclesiastical Polity, and rejoices that the latter part of that celebrated work "does not carry with it the weight of Hooker's plenary authority." He is not content with Bishop Warburton's Alliance of Church and State. "The propositions of that work generally," he says, "are to be received with qualification;" and he agrees with Bolingbroke in thinking that Warburton's whole theory rests on a fiction. He is still less satisfied with Paley's defence of the Church, which he pronounces to be "tainted by the original vice of false ethical principles," and "full of the seeds of evil." He conceives that Dr. Chalmers has taken a partial view of the subject, and "put forth much questionable matter." In truth, on almost every point on which we are opposed to Mr. Gladstone, we have on our side the authority of some divine, eminent as a defender of existing establishments.

Mr. Gladstone's whole theory rests on this great fundamental proposition, that the propagation of religious truth is one of the principal ends of government, as government. If Mr. Gladstone has not proved this proposition, his system vanishes at once.

We are desirous, before we enter on the discussion of this important question, to point out clearly a distinction which, though very obvious, seems to be overlooked by many excellent people. In their opinion, to say that the ends of government are temporal and not spiritual is tantamount to saying that the temporal welfare of man is of more importance than his spiritual welfare. But this is an entire mistake. The question is not whether spiritual interests be or be not superior in importance to temporal interests; but whether the machinery which happens at any moment to be employed for the purpose of protecting certain temporal interests of a society be necessarily such a machinery as is fitted to promote the spiritual interests of that society. Without a division of labour the world could not go on. It is of very much more importance that men should have food than that they should have pianofortes. Yet it by no means follows that every pianoforte-maker ought to add the business of a baker to his own; for, if he did so, we should have both much worse music and much worse bread. It is of much more importance that the knowledge of religious truth should be wisely diffused than that the art of sculpture should flourish among us. Yet it by no means follows that the Royal Academy ought to unite with its present functions those of the Society for promoting Christian Knowledge, to distribute theological tracts, to send forth missionaries, to turn out Nollekens for being a Catholic, Bacon for being a Methodist, and Flaxman for being a Swedenborgian. For the effect of such folly would be that we should have the worst possible academy of arts, and the worst possible society for the promotion of Christian knowledge. The community, it is plain, would be thrown into universal confusion, if it were supposed to be the duty of every association which is formed for one good object to promote every other good object.

As to some of the ends of civil government, all people are agreed. That it is designed to protect our persons and our property, that it is designed to compel us to satisfy our wants, not by rapine, but by industry, that it is designed to compel us to decide our differences, not by the strong hand, but by arbitration, that it is designed to direct our whole force, as that of one man, against any other society which may offer us injury, these are propositions which will hardly be disputed.

Now these are matters in which man, without any reference to any higher being or to any future state, is very deeply interested. Every human being, be he idolater, Mahometan, Jew, Papist, Socinian, Deist, or Atheist, naturally loves life, shrinks from pain, desires comforts which can be enjoyed only in communities where property is secure. To be murdered, to be tortured, to be robbed, to be sold into slavery, to be exposed to the outrages of gangs of foreign banditti calling themselves patriots, these are evidently evils from which men of every religion, and men of no religion, wish to be protected; and therefore it will hardly be disputed that men of every religion, and of no religion, have thus far a common interest in being well governed.

But the hopes and fears of man are not limited to this short life and to this visible world. He finds himself surrounded by the signs of a power and wisdom higher than his own; and, in all ages and nations, men of all orders of intellect, from Bacon and Newton down to the rudest tribes of cannibals, have believed in the existence of some superior mind. Thus far the voice of mankind is almost unanimous. But whether there be one God or many, what may be his natural and what his moral attributes, in what relation his creatures stand to him, whether he have ever disclosed himself to us by any other revelation than that which is written in all the parts of the glorious and well-ordered world which he has made, whether his revelation be contained in any permanent record, how that record should be interpreted, and whether it have pleased him to appoint any unerring interpreter on earth, these are questions respecting which there exists the widest diversity of opinion, and respecting which a large part of our race has, ever since the dawn of regular history, been deplorably in error.

Now here are two great objects: one is the protection of the persons and estates of citizens from injury; the other is the propagation of religious truth. No two objects more entirely distinct can well be imagined. The former belongs wholly to the visible and tangible world in which we live; the latter belongs to that higher world which is beyond the reach of our senses. The former belongs to this life; the latter to that which is to come. Men who are perfectly agreed as to the importance of the former object, and as to the way of attaining it, differ as widely as possible respecting the latter object. We must, therefore, pause before we admit that the persons, be they who they may, who are intrusted with power for the promotion of the former object, ought always to use that power for the promotion of the latter object.

Mr. Gladstone conceives that the duties of governments are paternal; a doctrine which we shall not believe till he can show us some government which loves its subjects as a father loves a child, and which is as superior in intelligence to its subjects as a father is to a child. He tells us, in lofty though somewhat indistinct language, that "Government occupies in moral the place of τὸ πᾶν in physical science." If government be indeed τὸ πᾶν in moral science, we do not understand why rulers should not assume all the functions which Plato assigned to them. Why should they not take away the child from the mother, select the nurse, regulate the school, overlook the playground, fix the hours of labour and of recreation, prescribe what ballads shall be sung, what tunes shall be played, what books shall be read, what physic shall be swallowed? Why should not they choose our wives, limit our expenses, and stint us to a certain number of dishes of meat, of glasses of wine, and of cups of tea? Plato, whose hardihood in speculation was perhaps more wonderful than any other peculiarity of his extra-ordinary mind, and who shrank from nothing to which his principles led, went this whole length. Mr. Gladstone is not so intrepid. He contents himself with laying down this proposition, that, whatever be the body which in any community is employed to protect the persons and property of men, that body ought also, in its corporate capacity, to profess a religion, to employ its power for the propagation of that religion, and to require conformity to that religion, as an indispensable qualification for all civil office. He distinctly declares that he does not in this proposition confine his view to orthodox governments, or even to Christian governments. The circumstance that a religion is false does not, he tells us, diminish the obligation of governors, as such, to uphold it. If they neglect to do so, "we cannot," he says, "but regard the fact as aggravating the case of the holders of such creed." "I do not scruple to affirm," he adds, "that, if a Mahometan conscientiously believes his religion to come from God, and to teach divine truth, he must believe that truth to be beneficial, and beneficial beyond all other things to the soul of man; and he must, therefore, and ought to desire its extension, and to use for its extension all proper and legitimate means; and that, if such Mahometan be a prince, he ought to count among those means the application of whatever influence or funds he may lawfully have at his disposal for such purposes."

Surely this is a hard saying. Before we admit that the Emperor Julian, in employing the influence and the funds at his disposal for the extinction of Christianity, was doing no more than his duty, before we admit that the Arian, Theodoric, would have committed a crime if he had suffered a single believer in the divinity of Christ to hold any civil employment in Italy, before we admit that the Dutch Government is bound to exclude from office all members of the Church of England, the King of Bavaria to exclude from office all Protestants, the Great Turk to exclude from office all Christians, the King of Ava to exclude from office all who hold the unity of God, we think ourselves entitled to demand very full and accurate demonstration. When the consequences of a doctrine are so startling, we may well require that its foundations shall be very solid.

The following paragraph is a specimen of the arguments by which Mr. Gladstone has, as he conceives, established his great fundamental proposition:—

"We may state the same proposition in a more general form, in which it surely must command universal assent. Wherever there is power in the universe, that power is the property of God, the King of that universe—his property of right, however for a time withholden or abused. Now this property is, as it were, realized, is used according to the will of the owner, when it is used for the purposes he has ordained, and in the temper of mercy, justice, truth, and faith, which he has taught us. But those principles never can be truly, never can be permanently, entertained in the human breast, except by a continual reference to their source, and the supply of the Divine grace. The powers, therefore, that dwell in individuals acting as a government, as well as those that dwell in individuals acting for themselves, can only be secured for right uses by applying to them a religion."

Here are propositions of vast and indefinite extent, conveyed in language which has a certain obscure dignity and sanctity, attractive, we doubt not, to many minds. But the moment that we examine these propositions closely, the moment that we bring them to the test by running over but a very few of the particulars which are included in them, we find them to be false and extravagant. The doctrine which "must surely command universal assent" is this, that every association of human beings which exercises any power whatever, that is to say, every association of human beings, is bound, as such association, to profess a religion. Imagine the effect which would follow if this principle were really in force during four-and-twenty hours. Take one instance out of a million. A stage-coach company has power over its horses. This power is the property of God. It is used according to the will of God when it is used with mercy. But the principle of mercy can never be truly or permanently entertained in the human breast without continual reference to God. The powers, therefore, that dwell in individuals, acting as a stage-coach company, can only be secured for right uses by applying to them a religion. Every stage-coach company ought, therefore, in its collective capacity, to profess some one faith, to have its articles, and its public worship, and its tests. That this conclusion, and an infinite number of other conclusions equally strange, follow of necessity from Mr. Gladstone's principle, is as certain as it is that two and two make four. And, if the legitimate conclusions be so absurd, there must be something unsound in the principle.

We will quote another passage of the same sort:—

"Why, then, we now come to ask, should the governing body in a state profess a religion? First, because it is composed of individual men; and they, being appointed to act in a definite moral capacity, must sanctify their acts done in that capacity by the offices of religion; inasmuch as the acts cannot otherwise be acceptable to God, or anything but sinful and punishable in themselves. And whenever we turn our face away from God in our conduct, we are living atheistically. . . . . In fulfilment, then, of his obligations as an individual, the statesman must be a worshipping man. But his acts are public—the powers and instruments with which he works are public—acting under and by the authority of the law, he moves at his word ten thousand subject arms; and because such energies are thus essentially public, and wholly out of the range of mere individual agency; they must be sanctified not only by the private personal prayers and piety of those who fill public situations, but also by public acts of the men composing the public body. They must offer prayer and praise in their public and collective character—in that character wherein they constitute the organ of the nation, and wield its collective force. Wherever there is a reasoning agency, there is a moral duty and responsibility involved in it. The governors are reasoning agents for the nation, in their conjoint acts as such. And therefore there must be attached to this agency, as that without which none of our responsibilities can be met, a religion. And this religion must be that of the conscience of the governor, or none."

Here again we find propositions of vast sweep, and of sound so orthodox and solemn, that many good people, we doubt not, have been greatly edified by it. But let us examine the words closely; and it will immediately become plain that, if these principles be once admitted, there is an end of all society. No combination can be formed for any purpose of mutual help, for trade, for public works, for the relief of the sick or the poor, for the promotion of art or science, unless the members of the combination agree in their theological opinions. Take any such combination at random, the London and Birmingham Railway Company, for example, and observe to what consequences Mr. Gladstone's arguments inevitably lead. "Why should the Directors of the Railway Company, in their collective capacity, profess a religion? First, because the direction is composed of individual men appointed to act in a definite moral capacity, bound to look carefully to the property, the limbs, and the lives of their fellow-creatures, bound to act diligently for their constituents, bound to govern their servants with humanity and justice, bound to fulfil with fidelity many important contracts. They must, therefore, sanctify their acts by the offices of religion, or these acts will be sinful and punishable in themselves. In fulfilment, then, of his obligations as an individual, the Director of the London and Birmingham Railway Company must be a worshipping man. But his acts are public. He acts for a body. He moves at his word ten thousand subject arms. And because these energies are out of the range of his mere individual agency, they must be sanctified by public acts of devotion. The Railway Directors must offer prayer and praise in their public and collective character, in that character wherewith they constitute the organ of the Company, and wield its collected power. Wherever there is reasoning agency, there is moral responsibility. The Directors are reasoning agents for the Company. And therefore there must be attached to this agency, as that without which none of our responsibilities can be met, a religion. And this religion must be that of the conscience of the Director himself, or none. There must be public worship and a test. No Jew, no Socinian, no Presbyterian, no Catholic, no Quaker, must be permitted to be the organ of the Company, and to wield its collected force." Would Mr. Gladstone really defend this proposition? We are sure that he would not; but we are sure that to this proposition, and to innumerable similar propositions, his reasoning inevitably leads.

Again,—

"National will and agency are indisputably one, binding either a dissentient minority or the subject body, in a manner that nothing but the recognition of the doctrine of national personality can justify. National honour and good faith are words in every one's mouth. How do they less imply a personality in nations than the duty towards God, for which we now contend? They are strictly and essentially distinct from the honour and good faith of the individuals composing the nation. France is a person to us, and we to her. A wilful injury done to her is a moral act, and a moral act quite distinct from the acts of all the individuals composing the nation. Upon broad facts like these we may rest, without resorting to the more technical proof which the laws afford in their manner of dealing with corporations. If, then, a nation have unity of will, have pervading sympathies, have capability of reward and suffering contingent upon its acts, shall we deny its responsibility; its need of a religion to meet that responsibility? . . . . A nation, then, having a personality, lies under the obligation, like the individuals composing its governing body, of sanctifying the acts of that personality by the offices of religion, and thus we have a new and imperative ground for the existence of a state religion."

A new ground we have here, certainly, but whether very imperative may be doubted. Is it not perfectly clear, that this argument applies with exactly as much force to every combination of human beings for a common purpose, as to governments? Is there any such combination in the world, whether technically a corporation or not, which has not this collective personality from which Mr. Gladstone deduces such extraordinary consequences? Look at banks, insurance offices, dock companies, canal companies, gas companies, hospitals, dispensaries, associations for the relief of the poor, associations for apprehending malefactors, associations of medical pupils for procuring subjects, associations of country gentlemen for keeping fox-hounds, book societies, benefit societies, clubs of all ranks, from those which have lined Pall-Mall and St. James's Street with their palaces, down to the Free-and-easy which meets in the shabby parlour of a village inn. Is there a single one of these combinations to which Mr. Gladstone's argument will not apply as well as to the State? In all these combinations, in the Bank of England, for example, or in the Athenæum club, the will and agency of the society are one, and bind the dissentient minority. The Bank and the Athenæum have a good faith and a justice different from the good faith and justice of the individual members. The Bank is a person to those who deposit bullion with it. The Athenæum is a person to the butcher and the wine-merchant. If the Athenæum keeps money at the Bank, the two societies are as much persons to each other as England and France. Either society may pay its debts honestly; either may try to defraud its creditors; either may increase in prosperity; either may fall into difficulties. If, then, they have this unity of will; if they are capable of doing and suffering good and evil, can we, to use Mr. Gladstone's words, "deny their responsibility, or their need of a religion to meet that responsibility?" Joint-stock banks, therefore, and clubs, "having a personality, lie under the necessity of sanctifying that personality by the offices of religion;" and thus we have "a new and imperative ground" for requiring all the directors and clerks of joint-stock banks, and all the officers of clubs, to qualify by taking the sacrament.

The truth is that Mr. Gladstone has fallen into an error very common among men of less talents than his own. It is not unusual for a person who is eager to prove a particular proposition to assume a *major* of huge extent, which includes that particular proposition, without ever reflecting that it includes a great deal more. The fatal facility with which Mr. Gladstone multiplies expressions stately and sonorous, but of indeterminate meaning, eminently qualifies him to practise this sleight on himself and on his readers. He lays down broad general doctrines about power, when the only power of which he is thinking is the power of governments, and about conjoint action, when the only conjoint action of which he is thinking is the conjoint action of citizens in a state. He first resolves on his conclusion. He then makes a *major* of most comprehensive dimensions, and, having satisfied himself that it contains his conclusion, never troubles himself about what else it may contain: and, as soon as we examine it, we find that it contains an infinite number of conclusions, every one of which is a monstrous absurdity.

It is perfectly true that it would be a very good thing if all the members of all the associations in the world were men of sound religious views. We have no doubt that a good Christian will be under the guidance of Christian principles, in his conduct as director of a canal company or steward of a charity dinner. If he were, to recur to a case which we before put, a member of a stage-coach company, he would, in that capacity, remember that "a righteous man regardeth the life of his beast." But it does not follow that every association of men must therefore, as such association, profess a religion. It is evident that many great and useful objects can be attained in this world only by cooperation. It is equally evident that there cannot be efficient cooperation, if men proceed on the principle that they must not cooperate for one object unless they agree about other objects. Nothing seems to us more beautiful or admirable in our social system than the facility with which thousands of people, who perhaps agree only on a single point, can combine their energies for the purpose of carrying that single point. We see daily instances of this. Two men, one of them obstinately prejudiced against missions, the other president of a missionary society, sit together at the board of a hospital, and heartily concur in measures for the health and comfort of the patients. Two men, one of whom is a zealous supporter and the other a zealous opponent of the system pursued in Lancaster's schools, meet at the Mendicity Society, and act together with the utmost cordiality. The general rule we take to be undoubtedly this, that it is lawful and expedient for men to unite in an association for the promotion of a good object, though they may differ with respect to other objects of still higher importance.

It will hardly be denied that the security of the persons and property of men is a good object, and that the best way, indeed the only way, of promoting that object is to combine men together in certain great corporations which are called States. These corporations are very variously, and, for the most part, very imperfectly organized. Many of them abound with frightful abuses. But it seems reasonable to believe that the worst that ever existed was, on the whole, preferable to complete anarchy.

Now, reasoning from analogy, we should say that these great corporations would, like all other associations, be likely to attain their end most perfectly if that end were kept singly in view; and that to refuse the services of those who are admirably qualified to promote that end, because they are not also qualified to promote some other end, however excellent, seems at first sight as unreasonable as it would be to provide that nobody who was not a fellow of the Society of Antiquaries should be a governor of the Eye Infirmary; or that nobody who was not a member of the Society for promoting Christianity among the Jews should be a trustee of the Literary Fund.

It is impossible to name any collection of human beings to which Mr. Gladstone's reasonings would apply more strongly than to an army. Where shall we find more complete unity of action than in an army? Where else do so many human beings implicitly obey one ruling mind? What other mass is there which moves so much like one man? Where is such tremendous power intrusted to those who command? Where is so awful a responsibility laid upon them? If Mr. Gladstone has made out, as he conceives, an imperative necessity for a State Religion, much more has he made it out to be imperatively necessary that every army should, in its collective capacity, profess a religion. Is he prepared to adopt this consequence?

On the morning of the thirteenth of August, in the year 1704, two great captains, equal in authority, united by close private and public ties, but of different creeds, prepared for a battle, on the event of which were staked the liberties of Europe. Marlborough had passed a part of the night in prayer, and before daybreak received the sacrament according to the rites of the Church of England. He then hastened to join Eugene, who had probably just confessed himself to a Popish priest. The generals consulted together, formed their plan in concert, and repaired each to his own post. Marlborough gave orders for public prayers. The English chaplains read the service at the head of the English regiments. The Calvinistic chaplains of the Dutch army, with heads on which hand of Bishop had never been laid, poured forth their supplications in front of their countrymen. In the mean time, the Danes might listen to their Lutheran ministers; and Capuchins might encourage the Austrian squadrons, and pray to the Virgin for a blessing on the arms of the Holy Roman Empire. The battle commences, and these men of various religions all act like members of one body. The Catholic and the Protestant general exert themselves to assist and to surpass each other. Before sunset the Empire is saved. France has lost in a day the fruits of eighty years of intrigue and of victory. And the allies, after conquering together, return thanks to God separately, each after his own form of worship. Now, is this practical atheism? Would any man in his senses say, that, because the allied army had unity of action and a common interest, and because a heavy responsibility lay on its Chiefs, it was therefore imperatively necessary that the Army should, as an Army, have one established religion, that Eugene should be deprived of his command for being a Catholic, that all the Dutch and Austrian colonels should be broken for not subscribing the Thirty-nine Articles? Certainly not. The most ignorant grenadier on the field of battle would have seen the absurdity of such a proposition. "I know," he would have said, "that the Prince of Savoy goes to mass, and that our Corporal John cannot abide it; but what has the mass to do with the taking of the village of Blenheim? The prince wants to beat the French, and so does Corporal John. If we stand by each other we shall most likely beat them. If we send all the Papists and Dutch away, Tallard will have every man of us." Mr. Gladstone himself, we imagine, would admit that our honest grenadier would have the best of the argument; and if so, what follows? Even this: that all Mr. Gladstone's general principles about power, and responsibility, and personality, and conjoint action, must be given up; and that, if his theory is to stand at all, it must stand on some other foundation.

We have now, we conceive, shown that it may be proper to form men into combinations for important purposes, which combinations shall have unity and common interests, and shall be under the direction of rulers intrusted with great power and lying under solemn responsibility; and yet that it may be highly improper that these combinations should, as such, profess any one system of religious beliefs, or perform any joint act of religious worship. How, then, is it proved that this may not be the case with some of those great combinations which we call States? We firmly believe that it is the case with some states. We firmly believe that there are communities in which it would be as absurd to mix up theology with government, as it would have been in the right wing of the allied army at Blenheim to commence a controversy with the left wing, in the middle of the battle, about purgatory and the worship of images.

It is the duty, Mr. Gladstone tell us, of the persons, be they who they may, who hold supreme power in the state, to employ that power in order to promote whatever they may deem to be theological truth. Now surely, before he can call on us to admit this proposition, he is bound to prove that these persons are likely to do more good than harm by so employing their power. The first question is, whether a government, proposing to itself the propagation of religious truth, as one of its principal ends, is more likely to lead the people right than to lead them wrong? Mr. Gladstone evades this question; and perhaps it was his wisest course to do so.

"If," says he, "the government be good, let it have its natural duties and powers at its command; but, if not good, let it be made so. . . . We follow, therefore, the true course in looking first for the true ἰδέα, or abstract conception of a government, of course with allowance for the evil and frailty that are in man, and then in examining whether there be comprised in that ἰδέα a capacity and consequent duty on the part of a government to lay down any laws, or devote any means for the purposes of religion,—in short, to exercise a choice upon religion."

Of course, Mr. Gladstone has a perfect right to argue any abstract question, provided he will constantly bear in mind that it is only an abstract question that he is arguing. Whether a perfect government would or would not be a good machinery for the propagation of religious truth is certainly a harmless, and may, for aught we know, be an edifying subject of enquiry. But it is very important that we should remember that there is not, and never has been, any such government in the world. There is no harm at all in enquiring what course a stone thrown into the air would take, if the law of gravitation did not operate. But the consequences would be unpleasant, if the enquirer, as soon as he had finished his calculation, were to begin to throw stones about in all directions, without considering that his conclusion rests on a false hypothesis, and that his projectiles, instead of flying away through infinite space, will speedily return in parabolas, and break the windows and heads of his neighbours.

It is very easy to say that governments are good, or, if not good, ought to be made so. But what is meant by good government? And how are all the bad governments in the world to be made good? And of what value is a theory which is true only on a supposition in the highest degree extravagant?

We do not, however, admit that, if a government were, for all its temporal ends, as perfect as human frailty allows, such government would, therefore, be necessarily qualified to propagate true religion. For we see that the fitness of governments to propagate true religion is by no means proportioned to their fitness for the temporal ends of their institution. Looking at individuals, we see that the princes under whose rule nations have been most ably protected from foreign and domestic disturbance, and have made the most rapid advances in civilisation, have been by no means good teachers of divinity. Take, for example, the best French sovereign, Henry the Fourth, a king who restored order, terminated a terrible civil war, brought the finances into an excellent condition, made his country respected throughout Europe, and endeared himself to the great body of the people whom he ruled. Yet this man was twice a Huguenot, and twice a Papist. He was, as Davila hints, strongly suspected of having no religion at all in theory; and was certainly not much under religious restraints in his practice. Take the Czar Peter, the Empress Catharine, Frederick the Great. It will surely not be disputed that these sovereigns, with all their faults, were, if we consider them with reference merely to the temporal ends of government, above the average of merit. Considered as theological guides, Mr. Gladstone would probably put them below the most abject drivellers of the Spanish branch of the house of Bourbon. Again, when we pass from individuals to systems, we by no means find that the aptitude of governments for propagating religious truth is proportioned to their aptitude for secular functions. Without being blind admirers either of the French or of the American institutions, we think it clear that the persons and property of citizens are better protected in France and in New England than in almost any society that now exists, or that has ever existed; very much better, certainly, than in the Roman empire under the orthodox rule of Constantine and Theodosius. But neither the government of France, nor that of New England, is so organized as to be fit for the propagation of theological doctrines. Nor do we think it improbable that the most serious religious errors might prevail in a state which, considered merely with reference to temporal objects, might approach far nearer than any that has ever been known to the ἰδέα of what a state should be.

But we shall leave this abstract question, and look at the world as we find it. Does, then, the way in which governments generally obtain their power make it at all probable that they will be more favourable to orthodoxy than to heterodoxy? A nation of barbarians pours down on a rich and unwarlike empire, enslaves the people, portions out the land, and blends the institutions which it finds in the cities with those which it has brought from the woods. A handful of daring adventurers from a civilised nation wander to some savage country, and reduce the aboriginal race to bondage. A successful general turns his arms against the state which he serves. A society, made brutal by oppression, rises madly on its masters, sweeps away all old laws and usages, and, when its first paroxysm of rage is over, sinks down passively under any form of polity which may spring out of the chaos. A chief of a party, as at Florence, becomes imperceptibly a sovereign and the founder of a dynasty. A captain of mercenaries, as at Milan, seizes on a city, and by the sword makes himself its ruler. An elective senate, as at Venice, usurps permanent and hereditary power. It is in events such as these that governments have generally originated; and we can see nothing in such events to warrant us in believing that the governments thus called into existence will be peculiarly well fitted to distinguish between religious truth and heresy.

When, again, we look at the constitutions of governments which have become settled, we find no great security for the orthodoxy of rulers. One magistrate holds power because his name was drawn out of a purse; another, because his father held it before him. There are representative systems of all sorts, large constituent bodies, small constituent bodies, universal suffrage, high pecuniary qualifications. We see that, for the temporal ends of government, some of these constitutions are very skilfully constructed, and that the very worst of them is preferable to anarchy. We see some sort of connexion between the very worst of them, and the temporal well-being of society. But it passes our understanding to comprehend what connexion any one of them has with theological truth.

And how stands the fact? Have not almost all the governments in the world always been in the wrong on religious subjects? Mr. Gladstone, we imagine, would say that, except in the time of Constantine, of Jovian, and of a very few of their successors, and occasionally in England since the Reformation, no government has ever been sincerely friendly to the pure and apostolical Church of Christ. If, therefore, it be true that every ruler is bound in conscience to use his power for the propagation of his own religion, it will follow that, for one ruler who has been bound in conscience to use his power for the propagation of truth, a thousand have been bound in conscience to use their power for the propagation of falsehood. Surely this is a conclusion from which common sense recoils. Surely, if experience shows that a certain machine, when used to produce a certain effect, does not produce that effect once in a thousand times, but produces, in the vast majority of cases, an effect directly contrary, we cannot be wrong in saying that it is not a machine of which the principal end is to be so used.

If, indeed, the magistrate would content himself with laying his opinions and reasons before the people, and would leave the people, uncorrupted by hope or fear, to judge for themselves, we should see little reason to apprehend that his interference in favour of error would be seriously prejudicial to the interests of truth. Nor do we, as will hereafter be seen, object to his taking this course, when it is compatible with the efficient discharge of his more especial duties. But this will not satisfy Mr. Gladstone. He would have the magistrate resort to means which have a great tendency to make malcontents, to make hypocrites, to make careless nominal conformists, but no tendency whatever to produce honest and rational conviction. It seems to us quite clear that an enquirer who has no wish, except to know the truth, is more likely to arrive at the truth than an enquirer who knows that, if he decides one way, he shall be rewarded, and that, if he decides the other way, he shall be punished. Now, Mr. Gladstone would have governments propagate their opinions by excluding all dissenters from all civil offices. That is to say, he would have governments propagate their opinions by a process which has no reference whatever to the truth or falsehood of those opinions, by arbitrarily uniting certain worldly advantages with one set of doctrines, and certain worldly inconveniences with another set. It is of the very nature of argument to serve the interest of truth; but if rewards and punishments serve the interest of truth, it is by mere accident. It is very much easier to find arguments for the Divine authority of the Gospel than for the Divine authority of the Koran. But it is just as easy to bribe or rack a Jew into Mahometanism as into Christianity.

From racks, indeed, and from all penalties directed against the persons, the property, and the liberty of heretics, the humane spirit of Mr. Gladstone shrinks with horror. He only maintains that conformity to the religion of the state ought to be an indispensable qualification for office; and he would, unless we have greatly misunderstood him, think it his duty, if he had the power, to revive the Test Act, to enforce it rigorously, and to extend it to important classes who were formerly exempt from its operation.

This is indeed a legitimate consequence of his principles. But why stop here? Why not roast dissenters at slow fires? All the general reasonings on which this theory rests evidently lead to sanguinary persecution. If the propagation of religious truth be a principal end of government, as government; if it be the duty of a government to employ for that end its constitutional power; if the constitutional power of governments extends, as it most unquestionably does, to the making of laws for the burning of heretics; if burning be, as it most assuredly is, in many cases, a most effectual mode of suppressing opinions; why should we not burn? If the relation in which government ought to stand to the people be, as Mr. Gladstone tell us, a paternal relation, we are irresistibly led to the conclusion that persecution is justifiable. For the right of propagating opinions by punishment is one which belongs to parents as clearly as the right to give instruction. A boy is compelled to attend family worship: he is forbidden to read irreligious books: if he will not learn his catechism, he is sent to bed without his supper: if he plays truant at church-time, a task is set him. If he should display the precocity of his talents by expressing impious opinions before his brothers and sisters, we should not much blame his father for cutting short the controversy with a horsewhip. All the reasons which lead us to think that parents are peculiarly fitted to conduct the education of their children, and that education is a principal end of the parental relation, lead us also to think, that parents ought to be allowed to use punishment, if necessary, for the purpose of forcing children, who are incapable of judging for themselves, to receive religious instruction and to attend religious worship. Why, then, is this prerogative of punishment, so eminently paternal, to be withheld from a paternal government? It seems to us, also, to be the height of absurdity to employ civil disabilities for the propagation of an opinion, and then to shrink from employing other punishments for the same purpose. For nothing can be clearer than that, if you punish at all, you ought to punish enough. The pain caused by punishment is pure unmixed evil, and never ought to be inflicted, except for the sake of some good. It is mere foolish cruelty to provide penalties which torment the criminal without preventing the crime. Now it is possible, by sanguinary persecution unrelentingly inflicted, to suppress opinions. In this way the Albigenses were put down. In this way the Lollards were put down. In this way the fair promise of the Reformation was blighted in Italy and Spain. But we may safely defy Mr. Gladstone to point out a single instance in which the system which he recommends has succeeded.

And why should he be so tender-hearted? What reason can he give for hanging a murderer, and suffering a heresiarch to escape without even a pecuniary mulct? Is the heresiarch a less pernicious member of society than the murderer? Is not the loss of one soul a greater evil than the extinction of many lives? And the number of murders committed by the most profligate bravo that ever let out his poniard to hire in Italy, or by the most savage buccaneer that ever prowled on the Windward Station, is small indeed, when compared with the number of souls which have been caught in the snares of one dexterous heresiarch. If, then, the heresiarch causes infinitely greater evils than the murderer, why is he not as proper an object of penal legislation as the murderer? We can give a reason, a reason, short, simple, decisive, and consistent. We do not extenuate the evil which the heresiarch produces; but we say that it is not evil of that sort against which it is the end of government to guard. But how Mr. Gladstone, who considers the evil which the heresiarch produces as evil of the sort against which it is the end of government to guard, can escape from the obvious consequence of his doctrine, we do not understand. The world is full of parallel cases. An orange-woman stops up the pavement with her wheel-barrow; and a policeman takes her into custody. A miser who has amassed a million suffers an old friend and benefactor to die in a work-house, and cannot be questioned before any tribunal for his baseness and ingratitude. Is this because legislators think the orange-woman's conduct worse than the miser's? Not at all. It is because the stopping up of the pathway is one of the evils against which it is the business of the public authorities to protect society, and heartlessness is not one of those evils. It would be the height of folly to say that the miser ought, indeed, to be punished, but that he ought to be punished less severely than the orange-woman.

The heretical Constantius persecutes Athanasius; and why not? Shall Cæsar punish the robber who has taken one purse, and spare the wretch who has taught millions to rob the Creator of his honour, and to bestow it on the creature? The orthodox Theodosius persecutes the Arians, and with equal reason. Shall an insult offered to the Cæsarean majesty be expiated by death; and shall there be no penalty for him who degrades to the rank of a creature the almighty, the infinite Creator? We have a short answer for both: "To Cæsar the things which are Cæsar's. Cæsar is appointed for the punishment of robbers and rebels. He is not appointed for the purpose of either propagating or exterminating the doctrine of the consubstantiality of the Father and the Son." "Not so," says Mr. Gladstone. "Cæsar is bound in conscience to propagate whatever he thinks to be the truth as to this question. Constantius is bound to establish the Arian worship throughout the empire, and to displace the bravest captains of his legions, and the ablest ministers of his treasury, if they hold the Nicene faith. Theodosius is equally bound to turn out every public servant whom his Arian predecessors have put in. But if Constantius lays on Athanasius a fine of a single *aureus*, if Theodosius imprisons an Arian presbyter for a week, this is most unjustifiable oppression." Our readers will be curious to know how this distinction is made out.

The reasons which Mr. Gladstone gives against persecution affecting life, limb, and property, may be divided into two classes; first, reasons which can be called reasons only by extreme courtesy, and which nothing but the most deplorable necessity would ever have induced a man of his abilities to use; and, secondly, reasons which are really reasons, and which have so much force that they not only completely prove his exception, but completely upset his general rule. His artillery on this occasion is composed of two sorts of pieces, pieces which will not go off at all, and pieces which go off with a vengeance, and recoil with most crushing effect upon himself.

"We, as fallible creatures," says Mr. Gladstone, "have no right, from any bare speculations of our own, to administer pains and penalties to our fellow-creatures, whether on social or religious grounds. We have the right to enforce the laws of the land by such pains and penalties, because it is expressly given by Him who has declared that the civil rulers are to bear the sword for the punishment of evil-doers, and for the encouragement of them that do well. And so, in things spiritual, had it pleased God to give to the Church or the State this power, to be permanently exercised over their members, or mankind at large, we should have the right to use it; but it does not appear to have been so received, and, consequently, it should not be exercised."

We should be sorry to think that the security of our lives and property from persecution rested on no better ground than this. Is not a teacher of heresy an evil-doer? Has not heresy been condemned in many countries, and in our own among them, by the laws of the land, which, as Mr. Gladstone says, it is justifiable to enforce by penal sanctions? If a heretic is not specially mentioned in the text to which Mr. Gladstone refers, neither is an assassin, a kidnapper, or a highwayman: and if the silence of the New Testament as to all interference of governments to stop the progress of heresy be a reason for not fining or imprisoning heretics, it is surely just as good a reason for not excluding them from office.

"God," says Mr. Gladstone, "has seen fit to authorize the employment of force in the one case and not in the other; for it was with regard to chastisement inflicted by the sword for an

insult offered to himself, that the Redeemer declared his kingdom
not to be of this world;—meaning, apparently in an especial
manner, that it should be otherwise than after this world's fashion,
in respect to the sanctions by which its laws should be maintained."

Now here Mr. Gladstone, quoting from memory, has fallen
into an error. The very remarkable words which he cites do not
appear to have had any reference to the wound inflicted by Peter
on Malchus. They were addressed to Pilate, in answer to the
question, "Art thou the King of the Jews?" We cannot help
saying that we are surprised that Mr. Gladstone should not have
more accurately verified a quotation on which, according to him,
principally depends the right of a hundred millions of his fellow-
subjects, idolaters, Mussulmans, Catholics, and dissenters, to their
property, their liberty, and their lives.

Mr. Gladstone's humane interpretations of Scripture are lam-
entably destitute of one recommendation, which he considers as
of the highest value: they are by no means in accordance with
the general precepts or practice of the Church, from the time
when the Christians became strong enough to persecute down to a
very recent period. A dogma favourable to toleration is certainly
not a dogma *quod semper, quod ubique, quod omnibus*. Bossuet
was able to say, we fear with too much truth, that on one point
all Christians had long been unanimous, the right of the civil
magistrate to propagate truth by the sword; that even heretics
had been orthodox as to this right, and that the Anabaptists and
Socinians were the first who called it in question. We will not
pretend to say what is the best explanation of the text under consideration; but we are sure that Mr. Gladstone's is the worst.
According to him, government ought to exclude dissenters from
office, but not to fine them, because Christ's kingdom is not of
this world. We do not see why the line may not be drawn at a
hundred other places as well as at that which he has chosen. We
do not see why Lord Clarendon, in recommending the act of 1664
against conventicles, might not have said, "It hath been thought
by some that this *classis* of men might with advantage be not
only imprisoned, but pilloried. But methinks, my Lords, we are
inhibited from the punishment of the pillory by that Scripture,
'My kingdom is not of this world.' " Archbishop Laud, when he
sate on Burton in the Star-Chamber, might have said, "I pronounce
for the pillory; and, indeed, I could wish that all such wretches
were delivered to the fire, but that our Lord hath said that his kingdom is not of this world." And Gardiner might have written to
the Sheriff of Oxfordshire: "See that execution be done without

fail on Master Ridley and Master Latimer, as you will answer the same to the Queen's grace at your peril. But if they shall desire to have some gunpowder for the shortening of their torment, I see not but you may grant it, as it is written, *Regnum meum non est de hoc mundo*; that is to say, My kingdom is not of this world."

But Mr. Gladstone has other arguments against persecution, arguments which are of so much weight, that they are decisive not only against persecution, but against his whole theory. "The government," he says, "is incompetent to exercise minute and constant supervision over religious opinion." And hence he infers, that "a government exceeds its province when it comes to adapt a scale of punishments to variations in religious opinion, according to their respective degrees of variation from the established creed. To decline affording countenance to sects is a single and simple rule. To punish their professors, according to their several errors, even were there no other objection, is one for which the state must assume functions wholly ecclesiastical, and for which it is not intrinsically fitted."

This is, in our opinion, quite true. But how does it agree with Mr. Gladstone's theory? What! The government incompetent to exercise even such a degree of supervision over religious opinion as is implied by the punishment of the most deadly heresy! The government incompetent to measure even the grossest deviations from the standard of truth! The government not intrinsically qualified to judge of the comparative enormity of any theological errors! The government so ignorant on these subjects that it is compelled to leave, not merely subtle heresies, discernible only by the eye of a Cyril or a Bucer, but Socinianism, Deism, Mahometanism, Idolatry, Atheism, unpunished! To whom does Mr. Gladstone assign the office of selecting a religion for the state, from among hundreds of religions, every one of which lays claim to truth? Even to this same government, which he now pronounces to be so unfit for theological investigations that it cannot venture to punish a man for worshipping a lump of stone with a score of heads and hands! We do not remember ever to have fallen in with a more extraordinary instance of inconsistency. When Mr. Gladstone wishes to prove that the government ought to establish and endow a religion, and to fence it with a test act, government is τὸ πᾶν in the moral world. Those who would confine it to secular ends take a low view of its nature. A religion must be attached to its agency; and this religion must be that of the conscience of the governor, or none. It is for the Governor to decide between

Papists and Protestants, Jansenists and Molinists, Arminians and Calvinists, Episcopalians and Presbyterians, Sabellians and Tritheists, Homoousians and Homoiousians, Nestorian sand Eutychians, Monothelites and Monophysites, Pædobaptists and Anabaptists. It is for him to rejudge the Acts of Nice and Rimini, of Ephesus and Chalcedon, of Constantinople and St. John Lateran, of Trent and Dort. It is for him to arbitrate between the Greek and the Latin procession, and to determine whether that mysterious *filioque* shall or shall not have a place in the national creed. When he has made up his mind, he is to tax the whole community in order to pay people to teach his opinion, whatever it may be. He is to rely on his own judgment, though it may be opposed to that of nine tenths of the society. He is to act on his own judgment, at the risk of exciting the most formidable discontents. He is to inflict, perhaps on a great majority of the population, what, whether Mr. Gladstone may choose to call it persecution or not, will always be felt as persecution by those who suffer it. He is, on account of differences often too slight for vulgar comprehension, to deprive the state of the services of the ablest men. He is to debase and enfeeble the community which he governs, from a nation into a sect. In our own country, for example, millions of Catholics, millions of Protestant Dissenters, are to be excluded from all power and honours. A great hostile fleet is on the sea; but Nelson is not to command in the Channel if in the mystery of the Trinity he confounds the persons. An invading army has landed in Kent; but the Duke of Wellington is not to be at the head of our forces if he divides the substance. And, after all this, Mr. Gladstone tells us, that it would be wrong to imprison a Jew, a Mussulman, or a Budhist, for a day; because really a government cannot understand these matters, and ought not to meddle with questions which belong to the Church. A singular theologian, indeed, this government! So learned that it is competent to exclude Grotius from office for being a Semi-Pelagian, so unlearned that it is incompetent to fine a Hindoo peasant a rupee for going on a pilgrimage to Juggernaut!

"To solicit and persuade one another," says Mr. Gladstone, "are privileges which belong to us all; and the wiser and better man is bound to advise the less wise and good: but he is not only not bound, he is not allowed, speaking generally, to coerce him. It is untrue, then, that the same considerations which bind a government to submit a religion to the free choice of the people would therefore justify their enforcing its adoption."

Granted. But it is true that all the same considerations which would justify a government in propagating a religion by means of civil disabilities would justify the propagating of that religion by penal laws. To solicit! Is it solicitation to tell a Catholic Duke, that he must abjure his religion or walk out of the House of Lords? To persuade! Is it persuasion to tell a barrister of distinguished eloquence and learning that he shall grow old in his stuff gown, while his pupils are seated above him in ermine, because he cannot digest the damnatory clauses of the Athanasian creed? Would Mr. Gladstone think that a religious system which he considers as false, Socinianism for example, was submitted to his free choice, if it were submitted in these terms. "If you obstinately adhere to the faith of the Nicene fathers, you shall not be burned in Smith-field; you shall not be sent to Dorchester gaol; you shall not even pay double land-tax. But you shall be shut out from all situations in which you might exercise your talents with honour to yourself and advantage to the country. The House of Commons, the bench of magistracy, are not for such as you. You shall see younger men, your inferiors in station and talents, rise to the highest dignities and attract the gaze of nations, while you are doomed to neglect and obscurity. If you have a son of the highest promise, a son such as other fathers would contemplate with delight, the development of his fine talents and of his generous ambition shall be a torture to you. You shall look on him as a being doomed to lead, as you have led, the abject life of a Roman or a Neapolitan in the midst of the great English people. All those high honours, so much more precious than the most costly gifts of despots, with which a free country decorates its illustrious citizens, shall be to him, as they have been to you, objects not of hope and virtuous emulation, but of hopeless, envious pining. Educate him, if you wish him to feel his degradation. Educate him, if you wish to stimulate his craving for what he never must enjoy. Educate him, if you would imitate the barbarity of that Celtic tyrant who fed his prisoners on salted food till they called eagerly for drink, and then let down an empty cup into the dungeon and left them to die of thirst." Is this to solicit, to persuade, to submit religion to the free choice of man? Would a fine of a thousand pounds, would imprisonment in Newgate for six months, under circumstances not disgraceful, give Mr. Gladstone the pain which he would feel, if he were to be told that he was to be dealt with in the way in which he would himself deal with more than one half of his countrymen?

We are not at all surprised to find such inconsistency even in a man of Mr. Gladstone's talents. The truth is, that every man is, to a great extent, the creature of the age. It is to no purpose that he resists the influence which the vast mass, in which he is but an atom, must exercise on him. He may try to be a man of the tenth century: but he cannot. Whether he will or no, he must be a man of the nineteenth century. He shares in the motion of the moral as well as in that of the physical world. He can no more be as intolerant as he would have been in the days of the Tudors than he can stand in the evening exactly where he stood in the morning. The globe goes round from west to east; and he must go round with it. When he says that he is where he was, he means only that he has moved at the same rate with all around him. When he says that he has gone a good way to the westward, he means only that he has not gone to the eastward quite so rapidly as his neighbours. Mr. Gladstone's book is, in this respect, a very gratifying performance. It is the measure of what a man can do to be left behind by the world. It is the strenuous effort of a very vigorous mind to keep as far in the rear of the general progress as possible. And yet, with the most intense exertion, Mr. Gladstone cannot help being, on some important points, greatly in advance of Locke himself: and, with whatever admiration he may regard Laud, it is well for him, we can tell him, that he did not write in the days of that zealous primate, who would certainly have refuted the expositions of Scripture which we have quoted by one of the keenest arguments that can be addressed to human ears.

This is not the only instance in which Mr. Gladstone has shrunk in a very remarkable manner from the consequences of his own theory. If there be in the whole world a state to which this theory is applicable, that state is the British Empire in India. Even we, who detest paternal governments in general, shall admit that the duties of the government of India are, to a considerable extent, paternal. There, the superiority of the governors to the governed in moral science is unquestionable. The conversion of the whole people to the worst form that Christianity ever wore in the darkest ages would be a most happy event. It is not necessary that a man should be a Christian to wish for the propagation of Christianity in India. It is sufficient that he should be an European not much below the ordinary European level of good sense and humanity. Compared with the importance of the interests at stake, all those Scotch and Irish questions which occupy so large a portion of Mr. Gladstone's book sink into insignificance. In no part of the world, since the days of Theodosius, has so large a heathen population been subject to a Christian government. In no part of the world is heathenism more cruel, more licentious, more fruitful of absurd rites and pernicious laws. Surely, if it be the duty of government to use its power and its revenue in order to bring seven millions of Irish Catholics over to the Protestant Church, it is *a fortiori* the duty of the government to use its power and its revenue in order to make seventy millions of idolaters Christians. If it be a sin to suffer John Howard or William Penn to hold any office in England, because they are not in communion with the Established Church, it must be a crying sin indeed to admit to high situations men who bow down, in temples covered with emblems of vice, to the hideous images of sensual or malevolent gods.

But no. Orthodoxy, it seems, is more shocked by the priests of Rome than by the priests of Kalee. The plain red-brick building, the Cave of Adullam, or Ebenezer Chapel, where uneducated men hear a half educated man talk of the Christian law of love and the Christian hope of glory, is unworthy of the indulgence which is reserved for the shrine where the Thug suspends a portion of the spoils of murdered travellers, and for the car which grinds its way through the bones of self-immolated pilgrims. "It would be," says Mr. Gladstone, "an absurd exaggeration to maintain it as the part of such a government as that of the British in India to bring home to the door of every subject at once the ministrations of a new and totally unknown religion." The government ought indeed to desire to propagate Christianity. But the extent to which they must do so must be "limited by the degree in which the people are found willing to receive it." He proposes no such limitation in the case of Ireland. He would give the Irish a Protestant Church whether they like it or not. "We believe," says he, "that that which we place before them is, whether they know it or not, calculated to be beneficial to them; and that, if they know it not now, they will know it when it is presented to them fairly. Shall we, then, purchase their applause at the expense of their substantial, nay, their spiritual interests?"

And why does Mr. Gladstone allow to the Hindoo a privilege which he denies to the Irishman? Why does he reserve his greatest liberality for the most monstrous errors? Why does he pay most respect to the opinion of the least enlightened people? Why does he withhold the right to exercise paternal authority from that one government which is fitter to exercise paternal authority than any government that ever existed in the world? We will give the reason in his own words.

"In British India," he says, "a small number of persons advanced to a higher grade of civilisation, exercise the powers of government over an immensely greater number of less cultivated persons, not by coercion, but under free stipulation with the governed. Now, the rights of a government, in circumstances thus peculiar, obviously depend neither upon the unrestricted theory of paternal principles, nor upon any primordial or fictitious contract of indefinite powers, but upon an express and known treaty, matter of positive agreement, not of natural ordinance."

Where Mr. Gladstone has seen this treaty we cannot guess; for, though he calls it a "known treaty," we will stake our credit that it is quite unknown both at Calcutta and Madras, both in Leadenhall Street and Cannon Row, that it is not to be found in any of the enormous folios of papers relating to India which fill the book-cases of members of Parliament, that it has utterly escaped the researches of all the historians of our Eastern empire, that, in the long and interesting debates of 1813 on the admission of missionaries to India, debates of which the most valuable part has been excellently preserved by the care of the speakers, no allusion to this important instrument is to be found. The truth is that this treaty is a nonentity. It is by coercion, it is by the sword, and not by free stipulation with the governed, that England rules India; nor is England bound by any contract whatever not to deal with Bengal as she deals with Ireland. She may set up a Bishop of Patna, and a Dean of Hoogley; she may grant away the public revenue for the maintenance of prebendaries of Benares and canons of Moorshedabad; she may divide the country into parishes, and place a rector with a stipend in every one of them; and all this without infringing any positive agreement. If there be such a treaty, Mr. Gladstone can have no difficulty in making known its date, its terms, and, above all, the precise extent of the territory within which we have sinfully bound ourselves to be guilty of practical atheism. The last point is of great importance. For, as the provinces of our Indian empire were acquired at different times, and in very different ways, no single treaty, indeed no ten treaties, will justify the system pursued by our government there.

The plain state of the case is this. No man in his senses would dream of applying Mr. Gladstone's theory to India, because, if so applied, it would inevitably destroy our empire, and, with our empire, the best chance of spreading Christianity among the natives. This Mr. Gladstone felt. In some way or other his theory was to be saved, and the monstrous consequences avoided.

Of intentional misrepresentation we are quite sure that he is incapable. But we cannot acquit him of that unconscious disingenuousness from which the most upright man, when strongly attached to an opinion, is seldom wholly free. We believe that he recoiled from the ruinous consequences which his system would produce, if tried in India; but that he did not like to say so, lest he should lay himself open to the charge of sacrificing principle to expediency, a word which is held in the utmost abhorrence by all his school. Accordingly, he caught at the notion of a treaty, a notion which must, we think, have originated in some rhetorical expression which he has imperfectly understood. There is one excellent way of avoiding the drawing of a false conclusion from a false *major*; and that is by having a false *minor*. Inaccurate history is an admirable corrective of unreasonable theory. And thus it is in the present case. A bad general rule is laid down, and obstinately maintained, wherever the consequences are not too monstrous for human bigotry. But when they become so horrible that even Christ Church shrinks, that even Oriel stands aghast, the rule is evaded by means of a fictitious contract. One imaginary obligation is set up against another. Mr. Gladstone first preaches to governments the duty of undertaking an enterprise just as rational as the Crusades, and then dispenses them from it on the ground of a treaty which is just as authentic as the donation of Constantine to Pope Sylvester. His system resembles nothing so much as a forged bond with a forged release indorsed on the back of it.

With more show of reason he rests the claims of the Scotch Church on a contract. He considers that contract, however, as most unjustifiable, and speaks of the setting up of the Kirk as a disgraceful blot on the reign of William the Third. Surely it would be amusing, if it were not melancholy, to see a man of virtue and abilities unsatisfied with the calamities which one Church, constituted on false principles, has brought upon the empire, and repining that Scotland is not in the same state with Ireland, that no Scottish agitator is raising rent and putting county members in and out, that no Presbyterian association is dividing supreme power with the government, that no meetings of precursors and repealers are covering the side of the Calton Hill, that twenty-five thousand troops are not required to maintain order on the north of the Tweed, that the anniversary of the Battle of Bothwell Bridge is not regularly celebrated by insult, riot, and murder. We could hardly find a stronger argument against Mr. Gladstone's system than that which Scotland furnishes. The policy which has been followed in that country has been directly opposed to the policy which he recommends. And the consequence is that Scotland, having been one of the rudest, one of the poorest, one of the most turbulent countries in Europe, has become one of the most highly civilised, one of the most flourishing, one of the most tranquil. The atrocities which were of common occurrence while an unpopular church was dominant are unknown. In spite of a mutual aversion as bitter as ever separated one people from another, the two kingdoms which compose our island have been indissolubly joined together. Of the ancient national feeling there remains just enough to be ornamental and useful; just enough to inspire the poet, and to kindle a generous and friendly emulation in the bosom of the soldier. But for all the ends of government the nations are one. And why are they so? The answer is simple. The nations are one for all the ends of government, because in their union the true ends of government alone were kept in sight. The nations are one, because the Churches are two.

Such is the union of England with Scotland, an union which resembles the union of the limbs of one healthful and vigorous body, all moved by one will, all cooperating for common ends. The system of Mr. Gladstone would have produced an union which can be compared only to that which is the subject of a wild Persian fable. King Zohak,—we tell the story as Mr. Southey tells it to us,—gave the devil leave to kiss his shoulders. Instantly two serpents sprang out, who, in the fury of hunger, attacked his head, and attempted to get at his brain. Zohak pulled them away, and tore them with his nails. But he found that they were inseparable parts of himself, and that what he was lacerating was his own flesh. Perhaps we might be able to find, if we looked round the world, some political union like this, some hideous monster of a state, cursed with one principle of sensation and two principles of volition, self-loathing and self-torturing, made up of parts which are driven by a frantic impulse to inflict mutual pain, yet are doomed to feel whatever they inflict, which are divided by an irreconcileable hatred, yet are blended in an indissoluble identity. Mr. Gladstone, from his tender concern for Zohak, is unsatisfied because the devil has as yet kissed only one shoulder, because there is not a snake mangling and mangled on the left to keep in countenance his brother on the right.

But we must proceed in our examination of his theory. Having, as he conceives, proved that it is the duty of every government to profess some religion or other, right or wrong, and to establish that religion, he then comes to the question what religion a government ought to prefer, and he decides this question in favour of the form of Christianity established in England. The Church of England is, according to him, the pure Catholic Church of Christ, which possesses the apostolical succession of ministers, and within whose pale is to be found that unity which is essential to truth. For her decisions he claims a degree of reverence far beyond what she has ever, in any of her formularies, claimed for herself; far beyond what the moderate school of Bossuet demands for the Pope; and scarcely short of what that school would ascribe to Pope and General Council together. To separate from her communion is schism. To reject her traditions or interpretations of Scripture is sinful presumption.

Mr. Gladstone pronounces the right of private judgment, as it is generally understood throughout Protestant Europe, to be a monstrous abuse. He declares himself favourable, indeed, to the exercise of private judgment, after a fashion of his own. We have, according to him, a right to judge all the doctrines of the Church of England to be sound, but not to judge any of them to be unsound. He has no objection, he assures us, to active enquiry into religious questions. On the contrary, he thinks such enquiry highly desirable, as long as it does not lead to diversity of opinion; which is much the same thing as if he were to recommend the use of fire that will not burn down houses, or of brandy that will not make men drunk. He conceives it to be perfectly possible for mankind to exercise their intellects vigorously and freely on theological subjects, and yet to come to exactly the same conclusions with each other and with the Church of England. And for this opinion he gives, as far as we have been able to discover, no reason whatever, except that every body who vigorously and freely exercises his understanding on Euclid's Theorems assents to them. "The activity of private judgment," he truly observes, "and the unity and strength of conviction in mathematics vary directly as each other." On this unquestionable fact he constructs a somewhat questionable argument. Every body who freely inquires agrees, he says, with Euclid. But the Church is as much in the right as Euclid. Why, then, should not every free inquirer agree with the Church? We could put many similar questions. Either the affirmative or the negative of the proposition that King Charles wrote the *Icon Basilike* is as true as that two sides of a triangle are greater than the third side. Why, then, do Dr. Wordsworth and Mr. Hallam agree in thinking two sides of a triangle greater than the third side, and yet differ about the genuineness of the *Icon Basilike*? The state of the exact sciences proves, says Mr. Gladstone, that, as respects religion, "the association of these two ideas, activity of enquiry, and variety of conclusion, is a fallacious one." We might just as well turn the argument the other way, and infer from the variety of religious opinions that there must necessarily be hostile mathematical sects, some affirming, and some denying, that the square of the hypothenuse is equal to the squares of the sides. But we do not think either the one analogy or the other of the smallest value. Our way of ascertaining the tendency of free enquiry is simply to open our eyes and look at the world in which we live; and there we see that free enquiry on mathematical subjects produces unity, and that free enquiry on moral subjects produces discrepancy. There would undoubtedly be less discrepancy if enquirers were more diligent and candid. But discrepancy there will be among the most diligent and candid, as long as the constitution of the human mind, and the nature of moral evidence, continue unchanged. That we have not freedom and unity together is a very sad thing; and so it is that we have not wings. But we are just as likely to see the one defect removed as the other. It is not only in religion that this discrepancy is found. It is the same with all matters which depend on moral evidence, with judicial questions, for example, and with political questions. All the judges will work a sum in the rule of three on the same principle, and bring out the same conclusion. But it does not follow that, however honest and laborious they may be, they will all be of one mind on the Douglas case. So it is vain to hope that there may be a free constitution under which every representative will be unanimously elected, and every law unanimously passed; and it would be ridiculous for a statesman to stand wondering and bemoaning himself, because people who agree in thinking that two and two make four cannot agree about the new poor law, or the administration of Canada.

There are two intelligible and consistent courses which may be followed with respect to the exercise of private judgment; the course of the Romanist, who interdicts private judgment because of its inevitable inconveniences; and the course of the Protestant, who permits private judgment in spite of its inevitable inconveniences. Both are more reasonable than Mr. Gladstone, who would have private judgment without its inevitable inconveniences. The Romanist produces repose by means of stupefaction. The Protestant encourages activity, though he knows that, where there is much activity, there will be some aberration. Mr. Gladstone wishes for the unity of the fifteenth century with the active and searching spirit of the sixteenth. He might as well wish to be in two places at once.

When Mr. Gladstone says that we "actually require discrepancy of opinion—require and demand error, falsehood, blindness, and plume ourselves on such discrepancy as attesting a freedom which is only valuable when used for unity in the truth," he expresses himself with more energy than precision. Nobody loves discrepancy for the sake of discrepancy. But a person who conscientiously believes that free enquiry is, on the whole, beneficial to the interests of truth, and that, from the imperfection of the human faculties, wherever there is much free enquiry there will be some discrepancy, may, without impropriety, consider such discrepancy, though in itself an evil, as a sign of good. That there are ten thousand thieves in London is a very melancholy fact. But, looked at in one point of view, it is a reason for exultation. For what other city could maintain ten thousand thieves? What must be the mass of wealth, where the fragments gleaned by lawless pilfering rise to so large an amount? St. Kilda would not support a single pickpocket. The quantity of theft is, to a certain extent, an index of the quantity of useful industry and judicious speculation. And just as we may, from the great number of rogues in a town, infer that much honest gain is made there; so may we often, from the quantity of error in a community, draw a cheering inference as to the degree in which the public mind is turned to those enquiries which alone can lead to rational convictions of truth.

Mr. Gladstone seems to imagine that most Protestants think it possible for the same doctrine to be at once true and false; or that they think it immaterial whether, on a religious question, a man comes to a true or a false conclusion. If there be any Protestants who hold notions so absurd, we abandon them to his censure.

The Protestant doctrine touching the right of private judgment, that doctrine, which is the common foundation of the Anglican, the Lutheran, and the Calvinistic Churches, that doctrine by which every sect of dissenters vindicates its separation, we conceive not to be this, that opposite opinions may both be true; nor this, that truth and falsehood are both equally good; nor yet this, that all speculative error is necessarily innocent; but this, that there is on the face of the earth no visible body to whose decrees men are bound to submit their private judgment on points of faith.

Is there always such a visible body? Was there such a visible body in the year 1500? If not, why are we to believe that there is such a body in the year 1839? If there was such a body in the year 1500, what was it? Was it the Church of Rome? And how can the Church of England be orthodox now, if the Church of Rome was orthodox then?

"In England," says Mr. Gladstone, "the case was widely different from that of the Continent. Her reformation did not destroy, but successfully maintained, the unity and succession of the Church in her apostolical ministry. We have, therefore, still among us the ordained hereditary witnesses of the truth, conveying it to us through an unbroken series from our Lord Jesus Christ and his apostles. This is to us the ordinary voice of authority; of authority equally reasonable and equally true, whether we will hear, or whether we will forbear."

Mr. Gladstone's reasoning is not so clear as might be desired. We have among us, he says, ordained hereditary witnesses of the truth, and their voice is to us the voice of authority. Undoubtedly, if they are witnesses of the truth, their voice is the voice of authority. But this is little more than saying that the truth is the truth. Nor is truth more true because it comes in an unbroken series from the apostles. The Nicene faith is not more true in the mouth of the Archbishop of Canterbury, than in that of a Moderator of the General Assembly. If our respect for the authority of the Church is to be only consequent upon our conviction of the truth of her doctrines, we come at once to that monstrous abuse, the Protestant exercise of private judgment. But if Mr. Gladstone means that we ought to believe that the Church of England speaks the truth, because she has the apostolical succession, we greatly doubt whether such a doctrine can be maintained. In the first place, what proof have we of the fact? We have, indeed, heard it said that Providence would certainly have interfered to preserve the apostolical succession in the true Church. But this is an argument fitted for understandings of a different kind from Mr. Gladstone's. He will hardly tell us that the Church of England is the true Church because she has the succession; and that she has the succession because she is the true Church.

What evidence, then, have we for the fact of the apostolical succession? And here we may easily defend the truth against Oxford with the same arguments with which, in old times, the truth was defended by Oxford against Rome. In this stage of our combat with Mr. Gladstone, we need few weapons except those which we find in the well furnished and well ordered armoury of Chillingworth.

The transmission of orders from the Apostles to an English clergyman of the present day must have been through a very great number of intermediate persons. Now, it is probable that no clergyman in the Church of England can trace up his spiritual genealogy from bishop to bishop, so far back as the time of the Conquest. There remain many centuries during which the history of the transmission of his orders is buried in utter darkness. And whether he be a priest by succession from the Apostles depends on the question, whether, during that long period, some thousands of events took place, any one of which may, without any gross improbability, be supposed not to have taken place. We have no; a tittle of evidence for any one of these events. We do not even know the names or countries of the men to whom it is taken for granted that these events happened. We do not know whether the spiritual ancestors of any one of our contemporaries were Spanish or Armenian, Arian or Orthodox. In the utter absence of all particular evidence, we are surely entitled to require that there should be very strong evidence indeed that the strictest regularity was observed in every generation, and that episcopal functions were exercised by none who were not bishops by succession from the Apostles. But we have no such evidence. In the first place, we have not full and accurate information touching the polity of the Church during the century which followed the persecution of Nero. That, during this period, the overseers of all the little Christian societies scattered through the Roman empire held their spiritual authority by virtue of holy orders derived from the Apostles, cannot be proved by contemporary testimony, or by any testimony which can be regarded as decisive. The question, whether the primitive ecclesiastical constitution bore a greater resemblance to the Anglican or to the Calvinistic model has been fiercely disputed. It is a question on which men of eminent parts, learning, and piety, have differed, and do to this day differ very widely. It is a question on which at least a full half of the ability and erudition of Protestant Europe has, ever since the Reformation, been opposed to the Anglican pretensions. Mr. Gladstone himself, we are persuaded, would have the candour to allow that, if no evidence were admitted but that which is furnished by the genuine Christian literature of the first two centuries, judgment would not go in favour of prelacy. And if he looked at the subject as calmly as he would look at a controversy respecting the Roman *Comitia* or the Anglo-Saxon Wittenagemote, he would probably think that the absence of contemporary evidence during so long a period was a defect which later attestations, however numerous, could but very imperfectly supply. It is surely impolitic to rest the doctrines of the English Church on a historical theory which, to ninety-nine Protestants out of a hundred, would seem much more questionable than any of those doctrines. Nor is this all. Extreme obscurity overhangs the history of the middle ages; and the facts which are discernible through that obscurity prove that the Church was exceedingly ill regulated. We read of sees of the highest dignity openly sold, transferred backwards and forwards by popular tumult, bestowed sometimes by a profligate woman on her paramour, sometimes by a warlike baron on a kinsman still a stripling. We read of bishops of ten years old, of bishops of five years old, of many popes who were mere boys, and who rivalled the frantic dissoluteness of Caligula, nay, of a female pope. And though this last story, once believed throughout all Europe, has been disproved by the strict researches of modern criticism, the most discerning of those who reject it have admitted that it is not intrinsically improbable. In our own island, it was the complaint of Alfred that not a single priest, south of the Thames, and very few on the north, could read either Latin or English. And this illiterate clergy exercised their ministry amidst a rude and half heathen population, in which Danish pirates, unchristened, or christened by the hundred on a field of battle, were mingled with a Saxon peasantry scarcely better instructed in religion. The state of Ireland was still worse. "Tota illa per universam Hiberniam dissolutio ecclesiasticæ disciplinæ, illa ubique pro consuetudine Christiana sæva subintroducta barbaries," are the expressions of St. Bernard. We are, therefore, at a loss to conceive how any clergyman can feel confident that his orders have come down correctly. Whether he be really a successor of the Apostles depends on an immense number of such contingencies as these; whether, under King Ethelwolf, a stupid priest might not, while baptizing several scores of Danish prisoners who had just made their option between the font and the gallows, inadvertently omit to perform the rite on one of these graceless proselytes; whether, in the seventh century, an impostor, who had never received consecration, might not have passed himself off as a bishop on a rude tribe of Scots; whether a lad of twelve did really, by a ceremony huddled over when he was too drunk to know what he was about, convey the episcopal character to a lad of ten.

Since the first century, not less, in all probability, than a hundred thousand persons have exercised the functions of bishops. That many of these have not been bishops by apostolical succession is quite certain. Hooker admits that deviations from the general rule have been frequent, and, with a boldness worthy of his high and statesman-like intellect, pronounces them to have been often justifiable. "There may be," says he, "sometimes very just and sufficient reason to allow ordination made without a bishop. Where the Church must needs have some ordained, and neither hath nor can have possibly a bishop to ordain, in case of such necessity the ordinary institution of God hath given *oftentimes*, and may give place. And therefore we are not simply without exception to urge a lineal descent of power from the Apostles by continued succession of bishops in every effectual ordination." There can be little doubt, we think, that the succession, if it ever existed, has often been interrupted in ways much less respectable. For example, let us suppose, and we are sure that no well informed person will think the supposition by any means improbable, that, in the third century, a man of no principle and some parts, who has, in the course of a roving and discreditable life, been a catechumen at Antioch, and has there become familiar with Christian usages and doctrines, afterwards rambles to Marseilles, where he finds a Christian society, rich, liberal, and simple-hearted. He pretends to be a Christian, attracts notice by his abilities and affected zeal, and is raised to the episcopal dignity without having ever been baptized. That such an event might happen, nay, was very likely to happen, cannot well be disputed by any one who has read the Life of Peregrinus. The very virtues, indeed, which distinguished the early Christians, seem to have laid them open to those arts which deceived

> "Uriel, though Regent of the Sun, and held
> The sharpest-sighted spirit of all in Heaven."

Now, this unbaptized impostor is evidently no successor of the Apostles. He is not even a Christian; and all orders derived through such a pretended bishop are altogether invalid. Do we know enough of the state of the world and of the Church in the third century to be able to say with confidence that there were not at that time twenty such pretended bishops? Every such case makes a break in the apostolical succession.

Now, suppose that a break, such as Hooker admits to have been both common and justifiable, or such as we have supposed to be produced by hypocrisy and cupidity, were found in the chain which connected the Apostles with any of the missionaries who first spread Christianity in the wilder parts of Europe, who can say how extensive the effect of this single break may be? Suppose that St. Patrick, for example, if ever there was such a man, or Theodore of Tarsus, who is said to have consecrated in the seventh century the first bishops of many English sees, had not the true apostolical orders, is it not conceivable that such a circumstance may affect the orders of many clergymen now living? Even if it were possible, which it assuredly is not, to prove that the Church had the apostolical orders in the third century, it would be impossible to prove that those orders were not in the twelfth century so far lost that no ecclesiastic could be certain of the legitimate descent of his own spiritual character. And if this were so, no subsequent precautions could repair the evil.

Chillingworth states the conclusion at which he had arrived on this subject in these very remarkable words: "That of ten thousand probables no one should be false; that of ten thousand requisites, whereof any one may fail, not one should be wanting, this to me is extremely improbable, and even cousin-german to impossible. So that the assurance hereof is like a machine composed of an innumerable multitude of pieces, of which it is strangely unlikely but some will be out of order; and yet, if any one be so, the whole fabric falls of necessity to the ground: and he that shall put them together, and maturely consider all the possible ways of lapsing and nullifying a priesthood in the Church of Rome, will be very inclinable to think that it is a hundred to one, that among a hundred seeming priests, there is not one true one; nay, that it is not a thing very improbable that, amongst those many millions which make up the Romish hierarchy, there are not twenty true." We do not pretend to know to what precise extent the canonists of Oxford agree with those of Rome as to the circumstances which nullify orders. We will not, therefore, go so far as Chillingworth. We only say that we see no satisfactory proof of the fact, that the Church of England possesses the apostolical succession. And, after all, if Mr. Gladstone could prove the apostolical succession, what would the apostolical succession prove? He says that "we have among us the ordained hereditary witnesses of the truth, conveying it to us through an *unbroken* series from our Lord Jesus Christ and his Apostles." Is this the fact? Is there any doubt that the orders of the Church of England are generally derived from the Church of Rome? Does not the Church of England declare, does not Mr. Gladstone himself admit, that the Church of Rome teaches much error and condemns much truth? And is it not quite clear, that as far as the doctrines of the Church of England differ from those of the Church of Rome, so far the Church of England conveys the truth through a broken series?

That the founders, lay and clerical, of the Church of England, corrected all that required correction in the doctrines of the

Church of Rome, and nothing more, may be quite true. But we never can admit the circumstance that the Church of England possesses the apostolical succession as a proof that she is thus perfect. No stream can rise higher than its fountain. The succession of ministers in the Church of England, derived as it is through the Church of Rome, can never prove more for the Church of England than it proves for the Church of Rome. But this is not all. The Arian Churches which once predominated in the kingdoms of the Ostrogoths, the Visigoths, the Burgundians, the Vandals, and the Lombards, were all episcopal churches, and all had a fairer claim than that of England to the apostolical succession, as being much nearer to the apostolical times. In the East, the Greek Church, which is at variance on points of faith with all the Western Churches, has an equal claim to this succession. The Nestorian, the Eutychian, the Jacobite Churches, all heretical, all condemned by councils, of which even Protestant divines have generally spoken with respect, had an equal claim to the apostolical succession. Now if, of teachers having apostolical orders, a vast majority have taught much error, if a large proportion have taught deadly heresy, if, on the other hand, as Mr. Gladstone himself admits, churches not having apostolical orders, that of Scotland for example, have been nearer to the standard of orthodoxy than the majority of teachers who have had apostolical orders, how can he possibly call upon us to submit our private judgment to the authority of a Church, on the ground that she has these orders?

Mr. Gladstone dwells much on the importance of unity in doctrine. Unity, he tells us, is essential to truth. And this is most unquestionable. But when he goes on to tell us that this unity is the characteristic of the Church of England, that she is one in body and in spirit, we are compelled to differ from him widely. The apostolical succession she may or may not have. But unity she most certainly has not, and never has had. It is matter of perfect notoriety, that her formularies are framed in such a manner as to admit to her highest offices men who differ from each other more widely than a very high Churchman differs from a Catholic, or a very low Churchman from a Presbyterian; and that the general leaning of the Church, with respect to some important questions, has been sometimes one way and sometimes another. Take, for example, the questions agitated between the Calvinists and the Arminians. Do we find in the Church of England, with respect to those questions, that unity which is essential to truth? Was it ever found in the Church? Is it not certain that, at the end of the sixteenth century, the rulers of the Church held doctrines as Calvinistic as ever were held by any Cameronian, and not only held them, but persecuted every body who did not hold them? And is it not equally certain, that the rulers of the Church have, in very recent times, considered Calvinism as a disqualification for high preferment, if not for holy orders? Look at the questions which Archbishop Whitgift propounded to Barret, questions framed in the very spirit of William Huntington, S.S.[1] And then look at the eighty-seven questions which Bishop Marsh, within our own memory, propounded to candidates for ordination. We should be loth to say that either of these celebrated prelates had intruded himself into a Church whose doctrines he abhorred, and that he deserved to be stripped of his gown. Yet it is quite certain, that one or other of them must have been very greatly in error. John Wesley again, and Cowper's friend, John Newton, were both presbyters of this Church. Both were men of talents. Both we believe to have been men of rigid integrity, men who would not have subscribed a Confession of Faith which they disbelieved for the richest bishopric in the empire. Yet, on the subject of predestination, Newton was strongly attached to doctrines which Wesley designated as "blasphemy, which might make the ears of a Christian to tingle." Indeed, it will not be disputed that the clergy of the Established Church are divided as to these questions, and that her formularies are not found practically to exclude even scrupulously honest men of both sides from her altars. It is notorious that some of her most distinguished rulers think this latitude a good thing, and would be sorry to see it restricted in favour of either opinion. And herein we most cordially agree with them. But what becomes of the unity of the Church, and of that truth to which unity is essential? Mr. Gladstone tells us that the *Regium Donum* was given originally to orthodox Presbyterian ministers, but that part of it is now received by their heterodox successors. "This," he says, "serves to illustrate the difficulty in which governments entangle themselves, when they covenant with arbitrary systems of opinion, and not with the Church alone. The opinion passes away, but the gift remains." But is it not clear, that if a strong Supralapsarian had, under Whitgift's primacy, left a large estate at the disposal of the bishops for ecclesiastical purposes, in the hope that the rulers of the Church would abide by Whitgift's theology, he would really have been giving his substance

---

[1] One question was, whether God had from eternity reprobated certain; and why. The answer which contented the Archbishop was, "Affirmative, et quia voluit."

for the support of doctrines which he detested? The opinion would have passed away, and the gift would have remained.

This is only a single instance. What wide differences of opinion respecting the operation of the sacraments are held by bishops, doctors, presbyters of the Church of England, all men who have conscientiously declared their assent to her articles, all men who are, according to Mr. Gladstone, ordained hereditary witnesses of the truth, all men whose voices make up, what he tells us, is the voice of true and reasonable authority! Here, again, the Church has not unity; and as unity is the essential condition of truth, the Church has not the truth.

Nay, take the very question which we are discussing with Mr. Gladstone. To what extent does the Church of England allow of the right of private judgment? What degree of authority does she claim for herself in virtue of the apostolical succession of her ministers? Mr. Gladstone, a very able and a very honest man, takes a view of this matter widely differing from the view taken by others whom he will admit to be as able and as honest as himself. People who altogether dissent from him on this subject eat the bread of the Church, preach in her pulpits, dispense her sacraments, confer her orders, and carry on that apostolical succession, the nature and importance of which, according to him, they do not comprehend. Is this unity? Is this truth?

It will be observed that we are not putting cases of dishonest men who, for the sake of lucre, falsely pretend to believe in the doctrines of an establishment. We are putting cases of men as upright as ever lived, who, differing on theological questions of the highest importance, and avowing that difference, are yet priests and prelates of the same Church. We therefore say that, on some points which Mr. Gladstone himself thinks of vital importance, the Church has either not spoken at all, or, what is for all practical purposes the same thing, has not spoken in language to be understood even by honest and sagacious divines. The religion of the Church of England is so far from exhibiting that unity of doctrine which Mr. Gladstone represents as her distinguishing glory that it is, in fact, a bundle of religious systems without number. It comprises the religious system of Bishop Tomline, and the religious system of John Newton, and all the religious systems which lie between them. It comprises the religious system of Mr. Newman, and the religious system of the Archbishop of Dublin, and all the religious systems which lie between them. All these different opinions are held, avowed, preached, printed, within the pale of the Church, by men of unquestioned integrity and understanding.

Do we make this diversity a topic of reproach to the Church of England? Far from it. We would oppose with all our power every attempt to narrow her basis. Would to God that, a hundred and fifty years ago, a good king and a good primate had possessed the power as well as the will to widen it! It was a noble enterprise, worthy of William and of Tillotson. But what becomes of all Mr. Gladstone's eloquent exhortations to unity? Is it not mere mockery to attach so much importance to unity in form and name, where there is so little in substance, to shudder at the thought of two churches in alliance with one state, and to endure with patience the spectacle of a hundred sects battling within one church? And is it not clear that Mr. Gladstone is bound, on all his own principles, to abandon the defence of a church in which unity is not found? Is it not clear that he is bound to divide the House of Commons against every grant of money which may be proposed for the clergy of the Established Church in the colonies? He objects to the vote for Maynooth, because it is monstrous to pay one man to teach truth, and another to denounce that truth as falsehood. But it is a mere chance whether any sum which he votes for the English Church in any colony will go to the maintenance of an Arminian or a Calvinist, of a man like Mr. Froude, or of a man like Dr. Arnold. It is a mere chance, therefore, whether it will go to support a teacher of truth, or one who will denounce that truth as falsehood.

This argument seems to us at once to dispose of all that part of Mr. Gladstone's book which respects grants of public money to dissenting bodies. All such grants he condemns. But surely, if it be wrong to give the money of the public for the support of those who teach any false doctrine, it is wrong to give that money for the support of the ministers of the Established Church. For it is quite certain that, whether Calvin or Arminius be in the right, whether Laud or Burnet be in the right, a great deal of false doctrine is taught by the ministers of the Established Church. If it be said that the points on which the clergy of the Church of England differ ought to be passed over, for the sake of the many important points on which they agree, why may not the same argument be maintained with respect to other sects which hold in common with the Church of England the fundamental doctrines of Christianity? The principle, that a ruler is bound in conscience to propagate religious truth, and to propagate no religious doctrine which is untrue, is abandoned as soon as it is admitted that a gentleman of Mr. Gladstone's opinions may lawfully vote the public money to a chaplain whose opinions are those of Paley or of Simeon. The whole question then becomes one of degree. Of course no individual and no government can justifiably propagate error for the sake of propagating error. But both individuals and governments must work with such machinery as they have; and no human machinery is to be found which will impart truth without some alloy of error. We have shown irrefragably, as we think, that the Church of England does not afford such a machinery. The question then is this; with what degree of imperfection in our machinery must we put up? And to this question we do not see how any general answer can be given. We must be guided by circumstances. It would, for example, be very criminal in a Protestant to contribute to the sending of Jesuit missionaries among a Protestant population. But we do not conceive that a Protestant would be to blame for giving assistance to Jesuit missionaries who might be engaged in converting the Siamese to Christianity. That tares are mixed with the wheat is matter of regret; but it is better that wheat and tares should grow together than that the promise of the year should be blighted.

Mr. Gladstone, we see with deep regret, censures the British Government in India for distributing a small sum among the Catholic priests who minister to the spiritual wants of our Irish soldiers. Now, let us put a case to him. A Protestant gentleman is attended by a Catholic servant, in a part of the country where there is no Catholic congregation within many miles. The servant is taken ill, and is given over. He desires, in great trouble of mind, to receive the last sacraments of his Church. His master sends off a messenger in a chaise and four, with orders to bring a confessor from a town at a considerable distance. Here a Protestant lays out money for the purpose of causing religious instruction and consolation to be given by a Catholic priest. Has he committed a sin? Has he not acted like a good master and a good Christian? Would Mr. Gladstone accuse him of "laxity of religious principle," of "confounding truth with falsehood," of "considering the support of religion as a boon to an individual, not as a homage to truth?" But how if this servant had, for the sake of his master, undertaken a journey which removed him from the place where he might easily have obtained religious attendance? How if his death were occasioned by a wound received in defending his master? Should we not then say that the master had only fulfilled a sacred obligation of duty? Now, Mr. Gladstone himself owns that "nobody can think that the personality of the state is more stringent, or entails stronger obligations, than that of the individual." How then stands the case of the Indian Government? Here is a poor fellow, enlisted in Clare or Kerry, sent over fifteen thousand miles of sea, quartered in a depressing and pestilential climate. He fights for the Government; he conquers for it; he is wounded; he is laid on his pallet, withering away with fever, under that terrible sun, without a friend near him. He pines for the consolations of that religion which, neglected perhaps in the season of health and vigour, now comes back to his mind, associated with all the overpowering recollections of his earlier days, and of the home which he is never to see again. And because the state for which he dies sends a priest of his own faith to stand at his bedside, and to tell him, in language which at once commands his love and confidence, of the common Father, of the common Redeemer, of the common hope of immortality, because the state for which he dies does not abandon him in his last moments to the care of heathen attendants, or employ a chaplain of a different creed to vex his departing spirit with a controversy about the Council of Trent, Mr. Gladstone finds that India presents "a melancholy picture," and that there is "a large allowance of false principle" in the system pursued there. Most earnestly do we hope that our remarks may induce Mr. Gladstone to reconsider this part of his work, and may prevent him from expressing in that high assembly, in which he must always be heard with attention, opinions so unworthy of his character.

We have now said almost all that we think it necessary to say respecting Mr. Gladstone's theory. And perhaps it would be safest for us to stop here. It is much easier to pull down than to build up. Yet, that we may give Mr. Gladstone his revenge, we will state concisely our own views respecting the alliance of Church and State.

We set out in company with Warburton, and remain with him pretty sociably till we come to his contract; a contract which Mr. Gladstone very properly designates as a fiction. We consider the primary end of government as a purely temporal end, the protection of the persons and property of men.

We think that government, like every other contrivance of human wisdom, from the highest to the lowest, is likely to answer its main end best when it is constructed with a single view to that end. Mr. Gladstone, who loves Plato, will not quarrel with us for illustrating our proposition, after Plato's fashion, from the most familiar objects. Take cutlery, for example. A blade which is designed both to shave and to carve will certainly not shave so well as a razor, or carve so well as a carving-knife. An academy of painting, which should also be a bank, would, in all probability, exhibit very bad pictures and discount very bad bills. A gas company, which should also be an infant school society, would, we apprehend, light the streets ill, and teach the children ill. On this principle, we think that government should be organized solely with a view to its main end; and that no part of its efficiency for that end should be sacrificed in order to promote any other end however excellent.

But does it follow from hence that governments ought never to pursue any end other than their main end? In no wise. Though it is desirable that every institution should have a main end, and should be so formed as to be in the highest degree efficient for that main end; yet if, without any sacrifice of its efficiency for that end, it can pursue any other good end, it ought to do so. Thus, the end for which a hospital is built is the relief of the sick, not the beautifying of the street. To sacrifice the health of the sick to splendour of architectural effect, to place the building in a bad air only that it may present a more commanding front to a great public place, to make the wards hotter or cooler than they ought to be, in order that the columns and windows of the exterior may please the passers-by, would be monstrous. But if, without any sacrifice of the chief object, the hospital can be made an ornament to the metropolis, it would be absurd not to make it so.

In the same manner, if a government can, without any sacrifice of its main end, promote any other good work, it ought to do so. The encouragement of the fine arts, for example, is by no means the main end of government; and it would be absurd, in constituting a government, to bestow a thought on the question, whether it would be a government likely to train Raphaels and Domenichinos. But it by no means follows that it is improper for a government to form a national gallery of pictures. The same may be said of patronage bestowed on learned men, of the publication of archives, of the collecting of libraries, menageries, plants, fossils, antiques, of journeys and voyages for purposes of geographical discovery or astronomical observation. It is not for these ends that government is constituted. But it may well happen that a government may have at its command resources which will enable it, without any injury to its main end, to pursue these collateral ends far more effectually than any individual or any voluntary association could do. If so, government ought to pursue these collateral ends.

It is still more evidently the duty of government to promote, always in subordination to its main end, every thing which is useful as a means for the attaining of that main end. The improvement of steam navigation, for example, is by no means a primary object of government. But as steam vessels are useful for the purpose of national defence, and for the purpose of facilitating intercourse between distant provinces, and of thereby consolidating the force of the empire, it may be the bounden duty of government to encourage ingenious men to perfect an invention which so directly tends to make the state more efficient for its great primary end.

Now, on both these grounds, the instruction of the people may with propriety engage the care of the government. That the people should be well educated is in itself a good thing; and the state ought therefore to promote this object, if it can do so without any sacrifice of its primary object. The' education of the people, conducted on those principles of morality which are common to all the forms of Christianity, is highly valuable as a means of promoting the main object for which government exists, and is on this ground well deserving the attention of rulers. We will not at present go into the general question of education; but will confine our remarks to the subject which is more immediately before us, namely, the religious instruction of the people.

We may illustrate our view of the policy which governments ought to pursue with respect to religious instruction, by recurring to the analogy of a hospital. Religious instruction is not the main end for which a hospital is built; and to introduce into a hospital any regulations prejudicial to the health of the patients, on the plea of promoting their spiritual improvement, to send a ranting preacher to a man who has just been ordered by the physician to lie quiet and try to get a little sleep, to impose a strict observance of Lent on a convalescent who has been advised to eat heartily of nourishing food, to direct, as the bigoted Pius the Fifth actually did, that no medical assistance should be given to any person who declined spiritual attendance, would be the most extravagant folly. Yet it by no means follows that it would not be right to have a chaplain to attend the sick, and to pay such a chaplain out of the hospital funds. Whether it will be proper to have such a chaplain at all, and of what religious persuasion such a chaplain ought to be, must depend on circumstances. There may be a town in which it would be impossible to set up a good hospital without the help of people of different opinions: and religious parties may run so high that, though people of different opinions are willing to contribute for the relief of the sick, they will not concur in the choice of any one chaplain. The high Churchmen insist that, if there is a paid chaplain, he shall be a high Churchman. The Evangelicals stickle for an Evangelical. Here it would evidently be absurd and cruel to let an useful and humane design, about which all are agreed, fall to the ground, because all cannot agree about something else. The governors must either appoint two chaplains, and pay them both; or they must appoint none; and every one of them must, in his individual capacity, do what he can for the purpose of providing the sick with such religious instruction and consolation as will, in his opinion, be most useful to them.

We should say the same of government. Government is not an institution for the propagation of religion, any more than St. George's Hospital is an institution for the propagation of religion: and the most absurd and pernicious consequences would follow, if Government should pursue, as its primary end, that which can never be more than its secondary end, though intrinsically more important than its primary end. But a government which considers the religious instruction of the people as a secondary end, and follows out that principle faithfully, will, we think, be likely to do much good and little harm.

We will rapidly run over some of the consequences to which this principle leads, and point out how it solves some problems which, on Mr. Gladstone's hypothesis, admit of no satisfactory solution.

All persecution directed against the persons or property of men is, on our principle, obviously indefensible. For the protection of the persons and property of men being the primary end of government, and religious instruction only a secondary end, to secure the people from heresy by making their lives, their limbs, or their estates insecure, would be to sacrifice the primary end to the secondary end. It would be as absurd as it would be in the governors of a hospital to direct that the wounds of all Arian and Socinian patients should be dressed in such a way as to make them fester.

Again, on our principles, all civil disabilities on account of religious opinions are indefensible. For all such disabilities make government less efficient for its main end: they limit its choice of able men for the administration and defence of the state; they alienate from it the hearts of the sufferers; they deprive it of a part of its effective strength in all contests with foreign nations. Such a course is as absurd as it would be in the governors of an hospital to reject an able surgeon because he is an universal Restitutionist, and to send a bungler to operate because he is perfectly orthodox.

Again, on our principles, no government ought to press on the people religious instruction, however sound, in such a manner as to excite among them discontents dangerous to public order. For here again government would sacrifice its primary end to an end intrinsically indeed of the highest importance, but still only a secondary end of government, as government. This rule at once disposes of the difficulty about India, a difficulty of which Mr. Gladstone can get rid only by putting in an imaginary discharge in order to set aside an imaginary obligation. There is assuredly no country where it is more desirable that Christianity should be propagated. But there is no country in which the government is so completely disqualified for the task. By using our power in order to make proselytes, we should produce the dissolution of society, and bring utter ruin on all those interests for the protection of which government exists. Here the secondary end is, at present, inconsistent with the primary end, and must therefore be abandoned. Christian instruction given by individuals and voluntary societies may do much good. Given by the Government it would do unmixed harm. At the same time, we quite agree with Mr. Gladstone in thinking that the English authorities in India ought not to participate in any idolatrous rite; and indeed we are fully satisfied that all such participation is not only unchristian, but also unwise and most undignified.

Supposing the circumstances of a country to be such, that the government may with propriety, on our principles, give religious instruction to a people; we have next to inquire, what religion shall be taught. Bishop Warburton answers, the religion of the majority. And we so far agree with him, that we can scarcely conceive any circumstances in which it would be proper to establish, as the one exclusive religion of the state, the religion of the minority. Such a preference could hardly be given without exciting most serious discontent, and endangering those interests, the protection of which is the first object of government. But we never can admit that a ruler can be justified in helping to spread a system of opinions solely because that system is pleasing to the majority. On the other hand, we cannot agree with Mr. Gladstone, who would of course answer that the only religion which a ruler ought to propagate is the religion of his own conscience. In truth, this is an impossibility. And, as we have shown, Mr. Gladstone himself, whenever he supports a grant of money to the Church of England, is really assisting to propagate, not the precise religion of his own conscience, but some one or more, he knows not how many or which, of the innumerable religions which lie between the confines of Pelagianism and those of Antinomianism, and between the confines of Popery and those of Presbyterianism. In our opinion, that religious instruction which the ruler ought, in his public capacity, to patronise, is the instruction from which he, in his conscience, believes that the people will learn most good with the smallest mixture of evil. And thus it is not necessarily his own religion that he will select. He will, of course, believe that his own religion is unmixedly good. But the question which he has to consider is, not how much good his religion contains, but how much good the people will learn, if instruction is given them in that religion. He may prefer the doctrines and government of the Church of England to those of the Church of Scotland. But if he knows that a Scotch congregation will listen with deep attention and respect while an Erskine or a Chalmers sets before them the fundamental doctrines of Christianity, and that a glimpse of a surplice or a single line of a liturgy would be the signal for hooting and riot, and would probably bring stools and brick-bats about the ears of the minister, he acts wisely if he conveys religious knowledge to the Scotch rather by means of that imperfect Church, as he may think it, from which they will learn much, than by means of that perfect Church from which they will learn nothing. The only end of teaching is, that men may learn; and it is idle to talk of the duty of teaching truth in ways which only cause men to cling more firmly to falsehood.

On these principles we conceive that a statesman, who might be far indeed from regarding the Church of England with the reverence which Mr. Gladstone feels for her, might yet firmly oppose all attempts to destroy her. Such a statesman may be too well acquainted with her origin to look upon her with superstitious awe. He may know that she sprang from a compromise huddled up between the eager zeal of reformers and the selfishness of greedy, ambitious, and time-serving politicians. He may find in every page of her annals ample cause for censure. He may feel that he could not, with ease to his conscience, subscribe all her articles. He may regret that all the attempts which have been made to open her gates to large classes of non-conformists should have failed. Her episcopal polity he may consider as of purely human institution. He cannot defend her on the ground that she possesses the apostolical succession; for he does not know whether that succession may not be altogether a fable. He cannot defend her on the ground of her unity: for he knows that her frontier sects are much more remote from each other, than one frontier is from the Church of Rome, or the other from the Church of Geneva. But he may think that she teaches more truth with less alloy of error than would be taught by those who, if she were swept away, would occupy the vacant space. He may think that the effect produced by her beautiful services and by her pulpits on the national mind, is, on the whole, highly beneficial. He may think that her civilising influence is usefully felt in remote districts. He may think that, if she were destroyed, a large portion of those who now compose her congregations would neglect all religious duties; and that a still larger portion would fall under the influence of spiritual mountebanks, hungry for gain, or drunk with fanaticism. While he would with pleasure admit that all the qualities of Christian pastors are to be found in large measure within the existing body of Dissenting ministers, he would perhaps be inclined to think that the standard of intellectual and moral character among that exemplary class of men may have been raised to its present high point and maintained there by the indirect influence of the Establishment. And he may be by no means satisfied that, if the Church were at once swept away, the place of our Sumners and Whateleys would be supplied by Doddridges and Halls. He may think that the advantages which we have described are obtained, or might, if the existing system were slightly modified, be obtained, without any sacrifice of the paramount objects which all governments ought to have chiefly in view. Nay, he may be of opinion that an institution, so deeply fixed in the hearts and minds of millions, could not be subverted without loosening and shaking all the foundations of civil society. With at least equal ease he would find reasons for supporting the Church of Scotland. Nor would he be under the necessity of resorting to any contract to justify the connection of two religious establishments with one government. He would think scruples on that head frivolous in any person who is zealous for a Church, of which both Dr. Herbert Marsh and Dr. Daniel Wilson are bishops. Indeed he would gladly follow out his principles much further. He would have been willing to vote in 1825 for Lord Francis Egerton's resolution, that it is expedient to give a public maintenance to the Catholic clergy of Ireland; and he would deeply regret that no such measure was adopted in 1829.

In this way, we conceive, a statesman might, on our principles, satisfy himself that it would be in the highest degree inexpedient to abolish the Church, either of England or of Scotland.

But if there were, in any part of the world, a national church regarded as heretical by four-fifths of the nation committed to its care, a church established and maintained by the sword, a church producing twice as many riots as conversions, a church which, though possessing great wealth and power, and though long backed by persecuting laws, had, in the course of many generations, been found unable to propagate its doctrines, and barely able to maintain its ground, a church so odious, that fraud and violence, when used against its clear rights of property, were generally regarded as fair play, a church, whose ministers were preaching to desolate walls, and with difficulty obtaining their lawful subsistence by the help of bayonets, such a church, on our principles, could not, we must own, be defended. We should say that the state which allied itself with such a church postponed the primary end of government to the secondary; and that the consequences had been such as any sagacious observer would have predicted. Neither the primary nor the secondary end is attained. The temporal and spiritual interests of the people suffer alike. The minds of men, instead of being drawn to the church, are alienated from the state. The magistrate, after sacrificing order, peace, union, all the interests which it is his first duty to protect, for the purpose of promoting pure religion, is forced, after the experience of centuries, to admit that he has really been promoting error. The sounder the doctrines of such a church, the more absurd and noxious the superstition by which those doctrines are opposed, the stronger are the arguments against the policy which has deprived a good cause of its natural advantages. Those who preach to rulers the duty of employing power to propagate truth would do well to remember that falsehood, though no match for truth alone, has often been found more than a match for truth and power together.

A statesman, judging on our principles, would pronounce without hesitation that a church, such as we have last described, never ought to have been set up. Further than this we will not venture to speak for him. He would doubtless remember that the world is full of institutions which, though they never ought to have been set up, yet, having been set up, ought not to be rudely pulled down; and that it is often wise in practice to be content with the mitigation of an abuse which, looking at it in the abstract, we might feel impatient to destroy.

We have done; and nothing remains but that we part from Mr. Gladstone with the courtesy of antagonists who bear no malice. We dissent from his opinions; but we admire his talents; we respect his integrity and benevolence; and we hope that he will not suffer political avocations so entirely to engross him, as to leave him no leisure for literature and philosophy.

SPEECHES

AND

THE MINUTE ON INDIAN EDUCATION

MACAULAY'S collected speeches first appeared in an unauthorised and inaccurate edition published in 1853 by Henry Vizetelly in two volumes, which were also issued simultaneously in New York. This was quite legal; Hansard had given his licence and most of the speeches had already been printed in newspapers, but Macaulay pronounced it "a gross injury to me and a gross fraud on the public," and hastened to bring out his own: *Speeches of the Right Honorable T. B. Macaulay, M.P. Corrected by Himself*, which was published in one volume by Longman in 1854 and is the text used here.

The Minute on Indian Education follows the text of the Cambridge University Library copy of *Macaulay's Minutes on Education in India . . . now first collected from Records in the Department of Public Instruction*, Calcutta, 1862. This is an extremely rare book of which there is no copy in the British Museum, and the Minute has so far been generally available only in Sir George Otto Trevelyan's *The Competition Wallah*, 1864, and in the present editor's selection of the Speeches in the World's Classics, 1935, from which the editorial notes are here reprinted by kind permission of the Oxford University Press.

All Macaulay's own notes have been retained.

PARLIAMENTARY REFORM. I

A SPEECH DELIVERED IN THE HOUSE OF COMMONS ON THE 2ND OF
MARCH, 1831

On Tuesday, the first of March, 1831, Lord John Russell moved the
House of Commons for leave to bring in a Bill to amend the representation of the people in England and Wales. The discussion occupied
seven nights. At length, on the morning of Thursday, the tenth of
March, the motion was carried without a division. The following Speech
was made on the second night of the debate.

It is a circumstance, Sir, of happy augury for the motion before
the House, that almost all those who have opposed it have declared
themselves hostile on principle to Parliamentary Reform.   Two
Members, I think, have confessed that, though they disapprove of
the plan now submitted to us, they are forced to admit the necessity
of a change in the Representative system. Yet even those gentlemen
have used, as far as I have observed, no arguments which would not
apply as strongly to the most moderate change as to that which has
been proposed by His Majesty's Government. I say, Sir, that I
consider this as a circumstance of happy augury. For what I feared
was, not the opposition of those who are averse to all Reform, but
the disunion of reformers. I knew that, during three months, every
reformer had been employed in conjecturing what the plan of the
Government would be. I knew that every reformer had imagined
in his own mind a scheme differing doubtless in some points from
that which my noble friend, the Paymaster of the Forces, has developed. I felt therefore great apprehension that one person would be
dissatisfied with one part of the bill, that another person would
be dissatisfied with another part, and that thus our whole strength
would be wasted in internal dissensions. That apprehension is now
at an end. I have seen with delight the perfect concord which pre-
vails among all who deserve the name of reformers in this House;
and I trust that I may consider it as an omen of the concord which

will prevail among reformers throughout the country. I will not, Sir, at present express any opinion as to the details of the bill; but, having during the last twenty-four hours given the most diligent consideration to its general principles, I have no hesitation in pronouncing it a wise, noble, and comprehensive measure, skilfully framed for the healing of great distempers, for the securing at once of the public liberties and of the public repose, and for the reconciling and knitting together of all the orders of the State.

The honorable Baronet who has just sate down[1] has told us, that the Ministers have attempted to unite two inconsistent principles in one abortive measure. Those were his very words. He thinks, if I understand him rightly, that we ought either to leave the representative system such as it is, or to make it perfectly symmetrical. I think, Sir, that the Ministers would have acted unwisely if they had taken either course. Their principle is plain, rational, and consistent. It is this, to admit the middle class to a large and direct share in the representation, without any violent shock to the institutions of our country. I understand those cheers: but surely the gentlemen who utter them will allow that the change which will be made in our institutions by this bill is far less violent than that which, according to the honorable Baronet, ought to be made if we make any Reform at all. I praise the Ministers for not attempting, at the present time, to make the representation uniform. I praise them for not effacing the old distinction between the towns and the counties, and for not assigning Members to districts, according to the American practice, by the Rule of Three. The Government has, in my opinion, done all that was necessary for the removing of a great practical evil, and no more than was necessary.

I consider this, Sir, as a practical question. I rest my opinion on no general theory of government. I distrust all general theories of government. I will not positively say, that there is any form of polity which may not, in some conceivable circumstances, be the best possible. I believe that there are societies in which every man may safely be admitted to vote. Gentlemen may cheer, but such is my opinion. I say, Sir, that there are countries in which the condition of the labouring classes is such that they may safely be intrusted with the right of electing Members of the Legislature. If the labourers of England were in that state in which I, from my soul, wish to see them, if employment were always plentiful, wages always high, food always cheap, if a large family were considered not as an encumbrance but as a blessing, the principal objections to Universal Suffrage would, I think, be removed. Universal

[1] Sir John Walsh.

Suffrage exists in the United States without producing any very frightful consequences; and I do not believe, that the people of those States, or of any part of the world, are in any good quality naturally superior to our own countrymen. But, unhappily, the labouring classes in England, and in all old countries, are occasionally in a state of great distress. Some of the causes of this distress are, I fear, beyond the control of the Government. We know what effect distress produces, even on people more intelligent than the great body of the labouring classes can possibly be. We know that it makes even wise men irritable, unreasonable, credulous, eager for immediate relief, heedless of remote consequences. There is no quackery in medicine, religion, or politics, which may not impose even on a powerful mind, when that mind has been disordered by pain or fear. It is therefore no reflection on the poorer class of Englishmen, who are not, and who cannot in the nature of things be, highly educated, to say that distress produces on them its natural effects, those effects which it would produce on the Americans, or on any other people, that it blinds their judgment, that it inflames their passions, that it makes them prone to believe those who flatter them, and to distrust those who would serve them. For the sake, therefore, of the whole society, for the sake of the labouring classes themselves, I hold it to be clearly expedient that, in a country like this, the right of suffrage should depend on a pecuniary qualification.

But, Sir, every argument which would induce me to oppose Universal Suffrage, induces me to support the plan which is now before us. I am opposed to Universal Suffrage, because I think that it would produce a destructive revolution. I support this plan, because I am sure that it is our best security against a revolution. The noble Paymaster of the Forces hinted, delicately indeed and remotely, at this subject. He spoke of the danger of disappointing the expectations of the nation; and for this he was charged with threatening the House. Sir, in the year 1817, the late Lord Londonderry proposed a suspension of the Habeas Corpus Act. On that occasion he told the House that, unless the measures which he recommended were adopted, the public peace could not be preserved. Was he accused of threatening the House? Again, in the year 1819, he proposed the laws known by the name of the Six Acts. He then told the House that, unless the executive power were reinforced, all the institutions of the country would be overturned by popular violence. Was he then accused of threatening the House? Will any gentleman say that it is parliamentary and decorous to urge the danger arising from popular discontent as an argument for severity; but that it is unparliamentary and indecorous to urge that same danger as an argument for conciliation? I, Sir, do entertain great apprehension for the fate of my country. I do in my conscience believe that, unless the plan proposed, or some similar plan, be speedily adopted, great and terrible calamities will befal us. Entertaining this opinion, I think myself bound to state it, not as a threat, but as a reason. I support this bill because it will improve our institutions; but I support it also because it tends to preserve them. That we may exclude those whom it is necessary to exclude, we must admit those whom it may be safe to admit. At present we oppose the schemes of revolutionists with only one half, with only one quarter of our proper force. We say, and we say justly, that it is not by mere numbers, but by property and intelligence, that the nation ought to be governed. Yet, saying this, we exclude from all share in the government great masses of property and intelligence, great numbers of those who are most interested in preserving tranquillity, and who know best how to preserve it. We do more. We drive over to the side of revolution those whom we shut out from power. Is this a time when the cause of law and order can spare one of its natural allies?

My noble friend, the Paymaster of the Forces, happily described the effect which some parts of our representative system would produce on the mind of a foreigner, who had heard much of our freedom and greatness. If, Sir, I wished to make such a foreigner clearly understand what I consider as the great defects of our system, I would conduct him through that immense city which lies to the north of Great Russell Street and Oxford Street, a city superior in size and in population to the capitals of many mighty kingdoms; and probably superior in opulence, intelligence, and general respectability, to any city in the world. I would conduct him through that interminable succession of streets and squares, all consisting of well built and well furnished houses. I would make him observe the brilliancy of the shops, and the crowd of well appointed equipages. I would show him that magnificent circle of palaces which surrounds the Regent's Park. I would tell him, that the rental of this district was far greater than that of the whole kingdom of Scotland, at the time of the Union. And then I would tell him, that this was an unrepresented district. It is needless to give any more instances. It is needless to speak of Manchester, Birmingham, Leeds, Sheffield, with no representation, or of Edinburgh and Glasgow with a mock representation. If a property tax were now imposed on the principle that no person who

had less than a hundred and fifty pounds a year should contribute,
I should not be surprised to find that one half in number and
value of the contributors had no votes at all; and it would, beyond
all doubt, be found that one fiftieth part in number and value of
the contributors had a larger share of the representation than the
other forty nine fiftieths. This is not government by property.
It is government by certain detached portions and fragments of
property, selected from the rest, and preferred to the rest, on no
rational principle whatever.

To say that such a system is ancient is no defence. My honorable
friend, the Member for the University of Oxford,[1] challenges us to
show, that the Constitution was ever better than it is. Sir, we are
legislators, not antiquaries. The question for us is, not whether
the Constitution was better formerly, but whether we can make it
better now. In fact, however, the system was not in ancient times
by any means so absurd as it is in our age. One noble Lord[2] has
to-night told us that the town of Aldborough, which he represents,
was not larger in the time of Edward the First than it is at present.
The line of its walls, he assures us, may still be traced. It is now
built up to that line. He argues, therefore, that as the founders of
our representative institutions gave Members to Aldborough when
it was as small as it now is, those who would disfranchise it on
account of its smallness have no right to say that they are recurring
to the original principle of our representative institutions. But
does the noble Lord remember the change which has taken place
in the country during the last five centuries? Does he remember
how much England has grown in population, while Aldborough
has been standing still? Does he consider, that in the time of
Edward the First the kingdom did not contain two millions of
inhabitants? It now contains nearly fourteen millions. A hamlet
of the present day would have been a town of some importance
in the time of our early Parliaments. Aldborough may be absolutely as considerable a place as ever. But compared with the
kingdom, it is much less considerable, by the noble Lord's own
showing, than when it first elected burgesses. My honorable
friend, the Member for the University of Oxford, has collected
numerous instances of the tyranny which the kings and nobles
anciently exercised, both over this House and over the electors.
It is not strange that, in times when nothing was held sacred, the
rights of the people, and of the representatives of the people,
should not have been held sacred. The proceedings which my
honorable friend has mentioned, no more prove that, by the

[1] Sir Robert Harry Inglis.   [2] Lord Stormont.

ancient constitution of the realm, this House ought to be a tool of the king and of the aristocracy, than the Benevolences and the Shipmoney prove their own legality, or than those unjustifiable arrests, which took place long after the ratification of the great Charter, and even after the Petition of Right, prove that the subject was not anciently entitled to his personal liberty. We talk of the wisdom of our ancestors: and in one respect at least they were wiser than we. They legislated for their own times. They looked at the England which was before them. They did not think it necessary to give twice as many Members to York as they gave to London, because York had been the capital of Britain in the time of Constantius Chlorus; and they would have been amazed indeed if they had foreseen, that a city of more than a hundred thousand inhabitants would be left without Representatives in the nineteenth century, merely because it stood on ground which, in the thirteenth century, had been occupied by a few huts. They framed a representative system, which, though not without defects and irregularities, was well adapted to the state of England in their time. But a great revolution took place. The character of the old corporations changed. New forms of property came into existence. New portions of society rose into importance. There were in our rural districts rich cultivators, who were not freeholders. There were in our capital rich traders, who were not liverymen. Towns shrank into villages. Villages swelled into cities larger than the London of the Plantagenets. Unhappily, while the natural growth of society went on, the artificial polity continued unchanged. The ancient form of the representation remained; and precisely because the form remained, the spirit departed. Then came that pressure almost to bursting, the new wine in the old bottles, the new society under the old institutions. It is now time for us to pay a decent, a rational, a manly reverence to our ancestors, not by superstitiously adhering to what they, in other circumstances, did, but by doing what they, in our circumstances, would have done. All history is full of revolutions, produced by causes similar to those which are now operating in England. A portion of the community which had been of no account expands and becomes strong. It demands a place in the system, suited, not to its former weakness, but to its present power. If this is granted, all is well. If this is refused, then comes the struggle between the young energy of one class and the ancient privileges of another. Such was the struggle between the Plebeians and the Patricians of Rome. Such was the struggle of the Italian allies for admission to the full rights of Roman citizens. Such was the struggle of our North American colonies against the mother country. Such was the struggle which the Third Estate of France maintained against the aristocracy of birth. Such was the struggle which the Roman Catholics of Ireland maintained against the aristocracy of creed. Such is the struggle which the free people of colour in Jamaica are now maintaining against the aristocracy of skin. Such, finally, is the struggle which the middle classes in England are maintaining against an aristocracy of mere locality, against an aristocracy the principle of which is to invest a hundred drunken potwallopers in one place, or the owner of a ruined hovel in another, with powers which are withheld from cities renowned to the furthest ends of the earth, for the marvels of their wealth and of their industry.

But these great cities, says my honorable friend, the Member for the University of Oxford, are virtually, though not directly, represented. Are not the wishes of Manchester, he asks, as much consulted as those of any town which sends Members to Parliament? Now, Sir, I do not understand how a power which is salutary when exercised virtually can be noxious when exercised directly. If the wishes of Manchester have as much weight with us as they would have under a system which should give Representation to Manchester, how can there be any danger in giving Representatives to Manchester? A virtual Representative is, I presume, a man who acts as a direct Representative would act: for surely it would be absurd to say that a man virtually represents the people of Manchester, who is in the habit of saying No, when a man directly representing the people of Manchester would say Aye. The utmost that can be expected from virtual Representation is that it may be as good as direct Representation. If so, why not grant direct Representation to places which, as every body allows, ought, by some process or other, to be represented?

If it be said that there is an evil in change as change, I answer that there is also an evil in discontent as discontent. This, indeed, is the strongest part of our case. It is said that the system works well. I deny it. I deny that a system works well, which the people regard with aversion. We may say here, that it is a good system and a perfect system. But if any man were to say so to any six hundred and fifty-eight respectable farmers or shopkeepers, chosen by lot in any part of England, he would be hooted down, and laughed to scorn. Are these the feelings with which any part of the government ought to be regarded? Above all, are these the feelings with which the popular branch of the legislature ought to be regarded? It is almost as essential to the utility of a House of Commons, that it should possess the confidence of the people, as that it should deserve that confidence. Unfortunately, that which is in theory the popular part of our government, is in practice the unpopular part. Who wishes to dethrone the King? Who wishes to turn the Lords out of their House? Here and there a crazy radical, whom the boys in the street point at as he walks along. Who wishes to alter the constitution of this House? The whole people. It is natural that it should be so. The House of Commons is, in the language of Mr. Burke, a check, not on the people, but for the people. While that check is efficient, there is no reason to fear that the King or the nobles will oppress the people. But if that check requires checking, how is it to be checked? If the salt shall lose its savour, wherewith shall we season it? The distrust with which the nation regards this House may be unjust. But what then? Can you remove that distrust? That it exists cannot be denied. That it is an evil cannot be denied. That it is an increasing evil cannot be denied. One gentleman tells us that it has been produced by the late events in France and Belgium; another, that it is the effect of seditious works which have lately been published. If this feeling be of origin so recent, I have read history to little purpose. Sir, this alarming discontent is not the growth of a day or of a year. If there be any symptoms by which it is possible to distinguish the chronic diseases of the body politic from its passing inflammations, all those symptoms exist in the present case. The taint has been gradually becoming more extensive and more malignant, through the whole lifetime of two generations. We have tried anodynes. We have tried cruel operations. What are we to try now? Who flatters himself that he can turn this feeling back? Does there remain any argument which escaped the comprehensive intellect of Mr. Burke, or the subtlety of Mr. Windham? Does there remain any species of coercion which was not tried by Mr. Pitt and by Lord Londonderry? We have had laws. We have had blood. New treasons have been created. The Press has been shackled. The Habeas Corpus Act has been suspended. Public meetings have been prohibited. The event has proved that these expedients were mere palliatives. You are at the end of your palliatives. The evil remains. It is more formidable than ever. What is to be done?

Under such circumstances, a great plan of reconciliation, pre-pared by the Ministers of the Crown, has been brought before us in a manner which gives additional lustre to a noble name, inseparably associated during two centuries with the dearest liberties of the English people. I will not say, that this plan is in all its details precisely such as I might wish it to be; but it is founded on a great and a sound principle. It takes away a vast power from a few. It distributes that power through the great mass of the middle order. Every man, therefore, who thinks as I think is bound to stand firmly by Ministers who are resolved to stand or fall with this measure. Were I one of them, I would sooner, infinitely sooner, fall with such a measure than stand by any other means that ever supported a Cabinet.

My honorable friend, the Member for the University of Oxford, tells us, that if we pass this law, England will soon be a republic. The reformed House of Commons will, according to him, before it has sate ten years, depose the King, and expel the Lords from their House. Sir, if my honorable friend could prove this, he would have succeeded in bringing an argument for democracy, infinitely stronger than any that is to be found in the works of Paine. My honorable friend's proposition is in fact this; that our monarchical and aristocratical institutions have no hold on the public mind of England; that these institutions are regarded with aversion by a decided majority of the middle class. This, Sir, I say, is plainly deducible from his proposition; for he tells us that the Representatives of the middle class will inevitably abolish royalty and nobility within ten years: and there is surely no reason to think that the Representatives of the middle class will be more inclined to a democratic revolution than their constituents. Now, Sir, if I were convinced that the great body of the middle class in England look with aversion on monarchy and aristocracy, I should be forced, much against my will, to come to this conclusion, that monarchical and aristocratical institutions are unsuited to my country. Monarchy and aristocracy, valuable and useful as I think them, are still valuable and useful as means, and not as ends. The end of government is the happiness of the people: and I do not conceive that, in a country like this, the happiness of the people can be promoted by a form of government in which the middle classes place no confidence, and which exists only because the middle classes have no organ by which to make their sentiments known. But, Sir, I am fully convinced that the middle classes sincerely wish to uphold the Royal prerogatives and the constitutional rights of the Peers. What facts does my honorable friend produce in support of his opinion? One fact only; and that a fact which has absolutely nothing to do with the question. The effect of this Reform, he tells us, would be to make the House of Commons allpowerful. It was allpowerful once before, in the beginning of 1649. Then it cut off the head of the King, and abolished the House of Peers. Therefore, if it again has the supreme power, it will act in the same manner. Now, Sir, it was not the House of Commons that cut off the head of Charles the First; nor was the House of Commons then allpowerful. It had been greatly reduced in numbers by successive expulsions. It was under the absolute dominion of the army. A majority of the House was willing to take the terms offered by the King. The soldiers turned out the majority; and the minority, not a sixth part of the whole House, passed those votes of which my honorable friend speaks, votes of which the middle classes disapproved then, and of which they disapprove still.

My honorable friend, and almost all the gentlemen who have taken the same side with him in this Debate, have dwelt much on the utility of close and rotten boroughs. It is by means of such boroughs, they tell us, that the ablest men have been introduced into Parliament. It is true that many distinguished persons have represented places of this description. But, Sir, we must judge of a form of government by its general tendency, not by happy accidents. Every form of government has its happy accidents. Despotism has its happy accidents. Yet we are not disposed to abolish all constitutional checks, to place an absolute master over us, and to take our chance whether he may be a Caligula or a Marcus Aurelius. In whatever way the House of Commons may be chosen, some able men will be chosen in that way who would not be chosen in any other way. If there were a law that the hundred tallest men in England should be Members of Parliament, there would probably be some able men among those who would come into the House by virtue of this law. If the hundred persons whose names stand first in the alphabetical list of the Court Guide were made Members of Parliament, there would probably be able men among them. We read in ancient history, that a very able king was elected by the neighing of his horse: but we shall scarcely, I think, adopt this mode of election. In one of the most celebrated republics of antiquity, Athens, Senators and Magistrates were chosen by lot; and sometimes the lot fell fortunately. Once, for example, Socrates was in office. A cruel and unjust proposition was made by a demagogue. Socrates resisted it at the hazard of his own life. There is no event in Grecian history more interesting than that memorable resistance. Yet who would have officers appointed by lot, because the accident of the lot may have given to a great and good man a power which he would probably never have attained in any other way? We must judge, as I said, by the general tendency of a system. No person can doubt that a House of Commons, chosen freely by the middle classes, will contain many very able men. I do not say, that precisely the same able men who would find their way into the present House of Commons will find their way into the reformed House: but that is not the question. No particular man is necessary to the State. We may depend on it that, if we provide the country with popular institutions, those institutions will provide it with great men.

There is another objection, which, I think, was first raised by the honorable and learned Member for Newport.[1] He tells us that the elective franchise is property; that to take it away from a man who has not been judicially convicted of malpractices is robbery; that no crime is proved against the voters in the close boroughs; that no crime is even imputed to them in the preamble of the bill; and that therefore to disfranchise them without compensation would be an act of revolutionary tyranny. The honorable and learned gentleman has compared the conduct of the present Ministers to that of those odious tools of power, who, towards the close of the reign of Charles the Second, seized the charters of the Whig Corporations. Now, there was another precedent, which I wonder that he did not recollect, both because it is much more nearly in point than that to which he referred, and because my noble friend, the Paymaster of the Forces, had previously alluded to it. If the elective franchise is property, if to disfranchise voters without a crime proved, or a compensation given, be robbery, was there ever such an act of robbery as the disfranchising of the Irish forty shilling freeholders? Was any pecuniary compensation given to them? Is it declared in the preamble of the bill which took away their franchise, that they had been convicted of any offence? Was any judicial inquiry instituted into their conduct? Were they even accused of any crime? Or if you say that it was a crime in the electors of Clare to vote for the honorable and learned gentleman[2] who now represents the county of Waterford, was a Protestant freeholder in Louth to be punished for the crime of a Catholic freeholder in Clare? If the principle of the honorable and learned Member for Newport be sound, the franchise of the Irish peasant was property. That franchise the Ministers under whom the honorable and learned Member held office did not scruple to take away. Will he accuse those Ministers of robbery? If not, how can he bring such an accusation against their successors?

Every gentleman, I think, who has spoken from the other side of the House, has alluded to the opinions which some of His Majesty's Ministers formerly entertained on the subject of Reform.

[1] Mr. Horace Twiss.   [2] [Daniel O'Connell.]

It would be officious in me, Sir, to undertake the defence of gentlemen who are so well able to defend themselves. I will only say that, in my opinion, the country will not think worse either of their capacity or of their patriotism, because they have shown that they can profit by experience, because they have learned to see the folly of delaying inevitable changes. There are others who ought to have learned the same lesson. I say, Sir, that there are those who, I should have thought, must have had enough to last them all their lives of that humiliation which follows obstinate and boastful resistance to changes rendered necessary by the progress of society, and by the development of the human mind. Is it possible that those persons can wish again to occupy a position which can neither be defended nor surrendered with honour? I well remember, Sir, a certain evening in the month of May, 1827. I had not then the honour of a seat in this House; but I was an attentive observer of its proceedings. The right honorable Baronet opposite,[1] of whom personally I desire to speak with that high respect which I feel for his talents and his character, but of whose public conduct I must speak with the sincerity required by my public duty, was then, as he is now, out of office. He had just resigned the seals of the Home Department, because he conceived that the recent ministerial arrangements had been too favourable to the Catholic claims. He rose to ask whether it was the intention of the new Cabinet to repeal the Test and Corporation Acts, and to reform the Parliament. He bound up, I well remember, those two questions together; and he declared that, if the Ministers should either attempt to repeal the Test and Corporation Acts, or bring forward a measure of Parliamentary Reform, he should think it his duty to oppose them to the utmost. Since that declaration was made four years have elapsed; and what is now the state of the three questions which then chiefly agitated the minds of men? What is become of the Test and Corporation Acts? They are repealed. By whom? By the right honorable Baronet. What has become of the Catholic disabilities? They are removed. By whom? By the right honorable Baronet. The question of Parliamentary Reform is still behind. But signs, of which it is impossible to misconceive the import, do most clearly indicate that, unless that question also be speedily settled, property, and order, and all the institutions of this great monarchy, will be exposed to fearful peril. Is it possible that gentlemen long versed in high political affairs cannot read these signs? Is it possible that they can really believe that the Representative system of England, such as it

[1] Sir Robert Peel.

now is, will last till the year 1860? If not, for what would they have us wait? Would they have us wait merely that we may show to all the world how little we have profited by our own recent experience? Would they have us wait, that we may once again hit the exact point where we can neither refuse with authority, nor concede with grace? Would they have us wait, that the numbers of the discontented party may become larger, its demands higher, its feelings more acrimonious, its organisation more complete? Would they have us wait till the whole tragicomedy of 1827 has been acted over again; till they have been brought into office by a cry of "No Reform," to be reformers, as they were once before brought into office by a cry of "No Popery," to be emancipators? Have they obliterated from their minds—gladly, perhaps, would some among them obliterate from their minds—the transactions of that year? And have they forgotten all the transactions of the succeeding year? Have they forgotten how the spirit of liberty in Ireland, debarred from its natural outlet, found a vent by forbidden passages? Have they forgotten how we were forced to indulge the Catholics in all the licence of rebels, merely because we chose to withhold from them the liberties of subjects? Do they wait for associations more formidable than that of the Corn Exchange, for contributions larger than the Rent, for agitators more violent than those who, three years ago, divided with the King and the Parliament the sovereignty of Ireland? Do they wait for that last and most dreadful paroxysm of popular rage, for that last and most cruel test of military fidelity? Let them wait, if their past experience shall induce them to think that any high honor or any exquisite pleasure is to be obtained by a policy like this. Let them wait, if this strange and fearful infatuation be indeed upon them, that they should not see with their eyes, or hear with their ears, or understand with their heart. But let us know our interest and our duty better. Turn where we may, within, around, the voice of great events is proclaiming to us, Reform, that you may preserve. Now, therefore, while every thing at home and abroad forebodes ruin to those who persist in a hopeless struggle against the spirit of the age, now, while the crash of the proudest throne of the continent is still resounding in our ears, now, while the roof of a British palace affords an ignominious shelter to the exiled heir of forty kings, now, while we see on every side ancient institutions subverted, and great societies dissolved, now, while the heart of England is still sound, now, while old feelings and old associations retain a power and a charm which may too soon pass away, now, in this your accepted time, now, in this your day of salvation, take counsel, not of prejudice, not of party spirit, not of the ignominious pride of a fatal consistency, but of history, of reason, of the ages which are past, of the signs of this most portentous time. Pronounce in a manner worthy of the expectation with which this great debate has been anticipated, and of the long remembrance which it will leave behind. Renew the youth of the State. Save property, divided against itself. Save the multitude, endangered by its own ungovernable passions. Save the aristocracy, endangered by its own unpopular power. Save the greatest, and fairest, and most highly civilised community that ever existed, from calamities which may in a few days sweep away all the rich heritage of so many ages of wisdom and glory. The danger is terrible. The time is short. If this bill should be rejected, I pray to God that none of those who concur in rejecting it may ever remember their votes with unavailing remorse, amidst the wreck of laws, the confusion of ranks, the spoliation of property, and the dissolution of social order.

PARLIAMENTARY REFORM. II

A SPEECH DELIVERED IN THE HOUSE OF COMMONS ON THE 20TH OF SEPTEMBER, 1831

On Monday, the nineteenth of September, 1831, the Bill to amend the representation of the people in England and Wales was read a third time, at an early hour and in a thin house, without any debate. But on the question whether the Bill should pass a discussion arose which lasted three nights. On the morning of the twenty-second of September the House divided; and the Bill passed by 345 votes to 236. The following Speech was made on the second night of the debate.

IT is not without great diffidence, Sir, that I rise to address you on a subject which has been nearly exhausted. Indeed, I should not have risen had I not thought that, though the arguments on this question are for the most part old, our situation at present is in a great measure new. At length the Reform Bill, having passed without vital injury through all the dangers which threatened it, during a long and minute discussion, from the attacks of its enemies and from the dissensions of its friends, comes before us for our final ratification, altered, indeed, in some of its details for the better, and in some for the worse, but in its great principles still the same bill which, on the first of March, was proposed to the late Parliament, the same bill which was received with joy and gratitude by the whole nation, the same bill which, in an instant, took away the power of interested agitators, and united in one firm body all the sects of sincere Reformers, the same bill which, at the late election, received the approbation of almost every great constituent body in the empire. With a confidence which discussion has only strengthened, with an assured hope of great public blessings if the wish of the nation shall be gratified, with a deep and solemn apprehension of great public calamities if that wish shall be disappointed, I, for the last time, give my most hearty assent to this noble law, destined, I trust, to be the parent of many good laws, and, through a long series of years, to secure the repose and promote the prosperity of my country.

When I say that I expect this bill to promote the prosperity of the country, I by no means intend to encourage those chimerical hopes which the honorable and learned Member for Rye,[1] who has so much distinguished himself in this debate, has imputed to the Reformers. The people, he says, are for the bill, because they expect that it will immediately relieve all their distresses. Sir, I believe that very few of that large and respectable class which we are now about to admit to a share of political power entertain any such absurd expectation. They expect relief, I doubt not; and I doubt not that they will find it; but sudden relief they are far too wise to expect. The bill, says the honorable and learned gentleman, is good for nothing: it is merely theoretical: it removes no real and sensible evil: it will not give the people more work, or higher wages, or cheaper bread. Undoubtedly, Sir, the bill will not immediately give all those things to the people. But will any institutions give them all those things? Do the present institutions of the country secure to them those advantages? If we are to pronounce the Reform Bill good for nothing, because it will not at once raise the nation from distress to prosperity, what are we to say of that system under which the nation has been of late sinking from prosperity into distress? The defect is not in the Reform Bill, but in the very nature of government. On the physical condition of the great body of the people, government acts not as a specific, but as an alterative. Its operation is powerful, indeed, and certain, but gradual and indirect. The business of government is not directly to make the people rich, but to protect them in making themselves rich; and a government which attempts more than this is precisely the government which is likely to perform less. Governments do not and cannot support the people. We have no miraculous powers: we have not the rod of the Hebrew lawgiver: we cannot rain down bread on the multitude from Heaven: we

[1] Mr. Pemberton.

cannot smite the rock and give them to drink. We can give them only freedom to employ their industry to the best advantage, and security in the enjoyment of what their industry has acquired. These advantages it is our duty to give at the smallest possible cost. The diligence and forethought of individuals will thus have fair play; and it is only by the diligence and forethought of individuals that the community can become prosperous. I am not aware that His Majesty's Ministers, or any of the supporters of this bill, have encouraged the people to hope, that Reform will remove distress, in any other way than by this indirect process. By this indirect process the bill will, I feel assured, conduce to the national prosperity. If it had been passed fifteen years ago, it would have saved us from our present embarrassments. If we pass it now, it will gradually extricate us from them. It will secure to us a House of Commons, which, by preserving peace, by destroying monopolies, by taking away unnecessary public burthens, by judiciously distributing necessary public burthens, will, in the progress of time, greatly improve our condition. This it will do; and those who blame it for not doing more blame it for not doing what no Constitution, no code of laws, ever did or ever will do; what no legislator, who was not an ignorant and unprincipled quack, ever ventured to promise.

But chimerical as are the hopes which the honorable and learned Member for Rye imputes to the people, they are not, I think, more chimerical than the fears which he has himself avowed. Indeed, those very gentlemen who are constantly telling us that we are taking a leap in the dark, that we pay no attention to the lessons of experience, that we are mere theorists, are themselves the despisers of experience, are themselves the mere theorists. They are terrified at the thought of admitting into Parliament members elected by ten pound householders. They have formed in their own imaginations a most frightful idea of these members. My honorable and learned friend, the Member for Cockermouth,[1] is certain that these members will take every opportunity of promoting the interests of the journeyman in opposition to those of the capitalist. The honorable and learned Member for Rye is convinced that none but persons who have strong local connections, will ever be returned for such constituent bodies. My honorable friend, the Member for Thetford,[2] tells us, that none but mob orators, men who are willing to pay the basest court to the multitude, will have any chance. Other speakers have gone still further, and have described to us the future borough members as so many

---

[1] Sir James Scarlett.   [2] Mr. Alexander Baring.

Marats and Santerres, low, fierce, desperate men, who will turn
the House into a bear garden, and who will try to turn the monarchy into a republic, mere agitators, without honor, without
sense, without education, without the feelings or the manners of
gentlemen. Whenever, during the course of the fatiguing discussions by which we have been so long occupied, there has been a
cry of "question," or a noise at the bar, the orator who has been
interrupted has remarked, that such proceedings will be quite
in place in the Reformed Parliament, but that we ought to remember that the House of Commons is still an assembly of
gentlemen. This, I say, is to set up mere theory, or rather mere
prejudice, in opposition to long and ample experience. Are the
gentlemen who talk thus ignorant that we have already the means
of judging what kind of men the ten pound householders will send
up to Parliament? Are they ignorant that there are even now large
towns with very popular franchises, with franchises even more
democratic than those which will be bestowed by the present bill?
Ought they not, on their own principles, to look at the results of
the experiments which have already been made, instead of predicting frightful calamities at random? How do the facts which
are before us agree with their theories? Nottingham is a city with
a franchise even more democratic than that which this bill establishes. Does Nottingham send hither mere vulgar demagogues?
It returns two distinguished men, one an advocate, the other a
soldier, both unconnected with the town. Every man paying scot
and lot has a vote at Leicester. This is a lower franchise than the
ten pound franchise. Do we find that the Members for Leicester
are the mere tools of the journeymen? I was at Leicester during
the contest of 1826; and I recollect that the suffrages of the scot
and lot voters were pretty equally divided between two candidates,
neither of them connected with the place, neither of them a slave
of the mob, one a Tory Baronet from Derbyshire, the other a
most respectable and excellent friend of mine, connected with the
manufacturing interest, and also an inhabitant of Derbyshire.
Look at Norwich. Look at Northampton, with a franchise more
democratic than even the scot and lot franchise. Northampton
formerly returned Mr. Perceval, and now returns gentlemen of
high respectability, gentlemen who have a great stake in the
prosperity and tranquillity of the country. Look at the metropolitan districts. This is an *a fortiori* case. Nay it is—the expression, I fear, is awkward—an *a fortiori* case at two removes. The
ten pound householders of the metropolis are persons in a lower
station of life than the ten pound householders of other towns.

The scot and lot franchise in the metropolis is again lower than the ten pound franchise. Yet have Westminster and Southwark been in the habit of sending us members of whom we have had reason to be ashamed, of whom we have not had reason to be proud? I do not say that the inhabitants of Westminster and Southwark have always expressed their political sentiments with proper moderation. That is not the question. The question is this: what kind of men have they elected? The very principle of all Representative government is, that men who do not judge well of public affairs may be quite competent to choose others who will judge better. Whom, then, have Westminster and Southwark sent us during the last fifty years, years full of great events, years of intense popular excitement? Take any one of those nomination boroughs, the patrons of which have conscientiously endeavoured to send fit men into this House. Compare the Members for that borough with the Members for Westminster and Southwark; and you will have no doubt to which the preference is due. It is needless to mention Mr. Fox, Mr. Sheridan, Mr. Tierney, Sir Samuel Romilly. Yet I must pause at the name of Sir Samuel Romilly. Was he a mob orator? Was he a servile flatterer of the multitude? Sir, if he had any fault, if there was any blemish on that most serene and spotless character, that character which every public man, and especially every professional man engaged in politics, ought to propose to himself as a model, it was this, that he despised popularity too much and too visibly. The honorable Member for Thetford told us that the honorable and learned Member for Rye, with all his talents, would have no chance of a seat in the Reformed Parliament, for want of the qualifications which succeed on the hustings. Did Sir Samuel Romilly ever appear on the hustings of Westminster? He never solicited one vote; he never showed himself to the electors, till he had been returned at the head of the poll. Even then, as I have heard from one of his nearest relatives, it was with reluctance that he submitted to be chaired. He shrank from being made a show. He loved the people, and he served them; but Coriolanus himself was not less fit to canvass them. I will mention one other name, that of a man of whom I have only a childish recollection, but who must have been intimately known to many of those who hear me, Mr. Henry Thornton. He was a man eminently upright, honorable, and religious, a man of strong understanding, a man of great political knowledge; but, in all respects, the very reverse of a mob orator. He was a man who would not have yielded to what he considered as unreasonable clamour, I will not say to save his seat, but to save his life. Yet he continued to represent South-wark, Parliament after Parliament, for many years. Such has been the conduct of the scot and lot voters of the metropolis; and there is clearly less reason to expect democratic violence from ten pound householders than from scot and lot householders; and from ten pound householders in the country towns than from ten pound householders in London. Experience, I say, therefore, is on our side; and on the side of our opponents nothing but mere con-jecture and mere assertion.

Sir, when this bill was first brought forward, I supported it, not only on the ground of its intrinsic merits, but, also, because I was convinced that to reject it would be a course full of danger. I believe that the danger of that course is in no respect diminished. I believe, on the contrary, that it is increased. We are told that there is a reaction. The warmth of the public feeling, it seems, has abated. In this story both the sections of the party opposed to Reform are agreed; those who hate Reform, because it will remove abuses, and those who hate it, because it will avert anarchy; those who wish to see the electing body controlled by ejectments, and those who wish to see it controlled by riots. They must now, I think, be undeceived. They must have already discovered that the surest way to prevent a reaction is to talk about it, and that the enthusiasm of the people is at once rekindled by any indiscreet mention of their seeming coolness. This, Sir, is not the first reaction which the sagacity of the Opposition has discovered since the Reform Bill was brought in. Every gentleman who sat in the late Parliament, every gentleman who, during the sitting of the late Parliament, paid attention to political speeches and publications, must remember how, for some time before the debate on General Gascoyne's motion, and during the debate on that motion, and down to the very day of the dissolution, we were told that public feeling had cooled. The right honorable Baronet, the Member for Tamworth, told us so. All the literary organs of the Opposition, from the Quarterly Review down to the Morning Post, told us so. All the Members of the Opposition with whom we conversed in private told us so. I have in my eye a noble friend of mine, who assured me, on the very night which preceded the dissolution, that the people had ceased to be zealous for the Ministerial plan, and that we were more likely to lose than to gain by the elections. The appeal was made to the people; and what was the result? What sign of a reaction appeared among the Livery of London? What sign of a reaction did the honorable Baronet who now represents Okehampton find among the freeholders of Cornwall?[1] How was it with the large represented towns? Had Liverpool cooled? or Bristol? or Leicester? or Coventry? or Nottingham? or Norwich? How was it with the great seats of manufacturing industry, Yorkshire, and Lancashire, and Staffordshire, and Warwickshire, and Cheshire? How was it with the agricultural districts, Northumberland and Cumberland, Leicestershire and Lincolnshire, Kent and Essex, Oxfordshire, Hampshire, Somersetshire, Dorsetshire, Devonshire? How was it with the strongholds of aristocratical influence, Newark, and Stamford, and Hertford, and St. Alban's? Never did any people display, within the limits prescribed by law, so generous a fervour, or so steadfast a determination, as that very people whose apparent languor had just before inspired the enemies of Reform with a delusive hope.

Such was the end of the reaction of April; and, if that lesson shall not profit those to whom it was given, such and yet more signal will be the end of the reaction of September. The two cases are strictly analogous. In both cases the people were eager when they believed the bill to be in danger, and quiet when they believed it to be in security. During the three or four weeks which followed the promulgation of the Ministerial plan, all was joy, and gratitude, and vigorous exertion. Everywhere meetings were held: everywhere resolutions were passed: from every quarter were sent up petitions to this House, and addresses to the Throne: and then the nation, having given vent to its first feelings of delight, having clearly and strongly expressed its opinions, having seen the principle of the bill adopted by the House of Commons on the second reading, became composed, and awaited the result with a tranquillity which the Opposition mistook for indifference. All at once the aspect of affairs changed. General Gascoyne's amendment was carried: the bill was again in danger: exertions were again necessary. Then was it well seen whether the calmness of the public mind was any indication of indifference. The depth and sincerity of the prevailing sentiments were proved, not by mere talking, but by actions, by votes, by sacrifices. Intimidation was defied: expenses were rejected: old ties were broken: the people struggled manfully: they triumphed gloriously: they placed the bill in perfect security, as far as this House was concerned; and they returned to their repose. They are now, as they were on the eve of General Gascoyne's motion, awaiting the issue of the deliberations of Parliament, without any indecent show of violence, but with anxious interest and immovable resolution. And because

[1] Sir Richard Vyvyan.

they are not exhibiting that noisy and rapturous enthusiasm which is in its own nature transient, because they are not as much excited as on the day when the plan of the Government was first made known to them, or on the day when the late Parliament was dissolved, because they do not go on week after week, hallooing and holding meetings, and marching about with flags, and making bonfires, and illuminating their houses, we are again told that there is a reaction. To such a degree can men be deceived by their wishes, in spite of their own recent experience. Sir, there is no reaction; and there will be no reaction. All that has been said on this subject convinces me only that those who are now, for the second time, raising this cry, know nothing of the crisis in which they are called on to act, or of the nation which they aspire to govern. All their opinions respecting this bill are founded on one great error. They imagine that the public feeling concerning Reform is a mere whim which sprang up suddenly out of nothing, and which will as suddenly vanish into nothing. They, therefore, confidently expect a reaction. They are always looking out for a reaction. Everything that they see, or that they hear, they construe into a sign of the approach of this reaction. They resemble the man in Horace, who lies on the bank of the river, expecting that it will every moment pass by and leave him a clear passage, not knowing the depth and abundance of the fountain which feeds it, not knowing that it flows, and will flow on for ever. They have found out a hundred ingenious devices by which they deceive themselves. Sometimes they tell us that the public feeling about Reform was caused by the events which took place at Paris about fourteen months ago; though every observant and impartial man knows, that the excitement which the late French revolution produced in England was not the cause but the effect of that progress which liberal opinions had made amongst us. Sometimes they tell us that we should not have been troubled with any complaints on the subject of the Representation, if the House of Commons had agreed to a certain motion, made in the Session of 1830, for inquiry into the causes of the public distress. I remember nothing about that motion, except that it gave rise to the dullest debate ever known; and the country, I am firmly convinced, cared not one straw about it. But is it not strange that men of real ability can deceive themselves so grossly, as to think that any change in the government of a foreign nation, or the rejection of any single motion, however popular, could all at once raise up a great, rich, enlightened nation, against its ancient institutions? Could such small drops have produced an overflowing, if the vessel had not already been filled to the very brim? These explanations are incredible, and if they were credible, would be anything but consolatory. If it were really true that the English people had taken a sudden aversion to a representative system which they had always loved and admired, because a single division in Parliament had gone against their wishes, or because, in a foreign country, in circumstances bearing not the faintest analogy to those in which we are placed, a change of dynasty had happened, what hope could we have for such a nation of madmen? How could we expect that the present form of government, or any form of government, would be durable amongst them?

Sir, the public feeling concerning Reform is of no such recent origin, and springs from no such frivolous causes. Its first faint commencement may be traced far, very far, back in our history. During seventy years that feeling has had a great influence on the public mind. Through the first thirty years of the reign of George the Third, it was gradually increasing. The great leaders of the two parties in the State were favourable to Reform. Plans of reform were supported by large and most respectable minorities in the House of Commons. The French Revolution, filling the higher and middle classes with an extreme dread of change, and the war calling away the public attention from internal to external politics, threw the question back; but the people never lost sight of it. Peace came, and they were at leisure to think of domestic improvements. Distress came, and they suspected, as was natural, that their distress was the effect of unfaithful stewardship and unskilful legislation. An opinion favourable to Parliamentary Reform grew up rapidly, and became strong among the middle classes. But one tie, one strong tie, still bound those classes to the Tory party. I mean the Catholic Question. It is impossible to deny that, on that subject, a large proportion, a majority, I fear, of the middle class of Englishmen, conscientiously held opinions opposed to those which I have always entertained, and were disposed to sacrifice every other consideration to what they regarded as a religious duty. Thus the Catholic Question hid, so to speak, the question of Parliamentary Reform. The feeling in favour of Parliamentary Reform grew, but it grew in the shade. Every man, I think, must have observed the progress of that feeling in his own social circle. But few Reform meetings were held, and few petitions in favour of Reform presented. At length the Catholics were emancipated; the solitary link of sympathy which attached the people to the Tories was broken; the cry of "No Popery" could no longer be opposed to the cry of "Reform." That which, in the opinion of the two great parties in Parliament, and of a vast portion of the community, had been the first question, suddenly disappeared; and the question of Parliamentary Reform took the first place. Then was put forth all the strength which had been growing in silence and obscurity. Then it appeared that Reform had on its side a coalition of interests and opinions unprecedented in our history, all the liberality and intelligence which had supported the Catholic claims, and all the clamour which had opposed them.

This, I believe, is the true history of that public feeling on the subject of Reform which has been ascribed to causes quite inadequate to the production of such an effect. If ever there was in the history of mankind a national sentiment which was the very opposite of a caprice, with which accident had nothing to do, which was produced by the slow, steady, certain progress of the human mind, it is the sentiment of the English people on the subject of Reform. Accidental circumstances may have brought that feeling to maturity in a particular year, or a particular month. That point I will not dispute; for it is not worth disputing. But those accidental circumstances have brought on Reform, only as the circumstance that, at a particular time, indulgences were offered for sale in a particular town in Saxony, brought on the great separation from the Church of Rome. In both cases the public mind was prepared to move on the slightest impulse.

Thinking thus of the public opinion concerning Reform, being convinced that this opinion is the mature product of time and of discussion, I expect no reaction. I no more expect to see my countrymen again content with the mere semblance of a Representation, than to see them again drowning witches or burning heretics, trying causes by red hot ploughshares, or offering up human sacrifices to wicker idols. I no more expect a reaction in favour of Gatton and Old Sarum, than a reaction in favour of Thor and Odin. I should think such a reaction almost as much a miracle, as that the shadow should go back upon the dial. Revolutions produced by violence are often followed by reactions; the victories of reason once gained, are gained for eternity.

In fact, if there be, in the present aspect of public affairs, any sign peculiarly full of evil omen to the opponents of Reform, it is that very calmness of the public mind on which they found their expectation of success. They think that it is the calmness of indifference. It is the calmness of confident hope; and in proportion to the confidence of hope will be the bitterness of disappointment. Disappointment, indeed, I do not anticipate. That we are certain of success in this House is now acknowledged; and our opponents have, in consequence, during the whole of this Session, and particularly during the present debate, addressed their arguments and exhortations rather to the Lords than to the assembly of which they are themselves Members. Their principal argument has always been, that the bill will destroy the peerage. The honorable and learned Member for Rye has, in plain terms, called on the Barons of England to save their order from democratic encroachments, by rejecting this measure. All these arguments, all these appeals, being interpreted, mean this: "Proclaim to your countrymen that you have no common interests with them, no common sympathies with them; that you can be powerful only by their weakness, and exalted only by their degradation; that the corruption which disgusts them, and the oppression against which their spirit rises up, are indispensable to your authority; that the freedom and purity of election are incompatible with the very existence of your House. Give them clearly to understand that your power rests, not, as they have hitherto imagined, on their rational convictions, or on their habitual veneration, or on your own great property, but on a system fertile of political evils, fertile also of low iniquities of which ordinary justice takes cognisance. Bind up, in inseparable union, the privileges of your estate with the grievances of ours: resolve to stand or fall with abuses visibly marked out for destruction: tell the people that they are attacking you in attacking the three holes in the wall,[1] and that they shall never get rid of the three holes in the wall till they have got rid of you; that a hereditary peerage, and a representative assembly, can coexist only in name, and that, if they will have a real House of Peers, they must be content with a mock House of Commons." This, I say, is the advice given to the Lords by those who call themselves the friends of aristocracy. That advice so pernicious will not be followed, I am well assured; yet I cannot but listen to it with uneasiness. I cannot but wonder that it should proceed from the lips of men who are constantly lecturing us on the duty of consulting history and experience. Have they never heard what effects counsels like their own, when too faithfully followed, have produced? Have they never visited that neighbouring country, which still presents to the eye, even of a passing stranger, the signs of a great dissolution and renovation of society? Have they never walked by those stately mansions, now sinking into decay, and portioned out into lodging rooms, which line the silent streets of the Faubourg St. Germain? Have

---

[1] [At Midhurst the sites of the burgage tenement (which carried votes) were marked by inscribed stones sunk in the wall.]

they never seen the ruins of those castles whose terraces and gardens overhang the Loire? Have they never heard that from those magnificent hotels, from those ancient castles, an aristocracy as splendid, as brave, as proud, as accomplished as ever Europe saw, was driven forth to exile and beggary, to implore the charity of hostile Governments and hostile creeds, to cut wood in the back settlements of America, or to teach French in the schoolrooms of London? And why were those haughty nobles destroyed with that utter destruction? Why were they scattered over the face of the earth, their titles abolished, their escutcheons defaced, their parks wasted, their palaces dismantled, their heritage given to strangers? Because they had no sympathy with the people, no discernment of the signs of their time; because, in the pride and narrowness of their hearts, they called those whose warnings might have saved them theorists and speculators; because they refused all concession till the time had arrived when no concession would avail. I have no apprehension that such a fate awaits the nobles of England. I draw no parallel between our aristocracy and that of France. Those who represent the peerage as a class whose power is incompatible with the just influence of the people in the State, draw that parallel, and not I. They do all in their power to place the Lords and Commons of England in that position with respect to each other in which the French gentry stood with respect to the Third Estate. But I am convinced that these advisers will not succeed. We see, with pride and delight, among the friends of the people, the Talbots, the Cavendishes, the princely house of Howard. Foremost among those who have entitled themselves, by their exertions in this House, to the lasting gratitude of their countrymen, we see the descendants of Marlborough, of Russell, and of Derby. I hope, and firmly believe, that the Lords will see what their interest and their honor require. I hope, and firmly believe, that they will act in such a manner as to entitle themselves to the esteem and affection of the people. But if not, let not the enemies of Reform imagine that their reign is straightway to recommence, or that they have obtained anything more than a short and uneasy respite. We are bound to respect the constitutional rights of the Peers; but we are bound also not to forget our own. We, too, have our privileges: we, too, are an estate of the realm. A House of Commons strong in the love and confidence of the people, a House of Commons which has nothing to fear from a dissolution, is something in the government. Some persons, I well know, indulge a hope that the rejection of the bill will at once restore the domination of that party which fled from power last November, leaving everything abroad and everything at home in confusion; leaving the European system, which it had built up at a vast cost of blood and treasure, falling to pieces in every direction; leaving the dynasties which it had restored, hastening into exile; leaving the nations which it had joined together, breaking away from each other; leaving the fundholders in dismay; leaving the peasantry in insurrection; leaving the most fertile counties lighted up with the fires of incendiaries; leaving the capital in such a state, that a royal procession could not safely pass through it. Dark and terrible, beyond any season within my remembrance of political affairs, was the day of their flight. Far darker and far more terrible will be the day of their return. They will return in opposition to the whole British nation, united as it was never before united on any internal question; united as firmly as when the Armada was sailing up the channel; united as firmly as when Bonaparte pitched his camp on the cliffs of Boulogne. They will return pledged to defend evils which the people are resolved to destroy. They will return to a situation in which they can stand only by crushing and trampling down public opinion, and from which, if they fall, they may, in their fall, drag down with them the whole frame of society. Against such evils, should such evils appear to threaten the country, it will be our privilege and our duty to warn our gracious and beloved Sovereign. It will be our privilege and our duty to convey the wishes of a loyal people to the throne of a patriot king. At such a crisis the proper place for the House of Commons is in front of the nation; and in that place this House will assuredly be found. Whatever prejudice or weakness may do elsewhere to ruin the empire, here, I trust, will not be wanting the wisdom, the virtue, and the energy that may save it.

GOVERNMENT OF INDIA

A SPEECH DELIVERED IN THE HOUSE OF COMMONS ON THE 10TH OF JULY, 1833

On Wednesday, the tenth of July, 1833, Mr. Charles Grant, President of the Board of Control, moved that the Bill for effecting an arrangement with the India Company, and for the better government of His Majesty's Indian territories, should be read a second time. The motion was carried without a division, but not without a long debate, in the course of which the following Speech was made.

HAVING, while this bill was in preparation, enjoyed the fullest and kindest confidence of my right honorable friend, the President of the Board of Control, agreeing with him completely in all those views which on a former occasion he so luminously and eloquently developed, having shared his anxieties, and feeling that in some degree I share his responsibility, I am naturally desirous to obtain the attention of the House while I attempt to defend the principles of the proposed arrangement. I wish that I could promise to be very brief; but the subject is so extensive that I will only promise to condense what I have to say as much as I can.

I rejoice, Sir, that I am completely dispensed, by the turn which our debates have taken, from the necessity of saying anything in favour of one part of our plan, the opening of the China trade. No voice, I believe, has yet been raised here in support of the monopoly. On that subject all public men of all parties seem to be agreed. The resolution proposed by the Ministers has received the unanimous assent of both Houses, and the approbation of the whole kingdom. I will not, therefore, Sir, detain you by vindicating what no gentleman has yet ventured to attack, but will proceed to call your attention to those effects which this great commercial revolution necessarily produced on the system of Indian government and finance.

The China trade is to be opened. Reason requires this. Public opinion requires it. The Government of the Duke of Wellington felt the necessity as strongly as the Government of Lord Grey. No Minister, Whig or Tory, could have been found to propose a renewal of the monopoly. No parliament, reformed or unreformed, would have listened to such a proposition. But though the opening of the trade was a matter concerning which the public had long made up its mind, the political consequences which must necessarily follow from the opening of the trade seem to me to be even now little understood. The language which I have heard in almost every circle where the subject was discussed was this: "Take away the monopoly, and leave the government of India to the Company:" a very short and convenient way of settling one of the most complicated questions that ever a legislature had to consider. The honorable Member for Sheffield,[1] though not disposed to retain the Company as an organ of Government, has repeatedly used language which proves that he shares in the general misconception. The fact is that the abolition of the monopoly rendered it absolutely necessary to make a fundamental change in the constitution of that great Corporation.

The Company had united in itself two characters, the character of trader and the character of sovereign. Between the trader and the sovereign there was a long and complicated account,

Mr. Buckingham.

almost every item of which furnished matter for litigation. While the monopoly continued, indeed, litigation was averted. The effect of the monopoly was, to satisfy the claims both of commerce and of territory, at the expense of a third party, the English people; to secure at once funds for the dividend of the stockholder and funds for the government of the Indian Empire, by means of a heavy tax on the tea consumed in this country. But when the third party would no longer bear this charge, all the great financial questions which had, at the cost of that third party, been kept in abeyance, were opened in an instant. The connection between the Company in its mercantile capacity, and the same Company in its political capacity, was dissolved. Even if the Company were permitted, as has been suggested, to govern India and at the same time to trade with China, no advances would be made from the profits of its Chinese trade for the support of its Indian government. It was in consideration of the exclusive privilege that the Company had hitherto been required to make those advances; it was by the exclusive privilege that the Company had been enabled to make them. When that privilege was taken away, it would be unreasonable in the Legislature to impose such an obligation, and impossible for the Company to fulfil it. The whole system of loans from commerce to territory, and repayments from territory to commerce, must cease. Each party must rest altogether on its own resources. It was therefore absolutely necessary to ascertain what resources each party possessed, to bring the long and intricate account between them to a close, and to assign to each a fair portion of assets and liabilities. There was vast property. How much of that property was applicable to purposes of state? How much was applicable to a dividend? There were debts to the amount of many millions. Which of these were the debts of the government that ruled at Calcutta? Which of the great mercantile house that bought tea at Canton? Were the creditors to look to the land revenues of India for their money? Or were they entitled to put executions into the warehouses behind Bishopsgate Street?

There were two ways of settling these questions; adjudication and compromise. The difficulties of adjudication were great; I think insuperable. Whatever acuteness and diligence could do has been done. One person in particular, whose talents and industry peculiarly fitted him for such investigations, and of whom I can never think without regret, Mr. Hyde Villiers,[1] devoted himself to the examination with an ardour and a perseverance

---

[1] [1801–32, a Cambridge friend of Macaulay's, became in 1832 Secretary to the Board of Control (India).]

which, I believe, shortened a life most valuable to his country and to his friends. The assistance of the most skilful accountants has been called in. But the difficulties are such as no accountant, however skilful, could possibly remove. The difficulties are not arithmetical, but political. They arise from the constitution of the Company, from the long and intimate union of the commercial and imperial characters in one body. Suppose that the treasurer of a charity were to mix up the money which he receives on account of the charity with his own private rents and dividends, to pay the whole into his bank to his own private account, to draw it out again by cheques in exactly the same form when he wanted it for his private expenses, and when he wanted it for the purposes of his public trust. Suppose that he were to continue to act thus till he was himself ignorant whether he were in advance or in arrear; and suppose that many years after his death a question were to arise whether his estate were in debt to the charity or the charity in debt to his estate. Such is the question which is now before us, with this important difference; that the accounts of an individual could not be in such a state unless he had been guilty of fraud, or of that gross negligence which is scarcely less culpable than fraud, and that the accounts of the Company were brought into this state by circumstances of a very peculiar kind, by circumstances unparalleled in the history of the world.

It is a mistake to suppose that the Company was a merely commercial body till the middle of the last century. Commerce was its chief object; but in order to enable it to pursue that object, it had been, like the other Companies which were its rivals, like the Dutch India Company, like the French India Company, invested from a very early period with political functions. More than a hundred and twenty years ago, the Company was in miniature precisely what it now is. It was intrusted with the very highest prerogatives of sovereignty. It had its forts, and its white captains, and its black sepoys; it had its civil and criminal tribunals; it was authorised to proclaim martial law; it sent ambassadors to the native governments, and concluded treaties with them; it was Zemindar of several districts, and within those districts, like other Zemindars of the first class, it exercised the powers of a sovereign, even to the infliction of capital punishment on the Hindoos within its jurisdiction. It is incorrect, therefore, to say, that the Company was at first a mere trader, and has since become a sovereign. It was at first a great trader and a petty prince. The political functions at first attracted little notice, because they were merely auxiliary to the commercial functions. By degrees, however, the political functions became more and more important. The Zemindar became a great nabob, became sovereign of all India; the two hundred sepoys became two hundred thousand. This change was gradually wrought, and was not immediately comprehended. It was natural that, while the political functions of the Company were merely auxiliary to its commerce, the political accounts should have been mixed up with the commercial accounts. It was equally natural that this mode of keeping accounts, having once been established, should have remained unaltered; and the more so, as the change in the situation of the Company, though rapid, was not sudden. It is impossible to name any one day, or any one year, as the day or the year when the Company became a great potentate. It has been the fashion indeed to fix on the year 1765, the year in which the Mogul issued a commission authorising the Company to administer the revenues of Bengal, Bahar, and Orissa, as the precise date of the accession of this singular body to sovereignty. I am utterly at a loss to understand why this epoch should be selected. Long before 1765 the Company had the reality of political power. Long before that year, they made a nabob of Arcot; they made and unmade nabobs of Bengal; they humbled the Vizier of Oude; they braved the Emperor of Hindostan himself; more than half the revenues of Bengal were under one pretence or another administered by them. And after the grant, the Company was not, in form and name, an independent power. It was merely a minister of the Court of Delhi. Its coinage bore the name of Shah Alum. The inscription which, down to the time of the Marquess of Hastings, appeared on the seal of the Governor General, declared that great functionary to be the slave of the Mogul. Even to this day we have never formally deposed the king of Delhi. The Company contents itself with being Mayor of the Palace, while the *Roi Fainéant* is suffered to play at being a sovereign. In fact, it was considered, both by Lord Clive and by Warren Hastings, as a point of policy to leave the character of the Company thus undefined, in order that the English might treat the princes in whose names they governed as realities or nonentities, just as might be most convenient.

Thus the transformation of the Company from a trading body, which possessed some sovereign prerogatives for the purposes of trade, into a sovereign body, the trade of which was auxiliary to its sovereignty, was effected by degrees and under disguise. It is not strange, therefore, that the mercantile and political transactions of this great corporation should be entangled together in inextricable complication. The commercial investments have been purchased out of the revenues of the empire. The expenses of war and government have been defrayed out of the profits of the trade. Commerce and territory have contributed to the improvement of the same spot of land, to the repairs of the same building. Securities have been given in precisely the same form, for money which has been borrowed for purposes of State, and for money which has been borrowed for purposes of traffic. It is easy, indeed,— and this is a circumstance which has, I think, misled some gentlemen,—it is easy to see what part of the assets of the Company appears in a commercial form, and what part appears in a political or territorial form. But this is not the question. Assets which are commercial in form may be territorial as respects the right of property; assets which are territorial in form may be commercial as respects the right of property. A chest of tea is not necessarily commercial property; it may have been bought out of the territorial revenue. A fort is not necessarily territorial property; it may stand on ground which the Company bought a hundred years ago out of their commercial profits. Adjudication, if by adjudication be meant decision according to some known rule of law, was out of the question. To leave matters like these to be determined by the ordinary maxims of our civil jurisprudence would have been the height of absurdity and injustice. For example, the home bond debt of the Company, it is believed, was incurred partly for political and partly for commercial purposes. But there is no evidence which would enable us to assign to each branch its proper share. The bonds all run in the same form; and a court of justice would, therefore, of course, either lay the whole burthen on the proprietors, or lay the whole on the territory. We have legal opinions, very respectable legal opinions, to the effect, that in strictness of law the territory is not responsible, and that the commercial assets are responsible for every farthing of the debts which were incurred for the government and defence of India. But though this may be, and I believe is, law, it is, I am sure, neither reason nor justice. On the other hand, it is urged by the advocates of the Company, that some valuable portions of the territory are the property of that body in its commercial capacity; that Calcutta, for example, is the private estate of the Company; that the Company holds the island of Bombay, in free and common socage, as of the Manor of East Greenwich. I will not pronounce any opinion on these points. I have considered them enough to see that there is quite difficulty enough in them to exercise all the ingenuity of all the lawyers in the kingdom for twenty years. But the fact is, Sir, that the municipal law was not made for controversies of this description. The existence of such a body as this gigantic corporation, this political monster of two natures, subject in one hemisphere, sovereign in another, had never been contemplated by the legislators or judges of former ages. Nothing but grotesque absurdity and atrocious injustice could have been the effect, if the claims and liabilities of such a body had been settled according to the rules of Westminster Hall, if the maxims of conveyancers had been applied to the titles by which flourishing cities and provinces are held, or the maxims of the law merchant to those promissory notes which are the securities for a great National Debt, raised for the purpose of exterminating the Pindarrees[1] and humbling the Burmese.

It was, as I have said, absolutely impossible to bring the question between commerce and territory to a satisfactory adjudication; and I must add that, even if the difficulties which I have mentioned could have been surmounted, even if there had been reason to hope that a satisfactory adjudication could have been obtained, I should still have wished to avoid that course. I think it desirable that the Company should continue to have a share in the government of India; and it would evidently have been impossible, pending a litigation between commerce and territory, to leave any political power to the Company. It would clearly have been the duty of those who were charged with the superintendence of India, to be the patrons of India throughout that momentous litigation, to scrutinise with the utmost severity every claim which might be made on the Indian revenues, and to oppose, with energy and perseverance, every such claim, unless its justice were manifest. If the Company was to be engaged in a suit for many millions, in a suit which might last for many years, against the Indian territory, could we entrust the Company with the government of that territory? Could we put the plaintiff in the situation of *prochain ami* of the defendant? Could we appoint governors who would have had an interest opposed in the most direct manner to the interest of the governed, whose stock would have been raised in value by every decision which added to the burthens of their subjects, and depressed by every decision which diminished those burthens? It would be absurd to suppose that they would efficiently defend our Indian Empire against the claims which they were themselves bringing against it; and it would be equally absurd to give the government of the Indian Empire to those who could not be trusted to defend its interests.

Seeing, then, that it was most difficult, if not wholly impossible,

[1] [Pindaris: mounted freebooters of Central India, crushed by Lord Hastings 1816–18; the Burma Campaign was in 1825–6.]

to resort to adjudication between commerce and territory, seeing that, if recourse were had to adjudication, it would be necessary to make a complete revolution in the whole constitution of India, the Government has proposed a compromise. That compromise, with some modifications which did not in the slightest degree affect its principle, and which, while they gave satisfaction to the Company, will eventually lay no additional burthen on the territory, has been accepted. It has, like all other compromises, been loudly censured by violent partisans on both sides. It has been represented by some as far too favorable to the Company, and by others as most unjust to the Company. Sir, I own that we cannot prove that either of these accusations is unfounded. It is of the very essence of our case that we should not be able to show that we have assigned, either to commerce or to territory, its precise due. For our principal reason for recommending a compromise was our full conviction that it was absolutely impossible to ascertain with precision what was due to commerce and what was due to territory. It is not strange that some people should accuse us of robbing the Company, and others of conferring a vast boon on the Company, at the expense of India: for we have proposed a middle course, on the very ground that there was a chance of a result much more favorable to the Company than our arrangement, and a chance also of a result much less favorable. If the questions pending between the Company and India had been decided as the ardent supporters of the Company predicted, India would, if I calculate rightly, have paid eleven millions more than she will now have to pay. If those questions had been decided as some violent enemies of the Company predicted, that great body would have been utterly ruined. The very meaning of compromise is that each party gives up his chance of complete success, in order to be secured against the chance of utter failure. And, as men of sanguine minds always overrate the chances in their own favour, every fair compromise is sure to be severely censured on both sides. I conceive that, in a case so dark and complicated as this, the compromise which we recommend is sufficiently vindicated, if it cannot be proved to be unfair. We are not bound to prove it to be fair. For it would have been unnecessary for us to resort to compromise at all, if we had been in possession of evidence which would have enabled us to pronounce, with certainty, what claims were fair and what were unfair. It seems to me that we have acted with due consideration for every party. The dividend which we give to the proprietors is precisely the same dividend which they have been receiving during forty years, and which they have expected to receive permanently. The price of their stock bears at present the same proportion to the price of other stock which it bore four or five years ago, before the anxiety and excitement which the late negotiations naturally produced had begun to operate. As to the territory on the other hand, it is true that, if the assets which are now in a commercial form should not produce a fund sufficient to pay the debts and dividend of the Company, the territory must stand to the loss and pay the difference. But in return for taking this risk, the territory obtains an immediate release from claims to the amount of many millions. I certainly do not believe that all those claims could have been substantiated; but I know that very able men think differently. And, if only one-fourth of the sum demanded had been awarded to the Company, India would have lost more than the largest sum which, as it seems to me, she can possibly lose under the proposed arrangement.

In a pecuniary point of view, therefore, I conceive that we can defend the measure as it affects the territory. But to the territory the pecuniary question is of secondary importance. If we have made a good pecuniary bargain for India, but a bad political bargain, if we have saved three or four millions to the finances of that country, and given to it, at the same time, pernicious institutions, we shall indeed have been practising a most ruinous parsimony. If, on the other hand, it shall be found that we have added fifty or a hundred thousand pounds a-year to the expenditure of an empire which yields a revenue of twenty millions, but that we have at the same time secured to that empire, as far as in us lies, the blessings of good government, we shall have no reason to be ashamed of our profusion. I hope and believe that India will have to pay nothing. But on the most unfavorable supposition that can be made, she will not have to pay so much to the Company as she now pays annually to a single state pageant, to the titular Nabob of Bengal, for example, or the titular King of Delhi. What she pays to these nominal princes, who, while they did anything, did mischief, and who now do nothing, she may well consent to pay to her real rulers, if she receives from them, in return, efficient protection and good legislation.

We come then to the great question. Is it desirable to retain the Company as an organ of government for India? I think that it is desirable. The question is, I acknowledge, beset with difficulties. We have to solve one of the hardest problems in politics. We are trying to make brick without straw, to bring a clean thing out of an unclean, to give a good government to a people to whom we cannot give a free government. In this country, in any neighbouring country, it is easy to frame securities against oppression. In Europe, you have the materials of good government everywhere ready to your hands. The people are everywhere perfectly competent to hold some share, not in every country an equal share, but some share, of political power. If the question were, What is the best mode of securing good government in Europe? the merest smatterer in politics would answer, representative institutions. In India you cannot have representative institutions. Of all the innumerable speculators who have offered their suggestions on Indian politics, not a single one, as far as I know, however democratical his opinions may be, has ever maintained the possibility of giving, at the present time, such institutions to India. One gentleman, extremely well acquainted with the affairs of our Eastern Empire, a most valuable servant of the Company, and the author of a History of India, which, though certainly not free from faults, is, I think, on the whole, the greatest historical work which has appeared in our language since that of Gibbon, I mean Mr. Mill, was examined on this point. That gentleman is well known to be a very bold and uncompromising politician. He has written strongly, far too strongly I think, in favour of pure democracy. He has gone so far as to maintain that no nation which has not a representative legislature, chosen by universal suffrage, enjoys security against oppression. But when he was asked before the Committee of last year, whether he thought representative government practicable in India, his answer was, "utterly out of the question." This, then, is the state in which we are. We have to frame a good government for a country into which, by universal acknowledgment, we cannot introduce those institutions which all our habits, which all the reasonings of European philosophers, which all the history of our own part of the world would lead us to consider as the one great security for good government. We have to engraft on despotism those blessings which are the natural fruits of liberty. In these circumstances, Sir, it behoves us to be cautious, even to the verge of timidity. The light of political science and of history are withdrawn: we are walking in darkness: we do not distinctly see whither we are going. It is the wisdom of a man, so situated, to feel his way, and not to plant his foot till he is well assured that the ground before him is firm.

Some things, however, in the midst of this obscurity, I can see with clearness. I can see, for example, that it is desirable that the authority exercised in this country over the Indian government should be divided between two bodies, between a minister or a board appointed by the Crown, and some other body independent of the Crown. If India is to be a dependency of England, to be at war with our enemies, to be at peace with our allies, to be protected by the English navy from maritime aggression, to have a portion of the English army mixed with its sepoys, it plainly follows that the King, to whom the Constitution gives the direction of foreign affairs, and the command of the military and naval forces, ought to have a share in the direction of the Indian government. Yet, on the other hand, that a revenue of twenty millions a year, an army of two hundred thousand men, a civil service abounding with lucrative situations, should be left to the disposal of the Crown without any check whatever, is what no Minister, I conceive, would venture to propose. This House is indeed the check provided by the Constitution on the abuse of the royal prerogative. But that this House is, or is likely ever to be, an efficient check on abuses practised in India, I altogether deny. We have, as I believe we all feel, quite business enough. If we were to undertake the task of looking into Indian affairs as we look into British affairs, if we were to have Indian budgets and Indian estimates, if we were to go into the Indian currency question and the Indian Bank Charter, if to our disputes about Belgium and Holland, Don Pedro and Don Miguel, were to be added disputes about the debts of the Guicowar and the disorders of Mysore, the ex-king of the Afghans and the Maharajah Runjeet Sing; if we were to have one night occupied by the embezzlements of the Benares mint, and another by the panic in the Calcutta money market; if the questions of Suttee or no Suttee, Pilgrim tax or no Pilgrim tax, Ryotwary or Zemindary, half Batta or whole Batta, were to be debated at the same length at which we have debated Church reform and the assessed taxes, twenty-four hours a day and three hundred and sixty-five days a year would be too short a time for the discharge of our duties. The House, it is plain, has not the necessary time to settle these matters; nor has it the necessary knowledge; nor has it the motives to acquire that knowledge. The late change in its constitution has made it, I believe, a much more faithful representative of the English people. But it is as far as ever from being a representative of the Indian people. A broken head in Cold Bath Fields[1] produces a greater sensation among us than three pitched battles in India. A few weeks ago we had to decide on a claim[2] brought by an individual against the revenues of India.

[1] [A Liberty or Death meeting on May 12th this year. A policeman was killed and the jury found it Justifiable Homicide.]

[2] [Hutchinson's Claim Bill, against the Rajah of Travancore, lost on second reading. A pepper speculation.]

If it had been an English question the walls would scarcely have held the Members who would have flocked to the division. It was an Indian question; and we could scarcely, by dint of supplication, make a House. Even when my right honorable friend, the President of the Board of Control, gave his able and interesting explanation of the plan which he intended to propose for the government of a hundred millions of human beings, the attendance was not so large as I have often seen it on a turnpike bill or a railroad bill.

I then take these things as proved, that the Crown must have a certain authority over India, that there must be an efficient check on the authority of the Crown, and that the House of Commons cannot be that efficient check. We must then find some other body to perform that important office. We have such a body, the Company. Shall we discard it?

It is true that the power of the Company is an anomaly in politics. It is strange, very strange, that a joint stock society of traders, a society, the shares of which are daily passed from hand to hand, a society, the component parts of which are perpetually changing, a society, which, judging *a priori* from its constitution, we should have said was as little fitted for imperial functions as the Merchant Tailors' Company or the New River Company, should be intrusted with the sovereignty of a larger population, the disposal of a larger clear revenue, the command of a larger army, than are under the direct management of the Executive Government of the United Kingdom. But what constitution can we give to our Indian Empire which shall not be strange, which shall not be anomalous? That Empire is itself the strangest of all political anomalies. That a handful of adventurers from an island in the Atlantic should have subjugated a vast country divided from the place of their birth by half the globe; a country which at no very distant period was merely the subject of fable to the nations of Europe; a country never before violated by the most renowned of Western Conquerors; a country which Trajan never entered; a country lying beyond the point where the phalanx of Alexander refused to proceed; that we should govern a territory ten thousand miles from us, a territory larger and more populous than France, Spain, Italy, and Germany put together, a territory, the present clear revenue of which exceeds the present clear revenue of any state in the world, France excepted; a territory, inhabited by men differing from us in race, colour, language, manners, morals, religion; these are prodigies to which the world has seen nothing similar. Reason is confounded. We interrogate the past in vain.

General rules are useless where the whole is one vast exception. The Company is an anomaly; but it is part of a system where everything is anomaly. It is the strangest of all governments; but it is designed for the strangest of all Empires.

If we discard the Company, we must find a substitute: and, take what substitute we may, we shall find ourselves unable to give any reason for believing that the body which we have put in the room of the Company is likely to acquit itself of its duties better than the Company. Commissioners appointed by the King during pleasure would be no check on the Crown; Commissioners appointed by the King or by Parliament for life would always be appointed by the political party which might be uppermost, and if a change of administration took place, would harass the new Government with the most vexatious opposition. The plan suggested by the right honorable Gentleman, the Member for Montgomeryshire,[1] is I think the very worst that I have ever heard. He would have Directors nominated every four years by the Crown. Is it not plain that these Directors would always be appointed from among the supporters of the Ministry for the time being; that their situations would depend on the permanence of that Ministry; that therefore all their power and patronage would be employed for the purpose of propping that Ministry, and, in case of a change, for the purpose of molesting those who might succeed to power; that they would be subservient while their friends were in, and factious when their friends were out? How would Lord Grey's Ministry have been situated if the whole body of Directors had been nominated by the Duke of Wellington in 1830? I mean no imputation on the Duke of Wellington. If the present Ministers had to nominate Directors for four years, they would, I have no doubt, nominate men who would give no small trouble to the Duke of Wellington if he were to return to office. What we want is a body independent of the Government, and no more than independent, not a tool of the Treasury, not a tool of the opposition. No new plan which I have heard proposed would give us such a body. The Company, strange as its constitution may be, is such a body. It is, as a corporation, neither Whig nor Tory, neither high-church nor low-church. It cannot be charged with having been for or against the Catholic Bill, for or against the Reform Bill. It has constantly acted with a view, not to English politics, but to Indian politics. We have seen the country convulsed by faction. We have seen Ministers driven from office by this House, Parliament dissolved in anger, general elections

[1] Mr. Charles Wynn.

of unprecedented turbulence, debates of unprecedented interest. We have seen the two branches of the Legislature placed in direct opposition to each other. We have seen the advisers of the Crown dismissed one day, and brought back the next day on the shoulders of the people. And amidst all these agitating events the Company has preserved strict and unsuspected neutrality. This is, I think, an inestimable advantage; and it is an advantage which we must altogether forego, if we consent to adopt any of the schemes which I have heard proposed on the other side of the House.

We must judge of the Indian government, as of all other governments, by its practical effects. According to the honorable Member for Sheffield, India is ill governed; and the whole fault is with the Company. Innumerable accusations, great and small, are brought by him against the Directors. They are fond of war: they are fond of dominion: the taxation is burthensome: the laws are undigested: the roads are rough: the post goes on foot: and for everything the Company is answerable. From the dethronement of the Mogul princes to the mishaps of Sir Charles Metcalfe's courier, every disaster that has taken place in the East during sixty years is laid to the charge of this Corporation. And the inference is, that all the power which they possess ought to be taken out of their hands, and transferred at once to the Crown.

Now, Sir, it seems to me that, for all the evils which the honorable Gentleman has so pathetically recounted, the Ministers of the Crown are as much to blame as the Company; nay, much more so: for the Board of Control could, without the consent of the Directors, have redressed those evils; and the Directors most certainly could not have redressed them without the consent of the Board of Control. Take the case of that frightful grievance which seems to have made the deepest impression on the mind of the honorable Gentleman, the slowness of the mail. Why, Sir, if my right honorable friend, the President of our Board, thought fit, he might direct me to write to the Court and require them to frame a dispatch on that subject. If the Court disobeyed, he might himself frame a dispatch ordering Lord William Bentinck to put the dawks all over Bengal on horseback. If the Court refused to send out this dispatch, the Board could apply to the King's Bench for a Mandamus. If, on the other hand, the Directors wished to accelerate the journeys of the mail, and the Board were adverse to the project, the Directors could do nothing at all. For all measures of internal policy the servants of the King are at least as deeply responsible as the Company. For all measures of foreign policy the servants of the King, and they alone, are responsible.

I was surprised to hear the honorable Gentleman accuse the Directors of insatiable ambition and rapacity, when he must know that no act of aggression on any native state can be committed by the Company without the sanction of the Board, and that, in fact, the Board has repeatedly approved of warlike measures, which were strenuously opposed by the Company. He must know, in particular, that, during the energetic and splendid administration of the Marquess Wellesley, the Company was all for peace, and the Board all for conquest. If a line of conduct which the honorable Gentleman thinks unjustifiable has been followed by the Ministers of the Crown in spite of the remonstrances of the Directors, this is surely a strange reason for turning off the Directors, and giving the whole power unchecked to the Crown.

The honorable Member tells us that India, under the present system, is not so rich and flourishing as she was two hundred years ago. Really, Sir, I doubt whether we are in possession of sufficient data to enable us to form a judgment on that point. But the matter is of little importance. We ought to compare India under our Government, not with India under Acbar and his immediate successors, but with India as we found it. The calamities through which that country passed during the interval between the fall of the Mogul power and the establishment of the English supremacy were sufficient to throw the people back whole centuries. It would surely be unjust to say, that Alfred was a bad king because Britain, under his government, was not so rich or so civilised as in the time of the Romans.

In what state, then, did we find India? And what have we made India? We found society throughout that vast country in a state to which history scarcely furnishes a parallel. The nearest parallel would, perhaps, be the state of Europe during the fifth century. The Mogul empire in the time of the successors of Aurungzebe, like the Roman empire in the time of the successors of Theodosius, was sinking under the vices of a bad internal administration, and under the assaults of barbarous invaders. At Delhi, as at Ravenna, there was a mock sovereign, immured in a gorgeous state prison. He was suffered to indulge in every sensual pleasure. He was adored with servile prostrations. He assumed and bestowed the most magnificent titles. But, in fact, he was a mere puppet in the hands of some ambitious subject. While the Honorii and Augustuli of the East, surrounded by their fawning eunuchs, revelled and dozed without knowing or caring what might pass beyond the walls of their palace gardens, the provinces had ceased to respect a government which could neither punish nor protect them. Society was a chaos. Its restless and shifting elements formed themselves every moment into some new combination, which the next moment dissolved. In the course of a single generation a hundred dynasties grew up, flourished, decayed, were extinguished, were forgotten. Every adventurer who could muster a troop of horse might aspire to a throne. Every palace was every year the scene of conspiracies, treasons, revolutions, parricides. Meanwhile a rapid succession of Alarics and Attilas passed over the defenceless empire. A Persian invader penetrated to Delhi, and carried back in triumph the most precious treasures of the House of Tamerlane. The Afghan soon followed, by the same track, to glean whatever the Persian had spared. The Jauts established themselves on the Jumna. The Seiks devasted Lahore. Every part of India, from Tanjore to the Himalayas, was laid under contribution by the Mahrattas. The people were ground down to the dust by the oppressor without and the oppressor within, by the robber from whom the Nabob was unable to protect them, by the Nabob who took whatever the robber had left to them. All the evils of despotism, and all the evils of anarchy, pressed at once on that miserable race. They knew nothing of government but its exactions. Desolation was in their imperial cities, and famine all along the banks of their broad and redundant rivers. It seemed that a few more years would suffice to efface all traces of the opulence and civilisation of an earlier age.

Such was the state of India when the Company began to take part in the disputes of its ephemeral sovereigns. About eighty years have elapsed since we appeared as auxiliaries in a contest between two rival families for the sovereignty of a small corner of the Peninsula. From that moment commenced a great, a stupendous process, the reconstruction of a decomposed society. Two generations have passed away; and the process is complete. The scattered fragments of the empire of Aurungzebe have been united in an empire stronger and more closely knit together than that which Aurungzebe ruled. The power of the new sovereigns penetrates their dominions more completely, and is far more implicitly obeyed, than was that of the proudest princes of the Mogul dynasty.

It is true, that the early history of this great revolution is chequered with guilt and shame. It is true that the founders of our Indian empire too often abused the strength which they derived from superior energy and superior knowledge. It is true that, with some of the highest qualities of the race from which they sprang, they combined some of the worst defects of the race over which they ruled. How should it have been otherwise? Born in humble stations, accustomed to earn a slender maintenance by obscure industry, they found themselves transformed in a few months from clerks drudging over desks, or captains in marching regiments, into statesmen and generals, with armies at their command, with the revenues of kingdoms at their disposal, with power to make and depose sovereigns at their pleasure. They were what it was natural that men should be who had been raised by so rapid an ascent to so dizzy an eminence, profuse and rapacious, imperious and corrupt.

It is true, then, that there was too much foundation for the representations of those satirists and dramatists who held up the character of the English Nabob to the derision and hatred of a former generation. It is true that some disgraceful intrigues, some unjust and cruel wars, some instances of odious perfidy and avarice stain the annals of our Eastern empire. It is true that the duties of government and legislation were long wholly neglected or carelessly performed. It is true that when the conquerors at length began to apply themselves in earnest to the discharge of their high functions, they committed the errors natural to rulers who were but imperfectly acquainted with the language and manners of their subjects. It is true that some plans, which were dictated by the purest and most benevolent feelings, have not been attended by the desired success. It is true that India suffers to this day from a heavy burthen of taxation and from a defective system of law. It is true, I fear, that in those states which are connected with us by subsidiary alliance, all the evils of oriental despotism have too frequently shown themselves in their most loathsome and destructive form.

All this is true. Yet in the history and in the present state of our Indian empire I see ample reason for exultation and for a good hope.

I see that we have established order where we found confusion. I see that the petty dynasties which were generated by the corruption of the great Mahometan empire, and which, a century ago, kept all India in constant agitation, have been quelled by one overwhelming power. I see that the predatory tribes which, in the middle of the last century, passed annually over the harvests of India with the destructive rapidity of a hurricane, have quailed before the valour of a braver and sterner race, have been vanquished, scattered, hunted to their strongholds, and either extirpated by the English sword, or compelled to exchange the pursuits of rapine for those of industry.

I look back for many years; and I see scarcely a trace of the vices which blemished the splendid fame of the first conquerors of Bengal. I see peace studiously preserved. I see faith inviolably maintained towards feeble and dependent states. I see confidence gradually infused into the minds of suspicious neighbours. I see the horrors of war mitigated by the chivalrous and Christian spirit of Europe. I see examples of moderation and clemency such as I should seek in vain in the annals of any other victorious and dominant nation. I see captive tyrants, whose treachery and cruelty might have excused a severe retribution, living in security, comfort, and dignity, under the protection of the government which they laboured to destroy.

I see a large body of civil and military functionaries resembling in nothing but capacity and valour those adventurers who, seventy years ago, came hither, laden with wealth and infamy, to parade before our fathers the plundered treasures of Bengal and Tanjore. I reflect with pride that to the doubtful splendour which surrounds the memory of Hastings and of Clive, we can oppose the spotless glory of Elphinstone and Munro.[1] I contemplate with reverence and delight the honorable poverty which is the evidence of rectitude firmly maintained amidst strong temptations. I rejoice to see my countrymen, after ruling millions of subjects, after commanding victorious armies, after dictating terms of peace at the gates of hostile capitals, after administering the revenues of great provinces, after judging the causes of wealthy Zemindars, after residing at the Courts of tributary Kings, return to their native land with no more than a decent competence.

I see a government anxiously bent on the public good. Even in its errors I recognise a paternal feeling towards the great people committed to its charge. I see toleration strictly maintained: yet I see bloody and degrading superstitions gradually losing their power. I see the morality, the philosophy, the taste of Europe, beginning to produce a salutary effect on the hearts and understandings of our subjects. I see the public mind of India, that public mind which we found debased and contracted by the worst forms of political and religious tyranny, expanding itself to just and noble views of the ends of government and of the social duties of man.

I see evils: but I see the government actively employed in the work of remedying those evils. The taxation is heavy; but the work of retrenchment is unsparingly pursued. The mischiefs arising from the system of subsidiary alliance are great: but the rulers of India are fully aware of those mischiefs, and are engaged

[1] [Governors of Bombay and Madras.]

in guarding against them. Wherever they now interfere for the purpose of supporting a native government, they interfere also for the purpose of reforming it.

Seeing these things, then, am I prepared to discard the Company as an organ of government? I am not. Assuredly I will never shrink from innovation where I see reason to believe that innovation will be improvement. That the present Government does not shrink from innovations which it considers as improvements the bill now before the House sufficiently shows. But surely the burthen of the proof lies on the innovators. They are bound to show that there is a fair probability of obtaining some advantage before they call upon us to take up the foundations of the Indian government. I have no superstitious veneration for the Court of Directors or the Court of Proprietors. Find me a better Council: find me a better constituent body: and I am ready for a change. But of all the substitutes for the Company which have hitherto been suggested, not one has been proved to be better than the Company; and most of them I could, I think, easily prove to be worse. Circumstances might force us to hazard a change. If the Company were to refuse to accept of the government unless we would grant pecuniary terms which I thought extravagant, or unless we gave up the clauses in this bill which permit Europeans to hold landed property and natives to hold office, I would take them at their word. But I will not discard them in the mere rage of experiment.

Do I call the government of India a perfect government? Very far from it. No nation can be perfectly well governed till it is competent to govern itself. I compare the Indian government with other governments of the same class, with despotisms, with military despotisms, with foreign military despotisms; and I find none that approaches it in excellence. I compare it with the government of the Roman provinces, with the government of the Spanish colonies; and I am proud of my country and my age. Here are a hundred millions of people under the absolute rule of a few strangers, differing from them physically, differing from them morally, mere Mamelukes, not born in the country which they rule, not meaning to lay their bones in it. If you require me to make this government as good as that of England, France, or the United States of America, I own frankly that I can do no such thing. Reasoning *a priori*, I should have come to the conclusion that such a government must be a horrible tyranny. It is a source of constant amazement to me that it is so good as I find it to be. I will not, therefore, in a case in which I have neither principles nor precedents to guide me, pull down the existing system on account of its theoretical defects. For I know that any system which I could put in its place would be equally condemned by theory, while it would not be equally sanctioned by experience.

Some change in the constitution of the Company was, as I have shown, rendered inevitable by the opening of the China Trade; and it was the duty of the Government to take care that the change should not be prejudicial to India. There were many ways in which the compromise between commerce and territory might have been effected. We might have taken the assets, and paid a sum down, leaving the Company to invest that sum as they chose. We might have offered English security with a lower interest. We might have taken the course which the late ministers designed to take. They would have left the Company in possession of the means of carrying on its trade in competition with private merchants. My firm belief is that, if this course had been taken, the Company must, in a very few years, have abandoned the trade, or the trade would have ruined the Company. It was not, however, solely or principally by regard for the interest of the Company, or of English merchants generally, that the Government was guided on this occasion. The course which appeared to us the most likely to promote the interests of our Eastern Empire was to make the proprietors of India stock creditors of the Indian territory. Their interest will thus be in a great measure the same with the interest of the people whom they are to rule. Their income will depend on the revenues of their empire. The revenues of their empire will depend on the manner in which the affairs of that empire are administered. We furnish them with the strongest motives to watch over the interests of the cultivator and the trader, to maintain peace, to carry on with vigour the work of retrenchment, to detect and punish extortion and corruption. Though they live at a distance from India, though few of them have ever seen or may ever see the people whom they rule, they will have a great stake in the happiness of their subjects. If their misgovernment should produce disorder in the finances, they will themselves feel the effects of that disorder in their own household expenses. I believe this to be, next to a representative constitution, the constitution which is the best security for good government. A representative constitution India cannot at present have. And we have therefore, I think, given her the best constitution of which she is capable.

One word as to the new arrangement which we propose with respect to the patronage. It is intended to introduce the principle of competition in the disposal of writerships; and from this change

I cannot but anticipate the happiest results. The civil servants of the Company are undoubtedly a highly respectable body of men; and in that body, as in every large body, there are some persons of very eminent ability. I rejoice most cordially to see this. I rejoice to see that the standard of morality is so high in England, that intelligence is so generally diffused through England, that young persons who are taken from the mass of society, by favour and not by merit, and who are therefore only fair samples of the mass, should, when placed in situations of high importance, be so seldom found wanting. But it is not the less true that India is entitled to the service of the best talents which England can spare. That the average of intelligence and virtue is very high in this country is matter for honest exultation. But it is no reason for employing average men where you can obtain superior men. Consider too, Sir, how rapidly the public mind of India is advancing, how much attention is already paid by the higher classes of the natives to those intellectual pursuits on the cultivation of which the superiority of the European race to the rest of mankind principally depends. Surely, in such circumstances, from motives of selfish policy, if from no higher motive, we ought to fill the magistracies of our Eastern Empire with men who may do honor to their country, with men who may represent the best part of the English nation. This, Sir, is our object; and we believe that by the plan which is now proposed this object will be attained. It is proposed that for every vacancy in the civil service four candidates shall be named, and the best candidate selected by examination. We conceive that, under this system, the persons sent out will be young men above par, young men superior either in talents or in diligence to the mass. It is said, I know, that examinations in Latin, in Greek, and in mathematics, are no tests of what men will prove to be in life. I am perfectly aware that they are not infallible tests: but that they are tests I confidently maintain. Look at every walk of life, at this House, at the other House, at the Bar, at the Bench, at the Church, and see whether it be not true that those who attain high distinction in the world were generally men who were distinguished in their academic career. Indeed, Sir, this objection would prove far too much even for those who use it. It would prove that there is no use at all in education. Why should we put boys out of their way? Why should we force a lad, who would much rather fly a kite or trundle a hoop, to learn his Latin Grammar? Why should we keep a young man to his Thucydides or his Laplace, when he would much rather be shooting? Education would be mere useless torture, if, at two or three and twenty, a man who had neglected his studies were exactly on a par with a man who had applied himself to them, exactly as likely to perform all the offices of public life with credit to himself and with advantage to society. Whether the English system of education be good or bad is not now the question. Perhaps I may think that too much time is given to the ancient languages and to the abstract sciences. But what then? Whatever be the languages, whatever be the sciences, which it is, in any age or country, the fashion to teach, the persons who become the greatest proficients in those languages and those sciences will generally be the flower of the youth, the most acute, the most industrious, the most ambitious of honorable distinctions. If the Ptolemaic system were taught at Cambridge instead of the Newtonian, the senior wrangler would nevertheless be in general a superior man to the wooden spoon. If, instead of learning Greek, we learned the Cherokee, the man who understood the Cherokee best, who made the most correct and melodious Cherokee verses, who comprehended most accurately the effect of the Cherokee particles, would generally be a superior man to him who was destitute of these accomplishments. If astrology were taught at our Universities, the young man who cast nativities best would generally turn out a superior man. If alchymy were taught, the young man who showed most activity in the pursuit of the philosopher's stone would generally turn out a superior man.

I will only add one other observation on this subject. Although I am inclined to think that too exclusive an attention is paid in the education of young English gentlemen to the dead languages, I conceive that when you are choosing men to fill situations for which the very first and most indispensable qualification is familiarity with foreign languages, it would be difficult to find a better test of their fitness than their classical acquirements.

Some persons have expressed doubts as to the possibility of procuring fair examinations. I am quite sure that no person who has been either at Cambridge or at Oxford can entertain such doubts. I feel, indeed, that I ought to apologise for even noticing an objection so frivolous.

Next to the opening of the China Trade, Sir, the change most eagerly demanded by the English people was, that the restrictions on the admission of Europeans to India should be removed. In this change there are undoubtedly very great advantages. The chief advantage is, I think, the improvement which the minds of our native subjects may be expected to derive from free intercourse with a people far advanced beyond themselves in intellectual cultivation. I cannot deny, however, that the advantages are attended with some danger.

The danger is that the new comers, belonging to the ruling nation, resembling in colour, in language, in manners, those who hold supreme military and political power, and differing in all these respects from the great mass of the population, may consider themselves as a superior class, and may trample on the indigenous race. Hitherto there have been strong restraints on Europeans resident in India. Licences were not easily obtained. Those residents who were in the service of the Company had obvious motives for conducting themselves with propriety. If they incurred the serious displeasure of the Government, their hopes of promotion were blighted. Even those who were not in the public service were subject to the formidable power which the Government possessed of banishing them at its pleasure.

The licence of the Government will now no longer be necessary to persons who desire to reside in the settled provinces of India. The power of arbitrary deportation is withdrawn. Unless, therefore, we mean to leave the natives exposed to the tyranny and insolence of every profligate adventurer who may visit the East, we must place the European under the same power which legislates for the Hindoo. No man loves political freedom more than I. But a privilege enjoyed by a few individuals, in the midst of a vast population who do not enjoy it, ought not to be called freedom. It is tyranny. In the West Indies I have not the least doubt that the existence of the Trial by Jury and of Legislative Assemblies has tended to make the condition of the slaves worse than it would otherwise have been. Or, to go to India itself for an instance, though I fully believe that a mild penal code is better than a severe penal code, the worst of all systems was surely that of having a mild code for the Brahmins, who sprang from the head of the Creator, while there was a severe code for the Sudras, who sprang from his feet. India has suffered enough already from the distinction of castes, and from the deeply rooted prejudices which that distinction has engendered. God forbid that we should inflict on her the curse of a new caste, that we should send her a new breed of Brahmins, authorised to treat all the native population as Parias!

With a view to the prevention of this evil, we propose to give to the Supreme Government the power of legislating for Europeans as well as for natives. We propose that the regulations of the Government shall bind the King's Court as they bind all other courts, and that registration by the Judges of the King's Courts shall no longer be necessary to give validity to those regulations within the towns of Calcutta, Madras, and Bombay.

I could scarcely, Sir, believe my ears when I heard this part of our plan condemned in another place. I should have thought that it would have been received with peculiar favour in that quarter where it has met with the most severe condemnation. What, at present, is the case? If the Supreme Court and the Government differ on a question of jurisdiction, or on a question of legislation within the towns which are the seats of Government, there is absolutely no umpire but the Imperial Parliament. The device of putting one wild elephant between two tame elephants was ingenious; but it may not always be practicable. Suppose a tame elephant between two wild elephants, or suppose that the whole herd should run wild together. The thing is not without example. And is it not most unjust and ridiculous that, on one side of a ditch, the edict of the Governor General should have the force of law, and that on the other side it should be of no effect unless registered by the Judges of the Supreme Court? If the registration be a security for good legislation, we are bound to give that security to all classes of our subjects. If the registration be not a security for good legislation, why give it to any? Is the system good? Extend it. Is it bad? Abolish it. But in the name of common sense do not leave it as it is. It is as absurd as our old law of sanctuary. The law which authorises imprisonment for debt may be good or bad. But no man in his senses can approve of the ancient system under which a debtor who might be arrested in Fleet Street was safe as soon as he had scampered into Whitefriars. Just in the same way, doubts may fairly be entertained about the expediency of allowing four or five persons to make laws for India; but to allow them to make laws for all India without the Mahratta ditch, and to except Calcutta, is the height of absurdity.

I say, therefore, that either you must enlarge the power of the Supreme Court, and give it a general veto on laws, or you must enlarge the power of the Government, and make its regulations binding on all Courts without distinction. The former course no person has ventured to propose. To the latter course objections have been made; but objections which to me, I must own, seem altogether frivolous.

It is acknowledged that of late years inconvenience has arisen from the relation in which the Supreme Court stands to the Government. But, it is said, that Court was originally instituted for the protection of natives against Europeans. The wise course would therefore be to restore its original character.

Now, Sir, the fact is, that the Supreme Court has never been so mischievous as during the first ten years of its power, or so respectable as it has lately been. Everybody who knows anything of its early history knows, that, during a considerable time, it was the terror of Bengal, the scourge of the native population, the screen of European delinquents, a convenient tool of the Government for all purposes of evil, an insurmountable obstacle to the Government in all undertakings for the public good; that its proceedings were made up of pedantry, cruelty, and corruption; that its disputes with the Government were at one time on the point of breaking up the whole fabric of society; and that a convulsion was averted only by the dexterous policy of Warren Hastings, who at last bought off the opposition of the Chief Justice for eight thousand pounds a year. It is notorious that, while the Supreme Court opposed Hastings in all his best measures, it was a thoroughgoing accomplice in his worst; that it took part in the most scandalous of those proceedings which, fifty years ago, roused the indignation of Parliament and of the country; that it assisted in the spoliation of the princesses of Oude; that it passed sentence of death on Nuncomar. And this is the Court which we are to restore from its present state of degeneracy to its original purity. This is the protection which we are to give to the natives against the Europeans. Sir, so far is it from being true that the character of the Supreme Court has deteriorated, that it has, perhaps, improved more than any other institution in India. But the evil lies deep in the nature of the institution itself. The Judges have in our time deserved the greatest respect. Their judgment and integrity have done much to mitigate the vices of the system. The worst charge that can be brought against any of them is that of pertinacity, disinterested, conscientious pertinacity, in error. The real evil is the state of the law. You have two supreme powers in India. There is no arbitrator except a Legislature fifteen thousand miles off. Such a system is on the face of it an absurdity in politics. My wonder is, not that this system has several times been on the point of producing fatal consequences to the peace and resources of India;—those, I think, are the words in which Warren Hastings described the effect of the contest between his Government and the Judges;—but that it has not actually produced such consequences. The most distinguished members of the Indian Government, the most distinguished Judges of the Supreme Court, call upon you to reform this system. Sir Charles Metcalfe, Sir Charles Grey, represent with equal urgency the expediency of having one single paramount council armed with legislative power. The admission of Europeans to India renders it absolutely necessary not to delay our decision. The effect of that admission would be to raise a hundred questions, to produce a hundred contests between the Council and the judicature. The Government would be paralysed at the precise moment at which all its energy was required. While the two equal powers were acting in opposite directions, the whole machine of the state would stand still. The Europeans would be uncontrolled. The natives would be unprotected. The consequences I will not pretend to foresee. Everything beyond is darkness and confusion.

Having given to the Government supreme legislative power, we next propose to give to it for a time the assistance of a Commission for the purpose of digesting and reforming the laws of India, so that those laws may, as soon as possible, be formed into a code. Gentlemen of whom I wish to speak with the highest respect have expressed a doubt whether India be at present in a fit state to receive a benefit which is not yet enjoyed by this free and highly civilised country. Sir, I can allow to this argument very little weight beyond that which it derives from the personal authority of those who use it. For in the first place, our freedom and our high civilisation make this improvement, desirable as it must always be, less indispensably necessary to us than to our Indian subjects; and in the next place our freedom and civilisation, I fear, make it far more difficult for us to obtain this benefit for ourselves than to bestow it on them.

I believe that no country ever stood so much in need of a code of laws as India; and I believe also that there never was a country in which the want might so easily be supplied. I said that there were many points of analogy between the state of that country after the fall of the Mogul power, and the state of Europe after the fall of the Roman empire. In one respect the analogy is very striking. As there were in Europe then, so there are in India now, several systems of law widely differing from each other, but coexisting and coequal. The indigenous population has its own laws. Each of the successive races of conquerors has brought with it its own peculiar jurisprudence: the Mussulman his Koran and the innumerable commentators on the Koran; the Englishman his Statute Book and his Term Reports. As there were established in Italy, at one and the same time, the Roman law, the Lombard law, the Ripuarian law, the Bavarian law, and the Salic law, so we have now in our Eastern empire Hindoo law, Mahometan law, Parsee law, English law, perpetually mingling with each other and disturbing each other, varying with the person, varying with the place. In one and the same cause the process and pleadings are in the fashion of one nation, the judgment is according to the laws of another. An issue is evolved according to the rules of Westminster, and decided according to those of Benares. The only Mahometan book in the nature of a code is the Koran; the only Hindoo book the Institutes. Every body who knows those books knows that they provide for a very small part of the cases which must arise in every community. All beyond them is comment and tradition. Our regulations in civil matters do not define rights, but merely establish remedies. If a point of Hindoo law arises, the Judge calls on the Pundit for an opinion. If a point of Mahometan law arises, the Judge applies to the Cauzee. What the integrity of these functionaries is, we may learn from Sir William Jones. That eminent man declared that he could not answer it to his conscience to decide any point of law on the faith of a Hindoo expositor. Sir Thomas Strange confirms this declaration. Even if there were no suspicion of corruption on the part of the interpreters of the law, the science which they profess is in such a state of confusion that no reliance can be placed on their answers. Sir Francis Macnaghten tells us, that it is a delusion to fancy that there is any known and fixed law under which the Hindoo people live; that texts may be produced on any side of any question; that expositors equal in authority perpetually contradict each other; that the obsolete law is perpetually confounded with the law actually in force, and that the first lesson to be impressed on a functionary who has to administer Hindoo law is that it is vain to think of extracting certainty from the books of the jurist. The consequence is that in practice the decisions of the tribunals are altogether arbitrary. What is administered is not law, but a kind of rude and capricious equity. I asked an able and excellent judge lately returned from India how one of our Zillah Courts[1] would decide several legal questions of great importance, questions not involving considerations of religion or of caste, mere questions of commercial law. He told me, that it was a mere lottery. He knew how he should himself decide them. But he knew nothing more. I asked a most distinguished civil servant of the Company, with reference to the clause in this Bill on the subject of slavery, whether at present, if a dancing girl ran away from her master, the judge would force her to go back. "Some judges," he said, "send a girl back. Others set her at liberty. The whole is a mere matter of chance. Everything depends on the temper of the individual judge."

[1] [An administrative district: the jurisdiction of a collector.]

Even in this country, we have had complaints of judge-made law; even in this country, where the standard of morality is higher than in almost any other part of the world; where, during several generations, not one depositary of our legal traditions has incurred the suspicion of personal corruption; where there are popular institutions; where every decision is watched by a shrewd and learned audience; where there is an intelligent and observant public; where every remarkable case is fully reported in a hundred newspapers; where, in short, there is everything which can mitigate the evils of such a system. But judge-made law, where there is an absolute government and a lax morality, where there is no bar and no public, is a curse and a scandal not to be endured. It is time that the magistrate should know what law he is to administer, and the subject should know under what law he is to live. We do not mean that all the people of India should live under the same law: far from it: there is not a word in the bill, there was not a word in my right honorable friend's speech, susceptible of such an interpretation. We know how desirable that object is; but we also know that it is unattainable. We know that respect must be paid to feelings generated by differences of religion, of nation, and of caste. Much, I am persuaded, may be done to assimilate the different systems of law without wounding those feelings. But, whether we assimilate those systems or not, let us ascertain them; let us digest them. We propose no rash innovation; we wish to give no shock to the prejudices of any part of our subjects. Our principle is simply this; uniformity where you can have it; diversity where you must have it; but in all cases certainty.

As I believe that India stands more in need of a code[1] than any other country in the world, I believe also that there is no country on which that great benefit can more easily be conferred. A code is almost the only blessing, perhaps it is the only blessing, which absolute governments are better fitted to confer on a nation than popular governments. The work of digesting a vast and artificial system of unwritten jurisprudence is far more easily performed, and far better performed, by few minds than by many, by a Napoleon than by a Chamber of Deputies and a Chamber of Peers, by a government like that of Prussia or Denmark than by a government like that of England. A quiet knot of two or three veteran jurists is an infinitely better machinery for such a purpose than a large popular assembly divided, as such assemblies almost always are, into adverse factions. This seems to me, therefore, to be pre-

[1] [The code was mainly drafted by Macaulay himself as Legal Member of the Council 1834-8.]

cisely that point of time at which the advantage of a complete written code of laws may most easily be conferred on India. It is a work which cannot be well performed in an age of barbarism, which cannot without great difficulty be performed in an age of freedom. It is a work which especially belongs to a government like that of India, to an enlightened and paternal despotism.

I have detained the House so long, Sir, that I will defer what I had to say on some parts of this measure, important parts, indeed, but far less important, as I think, than those to which I have adverted, till we are in Committee. There is, however, one part of the bill on which, after what has recently passed elsewhere, I feel myself irresistibly impelled to say a few words. I allude to that wise, that benevolent, that noble clause, which enacts that no native of our Indian empire shall, by reason of his colour, his descent, or his religion, be incapable of holding office. At the risk of being called by that nickname which is regarded as the most opprobrious of all nicknames by men of selfish hearts and contracted minds, at the risk of being called a philosopher,[1] I must say that, to the last day of my life, I shall be proud of having been one of those who assisted in the framing of the bill which contains that clause. We are told that the time can never come when the natives of India can be admitted to high civil and military office. We are told that this is the condition on which we hold our power. We are told, that we are bound to confer on our subjects every benefit—which they are capable of enjoying?—no; —which it is in our power to confer on them?—no;—but which we can confer on them without hazard to the perpetuity of our own domination. Against that proposition I solemnly protest as inconsistent alike with sound policy and sound morality.

I am far, very far, from wishing to proceed hastily in this most delicate matter. I feel that, for the good of India itself, the admission of natives to high office must be effected by slow degrees. But that, when the fulness of time is come, when the interest of India requires the change, we ought to refuse to make that change lest we should endanger our own power, this is a doctrine of which I cannot think without indignation. Governments, like men, may buy existence too dear. "Propter vitam vivendi perdere causas," is a despicable policy both in individuals and in states. In the present case, such a policy would be not only despicable, but absurd. The mere extent of empire is not necessarily an advantage.

[1] [This echoes Canning's defence of Huskisson in 1826. "Why is it to be supposed that to apply the refinement of philosophy to the affairs of common life indicates obduracy of feeling or obtuseness of sensibility?"]

To many governments it has been cumbersome; to some it has been fatal. It will be allowed by every statesman of our time that the prosperity of a community is made up of the prosperity of those who compose the community, and that it is the most childish ambition to covet dominion which adds to no man's comfort or security. To the great trading nation, to the great manufacturing nation, no progress which any portion of the human race can make in knowledge, in taste for the conveniences of life, or in the wealth by which those conveniences are produced, can be matter of indifference. It is scarcely possible to calculate the benefits which we might derive from the diffusion of European civilisation among the vast population of the East. It would be, on the most selfish view of the case, far better for us that the people of India were well governed and independent of us, than ill governed and subject to us; that they were ruled by their own kings, but wearing our broadcloth, and working with our cutlery, than that they were performing their salams to English collectors and English magistrates, but were too ignorant to value, or too poor to buy, English manufactures. To trade with civilised men is infinitely more profitable than to govern savages. That would, indeed, be a doting wisdom, which, in order that India might remain a dependency, would make it an useless and costly dependency, which would keep a hundred millions of men from being our customers in order that they might continue to be our slaves.

It was, as Bernier tells us, the practice of the miserable tyrants whom he found in India, when they dreaded the capacity and spirit of some distinguished subject, and yet could not venture to murder him, to administer to him a daily dose of the pousta, a preparation of opium, the effect of which was in a few months to destroy all the bodily and mental powers of the wretch who was drugged with it, and to turn him into a helpless idiot. The detestable artifice, more horrible than assassination itself, was worthy of those who employed it. It is no model for the English nation. We shall never consent to administer the pousta to a whole community, to stupify and paralyse a great people whom God has committed to our charge, for the wretched purpose of rendering them more amenable to our control. What is power worth if it is founded on vice, on ignorance, and on misery; if we can hold it only by violating the most sacred duties which as governors we owe to the governed, and which, as a people blessed with far more than an ordinary measure of political liberty and of intellectual light, we owe to a race debased by three thousand years of despotism and priest-craft? We are free, we are civilised, to little purpose, if we grudge to any portion of the human race an equal measure of freedom and civilisation.

Are we to keep the people of India ignorant in order that we may keep them submissive? Or do we think that we can give them knowledge without awakening ambition? Or do we mean to awaken ambition and to provide it with no legitimate vent? Who will answer any of these questions in the affirmative? Yet one of them must be answered in the affirmative, by every person who maintains that we ought permanently to exclude the natives from high office. I have no fears. The path of duty is plain before us: and it is also the path of wisdom, of national prosperity, of national honor.

The destinies of our Indian empire are covered with thick darkness. It is difficult to form any conjecture as to the fate reserved for a state which resembles no other in history, and which forms by itself a separate class of political phenomena. The laws which regulate its growth and its decay are still unknown to us. It may be that the public mind of India may expand under our system till it has outgrown that system; that by good government we may educate our subjects into a capacity for better government; that, having become instructed in European knowledge, they may, in some future age, demand European institutions. Whether such a day will ever come I know not. But never will I attempt to avert or to retard it. Whenever it comes, it will be the proudest day in English history. To have found a great people sunk in the lowest depths of slavery and superstition, to have so ruled them as to have made them desirous and capable of all the privileges of citizens, would indeed be a title to glory all our own. The sceptre may pass away from us. Unforeseen accidents may derange our most profound schemes of policy. Victory may be inconstant to our arms. But there are triumphs which are followed by no reverse. There is an empire exempt from all natural causes of decay. Those triumphs are the pacific triumphs of reason over barbarism; that empire is the imperishable empire of our arts and our morals, our literature and our laws.

INDIAN EDUCATION

MINUTE OF THE 2ND OF FEBRUARY, 1835

[On his arrival in India, as a Member of the Supreme Council, Macaulay was appointed President of the Committee of Public Instruction, which he found irreconcilably split into two factions: the orientalists and those who wanted to teach the Indians Western learning. He addressed this minute to the Governor General, Lord Bentinck, who, on 7 March, pronounced in favour of "the promotion of European literature and science among the natives of India."]

As it seems to be the opinion of some of the gentlemen who compose the Committee of Public Instruction, that the course which they have hitherto pursued was strictly prescribed by the British Parliament in 1813, and as, if that opinion be correct, a legislative act will be necessary to warrant a change, I have thought it right to refrain from taking any part in the preparation of the adverse statements which are now before us, and to reserve what I had to say on the subject till it should come before me as a member of the Council of India.

It does not appear to me that the Act of Parliament can, by any art of construction, be made to bear the meaning which has been assigned to it. It contains nothing about the particular languages or sciences which are to be studied. A sum is set apart "for the revival and promotion of literature and the encouragement of the learned natives of India, and for the introduction and promotion of a knowledge of the sciences among the inhabitants of the British territories." It is argued, or rather taken for granted, that by literature, the Parliament can have meant only Arabic and Sanscrit literature, that they never would have given the honorable appellation of "a learned native" to a native who was familiar with the poetry of Milton, the Metaphysics of Locke, and the Physics of Newton; but that they meant to designate by that name only such persons as might have studied in the sacred books of the Hindoos all the uses of cusa-grass, and all the mysteries of absorption into the Deity. This does not appear to be a very satisfactory interpretation. To take a parallel case; suppose that the Pacha of Egypt, a country once superior in knowledge to the nations of Europe, but now sunk far below them, were to appropriate a sum for the purpose of "reviving and promoting literature, and encouraging learned natives of Egypt," would anybody infer that he meant the youth of his pachalic to give years to the study of hieroglyphics, to search into all the doctrines disguised under the fable of Osiris, and to ascertain with all possible accuracy the ritual with which cats and onions were anciently adored? Would he be justly charged with inconsistency, if, instead of employing his young subjects in deciphering obelisks, he were to order them to be instructed in the English and French languages, and in all the sciences to which those languages are the chief keys?

The words on which the supporters of the old system rely do not bear them out, and other words follow which seem to be quite decisive on the other side. This lac of rupees is set apart, not only for "reviving literature in India," the phrase on which their whole interpretation is founded, but also for "the introduction and promotion of a knowledge of the sciences among the inhabitants of the British territories,"—words which are alone sufficient to authorise all the changes for which I contend.

If the Council agree in my construction, no legislative Act will be necessary. If they differ from me, I will prepare a short Act rescinding that clause of the Charter of 1813, from which the difficulty arises.

The argument which I have been considering, affects only the form of proceeding. But the admirers of the Oriental system of education have used another argument, which, if we admit it to be valid, is decisive against all change. They conceive that the public faith is pledged to the present system, and that to alter the appropriation of any of the funds which have hitherto been spent in encouraging the study of Arabic and Sanscrit, would be down-right spoliation. It is not easy to understand by what process of reasoning they can have arrived at this conclusion. The grants which are made from the public purse for the encouragement of literature differed in no respect from the grants which are made from the same purse for other objects of real or supposed utility. We found a sanatarium on a spot which we suppose to be healthy. Do we thereby pledge ourselves to keep a sanatarium there, if the result should not answer our expectation? We commence the erection of a pier. Is it a violation of the public faith to stop the works, if we afterwards see reason to believe that the building will be useless? The rights of property are undoubtedly sacred. But nothing endangers those rights so much as the practice, now unhappily too common, of attributing them to things to which they do not belong. Those who would impart to abuses the sanctity of property are in truth imparting to the institution of property the unpopularity and the fragility of abuses. If the Government has given to any person a formal assurance; nay, if the Government has excited in any person's mind a reasonable expectation that he shall receive a certain income as a teacher or a learner of Sanscrit or Arabic, I would respect that person's pecuniary interests—I would rather err on the side of liberality to individuals than suffer the public faith to be called in question. But to talk of a Government pledging itself to teach certain languages and certain sciences, though those languages may become useless, though those sciences may be exploded, seems to me quite unmeaning. There is not a single word in any public instructions, from which it can be inferred that the Indian Government ever intended to give any pledge on this subject, or ever considered the destination of these funds as unalterably fixed. But had it been otherwise, I should have denied the competence of our predecessors to bind us by any pledge on such a subject. Suppose that a Government had in the last century enacted in the most solemn manner that all its subjects should, to the end of time, be inoculated for the small-pox: would that Government be bound to persist in the practice after Jenner's discovery? These promises, of which nobody claims the performance, and from which nobody can grant a release; these vested rights, which vest in nobody; this property without proprietors; this robbery, which makes nobody poorer, may be comprehended by persons of higher faculties than mine.— I consider this plea merely as a set form of words, regularly used both in England and in India, in defence of every abuse for which no other plea can be set up.

I hold this lac of rupees to be quite at the disposal of the Governor General in Council, for the purpose of promoting learning in India, in any way which may be thought most advisable. I hold his Lordship to be quite as free to direct that it shall no longer be employed in encouraging Arabic and Sanscrit, as he is to direct that the reward for killing tigers in Mysore shall be diminished, or that no more public money shall be expended on the chanting at the cathedral.

We now come to the gist of the matter. We have a fund to be employed as Government shall direct for the intellectual improvement of the people of this country. The simple question is, what is the most useful way of employing it?

All parties seem to be agreed on one point, that the dialects commonly spoken among the natives of this part of India, contain neither literary nor scientific information, and are, moreover, so poor and rude that, until they are enriched from some other quarter, it will not be easy to translate any valuable work into them. It seems to be admitted on all sides, that the intellectual improvement of those classes of the people who have the means of pursuing higher studies can at present be effected only by means of some language not vernacular amongst them.

What then shall that language be? One-half of the Committee maintain that it should be the English. The other half strongly recommend the Arabic and Sanscrit. The whole question seems to me to be, which language is the best worth knowing?

I have no knowledge of either Sanscrit or Arabic.—But I have done what I could to form a correct estimate of their value. I have read translations of the most celebrated Arabic and Sanscrit works. I have conversed both here and at home with men distinguished by their proficiency in the Eastern tongues. I am quite ready to take the Oriental learning at the valuation of the Orientalists themselves. I have never found one among them who could deny that a single shelf of a good European library was worth the whole native literature of India and Arabia. The intrinsic superiority of the Western literature is, indeed, fully admitted by those members of the Committee who support the Oriental plan of education.

It will hardly be disputed, I suppose, that the department of literature in which the Eastern writers stand highest is poetry. And I certainly never met with any Orientalist who ventured to maintain that the Arabic and Sanscrit poetry could be compared to that of the great European nations. But when we pass from works of imagination to works in which facts are recorded, and general principles investigated, the superiority of the Europeans becomes absolutely immeasurable. It is, I believe, no exaggeration to say, that all the historical information which has been collected from all the books written in the Sanscrit language is less valuable than what may be found in the most paltry abridgments used at preparatory schools in England. In every branch of physical or moral philosophy, the relative position of the two nations is nearly the same.

How, then, stands the case? We have to educate a people who cannot at present be educated by means of their mother-tongue. We must teach them some foreign language. The claims of our own language it is hardly necessary to recapitulate. It stands preeminent even among the languages of the west. It abounds with works of imagination not inferior to the noblest which Greece has bequeathed to us; with models of every species of eloquence; with historical compositions, which, considered merely as narratives, have seldom been surpassed, and which, considered as vehicles of ethical and political instruction, have never been equalled; with just and lively representations of human life and human nature; with the most profound speculations on metaphysics, morals, government, jurisprudence, and trade; with full and correct information respecting every experimental science which tends to preserve the health, to increase the comfort, or to expand the intellect of man. Whoever knows that language has ready access to all the vast intellectual wealth, which all the wisest nations of the earth have created and hoarded in the course of ninety generations. It may safely be said, that the literature now extant in that language is of far greater value than all the literature which three hundred years ago was extant in all the languages of the world together. Nor is this all. In India, English is the language spoken by the ruling class. It is spoken by the higher class of natives at the seats of Government. It is likely to become the language of commerce throughout the seas of the East. It is the language of two great European communities which are rising, the one in the south of Africa, the other in Australasia; communities which are every year becoming more important, and more closely connected with our Indian empire. Whether we look at the intrinsic value of our literature, or at the particular situation of this country, we shall see the strongest reason to think that, of all foreign tongues, the English tongue is that which would be the most useful to our native subjects.

The question now before us is simply whether, when it is in our power to teach this language, we shall teach languages in which, by universal confession, there are no books on any subject which deserve to be compared to our own; whether, when we can teach European science, we shall teach systems which, by universal confession, whenever they differ from those of Europe, differ for the worse; and whether, when we can patronise sound Philosophy and true History, we shall countenance, at the public expense, medical doctrines, which would disgrace an English farrier,—Astronomy, which would move laughter in girls at an English boarding school,—History, abounding with kings thirty feet high, and reigns thirty thousand years long,—and Geography, made up of seas of treacle and seas of butter.

We are not without experience to guide us. History furnishes several analogous cases, and they all teach the same lesson. There are in modern times, to go no further, two memorable instances of a great impulse given to the mind of a whole society,—of prejudices overthrown,—of knowledge diffused,—of taste purified,—of arts and sciences planted in countries which had recently been ignorant and barbarous.

The first instance to which I refer, is the great revival of letters among the Western nations at the close of the fifteenth and the beginning of the sixteenth century. At that time almost every thing that was worth reading was contained in the writings of the ancient Greeks and Romans. Had our ancestors acted as the Committee of Public Instruction has hitherto acted; had they neglected the language of Cicero and Tacitus; had they confined their attention to the old dialects of our own island; had they printed nothing and taught nothing at the universities but Chronicles in Anglo-Saxon, and Romances in Norman-French, would England have been what she now is? What the Greek and Latin were to the contemporaries of More and Ascham, our tongue is to the people of India. The literature of England is now more valuable than that of classical antiquity. I doubt whether the Sanscrit literature be as valuable as that of our Saxon and Norman progenitors. In some departments,—in History, for example, I am certain that it is much less so.

Another instance may be said to be still before our eyes. Within the last hundred and twenty years, a nation which has previously been in a state as barbarous as that in which our ancestors were before the crusades, has gradually emerged from the ignorance in which it was sunk, and has taken its place among civilized communities.—I speak of Russia. There is now in that country a large educated class, abounding with persons fit to serve the state in the highest functions, and in no wise inferior to the most accomplished men who adorn the best circles of Paris and London. There is reason to hope that this vast empire, which in the time of our grandfathers was probably behind the Punjab, may, in the time of our grandchildren, be pressing close on France and Britain in the career of improvement. And how was this change effected? Not by flattering national prejudices: not by feeding the mind of the young Muscovite with the old women's stories which his rude fathers had believed: not by filling his head with lying legends about St. Nicholas: not by encouraging him to study the great question, whether the world was or was not created on the 13th of September: not by calling him "a learned native," when he has mastered all these points of knowledge: but by teaching him those foreign languages in which the greatest mass of information had been laid up, and thus putting all that information within his reach. The languages of Western Europe civilized Russia. I cannot doubt that they will do for the Hindoo what they have done for the Tartar.

And what are the arguments against that course which seems to be alike recommended by theory and by experience? It is said that we ought to secure the co-operation of the native public, and that we can do this only by teaching Sanscrit and Arabic.

I can by no means admit that when a nation of high intellectual attainments undertakes to superintend the education of a nation comparatively ignorant, the learners are absolutely to prescribe the course which is to be taken by the teachers. It is not necessary, however, to say any thing on this subject. For it is proved by unanswerable evidence that we are not at present securing the co-operation of the natives. It would be bad enough to consult their intellectual taste at the expense of their intellectual health. But we are consulting neither,—we are withholding from them the learning for which they are craving, we are forcing on them the mock-learning which they nauseate.

This is proved by the fact that we are forced to pay our Arabic and Sanscrit students, while those who learn English are willing to pay us. All the declamations in the world about the love and reverence of the natives for their sacred dialects will never, in the mind of any impartial person, outweigh the undisputed fact, that we cannot find, in all our vast empire, a single student who will let us teach him those dialects unless we will pay him.

I have now before me the accounts of the Madrassa for one month,—the month of December, 1833. The Arabic students appear to have been seventy-seven in number. All receive stipends from the public. The whole amount paid to them is above 500 rupees a month. On the other side of the account stands the following item: Deduct amount realized from the out-students of English for the months of May, June and July last, 103 rupees.

I have been told that it is merely from want of local experience that I am surprised at these phenomena, and that it is not the fashion for students in India to study at their own charges. This only confirms me in my opinion. Nothing is more certain than that it never can in any part of the world be necessary to pay men for doing what they think pleasant and profitable. India is no exception to this rule. The people of India do not require to be paid for eating rice when they are hungry, or for wearing woollen cloth in the cold season. To come nearer to the case before us, the children who learn their letters and a little elementary Arithmetic from the village school-master are not paid by him. He is paid for teaching them. Why then is it necessary to pay people to learn Sanscrit and Arabic? Evidently because it is universally felt that the Sanscrit and Arabic are languages, the knowledge of which does not compensate for the trouble of acquiring them. On all such subjects the state of the market is the decisive test.

Other evidence is not wanting, if other evidence were required. A petition was presented last year to the Committee by several ex-students of the Sanscrit College. The petitioners stated that they had studied in the college ten or twelve years; that they had made themselves acquainted with Hindoo literature and science; that they had received certificates of proficiency: and what is the fruit of all this! "Notwithstanding such testimonials," they say, "we have but little prospect of bettering our condition without the kind assistance of your Honorable Committee, the indifference with which we are generally looked upon by our countrymen leaving no hope of encouragement and assistance from them." They therefore beg that they may be recommended to the Governor General for places under the Government, not places of high dignity or emolument, but such as may just enable them to exist. "We want means," they say, "for a decent living, and for our progressive improvement, which, however, we cannot obtain without the assistance of Government, by whom we have been educated and maintained from childhood." They conclude by representing, very pathetically, that they are sure that it was never the intention of Government, after behaving so liberally to them during their education, to abandon them to destitution and neglect.

I have been used to see petitions to Government for compensation. All these petitions, even the most unreasonable of them, proceeded on the supposition that some loss had been sustained—that some wrong had been inflicted. These are surely the first petitioners who ever demanded compensation for having been educated gratis,—for having been supported by the public during twelve years, and then sent forth into the world well furnished with literature and science. They represent their education as an injury which gives them a claim on the Government for redress, as an injury for which the stipends paid to them during the infliction were a very inadequate compensation. And I doubt not that they are in the right. They have wasted the best years of life in learning what procures for them neither bread nor respect. Surely we might, with advantage, have saved the cost of making these persons useless and miserable; surely, men may be brought up to be burdens to the public and objects of contempt to their neighbours at a somewhat smaller charge to the state. But such is our policy. We do not even stand neuter in the contest between truth and falsehood. We are not content to leave the natives to the influence of their own hereditary prejudices. To the natural difficulties which obstruct the progress of sound science in the East, we add fresh difficulties of our own making. Bounties and premiums, such as ought not to be given even for the propagation of truth, we lavish on false taste and false philosophy.

By acting thus we create the very evil which we fear. We are making that opposition which we do not find. What we spend on the Arabic and Sanscrit colleges is not merely a dead loss to the cause of truth; it is bounty-money paid to raise up champions of error. It goes to form a nest, not merely of helpless place-hunters, but of bigots prompted alike by passion and by interest to raise a cry against every useful scheme of education. If there should be any opposition among the natives to the change which I recommend, that opposition will be the effect of our own system. It will be headed by persons supported by our stipends and trained in our colleges. The longer we persevere in our present course, the more formidable will that opposition be. It will be every year reinforced by recruits whom we are paying. From the native society left to itself, we have no difficulties to apprehend; all the murmuring will come from that oriental interest which we have, by artificial means, called into being, and nursed into strength.

There is yet another fact, which is alone sufficient to prove that the feeling of the native public, when left to itself, is not such as the supporters of the old system represent it to be. The Committee have thought fit to lay out above a lac of rupees in printing Arabic and Sanscrit books. Those books find no purchasers. It is very rarely that a single copy is disposed of. Twenty-three thousand volumes, most of them folios and quartos, fill the libraries, or rather the lumber-rooms, of this body. The Committee contrive to get rid of some portion of their vast stock of oriental literature by giving books away. But they cannot give so fast as they print. About twenty thousand rupees a year are spent in adding fresh masses of waste paper to a hoard which, I should think, is already sufficiently ample. During the last three years, about sixty thousand rupees have been expended in this manner. The sale of Arabic and Sanscrit books, during those three years, has not yielded quite one thousand rupees. In the mean time the School-book Society is selling seven or eight thousand English volumes every year, and not only pays the expenses of printing, but realises a profit of 20 per cent. on its outlay.

The fact that the Hindoo law is to be learned chiefly from Sanscrit books, and the Mahomedan law from Arabic books, has been much insisted on, but seems not to bear at all on the question. We are commanded by Parliament to ascertain and digest the laws of India. The assistance of a law Commission has been given to us for that purpose. As soon as the code is promulgated, the Shasster and the Hedaya will be useless to a Moonsiff or Sudder Ameen. I hope and trust that before the boys who are now entering at the Madrassa and the Sanscrit college have completed their studies, this great work will be finished. It would be manifestly absurd to educate the rising generation with a view to a state of things which we mean to alter before they reach manhood.

But there is yet another argument which seems even more untenable. It is said that the Sanscrit and Arabic are the languages in which the sacred books of a hundred millions of people are written, and that they are, on that account, entitled to peculiar encouragement. Assuredly it is the duty of the British Government in India to be not only tolerant, but neutral on all religious questions. But to encourage the study of a literature admitted to be of small intrinsic value, only because that literature inculcates the most serious errors on the most important subjects, is a course hardly reconcileable with reason, with morality, or even with that very neutrality which ought, as we all agree, to be sacredly preserved. It is confessed that a language is barren of useful knowledge. We are to teach it because it is fruitful of monstrous superstitions. We are to teach false History, false Astronomy, false Medicine, because we find them in company with a false religion. We abstain, and I trust shall always abstain, from giving any public encouragement to those who are engaged in the work of converting natives to Christianity. And while we act thus, can we reasonably and decently bribe men out of the revenues of the state to waste their youth in learning how they are to purify themselves after touching an ass, or what text of the Vedas they are to repeat to expiate the crime of killing a goat?

It is taken for granted by the advocates of Oriental learning, that no native of this country can possibly attain more than a mere smattering of English. They do not attempt to prove this; but they perpetually insinuate it. They designate the education which their opponents recommend as a mere spelling book education. They assume it as undeniable, that the question is between a profound knowledge of Hindoo and Arabian literature and science on the one side, and a superficial knowledge of the rudiments of English on the other. This is not merely an assumption, but an assumption contrary to all reason and experience. We know that foreigners of all nations do learn our language sufficiently to have access to all the most abstruse knowledge which it contains, sufficiently to relish even the more delicate graces of our most idiomatic writers. There are in this very town natives who are quite competent to discuss political or scientific questions with fluency and precision in the English language. I have heard the very question on which I am now writing discussed by native gentlemen with a liberality and an intelligence which would do credit to any member of the Committee of Public Instruction. Indeed it is unusual to find, even in the literary circles of the continent, any foreigner who can express himself in English with so much facility and correctness as we find in many Hindoos. Nobody, I suppose, will contend that English is so difficult to a Hindoo as Greek to an Englishman. Yet an intelligent English youth, in a much smaller number of years than our unfortunate pupils pass at the Sanscrit college, becomes able to read, to enjoy, and even to imitate, not unhappily, the compositions of the best Greek Authors. Less than half the time which enables an English youth to read Herodotus and Sophocles, ought to enable a Hindoo to read Hume and Milton.

To sum up what I have said, I think it clear that we are not fettered by the Act of Parliament of 1813; that we are not fettered by any pledge expressed or implied; that we are free to employ our funds as we choose; that we ought to employ them in teaching what is best worth knowing; that English is better worth knowing than Sanscrit or Arabic; that the natives are desirous to be taught English, and are not desirous to be taught Sanscrit or Arabic; that neither as the languages of law, nor as the languages of religion, have the Sanscrit and Arabic any peculiar claim to our engagement; that it is possible to make natives of this country thoroughly good English scholars, and that to this end our efforts ought to be directed.

In one point I fully agree with the gentlemen to whose general views I am opposed. I feel with them, that it is impossible for us, with our limited means, to attempt to educate the body of the people. We must at present do our best to form a class who may be interpreters between us and the millions whom we govern; a class of persons, Indian in blood and colour, but English in taste, in opinions, in morals, and in intellect. To that class we may leave it to refine the vernacular dialects of the country, to enrich those dialects with terms of science borrowed from the Western nomenclature, and to render them by degrees fit vehicles for conveying knowledge to the great mass of the population.

I would strictly respect all existing interests. I would deal even generously with all individuals who have had fair reason to expect a pecuniary provision. But I would strike at the root of the bad system which has hitherto been fostered by us. I would at once stop the printing of Arabic and Sanscrit books, I would abolish the Madrassa and the Sanscrit college at Calcutta. Benares is the great seat of Brahmanical learning; Delhi, of Arabic learning. If we retain the Sanscrit college at Benares and the Mahometan college at Delhi, we do enough, and much more than enough in my opinion, for the Eastern languages. If the Benares and Delhi colleges should be retained, I would at least recommend that no stipends shall be given to any students who may hereafter repair thither, but that the people shall be left to make their own choice between the rival systems of education without being bribed by us to learn what they have no desire to know. The funds which would thus be placed at our disposal would enable us to give larger encouragement to the Hindoo college at Calcutta, and to establish in the principal cities throughout the Presidencies of Fort William and Agra schools in which the English language might be well and thoroughly taught.

If the decision of his Lordship in Council should be such as I anticipate, I shall enter on the performance of my duties with the greatest zeal and alacrity. If, on the other hand, it be the opinion of the Government that the present system ought to remain unchanged, I beg that I may be permitted to retire from the chair of the Committee. I feel that I could not be of the smallest use there—I feel, also, that I should be lending my countenance to what I firmly believe to be a mere delusion. I believe that the present system tends, not to accelerate the progress of truth, but to delay the natural death of expiring errors. I conceive that we have at present no right to the respectable name of a Board of Public Instruction. We are a Board for wasting public money, for printing books which are of less value than the paper on which they are printed was while it was blank; for giving artificial encouragement to absurd history, absurd metaphysics, absurd physics, absurd theology; for raising up a breed of scholars who find their scholarship an encumbrance and a blemish, who live on the public while they are receiving their education, and whose education is so utterly useless to them that when they have received it they must either starve or live on the public all the rest of their lives. Entertaining these opinions, I am naturally desirous to decline all share in the responsibility of a body, which unless it alters its whole mode of proceeding, I must consider not merely as useless, but as positively noxious.

COPYRIGHT. I

A SPEECH DELIVERED IN THE HOUSE OF COMMONS ON THE
5TH OF FEBRUARY, 1841

On the twenty-ninth of January, 1841, Mr. Serjeant Talfourd[1] obtained leave to bring in a bill to amend the law of copyright. The object
of this bill was to extend the term of copyright in a book to sixty years,
reckoned from the death of the writer.
On the fifth of February Mr. Serjeant Talfourd moved that the bill
should be read a second time. In reply to him the following Speech was
made. The bill was rejected by 45 votes to 38.

[*Note:* The law and its amendment may be summarised thus:
Existing law: Copyright for life *or* 28 years, whichever longer.
Talfourd: Copyright for life *and* 60 years.
Mahon: Copyright for life *and* 25 years.
Macaulay: Copyright for life *or* 42 years, whichever longer.]

THOUGH, Sir, it is in some sense agreeable to approach a subject
with which political animosities have nothing to do, I offer myself
to your notice with some reluctance. It is painful to me to take a
course which may possibly be misunderstood or misrepresented
as unfriendly to the interests of literature and literary men. It is
painful to me, I will add, to oppose my honorable and learned
friend on a question which he has taken up from the purest
motives, and which he regards with a parental interest. These
feelings have hitherto kept me silent when the law of copyright
has been under discussion. But as I am, on full consideration,
satisfied that the measure before us will, if adopted, inflict grievous
injury on the public, without conferring any compensating advantage on men of letters, I think it my duty to avow that opinion and
to defend it.

The first thing to be done, Sir, is to settle on what principles
the question is to be argued. Are we free to legislate for the public
good, or are we not? Is this a question of expediency, or is it a
question of right? Many of those who have written and petitioned
against the existing state of things treat the question as one of
right. The law of nature, according to them, gives to every man a
sacred and indefeasible property in his own ideas, in the fruits
of his own reason and imagination. The legislature has indeed
the power to take away this property, just as it has the power to

---

[1] [Talfourd's first Copyright Bill was introduced in 1837 and was
rewarded with the dedication of *Pickwick*. In 1841 he unsuccessfully
defended Moxon for publishing a blasphemous libel, *Queen Mab*.]

pass an act of attainder for cutting off an innocent man's head without a trial. But, as such an act of attainder would be legal murder, so would an act invading the right of an author to his copy be, according to these gentlemen, legal robbery.

Now, Sir, if this be so, let justice be done, cost what it may. I am not prepared like my honorable and learned friend, to agree to a compromise between right and expediency, and to commit an injustice for the public convenience. But I must say, that his theory soars far beyond the reach of my faculties. It is not necessary to go, on the present occasion, into a metaphysical inquiry about the origin of the right of property; and certainly nothing but the strongest necessity would lead me to discuss a subject so likely to be distasteful to the House. I agree, I own, with Paley in thinking that property is the creature of the law, and that the law which creates property can be defended only on this ground, that it is a law beneficial to mankind. But it is unnecessary to debate that point. For, even if I believed in a natural right of property, independent of utility and anterior to legislation, I should still deny that this right could survive the original proprietor. Few, I apprehend, even of those who have studied in the most mystical and sentimental schools of moral philosophy, will be disposed to maintain that there is a natural law of succession older and of higher authority than any human code. If there be, it is quite certain that we have abuses to reform much more serious than any connected with the question of copyright. For this natural law can be only one; and the modes of succession in the Queen's dominions are twenty. To go no further than England, land generally descends to the eldest son. In Kent the sons share and share alike. In many districts the youngest takes the whole. Formerly a portion of a man's personal property was secured to his family; and it was only of the residue that he could dispose by will. Now he can dispose of the whole by will: but you limited his power, a few years ago, by enacting that the will should not be valid unless there were two witnesses. If a man dies intestate, his personal property generally goes according to the statute of distributions; but there are local customs which modify that statute. Now which of all these systems is conformed to the eternal standard of right? Is it primogeniture, or gavelkind, or borough English? Are wills *jure divino*? Are the two witnesses *jure divino*? Might not the *pars rationabilis* of our old law have a fair claim to be regarded as of celestial institution? Was the statute of distributions enacted in Heaven long before it was adopted by Parliament? Or is it to Custom of York, or to Custom of London, that this preeminence belongs? Surely, Sir, even those who hold that there is a natural right of property must admit that rules prescribing the manner in which the effects of deceased persons shall be distributed are purely arbitrary, and originate altogether in the will of the legislature. If so, Sir, there is no controversy between my honorable and learned friend and myself as to the principles on which this question is to be argued. For the existing law gives an author copyright during his natural life; nor do I propose to invade that privilege, which I should, on the contrary, be prepared to defend strenuously against any assailant. The only point in issue between us is, how long after an author's death the State shall recognise a copyright in his representatives and assigns; and it can, I think, hardly be disputed by any rational man that this is a point which the legislature is free to determine in the way which may appear to be most conducive to the general good.

We may now, therefore, I think, descend from these high regions, where we are in danger of being lost in the clouds, to firm ground and clear light. Let us look at this question like legislators, and after fairly balancing conveniences and inconveniences, pronounce between the existing law of copyright and the law now proposed to us. The question of copyright, Sir, like most questions of civil prudence, is neither black nor white, but grey. The system of copyright has great advantages and great disadvantages; and it is our business to ascertain what these are, and then to make an arrangement under which the advantages may be as far as possible secured, and the disadvantages as far as possible excluded. The charge which I bring against my honorable and learned friend's bill is this, that it leaves the advantages nearly what they are at present, and increases the disadvantages at least four fold.

The advantages arising from a system of copyright are obvious. It is desirable that we should have a supply of good books: we cannot have such a supply unless men of letters are liberally remunerated; and the least objectionable way of remunerating them is by means of copyright. You cannot depend for literary instruction and amusement on the leisure of men occupied in the pursuits of active life. Such men may occasionally produce compositions of great merit. But you must not look to such men for works which require deep meditation and long research. Works of that kind you can expect only from persons who make literature the business of their lives. Of these persons few will be found among the rich and the noble. The rich and the noble are not impelled to intellectual exertion by necessity. They may be impelled to intellectual exertion by the desire of distinguishing themselves, or by the desire of benefiting the community. But it is generally within these walls that they seek to signalise themselves and to serve their fellow creatures. Both their ambition and their public spirit, in a country like this, naturally take a political turn. It is then on men whose profession is literature, and whose private means are not ample, that you must rely for a supply of valuable books. Such men must be remunerated for their literary labour. And there are only two ways in which they can be remunerated. One of those ways is patronage; the other is copyright.

There have been times in which men of letters looked, not to the public, but to the government, or to a few great men, for the reward of their exertions. It was thus in the time of Mæcenas and Pollio at Rome, of the Medici at Florence, of Lewis the Fourteenth in France, of Lord Halifax and Lord Oxford in this country. Now, Sir, I well know that there are cases in which it is fit and graceful, nay, in which it is a sacred duty to reward the merits or to relieve the distresses of men of genius by the exercise of this species of liberality. But these cases are exceptions. I can conceive no system more fatal to the integrity and independence of literary men than one under which they should be taught to look for their daily bread to the favour of ministers and nobles. I can conceive no system more certain to turn those minds which are formed by nature to be the blessings and ornaments of our species into public scandals and pests.

We have, then, only one resource left. We must betake ourselves to copyright, be the inconveniences of copyright what they may. Those inconveniences, in truth, are neither few nor small. Copyright is monopoly, and produces all the effects which the general voice of mankind attributes to monopoly. My honorable and learned friend talks very contemptuously of those who are led away by the theory that monopoly makes things dear. That monopoly makes things dear is certainly a theory, as all the great truths which have been established by the experience of all ages and nations, and which are taken for granted in all reasonings, may be said to be theories. It is a theory in the same sense in which it is a theory, that day and night follow each other, that lead is heavier than water, that bread nourishes, that arsenic poisons, that alcohol intoxicates. If, as my honorable and learned friend seems to think, the whole world is in the wrong on this point, if the real effect of monopoly is to make articles good and cheap why does he stop short in his career of change? Why does he limit the operation of so salutary a principle to sixty years? Why does he consent to anything short of a perpetuity? He told us that in consenting to anything short of a perpetuity he was making a compromise between extreme right and expediency. But if his opinion about monopoly be correct, extreme right and expediency would coincide. Or rather why should we not restore the monopoly of the East India trade to the East India Company? Why should we not revive all those old monopolies which, in Elizabeth's reign, galled our fathers so severely that, maddened by intolerable wrong, they opposed to their sovereign a resistance before which her haughty spirit quailed for the first and for the last time? Was it the cheapness and excellence of commodities that then so violently stirred the indignation of the English people? I believe, Sir, that I may safely take it for granted that the effect of monopoly generally is to make articles scarce, to make them dear, and to make them bad. And I may with equal safety challenge my honorable friend to find out any distinction between copyright and other privileges of the same kind; any reason why a monopoly of books should produce an effect directly the reverse of that which was produced by the East India Company's monopoly of tea, or by Lord Essex's monopoly of sweet wines. Thus, then, stands the case. It is good that authors should be remunerated; and the least exceptionable way of remunerating them is by a monopoly. Yet monopoly is an evil. For the sake of the good we must submit to the evil; but the evil ought not to last a day longer than is necessary for the purpose of securing the good.

Now, I will not affirm, that the existing law is perfect, that it exactly hits the point at which the monopoly ought to cease; but this I confidently say, that the existing law is very much nearer that point than the law proposed by my honorable and learned friend. For consider this; the evil effects of the monopoly are proportioned to the length of its duration. But the good effects for the sake of which we bear with the evil effects are by no means proportioned to the length of its duration. A monopoly of sixty years produces twice as much evil as a monopoly of thirty years, and thrice as much evil as a monopoly of twenty years. But it is by no means the fact that a posthumous monopoly of sixty years gives to an author thrice as much pleasure and thrice as strong a motive as a posthumous monopoly of twenty years. On the contrary, the difference is so small as to be hardly perceptible. We all know how faintly we are affected by the prospect of very distant advantages, even when they are advantages which we may reasonably hope that we shall ourselves enjoy. But an advantage that is to be enjoyed more than half a century after we are dead, by somebody, we know not by whom, perhaps by somebody unborn, by somebody utterly unconnected with us, is really no motive at all to action. It is very probable, that in the course of some generations, land in the unexplored and unmapped heart of the Australasian continent, will be very valuable. But there is none of us who would lay down five pounds for a whole province in the heart of the Australasian continent. We know, that neither we, nor anybody for whom we care, will ever receive a farthing of rent from such a province. And a man is very little moved by the thought that in the year 2000 or 2100, somebody who claims through him will employ more shepherds than Prince Esterhazy, and will have the finest house and gallery of pictures at Victoria or Sydney. Now, this is the sort of boon which my honorable and learned friend holds out to authors. Considered as a boon to them, it is a mere nullity; but, considered as an impost on the public, it is no nullity, but a very serious and pernicious reality. I will take an example. Dr. Johnson died fifty-six years ago. If the law were what my honorable and learned friend wishes to make it, somebody would now have the monopoly of Dr. Johnson's works. Who that somebody would be it is impossible to say; but we may venture to guess. I guess, then, that it would have been some bookseller, who was the assign of another bookseller, who was the grandson of a third bookseller, who had bought the copyright from Black Frank, the Doctor's servant and residuary legatee, in 1785 or 1786. Now, would the knowledge that this copyright would exist in 1841 have been a source of gratification to Johnson? Would it have stimulated his exertions? Would it have once drawn him out of his bed before noon? Would it have once cheered him under a fit of the spleen? Would it have induced him to give us one more allegory, one more life of a poet, one more imitation of Juvenal? I firmly believe not. I firmly believe that a hundred years ago, when he was writing our debates for the Gentleman's Magazine, he would very much rather have had twopence to buy a plate of shin of beef at a cook's shop underground. Considered as a reward to him, the difference between a twenty years' term and a sixty years' term of posthumous copyright would have been nothing or next to nothing. But is the difference nothing to us? I can buy Rasselas for sixpence; I might have had to give five shillings for it. I can buy the Dictionary, the entire genuine Dictionary, for two guineas, perhaps for less; I might have had to give five or six guineas for it. Do I grudge this to a man like Dr. Johnson? Not at all. Show me that the prospect of this boon roused him to any vigorous effort, or sustained his spirits under depressing circumstances, and I am quite willing to pay the price of such an object, heavy as that price is. But what I do complain of is that my circumstances are to be worse, and Johnson's none the better; that I am to give five pounds for what to him was not worth a farthing.

The principle of copyright is this. It is a tax on readers for the purpose of giving a bounty to writers. The tax is an exceedingly bad one; it is a tax on one of the most innocent and most salutary of human pleasures; and never let us forget, that a tax on innocent pleasures is a premium on vicious pleasures. I admit, however, the necessity of giving a bounty to genius and learning. In order to give such a bounty, I willingly submit even to this severe and burdensome tax. Nay, I am ready to increase the tax, if it can be shown that by so doing I should proportionally increase the bounty. My complaint is, that my honorable and learned friend doubles, triples, quadruples, the tax, and makes scarcely any perceptible addition to the bounty. Why, Sir, what is the additional amount of taxation which would have been levied on the public for Dr. Johnson's works alone, if my honorable and learned friend's bill had been the law of the land? I have not data sufficient to form an opinion. But I am confident that the taxation on his Dictionary alone would have amounted to many thousands of pounds. In reckoning the whole additional sum which the holders of his copyrights would have taken out of the pockets of the public during the last half century at twenty thousand pounds, I feel satisfied that I very greatly underrate it. Now, I again say that I think it but fair that we should pay twenty thousand pounds in consideration of twenty thousand pounds' worth of pleasure and encouragement received by Dr. Johnson. But I think it very hard that we should pay twenty thousand pounds for what he would not have valued at five shillings.

My honorable and learned friend dwells on the claims of the posterity of great writers. Undoubtedly, Sir, it would be very pleasing to see a descendant of Shakespeare living in opulence on the fruits of his great ancestor's genius. A house maintained in splendour by such a patrimony would be a more interesting and striking object than Blenheim is to us, or than Strathfieldsaye will be to our children. But, unhappily, it is scarcely possible that, under any system, such a thing can come to pass. My honorable and learned friend does not propose that copyright shall descend to the eldest son, or shall be bound up by irrevocable entail. It is to be merely personal property. It is therefore highly improbable that it will descend during sixty years or half that term from parent

M—24

to child. The chance is that more people than one will have an interest in it. They will in all probability sell it and divide the proceeds. The price which a bookseller will give for it will bear no proportion to the sum which he will afterwards draw from the public, if his speculation proves successful. He will give little, if any thing, more for a term of sixty years than for a term of thirty or five and twenty. The present value of a distant advantage is always small; but when there is great room to doubt whether a distant advantage will be any advantage at all, the present value sinks to almost nothing. Such is the inconstancy of the public taste that no sensible man will venture to pronounce, with confidence, what the sale of any book published in our days will be in the years between 1890 and 1900. The whole fashion of thinking and writing has often undergone a change in a much shorter period than that to which my honorable and learned friend would extend posthumous copyright. What would have been considered the best literary property in the earliest part of Charles the Second's reign? I imagine Cowley's poems. Overleap sixty years, and you are in the generation of which Pope asked, "who now reads Cowley?" What works were ever expected with more impatience by the public than those of Lord Bolingbroke, which appeared, I think, in 1754. In 1814, no bookseller would have thanked you for the copyright of them all, if you had offered it to him for nothing. What would Paternoster Row give now for the copyright of Hayley's Triumphs of Temper, so much admired within the memory of many people still living? I say, therefore, that, from the very nature of literary property, it will almost always pass away from an author's family; and I say, that the price given for it to the family will bear a very small proportion to the tax which the purchaser, if his speculation turns out well, will in the course of a long series of years levy on the public.

If, Sir, I wished to find a strong and perfect illustration of the effects which I anticipate from long copyright, I should select,— my honorable and learned friend will be surprised,—I should select the case of Milton's granddaughter. As often as this bill has been under discussion, the fate of Milton's granddaughter has been brought forward by the advocates of monopoly. My honorable and learned friend has repeatedly told the story with great eloquence and effect. He has dilated on the sufferings, on the abject poverty, of this illfated woman, the last of an illustrious race. He tells us that, in the extremity of her distress, Garrick gave her a benefit, that Johnson wrote a prologue, and that the public contributed some hundreds of pounds. Was it fit, he asks, that she should receive, in this eleemosynary form, a small portion of what was in truth a debt? Why, he asks, instead of obtaining a pittance from charity, did she not live in comfort and luxury on the proceeds of the sale of her ancestor's works? But, Sir, will my honorable and learned friend tell me that this event, which he has so often and so pathetically described, was caused by the shortness of the term of copyright? Why, at that time, the duration of copyright was longer than even he, at present, proposes to make it. The monopoly lasted not sixty years, but for ever. At the time at which Milton's granddaughter asked charity, Milton's works were the exclusive property of a bookseller. Within a few months of the day on which the benefit was given at Garrick's theatre, the holder of the copyright of Paradise Lost,—I think it was Tonson, —applied to the Court of Chancery for an injunction against a bookseller, who had published a cheap edition of the great epic poem, and obtained the injunction. The representation of Comus was, if I remember rightly, in 1750; the injunction in 1752. Here, then, is a perfect illustration of the effect of long copyright. Milton's works are the property of a single publisher. Everybody who wants them must buy them at Tonson's shop, and at Tonson's price. Whoever attempts to undersell Tonson is harassed with legal proceedings. Thousands who would gladly possess a copy of Paradise Lost, must forego that great enjoyment. And what, in the meantime, is the situation of the only person for whom we can suppose that the author, protected at such a cost to the public, was at all interested? She is reduced to utter destitution. Milton's works are under a monopoly. Milton's granddaughter is starving. The reader is pillaged; but the writer's family is not enriched. Society is taxed doubly. It has to give an exorbitant price for the poems; and it has at the same time to give alms to the only sur- viving descendant of the poet.

But this is not all. I think it right, Sir, to call the attention of the House to an evil which is perhaps more to be apprehended when an author's copyright remains in the hands of his family, than when it is transferred to booksellers. I seriously fear that, if such a measure as this should be adopted, many valuable works will be either totally suppressed or grievously mutilated. I can prove that this danger is not chimerical; and I am quite certain that, if the danger be real, the safeguards which my honorable and learned friend has devised are altogether nugatory. That the danger is not chimerical may easily be shown. Most of us, I am sure, have known persons who, very erroneously as I think, but from the best motives, would not choose to reprint Fielding's novels, or Gibbon's History of the Decline and Fall of the Roman Empire. Some gentlemen may perhaps be of opinion, that it would be as well if Tom Jones and Gibbon's History were never reprinted. I will not, then, dwell on these or similar cases. I will take cases respecting which it is not likely that there will be any difference of opinion here; cases, too, in which the danger of which I now speak is not matter of supposition, but matter of fact. Take Richardson's novels. Whatever I may, on the present occasion, think of my honorable and learned friend's judgment as a legislator, I must always respect his judgment as a critic. He will, I am sure, say that Richardson's novels are among the most valuable, among the most original works in our language. No writings have done more to raise the fame of English genius in foreign countries. No writings are more deeply pathetic. No writings, those of Shakespeare excepted, show more profound knowledge of the human heart. As to their moral tendency, I can cite the most respectable testimony. Dr. Johnson describes Richardson as one who had taught the passions to move at the command of virtue. My dear and honored friend, Mr. Wilberforce, in his celebrated religious treatise, when speaking of the unchristian tendency of the fashionable novels of the eighteenth century, distinctly excepts Richardson from the censure. Another excellent person whom I can never mention without respect and kindness, Mrs. Hannah More, often declared in conversation, and has declared in one of her published poems, that she first learned from the writings of Richardson those principles of piety by which her life was guided. I may safely say that books celebrated as works of art through the whole civilised world, and praised for their moral tendency by Dr. Johnson, by Mr. Wilberforce, by Mrs. Hannah More, ought not to be suppressed. Sir, it is my firm belief, that if the law had been what my honorable and learned friend proposes to make it, they would have been suppressed. I remember Richardson's grandson well; he was a clergyman in the city of London; he was a most upright and excellent man; but he had conceived a strong prejudice against works of fiction. He thought all novel-reading not only frivolous but sinful. He said,—this I state on the authority of one of his clerical brethren who is now a bishop,—he said that he had never thought it right to read one of his grandfather's books. Suppose, Sir, that the law had been what my honorable and learned friend would make it. Suppose that the copyright of Richardson's novels had descended, as might well have been the case, to this gentleman. I firmly believe, that he would have thought it sinful to give them a wide circulation. I firmly believe, that he would not for a hundred thousand pounds have deliberately done what he thought sinful. He would not have reprinted them. And what protection does my honorable and learned friend give to the public in such a case? Why, Sir, what he proposes is this: if a book is not reprinted during five years, any person who wishes to reprint it may give notice in the London Gazette: the advertisement must be repeated three times: a year must elapse; and then, if the proprietor of the copyright does not put forth a new edition, he loses his exclusive privilege. Now, what protection is this to the public? What is a new edition? Does the law define the number of copies that make an edition? Does it limit the price of a copy? Are twelve copies on large paper, charged at thirty guineas each, an edition? It has been usual, when monopolies have been granted, to prescribe numbers and to limit prices. But I do not find that my honorable and learned friend proposes to do so in the present case. And, without some such provision the security which he offers is manifestly illusory. It is my conviction that, under such a system as that which he recommends to us, a copy of Clarissa would have been as rare as an Aldus or a Caxton.

I will give another instance. One of the most instructive, interesting, and delightful books in our language is Boswell's Life of Johnson. Now it is well known that Boswell's eldest son considered this book, considered the whole relation of Boswell to Johnson, as a blot in the escutcheon of the family. He thought, not perhaps altogether without reason, that his father had exhibited himself in a ludicrous and degrading light. And thus he became so sore and irritable that at last he could not bear to hear the Life of Johnson mentioned. Suppose that the law had been what my honorable and learned friend wishes to make it. Suppose that the copyright of Boswell's Life of Johnson had belonged, as it well might, during sixty years, to Boswell's eldest son. What would have been the consequence? An unadulterated copy of the finest biographical work in the world would have been as scarce as the first edition of Camden's Britannia.

These are strong cases. I have shown you that, if the law had been what you are now going to make it, the finest prose work of fiction in the language, the finest biographical work in the language, would very probably have been suppressed. But I have stated my case weakly. The books which I have mentioned are singularly inoffensive books, books not touching on any of those questions which drive even wise men beyond the bounds of wisdom. There are books of a very different kind, books which are the rallying points of great political and religious parties. What is likely to happen if the copyright of one of these books should by descent or transfer come into the possession of some hostile zealot? I will take a single instance. It is only fifty years since John Wesley died; and all his works, if the law had been what my honorable and learned friend wishes to make it, would now have been the property of some person or other. The sect founded by Wesley is the most numerous, the wealthiest, the most powerful, the most zealous of sects. In every parliamentary election it is a matter of the greatest importance to obtain the support of the Wesleyan Methodists. Their numerical strength is reckoned by hundreds of thousands. They hold the memory of their founder in the greatest reverence; and not without reason, for he was unquestionably a great and good man. To his authority they constantly appeal. His works are in their eyes of the highest value. His doctrinal writings they regard as containing the best system of theology ever deduced from Scripture. His journals, interesting even to the common reader, are peculiarly interesting to the Methodist: for they contain the whole history of that singular polity which, weak and despised in its beginning, is now, after the lapse of a century, so strong, so flourishing, and so formidable. The hymns to which he gave his Imprimatur are a most important part of the public worship of his followers. Now, suppose that the copyright of these works should belong to some person who holds the memory of Wesley and the doctrines and discipline of the Methodists in abhorrence. There are many such persons. The Ecclesiastical Courts are at this very time sitting on the case of a clergyman of the Established Church who refused Christian burial to a child baptized by a Methodist preacher. I took up the other day a work which is considered as among the most respectable organs of a large and growing party in the Church of England, and there I saw John Wesley designated as a forsworn priest. Suppose that the works of Wesley were suppressed. Why, Sir, such a grievance would be enough to shake the foundations of Government. Let gentlemen who are attached to the Church reflect for a moment what their feelings would be if the Book of Common Prayer were not to be reprinted for thirty or forty years, if the price of a Book of Common Prayer were run up to five or ten guineas. And then let them determine whether they will pass a law under which it is possible, under which it is probable, that so intolerable a wrong may be done to some sect consisting perhaps of half a million of persons.

I am so sensible, Sir, of the kindness with which the House has listened to me, that I will not detain you longer. I will only say this, that if the measure before us should pass, and should produce one tenth part of the evil which it is calculated to produce, and which I fully expect it to produce, there will soon be a remedy, though of a very objectionable kind. Just as the absurd acts which prohibited the sale of game were virtually repealed by the poacher, just as many absurd revenue acts have been virtually repealed by the smuggler, so will this law be virtually repealed by piratical booksellers. At present the holder of copyright has the public feeling on his side. Those who invade copyright are regarded as knaves who take the bread out of the mouths of deserving men. Every body is well pleased to see them restrained by the law, and compelled to refund their illgotten gains. No tradesmen of good repute will have anything to do with such disgraceful transactions. Pass this law: and that feeling is at an end. Men very different from the present race of piratical booksellers will soon infringe this intolerable monopoly. Great masses of capital will be constantly employed in the violation of the law. Every art will be employed to evade legal pursuit; and the whole nation will be in the plot. On which side indeed should the public sympathy be when the question is whether some book as popular as Robinson Crusoe, or the Pilgrim's Progress, shall be in every cottage, or whether it shall be confined to the libraries of the rich, for the advantage of the greatgrandson of a bookseller who, a hundred years before, drove a hard bargain for the copyright with the author when in great distress? Remember too that, when once it ceases to be considered as wrong and discreditable to invade literary property, no person can say where the invasion will stop. The public seldom make nice distinctions. The wholesome copyright which now exists will share in the disgrace and danger of the new copyright which you are about to create. And you will find that, in attempting to impose unreasonable restraints on the reprinting of the works of the dead, you have, to a great extent, annulled those restraints which now prevent men from pillaging and defrauding the living. If I saw, Sir, any probability that this bill could be so amended in the Committee that my objections might be removed, I would not divide the House in this stage. But I am so fully convinced that no alteration which would not seem insupportable to my honorable and learned friend, could render his measure supportable to me, that I must move, though with regret, that this bill be read a second time this day six months.

COPYRIGHT. II

A SPEECH DELIVERED IN A COMMITTEE OF THE HOUSE OF COMMONS
ON THE 6TH OF APRIL, 1842

On the third of March, 1842, Lord Mahon obtained permission to bring in a bill to amend the Law of Copyright. This bill extended the term of Copyright in a book to twenty-five years, reckoned from the death of the author.

On the sixth of April the House went into Committee on the bill, and Mr. Greene took the Chair. Several divisions took place, of which the result was that the plan suggested in the following Speech was, with some modifications, adopted.

MR. GREENE,

I have been amused and gratified by the remarks which my noble friend[1] has made on the arguments by which I prevailed on the last House of Commons to reject the bill introduced by a very able and accomplished man, Mr. Serjeant Talfourd. My noble friend has done me a high and rare honor. For this is, I believe, the first occasion on which a speech made in one Parliamant has been answered in another. I should not find it difficult to vindicate the soundness of the reasons which I formerly urged, to set them in a clearer light, and to fortify them by additional facts. But it seems to me that we had better discuss the bill which is now on our table than the bill which was there fourteen months ago. Glad I am to find that there is a very wide difference between the two bills, and that my noble friend, though he has tried to refute my arguments, has acted as if he had been convinced by them. I objected to the term of sixty years as far too long. My noble friend has cut that term down to twenty-five years. I warned the House that, under the provisions of Mr. Serjeant Talfourd's bill, valuable works might not improbably be suppressed by the representatives of authors. My noble friend has prepared a clause which, as he thinks, will guard against that danger. I will not therefore waste the time of the Committee by debating points which he has conceded, but will proceed at once to the proper business of this evening.

Sir, I have no objection to the principle of my noble friend's bill. Indeed, I had no objection to the principle of the bill of last year. I have long thought that the term of copyright ought to be extended. When Mr. Serjeant Talfourd moved for leave to bring in his bill, I did not oppose the motion. Indeed, I meant to vote

[1] Lord Mahon.

for the second reading, and to reserve what I had to say for the Committee. But the learned Serjeant left me no choice. He, in strong language, begged that nobody who was disposed to reduce the term of sixty years would divide with him. "Do not," he said, "give me your support if all that you mean to grant to men of letters is a miserable addition of fourteen or fifteen years to the present term. I do not wish for such support. I despise it." Not wishing to obtrude on the learned Serjeant a support which he despised, I had no course left but to take the sense of the House on the second reading. The circumstances are now different. My noble friend's bill is not at present a good bill; but it may be improved into a very good bill; nor will he, I am persuaded, withdraw it if it should be so improved. He and I have the same object in view; but we differ as to the best mode of attaining that object. We are equally desirious to extend the protection now enjoyed by writers. In what way it may be extended with most benefit to them and with least inconvenience to the public, is the question.

The present state of the law is this. The author of a work has a certain copyright in that work for a term of twenty-eight years. If he should live more than twenty-eight years after the publication of the work, he retains the copyright to the end of his life.

My noble friend does not propose to make any addition to the term of twenty-eight years. But he proposes that the copyright shall last twenty-five years after the author's death. Thus my noble friend makes no addition to that term which is certain, but makes a very large addition to that term which is uncertain.

My plan is different. I would make no addition to the uncertain term; but I would make a large addition to the certain term. I propose to add fourteen years to the twenty-eight years which the law now allows to an author. His copyright will, in this way, last till his death, or till the expiration of forty-two years, whichever shall first happen. And I think that I shall be able to prove to the satisfaction of the Committee that my plan will be more beneficial to literature and to literary men than the plan of my noble friend.

It must surely, Sir, be admitted that the protection which we give to books ought to be distributed as evenly as possible, that every book should have a fair share of that protection, and no book more than a fair share. It would evidently be absurd to put tickets into a wheel, with different numbers marked upon them, and to make writers draw, one a term of twenty-eight years, another a term of fifty, another a term of ninety. And yet this sort of lottery is what my noble friend proposes to establish. I know that we cannot altogether exclude chance. You have two terms of copyright; one certain, the other uncertain; and we cannot, I admit, get rid of the uncertain term. It is proper, no doubt, that an author's copyright should last during his life. But, Sir, though we cannot altogether exclude chance, we can very much diminish the share which chance must have in distributing the recompense which we wish to give to genius and learning. By every addition which we make to the certain term we diminish the influence of chance; by every addition which we make to the uncertain term we increase the influence of chance. I shall make myself best understood by putting cases. Take two eminent female writers, who died within our own memory, Madame D'Arblay and Miss Austen. As the law now stands, Miss Austen's charming novels would have only from twenty-eight to thirty-three years of copyright. For that extraordinary woman died young: she died before her genius was fully appreciated by the world. Madame D'Arblay outlived the whole generation to which she belonged. The copyright of her celebrated novel, Evelina, lasted, under the present law, sixty-two years. Surely this inequality is sufficiently great, sixty-two years of copyright for Evelina, only twenty-eight for Persuasion. But to my noble friend this inequality seems not great enough. He proposes to add twenty-five years to Madame D'Arblay's term, and not a single day to Miss Austen's term. He would give to Persuasion a copyright of only twenty-eight years, as at present, and to Evelina a copyright more than three times as long, a copyright of eighty-seven years. Now, is this reasonable? See, on the other hand, the operation of my plan. I make no addition at all to Madame D'Arblay's term of sixty-two years, which is, in my opinion, quite long enough; but I extend Miss Austen's term to forty-two years, which is, in my opinion, not too much. You see, Sir, that at present chance has too much sway in this matter; that at present the protection which the state gives to letters is very unequally given. You see that if my noble friend's plan be adopted, more will be left to chance than under the present system, and you will have such inequalities as are unknown under the present system. You see also that, under the system which I recommend, we shall have, not perfect certainty, not perfect equality, but much less uncertainty and inequality than at present.

But this is not all. My noble friend's plan is not merely to institute a lottery in which some writers will draw prizes and some will draw blanks. It is much worse than this. His lottery is so contrived that, in the vast majority of cases, the blanks will fall to the best books, and the prizes to books of inferior merit.

Take Shakspeare., My noble friend gives a longer protection than I should give to Love's Labour's Lost, and Pericles, Prince of Tyre; but he gives a shorter protection than I should give to Othello and Macbeth.

Take Milton. Milton died in 1674. The copyrights of Milton's great works would, according to my noble friend's plan, expire in 1699. Comus appeared in 1634, the Paradise Lost in 1668. To Comus, then, my noble friend would give sixty-five years of copyright, and to the Paradise Lost only thirty-one years. Is that reasonable? Comus is a noble poem: but who would rank it with the Paradise Lost? My plan would give forty-two years both to the Paradise Lost and to Comus.

Let us pass on from Milton to Dryden. My noble friend would give more than sixty years of copyright to Dryden's worst works; to the encomiastic verses on Oliver Cromwell, to the Wild Gallant, to the Rival Ladies, to other wretched pieces as bad as anything written by Flecknoe or Settle: but for Theodore and Honoria, for Tancred and Sigismunda, for Cimon and Iphigenia, for Palamon and Arcite, for Alexander's Feast, my noble friend thinks a copyright of twenty-eight years sufficient. Of all Pope's works, that to which my noble friend would give the largest measure of protection is the volume of Pastorals, remarkable only as the production of a boy. Johnson's first work was a Translation of a Book of Travels in Abyssinia, published in 1735. It was so poorly executed that in his later years he did not like to hear it mentioned. Boswell once picked up a copy of it, and told his friend that he had done so. "Do not talk about it," said Johnson: "it is a thing to be forgotten." To this performance my noble friend would give protection during the enormous term of seventy-five years. To the Lives of the Poets he would give protection during about thirty years. Well; take Henry Fielding; it matters not whom I take, but take Fielding. His early works are read only by the curious, and would not be read even by the curious, but for the fame which he acquired in the later part of his life by works of a very different kind. What is the value of the Temple Beau, of the Intriguing Chambermaid, of half a dozen other plays of which few gentlemen have even heard the names? Yet to these worthless pieces my noble friend would give a term of copyright longer by more than twenty years than that which he would give to Tom Jones and Amelia.

Go on to Burke. His little tract, entitled The Vindication of Natural Society, is certainly not without merit; but it would not be remembered in our days if it did not bear the name of Burke. To this tract my noble friend would give a copyright of near seventy years. But to the great work on the French Revolution, to the Appeal from the New to the Old Whigs, to the letters on the Regicide Peace, he would give a copyright of thirty years or little more.

And, Sir, observe that I am not selecting here and there extra-ordinary instances in order to make up the semblance of a case. I am taking the greatest names of our literature in chronological order. Go to other nations; go to remote ages; you will still find the general rule the same. There was no copyright at Athens or Rome; but the history of the Greek and Latin literature illustrates my argument quite as well as if copyright had existed in ancient times. Of all the plays of Sophocles, the one to which the plan of my noble friend would have given the most scanty recompence would have been that wonderful masterpiece, the Œdipus at Colonos. Who would class together the Speech of Demosthenes against his Guardians, and the Speech for the Crown? My noble friend, indeed, would not class them together. For to the Speech against the Guardians he would give a copyright of near seventy years; and to the incomparable Speech for the Crown a copy-right of less than half that length. Go to Rome. My noble friend would give more than twice as long a term to Cicero's juvenile declamation in defence of Roscius Amerinus as to the Second Philippic. Go to France; my noble friend would give a far longer term to Racine's Frères Ennemis than to Athalie, and to Molière's Étourdi than to Tartuffe. Go to Spain. My noble friend would give a longer term to forgotten works of Cervantes, works which nobody now reads, than to Don Quixote. Go to Germany. Accord-ing to my noble friend's plan, of all the works of Schiller the Robbers would be the most favoured: of all the works of Goethe, the Sorrows of Werter would be the most favoured. I thank the Committee for listening so kindly to this long enumeration. Gentlemen will perceive, I am sure, that it is not from pedantry that I mention the names of so many books and authors. But just as, in our debates on civil affairs, we constantly draw illustrations from civil history, we must, in a debate about literary property, draw our illustrations from literary history. Now, Sir, I have, I think, shown from literary history that the effect of my noble friend's plan would be to give to crude and imperfect works, to third-rate and fourth-rate works, a great advantage over the highest productions of genius. It is impossible to account for the facts which I have laid before you by attributing them to mere accident. Their number is too great, their character too uniform. We must seek for some other explanation; and we shall easily find one

It is the law of our nature that the mind shall attain its full power by slow degrees; and this is especially true of the most vigorous minds. Young men, no doubt, have often produced works of great merit; but it would be impossible to name any writer of the first order whose juvenile performances were his best. That all the most valuable books of history, of philology, of physical and metaphysical science, of divinity, of political economy, have been produced by men of mature years will hardly be disputed. The case may not be quite so clear as respects works of the imagination. And yet I know no work of the imagination of the very highest class that was ever, in any age or country, produced by a man under thirty-five. Whatever powers a youth may have received from nature, it is impossible that his taste and judgment can be ripe, that his mind can be richly stored with images, that he can have observed the vicissitudes of life, that he can have studied the nicer shades of character. How, as Marmontel very sensibly said, is a person to paint portraits who has never seen faces? On the whole I believe that I may, without fear of contradiction, affirm this, that of the good books now extant in the world more than nineteen-twentieths were published after the writers had attained the age of forty. If this be so, it is evident that the plan of my noble friend is framed on a vicious principle. For, while he gives to juvenile productions a very much larger protection than they now enjoy, he does comparatively little for the works of men in the full maturity of their powers, and absolutely nothing for any work which is published during the last three years of the life of the writer. For, by the existing law, the copyright of such a work lasts twenty-eight years from the publication; and my noble friend gives only twenty-five years to be reckoned from the writer's death.

What I recommend is that the certain term, reckoned from the date of publication, shall be forty-two years instead of twenty-eight years. In this arrangement there is no uncertainty, no inequality. The advantage which I propose to give will be the same to every book. No work will have so long a copyright as my noble friend gives to some books, or so short a copyright as he gives to others. No copyright will last ninety years. No copyright will end in twenty-eight years. To every book published in the course of the last seventeen years of a writer's life I give a longer term of copyright than my noble friend gives; and I am confident that no person versed in literary history will deny this,—that in general the most valuable works of an author are published in the course of the last seventeen years of his life. I will rapidly enumerate a few, and but a few, of the great works of English writers to which my plan is more favorable than my noble friend's plan. To Lear, to Macbeth, to Othello, to the Fairy Queen, to the Paradise Lost, to Bacon's Novum Organum and De Augmentis, to Locke's Essay on the Human Understanding, to Clarendon's History, to Hume's History, to Gibbon's History, to Smith's Wealth of Nations, to Addison's Spectators, to almost all the great works of Burke, to Clarissa and Sir Charles Grandison, to Joseph Andrews, Tom Jones and Amelia, and, with the single exception of Waverley, to all the novels of Sir Walter Scott, I give a longer term of copyright than my noble friend gives. Can he match that list? Does not that list contain what England has produced greatest in many various ways, poetry, philosophy, history, eloquence, wit, skilful portraiture of life and manners? I confidently therefore call on the Committee to take my plan in preference to the plan of my noble friend. I have shown that the protection which he proposes to give to letters is unequal, and unequal in the worst way. I have shown that his plan is to give protection to books in inverse proportion to their merit. I shall move when we come to the third clause of the bill to omit the words "twenty-five years," and in a subsequent part of the same clause I shall move to substitute for the words "twenty-eight years" the words "forty-two years." I earnestly hope that the Committee will adopt these amendments; and I feel the firmest conviction that my noble friend's bill, so amended, will confer a great boon on men of letters with the smallest possible inconvenience to the public.

MAYNOOTH

A SPEECH DELIVERED IN THE HOUSE OF COMMONS ON THE 14TH OF APRIL, 1845

On Saturday the eleventh of April, 1845, Sir Robert Peel moved the second reading of the Maynooth College Bill. After a debate of six nights the motion was carried by 323 votes to 176. On the second night the following Speech was made.

I DO not mean, Sir, to follow the honorable gentleman who has just sate down into a discussion on an amendment which is not now before us. When my honorable friend the Member for Sheffield shall think it expedient to make a motion on that important subject to which he has repeatedly called the attention of the House, I may, perhaps, ask to be heard. At present I shall content myself with explaining the reasons which convince me that it is my duty to vote for the second reading of this bill; and I cannot, I think, better explain those reasons than by passing in review, as rapidly as I can, the chief objections which have been made to the bill here and elsewhere.

The objectors, Sir, may be divided into three classes. The first class consists of those persons who object, not to the principle of the grant to Maynooth College, but merely to the amount. The second class consists of persons who object on principle to all grants made to a church which they regard as corrupt. The third class consists of persons who object on principle to all grants made to churches, whether corrupt or pure.

Now, Sir, of these three classes the first is evidently that which takes the most untenable ground. How any person can think that Maynooth College ought to be supported by public money, and yet can think this bill too bad to be suffered to go into Committee, I do not well understand. I am forced however to believe that there are many such persons. For I cannot but remember that the old annual vote attracted scarcely any notice; and I see that this bill has produced violent excitement. I cannot but remember that the old annual vote used to pass with very few dissentients; and I see that great numbers of gentlemen, who never were among those dissentients, have crowded down to the House in order to divide against this bill. It is indeed certain that a large proportion, I believe a majority, of those members who cannot, as they assure us, conscientiously support the plan proposed by the right honorable Baronet at the head of the Government, would without the smallest scruple have supported him if he had in this, as in former years, asked us to give nine thousand pounds for twelve months. So it is: yet I cannot help wondering that it should be so. For how can any human ingenuity turn a question between nine thousand pounds and twenty-six thousand pounds, or between twelve months and an indefinite number of months, into a question of principle. Observe: I am not now answering those who maintain that nothing ought to be given out of the public purse to a corrupt church; nor am I now answering those who maintain that nothing ought to be given out of the public purse to any church whatever. They, I admit, oppose this bill on principle. I perfectly understand, though I do not myself hold, the opinion of the zealous voluntary who says, "Whether the Roman Catholic Church teaches truth or error, she ought to have no assistance from the State." I also perfectly understand, though I do not myself hold, the opinion of the zealous Protestant who says,

"The Roman Catholic Church teaches error, and therefore ought to have no assistance from the State." But I cannot understand the reasoning of the man who says, "In spite of the errors of the Roman Catholic Church, I think that she ought to have some assistance from the State; but I am bound to mark my abhorrence of her errors by doling out to her a miserable pittance. Her tenets are so absurd and noxious that I will pay the professor who teaches them wages less than I should offer to my groom. Her rites are so superstitious that I will take care that they shall be performed in a chapel with a leaky roof and a dirty floor. By all means let us keep her a college, provided only that it be a shabby one. Let us support those who are intended to teach her doctrines and to administer her sacraments to the next generation, provided only that every future priest shall cost us less than a foot soldier. Let us board her young theologians; but let their larder be so scantily supplied that they may be compelled to break up before the regular vacation from mere want of food. Let us lodge them; but let their lodging be one in which they may be packed like pigs in a stye, and be punished for their heterodoxy by feeling the snow and the wind through the broken panes." Is it possible to conceive anything more absurd or more disgraceful? Can anything be clearer than this, that whatever it is lawful to do it is lawful to do well. If it be right that we should keep up this college at all, it must be right that we should keep it up respectably. Our national dignity is concerned. For this institution, whether good or bad, is, beyond all dispute, a very important institution. Its office is to form the character of those who are to form the character of millions. Whether we ought to extend any patronage to such an institution is a question about which wise and honest men may differ. But that, if we do extend our patronage to such an institution, our patronage ought to be worthy of the object, and worthy of the greatness of our country, is a proposition from which I am astonished to hear any person dissent.

It is, I must say, with a peculiarly bad grace that one of the members for the University to which I have the honor to belong,[1] a gentleman who never thought himself bound to say a word or to give a vote against the grant of nine thousand pounds, now vehemently opposes the grant of twenty-six thousand pounds as exorbitant. When I consider how munificently the colleges of Cambridge and Oxford are endowed, and with what pomp religion and learning are there surrounded; when I call to mind the long

[1] The Honorable Charles Law, member for the University of Cambridge.

streets of palaces, the towers and oriels, the venerable cloisters, the trim gardens, the organs, the altar pieces, the solemn light of the stained windows, the libraries, the museums, the galleries of painting and sculpture; when I call to mind also the physical comforts which are provided both for instructors and for pupils; when I reflect that the very sizars and servitors are far better lodged and fed than those students who are to be, a few years hence, the priests and bishops of the Irish people; when I think of the spacious and stately mansions of the heads of houses, of the commodious chambers of the fellows and scholars, of the refectories, the combination rooms, the bowling greens, the stabling, of the state and luxury of the great feast days, of the piles of old plate on the tables, of the savoury steam of the kitchens, of the multitudes of geese and capons which turn at once on the spits, of the oceans of excellent ale in the butteries; and when I remember from whom all this splendour and plenty is derived; when I remember what was the faith of Edward the Third and of Henry the Sixth, of Margaret of Anjou and Margaret of Richmond, of William of Wykeham and William of Waynefleet, of Archbishop Chicheley and Cardinal Wolsey; when I remember what we have taken from the Roman Catholics, King's College, New College, Christ Church, my own Trinity; and when I look at the miserable Dotheboys Hall[1] which we have given them in exchange, I feel, I must own, less proud than I could wish of being a Protestant and a Cambridge man.

Some gentlemen, it is true, have made an attempt to show that there is a distinction of principle between the old grant which they have always supported and the larger grant which they are determined to oppose. But never was attempt more unsuccessful. They say that, at the time of the Union, we entered into an implied contract with Ireland to keep up this college. We are therefore, they argue, bound by public faith to continue the old grant; but we are not bound to make any addition to that grant. Now, Sir, on this point, though on no other, I do most cordially agree with those petitioners who have, on this occasion, covered your table with such huge bales of spoiled paper and parchment. I deny the existence of any such contract. I think myself perfectly free to vote for the abolition of this college, if I am satisfied that it is a pernicious institution; as free as I am to vote against any item of the ordnance estimates; as free as I am to vote for a reduction of the number of marines. It is strange, too, that those who appeal to this imaginary contract should not perceive that, even if their fiction be admitted as true, it will by no means get them out of their

[1] [*Nicholas Nickleby* appeared in 1838.]

difficulty. Tell us plainly what are the precise terms of the contract which you suppose Great Britain to have made with Ireland about this college. Whatever the terms be, they will not serve your purpose. Was the contract this, that the Imperial Parliament would do for the college what the Irish Parliament had been used to do? Or was the contract this, that the Imperial Parliament would keep the college in a respectable and efficient state? If the former was the contract, nine thousand pounds would be too much. If the latter was the contract, you will not, I am confident, be able to prove that twenty-six thousand pounds is too little.

I have now, I think, said quite as much as need be said in answer to those who maintain that we ought to give support to this college, but that the support ought to be niggardly and precarious. I now come to another and a much more formidable class of objectors. Their objections may be simply stated thus. No man can justifiably, either as an individual or as a trustee for the public, contribute to the dissemination of religious error. But the Church of Rome teaches religious error. Therefore we cannot justifiably contribute to the support of an institution of which the object is the dissemination of the doctrines of the Church of Rome. Now, Sir, I deny the major of this syllogism. I think that there are occasions on which we are bound to contribute to the dissemination of doctrines with which errors are inseparably intermingled. Let me be clearly understood. The question is not whether we should teach truth or teach error, but whether we should teach truth adulterated with error, or teach no truth at all. The constitution of the human mind is such that it is impossible to provide any machinery for the dissemination of truth which shall not, with the truth, disseminate some error. Even those rays which come down to us from the great source of light, pure as they are in themselves, no sooner enter that gross and dark atmosphere in which we dwell than they are so much refracted, discoloured, and obscured, that they too often lead us astray. It will be generally admitted that, if religious truth can be anywhere found untainted by error, it is in the Scriptures. Yet is there actually on the face of the globe a single copy of the Scriptures of which it can be said that it contains truth absolutely untainted with error? Is there any manuscript, any edition of the Old or New Testament in the original tongues, which any scholar will pronounce faultless? But to the vast majority of Christians the original tongues are and always must be unintelligible. With the exception of perhaps one man in ten thousand, we must be content with translations. And is there any translation in which there are not numerous mistakes?

Are there not numerous mistakes even in our own authorised version, executed as that version was with painful diligence and care, by very able men and under very splendid patronage? Of course mistakes must be still more numerous in those translations which pious men have lately made into Bengalee, Hindostanee, Tamul, Canarese, and other Oriental tongues. I admire the zeal, the industry, the energy of those who, in spite of difficulties which to ordinary minds would seem insurmountable, accomplished that arduous work. I applaud those benevolent societies which munificently encouraged that work. But I have been assured by good judges that the translations have many faults. And how should it have been otherwise? How should an Englishman produce a faultless translation from the Hebrew into the Cingalese? I say, therefore, that even the Scriptures, in every form in which men actually possess them, contain a certain portion of error. And, if this be so, how can you look for pure undefecated truth in any other composition? You contribute, without any scruple, to the printing of religious tracts, to the establishing of Sunday Schools, to the sending forth of missionaries. But are your tracts perfect? Are your schoolmasters infallible? Are your missionaries inspired? Look at the two churches which are established in this island. Will you say that they both teach truth without any mixture of error? That is impossible. For they teach different doctrines on more than one important subject. It is plain, therefore, that if, as you tell us, it be a sin in a state to patronise an institution which teaches religious error, either the Church of England or the Church of Scotland ought to be abolished. But will anybody even venture to affirm that either of those churches teaches truth without any mixture of error? Have there not long been in the Church of Scotland two very different schools of theology? During many years, Dr. Robertson, the head of the moderate party, and Dr. Erskine, the head of the Calvinistic party, preached under the same roof, one in the morning, the other in the evening. They preached two different religions, so different that the followers of Robertson thought the followers of Erskine fanatics, and the followers of Erskine thought the followers of Robertson Arians or worse. And is there no mixture of error in the doctrine taught by the clergy of the Church of England? Is not the whole country at this moment convulsed by disputes as to what the doctrine of the Church on some important subjects really is? I shall not take on myself to say who is right and who is wrong. But this I say with confidence, that, whether the Tractarians or the Evangelicals be in the right, many hundreds of those divines who every Sunday occupy the pulpits of our parish churches must be very much in the wrong.

Now, Sir, I see that many highly respectable persons, who think it a sin to contribute to the teaching of error at Maynooth College, think it not merely lawful, but a sacred duty, to contribute to the teaching of error in the other cases which I have mentioned. They know that our version of the Bible contains some error. Yet they subscribe to the Bible Society. They know that the Serampore translations contain a still greater quantity of error. Yet they give largely towards the printing and circulating of those translations. My honorable friend the Member for the University of Oxford will not deny that there is among the clergy of the Church of England a Puritan party, and also an Antipuritan party, and that one of these parties must teach some error. Yet he is constantly urging us to grant to this Church an additional endowment of I know not how many hundreds of thousands of pounds. He would doubtless defend himself by saying that nothing on earth is perfect; that the purest religious society must consist of human beings, and must have those defects which arise from human infirmities; and that the truths held by the established clergy, though not altogether unalloyed with error, are so precious, that it is better that they should be imparted to the people with the alloy than that they should not be imparted at all. Just so say I. I am sorry that we cannot teach pure truth to the Irish people. But I think it better that they should have important and salutary truth, polluted by some error, than that they should remain altogether uninstructed. I heartily wish that they were Protestants. But I had rather that they should be Roman Catholics than that they should have no religion at all. Would you, says one gentleman, teach the people to worship Jugernaut or Kalee? Certainly not. My argument leads to no such conclusion. The worship of Jugernaut and Kalee is a curse to mankind. It is much better that people should be without any religion than that they should believe in a religion which enjoins prostitution, suicide, robbery, assassination. But will any Protestant deny that it is better that the Irish should be Roman Catholics than that they should live and die like the beasts of the field, indulge their appetites without any religious restraint, suffer want and calamity without any religious consolation, and go to their graves without any religious hope? These considerations entirely satisfy my mind. Of course I would not propagate error for its own sake. To do so would be not merely wicked, but diabolical. But, in order that I may be able to propagate truth, I consent to propagate that portion of error which adheres to truth, and which cannot be separated from truth. I wish Christianity to have a great influence on the peasantry of Ireland. I see no probability that Christianity will have that influence except in one form. That form I consider as very corrupt. Nevertheless, the good seems to me greatly to predominate over the evil; and therefore, being unable to get the good alone, I am content to take the good and the evil together.

I now come to the third class of our opponents. I mean those who take their stand on the voluntary principle. I will not, on this occasion, inquire whether they are right in thinking that governments ought not to contribute to the support of any religion, true or false. For it seems to me that, even if I were to admit that the general rule is correctly laid down by them, the present case would be an exception to that rule. The question on which I am about to vote is not whether the State shall or shall not give any support to religion in Ireland. The State does give such support, and will continue to give such support, whatever may be the issue of this debate. The only point which we have now to decide is whether, while such support is given, it shall be given exclusively to the religion of the minority. Here is an island with a population of near eight millions, and with a wealthy established church, the members of which are little more than eight hundred thousand. There is an archbishop with ten thousand a year. If I recollect rightly, seventy thousand pounds are divided among twelve prelates. At the same time the Protestant dissenters in the north of Ireland receive, in another form, support from the State. But the great majority of the population, the poorest part of the population, the part of the population which is most in need of assistance, the part of the population which holds that faith for the propagation of which the tithes were originally set apart, and the church lands originally given, is left to maintain its own priests. Now is not this a case which stands quite by itself? And may not even those who hold the general proposition, that every man ought to pay his own spiritual pastor, yet vote, without any inconsistency, for this bill? I was astonished to hear the honorable Member for Shrewsbury[1] tell us that, if we make this grant, it will be impossible for us to resist the claims of any dissenting sect. He particularly mentioned the Wesleyan Methodists. Are the cases analogous? Is there the slightest resemblance between them? Let the honorable gentleman show me that of the sixteen millions of people who inhabit England thirteen millions are Wesleyan Methodists. Let him show me that the members of the Established Church in

[1] Mr. Disraeli.

England are only one tenth of the population. Let him show me that English dissenters who are not Wesleyan Methodists receive a Regium Donum. Let him show me that immense estates bequeathed to John Wesley for the propagation of Methodism have, by Act of Parliament, been taken from the Methodists and given to the Church. If he can show me this, I promise him that, whenever the Wesleyan Methodists shall ask for twenty-six thousand pounds a year to educate their ministers, I shall be prepared to grant their request. But neither the case of the Methodists, nor any other case which can be mentioned, resembles the case with which we have to do. Look round Europe, round the world, for a parallel; and you will look in vain. Indeed the state of things which exists in Ireland never could have existed had not Ireland been closely connected with a country, which possessed a great superiority of power, and which abused that superiority. The burden which we are now, I hope, about to lay on ourselves is but a small penalty for a great injustice. Were I a staunch voluntary, I should still feel that, while the church of eight hundred thousand people retains its great endowments, I should not be justified in refusing this small boon to the church of eight millions.

To sum up shortly what I have said; it is clear to me in the first place that, if we have no religious scruple about granting to this College nine thousand pounds for one year, we ought to have no religious scruple about granting twenty-six thousand pounds a year for an indefinite term.

Secondly, it seems to me that those persons who tell us that we ought never in any circumstances to contribute to the propagation of error do in fact lay down a rule which would altogether interdict the propagation of truth.

Thirdly, it seems to me that, even on the hypothesis that the voluntary principle is the sound principle, the present case is an excepted case, to which it would be unjust and unwise to apply that principle.

So much, Sir, as to this bill: and now let me add a few words about those by whom it has been framed and introduced. We were exhorted, on the first night of this debate, to vote against the bill, without inquiring into its merits, on the ground that, good or bad, it was proposed by men who could not honestly and honorably propose it. A similar appeal has been made to us this evening. In these circumstances, Sir, I must, not I hope from party spirit, not, I am sure, from personal animosity, but from a regard for the public interest, which must be injuriously affected by everything which tends to lower the character of public men, say plainly what I think of the conduct of Her Majesty's Ministers. Undoubtedly it is of the highest importance that we should legislate well. But it is also of the highest importance that those who govern us should have, and should be known to have, fixed principles, and should be guided by those principles both in office and in opposition. It is of the highest importance that the world should not be under the impression that a statesman is a person who, when he is out, will profess and promise anything in order to get in, and who, when he is in, will forget all that he professed and promised when he was out. I need not, I suppose, waste time in proving that a law may be in itself an exceedingly good law, and yet that it may be a law which, when viewed in connection with the former conduct of those who proposed it, may prove them to be undeserving of the confidence of their country. When this is the case, our course is clear. We ought to distinguish between the law and its authors. The law we ought, on account of its intrinsic merits, to support. Of the authors of the law, it may be our duty to speak in terms of censure.

In such terms I feel it to be my duty to speak of Her Majesty's present advisers. I have no personal hostility to any of them; and that political hostility which I do not disavow has never prevented me from doing justice to their abilities and virtues. I have always admitted, and I now most willingly admit, that the right honorable Baronet at the head of the Government possesses many of the qualities of an excellent minister, eminent talents for debate, eminent talents for business, great experience, great information, great skill in the management of this House. I will go further, and say that I give him full credit for a sincere desire to promote the welfare of his country. Nevertheless, it is impossible for me to deny that there is too much ground for the reproaches of those who, having, in spite of a bitter experience, a second time trusted him, now find themselves a second time deluded. I cannot but see that it has been too much his practice, when in opposition, to make use of passions with which he has not the slightest sympathy, and of prejudices which he regards with profound contempt. As soon as he is in power a change takes place. The instruments which have done his work are flung aside. The ladder by which he has climbed is kicked down. I am forced to say that the right honorable Baronet acts thus habitually and on system. The instance before us is not a solitary instance. I do not wish to dwell on the events which took place seventeen or eighteen years ago, on the language which the right honorable Baronet held about the Catholic question when he was out of power in 1827, and on the change which twelve months of power produced. I will only say that one such change was quite enough for one life. Again the right honorable Baronet was in opposition; and again he employed his old tactics. I will not minutely relate the history of the manœuvres by which the Whig Government was overthrown. It is enough to say that many powerful interests were united against that Government under the leading of the right honorable Baronet, and that of those interests there is not one which is not now disappointed and complaining. To confine my remarks to the subject immediately before us,—can any man deny that, of all the many cries which were raised against the late administration, that which most strongly stirred the public mind was the cry of No Popery? Is there a single gentleman in the House who doubts that, if, four years ago, my noble friend the Member for the City of London had proposed this bill, he would have been withstood by every member of the present Cabinet? Four years ago, Sir, we were discussing a very different bill. The party which was then in opposition, and which is now in place, was attempting to force through Parliament a law, which bore indeed a specious name, but of which the effect would have been to disfranchise the Roman Catholic electors of Ireland by tens of thousands. It was in vain that we argued, that we protested, that we asked for the delay of a single session, for delay till an inquiry could be made, for delay till a Committee should report. We were told that the case was one of extreme urgency, that every hour was precious, that the House must, without loss of time, be purged of the minions of Popery. These arts succeeded. A change of administration took place. The right honorable Baronet came into power. He has now been near four years in power. He has had a Parliament which would, beyond all doubt, have passed eagerly and gladly that Registration Bill which he and his colleagues had pretended that they thought indispensable to the welfare of the State. And where is that bill now? Flung away; condemned by its own authors; pronounced by thém to be so oppressive, so inconsistent with all the principles of representative Government, that, though they had vehemently supported it when they were on your left hand, they could not think of proposing it from the Treasury Bench. And what substitute does the honorable Baronet give his followers to console them for the loss of their favourite Registration Bill? Even this bill for the endowment of Maynooth College. Was such a feat of legerdemain ever seen? And can we wonder that the eager, honest, hotheaded Protestants, who raised you to power in the confident hope that you would curtail the privileges of the Roman

Catholics, should stare and grumble when you propose to give public money to the Roman Catholics? Can we wonder that, from one end of the country to the other, everything should be ferment and uproar, that petitions should, night after night, whiten all our benches like a snowstorm? Can we wonder that the people out of doors should be exasperated by seeing the very men who, when we were in office, voted against the old grant to Maynooth, now pushed and pulled into the House by your whippers-in to vote for an increased grant? The natural consequences follow. All those fierce spirits, whom you hallooed on to harass us, now turn round and begin to worry you. The Orangeman raises his war-whoop: Exeter Hall sets up its bray: Mr. Macneile[1] shudders to see more costly cheer than ever provided for the priests of Baal at the table of the Queen; and the Protestant Operatives of Dublin call for impeachments in exceedingly bad English. But what did you expect? Did you think, when, to serve your turn, you called the Devil up, that it was as easy to lay him as to raise him? Did you think, when you went on, session after session, thwarting and reviling those whom you knew to be in the right, and flattering all the worst passions of those whom you knew to be in the wrong, that the day of reckoning would never come? It has come. There you sit, doing penance for the disingenuousness of years. If it be not so, stand up manfully, and clear your fame before the House and the country. Show us that some steady principle has guided your conduct with respect to Irish affairs? Show us how if you are honest in 1845, you can have been honest in 1841. Explain to us why, after having goaded Ireland to madness for the purpose of ingratiating yourselves with the English, you are now setting England on fire for the purpose of ingratiating yourselves with the Irish. Give us some reason which shall prove that the policy which you are following, as Ministers, is entitled to support, and which shall not equally prove you to have been the most factious and unprincipled opposition that ever this country saw.

But, Sir, am I, because I think thus of the conduct of Her Majesty's Ministers, to take the counsel of the honorable Member for Shrewsbury and to vote against their bill? Not so. I know well that the fate of this bill and the fate of the administration are in our hands. But far be it from us to imitate the arts by which we were overthrown. The spectacle exhibited on the bench opposite will do quite mischief enough. That mischief will not be lessened, but doubled, if there should be an answering display

[1] [Hugh McNeile finally became Dean of Ripon on the recommendation of Disraeli (1868), overriding the Queen's doubts.]

of inconsistency on this side of the House. If this bill, having been introduced by Tories, shall be rejected by Whigs, both the great parties in the State will be alike discredited. There will be one vast shipwreck of all the public character in the country. Therefore, making up my mind to sacrifices which are not unattended with pain, and repressing some feelings which stir strongly within me, I have determined to give my strenuous support to this bill. Yes, Sir, to this bill, and to every bill which shall seem to me likely to promote the real Union of Great Britain and Ireland, I will give my support, regardless of obloquy, regardless of the risk which I may run of losing my seat in Parliament. For such obloquy I have learned to consider as true glory; and as to my seat, I am determined that it never shall be held by an ignominious tenure; and I am sure that it can never be lost in a more honorable cause.

THE TEN HOURS BILL

A SPEECH DELIVERED IN THE HOUSE OF COMMONS ON THE 22ND OF MAY, 1846

On the twenty-ninth of April, 1846, Mr. Fielden, Member for Oldham, moved the second reading of a bill for limiting the labour of young persons in factories to ten hours a day. The debate was adjourned, and was repeatedly resumed at long intervals. At length on the twenty-second of May the bill was rejected by 203 votes to 193.[1] On that day the following Speech was made.

IT is impossible, Sir, that I can remain silent after the appeal which has been made to me in so pointed a manner by my honorable friend the Member for Sheffield.[2] And, even if that appeal had not been made to me, I should have been very desirous to have an opportunity of explaining the grounds on which I shall vote for the second reading of this bill.

It is, I hope, unnecessary for me to assure my honorable friend that I utterly disapprove of those aspersions which have, both in this House and out of it, been thrown on the owners of factories. For that valuable class of men I have no feeling but respect and good will. I am convinced that with their interests the interests of the whole community, and especially of the labouring classes, are inseparably bound up. I can also with perfect sincerity declare that the vote which I shall give to-night will not be a factious vote. In no circumstances indeed should I think that the laws

---

[1] [The bill was carried in 1847.]   [2] Mr. Ward.

of political hostility warranted me in treating this question as a party question. But at the present moment I would much rather strengthen than weaken the hands of Her Majesty's Ministers.[1] It is by no means pleasant to me to be under the necessity of opposing them. I assure them, I assure my friends on this side of the House with whom I am so unfortunate as to differ, and especially my honorable friend the Member for Sheffield who spoke, I must say, in rather too plaintive a tone, that I have no desire to obtain credit for humanity at their expense. I fully believe that their feeling towards the labouring people is quite as kind as mine. There is no difference between us as to ends; there is an honest difference of opinion as to means: and we surely ought to be able to discuss the points on which we differ without one angry emotion or one acrimonious word.

The details of the bill, Sir, will be more conveniently and more regularly discussed when we consider it in Committee. Our business at present is with the principle: and the principle, we are told by many gentlemen of great authority, is unsound. In their opinion, neither this bill, nor any other bill regulating the hours of labour, can be defended. This, they say, is one of those matters about which we ought not to legislate at all; one of those matters which settle themselves far better than any government can settle them. Now it is most important that this point should be fully cleared up. We certainly ought not to usurp functions which do not properly belong to us: but, on the other hand, we ought not to abdicate functions which do properly belong to us. I hardly know which is the greater pest to society, a paternal government, that is to say a prying, meddlesome government, which intrudes itself into every part of human life, and which thinks that it can do everything for everybody better than anybody can do anything for himself; or a careless, lounging government, which suffers grievances, such as it could at once remove, to grow and multiply, and which to all complaint and remonstrance has only one answer: "We must let things alone: we must let things take their course: we must let things find their level." There is no more important problem in politics than to ascertain the just mean between these two most pernicious extremes, to draw correctly the line which divides those cases in which it is the duty of the State to interfere from those cases in which it is the duty of the State to abstain from interference. In old times the besetting sin of rulers was undoubtedly an inordinate disposition to meddle. The lawgiver

[1] [Because the bill repealing the Corn Laws was at that moment before the Lords.]

was always telling people how to keep their shops, how to till their fields, how to educate their children, how many dishes to have on their tables, how much a yard to give for the cloth which made their coats. He was always trying to remedy some evil which did not properly fall within his province; and the consequence was that he increased the evils which he attempted to remedy. He was so much shocked by the distress inseparable from scarcity that he made statutes against forestalling and regrating, and so turned the scarcity into a famine. He was so much shocked by the cunning and hardheartedness of moneylenders that he made laws against usury; and the consequence was that the borrower, who, if he had been left unprotected, would have got money at ten per cent., could hardly, when protected, get it at fifteen per cent. Some eminent political philosophers of the last century exposed with great ability the folly of such legislation, and, by doing so, rendered a great service to mankind. There has been a reaction, a reaction which has doubtless produced much good, but which, like most reactions, has not been without evils and dangers. Our statesmen cannot now be accused of being busy-bodies. But I am afraid that there is, even in some of the ablest and most upright among them, a tendency to the opposite fault. I will give an instance of what I mean. Fifteen years ago it became evident that railroads would soon, in every part of the kingdom, supersede to a great extent the old highways. The tracing of the new routes which were to join all the chief cities, ports, and naval arsenals of the island was a matter of the highest national importance. But, unfortunately, those who should have acted for the nation refused to interfere. Consequently, numerous questions which were really public, questions which concerned the public convenience, the public prosperity, the public security, were treated as private questions. That the whole society was interested in having a good system of internal communication seemed to be forgotten. The speculator who wanted a large dividend on his shares, the landowner who wanted a large price for his acres, obtained a full hearing. But nobody applied to be heard on behalf of the community. The effects of that great error we feel, and we shall not soon cease to feel. Unless I am greatly mistaken, we are in danger of committing to-night an error of the same kind. The honorable Member for Montrose[1] and my honorable friend the Member for Sheffield think that the question before us is merely a question between the old and the new theories of commerce. They cannot understand how any friend of free trade can wish the

[1] Mr. Hume.

Legislature to interfere between the capitalist and the labourer. They say, "You do not make a law to settle the price of gloves, or the texture of gloves, or the length of credit which the glover shall give. You leave it to him to determine whether he will charge high or low prices, whether he will use strong or flimsy materials, whether he will trust or insist on ready money. You acknowledge that these are matters which he ought to be left to settle with his customers, and that we ought not to interfere. It is possible that he may manage his shop ill. But it is certain that we shall manage it ill. On the same grounds on which you leave the seller of gloves and the buyer of gloves to make their own contract, you ought to leave the seller of labour and the buyer of labour to make their own contract."

I have a great respect, Sir, for those who reason thus: but I cannot see this matter in the light in which it appears to them; and, though I may distrust my own judgment, I must be guided by it. I am, I believe, as strongly attached as any member of this House to the principle of free trade, rightly understood. Trade, considered merely as trade, considered merely with reference to the pecuniary interest of the contracting parties, can hardly be too free. But there is a great deal of trade which cannot be considered merely as trade, and which affects higher than pecuniary interests. And to say that Government never ought to regulate such trade is a monstrous proposition, a proposition at which Adam Smith would have stood aghast. We impose some restrictions on trade for purposes of police. Thus, we do not suffer everybody who has a cab and a horse to ply for passengers in the streets of London. We do not leave the fare to be determined by the supply and the demand. We do not permit a driver to extort a guinea for going half a mile on a rainy day when there is no other vehicle on the stand. We impose some restrictions on trade for the sake of revenue. Thus, we forbid a farmer to cultivate tobacco on his own ground. We impose some restrictions on trade for the sake of national defence. Thus we compel a man who would rather be ploughing or weaving to go into the militia; and we fix the amount of pay which he shall receive without asking his consent. Nor is there in all this anything inconsistent with the soundest political economy. For the science of political economy teaches us only that we ought not on commercial grounds to interfere with the liberty of commerce; and we, in the cases which I have put, interfere with the liberty of commerce on higher than commercial grounds.

And now, Sir, to come closer to the case with which we have to

deal, I say, first, that where the health of the community is concerned, it may be the duty of the State to interfere with the contracts of individuals; and to this proposition I am quite sure that
Her Majesty's Government will cordially assent. I have just read
a very interesting report signed by two members of that Government, the Duke of Buccleuch, and the noble earl who was lately
Chief Commissioner of the Woods and Forests, and who is now
Secretary for Ireland[1]; and, since that report was laid before the
House, the noble earl himself has, with the sanction of the Cabinet,
brought in a bill for the protection of the public health. By this
bill it is provided that no man shall be permitted to build a house
on his own land in any great town without giving notice to certain
Commissioners. No man is to sink a cellar without the consent
of these Commissioners. The house must not be of less than a
prescribed width. No new house must be built without a drain.
If an old house has no drain, the Commissioners may order the
owner to make a drain. If he refuses, they make a drain for him,
and send him in the bill. They may order him to whitewash his
house. If he refuses, they may send people with pails and brushes
to whitewash it for him, at his charge. Now, suppose that some
proprietor of houses at Leeds or Manchester were to expostulate
with the Government in the language in which the Government
has expostulated with the supporters of this bill for the regulation
of factories. Suppose that he were to say to the noble earl, "Your
lordship professes to be a friend to free trade. Your lordship's
doctrine is that everybody ought to be at liberty to buy cheap and
to sell dear. Why then may not I run up a house as cheap as I
can, and let my rooms as dear as I can? Your lordship does not
like houses without drains. Do not take one of mine then. You
think my bedrooms filthy. Nobody forces you to sleep in them.
Use your own liberty: but do not restrain that of your neighbours.
I can find many a family willing to pay a shilling a week for leave
to live in what you call a hovel. And why am not I to take the
shilling which they are willing to give me? And why are not they
to have such shelter as, for that shilling, I can afford them? Why
did you send a man without my consent to clean my house, and
then force me to pay for what I never ordered? My tenants
thought the house clean enough for them; or they would not have
been my tenants: and, if they and I were satisfied, why did you,
in direct defiance of all the principles of free trade, interfere
between us?" This reasoning, Sir, is exactly of a piece with the
reasoning of the honorable Member for Montrose, and of my

[1] The Earl of Lincoln.

honorable friend the Member for Sheffield. If the noble earl will allow me to make a defence for him, I believe that he would answer the objection thus: "I hold," he would say, "the sound doctrine of free trade. But your doctrine of free trade is an exaggeration, a caricature of the sound doctrine; and by exhibiting such caricature you bring discredit on the sound doctrine. We should have nothing to do with the contracts between you and your tenants, if those contracts affected only pecuniary interests. But higher than pecuniary interests are at stake. It concerns the commonwealth that the great body of the people should not live in a way which makes life wretched and short, which enfeebles the body and pollutes the mind. If, by living in houses which resemble hogstyes, great numbers of our countrymen have contracted the tastes of hogs, if they have become so familiar with filth and stench and contagion, that they burrow without reluctance in holes which would turn the stomach of any man of cleanly habits, that is only an additional proof that we have too long neglected our duties, and an additional reason for our now performing them."

Secondly, I say that where the public morality is concerned it may be the duty of the State to interfere with the contracts of individuals. Take the traffic in licentious books and pictures. Will anybody deny that the State may, with propriety, interdict that traffic? Or take the case of lotteries. I have, we will suppose, an estate for which I wish to get twenty thousand pounds. I announce my intention to issue a thousand tickets at twenty pounds each. The holder of the number which is first drawn is to have the estate. But the magistrate interferes; the contract between me and the purchasers of my tickets is annulled; and I am forced to pay a heavy penalty for having made such a contract. I appeal to the principle of free trade, as expounded by the honorable gentlemen the Members for Montrose and Sheffield. I say to you, the legislators who have restricted my liberty, "What business have you to interfere between a buyer and a seller? If you think the speculation a bad one, do not take tickets. But do not interdict other people from judging for themselves." Surely you would answer, "You would be right if this were a mere question of trade: but it is a question of morality. We prohibit you from disposing of your property in this particular mode, because it is a mode which tends to encourage a most pernicious habit of mind, a habit of mind incompatible with all the qualities on which the well being of individuals and of nations depends."

It must then, I think, be admitted that, where health is concerned, and where morality is concerned, the State is justified in interfering with the contracts of individuals. And, if this be admitted, it follows that the case with which we now have to do is a case for interference.

Will it be denied that the health of a large part of the rising generation may be seriously affected by the contracts which this bill is intended to regulate? Can any man who has read the evidence which is before us, can any man who has ever observed young people, can any man who remembers his own sensations when he was young, doubt that twelve hours a day of labour in a factory is too much for a lad of thirteen?

Or will it be denied that this is a question in which public morality is concerned? Can any one doubt,—none, I am sure, of my friends around me doubts,—that education is a matter of the highest importance to the virtue and happiness of a people? Now we know that there can be no education without leisure. It is evident that, after deducting from the day twelve hours for labour in a factory, and the additional hours necessary for exercise, refreshment, and repose, there will not remain time enough for education.

I have now, I think, shown that this bill is not in principle objectionable; and yet I have not touched the strongest part of our case. I hold that, where public health is concerned, and where public morality is concerned, the State may be justified in regulating even the contracts of adults. But we propose to regulate only the contracts of infants. Now was there ever a civilised society in which the contracts of infants were not under some regulation? Is there a single member of this House who will say that a wealthy minor of thirteen ought to be at perfect liberty to execute a conveyance of his estate, or to give a bond for fifty thousand pounds? If anybody were so absurd as to say, "What has the Legislature to do with the matter? Why cannot you leave trade free? Why do you pretend to understand the boy's interest better than he understands it?"—you would answer; "When he grows up, he may squander his fortune away if he likes: but at present the State is his guardian; and he shall not ruin himself till he is old enough to know what he is about." The minors whom we wish to protect have not indeed large property to throw away: but they are not the less our wards. Their only inheritance, the only fund to which they must look for their subsistence through life, is the sound mind in the sound body. And is it not our duty to prevent them from wasting that most precious wealth before they know its value?

But, it is said, this bill, though it directly limits only the labour of infants, will, by an indirect operation, limit also the labour of adults. Now, Sir, though I am not prepared to vote for a bill directly limiting the labour of adults, I will plainly say that I do not think that the limitation of the labour of adults would necessarily produce all those frightful consequences which we have heard predicted. You cheer me in very triumphant tones, as if I had uttered some monstrous paradox. Pray, does it not occur to any of you that the labour of adults is now limited in this country? Are you not aware that you are living in a society in which the labour of adults is limited to six days in seven? It is you, not I, who maintain a paradox opposed to the opinions and the practices of all nations and ages. Did you ever hear of a single civilised State since the beginning of the world in which a certain portion of time was not set apart for the rest and recreation of adults by public authority? In general, this arrangement has been sanctioned by religion. The Egyptians, the Jews, the Greeks, the Romans, had their holidays: the Hindoo has his holidays: the Mussulman has his holidays: there are holidays in the Greek Church, holidays in the Church of Rome, holidays in the Church of England. Is it not amusing to hear a gentleman pronounce with confidence that any legislation which limits the labour of adults must produce consequences fatal to society, without once reflecting that in the society in which he lives, and in every other society that exists, or ever has existed, there has been such legislation without any evil consequence? It is true that a Puritan Government in England, and an Atheistical Government in France, abolished the old holidays as superstitious. But those governments felt it to be absolutely necessary to institute new holidays. Civil festivals were substituted for religious festivals. You will find among the ordinances of the Long Parliament a law providing that, in exchange for the days of rest and amusement which the people had been used to enjoy at Easter, Whitsuntide, and Christmas, the second Tuesday of every month should be given to the working man, and that any apprentice who was forced to work on the second Tuesday of any month might have his master up before a magistrate. The French Jacobins decreed that the Sunday should no longer be a day of rest; but they instituted another day of rest, the Decade. They swept away the holidays of the Roman Catholic Church; but they instituted another set of holidays, the Sansculottides, one sacred to Genius, one to Industry, one to Opinion, and so on. I say, therefore, that the practice of limiting by law the time of the labour of adults is so far from being, as some gentlemen seem to think, an unheard of and monstrous practice, that it is a practice as universal as cookery, as the wearing of clothes, as the use of domestic animals.

And has this practice been proved by experience to be pernicious? Let us take the instance with which we are most familiar. Let us inquire what has been the effect of those laws which, in our own country, limit the labour of adults to six days in every seven. It is quite unnecessary to discuss the question whether Christians be or be not bound by a divine command to observe the Sunday. For it is evident that, whether our weekly holiday be of divine or of human institution, the effect on the temporal interests of society will be exactly the same. Now, is there a single argument in the whole Speech of my honorable friend the Member for Sheffield which does not tell just as strongly against the laws which enjoin the observance of the Sunday as against the bill on our table? Surely, if his reasoning is good for hours, it must be equally good for days.

He says, "If this limitation be good for the working people, rely on it that they will find it out, and that they will themselves establish it without any law." Why not reason in the same way about the Sunday? Why not say, "If it be a good thing for the people of London to shut their shops one day in seven, they will find it out, and will shut their shops without a law?" Sir, the answer is obvious. I have no doubt that, if you were to poll the shopkeepers of London, you would find an immense majority, probably a hundred to one, in favour of closing shops on the Sunday; and yet it is absolutely necessary to give to the wish of the majority the sanction of a law; for, if there were no such law, the minority, by opening their shops, would soon force the majority to do the same.

But, says my honorable friend, you cannot limit the labour of adults unless you fix wages. This proposition he lays down repeatedly, assures us that it is incontrovertible, and indeed seems to think it self-evident; for he has not taken the trouble to prove it. Sir, my answer shall be very short. We have, during many centuries, limited the labour of adults to six days in seven; and yet we have not fixed the rate of wages.

But, it is said, you cannot legislate for all trades; and therefore you had better not legislate for any. Look at the poor sempstress. She works far longer and harder than the factory child. She sometimes plies her needle fifteen, sixteen hours in the twenty-four. See how the housemaid works, up at six every morning, and toiling up stairs and down stairs till near midnight. You own that you cannot do anything for the sempstress and the house-maid. Why then trouble yourself about the factory child? Take care that by protecting one class you do not aggravate the hard-ships endured by the classes which you cannot protect. Why, Sir, might not all this be said, word for word, against the laws which enjoin the observance of the Sunday? There are classes of people whom you cannot prevent from working on the Sunday. There are classes of people whom, if you could, you ought not to prevent from working on the Sunday. Take the sempstress, of whom so much has been said. You cannot keep her from sewing and hem-ming all Sunday in her garret. But you do not think that a reason for suffering Covent Garden Market, and Leadenhall Market, and Smithfield Market, and all the shops from Mile End to Hyde Park to be open all Sunday. Nay, these factories about which we are debating,—does anybody propose that they shall be allowed to work all Sunday? See then how inconsistent you are. You think it unjust to limit the labour of the factory child to ten hours a day, because you cannot limit the labour of the sempstress. And yet you see no injustice in limiting the labour of the factory child, aye, and of the factory man, to six days in the week, though you cannot limit the labour of the sempstress.

But, you say, by protecting one class we shall aggravate the sufferings of all the classes which we cannot protect. You say this; but you do not prove it; and all experience proves the con-trary. We interfere on the Sunday to close the shops. We do not interfere with the labour of the housemaid. But are the house-maids of London more severely worked on the Sunday than on other days? The fact notoriously is the reverse. For your legisla-tion keeps the public feeling in a right state, and thus protects indirectly those whom it cannot protect directly.

Will my honorable friend the Member for Sheffield maintain that the law which limits the number of working days has been injurious to the working population? I am certain that he will not. How then can he expect me to believe that a law which limits the number of working hours must necessarily be injurious to the working population? Yet he and those who agree with him seem to wonder at our dulness because we do not at once admit the truth of the doctrine which they propound on this subject. They reason thus. We cannot reduce the number of hours of labour in factories without reducing the amount of production. We cannot reduce the amount of production without reducing the remunera-tion of the labourer. Meanwhile, foreigners, who are at liberty to work till they drop down dead at their looms, will soon beat us out of all the markets of the world. Wages will go down fast. The condition of our working people will be far worse than it is; and our unwise interference will, like the unwise interference of our ancestors with the dealings of the corn factor and the money lender, increase the distress of the very class which we wish to relieve.

Now, Sir, I fully admit that there might be such a limitation of the hours of labour as would produce the evil consequences with which we are threatened: and this, no doubt, is a very good reason for legislating with great caution, for feeling our way, for looking well to all the details of this bill. But it is certainly not true that every limitation of the hours of labour must produce these consequences. And I am, I must say, surprised when I hear men of eminent ability and knowledge lay down the proposition that a diminution of the time of labour must be followed by a diminution of the wages of labour, as a proposition universally true, as a proposition capable of being strictly demonstrated, as a proposition about which there can be no more doubt than about any theorem in Euclid. Sir, I deny the truth of the proposition; and for this plain reason. We have already, by law, greatly reduced the time of labour in the factories. Thirty years ago, the late Sir Robert Peel[1] told the House that it was a common practice to make children of eight years of age toil in mills fifteen hours a day. A law has since been made which prohibits persons under eighteen years of age from working in mills more than twelve hours a day. That law was opposed on exactly the same grounds on which the bill before us is opposed. Parliament was told then, as it is told now, that with the time of labour the quantity of production would decrease, that with the quantity of production the wages would decrease, that our manufacturers would be unable to contend with foreign manufacturers, and that the condition of the labouring population instead of being made better by the interference of the Legislature would be made worse. Read over those debates; and you may imagine that you are reading the debate of this evening. Parliament disregarded these prophecies. The time of labour was limited. Have wages fallen? Has the cotton trade left Manchester for France or Germany? Has the condition of the working people become more miserable? Is it not universally acknowledged that the evils which were so confidently predicted have not come to pass? Let me be understood. I am not arguing that, because a law which reduced the hours of daily labour from fifteen to twelve did not reduce wages, a law reducing those hours

[1] [The first Factory Act was introduced by Peel's father in 1802.]

from twelve to ten or eleven cannot possibly reduce wages. That would be very inconclusive reasoning. What I say is this, that, since a law which reduced the hours of daily labour from fifteen to twelve has not reduced wages, the proposition that every reduction of the hours of labour must necessarily reduce wages is a false proposition. There is evidently some flaw in that demonstration which my honorable friend thinks so complete; and what the flaw is we may perhaps discover if we look at the analogous case to which I have so often referred.

Sir, exactly three hundred years ago, great religious changes were taking place in England. Much was said and written, in that inquiring and innovating age, about the question whether Christians were under a religious obligation to rest from labour on one day in the week; and it is well known that the chief Reformers, both here and on the continent, denied the existence of any such obligation. Suppose then that, in 1546, Parliament had made a law that there should thenceforth be no distinction between the Sunday and any other day. Now, Sir, our opponents, if they are consistent with themselves, must hold that such a law would have immensely increased the wealth of the country and the remuneration of the working man. What an effect, if their principles be sound, must have been produced by the addition of one sixth to the time of labour! What an increase of production! What a rise of wages! How utterly unable must the foreign artisan, who still had his days of festivity and of repose, have found himself to maintain a competition with a people whose shops were open, whose markets were crowded, whose spades, and axes, and planes, and hods, and anvils, and looms were at work from morning till night on three hundred and sixty-five days a year! The Sundays of three hundred years make up fifty years of our working days. We know what the industry of fifty years can do. We know what marvels the industry of the last fifty years has wrought. The arguments of my honorable friend irresistibly lead us to this conclusion, that if, during the last three centuries, the Sunday had not been observed as a day of rest, we should have been a far richer, a far more highly civilised people than we now are, and that the labouring class especially would have been far better off than at present. But does he, does any Member of the House, seriously believe that this would have been the case? For my own part, I have not the smallest doubt that, if we and our ancestors had, during the last three centuries, worked just as hard on the Sundays as on the week days, we should have been at this moment a poorer people and a less civilised people than we are; that there would have been less production than there has been, that the wages of the labourer would have been lower than they are, and that some other nation would have been now making cotton stuffs and woollen stuffs and cutlery for the whole world.

Of course, Sir, I do not mean to say that a man will not produce more in a week by working seven days than by working six days. But I very much doubt whether, at the end of a year, he will generally have produced more by working seven days a week than by working six days a week; and I firmly believe that, at the end of twenty years, he will have produced much less by working seven days a week than by working six days a week. In the same manner I do not deny that a factory child will produce more, in a single day, by working twelve hours than by working ten hours, and by working fifteen hours than by working twelve hours. But I do deny that a great society in which children work fifteen, or even twelve hours a day, will, in the lifetime of a generation, produce as much as if those children had worked less. If we consider man merely in a commercial point of view, if we consider him merely as a machine for the production of worsted and calico, let us not forget what a piece of mechanism he is, how fearfully and wonderfully made. We do not treat a fine horse or a sagacious dog exactly as we treat a spinning jenny. Nor will any slaveholder, who has sense enough to know his own interest, treat his human chattels exactly as he treats his horses and his dogs. And would you treat the free labourer of England like a mere wheel or pulley? Rely on it that intense labour, beginning too early in life, continued too long every day, stunting the growth of the body, stunting the growth of the mind, leaving no time for healthful exercise, leaving no time for intellectual culture, must impair all those high qualities which have made our country great. Your overworked boys will become a feeble and ignoble race of men, the parents of a more feeble and more ignoble progeny; nor will it be long before the deterioration of the labourer will injuriously affect those very interests to which his physical and moral energies have been sacrificed. On the other hand, a day of rest recurring in every week, two or three hours of leisure, exercise, innocent amusement or useful study, recurring every day, must improve the whole man, physically, morally, intellectually; and the improvement of the man will improve all that the man produces. Why is it, Sir, that the Hindoo cotton manufacturer[1], close to whose door

[1] [In Chapter III of his History, Macaulay records that in 1680, Mr. Bassett, M.P. for Barnstaple, pointed out that the English workman at a shilling a day could not compete with the Bengalee at a copper piece.]

the cotton grows, cannot, in the bazaar of his own town, maintain a competition with the English cotton manufacturer, who has to send thousands of miles for the raw material, and who has then to send the wrought material thousands of miles to market? You will say that it is owing to the excellence of our machinery. And to what is the excellence of our machinery owing? How many of the improvements which have been made in our machinery do we owe to the ingenuity and patient thought of working men? Adam Smith tells us in the first chapter of his great work, that you can hardly go to a factory without seeing some very pretty machine, —that is his expression,—devised by some labouring man. Hargraves, the inventor of the spinning jenny, was a common artisan. Crompton, the inventor of the mule jenny, was a working man. How many hours of the labour of children would do so much for our manufacturers as one of these improvements has done? And in what sort of society are such improvements most likely to be made? Surely in a society in which the faculties of the working people are developed by education. How long will you wait before any negro, working under the lash in Louisiana, will contrive a better machinery for squeezing the sugar canes? My honorable friend seems to me, in all his reasonings about the commercial prosperity of nations, to overlook entirely the chief cause on which that prosperity depends. What is it, Sir, that makes the great difference between country and country? Not the exuberance of soil; not the mildness of climate; not mines, nor havens, nor rivers. These things are indeed valuable when put to their proper use by human intelligence: but human intelligence can do much without them; and they without human intelligence can do nothing. They exist in the highest degree in regions of which the inhabitants are few, and squalid, and barbarous, and naked, and starving; while on sterile rocks, amidst unwholesome marshes, and under inclement skies, may be found immense populations, well fed, well lodged, well clad, well governed. Nature meant Egypt and Sicily to be the gardens of the world. They once were so. Is it anything in the earth or in the air that makes Scotland more prosperous than Egypt, that makes Holland more prosperous than Sicily? No; it was the Scotchman that made Scotland: it was the Dutchman that made Holland. Look at North America. Two centuries ago the sites on which now arise mills, and hotels, and banks, and colleges, and churches, and the Senate Houses of flourishing commonwealths, were deserts abandoned to the panther and the bear. What has made the change? Was it the rich mould, or the redundant rivers? No:

the prairies were as fertile, the Ohio and the Hudson were as broad and as full then as now. Was the improvement the effect of some great transfer of capital from the old world to the new? No: the emigrants generally carried out with them no more than a pittance; but they carried out the English heart, and head, and arm; and the English heart and head and arm turned the wilderness into cornfield and orchard, and the huge trees of the primeval forest into cities and fleets. Man, man is the great instrument that produces wealth. The natural difference between Campania and Spitzbergen is trifling when compared with the difference between a country inhabited by men full of bodily and mental vigour, and a country inhabited by men sunk in bodily and mental decrepitude. Therefore it is that we are not poorer but richer, because we have, through many ages, rested from our labour one day in seven. That day is not lost. While industry is suspended, while the plough lies in the furrow, while the Exchange is silent, while no smoke ascends from the factory, a process is going on quite as important to the wealth of nations as any process which is performed on more busy days. Man, the machine of machines, the machine compared with which all the contrivances of the Watts and the Arkwrights are worthless, is repairing and winding up, so that he returns to his labours on the Monday with clearer intellect, with livelier spirits, with renewed corporal vigour. Never will I believe that what makes a population stronger, and healthier, and wiser, and better, can ultimately make it poorer. You try to frighten us by telling us that, in some German factories, the young work seventeen hours in the twenty-four, that they work so hard that among thousands there is not one who grows to such a stature that he can be admitted into the army; and you ask whether, if we pass this bill, we can possibly hold our own against such competition as this? Sir, I laugh at the thought of such competition. If ever we are forced to yield the foremost place among commercial nations, we shall yield it, not to a race of degenerate dwarfs, but to some people preeminently vigorous in body and in mind.

For these reasons, Sir, I approve of the principle of this bill, and shall, without hesitation, vote for the second reading. To what extent we ought to reduce the hours of labour is a question of more difficulty. I think that we are in the situation of a physician who has satisfied himself that there is a disease, and that there is a specific medicine for the disease, but who is not certain what quantity of that medicine the patient's constitution will bear. Such a physician would probably administer his remedy by small doses, and carefully watch its operation. I cannot help thinking that, by at once reducing the hours of labour from twelve to ten, we should hazard too much. The change is great, and ought to be cautiously and gradually made. Suppose that there should be an immediate fall of wages, which is not impossible. Might there not be a violent reaction? Might not the public take up a notion that our legislation had been erroneous in principle, though, in truth, our error would have been an error, not of principle, but merely of degree? Might not Parliament be induced to retrace its steps? Might we not find it difficult to maintain even the present limitation? The wisest course would, in my opinion, be to reduce the hours of labour from twelve to eleven, to observe the effect of that experiment, and if, as I hope and believe, the result should be satisfactory, then to make a further reduction from eleven to ten. This is a question, however, which will be with more advantage considered when we are in Committee.

One word, Sir, before I sit down, in answer to my noble friend near me.[1] He seems to think that this bill is ill timed. I own that I cannot agree with him. We carried up on Monday last to the bar of the Lords a bill which will remove the most hateful and pernicious restriction that ever was laid on trade. Nothing can be more proper than to apply, in the same week, a remedy to a great evil of a directly opposite kind. As lawgivers, we have two great faults to confess and to repair. We have done that which we ought not to have done. We have left undone that which we ought to have done. We have regulated that which we should have left to regulate itself. We have left unregulated that which we were bound to regulate. We have given to some branches of industry a protection which has proved their bane. We have withheld from public health and public morals the protection which was their due. We have prevented the labourer from buying his loaf where he could get it cheapest; but we have not prevented him from ruining his body and mind by premature and immoderate toil. I hope that we have seen the last both of a vicious system of interference and of a vicious system of non-interference, and that our poorer countrymen will no longer have reason to attribute their sufferings either to our meddling or to our neglect.

[1] Lord Morpeth.

EDUCATION

A SPEECH DELIVERED IN THE HOUSE OF COMMONS ON THE 19TH OF APRIL, 1847

In the year 1847 the Government asked from the House of Commons a grant of one hundred thousand pounds for the education of the people. On the nineteenth of April, Lord John Russell, having explained the reasons for this application, moved the order of the day for a Committee of Supply. Mr. Thomas Duncombe, Member for Finsbury, moved the following amendment:

"That previous to any grant of public money being assented to by this House, for the purpose of carrying out the scheme of national education, as developed in the Minutes of the Committee of Council on Education in August and December last, which minutes have been presented to both Houses of Parliament by command of Her Majesty, a select Committee be appointed to inquire into the justice and expediency of such a scheme, and its probable annual cost; also to inquire whether the regulations attached thereto do not unduly increase the influence of the Crown, invade the constitutional functions of Parliament, and interfere with the religious convictions and civil rights of Her Majesty's subjects."

In opposition to this amendment, the following speech was made. After a debate of three nights, Mr. Thomas Duncombe obtained permission to withdraw the latter part of his amendment. The first part was put, and negatived by 372 votes to 47.

You will not wonder, Sir, that I am desirous to catch your eye this evening. The first duty which I performed, as a Member of the Committee of Council[1] which is charged with the superintendence of public instruction, was to give my hearty assent to the plan which the honorable Member for Finsbury calls on the House to condemn. I am one of those who have been accused in every part of the kingdom, and who are now accused in Parliament, of aiming, under specious pretences, a blow at the civil and religious liberties of the people. It is natural therefore that I should seize the earliest opportunity of vindicating myself from so grave a charge.

The honorable Member for Finsbury must excuse me if, in the remarks which I have to offer to the House, I should not follow very closely the order of his speech. The truth is that a mere answer to his speech would be no defence of myself or of my colleagues. I am surprised, I own, that a man of his acuteness

---

[1] [Macaulay was Paymaster-General (a sinecure office) in Lord John Russell's administration 1846–7; he was then defeated at the General Election and retired from active public life.]

and ability should, on such an occasion, have made such a speech. The country is excited from one end to the other by a great question of principle. On that question the Government has taken one side. The honorable Member stands forth as the chosen and trusted champion of a great party which takes the other side. We expected to hear from him a full exposition of the views of those in whose name he speaks. But, to our astonishment, he has scarcely even alluded to the controversy which has divided the whole nation. He has entertained us with sarcasms and personal anecdotes: he has talked much about matters of mere detail: but I must say that, after listening with close attention to all that he has said, I am quite unable to discover whether, on the only important point which is in issue, he agrees with us or with that large and active body of Nonconformists which is diametrically opposed to us. He has sate down without dropping one word from which it is possible to discover whether he thinks that education is or that it is not a matter with which the State ought to interfere. Yet that is the question about which the whole nation has, during several weeks, been writing, reading, speaking, hearing, thinking, petitioning, and on which it is now the duty of Parliament to pronounce a decision. That question once settled, there will be, I believe, very little room for dispute. If it be not competent to the State to interfere with the education of the people, the mode of interference recommended by the Committee of Council must of course be condemned. If it be the right and the duty of the State to make provision for the education of the people, the objections made to our plan will, in a very few words, be shown to be frivolous.

I shall take a course very different from that which has been taken by the honorable gentleman. I shall in the clearest manner profess my opinion on that great question of principle which he has studiously evaded; and for my opinion I shall give what seem to me to be unanswerable reasons.

I believe, Sir, that it is the right and the duty of the State to provide means of education for the common people. This proposition seems to me to be implied in every definition that has ever yet been given of the functions of a government. About the extent of those functions there has been much difference of opinion among ingenious men. There are some who hold that it is the business of a government to meddle with every part of the system of human life, to regulate trade by bounties and prohibitions, to regulate expenditure by sumptuary laws, to regulate literature by a censorship, to regulate religion by an inquisition. Others go to the opposite extreme, and assign to Government a very narrow sphere of action. But the very narrowest sphere that ever was assigned to governments by any school of political philosophy is quite wide enough for my purpose. On one point all the disputants are agreed. They unanimously acknowledge that it is the duty of every government to take order for giving security to the persons and property of the members of the community.

This being admitted, can it be denied that the education of the common people is a most effectual means of securing our persons and our property? Let Adam Smith answer that question for me. His authority, always high, is, on this subject, entitled to peculiar respect, because he extremely disliked busy, prying, interfering governments. He was for leaving literature, arts, sciences, to take care of themselves. He was not friendly to ecclesiastical establishments. He was of opinion, that the State ought not to meddle with the education of the rich. But he has expressly told us that a distinction is to be made, particularly in a commercial and highly civilised society, between the education of the rich and the education of the poor. The education of the poor, he says, is a matter which deeply concerns the commonwealth. Just as the magistrate ought to interfere for the purpose of preventing the leprosy from spreading among the people, he ought to interfere for the purpose of stopping the progress of the moral distempers which are inseparable from ignorance. Nor can this duty be neglected without danger to the public peace. If you leave the multitude uninstructed, there is serious risk that religious animosities may produce the most dreadful disorders. The most dreadful disorders! Those are Adam Smith's own words; and prophetic words they were. Scarcely had he given this warning to our rulers when his prediction was fulfilled in a manner never to be forgotten. I speak of the No Popery riots of 1780. I do not know that I could find in all history a stronger proof of the proposition, that the ignorance of the common people makes the property, the limbs, the lives of all classes insecure. Without the shadow of a grievance, at the summons of a madman, a hundred thousand people rise in insurrection. During a whole week, there is anarchy in the greatest and wealthiest of European cities. The parliament is besieged. Your predecessor sits trembling in his chair, and expects every moment to see the door beaten in by the ruffians whose roar he hears all round the house. The peers are pulled out of their coaches. The bishops in their lawn are forced to fly over the tiles. The chapels of foreign ambassadors, buildings made sacred by the law of nations, are destroyed. The house of the Chief Justice is demolished. The little children of the Prime Minister are taken out of their beds and laid in their night clothes on the table of the Horse Guards, the only safe asylum from the fury of the rabble. The prisons are opened. Highwaymen, housebreakers, murderers, come forth to swell the mob by which they have been set free. Thirty-six fires are blazing at once in London. Then comes the retribution. Count up all the wretches who were shot, who were hanged, who were crushed, who drank themselves to death at the rivers of gin which ran down Holborn Hill; and you will find that battles have been lost and won with a smaller sacrifice of life. And what was the cause of this calamity, a calamity which, in the history of London ranks with the great plague and the great fire? The cause was the ignorance of a population which had been suffered, in the neighbourhood of palaces, theatres, temples, to grow up as rude and stupid as any tribe of tattooed cannibals in New Zealand, I might say as any drove of beasts in Smithfield Market.

The instance is striking: but it is not solitary. To the same cause are to be ascribed the riots of Nottingham, the sack of Bristol, all the outrages of Ludd, and Swing, and Rebecca, beautiful and costly machinery broken to pieces in Yorkshire, barns and haystacks blazing in Kent, fences and buildings pulled down in Wales. Could such things have been done in a country in which the mind of the labourer had been opened by education, in which he had been taught to find pleasure in the exercise of his intellect, taught to revere his Maker, taught to respect legitimate authority, and taught at the same time to seek the redress of real wrongs by peaceful and constitutional means?

This then is my argument. It is the duty of Government to protect our persons and property from danger. The gross ignorance of the common people is a principal cause of danger to our persons and property. Therefore, it is the duty of the Government to take care that the common people shall not be grossly ignorant.

And what is the alternative? It is universally allowed that, by some means, Government must protect our persons and property. If you take away education, what means do you leave? You leave means such as only necessity can justify, means which inflict a fearful amount of pain, not only on the guilty, but on the innocent who are connected with the guilty. You leave guns and bayonets, stocks and whipping-posts, treadmills, solitary cells, penal colonies, gibbets. See then how the case stands. Here is an end which, as we all agree, governments are bound to attain. There are only two ways of attaining it. One of those ways is by making men better, and wiser, and happier. The other way is by making them infamous and miserable. Can it be doubted which way we ought to prefer? Is it not strange, is it not almost incredible, that pious and benevolent men should gravely propound the doctrine that the magistrate is bound to punish and at the same time bound not to teach? To me it seems quite clear that whoever has a right to hang has a right to educate. Can we think without shame and remorse that more than half of those wretches who have been tied up at Newgate in our time might have been living happily, that more than half of those who are now in our gaols might have been enjoying liberty and using that liberty well, that such a hell on earth as Norfolk Island need never have existed, if we had expended in training honest men but a small part of what we have expended in hunting and torturing rogues.

I would earnestly entreat every gentleman to look at a report which is contained in the Appendix to the First Volume of the Minutes of the Committee of Council. I speak of the report made by Mr. Seymour Tremenheare on the state of that part of Monmouthshire which is inhabited by a population chiefly employed in mining. He found that, in this district, towards the close of 1839, out of eleven thousand children who were of an age to attend school, eight thousand never went to any school at all, and that most of the remaining three thousand might almost as well have gone to no school as to the squalid hovels in which men who ought themselves to have been learners pretended to teach. In general these men had only one qualification for their employment; and that was their utter unfitness for every other employment. They were disabled miners, or broken hucksters. In their schools all was stench, and noise, and confusion. Now and then the clamour of the boys was silenced for two minutes by the furious menaces of the master; but it soon broke out again. The instruction given was of the lowest kind. Not one school in ten was provided with a single map. This is the way in which you suffered the minds of a great population to be formed. And now for the effects of your negligence. The barbarian inhabitants of this region rise in an insane rebellion against the Government. They come pouring down their valleys to Newport. They fire on the Queen's troops. They wound a magistrate. The soldiers fire in return; and too many of these wretched men pay with their lives the penalty of their crime. But is the crime theirs alone? Is it strange that they should listen to the only teaching that they had? How can you, who took no pains to instruct them, blame them for giving ear to the demagogue who took pains to delude them? We put them down, of course. We punished them. We had no choice. Order must be maintained; property must be protected; and, since we had omitted to take the best way of keeping these people quiet, we were under the necessity of keeping them quiet by the dread of the sword and the halter. But could any necessity be more cruel? And which of us would run the risk of being placed under such necessity a second time?

I say, therefore, that the education of the people is not only a means, but the best means, of attaining that which all allow to be a chief end of government; and, if this be so, it passes my faculties to understand how any man can gravely contend that Government has nothing to do with the education of the people.

My confidence in my opinion is strengthened when I recollect that I hold that opinion in common with all the greatest lawgivers, statesmen, and political philosophers of all nations and ages, with all the most illustrious champions of civil and spiritual freedom, and especially with those men whose names were once held in the highest veneration by the Protestant Dissenters of England. I might cite many of the most venerable names of the old world; but I would rather cite the example of that country which the supporters of the Voluntary system here are always recommending to us as a pattern. Go back to the days when the little society which has expanded into the opulent and enlightened commonwealth of Massachusetts began to exist. Our modern Dissenters will scarcely, I think, venture to speak contumeliously of those Puritans whose spirit Laud and his High Commission Court could not subdue, of those Puritans who were willing to leave home and kindred, and all the comforts and refinements of civilised life, to cross the ocean, to fix their abode in forests among wild beasts and wild men, rather than commit the sin of performing, in the House of God, one gesture which they believed to be displeasing to Him. Did those brave exiles think it inconsistent with civil or religious freedom that the State should take charge of the education of the people? No, Sir; one of the earliest laws enacted by the Puritan colonists was that every township, as soon as the Lord had increased it to the number of fifty houses, should appoint one to teach all children to write and read, and that every township of a hundred houses should set up a grammar school. Nor have the descendants of those who made this law ever ceased to hold that the public authorities were bound to provide the means of public instruction. Nor is this doctrine confined to New England. "Educate the people" was the first admonition addressed by Penn to the colony which he founded. "Educate the people" was the legacy of Washington to the nation which he had saved. "Educate the people" was the unceasing exhortation of Jefferson; and I quote Jefferson with peculiar pleasure, because, of all the eminent men that have ever lived, Adam Smith himself not excepted, Jefferson was the one who most abhorred everything like meddling on the part of governments. Yet the chief business of his later years was to establish a good system of State education in Virginia.

And, against such authority as this, what have you who take the other side to show? Can you mention a single great philosopher, a single man distinguished by his zeal for liberty, humanity, and truth, who, from the beginning of the world down to the time of this present Parliament, ever held your doctrines? You can oppose to the unanimous voice of all the wise and good, of all ages, and of both hemispheres, nothing but a clamour which was first heard a few months ago, a clamour in which you cannot join without condemning, not only all whose memory you profess to hold in reverence, but even your former selves.

This new theory of politics has at least the merit of originality. It may be fairly stated thus. All men have hitherto been utterly in the wrong as to the nature and objects of civil government. The great truth, hidden from every preceding generation, and at length revealed, in the year 1846, to some highly respectable ministers and elders of dissenting congregations, is this. Government is simply a great hangman. Government ought to do nothing except by harsh and degrading means. The one business of Government is to handcuff, and lock up, and scourge, and shoot, and stab, and strangle. It is odious tyranny in a government to attempt to prevent crime by informing the understanding and elevating the moral feeling of a people. A statesman may see hamlets turned, in the course of one generation, into great seaport towns and manufacturing towns. He may know that on the character of the vast population which is collected in those wonderful towns, depends the prosperity, the peace, the very existence of society. But he must not think of forming that character. He is an enemy of public liberty if he attempts to prevent those hundreds of thousands of his countrymen from becoming mere Yahoos. He may, indeed, build barrack after barrack to overawe them. If they break out into insurrection, he may send cavalry to sabre them: he may mow them down with grape shot: he may hang them, draw them, quarter them, anything but teach them. He may see, and may shudder as he sees, throughout large rural districts, millions of infants growing up from infancy to manhood as ignorant, as mere slaves of sensual appetite, as the beasts that perish. No matter. He is a traitor to the cause of civil and religious freedom if he does not look on with folded arms, while absurd hopes and evil passions ripen in that rank soil. He must wait for the day of his harvest. He must wait till the Jaquerie comes, till farm houses are burning, till threshing machines are broken in pieces; and then begins his business, which is simply to send one poor ignorant savage to the county `gaol, and another to the antipodes, and a third to the gallows.

Such, Sir, is the new theory of government which was first propounded, in the year 1846, by some men of high note among the Nonconformists of England. It is difficult to understand how men of excellent abilities and excellent intentions,—and there are, I readily admit, such men among those who hold this theory,— can have fallen into so absurd and pernicious an error. One explanation only occurs to me. This is, I am inclined to believe, an instance of the operation of the great law of reaction. We have just come victorious out of a long and fierce contest for the liberty of trade. While that contest was undecided, much was said and written about the advantages of free competition, and about the danger of suffering the State to regulate matters which should be left to individuals. There has consequently arisen in the minds of persons who are led by words, and who are little in the habit of making distinctions, a disposition to apply to political questions and moral questions principles which are sound only when applied to commercial questions. These people, not content with having forced the Government to surrender a province wrongfully usurped, now wish to wrest from the Government a domain held by a right which was never before questioned, and which cannot be questioned with the smallest show of reason. "If," they say, "free competition is a good thing in trade, it must surely be a good thing in education. The supply of other commodities, of sugar, for example, is left to adjust itself to the demand; and the consequence is, that we are better supplied with sugar than if the Government undertook to supply us. Why then should we doubt that the supply of instruction will, without the intervention of the Government, be found equal to the demand?"

Never was there a more false analogy. Whether a man is well supplied with sugar is a matter which concerns himself alone. But whether he is well supplied with instruction is a matter which concerns his neighbours and the State. If he cannot afford to pay for sugar, he must go without sugar. But it is by no means fit that, because he cannot afford to pay for education, he should go without education. Between the rich and their instructors there may, as Adam Smith says, be free trade. The supply of music masters and Italian masters may be left to adjust itself to the demand. But what is to become of the millions who are too poor to procure without assistance the services of a decent schoolmaster? We have indeed heard it said that even these millions will be supplied with teachers by the free competition of benevolent individuals who will vie with each other in rendering this service to mankind. No doubt there are many benevolent individuals who spend their time and money most laudably in setting up and supporting schools; and you may say, if you please, that there is, among these respectable persons, a competition to do good. But do not be imposed upon by words. Do not believe that this competition resembles the competition which is produced by the desire of wealth and by the fear of ruin. There is a great difference, be assured, between the rivalry of philanthropists and the rivalry of grocers. The grocer knows that, if his wares are worse than those of other grocers, he shall soon go before the Bankrupt Court, and his wife and children will have no refuge but the workhouse: he knows that, if his shop obtains an honorable celebrity, he shall be able to set up a carriage and buy a villa: and this knowledge impels him to exertions compared with which the exertions of even very charitable people to serve the poor are but languid. It would be strange infatuation indeed to legislate on the supposition that a man cares for his fellow creatures as much as he cares for himself.

Unless, Sir, I greatly deceive myself, those arguments, which show that the Government ought not to leave to private people the task of providing for the national defence, will equally show that the Government ought not to leave to private people the task of providing for national education. On this subject, Mr. Hume has laid down the general law with admirable good sense and perspicuity. I mean David Hume, not the Member for Montrose, though that honorable gentleman will, I am confident, assent to the doctrine propounded by his illustrious namesake. David Hume, Sir, justly says that most of the arts and trades which exist in the world produce so much advantage and pleasure to individuals, that the magistrate may safely leave it to individuals to encourage those arts and trades. But he adds that there are callings which, though they are highly useful, nay, absolutely necessary to society, yet do not administer to the peculiar pleasure or profit of any individual. The military calling is an instance. Here, says Hume, the government must interfere. It must take on itself to regulate these callings, and to stimulate the industry of the persons who follow these callings by pecuniary and honorary rewards.

Now, Sir, it seems to me that, on the same principle on which Government ought to superintend and to reward the soldier, Government ought to superintend and to reward the schoolmaster. I mean, of course, the schoolmaster of the common people. That his calling is useful, that his calling is necessary, will hardly be denied. Yet it is clear that his services will not be adequately remunerated if he is left to be remunerated by those whom he teaches, or by the voluntary contributions of the charitable. Is this disputed? Look at the facts. You tell us that schools will multiply and flourish exceedingly, if the Government will only abstain from interfering with them. Has not the Government long abstained from interfering with them? Has not everything been left, through many years, to individual exertion? If it were true that education, like trade, thrives most where the magistrate meddles least, the common people of England would now be the best educated in the world. Our schools would be model schools. Every one would have a well chosen little library, excellent maps, a small but neat apparatus for experiments in natural philosophy. A grown person unable to read and write would be pointed at like Giant O'Brien or the Polish Count. Our schoolmasters would be as eminently expert in all that relates to teaching as our cutlers, our cottonspinners, our engineers are allowed to be in their respective callings. They would, as a class, be held in high consideration; and their gains would be such that it would be easy to find men of respectable character and attainments to fill up vacancies.

Now, is this the case? Look at the charges of the judges, at the resolutions of the grand juries, at the reports of public officers, at the reports of voluntary associations. All tell the same sad and ignominious story. Take the reports of the Inspectors of Prisons. In the House of Correction at Hertford, of seven hundred prisoners one half could not read at all; only eight could read and write well. Of eight thousand prisoners who had passed through Maidstone gaol only fifty could read and write well. In Coldbath Fields Prison, the proportion that could read and write well seems to have been still smaller. Turn from the registers of prisoners to the registers of marriages. You will find that about a hundred and thirty thousand couples were married in the year 1844. More than forty thousand of the bridegrooms and more than sixty thousand of the brides did not sign their names, but made their marks. Nearly one third of the men and nearly one half of the women, who are in the prime of life, who are to be the parents of the Englishmen of the next generation, who are to bear a chief part in forming the minds of the Englishmen of the next generation, cannot write their own names. Remember, too, that, though people who cannot write their own names must be grossly ignorant, people may write their own names and yet have very little knowledge. Tens of thousands who were able to write their names had in all probability received only the wretched education of a common day school. We know what such a school too often is; a room crusted with filth, without light, without air, with a heap of fuel in one corner and a brood of chickens in another; the only machinery of instruction a dogeared spellingbook and a broken slate; the masters the refuse of all other callings, discarded footmen, ruined pedlars, men who cannot work a sum in the rule of three, men who cannot write a common letter without blunders, men who do not know whether the earth is a sphere or a cube, men who do not know whether Jerusalem is in Asia or America. And to such men, men to whom none of us would entrust the key of his cellar, we have entrusted the mind of the rising generation, and, with the mind of the rising generation, the freedom, the happiness, the glory of our country.

Do you question the accuracy of this description? I will produce evidence to which I am sure that you will not venture to take an exception. Every gentleman here knows, I suppose, how important a place the Congregational Union holds among the Nonconformists, and how prominent a part Mr. Edward Baines has taken in opposition to State education. A Committee of the Congregational Union drew up last year a report on the subject of education. That report was received by the Union; and the person who moved that it should be received was Mr. Edward Baines. That report contains the following passage: "If it were necessary to disclose facts to such an assembly as this, as to the ignorance and debasement of the neglected portions of our population in towns and rural districts, both adults and juvenile, it could easily be done. Private information communicated to the Board, personal observation and investigation of the various localities, with the published documents of the Registrar General, and the reports of the state of prisons in England and Wales, published by order of the House of Commons, would furnish enough to make us modest in speaking of what has been done for the humbler classes, and make us ashamed that the sons of the soil of England should have been so long neglected, and should present to the enlightened traveller from other shores such a sad spectacle of neglected cultivation, lost mental power, and spiritual degradation." Nothing can be more just. All the information which I have been able to obtain bears out the statements of the

Congregational Union. I do believe that the ignorance and degradation of a large part of the community to which we belong ought to make us ashamed of ourselves. I do believe that an enlightened traveller from New York, from Geneva, or from Berlin, would be shocked to see so much barbarism in the close neighbourhood of so much wealth and civilisation. But is it not strange that the very gentlemen who tell us in such emphatic language that the people are shamefully ill educated, should yet persist in telling us that under a system of free competition the people are certain to be excellently educated? Only this morning the opponents of our plan circulated a paper in which they confidently predict that free competition will do all that is necessary, if we will only wait with patience. Wait with patience! Why, we have been waiting ever since the Heptarchy. How much longer are we to wait! Till the year 2847? Or till the year 3847? That the experiment has as yet failed you do not deny. And why should it have failed? Has it been tried in unfavourable circumstances? Not so; it has been tried in the richest, and in the freest, and in the most charitable country in all Europe. Has it been tried on too small a scale? Not so: millions have been subjected to it. Has it been tried during too short a time? Not so: it has been going on during ages. The cause of the failure then is plain. Our whole system has been unsound. We have applied the principle of free competition to a case to which that principle is not applicable.

But, Sir, if the state of the southern part of our island has furnished me with one strong argument, the state of the northern part furnishes me with another argument, which is, if possible, still more decisive. A hundred and fifty years ago England was one of the best governed and most prosperous countries in the world: Scotland was perhaps the rudest and poorest country that could lay any claim to civilisation. The name of Scotchman was then uttered in this part of the island with contempt. The ablest Scotch statesmen contemplated the degraded state of their poorer countrymen with a feeling approaching to despair. It is well known that Fletcher of Saltoun, a brave and accomplished man, a man who had drawn his sword for liberty, who had suffered proscription and exile for liberty, was so much disgusted and dismayed by the misery, the ignorance, the idleness, the lawlessness of the common people, that he proposed to make many thousands of them slaves. Nothing, he thought, but the discipline which kept order and inforced exertion among the negroes of a sugar colony, nothing but the lash and the stocks, could reclaim the vagabonds who infested every part of Scotland from their indolent and predatory habits, and compel them to support themselves by steady labour. He therefore, soon after the Revolution, published a pamphlet, in which he earnestly, and, as I believe, from the mere impulse of humanity and patriotism, recommended to the Estates of the Realm this sharp remedy, which alone, as he conceived, could remove the evil. Within a few months after the publication of that pamphlet a very different remedy was applied. The Parliament which sate at Edinburgh passed an act for the establishment of parochial schools. What followed? An improvement such as the world had never seen took place in the moral and intellectual character of the people. Soon, in spite of the rigour of the climate, in spite of the sterility of the earth, Scotland became a country which had no reason to envy the fairest portions of the globe. Wherever the Scotchman went,—and there were few parts of the world to which he did not go,—he carried his superiority with him. If he was admitted into a public office, he worked his way up to the highest post. If he got employment in a brewery or a factory, he was soon the foreman. If he took a shop, his trade was the best in the street. If he enlisted in the army, he became a colour-serjeant. If he went to a colony, he was the most thriving planter there. The Scotchman of the seventeenth century had been spoken of in London as we speak of the Esquimaux. The Scotchman of the eighteenth century was an object, not of scorn, but of envy. The cry was that, wherever he came, he got more than his share; that, mixed with Englishmen or mixed with Irishmen, he rose to the top as surely as oil rises to the top of water. And what had produced this great revolution? The Scotch air was still as cold, the Scotch rocks were still as bare as ever. All the natural qualities of the Scotchman were still what they had been when learned and benevolent men advised that he should be flogged, like a beast of burden, to his daily task. But the State had given him an education. That education was not, it is true, in all respects what it should have been. But, such as it was, it had done more for the bleak and dreary shores of the Forth and the Clyde than the richest of soils and the most genial of climates had done for Capua and Tarentum. Is there one member of this House, however strongly he may hold the doctrine that the Government ought not to interfere with the education of the people, who will stand up and say that, in his opinion, the Scotch would now have been a happier and a more enlightened people if they had been left, during the last five generations, to find instruction for themselves?

I say then, Sir, that, if the science of Government be an experimental science, this question is decided. We are in a condition to perform the inductive process according to the rules laid down in the Novum Organum. We have two nations closely connected, inhabiting the same island, sprung from the same blood, speaking the same language, governed by the same Sovereign and the same Legislature, holding essentially the same religious faith, having the same allies and the same enemies. Of these two nations one was, a hundred and fifty years ago, as respects opulence and civilisation, in the highest rank among European communities, the other in the lowest rank. The opulent and highly civilised nation leaves the education of the people to free competition. In the poor and half barbarous nation the education of the people is undertaken by the State. The result is that the first are last and the last first. The common people of Scotland,—it is vain to disguise the truth,—have passed the common people of England. Free competition, tried with every advantage, has produced effects of which, as the Congregational Union tell us, we ought to be ashamed, and which must lower us in the opinion of every intelligent foreigner. State education, tried under every disadvantage, has produced an improvement to which it would be difficult to find a parallel in any age or country. Such an experiment as this would be regarded as conclusive in surgery or chemistry, and ought, I think, to be regarded as equally conclusive in politics.

These, Sir, are the reasons which have satisfied me that it is the duty of the State to educate the people. Being firmly convinced of that truth, I shall not shrink from proclaiming it here and elsewhere, in defiance of the loudest clamour that agitators can raise. The remainder of my task is easy. For, if the great principle for which I have been contending is admitted, the objections which have been made to the details of our plan will vanish fast. I will deal with those objections in the order in which they stand in the amendment moved by the honorable member for Finsbury.

First among his objections he places the cost. Surely, Sir, no person who admits that it is our duty to train the minds of the rising generation can think a hundred thousand pounds too large a sum for that purpose. If we look at the matter in the lowest point of view, if we consider human beings merely as producers of wealth, the difference between an intelligent and a stupid population, estimated in pounds, shillings, and pence, exceeds a hundredfold the proposed outlay. Nor is this all. For every pound that you have saved in education, you will spend five in prosecutions, in prisons, in penal settlements. I cannot believe that the

House, having never grudged anything that was asked for the purpose of maintaining order and protecting property by means of pain and fear, will begin to be niggardly as soon as it is proposed to effect the same objects by making the people wiser and better.

The next objection made by the honorable member to our plan is that it will increase the influence of the Crown. This sum of a hundred thousand pounds may, he apprehends, be employed in corruption and jobbing. Those schoolmasters who vote for ministerial candidates will obtain a share of the grant: those schoolmasters who vote for opponents of the ministry will apply for assistance in vain. Sir, the honorable member never would have made this objection if he had taken the trouble to understand the minutes which he has condemned. We propose to place this part of the public expenditure under checks which must make such abuses as the honorable Member anticipates morally impossible. Not only will there be those ordinary checks which are thought sufficient to prevent the misapplication of the many millions annually granted for the army, the navy, the ordance, the civil government: not only must the Ministers of the Crown come every year to this House for a vote, and be prepared to render an account of the manner in which they have laid out what had been voted in the preceding year; but, when they have satisfied the House, when they have got their vote, they will still be unable to distribute the money at their discretion. Whatever they may do for any schoolmaster must be done in concert with those persons who, in the district where the schoolmaster lives, take an interest in education, and contribute out of their private means to the expense of education. When the honorable gentleman is afraid that we shall corrupt the schoolmasters, he forgets, first, that we do not appoint the schoolmasters; secondly, that we cannot dismiss the schoolmasters; thirdly, that managers who are altogether independent of us can, without our consent, dismiss the schoolmasters; and fourthly that without the recommendation of those managers we can give nothing to the schoolmasters. Observe, too, that such a recommendation will not be one of those recommendations which goodnatured easy people are too apt to give to everybody who asks; nor will it at all resemble those recommendations which the Secretary of the Treasury is in the habit of receiving. For every pound which we pay on the recommendation of the managers, the managers themselves must pay two pounds. They must also provide the schoolmaster with a house out of their own funds before they can obtain for him a grant from the public funds.

What chance of jobbing is there here? It is common enough, no doubt, for a Member of Parliament who votes with Government to ask that one of those who zealously supported him at the last election may have a place in the Excise or the Customs. But such a member would soon cease to solicit if the answer were, "Your friend shall have a place of fifty pounds a year, if you will give him a house and settle on him an income of a hundred a year." What chance then, I again ask, is there of jobbing? What, say some of the dissenters of Leeds, is to prevent a Tory Government, a High Church Government, from using this parliamentary grant to corrupt the schoolmasters of our borough, and to induce them to use all their influence in favour of a Tory and High Church candidate? Why, Sir, the dissenters of Leeds themselves have the power to prevent it. Let them subscribe to the schools: let them take a share in the management of the schools: let them refuse to recommend to the Committee of Council any schoolmaster whom they suspect of having voted at any election from corrupt motives: and the thing is done. Our plan, in truth, is made up of checks. My only doubt is whether the checks may not be found too numerous and too stringent. On our general conduct there is the ordinary check, the parliamentary check. And, as respects those minute details which it is impossible that this House can investigate, we shall be checked, in every town and in every rural district, by boards consisting of independent men zealous in the cause of education.

The truth is, Sir, that those who clamour most loudly against our plan, have never thought of ascertaining what it is. I see that a gentleman, who ought to have known better, has not been ashamed publicly to tell the world that our plan will cost the nation two millions a year, and will paralyse all the exertions of individuals to educate the people. These two assertions are uttered in one breath. And yet, if he who made them had read our minutes before he railed at them, he would have seen that his predictions are contradictory; that they cannot both be fulfilled; that, if individuals do not exert themselves, the country will have to pay nothing; and that, if the country has to pay two millions, it will be because individuals have exerted themselves with such wonderful, such incredible, vigour, as to raise four millions by voluntary contributions.

The next objection made by the honorable Member for Finsbury is that we have acted unconstitutionally, and have incroached on the functions of Parliament. The Committee of Council he seems to consider as an unlawful assembly. He calls it sometimes a self elected body and sometimes a self appointed body. Sir, these are words without meaning. The Committee is no more a self elected body than the Board of Trade. It is a body appointed by the Queen; and in appointing it Her Majesty has exercised, under the advice of her responsible Ministers, a prerogative as old as the monarchy. But, says the honorable member, the constitutional course would have been to apply for an Act of Parliament. On what ground? Nothing but an Act of Parliament can legalise that which is illegal. But whoever heard of an Act of Parliament to legalise what was already beyond all dispute legal? Of course, if we wished to send aliens out of the country, or to detain disaffected persons in custody without bringing them to trial, we must obtain an Act of Parliament empowering us to do so. But why should we ask for an Act of Parliament to empower us to do what anybody may do, what the honorable Member for Finsbury may do? Is there any doubt that he or anybody else may subscribe to a school, give a stipend to a monitor, or settle a retiring pension on a preceptor who has done good service? What any of the Queen's subjects may do the Queen may do. Suppose that her privy purse were so large that she could afford to employ a hundred thousand pounds in this beneficent manner; would an Act of Parliament be necessary to enable her to do so? Every part of our plan may lawfully be carried into execution by any person, Sovereign or subject, who has the inclination and the money. We have not the money; and for the money we come, in a strictly constitutional manner, to the House of Commons. The course which we have taken is in conformity with all precedent, as well as with all principle. There are military schools. No Act of Parliament was necessary to authorise the establishing of such schools. All that was necessary was a grant of money to defray the charge. When I was Secretary at War it was my duty to bring under Her Majesty's notice the situation of the female children of her soldiers. Many such children accompanied every regiment, and their education was grievously neglected. Her Majesty was graciously pleased to sign a warrant by which a girls' school was attached to each corps. No Act of Parliament was necessary. For to set up a school where girls might be taught to read, and write, and sew, and cook, was perfectly legal already. I might have set it up myself, if I had been rich enough. All that I had to ask from Parliament was the money. But I ought to beg pardon for arguing a point so clear.

The next objection to our plans is that they interfere with the religious convictions of Her Majesty's subjects. It has been sometimes insinuated, but it has never been proved, that the Committee of Council has shown undue favour to the Established Church.

Sir, I have carefully read and considered the minutes; and I wish that every man who has exerted his eloquence against them had done the same. I say that I have carefully read and considered them, and that they seem to me to have been drawn up with exemplary impartiality. The benefits which we offer we offer to people of all religious persuasions alike. The dissenting managers of schools will have equal authority with the managers who belong to the Church. A boy who goes to meeting will be just as eligible to be a monitor, and will receive just as large a stipend, as if he went to the cathedral. The schoolmaster who is a nonconformist and the schoolmaster who is a conformist will enjoy the same emoluments, and will, after the same term of service, obtain, on the same conditions, the same retiring pension. I wish that some gentleman would, instead of using vague phrases about religious liberty and the rights of conscience, answer this plain question. Suppose that in one of our large towns there are four schools, a school connected with the Church, a school connected with the Independents, a Baptist school, and a Wesleyan school; what encouragement, pecuniary or honorary, will, by our plan, be given to the school connected with the Church, and withheld from any of the other three schools? Is it not indeed plain that, if by neglect or maladministration the Church school should get into a bad state, while the dissenting schools flourish, the dissenting schools will receive public money and the Church school will receive none?

It is true, I admit, that, in rural districts which are too poor to support more than one school, the religious community to which the majority belongs will have an advantage over other religious communities. But this is not our fault. If we are as impartial as it is possible to be, you surely do not expect more. If there should be a parish containing nine hundred churchmen and a hundred dissenters, if there should, in that parish, be a school connected with the Church, if the dissenters in that parish should be too poor to set up another school, undoubtedly the school connected with the Church will, in that parish, get all that we give; and the dissenters will get nothing. But observe that there is no partiality to the Church, as the Church, in this arrangement. The churchmen get public money, not because they are churchmen, but because they are the majority. The dissenters get nothing, not because they are dissenters, but because they are a small minority. There are districts where the case will be reversed, where there will be dissenting schools, and no Church schools. In such cases the dissenters will get what we have to give, and the churchmen will get nothing.

But, Sir, I ought not to say that a churchman gets nothing by a system which gives a good education to dissenters, or that a dissenter gets nothing by a system which gives a good education to churchmen. We are not, I hope, so much conformists, or so much nonconformists, as to forget that we are Englishmen and Christians. We all, Churchmen, Presbyterians, Independents, Baptists, Methodists, have an interest in this, that the great body of the people should be rescued from ignorance and barbarism. I mentioned Lord George Gordon's mob. That mob began, it is true, with the Roman Catholics: but, long before the tumults were over, there was not a respectable Protestant in London who was not in fear for his house, for his limbs, for his life, for the lives of those who were dearest to him. The honorable Member for Finsbury says that we call on men to pay for an education from which they derive no benefit. I deny that there is one honest and industrious man in the country who derives no benefit from living among honest and industrious neighbours rather than among rioters and vagabonds. This matter is as much a matter of common concern as the defence of our coast. Suppose that I were to say, "Why do you tax me to fortify Portsmouth? If the people of Portsmouth think that they cannot be safe without bastions and ravelins, let the people of Portsmouth pay the engineers and masons. Why am I to bear the charge of works from which I derive no advantage?" You would answer, and most justly, that there is no man in the island who does not derive advantage from these works, whether he resides within them or not. And, as every man, in whatever part of the island he may live, is bound to contribute to the support of those arsenals which are necessary for our common security, so is every man, to whatever sect he may belong, bound to contribute to the support of those schools on which, not less than on our arsenals, our common security depends.

I now come to the last words of the amendment. The honorable Member for Finsbury is apprehensive that our plan may interfere with the civil rights of Her Majesty's subjects. How a man's civil rights can be prejudiced by his learning to read and write, to multiply and divide, or even by his obtaining some knowledge of history and geography, I do not very well apprehend. One thing is clear, that persons sunk in that ignorance in which, as we are assured by the Congregational Union, great numbers of our countrymen are sunk, can be free only in name. It is hardly necessary for us to appoint a Select Committee for the purpose of inquiring whether knowledge be the ally or the enemy of liberty. He is, I must say, but a shortsighted friend of the common people who is eager to bestow on them a franchise which would make them allpowerful, and yet would withhold from them that instruction without which their power must be a curse to themselves and to the State.

This, Sir, is my defence. From the clamour of our accusers I appeal with confidence to the country to which we must, in no long time, render an account of our stewardship. I appeal with still more confidence to future generations, which, while enjoying all the blessings of an impartial and efficient system of public instruction, will find it difficult to believe that the authors of that system should have had to struggle with a vehement and pertinacious opposition, and still more difficult to believe that such an opposition was offered in the name of civil and religious freedom.

THE EXAMINATION OF EDWARD OXFORD
BY THE PRIVY COUNCIL

IN the Library of Trinity College, Cambridge, are eleven volumes of Macaulay's journals. Sir George Otto Trevelyan quotes a large number of extracts in his *Life and Letters of Lord Macaulay*, but they have never been published in full. In the volume which runs from 20 October 1838 to 3 May 1849 (press-mark: 0.15.1) are five loose four-page foolscap sheets containing a journal for 10 and 11 June 1840. The following extract consists of sheets 2, 3 and 4.

WEDNESDAY June 10. cont^d—Left the stupidest of all Committees at four PM—looked into the House—benches thin—nothing to do—home—read—dressed—to Lord Holland's—sent in Carlisle's Embassy to My Lady—went to My Lord in the Library—no Cabinet Minister but Clarendon yet come—I found them both in great agitation. The Queen had been fired at scarce an hour before on her way along Constitution Hill—The other Ministers dropped in, one by one, full of the story—The particulars not fully known—But she is perfectly safe—I went to Lady H's dressing-room at her summons to be thanked for the book— Clarendon came too—Luttrell and Miss Fox were drinking tea there—We told her of the attempt at assassination. She and every body greatly shocked—To dinner—Melbourne and Normanby not yet arrived. They came before dinner was over. The Queen well and cheerful. Much talk as to the course to be pursued. I went to the library and looked out half a dozen precedents just in point—Margaret Nicholson—Hadfield—Despard—Settled to have a Privy Council to morrow, nothing unforeseen preventing, and to examine this young ruffian—Nothing is yet known of him but that his name is Edward Oxford . . .

Thursday June 11.—1840—Read Capefigue—thought over Irish Reg^n Question and looked over my papers—Quite ready for debate on the principle if such a debate should come on; but I hardly expected it. Walked with Hannah Fanny & Baba in St James's Park—put down my name at Prince Albert's—To my office—Summons to Privy Council at two—Went to the Home Office. A singular scene—Great number of curious people about— great signs of anxiety. All the Cabinet Ministers but Ld Holland were present—The Under Sec^y for the Home Department—The Attorney General and Maule Solicitor for the Treasury. On the table lay in a heap the effects discovered in a box at the Prisoner's lodging—very singular and mysterious they were. There were two pistol cases which had evidently held the pistols which he fired at the Queen—One of the pistol-cases bore the letters E.R. What could that mean except Ernest Rex?—And yet how monstrously improbable!—There were three letters and another paper, all I think in one hand—The letters were signed Smith—an assumed name I suspect, and were dated from Young England. One of the letters spoke of the great news from Hanover. Another complimented Mr Oxford on his beautiful speaking at the Society. "We heard" says the writer "knocking at our door the other night. We put the crape on our faces, & made our swords and pistols ready. Some of us held the papers ready to be thrown into the fire. Others were prepared to burn the house. But it turned out to be nothing." "Lieutenant Mars," it was also said, "introduced to the society a fine tall gentlemanlike man whose name had not transpired, but who was supposed to be an Officer in the army."—

The fourth paper purported to contain the rules of a most extraordinary society to which this wretched boy appears to have belonged—They were to this effect—Every member to have a sword, two pistols and a rifle—No member to leave town for more than a month without communicating with the Society. Disguises to be provided for such members as should be sent abroad or into the country on business. The disguises to be sometimes those of merchants—sometimes of labourers sometimes of gentlemen. Every member who could raise 100 men to be a Captain. None to be admitted without an oath of allegiance to the cause. Fictitious names provided for all the officers. There was President Gowrie—an allusion, I imagine, to the famous conspiracy—then a set of the most absurd names for different dignitaries—Justinian—Aloman—Caloman—Ernest—Frederic—Godfrey, Gregory, Albany, Mars, Neptune, Hannibal, Oxonian, Milton. Then regulations of costume—who was to have three red bows and who two red bows. The crape veil of the assassin lay on the table and had two red bows—the badge of a captain in their hierarchy. I ought to say that the rules as well as the letters were ill spelt—and, I should say in foreign spelling. Master for example was spelt *mastre*—not an English blunder. There was something German too about the choice of names. The box had also contained the crape veil which I have mentioned—a sabre—a wretched thing brass-handled—a few books.—A testament was one—The others were a geographical dictionary and a pocket book which had contained the manuscript before mentioned.—I had doubted whether Oxford was not a *nom de guerre* like Oxonian. But in the first page of the Testament I found *given by Somebody to Mrs Hannah Oxford*. At last the prisoner was brought in. He looked young—

about seventeen—was short and slightly made—dark complexion
—and not exactly ugly—but with a singularly odious countenance
—Perhaps I fancied so, knowing what he had done. Yet I really
believe that I should have thought so if I had never heard any
thing about him. His face was constantly twitching—sometimes
into a sneer—sometimes into a sort of attempt at a grin perfectly
hideous. He stood with folded arms, resolutely enough, but a
little theatrically. One of his legs shook violently. That, and the
working of his face which seemed to try to express scorn, were the
only marks of feeling which he gave, except for one moment
which I will mention hereafter. Lord Normanby took the lead, as
belonged to his place, and with great—perhaps immoderate
severity—addressed the prisoner. I say immoderate not because
I think that rudeness or severity ought to have been shewn; but
because the greatest solemnity and gravity consistent with
humanity would have best befitted the occasion. The witnesses
were called in, & the Attorney conducted the examination. The
prisoner—like most ignorant foolish people whom I have seen in
his situation, appeared to think only of catching out the witnesses
in trifling contradictions immaterial to the question while he owned,
every time that he opened his lips, more than enough to hang him.
He gloried in puzzling one of them as to whether he held the
pistol, the second time of firing in his left hand or in his right—
"Do you know which is your right hand & which your left." and
such other foolish questions. But he was most affronting to Lord
Colchester—He called him Lord Tom Noodle, & so forth—The
evidence all hung together with discrepancies as slight as I ever
knew in such a case. There were three if not four distinct eye
witnesses to the crime. The property found in the prisoner's
box was identified—His brother in law with whom he lived was
called in—Then and only then the fellow who during the rest of
the examination behaved with hardened depravity shewed signs
of feeling. He turned away from his brother-in-law, looked much
agitated and declined to cross-examine. When the evidence had
been gone through and he was called on to offer any thing that
might be of use to him always under caution, he stepped forward,
talked of the variations of the witnesses one of whom called a
distance ten yards which another called twenty yards, and one of
who had said that he fired with his right hand when another said
that he had fired with his left—He then—as if to prevent these
variations supposing them material from doing him the smallest
good, said in the most audacious manner that he had fired twice,
that at the first fire Prince Albert sprang up and seemed ready to

jump out of the carriage—but thought better of it, and so forth.
As to his motive he declined saying any thing—We of course
committed him. And now what do you think of this strange
affair? I do not suspect [the King of Hanover. I do not even think
—in spite of some appearances]¹ that the Orange party, here
through even its lowest and vilest members is concerned in this
crime. On the other hand I think that Chartism has nothing to
do with it. It is at the same time clear that the fellow is not alone
—that he belongs to a villainous association. Of what nature?
I am writing in the dark. But what seems tolerably clear is that it
is an association under foreign management. It has altogether
a foreign—decidedly a German air.—The orthography of the
Secretary is foreign—the names and the general taste is foreign.
The allusion to Hanover and the ER are very remarkable. The
name Ernest in the list of fictitious appellations I do not think so
much of. It is only one of several common German names. But,
as at present advised, I suspect that a plot originating in Hanover
has been formed for the assassination of the Queen—that German
agents are at the head of the design—that they have played off
on this young villain, who seems to be of the genuine Ravaillac
breed, some delusion which has infatuated him. I should not
wonder if they had worked him up by democratic stimulants for a
purpose by no means democratic. The King of Hanover cannot
be implicated, one would think—But he may have German
dependants who would do anything to place him on the English
throne. Of one thing I am perfectly satisfied—that the wretch is
no more mad than I am. There must be no weak indulgence in
such a case.²

¹ [Crossed out.]
² [Oxford was found "Not guilty, on the ground of insanity," on 10
July 1840, and was sentenced to be confined during Her Majesty's
pleasure.]

POETRY

Lays of Ancient Rome was first published by Longman in 1842. Macaulay made a few small corrections in the third edition of 1843, and this text has been used for *Horatius* and *The Battle of the Lake Regillus*. In 1848 a "new edition" of the *Lays* appeared which also included *Ivry* and *The Armada* and provides the text for these two poems. *Ivry* had already been printed, but without the sixth stanza, as the second of two *Songs of the Huguenots* in *Knight's Quarterly Magazine* for January–April 1824. *The Armada* had appeared in *Friendship's Offering* in 1832. *The Marriage of Tirzah and Ahirad*, *The Last Buccaneer*, and *Epitaph on a Jacobite* are here printed from the posthumous *Miscellaneous Writings*, published by Longman in 1860.

Macaulay handed the manuscript of the *Epitaph* to his friend Stanhope across the table at a meeting of the Trustees of the British Museum. It is preserved at Chevening.

POETRY

LAYS OF ANCIENT ROME

HORATIUS

A LAY
MADE ABOUT THE YEAR OF THE CITY CCCLX

I

Lars Porsena of Clusium
  By the Nine Gods he swore
That the great house of Tarquin
  Should suffer wrong no more.
By the Nine Gods he swore it,
  And named a trysting day,
And bade his messengers ride forth,
East and west and south and north,
  To summon his array.

2

East and west and south and north
  The messengers ride fast,
And tower and town and cottage
  Have heard the trumpet's blast.
Shame on the false Etruscan
  Who lingers in his home,
When Porsena of Clusium
  Is on the march for Rome.

3

The horsemen and the footmen
  Are pouring in amain
From many a stately market-place;
  From many a fruitful plain;
From many a lonely hamlet,
  Which, hid by beech and pine,
Like an eagle's nest, hangs on the crest
  Of purple Apennine;

4

From lordly Volaterræ,
  Where scowls the far-famed hold
Piled by the hands of giants
  For godlike kings of old;
From seagirt Populonia,
  Whose sentinels descry
Sardinia's snowy mountain-tops
  Fringing the southern sky;

5

From the proud mart of Pisæ,
  Queen of the western waves,
Where ride Massilia's triremes
  Heavy with fair-haired slaves;
From where sweet Clanis wanders
  Through corn and vines and flowers;
From where Cortona lifts to heaven
  Her diadem of towers.

6

Tall are the oaks whose acorns
  Drop in dark Auser's rill;
Fat are the stags that champ the boughs
  Of the Ciminian hill;
Beyond all streams Clitumnus
  Is to the herdsman dear;
Best of all pools the fowler loves
  The great Volsinian mere.

7

But now no stroke of woodman
  Is heard by Auser's rill;
No hunter tracks the stag's green path
  Up the Ciminian hill;
Unwatched along Clitumnus
  Grazes the milk-white steer;
Unharmed the water fowl may dip
  In the Volsinian mere.

8

The harvests of Arretium,
  This year, old men shall reap;

This year, young boys in Umbro
   Shall plunge the struggling sheep;
And in the vats of Luna,
   This year, the must shall foam
Round the white feet of laughing girls,
   Whose sires have marched to Rome.

9

There be thirty chosen prophets,
   The wisest of the land,
Who always by Lars Pórsena
   Both morn and evening stand:
Evening and morn the Thirty
   Have turned the verses o'er,
Traced from the right on linen white
   By mighty seers of yore.

10

And with one voice the Thirty
   Have their glad answer given:
"Go forth, go forth, Lars Porsena;
   Go forth, beloved of Heaven;
Go, and return in glory
   To Clusium's royal dome;
And hang round Nurscia's altars
   The golden shields of Rome."

11

And now hath every city
   Sent up her tale of men;
The foot are fourscore thousand,
   The horse are thousands ten.
Before the gates of Sutrium
   Is met the great array.
A proud man was Lars Porsena
   Upon the trysting day.

12

For all the Etruscan armies
   Were ranged beneath his eye,
And many a banished Roman,
   And many a stout ally;

And with a mighty following
  To join the muster came
The Tusculan Mamilius,
  Prince of the Latian name.

13

But by the yellow Tiber
  Was tumult and affright:
From all the spacious champaign
  To Rome men took their flight.
A mile around the city,
  The throng stopped up the ways;
A fearful sight it was to see
  Through two long nights and days.

14

For aged folk on crutches,
  And women great with child,
And mothers sobbing over babes
  That clung to them and smiled,
And sick men borne in litters
  High on the necks of slaves,
And troops of sun-burned husbandmen
  With reaping-hooks and staves.

15

And droves of mules and asses
  Laden with skins of wine,
And endless flocks of goats and sheep,
  And endless herds of kine,
And endless trains of waggons
  That creaked beneath the weight
Of corn-sacks and of household goods,
  Choked every roaring gate.

16

Now, from the rock Tarpeian,
  Could the wan burghers spy
The line of blazing villages
  Red in the midnight sky.
The Fathers of the City,
  They sat all night and day,
For every hour some horseman came
  With tidings of dismay.

17

To eastward and to westward
　Have spread the Tuscan bands;
Nor house, nor fence, nor dovecote
　In Crustumerium stands.
Verbenna down to Ostia
　Hath wasted all the plain;
Astur hath stormed Janiculum,
　And the stout guards are slain.

18

I wis, in all the Senate,
　There was no heart so bold,
But sore it ached, and fast it beat,
　When that ill news was told.
Forthwith up rose the Consul,
　Up rose the Fathers all;
In haste they girded up their gowns,
　And hied them to the wall.

19

They held a council standing
　Before the River-Gate;
Short time was there, ye well may guess,
　For musing or debate.
Out spake the Consul roundly:
　"The bridge must straight go down;
For, since Janiculum is lost,
　Nought else can save the town."

20

Just then a scout came flying,
　All wild with haste and fear:
"To arms! to arms! Sir Consul;
　Lars Porsena is here."
On the low hills to westward
　The Consul fixed his eye,
And saw the swarthy storm of dust
　Rise fast along the sky.

21

And nearer fast and nearer
　Doth the red whirlwind come;

And louder still and still more loud,
From underneath that rolling cloud,
Is heard the trumpet's war-note proud,
    The trampling, and the hum.
And plainly and more plainly
    Now through the gloom appears,
Far to left and far to right,
In broken gleams of dark-blue light,
The long array of helmets bright,
    The long array of spears.

22

And plainly and more plainly,
    Above that glimmering line,
Now might ye see the banners
    Of twelve fair cities shine;
But the banner of proud Clusium
    Was highest of them all,
The terror of the Umbrian,
    The terror of the Gaul.

23

And plainly and more plainly
    Now might the burghers know,
By port and vest, by horse and crest,
    Each warlike Lucumo.
There Cilnius of Arretium
    On his fleet roan was seen;
And Astur of the four-fold shield,
Girt with the brand none else may wield,
Tolumnius with the belt of gold,
And dark Verbenna from the hold
    By reedy Thrasymene.

24

Fast by the royal standard,
    O'erlooking all the war,
Lars Porsena of Clusium
    Sate in his ivory car.
By the right wheel rode Mamilius,
    Prince of the Latian name;
And by the left false Sextus,
    That wrought the deed of shame.

25

But when the face of Sextus
  Was seen among the foes,
A yell that rent the firmament
  From all the town arose.
On the house-tops was no woman
  But spat towards him and hissed;
No child but screamed out curses,
  And shook its little fist.

26

But the Consul's brow was sad,
  And the Consul's speech was low,
And darkly looked he at the wall,
  And darkly at the foe.
"Their van will be upon us
  Before the bridge goes down;
And if they once may win the bridge,
  What hope to save the town?"

27

Then out spake brave Horatius,
  The Captain of the gate:
"To every man upon this earth
  Death cometh soon or late.
And how can man die better
  Than facing fearful odds,
For the ashes of his father
  And the temples of his Gods,

28

"And for the tender mother
  Who dandled him to rest,
And for the wife who nurses
  His baby at her breast,
And for the holy maidens
  Who feed the eternal flame,
To save them from false Sextus
  That wrought the deed of shame?

29

"Hew down the bridge, Sir Consul,
  With all the speed ye may;

I, with two more to help me,
  Will hold the foe in play.
In yon strait path a thousand
  May well be stopped by three.
Now who will stand on either hand,
  And keep the bridge with me?"

30

Then out spake Spurius Lartius;
  A Ramnian proud was he:
"Lo, I will stand at thy right hand,
  And keep the bridge with thee."
And out spake strong Herminius;
  Of Titian blood was he:
"I will abide on thy left side,
  And keep the bridge with thee."

31

"Horatius," quoth the Consul,
  "As thou sayest, so let it be."
And straight against that great array
  Forth went the dauntless Three.
For Romans in Rome's quarrel
  Spared neither land nor gold,
Nor son nor wife, nor limb nor life,
  In the brave days of old.

32

Then none was for a party;
  Then all were for the state;
Then the great man helped the poor,
  And the poor man loved the great:
Then lands were fairly portioned;
  Then spoils were fairly sold:
The Romans were like brothers
  In the brave days of old.

33

Now Roman is to Roman
  More hateful than a foe,
And the Tribunes beard the high,
  And the Fathers grind the low.

As we wax hot in faction,
In battle we wax cold:
Wherefore men fight not as they fought
In the brave days of old.

34

Now while the Three were tightening
Their harness on their backs,
The Consul was the foremost man
To take in hand an axe:
And Fathers mixed with Commons
Seized hatchet, bar, and crow,
And smote upon the planks above,
And loosed the props below.

35

Meanwhile the Tuscan army,
Right glorious to behold,
Came flashing back the noonday light,
Rank behind rank, like surges bright
Of a broad sea of gold.
Four hundred trumpets sounded
A peal of warlike glee,
As that great host, with measured tread,
And spears advanced, and ensigns spread,
Rolled slowly towards the bridge's head,
Where stood the dauntless Three.

36

The Three stood calm and silent
And looked upon the foes,
And a great shout of laughter
From all the vanguard rose:
And forth three chiefs came spurring
Before that deep array;
To earth they sprang, their swords they drew,
And lifted high their shields, and flew
To win the narrow way;

37

Aunus from green Tifernum,
Lord of the Hill of Vines;

And Seius, whose eight hundred slaves
   Sicken in Ilva's mines;
And Picus, long to Clusium
   Vassal in peace and war,
Who led to fight his Umbrian powers
From that grey crag where, girt with towers,
The fortress of Nequinum lowers
   O'er the pale waves of Nar.

38

Stout Lartius hurled down Aunus
   Into the stream beneath:
Herminius struck at Seius,
   And clove him to the teeth:
At Picus brave Horatius
   Darted one fiery thrust;
And the proud Umbrian's gilded arms
   Clashed in the bloody dust.

39

Then Ocnus of Falerii
   Rushed on the Roman Three;
And Lausulus of Urgo,
   The rover of the sea;
And Aruns of Volsinium,
   Who slew the great wild boar,
The great wild boar that had his den
Amidst the reeds of Cosa's fen,
And wasted fields, and slaughtered men,
   Along Albinia's shore.

40

Herminius smote down Aruns:
   Lartius laid Ocnus low:
Right to the heart of Lausulus
   Horatius sent a blow.
"Lie there," he cried, "fell pirate!
   No more, aghast and pale,
From Ostia's walls the crowd shall mark
The track of thy destroying bark.
No more Campania's hinds shall fly
To woods and caverns when they spy
   Thy thrice accursed sail."

41

But now no sound of laughter
  Was heard amongst the foes.
A wild and wrathful clamour
  From all the vanguard rose.
Six spears' lengths from the entrance
  Halted that deep array,
And for a space no man came forth
  To win the narrow way.

42

But hark! the cry is Astur:
  And lo! the ranks divide;
And the great Lord of Luna
  Comes with his stately stride.
Upon his ample shoulders
  Clangs loud the four-fold shield,
And in his hand he shakes the brand
  Which none but he can wield.

43

He smiled on those bold Romans
  A smile serene and high;
He eyed the flinching Tuscans,
  And scorn was in his eye.
Quoth he, "The she-wolf's litter
  Stand savagely at bay:
But will ye dare to follow,
  If Astur clears the way?"

44

Then, whirling up his broadsword
  With both hands to the height,
He rushed against Horatius,
  And smote with all his might.
With shield and blade Horatius
  Right deftly turned the blow.
The blow, though turned, came yet too nigh;
It missed his helm, but gashed his thigh:
The Tuscans raised a joyful cry
  To see the red blood flow.

45

He reeled, and on Herminius
    He leaned one breathing-space;
Then, like a wild cat mad with wounds,
    Sprang right at Astur's face.
Through teeth, and skull, and helmet,
    So fierce a thrust he sped,
The good sword stood a hand-breadth out
    Behind the Tuscan's head.

46

And the great Lord of Luna
    Fell at that deadly stroke,
As falls on Mount Alvernus
    A thunder-smitten oak.
Far o'er the crashing forest
    The giant arms lie spread;
And the pale augurs, muttering low,
    Gaze on the blasted head.

47

On Astur's throat Horatius
    Right firmly pressed his heel,
And thrice and four times tugged amain,
    Ere he wrenched out the steel.
"And see," he cried, "the welcome,
    Fair guests, that waits you here!
What noble Lucumo comes next
    To taste our Roman cheer?"

48

But at his haughty challenge
    A sullen murmur ran,
Mingled of wrath, and shame, and dread,
    Along that glittering van.
There lacked not men of prowess,
    Nor men of lordly race;
For all Etruria's noblest
    Were round the fatal place.

49

But all Etruria's noblest
    Felt their hearts sink to see

On the earth the bloody corpses,
　In the path the dauntless Three:
And, from the ghastly entrance
　Where those bold Romans stood,
All shrank, like boys who unaware,
Ranging the woods to start a hare,
Come to the mouth of the dark lair
Where, growling low, a fierce old bear
　Lies amidst bones and blood.

50

Was none who would be foremost
　To lead such dire attack;
But those behind cried "Forward!"
　And those before cried "Back!"
And backward now and forward
　Wavers the deep array;
And on the tossing sea of steel,
To and fro the standards reel;
And the victorious trumpet-peal
　Dies fitfully away.

51

Yet one man for one moment
　Strode out before the crowd;
Well known was he to all the Three,
　And they gave him greeting loud.
"Now welcome, welcome, Sextus!
　Now welcome to thy home!
Why dost thou stay, and turn away?
　Here lies the road to Rome."

52

Thrice looked he at the city;
　Thrice looked he at the dead;
And thrice came on in fury,
　And thrice turned back in dread:
And, white with fear and hatred,
　Scowled at the narrow way
Where, wallowing in a pool of blood,
　The bravest Tuscans lay.

53

But meanwhile axe and lever
  Have manfully been plied;
And now the bridge hangs tottering
  Above the boiling tide.
"Come back, come back, Horatius!"
  Loud cried the Fathers all.
"Back, Lartius! back, Herminius!
  Back, ere the ruin fall!"

54

Back darted Spurius Lartius;
  Herminius darted back:
And, as they passed, beneath their feet
  They felt the timbers crack.
But when they turned their faces,
  And on the farther shore
Saw brave Horatius stand alone,
  They would have crossed once more.

55

But with a crash like thunder
  Fell every loosened beam,
And, like a dam, the mighty wreck
  Lay right athwart the stream:
And a long shout of triumph
  Rose from the walls of Rome,
As to the highest turret-tops
  Was splashed the yellow foam.

56

And, like a horse unbroken
  When first he feels the rein,
The furious river struggled hard,
  And tossed his tawny mane;
And burst the curb, and bounded,
  Rejoicing to be free;
And whirling down, in fierce career,
Battlement, and plank, and pier,
  Rushed headlong to the sea.

57

Alone stood brave Horatius,
  But constant still in mind;

Thrice thirty thousand foes before,
  And the broad flood behind.
"Down with him!" cried false Sextus,
  With a smile on his pale face.
"Now yield thee," cried Lars Porsena,
  "Now yield thee to our grace."

58

Round turned he, as not deigning
  Those craven ranks to see;
Nought spake he to Lars Porsena,
  To Sextus nought spake he;
But he saw on Palatinus
  The white porch of his home;
And he spake to the noble river
  That rolls by the towers of Rome.

59

"Oh, Tiber! father Tiber!
  To whom the Romans pray,
A Roman's life, a Roman's arms,
  Take thou in charge this day!"
So he spake, and speaking sheathed
  The good sword by his side,
And with his harness on his back,
  Plunged headlong in the tide.

60

No sound of joy or sorrow
  Was heard from either bank;
But friends and foes in dumb surprise,
With parted lips and straining eyes,
  Stood gazing where he sank;
And when above the surges
  They saw his crest appear,
All Rome sent forth a rapturous cry,
And even the ranks of Tuscany
  Could scarce forbear to cheer.

61

But fiercely ran the current,
  Swollen high by months of rain:
And fast his blood was flowing;
  And he was sore in pain,

And heavy with his armour,
　　And spent with changing blows:
And oft they thought him sinking,
　　But still again he rose.

62

Never, I ween, did swimmer,
　　In such an evil case,
Struggle through such a raging flood
　　Safe to the landing place:
But his limbs were borne up bravely
　　By the brave heart within,
And our good father Tiber
　　Bare bravely up his chin.

63

"Curse on him!" quoth false Sextus;
　　"Will not the villain drown?
But for this stay, ere close of day
　　We should have sacked the town!"
"Heaven help him!" quoth Lars Porsena,
　　"And bring him safe to shore;
For such a gallant feat of arms
　　Was never seen before."

64

And now he feels the bottom;
　　Now on dry earth he stands;
Now round him throng the Fathers
　　To press his gory hands;
And now with shouts and clapping,
　　And noise of weeping loud,
He enters through the River-Gate,
　　Borne by the joyous crowd.

65

They gave him of the corn-land,
　　That was of public right,
As much as two strong oxen
　　Could plough from morn till night;
And they made a molten image,
　　And set it up on high,
And there it stands unto this day
　　To witness if I lie.

66

It stands in the Comitium,
    Plain for all folk to see;
Horatius in his harness,
    Halting upon one knee:
And underneath is written,
    In letters all of gold,
How valiantly he kept the bridge
    In the brave days of old.

67

And still his name sounds stirring
    Unto the men of Rome,
As the trumpet-blast that cries to them
    To charge the Volscian home;
And wives still pray to Juno
    For boys with hearts as bold
As his who kept the bridge so well
    In the brave days of old.

68

And in the nights of winter,
    When the cold north winds blow,
And the long howling of the wolves
    Is heard amidst the snow;
When round the lonely cottage
    Roars loud the tempest's din,
And the good logs of Algidus
    Roar louder yet within;

69

When the oldest cask is opened,
    And the largest lamp is lit,
When the chestnuts glow in the embers,
    And the kid turns on the spit;
When young and old in circle
    Around the firebrands close;
When the girls are weaving baskets,
    And the lads are shaping bows;

70

When the goodman mends his armour,
    And trims his helmet's plume;

When the goodwife's shuttle merrily
 Goes flashing through the loom;
With weeping and with laughter
 Still is the story told,
How well Horatius kept the bridge
 In the brave days of old.

THE BATTLE OF THE LAKE REGILLUS

A LAY SUNG AT THE FEAST OF CASTOR AND POLLUX
ON THE IDES OF QUINTILIS, IN THE YEAR OF THE CITY CCCCLI

1

Ho, trumpets, sound a war-note!
 Ho, lictors, clear the way!
The Knights will ride, in all their pride,
 Along the streets to-day.
To-day the doors and windows
 Are hung with garlands all,
From Castor in the Forum,
 To Mars without the wall.
Each Knight is robed in purple,
 With olive each is crown'd;
A gallant war-horse under each
 Paws haughtily the ground.
While flows the Yellow River,
 While stands the Sacred Hill,
The proud Ides of Quintilis
 Shall have such honour still.
Gay are the Martian Kalends:
 December's Nones are gay:
But the proud Ides, when the squadron rides,
 Shall be Rome's whitest day.

2

Unto the Great Twin Brethren
 We keep this solemn feast.
Swift, swift, the Great Twin Brethren
 Came spurring from the east.
They came o'er wild Parthenius
 Tossing in waves of pine,
O'er Cirrha's dome, o'er Adria's foam,
 O'er purple Apennine.

From where with flutes and dances
   Their ancient mansion rings,
In lordly Lacedæmon,
   The City of two kings,
To where, by Lake Regillus,
   Under the Porcian height,
All in the lands of Tusculum,
   Was fought the glorious fight.

3

Now on the place of slaughter
   Are cots and sheepfolds seen,
And rows of vines, and fields of wheat,
   And apple-orchards green:
The swine crush the big acorns
   That fall from Corne's oaks.
Upon the turf by the Fair Fount
   The reaper's pottage smokes.
The fisher baits his angle;
   The hunter twangs his bow;
Little they think on those strong limbs
   That moulder deep below.
Little they think how sternly
   That day the trumpets pealed;
How in the slippery swamp of blood
   Warrior and war-horse reeled;
How wolves came with fierce gallop,
   And crows on eager wings,
To tear the flesh of captains,
   And peck the eyes of kings;
How thick the dead lay scattered
   Under the Porcian height;
How through the gates of Tusculum
   Raved the wild stream of flight;
And how the Lake Regillus
   Bubbled with crimson foam,
What time the Thirty Cities
   Came forth to war with Rome.

4

But, Roman, when thou standest
   Upon that holy ground,
Look thou with heed on the dark rock
   That girds the dark lake round.

So shalt thou see a hoof-mark
    Stamped deep into the flint:
It was no hoof of mortal steed
    That made so strange a dint:
There to the Great Twin Brethren
    Vow thou thy vows, and pray
That they, in tempest and in fight,
    Will keep thy head alway.

5

Since last the Great Twin Brethren
    Of mortal eyes were seen,
Have years gone by an hundred
    And fourscore and thirteen.
That summer a Virginius
    Was Consul first in place;
The second was stout Aulus,
    Of the Posthumian race.
The Herald of the Latines
    From Gabii came in state:
The Herald of the Latines
    Passed through Rome's Eastern Gate:
The Herald of the Latines
    Did in our Forum stand;
And there he did his office,
    A sceptre in his hand.

6

"Hear, Senators and people
    Of the good town of Rome:
The Thirty Cities charge you
    To bring the Tarquins home:
And if ye still be stubborn,
    To work the Tarquins wrong,
The Thirty Cities warn you,
    Look that your walls be strong."

7

Then spake the Consul Aulus,
    He spake a bitter jest:
"Once the jays sent a message
    Unto the eagle's nest:—
Now yield thou up thine eyrie
    Unto the carrion-kite,

Or come forth valiantly, and face
 The jays in deadly fight.—
Forth looked in wrath the eagle;
 And carrion-kite and jay,
Soon as they saw his beak and claw,
 Fled screaming far away."

8

The Herald of the Latines
 Hath hied him back in state:
The Fathers of the City
 Are met in high debate.
Then spake the elder Consul,
 An ancient man and wise:
"Now hearken, Conscript Fathers,
 To that which I advise.
In seasons of great peril
 'Tis good that one bear sway;
Then choose we a Dictator,
 Whom all men shall obey.
Camerium knows how deeply
 The sword of Aulus bites;
And all our city calls him
 The man of seventy fights.
Then let him be Dictator
 For six months and no more,
And have a Master of the Knights,
 And axes twenty-four."

9

So Aulus was Dictator,
 The man of seventy fights;
He made Æbutius Elva
 His Master of the Knights.
On the third morn thereafter,
 At dawning of the day,
Did Aulus and Æbutius
 Set forth with their array.
Sempronius Atratinus
 Was left in charge at home
With boys, and with grey-headed men,
 To keep the walls of Rome.

Hard by the Lake Regillus
　　Our camp was pitched at night:
Eastward a mile the Latines lay,
　　Under the Porcian height.
Far over hill and valley
　　Their mighty host was spread;
And with their thousand watch-fires
　　The midnight sky was red.

10

Up rose the golden morning
　　Over the Porcian height,
The proud Ides of Quintilis
　　Marked evermore with white.
Not without secret trouble
　　Our bravest saw the foes,
For girt by threescore thousand spears,
　　The thirty standards rose.
From every warlike city
　　That boasts the Latian name,
Foredoomed to dogs and vultures,
　　That gallant army came;
From Setia's purple vineyards,
　　From Norba's ancient wall,
From the white streets of Tusculum,
　　The proudest town of all;
From where the Witch's Fortress
　　O'erhangs the dark-blue seas,
From the still glassy lake that sleeps
　　Beneath Aricia's trees—
Those trees in whose dim shadow
　　The ghastly priest doth reign,
The priest who slew the slayer,
　　And shall himself be slain;—
From the drear banks of Ufens,
　　Where flights of marsh-fowl play,
And buffaloes lie wallowing
　　Through the hot summer's day;
From the gigantic watch-towers,
　　No work of earthly men,
Whence Cora's sentinels o'erlook
　　The never-ending fen;

From the Laurentian jungle,
  The wild hog's reedy home;
From the green steeps whence Anio leaps
  In floods of snow-white foam.

11

Aricia, Cora, Norba,
  Velitræ, with the might
Of Setia and of Tusculum,
  Were marshalled on their right:
Their leader was Mamilius,
  Prince of the Latian name;
Upon his head a helmet
  Of red gold shone like flame:
High on a gallant charger
  Of dark-grey hue he rode;
Over his gilded armour
  A vest of purple flowed,
Woven in the land of sunrise
  By Syria's dark-browed daughters,
And by the sails of Carthage brought
  Far o'er the southern waters.

12

Lavinium and Laurentum
  Had on the left their post,
With all the banners of the marsh,
  And banners of the coast.
Their leader was false Sextus,
  That wrought the deed of shame:.
With restless pace and haggard face,
  To his last field he came.
Men said he saw strange visions,
  Which none beside might see;
And that strange sounds were in his ears,
  Which none might hear but he.
A woman fair and stately,
  But pale as are the dead,
Oft through the watches of the night
  Sate spinning by his bed.
And as she plied the distaff,
  In a sweet voice and low,
She sang of great old houses,
  And fights fought long ago.

So spun she, and so sang she,
   Until the east was grey;
Then pointed to her bleeding breast,
   And shrieked, and fled away.

13

But in the centre thickest
   Were ranged the shields of foes,
And from the centre loudest
   The cry of battle rose.
There Tibur marched and Pedum
   Beneath proud Tarquin's rule,
And Ferentinum of the rock,
   And Gabii of the pool.
There rode the Volscian succours:
   There, in a dark stern ring,
The Roman exiles gathered close
   Around the ancient king.
Though white as Mount Soracte,
   When winter nights are long,
His beard flowed down o'er mail and belt,
   His heart and hand were strong:
Under his hoary eye-brows
   Still flashed forth quenchless rage:
And, if the lance shook in his gripe,
   'Twas more with hate than age.
Close at his side was Titus
   .On an Apulian steed,
Titus, the youngest Tarquin,
   Too good for such a breed.

14

Now on each side the leaders
   Gave signal for the charge;
And on each side the footmen
   Strode on with lance and targe;
And on each side the horsemen
   Struck their spurs deep in gore,
And front to front the armies
   Met with a mighty roar:
And under that great battle
   The earth with blood was red;

And, like the Pomptine fog at morn,
  The dust hung overhead;
And louder still and louder,
  Rose from the darkened field
The braying of the war-horns,
  The clang of sword and shield,
The rush of squadrons sweeping
  Like whirlwinds o'er the plain,
The shouting of the slayers,
  And screeching of the slain.

15

False Sextus rode out foremost:
  His look was high and bold;
His corslet was of bison's hide,
  Plated with steel and gold.
As glares the famished eagle
  From the Digentian rock,
On a choice lamb that bounds alone
  Before Bandusia's flock,
Herminius glared on Sextus,
  And came with eagle speed;
Herminius on black Auster,
  Brave champion on brave steed;
In his right hand the broadsword
  That kept the bridge so well,
And on his helm the crown he won
  When proud Fidenæ fell.
Woe to the maid whose lover
  Shall cross his path to-day!
False Sextus saw, and trembled,
  And turned, and fled away.
As turns, as flies, the woodman
  In the Calabrian brake,
When through the reeds gleams the round eye
  Of that fell painted snake;
So turned, so fled, false Sextus,
  And hid him in the rear,
Behind the dark Lavinian ranks,
  Bristling with crest and spear.

16

Then far to north Æbutius,
  The Master of the Knights,

Gave Tubero of Norba
  To feed the Porcian kites.
Next under those red horse-hoofs
  Flaccus of Setia lay;
Better had he been pruning
  Among his elms that day.
Mamilius saw the slaughter,
  And tossed his golden crest,
And towards the Master of the Knights
  Through the thick battle pressed.
Æbutius smote Mamilius
  So fiercely on the shield,
That the great lord of Tusculum
  Well nigh rolled on the field.
Mamilius smote Æbutius,
  With a good aim and true,
Just where the neck and shoulder join,
  And pierced him through and through;
And brave Æbutius Elva
  Fell swooning to the ground:
But a thick wall of bucklers
  Encompassed him around.
His clients from the battle
  Bare him some little space;
And filled a helm from the dark lake,
  And bathed his brow and face;
And when at last he opened
  His swimming eyes to light,
Men say, the earliest word he spake
  Was, "Friends, how goes the fight?"

17

But meanwhile in the centre
  Great deeds of arms were wrought;
There Aulus the Dictator,
  And there Valerius fought.
Aulus, with his good broadsword,
  A bloody passage cleared
To where, amidst the thickest foes,
  He saw the long white beard.
Flât lighted that good broadsword
  Upon proud Tarquin's head.

He dropped the lance: he dropped the reins:
    He fell as fall the dead.
Down Aulus springs to slay him,
    With eyes like coals of fire;
But faster Titus hath sprung down,
    And hath bestrode his sire.
Latian captains, Roman knights,
    Fast down to earth they spring,
And hand to hand they fight on foot
    Around the ancient king.

First Titus gave tall Cæso
    A death wound in the face;
Tall Cæso was the bravest man
    Of the brave Fabian race:
Aulus slew Rex of Gabii,
    The priest of Juno's shrine:
Valerius smote down Julius,
    Of Rome's great Julian line;
Julius, who left his mansion
    High on the Velian hill,
And through all turns of weal and woe
    Followed proud Tarquin still.

Now right across proud Tarquin
    A corpse was Julius laid;
And Titus groaned with rage and grief,
    And at Valerius made.
Valerius struck at Titus,
    And lopped off half his crest;
But Titus stabbed Valerius
    A span deep in the breast.
Like a mast snapped by the tempest,
    Valerius reeled and fell.
Ah! woe is me for the good house
    That loves the people well!

Then shouted loud the Latines;
    And with one rush they bore
The struggling Romans backward
    Three lances' length and more:
And up they took proud Tarquin,
    And laid him on a shield,
And four strong yeomen bare him,
    Still senseless, from the field.

18

But fiercer grew the fighting
   Around Valerius dead;
For Titus dragged him by the foot,
   And Aulus by the head.
"On, Latines, on!" quoth Titus,
   "See how the rebels fly!"
"Romans, stand firm!" quoth Aulus,
   "And win this fight or die!
They must not give Valerius
   To raven and to kite;
For aye Valerius loathed the wrong,
   And aye upheld the right:
And for your wives and babies
   In the front rank he fell.
Now play the men for the good house
   That loves the people well!"

19

Then tenfold round the body
   The roar of battle rose,
Like the roar of a burning forest,
   When a strong northwind blows.
Now backward, and now forward,
   Rocked furiously the fray,
Till none could see Valerius,
   And none wist where he lay.
For shivered arms and ensigns
   Were heaped there in a mound,
And corpses stiff, and dying men
   That writhed and gnawed the ground;
And wounded horses kicking,
   And snorting purple foam:
Right well did such a couch befit
   A Consular of Rome.

20

But north looked the Dictator;
   North looked he long and hard;
And spake to Caius Cossus,
   The Captain of his Guard:

"Caius, of all the Romans
   Thou hast the keenest sight;
Say, what through yonder storm of dust
   Comes from the Latian right?"

21

Then answered Caius Cossus:
   "I see an evil sight;
The banner of proud Tusculum
   Comes from the Latian right;
I see the plumed horsemen;
   And far before the rest
I see the dark-grey charger,
   I see the purple vest;
I see the golden helmet
   That shines far off like flame;
So ever rides Mamilius,
   Prince of the Latian name."

22

"Now hearken, Caius Cossus:
   Spring on thy horse's back;
Ride as the wolves of Apennine
   Were all upon thy track!
Haste to our southward battle;
   And never draw thy rein
Until thou find Herminius,
   And bid him come amain."

23

So Aulus spake, and turned him
   Again to that fierce strife;
And Caius Cossus mounted,
   And rode for death and life.
Loud clanged beneath his horse-hoofs
   The helmets of the dead,
And many a curdling pool of blood
   Splashed him from heel to head.
So came he far to southward,
   Where fought the Roman host,
Against the banners of the marsh
   And banners of the coast.

Like corn before the sickle
 The stout Lavinians fell,
Beneath the edge of the true sword
 That kept the bridge so well.

24

"Herminius! Aulus greets thee;
 He bids thee come with speed,
To help our central battle;
 For sore is there our need.
There wars the youngest Tarquin,
 And there the Crest of Flame,
The Tusculan Mamilius,
 Prince of the Latian name.
Valerius hath fallen fighting
 In front of our array;
And Aulus of the seventy fields
 Alone upholds the day."

25

Herminius beat his bosom;
 But never a word he spake.
He clapped his hand on Auster's mane;
 He gave the reins a shake,
Away, away, went Auster,
 Like an arrow from the bow:
Black Auster was the fleetest steed
 From Aufidus to Po.

26

Right glad were all the Romans
 Who, in that hour of dread,
Against great odds bare up the war
 Around Valerius dead,
When from the south the cheering
 Rose with a mighty swell;
"Herminius comes, Herminius,
 Who kept the bridge so well!"

27

Mamilius spied Herminius,
 And dashed across the way.
"Herminius! I have sought thee
 Through many a bloody day.

One of us two, Herminius,
   Shall never more go home.
I will lay on for Tusculum,
   And lay thou on for Rome!"

28

All round them paused the battle,
   While met in mortal fray
The Roman and the Tusculan,
   The horses black and grey.
Herminius smote Mamilius
   Through breast-plate and through breast;
And fast flowed out the purple blood
   Over the purple vest.
Mamilius smote Herminius
   Through head-piece and through head;
And side by side those chiefs of pride
   Together fell down dead.
Down fell they dead together
   In a great lake of gore;
And still stood all who saw them fall
   While men might count a score.

29

Fast, fast, with heels wild spurning,
   The dark-grey charger fled:
He burst through ranks of fighting men;
   He sprang o'er heaps of dead.
His bridle far out-streaming,
   His flanks all blood and foam,
He sought the southern mountains,
   The mountains of his home.
The pass was steep and rugged,
   The wolves they howled and whined;
But he ran like a whirlwind up the pass,
   And he left the wolves behind.
Through many a startled hamlet
   Thundered his flying feet:
He rushed through the gate of Tusculum,
   He rushed up the long white street;
He rushed by tower and temple,
   And paused not from his race
Till he stood before his master's door
   In the stately market-place.

And straightway round him gathered
  A pale and trembling crowd,
And when they knew him, cries of rage
  Brake forth, and wailing loud:
And women rent their tresses
  For their great prince's fall;
And old men girt on their old swords,
  And went to man the wall.

30

But, like a graven image,
  Black Auster kept his place,
And ever wistfully he looked
  Into his master's face.
The raven-mane that daily,
  With pats and fond caresses,
The young Herminia washed and combed,
  And twined in even tresses,
And decked with coloured ribands
  From her own gay attire,
Hung sadly o'er her father's corpse
  In carnage and in mire.
Forth with a shout sprang Titus,
  And seized black Auster's rein.
Then Aulus sware a fearful oath,
  And ran at him amain.
"The furies of thy brother
  With me and mine abide,
If one of your accursed house
  Upon black Auster ride!"
As on an Alpine watch-tower
  From heaven comes down the flame,
Full on the neck of Titus
  The blade of Aulus came:
And out the red blood spouted,
  In a wide arch and tall,
As spouts a fountain in the court
  Of some rich Capuan's hall.
The knees of all the Latines
  Were loosened with dismay
When dead, on dead Herminius,
  The bravest Tarquin lay.

31

And Aulus the Dictator
    Stroked Auster's raven mane,
With heed he looked unto the girths,
    With heed unto the rein.
"Now bear me well, black Auster,
    Into yon thick array;
And thou and I will have revenge
    For thy good lord this day."

32

So spake he; and was buckling
    Tighter black Auster's band,
When he was aware of a princely pair
    That rode at his right hand.
So like they were, no mortal
    Might one from other know:
White as snow their armour was:
    Their steeds were white as snow.
Never on earthly anvil
    Did such rare armour gleam;
And never did such gallant steeds
    Drink of an earthly stream.

33

And all who saw them trembled,
    And pale grew every cheek;
And Aulus the Dictator
    Scarce gathered voice to speak.
"Say by what name men call you?
    What city is your home?
And wherefore ride ye in such guise
    Before the ranks of Rome?"

34

"By many names men call us;
    In many lands we dwell:
Well Samothracia knows us;
    Cyrene knows us well.
Our house in gay Tarentum
    Is hung each morn with flowers:
High o'er the masts of Syracuse
    Our marble portal towers:

But by the proud Eurotas
　Is our dear native home;
And for the right we come to fight
　Before the ranks of Rome."

35

So answered those strange horsemen,
　And each couched low his spear;
And forthwith all the ranks of Rome
　Were bold, and of good cheer:
And on the thirty armies
　Came wonder and affright,
And Ardea wavered on the left,
　And Cora on the right.
"Rome to the charge!" cried Aulus;
　"The foe begins to yield!
Charge for the hearth of Vesta!
　Charge for the Golden Shield!
Let no man stop to plunder,
　But slay, and slay, and slay;
The Gods who live for ever
　Are on our side to-day."

36

Then the fierce trumpet-flourish
　From earth to heaven arose,
The kites know well the long stern swell
　That bids the Romans close.
Then the good sword of Aulus
　Was lifted up to slay:
Then, like a crag down Apennine,
　Rushed Auster through the fray.
But under those strange horsemen
　Still thicker lay the slain;
And after those strange horses
　Black Auster toiled in vain.
Behind them Rome's long battle
　Came rolling on the foe,
Ensigns dancing wild above,
　Blades all in line below.
So comes the Po in flood-time
　Upon the Celtic plain:

So comes the squall, blacker than night,
  Upon the Adrian main.
Now, by our Sire Quirinus,
  It was a goodly sight
To see the thirty standards
  Swept down the tide of flight.
So flies the spray of Adria
  When the black squall doth blow;
So corn-sheaves in the flood-time
  Spin down the whirling Po.
False Sextus to the mountains
  Turned first his horse's head;
And fast fled Ferentinum,
  And fast Lanuvium fled.
The horsemen of Nomentum
  Spurred hard out of the fray;
The footmen of Velitræ
  Threw shield and spear away.
And underfoot was trampled,
  Amidst the mud and gore,
The banner of proud Tusculum,
  That never stooped before:
And down went Flavius Faustus,
  Who led his stately ranks
From where the apple blossoms wave
  On Anio's echoing banks,
And Tullus of Arpinum,
  Chief of the Volscian aids,
And Metius with the long fair curls,
  The love of Anxur's maids,
And the white head of Vulso,
  The great Arician seer,
And Nepos of Laurentum,
  The hunter of the deer;
And in the back false Sextus
  Felt the good Roman steel,
And wriggling in the dust he died,
  Like a worm beneath the wheel:
And fliers and pursuers
  Were mingled in a mass;
And far away the battle
  Went roaring through the pass.

37

Sempronius Atratinus
   Sate in the Eastern Gate.
Beside him were three Fathers,
   Each in his chair of state;
Fabius, whose nine stout grandsons
   That day were in the field,
And Manlius, eldest of the Twelve
   Who keep the Golden Shield;
And Sergius, the High Pontiff,
   For wisdom far renowned;
In all Etruria's colleges
   Was no such Pontiff found.
And all around the portal,
   And high above the wall,
Stood a great throng of people,
   But sad and silent all;
Young lads, and stooping elders
   That might not bear the mail,
Matrons with lips that quivered,
   And maids with faces pale.
Since the first gleam of day-light,
   Sempronius had not ceased
To listen for the rushing
   Of horse-hoofs from the east.
The mist of eve was rising,
   The sun was hastening down,
When he was aware of a princely pair
   Fast pricking towards the town.
So like they were, man never
   Saw twins so like before;
Red with gore their armour was,
   Their steeds were red with gore.

38

"Hail to the great Asylum!
   Hail to the hill-tops seven!
Hail to the fire that burns for aye,
   And the shield that fell from heaven!
This day, by Lake Regillus,
   Under the Porcian height,
All in the lands of Tusculum
   Was fought a glorious fight.

    To-morrow your Dictator
      Shall bring in triumph home
    The spoils of thirty cities
      To deck the shrines of Rome!"

39

Then burst from that great concourse
    A shout that shook the towers,
And some ran north, and some ran south,
    Crying, "The day is ours!"
But on rode these strange horsemen,
    With slow and lordly pace;
And none who saw their bearing
    Durst ask their name or race.
On rode they to the Forum,
    While laurel-boughs and flowers,
From house-tops and from windows,
    Fell on their crests in showers.
When they drew nigh to Vesta,
    They vaulted down amain,
And washed their horses in the well
    That springs by Vesta's fane.
And straight again they mounted,
    And rode to Vesta's door;
Then, like a blast, away they passed,
    And no man saw them more.

40

And all the people trembled,
    And pale grew every cheek;
And Sergius the High Pontiff
    Alone found voice to speak:
"The Gods who live for ever
    Have fought for Rome to-day!
These be the Great Twin Brethren
    To whom the Dorians pray.
Back comes the Chief in triumph,
    Who, in the hour of fight,
Hath seen the Great Twin Brethren
    In harness on his right.
Safe comes the ship to haven,
    Through billows and through gales,

If once the Great Twin Brethren
   Sit shining on the sails.
Wherefore they washed their horses
   In Vesta's holy well,
Wherefore they rode to Vesta's door,
   I know, but may not tell.
Here, hard by Vesta's temple,
   Build we a stately dome
Unto the Great Twin Brethren
   Who fought so well for Rome.
And when the months returning
   Bring back this day of fight,
The proud Ides of Quintilis,
   Marked evermore with white,
Unto the Great Twin Brethren
   Let all the people throng,
With chaplets and with offerings,
   With music and with song;
And let the doors and windows
   Be hung with garlands all,
And let the Knights be summoned
   To Mars without the wall:
Thence let them ride in purple
   With joyous trumpet-sound,
Each mounted on his war-horse,
   And each with olive crowned;
And pass in solemn order
   Before the sacred dome,
Where dwell the Great Twin Brethren
   Who fought so well for Rome."

MISCELLANEOUS POEMS

IVRY

A SONG OF THE HUGUENOTS

Now glory to the Lord of Hosts, from whom all glories are!
And glory to our Sovereign Liege, King Henry of Navarre!
Now let there be the merry sound of music and of dance,
Through thy corn-fields green, and sunny vines, oh pleasant land
    of France!
And thou, Rochelle, our own Rochelle, proud city of the waters,
Again let rapture light the eyes of all thy mourning daughters.
As thou wert constant in our ills, be joyous in our joy,
For cold, and stiff, and still are they who wrought thy walls annoy.
Hurrah! Hurrah! a single field hath turned the chance of war,
Hurrah! Hurrah! for Ivry, and Henry of Navarre.

Oh! how our hearts were beating, when, at the dawn of day,
We saw the army of the League drawn out in long array;
With all its priest-led citizens, and all its rebel peers,
And Appenzel's stout infantry, and Egmont's Flemish spears.
There rode the brood of false Lorraine, the curses of our land;
And dark Mayenne was in the midst, a truncheon in his hand:
And, as we looked on them, we thought of Seine's empurpled
    flood,
And good Coligni's hoary hair all dabbled with his blood;
And we cried unto the living God, who rules the fate of war,
To fight for his own holy name, and Henry of Navarre.

The King is come to marshal us, in all his armour drest,
And he has bound a snow-white plume upon his gallant crest.
He looked upon his people, and a tear was in his eye;
He looked upon the traitors, and his glance was stern and high.
Right graciously he smiled on us, as rolled from wing to wing,
Down all our line, a deafening shout, "God save our Lord the
    King."
"An if my standard-bearer fall, as fall full well he may,
For never saw I promise yet of such a bloody fray,
Press where ye see my white plume shine, amidst the ranks of war,
And be your oriflamme to-day the helmet of Navarre."

Hurrah! the foes are moving. Hark to the mingled din,
Of fife, and steed, and trump, and drum, and roaring culverin.
The fiery Duke is pricking fast across Saint André's plain,
With all the hireling chivalry of Guelders and Almayne.
Now by the lips of those ye love, fair gentlemen of France,
Charge for the golden lilies,—upon them with the lance.
A thousand spurs are striking deep, a thousand spears in rest,
A thousand knights are pressing close behind the snow-white crest;
And in they burst, and on they rushed, while, like a guiding star,
Amidst the thickest carnage blazed the helmet of Navarre.

Now, God be praised, the day is ours. Mayenne hath turned his rein.
D'Aumale hath cried for quarter. The Flemish count is slain.
Their ranks are breaking like thin clouds before a Biscay gale;
The field is heaped with bleeding steeds, and flags, and cloven mail.
And then we thought on vengeance, and, all along our van,
"Remember Saint Bartholomew," was passed from man to man.
But out spake gentle Henry, "No Frenchman is my foe:
Down, down, with every foreigner, but let your brethren go."
Oh! was there ever such a knight, in friendship or in war,
As our Sovereign Lord, King Henry, the soldier of Navarre?

Right well fought all the Frenchmen who fought for France to-day;
And many a lordly banner God gave them for a prey.
But we of the religion have borne us best in fight;
And the good Lord of Rosny hath ta'en the cornet white.
Our own true Maximilian the cornet white hath ta'en,
The cornet white with crosses black, the flag of false Lorraine.
Up with it high; unfurl it wide; that all the host may know
How God hath humbled the proud house which wrought his church such woe.
Then on the ground, while trumpets sound their loudest point of war,
›Fling the red shreds, a footcloth meet for Henry of Navarre.

Ho! maidens of Vienna; Ho! matrons of Lucerne;
Weep, weep, and rend your hair for those who never shall return.
Ho! Philip, send, for charity, thy Mexican pistoles,
That Antwerp monks may sing a mass for thy poor spearmen's souls.

Ho! gallant nobles of the League, look that your arms be bright;
Ho! burghers of Saint Genevieve, keep watch and ward to-night.
For our God hath crushed the tyrant, our God hath raised the
    slave,
And mocked the counsel of the wise, and the valour of the brave.
Then glory to his holy name, from whom all glories are;
And glory to our Sovereign Lord, King Henry of Navarre.

THE MARRIAGE OF TIRZAH AND AHIRAD

GENESIS VI. 3

It is the dead of night:
Yet more than noonday light
Beams far and wide from many a gorgeous hall.
    Unnumbered harps are tinkling,
    Unnumbered lamps are twinkling,
In the great city of the fourfold wall.
    By the brazen castle's moat,
    The sentry hums a livelier note.
    The ship-boy chaunts a shriller lay
    From the galleys in the bay.
    Shout, and laugh, and hurrying feet
    Sound from mart and square and street,
    From the breezy laurel shades,
    From the granite colonnades,
    From the golden statue's base,
    From the stately market-place,
    Where, upreared by captive hands,
    The great Tower of Triumph stands,
    All its pillars in a blaze
    With the many-coloured rays,
    Which lanthorns of ten thousand dyes
    Shed on ten thousand panoplies.
      But closest is the throng,
      And loudest is the song,
In that sweet garden by the river's side,
    The abyss of myrtle bowers,
    The wilderness of flowers,
Where Cain hath built the palace of his pride.
    Such palace ne'er shall be again
    Among the dwindling race of men.

From all its threescore gates the light
  Of gold and steel afar was thrown;
Two hundred cubits rose in height
  The outer wall of polished stone.
  On the top was ample space
  For a gallant chariot race.
  Near either parapet a bed
  Of the richest mould was spread,
Where amidst flowers of every scent and hue
Rich orange trees, and palms, and giant cedars grew.

  In the mansion's public court
    All is revel, song, and sport;
For there, till morn shall tint the east,
Menials and guards prolong the feast.
The boards with painted vessels shine;
The marble cisterns foam with wine.
A hundred dancing girls are there
With zoneless waists and streaming hair;
And countless eyes with ardour gaze,
  And countless hands the measure beat,
As mix and part in amorous maze
  Those floating arms and bounding feet.
But none of all the race of Cain,
  Save those whom he hath deigned to grace
With yellow robe and sapphire chain,
  May pass beyond that outer space.
  For now within the painted hall
  The Firstborn keeps high festival.
Before the glittering valves all night
  Their post the chosen captains hold.
Above the portal's stately height
  The legend flames in lamps of gold:
  "In life united and in death
    "May Tirzah and Ahirad be,
  The bravest he of all the sons of Seth,
    Of all the house of Cain the loveliest she."

  Through all the climates of the earth
  This night is given to festal mirth.
  The long continued war is ended.
  The long divided lines are blended.

Ahirad's bow shall now no more
Make fat the wolves with kindred gore.
The vultures shall expect in vain
Their banquet from the sword of Cain.
Without a guard the herds and flocks
Along the frontier moors and rocks
   From eve to morn may roam;
Nor shriek, nor shout, nor reddened sky,
Shall warn the startled hind to fly
   From his beloved home.
Nor to the pier shall burghers crowd
   With straining necks and faces pale,
And think that in each flitting cloud
   They see a hostile sail.
The peasant without fear shall guide
Down smooth canal or river wide
   His painted bark of cane,
Fraught, for some proud bazaar's arcades,
With chestnuts from his native shades,
   And wine, and milk, and grain.
Search round the peopled globe to-night,
   Explore each continent and isle,
There is no door without a light,
   No face without a smile.
The noblest chiefs of either race,
   From north and south, from west and east,
Crowd to the painted hall to grace
   The pomp of that atoning feast.
With widening eyes and labouring breath
Stand the fair-haired sons of Seth,
As bursts upon their dazzled sight
The endless avenue of light,
The bowers of tulip, rose, and palm,
The thousand cressets fed with balm,
The silken vests, the boards piled high
With amber, gold, and ivory,
The crystal founts whence sparkling flow
The richest wines o'er beds of snow,
The walls where blaze in living dyes
The king's three hundred victories.
The heralds point the fitting seat
To every guest in order meet,
And place the highest in degree

Nearest th' imperial canopy.
Beneath its broad and gorgeous fold,
With naked swords and shields of gold,
Stood the seven princes of the tribes of Nod.
Upon an ermine carpet lay
Two tiger cubs in furious play,
Beneath the emerald throne where sat the signed of God.

Over that ample forehead white
   The thousandth year returneth.
Still, on its commanding height,
With a fierce and blood-red light,
   The fiery token burneth.
Wheresoe'er that mystic star
Blazeth in the van of war,
   Back recoil before its ray
Shield and banner, bow and spear,
   Maddened horses break away
From the trembling charioteer.
   The fear of that stern king doth lie
   On all that live beneath the sky;
All shrink before the mark of his despair,
The seal of that great curse which he alone can bear.

Blazing in pearls and diamonds' sheen,
   Tirzah, the young Ahirad's bride,
Of humankind the destined queen,
   Sits by her great forefather's side.
The jetty curls, the forehead high,
   The swanlike neck, the eagle face,
The glowing cheek, the rich dark eye,
   Proclaim her of the elder race.
With flowing locks of auburn hue,
And features smooth, and eye of blue,
   Timid in love as brave in arms,
The gentle heir of Seth askance
Snatches a bashful, ardent glance
   At her majestic charms;
Blest when across that brow high musing flashes
   A deeper tint of rose,
Thrice blest when from beneath the silken lashes
   Of her proud eye she throws
The smile of blended fondness and disdain
Which marks the daughters of the house of Cain.

All hearts are light around the hall
Save his who is the lord of all.
The painted roofs, the attendant train,
The lights, the banquet, all are vain.
He sees them not. His fancy strays
To other scenes and other days.
A cot by a lone forest's edge,
   A fountain murmuring through the trees,
A garden with a wild flower hedge,
   Whence sounds the music of the bees,
A little flock of sheep at rest
Upon a mountain's swarthy breast.
On his rude spade he seems to lean
   Beside the well remembered stone,
Rejoicing o'er the promise green
   Of the first harvest man hath sown.
   He sees his mother's tears;
   His father's voice he hears,
Kind as when first it praised his youthful skill.
   And soon a seraph-child,
   In boyish rapture wild,
With a light crook comes bounding from the hill,
   Kisses his hands, and strokes his face,
   And nestles close in his embrace.
   In his adamantine eye
   None might discern his agony;
But they who had grown hoary next his side,
   And read his stern dark face with deepest skill,
Could trace strange meanings in that lip of pride,
   Which for one moment quivered and was still.
No time for them to mark or him to feel
   Those inward stings; for clarion, flute, and lyre,
   And the rich voices of a countless quire,
Burst on the ear in one triumphant peal.
In breathless transport sits the admiring throng,
As sink and swell the notes of Jubal's lofty song.

   "Sound the timbrel, strike the lyre,
   Wake the trumpet's blast of fire,
     Till the gilded arches ring.
   Empire, victory, and fame,
   Be ascribed unto the name

Of our father and our king.
Of the deeds which he hath done,
Of the spoils which he hath won,
    Let his grateful children sing.

"When the deadly fight was fought,
When the great revenge was wrought,
When on the slaughtered victims lay
The minion stiff and cold as they,
Doomed to exile, sealed with flame,
From the west the wanderer came.
Six score years and six he strayed
A hunter through the forest shade.
The lion's shaggy jaws he tore,
To earth he smote the foaming boar,
He crushed the dragon's fiery crest,
And scaled the condor's dizzy nest;
Till hardy sons and daughters fair
Increased around his woodland lair.
Then his victorious bow unstrung
On the great bison's horn he hung.
Giraffe and elk he left to hold
    The wilderness of boughs in peace,
And trained his youth to pen the fold,
    To press the cream, and weave the fleece.
As shrunk the streamlet in its bed,
    As black and scant the herbage grew,
O'er endless plains his flocks he led
    Still to new brooks and pastures new.
So strayed he till the white pavilions
Of his camp were told by millions,
Till his children's households seven
Were numerous as the stars of heaven.
Then he bade us rove no more;
    And in the place that pleased him best,
On the great river's fertile shore,
    He fixed the city of his rest.
He taught us then to bind the sheaves,
    To strain the palm's delicious milk,
And from the dark green mulberry leaves
    To cull the filmy silk.
Then first from straw-built mansions roamed
    O'er flower-beds trim the skilful bees;

Then first the purple wine vats foamed
  Around the laughing peasant's knees;
And olive-yards, and orchards green,
O'er all the hills of Nod were seen.

"Of our father and our king
Let his grateful children sing.
From him our race its being draws,
His are our arts, and his our laws.
Like himself he bade us be,
Proud, and brave, and fierce, and free.
True, through every turn of fate,
In our friendship and our hate.
Calm to watch, yet prompt to dare;
Quick to feel, yet firm to bear;
Only timid, only weak,
Before sweet woman's eye and cheek.
We will not serve, we will not know,
The God who is our father's foe.
In our proud cities to his name
No temples rise, no altars flame.
Our flocks of sheep, our groves of spice,
To him afford no sacrifice.
Enough that once the House of Cain
Hath courted with oblation vain
    The sullen power above.
Henceforth we bear the yoke no more;
The only gods whom we adore
    Are glory, vengeance, love.

"Of our father and our king
Let his grateful children sing.
What eye of living thing may brook
On his blazing brow to look?
What might of living thing may stand
Against the strength of his right hand?
First he led his armies forth
Against the Mammoths of the north,
What time they wasted in their pride
Pasture and vineyard far and wide.
Then the White River's icy flood
Was thawed with fire and dyed with blood.

And heard for many a league the sound
Of the pine forests blazing round,
And the death-howl and trampling din
Of the gigantic herd within.
From the surging sea of flame
Forth the tortured monsters came;
As of breakers on the shore
Was their onset and their roar;
As the cedar-trees of God
Stood the stately ranks of Nod.
One long night and one short day
The sword was lifted up to slay.

Then marched the firstborn and his sons
O'er the white ashes of the wood,
And counted of that savage brood
　　Nine times nine thousand skeletons.

"On the snow with carnage red
The wood is piled, the skins are spread.
A thousand fires illume the sky;
Round each a hundred warriors lie.
But, long ere half the night was spent,
Forth thundered from the golden tent
　　The rousing voice of Cain.
A thousand trumps in answer rang,
And fast to arms the warriors sprang
　　O'er all the frozen plain.
A herald from the wealthy bay
Hath come with tidings of dismay.
From the western ocean's coast
Seth hath led a countless host,
And vows to slay with fire and sword
All who call not on the Lord.
His archers hold the mountain forts;
His light armed ships blockade the ports;
　　His horsemen tread the harvest down.
On twelve proud bridges he hath passed
The river dark with many a mast,
And pitched his mighty camp at last
　　Before the imperial town.

"On the south and on the west,
Closely was the city prest.

Before us lay the hostile powers.
The breach was wide between the towers.
Pulse and meal within were sold
For a double weight of gold.
Our mighty father had gone forth
Two hundred marches to the north.
Yet in that extreme of ill
We stoutly kept his city still;
And swore beneath his royal wall,
Like his true sons, to fight and fall.

"Hark, hark, to gong and horn,
Clarion, and fife, and drum,
The morn, the fortieth morn,
Fixed for the great assault is come.
Between the camp and city spreads
A waving sea of helmed heads.
From the royal car of Seth
Was hung the blood-red flag of death:
At sight of that thrice-hallowed sign
Wide flew at once each banner's fold:
The captains clashed their arms of gold;
The war cry of Elohim rolled
Far down their endless line.
On the northern hills afar
Pealed an answering note of war.
Soon the dust in whirlwinds driven,
Rushed across the northern heaven.
Beneath its shroud came thick and loud
The tramp as of a countless crowd;
And at intervals were seen
Lance and hauberk glancing sheen;
And at intervals were heard
Charger's neigh and battle word.

"Oh what a rapturous cry
From all the city's thousand spires arose,
With what a look the hollow eye
Of the lean watchman glared upon the foes,
With what a yell of joy the mother pressed
The moaning baby to her withered breast,

When through the swarthy cloud that veiled the plain
Burst on his children's sight the flaming brow of Cain!''

There paused perforce that noble song;
For from all the joyous throng,
Burst forth a rapturous shout which drowned
Singer's voice and trumpet's sound.
Thrice that stormy clamour fell,
Thrice rose again with mightier swell.
The last and loudest roar of all
Had died along the painted wall.
The crowd was hushed; the minstrel train
Prepared to strike the chords again;
When on each ear distinctly smote
A low and wild and wailing note.
It moans again. In mute amaze
Menials, and guests, and harpers gaze.
They look above, beneath, around,
No shape doth own that mournful sound.
It comes not from the tuneful quire;
    It comes not from the feasting peers;
There is no tone of earthly lyre
    So soft, so sad, so full of tears.
Then a strange horror came on all
Who sate at that high festival.
The far famed harp, the harp of gold,
Dropped from Jubal's trembling hold.
Frantic with dismay the bride
Clung to her Ahirad's side.
And the corpse-like hue of dread
Ahirad's haughty face o'erspread.
Yet not even in that agony of awe
    Did the young leader of the fair-haired race
From Tirzah's shuddering grasp his hand withdraw
    Or turn his eyes from Tirzah's livid face.
    The tigers to their lord retreat,
    And crouch and whine beneath his feet.
Prone sink to earth the golden shielded seven.
    All hearts are cowed save his alone
    Who sits upon the emerald throne;
For he hath heard Elohim speak from heaven.
    Still thunders in his ear the peal;
    Still blazes on his front the seal:

And on the soul of the proud king
No terror of created thing
From sky, or earth, or hell, hath power
Since that unutterable hour.

He rose to speak, but paused, and listening stood,
Not daunted, but in sad and curious mood,
  With knitted brow, and searching eye of fire.
A deathlike silence sank on all around,
And through the boundless space was heard no
    sound,
  Save the soft tones of that mysterious lyre.
  Broken, faint, and low,
  At first the numbers flow.
Louder, deeper, quicker, still
  Into one fierce peal they swell,
And the echoing palace fill
  With a strange funereal yell.
A voice comes forth. But what, or where?
On the earth, or in the air?
Like the midnight winds that blow
Round a lone cottage in the snow,
With howling swell and sighing fall,
It wails along the trophied hall.
In such a wild and dreary moan
  The watches of the Seraphim
  Poured out all night their plaintive hymn
Before the eternal throne.
Then, when from many a heavenly eye
  Drops as of earthly pity fell
For her who had aspired too high,
  For him who loved too well.
When, stunned by grief, the gentle pair
From the nuptial garden fair,
Linked in a sorrowful caress,
Strayed through the untrodden wilderness:
And close behind their footsteps came
The desolating sword of flame,
And drooped the cedared alley's pride,
And fountains shrank, and roses died.

"Rejoice, oh Son of God, rejoice,"
Sang that melancholy voice,

"Rejoice, the maid is fair to see;
  The bower is decked for her and thee;
  The ivory lamps around it throw
  A soft and pure and mellow glow.
  Where'er the chastened lustre falls
  On roof or cornice, floor or walls,
  Woven of pink and rose appear
  Such words as love delights to hear.
The breath of myrrh, the lute's soft sound,
Float through the moonlight galleries round.
O'er beds of violet and through groves of spice,
  Lead thy proud bride into the nuptial bower;
For thou hast bought her with a fearful price,
  And she hath dowered thee with a fearful dower.
  The price is life. The dower is death.
    Accursed loss! Accursed gain!
  For her thou givest the blessedness of Seth,
    And to thine arms she brings the curse of Cain.
  Round the dark curtains of the fiery throne
    Pauses awhile the voice of sacred song:
  From all the angelic ranks goes forth a groan,
    'How long, O Lord, how long?
The still small voice makes answer, 'Wait and see,
Oh sons of glory, what the end shall be.'

"But, in the outer darkness of the place
Where God hath shown his power without his grace,
  Is laughter and the sound of glad acclaim,
    Loud as when, on wings of fire,
    Fulfilled of his malign desire,
  From Paradise the conquering serpent came.
The giant ruler of the morning star
    From off his fiery bed
    Lifts high his stately head,
Which Michael's sword hath marked with many a
    scar.
    At his voice the pit of hell
    Answers with a joyous yell,
    And flings her dusky portals wide
    For the bridegroom and the bride.

  "But louder still shall be the din
    In the halls of Death and Sin,

When the full measure runneth o'er,
When mercy can endure no more,
When he who vainly proffers grace,
Comes in his fury to deface
   The fair creation of his hand;
When from the heaven streams down amain
For forty days the sheeted rain;
And from his ancient barriers free,
With a deafening roar the sea
   Comes foaming up the land.
Mother, cast thy babe aside:
Bridegroom, quit thy virgin bride:
Brother, pass thy brother by:
'Tis for life, for life, ye fly.
Along the drear horizon raves
The swift advancing line of waves.
On: on: their frothy crests appear
Each moment nearer and more near.
Urge the dromedary's speed;
Spur to death the reeling steed;
If perchance ye yet may gain
The mountains that o'erhang the plain.

"Oh thou haughty land of Nod,
Hear the sentence of thy God.
Thou hast said 'Of all the hills
Whence, after autumn rains, the rills
   In silver trickle down,
The fairest is that mountain white
Which intercepts the morning light
   From Cain's imperial town.
On its first and gentlest swell
Are pleasant halls where nobles dwell;
And marble porticoes are seen
Peeping through terraced gardens green.
Above are olives, palms, and vines;
And higher yet the dark-blue pines;
And highest on the summit shines
   The crest of everlasting ice.
Here let the God of Abel own
That human art hath wonders shown
   Beyond his boasted paradise.'

"Therefore on that proud mountain's crown
    Thy few surviving sons and daughters
Shall see their latest sun go down
    Upon a boundless waste of waters.
None salutes and none replies;
    None heaves a groan or breathes a prayer;
They crouch on earth with tearless eyes,
    And clenched hands, and bristling hair.
The rain pours on: no star illumes
    The blackness of the roaring sky.
And each successive billow booms
    Nigher still and still more nigh.
And now upon the howling blast
The wreaths of spray come thick and fast;
And a great billow by the tempest curled
    Falls with a thundering crash; and all is o'er.
And what is left of all this glorious world?
    A sky without a beam, a sea without a shore.

"Oh thou fair land, where from their starry home
    Cherub and seraph oft delight to roam,
Thou city of the thousand towers,
    Thou palace of the golden stairs,
Ye gardens of perennial flowers,
    Ye moated gates, ye breezy squares;
Ye parks amidst whose branches high
Oft peers the squirrel's sparkling eye;
Ye vineyards, in whose trellised shade
Pipes many a youth to many a maid;
Ye ports where rides the gallant ship;
    Ye marts where wealthy burghers meet;
Ye dark green lanes which know the trip
    Of woman's conscious feet;
Ye grassy meads where, when the day is done,
    The shepherd pens his fold;
Ye purple moors on which the setting sun
    Leaves a rich fringe of gold;
Ye wintry deserts where the larches grow;
Ye mountains on whose everlasting snow
    No human foot hath trod;
    Many a fathom shall ye sleep
    Beneath the grey and endless deep,
In the great day of the revenge of God."

THE ARMADA

A FRAGMENT

ATTEND, all ye who list to hear our noble England's praise;
I tell of thrice famous deeds she wrought in ancient days,
When that great fleet invincible against her bore in vain
The richest spoils of Mexico, the stoutest hearts of Spain.

It was about the lovely close of a warm summer day,
There came a gallant merchant-ship full sail to Plymouth Bay;
Her crew hath seen Castile's black fleet, beyond Aurigny's isle,
At earliest twilight, on the waves lie heaving many a mile.
At sunrise she escaped their van, by God's especial grace;
And the tall Pinta, till the noon, had held her close in chase.
Forthwith a guard at every gun was placed along the wall;
The beacon blazed upon the roof of Edgecumbe's lofty hall;
Many a light fishing-bark put out to pry along the coast,
And with loose rein and bloody spur rode inland many a post.
With his white hair unbonneted, the stout old sheriff comes;
Behind him march the halberdiers; before him sound the drums;
His yeomen round the market cross make clear an ample space;
For there behoves him to set up the standard of Her Grace.
And haughtily the trumpets peal, and gaily dance the bells,
As slow upon the labouring wind the royal blazon swells.
Look how the Lion of the sea lifts up his ancient crown,
And underneath his deadly paw treads the gay lilies down.
So stalked he when he turned to flight, on that famed Picard field,
Bohemia's plume, and Genoa's bow, and Cæsar's eagle shield.
So glared he when at Agincourt in wrath he turned to bay,
And crushed and torn beneath his claws the princely hunters lay.
Ho! strike the flagstaff, sir Knight: ho! scatter flowers, fair maids:
Ho! gunners, fire a loud salute: ho! gallants, draw your blades:
Thou sun, shine on her joyously; ye breezes, waft her wide;
Our glorious SEMPER EADEM, the banner of our pride.

The freshening breeze of eve unfurled that banner's massy fold;
The parting gleam of sunshine kissed that haughty scroll of gold;
Night sank upon the dusky beach, and on the purple sea,
Such night in England ne'er had been, nor ne'er again shall be.
From Eddystone to Berwick bounds, from Lynn to Milford Bay,
That time of slumber was as bright and busy as the day;
For swift to east and swift to west the ghastly war-flame spread,

High on St. Michael's Mount it shone: it shone on Beachy Head.
Far on the deep the Spaniard saw, along each southern shire,
Cape beyond cape, in endless range, those twinkling points of fire.
The fisher left his skiff to rock on Tamar's glittering waves:
The rugged miners poured to war from Mendip's sunless caves:
O'er Longleat's towers, o'er Cranbourne's oaks, the fiery herald
     flew:
He roused the shepherds of Stonehenge, the rangers of Beaulieu.
Right sharp and quick the bells all night rang out from Bristol town,
And ere the day three hundred horse had met on Clifton down;
The sentinel on Whitehall gate looked forth into the night,
And saw o'erhanging Richmond Hill the streak of blood-red light.
Then bugle's note and cannon's roar the deathlike silence broke,
And with one start, and with one cry, the royal city woke.
At once on all her stately gates arose the answering fires;
At once the wild alarum clashed from all her reeling spires;
From all the batteries of the Tower pealed loud the voice of fear;
And all the thousand masts of Thames sent back a louder cheer:
And from the furthest wards was heard the rush of hurrying feet,
And the broad streams of pikes and flags rushed down each roaring
     street;
And broader still became the blaze, and louder still the din,
As fast from every village round the horse came spurring in:
And eastward straight from wild Blackheath the warlike errand
     went,
And roused in many an ancient hall the gallant squires of Kent.
Southward from Surrey's pleasant hills flew those bright couriers
     forth;
High on bleak Hampstead's swarthy moor they started for the north;
And on, and on, without a pause, untired they bounded still:
All night from tower to tower they sprang; they sprang from hill
     to hill:
Till the proud peak unfurled the flag o'er Darwin's rocky dales,
Till like volcanoes flared to heaven the stormy hills of Wales,
Till twelve fair counties saw the blaze on Malvern's lonely height,
Till streamed in crimson on the wind the Wrekin's crest of light,
Till broad and fierce the star came forth on Ely's stately fane,
And tower and hamlet rose in arms o'er all the boundless plain;
Till Belvoir's lordly terraces the sign to Lincoln sent,
And Lincoln sped the message on o'er the wide vale of Trent;
Till Skiddaw saw the fire that burned on Gaunt's embattled pile,
And the red glare on Skiddaw roused the burghers of Carlisle.

       *   *   *   *   *   *

THE LAST BUCCANEER

THE winds were yelling, the waves were swelling,
　　The sky was black and drear,
When the crew with eyes of flame brought the ship without
　　　a name
　　Alongside the last Buccaneer.

"Whence flies your sloop full sail before so fierce a gale,
　　When all others drive bare on the seas?
Say, come ye from the shore of the holy Salvador,
　　Or the gulf of the rich Caribbees?"

"From a shore no search hath found, from a gulf no line can
　　　sound,
　　Without rudder or needle we steer;
Above, below, our bark, dies the sea fowl and the shark,
　　As we fly by the last Buccaneer.

"To-night there shall be heard on the rocks of Cape de
　　　Verde
　　A loud crash, and a louder roar;
And to-morrow shall the deep, with a heavy moaning, sweep
　　The corpses and wreck to the shore."

The stately ship of Clyde securely now may ride
　　In the breath of the citron shades;
And Severn's towering mast securely now flies fast,
　　Through the sea of the balmy Trades.

From St. Jago's wealthy port, from Havannah's royal fort,
　　The seaman goes forth without fear;
For since that stormy night not a mortal hath had sight
　　Of the flag of the last Buccaneer.

EPITAPH ON A JACOBITE

To my true king I offered free from stain
Courage and faith; vain faith, and courage vain.
For him, I threw lands, honours, wealth, away,
And one dear hope, that was more prized than they.
For him I languished in a foreign clime,
Grey-haired with sorrow in my manhood's prime;
Heard on Lavernia Scargill's whispering trees,
And pined by Arno for my lovelier Tees;
Beheld each night my home in fevered sleep,
Each morning started from the dream to weep;
Till God, who saw me tried too sorely, gave
The resting place I asked, an early grave.
Oh thou, whom chance leads to this nameless stone,
From that proud country which was once mine own,
By those white cliffs I never more must see,
By that dear language which I spake like thee,
Forget all feuds, and shed one English tear
O'er English dust. A broken heart lies here.

Date Due